# The Western Heritage
## Volume II: Since 1648

## SIXTH EDITION

### DONALD KAGAN
Yale University

### STEVEN OZMENT
Harvard University

### FRANK M. TURNER
Yale University

Prentice Hall, Upper Saddle River, New Jersey 07458

Library of Congress Cataloging–in–Publication Data

The Library of Congress has catalogued the one volume edition as follows:

Kagan, Donald
The Western Heritage/ Donald Kagan, Steven Ozment, Frank M.
     Turner. —6th ed.
          p.    cm.
       Includes bibliographical references and index.
       ISBN 0-13-617383-7
       1. Civilization, Western.    I. Ozment, Steven E. II. Turner,
Frank M. (Frank Miller). (Date). III. Title
     CB245.K28  1998              97-23706
     909′.09812—dc21                     CIP

Editorial Director: Charlyce Jones Owen
Editor-in-Chief, Development: Susanna Lesan
Development Editor: Roberta Meyer
Director of Production and Manufacturing: Barbara Kittle
Production Editor: Barbara DeVries
Executive Manager, New Media: Alison Pendergast
Manufacturing Manager: Nick Sklitsis
Prepress and Manufacturing Buyer: Lynn Pearlman
Creative Design Director: Leslie Osher

Interior and Cover Designer: Maria Lange
Supervisor of Production Services: Lori Clinton
Electronic Page Layout: Rosemary Ross
Photo Director: Lorinda Morris-Nantz
Photo Research: Barbara Salz
Cartographer: Maryland Cartographics
Line Art Coordinator: Michele Giusti
Copy Editor: Susan Saslow

Cover Art: Guillaumin, Armand. *The Seine River at Rouen.* Musee de la Chartreuse, Douai, France.
     Giraudon/Art Resource, NY.

This book was set in 10/12 Trump Mediaeval by the HSS in-house formatting and
production services group and was printed and bound by RR Donnelley & Sons.
The cover was printed by The Lehigh Press, Inc.

Time Line photo credits appear on page xxxi and constitute a continuation of the copyright page.

Printed in the United States of America
10 9 8 7 6 5 4 3 2 1

ISBN 0-13-617432-9

Prentice-Hall International (UK) Limited, *London*
Prentice-Hall of Australia Pty. Limited, *Sydney*
Prentice-Hall Canada Inc., *Toronto*
Prentice-Hall Hispanoamericana, S.A., *Mexico*
Prentice-Hall of India Private Limited, *New Delhi*
Prentice-Hall of Japan, Inc. *Tokyo*
Simon & Schuster Asia Pte. Ltd., *Singapore*
Editora Prentice-Hall do Brasil, Ltda., *Rio de Janeiro*

# BRIEF CONTENTS

# DETAILED CONTENTS

## Europe in Transitition, 1300–1750                       **304**

## 12   The Age of Religious Wars

**15 Successful and Unsuccessful Paths to Power (1686–1740)** 512

**16 Society and Economy Under the Old Regime in the Eighteenth Century** 544

**17 Empire, War, and Colonial Rebellion** 578

## Enlightenment and Revolution 604

## Toward the Modern World       **796**

# DOCUMENTS

# MAPS

# THE WEST & THE WORLD

# POLITICAL TRANSFORMATIONS

# PREFACE

The heritage of Western civilization has perhaps never been the focus of so much interest and controversy as it is today. Many commentators criticize it, many praise it, but for all it is a subject of intense discussion. *The Western Heritage*, sixth edition, is designed to allow teachers to introduce students to the subject of that discussion. It presents an overview of Western civilization, including its strengths, its weaknesses, and the controversies surrounding it.

On campus after campus, every aspect of Western civilization has become an object of scrutiny and debate. Many participants in this debate fail to recognize that such self-criticism is characteristic of Western civilization and an important part of its heritage. We welcome the debate and hope that this book can help raise its quality.

The collapse of Communism has left the people of half of Europe struggling to reorganize their political institutions and their social and economic lives. The choices they are making and the future they are forging will reflect in large measure their understanding of their heritage. To follow and participate in that process we too need to understand that heritage.

## GOALS OF THE TEXT

Since *The Western Heritage* first appeared, we have sought to provide our readers with a work that does justice to the richness and variety of Western civilization. Events since then have only added urgency to our purpose.

Our primary goal has been to present a strong, clear narrative account of the central developments in Western history. We have also sought to call attention to certain critical themes:

- the development of political freedom, constitutional government, and concern for the rule of law and individual rights
- the shifting relations among religion, society, and the state
- the development of science and technology and their expanding impact on thought, social institutions, and everyday life

- the major religious and intellectual currents that have shaped Western culture

We believe that these themes have been fundamental in Western civilization, shaping the past and exerting a continuing influence on the present.

**Balanced and Flexible Presentation** In this edition as in past editions, our goal has been to present Western civilization fairly, accurately, and in a way that does justice to its great variety. History has many facets, no one of which alone can account for the others. Any attempt to tell the story of the West from a single overarching perspective, no matter how timely, is bound to neglect or suppress some important part of that story.

*The Western Heritage*, sixth edition, is designed to accommodate a variety of approaches to a course in Western civilization, allowing teachers to stress what is most important to them. Some teachers will ask students to read all the chapters. Others will select among them to reinforce assigned readings and lectures.

We do not believe that a history of the West should be limited to politics and international relations, but we share the conviction that internal and external political events have shaped the Western experience in fundamental and powerful ways. Recent events in central and eastern Europe and the former Soviet Union have strengthened that belief. We have also been told repeatedly by teachers that no matter what their own historical specialization, they believe that a political narrative gives students an effective tool to begin to organize their understanding of the past.

*The Western Heritage* also provides one of the richest accounts of the social history of the West available today, with strong coverage of family life, the roles of women, and the place of the family in relation to broader economic, political, and social developments. This coverage reflects the explosive growth in social historical research in the past quarter century, which has enriched virtually all areas of historical study.

Finally, no other survey text presents so full an account of the religious and intellectual development of the West. People may be political and social beings, but they are also reasoning and spiritual beings. What they think and believe are among the most important things we can know about them. Their ideas about God, society, law, gender, human nature, and the physical world have changed over the centuries and continue to change. We cannot fully grasp our own approach to the world without understanding the intellectual currents of the past and their influence on our thoughts and conceptual categories.

**Clarity and Accessibility** Good narrative history requires clear, vigorous prose. As in earlier editions, we have paid careful attention to the quality of our writing, subjecting every paragraph to critical scrutiny. Our goal was to make our presentation fully accessible to students without compromising vocabulary or conceptual level. We hope this effort will benefit both teachers and students.

**Recent Scholarship** As in previous editions, changes in this edition reflect our determination to incorporate the most recent developments in historical scholarship and the expanding concerns of professional historians.

**Pedagogical Features** This edition retains the pedagogical features of the last edition, including part-opening comparative timelines, a list of key topics at the beginning of each chapter, chapter review questions, and questions accompanying the more than 200 source documents in the text. Each of these features is designed to make the text more accessible to students and to reinforce key concepts.

- The *part-opening timelines*, which follow the essays that open each of the six parts of the book, summarize major events in politics and government, society and economy, and religion and culture side by side. Appropriate photographs have been added to each timeline.

- *Primary source documents*, more than one third new to this edition, acquaint students with the raw material of history and provide intimate contact with the people of the past and their concerns. *Questions* accompanying the source documents direct students toward important, thought-provoking issues and help them relate the documents to the material in the text. They can

be used to stimulate class discussion or as topics for essays and study groups.

- Each chapter includes an *outline*, a list of *key topics*, and an *introduction*. Together these features provide a succinct overview of each chapter.

- *Chronologies* follow each major section in a chapter, listing significant events and their dates.

- *Concluding sections* summarize the major themes of each chapter and provide a bridge to the next chapter.

- *Chapter review questions* help students review the material in a chapter and relate it to broader themes. They too can be used for class discussion and essay topics.

- *Suggested readings* lists following each chapter have been updated with new titles reflecting recent scholarship.

## CHANGES IN THE SIXTH EDITION

The sixth edition retains all of the major content changes that appear in the fifth edition. In addition, Chapter 30, *"Europe and the Soviet-American Rivalry"* has been reorganized to relate the various regional conflicts occurring outside of Europe, including the Mideast, Korea, and Vietnam, more closely to the Cold War conflict between the superpowers. Chapter 31, *"Toward a New Europe and the Twenty-first Century,"* reviews recent events in Eastern Europe. As in the fifth edition, questions appear with each document and after every chapter.

**New Features** New to the edition are two major features designed to expand students' understanding of the heritage of the West. These are a series of illustrated essays, *The West & the World*, and a series of maps with explanations focusing on key *Political Transformations*.

### The West & the World

The students reading this book are drawn from a wide variety of cultures and experiences. They live in a world characterized by highly interconnected economies and instant communication between cultures. In this emerging multicultural society it seems both appropriate and necessary to recognize the ways in which Western civilization has throughout its history interacted with other cultures, influencing other societies and being influenced by them. Examples of this two-way interaction, such as that with Islam, already appear in the main body of the text. In this new feature, we focus on six subjects, comparing Western institutions with those of other parts of the world, or discussing the ways in which developments in the West have influenced cultures in other areas of the globe. Topics for this feature are:

## ANCIENT SLAVERY (p. 150)
Slavery has arisen as a social and economic institution in virtually every world culture. This essay compares slavery in the ancient cultures of Mesopotamia, Egypt, China, India, Greece, and Rome. It also describes the role of slavery in the economies of ancient Greece and the ante-bellum American South. The latter comparison seems especially appropriate since in both instances, ancient and modern, the surrounding political structures were democratic.

## SOCIAL LIFE IN MALI (1200–1400) (p. 300)
Medieval Europe in many respects constituted an underdeveloped economy. Production was quite limited and was almost entirely agrarian. This essay explores the ways in which that society compares with Mali Society. It discusses Islamic influences on marriage customs, education, and daily life in the African setting, allowing students to draw comparisons with similar European institutions influenced by Christianity, as examined in the preceding chapter.

## THE FAMILY IN EUROPE
## AND CHINA (1400–1800) (p. 408)
Throughout the human experience, the family has been the most enduring of all institutions. Recent scholarship has greatly improved our understanding of the early modern European family. This essay draws upon that knowledge, enabling students to compare and contrast the European family of the era with family structures in China.

## THE ABOLITION OF SLAVERY
## IN THE TRANSATLANTIC ECONOMY (p. 754)
The abolition of chattel slavery in the transatlantic economy stands as one of the most remarkable social and economic developments of the eighteenth and nineteenth centuries. Never before had a society abolished slavery. This essay traces the history of that crusade, noting the manner in which it

influenced the societies of Africa, Latin America and North America.

## IMPERIALISM: ANCIENT AND MODERN (p. 958)
During the past two centuries no interaction of the West with the rest of the world was more important or of more enduring significance than the establishment of colonial empires in Asia and Africa. This essay recalls for students the earlier empires that were part of the Western experience, comparing the imperialism of the ancient world with that of the modern era.

## GLOBAL DEMOCRATIZATION (p. 1116)
With the collapse of communism in the past decade, democratization has made enormous gains in Europe and the former Soviet Union. This essay places the recent European experience in the context of the worldwide movement of the past half-century toward greater democratic political participation. It pays particular attention to the civil rights movement in the United States and to the movements toward democracy in Latin America.

### Political Transformations

This new map feature concentrates on six highly significant moments of political transformation in the history of the West. As with *The West & the World*, most *Political Transformations* emphasize the interaction of the West with other areas of the world. Each of the features provides a brief overview of the transformation illustrated by a map as well as in an illustrative document. The features will provide opportunities for study not only by individual students, but also for class discussion. The topics for this feature are:

- Greek Colonization from Spain to the Black Sea
- Muslim Conquests and Domination of the Mediterranean to about 750
- Voyages of Discovery and the Colonial Claims of Spain and Portugal
- The Congress of Vienna Redraws the Map of Europe
- The Mandate System: 1919 to World War II
- Decolonization in Asia and Africa

**Maps and Illustrations** The skillful use of color in the maps greatly improves their clarity and pedagogical usefulness. All 90 maps in the text have been carefully edited for accuracy. The text also contains almost 500 color and black and white illustrations. In this edition, we have added photographs to the timelines preceding each part of the book.

**A Note on Dates and Transliterations** With this edition of *The Western Heritage* we shift to the use of B.C.E. (before the common era) and C.E. (common era) instead of B.C. (before Christ) and A.D. *(anno domini,* the year of the Lord) to designate dates.

Also, we have followed the most accurate currently accepted English transliterations of Arabic words. For example, today Koran is being replaced by the more accurate *Qur'an;* similarly *Muhammad* is preferable to *Mohammed* and *Muslim* to *Moslem.*

**Ancillary Instructional Materials** *The Western Heritage* sixth edition comes with an extensive package of ancillary materials.

*For the Instructor:*

- **Instructor's Manual with Test Items** prepared by Perry M. Rogers, Ohio State University. The manual includes chapter summaries, key points and vital concepts, identification questions, multiple-choice questions, essay questions, and suggested films.
- **Transparency Acetates** of the four-color maps, charts, figures, and graphs in the text provide useful instructional aids for lectures.
- **Prentice Hall Custom Test,** available in Windows, DOS, and Macintosh format, provides the questions from the printed test item file for generating multiple versions of tests.
- **Administrative Handbook** by Jay Boggis provides instructors with resources for using *The Western Heritage* with Annenberg/CPB telecourse, *The Western Tradition.*

*For the Student:*

- **Study Guide, Volumes I** and **II** includes commentary, definitions, identifications, map exercises, short-answer exercises, and essay questions.
- **Map Workbook** gives the student the opportunity to increase their knowledge of geography through identification exercises.

- **Documents in Western Civilization, Volumes I** and **II,** provides over 100 additional primary source readings with questions for discussion.
- **Telecourse Study Guide, Volumes I and II,** by Jay Boggis correlates *The Western Heritage* with the Annenberg/CPB telecourse, *The Western Tradition.*

*Media Ancillaries:*

- **The Western Heritage, Interactive Edition, Version 2.0** takes students on an interactive journey through the evolution of Western civilization and its people. With over 600 study questions, quizzes, and comprehension exercises, this unique CD-ROM provides a highly visual multimedia learning experience that will engage and captivate students' imagination. Available for IBM/Mac.
- **The World Wide Web Companion Study Guide** *(http://www.prenhall.com/kagan)* directly complements *The Western Heritage* and correlates the text to related material on the Internet. Each "chapter" corresponds to the chapter in the textbook and consists of objectives, multiple choice quizzes, essay questions, chapter chat, web destinations, and help.

**Acknowledgments** We are grateful to the scholars and teachers whose thoughtful and often detailed comments helped shape this revision:

Lenard R. Berlanstein, University of Virginia, Charlottesville
Stephanie Christelow, Idaho State University
Samuel Willard Crompton, Holyoke Community College
Robert L. Ervin, San Jacinto Community College
Joseph Gonzales, Moorpark College
Victor Davis Hanson, California State University, Fresno
William I. Hitchcock, Yale University
Pardaic Kenny, University of Colorado, Boulder
Raymond F. Kierstead, Reed College
Eleanor McCluskey, Palm Beach Atlantic College and Broward Community College
Robert J. Mueller, Hastings College
John Nicols, University of Oregon, Eugene
Sandra J. Peacock, State University of New York, Binghamton
John Powell, Pennsylvania State University

Robert A. Schneider, Catholic University
Hugo Schwyzer, Pasadena City College
Sidney R. Sherter, Long Island University
Roger P. Snow, College of Great Falls

Finally, we would like to thank the dedicated people who helped produce this revision: our development editor, Roberta Meyer; our production editor, Barbara DeVries; Maria Lange who created the handsome new design of this edition; Rosemary Ross who formatted the pages; Lynn Pearlman, our manufacturing buyer; and Barbara Salz, the photo researcher.

D.K.
S.O.
F.M.T.

**The New York Times** and **Prentice Hall** are sponsoring **Themes of the Times:** a program designed to enhance access to current information of relevance in the classroom.

Through this program, the core subject matter provided in the text is supplemented by a collection of time-sensitive articles from one of the world's most distinguished newspapers, **The New York Times**. These articles demonstrate the vital, ongoing connection between what is learned in the classroom and what is happening in the world around us.

To enjoy the wealth of information of **The New York Times** daily, a reduced subscription rate is available. For information, call toll-free: 1–800–631–1222.

**Prentice Hall** and **The New York Times** are proud to co-sponsor **Themes of the Times.** We hope it will make the reading of both textbooks and newspapers a more dynamic, involving process.

# ABOUT THE AUTHORS

**Donald Kagan** is Hillhouse Professor of History and Classics at Yale University, where he has taught since 1969. He received the A.B. degree in history from Brooklyn College, the M.A. in classics from Brown University, and the Ph.D. in history from Ohio State University. During 1958–1959 he studied at the American School of Classical Studies as a Fulbright Scholar. He has received three awards for undergraduate teaching at Cornell and Yale. He is the author of a history of Greek political thought, *The Great Dialogue* (1965); a four-volume history of the Peloponnesian war, *The Origins of the Peloponnesian War* (1969); *The Archidamian War* (1974); *The Peace of Nicias and the Sicilian Expedition* (1981); *The Fall of the Athenian Empire* (1987); and a biography of Pericles, *Pericles of Athens and the Birth of Democracy* (1991); and *On the Origins of War* (1995). With Brian Tierney and L. Pearce Williams, he is the editor of *Great Issues in Western Civilization*, a collection of readings.

**Steven Ozment** is McLean Professor of Ancient and Modern History at Harvard University. He has taught Western Civilization at Yale, Stanford, and Harvard. He is the author of eight books. *The Age of Reform, 1250–1550* (1980) won the Schaff Prize and was nominated for the 1981 American Book Award. *Magdalena and Balthasar: An Intimate Portrait of Life in Sixteenth Century Europe* (1986), *Three Behaim Boys: Growing Up in Early Modern Germany* (1990), and *Protestants: The Birth of a Revolution* (1992) were selections of the History Book Club, as is also his most recent book, *The Bürgermeister's Daughter* (1996).

**Frank M. Turner** is John Hay Whitney Professor of History at Yale University, where he served as University Provost from 1988 to 1992. He received his B.A. degree at the College of William and Mary and his Ph.D. from Yale. He has received the Yale College Award for Distinguished Undergraduate Teaching. He has directed a National Endowment for the Humanities Summer Institute. His scholarly research has received the support of fellowships from the National Endowment for the Humanities and the Guggenheim Foundation. He is the author of *Between Science and Religion: The Reaction to Scientific Naturalism in Late Victorian England* (1974), *The Greek Heritage in Victorian Britain* (1981), which received the British Council Prize of the Conference on British Studies and the Yale Press Governors Award, and *Contesting Cultural Authority: Essays in Victorian Intellectual Life* (1993). He has also contributed numerous articles to journals and has served on the editorial advisory boards of *The Journal of Modern History, Isis, and Victorian Studies*.

# TIME LINE PHOTO CREDITS

*Time Line I:* page 2, (left) Gary Cralle/The Image Bank; (right) Winfield I. Parks, Jr./ National Geographic Image Collection; page 3, The Granger Collection; page 4, Battle of Alexander the Great at Issue. Roman mosaic. Museo Archeologico Nazionale, Naples, Italy. Scala/Art Resource, NY; page 5, Robert Frerck, Woodfin Camp & Associates.

*Time Line II:* page 198, New York University Institute of Fine Arts; page 199, Bayeux, Musee de l'Eveche. "With special authorization of the City of Bayeux." Giraudon/Art Resource.

*Time Line III:* page 306, George Gower (1540–96). "Elizabeth I, The Armada Portrait." The Bridgeman Art Library; page 307, The Granger Collection.

*Time Line IV:* page 607, Musee de la Legion d'Honneur.

*Time Line V:* page 798, Corbis-Bettmann; page 799, John Christen Johansen, *Signing of the Treaty of Versailles,* 1919, National Portrait Gallery, Smithsonian Institution, Washington, D.C./Art Resource, NY.

*Time Line VI:* page 1030, Franklin D. Roosevelt Library; page 1031, John Launois/Black Star.

*Charles I governed England from 1625 to 1649. His attempts to establish an absolutist government in matters of both church and state provoked clashes with the English Parliament and the outbreak of the Civil War in 1642. He was executed in 1649. [Daniel Mytens/The Granger Collection]*

# Paths to Constitutionalism and Absolutism:
## England and France in the Seventeenth Century

## KEY TOPICS

- The factors behind the divergent political paths of England and France in the seventeenth century
- The conflict between Parliament and the king over taxation and religion in early Stuart England, the English Civil War, and the abolition of the monarchy
- The Restoration and the development of Parliament's supremacy over the monarchy after the "Glorious Revolution"
- The establishment of an absolutist monarchy in France under Louis XIV
- The wars of Louis XIV

During the seventeenth century England and France moved in two very different political directions. By the close of the century, after decades of fierce civil and religious conflict that pitted Parliament and monarch against each other, England had developed into a parliamentary monarchy with a policy of religious toleration. Parliament, composed of the House of Lords and the House of Commons, shared responsibility for government with the monarch. It met regularly and the Commons, composed primarily of wealthy landed gentry, had to stand for election every three years. By contrast, France developed an abso-

lutist, centralized form of government dominated by a monarchy that shared little power with any other national institutions. Its authority resided rather in a complex set of relationships with local nobility, guilds, and towns and in its ability to support the largest standing army in Europe. In the seventeenth century France also abandoned Henry IV's policy of religious toleration and proscribed all but the Roman Catholic church.

These English and French forms of government became models for other nations. The French model, termed absolutism in the nineteenth century, would be imitated by other monarchies across the continent during the eighteenth century. The English model would later inspire the political creed known in the nineteenth century as liberalism. Like all such political labels, these terms, although useful, can conceal considerable complexity. English "parliamentary monarchs" did not share all power with Parliament; they controlled the army, foreign policy, and much patronage. Likewise the "absolute monarchs" of France and their later imitators elsewhere in Europe were not truly absolute; laws, traditions, and many local institutions and customs limited their power.

## Two Models of European Political Development

In the second half of the sixteenth century, changes in military organization, weapons, and tactics sharply increased the cost of warfare. Because traditional sources of revenue were inadequate to finance these growing costs—as well as the costs of government—monarchs sought new sources. Only monarchies that succeeded in building a secure financial base that was not deeply dependent on the support of noble estates, diets, or assemblies achieved absolute rule. The French monarchy succeeded in this effort after mid-century, whereas the English monarchy failed. The paths to that success and failure led to the two models of government—absolutism in France and parliamentary monarchy in England—that shaped subsequent political development in Europe.

In their pursuit of adequate income, English monarchs of the seventeenth century threatened the local political interests and economic well-being of the country's nobility and others of great landed and commercial wealth. These politically active groups, invoking traditional English liberties in their defense, effectively resisted the monarchs' attempted intrusions throughout the century.

The experience of Louis XIV, the French king, was different. During the second half of the seventeenth century, he would make the French nobility dependent upon his goodwill and patronage. In turn, he would support their local influence and their place in a firm social hierarchy. But even the French king's dominance of the nobility was not wholly complete. Louis accepted the authority of the noble-dominated *Parlement* of Paris to register royal decrees before they officially became law, and he permitted regional *parlements* to exercise considerable author-

ity over local administration and taxation. Funds from taxes levied by the central monarchy found their way into many local pockets.

Religious factors also affected the political destinies of England and France. A strong Protestant religious movement known as Puritanism arose in England and actively opposed the Stuart monarchy. Puritanism represented a nonpolitical force that sought at first to limit and eventually to overturn the English monarchy. Louis XIV, in contrast, crushed the Protestant communities of France. He was generally supported in these efforts by Roman Catholics, who saw religious uniformity enforced by the monarchy working to their advantage.

There were also major institutional differences between the two countries. In Parliament, England possessed a political institution that had long bargained with the monarch over political issues. In the early seventeenth century, to be sure, Parliament did not meet regularly and was not the strong institution it would become by the close of the century. Nor was there anything certain or inevitable about the transformation it underwent over the course of the century. The institutional basis for it, however, was in place. Parliament was there and expected to be consulted from time to time. Its members—nobility and gentry—had experience organizing and speaking, writing legislation, and criticizing royal policies. Furthermore, the English had a legal and political tradition based on concepts of liberty to which members of Parliament and their supporters throughout the country could and did appeal in their conflict with the monarchy.

For all intents, France lacked a similarly strong tradition of broad liberties, representation, and bargaining between the monarchy and other national institutions. The Estates General had met from time to time to grant certain revenues to the monarch, but it played no role after the early seventeenth century. It met in 1614, but thereafter the monarchy was able to find other sources of income, and the Estates General was not called again until the eve of the French Revolution in 1789. Consequently, whatever political forces might have wished to oppose or limit the monarchy lacked both an institutional base from which to operate and a tradition of meetings during which the necessary political skills might have been developed.

Finally, personalities played an important role. During the first half of the century, France profited from the guidance of two of its most able statesmen, Cardinals Richelieu and Mazarin. Mazarin trained Louis XIV to be a hard-working, if not always wise, monarch. Louis drew strong and capable ministers about himself. The four Stuart monarchs of England, on the other hand, had trouble simply making people trust them. They did not always keep their word. They acted on whim. They often displayed faulty judgment. In a political situation that demanded compromise, they rarely offered any. They offended significant groups of their subjects unnecessarily. In a nation that saw itself as strongly Protestant, they were suspected, sometimes accurately, of Catholic sympathies. Many of Charles's opponents in Parliament, of course, had flaws of their own, but the nature of the situation focused attention and criticism on the king.

In both England and France, the nobility and large landowners stood at the top of the social hierarchy and sought to protect their privileges and local interests. Important segments of the British nobility and landed classes came to distrust the Stuart monarchs, whom they believed sought to undermine their local political control and social standing. Parliamentary government was the result of the efforts of these English landed classes to protect their concerns and limit the power of the monarchy to interfere with life on the local level. The French nobility under Louis XIV, in contrast, eventually concluded that the best way to secure their own interests was to support his monarchy. He provided them with many forms of patronage, and he protected their tax exemptions, their wealth, and their local social standing.

The divergent developments of England and France in the seventeenth century would have surprised most people in 1600. It was not inevitable that the English monarchy would have to govern through Parliament or that the French monarchy would avoid dealing with national political institutions that could significantly limit its authority. The Stuart kings of England certainly aspired to the autocracy Louis XIV achieved, and some English political philosophers eloquently defended the divine right of kings and absolute rule. At the beginning of the seventeenth century, the English monarchy was strong. Queen Elizabeth, after a reign of almost forty-five years, was much revered. Parliament met only when called to provide financial support to the monarch. France, on the other hand, was emerging from the turmoil of its religious wars. The strife of that conflict had torn the society asunder. The monarchy was relatively weak. Henry IV,

who had become king in 1589, pursued a policy of religious toleration. The French nobles had significant military forces at their disposal and in the middle of the seventeenth century confronted the king with rebellion. These conditions would change dramatically in both nations by the late seventeenth century.

# Constitutional Crisis and Settlement in Stuart England

## James I

In 1603 James VI of Scotland (r. 1603–1625), the son of Mary Stuart, Queen of Scots, without opposition or incident succeeded the childless Elizabeth as James I of England. His was a difficult situation. The elderly queen had been very popular and was totally identified with the nation. James was not well known, would never be popular, and, as a Scot, was an outsider. He inherited not only the crown but also a large royal debt and a fiercely divided church—problems that his politically active subjects expected him to address. The new king strongly advocated the divine right of kings, a subject on which he had written a book—*A Trew Law of Free Monarchies*—in 1598. He expected to rule with a minimum of consultation beyond his own royal court.

James quickly managed to anger many of his new subjects, but he did not wholly alienate them. In this period Parliament met only when the monarch summoned it, which James hoped to do rarely. Its chief business was to grant certain sources of income. The real value of these revenues, however, had been falling during the past half century, limiting their importance and thus the importance of Parliament to the king. To meet his needs, James developed other sources of income, largely by levying—solely on the authority of ill-defined privileges claimed to be attached to the office of king—new custom duties known as *impositions*. These were a version of the older customs duties known as *tonnage* and *poundage*. Members of Parliament resented these independent efforts to raise revenues as an affront to their authority over the royal purse, but they did not seek a serious confrontation. Rather, throughout James's reign they wrangled and negotiated behind the scenes.

The religious problem also festered under James. Puritans within the Church of England had hoped

This elegant painting portrays a very quiet London of the mid-1630s. During the next sixty years it would suffer wrenching political turmoil and the devastation of a great fire. [Yale Center for British Art]

that James's experience with the Scottish Presbyterian church and his own Protestant upbringing would incline him to favor their efforts to further the reformation of the English church. Since the days of Elizabeth, they had sought to eliminate elaborate religious ceremonies and replace the hierarchical episcopal system of church governance with a more representative Presbyterian form like that of the Calvinist churches on the Continent.

In January 1604, the Puritans had their first direct dealing with the new king. James responded in that month to a statement of Puritan grievances, the so-called Millenary Petition, at a special religious conference at Hampton Court. The political implications of the demands in this petition concerned him, and their tone offended him. To the dismay of the Puritans, he firmly declared his intention to maintain and even enhance the Anglican episcopacy. "A Scottish presbytery," he snorted, "agreeth as well with monarchy as God and the devil. No bishops, no king." James was not simply being arbitrary. Elizabeth also had not accommodated the Puritan demands. To have done so would have created strife within the Church of England.

Both sides left the conference with their suspicions of one another largely confirmed. The Hampton Court conference did, however, sow one fruitful seed. A commission was appointed to render a new translation of the Bible. That mission was fulfilled in 1611 with the publication of the eloquent Authorized, or King James, Version.

James also offended the Puritans with his opposition to their narrow view of human life and social activities. The Puritans believed that Sunday should be a day taken up largely with religious observances and little leisure or recreation. James believed recreation and sports were innocent activities and good for his people. He also believed Puritan narrowness discouraged Roman Catholics from converting to the Church of England. Consequently, in 1618 he issued the *Book of Sports*, which permitted games on Sunday for people who attended Church of England services. The clergy refused to read his order from the pulpit, and he had to rescind it.

It was during James's reign that some religious dissenters began to leave England. In 1620 Puritan separatists founded Plymouth Colony in Cape Cod Bay in North America, preferring flight from England to Anglican conformity. Later in the 1620s, a larger, better financed group of Puritans left England to found the Massachusetts Bay Colony. In each case, the colonists believed that reformation

# King James I Defends Popular Recreation Against the Puritans

*The English Puritans believed in strict observance of the Sabbath, disapproving any sports, games, or general social conviviality on Sunday. James I thought these strictures prevented many Roman Catholics from joining the Church of England. In 1618 James ordered the clergy of the Church of England to read the* Book of Sports *from their pulpits. In this declaration, he permitted people to engage in certain sports and games after church services. His hope was to allow innocent recreations on Sunday while encouraging people to attend the Church of England. Despite the king's good intentions, the order offended the Puritans. The clergy resisted his order and he had to withdraw it.*

✦ *What motives of state might have led James I to issue this declaration? How does he attempt to make it favorable to the Church of England? Why might so many clergy have refused to read this statement to their congregations?*

With our own ears we heard the general complaint of our people, that they were barred from all lawful recreation and exercise upon the Sunday's afternoon, after the ending of all divine service, which cannot but produce two evils: the one the hindering of the conversion of many [Roman Catholic subjects], whom their priests will take occasion hereby to vex, persuading them that no honest mirth or recreation is lawful or tolerable in our religion, which cannot but breed a great discontentment in our people's hearts, especially as such as are peradventure upon the point of turning [to the Church of England]: the other inconvenience is, that this prohibition barreth the common and meaner sort of people from using such exercises as may make their bodies more able for war, when we or our successors shall have occasion to use them; and in place thereof sets up filthy tipplings and drunkenness, and breeds a number of idle and discontented speeches in their ale-houses. For when shall the common people have leave to exercise, if not upon the Sundays and holy days, seeing they must apply their labor and win their living in all working days? . . .

[A]s for our good people's lawful recreation, our pleasure likewise is, that after the end of divine service our good people be not disturbed, . . . or discouraged from any lawful recreation, such as dancing, either men or women; archery for men, leaping, vaulting, or any other such harmless recreation, or from having of Hay-games, Whitsun-ales, and Morris-dances; and the setting up of Maypoles and other sports therewith used; . . . but withal we do here account still as prohibited all unlawful games to be used upon Sundays only, as bear and bull-baitings . . . and at all times in the meaner sort of people by law prohibited, bowling.

And likewise we bar from this benefit and liberty all such known as recusants [Roman Catholics], either men or women, as will abstain from coming to church or divine service, being therefore unworthy of any lawful recreation after the said service, that will not first come to the church and serve God; prohibiting in like sort the said recreations to any that, though [they] conform in religion [i.e.; members of the Church of England], are not present in the church at the service of God, before their going to the said recreations.

*Henry Bettenson, ed.,* Documents of the Christian Church, *2nd ed. (London: Oxford University Press, 1963), pp. 400–403.*

had not gone far enough in England and that only in America could they worship freely and organize a truly reformed church.

Although James inherited a difficult situation, he also created special problems for himself. His court became a center of scandal and corruption. He governed by favorites, the most influential of whom was the duke of Buckingham, whom rumor made the king's homosexual lover. Buckingham controlled royal patronage and openly sold peerages and titles to the highest bidders—a practice that angered the nobility because it cheapened their rank. There had always been court favorites, but never before had a single person so controlled access to the monarch.

James's foreign policy also roused opposition. He regarded himself as a peacemaker. Peace reduced pressures on royal revenues and the need for larger debts. The less his demands for money, the less the king had to depend on the goodwill of Parliament. In 1604 he concluded a much-needed peace with Spain, England's chief adversary during the second half of the sixteenth century. His subjects viewed this peace as a sign of pro-Catholic sentiment. James further increased suspicions when he tried unsuccessfully to relax the penal laws against Catholics. The English had not forgotten the brutal reign of Mary Tudor and the acts of treason by Catholics during Elizabeth's reign. In 1618 James hesitated, not unwisely, to rush English troops to the aid of Protestants in Germany at the outbreak of the Thirty Years' War. This hesitation caused some to question his loyalty to the Anglican Church. These suspicions increased when he tried to arrange a marriage between his son Charles and the Spanish *Infanta* (the daughter of the king of Spain). In the king's last years, as his health failed and the reins of government passed increasingly to his son Charles and to Buckingham, parliamentary opposition and Protestant sentiment combined to undo his pro-Spanish foreign policy. In 1624, shortly before James's death, England entered a continental war against Spain largely in response to the pressures of members of Parliament.

## Charles I

Parliament had favored the war with Spain but would not adequately finance it because its members distrusted Buckingham. Unable to gain adequate funds from Parliament, Charles I (r. 1625–1649), like his father, resorted to extraparliamentary measures. He levied new tariffs and duties

and attempted to collect discontinued taxes. He even subjected the English people to a so-called forced loan (a tax theoretically to be repaid), imprisoning those who refused to pay. The government quartered troops in transit to war zones in private homes. All these actions intruded on life at the local level and challenged the power of the local nobles and landowners to control their districts.

When Parliament met in 1628, its members were furious. Taxes were being illegally collected for a war that was going badly for England and that now, through royal blundering, involved France as well as Spain. Parliament expressed its displeasure by making the king's request for new funds conditional on his recognition of the Petition of Right. This important declaration of constitutional freedom required that henceforth there should be no forced loans or taxation without the consent of Parliament, that no freeman should be imprisoned without due cause, and that troops should not be billeted in private homes. It was thus an expression of resentment and resistance to the intrusion of the monarchy on the local level. Though Charles agreed to the petition, there was little confidence that he would keep his word.

YEARS OF PERSONAL RULE In August 1628, Charles's chief minister, Buckingham, with whom Parliament had been in open dispute since 1626, was assassinated. His death, while sweet to many, did not resolve the hostility between the king and Parliament. In January 1629, Parliament further underscored its resolve to limit royal prerogative. It declared that religious innovations leading to "popery"—by this it meant Charles's high-church policies—and the levying of taxes without parliamentary consent were acts of treason. Perceiving that things were getting out of hand, Charles promptly dissolved Parliament and did not recall it again until 1640, when war with Scotland forced him to do so.

To conserve his limited resources, Charles made peace with France in 1629 and Spain in 1630. This policy again roused fears among some of his subjects that he was too friendly to Roman Catholic powers. The French and Roman Catholic background of Charles's wife furthered these suspicions. Part of her marriage contract permitted her to hear mass daily at the English court. Charles's attitude toward the Church of England also raised suspicions. He supported a group within the church, known as Arminians, who rejected many Puritan

# Parliament Presents Charles I with the Petition of Right

*After becoming monarch in 1625 Charles I (1625–1649) had imposed unparliamentary taxes, coerced freemen, and quartered troops in transit in private homes. These actions deeply offended Parliament, which in 1628 refused to grant him any funds until he rescinded those practices by recognizing the Petition of Right (June, 1628). The Petition constituted a general catalog of the offenses associated with the exercise of arbitrary royal authority.*

✦ *What limits does the Petition attempt to place on royal taxation? How did the Petition criticize arbitrary arrest? Why was the quartering of soldiers in private homes so offensive?*

[The Lords Spirit and Temporal, and commons in Parliament assembled] do humbly pray your Most Excellent Majesty, that no man hereafter be compelled to make or yield any gift, loan, benevolence, tax, or such like charge, without common consent by Act of parliament; and that none be called to make answer, to take such oath, or to give attendance, or be confined, or otherwise molested or disquieted concerning the same, or for refusal thereof; and that no freeman, in any such manner as in before-mentioned, be imprisoned or detained; and that your Majesty will be pleased to remove the said soldiers and mariners [who have been quartered in private homes], and that your people may not be so burdened in time to come; and that the foresaid commissions for proceeding by martial law, may be revoked and annulled; and that

hereafter no commissions of like nature may issue forth to any person or persons whatsoever, to be executed as aforesaid, lest by colour of them any of your Majesty's subjects be destroyed or put to death, contrary to the laws and franchise of the land

All which they most humble pray of your Most Excellent Majesty, as their rights and liberties according to the laws and statues of this realm.

The King's Reply: The King willeth that right be done according to the laws and customs of the realm; and that the statues be put in due execution, that his subjects may have no cause to complain of any wrong or oppressions, contrary to their just rights and liberties, to the preservation whereof he holds himself as well obliged as of his prerogative.

*Samuel R. Gardiner, ed.,* The Constitutional Documents of the Puritan Revolution *(Oxford: Clarendon Press, 1889), pp. 4–5.*

---

doctrines and favored elaborate, high-church practices. The Puritans were convinced these practices would bring a return to Roman Catholicism.

To allow Charles to rule without renegotiating financial arrangements with Parliament, his chief minister, Thomas Wentworth (after 1640, earl of Stafford), instituted a policy known as *thorough*. This policy imposed strict efficiency and administrative centralization in government. Its goal was absolute royal control of England. Its success depended on the king's ability to operate independently of Parliament, which no law required him to summon.

Charles's ministers exploited every legal fundraising device. They enforced previously neglected laws and extended existing taxes into new areas. For example, starting in 1634, they gradually extended inland to the whole of England a tax called *ship money*, normally levied only on coastal areas to pay for naval protection. A great landowner named John Hampden mounted a legal challenge to the extension of this tax. Although the king prevailed in what was a close legal contest, his victory was costly. It deepened the animosity toward him among the powerful landowners, who would elect and sit in Parliament should he need to summon it.

During these years of personal rule, Charles surrounded himself with an elaborate court and patronized some of the greatest artists of the day. Like his father, he sold noble titles and knighthoods, lessening their value and the social exclusiveness conferred on those who already possessed them. Nobles and great landowners feared that the growth of the court, the king's relentless pursuit of revenue, and the inflation of titles and honors would reduce their local influence and social standing. They also feared that the monarch might actually succeed in governing without ever again calling Parliament into session.

Charles might very well have ruled indefinitely without Parliament had not his religious policies provoked war with Scotland. James I had allowed a wide variety of religious observances in England, Scotland, and Ireland. Charles by contrast hoped to impose religious conformity at least within England and Scotland. William Laud (1573–1645), who was first Charles's religious advisor and, after 1633, archbishop of Canterbury, held a high-church view of Anglicanism. He favored powerful bishops, elaborate liturgy, and personal religious observance and devotion rather than the preaching and listening favored by the Puritans. As a member of the Court of High Commission, Laud had already radicalized the English Puritans by denying them the right to publish and preach. In 1637 Charles and Laud, against the opposition of the English Puritans as well as the Scots, tried to impose on Scotland the English episcopal system and a prayerbook almost identical to the Anglican *Book of Common Prayer*.

The Scots rebelled, and Charles, with insufficient resources for a war, was forced to call Parliament. The members of Parliament opposed his policies almost as much as they wanted to crush the rebellion. Led by John Pym (1584–1643), they refused even to consider funds for war until the king agreed to redress a long list of political and religious grievances. The king, in response, immediately dissolved Parliament—hence its name, the Short Parliament (April–May 1640). When the Presbyterian Scots invaded England and defeated an English army at the Battle of Newburn in the summer of 1640, Charles reconvened Parliament, this time on its terms, for a long and most fateful duration.

THE LONG PARLIAMENT   The landowners and the merchant classes represented by Parliament had resented the king's financial measures and paternalistic rule for some time. The Puritans in Parliament resented his religious policies and deeply distrusted the influence of the Roman Catholic queen. The Long Parliament (1640–1660) thus acted with widespread support and general unanimity when it convened in November 1640.

The House of Commons impeached both the earl of Stafford and Archbishop Laud. Disgraced and convicted by a parliamentary bill of attainder (a judgment of treason entailing loss of civil rights), Stafford was executed in 1641. Laud was imprisoned and also later executed (1645). Parliament abolished the Court of Star Chamber and the Court of High Commission, royal instruments of political and religious *thorough*, respectively. The levying of new taxes without consent of Parliament and the inland extension of ship money now became illegal. Finally, Parliament resolved that no more than three years should elapse between its meetings and that it could not be dissolved without its own consent. Parliament was determined that neither Charles nor any future English king could again govern without consulting it.

Despite its cohesion on these initial actions, Parliament was divided over the precise direction to take on religious reform. Both moderate Puritans (the Presbyterians) and more extreme Puritans (the Independents) wanted the complete abolition of the episcopal system and the *Book of Common Prayer*. The majority Presbyterians sought to reshape England religiously along Calvinist lines, with local congregations subject to higher representative governing bodies (presbyteries). Independents wanted a much more fully decentralized church with every congregation as its own final authority. Finally, many conservatives in both houses of Parliament were determined to preserve the English church in its current form. Their numbers fell dramatically after 1642, however, when many of them left the House of Commons with the outbreak of civil war.

These divisions further intensified in October 1641, when a rebellion erupted in Ireland and Parliament was asked to raise funds for an army to suppress it. Pym and his followers, loudly reminding the House of Commons of the king's past behavior, argued that Charles could not be trusted with an army and that Parliament should become the commander-in-chief of English armed forces. Parliamentary conservatives, on the other hand, were appalled by such a bold departure from tradition.

ERUPTION OF CIVIL WAR   Charles saw the division within Parliament as a chance to reassert his power.

On December 1, 1641, Parliament presented him with the "Grand Remonstrance," a more-than-200-article summary of popular and parliamentary grievances against the crown. In January 1642, he invaded Parliament with his soldiers. He intended to arrest Pym and the other leaders, but they had been forewarned and managed to escape. The king then withdrew from London and began to raise an army. Shocked by his action, a majority of the House of Commons passed the Militia Ordinance, which gave Parliament authority to raise an army of its own. The die was now cast. For the next four years (1642–1646), civil war engulfed England.

Charles assembled his forces at Nottingham, and the war began in August. It was fought over two main issues:

- Would an absolute monarchy or a parliamentary government rule England?
- Would English religion be controlled by the king's bishops and conform to high Anglican practice or adopt a decentralized, Presbyterian system of church governance?

Charles's supporters, known as Cavaliers, were located in the northwestern half of England. The parliamentary opposition, known as Roundheads because of their close-cropped hair, had its stronghold in the southeastern half of the country. Supporters of both sides included nobility, gentry, and townspeople. The chief factor distinguishing them was religion; the Puritans tended to favor Parliament.

## Oliver Cromwell and the Puritan Republic

Two factors led finally to Parliament's victory. The first was an alliance with Scotland consummated in 1643 when John Pym persuaded Parliament to accept the terms of the Solemn League and Covenant, an agreement that committed Parliament, with the Scots, to a Presbyterian system of church government. This policy meant for the Scots that they would never again be confronted with an attempt to impose the English prayerbook on their religious services. The second factor was the reorganization of the parliamentary army under Oliver Cromwell (1599–1658), a middle-aged country squire of iron discipline and strong Independent religious sentiment. Cromwell and his "godly men" favored neither the episcopal system of the king nor the pure Presbyterian system of the Solemn League and Covenant. They were willing to tolerate an

*Oliver Cromwell's New Model Army defeated the royalists in the English Civil War. After the execution of Charles I in 1649, Cromwell dominated the short-lived English republic, conquered Ireland and Scotland, and ruled as Lord Protector from 1653 until his death in 1658. [Historical Pictures/Stock Montage, Inc.]*

established majority church, but only if it also permitted Protestant dissenters to worship outside it.

The allies won the Battle of Marston Moor in 1644, the largest engagement of the war. In June 1645, Cromwell's newly reorganized forces, known as the New Model Army, fighting with disciplined fanaticism, won a decisive victory over the king at Naseby. (See Map 13–1.)

Defeated militarily, Charles tried again to take advantage of divisions within Parliament, this time seeking to win the Presbyterians and the Scots over to the royalist side. But Cromwell and his army firmly foiled him. In December 1648, Colonel Thomas Pride physically barred the Presbyterians, who made up a majority of Parliament, from taking

The English Civil War 1642-1646

- Controlled by the Parliamentarians, Beginning of 1645.
- Controlled by the Royalists, Beginning of 1645.
- Conquered by the Parliamentarians, in 1645.
- ✦ Battle Site

MAP 13–1  THE ENGLISH CIVIL WAR  *This map shows the rapid deterioration of the royalist position in 1645.*

politician. He was increasingly frustrated by what seemed to him to be pettiness and dawdling on the part of Parliament. When in 1653 the House of Commons entertained a motion to disband his expensive army of 50,000, Cromwell responded by marching in and disbanding Parliament. He ruled thereafter as Lord Protector.

This military dictatorship, however, proved no more effective than Charles's rule had been and became just as harsh and hated. Cromwell's great army and foreign adventures inflated his budget to three times that of Charles. Near chaos reigned in many places, and commerce suffered throughout England. Cromwell was as intolerant of Anglicans as Charles had been of Puritans. People deeply resented his Puritan prohibitions of drunkenness, theatergoing, and dancing. Political liberty vanished in the name of religious liberty.

Cromwell's challenge had been to devise a political structure to replace that of monarch and Parliament. He tried various arrangements, none of which worked. He quarreled with the various Parliaments elected while he was Lord Protector. By the time of his death in 1658, most of the English were ready to end the Puritan religious experiment and the republican political experiment and return to their traditional institutions of government. Negotiations between leaders of the army and the exiled Charles II (r. 1660–1685), son of Charles I, led to the restoration of the Stuart monarchy in 1660.

### Charles II and the Restoration of the Monarchy

Charles II returned to England amid great rejoicing. A man of considerable charm and political skill, Charles set a refreshing new tone after eleven years of somber Puritanism. His restoration returned England to the status quo of 1642, with a hereditary monarch once again on the throne, no legal requirement that he summon Parliament regularly, and the Anglican Church, with its bishops and prayerbook, supreme in religion.

The king, however, had secret Catholic sympathies and favored a policy of religious toleration. He wanted to allow all those outside the Church of England, Catholics as well as Puritans, to worship freely so long as they remained loyal to the throne. But in Parliament, even the ultraroyalist Anglicans did not believe patriotism and religion could be separated. Between 1661 and 1665, through a series of laws known as the Clarendon Code, Parliament

their seats. After "Pride's Purge," only a "rump" of fewer than fifty members remained. Though small in numbers, this Independent Rump Parliament did not hesitate to use its power. On January 30, 1649, after a trial by a special court, the Rump Parliament executed Charles as a public criminal and thereafter abolished the monarchy, the House of Lords, and the Anglican Church. What had begun as a civil war had at this point become a revolution.

From 1649 to 1660, England became officially a Puritan republic, although for much of that time it was dominated by Cromwell. During this period, Cromwell's army conquered Ireland and Scotland, creating the single political entity of Great Britain. Cromwell, however, was a military man and no

*The bleeding head of Charles I is exhibited to the crowd after his execution on a cold day in January 1649. The contemporary Dutch artist also professed to see the immediate ascension of Charles's soul to heaven. In fact, many saw the king as a martyr. [DYCK, Sir Anthony van (1599–1641) (after)* The Execution of King Charles I of England, *by Weesop (an eyewitness), 1649. Private Collection. The Bridgeman Art Collection.]*

excluded Roman Catholics, Presbyterians, and Independents from the religious and political life of the nation. These laws imposed penalties for attending non-Anglican worship services, required strict adherence to the *Book of Common Prayer* and the *Thirty-Nine Articles*, and demanded oaths of allegiance to the Church of England from all persons serving in local government.

At the time of the Restoration, England adopted Navigation Acts that required all imports to be carried either in English ships or in ships registered to the country from which the cargo originated. Dutch ships carried cargo from many nations, and such laws struck directly at Dutch dominance in the shipping industry. A series of naval wars between England and Holland ensued. Charles also attempted to tighten his grasp on the rich English colonies in North America and the Caribbean, many of which had been settled and developed by separatists who desired independence from English rule.

Although Parliament strongly supported the monarchy, Charles, following the pattern of his predecessors, required greater revenues than Parliament appropriated. These he obtained in part by increased customs duties. Because England and France were both at war with Holland, he also received aid from France. In 1670 England and France formally allied against the Dutch in the Treaty of Dover. In a secret portion of this treaty, Charles pledged to announce his conversion to Catholicism as soon as conditions in England permitted. In return for this announcement (which was never made), Louis XIV of France promised to pay a substantial subsidy to England.

In an attempt to unite the English people behind the war with Holland, and as a sign of good faith to Louis XIV, Charles issued a Declaration of Indulgence in 1672. This document suspended all laws against Roman Catholics and Protestant nonconformists. But again, the conservative Parliament proved less generous than the king and refused to grant money for the war until Charles rescinded the measure. After he did, Parliament passed the Test Act, which required all officials of the crown, civil and military, to swear an oath against the doctrine of transubstantiation—a requirement that no loyal Roman Catholic could honestly meet.

# A Portrait of Oliver Cromwell

*Oliver Cromwell was one of the most powerful and controversial personalities of seventeenth-century Britain. He became Lord Protector through his command of the army which had first championed the parliamentary cause and later disbanded Parliament. Royalist statesman and historian Edward Hyde, the earl of Clarendon (1609–1674) was an enemy of Cromwell. Yet, his portrait of Cromwell mixed criticism with grudging admiration for the Puritan leader.*

✦ *According to the earl of Clarendon, what were the chief features of Cromwell's personality? What was the character of his methods of governing? How did his position at home and abroad depend upon his military standing?*

He was one of those men whom his enemies cannot condemn without at the same time also praising. For he could never have done half that mischief without great parts of courage and industry and judgment. And he must have had a wonderful understanding of the nature and humours of men and a great dexterity in applying them . . . [to] raise himself to such a height. . . .

When he first appeared in the Parliament, he seemed to have a person in no degree gracious, no ornament of discourse, none of those talents which reconcile the affections of the standers-by; yet as he grew into his place and authority, his parts seemed to be renewed, as if he concealed faculties till he had occasion to use them. . . .

After he was confirmed and invested Protector . . . he consulted with very few . . . nor communicated any enterprise he resolved upon with more than those who were to have principal parts in the execution of it; nor to them sooner than was absolutely necessary. What he once resolved . . . he would not be dissuaded from, nor endure any contradiction. . . .

In all other matters which did not concern . . . his jurisdiction, he seemed to have great reverence for the law. . . . and as he proceeded with . . . indignation and haughtiness with those who were refractory and dared to contend with his greatness, so towards those who complied with his good pleasure, and courted his protection, he used a wonderful civility, generosity, and bounty.

To three nations [England, Ireland, and Scotland], which perfectly hated him, to an entire obedience to all his dictates; to awe and govern those nations by an army that was not devoted to him and wished his ruin; this was an instance of a very prodigious address. But his greatness at home was but a shadow of the glory he had abroad. It was hard to discover which feared him most, France, Spain, or the Netherlands. . . . As they did all sacrifice their honour and their interest to his pleasure, so there is nothing he could have demanded that any of them would have denied him.

James Harvey Robinson, ed., Readings in European History, *vol. 2 (Boston: Atheneum, 1906), pp. 248–250.*

---

Parliament had aimed the Test Act largely at the king's brother, James, duke of York, heir to the throne and a recent, devout convert to Catholicism. In 1678 a notorious liar named Titus Oates swore before a magistrate that Charles's Catholic wife, through her physician, was plotting with Jesuits and Irishmen to kill the king so James could assume the throne. The matter was taken before Parliament, where Oates was believed. In the ensuing hysteria, known as the Popish Plot, several people were tried and executed. Riding the crest of anti-Catholic sentiment and led by the earl of Shaftesbury (1621–1683), opposition members of Parliament, called Whigs, made an impressive but unsuccessful effort to enact a bill excluding James from succession to the throne.

*Charles II (r. 1660–1685) was a person of considerable charm and political skill. Here he is portrayed as the founder of the Royal Society. [Robert Harding Picture Library, London]*

More suspicious than ever of Parliament, Charles II turned again to increased customs duties and the assistance of Louis XIV for extra income. By these means he was able to rule from 1681 to 1685 without recalling Parliament. In these years, Charles suppressed much of his opposition. He drove the earl of Shaftesbury into exile, executed several Whig leaders for treason, and bullied local corporations into electing members of Parliament submissive to the royal will. When Charles died in 1685 (after a deathbed conversion to Catholicism), he left James the prospect of a Parliament filled with royal friends.

### James II and Renewed Fears of a Catholic England

James II (r. 1685–1688) did not know how to make the most of a good thing. He alienated Parliament by insisting on the repeal of the Test Act. When Parliament balked, he dissolved it and proceeded openly to appoint known Catholics to high posi-

tions in both his court and the army. In 1687 he issued a Declaration of Indulgence, which suspended all religious tests and permitted free worship. Local candidates for Parliament who opposed the declaration were removed from their offices by the king's soldiers and were replaced by Catholics. In June 1688, James went so far as to imprison seven Anglican bishops who had refused to publicize his suspension of laws against Catholics. Each of these actions represented a direct royal attack on the local power and authority of nobles, landowners, the church, and other corporate bodies whose members believed they possessed particular legal privileges. James was attacking English liberty and challenging all manner of social privileges and influence.

Under the guise of a policy of enlightened toleration, James was actually seeking to subject all English institutions to the power of the monarchy. His goal was absolutism, and even conservative, loyalist Tories, as the royal supporters were called, could not abide this policy. The English feared, with reason, that James planned to imitate the religious intolerance of Louis XIV, who had, in 1685, revoked the Edict of Nantes (which had protected French Protestants for almost a century) and imposed Catholicism on the entire nation, using his dragoons against those who protested or resisted.

James soon faced united opposition. When his Catholic second wife gave birth to a son and Catholic male heir to the throne on June 20, 1688, opposition turned to action. The English had hoped that James would die without a male heir so the throne would pass to Mary, his Protestant eldest daughter. Mary was the wife of William III of Orange, *stadtholder* of the Netherlands, great-grandson of William the Silent, and the leader of European opposition to Louis XIV's imperial designs. Within days of the birth of James's son, Whig and Tory members of Parliament formed a coalition and invited Orange to invade England to preserve "traditional liberties," that is, the Anglican Church and parliamentary government.

### The "Glorious Revolution"

William of Orange arrived with his army in November 1688 and was received without opposition by the English people. In the face of sure defeat, James fled to France and the protection of Louis XIV. With James gone, Parliament declared the throne vacant and on its own authority in 1689 proclaimed

*William and Mary became the monarchs of England in 1689. Their accession brought England's economic and military resources into the balance against the France of Louis XIV. [Robert Harding Picture Library, London]*

William and Mary the new monarchs, completing the successful bloodless "Glorious Revolution." William and Mary, in turn, recognized a Bill of Rights that limited the powers of the monarchy and guaranteed the civil liberties of the English privileged classes. Henceforth, England's monarchs would be subject to law and would rule by the consent of Parliament, which was to be called into session every three years. The Bill of Rights also pointedly prohibited Roman Catholics from occupying the English throne. The Toleration Act of 1689 permitted worship by all Protestants and outlawed Roman Catholics and anti-Trinitarians (those who denied the Christian doctrine of the Trinity).

The measure closing this century of strife was the Act of Settlement in 1701. This bill provided for the English crown to go to the Protestant House of Hanover in Germany if none of the children of Queen Anne (r. 1702–1714), the second daughter of James II and the last of the Stuart monarchs, was alive at her death. She outlived all of her children, and so in 1714, the elector of Hanover became King George I of England, the third foreign monarch to occupy the English throne in just over a century.

The Glorious Revolution of 1688 established a framework of government by and for the governed that seemed to bear out the arguments of John Locke's *Second Treatise of Government* (1690). In this work, Locke described the relationship of a king and his people as a bilateral contract. If the king broke that contract, the people, by whom Locke meant the privileged and powerful, had the right to depose him. Locke had written the essay before the revolution, but it came to be read as a justification for it. Although neither in fact nor in theory a "popular" revolution such as would occur in America and France a hundred years later, the Glorious Revolution did establish in England a permanent check on monarchical power by the classes represented in Parliament. At the same time, as will be seen in Chapter 15, in its wake the English government had achieved a secure financial base that would allow it to pursue a century of warfare.

# Rise of Absolute Monarchy in France

Seventeenth-century France, in contrast to England, saw both discontent among the nobility and religious pluralism smothered by the absolute monarchy and the closed Catholic state of Louis XIV (r. 1643–1715). An aggressive ruler who sought glory (*la gloire*) in foreign wars, Louis XIV subjected his subjects at home to "one king, one law, one faith."

Historians once portrayed Louis XIV's reign as a time when the rising central monarchy exerted far-reaching, direct control of the nation at all levels. A somewhat different picture has now emerged. Louis's predecessors and their chief ministers in the half century before his reign had already tried to impose direct rule, arousing discontent and, at mid-century, a rebellion among the nobility. Louis's genius was to make the monarchy the most important and powerful political institution in France while also assuring the nobles and other wealthy groups of their social standing and political and social influence on the local level. Rather than destroying existing local social and political institutions, Louis largely worked through them. Once nobles understood the king would support their local authority, they supported his central royal authority. In other words, the king and the nobles came to recognize that they needed each other. Nevertheless, Louis made it clear to all concerned that he was the senior partner in the relationship.

Louis's royal predecessors laid the institutional foundations for absolute monarchy and also taught him certain practices to avoid. Just as the emergence of a strong Parliament was not inevitable in England, neither was the emergence of an absolute monarchy in France.

## Henry IV and Sully

Coming to the throne after the French wars of religion, Henry IV (r. 1589–1610; see Chapter 12) sought to curtail the privileges of the French nobility. His targets were the provincial governors and the regional *parlements*, especially the powerful *Parlement* of Paris, where a divisive spirit lived on. Here were to be found the old privileged groups, tax-exempt magnates who were largely preoccupied with protecting their self-interests. During the reign of Louis XIII (r. 1610–1643), royal civil servants known as *intendants* subjected these privileged groups to stricter supervision, implementing the king's will with some success in the provinces. An important function of the *intendants* was to prevent abuses from the sale of royal offices that conferred the right to collect revenues, sell licenses, or carry out other remunerative forms of administration. It was usually nobles who acquired these lucrative offices, which was one reason for their ongoing influence.

After decades of religious and civil war, an economy more amenable to governmental regulation emerged during Henry IV's reign. Henry and his finance minister, the duke of Sully (1560–1641), established government monopolies on gunpowder, mines, and salt, preparing the way for the mercantilist policies of Louis XIV and his minister, Colbert. They began a canal system to link the Atlantic and the Mediterranean by joining the Saône, the Loire, the Seine, and the Meuse rivers. They introduced the royal *corvée*, a labor tax that created a national force of drafted workers used to improve roads and the conditions of internal travel. Sully even dreamed of organizing the whole of Europe politically and commercially into a kind of common market.

## Louis XIII and Richelieu

Henry IV was assassinated in 1610, and the following year Sully retired. Because Henry's son and successor, Louis XIII, was only nine years old at his father's death, the task of governing fell to the queen mother, Marie de Médicis (d. 1642). Finding herself in a vulnerable position, she sought security abroad by signing a ten-year mutual defense pact with France's archrival Spain in the Treaty of Fontainebleau (1611). This alliance also arranged for the later marriage of Louis XIII to the Spanish *Infanta* as well as for the marriage of the queen's daughter Elizabeth to the heir to the Spanish throne. The queen sought internal security against pressures from the French nobility by promoting the career of Cardinal Richelieu (1585–1642) as the king's chief adviser. Richelieu, loyal and shrewd, aspired to make France a supreme European power. He, more than any other person, was the secret of French success in the first half of the seventeenth century.

An apparently devout Catholic who also believed that the church best served both his own ambition

*Cardinal Richelieu laid the foundations for the political ascendancy of the French monarchy. [The National Gallery, London]*

and the welfare of France, Richelieu pursued a strongly anti-Habsburg policy. Although he supported the Spanish alliance of the queen and Catholic religious unity within France, he was determined to contain Spanish power and influence, even when that meant aiding and abetting Protestant Europe. It is an indication both of Richelieu's awkward political situation and of his diplomatic agility that he could, in 1631, pledge funds to the Protestant army of Gustavus Adolphus, the king of Sweden, while also insisting that Catholic Bavaria be spared from attack and that Catholics in conquered countries be permitted to practice their religion. One measure of the success of Richelieu's foreign policies can be seen in France's substantial gains in land and political influence when the Treaty of Westphalia (1648) ended hostilities in the Holy Roman Empire (see Chapter 12) and the Treaty of the Pyrenees (1659) sealed peace with Spain.

At home, Richelieu pursued centralizing policies utterly without qualm. Supported by the king, who let his chief minister make most decisions of state,

Richelieu stepped up the campaign against separatist provincial governors and parlements. He made it clear that there was only one law, that of the king, and none could stand above it. When disobedient nobles defied his edicts, they were imprisoned and even executed. Such treatment of the nobility won Richelieu much enmity, even from the queen mother, who, unlike Richelieu, was not always willing to place the larger interests of the state above the pleasure of favorite nobles.

Richelieu started the campaign against the Huguenots that would end in 1685 with Louis XIV's revocation of the Edict of Nantes. Royal armies conquered major Huguenot cities in 1629. The subsequent Peace of Alais (1629) truncated the Edict of Nantes by denying Protestants the right to maintain garrisoned cities, separate political organizations, and independent law courts. Only Richelieu's foreign policy, which involved France in ties with Protestant powers, prevented the earlier implementation of the policy of extreme intolerance that marked the reign of Louis XIV. In the same year that Richelieu rescinded the independent political status of the Huguenots in the Peace of Alais, he also entered negotiations to make Gustavus Adolphus his counterweight to the expansion of Habsburg power within the Holy Roman Empire. By 1635 the Catholic soldiers of France were fighting openly with Swedish Lutherans against the emperor's army in the final phase of the Thirty Years' War (see Chapter 12).

Richelieu employed the arts and the printing press to defend his actions and to indoctrinate the French people in the meaning of *raison d'état* ("reason of state"). This also set a precedent for Louis XIV, who made elaborate use of royal propaganda and spectacle to assert and enhance his power.

## Young Louis XIV and Mazarin

Although Richelieu helped lay the foundations for a much expanded royal authority, his immediate legacy was strong resentment of the monarchy among the French nobility and wealthy commercial groups. The crown's steady multiplication of royal offices, its replacement of local authorities by "state" agents, and its reduction of local sources of patronage undermined the traditional position of the privileged groups in French society. Among those affected were officers of the crown in the law courts and other royal institutions.

*This medallion shows Anne of Austria, the wife of Louis XIII, with her son, Louis XIV. She wisely placed political authority in the hands of Cardinal Mazarin, who prepared Louis to govern France. [Giraudon/Art Resource, N.Y.]*

When Louis XIII died in 1643, Louis XIV was only five years old. During his minority, the queen mother, Anne of Austria (d. 1666), placed the reins of government in the hands of Cardinal Mazarin (1602–1661), who continued Richelieu's determined policy of centralization. During Cardinal Mazarin's regency, long-building resentment produced a backlash. Between 1649 and 1652, in a series of widespread rebellions known as the *Fronde* (after the slingshot used by street boys), segments of the nobility and townspeople sought to reverse the drift toward absolute monarchy and to preserve local autonomy.

The *Parlement* of Paris initiated the revolt in 1649, and the nobility at large soon followed. Urging them on were the influential wives of princes whom Mazarin had imprisoned for treason. The many (the nobility) briefly triumphed over the one (the monarchy) when Mazarin released the imprisoned princes in February 1651. He and Louis XIV thereafter entered a short exile (Mazarin leaving France, Louis fleeing Paris). They returned in October 1652 after an interlude of inefficient and nearly anarchic rule by the nobility. The period of the Fronde convinced most French people that the rule of a strong king was preferable to the rule of many regional powers

with competing and irreconcilable claims. At the same time, Louis XIV and his later advisors learned that heavy-handed policies like those of Richelieu and Mazarin could endanger the monarchy. Louis would ultimately concentrate unprecedented authority in the monarchy, but his means would be more clever than those of his predecessors.

## The Years of Louis's Personal Rule

On the death of Mazarin, Louis XIV assumed personal control of the government. Unlike his royal predecessors, he appointed no single chief minister. One result was to make revolt more difficult. Rebellious nobles would now be challenging the king directly; they could not claim to be resisting only a bad minister.

Mazarin prepared Louis XIV well to rule France. The turbulent events of his youth also made an indelible impression on the king. Louis wrote in his memoirs that the *Fronde* caused him to loathe "kings of straw," and he followed two strategies to assure he would never become one.

First, Louis and his advisors became masters of propaganda and political image creation. Indoctrinated with a strong sense of the grandeur of his crown, Louis never missed an opportunity to impress it on the French people. When the *dauphin* (the heir to the French throne) was born in 1662, for example, Louis appeared for the celebration dressed as a Roman emperor.

Second, Louis made sure the French nobles and other major social groups would benefit from the growth of his own authority. Although he maintained control over foreign affairs and limited the influence of noble institutions on the monarchy, he never tried to abolish those institutions or limit their authority at the local level. The crown, for example, usually conferred informally with regional *parlements* before making rulings that would affect them. Likewise, the crown would rarely enact economic regulations without consulting local opinion. Local *parlements* enjoyed considerable latitude in all regional matters. In an exception to this pattern, Louis did clash with the *Parlement* of Paris, with which he had to register laws, and eventually in 1673 he curtailed much of its power. Many regional *parlements* and other regional authorities, however, had resented the power of that body.

Employing these strategies of propaganda and cooperation, Louis set out to anchor his rule in the principle of the divine right of kings, to domesticate the French nobility by binding them to the court rituals of Versailles, and to crush religious dissent.

### King by Divine Right

Reverence for the king and the personification of government in his person had been nurtured in France since Capetian times. It was a maxim of French law and popular opinion that "the king of France is emperor in his realm" and the king's wish the law of the land. Building on this reverence, Louis XIV defended absolute royal authority on the grounds of divine right.

An important source for Louis's concept of royal authority was his devout tutor, the political theorist Bishop Jacques-Bénigne Bossuet (1627–1704).

## Bishop Bossuet Defends the Divine Right of Kings

*The revolutions of the seventeenth century caused many to fear anarchy far more than tyranny, among them the influential French bishop Jacques-Bénigne Bossuet (1627–1704), the leader of French Catholicism in the second half of the seventeenth century. Louis XIV made him court preacher and tutor to his son, for whom Bossuet wrote a celebrated Universal History. In the following excerpt, Bossuet defends the divine right and absolute power of kings. He depicts kings as embracing in their person the whole body of the state and the will of the people they govern and, as such, as being immune from judgment by any mere mortal.*

✦ *Why might Bossuet have wished to make such extravagant claims for absolute royal power? How might these claims be transferred to any form of government? What are the religious bases for Bossuet's argument? How does this argument for absolute royal authority lead also to the need for a single uniform religion in France?*

The royal power is absolute. . . . The prince need render account of his acts to no one. "I counsel thee to keep the king's commandment, and that in regard of the oath of God. Be not hasty to go out of his sight; stand not on an evil thing for he doeth whatsoever pleaseth him. Where the word of a king is, there is power; and who may say unto him, What doest thou? Whoso keepeth the commandment shall feel no evil thing" [Eccles. 8:2–5]. Without this absolute authority the king could neither do good nor repress evil. It is necessary that his power be such that no one can hope to escape him, and finally, the only protection of individuals against the public authority should be their innocence. This confirms the teaching of St. Paul: "Wilt thou then not be afraid of the power? Do that which is good" [Rom. 13:3].

God is infinite, God is all. The prince, as prince, is not regarded as a private person: he is a public personage, all the state is in him; the will of all the people is included in his. As all perfection and all strength are united in God, so all the power of individuals is united in the person of the prince. What grandeur that a single man should embody so much! . . .

Behold an immense people united in a single person; behold this holy power, paternal and absolute; behold the secret cause which governs the whole body of the state, contained in a single head: you see the image of God in the king, and you have the idea of royal majesty. God is holiness itself, goodness itself, and power itself. In these things lies the majesty of God. In the image of these things lies the majesty of the prince.

*From* Politics Drawn from the Very Words of Holy Scripture, *as quoted in James Harvey Robinson, ed.,* Readings in European History, *vol. 2 (Boston: Athenaeum, 1906), pp. 275–276.*

An ardent champion of the Gallican liberties—the traditional rights of the French king and church in matters of ecclesiastical appointments and taxation—Bossuet defended what he called the "divine right of kings." In support of his claims he cited examples of Old Testament rulers divinely appointed by and answerable only to God. As medieval popes had insisted that only God could judge a pope, so Bossuet argued that none save God could judge the king. Kings may have remained duty-bound to reflect God's will in their rule—in this sense, Bossuet considered them always subject to a higher authority. Yet as God's regents on Earth they could not be bound to the dictates of mere princes and parliaments. Such assumptions lay behind Louis XIV's alleged declaration: *L'état, c'est moi* ("I am the state").

## Versailles

More than any other monarch of the day, Louis XIV used the physical setting of his royal court to exert political control. The palace court at Versailles on the outskirts of Paris became Louis's permanent residence after 1682. It was a true temple to royalty, architecturally designed and artistically decorated to proclaim the glory of the Sun King, as Louis was known. A spectacular estate with magnificent fountains and acres of orange groves, it became home to thousands of the more important nobles, royal officials, and servants. Although its physical maintenance and new additions, which continued throughout Louis's lifetime, consumed over half his annual revenues, Versailles paid significant political dividends.

Because Louis ruled personally, he was the chief source of favors and patronage in France. To emphasize his prominence, he organized life at court around every aspect of his own daily routine. He encouraged nobles to approach him directly, but required them to do so through elaborate court etiquette. Polite and fawning nobles sought his attention, entering their names on waiting lists to be in attendance at especially favored moments. The king's rising and dressing in particular were times of rare intimacy, when nobles could whisper their special requests in his ear. Fortunate nobles held his night candle as they accompanied him to his bed.

Although only five feet four inches in height, the king had presence and was always engaging in conversation. He turned his own sexuality to political

*Louis XIV of France (r. 1643–1715) was the dominant European monarch in the second half of the seventeenth century. The powerful centralized monarchy he created established the prototype for the mode of government later termed* absolutism. *[Giraudon/Art Resource, N.Y.]*

ends and encouraged the belief at court that it was an honor to lie with him. Married to the Spanish *Infanta* Marie Thérèse for political reasons in 1660, he kept many mistresses. After Marie's death in 1683, he settled down in a secret marriage to Madame de Maintenon and apparently became much less the philanderer.

Court life was a carefully planned and successfully executed effort to domesticate and trivialize the nobility. Barred by law from high government positions, the ritual and play kept them busy and dependent so they had little time to plot revolt. Dress codes and high-stakes gambling contributed to their indebtedness and dependency on the king. Members of the court spent the afternoons hunting, riding, or strolling about the lush gardens of Versailles. Evenings were given over to planned entertainment in the large salons (plays, concerts, gambling, and the like), followed by supper at 10:00

p.m. Even the king's retirement was part of the day's spectacle.

Moments near the king were important to most court nobles because they were effectively excluded from the real business of government. Louis ruled through powerful councils that controlled foreign affairs, domestic relations, and economic regulations. Each day after morning mass, which Louis always observed, he spent hours with the chief ministers of these councils, whom he chose from families long in royal service or from among people just beginning to rise in the social structure. Unlike the nobles at court, they had no real or potential power bases in the provinces and depended solely on the king for their standing in both government and society.

Some nobles, of course, did not attend Versailles. Some tended to their local estates and cultivated their local influence. Many others were simply too poor to cut a figure at court. All the nobility understood, however, that Louis, unlike Richelieu and Mazarin, would not threaten their local social standing. Louis supported France's traditional social structure and the social privileges of the nobility.

## Suppression of the Jansenists

Like Richelieu before him, Louis believed that political unity and stability required religious conformity. His first move in this direction, which came early in his personal reign, was against the Roman Catholic Jansenists.

The French crown and the French church had by long tradition—originating with the so-called Gallican liberties in the fourteenth century—jealously guarded their independence from Rome. A great influx of Catholic religious orders, the Jesuits prominent among them, followed Henry IV's conversion to Catholicism. Because of their leadership at the Council of Trent and their close connections

*Versailles, as painted in 1668 by Pierre Patel the Elder (1605–1676). The central building is the hunting lodge built for Louis XII earlier in the century. The wings that appear here were some of Louis XIV's first expansions. [Giraudon/Art Resource, N.Y.]*

to Spain, the Jesuits had been banned from France by Catherine de Médicis. Henry IV, however, lifted the ban in 1603, with certain conditions: He required members of the order to swear an oath of allegiance to the king, he limited the number of new colleges they could open, and he required them to have special licenses for public activities.

The Jesuits were not, however, easily harnessed. They rapidly monopolized the education of the upper classes, and their devout students promoted the religious reforms and doctrine of the Council of Trent throughout France. In a measure of their success, Jesuits served as confessors to Henry IV, Louis XIII, and Louis XIV.

Jansenism arose in the 1630s as part of an intra-Catholic opposition to the theology and the political influence of the Jesuits. Jansenists adhered to the Augustinian tradition that had also spawned many Protestant teachings. Serious and uncompromising, they particularly opposed Jesuit teachings about free will. They believed with Saint Augustine that original sin so corrupted humankind that individuals could do nothing good nor secure their own salvation without divine grace. The namesake of the movement, Cornelius Jansen (d. 1638), was a Flemish theologian and the bishop of Ypres. His posthumously published *Augustinus* (1640) assailed Jesuit teaching on grace and salvation.

A prominent Parisian family, the Arnaulds, became Jansenist allies, adding a political element to the Jansenists' theological objections to the Jesuits. Like many other French people, the Arnaulds believed the Jesuits had been behind the assassination of Henry IV in 1610.

The Arnaulds dominated Jansenist communities at Port-Royal and Paris during the 1640s. In 1643 Antoine Arnauld published a work entitled *On Frequent Communion*, in which he criticized the Jesuits for confessional practices that permitted the easy redress of almost any sin. The Jesuits, in turn, condemned the Jansenists as "crypto-Calvinists."

On May 31, 1653, Pope Innocent X declared heretical five Jansenist theological propositions on grace and salvation. In 1656 the pope banned Jansen's *Augustinus* and the Sorbonne censured Antoine Arnauld. In this same year, Antoine's friend, Blaise Pascal (1623–1662), the most famous of Jansen's followers, published the first of his *Provincial Letters* in defense of Jansenism. A deeply religious man, Pascal tried to reconcile the "reasons of the heart" with growing seventeenth-century reverence for the clear and distinct ideas of the mind

(see Chapter 14). He objected to Jesuit moral theology not only as being lax and shallow, but also because he felt its rationalism failed to do full justice to the religious experience.

In 1660 Louis permitted the papal bull *Ad Sacram Sedem* (1656) to be enforced in France, thus banning Jansenism. He also closed down the Port-Royal community. Thereafter, Jansenists either retracted their views or went underground. Much later, in 1710, Louis lent his support to a still more thorough purge of Jansenist sentiment.

Jansenism had offered the prospect of a Catholicism broad enough to appeal to France's Protestant Huguenots. By suppressing it, Louis also eliminated the best hope for bringing peaceful religious unity to his country.

## Louis's Early Wars

Louis's France was in many ways like much of the rest of contemporary Europe. It had a largely subsistence economy and its cities enjoyed only limited commercial prosperity. It did not, in other words, achieve the economic strength of a modern industrial economy. By the 1660s, however, France was superior to any other European nation in administrative bureaucracy, armed forces, and national unity. Louis had sufficient resources at his disposal to raise and maintain a large and powerful army, and by every external measure he was in a position to dominate Europe. He spent most of the rest of his reign attempting to do so.

GOVERNING FOR WARFARE Three remarkable French ministers established and supported Louis XIV's great war machine: Colbert, Louvois, and Vauban.

Jean-Baptiste Colbert (1619–1683), controller general of finances and Louis's most brilliant minister, created the economic base Louis needed to finance his wars. Colbert worked to centralize the French economy with the same rigor that Louis had worked to centralize the French government. Colbert tried, with modest success, to organize much economic activity under state supervision and, through tariffs, carefully regulated the flow of imports and exports. He sought to create new national industries and organized factories around a tight regimen of work and ideology. He simplified the administrative bureaucracy, abolished unnecessary positions, and reduced the number of tax-exempt nobles. He also increased the *taille*, a direct

*The policies of Jean-Baptiste Colbert (1619–1683) transformed France into a major commercial power. [Erich Lessing/Art Resource, N.Y.]*

tax on the peasantry and a major source of royal income.

This kind of close government control of the economy came to be known as *mercantilism* (a term invented by later critics of the policy). Its aim was to maximize foreign exports and internal reserves of bullion, the gold and silver necessary for making war. Modern scholars argue that Colbert overcontrolled the French economy and cite his "paternalism" as a major reason for the failure of French colonies in the New World. Be that as it may, his policies unquestionably transformed France into a major commercial power, with foreign bases in Africa, in India, and in the Americas, from Canada to the Caribbean.

Louis's army, about a quarter of a million strong, was the creation of Michel Tellier and his more famous son, the marquis of Louvois (1641–1691). Louis's war minister from 1677 to 1691, Louvois was a superior military tactician.

Before Louvois, the French army had been an amalgam of local recruits and mercenaries, uncoordinated groups whose loyalty could not always be counted on. Without regular pay or a way to supply their everyday needs, troops often lived by pillage. Louvois instituted good salaries and improved discipline, making soldiering a respectable profession. He limited military commissions and introduced a system of promotion by merit, bringing dedicated fighters into the ranks. Enlistment was for four years and was restricted to single men. *Intendants*, the king's ubiquitous civil servants, monitored conduct at all levels.

Because it was well disciplined, this new, large, and powerful standing army had considerable public support. Unlike its undisciplined predecessor, the new army no longer threatened the lives, homes, or well-being of the people it was supposed to protect. It thus provides an excellent example of the kinds of benefits many saw in the growing authority of the central monarchy.

What Louvois was to military organization, Sebastien Vauban (1633–1707) was to military engineering. He perfected the arts of fortifying and besieging towns. He also devised the system of trench warfare and developed the concept of defensive frontiers that remained basic to military tactics through World War I.

THE WAR OF DEVOLUTION   Louis's first great foreign adventure was the War of Devolution (1667–1668). It was fought, as would be the later and more devastating War of the Spanish Succession, over Louis's claim to the Spanish Belgian provinces through his wife, Marie Thérèse (1638–1683). According to the terms of the Treaty of the Pyrenees (1659), Marie had renounced her claim to the Spanish succession on condition that a 500,000-crown dowry be paid to Louis within eighteen months of the marriage, a condition that was not met. When Philip IV of Spain died in September 1665, he left all his lands to his sickly four-year-old son by a second marriage, Charles II (r. 1665–1700), and explicitly denied any lands to his daughter. Louis had always harbored the hope of turning the marriage to territorial gain and even before Philip's death had argued that Marie was entitled to a portion of the inheritance.

Louis had a legal argument on his side, which gave the war its name. He maintained that in certain regions of Brabant and Flanders, which were part of the Spanish inheritance, property "devolved" to the children of a first marriage rather than to those of a second. Therefore, Marie had a higher claim than Charles II to these regions. Although

*Throughout the age of the splendor at the court of Louis XIV millions of French peasants lived lives of poverty and hardship, as depicted in this 1640 painting,* Peasant Family *by Louis LeNain. [Erich Lessing/Art Resource, N.Y.]*

such regional laws could hardly bind the king of Spain, Louis was not deterred from sending his armies, under the viscount of Turenne, into Flanders and the Franche-Comté in 1667. In response to this aggression, England, Sweden, and the United Provinces of Holland formed the Triple Alliance, a force sufficient to compel Louis to agree to peace under the terms in the Treaty of Aix-la-Chapelle (1668). According to the treaty, he gained control of certain towns bordering the Spanish Netherlands. (See Map 13–2.)

INVASION OF THE NETHERLANDS   In 1670, with the signing of the Treaty of Dover, England and France became allies against the Dutch. Without the English, the Triple Alliance crumbled. This left Louis in a stronger position to invade the Netherlands for a second time, which he did in 1672. This time he aimed directly at Holland, which had organized the Triple Alliance in 1667, foiling French designs in Flanders. Dutch gloating after the Treaty of Aix-la-Chapelle had mightily offended Louis. Such cartoons as one depicting the sun (Louis was called the "Sun King") eclipsed by a great moon of Dutch cheese distressed him. Without neutralizing Holland, he knew he could never hope to acquire land in the Spanish Netherlands, much less fulfill his dreams of European hegemony.

Louis's successful invasion of the United Provinces in 1672 brought the downfall of Dutch statesmen Jan and Cornelius De Witt. Replacing them was the twenty-seven-year-old Prince of Orange, destined after 1689 to become King William III of England. Orange was the great-grandson of William the Silent, who had repulsed Philip II and dashed Spanish hopes of dominating the Netherlands in the sixteenth century.

Orange, an unpretentious Calvinist, who was in almost every way Louis's opposite, galvanized the seven provinces into a fierce fighting unit. In 1673 he united the Holy Roman Emperor, Spain, Lorraine, and Brandenburg in an alliance against Louis. His enemies now saw the French king as a "Christian Turk," a menace to the whole of western Europe, Catholic and Protestant alike. In the ensuing warfare, both sides experienced gains and losses. Louis lost his ablest generals, Turenne and Condé, in 1675, but a victory by Admiral Duquesne over the Dutch fleet in 1676 gave France control of the Mediterranean. The Peace of Nijmwegen, signed with different parties in successive years (1678, 1679), ended the hostilities of this second war. There were various minor territorial adjustments but no clear victor except the United Netherlands, which retained all of its territory.

## Revocation of the Edict of Nantes

In the decade after his invasion of the Netherlands, Louis made his second major move to assure religious conformity. Following the proclamation of the Edict of Nantes in 1598, relations between the great Catholic majority (nine-tenths of the French population) and the Protestant minority remained hostile. There were about 1.75 million Huguenots in France in the 1660s, but their numbers were declin-

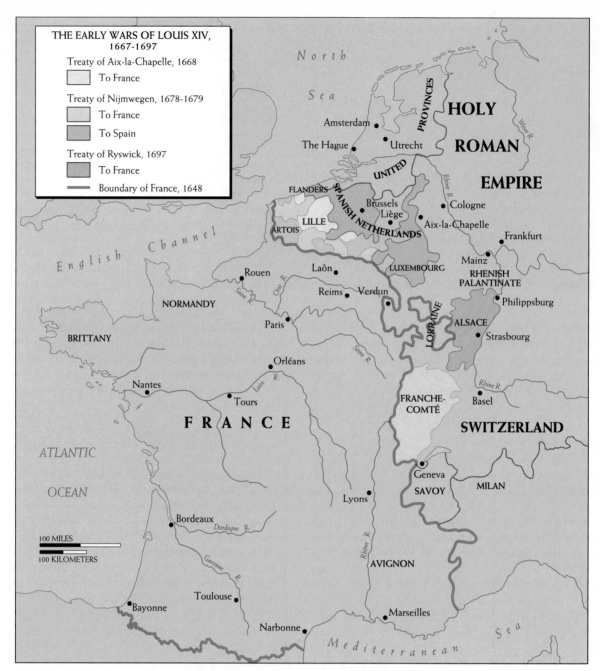

MAP 13–2  THE WARS OF LOUIS XIV  *This map shows the territorial changes result-ing from Louis XIV's first three major wars. The War of the Spanish Succession was yet to come.*

ing in the second half of the seventeenth century. The French Catholic Church had long denounced Calvinists as heretical and treasonous and had supported their persecution as both pious and patriotic.

Following the Peace of Nijmwegen in 1678–1679, which halted for the moment his aggression in Europe, Louis launched a methodical government campaign against the French Huguenots in a determined effort to unify France religiously. He hounded the Huguenots out of public life, banning them from government office and excluding them from such professions as printing and medicine. He

# Louis XIV Revokes the Edict of Nantes

*Believing that a country could not be under one king and one law unless it was also under one religious system, Louis XIV stunned much of Europe in October 1685 by revoking the Edict of Nantes, which had protected the religious freedoms and civil rights of French Protestants since 1598. Compare this document to the one in Chapter 15 in which the elector of Brandenburg welcomes displaced French Protestants into his domains.*

✦ *What specific actions does this declaration order against Protestants? Does it offer any incentives for Protestants to convert to Catholicism? How does this declaration compare with the English Test Act?*

Art. 1. Know that we . . . with our certain knowledge, full power and royal authority, have by this present, perpetual and irrevocable edict, suppressed and revoked the edict of the aforesaid king our grandfather, given at Nantes in the month of April, 1598, in all its extent . . . together with all the concessions made by [this] and other edicts, declarations, and decrees, to the people of the so-called Reformed religion, of whatever nature they be . . . and in consequence we desire . . . that all the temples of the people of the aforesaid so-called Reformed religion situated in our kingdom . . . should be demolished forthwith.

Art. 2. We forbid our subjects of the so-called Reformed religion to assemble any more for public worship of the above-mentioned religion. . . .

Art. 3. We likewise forbid all lords, of whatever rank they may be, to carry out heretical services in houses and fiefs . . . the penalty for . . . the said worship being confiscation of their body and possessions.

Art. 4. We order all ministers of the aforesaid so-called Reformed religion who do not wish to be converted and to embrace the Catholic, Apostolic, and Roman religion, to depart from our kingdom and the lands subject to us within fifteen days from the publication of our present edict . . . on pain of the galleys.

Art. 5. We desire that those among the said [Reformed] ministers who shall be converted [to the Catholic religion] shall continue to enjoy during their life, and their wives shall enjoy after their death as long as they remain widows, the same exemptions from taxation and billeting of soldiers, which they enjoyed while they fulfilled the function of ministers. . . .

Art. 8. With regard to children who shall be born to those of the aforesaid so-called Reformed religion, we desire that they be baptized by their parish priests. We command the fathers and mothers to send them to the churches for that purpose, on penalty of a fine of 500 livres or more if they fail to do so; and afterwards, the children shall be brought up in the Catholic, Apostolic, and Roman religion. . . .

Art. 10. All our subjects of the so-called Reformed religion, with their wives and children, are to be strongly and repeatedly prohibited from leaving our aforesaid kingdom . . . or of taking out . . . their possessions and effects. . . .

The members of the so-called Reformed religion, while awaiting God's pleasure to enlighten them like the others, can live in the towns and districts of our kingdom . . . and continue their occupation there, and enjoy their possessions . . . on condition . . . that they do not make public profession of [their religion].

*S. Z. Ehler and John B. Morrall, ed. and trans.,* Church and State Through the Centuries: A Collection of Historic Documents *(New York: Biblo and Tannen, 1967), pp. 209–213.*

used subsidies and selective taxation to encourage Huguenots to convert to Catholicism. And in 1681 he bullied them by quartering his troops in their towns. In the final stage of the persecution, Louis revoked the Edict of Nantes in October 1685. As a result, Protestant churches and schools were closed, Protestant ministers exiled, nonconverting laity forced to be galley slaves, and Protestant children ceremonially baptized by Catholic priests.

The revocation of the Edict of Nantes was a major blunder. Louis was afterwards viewed in Protestant countries as a new Philip II, intent on a Catholic reconquest of the whole of Europe, who must be resisted at all costs. The revocation prompted the voluntary emigration of more than a quarter million French people, who formed new communities and joined the resistance to France in England, Germany, Holland, and the New World. Thousands of French Huguenots served in the army of Louis's archfoe, William of Orange, later King William III of England. Many of those who remained in France became part of an uncompromising guerilla resistance to the king. Despite the many domestic and foreign liabilities it brought him, Louis, to his death, considered the revocation to be his most pious act, one that placed God in his debt.

## Louis's Later Wars

THE LEAGUE OF AUGSBURG AND THE NINE YEARS' WAR   After the Treaty of Nijmwegen, Louis maintained his army at full strength and restlessly probed beyond his perimeters. In 1681 his forces conquered the free city of Strasbourg, prompting new defensive coalitions to form against him. One of these, the League of Augsburg, created in 1686 to resist French expansion into Germany, had grown by 1689 to include England, Spain, Sweden, the United Provinces, and the electorates of Bavaria, Saxony, and the Palatinate. It also had the support of the Austrian emperor Leopold. Between 1689 and 1697, the league and France battled each other in the Nine Years' War. During the same period, England and France struggled for control of North America in what came to be known as King William's War.

The Nine Years' War ended when stalemate and exhaustion forced both sides to accept an interim settlement. The Peace of Ryswick, signed in September 1697, was a triumph for William of Orange, now William III of England, and Emperor Leopold. It secured Holland's borders and thwarted Louis's expansion into Germany.

WAR OF THE SPANISH SUCCESSION: TREATIES OF UTRECHT AND RASTADT   After Ryswick, Louis, who seemed to thrive on partial success, made still a fourth attempt to realize his grand design to dominate Europe. This time an unforeseen turn of events helped him. On November 1, 1700, Charles II of Spain, known as "the Sufferer" because of his genetic deformities and lingering illnesses, died.

Both Louis and the Austrian emperor Leopold had claims to the Spanish inheritance through their grandsons: Louis through his marriage to Marie Thérèse and Leopold through his marriage to her younger sister, Margaret Thérèse. Although Louis's grandson, Philip of Anjou, had the better claim (because Marie Thérèse was Margaret Thérèse's older sister), Marie Thérèse had renounced her right to the Spanish inheritance in the Treaty of the Pyrenees (1659), and the inheritance was expected to go to Leopold's grandson.

Louis nurtured fears that the Habsburgs would dominate Europe should they gain control of Spain as well as the Holy Roman Empire. Most of the nations of Europe, however, feared France more than the Habsburgs and determined to prevent a union of the French and Spanish crowns. As a result, before Charles II's death, negotiations began among the nations involved to partition his inheritance in a way that would preserve the existing balance of power.

Charles II upset these negotiations by leaving his entire inheritance to Philip of Anjou, Louis's grandson. At a stroke, Spain and its possessions had fallen to France. Although Louis had been party to the partition agreements that preceded Charles's death, he now saw God's hand in Charles's will; he chose to enforce its terms over those of the partition agreement. Philip of Anjou moved to Madrid and became Philip V of Spain. Louis, in what was interpreted as naked French aggression, sent his troops again into Flanders, this time to remove Dutch soldiers from Spanish territory in the name of the new French king of Spain. Louis also declared Spanish America open to French ships.

In September 1701, England, Holland, and the Holy Roman Empire formed the Grand Alliance to counter Louis. They sought to preserve the balance of power by once and for all securing Flanders as a neutral barrier between Holland and France and by gaining for the emperor his fair share of the Spanish inheritance. After the formation of the Grand Alliance, Louis increased the stakes of battle by recognizing the claim of James Edward, the son of James II of England, to the English throne.

In 1701 the thirteen-year War of the Spanish Succession (1701–1714) began, and once again total war enveloped western Europe. France, for the first time, went to war with inadequate finances, a poorly equipped army, and mediocre military leadership. The English, in contrast, had advanced weaponry (flintlock rifles, paper cartridges, and ring bayonets) and superior tactics (thin, maneuverable troop columns rather than the traditional deep ones). John Churchill, the duke of Marlborough, who succeeded William of Orange as military leader of the alliance, bested Louis's soldiers in every major engagement. He routed French armies at Blenheim in August 1704 and on the plain of Ramillies in 1706—two decisive battles of the war. In 1708–1709 famine, revolts, and uncollectible taxes tore France apart internally. Despair pervaded the French court. Louis wondered aloud how God could forsake one who had done so much for him.

Though ready to make peace in 1709, Louis could not bring himself to accept the stiff terms of the alliance. These included a demand that he transfer all Spanish possessions to the emperor's grandson Charles and remove Philip V from Madrid. Hostilities continued, and a clash of forces at Malplaquet (September 1709) left carnage on the battlefield unsurpassed until modern times.

France finally signed an armistice with England at Utrecht in July 1713 and concluded hostilities with Holland and the emperor in the Treaty of Rastadt in March 1714. This agreement confirmed Philip V as king of Spain but gave Gibraltar to England, making it a Mediterranean power. (See Map 13-3.) It also won Louis's recognition of the right of the House of Hanover to accede to the English throne.

Politically, the eighteenth century would belong to England as the sixteenth had belonged to Spain and the seventeenth to France. Although France remained intact and strong, the realization of Louis XIV's territorial ambitions had to await the rise of Napoleon Bonaparte. On his deathbed on September 1, 1715, Louis fittingly warned his heir, the *dauphin*, not to imitate his love of buildings and his liking for war.

### Louis XIV's Legacy

Louis XIV left France a mixed legacy. His wars had brought widespread death and destruction, and his

| The Reign of Louis XIV (1643–1715) | |
|---|---|
| 1643 | Louis ascends the French throne at the age of 5 |
| 1643–1661 | Cardinal Mazarin directs the French government |
| 1648 | Peace of Westphalia |
| 1649–1652 | The *Fronde* revolt |
| 1653 | The pope declares Jansenism a heresy |
| 1659 | Treaty of Pyrénees between France and Spain |
| 1660 | Papal ban on Jansenists enforced in France |
| 1661 | Louis commences personal rule |
| 1667–1668 | War of Devolution |
| 1670 | Secret Treaty of Dover between France and Great Britain |
| 1672–1679 | French war against the Netherlands |
| 1685 | Louis revokes the Edict of Nantes |
| 1689–1697 | War of the League of Augsburg |
| 1701 | Outbreak of the War of the Spanish Succession |
| 1713 | Treaty of Utrecht between France and Great Britain |
| 1714 | Treaty of Rastatt between France and Spain |
| 1715 | Death of Louis XIV |

armies had shelled civilian populations. Although the monarchy was still strong at his death, it was more feared than admired. Its finances were insecure and dependent on debt. Continued warfare in the eighteenth century would weaken its finances further, leading eventually to the crises that sparked the French Revolution. Louis's policies of centralization would later make it difficult for France to develop effective institutions of representation and self-government. The aristocracy, after its years of domestication at Versailles, would have difficulty providing the nation with effective leaders and ministers.

Yet Louis's reign also had a positive side. He may have loved war too much, but he also built the magnificent palace of Versailles and brought a new majesty to France. He skillfully manipulated the fractious French aristocracy and bourgeoisie, he elevated skilled and trustworthy ministers, councillors, and *intendants*, and he created a new French Empire by expanding trade into Asia and colonizing North America.

Louis's rule was not so absolute as to exert oppressive control over the daily lives of his sub-

MAP 13–3  EUROPE IN 1714    *The War of the Spanish Succession ended in the year before the death of the aged Louis XIV. By then France and Spain, although not united, were both ruled by members of the Bourbon family, and Spain had lost its non-Iberian possessions.*

jects as in the police states of the nineteenth and twentieth centuries. His absolutism functioned primarily in the classic areas of European state action—the making of war and peace, the regulation of religion, and the oversight of economic activity. Even at the height of his power, local institutions, some controlled by townspeople and others by nobles, continued to exert administrative authority at the local level. The king and his min-

isters supported the high status and tax exemptions of these local elites. But in contrast to the Stuart kings of England, Louis firmly prevented them from capturing or significantly limiting his authority on the national level. Not until the French monarchy was so weakened by financial crisis at the end of the eighteenth century would it succumb to demands for a more representative form of government.

*The foreign policy of Louis XIV brought warfare to all of Europe. This eighteenth-century painting by Benjamin West memorializes the British victory over France in the battle of La Hogue in 1692. [National Gallery of Art]*

✦

In the seventeenth century, England and France developed divergent forms of government. England became the model for parliamentary monarchy, France for absolute monarchy.

The politically active English elite—the nobility along with the wealthy landowning and commercial classes—struggled throughout the century to limit the authority of rulers—including Oliver Cromwell as well as the Stuart monarchs—over local interests. In the process, they articulated a political philosophy that stressed the need to prevent the central concentration of political power. The Bill of Rights of 1689 and the Toleration Act following the Glorious Revolution of William and Mary seemed to achieve the goals of this philoso-

phy. These acts brought neither democracy nor full religious freedom in a modern sense; the Bill of Rights protected only the privileged, not all the English people, and the Toleration Act outlawed Catholics and Unitarians. Still, they firmly established representative government in England and extended legal recognition, at least in principle, to a variety of religious beliefs. The Bill of Rights required the monarch to call Parliament regularly.

In France, by contrast, the monarchy remained supreme. Although the king had to mollify privileged local elites, by considering the interests of the nobility and the traditional rights of towns and regions, France had no national institution like Parliament through which he had to govern. Louis XIV was able, on his own authority, to fund the largest army in Europe. He could and did crush *religious dissent. His own propaganda and the fear of his adversaries may have led to an exaggerated view of Louis's power, but his reign nonetheless provided a model of effective centralized power that later continental rulers tried to follow.*

# Review Questions

1. By the end of the seventeenth century, England and France had different systems of government with different religious policies. What were the main differences? Similarities? Why did each nation develop as it did? How much did the particular personalities of the rulers of each nation determine the manner in which their political institutions emerged?

2. Why did the English king and Parliament come into conflict in the 1640s? What were the most important issues behind the war between them and who bears more responsibility for it? What role did religion play in the conflict?

3. What was the Glorious Revolution and why did it take place? What were James II's mistakes and what were the issues involved in the events of 1688? What kind of settlement emerged from the revolution? How did England in 1700 differ from England in 1600?

4. Discuss the development of absolutism in France. What policies of Henry IV and Louis XIII were essential in creating the absolute monarchy?

5. What were the chief ways Louis XIV consolidated his monarchy? What limits were there on his authority? What was Louis's religious policy?

6. Assess the success of Louis XIV's foreign policy. What were his aims? Were they realistic? To what extent did he attain them?

# Suggested Readings

M. ASHLEY, *England in the Seventeenth Century* (1980). Readable survey.

ROBERT ASHTON, *Counter-Revolution: The Second Civil War and Its Origins, 1646–1648* (1995). A major examination of the resumption of civil conflict in England that ended with the abolition of the monarchy, House of Lords, and established church.

W. BEIK, *Absolutism and Society in Seventeenth-Century France* (1985). An important study that questions the extent of royal power.

J. BERGIN, *Cardinal Richelieu: Power and the Pursuit of Wealth* (1985). Considers the role of finance and private wealth in the rise of Richelieu.

R. BONNEY, *Political Change in France Under Richelieu and Mazarin, 1624–1661* (1978). A careful examination of how these two cardinals lay the foundation for Louis XIV's absolutism.

R. BRIGGS, *Early Modern France, 1560–1715* (1977). A useful brief survey.

G. BURGESS, *Absolute Monarchy and the Stuart Constitution* (1996). A new study that challenges many of the traditional interpretive categories.

P. BURKE, *The Fabrication of Louis XIV* (1992). Examines the manner in which the public image of Louis XIV was forged in art.

P. COLLINSON, *The Religion of Protestants: The Church in English Society 1559–1625* (1982). The best introduction to Puritanism.

B. COWARD, *Cromwell* (1991). A brief biography.

R. S. DUNN, *The Age of Religious Wars, 1559–1715* (1979). Lucid survey setting the conflicting political systems of France and England in larger perspective.

D. HIRST, *Authority and Conflict: England 1603–1658* (1986). Scholarly survey integrating history and historiography.

R. HUTTON, *Charles the Second, King of England, Scotland, and Ireland* (1989). Replaces all previous biographies.

P. LAKE, *Anglicans and Puritans: Presbyterianism and English Conformist Thought from Whitgift to Hooker* (1988). An important study of religious thought.

R. LOCKYER, *Buckingham* (1984). Biography of the English court favorite.

R. METTAM, *Power and Faction in Louis XIV's France* (1988). Examines the political intricacies of the reign and suggests the limits to absolutism.

G. PARKER, *Europe in Crisis 1598–1648* (1979). Examines the entire scope of early seventeenth-century Europe.

O. RANUM, *The Fronde: A French Revolution, 1648–1652* (1993). The best recent work on the subject.

D. L. RUBIN (ED.), *The Sun King: The Ascendancy of French Culture During the Reign of Louis XIV* (1992). A collection of useful essays.

C. RUSSELL, *The Fall of the English Monarchies, 1637–1642* (1991). A major revisionist account, which should be read with Stone's book.

K. SHARPE, *The Personal Rule of Charles I* (1992). A major narrative work.

J. SPUR, *The Restoration Church of England, 1646–1689* (1992). Now the standard work on this subject.

L. STONE, *The Causes of the English Revolution 1529–1642* (1972). Brief survey stressing social history and ruminating over historians and historical method.

V. TAPIÉ, *France in the Age of Louis XIII and Richelieu* (1984). A narrative account.

G. Treasure, *Mazarin: The Crisis of Absolutism in France* (1996). An examination not only of Mazarin, but also of the larger national and international background.

N. Tyacke, *Anti-Calvinists: The Rise of English Armini-anism c. 1590–1640* (1987). The most important recent study of Archbishop Laud's policies and his predecessors.

D. Underdown, *Fire from Heaven: Life in an English Town in the Seventeenth Century* (1992). A lively account of the manner in which a single English town experienced the religious and political events of the century.

M. Walzer, *The Revolution of the Saints: A Study in the Origins of Radical Politics* (1965). Effort to relate ideas and politics that depicts Puritans as true revolutionaries.

J. B. Wolf, *Louis XIV* (1968). Very detailed political biography.

*Nicolaus Copernicus's revolutionary view of the universe, with the sun in the center, is summarized in this diagram from his* De Revolutionibus Orbium Coelestium *(On the Revolutions of Heavenly Bodies), published in 1543. [Library of the Collegium Maius. Collegium Maius, Cracow, Poland. Erich Lessing/Art Resource]*

# New Directions in Thought and Culture in the Sixteenth and Seventeenth Centuries

## K E Y   T O P I C S

- The astronomical theories of Copernicus, Brahe, Kepler, Galileo, and Newton and the emergence of the scientific worldview
- Witchcraft and witch hunts
- The literary imagination in a changing world
- The philosophical foundations of modern thought

The sixteenth and seventeenth centuries witnessed a sweeping change in the scientific view of the universe. An Earth-centered picture gave way to one in which the Earth was only another planet orbiting about the sun. The sun itself became one of millions of stars. This transformation of humankind's perception of its place in the larger scheme of things led to a profound rethinking of moral and religious matters as well as of scientific theory. Faith and reason needed new modes of reconciliation, as did faith and science. The new ideas and methods of science challenged modes of thought associated with medieval times and Scholasticism. The new outlook on physical nature touched the literary imagination, and religious thinkers had to reconsider many traditional ideas. Philosophers applied rational, scientific thought to the realm of politics. Some supported absolutism; others, parliamentary systems.

The new scientific concepts and the methods of their construction were so impressive that they set the standard for assessing the validity of knowledge in the Western world thereafter. Perhaps no single intellectual development proved to be more significant for the future of European and Western civilization.

Side by side with enlightenment and science, however, came a new wave of superstition and persecution. The

*changing world of religion and politics also created profound fear and anxiety among both the simple and the learned, resulting in Europe's worst witch hunts.*

# The Scientific Revolution

The process by which the new view of the universe and of scientific knowledge came to be established is normally termed the *Scientific Revolution*. This metaphor must be used carefully, however. The word *revolution* normally denotes rapid political change involving large numbers of people. The Scientific Revolution was not rapid, nor did it involve more than a few hundred human beings. It was a complex movement with many false starts and many brilliant people with wrong as well as useful ideas. It took place in the studies and the crude laboratories of thinkers in Poland, Italy, Bohemia, France, and Great Britain.

The Scientific Revolution stemmed from two major tendencies. The first, illustrated by Nicolaus Copernicus, was the imposition of important small changes on existing models of thought. The second, embodied by Francis Bacon, was the desire to pose new kinds of questions and to use new methods of investigation. In both cases, scientific thought changed current and traditional opinions in other fields.

## Nicolaus Copernicus: Rejection of an Earth-Centered Universe

Nicolaus Copernicus (1473–1543) was a Polish astronomer who enjoyed a high reputation throughout his life. He had been educated in Italy and corresponded with other astronomers throughout Europe. He had not been known, however, for strikingly original or unorthodox thought. In 1543, the year of his death, Copernicus published *On the Revolutions of the Heavenly Spheres*. Because he died near the time of publication, the fortunes of his work are not the story of one person's crusade for progressive science. Copernicus's book was "a revolution-making rather than a revolutionary text."[1] What Copernicus did was to provide an intellectual springboard for a complete criticism of

[1]Thomas S. Kuhn, *The Copernican Revolution: Planetary Astronomy in the Development of Western Thought* (New York: Vintage, 1959), p. 135.

the then-dominant view of the position of the Earth in the universe.

THE PTOLEMAIC SYSTEM   At the time of Copernicus, the standard explanation of the place of the Earth in the heavens was that associated with Ptolemy and his work entitled the *Almagest* (150 C.E.). Commentators on the original work had developed several alternative Ptolemaic systems over the centuries. Most of these assumed that the Earth was the center of the universe. Above the Earth lay a series of crystalline spheres, one of which contained the moon, another the sun, and still others the planets and the stars. This was the astronomy found in such works as Dante's *Divine Comedy*. At the outer regions of these spheres lay the realm of God and the angels. Aristotelian physics provided the intellectual underpinnings of the Ptolemaic systems. The Earth had to be the center because of its heaviness. The stars and the other heavenly bodies had to be enclosed in the crystalline spheres so that they could move. Nothing could move unless something was actually moving it. The state of rest was natural; motion was the condition that required explanation.

Numerous problems were associated with this system, and these had long been recognized. The most important was the observed motions of the planets, which included noncircular patterns around the Earth. At certain times the planets actually appeared to be going backward. The Ptolemaic systems explained these strange motions primarily through epicycles. An epicycle is an orbit upon an orbit, like a spinning jewel on a ring. The planets were said to make a second revolution in an orbit tangent to their primary orbit around the Earth. Other intellectual but nonobservational difficulties related to the immense speed at which the spheres had to move around the Earth. To say the least, the Ptolemaic systems were cluttered. They were effective, however, as long as one assumed Aristotelian physics and the Christian belief that the Earth rested at the center of the created universe.

COPERNICUS'S UNIVERSE   Copernicus's *On the Revolutions of the Heavenly Spheres* challenged this picture in the most conservative manner possible. It suggested that if the Earth were assumed to move about the sun in a circle, many of the difficulties with the Ptolemaic systems would disappear or become simpler. Although not wholly eliminated, the number of epicycles would be somewhat fewer. The motive behind this shift away from the Earth-centered universe was to find a solution to the problems of planetary motion. By allowing the Earth to move around the sun, Copernicus was able to construct a more mathematically elegant basis for astronomy. He had been discontented with the traditional system because it was mathematically clumsy and inconsistent. The primary appeal of his new system was its mathematical aesthetics. With

---

# Copernicus Ascribes Movement to the Earth

*Copernicus published* De Revolutionibus Orbium Caelestium *(On the Revolutions of the Heavenly Spheres) in 1543. In his preface, addressed to Pope Paul III, he explained what had led him to think that the Earth moved around the sun and what he thought were some of the scientific consequences of the new theory.*

✦ *How does Copernicus justify his argument to the pope? How important was historical precedent and tradition to the pope? Might Copernicus have thought that the pope would be especially susceptible to such argument, even though what Copernicus proposed (the movement of the Earth) contradicted the Bible?*

I may well presume, most Holy Father, that certain people, as soon as they hear that in this book about the Revolutions of the Spheres of the Universe I ascribe movement to the Earthly globe, will cry out that, holding such views, I should at once be hissed off the stage. . . .

So I should like your Holiness to know that I was induced to think of a method of computing the motions of the spheres by nothing else than the knowledge that the Mathematicians [who had previously considered the problem] are inconsistent in these investigations.

For, first, the mathematicians are so unsure of the movements of the Sun and Moon that they cannot even explain or observe the constant length of the seasonal year. Secondly, in determining the motions of these and of the other five planets, they use neither the same principles and hypotheses nor the same demonstrations of the apparent motions and revolutions. . . . Nor have they been able thereby to discern or deduce the principal thing—namely the shape of the Universe and the unchangeable symmetry of its parts. . . .

I pondered long upon this uncertainty of mathematical tradition in establishing the motions of the system of the spheres. At last I began to chafe

that philosophers could by no means agree on any one certain theory of the mechanism of the Universe, wrought for us by a supremely good and orderly Creator. . . . I therefore took pains to read again the works of all the philosophers on whom I could lay hand to seek out whether any of them had ever supposed that the motions of the spheres were other than those demanded by the [Ptolemaic] mathematical schools. I found first in Cicero that Hicetas [of Syracuse, fifth century B.C.] had realized that the Earth moved. Afterwards I found in Plutarch that certain others had held the like opinion. . . .

Thus assuming motions, which in my work I ascribe to the Earth, by long and frequent observations I have at last discovered that, if the motions of the rest of the planets be brought into relation with the circulation of the Earth and be reckoned in proportion to the circles of each planet, not only do their phenomena presently ensue, but the orders and magnitudes of all stars and spheres, nay the heavens themselves, become so bound together that nothing in any part thereof could be moved from its place without producing confusion of all the other parts of the Universe as a whole.

*As quoted in Thomas S. Kuhn,* The Copernican Revolution: Planetary Astronomy in the Development of Western Thought *(New York: Vintage Books, 1959), pp. 137–139, 141–142.*

---

the sun at the center of the universe, mathematical astronomy would make more sense. A change in the conception of the position of the Earth meant that the planets were actually moving in circular orbits and only seemed to be doing otherwise because of the position of the observers on Earth.

Except for this modification in the position of the Earth, Copernicus retained Ptolemaic ideas in most of the other parts of his book. The path of the planets remained circular. Genuine epicycles still existed in the heavens. His system was no more accurate than the existing ones for predicting the location of the planets. He had used no new evidence. The major impact of his work was to provide another way of confronting some of the difficulties inherent in Ptolemaic astronomy. It did not immediately replace the old astronomy, but it allowed other people who were also discontented with the Ptolemaic systems to think in new directions.

Copernicus's concern about the relationship between mathematics and the observed behavior of planets is an example of the single most important factor in the developing new science: the fusion of mathematics with empirical data and observation. Mathematics provided the model to which the new scientific thought would conform; new empirical evidence helped persuade the learned public of its validity.

## Tycho Brahe and Johannes Kepler: New Scientific Observations

The next major step toward the conception of a sun-centered system was taken by Tycho Brahe (1546–1601). He actually spent most of his life opposing Copernicus and advocating a different kind of Earth-centered system. He suggested that the moon and the sun revolved around the Earth and that the other planets revolved around the sun. In attacking Copernicus, however, he gave the latter's ideas more publicity. More important, this Danish astronomer's major weapon against Copernican astronomy was a series of new naked-eye astronomical observations. Brahe constructed the most accurate tables of observations that had been drawn up for centuries.

When Brahe died, these tables came into the possession of Johannes Kepler (1571–1630), a German astronomer. Kepler was a convinced Copernican, but his reasons for taking that position were not scientific. Kepler was deeply influenced by Renais-

Tycho Brahe in the Uranienburg observatory on the Danish island of Hven (1587). Brahe made the most important observations of the stars since antiquity. Kepler used his data to solve the problem of planetary motion in a way that supported Copernicus's sun-centered view of the universe. Ironically, Brahe himself had opposed Copernicus's view. [Bildarchiv Preussischer Kulturbesitz]

sance Neoplatonism, which held the sun in special honor. He was determined to find mathematical harmonies in Brahe's numbers that would support a sun-centered universe. After much work Kepler discovered that to keep the sun at the center of things, he must abandon the Copernican concept of circular orbits. The mathematical relationships that emerged from a consideration of Brahe's observations suggested that the orbits of the planets were elliptical. Kepler published his findings in his 1609 book, entitled *On the Motion of Mars*. He had solved the problem of planetary orbits by using Copernicus's sun-centered universe and Brahe's empirical data.

Kepler had also defined a new problem. None of the available theories could explain why the planetary orbits were elliptical. That solution awaited the work of Sir Isaac Newton.

### Galileo Galilei: A Universe of Mathematical Laws

From Copernicus to Brahe to Kepler, there had been little new information about the heavens that might not have been known to Ptolemy. In the same year that Kepler published his volume on Mars, however, an Italian scientist named Galileo Galilei (1564–1642) first turned a telescope on the heavens. Through that recently invented instrument he saw stars where none had been known to exist, mountains on the moon, spots moving across the sun, and moons orbiting Jupiter. The heavens were far more complex than anyone had formerly suspected. None of these discoveries proved that the Earth orbited the sun, but they did suggest the complete inadequacy of the Ptolemaic system. It simply could not accommodate itself to all these new phenomena. Some of Galileo's colleagues at the University of Padua were so unnerved that they refused to look through the telescope.

Galileo publicized his findings and arguments for the Copernican system in numerous works, the most famous of which was his *Dialogues on the Two Chief Systems of the World* (1632). This book brought down on him the condemnation of the Roman Catholic Church. He was compelled to recant his opinions. He is reputed, however, to have muttered after the recantation, *"E pur si muove,"* or "it [the Earth] still moves."

Galileo's discoveries and his popularization of the Copernican system were of secondary importance in his life work. His most important achievement was to articulate the concept of a universe totally subject to mathematical laws. More than any other writer of the century, he argued that nature in its most minute details displayed mathematical regularity:

Philosophy is written in that great book which ever lies before our eyes—I mean the universe—but we cannot understand it if we do not first learn the language and grasp the symbols in which it is written. This book is written in the mathematical language, and the symbols are triangles, circles, and other geometrical figures, without whose help it is impossible to comprehend a single

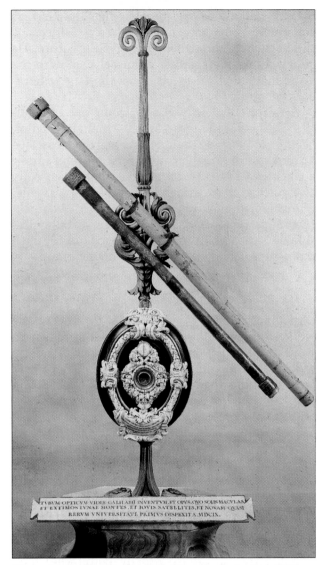

The telescope with which Galileo worked after 1609. He observed Earth's moon and the cyclical phases of the planet Venus and discovered the most prominent moons of Jupiter. These observations had revolutionary intellectual and theological implications in the seventeenth century. [Istituto e Museo de Storia della Scienza, Scala/Art Resource, N.Y.]

word of it; without which one wanders through a dark labyrinth.[2]

The universe was rational; however, its rationality was not that of scholastic logic but of mathe-

[2]Quoted in E. A. Burtt, *The Metaphysical Foundations of Modern Physical Science* (Garden City, N.Y.: Anchor-Doubleday, 1954), p. 75.

matics. Copernicus had thought that the heavens conformed to mathematical regularity; Galileo saw this regularity throughout all physical nature. He believed that the smallest atom behaved with the same mathematical precision as the largest heavenly sphere.

A world of quantity was replacing one of qualities. All aspects of the world—including color, beauty, and taste—would increasingly be described in terms of the mathematical relationships among quantities. Mathematical models would eventually be applied even to social relations. Nature was cold, rational, mathematical, and mechanistic. What was real and lasting was what was mathematically measurable. Few intellectual shifts have wrought such momentous changes for Western civilization.

## Isaac Newton: The Laws of Gravitation

Englishman Isaac Newton (1642–1727) drew on the work of his predecessors and his own brilliance to solve the major remaining problem of planetary motion and to establish a basis for physics that endured more than two centuries. The question that continued to perplex seventeenth-century scientists who accepted the theories of Copernicus, Kepler, and Galileo was how the planets and other heavenly bodies moved in an orderly fashion. The Ptolemaic and Aristotelian answer had been the crystalline spheres and a universe arranged in the order of the heaviness of its parts. Many unsatisfactory theories had been set forth to deal with the question.

In 1687 Newton published *The Mathematical Principles of Natural Philosophy*, better known by its Latin title of *Principia Mathematica*. Much of the research and thinking for this great work had taken place more than fifteen years earlier. Newton was heavily indebted to the work of Galileo and particularly to the latter's view that inertia applied to bodies both at rest and in motion. Galileo's mathematical bias permeated Newton's thought. Newton reasoned that the planets and all other physical objects in the universe moved through mutual attraction, or gravity. Every object in the universe affected every other object through gravity. The attraction of gravity explained why the planets moved in an orderly rather than a chaotic manner. He had found that "the force of gravity towards the whole planet did arise from and was compounded of the forces of gravity towards all its parts, and towards every one part was in the inverse

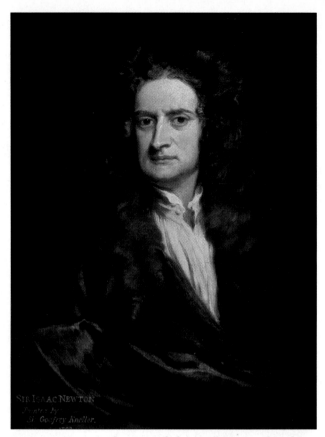

*Sir Isaac Newton discovered the mathematical and physical laws governing the force of gravity. Newton believed that religion and science were compatible and mutually supportive, and that the study of nature gave one a better understanding of the Creator. This portrait of Newton is by Sir Godfrey Kneller. [Bildarchiv Preussischer Kulturbesitz]*

proportion of the squares of the distances from the part."[3] Newton proved this relationship mathematically. He made no attempt to explain the nature of gravity itself.

Newton was a great mathematical genius, but he also upheld the importance of empirical data and observation. Like Francis Bacon (see pages 499–501), he believed that one must observe phenomena before attempting to explain them. The final test of any theory or hypothesis for him was whether it described what could actually be observed. He was a great opponent of the rationalism of the French philosopher Descartes (see pages 501–502), which he believed included insufficient guards against error. As Newton's own theory of universal gravi-

---

[3]Quoted in A. Rupert Hall, *From Galileo to Newton, 1630–1720* (London: Fontana, 1970), p. 300.

# Galileo Discusses the Relationship of Science and the Bible

*The religious authorities were often critical of the discoveries and theories of sixteenth- and seventeenth-century science. For years before his condemnation by the Roman Catholic Church in 1633, Galileo had contended that scientific theory and religious piety were compatible. In his* Letter to the Grand Duchess Christiana *(of Tuscany), written in 1615, he argued that God had revealed truth in both the Bible and physical nature and that the truth of physical nature did not contradict the Bible if the latter were properly understood.*

✦ *Is Galileo's argument based on science or theology? Did the church believe that nature was as much a revelation of God as the Bible? As Galileo describes them, which is the surer revelation of God, nature or the Bible? Why might the pope reject Galileo's argument?*

The reason produced for condemning the opinion that the Earth moves and the sun stands still is that in many places in the Bible one may read that the sun moves and the Earth stands still. . . .

With regard to this argument, I think in the first place that it is very pious to say and prudent to affirm that the holy Bible can never speak untruth—whenever its true meaning is understood. But I believe nobody will deny that it is often very abstruse, and may say things which are quite different from what its bare words signify. . . .

This being granted, I think that in discussions of physical problems we ought to begin not from the authority of scriptural passages, but from sense-experiences and necessary demonstrations; for the holy Bible and the phenomena of nature proceed alike from the divine Word, the former as the dictate of the Holy Ghost and the latter as the observant executrix of God's commands. It is necessary for the Bible, in order to be accommodated to the understanding of every man, to speak many things which appear to differ from the absolute truth so far as the bare meaning of the words is concerned. But Nature, on the other hand, is inexorable and immutable; she never transgresses the laws imposed upon her, or cares a whit whether her abstruse reasons and methods of operation are understandable to men. For that reason it appears that nothing physical which sense-experience sets before our eyes, or which necessary demonstrations prove to us, ought to be called in question (much less condemned) upon the testimony of biblical passages which may have some different meaning beneath their words. For the Bible is not chained in every expression to conditions as strict as those which govern all physical effects; nor is God any less excellently revealed in Nature's actions than in the sacred statements of the Bible. . . .

From this I do not mean to infer that we need not have an extraordinary esteem for the passages of holy Scripture. On the contrary, having arrived at any certainties in physics, we ought to utilize these as the most appropriate aids in the true exposition of the Bible and in the investigation of those meanings which are necessarily contained therein for these must be concordant with demonstrated truths. I should judge the authority of the Bible was designed to persuade men of those articles and propositions which, surpassing all human reasoning, could not be made credible by science, or by any other means than through the very mouth of the Holy Spirit. . . .

But I do not feel obliged to believe that the same God who has endowed us with senses, reason, and intellect has intended to forgo their use and by some other means to give us knowledge which we can attain by them.

Discoveries and Opinions of Galileo, *trans. and ed. by Stillman Drake (Garden City, N.Y.: Doubleday Anchor Books, 1957), pp. 181–183.*

tation became increasingly accepted, so too was Baconian empiricism.

### Newton's Reconciliation of Science and Faith

With the work of Newton, the natural universe became a realm of law and regularity. Beliefs in spirits and divinities were no longer necessary to explain its operation. Thus, the Scientific Revolution liberated human beings from the fear of a chaotic or haphazard universe. Most of the scientists were very devout people. They saw in the new picture of physical nature a new picture also of God. The Creator of this rational, lawful nature must also be rational. To study nature was to come to a better understanding of that Creator. Science and religious faith were not only compatible but mutually supporting. As Newton wrote, "The main Business of Natural Philosophy is to argue from Phaenomena without feigning Hypothesis, and to deduce Causes from Effects, till we come to the very first Cause, which certainly is not mechanical."[4]

This reconciliation of faith and science allowed the new physics and astronomy to spread rapidly. At the very time when Europeans were finally tiring of the wars of religion, the new science provided the basis for a view of God that might lead away from irrational disputes and wars over religious doctrine. Faith in a rational God encouraged faith in the rationality of human beings and in their capacity to improve their lot once liberated from the traditions of the past. The Scientific Revolution provided the great model for the desirability of

[4]Quoted in Franklin Baumer, *Main Currents of Western Thought*, 4th ed. (New Haven: Yale, 1978) p. 323.

change and of criticism of inherited views. The new science, however, caused some people to feel that the mystery had been driven from the universe and that the rational Creator was less loving and less near to humankind than the God of earlier ages.

## Continuing Superstition: Witch Hunts and Panics

The new science by no means swept away all other thought. Traditional beliefs and fears long retained their hold on the culture. During the sixteenth and seventeenth centuries many Europeans remained preoccupied with sin, death, and the Devil. Religious people, including many among the learned and many who were sympathetic to the emerging scientific ideas, continued to believe in the power of magic and the occult. Until the end of the seventeenth century almost all Europeans in one way or another believed in the power of demons.

Nowhere is the dark side of early modern thought and culture better seen than in the witch hunts and panics that erupted in almost every Western land. Between 1400 and 1700, courts sentenced an estimated 70,000–100,000 people to death for harmful magic (*malificium*) and diabolical witchcraft. In addition to inflicting harm on their neighbors, these witches were said to attend mass meetings known as *sabbats*, to which they were believed to fly. They were also accused of indulging in sexual orgies with the Devil, who appeared at such gatherings in animal form, most often as a he-goat. Still other charges against them were cannibalism (they were alleged to be especially fond of small Christian children) and a variety of ritual acts and practices designed to insult every Christian belief and value.

Where did such beliefs come from, and how could seemingly enlightened people believe them? Their roots were in both popular and elite cultures, especially in clerical culture.

### Village Origins

In village societies, so-called cunning folk played a positive role in helping people cope with calamity. People turned to them for help when such natural disasters as plague and famine struck or when such physical disabilities as lameness or inability to conceive offspring befell either humans or animals. The cunning folk provided consolation and gave people

# Newton Contemplates the Nature of God

*Isaac Newton believed there was a close relationship between his scientific theory and the truths of religion. He and many other scientists of his generation were convinced that the investigation of physical nature would lead to proofs of the existence of God. In this passage, taken from comments he added to later editions of the* Principia Mathematica, *Newton explains how the character of planetary motion leads one to conclude that God exists.*

♦ *How do Newton's arguments for God's existence compare with those of Thomas Aquinas (see Chapter 8, page 292)? If the pope could accept Aquinas's arguments, why not also those of Galileo and Newton? Why is Newton, like Copernicus and Galileo before him, so convinced that science and religion are in harmony? Are they still "medieval" men, or did the times in which they lived force them to argue this way to justify their work?*

The six primary planets are revolved about the sun in circles concentric with the sun. . . . Ten moons are revolved about the earth, Jupiter, and Saturn in circles concentric with them . . .; but it is not to be conceived that mere mechanical causes could give birth to so many regular motions. . . . This most beautiful system of sun, planets, and comets could only proceed from the counsel and dominion of an intelligent and powerful Being. And if the fixed stars are the centers of other like systems, these, being formed by the like wise counsel, must be all subject to the dominion of One, especially since the light of the fixed stars is of the same nature with the light of the sun and from every system light passes into all the other systems; and lest the systems of the fixed stars should, by their gravity, fall on each other, he hath placed those systems at immense distances from one another.

This Being governs all things, not as the soul of the world, but as Lord over all; and on account of his dominion he is wont to be called "Lord God." . . . The word "God" usually signifies "Lord," but every lord is not a God. It is the dominion of a spiritual being which constitutes a God: a true, supreme, or imaginary dominion makes a true, supreme, or imaginary god. And from his true dominion it follows that the true God is a living, intelligent, and powerful Being; and, from his other perfections, that he is supreme or most perfect. He is eternal and infinite, omnipotent, and omniscient; that is, his duration reaches from eternity to eternity; his presence from infinity to infinity; he governs all things and knows all things that are or can be done. He is not eternity and infinity, but eternal and infinite; he is not duration or space, but he endures and is present. He endures forever and is everywhere present; and, by existing always and everywhere, he constitutes duration and space. . . . We have ideas of his attributes, but what the real substance of anything is we know not. . . . We know him only by his most wise and excellent contrivances of things and final causes; we admire him for his perfections, but we reverence and adore him on account of his dominion, for we adore him as his servants; and a god without dominion, providence, and final causes is nothing else but Fate and Nature.

H. S. Thayer, ed., Newton's Philosophy of Nature: Selections from His Writings *(New York: Hafner Press, 1974), pp. 42–44.*

hope that such natural calamities might be averted or reversed by magical means. In this way they provided an important service and kept village life moving forward.

Possession of magical powers, for good or ill, made one an important person within village society. Not surprisingly, claims to such powers most often were made by the people most in need of security and influence, namely, the old and the impoverished, especially single or widowed women. Witch beliefs in village society may also have been a way of defying urban Christian society's attempts to impose its laws and institutions on the countryside. From this perspective, village Satanism became a fanciful substitute for an impossible social revolt, a way of spurning the values of one's new masters. It is also possible, although unlikely, that witch beliefs in rural society had a foundation in local fertility cults, whose semipagan practices, designed to ensure good harvests, may have acquired the features of diabolical witchcraft under church persecution.

## Influence of the Clergy

Popular belief in magic was the essential foundation of the great witch hunts of the sixteenth and seventeenth centuries. Had ordinary people not believed that certain gifted individuals could aid or harm others by magical means, and had they not been willing to make accusations, the hunts could never have occurred. Yet the contribution of learned

*Three witches suspected of practicing harmful magic are burned alive on a pyre in Baden. On the left, two of them are shown feasting and cavorting with demons at a sabbat. [Bildarchiv Preussischer Kulturbesitz]*

society was equally great. The Christian clergy also practiced magic, that of the holy sacraments, and the exorcism of demons had been one of their traditional functions within society. Fear of demons and the Devil, which the clergy actively encouraged, allowed the clergy to assert their moral authority over people and to enforce religious discipline and conformity.

In the late thirteenth century the church declared that only its priests possessed legitimate magical power. Since such power was not human, theologians reasoned, it had to come either from God or from the Devil. If it came from God, then it was properly confined to and exercised only on behalf of the church. Those who practiced magic outside the church evidently derived their power from the Devil. From such reasoning grew accusations of "pacts" between non-Christian magicians and Satan. This made the witch hunts a life-and-death struggle against Christian society's worst heretics and foes, those who had directly sworn allegiance to the Devil himself.

The church based its intolerance of magic outside its walls on sincere belief in and fear of the Devil. But attacking witches was also a way for established Christian society to extend its power and influence into new areas. To accuse, try, and execute witches was also a declaration of moral and political authority over a village or territory. As the cunning folk were local spiritual authorities, revered and feared by people, their removal became a major step in establishing a Christian beachhead in village society.

## Role of Women

A good 80 percent of the victims of witch hunts were women, the vast majority between forty-five and sixty years of age and single. This fact has suggested to some that misogyny fueled the witch hunts. Based in male hatred and sexual fear of women, and occurring at a time when women threatened to break out from under male control, witch hunts, it is argued, were simply woman hunts. Older single women may, however, have been vulnerable for more basic social reasons. They were a largely dependent social group in need of public assistance and natural targets for the peculiar "social engineering" of the witch hunts. Some accused witches were women who sought to protect and empower themselves within their communities by claiming supernatural powers.

It may be, however, that gender played a largely circumstantial role. Because of their economic straits, more women than men laid claim to the supernatural powers that made them influential in village society. For this reason, they found themselves on the front lines in disproportionate numbers when the church declared war against all who practiced magic without its blessing. Also, the involvement of many of these women in midwifery associated them with the deaths of beloved wives and infants and thus made them targets of local resentment and accusations. Both the church and midwives' neighbors were prepared to think and say the worst about these women. It was a deadly combination.

## Witch Panics

Why did the great witch panics occur in the second half of the sixteenth and early seventeenth centuries? The misfortune created by religious division and warfare were major factors. The new levels of violence exacerbated fears and hatreds and encouraged scapegoating. But political self-aggrandizement also played a role. As governments expanded and attempted to control their realms, they, like the Church, wanted to eliminate all competition for the loyalty of their subjects. Secular rulers as well as the pope could pronounce their competitors "devilish."

Some argue that the Reformation was responsible for the witch panics. Having weakened the traditional religious protections against demons and the Devil, while at the same time portraying them as still powerful, the Reformation is said to have forced people to protect themselves by executing perceived witches.

## End of the Witch Hunts

Why did the witch hunts come to an end in the seventeenth century? Many factors played a role. The emergence of a new, more scientific worldview made it difficult to believe in the powers of witches. When in the seventeenth century mind and matter came to be viewed as two independent realities, words and thoughts lost the ability to affect things. A witch's curse was merely words. With advances in medicine and the beginning of insurance companies, people learned to rely on themselves when faced with natural calamity and physical affliction

# Why More Women Than Men Are Witches

*A classic of misogyny,* The Hammer of Witches *(1486), written by two Dominican monks, Heinrich Krämer and Jacob Sprenger, was sanctioned by Pope Innocent VIII as an official guide to the church's detection and punishment of witches. Here Krämer and Sprenger explain why they believe that the great majority of witches are women rather than men.*

◆ *Why would two Dominican monks say such things about women? What are the biblical passages that they believe justify them? Do their descriptions have any basis in the actual behavior of women then? What is the rivalry between married and unmarried people that they refer to?*

Why are there more superstitious women than men? The first [reason] is that they are more credulous; and since the chief aim of the devil is to corrupt faith, therefore he rather attacks them. . . . The second reason is that women are naturally more impressionable and ready to receive the influence of a disembodied spirit. . . . The third reason is that they have slippery tongues and are unable to conceal from their fellow-women those things which by evil arts they know; and since they are weak, they find an easy and secret manner of vindicating themselves by witchcraft. . . . [Therefore] since women are feebler both in mind and body, it is not surprising that they should come more under the spell of witchcraft. For as regards intellect, or the understanding of spiritual things, they seem to be of a different nature from men, a fact which is vouched for by the logic of the authorities, backed by various examples from the Scriptures. . . .

But the natural reason [for woman's proclivity to witchcraft] is that she is more carnal than a man, as is clear from her many carnal abominations. And it should be noted that there was a defect in the formation of the first woman, since she was formed from a bent rib, that is, a rib of the breast, which is bent as it were in a contrary direction to a man. And since through this defect she is an imperfect animal, she always deceives. . . .

As to her other mental quality, her natural will, when she hates someone whom she formerly loved, then she seethes with anger and impatience in her whole soul, just as the tides of the sea are always heaving and boiling. . . .

Truly the most powerful cause which contributes to the increase of witches is the woeful rivalry between married folk and unmarried women and men. This [jealousy or rivalry exists] even among holy women, so what must it be among the others . . . ?

Just as through the first defect in their intelligence women are more prone [than men] to abjure the faith, so through their second defect of inordinate affections and passions they search for, brood over, and inflict various vengeances, either by witchcraft or by some other means. Wherefore it is no wonder that so great a number of witches exist in this sex. . . . [Indeed, witchcraft] is better called the heresy of witches than of wizards, since the name is taken from the more powerful party [that is, the greater number, who are women]. Blessed be the Highest who has so far preserved the male sex from so great a crime.

Malleus Maleficarum, *trans. by Montague Summers (Bungay, Suffolk: John Rodker, 1928), pp. 41–47.*

and no longer searched for supernatural causes and solutions. Witch hunts also tended to get out of hand. Accused witches sometimes alleged that important townspeople had also attended sabbats; even the judges could be so accused. At this point the trials ceased to serve the purposes of those who were conducting them. They not only became dysfunctional but threatened anarchy as well.

Although Protestants, like Catholics, hunted witches, the Reformation may also have contributed to an attitude of mind that put the Devil in a more manageable perspective. Protestants ridiculed the sacramental magic of the old church as superstition and directed their faith to a sovereign God absolutely supreme over time and eternity. Even the Devil was believed to serve God's purposes and acted only with his permission. Ultimately God was the only significant spiritual force in the universe. This belief made the Devil a less fearsome creature. "One little word can slay him," Luther wrote of the Devil in the great hymn of the Reformation.

Finally, the imaginative and philosophical literature of the sixteenth and seventeenth centuries (see below), while continuing to display concern for religion and belief in the supernatural, also suggested that human beings have a significant degree of control over their own lives and need not be constantly fearing demons and resorting to supernatural aid.

## Literary Imagination in Transition

The world of the new science developed in the midst of a society where medieval outlooks and religious values remained very much alive. Literary figures of the same period often reflected both the new and the old. In Cervantes one sees a brilliant writer raising questions about the adequacy of medieval values of chivalry and honor and probing the nature of human perceptions of reality. Shakespeare's dramas provide an insight into virtually the entire range of late sixteenth- and early seventeenth-century English worldviews. John Milton could attempt to justify the ways of the Christian God to doubting human beings and in the same work have characters debate the adequacy of the Ptolemaic and Copernican systems. During the same years that Newton reached his deepest insights about nature, John Bunyan could write one of the classic works of simple Christian piety. It is the combination of past and future worldviews that makes the thought of the seventeenth century so remarkable and rich.

### Miguel de Cervantes Saavedra: Rejection of Idealism

Spanish literature of the sixteenth and seventeenth centuries reflects the peculiar religious and politi-

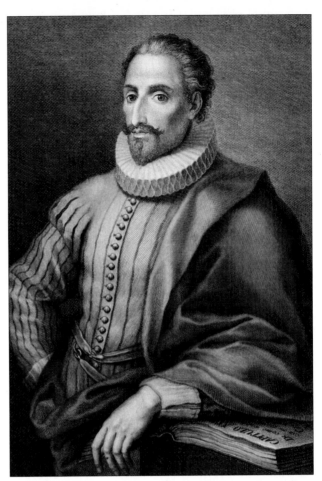

*Miguel de Cervantes Saavedra (1547–1616), the author of* Don Quixote, *considered by many to be Spain's greatest writer. [Art Resource, N.Y.]*

cal history of Spain in this period. Spain was a deeply Catholic country, and this was a major influence on its literature. Since the joint reign of Ferdinand and Isabella (1479–1504), the church had received the unqualified support of reigning political power. Although there was religious reform in Spain, a Protestant Reformation never occurred, thanks largely to the entrenched power of the church and the Inquisition.

A second influence on Spanish literature was the aggressive piety of Spanish rulers, and this intertwining of Catholic piety and political power underlay a third influence: preoccupation with medieval chivalric virtues—in particular, questions of honor and loyalty. The novels and plays of the period almost invariably focus on a special decision involving a character's reputation as his honor or loyalty is tested. In this regard Spanish literature may be said to have remained more Catholic and medieval than that of England and France, where major Protestant movements had occurred. Two of the most important Spanish writers in this period became priests (Lope de Vega and Pedro Calderón de la Barca). The one generally acknowledged to be the greatest Spanish writer of all time, Cervantes, was preoccupied in his work with the strengths and weaknesses of religious idealism.

Cervantes (1547–1616) had only a smattering of formal education. He educated himself by wide reading in popular literature and immersion in the "school of life." As a young man he worked in Rome for a Spanish cardinal. As a soldier he was decorated for gallantry in the Battle of Lepanto (1571). He also spent five years as a slave in Algiers after his ship was pirated in 1575. Later, while working as a tax collector, he was several times imprisoned for padding his accounts, and it was in prison that he began, in 1603, to write his most famous work, *Don Quixote*.

The first part of *Don Quixote* appeared in 1605. The intent of this work seems to have been to satirize the chivalric romances then popular in Spain. But Cervantes could not conceal his deep affection for the character he created as an object of ridicule, Don Quixote. The work is satire only on the surface and has remained as much an object of study by philosophers and theologians as by students of Spanish literature. Cervantes presented Don Quixote as a none-too-stable middle-aged man. Driven mad by reading too many chivalric romances, he had come to believe he was an aspiring knight who had to prove his worthiness by brave deeds. To this end, he donned a rusty suit of armor and chose for his inspiration a quite unworthy peasant girl (Dulcinea), whom he fancied to be a noble lady to whom he could, with honor, dedicate his life.

Don Quixote's foil—Sancho Panza, a clever, worldly-wise peasant who serves as his squire—watched with bemused skepticism as his lord did battle with a windmill (which he mistook for a dragon) and repeatedly made a fool of himself as he galloped across the countryside. The story ends tragically with Don Quixote's humiliating defeat by a well-meaning friend, who, disguised as a knight, bests Don Quixote in combat and forces him to renounce his quest for knighthood. The humiliated Don Quixote does not, however, come to his senses as a result. He returns sadly to his village to die a shamed and broken-hearted old man.

Throughout *Don Quixote*, Cervantes juxtaposes the down-to-Earth realism of Sancho Panza with the old-fashioned religious idealism of Don Quixote. The reader perceives that Cervantes admired the one as much as the other and meant to portray both as representing attitudes necessary for a happy life.

## William Shakespeare: Dramatist of the Age

There is much less factual knowledge about Shakespeare (1564–1616) than one would expect of the greatest playwright in the English language. He married at the early age of eighteen, in 1582, and he and his wife, Anne Hathaway, were the parents of three children (including twins) by 1585. He apparently worked as a schoolteacher for a time and in this capacity gained his broad knowledge of Renaissance learning and literature. His own reading and enthusiasm for the learning of his day are manifest in the many literary allusions that appear in his plays.

Shakespeare lived the life of a country gentleman. There is none of the Puritan distress over worldliness in his work. He took the new commercialism and the bawdy pleasures of the Elizabethan Age in stride and with amusement. He was a radical neither in politics nor religion. The few allusions in his works to the Puritans seem more critical than complimentary.

That Shakespeare was interested in politics is apparent from his historical plays and the references to contemporary political events that fill all his plays. He viewed government through the character of the individual ruler, whether Richard III or Elizabeth Tudor, not in terms of ideal systems or social goals. By modern standards he was a political conservative, accepting the social rankings and the power structure of his day and demonstrating unquestioned patriotism.

Shakespeare knew the theater as one who participated in every phase of its life—as a playwright, an actor, and part owner of a theater. He was a member and principal writer of a famous company of actors known as the King's Men. Between 1590 and 1610, many of his plays were performed at court, where he moved with comfort and received both Queen Elizabeth's and King James's enthusiastic patronage.

Elizabethan drama was already a distinctive form when Shakespeare began writing. Unlike French drama of the seventeenth century, which was dom-

A view of London indicating the Swan Theatre, where many of Shakespeare's plays were performed. [Folger Shakespeare Library]

inated by classical models, English drama developed in the sixteenth and seventeenth centuries as a blending of many forms: classical comedies and tragedies, medieval morality plays, and contemporary Italian short stories.

Two contemporaries, Thomas Kyd and Christopher Marlowe, influenced Shakespeare's tragedies. Kyd (1558–1594) wrote the first dramatic version of Hamlet. The tragedies of Marlowe (1564–1593) set a model for character, poetry, and style that only Shakespeare among the English playwrights of the period surpassed. Shakespeare synthesized the best past and current achievements. A keen student of human motivation and passion, he had a unique talent for getting into people's minds.

Shakespeare wrote histories, comedies, and tragedies. *Richard III* (1593), a very early play, stands out among the histories, although the picture it presents of Richard as an unprincipled villain has been characterized by some scholars as "Tudor propaganda." Shakespeare's comedies, although not attaining the heights of his tragedies, surpass his history plays in originality.

Shakespeare's tragedies are considered his unique achievement. Four of these were written within a three-year period: *Hamlet* (1603), *Othello* (1604), *King Lear* (1605), and *Macbeth* (1606). The most original of the tragedies, *Romeo and Juliet* (1597), transformed an old popular story into a moving drama of "star-cross'd lovers." Both Romeo and Juliet, denied a marriage by their warring families, die tragic deaths. Romeo, believing Juliet to be dead when she has merely taken a sleeping potion, poisons himself. When Juliet awakes to find Romeo dead, she kills herself with his dagger.

Throughout his lifetime and ever since, Shakespeare was immensely popular with both the playgoer and the play reader. The works of no other dramatist from his age are performed in theaters, and even on the screen, more regularly today.

## John Milton: Puritan Poet

John Milton (1608–1674) was the son of a devout Puritan father. As a student, he avidly read the Christian and pagan classics. In 1638 he traveled to Italy, where he found in the lingering Renaissance a very congenial intellectual atmosphere. The Phlegraean Fields near Naples, a volcanic region, later became the model for hell in *Paradise Lost*, and it is suspected by some scholars that the Villa d'Este provided the model for paradise in *Paradise Regained*. Milton remained throughout his life a man more at home in the Italian Renaissance, with its high ideals and universal vision, than in the war-torn England of the seventeenth century.

A man of deep inner conviction and principle, Milton believed that standing a test of character was the most important thing in a person's life. This belief informed his own personal life and is the subject of much of his literary work.

In 1639 Milton joined the Puritan struggle against Charles I and Archbishop Laud. Employing his writing talent, he defended the Presbyterian form of church government against the episcopacy and supported other Puritan reforms. After a month-long unsuccessful marriage in 1642 (a marriage later reconciled), he wrote several tracts in defense of the right to divorce. These writings became targets of a Parliamentary censorship law in 1643, against which Milton wrote an eloquent defense of freedom of the press entitled *Areopagitica* (1644).

Until the upheavals of the civil war moderated his views, Milton believed that government should have the least possible control over the private lives of individuals. When Parliament divided into Presbyterians and Independents, he took the side of the latter, who wanted to dissolve the national church altogether in favor of the local autonomy of individual congregations. He also defended the execution of Charles I in a tract entitled *On the Tenure of Kings and Magistrates*. After his intense labor on this tract, his eyesight failed. Milton was totally blind when he wrote his masterpieces.

*Paradise Lost*, completed in 1665 and published in 1667, is a study of the destructive qualities of pride and the redeeming possibilities of humility. It elaborates in traditional Christian language and concept the revolt of Satan in heaven and the fall of Adam on Earth. The motives of Satan and all who rebel against God intrigued Milton. His proud but

*John Milton (1608–1674). [Courtesy of the Prints Division, Library of Congress]*

tragic Satan, who preferred to reign in hell than to serve in heaven, is one of the great figures in world literature and represented for Milton the absolute corruption of potential greatness.

Milton wanted *Paradise Lost* to be for England what Homer's *Iliad* was for Greece and Vergil's *Aeneid* for Rome. In choosing biblical subject matter, he revealed the great influence of contemporary theology on his mind. Milton tended to agree with the Arminians, followers of the Dutch Protestant theologian Arminius (1560–1609), who, unlike the extreme Calvinists, did not believe that all worldly events, including the Fall of Man, were immutably fixed in the eternal decree of God. Milton shared the Arminian belief that human beings must take responsibility for their fate and that human efforts to improve character could, with God's grace, bring salvation.

Perhaps his own blindness, joined with the hope of making the best of the failed Puritan revolution, inclined Milton to sympathize with those who urged people to make the most of what they had, even in the face of defeat. That is a manifest concern of his last works, *Samson Agonistes*, which

# John Milton Defends Freedom to Print Books

*During the English Civil War, the Parliament passed a very strict censorship measure. In* Areopagitica *(1644), John Milton attacked this law and contributed one of the major defenses for the freedom of the press in the history of Western culture. In the following passage, he compares the life of a book with the life of a human being.*

◆ *Why does Milton think that it may be more dangerous and harmful to attack a book than to attack a person? Was life cheaper and intelligence rarer in his time? Does he have particular kinds of books in mind? What can a book do for society that people cannot?*

I deny not but that it is of greatest concern in the Church and Commonwealth to have a vigilant eye how books demean themselves as well as men; and thereafter to confine, imprison, and do sharpest justice on them as [if they were criminals]; for books are not absolutely dead things, but do contain a progeny of life in them to be as active as that soul was whose progeny they are; nay, they do preserve as in a vial the purest efficacy and extraction of that living intellect that bred them. . . . He who kills a man kills a reasonable creature, God's Image; but he who destroys a good book, kills reason itself, kills the Image of God, as it were. . . . Many a man lives [as] a burden to the Earth; but a good book is the precious life-blood of a master spirit, embalmed and treasured up on purpose to a life beyond life. It is true, no age can restore a life, whereof, perhaps there is no great loss; and revolutions of ages do not oft recover the loss of a rejected truth, for the want of which whole nations fare the worse. We should be wary, therefore, what persecution we raise against the living labours of public men, how we spill that seasoned life of man preserved and stored up in books; since we see a kind of homicide may be thus committed, sometimes a martyrdom, and if it extends to the whole impression, a kind of massacre, whereof the execution ends not in the slaying of an elemental life, but strikes at that ethereal . . . essence, the breath of reason itself; slays an immortality rather than a life.

J. A. St. John, ed., The Prose Works of John Milton *(London: H. G. Bohn, 1843–1853), 2:8–9.*

---

recounts the biblical story of Samson, and *Paradise Regained*, the story of Christ's temptation in the wilderness, both published in 1671.

## John Bunyan: Visions of Christian Piety

Bunyan (1628–1688) was the English author of two classics of sectarian Puritan spirituality: *Grace Abounding* (1666) and *The Pilgrim's Progress* (1678). A Bedford tinker, his works speak especially for the seventeenth-century working people and popular religious culture. He received only the most basic education before taking up his father's craft, and he served in Oliver Cromwell's revolutionary army for two years. The visionary fervor of the New Model Army influenced his work, which is filled with the language of battle.

After the restoration of the monarchy in 1660, Bunyan went to prison for his fiery preaching and remained there for twelve years. During these years, he wrote his famous autobiography, *Grace Abounding*, both a very personal statement and a model for the faithful. Like *The Pilgrim's Progress*, Bunyan's later masterpiece, *Grace Abounding* is Puritan piety at its most fervent. Puritans believed that individuals could do absolutely nothing to save themselves, and this made them extremely restless and introspective. People could only trust that God had placed them among the elect and try each day to live a life that reflected such favored status. So long

the Renaissance, reacting against the dogmatic thinking of medieval Scholasticism, had laid the groundwork for this change.

The revolution in scientific thought contributed directly to a major reconsideration of Western philosophy. Several of the most important figures in the Scientific Revolution, such as Descartes and

*The microscope of Robert Hooke (1635–1703). The microscope became the telescope's companion as a major optical instrument in the seventeenth century. Several scientists, including Galileo, had a hand in its development, but the Englishman Hooke and the Dutchman Anton von Leeuwenhoek (1632–1723) did the most to perfect it. [Historical Collections, National Museum of Health and Medicine, Armed Forces Institute of Pathology]*

as men and women struggled successfully against the flesh and the world, they had presumptive evidence that they were among God's elect. To falter or to become complacent in the face of temptation was to cast doubt on one's faith and salvation and even to raise the specter of eternal damnation.

This anxious questing for salvation is the subject of *The Pilgrim's Progress*, a work unique in its contribution to Western religious symbolism and imagery. It is the story of the journey of Christian and his friends Hopeful and Faithful to the Celestial City. It teaches that one must deny spouse, children, and all Earthly security and go in search of "Life, life, eternal life." During the long journey, the travelers must resist the temptations of Worldly-Wiseman and Vanity Fair, pass through the Slough of Despond, and endure a long dark night in Doubting Castle, their faith being tested at every turn. Bunyan later wrote a work tracing the progress of Christian's opposite, *The Life and Death of Mr. Badman* (1680), which told the story of a man so addicted to the bad habits of Restoration society, of which Bunyan strongly disapproved, that he journeyed steadfastly not to heaven but to hell.

## Philosophy in the Wake of Changing Science

By the end of the sixteenth century, many people, weary of religious strife, no longer embraced either the old Catholic or the new Protestant absolutes. The century that followed was a period of intellectual as well as political transition. The thinkers of

Bacon, were also philosophers discontented with the scholastic heritage. Bacon stressed the importance of empirical research. Descartes attempted to find certainty through the exploration of his thinking processes. Newton's interests likewise extended to philosophy; he wrote broadly on many topics, including scientific method and theology.

The new methods of science had a broad impact on philosophers. The emphasis that Galileo placed on mathematics spread to other areas of thought. Pascal, a gifted mathematician, became concerned about the issue of certain knowledge and religious faith. Spinoza would write his ethical discourses in the form of geometrical theorems. Hobbes produced a great political treatise through a mode of rational reasoning resembling mathematics. Locke would attempt to explore the human mind in a fashion that he believed resembled Newton's approach to the physical universe. Virtually all of these writers found a tension that they hoped to resolve between the new science and religious belief.

### Francis Bacon: Empirical Method

Bacon (1561–1626) was an Englishman of almost universal accomplishment. He was a lawyer, a high royal official, and the author of histories, moral essays, and philosophical discourses. Traditionally, he has been regarded as the father of empiricism and of experimentation in science. Much of this reputation is unearned. Bacon was not a scientist except in the most amateur fashion. His accomplishment was setting a tone and helping to create a climate conducive to scientific work.

In books such as *The Advancement of Learning* (1605), the *Novum Organum* (1620), and the *New Atlantis* (1627), Bacon attacked the scholastic belief that most truth had already been discovered and only required explanation, as well as the scholastic reverence for intellectual authority in general. He believed that scholastic thinkers paid too much attention to tradition and to the knowledge of the ancients. He urged contemporaries to strike out on their own in search of a new understanding of nature. He wanted seventeenth-century Europeans to have confidence in themselves and their own abilities rather than in the people and methods of the past. Bacon was one of the first major European writers to champion the desirability of innovation and change.

Bacon believed that human knowledge should produce useful results. In particular, knowledge of

*Sir Francis Bacon (1561–1626), champion of the inductive method of gaining knowledge. [By courtesy of the National Portrait Gallery, London]*

nature should be brought to the aid of the human condition. These goals required the modification or abandonment of scholastic modes of learning and thinking. Bacon contended, "The [scholastic] logic now in use serves more to fix and give stability to the errors which have their foundation in commonly received notions than to help the search after truth."[5] Scholastic philosophers could not escape from their syllogisms to examine the foundations of their thought and intellectual presuppositions. Bacon urged that philosophers and investigators of nature examine the evidence of their senses before constructing logical speculations. In a famous passage, he divided all philosophers into

[5]Quoted in Baumer, p. 281.

# Bacon Attacks the Idols That Harm Human Understanding

*Francis Bacon wanted the men and women of his era to have the courage to change the way they thought about physical nature. In this famous passage from the* Novum Organum *(1620), he attempted to explain why it is so difficult to ask new questions and seek new answers.*

✦ *Is Bacon's view of human nature pessimistic? Are people hopelessly trapped in overlapping worlds of self-interest and fantasy imposed by their nature and cultural traditions? How did Bacon expect people to overcome such formidable barriers?*

The idols and false notions which are now in possession of the human understanding and have taken deep root therein. . . . so beset men's minds that truth can hardly find entrance. . . . There are four classes of Idols which beset men's minds. To these for distinction's sake I have assigned names,—calling the first class *Idols of the Tribe*; the second, *Idols of the Cave*; the third, *Idols of the Marketplace*; the fourth, *Idols of the Theatre.*

. . . . . . . . . . . . . . . . . . . . . . . . . . . . . . . . . . .

The Idols of the Tribe have their foundation in human nature itself; and in the tribe or race of men. For it is a false assertion that the sense of man is the measure of things. On the contrary, all perceptions as well as the sense as of the mind are according to the measure of the universe. And the human understanding is like a false mirror, which, receiving rays irregularly, distorts and discolours the nature of things by mingling its own nature with it.

The Idols of the Cave are the idols of the individual man. For every one (besides the errors common to human nature in general) has a cave or den of his own, which refracts and discolours the light of nature; owing either to his own proper and peculiar nature; or to his education and conversation with others; or to the reading of books, and the authority of those whom he esteems and admires. . . .

There are also Idols formed by the intercourse and association of men with each other, which I call Idols of the Marketplace, on account of the commerce and consort of men there. For it is by discourse that men associate; and words are imposed according to the apprehension of the vulgar. And therefore the ill and unfit choice of words wonderfully obstructs the understanding. . . .

Lastly, there are Idols which have immigrated into men's minds from the various dogmas of philosophies, and also from wrong laws of demonstration. These I call Idols of the Theatre; because in my judgment all the received systems are but so many stage plays, representing worlds of their own creation after an unreal and scenic fashion.

Francis Bacon, Essays, Advancement of Learning, New Atlantis, and Other Pieces, *ed. by Richard Foster Jones (New York: Odyssey, 1937), pp. 278–280.*

"men of experiment and men of dogmas." He observed:

The men of experiment are like the ant, they only collect and use; the reasoners resemble spiders, who make cobwebs out of their own substance. But the bee takes a middle course: it gathers its material from the flowers of the garden and of the field, but transforms and digests it by a power of its own. Not unlike this is the true business of philosophy.[6]

[6]Quoted in Baumer, p. 288.

By directing scientists toward an examination of empirical evidence, Bacon hoped that they would achieve new knowledge and thus new capabilities for humankind.

Bacon compared himself with Columbus, plotting a new route to intellectual discovery. The comparison is significant, because it displays the consciousness of a changing world that appears so often in writers of the late sixteenth and early seventeenth centuries. They were rejecting the past not from simple hatred but rather from a firm understanding that the world was much more complicated than their medieval forebears had thought.

Neither Europe nor European thought could remain self-contained. Like the new worlds on the globe, new worlds of the mind were also emerging. Most of the people in Bacon's day, including the intellectuals, thought that the best era of human history lay in antiquity. Bacon dissented vigorously from that view. He looked to a future of material improvement achieved through the empirical examination of nature. His own theory of induction from empirical evidence was quite unsystematic, but his insistence on appeal to experience influenced others whose methods were more productive.

Bacon believed that science had a practical purpose and its goal was human improvement. Some scientific investigation does have this character. Much pure research does not. Bacon, however, linked science and material progress in the public mind. This was a powerful idea and has continued to influence Western civilization to the present day. It has made science and those who can appeal to the authority of science major forces for change and innovation. Thus, though not making any major scientific contribution himself, Bacon directed investigators of nature to a new method and a new purpose.

### René Descartes: The Method of Rational Deduction

Descartes (1596–1650) was a gifted mathematician who invented analytic geometry. His most important contribution, however, was to develop a scientific method that relied more on deduction than empirical observation and induction.

In 1637 he published his *Discourse on Method*, in which he attempted to provide a basis for all thinking founded on a mathematical model. The work appeared in French rather than in Latin because he wanted it to have wide circulation and

*René Descartes (1596–1650) believed that because the material world operated according to mathematical laws, it could be accurately understood by the exercise of human reason. [Erich Lessing/Art Resource, N.Y.]*

application. He began by saying that he would doubt everything except those propositions about which he could have clear and distinct ideas. This approach rejected all forms of intellectual authority except the conviction of his own reason. He concluded that he could not doubt his own act of thinking and his own existence. From this base he proceeded to deduce the existence of God. The presence of God was important to Descartes because God guaranteed the correctness of clear and distinct ideas. Because God was not a deceiver, the ideas of God-given reason could not be false.

On the basis of such assumptions, Descartes concluded that human reason could fully comprehend the world. He divided existing things into two basic categories: things thought and things occupying space—mind and body. Thinking was characteristic of the mind, and extension (things occupying space) was characteristic of the body. Within the material world, the world of extension, mathematical laws reigned supreme and could be grasped by reason. Because they were mathematical, they could be deduced from each other and constituted a complete system. The world of extension was the world of the scientist. It had no place for spirits, divinity, or anything nonmaterial. Descartes separated mind from body to banish such things from the realm of scientific speculation. Reason was to be applied only to the mechanical and mathematical realm of matter.

Descartes's emphasis on deduction and rational speculation exercised broad influence. His deductive methodology, however, eventually lost favor to scientific induction, in which the scientist draws generalizations from data derived from empirical observations.

### Blaise Pascal: Reason and Faith

Pascal (1623–1662) was a French mathematician and a physical scientist who surrendered all his

## Pascal Meditates on Human Beings as Thinking Creatures

*Pascal was both a religious and a scientific writer. Unlike other scientific thinkers of the seventeenth century, he was not overly optimistic about the ability of science to improve the human condition. But science and philosophy might help human beings to understand their situation better. In these passages from his* Pensées *(Thoughts), he ponders the uniqueness of human beings as thinking creatures.*

✦ *Is this an intellectual's view of human nature? Does the idea that man is a rational creature come from the belief that human reason is more noble than the universe? Does Pascal ignore human will and emotion, selfishness, and destructiveness?*

### 339
I can well conceive a man without hands, feet, head (for it is only experience which teaches us that the head is more necessary than feet). But I cannot conceive man without thought; he would be a stone or a brute.

### 344
Reason commands us far more imperiously than a master; for in disobeying the one we are unfortunate, and in disobeying the other we are fools.

### 346
Thought constitutes the greatness of man.

### 347
Man is but a reed, the most feeble thing in nature; but he is a thinking reed. The entire universe need not arm itself to crush him. A vapour, a drop of water suffices to kill him. But, if the universe were to crush him, man would still be more noble than that which killed him, because he knows that he dies and the advantage which the universe has over him; the universe knows nothing of this.

All our dignity consists, then, in thought. By it we must elevate ourselves, and not by space and time which we cannot fill. Let us endeavour, then, to think well; this is the principle of morality.

### 348
A thinking reed—It is not from space that I must seek my dignity, but from the government of my thought. I shall have no more if I possess worlds. By space the universe encompasses and swallows me up like an atom; by thought I comprehend the world.

*Blaise Pascal,* Pensées and The Provincial Letters *(New York: Modern Library, 1941), pp. 115–116.*

*Pascal invented this adding machine, the ancestor of mechanical calculators, around 1644. It has eight wheels with ten cogs each, corresponding to the numbers 0–9. The wheels move forward for addition, backward for subtract. [Bildarchiv Preussischer Kulturbesitz]*

wealth to pursue an austere, self-disciplined life. He aspired to write a work that would refute both dogmatism (which he saw epitomized by the Jesuits) and skepticism. Pascal considered the Jesuits' casuistry (i.e., arguments designed to minimize and excuse sinful acts) a distortion of Christian teaching. He rejected the skeptics of his age because they either denied religion altogether (atheists) or accepted it only as it conformed to reason (deists). He never produced a definitive refutation of the two sides. Rather he formulated his views on these matters in piecemeal fashion in a provocative collection of reflections on humankind and religion published posthumously under the title *Pensées*.

Pascal allied himself with the Jansenists, seventeenth-century Catholic opponents of the Jesuits. His sister was a member of the Jansenist community of Port-Royal, near Paris. The Jansenists shared with the Calvinists Saint Augustine's belief in human beings' total sinfulness, their eternal predestination by God, and their complete dependence on faith and grace for knowledge of God and salvation.

Pascal believed that reason and science were of no avail in matters of religion. Here only the reasons of the heart and a "leap of faith" could prevail. He saw two essential truths in the Christian religion: that a loving God, worthy of human attainment, exists, and that human beings, because they are corrupt by nature, are utterly unworthy of God. He believed that the atheists and the deists of his age had spurned the clear lesson of reason. For him rational analysis of the human condition revealed utter mortality and corruption and exposed the weakness of reason itself in resolving the problems of human nature and destiny. Reason properly drove those who truly heed it to faith in God and reliance on divine grace.

Pascal made a famous wager with the skeptics. It is a better bet, he argued, to believe that God exists and to stake everything on his promised mercy than not to do so. This is because if God does exist, everything will be gained by the believer, whereas, should he prove not to exist, the loss incurred by having believed in him is by comparison very slight.

Convinced that belief in God improved life psychologically and disciplined it morally (regardless of whether God proved in the end to exist), Pascal worked to strengthen traditional religious belief. He urged his contemporaries to seek self-understanding by "learned ignorance" and to discover humankind's greatness by recognizing its misery. He hoped thereby to counter what he believed to be the false optimism of the new rationalism and science.

## Baruch Spinoza: The World as Divine Substance

The most controversial thinker of the seventeenth century may have been Baruch Spinoza (1632–1677), the son of a Jewish merchant of Amsterdam. His philosophy caused his excommunication by his own synagogue in 1656. During his lifetime, both Jews and Protestants attacked him as an atheist.

Spinoza's most influential writing, the *Ethics*, appeared after his death in 1677. Religious leaders universally condemned it for its apparent espousal of pantheism (a doctrine equating God and nature). Spinoza so closely identified God and nature that little room seemed left either for divine revelation in scripture or for the personal immortality of the soul—a position equally repugnant to Jews and to Christians. The *Ethics* was written, in the spirit of the new science, as a geometrical system of definitions, axioms, and propositions. Spinoza divided the work into five parts, which dealt with God, the mind, emotions, human bondage, and human freedom.

The most controversial part of the *Ethics* deals with the nature of substance and of God. According to Spinoza, there is only one substance, which is self-caused, free, and infinite, and that substance is God. From this definition it follows that everything that exists is in God and cannot even be conceived

of apart from him. Such a doctrine was not literally pantheistic because God was still seen to be more than the created world that he, as primal substance, embraced. But in Spinoza's view, statements about the natural world were also statements about divine nature. Mind and matter are thus seen to be extensions of the infinite substance of God; what transpires in the world of people and nature is also an expression of the divine.

Such teaching seemed to portray the world as eternal and human actions as unfree and inevitable. Jews and Christians had traditionally condemned such teachings because they deny the creation of the world by God in time and destroy any voluntary basis for personal reward and punishment.

Although his contemporaries condemned him, Spinoza found enthusiastic supporters among many nineteenth-century thinkers who, unable to accept traditional religious language and doctrines, found in his teaching a congenial rational religion.

## Thomas Hobbes: Apologist for Absolutism

Thomas Hobbes (1588–1679) was the most original political philosopher of the seventeenth century. Although he never broke with the Church of England, he embraced basic Calvinist beliefs, particularly their low view of human nature and the ideal of a commonwealth based on a divine–human covenant.

An urbane and much-traveled man, Hobbes enthusiastically supported the new scientific movement. During the 1630s, he visited Paris, where he came to know Descartes, and he spent time with Galileo in Italy as well. He took special interest in the works of William Harvey (1578–1657), famous for his discovery of the circulation of blood through the body. Hobbes was also a superb classicist. His first published work was a translation of Thucydides' *History of the Peloponnesian War*, the first English translation of this work, still reprinted today.

The English civil war made Hobbes a political philosopher and inspired his *Leviathan* (1651). Written as the concluding part of a broad philosophical system that analyzed physical bodies and human nature, the work established Hobbes as a major European thinker.

Hobbes viewed people and society in a thoroughly materialistic and mechanical way. All psychological processes begin with and are derived

*A portrait of Thomas Hobbes (1588–1679), whose political treatise, Leviathan, portrayed rulers as absolute lords over their lands, incorporating in their persons the individual wills of all their people. [Bildarchiv Preussischer Kulturbesitz]*

The key to Hobbes's political philosophy can be found in a brilliant myth he created about the original state of humankind. According to this account, people in their natural state are inclined to "perpetual and restless desire" for power. Because all people want and, in their natural state, possess a natural right to everything, their equality breeds enmity, competition, diffidence, and perpetual quarreling—"a way of every man against every man." As Hobbes put it in a famous summary:

In such condition there is no place for industry, because the fruit thereof is uncertain; and consequently no culture of the Earth; no navigation nor use of the commodities that may be imported by sea; no commodious building; no instruments of moving and removing such things as require much force; no knowledge of the face of the Earth; no account of time; no arts; no letters; no society; and, which is worst of all, continual fear and danger of violent death; and the life of man solitary, poor, nasty, brutish, and short.[7]

Whereas earlier and later philosophers saw the original human state as a paradise from which humankind had fallen, Hobbes saw it as a corruption from which only society could deliver people. Contrary to Aristotle and Christian thinkers like Thomas Aquinas, Hobbes did not believe human beings were naturally sociable; they were self-centered beasts and utterly without a master until one was imposed by force.

People escape this terrible state of nature, according to Hobbes, only by entering a social contract, that is, by agreeing to live in a commonwealth tightly ruled by a recognized sovereign. They are driven to this solution by their desire for "commodious living" and fear of death. The social contract obliges every person, for the sake of peace and self-defense, to agree to set aside personal rights to all things and to be content with as much liberty against others as he or she would allow others against himself or herself. All agree to live according to a secularized version of the golden rule: "Do not that to another which you would not have done to yourself."[8]

Because words and promises are insufficient to guarantee this state, the social contract also establishes the coercive use of force to compel compliance. Believing the dangers of anarchy to be always

[7]Thomas Hobbes, *Leviathan* Parts I and II, ed. by H. W. Schneider (Indianapolis: Bobbs-Merrill, 1958), pp. 86, 106–107.
[8]Hobbes, p. 130.

from bare sensation, and all motivations are egoistical, intended to increase pleasure and minimize pain. The human power of reasoning, which Hobbes defined as the process of adding and subtracting the consequences of agreed-upon general names of things, develops only after years of concentrated industry. Human will he defined as simply "the last appetite before choice."

Despite this mechanistic view of human nature, Hobbes believed people could accomplish much by the reasoned use of science. Such progress, however, was contingent on their prior correct use of that greatest of human creations, the commonwealth, in which people were freely united by mutual agreement in one all-powerful sovereign government.

greater than those of tyranny, Hobbes thought that rulers should be absolute and unlimited in their power, once established in office. There is no room in Hobbes's political philosophy for protest in the name of individual conscience, nor for resistance to legitimate authority by private individuals. Contemporary Catholics and Puritans alike criticized these features of the *Leviathan*. To his critics, Hobbes pointed out the alternative:

The greatest that in any form of government can possibly happen to the people in general is scarce sensible in respect of the miseries and horrible calamities that accompany a civil war or that dissolute condition of masterless men, without subjection to laws and a coercive power to tie their hands from rapine and revenge.[9]

[9]Hobbes, p. 152.

It is puzzling why Hobbes believed that absolute rulers would be more benevolent and less egoistic than all other people. He simply placed the highest possible value on a strong, efficient ruler who could save human beings from the chaos attendant on the state of nature. In the end, it mattered little to Hobbes whether that ruler was Charles I, Oliver Cromwell, or Charles II, each of whom received Hobbes's enthusiastic support—once he was established in power.

## John Locke: Defender of Moderate Liberty

Locke (1632–1704) has proved to be the most influential political thinker of the seventeenth century. Although he was not as original as Hobbes, his political writings became a major source of the later

*The famous title page illustration for Hobbes's* Leviathan. *The ruler is pictured as absolute lord of his lands, but note that the ruler incorporates the mass of individuals whose self-interests are best served by their willing consent to accept him and cooperate with him. [New York Public Library]*

Enlightenment criticism of absolutism. They gave inspiration to both the American and the French revolutions.

Locke's sympathies lay with the Puritans and the parliamentary forces that challenged the Stuart monarchy. His father fought with the parliamentary army during the English civil war. Locke read deeply in the works of Francis Bacon, René Descartes, and Isaac Newton and was a close friend of the English physicist and chemist Robert Boyle (1627–1691). Some view Locke as synthesizing the rationalism of Descartes and the experimental science of Bacon, Newton, and Boyle.

Locke came for a brief period also under the influence of Hobbes. This ended, however, after his association with Anthony Ashley Cooper, the earl of Shaftesbury. Shaftesbury was considered by his contemporaries to be a radical in both religion and politics. He organized an unsuccessful rebellion against Charles II in 1682, after which both he and Locke, who lived with him, were forced to flee to Holland.

In his *Essay Concerning Human Understanding* (1690), Locke explored the function of the human mind. He portrayed it at birth as a blank tablet. There are no innate ideas, he argued; all knowledge is derived from direct sensual experience. What people know is not the external world in itself but the results of the interaction of the mind with the outside world.

Locke also denied the existence of innate moral norms. Moral ideas are the product of people's subordination of self-love to reason—a free act of self-discipline so that conflict in conscience may be avoided and happiness attained. Locke also believed the teachings of Christianity to be identical to what uncorrupted reason taught. A rational person would therefore always live according to Christian moral precepts. Although Locke firmly denied toleration to Catholics and atheists—both of whom were considered subversive in England—he otherwise sanctioned a variety of Protestant religious practice.

During the reign of Charles II, Locke wrote *Two Treatises of Government*. Here he opposed the argument, set forth by Sir Robert Filmer and Thomas Hobbes, that rulers are absolute in their power. Filmer was the author of *Patriarcha, or the Natural Power of Kings* (1680), which compared the rights of kings over their subjects to those of fathers over their children. Locke devoted his entire first treatise

*John Locke (1632–1704), defender of the rights of the people against rulers who think their power absolute. [By courtesy of the National Portrait Gallery, London]*

to a refutation of this argument, maintaining that both fathers and rulers were bound to the law of nature. The voice of reason teaches that "all mankind [are] equal and independent, [and] no one ought to harm another in his life, health, liberty, or possessions,"[10] inasmuch as all humans are made in the image of God. According to Locke, people enter into social contracts, empowering legislatures and monarchs to "umpire" their disputes, precisely to preserve their natural rights, not to give rulers an absolute power over them. Rulers are "entrusted" with the preservation of the law of nature and transgress it at their peril:

[10]John Locke, *The Second Treatise of Government*, ed. by T. P. Peardon (Indianapolis: Bobbs-Merrill, 1952), Ch. 2, secs. 4–6, pp. 4–6.

# John Locke Explores the Sources of Human Knowledge

*An Essay Concerning Human Understanding (1690) was probably the most influential philosophical work ever written in English. Locke's fundamental idea, which is explicated in the passage below, was that human knowledge is grounded in the experiences of the senses and in the reflection of the mind on those experiences. He rejected any belief in innate ideas. His emphasis on experience led to the wider belief that human beings are creatures of their environment. After Locke, numerous writers argued that human beings could be improved if the political and social environments in which they lived were reformed.*

✦ *How does Locke explain the manner in which the human mind comes to be furnished? What does Locke mean by* experience? *How does reflection deal with external sensations? What is the role that external environment plays in Locke's psychology?*

Let us then suppose the mind to be, as we say, white paper void of all characters, without any ideas. Whence comes it to be furnished? Whence comes it by that vast store which the busy and boundless fancy of man has painted on it with an almost endless variety? Whence has it all the materials of reason and knowledge? To this I answer, in one word, from experience; in that all our knowledge is founded, and from that it ultimately derives itself. Our observation, employed either about external sensible objects, or about the internal operations of our minds perceived and reflected on by ourselves, is that which supplies our understanding with all the materials of thinking. These two are the fountains of knowledge, from whence all the ideas we have, or can naturally have, do spring.

First, our senses, conversant about particular sensible objects, do convey into the mind several distinct perceptions of things, according to those various ways wherein those objects do affect them. And thus we come by those ideas we have of yellow, white, heat, cold, soft, hard, bitter, sweet, and all those which we call sen-

sible qualities. . . . This great source of most of the ideas we have, depending wholly upon our senses, and derived by them to the understanding, I call SENSATION.

Secondly, the other fountain from which experience furnisheth the understanding with ideas is the perception of the operations of our own minds within us, as it is employed about the ideas it has got . . . and such are perception, thinking, doubting, believing, reasoning, knowing, willing, and all the different actings of our own minds. . . . I call this REFLECTION, the ideas it affords being such only as the mind gets by reflecting on its own operations within itself. . . . These two, I say, viz., external material things as the objects of SENSATION, and the operations of our own minds within as the objects of REFLECTION, are to me the only originals from whence all our ideas take their beginnings. . . .

The understanding seems to me not to have the least glimmering of any ideas which it doth not receive from one of these two.

*John Locke,* An Essay Concerning Human Understanding, *vol. 1 (London: Everyman's Library, 1961), pp. 77–78.*

Whenever that end [the preservation of life, liberty, and property] is manifestly neglected or opposed, the trust must necessarily be forfeited and the power devolve into the hands of those that gave it, who may place it anew where they think best for their safety and security.[11]

From Locke's point of view, absolute monarchy was "inconsistent" with civil society and can be "no form of civil government at all."

Locke's main differences with Hobbes stemmed from the latter's negative views of human nature. Locke believed that the natural human state was one of perfect freedom and equality in which everyone enjoyed, in unregulated fashion, the natural rights of life, liberty, and property. Contrary to Hobbes, human beings in their natural state were creatures not of monomaniacal passion but of extreme goodwill and rationality. And they did not surrender their natural rights unconditionally when they entered the social contract. Rather they established a means whereby these rights could be better preserved. The warfare that Hobbes believed characterized the state of nature emerged for Locke only when rulers failed to preserve people's natural freedom and attempted to enslave them by absolute rule. The preservation and protection of human freedom, not its suppression, was government's mandate.

◆

*The Scientific Revolution and the thought of writers whose work was contemporaneous with it mark a major turning point in the history of Western thought and eventually had a worldwide impact. The scientific and political ideas of the late sixteenth and seventeenth centuries gradually overturned many of the most fundamental premises of the medieval worldview. The sun replaced the Earth as the center of the solar system. The solar system itself came to be viewed as one of many possible systems in the universe. The new knowledge of the physical universe provided occasions for challenges to the authority of the church and of scripture. Mathematics began to replace theology and metaphysics as the tool for understanding nature.*

*Parallel to these developments and sometimes related to them, political thought became much*

*less concerned with religious issues. Hobbes generated a major theory of political obligation with virtually no reference to God. Locke theorized about politics with a recognition of God but with little attention to scripture. Both Locke and Spinoza championed greater freedom of religious and political expression. Locke produced a psychology that emphasized the influence of environment on human character and action. All of these new ideas gradually displaced or reshaped theological and religious modes of thought and placed humankind and life on Earth at the center of Western thinking. Intellectuals in the West consequently developed greater self-confidence in their own capacity to shape the world and their own lives.*

*None of this came easily, however. The new science and enlightenment were accompanied by new anxieties that were reflected in a growing preoccupation with sin, death, and the Devil. The worst expression of this preoccupation was a succession of witch hunts and trials that took the lives of as many as 100,000 people between 1400 and 1700.*

## Review Questions

1. Discuss the contributions of Copernicus, Brahe, Kepler, Galileo, and Newton to the Scientific Revolution. Which do you think made the most important contributions and why? What did Francis Bacon contribute to the foundation of scientific thought?

2. How would you define the term *Scientific Revolution*? In what ways was it truly revolutionary? Which is more enduring, a political revolution or an intellectual one?

3. How did Isaac Newton reconcile his scientific discoveries with his faith in God? Compare his experience with that of Galileo or Pascal. Are reason and faith compatible?

4. Compare and contrast the political philosophies of Thomas Hobbes and John Locke. How did each view human nature? Would you rather live under a government designed by Hobbes or by Locke? Why?

5. How do you explain the phenomenon of witchcraft and witch hunts in an age of scientific enlightenment? Why did the witch panics occur in the late sixteenth and early seventeenth centuries? How might the Reformation have contributed to them?

[11]Locke, Ch. 13, sec. 149, p. 84.

**6.** How do the literary works of Cervantes, Shakespeare, and Milton reflect concern about the adequacy of past values and how did they shape the worldview of their own seventeenth century society?

## Suggested Readings

R. ASHCRAFT, *Revolutionary Politics and Locke's Two Treatises of Government* (1986). A major study emphasizing the radical side of Locke's thought.

M. BIAGIOLI, *Galileo Courtier: The Practice of Science in the Culture of Absolutism* (1993). A major revisionist work that emphasizes the role of the political setting on Galileo's career and thought.

H. BUTTERFIELD, *The Origins of Modern Science 1300–1800* (1949). A classic survey.

J. CAIRD, *Spinoza* (1971). Intellectual biography by a philosopher.

H. F. COHEN, *The Scientific Revolution: A Historiographical Inquiry* (1994). Supplants all previous discussions of the history and concept of the Scientific Revolution.

J. DUNN, *The Political Thought of John Locke; An Historical Account of the "Two Treatises of Government"* (1969). An excellent introduction.

M. DURAN, *Cervantes* (1974). Detailed biography.

M. A. FINOCCHIARO, *The Galileo Affair: A Documentary History* (1989). A collection of all the relevant documents and introductory commentary.

S. GAUKROGER, *Descartes: An Intellectual Biography* (1995). A major work that explores both the science and philosophy in Descartes's work.

A. GOLDGAR, *Impolite Learning: Conduct and Community in the Republic of Letters, 1680–1750* (1995). A lively survey of the structure of the European intellectual community.

A. R. HALL, *The Scientific Revolution 1500–1800: The Formation of the Modern Scientific Attitude* (1966). Traces undermining of traditional science and rise of new sciences.

I. HARRIS, *The Mind of John Locke: A Study of Political Theory in Its Intellectual Setting* (1994). The most comprehensive recent treatment.

C. HILL, *Milton and the English Revolution* (1977). A major biography.

M. HUNTER, *Science and Society in Restoration England* (1981). Examines the social relations of scientists and scientific societies.

M. JACOB, *The Newtonians and the English Revolution* (1976). A controversial book that attempts to relate science and politics.

D. JOHNSTON, *The Rhetoric of Leviathan: Thomas Hobbes and the Politics of Cultural Transformation* (1986). An important study that links Hobbes's thought to the rhetoric of the Renaissance.

R. KIECKHEFER, *European Witch Trials: Their Foundations in Popular and Learned Culture 1300–1500* (1976). Excellent background for understanding the great witch panic.

A. KORS AND E. PETERS (EDS.), *European Witchcraft, 1100–1700* (1972). Collection of major documents.

A. KOYRÉ, *From the Closed World to the Infinite Universe* (1957). Treated from perspective of the historian of ideas.

T. S. KUHN, *The Copernican Revolution* (1957). Remains the leading work on the subject.

C. LARNER, *Enemies of God: The Witchhunt in Scotland* (1981). Perhaps the most exemplary local study of the subject.

P. LASLETT, *Locke's Two Treatises of Government*, 2nd ed. (1970). Definitive texts with very important introductions.

B. LEVACK, *The Witch Hunt in Early Modern Europe* (1986). Lucid, up-to-date survey of research.

D. LINDBERG AND R. L. NUMBERS (EDS.), *God and Nature: Historical Essays on the Encounter Between Christianity and Science* (1986). The best collection of essays on the subject.

D. LINDBERG AND R. S. WESTMAN (EDS.), *Reappraisals of the Scientific Revolution* (1990). Important essays pointing the way toward new understandings of the subject.

J. MARTIN, *Francis Bacon, The State, and the Reform of Natural Philosophy* (1992). Relates Bacon's thought to his political goals.

O. MAYER, *Authority, Liberty, and Automatic Machinery in Early Modern Europe* (1986). A lively study that seeks to relate thought about machinery to thought about politics.

R. POPKIN, *The History of Scepticism from Erasmus to Spinoza* (1979). A classic study of the fear of loss of intellectual certainty.

P. REDONDI, *Galileo: Heretic* (1987). A controversial work that examines the relationship of Galileo's thought to the church's teaching on the Eucharist rather than to planetary motion.

S. SHAPIN AND S. SCHAFFER, *Leviathan and the Air-Pump: Hobbes, Boyle, and the Experimental Life* (1985). A study of the debate over the validity of scientific experiment during the age of the Scientific Revolution.

Q. SKINNER, *Reason and Rhetoric in the Philosophy of Hobbes* (1996). A major study by one of the leading scholars of Hobbes and early modern political thought.

L. STEWART, *The Rise of Public Science: Rhetoric, Technology, and Natural Philosophy in Newtonian Britain, 1660–1750* (1992). Examines the manner in which science became related to public life and economic development.

K. THOMAS, *Religion and the Decline of Magic* (1971). Provocative, much acclaimed work focused on popular culture.

R. S. WESTFALL, *Never at Rest: A Biography of Isaac Newton* (1981). The major study.

B. H. G. WORMALD, *Francis Bacon: History, Politics, and Science, 1561–1626* (1993). The most extensive recent study.

*Peter the Great (r. 1682–1725) seeking to make Russia a major military power, reorganized the country's political and economic structures. His reign saw Russia enter fully into European power politics. [The Apotheosis of Tsar Peter the Great 1682–1725 by unknown artist, 1710. Historical Museum, Moscow./E.T. Archive]*

# Successful and Unsuccessful Paths to Power (1686–1740)

**The Maritime Powers**
Spain
The Netherlands
France After Louis XIV
Great Britain: The Age of Walpole

**Central and Eastern Europe**
Sweden: The Ambitions of Charles XII
The Ottoman Empire

Poland: Absence of Strong Central Authority
The Habsburg Empire and the Pragmatic
   Sanction
Prussia and the Hohenzollerns

**The Entry of Russia into the European
Political Arena**
Birth of the Romanov Dynasty
Peter the Great

## K E Y   T O P I C S

- The decline of Spain and the Netherlands relative to France and England among the maritime powers
- French aristocratic resistance to the monarchy
- Early eighteenth-century British political stability
- The efforts of the Habsburgs to secure their holdings
- The emergence of Prussia as a major power under the Hohenzollerns
- The efforts of Peter the Great to transform Russia into a powerful centralized nation along Western lines

*The late seventeenth and early eighteenth centuries witnessed significant shifts of power and influence among the states of Europe. Nations that had been strong lost their status as significant military and economic units. Other countries that in some cases had figured only marginally in international relations came to the fore. Great Britain, France, Austria, Russia, and Prussia emerged during this period as the powers that would dominate Europe until at least World War I. Their political and economic dominance occurred at the expense of Spain, the United Netherlands, Poland, Sweden, and the Ottoman Empire. Equally essential to their rise was the weakness of the Holy Roman Empire after the Treaty of Westphalia (1648), which ended the Thirty Years' War.*

*The successful competitors for international power were those states that* created strong central political authorities. Far-sighted observers in the late seventeenth century already understood that in the future those domains that would become or remain great powers must imitate the political and military organization of Louis XIV's France. Strong monarchy alone could impose unity of purpose on the state. The turmoil of seventeenth-century civil wars and aristocratic revolts had impressed people with the value of a strong monarch as the guarantor of minimum domestic tranquility.*

*Imitation of French absolutism involved more than belief in a strong monarchy. It usually required building a standing army, organizing an efficient tax structure to support the army, and establishing a bureaucracy to collect the taxes. Moreover, the political classes of the country, especially the nobles, had to be converted to a sense* of duty and loyalty to the central government that was more intense than their loyalty to other competing political and social institutions.

The waning powers were those that failed to achieve such effective organization. They were unable to employ their political, economic, and human resources to resist external aggression or to overcome the forces of domestic dissolution. Internal and external failures were closely related. If a state did not maintain or establish a central political authority with sufficient power over the nobility, the cities, the guilds, and the church, it could not raise a strong army to defend its borders or its economic interests. More often than not, the key element leading to success or failure was the character, personality, and energy of the monarch.

# The Maritime Powers

In western Europe, Britain and France emerged as the dominant powers. This development represented a shift of influence away from Spain and the United Netherlands. Both the latter countries had been strong and important during the sixteenth and seventeenth centuries, but they became politically and militarily marginal during the eighteenth century. Neither, however, disappeared from the map, and both retained considerable economic vitality and influence. The difference was that France and Britain attained so much more power and economic strength.

## Spain

Spanish power had depended on the influx of wealth from the Americas and on the capacity of the Spanish monarchs to rule the still largely autonomous provinces of the Iberian Peninsula. The economic life of Spain was never healthy. Except for wool, it had virtually no exports to pay for its imports. Instead of promoting domestic industries, the Spanish government financed imports by using the gold and silver mined in its New World empire. This external source of wealth was uncertain because the treasure fleets from the New World (discussed more fully in Chapter 17) could be and sometimes were captured by pirates or hostile navies.

The political life of Spain was also weak. Within its divisions of Castile, Aragon, Navarre, the Basque provinces, and other districts, the royal government could not operate without the cooperation of strong local nobles and the church. From the defeat of the Armada in 1588 to the Treaty of the Pyrenees in 1659 after Spain's defeat by France, Spain suffered a series of foreign policy reverses that harmed the domestic prestige of the monarchy. Furthermore, between 1665 and 1700, the physically malformed, dull-witted, and sexually impotent Charles II was monarch. Throughout his reign, the provincial estates and the nobility increased their power. After his death, the other powers of Europe fought over who would succeed him in the War of the Spanish Succession (1701–1714).

The Treaty of Utrecht (1713), which ended the war, gave the Spanish crown to Philip V (r. 1700–1746), a grandson of Louis XIV. The new king should have tried to consolidate his internal power and protect Spanish overseas trade. However, his second wife, Elizabeth Farnese, used Spanish power to secure thrones for her two sons in Italy. Such diversions of government resources allowed the nobility and the provinces to continue to assert their privileges against the monarchy. Not until the reign of Charles III (r. 1759–1788) did Spain have a monarch concerned with efficient domestic and imperial administration and internal improvement. By the third quarter of the century, Spain was better governed, but it could no longer compete effectively in great power politics.

## The Netherlands

The decline of the United Provinces of the Netherlands occurred wholly within the eighteenth century. After the death of William III of Britain in 1702, the various local provinces successfully prevented the emergence of another strong *stadtholder*. Unified political leadership therefore vanished. During the earlier long wars of the Netherlands with Louis XIV and Britain, naval supremacy had slowly but steadily passed to the British. The fishing industry declined, and the Dutch lost their technological superiority in shipbuilding. Countries between which Dutch ships had once carried goods now traded directly with each other. For example, the British began to use their own vessels in the Baltic traffic with Russia.

Similar stagnation overtook the Dutch domestic industries, such as textile finishing, paper making, and glass blowing. The disunity of the provinces and the absence of vigorous leadership hastened this economic decline and prevented action that might have slowed or halted it.

*In the mid-eighteenth century, when this picture of the Amsterdam Exchange was painted, Amsterdam had replaced the cities of Italy and south Germany as the leading banking center of Europe. Amsterdam retained this position until the late eighteenth century. [Museum Boymans-van Beuningen, Rotterdam]*

What saved the United Provinces from becoming completely insignificant in European matters was their continued financial dominance. Well past the middle of the century, their banks continued to provide loans and financing for European trade.

### France After Louis XIV

Despite its military reverses in the War of the Spanish Succession, France remained a great power. It was less strong in 1715 than in 1680, but it still possessed the largest European population, an advanced if troubled economy, and the administrative structure bequeathed it by Louis XIV. Moreover, even if France and its resources had been drained by the last of Louis's wars, the other major states of Europe were similarly debilitated. What France required was economic recovery and consolidation, wiser political leadership, and a less ambitious foreign policy. It did enjoy a period of recovery, but its leadership was at best indifferent. Louis XIV was succeeded by his five-year-old great-grandson Louis XV (r. 1715–1774). The young boy's uncle, the duke of Orléans, became regent and remained so until his death in 1720. The regency, marked by financial and moral scandals, further undermined the faltering prestige of the monarchy.

*The impending collapse of John Law's bank triggered a financial panic throughout France. Desperate investors, such as those shown here in the city of Rennes, sought to exchange their paper currency for gold and silver before the bank's supply of precious metals was exhausted. [Musée de Bretagne, Rennes]*

JOHN LAW AND THE MISSISSIPPI BUBBLE   The duke of Orléans was a gambler, and for a time he turned over the financial management of the kingdom to John Law (1671–1729), a Scottish mathematician and fellow gambler. Law believed that an increase in the paper-money supply would stimulate France's economic recovery. With the permission of the regent, he established a bank in Paris that issued paper money. Law then organized a monopoly, called the Mississippi Company, on trading privileges with the French colony of Louisiana in North America.

The Mississippi Company also took over the management of the French national debt. The company issued shares of its own stock in exchange for government bonds, which had fallen sharply in value. To redeem large quantities of bonds, Law encouraged speculation in Mississippi Company stock. In 1719 the price of the stock rose handsomely. Smart investors, however, took their profits by selling their stock in exchange for paper money from Law's bank, which they then sought to exchange for gold. The bank, however, lacked enough gold to redeem all the paper money brought to it.

In February 1720, all gold payments were halted in France. Soon thereafter Law himself fled the country. The Mississippi Bubble, as the affair was called, had burst. The fiasco brought disgrace on the government that had sponsored Law. The Mississippi Company was later reorganized and functioned profitably, but fear of paper money and speculation marked French economic life for decades.

RENEWED AUTHORITY OF THE *PARLEMENTS* The duke of Orléans made a second decision that also lessened the power of the monarchy. He attempted to draw the French nobility once again into the decision-making processes of the government. Louis XIV had filled his ministries and bureaucracies with persons from nonnoble families. The regent, under pressure from the nobility, tried to restore a balance. He set up a system of councils on which nobles were to serve along with bureaucrats. The years of idle noble domestication at Versailles, however, had worked too well, and the nobility seemed to lack both the talent and the desire to govern. The experiment failed.

Despite this failure, the great French nobles did not surrender their ancient ambition to assert their rights, privileges, and local influence over those of the monarchy. The chief feature of eighteenth-century French political life was the attempt of the nobility to use its authority to limit the power of the monarchy. The most effective instrument in this process was the *parlements*, or courts dominated by the nobility.

The French *parlements* were different from the English Parliament. These French courts, the most important of which was the *Parlement* of Paris, could not legislate. Rather, they had the power to recognize or not to recognize the legality of an act or law promulgated by the monarch. By long tradition their formal approval had been required to make a royal law valid. Louis XIV had often restricted stubborn, uncooperative *parlements*. In another major political blunder, however, the duke of Orléans had formally approved the full reinstitution of the *parlements'* power to allow or disallow laws. Thereafter the growing financial and moral weakness of the monarchy allowed these aristocratic judicial institutions to reassert their authority. This situation meant that until the revolution in 1789 the *parlements* became natural centers for aristocratic resistance to royal authority.

ADMINISTRATION OF CARDINAL FLEURY In 1726 Cardinal Fleury (1653–1743) became the chief minister of the French court. He was the last of the great clerics who loyally and effectively served the French monarchy. Like his seventeenth-century pre-

*Cardinal Fleury (1653–1743) was the tutor and chief minister of Louis XV from 1726 to 1743. Fleury gave France a period of peace and prosperity, but was unable to solve the state's long-term financial problems. This portrait is by Hyacinthe Rigaud*

decessors, the cardinals Richelieu and Mazarin, Fleury was a realist. He understood the political ambition and incapacity of the nobility and worked quietly to block their undue influence. He was also aware of the precarious financial situation of the royal treasury.

The cardinal, who was seventy-three years old when he came to office, was determined to give the country a period of peace. He surrounded himself with able assistants who tried to solve France's financial problems. Part of the national debt was repudiated. New industries enjoying special privileges were established, and roads and bridges built. On the whole the nation prospered, but Fleury could never draw from the nobles or the church sufficient tax revenues to put the state on a stable financial footing.

Fleury died in 1743, having unsuccessfully attempted to prevent France from intervening in the

*Madame de Pompadour (1721–1764) was the mistress of Louis XV. She exercised considerable political influence at the court and was a notable patron of artists, craftspeople, and writers. This 1763 portrait is by Hubert Drouais (1727–1775) [H. Roger Viollet]*

war then raging between Austria and Prussia. The cost of this intervention was to undo all his financial pruning and planning.

Another failure must also be credited to this elderly cleric. Despite his best efforts, he had not trained Louis XV to become an effective monarch. Louis XV possessed most of the vices and almost none of the virtues of his great-grandfather Louis XIV. He wanted to hold on to absolute power but was unwilling to work the long hours required. He did not choose many wise advisers after Fleury. He was tossed about by the gossip and intrigues of the court. His personal life was scandalous. Louis XV was not an evil person but a mediocre one. And in a monarch, mediocrity was unfortunately often a greater fault than vice.

Despite this political drift, France remained a great power. France's army at mid-century was still the largest and strongest military force on the Continent. Its commerce and production expanded. Its colonies produced wealth and spurred domestic industries. Its cities grew and prospered. The wealth of the nation waxed as the absolutism of the monarchy waned. France did not lack sources of power and strength, but the political leadership could not organize, direct, or inspire its people.

## Great Britain: The Age of Walpole

In 1713 Britain had emerged as a victor over Louis XIV, but the nation required a period of recovery. As an institution, the British monarchy was not in the degraded state of the French monarchy, yet its stability was not certain.

THE HANOVERIAN DYNASTY    In 1714 the Hanoverian dynasty, as designated by the Act of Settlement (1701), came to the throne. Almost immediately, George I (r. 1714–1727) faced a challenge to his new title. The Stuart pretender James Edward (1688–1766), the son of James II, landed in Scotland in December 1715. His forces marched southward but met defeat less than two months later. Although militarily successful against the pretender, the new dynasty and its supporters saw the need for consolidation.

WHIGS AND TORIES    During the seventeenth century, England had been one of the most politically restive countries in Europe. The closing years of Queen Anne's reign (1702–1714) had seen sharp clashes between the political factions of Whigs and Tories over whether to end the war with France. The Tories had urged a rapid peace settlement and after 1710 had opened negotiations with France. During the same period, the Whigs were seeking favor from the elector of Hanover, the future George I, who would soon be their monarch. His concern for his domains in Hanover made him unsympathetic to the Tory peace policy. In the final months of Anne's reign, some Tories, fearing that they would lose power under the waiting Hanoverian dynasty, opened channels of communication with the Stuart pretender; and a few even rallied to his cause.

Under these circumstances, George I, on his arrival in Britain, clearly favored the Whigs. Previously the differences between the Whigs and the Tories had been vaguely related to principle. The Tories emphasized a strong monarchy, low taxes for landowners, and firm support of the Anglican Church. The Whigs supported monarchy but wanted Parliament to retain final sovereignty. They favored urban commercial interests as well as the prosperity of the landowners. They encouraged a policy of religious toleration toward the Protestant nonconformists in England. Socially both groups supported the status quo.

Neither group was organized like a modern political party. Outside Parliament, each party consisted of political networks based on local connections and economic influence. Each group acknowledged a few national spokespeople, who articulated positions and principles. After the Hanoverian accession and the eventual Whig success in achieving the firm confidence of George I, the chief difference for almost forty years between the Whigs and the Tories was that one group had access to public office and patronage and the other did not. This early Hanoverian proscription of Tories from public life was one of the most prominent features of the age.

THE LEADERSHIP OF ROBERT WALPOLE The political situation after 1715 remained in flux, until Robert Walpole (1676–1745) took over the helm of government. Walpole had been active in the House of Commons since the reign of Queen Anne and had been a cabinet minister. What gave him special prominence under the new dynasty was a British financial scandal similar to the French Mississippi Bubble.

Management of the British national debt had been assigned to the South Sea Company, which exchanged government bonds for company stock. As in the French case, the price of the stock soared,

*Sir Robert Walpole (1676–1745), far left, is shown talking with the Speaker of the House of Commons. Walpole, who dominated British political life from 1721 to 1742, is considered the first prime minister of Britain. [Mansell Collection]*

## Lady Mary Wortley Montagu Advises Her Husband on Election to Parliament

*In this letter of 1714, Lady Mary Wortley Montagu discussed with her husband the various paths that he might follow to gain election to the British House of Commons. Note her emphasis on knowing the right people and on having large amounts of money to spend on voters. Eventually, her husband was elected to Parliament in a borough that was controlled through government patronage.*

✦ *What are the various ways in which candidates and their supporters used money to campaign? What role did friendships play in the campaigning? How important do the political ideas or positions of the candidates seem to be? Women could not vote in eighteenth-century parliamentary elections. Is there some other influence they exert?*

You seem not to have received my letters, or not to have understood them: you had been chose undoubtedly at York, if you had declared in time; but there is not any gentleman or tradesman disengaged at this time; they are treating every night. Lord Carlisle and the Thompsons have given their interest to Mr. Jenkins. I agree with you of the necessity of your standing this Parliament, which, perhaps, may be more considerable than any that are to follow it; but, as you proceed, 'tis my opinion, you will spend your money and not be chose. I believe there is hardly a borough unengaged. I expect every letter should tell me you are sure of some place; and, as far as I can perceive you are sure of none. As it has been managed, perhaps it will be the best way to deposit a certain sum in some friend's hands, and buy some little Cornish borough: it would, undoubtedly, look better to be chose for a considerable town; but I take it to be now too late. If you have any thoughts of Newark, it will be absolutely necessary for you to enquire after Lord Lexington's interest; and your best way to apply yourself to Lord Holdernesse, who is both a Whig and an honest man. He is now in town, and you may enquire of him if Brigadier Sutton stands there; and if not, try to engage him for you. Lord Lexington is so ill at the Bath, that it is a doubt if he will live 'till the elections; and if he dies, one of his heiresses, and the whole interest of his estate, will probably fall on Lord Holdernesse.

'Tis a surprize to me, that you cannot make sure of some borough, when a number of your friends bring in so many Parliament-men without trouble or expense. 'Tis too late to mention it now, but you might have applied to Lady Winchester, as Sir Joseph Jekyl did last year, and by her interest the Duke of Bolton brought him in for nothing; I am sure she would be more zealous to serve me, than Lady Jekyl.

*Lord Wharncliffe, ed.,* Letters and Works of Lady Mary Wortley Montagu, *3rd ed., vol. 1 (London, 1861), p. 211.*

only to crash in 1720 when prudent investors sold their holdings and took their speculative profits. Parliament intervened and, under Walpole's leadership, adopted measures to honor the national debt. To most contemporaries, Walpole had saved the financial integrity of the country and had thus proved himself a person of immense administrative capacity and political ability.

George I gave Walpole his full confidence. For this reason Walpole has often been regarded as the first prime minister of Great Britain and the originator of the cabinet system of government. Walpole generally demanded that all the ministers in the cabinet agree on policy, but he could not prevent frequent public differences among them. Unlike a modern English prime minister, he was not chosen by the majority of the House of Commons. The real sources of his power were the personal support of the king, George I and later George II (r. 1727–1760), his ability to handle the House of Commons, and his iron-fisted control of government patronage. To oppose Walpole meant the almost certain loss of government patronage for oneself, one's family, or one's friends. Through the skillful use of patronage, Walpole bought support for himself and his policies from people who wanted to receive jobs, appointments, favors, and government contracts. Such corruption supplied the glue of political loyalty.

Walpole's favorite slogan was "*Quieta non movere*" (roughly, "Let sleeping dogs lie"). To that end, he pursued peace abroad and supported the status quo at home. In this regard he much resembled Cardinal Fleury.

*Lady Mary Wortley Montagu (1689–1762) was a famous writer of letters and an extremely well-traveled woman of the eighteenth century. As the previous document suggests, she was also a shrewd and toughminded political advisor to her husband. [National Portrait Gallery, London]*

This series of four Hogarth etchings satirizes the notoriously corrupt English electoral system. Hogarth shows the voters going to the polls after having been bribed and intoxicated with free gin. (Voting was then in public. The secret ballot was not introduced in England until 1872.) The fourth etching, "Chairing the Member," shows the triumphal procession of the victorious candidate, which is clearly turning into a brawl. [Metropolitan Museum of Art, Harris Brisbane Dick Fund, 1932. Acc. #32.35.(124)]

THE STRUCTURE OF PARLIAMENT   The structure of the eighteenth-century British House of Commons aided Walpole in his pacific policies. It was neither a democratic nor a representative body. Each of the counties into which Britain was divided elected two members. But if the more powerful landed families in a county agreed on the candidates, there was no contest. Most members, however, were elected from a variety of units called boroughs. A few boroughs were large enough for elections to be relatively democratic, but most had few electors. For example, a local municipal corporation or council of only a dozen members might have the right to elect a member of Parliament. In Old Sarum, one of the most famous corrupt, or "rotten," boroughs, the Pitt family simply bought up those pieces of property to which a vote was attached and thus in effect owned a seat in the House of Commons. Through proper electoral management, which involved favors to the electors, the House of Commons could be controlled.

The structure of Parliament and the manner in which the House of Commons was elected meant that the owners of property, especially wealthy nobles, dominated the government of England. They did not pretend to represent people and districts or to be responsive to what would later be called public opinion. They regarded themselves as representing various economic and social interests, such as the West Indian interest, the merchant interest, or the landed interest. These owners of property were suspicious of an administrative bureaucracy controlled by the crown or its ministers. To diminish royal influence, they or their agents served as local government administrators, judges, militia commanders, and tax collectors. In this sense, the British nobility and large landowners actually did govern the nation. And because they regarded the Parliament as the political sovereign, there was no absence of central political authority and direction. Consequently, the supremacy of Parliament gave Britain the unity that absolute monarchy provided elsewhere in Europe.

These parliamentary structures also helped to strengthen the financial position of the British government. The British monarch could not raise taxes the way his continental counterparts could, but the British government consisting of the monarch and Parliament could and did raise vast sums of tax revenue and loans to wage war throughout the eighteenth century. All Britons paid

| France and Great Britain in the Early Eighteenth Century | |
| --- | --- |
| 1713 | Treaty of Utrecht ends the War of the Spanish Succession |
| 1714 | George I becomes king of Great Britain and establishes the Hanoverian dynasty |
| 1715 | Louis XV becomes King of France |
| 1715–1720 | Regency of the duke of Orléans in France |
| 1720 | Mississippi Bubble bursts in France and South Sea Bubble bursts in Great Britain |
| 1720–1742 | Robert Walpole dominates British politics |
| 1726–1743 | Cardinal Fleury serves as Louis XV's chief minister |
| 1727 | George II becomes king of Great Britain |
| 1733 | Excise tax crisis in Britain |

taxes. There were virtually no exemptions. The British credit market was secure through the regulation of the Bank of England, founded in 1693. This strong system of finance and tax collection was one of the cornerstones of eighteenth-century British power.

FREEDOM OF POLITICAL LIFE   British political life was genuinely more free than that on the Continent. There were real limits on the power of Robert Walpole. Parliament could not wholly ignore popular political pressure. Even with the extensive use of patronage, many members of Parliament maintained independent views. Newspapers and public debate flourished. There was freedom of speech and association. There was no large standing army. Those Tories barred from political office and the Whig enemies of Walpole could and did openly oppose his policies—which would have been impossible on the Continent.

For example, in 1733 Walpole presented to the House of Commons a scheme to expand the scope of the excise tax, a tax that resembled a modern sales tax. The outcry in the press, on the public platform, and in the streets was so great that he eventually withdrew the measure. What the British regarded as their traditional political rights raised a real and potent barrier to the power of the government. Again in 1739 the public outcry over the alleged Spanish treatment of British merchants in the Caribbean pushed Britain into a war that Walpole opposed and deplored.

Walpole's ascendancy, which lasted until 1742, did little to raise the level of British political morality, but it brought a kind of stability that Britain had not enjoyed for a century. Its foreign trade grew steadily and spread from New England to India. Agriculture became more productive. All forms of economic enterprise seemed to prosper. The navy became stronger. As a result of this political stability and economic growth, Great Britain became a European power of the first order and stood at the beginning of its era as a world power. Its government and economy during the next generation became a model for all progressive Europeans.

# Central and Eastern Europe

The major factors in the shift of political influence among the maritime nations were naval strength, economic progress, foreign trade, and sound domestic administration. The conflicts among them occurred less in Europe than on the high seas and in their overseas empires. These nations existed in well-defined geographical areas with established borders. Their populations generally accepted the authority of the central government.

Central and eastern Europe were different. Except for the Baltic ports, the economy was agrarian. There were fewer cities and many more large estates populated by serfs. The states in this region did not possess overseas empires. Changes in the power structure normally involved changes in borders or, at least, in which prince ruled a particular area. Military conflicts took place at home rather than overseas.

The political structure of this region, which lay largely east of the Elbe River, was very "soft." The almost constant warfare of the seventeenth century had led to a habit of temporary and shifting political loyalties. The princes and aristocracies of small states and principalities were unwilling to subordinate themselves to a central monarchical authority. Consequently, the political life of the region and the kind of state that emerged there were different from those of western Europe.

Beginning in the last half of the seventeenth century, eastern and central Europe began to assume the political and social contours that would characterize it for the next two centuries. After the Peace of Westphalia, the Austrian Habsburgs rec-

*Charles XII of Sweden (r. 1697–1718) led his nation into a number of disastrous wars. These conflicts exhausted the country's resources, preventing Sweden from playing a major role in later eighteenth-century power politics. [H. Roger Viollet]*

ognized the basic weakness of the position of Holy Roman Emperor and began to consolidate their power outside Germany. At the same time, Prussia emerged as a factor in North German politics and as a major challenger to Habsburg domination of Germany. Most important, Russia at the opening of the eighteenth century became a military power of the first order. These three states (Austria, Prussia, and Russia) achieved their new status largely as a result of the political decay or military defeat of Sweden, Poland, and the Ottoman Empire.

## Sweden: The Ambitions of Charles XII

Under Gustavus Adolphus II (r. 1611–1632), Sweden had played an important role as a Protestant combatant in the Thirty Years' War. During the rest of the seventeenth century, Sweden had consolidated its control of the Baltic, thus preventing Russian possession of a Baltic port and permitting Polish and German access to the sea only on Swedish terms. The Swedes also possessed one of the better armies in Europe. Sweden's economy, however, based primarily on the export of iron, was not strong enough to ensure continued political success.

In 1697 Charles XII (r. 1697–1718) came to the throne. He was headstrong, to say the least, and perhaps insane. In 1700 Russia began a drive to the west against Swedish territory. The Russian goal was a foothold on the Baltic. In the resulting Great Northern War (1700–1721), Charles XII led a vigorous and often brilliant campaign, but one that eventually resulted in the defeat of Sweden. In 1700 he defeated the Russians at the Battle of Narva, but then he turned south to invade Poland. The conflict dragged on, and the Russians were able to strengthen their forces.

In 1708 the Swedish monarch began a major invasion of Russia but became bogged down in the harsh Russian winter. The next year his army was decisively defeated at the Battle of Poltava. Thereafter the Swedes could maintain only a holding action against their enemies. Charles himself sought refuge in Turkey and did not return to Sweden until 1714. He was killed four years later while fighting the Norwegians.

The Great Northern War came to a close in 1721. Sweden had exhausted its military and economic resources and had lost its monopoly on the Baltic coast. Russia had conquered a large section of the eastern Baltic, and Prussia had gained a part of Pomerania. Internally, after the death of Charles XII, the Swedish nobles were determined to reassert their power over the monarchy. They did so but then quarreled among themselves. Sweden played a very minor role in European affairs thereafter.

## The Ottoman Empire

At the southeastern extreme of Europe, the Ottoman Empire was a barrier to the territorial ambitions of the Austrian Habsburgs, Poland, and Russia. The empire in the late seventeenth century still controlled most of the Balkan Peninsula and the entire coastline of the Black Sea. In theory the empire existed to enhance the spread of Islam. Its population, however, was exceedingly diverse both ethnically and religiously. The empire ruled these people not on a territorial but on a religious basis. That is, it created units, called *millets*, that included all persons of a particular religious faith. Various laws and regulations applied to the per-

sons who belonged to a particular millet rather than to a particular administrative territory. Non-Islamic persons in the empire were known as *zimmis*. They could practice their religion, but they were second class citizens who could not rise in the service of the empire or profit much from its successes. This mode of government maintained the self-identity of these various peoples and allowed for little religious integration or interaction.

From the fifteenth century onward, the Ottoman Empire had tried to push further westward in Europe. The empire made its greatest military invasion into Europe in 1683, when it unsuccessfully besieged Vienna. In addition, many Christians in the Balkans and on the Aegean islands had converted to Islam. Many of these people had earlier been forced to convert to Roman Catholicism by the Venetians and welcomed the Turks and their faith as vehicles for political liberation. Much of the Islamic presence in the Balkans today dates to these conversions.

By the last third of the seventeenth century, however, the Ottomans had overextended themselves politically, economically, and militarily. From the mid-sixteenth century, the Ottoman rulers spent so much time at war that they could not attend to meetings of governmental bodies in Constantinople. As time passed, political groups in the capital resisted any substantial strengthening of the central government or of the role of the sultan. Rivalries for power among army leaders and nobles, as well as their flagrant efforts to enrich themselves, weakened the effectiveness of the government. In the outer provinces, such as Transylvania, Wallachia, and Moldavia (all parts of modern Romania), the empire depended on the goodwill of local rulers, who paid tribute but never submitted themselves fully to the imperial power. The empire's economy was weak, and its exports were primarily raw materials. Moreover, the actual conduct of most of its trade had been turned over to representatives of other nations.

By the early eighteenth century, the weakness of the Ottoman Empire meant that a political vacuum that would grow during the next two centuries had come into existence on the southeastern perimeter of Europe. The various European powers who had created strong armies and bureaucracies would begin to probe and eventually dismember the Ottoman Empire. In 1699 the Turks

John III Sobieski (1624–1696) was elected king of Poland in 1764. Sobieski led the Polish Army in repulsing the Turkish siege of Vienna in 1683, an event discussed in one of the documents in this chapter. Despite this victory Sobieski failed to establish a strong central monarchy in Poland. [Erich Lessing/Art Resource, N.Y.]

concluded a treaty with their longtime Habsburg enemy and surrendered all pretensions of control over and consequent receipt of revenues from Hungary, Transylvania, Croatia, and Slavonia. From this time onward, Russia also attempted to extend its territory and influence at the expense of the empire. By the early nineteenth century, many of the peoples who lived in the Balkans and around the Black Sea would seek to create their own national states. The retreat and decay of the Ottoman Empire and the scramble of other states and regional peoples to assume control of southeastern Europe would cause political and ethnic turmoil there from the eighteenth century to our own day.

## Poland: Absence of Strong Central Authority

In no other part of Europe was the failure to maintain a competitive political position so complete as in Poland. In 1683 King John III Sobieski (r. 1674–1696) had led a Polish army to rescue Vienna from the Turkish siege. Following that spectacular effort, however, Poland became a byword for the dangers of aristocratic independence. In Poland as nowhere else on the Continent, the nobility became the single most powerful political factor in the country. Unlike the British nobility and landowners, the Polish nobility would not even submit to a central authority of their own making. There was

# The King of Poland Frees Vienna from the Turks

*In 1683 the Ottoman Empire had laid siege to Vienna. The Habsburg monarchy found itself under enormous military pressure. The military forces of John III Sobieski, the king of Poland, rescued the city and repulsed the last great Turkish advance upon central Europe.*

✦ *What role did religious sentiments and prejudice play in this description? In that regard, how was the battle portrayed as a conflict between two different religions and two different cultures? How is the ruler of Austria portrayed so as to make the king of Poland the hero of the account? What factors appear to have led the leader of the Ottoman forces to retreat? What were the physical fruits of battle for the victors?*

The Victory which the King of Poland hath obtained over the Infidels, is so great and so compleat that past Ages can scarce parallel the fame; and perhaps future Ages will never see any thing like it. . . . On the one hand we see Vienna besieged by three hundred thousand Turks; reduced to the last extremity; its Outworks taken; the Enemy fixed to the Body of the Place; . . . : We see an Emperor [the Habsburg ruler] chased from his Capital; retired to a Corner of his Dominions; all his Country at the mercy of the Tartars, who have filled the Camp with an infinite Number of unfortunate Slaves that had been forcibly carried away out of Austria. On the other hand, we see the King of Poland, who goes out of his Kingdom, with part of his Army, and hastens to succour his . . . Allies, . . . to march against the Enemies of the Christian Religion willing to act in Person on this Occasion, as a true Buckler of Religion. . . .

The Battle was fought on the 12th, it lasted 14 or 15 Hours; the slaughter was horrible, and the loss of the Turks inestimable, for they left the Field of Battle, besides the Dead and Prisoners, all their Canon, Equipage, Tents and infinite Riches that they had been six Years gathering together throughout the whole Ottoman Empire. . . .

The Night was spent in slaughter, and the unhappy Remnant of this Army saved their Lives by flight, having abandoned all to the Victors; even an infinite Number of Waggons, loaden with Ammunition, and some Field pieces, that designed to have carried with them; and which were found the next Day upon the Road they had taken; which makes us suspect that they'll not be able to rally again, . . .

The King [of Poland] understood afterwards by Deserters, who come every hour in Troops to surrender themselves to him, as well as the Renegadoes, that the Visier [the Turkish leader], seeing the defeat of the Army, called his Sons to him, embraced them, bitterly bewailed their Misfortune, and turned towards the Han of the Tartars [an ally of the Turks], and said, 'And thou, wilt not thou succour me?' To whom the Tartar Prince replied, That he knew the King of Poland by more than one Proof, and that the Visier would be very happy if he could save himself by flight, as having no other way for his Security, and that he was going to show him Example.

The Grand Visier being thus abandoned, took the same way, and retired in Disorder with only one Horse. . . . The Booty that was taken in this Action is infinite and inestimable; The Field of Battle was sowed with Gold Sabres, . . . and such a prodigious Quantity of other things that the Pillage which has already lasted three Days, will scarce be over in a whole Week. . . .

*From* Polish Manuscripts: or the Secret History of the Reign of John Sobieski, the III of That Name, King of Poland, *trans. by M. Delerac (London: D. Rhodes, 1700), pp. 355–364, as quoted in Alfred J. Bannan and Achilles Edelenyi, eds.,* Documentary History of Eastern Europe *(New York: Twayne Publishers, Inc., 1970), pp. 112–116.*

no effective central authority in the form of either a king or a parliament.

The Polish monarchy was elective, but the deep distrust and divisions among the nobility prevented their electing a king from among themselves. Sobieski was a notable exception. Most of the Polish monarchs were foreigners and were the tools of foreign powers. The Polish nobles did have a central legislative body called the *Sejm*, or Diet. It included only the nobles and specifically excluded representatives from corporate bodies, such as the towns. In the Diet, however, there existed a practice known as the *liberum veto*, whereby the staunch opposition of any single member could require the body to disband. Such opposition was termed "exploding the Diet." This practice was most often the work of a group of dissatisfied nobles rather than of one person. Nonetheless, the requirement of unanimity was a major stumbling block to effective government.

Government as it was developing elsewhere in Europe simply was not tolerated in Poland. Localism reminiscent of the Middle Ages continued to hold sway as the nobles used all their energy to maintain their traditional "Polish liberties." There was no way to collect enough taxes to build up an army. The price of this noble liberty would eventually be the disappearance of Poland from the map of Europe during the latter half of the eighteenth century.

## The Habsburg Empire and the Pragmatic Sanction

The close of the Thirty Years' War marked a fundamental turning point in the history of the Austrian Habsburgs. Previously, in alliance with the Spanish branch of the family, they had hoped to dominate all of Germany and to return it to the Catholic fold. They did not achieve either goal, and the decline of Spanish power meant that in future diplomatic relations the Austrian Habsburgs were on their own. The Treaty of Westphalia in 1648 permitted Protestantism within the Holy Roman Empire and also recognized the political autonomy of more than 300 corporate German political entities within the empire. These included large units (such as Saxony, Hanover, Bavaria, and Brandenburg) and scores of small cities, bishoprics, principalities, and petty territories of independent knights.

After 1648 the Habsburgs retained a firm hold on the title of Holy Roman Emperor, but the effectiveness of the title depended less on force of arms than on the cooperation that the emperor could elicit from the various political bodies in the empire. The Diet of the empire sat at Regensburg from 1663 until the empire was dissolved in 1806. The Diet and the emperor generally regulated the daily economic and political life of Germany. The post-Westphalian Holy Roman Empire resembled Poland in its lack of central authority. Unlike its Polish neighbor, however, the Holy Roman Empire was reorganized from within as the Habsburgs attempted to regain their authority. As will be seen shortly, Prussia set out on its course toward European power at the same time.

CONSOLIDATION OF AUSTRIAN POWER  While concentrating on their hereditary Austrian holdings among the German states, the Habsburgs also began to consolidate their power and influence within their other hereditary possessions. (See Map 15–1.) These included, first, the Crown of Saint Wenceslas, encompassing the kingdom of Bohemia (in the modern Czech Republic and Slovakia) and the duchies of Moravia and Silesia and, second, the Crown of Saint Stephen, which included Hungary, Croatia, and Transylvania. In the middle of the seventeenth century, much of Hungary remained occupied by the Turks and was liberated only at the end of the century.

In the early eighteenth century, the family further extended its domains, receiving the former Spanish (thereafter Austrian) Netherlands, Lombardy in northern Italy, and briefly, the kingdom of Naples in southern Italy through the Treaty of Utrecht in 1713. During the eighteenth and nineteenth centuries, the Habsburgs' power and influence in Europe were based primarily on their territories outside Germany.

In the second half of the seventeenth century and later, the Habsburgs faced immense problems in these hereditary territories. In each they ruled by virtue of a different title and had to gain the cooperation of the local nobility. The most difficult province was Hungary, where the Magyar nobility seemed ever ready to rebel. There was almost no common basis for political unity among peoples of such diverse languages, customs, and geography. Even the Habsburg zeal for Roman Catholicism no longer proved a bond for unity as they confronted the equally zealous Calvinism of many of the Magyar nobles. The Habsburgs established various central councils to chart common policies for their

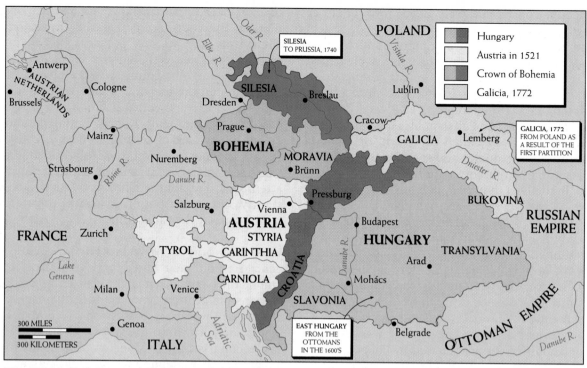

MAP 15–1  THE AUSTRIAN HABSBURG EMPIRE, 1521–1772  *The empire had three main units—Austria, Bohemia, and Hungary. Expansion was mainly eastward: East Hungary from the Ottomans (seventeenth century) and Galicia from Poland (1772). Meantime, Silesia was lost, but the Habsburgs retained German influence as Holy Roman emperors.*

far-flung domains. Virtually all of these bodies dealt with only part of the Habsburgs' holdings. Repeatedly, the Habsburgs had to bargain with nobles in one part of Europe to maintain their position in another.

Despite all these internal difficulties, Leopold I (r. 1657–1705) rallied his domains to resist the advances of the Turks and the aggression of Louis XIV. He achieved Ottoman recognition of his sovereignty over Hungary in 1699 and began the suppression of a long rebellion by his new Magyar subjects that lasted from 1703 to 1711. He also conquered much of the Balkan Peninsula and western Romania. These southeastward extensions allowed the Habsburgs to hope to develop Mediterranean trade through the port of Trieste. The expansion at the cost of the Ottoman Empire also helped them to compensate for their loss of domination over the Holy Roman Empire. Strength in the East gave them greater political leverage in Germany. Leopold I was succeeded by Joseph I (r. 1705–1711), who continued his policies.

THE HABSBURG DYNASTIC PROBLEM  When Charles VI (r. 1711–1740) succeeded Joseph, he had no male heir, and there was only the weakest of precedents for a female ruler of the Habsburg domains. Charles feared that on his death the Austrian Habsburg lands might fall prey to the surrounding powers, as had those of the Spanish Habsburgs in 1700. He was determined to prevent that disaster and to provide his domains with the semblance of legal unity. To those ends, he devoted most of his reign to seeking the approval of his family, the estates of his realms, and the major foreign powers for a document called the Pragmatic Sanction.

This instrument provided the legal basis for a single line of inheritance within the Habsburg dynasty through Charles VI's daughter Maria Theresa (r. 1740–1780). Other members of the Habsburg family recognized her as the rightful heir. The nobles of the various Habsburg domains did likewise after extracting various concessions from Charles. So, when Charles VI died in October 1740, he believed that he had secured legal unity for the Habsburg Empire and a safe succession for his daughter.

Charles VI had indeed established a permanent line of succession and the basis for future legal bonds within the Habsburg holdings. He had failed, however, to protect his daughter from foreign aggression, either through the Pragmatic Sanction or, more important, by leaving her a strong army and a full treasury. Less than two months after his death, the fragility of the foreign agreements became apparent. In December 1740, Frederick II of Prussia invaded the Habsburg province of Silesia. Maria Theresa had to fight to defend her inheritance.

## Prussia and the Hohenzollerns

The Habsburg achievement had been to draw together into an uncertain legal unity a collection of domains possessed through separate feudal titles. The achievement of the Hohenzollerns of Brandenburg-Prussia was to acquire a similar collection of titular holdings and then to forge them into a centrally administered unit. Despite the geographical separation of their territories and the paucity of their natural economic resources, they transformed feudal ties and structures into bureaucratic ones. They subordinated every social class and most economic pursuits to the strengthening of the institution that united their far-flung realms: the army. They thus made the term "Prussian" synonymous with administrative rigor and military discipline.

A STATE OF DISCONNECTED TERRITORIES  The rise of Prussia occurred within the German power vacuum created after 1648 by the Peace of Westphalia. It is the story of the extraordinary Hohenzollern family, which had ruled the German territory of Brandenburg since 1417. (See Map 15–2.) Through inheritance the family had acquired the duchy of Cleves and the counties of Mark and Ravensburg in 1609, the duchy of East Prussia in 1618, and the duchy of Pomerania in 1637. Except for Pomerania, none of these lands was contiguous with Brandenburg. East Prussia lay inside Poland and outside the authority of the Holy Roman Emperor. All of the territories lacked good natural resources, and many of them were devastated during the Thirty Years' War. At Westphalia the Hohenzollerns lost part of Pomerania to Sweden but were compensated by receiving three more bishoprics and the promise of the archbishopric of Magdeburg when it became vacant, as it did in

1680. By the late seventeenth century, the scattered Hohenzollern holdings represented a block of territory within the Holy Roman Empire second in size only to that of the Habsburgs.

Despite its size, the Hohenzollern conglomerate was weak. The areas were geographically separate, with no mutual sympathy or common concern among them. In each, local noble estates limited the power of the Hohenzollern prince. The various areas were also exposed to foreign aggression.

FREDERICK WILLIAM, THE GREAT ELECTOR  The person who began to forge these areas and nobles into a modern state was Frederick William (r. 1640–1688), who became known as the Great Elector (the ruler of Brandenburg was called an elector because he was one of the princes who elected the Holy Roman Emperor). He established himself and his successors as the central uniting power by breaking the local noble estates, organizing a royal bureaucracy, and establishing a strong army.

Between 1655 and 1660, Sweden and Poland engaged in a war that endangered the Great Elector's holdings in Pomerania and East Prussia. Frederick William had neither the military nor the financial resources to confront this threat. In 1655 the Brandenburg estates refused to grant his new taxes; however, he proceeded to collect the required taxes by military force. In 1659 a different grant of taxes, originally made in 1653, elapsed; Frederick William continued to collect them as well as those he had imposed by his own authority. He used the money to build up an army that allowed him to continue to enforce his will without the approval of the nobility. Similar threats and coercion took place against the nobles in his other territories.

There was, however, a political and social trade-off between the elector and his various nobles. These *Junkers*, or German noble landlords, were allowed almost complete control over the serfs on their estates. In exchange for their obedience to the Hohenzollerns, the Junkers received the right to demand obedience from their serfs. Frederick William also tended to choose as the local administrators of the tax structure men who would normally have been members of the noble estates. He thus co-opted potential opponents into his service. The taxes fell most heavily on the backs of the peasants and the urban classes.

As the years passed, sons of Junkers increasingly dominated the army officer corps, and this practice

# The Great Elector Welcomes Protestant Refugees from France

*The Hohenzollern dynasty of Brandenburg-Prussia pursued a policy of religious toleration. The family itself was Calvinist, whereas most of its subjects were Lutherans. When Louis XIV of France revoked the Edict of Nantes in 1685 (see the document in Chapter 13), Frederick William, the Great Elector, seized the opportunity to invite into his realms French Protestants. As his proclamation indicates, he wanted to attract persons with productive skills who could aid the economic development of his domains.*

✦ *In reading this document, do you believe religious or economic concerns more nearly led the Elector of Brandenburg to welcome the French Protestants? What specific privileges did the Elector extend to them? To what extent were these privileges a welcoming measure and to what extent were they inducements to emigrate to Brandenburg? In what kind of economic activity does the elector expect the French refugees to engage?*

We, Friedrich Wilhelm, by Grace of God Margrave of Brandenburg. . . .

Do hereby proclaim and make known to all and sundry that since the cruel persecutions and rigorous ill-treatment in which Our co-religionists of the Evangelical-Reformed faith have for some time past been subjected in the Kingdom of France, have caused many families to remove themselves and to betake themselves out of the said Kingdom into other lands, We now . . . have been moved graciously to offer them through this Edict . . . a secure and free refuge in all Our Lands and Provinces. . . .

Since Our Lands are not only well and amply endowed with all things necessary to support life, but also very well-suited to the reestablishment of all kinds of manufactures and trade and traffic by land and water, We permit, indeed, to those settling therein free choice to establish themselves where it is most convenient for their profession and way of living. . . .

The personal property which they bring with them, including merchandise and other wares, is to be totally exempt from any taxes, customs dues, licenses, or other imposts of any description, and not detained in any way. . . .

As soon as these Our French co-religionists of the Evangelical-Reformed faith have settled in any town or village, they shall be admitted to the domiciliary rights and craft freedoms customary there, gratis and without payments of any fee; and shall be entitled to the benefits, rights, and privileges enjoyed by Our other, native, subjects, residing there. . . .

Not only are those who wish to establish manufacture of cloth, stuffs, hats, or other objects in which they are skilled to enjoy all necessary freedoms, privileges and facilities, but also provision is to be made for them to be assisted and helped as far as possible with money and anything else which they need to realize their intention. . . .

Those who settle in the country and wish to maintain themselves by agriculture are to be given a certain plot of land to bring under cultivation and provided with whatever they need to establish themselves initially. . . .

C. A. Macartney, ed., The Habsburg and Hohenzollern Dynasties in the Seventeenth and Eighteenth Centuries (New York: Walker, 1970), pp. 270–273.

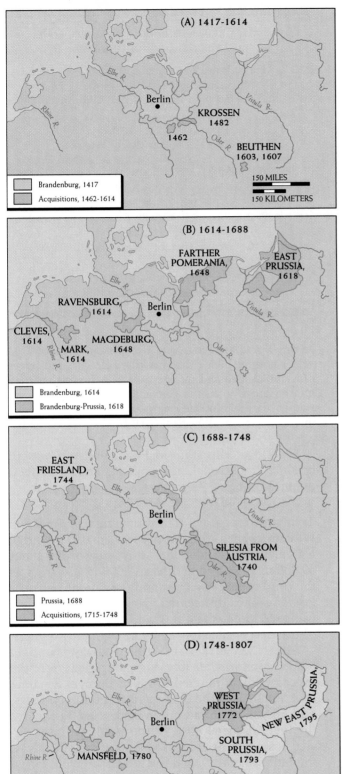

MAP 15–2   EXPANSION OF BRANDENBURG-PRUSSIA
*In the seventeenth-century, Brandenburg-Prussia expanded mainly by acquiring dynastic titles in geographically separated lands. In the eighteenth century, it expanded through aggression to the east, seizing Silesia in 1740 and various parts of Poland in 1772, 1793, and 1795.*

**(A) 1417-1614**

Berlin

KROSSEN
1482

1462

BEUTHEN
1603, 1607

150 MILES

150 KILOMETERS

Brandenburg, 1417

Acquisitions, 1462-1614

**(B) 1614-1688**

FARTHER POMERANIA,
1648

EAST PRUSSIA,
1618

RAVENSBURG,
1614

Berlin

CLEVES,
1614

MAGDEBURG,
1648

MARK,
1614

Brandenburg, 1614

Brandenburg-Prussia, 1618

**(C) 1688-1748**

EAST FRIESLAND,
1744

Berlin

SILESIA FROM AUSTRIA,
1740

Prussia, 1688

Acquisitions, 1715-1748

**(D) 1748-1807**

WEST PRUSSIA,
1772

NEW EAST PRUSSIA,
1795

Berlin

MANSFELD, 1780

SOUTH PRUSSIA,
1793

Prussia, 1748

Acquisitions, 1748-1772

Temporary Acquisitions,
1793-1795 to 1807.

became even more pronounced during the eighteenth century. All officials and army officers took an oath of loyalty directly to the elector. The army and the elector thus came to embody the otherwise absent unity of the state. The existence of the army made Prussia a valuable potential ally and a state with which other powers needed to curry favor.

FREDERICK WILLIAM I, KING OF PRUSSIA   Yet, even with the considerable accomplishments of the Great Elector, the house of Hohenzollern did not possess a crown. The achievement of a royal title was one of the few state-building accomplishments of Frederick I (r. 1688–1713). This son of the Great Elector was the least "Prussian" of his family during these crucial years. He built palaces, founded Halle University (1694), patronized the arts, and lived luxuriously. In 1701, however, at the outbreak of the War of the Spanish Succession, he put his army at the disposal of the Habsburg Holy Roman Emperor. In exchange for this loyal service, the emperor permitted Frederick to assume the title of "King in Prussia." Thereafter Frederick became Frederick I, and he passed the much-desired royal title to his son Frederick William I in 1713.

Frederick William I (r. 1713–1740) was both the most eccentric and one of the most effective Hohenzollerns. After giving his father a funeral that matched the luxury of his life, Frederick William I immediately imposed strict austerity. Some jobs were abolished, and other salaries lowered. His political aims seem to have been the consolidation of an obedient, compliant bureaucracy and a bigger army. He initiated a policy of *Kabinett* government, which meant that lower officials submitted all relevant documents to him in his office, or *Kabinett*. Then he alone examined the papers, made his decisions, and issued his orders. He thus skirted the influence of ministers and ruled alone.

Frederick William I organized the bureaucracy along military lines. He united all departments under the *General-Ober Finanz-Kriegs-und-Domänen-Direktorium*, more happily known to us as the General Directory. He imposed taxes on the nobility and changed most remaining feudal dues into money payments. He sought to transform feudal and administrative loyalties into a sense of duty to the monarch as a political institution rather than as a person. He once described the perfect royal servant as

| Austria and Prussia in the Late Seventeenth and Early Eighteenth Centuries | |
| --- | --- |
| 1640–1688 | Reign of Frederick William, the Great Elector |
| 1657–1705 | Leopold I rules Austria and resists the Turkish invasions |
| 1683 | Turkish siege of Vienna |
| 1688–1713 | Reign of Frederick I of Prussia |
| 1699 | Peace treaty between Turks and Habsburgs |
| 1711–1740 | Charles VI rules Austria and secures agreement to the Pragmatic Sanction |
| 1713–1740 | Frederick William I builds up the military power of Prussia |
| 1740 | Maria Theresa succeeds to the Habsburg throne |
| 1740 | Frederick II violates the Pragmatic Sanction by invading Silesia |

an intelligent, assiduous, and alert person who after God values nothing higher than his king's pleasure and serves him out of love and for the sake of honor rather than money and who in his conduct solely seeks and constantly bears in mind his king's service and interests, who, moreover, abhors all intrigues and emotional deterrents.[1]

Service to the state and the monarch was to become impersonal, mechanical, and, in effect, unquestioning.

THE PRUSSIAN ARMY   The discipline that Frederick William applied to the army was fanatical. During his reign the size of the army grew from about 39,000 in 1713 to more than 80,000 in 1740. It was the third or fourth largest army in Europe, whereas Prussia ranked thirteenth in population. Rather than using recruiters, the king made each canton or local district responsible for supplying a quota of soldiers.

After 1725 Frederick William always wore an officer's uniform. He formed one regiment from the tallest soldiers he could find in Europe. Separate laws applied to the army and to civilians. Laws, customs, and royal attention made the officer corps the highest social class of the state. Military service attracted the sons of Junkers. Thus, the army, the Junker nobility, and the monarchy were forged

---

[1]Quoted in Hans Rosenberg, *Bureaucracy, Aristocracy, and Autocracy* (Boston: Beacon Press, 1958), p. 93.

into a single political entity. Military priorities and values dominated Prussian government, society, and daily life as in no other state of Europe. It has often been said that whereas other nations possessed armies, the Prussian army possessed its nation.

Although Frederick William I built the best army in Europe, he avoided conflict. He wanted to drill his soldiers but not to order them into battle. Although he terrorized his family and associates and on occasion knocked out teeth with his walking stick, he was not militarily aggressive. The army was for him a symbol of Prussian power and unity, not an instrument to be used for foreign adventures or aggression.

At his death in 1740, he passed to his son Frederick II "the Great" (r. 1740–1786) this superb military machine, but he could not also pass on the wisdom to refrain from using it. Almost immediately on coming to the throne, Frederick II upset the Pragmatic Sanction and invaded Silesia. He thus crystallized the Austrian–Prussian rivalry for control of Germany that would dominate central European affairs for over a century.

*Though economically weak and with a small population, Prussia became an important state because it developed a large, well-trained army. Prussian troops were known for their discipline, the result of constant drill and harsh punishment. In this mid-eighteenth-century engraving one soldier is being whipped while another is about to run a gauntlet of other soldiers. [Bildarchiv Preussischer Kulturbesitz]*

# The Entry of Russia into the European Political Arena

Though ripe with consequences for the future, the rise of Prussia and the new consolidation of the Austrian Habsburg domains seemed to many at the time only another shift in the long-troubled German scene. The emergence of Russia, however, as an active European power was a wholly new factor in European politics. Previously Russia had been considered part of Europe only by courtesy. Geographically and politically it lay on the periphery. Hemmed in by Sweden on the Baltic and by the Ottoman Empire on the Black Sea, the country had no warm-water ports. Its chief outlet to the west was Archangel on the White Sea, which was ice free for only part of the year. There was little trade. What Russia did possess was a vast reserve of largely undeveloped natural and human resources.

## Birth of the Romanov Dynasty

The reign of Ivan the Terrible, which had begun so well and closed so frighteningly, was followed by anarchy and civil war known as the "Time of Troubles." In 1613, hoping to restore stability, an assembly of nobles elected as tsar a seventeen-year-old boy named Michael Romanov (r. 1613–1654). Thus began the dynasty that despite palace revolutions, military conspiracies, assassinations, and family strife ruled Russia until 1917.

Michael Romanov and his two successors, Alexis I (r. 1654–1676) and Theodore III (r. 1676–1682), brought stability and some bureaucratic centralization to Russia. The country remained, however, weak and impoverished. The bureaucracy after years of turmoil was still largely controlled by the *boyars*, the old nobility. This administrative apparatus could barely suppress a revolt of peasants and Cossacks (horsemen who lived on the steppe frontier) under Stepan Razin in 1670–1671. Furthermore, the government and the tsars faced the danger of mutiny from the *streltsy*, or guards of the Moscow garrison.

## Peter the Great

In 1682 another boy—ten years old at the time—ascended the fragile Russian throne as co-ruler with his half brother. His name was Peter (r. 1682–1725), and Russia would never be the same after him. He and the ill Ivan V had come to power on the shoulders of the *streltsy*, who expected to be rewarded for their support. Much violence and bloodshed had surrounded the disputed succession. Matters became even more confused when the boys' sister, Sophia, was named regent. Peter's followers overthrew her in 1689. From that date onward, Peter ruled personally, although in theory he shared the crown until Ivan died in 1696. The dangers and turmoil of his youth convinced Peter of two things. First, the power of the tsar must be made secure from the jealousy of the *boyars* and the greed of the *streltsy*. Second, the military power of Russia must be increased. In that respect he resembled Louis XIV of France, who had experienced the turmoil of the *Fronde* during his youth and resolved to establish a strong monarchy.

Western Europe, particularly its military resources, fascinated Peter I, who became known as Peter the Great. He was an imitator of the first

| Rise of Russian Power | |
|---|---|
| 1533–1584 | Reign of Ivan the Terrible |
| 1584–1613 | "Time of Troubles" |
| 1613 | Michael Romanov becomes tsar |
| 1682 | Peter the Great, age ten, becomes tsar |
| 1689 | Peter assumes personal rule |
| 1696 | Russia captures Azov on the Black Sea from the Turks |
| 1697 | European tour of Peter the Great |
| 1698 | Peter returns to Russia to put down the revolt of the *streltsy* |
| 1700 | The Great Northern War opens between Russia and Sweden; Russia defeated at Narva by Swedish Army of Charles XII |
| 1703 | Saint Petersburg founded |
| 1709 | Russia defeats Sweden at the Battle of Poltava |
| 1718 | Charles XII of Sweden dies |
| 1718 | Son of Peter the Great dies in prison under mysterious circumstances |
| 1721 | Peace of Nystad ends the Great Northern War |
| 1721 | Peter establishes a synod for the Russian church |
| 1722 | Peter issues the Table of Ranks |
| 1725 | Peter dies leaving an uncertain succession |

*After Peter the Great of Russia returned from his journey to western Europe, he personally cut off the traditional and highly prized long sleeves and beards of the Russian nobles. His action symbolized his desire to see Russia become more powerful and more modern. [The Granger Collection]*

order. The products and workers from the West who had filtered into Russia impressed and intrigued him. In 1697 he made a famous visit in transparent disguise to western Europe. There he dined and talked with the great and the powerful, who considered this almost seven-foot-tall ruler both crude and rude. His happiest moments on the trip were spent inspecting shipyards, docks, and the manufacture of military hardware.

Peter returned to Moscow determined to copy what he had seen abroad, for he knew that warfare would be necessary to make Russia a great power. The tsar's drive toward westernization, though unsystematic, had four general goals: taming the *boyars* and the *streltsy*, achieving secular control of the church, reorganizing the internal administration, and developing the economy. Peter pursued each of these goals ruthlessly. His effort was unprecedented in Russian history in both its intensity and scope.

TAMING THE *BOYARS* AND *STRELTSY* Peter made a sustained attack on the *boyars*. In 1698, immediately on his return from abroad, he personally shaved the long beards of the court *boyars* and sheared off the customary long, hand-covering sleeves of their shirts and coats, which had made them the butt of jokes throughout Europe. More important, he demanded that the nobles serve his state.

In 1722 Peter published a Table of Ranks that equated a person's social position and privileges with his rank in the bureaucracy or the army rather than with his position in the nobility. Peter thus intended to make the social standing of individual *boyars* a function of their willingness to

# Peter the Great Establishes Building Requirements in Saint Petersburg

*By constructing Saint Petersburg on the Gulf of Finland, Peter the Great tried to consolidate his military efforts in the Great Northern War. The city was to provide Russia with a permanent outlet to the West and to be the site of its new capital. The construction of this city consequently served symbolic political ends as well as military and economic ones. In this document, Peter explains how he expected the city to be constructed.*

✦ *Why might Peter have been so concerned that the work on the city progress rapidly? What are the difficulties in construction in Russia that this document reveals? What do those difficulties tell you about Russia's society and its economic resources? Why might Peter have been concerned that only houses face on the streets of the new city.*

1. On the City Island and the Admiralty Island in Saint Petersburg, as likewise on the banks of the greater Neva and its more important arms, wood buildings are forbidden, only adobe houses being allowed. The two above-mentioned islands and the embankments excepted, wood may be used for buildings, the plans to be obtained from the architect. . . . The roofs are to be covered either with two thicknesses of turf laid on rafters with cross-ribs (not on laths or boards), or with tiles. No other roof covering is allowed under penalty of severe fines. The streets should be bordered directly by the houses, not with fences or stables.

2. The most illustrious and mighty Peter the Great, Emperor and Autocrat of all Russia, has commanded his imperial decree to be proclaimed to people of all ranks. Whereas stone construction here is advancing very slowly, it being difficult to obtain stonemasons and other artisans of this craft even for good pay; for this reason all stone buildings of any description are forbidden in the whole state for a few years, until construction has suffi-ciently progressed here, under penalty of confiscation of the offender's property and exile. This decree is to be announced in all the cities and districts of the Saint Petersburg province, except this city, so that none may plead ignorance as an excuse.

3. The following is ordered: no building shall be undertaken in Petersburg on the grounds of houses, between neighboring back yards, until all the main and side streets are entirely built up. However, if after this any person needs more buildings, he may build on his grounds, along the neighbor's lot. No stables or barns may be built facing the street, but only inside the grounds. Along the streets and side streets all the space must be filled by residences, as ordered. In the locations where, as ordered by previous decrees, wooden houses may be built, they must be made of squared logs. If the logs are used as they are, the walls must be faced with boards and coated with red, or painted to look like brick.

*From Marthe Blinoff, ed.,* Life and Thought in Old Russia, *(University Park: The Pennsylvania State University Press, 1961), pp. 16–17.*

*Peter the Great built Saint Petersburg on the Gulf of Finland to provide Russia with better contact with western Europe. He moved Russia's capital there from Moscow in 1703. This is an eighteenth-century view of the city. [John R. Freeman]*

serve the central state. Unlike Prussian Junkers, however, the Russian nobility never became perfectly loyal to the state. They repeatedly sought to reassert their independence and their control of the Russian imperial court and to bargain with later tsars over local authority and the nobles' dominance of the serfs.

The *streltsy* fared less well than the *boyars*. In 1698 they had rebelled while Peter was on his European tour. On his return, he brutally suppressed the revolt. There were private tortures and public executions, in which Peter's own ministers took part. Almost 1,200 of the rebels were put to death, and their corpses remained on public display to discourage future disloyalty.

ACHIEVING SECULAR CONTROL OF THE CHURCH
Peter dealt with the potential independence of the Russian Orthodox Church with similar ruthlessness. Here again, he had to confront a problem that had arisen in the turbulent decades that had pre-

ceded his reign. The Russian church had long opposed the scientific as well as the theological thought of the West. In the mid-seventeenth century, a reformist movement led by Patriarch Nikon introduced certain changes into church texts and ritual. These reforms caused great unrest among the Old Believers, a group of Russian Christians who strongly opposed these changes. Although condemned by the hierarchy, the Old Believers persisted in their opposition. Thousands of them committed suicide rather than submit to the new rituals. The Old Believers represented a rejection of change and innovation; their opposition discouraged the church hierarchy from making any further substantial accommodations with modern thought.

In the future Peter wanted to avoid two kinds of difficulties with the church. First, the clergy must not be able to oppose change and westernization. Second, the hierarchy of the church must not be permitted to cause again the kind of controversy that had inspired the Old Believers. Consequently,

## Bishop Burnet Recalls the Visit of Peter the Great to England

*In 1797 and 1798 Peter the Great of Russia toured western Europe to discover how Russia must change its society and economy in order to become a great power. As this description indicates, English Bishop Gilbert Burnet found the tsar a curious person. He was deeply impressed by the tsar's difficult personality and by his determination to have his subjects learn the ways of western Europe.*

✦ *What qualities did Burnet admire and criticize in Peter the Great? How had some of these qualities been manifested in Peter's behavior as ruler of Russia? Why might Peter the Great have been so interested in ships and shipbuilding? What steps did the tsar take to allow his subjects to become familiar with other nations?*

He came this winter over to England, and stayed some months among us. . . . I had good interpreters, so I had much free discourse with him; he is a man of a very hot temper, soon inflamed, and very brutal in his passion; he raises his natural heat, by drinking much brandy, . . . he is subject to convulsive motions all over his body, and his head seems to be affected with these; he wants not capacity, and has a larger measure of knowledge, than might be expected from his education, which was very indifferent; a want of judgment, with an instability of temper, appear in him too often and too evidently; he is mechanically turned, and seems designed by nature rather to be a ship-carpenter, than a great prince. This was his chief study and exercise, while he stayed here: he wrought much with his own hands, and made all about him work at the models of ships. . . . He was . . . resolved to encourage learning, and to polish his people, by sending some of them to travel in other countries, and to draw strangers to come and live among them. . . . After I had seen him often, and had conversed much with him, I could not but adore the depth of the providence of God, that had raised up such a furious man to so absolute an authority over so great a part of the world.

Bishop Burnet's History of His Own Time *(Oxford: Clarendon Press, 1823), vol. 4, pp. 396–397.*

---

in 1721, Peter simply abolished the position of patriarch. In its place he established a synod headed by a layman, called the Procurator General, to rule the church in accordance with secular requirements. So far as transforming a traditional institution was concerned, this action toward the church was the most radical policy of Peter's reign. It produced still further futile opposition from the Old Believers, who saw the tsar as leading the church into new heresy.

REORGANIZING DOMESTIC ADMINISTRATION  In his reorganization of domestic administration, Peter looked to institutions then used in Sweden. These were "colleges," or bureaus, of several persons rather than departments headed by a single minister. These colleges, which he imposed on Russia, were to look after matters such as the collection of taxes, foreign relations, war, and economic affairs. This new organization was an attempt to breathe life into Russia's stagnant and inefficient administration.

In 1711 Peter created a central senate of nine members who were to direct the Moscow government when the tsar was away with the army. The purpose of these and other local administrative reforms was to establish a bureaucracy that could support an efficient army.

DEVELOPING THE ECONOMY AND WAGING WAR The economic development advocated by Peter the Great was closely related to his military needs. He encouraged the establishment of an iron industry in the Ural Mountains, and by mid-century Russia had become the largest iron producer in Europe. He sent promising young Russians abroad to acquire technical and organizational skills. He tried to attract West European craftspeople to live and work in Russia. Except for the striking growth of the iron industry, which nevertheless later languished, these efforts had only marginal success.

The goal of these internal reforms and political departures was to support a policy of warfare. Peter was determined to secure warm-water ports that would allow Russia to trade with the West and to have a greater impact on European affairs. This policy led him into wars with the Ottoman Empire and Sweden. His armies began fighting the Turks in 1695 and captured Azov on the Black Sea in 1696. It was a temporary victory, for in 1711 he was compelled to return the port.

Peter had more success against Sweden, where the inconsistency and irrationality of Charles XII were no small aid. In 1700 Russia invaded the Swedish Baltic possessions. The Swedish king's failure to follow up his victory at Narva in 1700 allowed Peter to regroup his forces and reserve his resources. In 1709, when Charles XII returned to fight Russia again, Peter was ready, and the Battle of Poltava sealed the fate of Sweden. In 1721 the Peace of Nystad, which ended the Great Northern War, confirmed the Russian conquest of Estonia, Livonia, and part of Finland. Henceforth Russia possessed warm-water ports and a permanent influence on European affairs.

At one point the domestic and foreign policies of Peter the Great literally intersected. This was at the spot on the Gulf of Finland where he founded his new capital city of Saint Petersburg. There he built government structures and compelled the *boyars* to construct town houses. He thus imitated those European monarchs who had copied Louis XIV by constructing smaller versions of Versailles. The founding of Saint Petersburg went beyond establishing a central imperial court, however. It symbolized a new Western orientation of Russia and Peter's determination to hold his position on the Baltic coast. He had begun the construction of the city and had moved the capital there in 1703, even before his victory over Sweden was assured.

Despite his notable success on the Baltic, Peter's reign ended with a great question mark. He had long quarreled with his only son, Alexis. Peter was jealous of the young man and feared he might undertake sedition. In 1718 Peter had his son imprisoned, and during this imprisonment, Alexis died mysteriously. Thereafter Peter claimed for himself the right to name a successor, but he could never bring himself to designate one either orally or in writing. Consequently, when he died in 1725, there was no firm policy on the succession to the throne. For more than thirty years, soldiers and nobles again determined who ruled Russia. Peter had laid the foundations of a modern Russia, but he had failed to lay the foundations of a stable state.

◆

*By the second quarter of the eighteenth century, the major European powers were not yet nation-states in which the citizens felt themselves united by a shared sense of community, culture, language, and history. They were still monarchies in which the personality of the ruler and the personal relationships of the great noble families exercised considerable influence over public affairs. The monarchs, except in Great Britain, had generally succeeded in making their power greater than the nobility's. The power of the aristocracy and its capacity to resist or obstruct the policies of the monarch were not destroyed, however. In Britain, of course, the nobility had tamed the monarchy, but even there tension between nobles and monarchs would continue throughout the rest of the century.*

*In foreign affairs the new arrangement of military and diplomatic power established early in the century prepared the way for two long conflicts. The first was a commercial rivalry for trade and overseas empire between France and Great Britain. During the reign of Louis XIV, these two nations had collided over the French bid for dominance in Europe. During the eighteenth century, they dueled for control of commerce on other continents. The second arena of warfare was in central Europe, where Austria and Prussia fought for the leadership of the German states.*

*Behind these international conflicts and the domestic rivalry of monarchs and nobles, however, the society of eighteenth-century Europe began to change. The character and the structures of the societies over which the monarchs ruled were beginning to take on some features associated with the modern age. These economic and social developments would eventually transform the life of Europe to a degree beside which the state building of the early eighteenth-century monarchs paled.*

# Review Questions

1. Explain why Britain and France remained leading powers in western Europe while Spain and the United Netherlands declined.

2. How did the structure of British government change under the political leadership of Robert Walpole? What were the chief sources of Walpole's political strength?

3. How was the Hohenzollern family able to forge a conglomerate of diverse land holdings into the state of Prussia? Who were the major personalities involved in this process and what were their individual contributions? Why was the military so important in Prussia?

4. Compare and contrast the varying success with which the Hohenzollerns and Habsburgs each handled their problems. Which family was more successful and why? Why were Sweden, the Ottoman Empire, and Poland each less successful?

5. How and why did Russia emerge as a great power? Discuss the character of Peter the Great. What were Russia's domestic problems before Peter came to power? What were his methods of reform? To what extent did he succeed? How were his reforms related to his military ambitions?

6. It has been said that Peter the Great was a rational ruler, interested in the welfare of his people. Do you agree with this statement? Why? Can you make a case for Peter as a bloody tyrant, concerned only with promoting his own glory?

# Suggested Readings

T. M. BARKER, *Army, Aristocracy, Monarchy: Essays in War, Society and Government in Austria, 1618–1780* (1982). Examines the intricate power relationships among these major institutions.

J. BLACK, *Eighteenth-Century Europe 1700–1789* (1990). An excellent survey.

J. BREWER, *The Sinews of Power: War, Money and the English State, 1688–1783* (1989). An extremely important study of the financial basis of English power.

R. BROWNING, *Political and Constitutional Ideas of the Court Whigs* (1982). An excellent overview of the ideology of Walpole's supporters.

F. L. CARSTEN, *The Origins of Prussia* (1954). Discusses the groundwork laid by the Great Elector in the seventeenth century.

J. C. D. CLARK, *English Society: 1688–1832: Social Structure and Political Practice during the Ancien Régime* (1985). An important, controversial work that emphasizes the role of religion in English political life.

A. COBBAN, *A History of Modern France*, 2nd ed., vol. 1 (1961). A lively and opinionated volume.

L. COLLEY, *In Defiance of Oligarchy: The Tory Party, 1714–60* (1982). An important study that challenges much conventional opinion about eighteenth-century British politics.

N. DAVIS, *God's Playground*, vol. 1 (1991). Excellent on prepartition Poland.

P. M. G. DICKSON, *Finance and Government Under Maria Theresa* (1987). A definitive work.

W. DOYLE, *The Old European Order, 1660–1800* (1992). The most thoughtful treatment of the subject.

P. DUKES, *The Making of Russian Absolutism: 1613–1801* (1982). An overview based on recent scholarship.

R. R. ERGANG, *The Potsdam Führer* (1941). The biography of Frederick William I.

R. J. W. EVANS, *The Making of the Habsburg Monarchy, 1550–1700: An Interpretation* (1979). Places much emphasis on intellectual factors and the role of religion.

F. FORD, *Robe and Sword: The Regrouping of the French Aristocracy After Louis XIV* (1953). An important book for political, social, and intellectual history.

J. M. HITTLE, *The Service City: State and Townsmen in Russia, 1600–1800* (1979). Examines the relationship of cities in Russia to the growing power of the central government.

H. HOLBORN, *A History of Modern Germany, 1648–1840* (1966). The most comprehensive survey in English.

R. A. KANN AND Z. V. DAVID, *The Peoples of the Eastern Habsburg Lands, 1526–1918* (1984). A helpful overview of the subject.

D. MCKAY AND H. M. SCOTT, *The Rise of the Great Powers 1648–1815* (1983). Now the standard survey.

W. H. MCNEIL, *Europe's Steppe Frontier, 1500–1800* (1964). An interpretive essay on the history of southeastern Europe.

R. K. MASSIE, *Peter the Great: His Life and His World* (1980). A good popular biography.

L. B. NAMIER AND J. BROOKE, *The History of Parliament: The House of Commons, 1754–1790*, 3 vols. (1964). A detailed examination of the unreformed British House of Commons and electoral system.

J. B. OWEN, *The Eighteenth Century* (1974). An excellent introduction to England in this period.

G. PARKER, *The Military Revolution: Military Innovation and the Rise of the West (1500–1800)* (1988). A major work in every respect.

J. H. PLUMB, *Sir Robert Walpole*, 2 vols. (1956, 1961). A masterful biography ranging across the sweep of European politics.

J. H. PLUMB, *The Growth of Political Stability in England, 1675–1725* (1969). An important interpretive work.

N. V. RIASANOVSKY, *The Image of Peter the Great in Russian History and Thought* (1985). Examines the legacy of Peter in Russian history.

N. V. RIASANOVSKY, *A History of Russia*, 5th ed. (1992). The best one-volume introduction.

H. ROSENBERG, *Bureaucracy, Aristocracy, and Autocracy: The Prussian Experience, 1660–1815* (1960). Emphasizes the organization of Prussian administration.

P. F. SUGAR, *Southeastern Europe Under Ottoman Rule, 1354–1804* (1977). An extremely clear presentation.

E. N. WILLIAMS, *The Ancien Régime in Europe* (1972). A state-by-state survey of very high quality.

*During the eighteenth century, most goods were produced in small workshops such as this iron forge painted by Joseph Wright of Derby (1734–1797), or in the homes of artisans. Not until very late in the century, with the early stages of industrialization, did a few factories appear. In the small early workshops it would not have been uncommon for the family of the owner to visit, as portrayed in this painting. [The Bridgeman Art Library/Broadlands Trust, Hants]*

# Society and Economy
# Under the Old Regime
# in the Eighteenth Century

# K E Y   T O P I C S

- The varied privileges and powers of Europe's aristocracies in the Old
  Regime and their efforts to increase their wealth
- The plight of rural peasants
- Family structure and family economy
- The transformation of Europe's economy by the agricultural and
  industrial revolutions
- Urban growth and the social tensions that accompanied it
- The strains on the institutions of the Old Regime brought about by social
  change

During the French Revolution and the turmoil spawned by that upheaval, it became customary to refer to the patterns of social, political, and economic relationships that had existed in France before 1789 as the **ancien régime,** or the "old regime." The term has come to be applied generally to the life and institutions of prerevolutionary Europe. Politically, it meant the rule of theo-retically absolute monarchies with growing bureaucracies and aristocratically led armies. Economically, scarcity of food, predominance of agriculture, slow transport, a low level of iron production, comparatively unsophisticated financial institutions, and, in some cases, competitive commercial overseas empires characterized the Old Regime. Socially, men and women living during *the period saw themselves less as individuals than as members of distinct corporate bodies that possessed certain privileges or rights as a group.*

*Tradition, hierarchy, corporateness, and privilege were the chief social characteristics of the Old Regime. Yet it was by no means a static society. Change and innovation were fermenting in its midst. Farming became more commercialized, and both food production and the size of the population increased. The early stages of the Industrial Revolution made more consumer goods available, and domestic consumption expanded throughout the century. The colonies in the Americas provided strong demand for European goods and manufactures. Merchants in seaports and other cities were expanding their businesses. By preparing their states for war, European governments put new demands on the resources and the economic organizations of their nations. The spirit of rationality that had been so important to the Scientific Revolution of the seventeenth century continued to manifest itself in the economic life of the eighteenth century. The Old Regime itself fostered the changes that eventually transformed it into a different kind of society.*

# Major Features of Life in the Old Regime

Socially, prerevolutionary Europe was based on (1) aristocratic elites possessing a wide variety of inherited legal privileges; (2) established churches intimately related to the state and the aristocracy; (3) an urban labor force usually organized into guilds; and (4) a rural peasantry subject to high taxes and feudal dues. Of course, the men and women living during this period did not know it as the "Old Regime." Most of them earned their livelihoods and passed their lives as their forebears had done for generations before them and as they expected their children to do after them.

## Maintenance of Tradition

During the eighteenth century, the past weighed more heavily on people's minds than did the future. Few persons outside the government bureaucracies, the expanding merchant groups, and the movement for reform called the Enlightenment

(see Chapter 18) considered change or innovation desirable. This was especially true of social relationships. Both nobles and peasants, for different reasons, repeatedly called for the restoration of traditional, or customary, rights. The nobles asserted what they considered their ancient rights against the intrusion of the expanding monarchical bureaucracies. The peasants, through petitions and revolts, called for the revival or the maintenance of the customary manorial rights that allowed them access to particular lands, courts, or grievance procedures.

Except for the early industrial development in Britain and the accompanying expansion of personal consumption, the eighteenth-century economy was also predominantly traditional. The quality and quantity of the grain harvest remained the most important fact of life for most of the population and the gravest concern for governments.

## Hierarchy and Privilege

Closely related to this traditional social and economic outlook was the hierarchical structure of the society. The medieval sense of rank and degree not only persisted but became more rigid during the century. In several continental cities, sumptuary laws regulating the dress of the different classes remained on the books. These laws forbade persons in one class or occupation to wear clothes like those worn by their social superiors. These laws, which sought to make the social hierarchy easily visible, were largely ineffective by this time. What really enforced the hierarchy was the corporate nature of social relationships.

Each state or society was considered a community composed of numerous smaller communities. Eighteenth-century Europeans did not enjoy what Americans regard as "individual rights." Instead a person enjoyed such rights and privileges as were guaranteed to the particular communities or groups of which she or he was a part. The "community" might include the village, the municipality, the nobility, the church, the guild, a university, or the parish. In turn, each of these bodies enjoyed certain privileges, some great, some small. The privileges might involve exemption from taxation or from some especially humiliating punishment, the right to practice a trade or craft, the right of one's children to pursue a particular occupation, or, for the church, the right to collect the tithe.

# The Aristocracy

The eighteenth century was the great age of the aristocracy. The nobility constituted approximately 1 to 5 percent of the population of any given country. In every country, the nobility was the single wealthiest sector of the population, had the widest degree of social, political, and economic power, and set the tone of polite society. In most countries, the nobility had their own separate house in the parliament, estates, or diet. Only nobles had any kind of representation in Hungary and Poland. Land continued to provide the aristocracy with its largest source of income, but aristocrats did not merely own estates. Their influence was felt throughout social and economic life. In much of Europe, however, it was felt that manual labor was regarded as beneath a noble. In Spain, it was assumed that even the poorer nobles would lead lives of idleness. In other nations, however, the nobility often fostered economic innovation and embraced the commercial spirit. Such willingness to change helped protect the nobility's wealth.

## Varieties of Aristocratic Privilege

To be an aristocrat was a matter of birth and legal privilege. This much the aristocracy had in common across the Continent. In almost every other respect, they differed markedly from country to country.

BRITISH NOBILITY    The smallest, wealthiest, best-defined, and most socially responsible aristocracy resided in Great Britain. It consisted of about 400 families, and the eldest male members of each family sat in the House of Lords. Through the corruptions of the electoral system, these families also controlled many seats in the House of Commons. The estates of the British nobility ranged from a few thousand to fifty thousand acres, from which they received rents. The nobles owned about one-fourth of all the arable land in the country. Increasingly the British aristocracy invested its wealth in commerce, canals, urban real estate, mines, and even industrial ventures. Because only the eldest son inherited the title and the land, younger sons moved into commerce, the army, the professions, and the church. British landowners in both houses of Parliament levied taxes and also paid them. They had few significant legal privileges, but their direct or indirect control of local government gave them immense political power and social influence. The aristocracy dominated the society and politics of the English counties. Their country houses, many of which were built in the eighteenth century, were centers for local society.

FRENCH NOBILITY    The situation of the continental nobilities was less clear-cut. In France, the approximately 400,000 nobles were divided between nobles "of the sword," or those whose nobility was derived from military service, and those "of the robe," or those who had either acquired their titles by serving in the bureaucracy or had purchased them. The two groups had quarreled in the past but often cooperated during the eighteenth century to defend their common privileges.

*The foundation of aristocratic life was the possession of land. English aristocrats and large landowners controlled local government as well as the English Parliament. This painting of Robert Andrews and his wife by Thomas Gainsborough (1728–1788) shows an aristocratic couple on their estate. The gun and the hunting dog in this portrait suggest the importance landowners assigned to the virtually exclusive hunting privileges they enjoyed on their land. [The National Gallery, London]*

*Eighteen-century France had some of the best roads in the world, but they were often built with forced labor. French peasants were required to work part of each year on such projects. This system, called the* corvée, *was not abolished until the French Revolution in 1789. [Giraudon/Art Resource, N.Y.]*

The French nobles were also divided between those who held office or favor with the royal court at Versailles and those who did not. The court nobility reaped the immense wealth that could be gained from holding high office. The nobles' hold on such offices intensified during the century. By the late 1780s, appointments to the church, the army, and the bureaucracy, as well as other profitable positions, tended to go to the nobles already established in court circles. Whereas these well-connected aristocrats were rich, the provincial nobility, called *hobereaux*, were often little better off than wealthy peasants.

Despite differences in rank, origin, and wealth, certain hereditary privileges set all French aristocrats apart from the rest of society. They were exempt from many taxes. For example, most French nobles did not pay the *taille*, or land tax, the basic tax of the Old Regime. The nobles were technically liable for payment of the *vingtième*, or the "twentieth," which resembled an income tax, but they rarely had to pay it in full. The nobles were not liable for the royal *corvées*, or forced labor on public works, which fell on the peasants. In addition to these exemptions, French nobles could collect feudal dues from their tenants and enjoyed exclusive hunting and fishing privileges.

EASTERN EUROPEAN NOBILITIES  East of the Elbe River, the character of the nobility became even more complicated and repressive. Throughout the area, the military traditions of the aristocracy remained important. In Poland, there were thousands of nobles, or *szlachta*, who after 1741 were entirely

exempt from taxes. Until 1768 these Polish aristocrats possessed the right of life and death over their serfs. Most of the Polish nobility were relatively poor. A few rich nobles who had immense estates exercised political power in the fragile Polish state.

In Austria and Hungary, the nobility continued to possess broad judicial powers over the peasantry through their manorial courts. They also enjoyed various degrees of exemption from taxation. The wealthiest of them, Prince Esterhazy of Hungary, owned ten million acres of land.

In Prussia, after the accession of Frederick the Great in 1740, the position of the Junker nobles became much stronger. Frederick's various wars required their full support. He drew his officers almost wholly from the Junker class. Nobles also increasingly made up the bureaucracy. As in other parts of eastern Europe, the Prussian nobles had extensive judicial authority over the serfs.

In Russia, the eighteenth century saw what amounted to the creation of the nobility. Peter the Great's (r. 1682–1725) linking of state service and noble social status through the Table of Ranks (1722) established among Russian nobles a self-conscious class identity that had not previously existed. Thereafter they were determined to resist compulsory state service. In 1736 Empress Anna (r. 1730–1740) reduced such service to twenty-five years. In 1762 Peter III (r. 1762) exempted the greatest nobles entirely from compulsory service. In 1785, in the Charter of the Nobility, Catherine the Great (r. 1762–1796) legally defined noble rights and privileges in exchange for the assurance that the nobility would serve the state voluntarily. Noble privileges included the right of transmitting noble status to a nobleman's wife and children, the judicial protection of noble rights and property, considerable power over the serfs, and exemption from personal taxes.

### Aristocratic Resurgence

The Russian Charter of the Nobility constituted one aspect of the broader European-wide development termed the "aristocratic resurgence." The aristocratic resurgence was the nobility's reaction to the threat to their social position and privileges that they felt from the expanding power of the monarchies. This resurgence took several forms in the eighteenth century. First, all nobilities tried to preserve their exclusiveness by making it more difficult to become a noble. Second, they pushed to reserve appointments to the officer corps of the armies, the bureaucracies, the government ministries, and the church exclusively for nobles. By doing this, they hoped to control the power of the monarchies.

Third, the nobles attempted to use the authority of existing aristocratically controlled institutions against the power of the monarchies. These institutions included the British Parliament, the French courts, or *parlements*, and the local aristocratic estates and provincial diets in Germany and the Habsburg Empire. Fourth, the nobility sought to improve its financial position by gaining further exemptions from taxation or by collecting higher rents or long-forgotten feudal dues from the peasantry. The nobility tried to shore up its position by various appeals to traditional and often ancient privileges that had lapsed over time. This aristocratic challenge to the monarchies was a fundamental political fact of the day.

# The Land and Its Tillers

Land was the economic basis of eighteenth-century life and the foundation of the status and power of the nobility. Well over three-fourths of all Europeans lived in the country, and few of them ever traveled more than a few miles from their birthplace. Except for the nobility and the wealthier nonaristocratic landowners, most people who dwelled on the land were poor. They lived in various states of economic and social dependency, exploitation, and vulnerability.

### Peasants and Serfs

Rural social dependency related directly to the land. The nature of the dependency differed sharply for free peasants, such as English tenants and most French cultivators, and for the serfs of Germany, Austria, and Russia, who were legally bound to a particular plot of land and a particular lord. But everywhere, the class that owned most of the land also controlled the local government and the courts. For example, in Great Britain, all farmers and smaller tenants had the legal rights of English citizens. The justices of the peace, however, who presided over the county courts and who could call out the local militia, were always substantial landowners, as were the members of Parliament, who made the laws. In eastern Europe, the landowners presided over the manorial courts. On the Continent, the burden of taxation fell on the tillers of the soil.

Obligations of Peasants   Landlord power increased as one moved across Europe from west to east. Most French peasants owned some land, but there were a few serfs in eastern France. Nearly all French peasants were subject to certain feudal dues, called *banalités*. These included the required use-for-payment of the lord's, or *seigneur's*, mill to grind grain and his oven to bake bread. The *seigneur* could also require a certain number of days each year of the peasant's labor. This practice of forced labor was termed the *corvée*. Because even landowning French peasants rarely possessed enough land to support their families, they had to rent more land from the *seigneur* and were also subject to feudal dues attached to those plots. In Prussia and Austria, despite attempts by the monarchies late in the century to improve the lot of the serfs, the landlords continued to exercise almost complete control over them. In many of the Habsburg lands, law and custom required the serfs to provide service, or *robot*, to the lords.

Serfs were worst off in Russia. There nobles reckoned their wealth by the number of "souls," or, male serfs, owned rather than by the acreage the landlord possessed. Russian landlords, in effect, regarded serfs merely as economic commodities. They could demand as many as six days a week of labor, known as *barshchina*, from the serfs. Like Prussian and Austrian landlords, they enjoyed the right to punish their serfs. On their own authority, Russian landlords could even exile a serf to Siberia.

# An English Traveler Describes Serfdom in Eighteenth-Century Russia

*William Coxe was an Englishman who traveled widely in eastern Europe. His description of Russian serfdom portrays the brutality of the institution. It also illustrates his amazement at the absence in Russia of civil liberties such as he and more humble citizens enjoyed in England.*

✦ *What are the examples of a Russian master not being restrained by law in his treatment of his serfs? What rights did the serfs have in regard to possessing property acquired through their own industry? How did Russian masters improve the skills of their serfs for their own economic benefit?*

Peasants belonging to individuals are the private property of the landholders, as much as implements of agriculture, or herds of cattle; and the value of an estate is estimated, as in Poland, by the number of boors [serfs], and not by the number of acres. ... If the Polish boor is oppressed, and he escapes to another master, the latter is liable to no pecuniary penalty for harboring him; but in Russia the person who receives another's vassal is subject to a heavy fine. With respect to his own demands upon his peasants, the lord is restrained by no law, either in the exaction of any sum, or in the mode of employing them. He is absolute master of their time and labour: some he employs in agriculture: a few he makes his menial servants, and perhaps without wages; and from others he exacts an annual payment.

Each vassal, therefore, is rated according to the arbitrary will of his master. Some contribute four or five shillings a year; others, who are engaged in traffic or trade, are assessed proportion to their supposed profits. ... With regard to any capital which they may have acquired by their industry, it may be seized, and there can be no redress. ...

... [S]ome of the Russian nobility send their vassals to Moscow or Petersburg for the purpose of learning various handcraft trades: they either employ them on their own estates; let them out for hire; sell them at an advanced price; or receive from them an annual compensation for the permission of exercising trade for their own advantage.

*William Coxe,* Travels into Poland, Russia, Sweden, and Denmark, *4th ed., vol. 3 (London: T. Cadell, 1972, first printed 1784), pp. 174–181.*

Serfs had no legal recourse against the orders and whims of their lords. There was little difference between Russian serfdom and slavery.

In southeastern Europe, where the Ottoman Empire held sway, peasants were free though landlords tried to exert authority in every way. The domain of the landlords was termed a çift. The landlord was often an absentee who managed the estate through an overseer. During the seventeenth and eighteenth centuries, these landlords, like those elsewhere in Europe, often became more commercially oriented and turned to the production of commercial crops, such as cotton, vegetables, potatoes, and maize.

Scarcity of labor rather than recognition of legal rights supported the independence of the southeastern European peasants. A peasant might migrate from one landlord to another. Because the second landlord needed the peasant's labor, he had no reason to return him to the original landlord. During the seventeenth and eighteenth centuries, however, disorder originating in the capital of Constantinople (now Istanbul) spilled over into the Balkan Peninsula. In this climate, landlords increased their authority by offering their peasants protection from bandits or rebels who might destroy peasant villages. As in medieval times, the manor house or armed enclosure of a local landlord became the peasants' refuge. These landlords also owned all the housing and tools required by the peasants and furnished their seed grain. Consequently, despite legal independence, Balkan peasants under the Ottoman Empire became largely dependent upon the landlords, though never to the extent of serfs in eastern Europe or Russia.

PEASANT REBELLIONS    The Russian monarchy itself contributed to the further degradation of the serfs.

Peter the Great gave whole villages to favored nobles. Later in the century, Catherine the Great confirmed the authority of the nobles over their serfs in exchange for the landowners' political cooperation. Russia experienced vast peasant unrest with well over fifty peasant revolts occurring between 1762 and 1769. These culminated between 1773 and 1775 in Pugachev's Rebellion, when Emelyan Pugachev (1726–1775) promised the serfs land of their own and freedom from their lords. All

---

## Catherine the Great Issues a Proclamation Against Pugachev

*Against a background of long-standing human degradation and increasing landowner authority, a Don Cossack named Emelyan Pugachev led the greatest serf rebellion in Russian history from 1773 to 1775. Empress Catherine the Great's proclamation of 1773 argues that he was alienating the serfs from their natural and proper allegiance to her and their masters.*

✦ *How does the language of this proclamation seek to denigrate as well as to condemn Pugachev and his followers? What does the proclamation claim that Pugachev has been promising? On what grounds did Catherine expect her loyal subjects to resist Pugachev?*

By the grace of God, we Catherine II . . . make known to our faithful subjects, that we have learnt, with the utmost indignation and extreme affliction, that a certain Cossack, a deserter and fugitive from the Don, named Emelyan Pugachev, after having traversed Poland, has been collecting, for some time past, in the districts that border on the river Irghis, in the government of Orenburg, a troop of vagabonds like himself; that he continues to commit in those parts all kinds of excesses, inhumanly depriving the inhabitants of their possessions, and even of their lives. . . .

In a word, there is not a man deserving of the Russian name, who does not hold in abomination the odious and insolent like by which Pugachev fancies himself able to seduce and to deceive persons of a simple and credulous disposition, by promising to free them from the bonds of submission, and obedience to their sovereign, as if the Creation of the universe had established human

societies in such a manner as that they can subsist without an intermediate authority between the sovereign and the people.

Nevertheless, as the insolence of this vile refuse of the human race is attended with consequences pernicious to the provinces adjacent to that district; as the report of the flagrant enormities which he has committed, may affright those persons who are accustomed to imagine the misfortunes of others as ready to fall upon them, and as we watch with indefatigable care over the tranquillity of our faithful subjects, we inform them . . . that we have taken . . . such measures as are the best adapted to stifle the sedition . . .

We trust . . . that every true son of the country will unremittedly fulfill his duty, of the contributing to the maintenance of good order and of public tranquillity, by preserving himself from the snares of seduction, and by discharging his obedience to his lawful sovereign.

*William Tooke, Life of Catherine II, Empress of Russia, 4th ed., vol. 2 (London: T. N. Longman and O. Rees, 1800), pp. 460–461 (spelling modernized).*

of southern Russia was in turmoil until the government brutally suppressed the rebellion. Thereafter, any thought of liberalizing or improving the condition of the serfs was set aside for a generation.

Pugachev's was the largest peasant uprising of the eighteenth century, but smaller peasant revolts or disturbances took place in Bohemia in 1775, in Transylvania in 1784, in Moravia in 1786, and in Austria in 1789. There were almost no revolts in western Europe, but England experienced many rural riots. Rural rebellions were violent, but the peasants and serfs normally directed their wrath against property rather than persons. The rebels usually sought to reassert traditional or customary rights against practices that they perceived as innovations. Their targets were carefully chosen and included unfair pricing, onerous new or increased feudal dues, changes in methods of payment or land use, unjust officials, or extraordinarily brutal overseers and landlords. Peasant revolts were thus conservative in nature.

## Aristocratic Domination of the Countryside: The English Game Laws

One of the clearest examples of aristocratic domination of the countryside and of aristocratic manipulation of the law to its own advantage was English legislation on hunting.

Between 1671 and 1831, English landowners had the exclusive legal right to hunt game animals. These specifically included hares, partridges, pheasants, and moorfowl. Similar legislation covered other animals such as deer, the killing of which by an unauthorized person became a capital offense in the eighteenth century. By law, only persons owning a particular amount of landed property could hunt these animals. Excluded from the right to hunt were all persons renting land, wealthy city merchants who did not own land, and poor people in cities, villages, and the countryside. The poor were excluded because the elite believed that allowing the poor to enjoy the sport of hunting would undermine their work habits. The city merchants were excluded because the landed gentry in Parliament wanted to demonstrate visibly and legally the superiority of landed wealth over commercial wealth. Thus, the various game laws upheld the superior status of the aristocracy and the landed gentry.

The game laws represent a prime example of class legislation. The gentry who benefitted from the laws and whose parliamentary representatives had passed them also served as the local justices of the peace who administered the laws and punished their violation. The justices of the peace could levy fines and even have poachers impressed into the army. Gentry could also take civil legal action against wealthier poachers, such as rich farmers who rented land, and thus saddle them with immense legal fees. The gentry also employed gamekeepers to protect game from poachers. The gamekeepers were known to kill the dogs belonging to people suspected of poaching. By the middle of the century, gamekeepers had devised trapguns to shoot poachers who tripped their hidden levers.

A small industry arose to circumvent the game laws, however. Many poor people living either on an estate or in a nearby village would kill game for food. They believed that the game actually belonged to the community, and this poaching increased during hard times. Poaching was thus one way for the poor to find food.

Even more important was the black market in game animals sustained by the demand of urban people for this kind of luxury meat. Here arose the possibility of poaching for profit, and indeed, poaching technically meant the stealing or killing of game for sale. Local people from both the countryside and the villages would steal the game and then sell it to intermediaries called *higglers*. Later, coachmen took over this function. The higglers and the coachmen would smuggle the game into the cities, where poulterers would sell it at a premium price. Everyone involved made a bit of money along the way. During the second half of the century, English aristocrats began to construct large game preserves. The rural poor, who had lost their rights to communal land as a result of its enclosure by the large landowners, deeply resented these preserves, which soon became hunting grounds to organized gangs of poachers.

Penalties against poaching increased in the 1790s after the outbreak of the French Revolution, but so did the amount of poaching as the economic hardships caused by Britain's participation in the wars of the era put a greater burden on poor people and as the demand for food in English cities grew along with their population. By the 1820s, both landowners and reformers called for a change in the law. In 1831 Parliament rewrote the game laws, retaining the landowners' possession of the game but permitting them to allow other people to hunt it. Poaching continued, but the exclusive right of the landed classes to hunt game had ended.

# Family Structures and the Family Economy

In preindustrial Europe, the household was the basic unit of production and consumption. Few productive establishments employed more than a handful of people not belonging to the family of the owner, and those rare exceptions were in cities. The overwhelming majority of Europeans, however, lived in rural areas. There, as well as in small towns and cities, the household mode of organization predominated on farms, in artisans' workshops, and in small merchants' shops. With that mode of economic organization, there developed what is known as the *family economy*. Its structure as described here had prevailed over most of Europe for centuries.

## Households

What was a household in the preindustrial Europe of the Old Regime? There were two basic models, one characterizing northwestern Europe and the other eastern Europe.

NORTHWESTERN EUROPE  In northwestern Europe, the household almost invariably consisted of a married couple, their children through their early teenage years, and their servants. Except for the few wealthy people, households were small, usually consisting of not more than five or six members. Furthermore, in these households, more than two generations of a family rarely lived under the same roof. High mortality and late marriage prevented families of three generations. In other words, grandparents rarely lived in the same household as their grandchildren and families consisted of parents and children. The family structure of northwestern Europe was thus nuclear rather than extended.

This particular characteristic of the northwestern European household is one of the major discoveries of recent research into family history. Previously historians had assumed that before industrialization Europeans lived in extended familial settings with several generations living together in a household. Recent demographic investigation has sharply reversed this picture. Children lived with their parents only until their early teens. Then they normally left home, usually to enter the work force of young servants who lived and worked in another household. A child of a skilled artisan might remain with his or her parents to learn a valuable skill; but only rarely would more than one child do so because children's labor was more remunerative outside the home.

These young men and women who had left home would eventually marry and form an independent household of their own. This practice of moving away from home is known as *neolocalism*. These young people married relatively late. Men were usually over twenty-six, and women over twenty-three. The new couple usually had children as soon after marriage as possible. Frequently, the woman was already pregnant at marriage. Family and community pressure often compelled the man to marry her. In any case, premarital sexual relations were common, though illegitimate births were rare. The new couple would soon employ a servant, who, together with their growing children, would undertake whatever form of livelihood the household used to support itself.

The word *servant* in this context may be confusing. It does not refer to someone looking after the needs of wealthy people. Rather, in preindustrial Europe, a servant was a person—either male or female—who was hired, often under a clear contract, to work for the head of the household in exchange for room, board, and wages. The servant was usually young and by no means always socially inferior to his or her employer. Normally, the servant was an integral part of the household and ate with the family.

Young men and women became servants when their labor was no longer needed in their parents' household or when they could earn more money for their family outside the parental household. Being a servant for several years—often as many as eight or ten—allowed young people to acquire the productive skills and the monetary savings necessary to begin their own household. These years spent as servants largely account for the late age of marriage in northwestern Europe.

EASTERN EUROPE  As one moved eastward across the continent, the structure of the household and the pattern of marriage changed. There both men and women usually married before the age of twenty. Consequently, children were born to much younger parents. Often, especially among Russian serfs, wives were older than their husbands. Eastern European households were generally larger than those in the West. Often a rural Russian household consisted of more than nine and possibly more than twenty members, with three or perhaps even four generations of the same family living together. Early marriage made this situation more likely. In Russia, marrying involved not starting a new household but remaining in and expanding one already established.

The landholding structure in eastern Europe accounts, at least in part, for these patterns of marriage and the family. The lords of the manor who owned land wanted to ensure that it would be cultivated so they could receive their rents. Thus, for example, in Poland, landlords might forbid marriage between their own serfs and those from another estate. They might also require widows and widowers to remarry to assure adequate labor for a particular plot of land. Polish landlords also frowned on the hiring of free laborers—the equivalent of servants in the West—to help cultivate land. The landlords preferred to use other serfs. This practice inhibited the formation of independent households. In Russia, landlords ordered the families of young people in their villages to arrange marriages within a short, set time. These lords discouraged single-generation family households because the death or serious illness of one person in such a household might mean that the land assigned to it would go out of cultivation.

## The Family Economy

Throughout Europe, most people worked within the family economy. That is to say, the household was the basic unit of production and consumption. Almost everyone lived within a household of some kind because it was virtually impossible for ordinary people to support themselves independently. Indeed, except for members of religious orders, people living outside a household were viewed with great suspicion. They were considered potentially criminal or disruptive or, at least, potentially dependent on the charity of others. Everywhere beggars met deep hostility.

Depending on their ages and skills, everyone in the household worked. The need to survive poor harvests or economic slumps meant that no one could be idle. Within this family economy, all goods and income produced went to the benefit of the household rather than to the individual family member. On a farm much of the effort went directly into raising food or producing other agricultural goods that could be exchanged for food. Few western Europeans, however, had enough land to support their household from farming alone. Thus one or more family members might work

elsewhere and send wages home. For example, the father and older children might work as harvest pickers or might fish or might engage in other labor, either in the neighborhood or farther from home. If the father was such a migrant worker, the burden of farm work would fall on his wife and their younger children. This was not an uncommon pattern.

The family economy also dominated the life of skilled urban artisans. The father was usually the chief artisan. He normally employed one or more servants, but would expect his children to work in the enterprise also. His eldest child was usually trained in the trade. His wife often sold his wares or opened a small shop of her own. Wives of merchants also often ran their husbands' businesses, especially when the husband traveled to purchase new goods. In any case, everyone in the family was involved. If business was poor, family members would look for employment elsewhere, not to support themselves as individuals but to ensure the survival of the family unit.

In western Europe, the death of a father often brought disaster to the economy of the household. The continuing economic life of the family usually depended on his land or skills. The widow might take on the farm or the business, or his children might do so. The widow usually sought to remarry quickly to restore the labor and skills of a male to the household and to prevent herself from becoming dependent on relatives or charity.

The high mortality rate of the time meant that many households were reconstituted second family groups that included stepchildren. Because of the advanced age of the widow or economic hard times, however, some households might simply dissolve. The widow became dependent on charity or relatives. The children became similarly dependent or entered the workforce of servants earlier than they would otherwise. In other cases, the situation could be so desperate that they would resort to crime or to begging. The personal, emotional, and economic vulnerability of the family economy cannot be overemphasized.

In eastern Europe, the family economy functioned in the context of serfdom and landlord domination. Peasants clearly thought in terms of their families and expanding the land available for cultivation. The village structure may have mitigated the pressures of the family economy, as did the multigenerational family. Dependence on the available land was the chief fact of life. There were many fewer

# Rules Are Established for the Berlin Poor House

*Poverty was an enormous problem in eighteenth-century Europe, often forcing family members to work away from home and creating thousands of migrant workers and beggars. Governments were hostile to beggars and sometimes migrant workers, whom they regarded as a potential source of crime and disorder. Many of these concerns are evident in the regulations for the Berlin Poor House.*

✦ *What were the distinctions made between the poor who deserved sympathy and those who did not? How would such a distinction affect social policy? Why might beggars have been regarded as dangers to public order? What attitudes toward work are displayed in these regulations?*

Whereas His Majesty . . . has renewed the prohibition of begging in the streets and in houses and has made all giving of alms punishable; it is decided to inform the public of the present measures for the relief of the poor, and to acquaint it with the main outlines of the above order:

1. In the new workhouse, . . . the genuinely needy and the poor deserving sympathy shall be cared for better than hitherto, but the deliberate beggars shall more resolutely be made to work.

2. The past organization of this house has therefore been totally altered, so that all persons to be received in it shall be divided into two entirely separate main classes, differentiated both in the status of their work and its location, in their dormitory and in their board.

3. The first class is meant for the old and for other persons deserving help and sympathy, who cannot entirely live by their work and do not wish to beg. Those report to the Poor's Chest in the Town Hall of Berlin, with a certificate from the Minister of their Church, showing their hitherto unblemished character, and after their references have been checked, they shall be accepted. They spin in the house as much wool as their age and health permits, and if they spin more than the cost of their keep, the surplus shall be paid out to them. . . .

5. The second main class is destined for those who do not wish to make use of this benefaction, but would rather live by begging. These deliberate beggars will be arrested by the Poor Law Constables, if necessary with the assistance of the Police, irrespective of age or status, whether they be vagabonds, journeymen, citizens, discharged soldiers, their wives or children, and will be sent to the workhouse.

6. Those who are caught begging for the first time shall be put into this class for three months at least, for the second time, for a year, and for the third and later times for several years, according to circumstances, for life.

7. Similarly, this class is destined for those who after due process of law have been sent for punishment as runaway servants and apprentices, for a period of time determined by the Court.

8. All the persons under numbers 5, 6, and 7 shall be forced to spin and prepare wool, and shall be kept on a minimum standard, clearly differentiated from the first class, both in the status and quantity of their work in their board and their lodging.

9. The children shall be cared for separately, . . . and shall receive education for several hours a day. . . .

10. Before a beggar is discharged, he must, in order that he shall not again become a public nuisance, prove an occupation in prospect or the existence of relations or of other persons, who will look after him and will put him up at once. . . .

*Kruegeger, Geschichte der Manufacturen . . . , as quoted and translated in S. Pollard and C. Holmes, eds.,* Documents of European Economic History, *vol. I (London: Edward Arnold, 1968), pp. 166–167.*

(a)

(b)

These four scenes were painted by the English artist Francis Wheatley (1747–1801) near the close of the eighteenth century. They illustrate in a very idealized manner the life of a farm family in the morning (a), at noon (b), in the evening (c), and at night (d). Note the artist's assumptions about the division of labor by gender. Men work in the fields, women work in the home or look after the needs of men and children. As other illustrations in this chapter show, many eighteenth-century women in fact worked outside the home, but considerable social pressure was developing at this time to restrict them to domestic roles. These paintings are thus more prescriptive than descriptive, intended in part to persuade their viewers that women belonged in their separate family sphere. Many, perhaps most, families living in the countryside could not maintain the closeness that these paintings extol. To survive, many had to send members to work on other farms or even in other regions of the country following the harvest. [Yale Center for British Art, Paul Mellon Collection]

(c)

(d)

# Priscilla Wakefield Demands More Occupations Be Opened to Women

*At the end of the eighteenth century, several English women writers began to demand a wider life for women. Priscilla Wakefield was among such authors. She was concerned that women found themselves only able to pursue occupations that paid poorly. Often they were excluded from work on the grounds of their alleged physical weakness. She also believed that women should receive equal wages for equal work. Many of the issues she raised have yet to be adequately addressed on behalf of women.*

✦ *From reading this passage, what do you understand to have been the arguments at the end of the eighteenth century to limit the kinds of employment that women might enter? Why did women receive lower wages for work similar to or the same as that done by men? What occupations traditionally filled by men does Wakefield believe women might also pursue?*

Another heavy discouragement to the industry of women, is the inequality of the reward of their labor, compared with that of men; an injustice which pervades every species of employment performed by both sexes.

In employments which depend on bodily strength, the distinction is just; for it cannot be pretended that the generality of women can earn as much as men, when the produce of their labor is the result of corporeal exertion; but it is a subject of great regret, that this inequality should prevail even where an equal share of skill and application is exerted. Male stay-makers, mantua-makers, and hair-dressers, are better paid than female artists of the same professions; but surely it will never be urged as an apology for this disproportion, that women are not as capable of making stays, gowns, dressing hair, and similar arts, as men; if they are not superior to them, it can only be accounted for upon this principle, that the prices they receive for their labor are not sufficient to repay them for the expense of qualifying themselves for their business; and that they sink under the mortification of being regarded as artisans of inferior estimation. . . .

Besides these employments which are commonly performed by women, and those already shown to be suitable for such persons as are above the condition of hard labor, there are some professions and trades customarily in the hands of men, which might be conveniently exercised by either sex.—Watchmaking requiring more ingenuity than strength, seems peculiarly adapted to women; as do many parts of the business of stationer, particularly, ruling account books or making pens. The compounding of medicines in an apothecary's shop, requires no other talents than care and exactness; and if opening a vein occasionally be a indispensable requisite, a woman may acquire the capacity of doing it, for those of her own sex at least, without any reasonable objection. . . . Pastry and confectionery appear particularly consonant to the habits of women, though generally performed by men; perhaps the heat of the ovens, and the strength requisite to fill and empty them, may render male assistants necessary; but certain women are most eligible to mix up the ingredients, and prepare the various kinds of cakes for baking.—Light turnery and toy-making depend more upon dexterity and invention than force, and are therefore suitable work for women and children. . . .

Farming, as far as respects the theory, is commensurate with the powers of the female mind: nor is the practice of inspecting agricultural processes incompatible with the delicacy of their frames if their constitution be good.

*Priscilla Wakefield,* Reflections on the Present Condition of the Female Sex *(1798), (London, 1817), pp. 125–127, as quoted in Bridget Hill, ed.,* Eighteenth-Century Women: An Anthology *(London: George Allen & Unwin, 1984), pp. 227–228.*

artisan and merchant households, and there was far less geographical mobility than in western Europe.

## Women and the Family Economy

The family economy established many of the chief constraints on the lives and personal experiences of women in preindustrial society. Most of the historical research that has been undertaken on this subject relates to western Europe. There, a woman's life experience was largely the function of her capacity to establish and maintain a household. For women, marriage was an economic necessity as well as an institution that fulfilled sexual and psychological needs. Outside a household a woman's life was vulnerable and precarious. Some women succeeded in becoming economically independent. They were the exception. Normally, unless she were an aristocrat or a member of a religious order, a woman probably could not support herself solely by her own efforts. Consequently, a woman devoted much of her life first to maintaining her parents' household and then to devising some means of getting her own household to live in as an adult. Bearing and rearing children were usually subordinate to these goals.

By the age of seven, a girl would have begun to help with the household work. On a farm, this might mean looking after chickens, watering animals, or carrying food to adults working the land. In an urban artisan's household, she would do light work, perhaps cleaning or carrying and later sewing or weaving. The girl would remain in her parents' home as long as she made a real contribution to the family enterprise or as long as her labor elsewhere was not more remunerative to the family.

An artisan's daughter might not leave home until marriage because at home she could learn increasingly valuable skills associated with the trade. The situation was different for the much larger number of girls growing up on farms. Their parents and brothers could often do all the necessary farm work, and a girl's labor at home quickly became of little value to her family. She would then leave home, usually between the ages of twelve and fourteen. She might take up residence on another farm, but more likely she would migrate to a nearby town or city. She would rarely travel more than thirty miles from her parents' household. She would then normally become a servant, once again living in a household, but this time in the household of an employer.

Having migrated from home, the young woman's chief goal was to accumulate enough capital for a dowry. Her savings would make her eligible for marriage because they would allow her to make the necessary contribution to form a household with her husband. Marriage within the family economy was a joint economic undertaking, and the wife was expected to make an immediate contribution of capital for establishing the household. A young woman might well work for ten years or more to accumulate a dowry. This practice meant that marriage was usually postponed until her mid- to late twenties.

Within marriage, earning enough money or producing enough farm goods to ensure an adequate food supply dominated women's concerns. Domestic duties, childbearing, and child rearing were subordinate to economic pressures. Consequently, couples tried to limit the number of children, usually through the practice of *coitus interruptus*, the withdrawal of the male before ejaculation. Parents often placed young children with wet nurses so the mother could continue to make her economic contribution to the household. The wet nurse, in turn, contributed to the economic welfare of her own household. The child would be fully reintegrated into its own family when it was weaned and would then be expected to aid the family at an early age.

The work of married women differed markedly between city and country and was in many ways a function of their husbands' occupations. If the peasant household had enough land to support itself, the wife spent much of her time quite literally carrying things for her husband—water, food, seed, harvested grain, and the like. There were few such adequate landholdings, however. If the husband had to do work besides farming, such as fishing or migrant labor, the wife might actually be in charge of the farm and do the ploughing, planting, and harvesting. In the city, the wife of an artisan or a merchant might well be in charge of the household finances and actively participate in managing the trade or manufacturing enterprise. When her husband died, she might take over the business and perhaps hire an artisan. Finally, if economic disaster struck the family, it was usually the wife who organized what Olwen Hufton has called the "economy of expedients,"[1] within which family members might be sent off to find work elsewhere or even to beg in the streets.

Through all this economic activity women found many occupations and professions closed to them

[1] Olwen Hufton, "Women and the Family Economy in Eighteenth-Century France," *French Historical Studies*, 9 (1976): 19.

# An Edinburgh Physician Describes the Dangers of Childbirth

*Death in childbirth was a common occurrence throughout Europe until the twentieth century. This brief letter from an Edinburgh physician illustrates how devastating infectious diseases could be to women at the time of child-birth.*

✦ *How does this passage illustrate a health danger that only women confronted? How might the likelihood of the death of oneself or a spouse in childbirth have affected one's attitudes toward children? How does this passage illustrate limitations on knowledge about disease in the eighteenth century?*

We had puerperal fever in the infirmary last winter. It began about the end of February, when almost every woman, as soon as she was delivered, or perhaps about twenty-four hours after, was seized with it; and all of them died, though every method was tried to cure the disorder. What was singular, the women were in good health before they were brought to bed, though some of them had been long in the hospital before delivery. One woman had been dismissed from the ward before she was brought to bed; came into it some days after with her labor upon her; was easily delivered, and remained perfectly well for twenty-four hours, when she was seized with a shivering and the other symptoms of the fever. I caused her to be removed to another ward; yet notwithstanding all the care that was taken of her she died in the same manner as the others.

*From a letter to Mr. White from a Dr. Young of Edinburgh, 21 November, 1774, cited in C. White, Treatise on the Management of Pregnant and Lying-In Women (London, 1777), pp. 45–46, as quoted in Bridget Hill, ed., Eighteenth-Century Women: An Anthology (London: George Allen & Unwin, 1984), p. 102.*

because they were women. They labored with less education than men, because in this society women in all levels of life consistently found fewer opportunities for education than men. They often received lower wages than men for the same work.

## Children and the World of the Family Economy

For women of all social ranks, childbirth was a time of fear and personal vulnerability. Contagious diseases endangered both mother and child. Puerperal fever was frequent, as were other infections from unsterilized medical instruments. Not all midwives were skillful practitioners. Furthermore, most mothers and children immediately encountered immense poverty and wretched housing. Assuming that both mother and child survived, the mother might nurse the infant, but often the child would be sent to a wet nurse. Convenience may have led to this practice among the wealthy, but economic necessity dictated it for the poor. The structures and customs of the family economy did not permit a woman to devote herself entirely to rearing a child. The wet-nursing industry was well organized, with urban children being frequently transported to wet nurses in the country, where they would remain for months or even years.

Throughout Europe, the birth of a child was not always welcome. The child might represent another economic burden on an already hard-pressed household. Or it might be illegitimate. The number of illegitimate births seems to have increased during the eighteenth century, possibly because increased population migration led to fleeting romances.

Through at least the end of the seventeenth century, unwanted or illegitimate births could lead to infanticide, especially among the poor. The parents might smother the infant or expose it to the elements. These practices were one result of both the ignorance and the prejudice surrounding contraception.

The late seventeenth and the early eighteenth centuries saw a new interest in preserving the lives of abandoned children. Although foundling hospitals established to care for abandoned children had existed before, their size and number expanded during these years. Two of the most famous were the Paris Foundling Hospital (1670) and the London Foundling Hospital (1739). Such hospitals cared for thousands of European children, and the demands for their services increased during the eighteenth century. For example, early in the century, an average of 1,700 children a year were admitted to the Paris Foundling Hospital. In the peak year of 1772, however, that number rose to 7,676 children. Not all of those children came from Paris. Many had been brought to the city from the provinces, where local foundling homes and hospitals were overburdened. The London Foundling Hospital lacked the income to deal with all the children brought to it. In the middle of the eighteenth century, the hospital found itself compelled to choose children for admission by a lottery system.

Sadness and tragedy surrounded abandoned children. Most of them were illegitimate infants from across the social spectrum. Many, however, were left with the foundling hospitals because their parents could not support them. There was a close relationship between rising food prices and increasing numbers of abandoned children in Paris. Parents would sometimes leave personal tokens or saints' medals on the abandoned baby in the vain hope that they might one day be able to reclaim the child. Few children were reclaimed. Leaving a child at a foundling hospital did not guarantee its survival. In Paris, only about 10 percent of all abandoned children lived to the age of ten.

Despite all of these perils of early childhood, children did grow up and come of age across Europe. The world of the child may not have received the kind of attention that it does today, but during the eighteenth century, the seeds of that modern sensibility were sown. Particularly among the upper classes, new interest arose in the education of children. In most areas education remained firmly in the hands of the churches. As economic skills became more demanding, literacy became more valuable, and literacy rates rose during the century. Yet most Europeans remained illiterate. Not until the late nineteenth century was the world of childhood inextricably linked to the process of education. Then children would be reared to become members of a national citizenry. In the Old Regime, they were reared to make their contribution to the economy of their parents' family and then to set up their own households.

# The Revolution in Agriculture

Thus far this chapter has examined those groups who sought stability and who, except for certain members of the nobility, resisted change. Other groups, however, wished to pursue significant new directions in social and economic life. The remainder of this chapter will consider those forces and developments that would during the next century transform European life. These developments first appeared in agriculture.

The main goal of traditional peasant society was a stability that would ensure the local food supply. Despite differences in rural customs throughout Europe, the tillers resisted changes that might endanger the sure supply of food, which they generally believed that traditional cultivation would provide. The food supply was never certain, and the farther east one traveled, the more uncertain it became. Failure of the harvest meant not only hardship but death from either outright starvation or protracted debility. Often, people living in the countryside had more difficulty finding food than did city dwellers, whose local government usually stored reserve supplies of grain.

Poor harvests also played havoc with prices. Smaller supplies or larger demand raised grain prices. Even small increases in the cost of food could exert heavy pressure on peasant or artisan families. If prices increased sharply, many of those families fell back on poor relief from their local municipality or county or the Church.

Historians now believe that during the eighteenth century, bread prices slowly but steadily rose, spurred largely by population growth. Since bread was their main food, this inflation put pressure on all of the poor. Prices rose faster than urban wages and brought no appreciable advantage to the small peasant producer. On the other hand, the rise in grain prices benefitted landowners and those wealthier peasants who had surplus grain to sell.

The rising grain prices gave landlords an opportunity to improve their incomes and lifestyle. To achieve those ends, landlords in western Europe began a series of innovations in farm production that became known as the *Agricultural Revolution*.

Landlords commercialized agriculture and thereby challenged the traditional peasant ways of production. Peasant revolts and disturbances often resulted. The governments of Europe, hungry for new taxes and dependent on the goodwill of the nobility, used their armies and militias to smash peasants who defended the past.

NEW CROPS AND NEW METHODS The drive to improve agricultural production began during the sixteenth and seventeenth centuries in the Low Countries, where the pressures of the growing population and the shortage of land required changes in cultivation. Dutch landlords and farmers devised better ways to build dikes and to drain land, so that they could farm more extensive areas. They also experimented with new crops, such as clover and turnips, that would increase the supply of animal fodder and restore the soil. These improvements became so famous that early in the seventeenth century English landlords hired Cornelius Vermuyden, a Dutch drainage engineer, to drain thousands of acres of land around Cambridge.

English landlords provided the most striking examples of eighteenth-century agricultural improvement. They originated almost no genuinely new farming methods, but they popularized ideas developed in the previous century either in the Low Countries or in England. Some of these landlords and agricultural innovators became famous. For example, Jethro Tull (1674–1741) was willing to experiment himself and to finance the experiments of others. Many of his ideas, such as the rejection of manure as fertilizer, were wrong. Others, however, such as using iron plows to turn earth more deeply and planting wheat by a drill rather than by casting, were excellent. His methods permitted land to be cultivated for longer periods without having to be left fallow.

## Turgot Describes French Landholding

*The economy of Europe until the nineteenth century was overwhelmingly rural. That meant that economic growth and political stability depended largely on agricultural production. During the eighteenth century, many observers became keenly aware that different kinds of landholding led to different attitudes toward work and to different levels of production. Robert Jacques Turgot (1727–1781), who later became finance minister of France, analyzed these differences in an effort to reform French agriculture. He was especially concerned with arrangements that encouraged long-term investment. The métayer system, discussed by Turgot, was an arrangement whereby landowners arranged to have land farmed by peasants who received part of the harvest as payment for their working the land. The peasant had no long-term interest in improving the land. Virtually all observers regarded the system as inefficient.*

♦ *Why does Turgot clearly favor those farmers who can make investments in the land they rent from a proprietor? What are the structures of the métayer system? Why did it necessarily lead to poor investments and lesser harvests? What is Turgot's attitude toward work and entrepreneurship?*

1. What really distinguishes the area of large-scale farming from the areas of small-scale production is that in the former areas the proprietors find farmers who provide them with a permanent revenue from the land and who buy from them the right to cultivate it for a certain number of years. These farmers undertake all the expenses of cultivation, the ploughing, the sowing and the stocking of the farm with cattle, animals and tools. They are really agricultural entrepreneurs, who possess, like the entrepreneurs in all other branches of commerce, considerable funds, which they employ in the cultivation of land. . . .

Charles "Turnip" Townsend (1674–1738) encouraged other important innovations. He learned from the Dutch how to cultivate sandy soil with fertilizers. He also instituted crop rotation, using wheat, turnips, barley, and clover. This new system of rotation replaced the fallow field with one sown with a crop that both restored nutrients to the soil and supplied animal fodder. The additional fodder meant that more livestock could be raised. These fodders allowed animals to be fed during the winter and assured a year-round supply of meat. The larger number of animals increased the quantity of manure available as fertilizer for the grain crops. Consequently, in the long run, there was more food for both animals and human beings.

A third British agricultural improver was Robert Bakewell (1725–1795), who pioneered new methods of animal breeding that produced more and better animals and more milk and meat.

These and other innovations received widespread discussion in the works of Arthur Young (1741–1820), who edited the *Annals of Agriculture*. In 1793 he became secretary of the British Board of Agriculture. Young traveled widely across Europe, and his books are among the most important documents of life during the second half of the eighteenth century.

ENCLOSURE REPLACES OPEN-FIELD METHOD  Many of the agriculture innovations, which were adopted only slowly, were incompatible with the existing organization of land in England. Small cultivators who lived in village communities still farmed most of the soil. Each farmer tilled an assortment of unconnected strips. The two- or three-field systems of rotation left large portions of land fallow and unproductive each year. Animals grazed on the common land in the summer and on the stubble of

---

They have not only the brawn but also the wealth to devote to agriculture. They have to work, but unlike workers they do not have to earn their living by the sweat of their brow, but by the lucrative employment of their capital, just as the shipowners of Nantes and Bordeaux employ theirs in maritime commerce.

2. *Métayer* System The areas of small-scale farming, that is to say at least 4/7ths of the kingdom, are those where there are no agricultural entrepreneurs, where a proprietor who wishes to develop his land cannot find anyone to cultivate it except wretched peasants who have no resources other than their labor, where he is obliged to make, at his own expense, all the advances necessary for tillage, beasts, tools, sowing, even to the extent of advancing to his *métayer* the wherewithal to feed himself until the first harvest, where consequently a proprietor who did not have any property other than his estate would be obliged to allow it to lie fallow.

After having deducted the costs of sowing and feudal dues with which the property is burdened, the proprietor shares with the *métayer* what remains of the profits, in accordance with the agreement they have concluded. The proprietor runs all the risks of harvest failure and any loss of cattle:

he is the real entrepreneur. The *métayer* is nothing more than a mere workman, a farm hand to whom the proprietor surrenders a share of his profits instead of paying wages. But in his work the proprietor enjoys none of the advantages of the farmer who, working on his own behalf, works carefully and diligently; the proprietor is obliged to entrust all his advances to a man who may be negligent or a scoundrel and is answerable for nothing.

This *métayer*, accustomed to the most miserable existence and without the hope and even the desire to obtain a better living for himself, cultivates badly and neglects to employ the land for valuable and profitable production; by preference he occupies himself in cultivating those things whose growth is less troublesome and which provide him with more foodstuffs, such as buck wheat and chestnuts which do not require any attention. He does not worry very much about his livelihood; he knows that if the harvest fails, his master will be obliged to feed him in order not to see his land neglected.

*A. M. R. Turgot, Oeuvres, et documents les concernant, ed. by F. Schelle, 5 vols. (Paris, 1914), vol. II, pp. 448–450, as quoted and translated in S. Pollard and C. Holmes, eds., Documents of European Economic History, vol. I (London: Edward Arnold, 1968), pp. 38–39.*

the harvest in the winter. Until at least the middle of the eighteenth century, the decisions about what crops would be planted were made communally. The entire system discouraged improvement and favored the poorer farmers, who needed the common land and stubble fields for their animals. The village method precluded expanding the pasture land to raise more animals that would, in turn, produce more manure, which could be used for fertilizer. Thus, the methods of traditional production aimed at a steady, but not a growing, supply of food.

In 1700 approximately half the arable land in England was farmed by this open-field method. By the second half of the century, the rising price of wheat encouraged landlords to consolidate or enclose their lands to increase production. The enclosures were intended to use land more rationally and to achieve greater commercial profits. The process involved the fencing of common lands, the reclamation of previously untilled waste, and the transformation of strips into block fields. These procedures brought turmoil to the economic and social life of the countryside. Riots often ensued.

Because many English farmers either owned their strips or rented them in a manner that amounted to ownership, the larger landlords usually resorted to parliamentary acts to legalize the enclosure of the land, which they owned but rented to the farmers. Because the large landowners controlled Parliament, such measures passed easily. Between 1761 and 1792, almost 500,000 acres were enclosed through parliamentary act, compared with 75,000 acres between 1727 and 1760. In 1801 a general enclosure act streamlined the process.

The enclosures were controversial at the time and have remained so among historians. They permitted the extension of both farming and innovation and thus increased food production on larger agricultural units. They also disrupted small traditional communities; they forced off the land independent farmers, who had needed the common pasturage, and poor cottagers, who had lived on the reclaimed waste land. The enclosures, however, did not depopulate the countryside. In some counties where the enclosures took place, the population increased. New soil had come into production, and services subsidiary to farming also expanded.

The enclosures did not create the labor force for the British Industrial Revolution. What the enclosures most conspicuously displayed was the introduction of the entrepreneurial or capitalistic attitude of the urban merchant into the countryside.

This commercialization of agriculture, which spread from Britain slowly across the Continent during the next century, strained the paternal relationship between the governing and governed classes. Previously, landlords often had looked after the welfare of the lower orders through price controls or waiving rents during depressed periods. As the landlords became increasingly concerned about profits, they began to leave the peasants to the mercy of the marketplace.

LIMITED IMPROVEMENTS IN EASTERN EUROPE Improving agriculture tended to characterize farm production west of the Elbe. Dutch farming was quite efficient. In France, despite the efforts of the government to improve agriculture, enclosures were restricted. Yet there was much discussion in France about improving agricultural methods. These new procedures benefitted the ruling classes because better agriculture increased their incomes and assured a larger food supply, which discouraged social unrest.

In Prussia, Austria, Poland, and Russia, agricultural improvement was limited. Nothing in the relationship of the serfs to their lords encouraged innovation. In eastern Europe, the chief method of increasing production was to bring previously untilled lands under the plow. The landlords or their agents rather than the villages normally directed farm management. By extending tillage, the great landlords sought to squeeze more labor from their serfs rather than greater productivity from the soil. Eastern European landlords, like their western counterparts, sought to increase their profits, but they were much less ambitious and successful. The only significant nutritional gain achieved through their efforts was the introduction of maize and the potato. Livestock production did not increase significantly.

## Population Expansion

The population explosion with which the entire world must contend today had its origins in the eighteenth century. Before this time, Europe's population had experienced dramatic increases, but plagues, wars, or famine had redressed the balance. Beginning in the second quarter of the eighteenth century, the population began to increase steadily. The need to feed this population caused food prices to rise, which spurred agricultural innovation. The need to provide everyday consumer goods for the expanding numbers of people fueled the demand side of the Industrial Revolution.

Our best estimates are that in 1700 Europe's population, excluding the European provinces of the Ottoman Empire, was between 100 million and 120 million people. By 1800 the figures had risen to almost 190 million, and by 1850 to 260 million. The population of England and Wales rose from 6 million in 1750 to more than 10 million in 1800. France grew from 18 million in 1715 to about 26 million in 1789. Russia's population increased from 19 million in 1722 to 29 million in 1766. Such extraordinary, sustained growth put new demands on all resources and considerable pressure on existing social organization.

The population expansion occurred across the Continent in both the country and the cities. Only a limited consensus exists among scholars about the causes of this growth. There was a clear decline in the death rate. There were fewer wars and somewhat fewer epidemics in the eighteenth century. Hygiene and sanitation also improved. Better medical knowledge and techniques were once thought to have contributed to the decline in deaths. This factor is now discounted because the more important medical advances came after the initial population explosion or would not have contributed directly to it.

Rather, changes in the food supply itself may have allowed population growth to be sustained. Improved and expanding grain production made one contribution. Another and even more important change was the cultivation of the potato. This tuber was a product of the New World and came into widespread European production during the eighteenth century. On a single acre enough potatoes could be raised to feed one peasant's family for an entire year. This more certain food supply enabled more children to survive to adulthood and rear children of their own.

The impact of the population explosion can hardly be overestimated. It created new demands for food, goods, jobs, and services. It provided a new pool of labor. Traditional modes of production and living had to be revised. More people lived in the countryside than could find employment there. Migration increased. There were also more people who might become socially and politically discontented. And because the population growth fed on itself, these pressures and demands continued to increase. The society and the social practices of the Old Regime literally outgrew their traditional bounds.

# The Industrial Revolution of the Eighteenth Century

The second half of the eighteenth century witnessed the beginning of the industrialization of the European economy. The Industrial Revolution constituted the achievement of sustained economic growth. Previously, production had been limited. The economy of a province or a country might grow, but growth soon reached a plateau. Since the late eighteenth century, however, the economy of Europe has managed to expand almost uninterrupted. Depressions and recessions have been temporary, and even during such economic downturns, the Western economy has continued to grow.

At considerable social cost, industrialization made possible the production of more goods and more services than ever before in human history. Industrialization in Europe eventually overcame the economy of scarcity. The new means of production demanded new kinds of skills, new discipline in work, and a large labor force. The goods produced met immediate consumer demand and also created new demands. In the long run, industrialization clearly raised the standard of living and overcame the poverty that most Europeans who lived during the eighteenth century and earlier had taken for granted. It gave human beings greater control over the forces of nature than they had ever known before; yet industrialism would also by the middle of the nineteenth century cause new and unanticipated problems with the environment.

During the eighteenth century, people did not call these economic developments a *revolution*. That term came to be applied to the British economic phenomena only after the French Revolution. Then continental writers observed that what had taken place in Britain was the economic equivalent of the political events in France, hence an *Industrial Revolution*. It was revolutionary less in its speed, which was on the whole rather slow, than in its implications for the future of European society.

## A Revolution in Consumption

The most familiar side of the Industrial Revolution was the invention of new machinery, the establishment of factories, and the creation of a new kind of workforce. Recent studies, however, have emphasized the demand side of the Industrial Revolution

*Consumption of all forms of consumer goods increased greatly in the eighteenth century. This engraving illustrates a shop, probably in Paris. Here women, working apparently for a woman manager, are making dresses and hats to meet the demands of the fashion trade. As the document on page 558 demonstrates, some women writers urged more such employment opportunities for women. [Bildarchiv Preussischer Kulturbesitz]*

and the vast increase in both the desire and the possibility of consuming goods and services that arose in the early eighteenth century.

The inventions of the Industrial Revolution increased the supply of consumer goods as never before in history. The supply of goods was only one side of the economic equation, however. The supply had been called forth by an unprecedented demand for humble goods of everyday life. Those goods included everyday consumer items such as clothing of all kinds, buttons, toys, china, furniture, rugs, kitchen utensils, candlesticks, brassware, silverware, pewterware, glassware, watches, jewelry, soap, beer, wines, and foodstuffs. It was the ever-increasing demand for these goods that sparked the ingenuity of designers and inventors. Furthermore, there seemed to be no limits to consumer demand.

Many social factors came into play to establish the markets for these consumer goods. During the seventeenth century, the Dutch had enjoyed enormous prosperity and had led the way in new forms of both everyday consumption and that of luxury goods. For reasons that are still not clear, during the eighteenth century, increasing numbers first of the English and then of people living on the Continent came to have more disposable income. This wealth may have resulted from the improvements in agriculture. Those incomes allowed people to buy consumer goods that previous generations had inher-

ited or did not possess. What is key to this change in consumption is that it depended primarily upon expanding the various domestic markets in Europe.

This revolution, if that is not too strong a term, in consumption was not automatic. People became persuaded that they needed or wanted new consumer goods. Often, entrepreneurs caused it to happen by developing new methods of marketing. An enterprising manufacturer such as the porcelain manufacturer Josiah Wedgwood (1730–1795) first attempted to find customers among the royal family and the aristocracy. Once he had gained their business with luxury goods, he would then produce a somewhat less expensive version of the chinaware for middle-class customers. He also used advertising. He opened showrooms in London and had salespeople traveling all over England with samples and catalogs of his wares. On the Continent, he equipped salespeople with bilingual catalogs. There seemed to be no limit to the markets for different kinds of consumer goods that could be stimulated by social emulation on the one hand and advertising on the other.

Furthermore, the process of change in style itself became institutionalized. New fashions and inventions were always better than old ones. If new kinds of goods could be produced, there usually was a market for them. If one product did not find a market, its failure provided a lesson for the development of a different new product.

This expansion of consumption quietly but steadily challenged the social assumptions of the day. Fashion publications made all levels of society aware of new styles. Clothing fashions could be copied. Servants could begin to dress well if not luxuriously. There were changes in the consumption of food and drink that also called forth demand for new kinds of dishware for the home. Tea and coffee became staples. The brewing industry became fully commercialized. Those developments entailed the need for new kinds of cups and mugs and many more of them.

There would always be critics of this consumer economy. The vision of luxury and comfort it offered contrasted with the asceticism of ancient Sparta and contemporary Christian ethics. Yet ever-increasing consumption and production of the goods of everyday life became a hallmark of modern Western society from the eighteenth century to our own day. It would be difficult to overestimate the importance of the desire for consumer goods and the increasing material standard of living that they made possible in Western history after the eighteenth century. The presence and accessibility of such goods became the hallmark of a nation's prosperity. It is perhaps relevant to note that it was the absence of such consumer goods as well as of civil liberties that during the 1980s led to such deep discontent with the communist regimes in Eastern Europe and the former Soviet Union.

## Industrial Leadership of Great Britain

Great Britain was the home of the Industrial Revolution and, until the middle of the nineteenth century, maintained the industrial leadership of Europe. Several factors contributed to the early start in Britain.

Great Britain took the lead in the consumer revolution that expanded the demand for goods that could be efficiently supplied. London was by far the largest city in Europe. It was the center of a world of fashion and taste to which hundreds of thousands if not millions of British citizens were exposed each year. In London, these people learned to want the consumer goods they saw on visits for business and pleasure. Newspapers thrived in Britain during the eighteenth century, allowing for advertising that increased consumer wants. The social structure of Britain allowed and even encouraged people to imitate the lifestyles of their social superiors. It seems to have been in Britain that a world of fashion first

developed that led people to want to accumulate goods. In addition to the domestic consumer demand, the British economy benefitted from demand from the colonies in North America.

Britain was also the single largest free-trade area in Europe. The British had good roads and waterways without internal tolls or other trade barriers. The country was endowed with rich deposits of coal and iron ore. Its political structure was stable, and property was absolutely secure. The sound systems of banking and public credit established a stable climate for investment. Taxation in Britain was heavy, but it was efficiently and fairly collected, largely from indirect taxes. Furthermore, British taxes received legal approval through Parliament with all social classes and all regions of the nation paying the same taxes. In contrast to the Continent, there was no pattern of privileged tax exemptions.

Finally, British society was mobile by the standards of the time. Persons who had money or could earn money could rise socially. The British aristocracy would receive into its midst people who had amassed large fortunes. Even persons of wealth not admitted to the aristocracy could enjoy their riches, receive social prominence, and exert political influence. No one of these factors preordained the British advance toward industrialism. Together, however, when added to the progressive state of British agriculture, they provided the nation with the marginal advantage to create a new mode of economic production.

## New Methods of Textile Production

The industry that pioneered the Industrial Revolution and met growing consumer demand was the production of textiles for clothing. It provides the key example of industrialism emerging to supply the demands of an ever-growing market for everyday goods. Furthermore, it illustrates the surprising fact that much of the earliest industrial change took place not in cities but in the countryside.

Although eighteenth-century society was primarily agricultural, manufacturing also permeated rural areas. The peasant family living in a one- or two-room cottage was the basic unit of production rather than the factory. The same peasants who tilled the land in spring and summer often spun thread or wove textiles in the winter.

Under what is termed the domestic, or putting-out, system, agents of urban textile merchants took wool or other unfinished fibers to the homes of peasants, who spun it into thread. The agent then transported the thread to other peasants, who wove it into the finished product. The merchant sold the wares. In thousands of peasant cottages from Ireland to Austria, there stood a spinning wheel or a handloom. Sometimes the spinners or weavers owned their own equipment, but more often than not by the middle of the century, the merchant capitalist owned the machinery as well as the raw material.

The domestic system of textile production was a basic feature of this family economy and would continue to be so in Britain and on the Continent well into the nineteenth century. By mid-century, however, a series of production bottlenecks had developed within the domestic system. The demand for cotton textiles was growing more rapidly than production, especially in Great Britain, which had a large domestic and North American market for cotton textiles. Inventors devised some of the most famous machines of the early Industrial Revolution in response to this consumer demand for cotton textiles.

THE SPINNING JENNY   Cotton textile weavers had the technical capacity to produce the quantity of fabric demanded. The spinners, however, did not have the equipment to produce as much thread as the weavers needed. James Kay's invention of the flying shuttle, which increased the productivity of the weavers, had created this imbalance during the 1730s. Thereafter, various groups of manufacturers and merchants offered prizes for the invention of a machine to eliminate this bottleneck.

About 1765 James Hargreaves (d. 1778) invented the spinning jenny. Initially, this machine allowed 16 spindles of thread to be spun, but by the close of the century its capacity had been increased to as many as 120 spindles.

THE WATER FRAME   The spinning jenny broke the bottleneck between the productive capacity of the spinners and the weavers, but it was still a piece of machinery used in the cottage. The invention that took cotton textile manufacture out of the home and put it into the factory was Richard Arkwright's (1732–1792) water frame, patented in 1769. This was a water-powered device designed to permit the production of a purely cotton fabric rather than a cotton fabric containing linen fiber for durability. Eventually Arkwright lost his patent rights, and other manufacturers could use his invention freely. As a result, many factories sprang up in the countryside near streams that provided the necessary waterpower. From the 1780s onward, the cotton industry could meet an ever-expanding demand. Cotton output increased by 800 percent between 1780 and 1800. By 1815 cotton composed 40 percent of the value of British domestic exports, and by 1830 just over 50 percent.

The Industrial Revolution had commenced in earnest by the 1780s, but the full economic and social ramifications of this unleashing of human productive capacity were not really felt until the early nineteenth century. The expansion of industry and the incorporation of new inventions often occurred rather slowly. For example, Edmund Cartwright (1743–1822) invented the power loom for machine weaving in the late 1780s. Yet not until the 1830s were there more power-loom weavers than handloom weavers in Britain. Nor did all the social ramifications of industrialism appear immediately. The first cotton mills used water power, were located in the country, and rarely employed more than two dozen workers. Not until the late-century application of the steam engine, perfected by James Watt (1736–1819) in 1769, to the running of textile machinery could factories easily be located in or near existing urban centers. The steam engine not only vastly increased and regularized the available energy but also made possible the combination of urbanization and industrialization.

## The Steam Engine

More than any other invention, the steam engine permitted industrialization to grow on itself and to expand into one area of production after another. This machine provided for the first time in human history a steady and essentially unlimited source of inanimate power. Unlike engines powered by water or the wind, the steam engine, driven by the burning of coal, provided a portable source of industrial power that did not fail or falter as the seasons of the year changed. Unlike human or animal power, the steam engine depended on mineral energy that did not tire during a day. Finally, the steam engine could be applied to many industrial and, eventually, transportation uses.

The first practical engine using steam power had been the invention of Thomas Newcomen (1663–1729) in the early eighteenth century. The piston of this device was moved when the steam that had been induced into the cylinder condensed, causing

the piston to fall. The Newcomen machine was large, inefficient in its use of energy because both the condenser and the cylinder were heated, and practically untransportable. Despite these problems, English mine operators used the Newcomen machines to pump water out of coal and tin mines. By the third quarter of the eighteenth century, almost 100 Newcomen machines were operating in the mining districts of England.

During the 1760s, James Watt, a Scottish engineer and machine maker, began to experiment with a model of a Newcomen machine at the University of Glasgow. He gradually understood that separating the condenser from the piston and the cylinder would achieve much greater efficiency. In 1769 he patented his new invention, but transforming his idea into application presented difficulties. His design required precise metalwork. Watt soon found a partner in Matthew Boulton (1728–1809), a successful toy and button manufacturer in Birmingham, the city with the most skilled metalworkers in Britain. Watt and Boulton, in turn, consulted with John Wilkinson (1728–1808), a cannon manufacturer, to find ways to drill the precise metal cylinders required by Watt's design. In 1776 the Watt steam engine found its first commercial application pumping water from mines in Cornwall.

The use of the steam engine spread slowly because until 1800 Watt retained the exclusive patent rights. He was also reluctant to make further changes in his invention that would permit the engine to operate more rapidly. Boulton eventually persuaded him to make modifications and improvements. These allowed the engines to be used not only for pumping but also for running cotton mills. By the early nineteenth century, the steam engine had become the prime mover for all industry. With its application to ships and then to wagons on iron rails, the steam engine also revolutionized transportation.

### Iron Production

The manufacture of high-quality iron has been basic to modern industrial development. It is the chief element of all heavy industry and land or sea transport. Iron has also been the material out of which most productive machinery itself has been manufactured. During the early eighteenth century, British ironmakers produced somewhat less than 25,000 tons annually. Three factors held back the production of the metal. First, charcoal rather than coke was used to smelt the ore. Charcoal, derived from wood, was becoming scarce and does not burn at as high a temperature as coke, derived from coal. Second, until the perfection of the steam engine, insufficient blasts could be achieved in the furnaces. Finally, the demand for iron was limited. The elimination of the first two problems also eliminated the third.

Eventually, British ironmakers began to use coke, and the steam engine provided new power for the blast furnaces. Coke was an abundant fuel because of Britain's large coal deposits. The existence of the steam engine both improved iron production and increased the demand for iron.

| Major Inventions in the Textile-Manufacturing Revolution | |
|---|---|
| 1733 | James Kay's flying shuttle |
| 1765 | James Hargreaves's spinning jenny (patented 1770) |
| 1769 | James Watt's steam engine patent |
| 1769 | Richard Arkwright's water frame patent |
| 1787 | Edmund Cartwright's power loom |

In 1784 Henry Cort (1740–1800) introduced a new puddling process, that is, a new method for melting and stirring the molten ore. Cort's process allowed more slag (the impurities that bubbled to the top of the molten metal) to be removed and a purer iron to be produced. Cort also developed a rolling mill that continuously shaped the still-molten metal into bars, rails, or other forms. Previously the metal had to be pounded into these forms.

All these innovations achieved a better, more versatile product at a lower cost. The demand for iron grew as its price became lower. By the early nineteenth century, the British produced over a million tons annually. The lower cost of iron, in turn, lowered the cost of steam engines and allowed them to be used more widely.

# Cities

Remarkable changes occurred in the pattern of city growth between 1500 and 1800. In 1500 within Europe (excluding Hungary and Russia) there were 156 cities with a population greater than 10,000. Only 4 of those cities—Paris, Milan, Venice, and Naples—had populations larger than 100,000. By 1800, 363 cities had 10,000 or more inhabitants, and 17 of them had populations larger than 100,000. The percentage of the European population living in urban areas had risen from just over 5 percent to just over 9 percent. There had also occurred a major shift in urban concentration from southern, Mediterranean Europe to the north.

## Patterns of Preindustrial Urbanization

The eighteenth century witnessed a considerable growth of towns, closely related to the tumult of the day and the revolutions with which the century closed. London grew from about 700,000 inhabi-

tants in 1700 to almost 1 million in 1800. By the time of the French Revolution, Paris had more than 500,000 inhabitants. Berlin's population tripled during the century, reaching 170,000 in 1800. Warsaw had 30,000 inhabitants in 1730, but almost 120,000 in 1794. Saint Petersburg, founded in 1703, numbered more than 250,000 inhabitants a century later. In addition to the growth of these capitals, the number of smaller cities of 20,000–50,000 people increased considerably. This urban growth must, however, be kept in perspective. Even in France and Great Britain, probably somewhat less than 20 percent of the population lived in cities. And the town of 10,000 inhabitants was much more common than the giant urban center.

These raw figures conceal significant changes that took place in how cities grew and how the population distributed itself. The major urban development of the sixteenth century had been followed by a leveling off and even a decline in the seventeenth. New growth began in the early eighteenth century and accelerated during the late eighteenth and the early nineteenth centuries. Between 1500 and 1750 the major urban expansion took place within already established and generally already large cities. After 1750 the pattern changed with the birth of new cities and the rapid growth of older smaller cities.

GROWTH OF CAPITALS AND PORTS   In particular, between 1600 and 1750, the cities that grew most vigorously were capitals and ports. This situation reflects the success of monarchical state building during those years and the consequent burgeoning of bureaucracies, armies, courts, and other groups who lived in the capitals. The growth of port cities, in turn, reflects the expansion of European overseas trade and most especially that of the Atlantic routes. Except for Manchester in England and Lyons in France, the new urban conglomerates were nonindustrial cities.

Furthermore, between 1600 and 1750, cities with populations of fewer than 40,000 inhabitants declined. These included older landlocked trading centers, medieval industrial cities, and ecclesiastical centers. They contributed less to the new political regimes, and the expansion of the putting-out system transferred to the countryside much production that had once occurred in medieval cities. Rural labor was cheaper than urban labor, and cities with concentrations of labor declined as production was moved from the urban workshop into the country.

EMERGENCE OF NEW CITIES AND GROWTH OF SMALL TOWNS In the middle of the eighteenth century, a new pattern emerged. The rate of growth of existing large cities declined, while new cities began to emerge and existing smaller cities began to grow. Several factors were at work in the process, which Jan De Vries has termed "an urban growth from below."[2] First, there was the general overall population increase. Second, the early stages of the Industrial Revolution, particularly in Britain, occurred in the countryside and fostered the growth of smaller towns and cities located near factories. Factory organization itself led to new concentrations of population.

Cities also grew as a result of the new prosperity of European agriculture even where there was little industrialization. Improved agricultural production promoted the growth of nearby market towns and other urban centers that served agriculture or allowed more prosperous farmers to have access to the consumer goods and recreation they wanted. This new pattern of urban growth—new cities and the expansion of smaller existing ones—would continue into the nineteenth century.

## Urban Classes

Social divisions were as marked in the cities of the eighteenth century as they were in the industrial centers of the nineteenth. Visible segregation often existed between the urban rich and the urban poor. The nobles and the upper middle class lived in fashionable town houses, often constructed around newly laid-out green squares. The poorest town dwellers usually congregated along the rivers. Small merchants and artisans lived above their shops. Whole families might live in a single room. Modern sanitary facilities were still unknown. There was little pure water. Cattle, pigs, goats, and other animals walked the streets with the people. All reports on the cities of Europe during this period emphasize both the striking grace and beauty of the dwellings of the wealthy and the dirt, filth, and stench that filled the streets.

Poverty was not just an urban problem; it was usually worse in the countryside. In the city, however, poverty was more visible in the form of crime, prostitution, vagrancy, begging, and alcoholism.

[2]Jan De Vries, "Patterns of Urbanization in Pre-Industrial Europe, 1500–1800," in H. Schmal, ed., *Patterns of Urbanization Since 1500* (London: Croom Helm, 1981), p. 103.

*The socially astute English artist William Hogarth created a series of engravings and etchings in which he commented on the evils of city life. This picture, from "A Harlot's Progress," is entitled "Ensnared by a Procuress" (1732). [The Trustees of the Weston Park Foundation/The Bridgeman Art Library]*

Many a young man or woman from the countryside migrated to the nearest city to seek a better life, only to discover poor housing, little food, disease, degradation, and finally death. It did not require the Industrial Revolution and the urban factories to make the cities into hellholes for the poor and the dispossessed. The full darkness of London life during the mid-century "gin age," when consumption of that liquor blinded and killed many poor people, is evident in the engravings of William Hogarth (1697–1764).

Also contrasting with the serenity of the aristocratic and upper-commercial-class lifestyle were the public executions that took place all over Europe, the breaking of men and women on instruments of torture in Paris, and the public floggings in Russia. Brutality condoned and carried out by the ruling classes was simply a fact of everyday life.

THE UPPER CLASSES At the top of the urban social structure stood a generally small group of nobles, large merchants, bankers, financiers, clergy, and government officials. These upper-classmen controlled the political and economic affairs of the town. Nor-

# Manchester's Calico Printers Protest the Use of New Machinery

*The introduction of the new machines associated with the Industrial Revolution stirred much protest. With machines able to duplicate the skills of laborers, workers feared the loss of jobs and the resulting loss of status when their chief means of livelihood lay in their possession of those displaced and now mechanized skills. The following letter was sent anonymously to a Manchester manufacturer by English workers. It shows the outrage of those workers, the intimidation they were willing to use as threats, and their own economic fears.*

✦ *How might new machines adversely affect the livelihood of workers? Did the workers have other complaints against Mr. Taylor in addition to the introduction of new machinery? How have these workers reached an agreement to protect the interests of James Hobson? How do the workers combine the threat of violent actions with claims that other actions they have taken are legal?*

Mr. Taylor, If you dont discharge James Hobson from the House of Correction we will burn your House about your Ears for we have sworn to stand by one another and you must immediately give over any more Mashen Work for we are determined there shall be no more of them made use of in the Trade and it will be madness for you to contend with the Trade as we are combined by Oath to fix Prices we can afford to pay him a Guinea Week and not hurt the fund if you was to keep him there till Dumsday therefore mind you comply with the above or by God we will keep our Words with you we will make some rare Bunfires in this Countey and at your Peril to call any more Meetings mind that we will make the Mosney Pepel shake in their Shoes we are determined to destroy all Sorts of Masheens for Printing in the Kingdom for there is more hands then is work for so no more from the ingerd Gurnemen Rember we are a great number sworn nor you must not advertise the Men that you say run away from you when your il Usage was the Cause of their going we will punish you for that our Meetings are legal for we want nothing but what is honest and to work for selvs and familers and you want to starve us but it is better for you and a few more which we have marked to die then such a Number of Pore Men and their famerles to be starved.

*London Gazette, 1786, p. 36, as reprinted in Douglas Hay, ed.,* Albion's Fatal Tree *(New York: Pantheon Books, 1975), p. 318.*

mally, they constituted a self-appointed and self-electing oligarchy that governed the city through its corporation or city council. These rights of self-government had normally been granted by some form of royal charter that gave the city corporation its authority and the power to select its own members. In a few cities on the Continent, artisan guilds controlled the corporations, but more generally the councils were under the influence of the local nobility and the wealthiest commercial people.

THE MIDDLE CLASS    Another group in the city was the prosperous but not always immensely wealthy merchants, tradespeople, bankers, and professional people. They were the most dynamic element of the urban population and constituted the persons traditionally regarded as the middle class, or bourgeoisie. The concept of the middle class was much less clear-cut than that of the nobility. The middle class itself was and would remain diverse and divided with persons employed in the professions often resentful of those who drew their incomes from commerce. Less wealthy members of the middle class of whatever occupation resented wealthier members who might be connected to the nobility through social or business relationships.

*This engraving illustrates a metalworking shop such as might have been found in almost any town of significance in Europe. Most of the people employed in the shop probably belonged to the same family. Note that two women are also working. The wife may very well have been the person in charge of keeping the accounts of the business. The two younger boys might be children of the owner or apprentices in the trade, or both. [Bildarchiv Preussischer Kulturbesitz]*

The middle class had less wealth than most nobles but more than urban artisans. Middle-class people lived in the cities and towns, and their sources of income had little or nothing to do with the land. In one way or another, they all benefitted from expanding trade and commerce whether as merchants, as lawyers, or as small factory owners. Theirs was a world in which the earning and saving of money allowed for rapid social mobility and change in lifestyle. They saw themselves as people willing to use their capital and energy to work, while they portrayed the nobility as idle. The members of the middle class tended to be economically aggressive and socially ambitious. People often made fun of them for these characteristics and were jealous of their success. The middle class normally supported reform, change, and economic growth. The bourgeoisie also wanted more rational regulations for trade and commerce, as did some of the more progressive aristocrats.

The middle class was made up of people whose lives fostered the revolution in consumption. On one hand, as owners of factories and of wholesale and retail businesses, they produced and sold goods for the expanding consumer market; on the other hand, members of the middle class were also among the chief consumers. It was to their homes that the vast array of new consumer goods made their way. They were also the people whose social values clearly embraced most fully the commercial spirit. They might not enjoy the titles or privileges of the nobility, but they could enjoy considerable material comfort and prosperity. It was this style of life that less well-off people could still emulate as they sought to acquire consumer goods for themselves.

During the eighteenth century, the relationship between the middle class and the aristocracy was complicated. On one hand, the nobles, especially in England and France, increasingly embraced the commercial spirit associated with the middle class by improving their estates and investing in cities. On the other hand, wealthy members of the middle class often tried to imitate the lifestyle of the nobility by purchasing landed estates. The aspirations of the middle class for social mobility, however, conflicted with the determination of the nobles to maintain and reassert their own privileges and to protect their own wealth. The middle-class commercial figures—traders, bankers, manufacturers, and lawyers—often found their pursuit of both profit and prestige blocked by the privileges of the nobility and its social exclusiveness, by the inefficiency of monarchical bureaucracies dominated by the nobility, or by aristocrats who controlled patronage and government contracts.

The bourgeoisie was not rising to challenge the nobility; rather, both were seeking to add new dimensions to their existing political power and social prestige. The tensions that arose between the nobles and the middle class during the eighteenth century normally involved issues of power sharing or access to political influence rather than clashes over values or goals associated with class.

The middle class in the cities also feared the lower urban classes as much as they envied the nobility. The lower orders were a potentially violent element in society, a potential threat to property, and, in their poverty, a drain on national resources. The lower classes, however, were much more varied than either the city aristocracy or the middle class cared to admit.

ARTISANS Shopkeepers, artisans, and wage earners were the single largest group in any city. They were grocers, butchers, fishmongers, carpenters, cabinetmakers, smiths, printers, handloom weavers, and tailors, to give a few examples. They had their own culture, values, and institutions. Like the peasants of the countryside, they were in many respects conservative. Their economic position was highly vulnerable. If a poor harvest raised the price of food, their own businesses suffered. These urban classes also contributed to the revolution in consumption, however. They could buy more goods than ever before, and many of them sought to the extent their incomes permitted to copy the domestic consumption of the middle class.

The lives of these artisans and shopkeepers centered on their work and their neighborhoods. They usually lived near or at their place of employment. Most of them worked in shops with fewer than a half dozen other artisans. Their primary institution had historically been the guild, but by the eighteenth century, the guilds rarely had the influence of their predecessors in medieval or early modern Europe.

Nevertheless, the guilds were not to be ignored. They played a conservative role. Rather than seeking economic growth or innovation, they tried to preserve the jobs and skills of their members. The guilds were still able in many countries to determine who could pursue a particular craft. To lessen competition, they attempted to prevent too many people from learning a particular skill.

The guilds also provided a framework for social and economic advancement. At an early age, a boy might become an apprentice to learn a craft or trade. After several years he would be made a journeyman. Still later, if successful and sufficiently competent, he might become a master. The artisan could also receive certain social benefits from the guilds. These might include aid for his family during sickness or the promise of admission for his son. The guilds were the chief protection for artisans against the operation of the commercial market. They were particularly strong in central Europe.

## The Urban Riot

The artisan class, with its generally conservative outlook, maintained a rather fine sense of social and economic justice. These ideals were based largely on traditional practices. If the collective sense of what was economically "just" was offended, arti-sans frequently manifested their displeasure by rioting. The most sensitive area was the price of bread, the staple food of the poor. If a baker or a grain merchant announced a price that was considered unjustly high, a bread riot might well ensue. Artisan leaders would confiscate the bread or grain and sell it for what the urban crowd considered a "just price." They would then give the money paid for the grain or bread to the baker or merchant.

The potential for bread riots restrained the greed of merchants. Such disturbances represented a collective method of imposing the "just price" in place of the price set by the commercial marketplace. Thus, bread and food riots, which occurred throughout Europe, were not irrational acts of screaming hungry people but highly ritualized social phenomena of the Old Regime and its economy of scarcity.

Other kinds of riots also characterized eighteenth-century society and politics. The riot was a way in which people who were excluded in every other way from the political processes could make their will known. Sometimes urban rioters were incited by religious bigotry. For example, in 1753 London Protestant mobs compelled the government ministry to withdraw an act to legalize Jewish naturalization. In 1780 the same rabidly Protestant spirit manifested itself in the Gordon riots. Lord George Gordon (1751–1793) had raised the specter of an imaginary Catholic plot after the government relieved military recruits from having to take specifically anti-Catholic oaths.

In these riots and in food riots, violence was normally directed against property rather than against people. The rioters themselves were not "riff-raff" but usually small shopkeepers, freeholders, artisans, and wage earners. They usually wanted only to restore a traditional right or practice that seemed endangered. Nevertheless, considerable turmoil and destruction could result from their actions.

During the last half of the century, urban riots increasingly involved political ends. Though often simultaneous with economic disturbances, the political riot always had nonartisan leadership or instigators. In fact, the "crowd" of the eighteenth century was often the tool of the upper classes. In Paris, the aristocratic *Parlement* often urged crowd action in their disputes with the monarchy. In Geneva, middle-class citizens supported artisan riots against the local urban oligarchy. In Great Britain in 1792, the government incited mobs to attack English sympathizers of the French Revolution. Such outbursts of popular unrest suggest that the crowd or mob first entered the European political and social arena well before the revolution in France.

## The Jewish Population: The Age of the Ghetto

Although the small Jewish communities of Amsterdam and other western European cities became famous for their intellectual life and financial institutions, the vast majority of European Jews lived in eastern Europe. In the eighteenth century and thereafter, the Jewish population of Europe was concentrated in Poland, Lithuania, and the Ukraine, where no fewer than three million Jews dwelled. There were perhaps as many as 150,000 Jews in the Habsburg lands, primarily Bohemia, around 1760. Fewer than 100,000 Jews lived in Germany. There were approximately 40,000 Jews in France. Much smaller Jewish populations resided in England and Holland, each of which had a Jewish population of fewer than 10,000. There were even smaller groups of Jews elsewhere.

In 1762 Catherine the Great of Russia specifically excluded Jews from a manifesto that welcomed foreigners to settle in Russia. She somewhat relaxed the exclusion a few years later. After the first partition of Poland of 1772, to be discussed in Chapter 18, Russia included a large Jewish population. There were also larger Jewish communities in Prussia and under Austrian rule.

Jews dwelled in most nations without enjoying the rights and privileges of other subjects of the monarchs unless such rights were specifically granted to them. They were regarded as a kind of resident alien whose residence might well be temporary or changed at the whim of local rulers or the monarchical government.

No matter where they dwelled, the Jews of Europe under the Old Regime lived apart in separate communities from non-Jewish Europeans. These communities might be distinct districts of cities known as ghettos or in primarily Jewish villages in the countryside. Jews were also treated as a distinct people religiously and legally. In Poland for much of the century, they were virtually self-governing. In other areas, they lived under the burden of discriminatory legislation. Except in England, Jews could not and did not mix in the mainstream of the societies in which they dwelled. This period, which really may be said to have begun with the expulsion of the Jews from Spain at the end of the fifteenth century, is known as the age of the ghetto or separate community.

During the seventeenth century, a few Jews had helped finance the wars of major rulers. These financiers often became close to the rulers and were known as "court Jews." Perhaps the most famous was Samuel Oppenheimer (1630–1703), who helped the Habsburgs finance their struggle against the Turks and the defense of Vienna. Even these privileged Jews, including Oppenheimer, however, often failed to have their loans repaid. The court Jews and their financial abilities became famous. They tended to marry among themselves.

The overwhelming majority of the Jewish population of Europe, however, lived in poverty. They occupied the most undesirable sections of cities or poor rural villages. They pursued money-lending in some cases, but often worked at the lowest occupations. Their religious beliefs, rituals, and community set them apart. Virtually all laws and social institutions kept them apart from their Christian neighbors in situations of social inferiority.

Under the Old Regime, it is important to emphasize, all of this discrimination was based on religious separateness. Jews who converted to Christianity were welcomed, even if not always warmly, into the major political and social institutions of gentile European society. Until the last two decades of the eighteenth century, in every part of Europe, however, those Jews who remained loyal to their faith were subject to various religious, civil, and social disabilities. They could not pursue the professions freely; often they could not change residence freely; and they stood outside the political structures of the nations in which they lived. Jews could be expelled from the cities where they lived, and their property could be confiscated. They were regarded as socially and religiously inferior. They could be required to listen to sermons that insulted them and their religion. Jews might find their children taken away from them and given Christian instruction. They knew that their non-Jewish neighbors might suddenly turn against them and kill them or their fellow religious believers.

As will be seen in subsequent chapters, the end of the Old Regime brought major changes in the lives of these Jews and in their relationship to the larger culture.

◆

*Near the close of the eighteenth century, European society was on the brink of a new era. That society had remained traditional and corporate largely* because of the economy of scarcity. Beginning in the eighteenth century, the commercial spirit and the values of the marketplace, although not new, were permitted fuller play than ever before in European history. The newly unleashed commercial spirit led increasingly to a conception of human beings as individuals rather than as members of communities. In particular that spirit manifested itself in agricultural and industrial revolutions, as well as in the drive toward greater consumption. Together those two vast changes in production overcame most of the scarcity that had haunted Europe and the West generally. The accompanying changes in landholding and production would bring major changes to the European social structure.

The expansion of population provided a further stimulus for change. More people meant more labor, more energy, and more minds contributing to the creation and solution of social difficulties. Cities had to accommodate themselves to expanding populations. Corporate groups, such as the guilds, had to confront the existence of a larger labor force. New wealth meant that birth would eventually become less and less a determining factor in social relationships, except in regard to the social roles assigned to the two sexes. Class structure and social hierarchy remained, but the boundaries became somewhat blurred.

Finally, the conflicting ambitions of monarchs, the nobility, and middle class generated innovation. In the pursuit of new revenues, the monarchs interfered with the privileges of the nobles. In the name of ancient rights, the nobles attempted to secure and expand their existing social privileges. The middle class, in all of its diversity, was growing wealthier from trade, commerce, and the practice of the professions. Its members wanted social prestige and influence equal to their wealth. They resented privileges, frowned on hierarchy, and rejected tradition.

All these factors meant that the society of the eighteenth century stood at the close of one era in European history and at the opening of another.

## Review Questions

1. Describe the life of an English aristocrat at the beginning of the eighteenth century and toward its close. How did the English aristocrat differ from the French aristocrat in this regard? What kind of privileges separated European aristocrats from other social groups?

2. How would you define the term *family economy*? What were some of the particular characteristics of the northwestern European household as opposed to that in eastern Europe? In what ways were the lives of women constrained by the family economy in preindustrial Europe?

3. What caused the Agricultural Revolution? How did technological innovations help change European agriculture? To what extent did the English aristocracy contribute to the Agricultural Revolution? What were some of the reasons for peasant revolts in Europe in the eighteenth century?

4. What factors explain the increase in Europe's population in the eighteenth century? What were the effects of the population explosion? How did population growth contribute to changes in consumption?

5. What caused the Industrial Revolution of the eighteenth century? What were some of the technological innovations and why were they important? Why did Great Britain take the lead in the Industrial Revolution? How did the consumer contribute to the Industrial Revolution?

6. Describe city life during the eighteenth century. Were all European cities of the same character? What changes had taken place in the distribution of population in cities and towns? Compare the lifestyle of the upper class with that of the middle and lower classes. What were some of the causes of urban riots?

## Suggested Readings

I. T. BEREND AND G. RANKI, *The European Periphery and Industrialization, 1780–1914* (1982). Examines the experience of eastern and Mediterranean Europe.

J. BLUM, *Lord and Peasant in Russia from the Ninth to the Nineteenth Century* (1961). A thorough and wide-ranging discussion.

J. BLUM, *The End of the Old Order in Rural Europe* (1978). The most comprehensive treatment of life in rural Europe, especially central and eastern, from the early eighteenth through the mid-nineteenth centuries.

F. BRAUDEL, *The Structures of Everyday Life: The Limits of the Possible*, trans. by M. Kochan (1982). A magisterial survey by the most important social historian of our time.

J. BREWER AND R. PORTER, *Consumption and the World of Goods* (1993). A large, wide-ranging collection of essays.

J. Cannon, *Aristocratic Century: The Peerage of Eighteenth-Century England* (1985). A useful treatment based on the most recent research.

P. Deane, *The First Industrial Revolution*, 2nd ed. (1979). A well-balanced and systematic treatment.

J. De Vries, *The Economy of Europe in an Age of Crisis, 1600–1750* (1976). An excellent overview that sets forth the main issues.

J. De Vries, *European Urbanization 1500–1800* (1984). The most important and far-ranging recent treatment of the subject.

W. Doyle, *The Old European Order: 1660–1800* (1992). The best one-volume treatment.

P. Earle, *The Making of the English Middle Class: Business, Community, and Family Life in London, 1660–1730* (1989). The most careful study of the subject.

M. W. Flinn, *The European Demographic System, 1500–1820* (1981). A major summary.

R. Forster and O. Ranum, *Deviants and Abandoned in French Society* (1978). This and the following volume contain important essays from the French journal *Annales*.

R. Forster and O. Ranum, *Medicine and Society in France* (1980).

D. V. Glass and D. E. C. Eversley (eds.), *Population in History: Essays in Historical Demography* (1965). Fundamental for understanding the eighteenth-century increase in population.

P. Goubert, *The Ancien Régime: French Society, 1600–1750*, trans. by S. Cox (1974). A superb account of the peasant social order.

D. Hay (ed.), *Albion's Fatal Tree: Crime and Society in Eighteenth-Century England* (1975). Separate essays on a previously little explored subject.

O. H. Hufton, *The Poor of Eighteenth-Century France, 1750–1789* (1975). A brilliant study of poverty and the family economy.

R. M. Isherwood, *Farce and Fantasy: Popular Entertainment in Eighteenth-Century Paris* (1986). A study that concentrates primarily on the theater and related spectacles.

C. Jones, *Charity and Bienfaisance: The Treatment of the Poor in the Montpellier Region, 1740–1815* (1982). An important local French study.

E. L. Jones, *Agriculture and Economic Growth in England, 1650–1815* (1968). A good introduction to an important subject.

A. Kahan, *The Plow, the Hammer, and the Knout: An Economic History of Eighteenth-Century Russia* (1985). An extensive and detailed treatment.

H. Kamen, *European Society, 1500–1700* (1985). The best one-volume treatment.

R. K. McClure, *Coram's Children: The London Foundling Hospital in the Eighteenth Century* (1981).

A moving work that deals with the plight of all concerned with the problem.

N. McKenderick (ed.), *The Birth of a Consumer Society: The Commercialization of Eighteenth-Century England* (1982). Deals with several aspects of the impact of commercialization.

F. E. Manuel, *The Broken Staff: Judaism Through Christian Eyes* (1992). An important discussion of Christian interpretations of Judaism.

M. A. Meyer, *The Origins of the Modern Jew: Jewish Identity and European Culture in Germany, 1749–1824* (1967). A general introduction organized around individual case studies.

P. B. Munsche, *Gentlemen and Poachers: The English Game Laws, 1671–1831* (1981). An excellent analysis of these laws.

S. Pollard, *The Genesis of Modern Management: A Study of the Industrial Revolution in Great Britain* (1965). Treats the issue of industrialization from the standpoint of factory owners.

S. Pollard, *Peaceful Conquest: The Industrialization of Europe, 1760–1970* (1981). A useful survey.

A. Ribeiro, *Dress in Eighteenth Century Europe, 1715–1789* (1985). An interesting examination of the social implication of style in clothing.

G. Rudé, *The Crowd in History 1730–1848* (1964). A pioneering study.

S. Schama, *The Embarrassment of Riches: An Interpretation of Dutch Culture in the Golden Age* (1987). A broad examination of the impact of wealth on the Dutch.

H. Schmal (ed.), *Patterns of European Urbanization Since 1500* (1981). Major revisionist essays.

L. Stone, *The Family, Sex and Marriage in England 1500–1800* (1977). A pioneering study of a subject receiving increasing interest from historians.

L. Stone, *An Open Elite?* (1985). Raises important questions about the traditional view of open access to social mobility in England.

T. Tackett, *Priest and Parish in Eighteenth-Century France: A Social and Political Study of the Curés in a Diocese of Dauphiné, 1750–1791* (1977). An important local study that displays the role of the church in the fabric of social life in the Old Regime.

R. Wall (ed.), *Family Forms in Historic Europe* (1983). Essays that cover the entire continent.

E. A. Wrigley and R. S. Schofield, *The Population History of England, 1541–1871: A Reconstruction* (1982). One of the most ambitious demographic studies ever undertaken.

E. A. Wrigley, *Continuity, Chance and Change: The Character of the Industrial Revolution in England* (1988). A major conceptual reassessment.

*The trade and empires of the eighteenth century were held together and protected by navies. These navies patrolled sea lanes to protect ships from pirates and smugglers and from attacks by hostile forces. In this painting (1735) by Peter Monamy, ships from the British sailing fleet rest in Lisbon harbor where they may well have stopped to take on supplies. Britain and Portugal were major trading partners, with British wool being exchanged for Portuguese wine. [Ackermann and Johnson Ltd., London/The Bridgeman Art Library]*

# Empire, War, and Colonial Rebellion

## K E Y   T O P I C S

- Europe's mercantilist empires
- Spain's vast colonial empire in the Americas
- The wars of the mid-eighteenth century in Europe and the colonies
- The struggle for independence in Britain's North American colonies

*The middle of the eighteenth century witnessed a renewal of European warfare on a worldwide scale. The conflict involved two separate but interrelated rivalries. Austria and Prussia fought for dominance in central Europe, while Great Britain and France dueled for commercial and colonial supremacy. The wars were long, extensive, and costly in both effort and money. They resulted in a new balance of power on the Continent and on the high seas. Prussia emerged as a great power, and Great Britain gained a world empire.*

*Moreover, the expense of these wars led every major European government after the Peace of Paris of 1763 to reconstruct its policies of taxation and finance. These revised fiscal programs produced internal conditions for the monarchies of Europe that had most significant results for the rest of the century. These included the American Revolution, enlightened absolutism on the Continent, a continuing financial crisis for the French* *monarchy, and reform of the Spanish Empire in South America.*

## Periods of European Overseas Empires

Since the Renaissance, European contacts with the rest of the world have gone through four distinct stages. The first was that of the European discovery, exploration, initial conquest, and settlement of the New World. This period had closed by the end of the seventeenth century.

The second era, which is largely the concern of this chapter, was one of colonial trade rivalry among Spain, France, and Great Britain. The Anglo-French side of the contest has often been compared to a second Hundred Years' War. During this second period, both the British colonies of the North American seaboard and the Spanish colonies of

Mexico and Central and South America emancipated themselves from European control. This era may be said to have closed during the 1820s.

The third stage of European contact with the non-European world occurred in the nineteenth century. During that period, European governments carved new formal empires involving the European administration of indigenous peoples in Africa and Asia. Those nineteenth-century empires also included new areas of European settlement, such as Australia, New Zealand, and South Africa. The bases of these empires were trade, national honor, and military strategy.

The last period of European empire occurred during the mid-twentieth century, with the decolonization of peoples who had previously lived under European colonial rule.

During the four-and-one-half centuries before decolonization, Europeans exerted political dominance over much of the rest of the world that was far disproportional to the geographical size or population of Europe. Europeans frequently treated other peoples as social, intellectual, and economic inferiors. They ravaged existing cultures because of greed, religious zeal, or political ambition. These actions are major facts of European history and significant factors in the contemporary relationship of Europe and its former colonies. What allowed the Europeans to exert such influence and domination for so long over so much of the world was not any innate cultural superiority but a technological supremacy related to naval power and gunpowder. Ships and guns allowed the Europeans to exercise their will almost wherever they chose.

# Eighteenth-Century Empires

Eighteenth-century European empires existed primarily to enrich trade. They were empires based on commerce, and the trade of these empires helped to establish the consumer revolution discussed in the previous chapter. Extensive trade rivalries sprang up around the world. Consequently, the protection of these empires required extensive naval power. Spain dominated the largest of these empires and constructed elaborate naval, commercial, and political structures to exploit and govern it. Finally, these empires depended largely upon slave labor. Indeed, the Atlantic slave trade itself represented one of the major ways in which European merchants enriched themselves. That trade in turn forcibly brought the peoples of Africa into the life and culture of the New World.

## Mercantile Empires

Navies and merchant shipping were the keystones of the mercantile empires that were meant to bring profit to a nation rather than to provide areas for settlement. The Treaty of Utrecht (1713) established the boundaries of empire during the first half of the century.

Except for Brazil, which was governed by Portugal, Spain controlled all of mainland South America. In North America, it ruled Florida, Mexico, California, and the Southwest. The Spanish also governed the islands of Cuba, Puerto Rico, and half of Hispaniola.

The British Empire consisted of the colonies along the North Atlantic seaboard, Nova Scotia, Newfoundland, Jamaica, and Barbados. Britain also possessed a few trading stations on the Indian subcontinent.

The French domains covered the Saint Lawrence River valley and the Ohio and Mississippi river valleys. They included the West Indian islands of Saint Domingue, Guadeloupe, and Martinique and also stations in India. To the French and British merchant communities, India appeared as a vast potential market for European goods as well as the source of calicos and spices that were much in demand in Europe.

The Dutch controlled Surinam, or Dutch Guiana, in South America, and various trading stations in Ceylon and Bengal. Most important, they controlled the trade with Java in what is now Indonesia. The Dutch had opened these markets largely in the seventeenth century and had created a vast trading empire far larger in extent, wealth, and importance than the geographical size of the United Netherlands would have led one to expect. The Dutch had been daring sailors and had made important technological innovations in sailing.

All of these powers also possessed numerous smaller islands in the Caribbean. So far as eighteenth-century developments were concerned, the major rivalries existed among the Spanish, the French, and the British.

MERCANTILIST GOALS  Where any formal economic theory lay behind the conduct of these empires, it was *mercantilism*, that practical creed of hardheaded businesspeople. The terms *mercantilism*

*The Dutch established a major trading base at Batavia in the East Indies. The city they called Batavia is now Djakarta, Indonesia. [Bildarchiv Preussischer Kulturbesitz]*

and *mercantile system* were invented by opponents of the system whereby governments heavily regulated trade and commerce in hope of increasing national wealth. Economic writers believed it necessary for a nation to gain a favorable trade balance of gold and silver bullion. They regarded bullion as the measure of a country's wealth, and a nation was truly wealthy only if it amassed more bullion than its rivals.

The mercantilist statesmen and traders regarded the world as an arena of scarce resources and economic limitation. The attitudes associated with mercantilist thinking assumed very modest levels of economic growth. Such thinking pre-dated the expansion of agricultural and later industrial productivity discussed in the previous chapter. Prior to the beginning of such sustained economic growth, the wealth of one nation was assumed to grow or to be increased largely at the direct cost of another nation. That is to say, the wealth of one state might expand only if its armies or navies conquered the domestic or colonial territory of another state and thus gained the productive capacity of that area or if a state expanded its trading monopoly over new territory or if, by smuggling, it could intrude upon the trading monopoly of another state.

From beginning to end, the economic well-being of the home country was the primary concern of mercantilist writers. Colonies were to provide markets and natural resources for the industries of the home country. In turn, the home country was to furnish military security and political administration for the colonies. For decades both sides assumed that the colonies were the inferior partner in the relationship. The home country and its colonies were to trade exclusively with each other. To that end, they tried to forge trade-tight systems of national commerce through navigation laws, tariffs, bounties to encourage production, and prohibitions against trading with the subjects of other monarchs. National monopoly was the ruling principle.

Mercantilist ideas had always been neater on paper than in practice. By the early eighteenth century, mercantilist assumptions were far removed from the economic realities of the colonies. The colonial and home markets simply did not mesh. Spain could not produce enough goods for South America. Economic production in the British North American colonies challenged English manufacturing and led to British attempts to limit certain colonial industries, such as iron and hat making.

Colonists of different countries wished to trade with each other. English colonists could buy sugar more cheaply from the French West Indies than from English suppliers. The traders and merchants of one nation always hoped to break the monopoly of another. For all these reasons the eighteenth century became the "golden age of smugglers."[1] The governments could not control the activities of all their subjects. Clashes among colonists could and did bring about conflict between governments.

[1]Walter Dorn, *Competition for Empire, 1740–1763* (New York: Harper, 1940), p. 266.

## The Mercantilist Position Stated

*One of the earliest discussions of the economic theory of mercantilism appeared in* England's Treasure by Forraign Trade *(1664) by Thomas Mun (1571–1641). In this passage from that work, Mun explained why it was necessary to the prosperity of the nation for more goods to be exported than imported. Although mercantilist theory later became more sophisticated, all writers in the eighteenth century emphasized the necessity of a favorable balance of trade.*

◆ *Why does Mun emphasize foreign trade rather than the development of a domestic market? Why might persons of Mun's day have put so much stress on the possession of gold and silver bullion? How does the outlook of this passage assume a world of scarce goods rather than one in which economies might grow through the production of new kinds of products?*

The ordinary means therefore to increase our wealth and treasure is by Forraign Trade wherein wee must ever observe this rule; to sell more to strangers yearly than wee consume of theirs in value. For suppose that when this Kingdom is plentifully served with the Cloth, Lead, Tinn, Iron, Fish and other native commodities, we doe yearly export the overplus to forraign countries to the value of twenty two hundred thousand pounds; by which means we are enabled beyond the Seas to buy and bring in forraign wares for our use and Consumptions, to the value of twenty hundred thousand pounds; By this order duly kept in our trading, we may rest assured that the Kingdom shall be enriched yearly two hundred thousand pounds, which must be brought to us in so much Treasure; because that part of our stock which is not returned to us in wares must necessarily be brought home in treasure [i.e., gold or silver bullion].

Thomas Mun, England's Treasure by Forraign Trade, *as quoted in Charles Wilson,* England's Apprenticeship, 1603–1763 *(London: Longman, 1965), p. 60.*

---

FRENCH–BRITISH RIVALRY Major flash points existed between France and Britain in North America. Their colonists quarreled endlessly with each other. Both groups of settlers coveted the lower Saint Lawrence River valley, upper New England, and later the Ohio River valley. There were other rivalries over fishing rights, fur trade, and alliances with Native American tribes.

India was another area of French-British rivalry. On the Indian subcontinent, both France and Britain traded through privileged, chartered companies that enjoyed a legal monopoly. The East India Company was the English institution; the French equivalent was the *Compagnie des Indes*. The trade of India and Asia figured only marginally in the economics of empire. Nevertheless, enterprising Europeans always hoped to develop profitable commerce with India. Others regarded India as a springboard into the even larger potential market of China. The original European footholds in India were trading posts called *factories*. They existed through privileges granted by various Indian governments.

Two circumstances in the middle of the eighteenth century changed this situation in India. First, the indigenous administration and government of several Indian states had decayed. Second, Joseph Dupleix (1697–1763) for the French and Robert Clive (1725–1774) for the British saw this developing power vacuum as opportunities for expanding the control of their respective companies. To maintain their own security and to expand their privileges, each of the two companies began in effect to take over the government of some regions. Each group of Europeans hoped to checkmate the other.

## The Spanish Colonial System

Spanish control of its American Empire involved both a system of government and one of monopolistic trade regulation. Both were more rigid in appearance than in practice. Actual government was often informal, and the trade monopoly was frequently breached.

COLONIAL GOVERNMENT    Because Queen Isabella of Castile (r. 1474–1504) had commissioned Columbus, the technical legal link between the New World and Spain was the crown of Castile. Its powers both at home and in America were subject to few limitations. The Castilian monarch assigned the government of America to the Council of the Indies, which, with the monarch, nominated the viceroys of New Spain (Mexico) and Peru. These viceroys served as the chief executives in the New World and carried out the laws promulgated by the Council of the Indies.

Each of the viceroyalties was divided into several subordinate judicial councils, known as *audiencias*. There was also a variety of local officers, the most important of which were the *corregidores*, who presided over municipal councils. All of these offices provided the monarchy with a vast array of patronage, usually bestowed on persons born in Spain. Virtually all power flowed from the top of this political structure downward; in effect, local initiative or self-government scarcely existed.

TRADE REGULATION    The colonial political structures functioned largely to support Spanish commercial self-interest. The *Casa de Contratación* (House of Trade) in Seville regulated all trade with the New World. Cadiz was the only port authorized for use in the American trade. The Casa de Contratación was the most influential institution of the Spanish Empire. Its members worked closely with the *Consulado* (Merchant Guild) of Seville and other groups involved with the American commerce in Cadiz.

A complicated system of trade and bullion fleets administered from Seville was the key for maintaining the trade monopoly. Each year, a fleet of commercial vessels (the flota) controlled by Seville merchants, escorted by warships, carried merchandise from Spain to a few specified ports in America. These included Portobello, Veracruz, and Cartagena. There were no authorized ports on the Pacific Coast.

Areas far to the south, such as Buenos Aires on the Rio de la Plata, received goods only after the shipments had been unloaded at one of the authorized ports. After selling their wares, the ships were loaded with silver and gold bullion, usually wintered in heavily fortified Caribbean ports, and then sailed back to Spain. The flota system always worked imperfectly, but trade outside it was illegal. Regulations prohibited the Spanish colonists within the American Empire from establishing direct trade with each other and from building their own shipping and commercial industry. Foreign merchants were also forbidden to breach the Spanish monopoly.

COLONIAL REFORM UNDER THE SPANISH BOURBON MONARCHS    A crucial change occurred in the Spanish colonial system in the early eighteenth century. The War of the Spanish Succession (1701–1714) and the Treaty of Utrecht (1713) replaced the Spanish Habsburgs with the Bourbons of France on the Spanish throne. Philip V (r. 1700–1746) and his successors tried to use French administrative skills to reassert the imperial trade monopoly, which had decayed under the last Spanish Habsburgs, and thus to improve the domestic economy and revive Spanish power in European affairs.

Under Philip V, Spanish coastal patrol vessels tried to suppress smuggling in American waters. An incident arising from this policy (to be discussed later in this chapter) led to war with England in 1739. In 1739 Philip established the viceroyalty of New Granada in the area that today includes Venezuela, Colombia, and Ecuador. The goal was to increase direct royal government in the area.

During the reign of Ferdinand VI (r. 1746–1759), the great mid-century wars exposed the vulnerability of the empire to naval attack and economic penetration. As an ally of France, Spain emerged as one of the defeated powers in 1763. Government circles became convinced that further changes in the colonial system had to be undertaken.

Charles III (r. 1759–1788), the most important of the royal imperial reformers, attempted to reassert Spain's control of the empire. Like his two Bourbon predecessors, Charles III emphasized royal ministers rather than councils. Thus, the role of both the Council of the Indies and the Casa de Contratación diminished. After 1765 Charles abolished the monopolies of Seville and Cadiz and permitted other Spanish cities to trade with America. He also opened more South American and Caribbean ports

# Visitors Describe the Portobello Fair

*The Spanish tried to restrict all trade within their Latin American empire to a few designated ports. Each year a fair was held in certain of these ports. The most famous of these was Portobello on the Isthmus of Panama. In the 1730s, two visitors saw the event and described it. This fair was the chief means of facilitating trade between the western coast of South America and Spain.*

✦ *What products were sold at this fair? How might the actual sale of gold bullion at this fair have led to attitudes such as were seen in the earlier document by Thomas Mun? How does this passage illustrate the inefficiency of monopoly trade in the Spanish empire and the many chances for smuggling?*

The town of Portobello, so thinly inhabited, by reason of its noxious air, the scarcity of provisions, and the soil, becomes, at the time of the [Spanish] galleons one of the most populous places in all South America. . . .

The ships are no sooner moored in the harbour, than the first work is, to erect, in the square, a tent made of the ship's sails, for receiving its cargo; at which the proprietors of the goods are present, in order to find their bales, by the marks which distinguish them. These bales are drawn on sledges, to their respective places by the crew of every ship, and the money given them is proportionally divided.

Whilst the seamen and European traders are thus employed, the land is covered with droves of mules from Panama, each drove consisting of above an hundred, loaded with chests of gold and silver, on account of the merchants of Peru. Some unload them at the exchange, others in the middle of the square; yet, amidst the hurry and confusion of such crowds, no theft, loss, or disturbance, is ever known. He who has seen this place during the tiempo muerto, or dead time, solitary, poor, and a perpetual silence reigning everywhere; the harbour quite empty, and every place wearing a melancholy aspect; must be filled with astonishment at the sudden change, to see the bustling multitudes, every house crowded, the square and streets encumbered with bales and chests of gold and silver of all kinds; the harbour full of ships and vessels, some bringing by the way of Rio de Chape the goods of Peru, such as cacao, quinquina, or Jesuit's bark, Vicuña wool, and bezoar stones; others coming from Carthagena, loaded with provisions; and thus a spot, at all times detested for its deleterious qualities, becomes the staple of the riches of the old and new world, and the scene of one of the most considerable branches of commerce in the whole earth.

The ships being unloaded, and the merchants of Peru, together with the president of Panama, arrived, the fair comes under deliberation. And for this purpose the deputies of the several parties repair on board the commodore of the galleons, where, in the presence of the commodore, and the president of Panama, . . . the prices of the several kinds of merchandizes are settled. . . . The purchases and sales, as likewise the exchanges of money, are transacted by brokers, both from Spain and Peru. After this, every one begins to dispose of his goods; the Spanish brokers embarking their chests of money, and those of Peru sending away the goods they have purchased, in vessels called chatas and bongos, up the river Chagres. And thus the fair of Portobello ends.

*George Juan and Antonio de Ulloa,* A Voyage to South America, *vol. 1 (London, 1772), pp. 103–110, as quoted in Benjamin Keen, ed.,* Readings in Latin-American Civilization 1492 to the Present *(New York: Houghton Mifflin, 1955), pp. 107–108.*

to trade and authorized some commerce between Spanish ports in America. In 1776 he organized a fourth viceroyalty in the region of Rio de la Plata, which included much of present-day Argentina, Uruguay, Paraguay, and Bolivia. (See Map 17–1.)

While relaxing Spanish trade with and in America, Charles III attempted to increase the efficiency of tax collection and to end bureaucratic corruption. To achieve those ends, he introduced the institution of the intendent into the Spanish Empire. These loyal, royal bureaucrats were patterned on the French intendants made so famous and effective as agents of the absolutism of Louis XIV.

These late-eighteenth-century Bourbon reforms did stimulate the imperial economy. Trade expanded and became more varied. These reforms, however, also brought the empire more fully under direct Spanish control. Many *peninsulares* (persons born in Spain) entered the New World to fill new posts. Expanding trade brought more Spanish merchants to Latin America. The economy remained export oriented, and economic life was still organized to benefit Spain. As a result of these policies, the *creoles* (persons of European descent born in the Spanish colonies) came to feel that they were second-class subjects. In time their resentment would provide a major source of the discontent leading to the wars of independence in the early nineteenth century. The imperial policies of Charles III were the Spanish equivalent of the new colonial measures undertaken by the British government after 1763, which led to the American Revolution.

## Black African Slavery, the Plantation System, and the Atlantic Economy

The heart of the eighteenth-century colonial rivalry lay in the West Indies. These islands, close to the American continents, were the jewels of empire. The West Indies raised tobacco, cotton, indigo, coffee, and, above all, sugar, for which there existed strong markets in Europe. These commodities were becoming part of daily life especially in western Europe; they represented one aspect of those major changes in consumption that marked eighteenth-century European culture. Sugar in particular had become a staple rather than a luxury. It was used in coffee, tea, and cocoa, for making candy and preserving fruits, and in the brewing industry. There seemed no limit to its uses, and no limit to consumer demand for it.

Slavery was basic to the economies of the West Indies, the Spanish and Portuguese settlements in South America, and the British colonies on the South Atlantic seaboard of North America. The major source of slaves was black West Africans.

Slavery had existed in various parts of Europe since ancient times. Before the eighteenth century, little or no moral or religious stigma attached to slave owning or slave trading. It had had a continuous existence in the Mediterranean world, where only the sources of slaves changed over the centuries. After the conquest of Constantinople in the mid-fifteenth century, the Ottoman Empire forbade the exportation of white slaves from regions under its control. The Portuguese had then begun to import African slaves into the Iberian Peninsula from the Canary Islands and West Africa. Black slaves from Africa were also not uncommon in other parts of the Mediterranean, and a few found their way into northern Europe. There they might be used as personal servants or displayed because of the novelty of their color in the courts of royalty or homes of the wealthy.

THE PLANTATION SYSTEM   Once the New World was discovered and settled, the conquering Spanish and Portuguese faced a severe shortage of labor. They and most of the French and English settlers who came later had no intention of undertaking manual work themselves. At first, they used Native Americans as laborers, but during the sixteenth and seventeenth centuries, disease killed hundreds of thousands of Native Americans. As a result labor soon became scarce. The Spanish and Portuguese then turned to the labor of imported African slaves. By the late sixteenth century, in the islands of the West Indies and the major cities of South America, black slaves equaled or surpassed the numbers of white European settlers.

On much of the South American continent dominated by Spain, the numbers of slaves declined during the late seventeenth century, and the institution became less fundamental there than elsewhere. Slavery continued to prosper, however, in Brazil and in the Caribbean. Later, slavery spread into the British North American colonies. The first slaves were brought to Jamestown in 1619. They soon became a fundamental institution in North American colonial life, where at one time or another slaves were held in all the colonies.

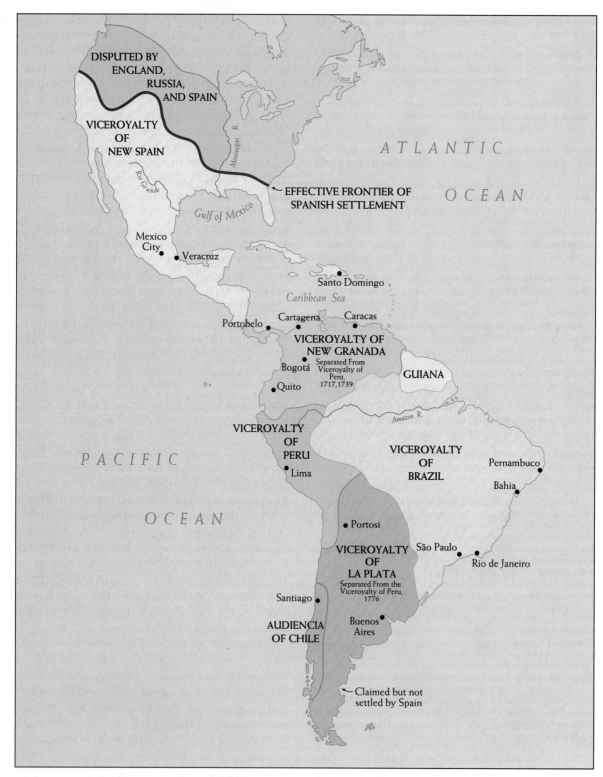

MAP 17–1    VICEROYALTIES IN LATIN AMERICA IN 1780    *The late-eighteenth century viceroyalties in Latin America display the effort of the Spanish Bourbon monarchy to establish more direct control of the continent. They sought this control through the introduction of more royal officials and by establishing more governmental districts.*

One of the forces that led to the spread of slavery in Brazil and the West Indies was the cultivation of sugar. Small landowners could not cultivate sugar because it required a large investment in land and equipment. Only slave labor could provide enough workers for the extremely large and profitable sugar plantations. By the close of the seventeenth century, the Caribbean islands were the world center for the production of sugar and the chief supplier for the ever growing consumer demand for the product. As the production of sugar expanded, so also did the demand for slaves and their consequent importation. By 1725, it has been estimated, almost 90 percent of the population of Jamaica was black slaves. The situation was similar throughout the West Indies. There and elsewhere, in Brazil and the southern British colonies, prosperity and slavery went hand in hand. The wealthiest and most prized of the colonies were those that raised staples such as sugar, rice, tobacco, or cotton by slave labor. In Brazil, slave labor sustained first sugar production and then late in the eighteenth century gold mining and coffee cultivation.

The plantation to which the slaves eventually arrived was always in a more or less isolated rural setting, but its products rapidly entered a larger integrated transatlantic economy. The plantation might raise food for its owners and their slaves, but the main production, whether sugar, tobacco, or later cotton and coffee, was intended for export. The production of the plantations was thus drawn into the world of transatlantic trade, manufacture, and consumption. In turn, the plantation owners imported virtually all the finished or manufactured goods used or consumed on the plantation from Europe.

Colonial trade followed roughly a geographic triangle. European goods were carried to Africa to be exchanged for slaves, who were then taken to the West Indies, where they were traded for sugar and other tropical products, which were then shipped to Europe. Not all ships covered all three legs of the triangle. Another major trade pattern existed between New England and the West Indies with New England fish or ship stores being traded for sugar.

Slavery and the slave trade touched most of the economy of the transatlantic world. The prosperity of such cities as Newport, Rhode Island, Liverpool, England, and Nantes, France, rested almost entirely on the slave trade. Cities in the British North American colonies profited from slavery sometimes by trading in slaves but more often by supplying other goods to the West Indian market. It was not the New World planters and slave traders alone, however, who were involved in the trade. Slavery touched most of the economy of the transatlantic world. All the shippers who handled cotton, tobacco, and sugar depended on slavery, though they might not have had direct contact with the institution, as did all the manufacturers and merchants who produced the finished products for the consumer market.

SLAVE EXPERIENCE The Spanish, Portuguese, Dutch, French, and English traders who participated in the slave trade forcibly transported several million (perhaps more than nine million) Africans to the New World. During the first four centuries of settlement, far more black slaves came involuntarily to the New World than did free European settlers. The conditions of their passage across the Atlantic were wretched. Quarters were unspeakably cramped; food was bad; disease was rampant. Many Africans died on the crossing. Yet the trade persisted because of the demand for labor in America, where it was cheaper to import new slaves than it was to rear slave children to adulthood. The mortality rate of slaves in the West Indies and elsewhere was very high. More and more new Africans had to be bought into slavery simply to keep a steady supply.

The life conditions of plantation slaves differed from colony to colony. Black slaves living in Portuguese areas had the fewest legal protections. In the Spanish colonies, the church attempted to provide some protection for black slaves but devoted more effort toward protecting the Native Americans. Slave codes were developed in the British and the French colonies during the seventeenth century, but they provided only the most limited protection. Virtually all slaveowners feared a slave revolt, and legislation and other regulations were intended to prevent one. All slave laws favored the master rather than the slave. Slave masters were permitted to whip slaves and inflict other exceedingly harsh corporal punishment. Furthermore, slaves were often forbidden to gather in large groups lest they plan a revolt. In most of these slave societies, the marriages of slaves were not recognized by law. The children of slaves continued to be slaves and were owned by the owner of their parents.

The daily life of most slaves during these centuries was one of hard agricultural labor, poor diet, and inadequate housing. Slave families could be

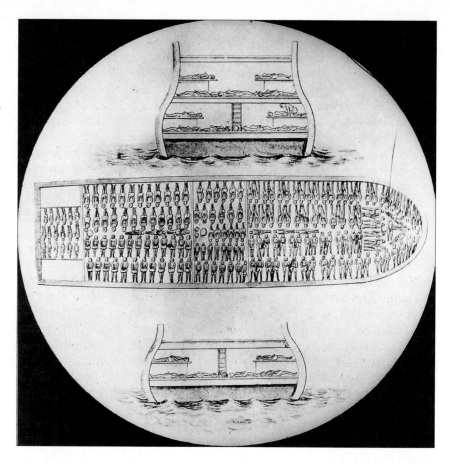

*African captives imported into the Americas were carried across the Atlantic in unspeakable conditions on ships designed to maximize the number of human beings carried as cargo. This cross-section illustrates how the human cargo was arranged. The following document describes the Atlantic passage. [Bildarchiv Preussischer Kulturbesitz]*

separated by the owner during his life or sold separately after his death. Their welfare and their lives were sacrificed to the continuing expansion of the sugar, rice, and tobacco plantations that made their owners wealthy and that produced goods for European consumers. Scholars have sometimes concluded that slaves in one area lived better than in another. Today, it is generally accepted that all the slaves in plantation societies led exposed and difficult lives with little variation among them.

The African slaves who were transported to the Americas, were, like the Native Americans, converted to Christianity. In the Spanish, French, and Portuguese domains, they became Roman Catholics, and in the English colonies they became Protestants of one denomination or another. In either case, although some African practices survived in muted forms, these practices were gradually separated from African religious belief. Although slaves did manage to mix Christianity with their previous African religions, their conversion to Christianity was nonetheless another exam-

ple, like that of the Native Americans, of the crushing of a set of non-European cultural values in the context of the New World economies and social structures.

The European settlers in the Americas and the slave traders also carried with them prejudices against black Africans. Many Europeans considered Africans to be savages or less than civilized. Still others looked down on them simply because they were slaves. Both Christians and Muslims had shared these attitudes in the Mediterranean world, where European slavery had for so long existed. Furthermore, many European languages and cultures attached negative connotations to the idea and image of blackness. In virtually all these plantation societies, race was an important element in keeping black slaves in a position of marked subservience. Although racial thinking in regard to slavery became important primarily in the nineteenth century, the fact of slaves being differentiated from the rest of the population by race as well as by their being chattel property was fundamental to the

# A Slave Trader Describes the Atlantic Passage

*During 1693 and 1694, Captain Thomas Phillips carried slaves from Africa to Barbados on the ship* Hannibal. *The financial backer of the voyage was the Royal African Company of London, which held an English crown monopoly on slave trading. Phillips sailed to the west coast of Africa, where he purchased the Africans who were sold into slavery by an African king. Then he set sail westward.*

✦ *Who are the various people described in this document who in one way or another were involved in or profited from the slave trade? What dangers did the Africans face on the voyage? What contemporary attitudes could have led this ship captain to treat and think of his human cargo simply as goods to be transported? What are the grounds of his self-pity for the difficulties he met?*

Having bought my complement of 700 slaves, 480 men and 220 women, and finish'd all my business at Whidaw [on the Gold Coast of Africa], I took my leave of the old king and his cappasheirs [attendants], and parted, with many affectionate expressions on both sides, being forced to promise him that I would return again the next year, with several things he desired me to bring from England. . . . I set sail the 27th of July in the morning, accompany'd with the East-India Merchant, who had bought 650 slaves, for the Island of St. Thomas . . . from which we took our departure on August 25th and set sail for Barbadoes.

We spent in our passage from St. Thomas to Barbadoes two months eleven days, from the 25th of August to the 4th of November following: in which time there happened such sickness and mortality among my poor men and Negroes. Of the first we buried 14, and of the last 320, which was a great detriment to our voyage, the Royal African Company losing ten pounds by every slave that died, and the owners of the ship ten pounds ten shillings, being the freight agreed on to be paid by the charter-party for every Negro delivered alive ashore to the African Company's agents at Barbadoes. . . . The loss in all amounted to near 6500 pounds sterling.

The distemper which my men as well as the blacks mostly died of was the white flux, which was so violent and inveterate that no medicine would in the least check it, so that when any of our men were seized with it, we esteemed him a dead man, as he generally proved. . . .

The Negroes are so incident to the small-pox that few ships that carry them escape without it, and sometimes it makes vast havock and destruction among them. But tho' we had 100 at a time sick of it, and that it went thro' the ship, yet we lost not above a dozen by it. All the assistance we gave the diseased was only as much water as they desir'd to drink, and some palm-oil to annoint their sores, and they would generally recover without any other helps but what kind nature gave them. . . .

But what the small pox spar'd, the flux swept off, to our great regret, after all our pains and care to give them their messes in due order and season, keeping their lodgings as clean and sweet as possible, and enduring so much misery and stench so long among a parcel of creatures nastier than swine, and after all our expectations to be defeated by their mortality. . . .

No gold-finders can endure so much noisome slavery as they do who carry Negroes; for those have some respite and satisfaction, but we endure twice the misery; and yet by their mortality our voyages are ruin'd, and we pine and fret ourselves to death, and take so much pains to so little purpose.

Thomas Phillips, "Journal," A Collection of Voyages and Travels, *vol. VI, ed. by Awnsham and John Churchill (London, 1746), as quoted in Thomas Howard, ed.,* Black Voyage: Eyewitness Accounts of the Atlantic Slave Trade *(Boston: Little, Brown and Company, 1971), pp. 85–87.*

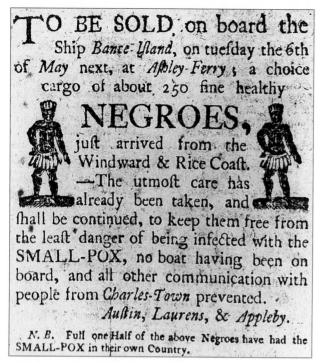

*Those Africans who survived the voyage across the Atlantic were immediately sold into slavery in the Americas. This slave-auction notice relates to a group of slaves whose ship had stopped at Charleston, South Carolina, and then landed elsewhere in the region to auction its human cargo. Notice the concern to assure potential buyers that the slaves were healthy. [The Bettmann Archive]*

system. All of these factors formed the racial prejudice that continues to plague society in the former slave-owning regions.

The plantations that stretched from the middle Atlantic colonies of North America through the West Indies and into Brazil constituted a vast corridor of slave societies in which social and economic subordination was based on both involuntary servitude and race. It had not existed before the European discovery and exploitation of the resources of the Americas. This kind of society in its extent and totality of dependence on slave labor and racial differences was novel in both European and world history. As already noted, its social and economic influence touched not only the plantation societies themselves but West Africa, western Europe, and New England. It existed from the sixteenth century through the second half of the nineteenth century, when slave emancipation had been completed through the Slave revolt of Saint Domingue (1794), British outlawing of the slave trade

(1807), the Latin American Wars of Independence, the Emancipation Proclamation of 1863 in the United States, and Brazilian emancipation of 1888. To the present day, every society where this form of plantation slavery once existed still contends with the long-term effects of that institution.

# Mid-Eighteenth-Century Wars

From the standpoint of international relations the state system of the middle of the eighteenth century was quite unstable and tended to lead the major states of Europe into periods of prolonged warfare. The statesmen of the period generally assumed that warfare could be used to further national interests. There were essentially no forces or set of powers who saw it in their interest to prevent war or to maintain peace. Because eighteenth-century wars before the French Revolution were fought by professional armies and navies, civilian populations were rarely drawn deeply into the conflicts. Wars were not associated with domestic political or social upheaval, and peace was not associated with the achievement of international stability. Consequently, periods of peace at the conclusion of a war were often viewed simply as times when a nation might become strong enough to recommence warfare at a later period for the purpose of seizing another nation's territory or of invading another empire's area of trading monopoly.

There were two fundamental areas of great power rivalry: the overseas empires and central and eastern Europe. Alliances and general strategic concerns repeatedly interrelated these regions of conflict.

## *The War of Jenkins's Ear*

In the middle of the eighteenth century, the West Indies had become a hotbed of trade rivalry. Spain attempted to tighten its monopoly, and English smugglers, shippers, and pirates attempted to pierce it. Matters came to a climax in the late 1730s.

The Treaty of Utrecht (1713) gave two special privileges to Great Britain in the Spanish Empire. The British received a thirty-year *asiento*, or contract, to furnish slaves to the Spanish. Britain also gained the right to send one ship each year to the trading fair at Portobello, a major Caribbean seaport on the Panamanian coast. These two privileges allowed British traders and smugglers potential inroads into the Spanish market. Little but friction

*Slaves in Brazil washing diamond ore to isolate gems. Notice the ratio of white overseers with whips to black slaves. [Bildarchiv Preussischer Kulturbesitz]*

arose from these rights. During the night offshore, British ships often resupplied the annual legal Portobello ship with additional goods as it lay in port. Much to the chagrin of the British, the Spanish government took its own alleged trading monopoly seriously and maintained coastal patrols, which boarded and searched English vessels to look for contraband.

In 1731, during one such boarding operation, there was a fight, and the Spaniards cut off the ear of an English captain named Robert Jenkins. Thereafter he carried about his severed ear preserved in a jar of brandy. This incident was of little importance until 1738, when Jenkins appeared before the British Parliament, reportedly brandishing his ear as an example of Spanish atrocities to British merchants in the West Indies. The British merchant and West Indies interests put great pressure on Parliament to relieve Spanish intervention in their trade. Sir Robert Walpole (1676–1745), the British prime minister, could not resist these pressures. In late 1739, Great Britain went to war with Spain. This war might have been a relatively minor incident, but because of developments in continental European politics, it became the opening encounter to a series of European wars fought across the world until 1815.

## The War of the Austrian Succession (1740–1748)

In December 1740, after being king of Prussia for less than seven months, Frederick II seized the Austrian province of Silesia in eastern Germany. The invasion shattered the provisions of the Pragmatic Sanction (see Chapter 15) and upset the continental balance of power as established by the Treaty of Utrecht. The young king of Prussia had treated the House of Habsburg simply as another German state rather than as the leading power in the region. Silesia itself rounded out Prussia's possessions, and Frederick was determined to keep his ill-gotten prize.

MARIA THERESA PRESERVES THE HABSBURG EMPIRE The Prussian seizure of Silesia could have marked the opening of a general hunting season on Habsburg holdings and the beginning of revolts by Habsburg subjects. Instead it led to new political allegiances. Maria Theresa's great achievement was not

*Maria Theresa of Austria provided the leadership that saved the Habsburg Empire from possible disintegration after the Prussian invasion of Silesia in 1740. [Kunsthistorisches Museum, Vienna]*

the reconquest of Silesia, which eluded her, but the preservation of the Habsburg Empire as a major political power.

Maria Theresa was then only twenty-three and had succeeded to the Habsburg realms only two months before the invasion. She won loyalty and support from her various subjects not merely through her heroism but more specifically by granting new privileges to the nobility. Most significant, the empress recognized Hungary as the most important of her crowns and promised the Magyars considerable local autonomy. She thus preserved the Habsburg state, but at considerable cost to the power of the central monarchy.

Hungary would continue to be, as it had been in the past, a particularly troublesome area in the Habsburg Empire. When the monarchy enjoyed periods of strength and security, guarantees made to Hungary could be ignored. At times of weakness, or when the Magyars could stir enough opposition, the monarchy promised new concessions.

FRANCE DRAWS GREAT BRITAIN INTO THE WAR  The war over the Austrian succession and the British–Spanish commercial conflict could have remained separate disputes. What quickly united them was the role of France. Just as British merchant interests had pushed Sir Robert Walpole into war, a group of aggressive court aristocrats compelled the elderly Cardinal Fleury (1653–1743), first minister of Louis XV, to abandon his planned naval attack on British trade and instead to support the Prussian aggression against Austria, the traditional enemy of France. This was among the more fateful decisions in French history.

In the first place, aid to Prussia consolidated a new and powerful state in Germany. That new power could, and indeed later did, endanger France. Second, the French move against Austria brought Great Britain into the Continental war, as Britain sought to assure that the Low Countries remained in the friendly hands of Austria, not France. In 1744 the British–French conflict expanded beyond the Continent, as France decided to support Spain against Britain in the New World. As a result, French military and economic resources were badly divided. France could not bring sufficient strength to the colonial struggle. Having chosen to continue the old struggle with Austria, France lost the struggle for the future against Great Britain. The war ended in stalemate in 1748 with the Treaty of Aix-la-Chapelle. Prussia retained Silesia, and Spain

renewed the *asiento* agreement with Great Britain. Most observers rightly thought the treaty was a truce rather than a permanent peace.

## The "Diplomatic Revolution" of 1756

Before the rivalries again erupted into war, a dramatic shift of alliances took place. In January 1756 Prussia and Great Britain signed the Convention of Westminster, a defensive alliance aimed at preventing the entry of foreign troops into the Germanies. Frederick II feared invasions by both Russia and France. The convention meant that Great Britain, the ally of Austria since the wars of Louis XIV, had now joined forces with Austria's major eighteenth-century enemy.

Maria Theresa was despondent over this development. It delighted her foreign minister, Prince Wenzel Anton Kaunitz (1711–1794), however. He had long hoped for an alliance with France to help dismember Prussia. The Convention of Westminster made possible this alliance, which would have been unthinkable a few years earlier. France was agreeable because Frederick had not consulted with its ministers before coming to his understanding with Britain. So, later in May 1756, France and Austria signed a defensive alliance. Kaunitz had succeeded in completely reversing the direction that French foreign policy had followed since the sixteenth century. France would now fight to restore Austrian supremacy in central Europe.

## The Seven Years' War (1756–1763)

Although the Treaty of Aix-la-Chapelle had brought peace in Europe, France and Great Britain continued to struggle unofficially on the colonial front. There were continual clashes between their settlers in the Ohio River valley and in upper New England. These were the prelude to what is known in American history as the French and Indian War. Once again, however, Frederick II precipitated a European war that extended into a colonial theater.

FREDERICK THE GREAT OPENS HOSTILITIES  In August 1756, Frederick II opened what would become the Seven Years' War by invading Saxony. Frederick considered this to be a preemptive strike against a conspiracy by Saxony, Austria, and France to destroy Prussian power. He regarded this invasion as a continuation of the defensive strategy of the Convention of Westminster. The invasion itself,

*William Pitt the Elder guided Great Britain to a stunning victory in the Seven Years' War. [National Portrait Gallery, London]*

**Conflicts of the Mid-Eighteenth Century**

| | |
|---|---|
| 1713 | Treaty of Utrecht |
| 1739 | Outbreak of War of Jenkins's Ear between England and Spain |
| 1740 | War of the Austrian Succession commences |
| 1748 | Treaty of Aix-la-Chapelle |
| 1756 | Convention of Westminster between England and Prussia |
| 1756 | Seven Years' War opens |
| 1757 | Battle of Plassey |
| 1759 | British forces capture Quebec |
| 1763 | Treaty of Hubertusburg |
| 1763 | Treaty of Paris |

however, created the very destructive alliance that Frederick feared. In the spring of 1757, France and Austria made a new alliance dedicated to the destruction of Prussia. They were eventually joined by Sweden, Russia, and many of the smaller German states.

Two factors in addition to Frederick's stubborn leadership (it was after this war that he came to be called Frederick the Great) saved Prussia. First, Britain furnished considerable financial aid. Second, in 1762 Empress Elizabeth of Russia died. Her successor was Tsar Peter III (he was murdered the same year), whose admiration for Frederick was boundless. He immediately made peace with Prussia, thus relieving Frederick of one enemy and allowing him to hold off Austria and France. The Treaty of Hubertusburg of 1763 ended the continental conflict with no significant changes in prewar borders. Silesia remained Prussian, and Prussia clearly stood among the ranks of the great powers.

WILLIAM PITT'S STRATEGY FOR WINNING NORTH AMERICA   The survival of Prussia was less impressive to the rest of Europe than the victories of Great Britain in every theater of conflict. The architect of these victories was William Pitt the Elder (1708–1778). Pitt was a person of colossal ego and administrative genius who had grown up in a commercial family. Although he had previously criticized British involvement with the Continent, once he became secretary of state in charge of the war in 1757, he reversed himself and pumped huge financial subsidies to Frederick the Great. He regarded the German conflict as a way to divert French resources and attention from the colonial struggle. He later boasted of having won America on the plains of Germany.

North America was the center of Pitt's real concern. Put quite simply, he wanted all of North America east of the Mississippi for Great Britain, and that was exactly what he won. He sent more than 40,000 regular English and colonial troops against the French in Canada. Never had so many soldiers been devoted to a field of colonial warfare. He achieved unprecedented cooperation with the American colonies, whose leaders realized that they might finally defeat their French neighbors.

The French government was unwilling and unable to direct similar resources against the English in America. Their military administration was corrupt; the military and political command in Canada were divided; and France could not adequately provision its North American forces. In September 1759, on the Plains of Abraham overlooking the valley of the Saint Lawrence River at Quebec City, the British army under General James Wolfe defeated the French under Lieutenant General Louis Joseph de Montcalm. The French Empire in Canada was ending.

Pitt's colonial vision, however, extended beyond the Saint Lawrence Valley and the Great Lakes Basin. The major islands of the French West Indies fell to British fleets. Income from the sale of captured sugar helped finance the British war effort. British slave interests captured the bulk of the French slave trade. Between 1755 and 1760 the value of the French colonial trade fell by more than 80 percent. In India, the British forces under the command of Robert Clive defeated the French in 1757 at the Battle of Plassey. This victory opened the way for the eventual conquest of Bengal in northeast India and later of all India by the British East India Company. Never had Great Britain or any other European power experienced such a complete worldwide military victory.

THE TREATY OF PARIS OF 1763   The Treaty of Paris of 1763 reflected somewhat less of a victory than Britain had won on the battlefield. Pitt was no longer in office. George III (r. 1760–1820) and Pitt had quarreled over policy, and the minister had departed. His replacement was the earl of Bute (1713–1792), a favorite of the new monarch. Bute was responsible for the peace settlement. Britain received all of Canada, the Ohio River valley, and the eastern half of the Mississippi River valley. Britain returned Pondicherry and Chandernagore in India and the West Indian sugar islands of Guadeloupe and Martinique to the French.

The Seven Years' War had been a vast conflict. Tens of thousands of soldiers and sailors had been killed or wounded. Major battles had been fought around the globe. At great internal sacrifice, Prussia had permanently wrested Silesia from Austria and had turned the Holy Roman Empire into an empty shell. Habsburg power now depended largely on the Hungarian domains. France, though still having sources of colonial income, was no longer a great colonial power. The Spanish Empire remained largely intact, but the British were still determined to penetrate its markets.

On the Indian subcontinent, the British East India Company was able to continue to impose its own authority on the decaying indigenous governments. The results of that situation would be felt until the middle of the twentieth century. In North America, the British government faced the task of organizing its new territories. From this time until World War II, Great Britain was a world power, not just a European one.

The quarter century of warfare also caused a long series of domestic crises among the European powers. The French defeat convinced many people in that nation of the necessity for political and administrative reform. The financial burdens of the wars had astounded all contemporaries. Every power had to begin to find ways to increase revenues to pay its war debt and to finance its preparation for the next combat. Nowhere did this search for revenue lead to more far-ranging consequences than in the British colonies in North America.

# The American Revolution and Europe

The revolt of the British colonies in North America was an event in both transatlantic and European history. It erupted from problems of revenue collection common to all the major powers after the Seven Years' War. The War of the American Revolution also continued the conflict between France and Great Britain. The French support of the Americans deepened the existing financial and administrative difficulties of the French monarchy.

## Resistance to the Imperial Search for Revenue

After the Treaty of Paris of 1763, the British government faced two imperial problems. The first was the sheer cost of empire, which the British felt they could no longer carry alone. The national debt had risen considerably, as had domestic taxation. Since the American colonies had been the chief beneficiaries of the conflict, the British felt that it was rational for the colonies henceforth to bear part of the cost of their protection and administration. The second problem was the vast expanse of new territory in North America that the British had to organize. This included all the land from the mouth of the Saint Lawrence River to the Mississippi River, with its French settlers and, more importantly, its Native American possessors. (See Map 17–2.)

The British drive for revenue began in 1764 with the passage of the Sugar Act under the ministry of George Grenville (1712–1770). The measure attempted to produce more revenue from imports into the colonies by the rigorous collection of what was actually a lower tax. Smugglers who violated the law were to be tried in admiralty courts without juries. The next year, Parliament passed the

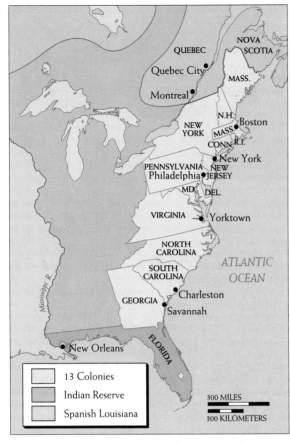

MAP 17–2 NORTH AMERICA IN 1763 *In the year of the victory over France, the English colonies lay along the Atlantic seaboard. The difficulties of organizing authority over the previous French territory in Canada and west of the Appalachian Mountains would contribute to the coming of the American Revolution.*

Stamp Act, which put a tax on legal documents and certain other items such as newspapers. The British considered these taxes legal because the decision to collect them had been approved by Parliament. They regarded them as just because the money was to be spent in the colonies.

The Americans responded that they alone through their assemblies had the right to tax themselves and that they were not represented in Parliament. Furthermore, the expenditure in the colonies of the revenue levied by Parliament did not reassure the colonists. They feared that if colonial government were financed from outside, they would lose control over it. In October 1765, the Stamp Act Congress met in America and drew up a protest to the crown. There was much disorder in the colonies, particularly in Massachusetts, roused by groups known as the Sons of Liberty. The colonists agreed to refuse to import British goods. In 1766 Parliament repealed the Stamp Act, but through the Declaratory Act said that it had the power to legislate for the colonies.

The Stamp Act crisis set the pattern for the next ten years. Parliament, under the leadership of a royal minister, would approve revenue or administrative legislation. The Americans would then resist by reasoned argument, economic pressure, and violence. Then the British would repeal the legislation, and the process would begin again. Each time, tempers on both sides became more frayed and positions more irreconcilable. With each clash the Americans more fully developed their own thinking about political liberty.

*"The Horse America throwing his Master," an eighteenth-century cartoon mocking George III about the rebellion of the American colonies. Although he tried to reassert some of the monarchical influence on Britain's politics that had eroded under George I and George II, the first two Hanoverian kings, George III never sought to make himself a tyrant as his critics charged. [The Granger Collection]*

# The Stamp Act Congress Addresses George III

*In 1765 the Stamp Act Congress met to protest the British imposition of taxes on the colonies. The resolutions of the Congress made it very clear that American leaders believed that Great Britain had no right to impose such taxation.*

✦ *What are the rights of English citizens that the Americans claim? How has the Stamp Act violated them? Why do they believe the British Parliament has no right to tax them? Do the colonists believe it possible for themselves to be represented in Parliament?*

The Members of this Congress, sincerely devoted, with the warmest sentiments of affection and duty to His Majesty's person and government . . . and with minds deeply impressed by a sense of the present and impending misfortunes of the British colonies on this continent; having considered as maturely as time will permit, the circumstances of the said colonies, esteem it our indispensable duty to make the following declarations of our humble opinion, respecting the most essential rights and liberties of the colonists, and of the grievances under which they labor, by reason of several late acts of Parliament.

I. That His Majesty's subjects in these colonies, own the same allegiance to the crown of Great Britain, that is owing from his subjects born within the realm, and all due subordination to that august body the Parliament of Great Britain.

II. That His Majesty's liege subjects in these colonies are entitled to all the inherent rights and liberties of his natural born subjects, within the kingdom of Great Britain.

III. That it is inseparably essential to the freedom of a people, and the undoubted right of Englishmen, that no taxes be imposed on them but with their own consent, given personally, or by their representatives.

IV. That the people of these colonies are not, and cannot, be represented in the House of Commons in Great Britain.

V. That the only representatives of the people of these colonies are persons chosen therein by themselves, and that no taxes ever have been, or can be constitutionally imposed on them, but by their respective legislatures.

VI. That all supplies to the crown being free gifts of the people, it is unreasonable and inconsistent with the principles and spirit of the British constitution, for the people of Great Britain to grant to His Majesty the property of the colonists.

VII. That trial by jury, is the inherent and invaluable right of every British subject in these colonies.

VIII. That the late act of Parliament entitled, An act for granting and supplying certain stamp duties, and other duties, in the British colonies and plantations, in America, etc. by imposing taxes on the inhabitants of these colonies, and the said act, and several other acts, by extending the jurisdiction of the courts of admiralty beyond its ancient limits, have a manifest tendency to subvert the rights and liberties of the colonists.

*Journal of the First Congress of the American Colonies . . . 1765 (New York, 1845), pp. 27–29, as quoted in Oscar Handlin, ed.,* Readings in American History *(New York: Alfred A. Knopf, 1957), pp. 116–117.*

## The Crisis and Independence

In 1767 Charles Townshend (1725–1767), as Chancellor of the Exchequer, the British finance minister, led Parliament to pass a series of revenue acts relating to colonial imports. The colonists again resisted. The ministry sent over its own customs agents to administer the laws. To protect these new officers, the British sent troops to Boston in 1768. The obvious tensions resulted. In March 1770, the Boston Massacre, in which British troops killed five citizens, took place. That same year, Parliament

This view of the "Boston Massacre" of March 5, 1770 by Paul Revere owes more to propaganda than fact. There was no order to fire and the innocent citizens portrayed here were really an angry, violent mob. [New-York Historical Society]

repealed all of the Townshend duties except the one on tea.

In May 1773, Parliament passed a new law relating to the sale of tea by the East India Company. The measure permitted the direct importation of tea into the American colonies. It actually lowered the price of tea while retaining the tax imposed without the colonists' consent. In some cities, the colonists refused to permit the unloading of the tea; in Boston, a shipload of tea was thrown into the harbor.

The British ministry of Lord North (1732–1792) was determined to assert the authority of Parliament over the resistant colonies. During 1774 Parliament passed a series of laws known in American history as the *Intolerable Acts*. These measures closed the port of Boston, reorganized the government of Massachusetts, allowed troops to be quartered in private homes, and removed the trials of royal customs officials to England. The same year, Parliament approved the Quebec Act for the future administration of Canada. It extended the boundaries of Quebec to include the Ohio River valley. The Americans regarded the Quebec Act as an attempt to prevent the extension of their mode of self-government westward beyond the Appalachian Mountains.

During these years, citizens critical of British policy had established committees of correspondence throughout the colonies. They made the various sections of the eastern seaboard aware of common problems and aided united action. In September 1774, these committees organized the gathering of the First Continental Congress in Philadelphia. This body hoped to persuade Parliament to restore self-government in the colonies and to abandon its attempt at direct supervision of colonial affairs. Conciliation, however, was not forthcoming. By April 1775, the Battles of Lexington and Concord had been fought. In June, the colonists suffered defeat at the Battle of Bunker Hill. Despite that defeat, the colonial assemblies soon began to meet under their own authority rather than under that of the king.

The Second Continental Congress gathered in May 1775. It still sought conciliation with Britain, but the pressure of events led it to begin to conduct the government of the colonies. By August 1775, George III had declared the colonies in rebellion. During the winter, Thomas Paine's (1737–1809) pamphlet *Common Sense* galvanized public opinion in favor of separation from Great Britain. A colonial army and navy were organized. In April 1776, the Continental Congress opened American ports to the trade of all nations. And on July 4, 1776, the Continental Congress adopted the Declaration of Independence. Thereafter, the War of the American Revolution continued until 1781, when the forces of George Washington defeated those of Lord Cornwallis at Yorktown. Early in 1778, however, the war had widened into a European conflict when Benjamin Franklin (1706–1790) persuaded the French government to support the rebellion. In 1779 the Spanish also came to the aid of the colonies. The 1783 Treaty of Paris concluded the conflict, and the thirteen American colonies had established their independence.

## American Political Ideas

The political ideas of the American colonists had largely arisen out of the struggle of seventeenth-century English aristocrats and gentry against the absolutism of the Stuart monarchs. The American colonists looked to the English Revolution of 1688 as having established many of their own fundamental political liberties as well as those of the English. The colonists claimed that, through the measures imposed from 1763 to 1776, George III and the British Parliament were attacking those liberties and dissolving the bonds of moral and political allegiance that had formerly united the two peoples. Consequently, the colonists employed a theory that had developed to justify an aristocratic rebellion to support their own popular revolution.

These Whig political ideas, largely derived from the writings of John Locke, were, however, only a part of the English ideological heritage that affected the Americans. Throughout the eighteenth century, they had become familiar with a series of British political writers called the *Commonwealthmen*. These writers held republican political ideas that had their intellectual roots in the most radical thought of the Puritan revolution. During the early eighteenth century, these writers, the most influential of whom were John Trenchard (1662–1723) and Thomas Gordon (d. 1750) in *Cato's Letters* (1720–1723), had relentlessly criticized the government patronage and parliamentary management of Sir Robert Walpole and his successors. They argued that such government was corrupt and that it

*Thomas Paine was the author of* Common Sense, *a political pamphlet published early in 1776 that helped galvanize American opinion in favor of independence.* [Bildarchiv Preussischer Kulturbesitz]

undermined liberty. They regarded much parliamentary taxation as simply a means of financing political corruption. They also considered standing armies instruments of tyranny. In Great Britain, this republican political tradition had only a marginal impact. The writers were largely ignored because most British subjects regarded themselves as the freest people in the world. Three thousand miles away, however, colonists read these radical books and pamphlets and often accepted them at face value. The policy of Great Britain toward America following the Treaty of Paris of 1763 and certain political events in Britain had made many colonists believe that the worst fears of the Commonwealthmen were coming true. All of these events coincided with the accession of George III to the throne.

## Events in Great Britain

George III (r. 1760–1820) believed that a few powerful Whig families and the ministries that they controlled had bullied and dominated his two immediate royal predecessors. George III also believed that he should have ministers of his own choice and that Parliament should function under royal rather than aristocratic management. When William Pitt resigned after a disagreement with George over war policy, the king appointed the earl of Bute as his first minister. In doing so, he ignored the great Whig families that had run the country since 1715. The king sought the aid of politicians whom the Whigs hated. Moreover, he tried to use the same kind of patronage techniques developed by Walpole to achieve royal control of the House of Commons.

Between 1761 and 1770, George tried one minister after another, but each in turn failed to gain enough support from the various factions in the House of Commons. Finally, in 1770 he turned to Lord North, who remained the king's first minister until 1782. The Whig families and other political spokespersons claimed that George III was attempting to impose a tyranny. What they meant was that the king was attempting to curb the power of a particular group of the aristocracy. George III certainly was seeking to restore more royal influence to the government of Great Britain, but he was not attempting to make himself a tyrant.

THE CHALLENGE OF JOHN WILKES    Then, in 1763, began the affair of John Wilkes (1725–1797). This

*This satirical portrait of John Wilkes is by William Hogarth. It depicts Wilkes with unattractive personal characteristics and questions the sincerity of his calls for liberty. [Charles Farrell Collection]*

London political radical and member of Parliament published a newspaper called *The North Briton*. In issue Number 45 of this paper, Wilkes strongly criticized Lord Bute's handling of the peace negotiations with France. Wilkes was arrested under the authority of a general warrant issued by the secretary of state. He pleaded the privileges of a member of Parliament and was released. The courts also later ruled that the vague kind of general warrant by which he had been arrested was illegal. The House of Commons, however, ruled that issue Number 45 of *The North Briton* constituted libel, and expelled Wilkes. He soon fled the country and was outlawed. Throughout these procedures there was widespread support for Wilkes, and many popular demonstrations were held in his cause.

In 1768 Wilkes returned to England and again stood for election to Parliament. He won the election, but the House of Commons, under the influence of George III's friends, refused to seat him. He was elected three more times. After the fourth election, the House of Commons simply ignored the results and seated the government-supported candidate. As had happened earlier in the decade, large, popular, unruly demonstrations of shopkeepers, artisans, and small property owners supported Wilkes. He also received aid from some aristocratic politicians who wished to humiliate George III. Wilkes himself contended during all his troubles that his was the cause of English liberty. "Wilkes and Liberty" became the slogan of all political radicals and many noble opponents of the monarch. Wilkes was finally seated in 1774, after having become the lord mayor of London.

The American colonists closely followed these developments. Events in Britain confirmed their fears about a monarchical and parliamentary conspiracy against liberty. The king, as their Whig friends told them, was behaving like a tyrant. The Wilkes affair displayed the arbitrary power of the monarch, the corruption of the House of Commons, and the contempt of both for popular electors. That same monarch and Parliament were attempting to overturn the traditional relationship of Great Britain to its colonies by imposing parliamentary taxes. The same government had then landed troops in Boston, changed the government of Massachusetts, and undermined the traditional right of jury trial. All of these events fulfilled too exactly the portrait of political tyranny that had developed over the years in the minds of articulate colonists.

MOVEMENT FOR PARLIAMENTARY REFORM  The political influences between America and Britain operated both ways. The colonial demand for no taxation without representation and the criticism of the adequacy of the British system of representation struck at the core of the eighteenth-century British political structure. British subjects at home who were no more directly represented in the House of Commons than were the Americans could adopt the colonial arguments. The colonial questioning of the taxing authority of the House of Commons was related to the protest of John Wilkes. Both the Americans and Wilkes were challenging the power of the monarch and the authority of Parliament. Moreover, both the colonial leaders and Wilkes appealed over the head of legally constituted political authorities to popular opinion and popular demonstrations. Both were protesting the power of a largely self-selected aristocratic political body. The British ministry was fully aware of these broader political implications of the American troubles.

# Major Cartwright Calls for the Reform of Parliament

*During the years of the American Revolution, there were many demands in England itself for a major reform of Parliament. In this pamphlet of 1777, Major John Cartwright (1740–1824) demanded that many more English citizens be allowed to vote for members of the House of Commons.*

✦ *What does Cartwright mean by "deep parliamentary corruption"? Does it extend beyond Parliament itself? Why are annual parliaments and equal representation a solution? Why are the claims of the few who now send representatives to Parliament rejected by Cartwright?*

Suffering as we do, from a deep parliamentary corruption, it is no time to tamper with silly correctives, and trifle away the life of public freedom: but we must go to the bottom of the stinking sore and cleanse it thoroughly: we must once more infuse into the constitution the vivifying spirit of liberty and expel the very last dregs of this poison. Annual parliaments with an equal representation of the commons are the only specifics in this case: and they would effect a radical cure. That a house of commons, formed as ours is, should maintain septennial elections, and laugh at every other idea is no wonder. The wonder is, that the British nation which, but the other day, was the greatest nation on earth, should be so easily laughed out of its liberties. . . .

Those who now claim the exclusive right of sending to parliament the 513 representatives for about six million souls (amongst whom are one million five hundred thousand males, competent as electors) consist of about two hundred and fourteen thousand persons; and 254 of these representatives are elected by 5,723. . . . Their pretended rights are many of them, derived from royal favour; some from ancient usage and prescription; and some indeed from act of parliament; but neither the most authentic acts of royalty, nor precedent, nor prescription, nor even parliament can establish any flagrant injustice; much less can they strip one million two hundred and eighty six thousand of an inalienable right, to vest it in a number amounting to only one seventh of that multitude. . . .

*John Cartwright,* Legislative Rights of the Commonality Vindicated *(1777), cited in S. Maccoby,* The English Radical Tradition, 1763–1914 *(London: Adam and Charles Black, 1966), pp. 32–33.*

---

The American colonists also demonstrated to Europe how a politically restive people in the Old Regime could fight tyranny and protect political liberty. They established revolutionary but orderly political bodies that could function outside the existing political framework: the congress and the convention. These began with the Stamp Act Congress of 1765 and culminated in the Constitutional Convention of 1787. The legitimacy of those congresses and conventions lay not in existing law but in the alleged consent of the governed. This approach represented a new way to found a government.

Toward the end of the War of the American Revolution, calls for parliamentary reform arose in Britain itself. The method proposed for changing the system was the extralegal Association Movement.

THE YORKSHIRE ASSOCIATION MOVEMENT By the close of the 1770s, many in Britain resented the mismanagement of the American war, the high taxes, and Lord North's ministry. In northern England in 1778, Christopher Wyvil (1740–1822), a landowner and retired clergyman, organized the Yorkshire Association Movement. Property owners, or freeholders, of Yorkshire met in a mass meeting to demand rather moderate changes in the corrupt system of parliamentary elections. They organized corresponding societies elsewhere. They intended that the association examine—and suggest reforms for—the entire government. The Association Movement was thus a popular attempt to establish an extralegal institution to reform the government.

The movement collapsed during the early 1780s because its supporters, unlike Wilkes and the American rebels, were not willing to appeal for broad popular support. Nonetheless, the agitation of the Association Movement provided many people with experience in political protest. Several of its younger figures lived to raise the issue of parliamentary reform after 1815.

Parliament was not insensitive to the demands of the Association Movement. In April 1780, the Commons passed a resolution that called for lessening the power of the crown. In 1782 Parliament adopted a measure for "economical" reform, which abolished some patronage at the disposal of the monarch. These actions, however, did not prevent George III from appointing a minister of his own choice. In 1783 shifts in Parliament obliged Lord North to form a ministry with Charles James Fox (1749–1806), a long-time critic of George III. The monarch was most unhappy with the arrangement.

In 1783 the king approached William Pitt the Younger (1759–1806), son of the victorious war minister, to manage the House of Commons. During the election of 1784, Pitt received immense patronage support from the crown and constructed a House of Commons favorable to the monarch. Thereafter, Pitt sought to formulate trade policies that would give his ministry broad popularity. He attempted in 1785 one measure of modest parliamentary reform. When it failed, the young prime minister, who had been only twenty-four at the time of his appointment, abandoned the cause of reform.

By the mid-1780s, George III had achieved a part of what he had sought since 1761. He had reasserted the influence of the monarchy in political affairs. It proved a temporary victory because his own mental illness, which would eventually require a regency, weakened the royal power. The cost of his years of dominance had been high, however. On both sides of the Atlantic, the issue of popular sovereignty had been raised and widely discussed. The American colonies had been lost. Economically, this loss did not prove disastrous. British trade with America after independence actually increased.

The Americans—through the state constitutions, the Articles of Confederation, and the federal Constitution adopted in 1788—had demonstrated to Europe the possibility of government without kings

---

> ### Events in Britain and America Relating to the American Revolution
>
> | | |
> |---|---|
> | 1760 | George III becomes king |
> | 1763 | Treaty of Paris concludes the Seven Years' War |
> | 1763 | John Wilkes publishes issue Number 45 of *The North Briton* |
> | 1764 | Sugar Act |
> | 1765 | Stamp Act |
> | 1766 | Sugar Act repealed and Declaratory Act passed |
> | 1767 | Townshend Acts |
> | 1768 | Parliament refuses to seat John Wilkes after his election |
> | 1770 | Lord North becomes George III's chief minister |
> | 1770 | Boston Massacre |
> | 1773 | Boston Tea Party |
> | 1774 | Intolerable Acts |
> | 1774 | First Continental Congress |
> | 1775 | Second Continental Congress |
> | 1776 | Declaration of Independence |
> | 1778 | France enters the war on the side of America |
> | 1778 | Yorkshire Association Movement founded |
> | 1781 | British forces surrender at Yorktown |
> | 1783 | Treaty of Paris concludes War of the American Revolution |

---

and hereditary nobilities. They had established the example of a nation in which written documents based on popular consent and popular sovereignty—rather than on divine law, natural law, tradition, or the will of kings—were the highest political and legal authority. The political novelty of these assertions should not be ignored.

As the crisis with Britain unfolded during the 1760s and 1770s, the American colonists had come to see themselves as first preserving traditional English liberties against the tyrannical crown and corrupt Parliament and then as developing a whole new sense of liberty. By the mid-1770s, the colonists had rejected monarchical government and embraced republican political ideals. They would govern themselves through elected assemblies without any presence of a monarchical authority. Once a constitution was adopted, they would insist on a bill of rights specifically protecting a whole series of civil liberties. The Americans would reject the aristocratic social hierarchy that had existed in the colonies. They would embrace democratic ideals even if the franchise remained limited. They would assert the equality of white male citizens not only before the law but in ordinary social relations. They would reject social status based on birth and inheritance and assert the necessity of the liberty for all citizens to improve their social standing and economic lot by engaging in free commercial activity. They did not free their slaves nor did they address issues of the rights of women or of Native Americans, but the American colonists of the eighteenth century in making their revolution produced a society more free than any the world had seen and one that would eventually expand the circle of political and social liberty. In all these respects, the American Revolution was a genuinely radical movement, whose influence would widen as Americans moved across the continent and as other peoples began to question traditional modes of European government.

◆

*Throughout the eighteenth century, the great European powers fought in two major arenas—their overseas commercial empires and central Europe.*

*In the New World, Britain, France, and Spain battled for commercial dominance. France and Britain also clashed over their spheres of influence in India. By the third quarter of the century, Britain had succeeded in ousting France from most of its major holdings in North America and from any significant presence in India. Spain, though no longer a military power of the first order, had managed to maintain its vast colonial empire in Latin America and a large measure of its monopoly over the region's trade.*

*On the Continent, France, Austria, and Prussia collided over conflicting territorial and dynastic ambitions. Britain became involved to protect its continental interests and to use the continental wars to divert France from the colonial arena. Prussia with British aid had emerged in 1763 as a major continental power. Austria had lost considerable territory to Prussia. France had accumulated a vast debt.*

*The mid-century conflicts in turn led to major changes in all the European states. Each of the monarchies needed more money and tried to govern itself more efficiently. This problem led Britain to attempt to tax the North American colonies, which led to a revolution and the colonies' independence. Already deeply in debt, the French monarchy aided the Americans, fell into a deeper financial crisis, and soon sharply clashed*

*with the nobility as royal ministers tried to find new revenues. That clash eventually unleashed the French Revolution. Spain moved to administer its Latin American empire more efficiently, which increased revolutionary discontent in the early nineteenth century. In preparation for future wars, the rulers of Prussia, Austria, and Russia pursued a mode of activist government known as Enlightened Absolutism. This will be examined in the next chapter. In that regard, the mid-eighteenth-century wars set in motion most of the major political developments of the next half century.*

# Review Questions

1. What were the fundamental ideas associated with mercantile theory? Did they work? Which European country was most successful in establishing a mercantile empire? Least successful? Why?
2. What were the main points of conflict between Britain and France in North America, the West Indies, and India? How did the triangles of trade function between the Americas, Europe, and Africa?
3. How was the Spanish colonial empire in the Americas organized and managed? What changes did the Bourbon monarchs institute in the Spanish Empire?
4. What was the nature of slavery in the Americas? How was it linked to the economies of the Americas, Europe, and Africa? What was the plantation system and how did it contribute to the inhumane treatment of slaves?
5. The Seven Years' War was a major conflict with battles fought around the globe. What were the results of this war? Which countries emerged in a stronger position and why?
6. Discuss the American Revolution in the context of European history. To what extent were the colonists influenced by European ideas and political developments? To what extent did their actions in turn influence Europe?

# Suggested Readings

B. BAILYN, *The Ideological Origins of the American Revolution* (1967). An important work illustrating the role of English radical thought in the perceptions of the American colonists.

B. BAILYN, *The Peopling of British North America: An Introduction* (1988). A study of the immigrants to the British colonies on the eve of the Revolution.

C. A. BAYLY, *Imperial Meridian: The British Empire and the World, 1780–1830* (1989). A major study of the empire after the loss of America.

C. BECKER, *The Declaration of Independence: A Study in the History of Political Ideas* (1922). Remains an important examination of the political and imperial theory of the Declaration.

L. BETHELL (ED.), *The Cambridge History of Latin America*, vols. 1 and 2 (1984). Excellent essays on the colonial era.

J. BLACK, *Pitt the Elder* (1992). The most recent biography.

J. BLACK, *European Warfare, 1660–1815* (1994). A major, wide-ranging synthesis.

C. BONWICK, *English Radicals and the American Revolution* (1977). Explores the relationship between English radical politics and events in America.

D. BRADING, *The First America* (1991). A major study of colonial Latin America.

J. BREWER, *Party Ideology and Popular Politics at the Accession of George III* (1976). An important series of essays on popular radicalism.

J. BREWER, *The Sinews of Power: War, Money, and the English State, 1688–1783* (1989). A study that emphasizes the financial power behind British military success.

J. BROOKE, *King George III* (1972). The best biography.

K. N. CHAUDHURI, *The Trading World of Asia and the English East India Company* (1978). Examines the impact of trade on both Asians and Europeans.

L. COLLEY, *Britons: Forging the Nation, 1707–1837* (1992). A major work with important discussions of the recovery from the loss of America.

P. CURTIN, *The Atlantic Slave Trade* (1969). The best work on the subject.

D. B. DAVIS, *The Problem of Slavery in Western Culture* (1966). A brilliant and far-ranging discussion.

D. B. DAVIS, *The Problem of Slavery in the Age of Revolution, 1770–1823* (1975). A major work on both European and American history.

R. DAVIS, *The Rise of the Atlantic Economies* (1973). A major synthesis.

W. DORN, *Competition for Empire, 1740–1763* (1940). Still one of the best accounts of the mid-century struggle.

C. GIBSON, *Spain in America* (1966). A splendidly clear and balanced discussion.

P. LANGFORD, *A Polite and Commercial People: England 1717–1783* (1989). An excellent survey of mid-century Britain based on the most recent scholarship covering social history as well as politics, the overseas wars, and the American Revolution.

J. LOCKHARDT AND S. B. SCHWARTZ, *Early Latin America: A History of Colonial Spanish America and Brazil* (1983). The new standard work.

J. R. MCNEIL, *Atlantic Empires of France and Spain: Louisbourg and Havana, 1700–1763* (1985). An examination of imperial policies for two key overseas outposts.

S. W. MINTZ, *Sweetness and Power: The Place of Sugar in Modern History* (1985). Traces the role of sugar in the world economy and how sugar has had an impact on world culture.

A. PAGDEN, *Lords of All the World: Ideologies of Empire in Spain, Britain, and France, 1492–1830* (1995). One of the few comparative studies of empire during this period.

J. H. PARRY, *Trade and Dominion: The European Overseas Empires in the Eighteenth Century* (1971). A comprehensive account with attention to the European impact on the rest of the world.

J. G. A. POCOCK, *The Machiavellian Moment: Florentine Political Thought and the Atlantic Republican Tradition* (1975). An important book that traces the origins of Anglo-American radicalism to Renaissance Florence.

C. D. RICE, *The Rise and Fall of Black Slavery* (1975). An excellent survey of the subject with careful attention to the numerous historiographical controversies.

J. C. RILEY, *The Seven Years' War and the Old Regime in France: The Economic and Financial Toll* (1986). A useful analysis of pressures that would undermine the French monarchy.

G. RUDÉ, *Wilkes and Political Liberty* (1962). A close analysis of popular political behavior.

K. W. SCHWEIZER, *Frederick the Great, William Pitt, and Lord Bute: The Anglo-Prussian Alliance, 1756–1763* (1991). The most recent study of this complex diplomacy.

I. K. STEELE, *The English Atlantic, 1675–1740: An Exploration of Communication and Community* (1986). An exploration of culture and commerce in the transatlantic world.

R. L. STEIN, *The French Sugar Business in the Eighteenth Century* (1988). A study that covers all aspects of the French sugar trade.

J. THORNTON, *Africa and Africans in the Making of the Atlantic World, 1400–1680* (1992). A discussion of the role of Africans in the emergence of the transatlantic economy.

J. WEST, *Gunpower, Government, and War in the Mid-Eighteenth Century* (1991). A study of how warfare touched much of government.

G. WILLS, *Inventing America: Jefferson's Declaration of Independence* (1978). An important study that challenges much of the analysis in the Becker volume.

G. S. WOOD, *The Creation of the American Republic, 1776–1787* (1969). A far-ranging work dealing with Anglo-American political thought.

G. S. WOOD, *The Radicalism of the American Revolution* (1991). A major interpretation.

# Enlightenment and Revolution

Between approximately 1750 and 1850, certain extraordinary changes occurred in Western civilization. Although of immediate significance primarily for the nations of Europe and the Americas, these developments in the long run had an immense worldwide impact. Eventually, all civilizations were to feel the influence of the European intellectual ferment and political turmoil of these years. Most of the intellectual, political, economic, and social characteristics associated with the modern world came into being during this era. Europe became the great exporter of ideas and technologies that in time transformed one area after another of human experience.

An intellectual movement known as the *Enlightenment*, characterized by ideals of reform and challenge to traditional cultural authority, captured the imagination of the reading public. The Enlightenment drew confidence from the scientific worldview that had emerged during the seventeenth century. Its exponents urged the application of the spirit of critical rationalism in one area of social and political life after another. They posed serious historical and moral questions to the Christian faith. They contended that laws of society and economics could be discovered and could then be used to improve the human condition. They embraced the idea of economic growth and development. They called for political reform and more efficient modes of government. They upheld the standard of rationality in order to cast doubt on traditional modes of thought and behavior that seemed to them less than rational. As a result of their labors, initially in Europe and ultimately throughout the world, the idea of change as a positive value, which has played so important a role in modern life, emerged for the first time.

For many people, however, change seemed to come too rapidly and violently when revolution erupted in France in 1789. Beginning as an aristocratic revolt against the monarchy, the revolution rapidly spread to every corner of French political and social life. The rights of man and citizen displaced those of the monarchy, the aristocracy, and the church. By 1792 the revolution had become a genuinely popular movement and had established a French republic whose armies challenged the other major European monarchies. The reign of terror that saw the execution of the French king unleashed civil violence unlike anything witnessed in Europe since the age of the religious wars. By the end of the 1790s, to restore order, French political leaders turned themselves over to the leadership of Napoleon. Thereafter, for more than a decade, his armies uprooted institutions of the Old Regime across the Continent. Only in 1815, after the Battle of Waterloo, was the power of France and Napoleon finally contained.

The French Revolution in one way or another served as a model for virtually all later popular revolutions. It unleashed new forces and political creeds in one area of the world after another. The French Revolution, with its broad popular base, brought the *people* to the forefront of world political history. In defining the early goals of the revolution—to establish a legal framework of limited monarchical power, secure citizen rights, and make possible relatively free economic activity—its supporters developed the political creed of *liberalism*.

The wars of the French Revolution and of Napoleon, stretching from 1792 to 1815, awakened the political force of *nationalism*, which has proved to be the single most powerful ideology of the modern world. Loyalty to the nation defined in ethnic terms of a common language, history, and culture replaced loyalty to dynasties. As a political ideology, nationalism could be used both to liberate a people from the domination of another nation and to justify wars of aggression. Nationalism was put to both uses in Europe and throughout the rest of the world in the two centuries following the revolution in France. Nationalism became a kind of secular religion that aroused a degree of loyalty and personal self-sacrifice previously prompted only by the great religious traditions.

Finally, between 1750 and 1850, Europe became not only an exporter of reform and revolution but also of manufactured commodities. The technology and the society associated with industrialism took root throughout the western portion of the Continent. Europeans achieved a productive capacity that, in cooperation with their naval power, permitted them to dominate the markets of the world. Thereafter, to be strong, independent, and modern seemed to require industrialization and imitation of the manufacturing techniques of Europe and, later, of the United States.

Industrialism and its society, however, fostered immense social problems, dislocations, and injustices. The major intellectual and political response to these was *socialism*, several varieties of which emerged from the European social and economic turmoil of the 1830s and 1840s. History eventually proved the most significant of these to be that espoused by Karl Marx, whose *Communist Manifesto* appeared in 1848.

Remarkable ironies are attached to the European achievements of the late eighteenth and the early nineteenth centuries. Enlightenment, revolution, and industrialism contributed to an awakening of European power that permitted the Continent to dominate the world for a time at the end of the nineteenth century. Yet those same movements produced various intellectual critiques, political ideas, and economic skills that twentieth-century non-European peoples would turn against their temporary European masters. It is for that reason that the Age of Enlightenment and revolution in the West proved so important, not only for Europe, but for the history of the entire modern world.  ✦

| | POLITICS AND GOVERNMENT | SOCIETY AND ECONOMY | RELIGION AND CULTURE |
|---|---|---|---|
| **1700–1789** | 1713 **Peace of Utrecht**<br>1713–1740 **Frederick William I builds Prussian military**<br>1720–1740 **Walpole in England, Fleury in France**<br>1739 **War of Jenkins's Ear**<br>1740 **Maria Theresa succeeds to Habsburg throne**<br>1740–1748 **War of the Austrian Succession** | 1715–1763 **Colonial rivalry in the Caribbean**<br>1733 **James Kay's flying shuttle** | 1721 **Montesquieu,** *Persian Letters*<br>1733 **Voltaire,** *Letters on the English*<br>1738 **Voltaire,** *Elements of the Philosophy of Newton*<br>1739 **Wesley begins field preaching**<br>1748 **Hume,** *Inquiry into Human Nature*<br>1748 **Montesquieu,** *Spirit of the Laws* |

Voltaire

| | POLITICS AND GOVERNMENT | SOCIETY AND ECONOMY | RELIGION AND CULTURE |
|---|---|---|---|
| | 1756–1763 **Seven Years' War**<br>1767 **Legislative Commission in Russia**<br>1772 **First Partition of Poland**<br>1775–1783 **American Revolution**<br>1785 **Catherine the Great of Russia issues Charter of Nobility** | 1750s **Agricultural Revolution in Britain**<br>1750–1840 **Growth of new cities**<br>1763 **British establish dominance in India**<br>1763–1789 **Enlightened absolutist rulers seek to spur economic growth**<br>1765 **James Hargreaves's spinning jenny**<br>1769 **Richard Arkwright's waterframe**<br>1771–1775 **Pugachev's Rebellion**<br>1780 **Gordon riots in London**<br>1787 **Edmund Cartwright's power loom** | 1750 **Rousseau,** *Discourse on the Moral Effects of the Arts and Sciences*<br>1751 **First volume of Diderot's** *Encyclopedia*<br>1762 **Rousseau,** *Social Contract and Émile*<br>1763 **Voltaire,** *Treatise on Toleration*<br>1774 **Goethe,** *Sorrows of Young Werther*<br>1776 **Smith,** *Wealth of Nations*<br>1779 **Lessing,** *Nathan the Wise*<br>1781 **Joseph II adopts toleration in Austria**<br>1781 **Kant,** *Critique of Pure Reason* |
| **1789–1815** | 1789 **Gathering of the Estates General at Versailles; fall of the Bastille; Declaration of the Rights of Man and Citizen**<br>1791 **French monarchy abolished**<br>1793 **Louis XVI executed**<br>1793–1794 **Reign of Terror** | 1789–1802 **Revolutionary legislation restructures French economic life** | 1789 **Blake,** *Songs of Innocence*<br>1790 **Civil Constitution of the Clergy; Burke,** *Reflections on the Revolution in France*<br>1792 **Wollstonecraft,** *Vindication of the Rights of Woman*<br>1793 **France proclaims Cult of Reason** |

| POLITICS AND GOVERNMENT | SOCIETY AND ECONOMY | RELIGION AND CULTURE |
|---|---|---|

**1789–1815 (cont.)**

**POLITICS AND GOVERNMENT**

1795 The Directory established in France

1799 Napoleon named First Consul in France

1803 War resumes between Britain and France

1804 Napoleonic Code; Napoleon crowned emperor

1805 Third Coalition formed against France; battles of Trafalgar and Austerlitz

1806 Napoleon establishes the Continental System

1807 Treaty of Tilsit between France and Russia

1808 Spanish resistance to Napoleon stiffens

1812 Napoleon invades Russia; meets defeat

1814 Napoleon abdicates; Congress of Vienna opens; Louis XVIII restored in France

**1815–1850**

1815 Napoleon defeated at Waterloo

1819 Carlsbad Decrees in Germanies; Peterloo Massacre and the Six Acts, Britain

1820 Spanish Revolution begins

1821 Greek Revolution begins

1823 France intervenes in Spanish Revolution

1825 Decembrist Revolt in Russia

1829 Catholic Emancipation Act in Great Britain

1830 Revolution in France, Belgium, and Poland; Serbia gains independence

1832 Great Reform Bill in Britain

1848 Revolutions sweep across Europe

**SOCIETY AND ECONOMY**

1794–1824 Wars of independence in Latin America break the colonial system

Napoleon Bonaparte

1810 Abolition of serfdom in Prussia

1800–1850 British industrial dominance

1825 Stockton and Darlington Railway opens

1828–1850 First European police departments

1830–1850 Railway building in western Europe

1833 English Factory Act to protect children

1834 German *Zollverein* established

1842 Chadwick, *Report on the Sanitary Condition of the Labouring Population*

1846 Corn Laws repealed in Britain

1847 Ten Hour Act passed in Britain

1848 Serfdom abolished in Austria and Hungary

**RELIGION AND CULTURE**

1794 France proclaims Cult of the Supreme Being

1798 Wordsworth and Coleridge, *Lyrical Ballads*; Malthus, *Essay on the Principle of Population*

1799 Schleiermacher, *Speeches on Religion to Its Cultured Despisers*

1802 Chateaubriand, *Genius of Christianity*

1802 Napoleon, Concordat with the Papacy

1806 Hegel, *Phenomenology of Mind*

1807 Fichte, *Addresses to the German Nation*

1808 Goethe, *Faust*, Part I

1812 Byron, *Childe Harold's Pilgrimage*

1817 Ricardo, *Principles of Political Economy*

1819 Byron, *Don Juan*

1829 Catholic Emancipation Act in Great Britain

1830–1842 Comte, *The Positive Philosophy*

1830 Lyell, *Principles of Geology*

1833 Russia begins "Official Nationality" policy

1835 Strauss, *Life of Jesus*

1840 Villermé, *Catalogue of the Physical and Moral State of Workers*

1843 Kierkegaard, *Fear and Trembling*

1848 Marx and Engels, *Communist Manifesto*

*Philosopher, dramatist, poet, historian, and popularizer of scientific ideas, Voltaire (1694–1778) was the most famous and influential of the eighteenth-century philosophes. His sharp satire and criticism of religious institutions opened the way for a more general critique of the European political and social status quo. [Private Collection, Musee de la Ville de Paris, Musee Carnavalet, Paris, France. Giraudon/Art Resource]*

# The Age of Enlightenment: Eighteenth-Century Thought

## KEY TOPICS

- The intellectual and social background of the Enlightenment
- The *philosophes* of the Enlightenment and their agenda of intellectual and political reform
- Efforts of "enlightened" monarchs in central and eastern Europe to increase the economic and military strength of their domains
- The partition of Poland by Prussia, Russia, and Austria

During the eighteenth century, the conviction began to spread throughout the literate sectors of European society that change and reform were both possible and desirable. This attitude is now commonplace, but it came into its own only after 1700. It represents one of the primary intellectual inheritances from that age. The movement of people and ideas that fostered such thinking is called the Enlightenment.

Its leading voices combined confidence in the human mind inspired by the Scientific Revolution and faith in the power of rational criticism to challenge the intellectual authority of tradition and the Christian past. These writers stood convinced that human beings could comprehend the operation of physical nature and mold it to the ends of material and moral improvement, economic growth, and political reform. The rationality of the physical universe became a standard against which the customs and traditions of society could be measured and criticized. Such criticism penetrated every corner of contemporary society, politics, and religious opinion. As a result, the spirit of innovation and improvement came to characterize modern Europe and Western society.

Some of the ideas and outlooks of the Enlightenment had a direct impact on several rulers in central and eastern

*Europe. These rulers, whose policies became known by the term* enlightened absolutism, *sought to centralize their authority so as to reform their countries. They often attempted to restructure religious authority and to sponsor economic growth. Although they were often associated with the writers of the Enlightenment, many of their policies were in direct opposition to enlightened ideals. Nonetheless, both the Enlightenment writers and these monarchs were forces for modernization in European life.*

## Formative Influences

The Newtonian worldview, the stability and prosperity of Great Britain after 1688, the need for reform in France after the wars of Louis XIV, and the consolidation of what is known as a *print culture* were the chief factors that fostered the ideas of the Enlightenment and the call for reform throughout Europe.

### Ideas of Newton and Locke

Isaac Newton (1642–1727) and John Locke (1632–1704) were the major intellectual forerunners of the Enlightenment. Newton's formulation of the law of universal gravitation exemplified the power of the human mind. By example and in his writing, he encouraged Europeans to approach the study of nature directly and to avoid metaphysics and supernaturalism. Newton had always insisted on empirical support for his general laws and constantly used empirical experience to check his rational speculations. This emphasis on concrete experience became a key feature of Enlightenment thought.

Newton also seemed to have revealed a pattern of rationality in the physical world. During the eighteenth century, thinkers began to apply this insight to society. If nature was rational, they reasoned, society too should be organized rationally.

As noted in Chapter 14, Newton's success in physics inspired his countryman John Locke to explain human psychology in terms of experience. In *An Essay Concerning Human Understanding* (1690), Locke argued that all humans enter the world a *tabula rasa*, or blank page. Personality is the product of the sensations that impinge on an individual from the external world throughout his or her life. Thus, experience, and only experience, shapes character. The implication of this theory

*This elaborate eighteenth-century engraving pays homage to Isaac Newton. Newton was a major intellectual influence on the Enlightenment. This engraving is in the collection of the British Museum. [Corbis-Bettmann]*

was that human nature is changeable and can be molded by modifying the surrounding physical and social environment. Locke's was a reformer's psychology. It suggested the possibility of improving the human condition. Locke's psychology also, in effect, rejected the Christian doctrine that human beings are permanently flawed by sin. Human beings need not wait for the grace of God or other divine aid to better their lives. They could take charge of their own destiny.

### The Example of British Toleration and Stability

Newton's physics and Locke's psychology provided the theoretical basis for a reformist approach to society. The domestic stability of Great Britain after the Revolution of 1688 furnished a living example of a society in which enlightened reforms appeared to function for the benefit of all. England permitted religious toleration to all except Unitarians and Roman Catholics, and even they were not actually persecuted. Relative freedom of the press and free speech prevailed. The authority of the monarchy was limited, and political sovereignty resided in Parliament. The courts protected citizens from arbitrary government action. The army was small. In the view of reformist observers on the Continent, these liberal policies had produced not disorder and instability but prosperity, stability, and a loyal citizenry. This view may have been idealized, but England was nonetheless significantly freer than any other European nation at the time.

## Need for Reform in France

If the example of Great Britain suggested that change and freedom need not be disastrous, France seemed to illustrate those aspects of European politics and society that most demanded reform. Its legacy from Louis XIV was absolute monarchy, a large standing army, heavy taxation, and religious persecution. Louis's policies had ultimately brought defeat in war and left his people so miserable that many celebrated when he died. His successors continued to curb liberties. The regime restricted freedom of worship and censored the press and literary expression. Authors often had their works printed in Switzerland to avoid these restraints. Critics of the regime were subject to arbitrary arrest, although some of them reached accommodations with the authorities. State regulations hampered economic growth. Many aristocrats, regarding themselves as part of a military class, upheld traditional militaristic values.

Yet France, because it confronted its political thinkers so sharply with the need for reform, became a major center for the Enlightenment.

## The Emergence of a Print Culture

The Enlightenment was the first major intellectual movement of European history to flourish in a print culture, a culture in which books, journals, newspapers, and pamphlets had achieved a status of their own. Although printed books and pamphlets played a significant role during the Reformation and Counter-Reformation, the powerful messages of those movements were spread mostly by preaching. During the eighteenth century, the volume of printed material—books, journals, magazines, and daily newspapers—increased sharply throughout Europe, most notably in Britain. Prose came to be valued as highly as poetry and the novel emerged as a distinct genre. The printed word had become the chief vehicle for the communication of ideas and would remain so until the electronic revolution of our own day.

A growing concern with everyday life and material concerns—with secular as opposed to religious issues—accompanied this expansion of printed forms. Toward the end of the seventeenth century, half the books published in Paris were religious; by the 1780s, only about 10 percent were.

Books were not inexpensive in this era, but they, and the ideas they conveyed, circulated in a variety of ways to reach a broad public. Private and public libraries grew in number, allowing single copies to reach many readers. Authors might also publish the same material in different formats. The English essayist, critic, and dictionary author Samuel Johnson (1709–1784), for example, published as books collections of essays that had first appeared in newspapers or journals.

Familiarity with books and secular ideas came increasingly to be expected within aristocratic and middle-class society. Popular publications, such as *The Spectator*, begun in 1711 by Joseph Addison (1672–1719) and Richard Steele (1672–1729), fostered the value of polite conversation and the reading of books. Coffee houses became centers for the discussion of writing and ideas. The lodges of Freemasons, the meeting places for members of a movement that began in Britain and spread to the Continent, provided another site for the consideration of secular ideas in secular books.

The expanding market for printed matter allowed writers to earn a living from their work for the first time, making authorship an occupation. Parisian ladies sought out popular writers for their fashionable salons. Some writers, notably Alexander Pope (1688–1744) and Voltaire, grew wealthy, providing an example for their aspiring young colleagues. In a challenge to older aristocratic values, status for authors in this new print culture was based on merit and commercial competition, not heredity and patronage.

A division, however, soon emerged between high and low literary culture. Successful authors of the Enlightenment addressed themselves to monarchs, nobles, the upper middle classes, and professional groups and were read and accepted in these upper levels of society. Other authors found social and economic disappointment. They lived marginally,

*The world of the Enlightenment has often been portrayed as entirely optimistic. Such was hardly the case. Some people feared that the expansion of knowledge might bring danger as well as liberation. In this famous painting of a bird in an air pump, Joseph Wright of Derby captures some of that uncertainty. The scene is suffused in light, a metaphor for scientific enlightenment, but the bird will probably die as a result of the experiment. The people gathered around it are clearly having varied reactions to what they are witnessing. [The National Gallery, London]*

writing professionally for whatever newspaper or journal would pay for their pages. Many of these lesser writers grew resentful, blaming a corrupt society for their lack of success. From their anger, they often espoused radical ideas or carried Enlightenment ideas to radical extremes, transmitting them in this embittered form to their often lower-class audience. The new print culture thus circulated the ideas of the Enlightenment to virtually all literate groups in society.

An expanding literate public and the growing influence of secular printed materials created a new and increasingly influential social force called *public opinion*. This force—the collective effect on political and social life of views circulated in print and discussed in the home, the workplace, and centers of leisure—seems not to have existed as a vital force before the middle of the eighteenth century. Books and newspapers could have thousands of readers, who in effect supported the writers whose works they bought, discussing their ideas and circulating them widely. The writers, in turn, had to answer only to their readers. The result changed the cultural and political climate in Europe. In 1775 a new member of the French Academy declared:

A tribunal has arisen independent of all powers and that all powers respect, that appreciates all talents, that pronounces on all people of merit. And in an enlightened century, in a century in which each citizen can speak to

the entire nation by way of print, those who have a talent for instructing men and a gift for moving them—in a word, men of letters—are, amid the public dispersed, what the orators of Rome and Athens were in the middle of the public assembled.[1]

Governments could no longer operate wholly in secret or with disregard to the larger public sphere. They, as well as their critics, had to explain and discuss their views and policies openly.

Continental European governments sensed the political power of the new print culture. They regulated the book trade, censored books and newspapers, confiscated offending titles, and imprisoned offending authors. The eventual expansion of freedom of the press represented also an expansion of the print culture—with its independent readers, authors, and publishers—and the challenge it represented to traditional intellectual, social, and political authorities.

## The *Philosophes*

The writers and critics who forged the new attitudes favorable to change, who championed reform, and who flourished in the emerging print culture

[1]Chrétien-Guillaume Malesherbes, as quoted in Roger Chartier, *The Cultural Origins of the French Revolution*, trans. by Lydia G. Cochran (Durham, N.C.: Duke University Press, 1991), pp. 30–31.

were the *philosophes*. Not usually philosophers in a formal sense, they sought rather to apply the rules of reason and common sense to nearly all the major institutions and social practices of the day. The most famous of their number included Voltaire, Montesquieu, Diderot, Rousseau, Hume, Gibbon, Smith, Lessing, and Kant.

A few of these *philosophes* occupied professorships in universities. Most, however, were free agents who might be found in London coffee houses, Edinburgh drinking spots, the salons of fashionable Parisian ladies, the country houses of reform-minded nobles, or the courts of the most powerful monarchs on the Continent. In eastern Europe, they were often to be found in the royal bureaucracies. They were not an organized group; they disagreed on many issues. Their relationship with each other and with lesser figures of the same turn of mind has quite appropriately been compared with that of a family, in which despite quarrels and tensions a basic unity still remains.[2]

The chief bond among the *philosophes* was their common desire to reform thought, society, and government for the sake of human liberty. As Peter Gay has suggested, this goal included "freedom from arbitrary power, freedom of speech, freedom of trade, freedom to realize one's talents, freedom of aesthetic response, freedom, in a word, of moral man to make his way in the world."[3] No other single set of ideas has done so much to shape the modern world. The literary vehicles through which the *philosophes* delivered their message included books, pamphlets, plays, novels, philosophical treatises, encyclopedias, newspapers, and magazines. During the Reformation and the religious wars, writers had used the printed word to debate the proper mode of faith in God. The *philosophes* of the Enlightenment employed the printed word to proclaim a new faith in the capacity of humankind to improve itself without the aid of God.

Many of the *philosophes* were of middle-class origins. The bulk of their readership was also drawn from the prosperous commercial and professional people of the eighteenth-century towns and cities. These people discussed the reformers' writings and ideas in local philosophical societies, Freemason lodges, and clubs. They had enough income and leisure time to buy and read the *philosophes'* works.

[2]Peter Gay, *The Enlightenment: An Interpretation*, vol. 1 (New York: Knopf, 1967), p. 4.
[3]Gay, p. 3.

Although the writers of the Enlightenment did not consciously champion the goals or causes of the middle class, they did provide an intellectual ferment and a major source of ideas that could be used to undermine existing social practices and political structures. They taught their contemporaries how to pose pointed, critical questions. Moreover, the *philosophes* generally supported the economic growth, the expansion of trade, and the improvement of transport, which were transforming the society and the economy of the eighteenth century and enlarging the middle class.

The Enlightenment evolved over the course of the century and involved writers living at different times in various countries. Its early exponents popularized the rationalism and scientific ideas of the seventeenth century. (See Chapter 14.) They worked to expose contemporary social and political abuses and argued that reform was necessary and possible. Their progress in this cause was anything but steady. Among the obstacles they met were vested interests, political oppression, and religious condemnation.

Yet, by mid-century, they had brought enlightened ideas to the European public in a variety of formats. The *philosophes'* "family" had come into being. They corresponded with each other, wrote for each other as well as for the public, and defended each other against the political and religious authorities.

By the second half of the century, they were sufficiently safe to quarrel among themselves on occasion. They had stopped talking in generalities, and their major advocates were addressing specific abuses. Their books and articles had become more specialized and more practical. They had become more concerned with politics than with religion. Having convinced Europeans that change was a good idea, they began to suggest exactly what changes were most desirable. They had become honored figures.

## Voltaire's Agenda of Intellectual Reform

One of the earliest and by far the most influential of the *philosophes* was François Marie Arouet, known to posterity as Voltaire (1694–1778). During the 1720s, Voltaire had offended the French authorities by certain of his writings. He was arrested and put in prison for a brief time.

Later Voltaire went to England, visiting its best literary circles, observing its tolerant intellectual and religious climate, relishing the freedom he felt in its moderate political atmosphere, and admiring its science and economic prosperity. In 1733 he published *Letters on the English*, which appeared in French the next year. The book praised the virtues of the English and indirectly criticized the abuses of French society. In 1738 he published *Elements of the Philosophy of Newton*, which popularized the thought of the great scientist. Both works were well received and gave Voltaire a reputation as an important writer.

Thereafter Voltaire lived part of the time in France and part near Geneva, just across the French border, where the royal authorities could not bother him. He wrote essays, history, plays, stories, and letters that made him the literary dictator of Europe. He used the bitter venom of his satire and sarcasm against one evil after another in French and European life. In his most famous satire, *Candide* (1759), he attacked war, religious persecution, and what he regarded as unwarranted optimism about the human condition.

Like most *philosophes*, Voltaire believed that improvement of human society was necessary and possible. But he was never certain that reform, if achieved, would be permanent. The optimism of the Enlightenment was a tempered hopefulness rather than a glib certainty. An undercurrent of pessimism characterized most of the works of the period.

### The Encyclopedia

The mid-century witnessed the publication of the *Encyclopedia*, one the greatest monuments of the Enlightenment. Under the heroic leadership of Denis Diderot (1713–1784), and Jean le Rond d'Alembert (1717–1783), the first volume appeared in 1751. Numbering seventeen volumes of text and eleven of plates (illustrations), the project reached completion in 1772.

The *Encyclopedia*, in part a collective plea for freedom of expression, reached fruition only after many attempts to censor it and to halt its publication. It was the product of the collective effort of more than 100 authors, and its editors had at one time or another solicited articles from all the major French *philosophes*. It included the most advanced critical ideas of the time on religion, government, and philosophy. To avoid official censure, these ideas often had to be hidden in obscure articles or under the cover of irony. The *Encyclopedia* also

included important articles and illustrations on manufacturing, canal building, ship construction, and improved agriculture, making it an important source of knowledge about eighteenth-century social and economic life.

Between 14,000 and 16,000 copies of various editions of the *Encyclopedia* were sold before 1789. The project had been designed to secularize learning and to undermine intellectual assumptions that lingered from the Middle Ages and the Reformation. The articles on politics, ethics, and society ignored divine law and concentrated on humanity and its immediate well-being. The Encyclopedists looked to antiquity rather than to the Christian centuries for their intellectual and ethical models. For them, the future welfare of humankind lay not in pleasing God or following divine commandments but rather in harnessing the power and resources of the Earth and in living at peace with one's fellow human beings. The good life lay here and now and was to be achieved through the application of reason to human relationships. With the publication of the *Encyclopedia*, Enlightenment thought became more fully diffused over the Continent, penetrating German and Russian intellectual and political circles.

## The Enlightenment and Religion

For many but not all *philosophes* of the eighteenth century, ecclesiastical institutions were the chief impediment to human improvement and happiness. Voltaire's cry, "Crush the Infamous Thing," summed up the attitude of a number of *philosophes* toward the church and Christianity. Almost all varieties of Christianity, but especially Roman Catholicism, felt their criticism.

The critical *philosophes* complained that the churches hindered the pursuit of a rational life and the scientific study of humanity and nature. The clergy taught that humans were basically depraved, becoming worthy only through divine grace. According to the doctrine of original sin, Protestant or Catholic, meaningful improvement in human nature on Earth was impossible. Religion thus turned attention away from this world to the world to come. For example, the *philosophes* argued that the Calvinist doctrine of predestination denied a relationship between virtuous actions in this life and the fate of the soul after death. Mired in conflicts over obscure doctrinal differences, the churches promoted intolerance and bigotry, inciting torture, war, and other forms of human suffering.

With this attack, the *philosophes* were challenging not only a set of ideas but also some of Europe's most powerful institutions. The churches were deeply enmeshed in the power structure of the old regime. They owned large amounts of land and collected tithes from peasants before any secular authority collected its taxes. Most clergy were legally exempt from taxes and made only annual voluntary grants to the government. The upper clergy in most countries were relatives of aristocrats. Clerics were actively involved in politics, serving in the British House of Lords and advising princes on the Continent. In Protestant countries, the leading local landowner usually appointed the clergyman of a particular parish. Across the Continent, membership in the predominant denomination of the kingdom gave certain subjects political advantages. Nonmembership often excluded other subjects from political participation. Clergy of all faiths preached the sinfulness of political disobedience. They provided intellectual justification for the social and political status quo, and they were active agents of religious and literary censorship.

## Deism

The *philosophes*, although critical of many religious institutions and frequently anticlerical, were not opposed to all religion. In Scotland, for example, the enlightened historian William Robertson (1721–1793) was the head of the Scottish Kirk. In England, clergy of the established church did much to popularize the thought of Newton. What the *philosophes* sought, however, was religion without fanaticism and intolerance, a religious life that would not substitute church authority for the authority of human reason. The Newtonian worldview had convinced many writers that nature was rational. Therefore, the God who had created nature must also be rational, and the religion through which that God was worshiped should be rational. Most of them believed that the life of religion and of reason could be combined, giving rise to a movement known as *deism*.

The title of one of the earliest deist works, *Christianity Not Mysterious* (1696) by John Toland (1670–1722), indicates the general tenor of this religious outlook. Toland and later deist writers promoted religion as a natural and rational, rather than a supernatural and mystical, phenomenon. In this respect they differed from Newton and Locke, both

of whom regarded themselves as distinctly Christian. Newton believed God could interfere with the natural order, whereas the deists regarded God as a kind of divine watchmaker who had created the mechanism of nature, set it in motion, and then departed. Most of the deist writers were also strongly anticlerical and for that reason regarded as radical.

There were two major points in the deists' creed. The first was a belief in the existence of God, which they thought could be empirically justified by the contemplation of nature. Joseph Addison's poem on the spacious firmament (1712) illustrates this idea:

The spacious firmament on high,
With all the blue ethereal sky,
And spangled heav'n, a shining frame,
Their great Original proclaim:
Th' unwearied Sun, from day to day,
Does his Creator's power display,
And publishes to every land
The work of an Almighty hand.

Because nature provided evidence of a rational God, that deity must also favor rational morality. So the second point in the deists' creed was a belief in life after death, when rewards and punishments would be meted out according to the virtue of the lives people led on this Earth.

Deism was empirical, tolerant, reasonable, and capable of encouraging virtuous living. Voltaire declared:

The great name of Deist, which is not sufficiently revered, is the only name one ought to take. The only gospel one ought to read is the great book of Nature, written by the hand of God and sealed with his seal. The only religion that ought to be professed is the religion of worshiping God and being a good man.[4]

Deists hoped that wide acceptance of their faith would end rivalry among the various Christian sects and with it religious fanaticism, conflict, and persecution. They also felt deism would remove the need for priests and ministers, who, in their view, were often responsible for fomenting religious differences and denominational hatred.

## Toleration

According to the *philosophes*, religious toleration was a primary social condition for the virtuous life. Again Voltaire took the lead in championing this cause. In 1762 the Roman Catholic political author-

[4]Quoted in J. H. Randall, *The Making of the Modern Mind*, rev. ed. (New York: Houghton Mifflin, 1940), p. 292.

ities in Toulouse ordered the execution of a Huguenot named Jean Calas. He stood accused of having murdered his son to prevent him from converting to Roman Catholicism. Calas was viciously tortured and publicly strangled without ever confessing his guilt. The confession would not have saved his life, but it would have given the Catholics good propaganda to use against Protestants.

Voltaire learned of the case only after Calas's death. He made the dead man's cause his own. In 1763 he published his *Treatise on Tolerance* and hounded the authorities for a new investigation. Finally, in 1765 the judicial decision against the unfortunate man was reversed. For Voltaire, the case illustrated the fruits of religious fanaticism and the need for rational reform of judicial processes. Somewhat later in the century, the German playwright and critic Gotthold Lessing (1729–1781) wrote *Nathan the Wise* (1779), a plea for toleration not only of different Christian sects but also of religious faiths other than Christianity.

The premise behind all of these calls for toleration was, in effect, that life on Earth and human relationships should not be subordinated to religion. Secular values and considerations were more important than religious ones.

### Radical Enlightenment Criticism of Religion

Some *philosophes* went beyond the formulation of a rational religious alternative to Christianity and the advocacy of toleration to attack the churches and the clergy with great vehemence. Voltaire repeatedly questioned the truthfulness of priests and the morality of the Bible. In his *Philosophical Dictionary* (1764) he humorously pointed out inconsistencies in biblical narratives and immoral acts of the biblical heroes. The Scottish philosopher David Hume (1711–1776), in "Of Miracles," a chapter in his *Inquiry into Human Nature* (1748), argued that no empirical evidence supported the belief in divine miracles central to much of Christianity. For Hume, the greatest miracle was that people believed in miracles. In *The Decline and Fall of the Roman Empire* (1776), Edward Gibbon (1737–1794), the English historian, explained the rise of Christianity in terms of natural causes rather than the influence of miracles and piety.

A few *philosophes* went further. Baron d'Holbach (1723–1789) and Julien Offray de La Mettrie (1709–1751) embraced positions very near to atheism and materialism. Theirs was distinctly a minority posi-

tion, however. Most of the *philosophes* sought not the abolition of religion but its transformation into a humane force that would encourage virtuous living.

The *philosophes'* criticisms of traditional religion nonetheless often reflected an implicit contempt not only for Christianity but also, and sometimes more vehemently, for Judaism. Their attack on the veracity of biblical miracles and biblical history undermined the authority of the Hebrew scriptures as well as the Christian, and their satirical barbs were aimed most often at personalities from the Hebrew scriptures. Some *philosophes* characterized Judaism as a more primitive faith than Christianity. The Enlightenment view of religion thus served in some ways to further stigmatize Jews and Judaism in the eyes of non-Jewish Europeans.

## The Enlightenment and Society

Although the *philosophes* wrote much on religion, humanity was the center of their interest. As one writer in the *Encyclopedia* observed, "Man is the unique point to which we must refer everything,

*David Hume (1711–1776), the Scottish philosopher, argued against belief in miracles and, by implication, against belief in Christianity itself. [The Bettmann Archive]*

# Voltaire Attacks Religious Fanaticism

*The chief complaint of the* philosophes *against Christianity was that it bred a fanaticism that led people to commit crimes in the name of religion. In this passage from Voltaire's* Philosophical Dictionary *(1764), he directly reminds his readers of the intolerance of the Reformation era and indirectly referred to examples of contemporary religious excesses. He argues that the philosophical spirit can overcome fanaticism and foster toleration and more humane religious behavior. Shocking many of his contemporaries, he praises the virtues of Confucianism over those of Christianity.*

✦ *What concrete examples of religious fanaticism might Voltaire have had in mind? Why does Voltaire contend that neither religion nor laws can contain religious fanaticism? Why does Voltaire admire the Chinese?*

Fanaticism is to superstition what delirium is to fever and rage to anger. The man visited by ecstasies and visions, who takes dreams for realities and his fancies for prophecies, is an enthusiast; the man who supports his madness with murder is a fanatic. . . .

The most detestable example of fanaticism was that of the burghers of Paris who on St. Bartholomew's Night [1572] went about assassinating and butchering all their fellow citizens who did not go to mass, throwing them out of windows, cutting them in pieces.

Once fanaticism has corrupted a mind, the malady is almost incurable. . . .

The only remedy for this epidemic malady is the philosophical spirit which, spread gradually, at last tames men's habits and prevents the disease from starting; for once the disease has made any progress, one must flee and wait for the air to clear itself. Laws and religion are not strong enough against the spiritual pest; religion, far from being healthy food for infected brains, turns to poison in them. . . .

Even the law is impotent against these attacks of rage; it is like reading a court decree to a raving maniac. These fellows are certain that the holy spirit with which they are filled is above the law, that their enthusiasm is the only law they must obey.

What can we say to a man who tells you that he would rather obey God than men, and that therefore he is sure to go to heaven for butchering you?

Ordinarily fanatics are guided by rascals, who put the dagger into their hands; these latter resemble that Old Man of the Mountain who is supposed to have made imbeciles taste the joys of paradise and who promised them an eternity of the pleasures of which he had given them a foretaste, on condition that they assassinated all those he would name to them. There is only one religion in the world that has never been sullied by fanaticism, that of the Chinese men of letters. The schools of philosophy were not only free from this pest, they were its remedy; for the effect of philosophy is to make the soul tranquil, and fanaticism is incompatible with tranquility. If our holy religion has so often been corrupted by this infernal delirium, it is the madness of men which is at fault.

*Voltaire,* Philosophical Dictionary, *trans. by P. Gay (New York: Basic Books, 1962), pp. 267–269.*

if we wish to interest and please amongst considerations the most arid and details the most dry."[5]

[5]Quoted in F. L. Baumer, *Main Currents of Western Thought,* 4th ed. (New Haven, Conn.: Yale University Press, 1978), p. 374.

The *philosophes* believed that the application of human reason to society would reveal laws in human relationships similar to those found in physical nature. At the same time, the use of the word *man* in this passage was not simply an accident of language. Most *philosophes* were thinking primarily of men, not women, when they framed their reformist ideas. With a few exceptions, as will be seen later in this chapter, they had little interest in expanding women's intellectual and social opportunities.

Although the term did not appear until later, the idea of social science originated with the Enlightenment. *Philosophes* hoped to end human cruelty by discovering social laws and making people aware of them. These concerns are most evident in the *philosophes'* work on law and prisons.

### Beccaria and Reform of Criminal Law

In 1764 Cesare Beccaria (1738–1794), an Italian *philosophe*, published *On Crimes and Punishments*, in which he applied critical analysis to the problem of making punishments both effective and just. He wanted the laws of monarchs and legislatures—that is, positive law—to conform with the rational laws of nature. He rigorously and eloquently attacked both torture and capital punishment. He thought that the criminal justice system should ensure speedy trial and certain punishment, and that the intent of punishment should be to deter further crime. The purpose of laws was not to impose the will of God or some other ideal of perfection; its purpose was to secure the greatest good or happiness for the greatest number of human beings. This utilitarian philosophy based on happiness in this life permeated most of Enlightenment writing on practical reforms.

### The Physiocrats and Economic Freedom

Economic policy was another area where the *philosophes* saw existing legislation and administration preventing the operation of natural social laws. They believed that mercantilist legislation (designed to protect a country's trade from external competition) and the regulation of labor by governments and guilds actually hampered the expansion of trade, manufacture, and agriculture. In France, these economic reformers were called the *physiocrats*. Their leading spokespeople were François Quesnay (1694–1774) and Pierre Dupont de Nemours (1739–1817).

The physiocrats believed that the primary role of government was to protect property and to permit its owners to use it freely. They particularly felt that all economic production depended on sound

agriculture. They favored the consolidation of small peasant holdings into larger, more efficient farms. Here as elsewhere there was a close relationship between the rationalism of the Enlightenment and the spirit of improvement at work in eighteenth-century European economic life.

### Adam Smith and The Wealth of Nations

The most important economic work of the Enlightenment was Adam Smith's (1723–1790) *Inquiry into the Nature and Causes of the Wealth of Nations* (1776). Smith, who was for a time a professor at Glasgow, believed that economic liberty was the foundation of a natural economic system. As a result, he urged that the mercantile system of England—including the navigation acts, the bounties, most tariffs, special trading monopolies, and the domestic regulation of labor and manufacture—be abolished. These regulations were intended to preserve the wealth of the nation, to capture wealth from other nations, and to maximize the work available for the nation's laborers. Smith argued, however, that they hindered the expansion of wealth and production. The best way to encourage economic growth, he maintained, was to unleash individuals to pursue their own selfish economic interest. As self-interested individuals sought to enrich themselves by meeting the needs of others in the marketplace, the economy would expand. Consumers would find their wants met as manufacturers and merchants competed for their business.

It was a basic assumption of mercantilism that the Earth's resources are limited and scarce, so that one nation can only acquire wealth at the expense of others. Smith's book challenged this assumption. He saw the resources of nature—water, air, soil, and minerals—as boundless. To him, they demanded exploitation for the enrichment and comfort of humankind. In effect, Smith was saying that the nations and peoples of Europe need not be poor.

The idea that humans should exploit nature's infinite bounty for their benefit, which dominated Western economic activity until recently, thus stemmed directly from the Enlightenment. When Smith wrote, the population of the world was smaller, its people poorer, and the quantity of undeveloped resources per capita much greater than now. For people of the eighteenth century, true improvement of the human condition seemed to lie in the uninhibited exploitation of natural resources.

Smith is usually regarded as the founder of *laissez-faire* economic thought and policy, which favors a limited role for the government in economic life. The *Wealth of Nations* was, however, a complex book. Smith was no simple dogmatist. For example, he did not oppose all government activity touching the economy. The state, he argued, should provide schools, armies, navies, and roads. It should also undertake certain commercial ventures, such as the opening of dangerous new trade routes that were economically desirable but too expensive or risky for private enterprise.

# Political Thought of the *Philosophes*

Nowhere was the *philosophes'* appreciation of the complexity of the problems of contemporary society clearer than their political thought. Nor did any other area of their reformist enterprise so clearly illustrate the tension and conflict within the "family" of the Enlightenment. Most *philosophes* were discontented with certain political features of their countries, but they were especially discontented in France. There the corruptness of the royal court, the blundering of the bureaucracy, the less than glorious mid-century wars, and the power of the church compounded all problems. Consequently, the most important political thought of the Enlightenment occurred in France. The French *philosophes*, however, stood quite divided as to the proper solution to their country's problems. Their attitudes spanned a wide political spectrum from aristocratic reform to democracy to absolute monarchy.

## Montesquieu *and* Spirit of the Laws

Charles Louis de Secondat, Baron de Montesquieu (1689–1755), was a lawyer, noble of the robe, and a member of a provincial *parlement*. He also belonged to the Bordeaux Academy of Science, before which he presented papers on scientific topics.

Although living comfortably within the bosom of French society, he saw the need for reform. In 1721 he published *The Persian Letters* to satirize contemporary institutions. The book consisted of letters purportedly written by two Persians visiting Europe. They explained to friends at home how European behavior contrasted with Persian life and customs. Behind the humor lay the cutting edge of criticism and an exposition of the cruelty and irrationality of much contemporary European life.

In his most enduring work, *Spirit of the Laws* (1748), Montesquieu held up the example of the British constitution as the wisest model for regulating the power of government. With his interest in science, his hope for reform, and his admiration for Britain, he embodied all the major elements of the Enlightenment mind.

Montesquieu's *Spirit of the Laws*, perhaps the single most influential book of the century, exhibits the internal tensions of the Enlightenment. In it, Montesquieu pursued an empirical method, taking illustrative examples from the political experience of both ancient and modern nations. From these he concluded there could be no single set of political laws that applied to all peoples at all times and in all places. The good political life depended rather on the relationship among many political variables. Whether the best form of government for a country was a monarchy or a republic, for example, depended on its size, population, social and reli-

*Charles de Secondat, Baron de Montesquieu (1689–1755), was the author of* Spirit of the Laws, *possibly the most influential work of political thought of the eighteenth century. [Bettmann/Hulton]*

# Montesquieu Defends the Separation of Powers

*Spirit of the Laws (1748) was probably the most influential political work of the Enlightenment. In this passage Montesquieu explains how the division of powers within a government would make that government more moderate and would protect the liberty of its subjects. This idea was adopted by the writers of the United States Constitution when they devised the checks and balances of the three branches of government.*

✦ *What did Montesquieu mean by "moderate governments," and why did he associate political liberty with such governments? What might he have seen as such a government in his own day? How does Montesquieu define the liberty of a subject? Why does he regard a situation where the power of government is not divided as one where there can be no liberty?*

Democratic and aristocratic states are not in their own nature free. Political liberty is to be found only in moderate governments; and even in these it is not always found. It is there only when there is no abuse of power. But constant experience shows us that every man invested with power is apt to abuse it, and to carry his authority as far as it will go. . . .

To prevent this abuse, it is necessary from the very nature of things that power should be a check to power. . . .

In every government there are three sorts of power: the legislative; the executive in respect to things dependent on the law of nations; and the executive in regard to matters that depend on the civil law [the realm of the judiciary]. . . .

The political liberty of the subject is a tranquillity of mind arising from the opinion each person has of his safety. In order to have this liberty, it is requisite that government be so constituted as one man need not be afraid of another.

When the legislative and executive powers are united in the same person, or in the same body of magistrates, there can be no liberty; because apprehensions may arise, lest the same monarchy or senate should enact tyrannical laws, to execute them in a tyrannical manner.

Again, there is no liberty, if the judiciary power be not separated from the legislative and executive. Were it joined with the legislative, the life and liberty of the subject would be exposed to arbitrary control; for the judge would be then the legislator. Were it joined to the executive power, the judge might behave with violence and oppression.

There would be an end of everything, were the same man or the same body, whether of the nobles or of the people, to exercise those three powers, that of enacting laws, that of executing the public resolutions, and of trying the causes of individuals.

*Baron de Montesquieu, Spirit of the Laws, trans. by Thomas Nugent, (New York: Hafner Press, 1949), pp. 150–152.*

gious customs, economic structure, traditions, and climate. Only a careful examination and evaluation of these elements could reveal what mode of government would prove most beneficial to a particular people.

So far as France was concerned, Montesquieu had some definite ideas. He believed in a monarchical government tempered and limited by various sets of intermediary institutions. These included the aristocracy, the towns, and the other corporate bodies that enjoyed liberties the monarch had to respect. These corporate bodies might be said to represent various segments of the general population and thus of public opinion. In France, he regarded the aristocratic courts, or *parlements*, as the major example of an intermediary association. Their role was to limit the power of the monarchy and thus to preserve the liberty of its subjects.

In championing these aristocratic bodies and the general role of the aristocracy, Montesquieu was a political conservative. He adopted this conservatism in the hope of achieving reform, however, for he believed the oppressive and inefficient absolutism of the monarchy accounted for the degradation of French life.

One of Montesquieu's most influential ideas was that of the division of power in government. For his model of a government with authority wisely separated among different branches, he took contemporary Great Britain. There, he believed, executive power resided in the king, legislative power in the Parliament, and judicial power in the courts. He thought any two branches could check and balance the power of the other. His perception of the eighteenth-century British constitution was incorrect because he failed to see how patronage and electoral corruption allowed a handful of powerful aristocrats to dominate the government. Moreover, he was also unaware of the emerging cabinet system, which was slowly making the executive power a creature of the Parliament.

Nevertheless, Montesquieu's analysis illustrated his strong sense that monarchs should be subject to constitutional limits on their power and that a separate legislature, not the monarch, should formulate laws. For this reason, although he set out to defend the political privileges of the French aristocracy, Montesquieu's ideas had a profound and still-lasting effect on the constitutional form of liberal democracies of the next two centuries.

### Rousseau: A Radical Critique of Modern Society

Jean-Jacques Rousseau (1712–1778) held a view of the exercise and reform of political power quite different from Montesquieu's. Rousseau was a strange, isolated genius who never felt particularly comfortable with the other *philosophes*. His own life was troubled. He could form few close friendships. He sired numerous children whom he abandoned to foundling hospitals. Yet perhaps more than any other writer of the mid-eighteenth century, he transcended the political thought and values of his own time. Rousseau had a deep antipathy toward the world and the society in which he lived. It seemed to him impossible for human beings living according to contemporary commercial values to achieve moral, virtuous, or sincere lives. In 1750, in his *Discourse on the Moral Effects of the Arts and Sci-*ences, he contended that the process of civilization and enlightenment had corrupted human nature. In 1755, in his *Discourse on the Origin of Inequality*, Rousseau blamed much of the evil in the world on the uneven distribution of property.

In both works Rousseau brilliantly and directly challenged the social fabric of the day. He drew into question the concepts of material and intellectual progress and the morality of a society in which commerce and industry were regarded as the most important human activities. He felt that the real purpose of society was to nurture better people. In this respect Rousseau's vision of reform was much more radical than that of other contemporary writers. The other *philosophes* believed that life would improve if people could enjoy more of the fruits of the Earth or could produce more goods. Rousseau raised the more fundamental question of what constitutes the good life. This question has haunted European social thought ever since the eighteenth century.

*Jean-Jacques Rousseau (1712–1778) raised some of the most profound social and ethical questions of the Enlightenment. This portrait is by Maurice Quentin. [Bildarchiv Preussischer Kulturbesitz]*

Rousseau carried these same concerns into his political thought. His most extensive discussion of politics appeared in *The Social Contract* (1762). Although the book attracted rather little immediate attention, by the end of the century it was widely read in France. The *Social Contract*, compared with Montesquieu's *Spirit of the Laws*, is a very abstract book. It does not propose specific reforms but outlines the kind of political structure that Rousseau believed would overcome the evils of contemporary politics and society.

In the tradition of John Locke, most eighteenth-century political thinkers regarded human beings as individuals and society as a collection of individuals pursuing personal, selfish goals. These writers wished to liberate individuals from the undue bonds of government. Rousseau picked up the stick from the other end. His book opens with the declaration, "All men are born free, but everywhere they are in chains."[6] The rest of the volume is a defense of the chains of a properly organized society over its members.

Rousseau suggested that society is more important than its individual members, because they are what they are only because of their relationship to the larger community. Independent human beings living alone can achieve very little. Through their relationship to the larger community, they become moral creatures capable of significant action. The question then becomes what kind of community allows people to behave morally. In his two previous discourses, Rousseau had explained that contemporary European society was not such a community. It was merely an aggregate of competing individuals whose chief social goal was to preserve selfish independence in spite of all potential social bonds and obligations.

Rousseau envisioned a society in which each person could maintain personal freedom while behaving as a loyal member of the larger community. Drawing on the traditions of Plato and Calvin, he defined *freedom* as obedience to law. In his case, the law to be obeyed was that created by the general will. In a society with virtuous customs and morals in which citizens have adequate information on important issues, the concept of the general will is normally equivalent to the will of a majority of voting citizens. Democratic participation in decision making would bind the individual citizen

[6]Jean-Jacques Rousseau, *The Social Contract and Discourses*, trans. by G. D. H. Cole (New York: Dutton, 1950), p. 3.

to the community. Rousseau believed that the general will, thus understood, must always be right and that to obey the general will is to be free. This argument led him to the notorious conclusion that under certain circumstances some people must be forced to be free. Rousseau's politics thus constituted a justification for radical direct democracy and for collective action against individual citizens.

Rousseau had in effect launched an assault on the eighteenth-century cult of the individual and the fruits of selfishness. He stood at odds with the commercial spirit that was transforming the society in which he lived. Rousseau would have disapproved of the main thrust of Adam Smith's *Wealth of Nations*, which he may or may not have read, and would no doubt have preferred a study on the virtue of nations. Smith wanted people to be prosperous; Rousseau wanted them to be good even if being good meant that they might remain poor. He saw human beings not as independent individuals but as creatures enmeshed in necessary social relationships. He believed that loyalty to the community should be encouraged. As one device to that end, he suggested a civic religion based on the creed of deism. Such a shared religious faith would help unify a society.

Rousseau's chief source of intellectual inspiration was Plato and the ancient Greek *polis*. Especially in Sparta, he thought he had discovered human beings dwelling in a moral society inspired by a common purpose. He hoped that modern human beings might also create such a moral commonwealth in which virtuous living would be valued over commercial profit.

Rousseau had only a marginal impact on his own time. The other *philosophes* questioned his critique of material improvement. Aristocrats and royal ministers could hardly be expected to welcome his proposal for radical democracy. Too many people were either making or hoping to make money to appreciate his criticism of commercial values. He proved, however, to be a figure to whom later generations returned. Many leaders in the French Revolution were familiar with his writing, and he influenced most writers in the nineteenth and twentieth centuries who were critical of the general tenor and direction of Western culture. Rousseau hated much about the emerging modern society in Europe, but he contributed much to modernity by exemplifying for later generations the critic who dared to call into question the very foundations of social thought and action.

## Women in the Thought and Practice of the Enlightenment

Women, especially in France, helped significantly to promote the careers of the *philosophes*. In Paris, the salons of women such as Marie-Thérèse Geoffrin (1699–1777), Julie de Lespinasse (1733–1776), and Claudine de Tencin (1689–1749) gave the *philosophes* access to useful social and political contacts and a receptive environment in which to circulate their ideas. Association with a fashionable salon brought *philosophes* increased social status and added luster and respectability to their ideas. They clearly enjoyed the opportunity to be the center of attention that a salon provided, and their presence at them could boost the sales of their works. The women who organized the salons were well-connected to major political figures who could help protect the *philosophes* and secure them pensions. The marquise de Pompadour, the mistress of Louis XV (1721–1764), played a key role in overcoming efforts to censor the *Encyclopedia*. She also helped block the circulation of works attacking the *philosophes*. Other salon hostesses purchased the writings of the *philosophes* and distributed them among their friends. Madame de Tencin was responsible for promoting Montesquieu's *Spirit of the Laws* in this way.

Despite this help and support from the learned women of Paris, the *philosophes* were on the whole not strong feminists. Many urged better and broader education for women. They criticized the education women did receive as overly religious, and they tended to reject ascetic views of sexual relations. But in general they displayed rather traditional views toward women and advocated no radical changes in the social condition of women.

Montesquieu, for example, illustrates some of these tensions in the views of Enlightenment writers toward women. He maintained in general that the status of women in a society was the result of climate, the political regime, culture, and women's physiological nature. He believed women were not naturally inferior to men and should have a wider role in society. He showed himself well aware of the kinds of personal, emotional, and sexual repression European women endured in his day. He sympathetically observed the value placed on women's appearance and the prejudice women met as they aged. In *The Persian Letters*, he included a long exchange about the repression of women in a Persian harem, condemning by implication the restrictions on women in European society. Yet there were limits to Montesquieu's willingness to consider social change in regard to the role of women in European life. Although in the *Spirit of the Laws* he indicated a belief in the equality of the sexes, he still retained a traditional view of marriage and family and expected men to dominate those institutions. Furthermore, although he supported the right of women to divorce and opposed laws directly oppressive of women, he upheld the ideal of female chastity.

The salon of Mme. Marie-Thérèse Geoffrin (1699–1777) was one of the most important gathering spots for Enlightenment writers during the middle of the eighteenth century. Well-connected women such as Mme. Geoffrin were instrumental in helping the philosophes *they patronized to bring their ideas to the attention of influential people in French society and politics.* [Giraudon/Art Resource, N.Y.]

# Rousseau Argues for Separate Spheres for Men and Women

*Rousseau published* Émile, *a novel about education, in 1762. In it he made one of the strongest and most influential arguments of the eighteenth century for distinct social roles for men and women. Furthermore, he portrayed women as fundamentally subordinate to men. In the next document, Mary Wollstonecraft, a contemporary, presents a rebuttal.*

✦ *How does Rousseau move from the physical differences between men and women to an argument for distinct social roles and social spheres? What would be the proper kinds of social activities for women in Rousseau's vision? What kind of education would he think appropriate for women?*

There is no parity between the two sexes in regard to the consequences of sex. The male is male only at certain moments. The female is female her whole life or at least during her whole youth. Everything constantly recalls her sex to her; and, to fulfill its functions well, she needs a constitution which corresponds to it. She needs care during her pregnancy; she needs rest at the time of childbirth; she needs a soft and sedentary life to suckle her children; she needs patience and gentleness, a zeal and an affection that nothing can rebuff in order to raise her children. She serves as the link between them and their father; she alone makes him love them and gives him the confidence to call them his own. How much tenderness and care is required to maintain the union of the whole family! And, finally, all this must come not from virtues but from tastes, or else the human species would soon be extinguished.

The strictness of the relative duties of the two sexes is not and cannot be the same. When woman complains on this score about unjust man-made inequality, she is wrong. This inequality is not a human institution—or, at least, it is the work not of prejudice but of reason. It is up to the sex that nature has charged with the bearing of children to be responsible for them to the other sex. Doubtless it is not permitted to any one to violate his faith, and every unfaithful husband who deprives his wife of the only reward of the austere duties of her sex is an unjust and barbarous man. But the unfaithful woman does more; she dissolves the family and breaks all the bonds of nature. . . .

Once it is demonstrated that man and woman are not and ought not be constituted in the same way in either character or temperament, it follows that they ought not to have the same education. In following nature's directions, man and woman ought to act in concert, but they ought not to do the same things. The goal of their labors is common, but their labors themselves are different, and consequently so are the tastes directing them. . . .

The good constitution of children initially depends on that of their mothers. The first education of men depends on the care of women. Men's morals, their passions, their tastes, their pleasures, their very happiness also depend on women. Thus the whole education of women ought to relate to men. To please men, to be useful to them, to make herself loved and honored by them, to raise them when young, to care for them when grown, to counsel them, to console them, to make their lives agreeable and sweet—these are the duties of women at all times, and they ought to be taught from childhood. So long as one does not return to this principle, one will deviate from the goal, and all the precepts taught to women will be of no use for their happiness or for ours.

*Jean-Jacques Rousseau,* Émile; or, On Education, *trans. by Allan Bloom (New York: Basic Books, Inc., 1979), pp. 361, 363, 365.*

The views about women expressed in the *Encyclopedia* were less generous than those of Montesquieu. It suggested some ways to improve women's lives, but in general it did not include the condition of women as a focus of reform. The editors, Diderot and d'Alembert, recruited men almost exclusively as contributors, and there is no indication they saw a need to include many articles by women. Most of the articles that dealt with women specifically or that discussed women in connection with other subjects often emphasized their physical weakness and inferiority, usually attributed to menstruation or childbearing. Contributors disagreed on the social equality of women. Some favored it, others opposed it, and still others were indifferent. The articles conveyed a general sense that women were reared to be frivolous and unconcerned with important issues. The Encyclopedists discussed women primarily in a family context—as daughters, wives, and mothers—and presented motherhood as their most important occupation. And on sexual behavior, the Encyclopedists upheld an unquestioned double standard.

In contrast to the articles, however, illustrations in the *Encyclopedia* showed women deeply involved in the economic activities of the day. The illustrations also showed the activities of lower- and working-class women, about whom the articles have little to say.

One of the most surprising and influential analyses of the position of women came from Jean-Jacques Rousseau. This most radical of all Enlightenment political theorists urged a very traditional and conservative role for women. In his novel *Émile* (1762) (discussed again in Chapter 20), he set forth a radical version of the view that men and women occupy separate spheres. He declared that women should be educated for a position subordinate to men, emphasizing especially women's function in bearing and rearing children. In his vision there was little else for women to do but make themselves pleasing to men. He portrayed them as weaker and inferior to men in virtually all respects except perhaps for their capacity for feeling and giving love. He excluded them from political life. The world of citizenship, political action, and civic virtue was to be populated by men. Women were assigned the domestic sphere alone. Many of these attitudes were not new—some have roots as ancient as Roman law—but Rousseau's powerful presentation and the influence of his other writings gave them

| | Major Works of the Enlightenment and Their Publication Dates |
|---|---|
| 1687 | Newton's *Principia Mathematica* |
| 1690 | Locke's *Essay Concerning Human Understanding* |
| 1696 | Toland's *Christianity Not Mysterious* |
| 1721 | Montesquieu's *Persian Letters* |
| 1733 | Voltaire's *Letters on the English* |
| 1738 | Voltaire's *Elements of the Philosophy of Newton* |
| 1748 | Montesquieu's *Spirit of the Laws* |
| 1748 | Hume's *Inquiry into Human Nature*, with the chapter "Of Miracles" |
| 1750 | Rousseau's *Discourse on the Moral Effects of the Arts and Sciences* |
| 1751 | First volume of the *Encyclopedia*, edited by Diderot |
| 1755 | Rousseau's *Discourse on the Origin of Inequality* |
| 1759 | Voltaire's *Candide* |
| 1762 | Rousseau's *Social Contract* and *Émile* |
| 1763 | Voltaire's *Treatise on Toleration* |
| 1764 | Voltaire's *Philosophical Dictionary* |
| 1764 | Beccaria's *On Crimes and Punishments* |
| 1776 | Gibbon's *Decline and Fall of the Roman Empire* |
| 1776 | Smith's *Wealth of Nations* |
| 1779 | Lessing's *Nathan the Wise* |
| 1792 | Wollstonecraft's *Vindication of the Rights of Woman* |

new life in the late eighteenth century. Rousseau deeply influenced many leaders of the French Revolution, who, as will be seen in the next chapter, often incorporated his view on gender roles in the policies they implemented.

Paradoxically, in spite of these views and in spite of his own ill treatment of the many women who bore his many children, Rousseau achieved a vast following among women in the eighteenth century. He is credited with persuading thousands of upper-class women to breast-feed their own children rather than putting them out to wet nurses. One explanation for this influence is that his writings, although they did not advocate liberating women or expanding their social or economic roles, did stress the importance of their emotions and subjective feelings. He portrayed the domestic life and the role of wife and mother as a noble and fulfilling vocation, giving middle- and upper-class women

# Mary Wollstonecraft Criticizes Rousseau's View of Women

*Mary Wollstonecraft published* A Vindication of the Rights of Woman *in 1792, thirty years after Rousseau's* Émile *had appeared. In this pioneering feminist work, she criticizes and rejects Rousseau's argument for distinct and separate spheres for men and women. She portrays that argument as defending the continued bondage of women to men and as hindering the wider education of the entire human race.*

✦ *What specific criticisms does Wollstonecraft direct against Rousseau's views? Why does Wollstonecraft put so much emphasis on a new kind of education for women?*

The most perfect education . . . is such an exercise of the understanding as is best calculated to strengthen the body and form the heart. Or, in other words, to enable the individual to attain such habits of virtue as will render it independent. In fact, it is a farce to call any being virtuous whose virtues do not result from the exercise of its own reason. This was Rousseau's opinion respecting men: I extend it to women. . . .

I may be accused of arrogance; still I must declare what I firmly believe, that all the writers who have written on the subject of female education and manners from Rousseau to Dr. Gregory [a Scottish physician], have contributed to render women more artificial, weak characters, than they would other wise have been; and, consequently, more useless members of society. . . .

. . . Strengthen the female mind by enlarging it, and there will be an end to blind obedience; but, as blind obedience is ever sought for by power, tyrants and sensualists are in the right when they endeavour to keep women in the dark, because the former only wants slaves, and the latter a play-thing. The sensualist, indeed, has been the most dangerous of tyrants, and women have been duped by their lovers, as princes by their ministers, whilst dreaming that they reigned over them.

a sense that their daily occupations had purpose. He assigned them a degree of influence in the domestic sphere that they could not have competing with men outside it.

In 1792, in *A Vindication of the Rights of Woman*, Mary Wollstonecraft (1759–1797) brought Rousseau before the judgment of the rational Enlightenment ideal of progressive knowledge. The immediate incentive for this essay was her opposition to certain policies of the French Revolution, unfavorable to women, which were inspired by Rousseau. Wollstonecraft (who, like so many women of her day, died of puerperal fever shortly after childbirth) accused Rousseau and others after him who upheld traditional roles for women of attempting to narrow women's vision and limit their experience. She argued that to confine women to the separate domestic sphere because of supposed limitations of their physiological nature was to make them the sensual slaves of men. Confined in this separate sphere, they were the victims of male tyranny, their obedience was blind, and they could never achieve their own moral or intellectual identity. Denying good education to women would impede the progress of all humanity. With these arguments, Wollstonecraft was demanding for women the kind of liberty that male writers of the Enlightenment had been championing for men for more than a century. In doing so, she placed herself among the *philosophes* and broadened the agenda of the Enlightenment to include the rights of women as well as those of men.

... Rousseau declares that a woman should never, for a moment, feel herself independent, that she should be governed by fear to exercise her natural cunning, and made a coquetish slave in order to render her a more alluring object of desire, a sweeter companion to man, whenever he chooses to relax himself. He carries the arguments, which he pretends to draw from the indications of nature, still further, and insinuates that truth and fortitude, the corner stones of all human virtue, should be cultivated with certain restrictions, because, with respect to the female character, obedience is the grand lesson which ought to be impressed with unrelenting rigour.

What nonsense! when will a great man arise with sufficient strength of mind to put away the fumes which pride and sensuality have thus spread over the subject! If women are by nature inferior to men, their virtues must be the same in quality, if not in degree, or virtue is a relative idea; consequently, their conduct should be founded on the same principles, and have the same aim.

Connected with man as daughters, wives, and mothers, their moral character may be estimated by their manner of fulfilling those simple duties; but the end, the grand end of their exertions should be to unfold their own faculties and acquire the dignity of conscious virtue....

But avoiding ... any direct comparison of the two sexes collectively, or frankly acknowledging the inferiority of women, according to the present appearance of things, I shall only insist that men have increased that inferiority till women are almost sunk below the standard of rational creatures. Let their faculties have room to unfold, and their virtues to gain strength, and then determine where the whole sex must stand in the intellectual scale....

... I ... will venture to assert, that till women are more rationally educated, the progress of human virtue and improvement in knowledge must receive continual checks....

The mother, who wishes to give true dignity of character to her daughter, must, regardless of the sneers of ignorance, proceed on a plan diametrically opposite to that which Rousseau has recommended with all the deluding charms of eloquence and philosophical sophistry: for his eloquence renders absurdities plausible, and his dogmatic conclusions puzzle, without convincing, those who have not ability to refute them.

*Mary Wollstonecraft, A Vindication of the Rights of Woman, ed. by Carol H. Poston (New York: W. W. Norton & Co., Inc., 1975), pp. 21, 22, 24–26, 35, 40, 41.*

# Enlightened Absolutism

Most of the *philosophes* favored neither Montesquieu's reformed and revived aristocracy nor Rousseau's democracy as a solution to contemporary political problems. Like other thoughtful people of the day in other stations and occupations, they looked to the existing monarchies. Voltaire was a very strong monarchist. He and others—such as Diderot, who visited Catherine II of Russia, and the physiocrats, some of whom were ministers to the French kings—did not wish to limit the power of monarchs. Rather, they sought to redirect that power toward the rationalization of economic and political structures and the liberation of intellectual life. Most

*philosophes* were not opposed to power if they could find a way of using it for their own purposes.

During the last third of the century, it seemed to some observers that several European rulers had actually embraced many of the reforms set forth by the *philosophes*. *Enlightened absolutism* is the term used to describe this phenomenon. The phrase indicates monarchical government dedicated to the rational strengthening of the central absolutist administration at the cost of other lesser centers of political power. The monarchs most closely associated with it are Frederick II of Prussia, Joseph II of Austria, and Catherine II of Russia.

Frederick II corresponded with the *philosophes*, for a time provided Voltaire with a place at his court, and even wrote history and political tracts. Catherine II, adept at what would later be called *public relations*, consciously sought to create the image of being enlightened. She read the works of the *philosophes*, became a friend of Diderot and Voltaire, and made frequent references to their ideas, all in the hope that her nation might seem more modern and Western. Joseph II continued numerous initiatives begun by his mother, Maria Theresa. He imposed a series of religious, legal, and social reforms that contemporaries believed he had derived from suggestions of the *philosophes*.

The relationship between these rulers and the writers of the Enlightenment was, however, more complicated than these appearances suggest. The humanitarian and liberating zeal of the Enlightenment writers was only part of what motivated the policies of the rulers. Frederick II, Joseph II, and Catherine II were also determined that their nations would play major diplomatic and military roles in Europe. In no small measure, they adopted Enlightenment policies favoring the rational economic and social integration of their realms because these policies also increased their military strength. As explained in Chapter 17, all the states of Europe had emerged from the Seven Years' War knowing they would need stronger armies for future wars and increased revenue to finance those armies. The search for new revenues and internal political support was one of the incentives prompt-ing the "enlightened" reforms of the monarchs of Russia, Prussia, and Austria. Consequently, they and their advisers used rationality to pursue many goals admired by the *philosophes* but also to further what the *philosophes* considered irrational militarism.

### Frederick the Great of Prussia

Frederick II, the Great (r. 1740–1786) sought the recovery and consolidation of Prussia in the wake of its suffering and near defeat in the mid-century wars. He succeeded, at great military and financial cost, in retaining Silesia, which he had seized from Austria in 1740, and worked to promote it as a manufacturing district. Like his Hohenzollern forebears, he continued to import workers from outside Prussia. He directed new attention to Prussian agriculture. Under state supervision, swamps were drained, new crops introduced, and peasants encouraged and sometimes compelled to migrate where they were needed. For the first time in Prussia, potatoes and turnips came into general production. Frederick also established a land-mortgage credit Association to help landowners raise money for agricultural improvements.

The impetus for these economic policies came from the state. The monarchy and its bureaucracy were the engine for change. Most Prussians, however, did not prosper under Frederick's reign. The

*Frederick II, the Great (r. 1740–1786), sought to create prosperity for all parts of the Prussian economy and would make personal visits to factories and shops to inspect the goods being made and sold in his kingdom. Here he visits a fashionable shop. [Bildarchiv Preussischer Kulturbesitz]*

burden of taxation continued to fall disproportionally on peasants and townspeople.

Frederick's noneconomic policies met with somewhat more success. Continuing the Hohenzollern policy of toleration, he allowed Catholics and Jews to settle in his predominantly Lutheran country, and he protected the Catholics living in Silesia. This policy permitted the state to benefit from the economic contribution of foreign workers. Frederick, however, virtually always appointed Protestants to major positions in the government and army.

Frederick also ordered a new codification of Prussian law, completed after his death. His object was to rationalize the existing legal system, making it more efficient, eliminating regional peculiarities, and reducing aristocratic influence. Frederick shared this concern for legal reform with the other enlightened monarchs, who saw it as a means of extending and strengthening royal power.

Reflecting an important change in the European view of the ruler, Frederick liked to describe himself as "the first servant of the State." The impersonal state was beginning to replace the personal monarchy. Kings might come and go, but the apparatus of government—the bureaucracy, the armies, the laws, the courts, and the combination of power, service, and protection that compelled citizen loyalty—remained. The state as an entity separate from the personality of the ruler came into its own after the French Revolution, but it was born in the monarchies of the old regime.

## Joseph II of Austria

No eighteenth-century ruler so embodied rational, impersonal force as the emperor Joseph II of Austria. He was the son of Maria Theresa and co-ruler with her from 1765 to 1780. During the next ten years he ruled alone. He was an austere and humorless person. During much of his life, he slept on straw and ate little but beef. He prided himself on a narrow, passionless rationality, which he sought to impose by his own will on the various Habsburg domains. Despite his eccentricities and the coldness of his personality, Joseph II sincerely wished to improve the lot of his people. He was much less a political opportunist and cynic than either Frederick the Great of Prussia or Catherine the Great of Russia. The ultimate result of his well-intentioned efforts was a series of aristocratic and peasant rebellions extending from Hungary to the Austrian Netherlands.

*Joseph II of Austria (r. 1765–1790), shown here in the center, with his brother Leopold (later Leopold II) on his right, attempted to impose exceedingly rational policies on the Habsburg Empire. Joseph urged religious toleration and confiscated church lands. His attempts to tax the nobility stirred up a revolt that Leopold settled after Joseph's death by rescinding his policies. [Kunsthistorisches Museum, Vienna]*

CENTRALIZATION OF AUTHORITY As explained in Chapter 15, of all the rising states of the eighteenth century, Austria was the most diverse in its people and problems. Robert Palmer likened it to "a vast holding company."[7] The Habsburgs never succeeded in creating either a unified administrative structure or a strong aristocratic loyalty. To preserve the monarchy during the War of the Austrian Succession (1740–1748), Maria Theresa had guaranteed the aristocracy considerable independence, especially in Hungary.

[7]Robert R. Palmer, *The Age of Democratic Revolution*, vol. 1 (Princeton, N.J.: Princeton University Press, 1959), p. 103.

# Maria Theresa and Joseph II of Austria Debate the Question of Toleration

*In 1765 Joseph, the eldest son of the Empress Maria Theresa, had become co-regent with his mother. He began to believe that some measure of religious toleration should be introduced into the Habsburg realms. Maria Theresa, whose opinions on many political issues were quite advanced, adamantly refused to consider adopting a policy of toleration. This exchange of letters sets forth their sharply differing positions. The toleration of Protestants in dispute related only to Lutherans and Calvinists. Maria Theresa died in 1780; the next year Joseph issued an edict of toleration.*

✦ *How does Joseph define* toleration, *and why does Maria Theresa believe it is the same as* religious indifference? *Why does Maria Theresa fear that toleration will bring about political as well as religious turmoil? Why does Maria Theresa think the belief in toleration has come from Joseph's acquaintance with wicked books?*

### Joseph to Maria Theresa, July 20, 1777

It is only the word "toleration" which has caused the misunderstanding. You have taken it in quite a different meaning [from mine expressed in an earlier letter]. God preserve me from thinking it a matter of indifference whether the citizens turn Protestant or remain Catholic, still less, whether they cleave to, or at least observe, the cult which they have inherited from their fathers! I would give all I possess if all the Protestants of your states would go over to Catholicism.

The word "toleration," as I understand it, means only that I would employ any persons, without distinction of religion, in purely temporal matters, allow them to own property, practice trades, be citizens, if they were qualified and if

During and after the conflict, however, Maria Theresa took steps to strengthen the power of the crown outside of Hungary, building more of a bureaucracy than had previous Habsburg rulers. In Austria and Bohemia, through major administrative reorganization, she imposed a much more efficient system of tax collection that extracted funds even from the clergy and the nobles. She also established several central councils to deal with governmental problems. To assure her government a sufficient supply of educated officials, she sought to bring all educational institutions into the service of the crown. She also expanded primary education on the local level.

Maria Theresa was concerned about the welfare of the peasants and serfs. She brought them some assistance by extending the authority of the royal bureaucracy over local nobles and decreeing limits on the amount of labor, or *robot*, landowners could demand from peasants. Her concern was not par-ticularly humanitarian; rather, it arose from her desire to assure a good pool from which to draw military recruits. In all these policies and in her general desire to stimulate prosperity and military strength by royal initiative, Maria Theresa anticipated the policies of her son.

Joseph II was more determined than his mother and his projected reforms were more wide-ranging. He aimed to extend the borders of his territories in the direction of Poland, Bavaria, and the Ottoman Empire. His greatest ambition, however, was to increase the authority of the Habsburg emperor over his various realms. He sought to overcome the pluralism of the Habsburg holdings by imposing central authority in areas of political and social life where Maria Theresa had wisely chosen not to exert authority.

In particular, Joseph sought to reduce Hungarian autonomy. To avoid having to guarantee Hungary's existing privileges or extend new ones at the time of

this would be of advantage to the State and its industry. Those who, unfortunately, adhere to a false faith, are far further from being converted if they remain in their own country than if they migrate into another, in which they can hear and see the convincing truths of the Catholic faith. Similarly, the undisturbed practice of their religion makes them far better subjects and causes them to avoid irreligion, which is a far greater danger to our Catholics than if one lets them see others practice their religion unimpeded.

### Maria Theresa to Joseph, Late July, 1777

Without a dominant religion? Toleration, indifference are precisely the true means of undermining everything, taking away every foundation; we others will then be the greatest losers. . . . He is no friend of humanity, as the popular phrase is, who allows everyone his own thoughts. I am speaking only in the political sense, not as a Christian; nothing is so necessary and salutary as religion. Will you allow everyone to fashion his own religion as he pleases? No fixed cult, no subordination to the Church—what will then become of us? The result will not be quiet and contentment; its outcome will be the rule of the stronger and more unhappy times like those which we have already seen. A manifesto by you to this effect can produce the utmost distress and make you responsible for many thousands of souls. And what are my own sufferings, when I see you entangled in opinions so erroneous? What is at stake is not only the welfare of the State but your own salvation. . . . Turning your eyes and ears everywhere, mingling your spirit of contradiction with the simultaneous desire to create something, you are ruining yourself and dragging the Monarchy down with you into the abyss. . . . I only wish to live so long as I can hope to descend to my ancestors with the consolation that my son will be as great, as religious as his forebears, that he will return from his erroneous views, from those wicked books whose authors parade their cleverness at the expense of all that is most holy and most worthy of respect in the world, who want to introduce an imaginary freedom which can never exist and which degenerates into license and into complete revolution.

*As quoted in C. A. Macartney, ed., The Habsburg and Hohenzollern Dynasties in the Seventeenth and Eighteenth Centuries (New York: Walker, 1970), pp. 151–153.*

his coronation, he refused to have himself crowned king of Hungary and even had the Crown of Saint Stephen sent to the Imperial Treasury in Vienna. He reorganized local government in Hungary to increase the authority of his own officials. He also required the use of German in all governmental matters. The Magyar nobility resisted these measures, and in 1790 Joseph had to rescind most of them.

ECCLESIASTICAL POLICIES   Another target of Joseph's assertion of royal absolutism was the church. From the reign of Charles V in the sixteenth century to that of Maria Theresa, the Habsburgs had been the most important dynastic champion of Roman Catholicism. Maria Theresa was devout, but she had not allowed the church to limit her authority. Although she had attempted to discourage certain of the more extreme modes of Roman Catholic popular religious piety, such as public flagellation, she adamantly opposed toleration.

Joseph II was also a practicing Catholic, but from the standpoint of both enlightenment and pragmatic politics, he favored a policy of toleration. In October 1781, Joseph issued a toleration patent or decree, that extended freedom of worship to Lutherans, Calvinists, and the Greek Orthodox. They were permitted to have their own places of worship, to sponsor schools, to enter skilled trades, and to hold academic appointments and positions in the public service. From 1781 through 1789, Joseph issued a series of patents and other enactments that relieved the Jews in his realms of certain taxes and signs of personal degradation. He also extended to them the right of private worship. Although these actions benefitted the Jews, they did not grant them full equality with other Habsburg subjects.

Joseph also sought to bring the various institutions of the Roman Catholic Church directly under royal control. He forbade direct communication between the bishops of his realms and the pope.

Viewing religious orders as unproductive, he dissolved more than 600 monasteries and confiscated their lands. He excepted, however, certain orders that ran schools or hospitals. He dissolved the traditional Roman Catholic seminaries, which instilled in priests too great a loyalty to the papacy and too little concern for their future parishioners. In their place he sponsored eight general seminaries where the training emphasized parish duties. He also issued decrees creating new parishes in areas with a shortage of priests, funding them with money from the confiscated monasteries. In effect, Joseph's policies made Roman Catholic priests the employees of the state, ending the influence of the Roman Catholic Church as an independent institution in Habsburg lands. In many respects the ecclesiastical policies of Joseph II, known as *Josephinism*, prefigured those of the French Revolution.

ECONOMIC AND AGRARIAN REFORM  Like Frederick of Prussia, Joseph sought to improve the economic life of his domains. He abolished many internal tariffs and encouraged road building and the improvement of river transport. He went on personal inspection tours of farms and manufacturing districts. Joseph also reconstructed the judicial system to make laws more uniform and rational and to lessen the influence of local landlords. National courts with power over the landlord courts were established. All of these improvements were expected to bring new unity to the state and more taxes into the imperial coffers in Vienna.

Joseph's policies toward serfdom and the land were a far-reaching extension of those Maria Theresa had initiated. Over the course of his reign he introduced a series of reforms that touched the very heart of the rural social structure. He did not seek to abolish the authority of landlords over their peasants, but he did seek to make that authority more moderate and subject to the oversight of royal officials. He abolished serfdom as a legally sanctioned state of servitude. He granted peasants a wide array of personal freedoms, including the right to marry, to engage in skilled work, and to have their children trained in skilled work without the landlord's permission.

Joseph reformed the procedures of the manorial courts and opened avenues of appeal to royal officials. He also encouraged landlords to change land leases so it would be easier for peasants to inherit them or to transfer them to other peasants. His goal in all of these efforts to reduce traditional burdens on peasants was to make them more productive and industrious farmers.

Near the end of his reign, Joseph proposed a new and daring system of land taxation. He decreed in 1789 that all proprietors of the land were to be taxed regardless of social status. No longer were the peasants alone to bear the burden of taxation. He abolished *robot* and commuted it into a monetary tax, only part of which was to go to the landlord, the rest reverting to the state. Resistant nobles blocked the implementation of this decree, and after Joseph died in 1790 it did not go into effect. This and other of Joseph's earlier measures, however, brought turmoil throughout the Habsburg realms. Peasants revolted over disagreements about the interpretation of their newly granted rights. The nobles of the various realms protested the taxation scheme. The Hungarian Magyars resisted Joseph's centralization measures and forced him to rescind them.

On Joseph's death, the crown went to his brother Leopold II (r. 1790–1792). Although sympathetic to Joseph's goals, Leopold found himself forced to repeal many of the most controversial decrees, such as that on taxation. In other areas, Leopold thought his brother's policies simply wrong. For example, he returned much political and administrative power to local nobles because he thought it expedient for them to have a voice in government. Still, he did not repudiate his brother's policies wholesale. He retained, in particular, Joseph's religious policies and maintained political centralization to the extent he thought possible.

## Catherine the Great of Russia

Joseph II never grasped the practical necessity of forging political constituencies to support his policies. Catherine II (r. 1762–1796), who had been born a German princess but who became empress of Russia, understood only too well the fragility of the Romanov dynasty's base of power.

After the death of Peter the Great in 1725, the court nobles and the army repeatedly determined the Russian succession. As a result, the crown fell primarily into the hands of people with little talent. Peter's wife, Catherine I, ruled for two years (1725–1727) and was succeeded for three years by Peter's grandson, Peter II. In 1730 the crown devolved on Anna, a niece of Peter the Great. During 1740 and 1741, a child named Ivan VI, who was less than a year old, was the nominal ruler. Finally, in 1741 Peter the Great's daughter Eliza-

Catherine the Great, here portrayed as a young princess, ascended to the Russian throne after the murder of her husband. She tried initially to enact major reforms but she never intended to abandon absolutism. She assured nobles of their rights and by the end of her reign had imposed press censorship. [The Bettmann Archive]

beth came to the throne. She held the title of empress until 1762, but her reign was not notable for new political departures or sound administration. Her court was a shambles of political and romantic intrigue. Much of the power possessed by the tsar at the opening of the century had vanished.

At her death in 1762, Elizabeth was succeeded by Peter III, one of her nephews. He was a weak ruler whom many contemporaries considered mad. He immediately exempted the nobles from compulsory military service and then rapidly made peace with Frederick the Great, for whom he held unbounded admiration. That decision probably saved Prussia from military defeat in the Seven Years' War. The one positive feature of this unbalanced creature's life was his marriage in 1745 to a young German princess born in Anhalt Zerbst. This was the future Catherine the Great.

For almost twenty years Catherine lived in misery and frequent danger at the court of Elizabeth. During that time she befriended important nobles and read widely in the books of the *philosophes*. She was a shrewd person whose experience in a court crawling with rumors, intrigue, and conspiracy had taught her how to survive. She exhibited neither love nor fidelity toward her demented husband. A few months after his accession as tsar, Peter was deposed and murdered with Catherine's approval, if not her aid, and she was immediately proclaimed empress.

Catherine's familiarity with the Enlightenment and the general culture of western Europe convinced her that Russia was very backward and that it must make major reforms if it was to remain a great power. She understood that any major reform must have a wide base of political and social support, especially since she had assumed the throne through a palace coup. In 1767 she summoned a legislative commission to advise her on revisions in the law and government of Russia. There were more than 500 delegates, drawn from all sectors of Russian life. Before the commission convened, Catherine issued a set of instructions, partly written by herself. They contained many ideas drawn from the political writings of the philosophes. The commission considered the instructions as well as other ideas and complaints raised by its members.

The revision of Russian law, however, did not occur for more than half a century. In 1768 Catherine dismissed the commission before several of its key committees had reported. Yet the meeting had not been useless, for a vast amount of information had been gathered about the conditions of local administration and economic life throughout the realm. The inconclusive debates and the absence of programs from the delegates themselves suggested that most Russians saw no alternative to an autocratic monarchy. For her part, Catherine had no intention of departing from absolutism.

# Alexander Radishchev
## Attacks Russian Censorship

*Alexander Radishchev (1749–1802) was an enlightened Russian landowner who published* A Journey from Saint Petersburg to Moscow *in 1790. The book criticized many aspects of Russian political and social life, including the treatment of serfs. Shortly after its publication, Catherine the Great, fearing that the kind of unrest associated with the French Revolution might spread to Russia, had Radishchev arrested. He was tried and sentenced to death, but Catherine commuted the sentence to a period of Siberian exile. All but eighteen copies of his book were destroyed. It was not published in Russia again until 1905. These passages criticizing censorship illustrate how a writer filled with the ideas of the Enlightenment could question some of the fundamental ways in which an enlightened absolutist ruler, such as Catherine, governed.*

✦ *How does Radishchev satirize censorship and the censors? Why does he contend that public opinion rather than the government will act as an adequate censor? Would work censored by public opinion be truly free from censorship? Why might Catherine the Great or other enlightened absolutist rulers have feared opinions like these?*

Having recognized the usefulness of printing, the government has made it open to all; having further recognized that control of thought might invalidate its good intention in granting freedom to set up presses, it turned over the censorship or inspection of printed works to the Department of Public Morals. Its duty in this matter can only be the prohibition of the sale of objectionable works. But even this censorship is superfluous. A single stupid official in the Department of Public Morals may do the greatest harm to enlightenment and may for years hold back the progress of

---

LIMITED ADMINISTRATIVE REFORM    Catherine proceeded to carry out limited reforms on her own authority. She gave strong support to the rights and local power of the nobility. In 1777 she reorganized local government to solve problems brought to light by the legislative commission. She put most local offices in the hands of nobles rather than creating a royal bureaucracy. In 1785 Catherine issued the Charter of the Nobility, which guaranteed many noble rights and privileges. In part, the empress had no choice but to favor the nobles. They had the capacity to topple her from the throne. There were too few educated subjects in her realm to establish an independent bureaucracy, and the treasury could not afford an army strictly loyal to the crown. So Catherine wisely made a virtue of necessity. She strengthened the stability of her crown by making convenient friends with her nobles.

ECONOMIC GROWTH    Part of Catherine's program was to continue the economic development begun under Peter the Great. She attempted to suppress internal barriers to trade. Exports of grain, flax, furs, and naval stores grew dramatically. She also favored the expansion of the small Russian urban middle class so vital to trade. And through all of these departures Catherine tried to maintain ties of friendship and correspondence with the *philosophes*. She knew that if she treated them kindly, they would be sufficiently flattered to give her a progressive reputation throughout Europe.

TERRITORIAL EXPANSION    Catherine's limited administrative reforms and her policy of economic growth had a counterpart in the diplomatic sphere. The Russian drive for warm-water ports continued. (See

reason: he may prohibit a useful discovery, a new idea, and may rob everyone of something great. Here is an example on a small scale. A translation of a novel is brought to the Department of Public Morals for its imprimatur. The translator, following the author in speaking of love calls it "the tricky god." The censor in uniform and in the fullness of piety strikes out the expression saying, "It is improper to call a divinity tricky." He who does not understand should not interfere. . . .

Let anyone print anything that enters his head. If anyone finds himself insulted in print, let him get his redress at law. I am not speaking in jest. Words are not always deeds, thoughts are not crimes. These are the rules in the Instruction for a New Code of Laws. But an offense in words or in print is always an offense. Under the law no one is allowed to libel another, and everyone has the right to bring suit. But if one tells the truth about another, that cannot, according to the law, be considered a libel. What harm can there be if books are printed without a police stamp? Not only will there be no harm; there will be an advantage, an advantage from the first to the last, from the least to the greatest, from the Tsar to the last citizen. . . .

I will close with this: the censorship of what is printed belongs properly to society, which gives the author a laurel wreath or uses his sheets for wrapping paper. Just so, it is the public that gives its approval to a theatrical production, and not the director of the theater. Similarly the Censor can give neither glory nor dishonor to the publication of a work. The curtain rises, and every one eagerly watches the performance. If they like it, they applaud; if not, they stamp and hiss. Leave what is stupid to the judgment of public opinion, stupidity will find a thousand censors. The most vigilant policy cannot check worthless ideas as well as a disgusted public. They will be heard just once; they will die, never to rise again. But once we have recognized the uselessness of the censorship, or, rather, its harmfulness in the realm of knowledge, we must also recognize the vast and boundless usefulness of freedom of the press.

*Alexander Radishchev*, A Journey from Saint Petersburg to Moscow *(Cambridge, Mass.: Harvard University Press, 1958), pp. 9–19, as quoted in Thomas Riha, ed.,* Readings in Russian Civilization, *2nd ed., rev., vol. II (Chicago: The University of Chicago Press, 1969), pp. 269–271.*

Map 18–1, on page 636.) This goal required warfare with the Turks. In 1769, as a result of a minor Russian incursion, the Ottoman Empire declared war on Russia. The Russians responded in a series of strikingly successful military moves.

During 1769 and 1770, the Russian fleet sailed all the way from the Baltic Sea into the eastern Mediterranean. The Russian army won several major victories that by 1771 gave Russia control of Ottoman provinces on the Danube River and the Crimean coast of the Black Sea. The conflict dragged on until 1774, when it was closed by the Treaty of Kuchuk-Kainardji. The treaty gave Russia a direct outlet on the Black Sea, free navigation rights in its waters, and free access through the Bosporus. Moreover, the province of the Crimea became an independent state, which Catherine painlessly annexed in 1783.

## The Partition of Poland

These Russian military successes obviously brought Catherine much domestic political support, but they made the other states of eastern Europe uneasy. These anxieties were overcome by an extraordinary division of Polish territory known as the First Partition of Poland.

The Russian victories along the Danube River were most unwelcome to Austria, which also harbored ambitions of territorial expansion in that direction. At the same time, the Ottoman Empire was pressing Prussia for aid against Russia. Frederick the Great made a proposal to Russia and Austria that would give each something it wanted, prevent conflict among the powers, and save appearances. After long, complicated, secret negotiations the three powers agreed that Russia would

**MAP 18–1** **EXPANSION OF RUSSIA 1689–1796** *The overriding territorial aim of Peter the Great in the first quarter and of Catherine the Great in the latter half of the eighteenth century was to secure year-round navigable outlets to the sea for the vast Russian Empire, hence Peter's push to the Baltic Sea and Catherine's to the Black Sea. Catherine also managed to acquire large areas of Poland through the partitions of that country.*

| Russia from Peter the Great Through Catherine the Great | |
|---|---|
| 1725 | Death of Peter the Great |
| 1725–1727 | Catherine I |
| 1727–1730 | Peter II |
| 1730–1741 | Anna |
| 1740–1741 | Ivan VI |
| 1741–1762 | Elizabeth |
| 1762 | Peter III |
| 1762 | Catherine II (the Great) becomes empress |
| 1767 | Legislative commission summoned |
| 1769 | War with Turkey begins |
| 1771–1775 | Pugachev's Rebellion |
| 1772 | First Partition of Poland |
| 1774 | Treaty of Kuchuk-Kainardji ends war with Turkey |
| 1775 | Reorganization of local government |
| 1783 | Russia annexes the Crimea |
| 1785 | Catherine issues the Charter of the Nobility |
| 1793 | Second Partition of Poland |
| 1795 | Third Partition of Poland |
| 1796 | Death of Catherine the Great |

abandon the conquered Danubian provinces. In compensation Russia received a large portion of Polish territory with almost two million inhabitants. As a reward for remaining neutral, Prussia annexed most of the territory between East Prussia and Prussia proper. This land allowed Frederick to unite two previously separate sections of his realm. Finally, Austria took Galicia, with its important salt mines, and other Polish territory with more than two and one-half million inhabitants. (See Map 18–2.)

In September 1772, the helpless Polish aristocracy, paying the price for maintaining internal liberties at the expense of developing a strong central government, ratified this seizure of nearly one-third of Polish territory. The loss was not necessarily fatal to Poland's continued existence, and it inspired a revival of national feeling. Real attempts were made to adjust the Polish political structures to the realities of the time. These proved, however, to be too little and too late. The political and military strength of Poland could not match that of its stronger, more ambitious neighbors. The partition of Poland clearly demonstrated that any nation that had not established a strong monarchy, bureaucracy, and army could no longer compete within the European state system. It also demonstrated that the major powers in eastern Europe were prepared to settle their own rivalries at the expense of such a weak state. But if such territory from a weaker state had not been available, the tendency of the international rivalries would have been to warfare.

Russia and Prussia partitioned Poland again in 1793, and Russia, Prussia, and Austria partitioned it a third time in 1795, removing it from the map of Europe for more than a century. Each time, the great powers contended that they were saving themselves, and by implication the rest of Europe, from

MAP 18–2   PARTITIONS OF POLAND, 1772; 1793;
1795  *The callous eradication of Poland from the
map displayed eighteenth-century power politics
at its most extreme. Poland, without strong central governmental institutions, fell victim to those
states in central and eastern Europe that had
developed such institutions.*

Polish anarchy. The fact of the matter was that
Poland's political weakness left it vulnerable to
plunderous aggression. The partitions of 1793 and
1795 took place in the shadow of the French Revolution, which left the absolute monarchies of eastern Europe concerned for their own stability. As a
result, they reacted harshly even to minor attempts
at reform by the Polish nobles, fearing they might
infect their own domains.

## The End of the Eighteenth Century in Central and Eastern Europe

During the last two decades of the eighteenth century, all three regimes based on enlightened absolutism became more conservative and politically
repressive. In Prussia and Austria, the innovations of
the rulers stirred resistance among the nobility. In
Russia, fear of peasant unrest was the chief factor.

Frederick the Great of Prussia grew remote
during his old age, leaving the aristocracy to fill
important military and administrative posts. A
reaction to Enlightenment ideas also set in among
Prussian Lutheran writers.

In Austria, Joseph II's plans to restructure society
and administration in his realms provoked growing
frustration and political unrest, with the nobility
calling for an end to innovation. In response, Joseph
turned increasingly to censorship and his secret
police.

Russia faced a peasant uprising, the Pugachev
Rebellion, between 1773 and 1775, and Catherine
the Great never fully recovered from the fears of
social and political upheaval it raised. Once the
French Revolution broke out in 1789, the Russian
empress censored books based on Enlightenment
thought and sent offensive authors into Siberian
exile.

By the close of the century, fear of and hostility
to change permeated the ruling classes of central
and eastern Europe. This reaction had begun before
1789, but the events in France bolstered and sustained it for almost half a century. Paradoxically,
nowhere did the humanity and liberalism of the
Enlightenment encounter greater rejection than in
those states that had been governed by "enlightened" rulers.

Although the enlightened absolute monarchs
lacked the humanity of the *philosophes*, they had
embraced the Enlightenment spirit of innovation.
They wanted to change the political, social, and
economic structures of their realms. From the close
of the Seven Years' War (1763) until the opening of
the French Revolution in 1789, the monarchies of
both western and eastern Europe had been the
major agents of institutional change. In every case
they provoked aristocratic, and sometimes popular, resistance and resentment. George III of Britain
fought for years with Parliament and lost the
colonies of North America in the process. Frederick II of Prussia succeeded with his program of
reform only because he accepted new aristocratic
influence over the bureaucracy and the army.
Catherine II of Russia had to come to terms with
Russia's nobility. Joseph II, who did not consult
with the nobility of his domains, left those
domains in turmoil.

These monarchs pushed for innovations from a desire for increased revenue. In France also, the royal drive for adequate fiscal resources led to aristocratic resistance. In France, however, neither the monarchy nor the aristocracy could control the social and political forces their quarrel unleashed.

◆

*The writers of the Enlightenment, known as* philosophes, *charted a major new path in modern European and Western thought. They operated within a print culture that made public opinion into a distinct cultural force. Admiring Newton and the achievements of physical science, they tried to apply reason and the principles of science to the cause of social reform. They believed also that passions and feelings were essential parts of human nature. Throughout their writings they championed reasonable moderation in social life. More than any other previous group of Western thinkers, they strongly opposed the authority of the established churches and especially of Roman Catholicism. Most of them championed some form of religious toleration. They also sought to achieve a science of society that could discover how to maximize human productivity and material happiness. The great dissenter among them was Rousseau, who also wished to reform society but in the name of virtue rather than material happiness.*

*The political influence of these writers went in several directions. The founding fathers of the American republic looked to them for political guidance, as did moderate liberal reformers throughout Europe, especially within royal bureaucracies. The autocratic rulers of eastern Europe consulted the* philosophes *in the hope that Enlightenment ideas might allow them to rule more efficiently. The revolutionaries in France would honor them. This diverse assortment of followers illustrates the diverse character of the* philosophes *themselves. It also shows that Enlightenment thought cannot be reduced to a single formula. Rather it should be seen as an outlook that championed change and reform, giving central place to humans and their welfare on Earth rather than to God and the hereafter.*

## Review Questions

1. How did the Enlightenment change basic Western attitudes toward reform, faith, and reason?

What were the major formative influences on the *philosophes*? How important were Voltaire and the *Encyclopedia* in the success of the Enlightenment?

2. Why did the *philosophes* consider organized religion to be their greatest enemy? Discuss the basic tenets of deism. What criticism might a deist direct at traditional Christianity and how might she or he improve it?

3. What were the attitudes of the *philosophes* toward women? What was Rousseau's view of women? What were the separate spheres he imagined men and women occupying? What were Mary Wollstonecraft's criticisms of Rousseau's view?

4. Compare the arguments of the mercantilists with those of Adam Smith in his book, *The Wealth of Nations*. How did both sides view the Earth's resources? Why might Smith be regarded as an advocate of the consumer?

5. Discuss the political views of Montesquieu and Rousseau. Was Montesquieu's view of England accurate? Was Rousseau a child of the Enlightenment or its enemy? Which did Rousseau value more, the individual or society?

6. Were the enlightened monarchs true believers in the ideal of the *philosophes* or was their enlightenment a mere veneer? Were they really absolute in power? What motivated their reforms? What does the partition of Poland indicate about the spirit of enlightened absolutism?

## Suggested Readings

G. J. BARKER-BENFIELD, *The Culture of Sensibility: Sex and Society in Eighteenth-Century Britain* (1992). A broad exploration of the role of women in society and literature in the age of enlightenment.

R. P. BARTLETT, *Human Capital: The Settlement of Foreigners in Russia, 1762–1804* (1979). Examines Catherine's policy of attracting farmers and skilled workers to Russia.

D. BEALES, *Joseph II: In the Shadow of Maria Theresa, 1741–1780* (1987). The best treatment in English of the early political life of Joseph II.

C. BECKER, *The Heavenly City of the Eighteenth Century Philosophers* (1932). An influential but very controversial discussion.

C. B. A. BEHRENS, *Society, Government, and the Enlightenment: The Experiences of Eighteenth-Century France and Prussia* (1985). A wide-ranging comparative study.

D. D. BIEN, *The Calas Affair: Persecution, Toleration, and Heresy in Eighteenth-Century Toulouse* (1960). The standard treatment of the famous case.

R. Chartier, *The Cultural Origins of the French Revolution* (1991). A wide-ranging discussion of the emergence of the public sphere and the role of books and the book trade during the Enlightenment.

H. Chisick, *The Limits of Reform in the Enlightenment: Attitudes Toward the Education of the Lower Classes in Eighteenth-Century France* (1981). An attempt to examine the impact of the Enlightenment on nonelite classes.

R. Darnton, *The Literary Underground of the Old Regime* (1982). Essays on the world of printers, publishers, and booksellers.

R. Darnton, *The Forbidden Best-Sellers of Pre-Revolutionary France* (1995). An exploration of what books the French read and the efforts of the government to control the book trade.

T. S. Dock, *Women in the* Encyclopédie: *A Compendium* (1983). An analysis of the articles from the *Encyclopedia* that deal with women.

J. Gagliardo, *Enlightened Despotism* (1967). A discussion of the subject in its European context.

P. Gay, *The Enlightenment: An Interpretation*, 2 vols. (1966, 1969). The most important and far-reaching treatment.

P. Gay, *Voltaire's Politics* (1988). A wide-ranging discussion.

C. C. Gillispie, *Science and Polity in France at the End of the Old Regime* (1980). A major survey of the subject.

D. Goodman, *The Republic of Letters: A Cultural History of the French Enlightenment* (1994). Concentrates on the role of salons.

N. Hampson, *A Cultural History of the Enlightenment* (1969). A useful introduction.

M. C. Jacob, *The Radical Enlightenment: Pantheists, Freemasons, and Republicans* (1981). A treatment of frequently ignored figures in the Age of Enlightenment.

M. C. Jacob, *Living the Enlightenment: Freemasonry and Politics in Eighteenth-Century Europe* (1991). The best treatment in English of Freemasonry.

A. Kernan, *Printing Technology, Letters, and Samuel Johnson* (1987). A discussion of print culture and its impact on English letters.

R. Kreiser, *Miracles, Convulsions, and Ecclesiastical Politics in Early Eighteenth-Century Paris* (1978). An important study of the kind of religious life that the philosophes opposed.

J. B. Landes, *Women and the Public Sphere in the Age of the French Revolution* (1988). An extended essay on the role of women in public life during the eighteenth century.

C. A. Macartney, *The Habsburg Empire, 1790–1918* (1971). Provides useful coverage of major mid-eighteenth century developments.

I. de Madariaga, *Russia in the Age of Catherine the Great* (1981). The best discussion in English.

J. M. McManners, *Death and the Enlightenment: Changing Attitudes to Death Among Christians and Unbelievers in Eighteenth-Century France* (1982). Explores a wide spectrum of religious beliefs.

G. Ritter, *Frederick the Great* (trans. 1968). A useful biography.

R. O. Rockwood (ed.), *Carl Becker's Heavenly City Revisited* (1958). Important essays qualifying Becker's thesis.

J. Schwartz, *The Sexual Politics of Jean-Jacques Rousseau* (1984). A controversial reading of Rousseau's political thought organized around gender issues.

R. B. Sher, *Church and University in the Scottish Enlightenment: The Moderate Literati of Edinburgh* (1985). A major study that examines the role of religious moderates in aiding the goals of the Enlightenment.

J. N. Shklar, *Men and Citizens, a Study of Rousseau's Social Theory* (1969). A thoughtful and provocative overview of Rousseau's political thought.

D. Spadafora, *The Idea of Progress in Eighteenth Century Britain* (1990). A recent major study that covers many aspects of the Enlightenment in Britain.

S. I. Spencer, *French Women and the Age of Enlightenment* (1984). An outstanding collection of essays that cover the political, economic, and cultural roles of women.

J. Starobinski, *Jean-Jacques Rousseau: Transparency and Obstruction* (1971). A powerful analysis of Rousseau.

R. E. Sullivan, *John Toland and the Deist Controversy: A Study in Adaptation* (1982). An important and informative discussion.

A. M. Wilson, *Diderot* (1972). A splendid biography of the person behind the *Encyclopedia* and other major Enlightenment publications.

L. Wolff, *Inventing Eastern Europe: The Map of Civilization on the Mind of the Enlightenment* (1994). A remarkable study of the manner in which Enlightenment writers recast the understanding of this part of the continent.

*The Declaration of the Rights of Man and Citizen promulgated by the National Assembly in August, 1789, constituted the cornerstone of the new political order being established by the French Revolution. It declared equality of civil rights, protected property, and recognized the political sovereignty of the nation. It was published repeatedly in a wide variety of formats surrounded by symbols of the nation and of the revolution [Giraudon/Art Resource]*

# The French Revolution

## KEY TOPICS

- The financial crisis that impelled the French monarchy to call the Estates General
- The transformation of the Estates General into the National Assembly, the Declaration of the Rights of Man and Citizen, and the reconstruction of the political and ecclesiastical institutions of France
- The second revolution, the end of the monarchy, and the turn to more radical reforms
- The war between France and the rest of Europe
- The Reign of Terror, the Thermidorian Reaction, and the establishment of the Directory

*In the spring of 1789, the long-festering conflict between the French monarchy and the aristocracy erupted into a new political crisis. This dispute, unlike earlier ones, quickly outgrew the issues of its origins and produced the wider disruption known as the French Revolution. Before the turmoil settled, small-town provincial lawyers and Parisian street orators exercised more influence over the fate of the Continent than did aristocrats, royal ministers, or monarchs. Armies commanded by people of low birth and filled by conscripted village youths emerged victorious over forces composed of professional soldiers led by officers of noble birth. The very existence of the Roman Catholic faith in France was challenged. Politically and socially neither France nor Europe would ever be the same after these events.*

# The Crisis of the French Monarchy

Although the French Revolution was a turning point in modern European history, it grew out of the tensions and problems that characterized practically all late-eighteenth-century states. The French monarchy emerged from the Seven Years' War (1756–1763) both defeated and in debt and was unable afterward to put its finances on a sound basis. French support of the American revolt against Great Britain further deepened the financial difficulties of the government. On the eve of the revolution, the interest and payments on the royal debt amounted to just over one-half of the entire budget. Given the economic vitality of the nation, the debt was neither overly large nor disproportionate to the debts of other European powers. The problem lay with the inability of the royal government to tap the wealth of the French nation through taxes to service and repay the debt. Paradoxically France was a rich nation with an impoverished government.

## The Monarchy Seeks New Taxes

The debt was symptomatic of the failure of the late eighteenth-century French monarchy to come to terms with the resurgent social and political power of aristocratic institutions and in particular the *parlements*. For twenty-five years after the Seven Years' War there was a stand-off between them as one royal minister after another attempted to devise new tax schemes that would tap the wealth of the nobility, only to be confronted by the opposition of both the Parlement of Paris and provincial *parlements*. Both Louis XV (r. 1715–1774) and Louis XVI (r. 1774–1792) lacked the character and the resolution to carry the dispute to a successful conclusion. The moral and political corruption of both their courts and the indecision of Louis XVI meant that the monarchy could not rally the French public to its side. In place of a consistent policy to deal with the growing debt and aristocratic resistance to change, the monarchy gave way to hesitancy, retreat, and even duplicity.

In 1770 Louis XV appointed René Maupeou (1714–1792) as chancellor. The new minister was determined to break the *parlements* and increase taxes on the nobility. He abolished the *parlements* and exiled their members to different parts of the country. He then began an ambitious program of reform and efficiency. What ultimately doomed Maupeou's policy was less the resistance of the nobility than the death of Louis XV in 1774. His successor, Louis XVI, in an attempt to regain what he conceived to be popular support, restored all the *parlements* and confirmed their old powers.

France's successful intervention on behalf of the American colonists against the British did nothing to relieve the government's financial difficulties. By 1781, as a result of the aid to America, its debt was larger and its sources of revenues were unchanged. The new director-general of finances, Jacques Necker (1732–1804), a Swiss banker, then produced a public report that suggested that the situation was not so bad as had been feared. He argued that if the expenditures for the American war were removed, the budget was in surplus. Necker's report also revealed that a large portion of royal expenditures went to pensions for aristocrats and other royal court favorites. This revelation angered court aristocratic circles, and Necker soon left office. His financial sleight of hand, nonetheless, made it more difficult for later government officials to claim a real need to raise new taxes.

The monarchy hobbled along until 1786. By this time, Charles Alexandre de Calonne (1734–1802) was the minister of finance. Calonne proposed to encourage internal trade, to lower some taxes, such as the *gabelle* on salt, and to transform peasants' services to money payments. More important, Calonne urged the introduction of a new land tax that would require payments from all landowners regardless of their social status. If this tax had been imposed, the monarchy could have abandoned other indirect taxes. The government would also have had less need to seek additional taxes that required approval from the aristocratically dominated *parlements*. Calonne also intended to establish new local assemblies to approve land taxes; in these assemblies the voting power would have depended on the amount of land owned rather than on the social status of the owner. All these proposals would have undermined both the political and the social power of the French aristocracy.

## The Aristocracy and the Clergy Resist Taxation

Calonne's policies and the country's fiscal crisis made a new clash with the nobility unavoidable, and the monarchy had very little room to maneuver. The creditors were at the door; the treasury was nearly empty. In 1787 Calonne met with an Assembly of Notables drawn from the upper ranks

*This late-eighteenth-century cartoon satirizes the French social structure. It shows a poor man in chains, who represents the vast majority of the population, supporting an aristocrat, a bishop, and a noble of the robe. The aristocrat is claiming feudal rights, the bishop holds papers associating the church with religious persecution and clerical privileges, and the noble of the robe holds a document listing the rights of the noble-dominated* parlements. *[The Bettmann Archive]*

of the aristocracy and the church to seek support and approval for his plan. The assembly adamantly refused any such action; rather, it demanded that the aristocracy be allowed a greater share in the direct government of the kingdom. The notables called for the reappointment of Necker, who they believed had left the country in sound fiscal condition. Finally, they claimed that they had no right to consent to new taxes and that such a right was vested only in the medieval institution of the Estates General of France, which had not met since 1614. The notables believed that calling the Estates General, which had been traditionally organized to allow aristocratic and church dominance, would produce a victory for the nobility over the monarchy.

Again Louis XVI backed off. He dismissed Calonne and replaced him with Étienne Charles Loménie de Brienne (1727–1794), archbishop of Toulouse and the chief opponent of Calonne at the Assembly of Notables. Once in office Brienne

found, to his astonishment, that the situation was as bad as his predecessor had asserted. Brienne himself now sought to impose the land tax. The *Parlement* of Paris, however, took the new position that it lacked authority to authorize the tax and said that only the Estates General could do so. Shortly thereafter Brienne appealed to the Assembly of the Clergy to approve a large subsidy to allow funding of that part of the debt then coming due for payment. The clergy, like the *Parlement* dominated by aristocrats, not only refused the subsidy but also reduced their existing contribution, or *don gratuit*, to the government.

As these unfruitful negotiations were taking place at the center of political life, local aristocratic *parlements* and estates in the provinces were making their own demands. They wanted a restoration of the privileges they had enjoyed during the early seventeenth century, before Richelieu and Louis XIV had crushed their independence. Consequently, in July 1788, the king, through Brienne,

*Well-meaning but weak and vacillating, Louis XVI (r. 1774–1792) stumbled from concession to concession until he finally lost all power to save his throne. [Giraudon/Art Resource, N.Y.]*

agreed to convoke the Estates General the next year. Brienne resigned and Necker replaced him. The institutions of the aristocracy—and to a lesser degree, of the church—had brought the French monarchy to its knees. In the country of its origin, royal absolutism had been defeated.

## The Revolution of 1789

The year 1789 proved to be one of the most remarkable in the history of both France and Europe. The French aristocracy had forced Louis XVI to call the Estates General into session. Yet the aristocrats' triumph proved to be quite brief. From the moment the monarch summoned the Estates General, the political situation in France drastically changed. Social and political forces that neither the nobles nor the king could control were immediately unleashed.

From that calling of the Estates General to the present, historians have heatedly debated the meaning of the event and the turmoil that followed over the next decade. Many historians long believed that the calling and gathering of the Estates General unleashed a clash between the bourgeoisie and the aristocracy that had been building in the decades before 1789. More recently other historians have countered that the two groups actually had much in common by 1789 and that many members of both the bourgeoisie and the aristocracy resented and opposed the clumsy absolutism of the late-eighteenth-century monarchy. This second group of historians contends that the fundamental issue of 1789 was the determination of various social groups to reorganize the French government to assure the future political influence of all forms of wealth.

As this complicated process was being worked out, the argument goes, distrust arose between the aristocracy and increasingly radical middle-class leaders. The latter then turned to the tradespeople of Paris, building alliances with them to achieve their goals. That alliance radicalized the revolution. When in the mid-1790s revolutionary policies and actions became too radical, aristocratic and middle-class leaders once again cooperated to reassert the security of all forms of private wealth and property. According to this view, there did exist conflict among different social groups during the years of the revolution, but its causes were immediate, not hidden in the depths of French economic and social development.

Other historians also look to the influence of immediate rather than long-term causes. They believe that the faltering of the monarchy and the confusion following the calling, election, and organization of the Estates General created a political vacuum. Various leaders and social groups, often using the political vocabulary of the Enlightenment, stepped into that vacuum, challenging each other for dominance. The precedent for such public debate had been set during the years of conflict between the monarchy and the *parlements* when the latter had begun to challenge the former as the true representative of the nation. These debates and conflicts over the language, and hence values, of political life and activity had been made possible by the emergence of the new print culture with its reading public and numerous channels for the circulation of books, pamphlets, and newspapers. Emerging from this culture were a large number of often-unemployed authors who were resentful of their situation and ready to use their skills to radicalize the discussion. The result was a political debate wider than any before in European history. The events of the era represented a continuing effort to dominate public opinion about the future course of the nation. The French Revolution, according to this view, thus illustrates the character of a new political culture created by changes in the technology and distribution of print communication.

Yet another group of historians maintains that the events of 1789 through 1795 are only one chapter in a longer-term political reorganization of France following the paralysis of monarchical government, a process that was not concluded until the establishment of the Third Republic in the 1870s. According to this interpretation, the core accomplishment of the revolution of the 1790s was to lay the foundations for a republic that could assure both individual liberty and the safety of property. It was not until the last quarter of the nineteenth century, however, that such a republic actually came into existence.

To some extent, how convincing one finds each of these interpretations depends on which years or even months of the revolution one examines. The various interpretations are not, in any case, always mutually exclusive. Certainly, the weakness and ultimate collapse of the monarchy influenced events more than was once acknowledged. All sides did indeed make use of the new formats and institutions of the print culture. Individual leaders shifted their positions and alliances quite frequently, sometimes out of principle, more often for political expediency. Furthermore, the actual political situation differed from city to city and from region to region. The controversial and divisive religious policies of the revolutionary government itself were often determining factors in the attitudes that French citizens assumed toward the revolution. What does seem clear is that much of the earlier consensus—that the revolution arose almost entirely from conflict between the aristocracy and bourgeoisie—no longer stands except with many qualifications. The interpretive situation is now much more complicated, and a new consensus has yet to emerge.

## The Estates General Becomes the National Assembly

Almost immediately after the Estates General was called, the three groups, or Estates, represented within it clashed with each other. The First Estate was the clergy, the Second Estate the nobility, and the Third Estate theoretically everyone else in the kingdom, although its representatives were drawn primarily from wealthy members of the commercial and professional middle classes. All the representatives in the Estates General were men. During the widespread public discussions preceding the meeting of the Estates General, representatives of the Third Estate made it clear that they would not permit the monarchy and the aristocracy to decide the future of the nation.

A comment by the Abbé Siéyès (1748–1836) in a pamphlet published in 1789 captures the spirit of the Third Estate's representatives: "What is the Third Estate? Everything. What has it been in the political order up to the present? Nothing. What does it ask? To become something."[1]

DEBATE OVER ORGANIZATION AND VOTING   The initial split between the aristocracy and the Third Estate occurred before the Estates General gathered. The public debate over the proper organiza-

[1]Quoted in Leo Gershoy, *The French Revolution and Napoleon* (New York: Appleton-Century-Crofts, 1964), p. 102.

*The Estates General opened at Versailles in 1789 with much pomp and splendor. This print shows the representatives of the three estates seated in the hall and Louis XVI on a throne at its far end. [Giraudon/Art Resource, N.Y.]*

tion of the body drew the lines of basic disagreement. The aristocracy made two moves to limit the influence of the Third Estate. First, they demanded an equal number of representatives for each estate. Second, in September 1788, the *Parlement* of Paris ruled that voting in the Estates General should be conducted by order rather than by head—that is, each estate, or order, should have one vote, rather than each member. This procedure would ensure that the aristocratic First and Second Estates could always outvote the Third. Both moves exposed the hollowness of the aristocracy's alleged concern for French liberty and revealed it as a group determined to maintain its privileges. Spokespeople for the Third Estate denounced the arrogant claims of the aristocracy. Although the aristocracy and the Third Estate shared many economic interests and goals and some intermarriage had occurred throughout the country between nobles and the elite of the Third Estate, a fundamental social distance separated the members of the two orders. There were far more examples of

enormous wealth and military experience among the nobility than among the Third Estate; the latter also had experienced various forms of political and social discrimination from the nobility. The resistance of the nobility to voting by head simply confirmed the suspicions and resentments of the members of the Third Estate, who were overwhelmingly lawyers of substantial but not enormous economic means.

The royal council eventually decided that the cause of the monarchy and fiscal reform would best be served by a strengthening of the Third Estate. In December 1788, the council announced that the Third Estate would elect twice as many representatives as either the nobles or the clergy. This so-called doubling of the Third Estate meant that it could easily dominate the Estates General if voting were allowed by head rather than by order. It was correctly assumed that liberal nobles and clergy would support the Third Estate, confirming that despite social differences these groups shared important interests and reforming goals. The method of voting was settled by the king only after the Estates General had gathered at Versailles in May 1789.

THE CAHIERS DE DOLÉANCES   When the representatives came to the royal palace, they brought with them *cahiers de doléances*, or lists of grievances, registered by the local electors, to be presented to the king. Many of these have survived and provide considerable information about the state of the country on the eve of the revolution. These documents recorded criticisms of government waste, indirect taxes, church taxes and corruption, and the hunting rights of the aristocracy. They included calls for periodic meetings of the Estates General, more equitable taxes, more local control of administration, unified weights and measures to facilitate trade and commerce, and a free press. The overwhelming demand of the *cahiers* was for equality of rights among the king's subjects.

These complaints and demands could not, however, be discussed until the questions of organization and voting had been decided. From the beginning, the Third Estate, whose members consisted largely of local officials, professionals, and other persons of property, refused to sit as a separate order as the king desired. For several weeks there was a stand-off. Then, on June 1, the Third Estate invited the clergy and the nobles to join them in organizing a new legislative body. A few members of the lower clergy did so. On June 17, that body declared itself the National Assembly.

THE TENNIS COURT OATH   Three days later, finding themselves accidentally locked out of their usual meeting place, the National Assembly moved to a nearby tennis court. There its members took an oath to continue to sit until they had given France a constitution. This was the famous Tennis Court Oath. Louis XVI ordered the National Assembly to

*This painting of the Tennis Court Oath, June 20, 1789, is by Jacques-Louis David (1748–1825). In the center foreground are members of different Estates joining hands in cooperation as equals. The presiding officer is Jean-Sylvain Bailly, soon to become mayor of Paris. [Giraudon/Art Resource, N.Y.]*

# The Third Estate of a French City Petitions the King

*The cahiers de doléances were the lists of grievances brought to Versailles in 1789 by members of the Estates General. This particular cahier originated in Dourdan, a city of central France, and reflects the complaints of the Third Estate. The first two articles refer to the organization of the Estates General. The other articles ask that the king grant various forms of equality before the law and in matters of taxation. These demands for equality appeared in practically all the cahiers of the Third Estate.*

✦ *Which of the following petitions relate to political rights and which to economic equality? The slogan most associated with the French Revolution was "Liberty, Equality, Fraternity." Which of these petitions represents each of those values?*

The order of the third estate of the City . . . of Dourdan . . . supplicates [the king] to accept the grievances, complaints, and remonstrances which it is permitted to bring to the foot of the throne, and to see therein only the expression of its zeal and the homage of its obedience.

It wishes:

1. That his subjects of the third estate, equal by such status to all other citizens, present themselves before the common father without other distinction which might degrade them.

2. That all the orders, already united by duty and common desire contribute equally to the needs of the State, also deliberate in common concerning its needs.

3. That no citizen lose his liberty except according to law: that, consequently, no one be arrested by virtue of special orders, or, if imperative circumstances necessitate such orders, that the prisoner be handed over to regular courts of justice within forty-eight hours at the latest.

12. That every tax, direct or indirect, be granted only for a limited time, and that every collection beyond such term be regarded as peculation, and punished as such.

15. That every personal tax be abolished; that thus the *capitation* [a poll tax] and the *taille* [tax from which nobility and clergy were exempt] and its accessories be merged with the *vingtièmes* [an income tax] in a tax on land and real or nominal property.

16. That such tax be borne equally, without distinction, by all classes of citizens and by all kinds of property, even feudal . . . rights.

17. That the tax substituted for the *corvée* be borne by all classes of citizens equally and without distinction. That said tax, at present beyond the capacity of those who pay it and the needs to which it is destined, be reduced by at least one-half.

*John Hall Stewart,* A Documentary Survey of the French Revolution *(New York: Macmillan, 1951), pp. 76–77.*

desist from their actions, but shortly afterward a majority of the clergy and a large group of nobles joined the assembly.

On June 27, the king capitulated and formally requested the First and Second Estates to meet with the National Assembly, where voting would occur by head rather than by order. Had nothing further occurred, the government of France would have been transformed. Government by privileged orders had ended. The National Assembly, which renamed itself the National Constituent Assembly, was composed of people from all three orders, who shared liberal goals for the administrative, constitutional, and economic reform of the country. The revolution in France against government by privileged hereditary orders had begun.

### Fall of the Bastille

Two new forces soon intruded on the scene. The first was Louis XVI himself, who attempted to regain the political initiative by mustering royal troops near Versailles and Paris. It appeared that he might, following the advice of Queen Marie Antoinette (1755–1793), his brothers, and the most conservative nobles, be contemplating disruption of the National Constituent Assembly. On July 11, without consulting assembly leaders, Louis abruptly dismissed his minister of finance, Necker. These actions marked the beginning of a steady, but consistently poorly executed, royal attempt to undermine the assembly and halt the revolution. Most of the National Constituent Assembly wished to establish some form of constitutional monarchy, but from the start Louis's refusal to cooperate thwarted that effort. The king fatally decided to throw his lot in with the conservative aristocracy against the emerging forces of reform drawn from across the social and political spectrum.

The second new factor to impose itself on the events at Versailles was the populace of Paris. The mustering of royal troops created anxiety in the city, where throughout the winter and spring of 1789 there had been several bread riots. The Parisians who had elected their representatives to the Third Estate had continued to meet after the elections. By June they were organizing a citizen militia and collecting arms. They regarded the dismissal of Necker as the opening of a royal offensive against the National Constituent Assembly and the city.

On July 14, somewhat more than 800 people, most of them small shopkeepers, tradespeople, artisans, and wage earners, marched to the Bastille in search of weapons for the militia. This great fortress, with ten-foot-thick walls, had once held political prisoners. Through miscalculations and ineptitude on the part of the governor of the fortress, the troops in the Bastille fired into the crowd, killing ninety-eight people and wounding many others. Thereafter the crowd stormed the fortress and eventually gained entrance. They released the seven prisoners, none of whom was there for political reasons, and killed several troops and the governor. They found no weapons.

On July 15, the militia of Paris, by then called the National Guard, offered its command to the marquis de Lafayette (1757–1834). This hero of the American Revolution gave the guard a new insignia: the red and blue stripes of Paris separated by the white stripe of the king. This emblem became the revolutionary *cockade* (badge) and eventually the flag of revolutionary France.

The attack on the Bastille marked the first of many crucial *journées*, days on which the populace of Paris redirected the course of the revolution. The fall of the fortress signaled that the National Constituent Assembly alone would not decide the political future of the nation. As the news of the taking of the Bastille spread, similar disturbances took place in provincial cities. A few days later, Louis XVI again bowed to the force of events and personally visited Paris, where he wore the revolutionary *cockade* and recognized the organized electors as the legitimate government of the city. The king also recognized the National Guard. The citizens of Paris were, for the time being, satisfied. They also had established themselves as an independent political force with which other political groups might ally for their own purposes.

### The "Great Fear" and the Surrender of Feudal Privileges

Simultaneous with the popular urban disturbances, a movement known as the "Great Fear" swept across much of the French countryside. Rumors had spread that royal troops would be sent into the rural districts. The result was an intensification of the peasant disturbances that had begun during the spring. The Great Fear saw the burning of *châteaux*, the destruction of records and documents, and the

*On July 14, 1789, crowds stormed the Bastille, a prison in Paris. This event, whose only practical effect was to free a few prisoners, marked the first time the populace of Paris redirected the course of the revolution. [Giraudon/Art Resource, N.Y.]*

refusal to pay feudal dues. The peasants were determined to take possession of food supplies and land that they considered rightfully theirs. They were reclaiming rights and property that they had lost through the aristocratic resurgence of the last quarter century, as well as venting their general anger against the injustices of rural life.

On the night of August 4, 1789, aristocrats in the National Constituent Assembly attempted to halt the spreading disorder in the countryside. By prearrangement, several liberal nobles and clerics rose in the assembly and renounced their feudal rights, dues, and tithes. In a scene of great emotion, hunt-ing and fishing rights, judicial authority, and special exemptions were surrendered. These nobles gave up what they had already lost and what they could not have regained without civil war in the rural areas. Later they would also, in many cases, receive compensation for their losses. Nonetheless, after the night of August 4, all French citizens were subject to the same and equal laws. That dramatic session of the assembly paved the way for the legal and social reconstruction of the nation. Without those renunciations, the constructive work of the National Constituent Assembly would have been much more difficult.

Both the attack on the Bastille and the Great Fear displayed characteristics of the rural and urban riots that had occurred often in eighteenth-century France. Louis XVI first thought that the turmoil over the Bastille was simply another bread riot. Indeed, the popular disturbances were only partly related to the events at Versailles. A deep economic downturn had struck France in 1787 and continued into 1788. The harvests for both years had been poor, and food prices in 1789 were higher than at any time since 1703. Wages had not kept up with the rise in prices. Throughout the winter of 1788–1789, an unusually cold one, many people suffered from hunger. Several cities had experienced wage and food riots. These economic problems helped the revolution reach the vast proportions it did.

The political, social, and economic grievances of many sections of the country became combined. The National Constituent Assembly could look to the popular forces as a source of strength against the king and the conservative aristocrats. When the

## The National Assembly Decrees Civic Equality in France

*These famous decrees of August 4, 1789, in effect created civic equality in France. The special privileges previously possessed or controlled by the nobility were removed.*

✦ *What institutions and privileges are included in "the feudal regime"? How do these decrees recognize that the abolition of some privileges and former tax arrangements will require new kinds of taxes and government financing to support religious, educational, and other institutions?*

1. The National Assembly completely abolishes the feudal regime. It decrees that, among the rights and dues . . . all those originating in real or personal serfdom, personal servitude, and those which represent them, are abolished without indemnification; all others are declared redeemable, and that the price and mode of redemption shall be fixed by the National Assembly. . . .

2. The exclusive right to maintain pigeon-houses and dove-cotes is abolished. . . .

3. The exclusive right to hunt and to maintain unenclosed warrens is likewise abolished. . . .

4. All manorial courts are suppressed without indemnification.

5. Tithes of every description and the dues which have been substituted for them . . . are abolished, on condition, however, that some other method be devised to provide for the expenses of divine worship, the support of the officiating clergy, the relief of the poor, repairs and rebuilding of churches and parsonages, and for all establishments, seminaries, schools, academies, asylums, communities, and other institutions, for the maintenance of which they are actually devoted. . . .

. . . . . . . . . . . . . . . . . . . . . . . . . . . . . .

7. The sale of judicial and municipal offices shall be suppressed forthwith. . . .

8. Pecuniary privileges, personal or real, in the payment of taxes are abolished forever. . . .

. . . . . . . . . . . . . . . . . . . . . . . . . . . . . .

11. All citizens, without distinction of birth, are eligible to any office or dignity, whether ecclesiastical, civil or military. . . .

*Frank Maloy Anderson, ed. and trans.,* The Constitutions and Other Select Documents Illustrative of the History of France, 1789–1907, *2nd. ed., rev. and enl. (Minneapolis: H. W. Wilson, 1908), pp. 11–13.*

various elements of the assembly later fell into quarrels among themselves, the resulting factions appealed for support to the politically sophisticated and well-organized shopkeeping and artisan classes. They, in turn, would demand a price for their cooperation.

## The Declaration of the Rights of Man and Citizen

In late August 1789, the National Constituent Assembly decided that before writing a new constitution, it should set forth a statement of broad political principles. On August 27, the assembly issued the Declaration of the Rights of Man and Citizen. This declaration drew upon much of the political language of the Enlightenment and was also influenced by the Declaration of Rights adopted by Virginia in America in June 1776.

*Civic equality was one of the hallmarks of the revolutionary era. This figure of Equality holds in her hand a copy of the Declaration of the Rights of Man and Citizen. [The Bettmann Archive]*

The French declaration proclaimed that all men were "born and remain free and equal in rights." The natural rights so proclaimed were "liberty, property, security, and resistance to oppression." Governments existed to protect those rights. All political sovereignty resided in the nation and its representatives. All citizens were to be equal before the law and were to be "equally admissible to all public dignities, offices, and employments, according to their capacity, and with no other distinction than that of their virtues and talents." There were to be due process of law and presumption of innocence until proof of guilt. Freedom of religion was affirmed. Taxation was to be apportioned equally according to capacity to pay. Property constituted "an inviolable and sacred right."[2]

Although these statements were rather abstract, almost all of them were directed against specific abuses of the old aristocratic and absolutist regime. If any two principles of the future governed the declaration, they were civic equality and protection of property. The Declaration of the Rights of Man and Citizen has often been considered the death certificate of the Old Regime.

It was not accidental that the Declaration of the Rights of Man and Citizen specifically applied to men and not to women. As discussed in the previous chapter, much of the political language of the Enlightenment, and most especially that associated with Rousseau, separated men and women into distinct gender spheres. According to this view, which influenced the legislation of the revolutionary era, men were suited for citizenship, women for motherhood and the domestic life. Nonetheless, in the charged atmosphere of the summer of 1789, many politically active and informed French women hoped the guarantees of the declaration would be extended to them. Their issues of particular concern related to property, inheritance, family, and divorce. Some people saw in the declaration a framework within which women might eventually enjoy the rights and protection of citizenship.

### The Royal Family Forced to Return to Paris

Louis XVI stalled before ratifying both the declaration and the aristocratic renunciation of feudalism.

[2]Quoted in Georges Lefebvre, *The Coming of the French Revolution*, trans. by R. R. Palmer (Princeton, N.J.: Princeton University Press, 1967), pp. 221–223.

*The women of Paris marched to Versailles on October 5, 1789. The following day the royal family was forced to return to Paris with them. Henceforth, the French government would function under the constant threat of mob violence. [Giraudon/Art Resource]*

The longer he hesitated, the stronger grew suspicions that he might again try to resort to the use of troops. Moreover, bread continued to be scarce. On October 5, a crowd of as many as 7,000 Parisian women armed with pikes, guns, swords, and knives marched to Versailles demanding more bread. They milled about the palace, and many stayed the night. Intimidated by these Parisian women, the king agreed to sanction the decrees of the assembly. The next day he and his family appeared on a balcony before the crowd. The Parisians, however, were deeply suspicious of the monarch and believed that he must be kept under the watchful eye of the people. They demanded that Louis and his family return to Paris. The monarch had no real choice in the matter. On October 6, 1789, his carriage followed the crowd into the city, where he and his family settled in the palace of the Tuileries.

The march of the women of Paris was the first example of a popular insurrection employing the language of popular sovereignty directed against the monarch. The National Constituent Assembly also soon moved into Paris. Thereafter, both Paris and France remained relatively stable and peaceful until the summer of 1792.

## The Reconstruction of France

Once established in Paris, the National Constituent Assembly set about reorganizing France. In government, it pursued a policy of constitutional monarchy; in administration, rationalism; in economics, unregulated freedom; and in religion, anticlericalism. Throughout its proceedings the assembly was determined to protect property in all its forms. In those policies the aristocracy and the middle-class elite stood united. The assembly also sought to limit the impact on national life of the unpropertied elements of the nation and even of possessors of small amounts of property. Although championing civic equality before the law, the assembly spurned social equality and extensive democracy. In all these ways the assembly charted a general course that, to a greater or lesser degree, nineteenth-century liberals across Europe would follow.

## Political Reorganization

The Constitution of 1791, the product of the National Constituent Assembly's deliberations, established a constitutional monarchy. The major political authority of the nation would be a unicameral Legislative Assembly, in which all laws would originate. The monarch was allowed a suspensive veto that could delay but not halt legislation. Powers of war and peace were vested in the assembly.

ACTIVE AND PASSIVE CITIZENS The constitution provided for an elaborate system of indirect elections intended to thwart direct popular pressure on the government. The citizens of France were divided into active and passive categories. Only active citizens—that is, men paying annual taxes equal to three days of local labor wages—could vote. They chose electors, who then in turn voted for the members of the legislature. At the level of electors or members, still further property qualifications were imposed. Only about fifty thousand citizens of a population of about twenty-five million could qualify as electors or members of the Legislative Assembly. Women could neither vote nor hold office.

These constitutional arrangements effectively transferred political power from aristocratic wealth to all forms of propertied wealth in the nation. Political authority would no longer be achieved through hereditary privilege or through purchase of titles, but through the accumulation of land and commercial property. These new political arrangements based on property rather than birth recognized the new complexities of French society that had developed over the past century and allowed more social and economic interests to have a voice in the governing of the nation.

The laws that excluded women from both voting and holding office did not pass unnoticed. In 1791 Olympe de Gouges (d. 1793), a butcher's daughter from Montauban who became a major revolutionary radical in Paris, composed a *Declaration of the Rights of Woman*, which she ironically addressed to Queen Marie Antoinette. Much of the document reprinted the Declaration of the Rights of Man and Citizen adding the word *woman* to the various original clauses. That strategy demanded that women be regarded as citizens and not merely as daughters, sisters, wives, and mothers of citizens. Olympe de Gouges further outlined rights that would permit women to own property and require men to recognize the paternity of their children. She called for equality of the sexes in marriage and improved education for women. She declared, "Women, wake up; the tocsin of reason is being heard throughout the whole universe; discover your rights."[3] Her declaration illustrated how the simple listing of rights in the Declaration of the Rights of Man and Citizen created a structure of universal civic expectations even for those it did not cover. The National Assembly had established a set of values against which it was itself to be measured. It provided criteria for liberty, and those to whom it had not extended full liberties could demand to know why and could claim that the revolution was incomplete until they enjoyed those freedoms.

DEPARTMENTS REPLACE PROVINCES In reconstructing the local and judicial administration, the National Constituent Assembly applied the rational spirit of the Enlightenment. It abolished the ancient French provinces, such as Burgundy and Brittany, and established in their place eighty-three departments, or "*départements*," of generally equal size named after rivers, mountains, and other geographical features. (See Map 19–1.) The departments in turn were subdivided into districts, cantons, and communes. Most local elections were also indirect. The departmental reconstruction proved to be a permanent achievement of the assembly. The departments exist to the present day.

All the ancient judicial courts, including the seigneurial courts and the *parlements*, were also abolished. Uniform courts with elected judges and prosecutors were organized in their place. Procedures were simplified, and the most degrading punishments were removed from the books.

## Economic Policy

In economic matters the National Constituent Assembly continued the policies formerly advo-

3Quoted in Sara E. Melzer and Leslie W. Rabine, eds., *Rebel Daughters: Women and the French Revolution* (New York: Oxford University Press, 1992), p. 88.

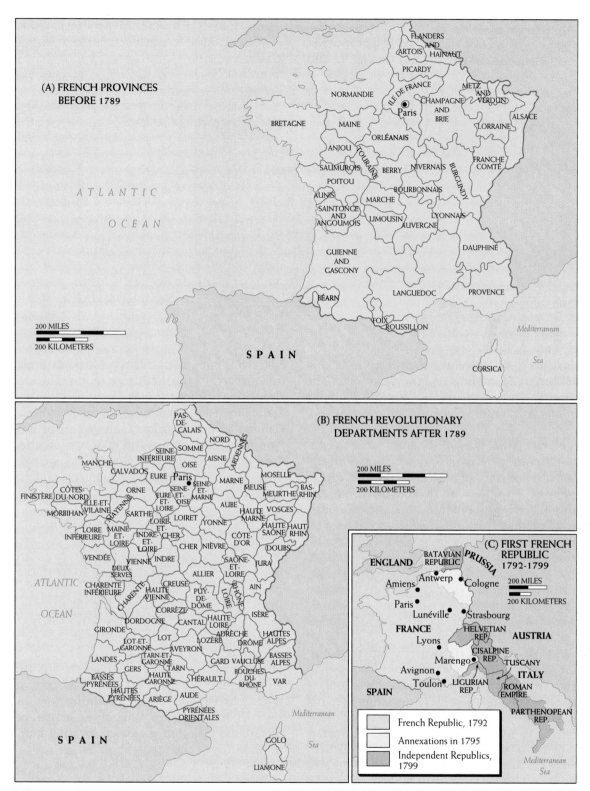

**MAP 19-1  FRENCH PROVINCES AND THE REPUBLIC**  *In 1789 the National Constituent Assembly redrew the map of France. The ancient provinces (A) were replaced with a larger number of new, smaller departments (B). This redrawing of the map was part of the assembly's effort to impose greater administrative rationality in France. The borders of the republic (C) changed as the French army conquered new territory.*

cated by Louis XVI's reformist ministers. It suppressed the guilds and liberated the grain trade. The assembly established the metric system to provide the nation with uniform weights and measures.

WORKERS' ORGANIZATIONS FORBIDDEN   These policies of economic freedom and uniformity disappointed both peasants and urban workers caught in the cycle of inflation. By decrees in 1789, the assembly placed the burden of proof on the peasants to rid themselves of the residual feudal dues for which compensation was to be paid. On June 14, 1791, the assembly crushed the attempts of urban workers to protect their wages by enacting the Chapelier Law, which forbade workers' associations. Peasants and workers were henceforth to be left to the freedom and mercy of the marketplace.

CONFISCATION OF CHURCH LANDS   While these various reforms were being put into effect, the original financial crisis that had occasioned the calling of the Estates General persisted. The assembly did not repudiate the royal debt, because it was owed to the bankers, the merchants, and the commercial traders of the Third Estate. The National Constituent Assembly had suppressed many of the old, hated indirect taxes and had substituted new land taxes, but these proved insufficient. Moreover, there were not enough officials to collect them. The continuing financial problem led the assembly to take what

may well have been, for the future of French life and society, its most decisive action. The assembly decided to finance the debt by confiscating and then selling the land and property of the Roman Catholic Church in France. The results were further inflation, religious schism, and civil war. In effect, the National Constituent Assembly had opened a new chapter in the relations of church and state in Europe.

THE ASSIGNATS   Having chosen to plunder the land of the church, in December 1789 the assembly authorized the issuance of *assignats*, or government bonds. Their value was guaranteed by the revenue to be generated from the sale of church property. Initially a limit was set on the quantity of *assignats* to be issued. The bonds, however, proved so acceptable to the public that they began to circulate as currency. The assembly decided to issue an ever larger number of them to liquidate the national debt and to create a large body of new property owners with a direct stake in the revolution. Within a few months, however, the value of the *assignats* began to fall and inflation increased, putting new stress on the lives of the urban poor.

### The Civil Constitution of the Clergy

The confiscation of church lands required an ecclesiastical reconstruction. In July 1790, the National

# The Revolutionary Government Forbids Worker Organizations

*The Chapelier Law of June 14, 1791, was one of the most important pieces of revolutionary legislation. It abolished the kinds of labor organizations that had protected skilled workers under the Old Regime. The principles of this legislation prevented effective labor organization in France for well over half a century.*

✦ *Why are workers' organizations declared to be contrary to the principles of liberty? Why were guilds seen as one of the undesirable elements of the Old Regime? What are the coercive powers that are to be brought to bear against workers' organizations? In light of this legislation, what courses of actions were left open to workers as they confronted the operation of the market economy?*

1. Since the abolition of all kinds of corporations of citizens of the same occupation and profession is one of the fundamental bases of the French Constitution, reestablishment thereof under any pretext or form whatsoever is forbidden.

2. Citizens of the same occupation or profession, entrepreneurs, those who maintain open shop, workers, and journeymen of any craft whatsoever may not, when they are together, name either president, secretaries, or trustees, keep accounts, pass decrees or resolutions, or draft regulations concerning their alleged common interests.

. . . . . . . . . . . . . . . . . . . . . . . . . . . . . . .

4. If, contrary to the principles of liberty and the Constitution, some citizens associated in the same professions, arts, and crafts hold deliberations or make agreements among themselves tending to refuse by mutual consent or to grant only at a determined price the assistance of their industry or their labor, such deliberations and agreements, whether accom-panied by oath or not, are declared unconstitutional, in contempt of liberty and the Declaration of the Rights of Man, and noneffective; administrative and municipal bodies shall be required so to declare them. . . .

. . . . . . . . . . . . . . . . . . . . . . . . . . . . . . .

8. All assemblies composed of artisans, workers, journeymen, day laborers, or those incited by them against the free exercise of industry and labor appertaining to every kind of person and under all circumstances arranged by private contract, or against the action of police and the execution of judgments rendered in such connection, as well as against public bids and auctions of divers enterprises, shall be considered as seditious assemblies, and as such shall be dispersed by the depositories of the public force, upon legal requisitions made thereupon, and shall be punished according to all the rigor of the laws concerning authors, instigators, and leaders of the said assemblies, and all those who have committed assaults and acts of violence.

*John Hall Stewart,* A Documentary Survey of the French Revolution *(New York: Macmillan, 1951), pp. 165–166.*

Constituent Assembly issued the Civil Constitution of the Clergy, which transformed the Roman Catholic Church in France into a branch of the secular state. This legislation reduced the number of bishoprics from 135 to 83 and brought the borders of the dioceses into conformity with those of the new departments. It also provided for the election of priests and bishops, who henceforth became salaried employees of the state. The assembly consulted neither the pope nor the French clergy about these broad changes. The king approved the measure only with the greatest reluctance.

The Civil Constitution of the Clergy was the major blunder of the National Constituent Assembly. It created embittered relations between the French church and state that have persisted to the present day. The measure immediately created immense opposition within the French church even from bishops who had long championed Gallican liberties over papal domination. In the face of this resistance, the assembly unwisely ruled that all clergy must take an oath to support the Civil Constitution. Only seven bishops and about half the clergy did so. In reprisal, the assembly designated the clergy who had not taken the oath as "refractory" and removed them from their clerical functions.

Further reaction was swift. Refractory priests attempted to celebrate mass. In February 1791, the pope condemned not only the Civil Constitution of the Clergy but also the Declaration of the Rights of Man and Citizen. That condemnation marked the opening of a Roman Catholic offensive against liberalism and the revolution that continued throughout the nineteenth century. Within France itself, the pope's action created a crisis of conscience and political loyalty for all sincere Catholics. Religious devotion and revolutionary loyalty became incompatible for many people. French citizens were divided between those who supported the constitutional priests and those who resorted to the refractory clergy. Louis XVI and his family favored the refractory clergy.

### Counterrevolutionary Activity

The revolution had other enemies besides the pope and the devout Catholics. As it became clear that the old political and social order was undergoing fundamental and probably permanent change, many aristocrats left France. Known as the *émigrés*, they settled in countries near the French border, where they sought to foment counterrevolution. Among the most important of their number was the king's younger brother, the count of Artois (1757–1836). In the summer of 1791, his agents and the queen persuaded Louis XVI to attempt to flee the country.

FLIGHT TO VARENNES   On the night of June 20, 1791, Louis and his immediate family, disguised as servants, left Paris. They traveled as far as Varennes on their way to Metz. At Varennes the king was recognized, and his flight was halted. On June 24, a company of soldiers escorted the royal family back to Paris. The leaders of the National Constituent Assembly, determined to save the constitutional monarchy, announced that the king had been abducted from the capital. Such a convenient public fiction could not cloak the realities that the chief counterrevolutionary in France now sat on the throne and that the constitutional monarchy might not last long.

DECLARATION OF PILLNITZ   Two months later, on August 27, 1791, under pressure from a group of *émigrés*, Emperor Leopold II of Austria, who was the brother of Marie Antoinette, and Frederick William II (r. 1786–1797), the king of Prussia, issued the Declaration of Pillnitz. The two monarchs promised to intervene in France to protect the royal family and to preserve the monarchy if the other major European powers agreed. This provision rendered the statement meaningless because at the time Great Britain would not have given its consent. The declaration was not, however, so read in France, where the revolutionaries saw the nation surrounded by aristocratic and monarchical foes.

The National Constituent Assembly drew to a close in September 1791. Its task of reconstructing the government and the administration of France had been completed. One of its last acts was the passage of a measure that forbade any of its own members to sit in the Legislative Assembly then being elected. The new body met on October 1 and had to confront the immense problems that had emerged during the earlier part of the year. Within the Legislative Assembly major political divisions also soon developed over the future course of the nation and the revolution. Those groups whose

*In June 1791, Louis XVI and his family attempted to flee France. They were recognized in the town of Varennes, where their flight was halted and they were returned to Paris. This ended any realistic hope for a constitutional monarchy. [The Bettmann Archive]*

members had been assigned to passive citizenship began to demand full political participation in the nation.

## A Second Revolution

By the autumn of 1791, the government of France had been transformed into a constitutional monarchy. Virtually all the other administrative and religious structures of the nation had also been reformed. The situation both inside and outside France, however, remained unstable. Louis XVI had reluctantly accepted the constitution on July 14, 1790. French aristocrats resented their loss of position and plotted to overthrow the new order. In the west of France, peasants resisted the revolutionary changes especially as they affected the church. In Paris, many groups of workers believed the revolution had not gone far enough. Furthermore, during these same months women's groups in Paris began to organize both to support the revolution and to demand a wider civil role and civic protection for women. Radical members of the new Legislative Assembly also believed the revolution should go further. The major foreign powers saw the French Revolution as dangerous to their own domestic political order. By the spring of 1792, all these unstable elements had begun to overturn the first revolutionary settlement and led to a second series of revolutionary changes far more radical and democratically extensive than the first.

## End of the Monarchy

The issues raised by the Civil Constitution of the Clergy and Louis XVI's uncertain trustworthiness undermined the unity of the newly organized nation. Factionalism plagued the Legislative Assembly throughout its short life (1791–1792). Ever since the original gathering of the Estates General, deputies from the Third Estate had organized themselves into clubs composed of politically like-minded persons. The most famous and best organized of these were the Jacobins, whose name derived from the fact that Dominican friars were called Jacobins, and the group met in a Dominican monastery in Paris. The Jacobins had also established a network of local clubs throughout the provinces. They had been the most advanced political group in the National Constituent Assembly and had pressed for a republic rather than a constitutional monarchy. Their political language and rhetoric were drawn from the most radical thought of the Enlightenment. That thought and language became all the more effective because the events of 1789–1791 had destroyed the old political framework and the old monarchical political vocabulary was less and less relevant. The political language and rhetoric of a republic filled that vacuum and for a time supplied the political values of the day. The events of the summer of 1791 led to the reassertion of demands for establishing a republic.

In the Legislative Assembly, a group of Jacobins known as the Girondists (because many of them came from the department of the Gironde) assumed

---

# French Women Petition to Bear Arms

*The issue of women serving in the revolutionary French military appeared early in the revolution. In March 1791, Pauline Léon presented a petition to the National Assembly on behalf of more than 300 Parisian women asking the right to bear arms and train for military service for the revolution. Similar requests were made during the next two years. Some women did serve in the military, but in 1793 legislation specifically forbade women from participating in military service. The ground for that refusal was the argument that women belonged in the domestic sphere and military service would lead them to abandon family duties.*

✦ Citoyenne *is the feminine form of the French word for* citizen. *How does this petition seek to challenge the concept of citizenship in the Declaration of the Rights of Man and Citizen? How do these petitioners relate their demand to bear arms to their role as women in French society? How do the petitioners relate their demands to the use of all national resources against the enemies of the revolution?*

Patriotic women come before you to claim the right which any individual has to defend his life and liberty.

. . . We are *citoyennes*, [female citizens], and we cannot be indifferent to the fate of the fatherland.

. . . Yes, Gentlemen, we need arms, and we come to ask your permission to procure them. May our weakness be no obstacle; courage and intrepidity will supplant it, and the love of the fatherland and hatred of tyrants will allow us to brave all dangers with ease. . . .

No, Gentlemen, We will [use arms] only to defend ourselves the same as you; you cannot refuse us, and society cannot deny the right nature gives us, unless you pretend the Declaration of Rights does not apply to women and that they

---

leadership.[4] They were determined to oppose the forces of counterrevolution. They passed one measure ordering the *émigrés* to return or suffer loss of property and another requiring the refractory clergy to support the Civil Constitution or lose their state pensions. The king vetoed both acts.

Furthermore, on April 20, 1792, the Girondists led the Legislative Assembly to declare war on Austria, by this time governed by Francis II (r. 1792–1835) and allied to Prussia. The Girondists believed that the pursuit of the war would preserve the revolution from domestic enemies and bring the most advanced revolutionaries to power. Paradoxically, Louis XVI and other monarchists also favored the war. They thought that the conflict would strengthen the executive power (the monarchy). The king also entertained the hope that foreign armies might defeat French forces and restore the Old Regime. Both sides were playing dangerously foolish politics.

The war radicalized the revolution and led to what is usually called the *second revolution*, which overthrew the constitutional monarchy and established a republic. Both the country and the revolution seemed in danger. As early as March 1791, a group of women led by Pauline Léon had petitioned the Legislative Assembly for the right to bear arms and to fight for the protection of the revolution. Earlier she had led an effort to allow women to serve in the National Guard. These demands to serve, voiced in the universal language of citizenship, illustrated how the words and rhetoric of the revolution could be used to challenge traditional social roles and the concept of separate social spheres for

[4]The Girondists are also frequently called the Brissotins after Jacques-Pierre Brissot (1754–1793), their chief spokesperson in early 1792.

---

should let their throats be cut like lambs, without the right to defend themselves. For can you believe the tyrants would spare us? . . . Why then not terrorize aristocracy and tyranny with all the resources of civic effort and the pure zeal, zeal which cold men can well call fanaticism and exaggeration, but which is only the natural result of a heart burning with love for the public weal? . . .

. . . If, for reasons we cannot guess, you refuse our just demands, these women you have raised to the ranks of *citoyennes* by granting that title to their husbands, these women who have sampled the promises of liberty, who have conceived the hope of placing free men in the world, and who have sworn to live free or die—such women, I say, will never consent to concede the day to slaves; they will die first. They will uphold their oath, and a dagger aimed at their breasts will deliver them from the misfortunes of slavery! They will die, regretting not life, but the uselessness of their death; regretting moreover, not having been able to drench their hands in the impure blood of the enemies of the fatherland and to avenge some of their own!

But, Gentlemen, let us cast our eyes away from these cruel extremes. Whatever the rages and plots of aristocrats, they will not succeed in vanquishing a whole people of united brothers armed to defend their rights. We also demand only the honor of sharing their exhaustion and glorious labors and of making tyrants see that women also have blood to shed for the service of the fatherland in danger.

Gentlemen, here is what we hope to obtain from your justice and equity:

1. Permission to procure pikes, pistols, and sabres (even muskets for those who are strong enough to use them), within police regulations.

2. Permission to assemble on festival days and Sundays on the *Champ de la Fédération*, or in other suitable places, to practice maneuvers with these arms.

3. Permission to name the former French Guards to command us, always in conformity with the rules which the mayor's wisdom prescribes for good order and public calm.

*From Pauline Léon, Adresse individuelle à l'Assemblée nationale, par des citoyennes de la Capitale, le 6 mars 1791 (Paris, n.d.), as quoted and translated in Darline Gay Levy, Harriet Branson Applewhite, and Mary Durham Johnson, eds., Women in Revolutionary Paris, 1789–1795 (Urbana: University of Illinois Press, 1979), pp. 72–73.*

men and women. Furthermore, the pressure of war raised the possibility that the military needs of the nation could not be met if the ideal of separate spheres were honored. Once the war began, some French women did enlist in the army and served with distinction.

Initially the war effort went quite poorly. In July 1792, the duke of Brunswick, commander of the Prussian forces, issued a manifesto promising the destruction of Paris if harm came to the French royal family. This statement stiffened support for the war and increased the already significant distrust of the king.

Late in July, under radical working-class pressure, the government of Paris passed from the elected council to a committee, or *commune*, of representatives from the sections (municipal wards) of the city. On August 10, 1792, a very large Parisian crowd invaded the Tuileries palace and forced Louis XVI and Marie Antoinette to take refuge in the Legislative Assembly itself. The crowd fought with the royal Swiss guards. When Louis was finally able to call off the troops, several hundred of them and many Parisian citizens lay dead. The monarchy itself was also a casualty of that melee. Thereafter the royal family was imprisoned in comfortable quarters, but the king was allowed to perform none of his political functions. The recently established constitutional monarchy no longer had a monarch.

## The Convention and the Role of the Sans-culottes

Early in September the Parisian crowd again made its will felt. During the first week of the month, in what are known as the September Massacres, the Paris Commune summarily executed or murdered about 1,200 people who were in the city jails. Many of these people were aristocrats or priests, but the majority were simply common criminals. The crowd had assumed that the prisoners were all counterrevolutionaries.

The Paris Commune then compelled the Legislative Assembly to call for the election by universal male suffrage of a new assembly to write a democratic constitution. That body, called the *Convention* after its American counterpart of 1787, met on September 21, 1792. The previous day the French army had halted the Prussian advance at the Battle of Valmy in eastern France. The victory of democratic forces at home had been confirmed by victory on the battlefield. As its first act, the Convention declared France a republic, that is, a nation governed by an elected assembly without a monarch.

GOALS OF THE *SANS-CULOTTES*  The second revolution had been the work of Jacobins more radical than the Girondists and of the people of Paris known as the *sans-culottes*. The name of this group means "without breeches" and derived from the long trousers that, as working people, they wore instead of aristocratic knee breeches. The *sans-culottes* were shopkeepers, artisans, wage earners, and, in a few cases, factory workers. The persistent food shortages and the revolutionary inflation had made their difficult lives even more burdensome. The politics of the Old Regime had ignored them, and the policies of the National Constituent Assembly had left them victims of unregulated economic liberty. The government, however, required their labor and their lives if the war was to succeed. From the summer of 1792 until the summer of 1794, their attitudes, desires, and ideals were the primary factors in the internal development of the revolution.

The *sans-culottes* generally knew what they wanted. The Parisian tradespeople and artisans sought immediate relief from food shortages and rising prices through price controls. They believed that all people had a right to subsistence and profoundly resented most forms of social inequality. This attitude made them intensely hostile to the aristocracy and the original leaders of the revolution of 1789, who they believed simply wanted to share political power, social prestige, and economic security with the aristocracy. The *sans-culottes'* hatred of inequality did not take them so far as to demand the abolition of property. Rather, they advocated a community of small property owners who would also participate in the political nation.

In politics they were antimonarchical, strongly republican, and suspicious even of representative government. They believed that the people should make the decisions of government to as great an extent as possible. In Paris, where their influence was most important, the *sans-culottes* had gained their political experience in meetings of the Paris sections. Those gatherings exemplified direct community democracy and were not unlike a New England town meeting. The economic hardship of their lives made them impatient to see their demands met.

THE POLICIES OF THE JACOBINS The goals of the *sans-culottes* were not wholly compatible with those of the Jacobins. The latter were republicans who sought representative government. Jacobin hatred of the aristocracy and hereditary privilege did not extend to a general suspicion of wealth. Basically, the Jacobins favored an unregulated economy. From the time of Louis XVI's flight to Varennes onward, however, the more extreme Jacobins began to cooperate with leaders of the Parisian *sans-culottes* and the Paris Commune for the overthrow of the monarchy. Once the Convention began its deliberations, these Jacobins, known as the *Mountain* because of their seats high in the assembly hall, worked with the *sans-culottes* to carry the revolution forward and to win the war. This willingness to cooperate with the forces of the popular revolution separated the Mountain from the Girondists, who were also members of the Jacobin Club.

EXECUTION OF LOUIS XVI By the spring of 1793, several issues had brought the Mountain and its *sans-culottes* allies to domination of the Convention and the revolution. In December 1792, Louis XVI was put on trial as mere "Citizen Capet," the family name of extremely distant forebears of the royal family. The Girondists looked for some way to spare his life, but the Mountain defeated the effort. Louis was convicted, by a very narrow majority, of conspiring against the liberty of the people and the security of the state. He was condemned to death and was beheaded on January 21, 1793.

The next month the Convention declared war on Great Britain, Holland, and Spain. Soon thereafter

*On August 10, 1792, the Swiss Guards of Louis XVI fought Parisians who attacked the Tuileries Palace. Several hundred troops and citizens were killed, and Louis XVI and his family were forced to take refuge with the Legislative Assembly. After this event, the monarch virtually ceased to influence events in France. [Giraudon/Art Resource, N.Y.]*

## A Pamphleteer Describes a Sans-culotte

*This pamphlet is a 1793 description of a* sans-culotte *written either by one or by a sympathizer. It describes the* sans-culotte *as a hard-working, useful, patriotic citizen who bravely sacrifices himself to the war effort. It contrasts those virtues to the lazy and unproductive luxury of the noble and the personally self-interested plottings of the politician.*

✦ *What social resentments appear in this description? How could these social resentments be used to create solidarity among the* sans-culottes *to defend the revolution? How does this document relate civic virtue to work? Do you see any relationship between the social views expressed in this document and the abolition of workers' organizations in a previous document? Where does this document suggest the* sans-culotte *may need to confront enemies of the republic?*

A *sans-culotte* you rogues? He is someone who always goes on foot, who has no millions as you would all like to have, no chateaux, no valets to serve him, and who lives simply with his wife and children, if he has any, on a fourth or fifth story.

He is useful, because he knows how to work in the field, to forge iron, to use a saw, to use a file, to roof a house, to make shoes, and to shed his last drop of blood for the safety of the Republic.

And because he works, you are sure not to meet his person in the Café de Chartres, or in the gaming houses where others conspire and game; nor at the National theatre . . . nor in the literary clubs. . . .

In the evening he goes to his section, not powdered or perfumed, or smartly booted in the hope of catching the eye of the citizenesses in the galleries, but ready to support good proposals with all his might, and to crush those which come from the abominable faction of politicians.

Finally, a *sans-culotte* always has his sabre sharp, to cut off the ears of all enemies of the Revolution; sometimes he even goes out with his pike; but at the first sound of the drum he is ready to leave for the Vendée, for the army of the Alps or for the army of the North. . . .

"Reply to an Impertinent Question: What is a *Sans-culotte?*" *April 1793. Reprinted in Walter Markov and Albert Soboul, eds.,* Die Sansculotten von Paris, *and republished trans. by Clive Emsley in Merryn Williams, ed.,* Revolutions: 1775–1830 *(Baltimore: Penguin Books, in association with the Open University, 1971), pp. 100–101.*

---

the Prussians renewed their offensive and drove the French out of Belgium. To make matters worse, General Dumouriez (1739–1823), the Girondist victor of Valmy, deserted to the enemy. Finally, in March 1793, a royalist revolt led by aristocratic officers and priests erupted in the Vendée in western France and roused much popular support. Thus, the revolution found itself at war with most of Europe and much of the French nation. The Girondists had led the country into the war but had proved themselves incapable either of winning it or of suppressing the enemies of the revolution at home. The

Mountain stood ready to take up the task. Every major European power was now hostile to the revolution.

## Europe at War with the Revolution

Initially the rest of Europe had been ambivalent toward the revolutionary events in France. Those people who favored political reform regarded the revolution as wisely and rationally reorganizing a

*Louis XVI was executed on January 21, 1793. [Giraudon/Art Resource, N.Y.]*

corrupt and inefficient government. The major foreign governments thought that the revolution meant that France would cease to be an important factor in European affairs for several years.

### Edmund Burke Attacks the Revolution

In 1790, however, the Irish-born writer and British statesman Edmund Burke (1729–1799) argued a different position in *Reflections on the Revolution in France*. Burke regarded the reconstruction of French administration as the application of a blind rationalism that ignored the historical realities of political development and the complexities of social relations. He also forecast further turmoil as people without political experience tried to govern France. As the revolutionaries proceeded to attack the church, the monarchy, and finally the rest of Europe, Burke's ideas came to have many admirers. His *Reflections* became the handbook of European conservatives for decades.

By the outbreak of the war with Austria in April 1792, the other European monarchies recognized the danger of both the ideas and the aggression of revolutionary France. The ideals of the Rights of Man and Citizen were highly exportable and applicable to the rest of Europe. In response, one government after another turned to repressive domestic policies.

### Suppression of Reform in Britain

In Great Britain, William Pitt the Younger (1759–1806), the prime minister, who had unsuccessfully supported moderate reform of Parliament during the 1780s, turned against both reform and popular movements. The government suppressed the London Corresponding Society, founded in 1792 as a working-class reform group. In Birmingham, the government sponsored mob action to drive Joseph Priestley (1733–1804), a famous chemist and a radical political thinker, out of the country. In early

*Edmund Burke (1729–1799) published* Reflections on the Revolution in France *in 1790. It became the most famous of all conservative denunciations of the revolution. [National Portrait Gallery, London]*

# Burke Denounces the Extreme Measures of the French Revolution

*Edmund Burke was undoubtedly the most important and articulate foreign critic of the French Revolution. His first critique* Reflections on the Revolution in France *appeared in 1790. He continued to attack the revolution in later years. In 1796 he published* Letters on a Regicide Peace *which opposed a peace treaty between Great Britain and revolutionary France. In that work he enumerated what he regarded as the most fundamental evils of the revolutionary government: the execution of the king, the confiscation of property of the church and nobles, and the policy of dechristianization.*

✦ *To which of the major events in the French Revolution does Burke make reference? Why by 1796 would Burke and others have attached so much importance to the religious policies of the revolution? Did Burke exaggerate the evils of the revolution? Who might have been persuaded by Burke's condemnation?*

A government of the nature of that set up at our very door has never been hitherto seen, or even imagined in Europe. . . . France, since her revolution, is under the sway of a sect, whose leaders have deliberately, at one stroke, demolished the whole body of that jurisprudence which France had pretty nearly in common with other civilized countries. . . .

Its foundation is laid in regicide, in Jacobinism, and in atheism, and it has joined to those principles a body of systematic manners, which secures their operation. . . .

I call a commonwealth *regicide*, which lays it down as a fixed law of nature, and a fundamental right of man, that all government, not being a democracy, is an usurpation. That all kings, as

1793, Pitt secured parliamentary approval for acts suspending habeas corpus and making it possible to commit treason in writing. With less success Pitt attempted to curb freedom of the press. All political groups who dared oppose the government faced being associated with revolutionary sedition.

## The End of Enlightened Absolutism in Eastern Europe

In eastern Europe, the revolution brought an end to enlightened absolutism. The aristocratic resistance to the reforms of Joseph II in the Habsburg lands led his brother, Leopold II, to come to terms with the landowners. Leopold's successor, Francis II (r. 1792–1835), became a major leader of the counterrevolution. In Prussia, Frederick William II (r. 1786–1797), the nephew of Frederick the Great, looked to the leaders of the Lutheran church and the aristocracy to discourage any potential popular

uprisings, such as those of the downtrodden Silesian weavers. In Russia, Catherine the Great burned the works of her one-time friend Voltaire. She also exiled Alexander Radishchev (1749–1802) to Siberia for publishing his *Journey from Saint Petersburg to Moscow*, a work critical of Russian social conditions. (See the document in Chapter 18, Alexander Radishchev Attacks Russian Censorship.)

In 1793 and 1795, the eastern powers once again combined against Poland. In that unhappy land, aristocratic reformers had finally achieved the abolition of the *liberum veto* and had organized a new constitutional monarchy in 1791. Russia and Prussia, which already had designs on Polish territory, saw or pretended to see a threat of revolution in the new Polish constitution. In 1793 they annexed large sections of the country; in 1795 Austria joined the two other powers in a final partition that removed Poland from the map of Europe until after World War I. The governments of eastern Europe had used the widely

such, are usurpers; and for being kings may and ought to be put to death, with their wives, families, and adherents. That commonwealth which acts uniformly upon those principles . . .—this I call regicide by establishment.

Jacobinism is the revolt of the enterprising talents of a country against its property. When private men form themselves into associations for the purpose of destroying the pre-existing laws and institutions of their country; when they secure to themselves an army, by dividing amongst the people of no property the estates of the ancient and lawful proprietors, when a state recognizes those acts; when it does not make confiscations for crimes, but makes crimes for confiscations; when it has its principal strength, and all its resources, in such a violation of property . . .—I call this *Jacobinism by establishment.*

I call it *atheism by establishment,* when any state, as such, shall not acknowledge the existence of God as a moral governor of the world; . . .—when it shall abolish the Christian religion by a regular decree;—when it shall persecute with a cold, unrelenting, steady cruelty, by every mode of confiscation, imprisonment, exile, and

death, all its ministers; —when it shall generally shut up or pull down churches; when the few buildings which remain of this kind shall be opened only for the purpose of making a profane apotheosis of monsters, whose vices and crimes have no parallel amongst men . . . When, in the place of that religion of social benevolence, and of individual self-denial, in mockery of all religion, they institute impious, blasphemous, indecent theatric rites, in honour of their vitiated, perverted reason, and erect altars to the personification of their own corrupted and bloody republic; . . . when wearied out with incessant martyrdom, and the cries of a people hungering and thirsting for religion, they permit it, only as a tolerated evil—I call this *atheism by establishment.*

When to these establishments of regicide, of Jacobinism, and of atheism, you add the *correspondent system of manners,* no doubt can be left on the mind of a thinking man concerning their determined hostility to the human race.

The Works of the Right Honourable Edmund Burke *(London: Henry G. Bohn, 1856), 5: 206–208.*

shared fear of further revolutionary disorder to justify old-fashioned eighteenth-century aggression.

## War with Europe

In a paradoxical fashion the very success of the revolution in France brought a rapid close to reform movements in the rest of Europe. The French invasion of the Austrian Netherlands and the revolutionary reorganization of that territory roused the rest of Europe to the point of active hostility. In November 1792, the Convention declared that it would aid all peoples who wished to cast off the burdens of aristocratic and monarchical oppression. The Convention had also proclaimed the Scheldt River in the Netherlands open to the commerce of all nations and thus had violated a treaty that Great Britain had made with Austria and Holland. The British were on the point of declaring war on France over this issue when the Convention in February 1793 issued its own declaration of hostilities.

By April 1793, when the Mountain began to direct the French government, the nation was at war with Austria, Prussia, Great Britain, Spain, Sardinia, and Holland. The governments of those nations, allied in what is known as the *First Coalition*, were attempting to protect their social structures, political systems, and economic interests against the aggression of the revolution.

# The Reign of Terror

The outbreak of war in the winter and spring of 1793 brought new, radical political actions within France. The government mobilized both itself and the nation for conflict. Throughout the nation there was the sense that a new kind of war had erupted. In this war the major issue was not protection of national borders as such but rather the defense of the bold new republican political and social order that had emerged during the past four years. The French people understood that the achievements of the revolution were in danger. To protect those achievements the government took extraordinary actions that touched almost every aspect of national life.

## The Republic Defended

To mobilize for war, the revolutionary government organized a collective executive in the form of powerful committees. These in turn sought to organize all French national life on a wartime footing. The result was an immense military effort dedicated to both the protection and advance of revolutionary ideals. Ironically, this war effort brought the suppression of many liberties within France itself and led ultimately to a destructive search for internal enemies of the revolution.

THE COMMITTEE OF PUBLIC SAFETY  In April 1793, the Convention established a Committee of General Security and a Committee of Public Safety to perform the executive duties of the government. The latter committee became more important and eventually enjoyed almost dictatorial power. The most prominent leaders of the Committee of Public Safety were Jaques Danton (1759–1794), who had provided heroic leadership in September 1792; Maximilien Robespierre (1758–1794), who became for a time the single most powerful member of the committee; and Lazare Carnot (1753–1823), who was in charge of the military. All of these men and the other figures on the committee were strong republicans who had opposed the weak policies of the Girondists. They conceived of their task as saving the revolution from mortal enemies at home and abroad. They enjoyed a working political relationship with the *sans-culottes* of Paris, but this was an alliance of expediency on the part of the committee.

THE LEVÉE EN MASSE  The major problem for the Convention was to wage the war and at the same time to secure domestic support for the effort. In early June 1793, the Parisian *sans-culottes* invaded the Convention and successfully demanded the expulsion of the Girondist members. That action further radicalized the Convention and gave the Mountain complete control. On June 22, the Convention approved a fully democratic constitution but delayed its implementation until the conclusion of the war emergency. In point of fact, it was never implemented. On August 23, Carnot began a mobilization for victory by issuing a *levée en masse*, a military requisition on the entire population, conscripting males into the army and directing economic production to military purposes. On September 17, a ceiling on prices was established in accord with *sans-culotte* demands. During these same months the armies of the revolution also successfully crushed many of the counterrevolutionary disturbances in the provinces.

# The French Convention Calls Up the Entire Nation

*This proclamation of the* levée en masse, *August 23, 1793, marked the first time in European history that all citizens of a nation were called to contribute to a war effort. The decree set the entire nation on a wartime footing under the centralized direction of the Committee of Public Safety.*

✦ *How did this declaration put the entire nation on a wartime footing? How does this remarkable call to patriotism and opposition to the enemies of the revolution turn extraordinary power over to the revolutionary government? How could the government believe it would receive the wartime support of the workers whose organizations it had forbidden (see the document entitled "The Revolutionary Government Forbids Worker Organizations," earlier in this chapter)?*

1. From this moment until that in which the enemy shall have been driven from the soil of the Republic, all Frenchmen are in permanent requisition for the service of the armies.

The young men shall go to battle; the married men shall forge arms and transport provisions; the women shall make tents and clothing and shall serve in the hospitals; the children shall turn old linen into lint; the aged shall betake themselves to the public places in order to arouse the courage of the warriors and preach the hatred of kings and the unity of the Republic.

2. The national buildings shall be converted into barracks, the public places into workshops for arms, the soil of the cellars shall be washed in order to extract therefrom the saltpetre.

3. The arms of the regulation calibre shall be reserved exclusively for those who shall march against the enemy; the service of the interior shall be performed with hunting pieces and side arms.

4. The saddle horses are put in requisition to complete the cavalry corps; the draught-horses, other than those employed in agriculture, shall convey the artillery and the provisions.

5. The Committee of Public Safety is charged to take all the necessary measures to set up without delay an extraordinary manufacture of arms of every sort which corresponds with the ardor and energy of the French people.

. . . . . . . . . . . . . . . . . . . . . . . . . . . . . . . .

8. The levy shall be general. . . .

*Frank Maloy Anderson, ed. and trans.,* The Constitutions and Other Select Documents Illustrative of the History of France, 1789–1907, *2nd ed., rev. and enl. (Minneaspolis: H. W. Wilson, 1908), pp. 184–185.*

---

Never before had Europe seen a nation organized in this way nor one defended by a citizen army. Other events within France astounded Europeans even more. The Reign of Terror had begun. Those months of quasi judicial executions and murders stretching from the autumn of 1793 to the mid-summer of 1794 are probably the most famous or infamous period of the revolution. They can be understood only in the context of the war on one hand and the revolutionary expectations of the Convention and the *sans-culottes* on the other.

### The "Republic of Virtue"

The presence of armies closing in on the nation made it easy to dispense with legal due process. The people who sat in the Convention and composed the Committee of Public Safety, however, did not see their actions simply in terms of expediency made necessary by war. They also believed they had created something new in world history, a "republic of virtue". In this republic, civic virtue would flourish in place of aristocratic and monarchical corruption. The republic of virtue manifested itself in many ways: in the renaming of streets from the egalitarian vocabulary of the revolution; in republican dress copied from that of the *sans-culottes* or the Roman Republic; in the absence of powdered wigs; in the suppression of plays that were insufficiently republican; and in a general attack against crimes, such as prostitution, that were supposedly characteristic of aristocratic society.

THE SOCIETY OF REVOLUTIONARY REPUBLICAN WOMEN Revolutionary women established their own distinct institutions during these months. In May 1793, Pauline Léon and Claire Lacombe founded the Society of Revolutionary Republican Women. Their purpose was to fight the internal enemies of the revolution. They saw themselves as militant citizens. Initially the Jacobin leaders welcomed the organization. Its members and other women filled the galleries of the Convention to hear the debates and cheer their favorite speakers. The Society became increasingly radical, however. Its members sought stricter

*Maximilien Robespierre (1758–1794) emerged as the most powerful revolutionary figure in 1793 and 1794, dominating the Committee of Public Safety. He considered the Terror essential for the success of the revolution. [Giraudon/Art Resource, N.Y.]*

controls on the price of food and other commodities, worked to ferret out food hoarders, and brawled with working market women thought to be insufficiently revolutionary. The women of the Society also demanded the right to wear the revolutionary cockade usually worn only by male citizens. By October 1793, the Jacobins in the Convention had begun to fear the turmoil the Society was causing and banned all women's clubs and societies. The debates over these decrees show that the Jacobins believed the Society opposed many of their economic policies, but the deputies used the Rousseauian language of separate spheres for men and women to justify their exclusion of women from active political life.

There were other examples of repression of women in 1793. Olympe de Gouges, author of the *Declaration of the Rights of Woman*, opposed the Terror and accused certain Jacobins of corruption. She was tried and guillotined in November 1793. The same year, women were formally excluded from serving in the French army. They were also excluded from the galleries of the Convention. In a very real sense the exclusion of women from public political life was a part of the establishment of the Jacobin republic of virtue, because in such a republic men would be active citizens in the military and political sphere and women would be active in the domestic sphere.

DECHRISTIANIZATION   The most dramatic departure of the republic of virtue, and one that illustrates the imposition of political values that would justify the Terror, was an attempt by the Convention to dechristianize France. In November 1793, the Convention proclaimed a new calendar dating from the first day of the French Republic. There were twelve months of thirty days with names associated with the seasons and climate. Every tenth day, rather than every seventh, was a holiday. Many of the most important events of the next few years became known by their dates on the revolutionary calendar.[5] In November 1793, the convention decreed the Cathedral of Notre Dame to be a "Temple of Reason." The legislature then sent trusted members, known as *deputies on mission*, into the provinces to enforce dechristianization by closing churches, persecuting clergy and believers, and occasionally forcing priests to marry. This religious policy roused much opposition and deeply separated the French provinces from the revolutionary government in Paris.

ROBESPIERRE   During the crucial months of late 1793 and early 1794, the person who emerged as the chief figure on the Committee of Public Safety was Robespierre. This complex figure has remained controversial to the present day. He was utterly selfless and from the earliest days of the revolution had favored a republic. The Jacobin Club provided his primary forum and base of power. A shrewd and sensitive politician, Robespierre had opposed the war in 1792 because he feared it might aid the monarchy. He largely depended on the support of the *sans-culottes* of Paris, but he continued to dress as he had before the revolution and opposed dechristianization as a political blunder. For him, the republic of virtue meant wholehearted support of republican government and the renunciation of selfish gains from political life. He once told the Convention:

If the mainspring of popular government in peacetime is virtue, amid revolution it is at the same time virtue and terror: virtue, without which terror is fatal; terror, without which virtue is impotent. Terror is nothing but prompt, severe, inflexible justice; it is therefore an emanation of virtue.[6]

Robespierre and those who supported his policies were among the first of a succession of secular ideologues of the left and the right who, in the name of humanity, would bring so much suffering to Europe in the following two centuries.

## Progress of the Terror

The Reign of Terror manifested itself through a series of revolutionary tribunals established by the Convention during the summer of 1793. The mandate of these tribunals was to try the enemies of the republic, but the definition of *enemy* was uncertain and shifted as the months passed. It included those who might aid other European powers, those who endangered republican virtue, and finally good republicans who opposed the policies of the domi-

---

[5]From summer to spring the months on the revolutionary calendar were *Messidor, Thermidor, Fructidor, Vendémiaire, Brumaire, Frimaire, Nivose, Pluviose, Ventose, Germinal, Floreal,* and *Prairial.*

[6]Quoted in Richard T. Bienvenu, *The Ninth of Thermidor: The Fall of Robespierre* (New York: Oxford University Press, 1968), p. 38.

nant faction of the government. In a very real sense the Terror of the revolutionary tribunals systematized and channeled the popular resentment that had manifested itself in the September Massacres of 1792.

The first victims of the Terror were Marie Antoinette, other members of the royal family, and some aristocrats, who were executed in October 1793. They were followed by certain Girondist politicians who had been prominent in the Legislative Assembly. These executions took place in the same weeks that the Convention had moved against the Society of Revolutionary Republican Women, whom it had also seen as endangering Jacobin control.

By the early months of 1794, the Terror had moved to the provinces, where the deputies on mission presided over the summary execution of thousands of people who had allegedly supported inter-

nal opposition to the revolution. One of the most infamous incidents occurred in Nantes, where several hundred people were simply tied to rafts and drowned in the river. The victims of the Terror were now coming from every social class, including the *sans-culottes*.

REVOLUTIONARIES TURN AGAINST THEMSELVES  In Paris during the late winter of 1794, Robespierre began to orchestrate the Terror against republican political figures of the left and right. On March 24, he secured the execution of certain extreme *sans-culottes* leaders known as the *enragés*. They had wanted further measures regulating prices, securing social equality, and pressing dechristianization. Robespierre then turned against more conservative republicans, including Danton. They were accused of being insufficiently militant on the war, profiting

*On the way to her execution in 1793, Marie Antoinette was sketched from life by Jacques-Louis David as she passed his window. [Giraudon/Art Resource, N.Y.]*

*The Girondists on the way to the Guillotine. The reign of terror commenced with the execution of aristocrats and members of the French royal family, but soon supporters of the revolution also became victims of the Terror. In October, 1793, a number of Girondist politicians were sentenced to death. [Archive Photos]*

monetarily from the revolution, and rejecting any link between politics and moral virtue. Danton was executed during the first week in April. In this fashion, Robespierre exterminated the leadership from both groups that might have threatened his position. Finally, on June 10, he secured passage of the Law of 22 *Prairial*, which permitted the revolutionary tribunal to convict suspects without hearing substantial evidence. The number of executions was growing steadily.

FALL OF ROBESPIERRE   In May 1794, at the height of his power, Robespierre, considering the worship of "Reason" too abstract for most citizens, abolished it and established the "Cult of the Supreme Being." This deistic cult reflected Rousseau's vision of a civic religion that would induce morality among

citizens. Robespierre, however, did not long preside over his new religion.

On July 26, he made an ill-tempered speech in the Convention declaring that other leaders of the government were conspiring against himself and the revolution. Such accusations against unnamed persons had usually preceded his earlier attacks. On July 27—the Ninth of *Thermidor*—members of the Convention, by prearrangement, shouted him down when he rose to make another speech. That night Robespierre was arrested, and the next day he was executed. The revolutionary *sans-culottes* of Paris would not save him because he had deprived them of their chief leaders. The other Jacobins turned against him because after Danton's death they feared becoming the next victims. Robespierre had destroyed rivals for leadership without creating sup-

# The Convention Establishes the Worship of the Supreme Being

*On May 7, 1794, the Convention passed an extraordinary piece of revolutionary legislation. It established the worship of the Supreme Being as a state cult. Although the law drew on the religious ideas of deism, the point of the legislation was to provide a religious basis for the new secular French state. The reader should pay particular attention to Article 7, which outlines the political and civic values that the Cult of the Supreme Being was supposed to nurture.*

✦ *How does this declaration reflect the ideas of the Enlightenment? Why has it been seen as establishing a* civil *religion? What personal and social values was this religion supposed to nurture?*

1. The French people recognize the existence of the Supreme Being and the immortality of the soul.

2. They recognize that the worship worthy of the Supreme Being is the observance of the duties of man.

3. They place in the forefront of such duties detestation of bad faith and tyranny, punishment of tyrants and traitors, succoring of unfortunates, respect of weak persons, defence of the oppressed, doing to others all the good that one can, and being just towards everyone.

4. Festivals shall be instituted to remind man of the concept of the Divinity and of the dignity of his being.

5. They shall take their names from the glorious events of our Revolution, or from the virtues most dear and most useful to man, or from the greatest benefits of nature.

. . . . . . . . . . . . . . . . . . . . . . . . . . . . . . . .

7. On the days of *décade* [the name given to a particular day in each month of the revolutionary calendar] it shall celebrate the following festivals:

To the Supreme Being and to nature; to the human race; to the French people; to the benefactors of humanity; to the martyrs of liberty; to liberty and equality; to the Republic; to the liberty of the world; to the love of the Patrie [Fatherland]; to the hatred of tyrants and traitors; to truth; to justice; to modesty; to glory and immortality; to friendship; to frugality; to courage; to good faith; to heroism; to disinterestedness; to stoicism; to love; to conjugal love; to paternal love; to maternal tenderness; to filial piety; to infancy; to youth; to manhood; to old age; to misfortune; to agriculture; to industry; to our forefathers; to posterity; to happiness.

John Hall Stewart, A Documentary Survey of the French Revolution *(New York: Macmillan, 1951), pp. 526–527.*

porters for himself. In that regard, he was the selfless creator of his own destruction.

The fall of Robespierre might simply have been one more shift in the turbulent politics of the revolution. Instincts of self-preservation rather than major policy differences motivated those who brought about his demise. They had generally supported the Terror and the executions. Yet within a short time the Reign of Terror, which ultimately claimed more than 25,000 victims, came to a close. The largest number of executions had involved peasants and *sans-culottes* who had joined rebellions against the revolutionary government. By the late summer of 1794, those provincial uprisings had been crushed, and the war against foreign enemies was also going well. Those factors, combined with

*The Festival of the Supreme Being, which took place in June 1794, inaugurated Robespierre's new civic religion. Its climax occurred when a statue of Atheism was burned and another statue of Wisdom rose from the ashes. [Giraudon/Art Resource, N.Y.]*

the feeling in Paris that the revolution had consumed enough of its own children, brought the Terror to an end.

# The Thermidorian Reaction

This tempering of the revolution, called the *Thermidorian Reaction*, began in July 1794. It consisted of the destruction of the machinery of terror and the institution of a new constitutional regime. It was the result of a widespread feeling that the revolution had become too radical. In particular, it displayed a weariness of the Terror and a fear that the *sans-culottes* were exerting far too much political influence.

## *The End of the Terror*

The influence of generally wealthy middle-class and professional people soon replaced that of the *sans-culottes*. Within days and weeks of Robespierre's execution, the Convention allowed the Girondists who had been in prison or hiding to return to their seats. There was a general amnesty for political prisoners. The Convention restructured the Committee of Public Safety and gave it much less power. The Convention also repealed the notorious Law of 22 *Prairial*. Some, though by no means all, of the people responsible for the Terror were removed from public life. Leaders of the Paris Commune and certain deputies on mission were executed. The Paris Commune itself was outlawed. The Paris Jacobin Club was closed, and Jacobin clubs in the provinces were forbidden to correspond with each other.

The executions of former terrorists marked the beginning of "the white terror." Throughout the country, people who had been involved in the Reign of Terror were attacked and often murdered. Jacobins were executed with little more due process than they had extended to their victims a few months earlier. The Convention itself approved some of these trials. In other cases, gangs of youths who had aristocratic connections or who had avoided serving in the army roamed the streets beating known Jacobins. In Lyons, Toulon, and Mar-

*The closing of the Jacobin Club in November 1794 was a major event in the Thermidorean Reaction that began with the fall of Robespierre. [Roger-Viollet, © Collection Violett]*

seilles, these "bands of Jesus" dragged suspected terrorists from prisons and murdered them much as alleged royalists had been murdered during the September Massacres of 1792.

The republic of virtue gave way, if not to one of vice, at least to one of frivolous pleasures. The dress of the *sans-culottes* and the Roman Republic disappeared among the middle class and the aristocracy. New plays appeared in the theaters, and prostitutes again roamed the streets of Paris. Families of victims of the Reign of Terror gave parties in which they appeared with shaved necks like the victims of the guillotine and red ribbons tied about them. Although the Convention continued to favor the Cult of the Supreme Being, it allowed Catholic services to be held. Many refractory priests returned to the country. One of the unanticipated results of the

Thermidorian Reaction was a genuine revival of Catholic worship.

The Thermidorian Reaction also saw the repeal of legislation that had been passed in 1792 making divorce more equitable for women. As this suggests, the reaction did not result in any extension of women's rights or an improvement in women's education. The Thermidorians and their successors had seen enough attempts at political and social change. They sought to return family life to its status before the outbreak of the revolution. Political authorities and the church articulated a firm determination to reestablish separate spheres for men and women and to reinforce traditional gender roles. As a result, French women may have had somewhat less freedom after 1795 than before 1789.

## The French Revolution

**1789**

| | |
|---|---|
| May 5 | The Estates General opens at Versailles |
| June 17 | The Third Estate declares itself the National Assembly |
| June 20 | The National Assembly takes the Tennis Court Oath |
| July 14 | Fall of the Bastille in the city of Paris |
| Late July | The Great Fear spreads in the countryside |
| August 4 | The nobles surrender their feudal rights in a meeting of the National Constituent Assembly |
| August 27 | Declaration of the Rights of Man and Citizen |
| October 5–6 | Parisian women march to Versailles and force Louis XVI and his family to return to Paris |

**1790**

| | |
|---|---|
| July 12 | Civil Constitution of the Clergy adopted |
| July 14 | A new political constitution is accepted by the king |

**1791**

| | |
|---|---|
| June 14 | Chapelier Law |
| June 20–24 | Louis XVI and his family attempt to flee France and are stopped at Varennes |
| August 27 | The Declaration of Pillnitz |
| October 1 | The Legislative Assembly meets |

**1792**

| | |
|---|---|
| April 20 | France declares war on Austria |
| August 10 | The Tuileries palace is stormed, and Louis XVI takes refuge with the Legislative Assembly |
| September 2–7 | The September Massacres |
| September 20 | France wins the Battle of Valmy |
| September 21 | The Convention meets, and the monarchy is abolished |

**1793**

| | |
|---|---|
| January 21 | King Louis XVI is executed |
| February 1 | France declares war on Great Britain |
| March | Counterrevolution breaks out in the Vendée |
| April | The Committee of Public Safety is formed |
| June 22 | The Constitution of 1793 is adopted but not implemented |
| July | Robespierre enters the Committee of Public Safety |
| August 23 | *Levée en masse* proclaimed |
| September 17 | Maximum prices set on food and other commodities |
| October 16 | Queen Marie Antoinette is executed |
| October 30 | Women's societies and clubs banned |
| November 10 | The Cult of Reason is proclaimed; the revolutionary calendar, beginning on September 22, 1792, is adopted |

**1794**

| | |
|---|---|
| March 24 | Execution of the leaders of the *sans-culottes* known as the *enragés* |
| April 6 | Execution of Danton |
| May 7 | Cult of the Supreme Being proclaimed |
| June 8 | Robespierre leads the celebration of the Festival of the Supreme Being |
| June 10 | The Law of 22 *Prairial* is adopted |
| July 27 | The Ninth of *Thermidor* and the fall of Robespierre |
| July 28 | Robespierre is executed |

**1795**

| | |
|---|---|
| August 22 | The Constitution of the Year III is adopted, establishing the Directory |

## *Establishment of the Directory*

The Thermidorian Reaction involved further political reconstruction. The fully democratic constitution of 1793, which had never gone into effect, was abandoned. The Convention issued in its place the Constitution of the Year III, which reflected the Thermidorian determination to reject both constitutional monarchy and democracy. The new document provided for a legislature of two houses. Members of the upper body, or Council of Elders, were to be men over forty years of age who were either husbands or widowers. The lower Council of Five Hundred was to consist of men of at least thirty who were either married or single. The executive body was to be a five-person Directory chosen by the Elders from a list submitted by the Council of Five Hundred. Property qualifications limited the franchise, except for soldiers, who even without property were permitted to vote.

The term *Thermidor* has come to be associated with political reaction. If the French Revolution had originated in political conflicts characteristic of the eighteenth century, however, it had by 1795 become something very different. A society and a political structure based on rank and birth had given way to one based on civic equality and social status based on property ownership. People who had never been allowed direct, formal access to political power had, to different degrees, been granted it. Their entrance in political life had given rise to questions of property distribution and economic regulations that could not again be ignored. Representation had been established as a principle of politics. Henceforth the question before France and eventually before all of Europe would be which new groups would be permitted representation. In the *levée en masse* the French had demonstrated to Europe the power of the secular ideal of nationhood.

The post-Thermidorian course of the French Revolution did not void these stunning changes in the political and social contours of Europe. What triumphed in the Constitution of the Year III was the revolution of the holders of property. For this reason the French Revolution has often been considered a victory of the bourgeoisie, or middle class. The property that won the day, however, was not industrial wealth but the wealth stemming from commerce, the professions, and from land. The largest new propertied class to emerge from the revolutionary turmoil was the peasantry, who, as a result of the destruction of aristocratic privileges, now owned their land. And unlike peasants liberated from traditional landholding in other parts of Europe during the next century, French peasants had to pay no monetary compensation.

## Removal of the Sans-culottes from Political Life

The most decisively reactionary element in the Thermidorian Reaction and the new constitution was the removal of the *sans-culottes* from political life. With the war effort succeeding, the Convention severed its ties with the *sans-culottes*. True to their belief in an unregulated economy, the Thermidorians repealed the ceiling on prices. As a result, the winter of 1794–1795 brought the worst food shortages of the period. There were many food riots, which the Convention put down with force to prove that the era of the *sans-culottes journées* had come to a close. Royalist agents, who aimed to restore the monarchy, tried to take advantage of their discontent. On October 5, 1795–13 *Vendémiaire*—the sections of Paris led by the royalists rose up against the Convention. The government turned the artillery against the royalist rebels. A general named Napoleon Bonaparte (1769–1821) commanded the cannon, and with a "whiff of grapeshot" he dispersed the crowd.

By the Treaty of Basel in March 1795, the Convention concluded peace with Prussia and Spain. The legislators, however, feared a resurgence of both radical democrats and royalists in the upcoming elections for the Council of Five Hundred. Consequently, the Convention ruled that at least two-thirds of the new legislature must have been members of the older body. The Thermidorians did not even trust the property owners as voters.

The next year, the newly established Directory again faced social unrest. In Paris, Gracchus Babeuf (1760–1797) led the Conspiracy of Equals. He and his followers called for more radical democracy and for more equality of property. They declared at one point, "The aim of the French Revolution is to destroy inequality and to re-establish the general welfare. ... The Revolution is not complete, because the rich monopolize all the property and govern exclusively, while the poor toil like slaves, languish in misery, and count for nothing in the *state*."[7] They were in a sense correct. The Directory fully intended to resist any further social changes in France that might endanger property. Babeuf was arrested, tried, and executed. This minor plot became famous many decades later when European socialists attempted to find their historical roots in the French Revolution.

The suppression of the *sans-culottes*, the narrow franchise of the constitution, the rule of the two-thirds, and the Catholic royalist revival presented the Directory with problems that it never suc-

[7]Quoted in John Hall Stewart, *A Documentary Survey of the French Revolution* (New York: Macmillan, 1966), pp. 656–657.

ceeded in overcoming. It lacked any broad base of meaningful political support. It particularly required active loyalty because France remained at war with Austria and Great Britain. Consequently, the Directory came to depend on the power of the army rather than on constitutional processes for governing the country. All the soldiers could vote. Moreover, within the army, created and sustained by the revolution, were officers who were eager for power and ambitious for political conquest. The results of the instability of the Directory and the growing role of the army held profound consequences not only for France but for the entire Western world.

◆

*The French Revolution is the central political event of modern European history. It unleashed political and social forces that shaped events in Europe and much of the rest of the world for the next two centuries. The revolution began with a clash between the monarchy and the nobility. Once the Estates General gathered, however, discontent could not be contained within the traditional boundaries of eighteenth-century political life. The Third Estate, in all of its diversity, demanded real influence in government. Initially, that meant the participation of middle-class members of the Estates General, but quite soon the people of Paris and the peasants of the countryside made their demands known. Thereafter, popular nationalism exerted itself on French political life and the destiny of Europe.*

*Revolutionary legislation and popular uprisings in Paris, the countryside, and other cities transformed the social as well as the political life of the nation. Nobles surrendered traditional social privileges. The church saw its property confiscated and its operations brought under state control. For a time there was an attempt to dechristianize the nation. Vast amounts of landed property changed hands, and France became a nation of peasant landowners. Urban workers lost much of the protection they had enjoyed under the guilds and became much more subject to the forces of the marketplace.*

*Great violence accompanied many of the revolutionary changes. The Reign of Terror took the lives of thousands. France also found itself at war with virtually all of the rest of Europe. Resentment, fear, and a new desire for stability brought the Terror to an end. That desire for stability, com-*

*bined with a determination to de[...] enemies of the revolution and to [...] would in turn work to the advant[...] Eventually Napoleon Bonaparte w[...] ership in the name of stability and [...]*

## Review Questions

1. It has been said that France was a rich nation with an impoverished government. Explain this statement. How did the financial weaknesses of the French monarchy lay the foundations of the revolution of 1789?

2. Discuss the role of Louis XVI in the French Revolution. What were some of Louis XVI's most serious mistakes? Had Louis been a more able ruler, could the French Revolution have been avoided, or might a constitutional monarchy have succeeded? Or did the revolution ultimately have little to do with the competence of the monarch?

3. How was the Estates General transformed into the National Assembly? How does the Declaration of the Rights of Man and Citizen reflect the social and political values of the eighteenth-century Enlightenment? What were the chief ways in which France and its government were reorganized in the early years of the revolution? Why has the Civil Constitution of the Clergy been called the greatest blunder of the National Assembly?

4. Why were some political factions dissatisfied with the constitutional settlement of 1791? What was the revolution of 1792 and why did it occur? Who were the *sans-culottes* and how did they become a factor in the politics of the period? How influential were they during the Terror in particular? Why did the *sans-culottes* and the Jacobins cooperate at first? Why did that cooperation end?

5. Why did France go to war with Austria in 1792? What were the benefits and drawbacks for France of fighting an external war while in the midst of a domestic political revolution? What were the causes of the Terror? How did the rest of Europe react to the French Revolution and the Terror?

6. A motto of the French Revolution was "equality, liberty and fraternity." How did the revolution both support and violate this motto? Did French women benefit from the revolution? Did French peasants benefit from it?

# Suggested Readings

... M. Baker and C. Lucas (eds.), *The French Revolution and the Creation of Modern Political Culture*, 3 vols. (1987). A splendid collection of important original articles on all aspects of politics during the revolution.

K. M. Baker, *Inventing the French Revolution: Essays on French Political Culture in the Eighteenth Century* (1990). Influential essays on political thought before and during the revolution.

T. C. W. Blanning (ed.), *The Rise and Fall of the French Revolution* (1996). A wide-ranging collection of essays illustrating the recent interpretive debates.

C. Blum, *Rousseau and the Republic of Virtue: The Language of Politics in the French Revolution* (1986). An exploration of the role of Rousseau's political ideals in the debates of the French Revolution.

R. Cobb, *The Police and the People: French Popular Protest, 1789–1820* (1970). An interesting and imaginative treatment of the question of social control during the revolution.

R. Cobb, *The People's Armies* (1987). The best treatment in English of the revolutionary army.

J. Egret, *The French Pre-Revolution, 1787–88* (1978). A useful survey of the coming crisis for the monarchy.

K. Epstein, *The Genesis of German Conservatism* (1966). A major study of antiliberal forces in Germany before and during the revolution.

F. Fehér, *The French Revolution and the Birth of Modernity* (1990). A wide-ranging collection of essays on political and cultural facets of the revolution.

A. Forrest, *The French Revolution and the Poor* (1981). A study that expands consideration of the revolution beyond the standard social boundaries.

F. Furet, *Interpreting the French Revolution* (1981). A collection of controversial revisionist essays that cast doubt on the role of class conflict in the revolution.

F. Furet, *Revolutionary France, 1770–1880* (1988). An important survey by an historian who argues the revolution must be seen in the perspective of an entire century.

J. Godechot, *The Taking of the Bastille, July 14, 1789* (1970). The best modern discussion of the subject and one that places the fall of the Bastille in the context of crowd behavior in the eighteenth century.

J. Godechot, *The Counter-Revolution: Doctrine and Action, 1789–1803* (1971). An examination of opposition to the revolution.

A. Goodwin, *The Friends of Liberty: The English Democratic Movement in the Age of the French Revolution* (1979). A major work that explores the impact of the French Revolution on English radicalism.

C. Hesse, *Publishing and Cultural Politics in Revolutionary Paris* (1991). Probes the world of print culture during the French Revolution.

L. Hunt, *Politics, Culture, and Class in the French Revolution* (1986). A series of essays that focus on the modes of symbolic expression for revolutionary values and political ideals.

E. Kennedy, *A Cultural History of the French Revolution* (1989). An important examination of the role of the arts, schools, clubs, and intellectual institutions.

M. Kennedy, *The Jacobin Clubs in the French Revolution: The First Years* (1982). A careful scrutiny of the organizations chiefly responsible for the radicalizing of the revolution.

M. Kennedy, *The Jacobin Clubs in the French Revolution: The Middle Years* (1988). A continuation of the previously listed study.

G. Lefebvre, *The French Revolution*, 2 vols. (1962–1964). The leading study of the scholar noted for his subtle class interpretation of the revolution.

D. G. Levy, H. B. Applewhite, and M. D. Johnson (eds. and Trans.), *Women in Revolutionary Paris, 1789–1795* (1979). A remarkable collection of documents on the subject.

G. Lewis and C. Lucas (eds.), *Beyond the Terror: Essays in French Regional and Social History, 1794–1815* (1983). Explorations of the counter-terror that followed in the wake of the Thermidorian Reaction.

M. Lyons, *France Under the Directory* (1975). A brief survey of the post-Thermidorian governmental experiment.

T. W. Margadant, *Urban Rivalries in the French Revolution* (1992). Examines the political tensions between the central government in Paris and the cities and towns of the provinces.

S. E. Melzer and L. W. Rabine (eds.), *Rebel Daughters: Women and the French Revolution* (1992). A collection of essays exploring various aspects of the role and image of women in the French Revolution.

C. C. O'Brien, *The Great Melody: A Thematic Biography of Edmund Burke* (1992). The best recent biography.

M. Ozouf, *Festivals and the French Revolution* (1988). A pioneering study of the role of public festivals in the revolution.

R. R. Palmer, *Twelve Who Ruled: The Committee of Public Safety During the Terror* (1941). A clear narrative and analysis of the policies and problems of the committee.

R. R. Palmer, *The Age of Democratic Revolution: A Political History of Europe and America, 1760–1800*, 2 vols. (1959, 1964). An impressive survey of the political turmoil in the transatlantic world.

C. Proctor, *Women, Equality, and the French Revolution* (1990). An examination of how the ideas of the Enlightenment and the attitudes of revolutionaries affected the legal status of women.

W. J. Sewell, Jr., *A Rhetoric of Bourgeois Revolution: The Abbé Siéyès and What is the Third Estate* (1994). An important study of the political thought of Siéyès.

A. Soboul, *The Parisian Sans-Culottes and the French Revolution, 1793–94* (1964). The best work on the subject.

A. Soboul, *The French Revolution* (trans., 1975). An important work by a Marxist scholar.

B. S. Stone, *The French Parlements and the Crisis of the Old Regime* (1988). A study that considers the role of the aristocratic courts in bringing on the collapse of monarchical government.

D. G. Sutherland, *France, 1789–1815: Revolution and Counterrevolution* (1986). A major synthesis based on recent scholarship in social history.

T. Tackett, *Religion, Revolution, and Regional Culture in Eighteenth-Century France: The Ecclesiastical Oath of 1791* (1986). The most important study of this topic.

T. Tackett, *Becoming a Revolutionary: The Deputies of the French National Assembly and the Emergence of a Revolutionary Culture (1789-1790)* (1996). The best study of the early months of the revolution.

J. M. Thompson, *Robespierre*, 2 vols. (1935). The best biography.

C. Tilly, *The Vendée* (1964). A significant sociological investigation.

D. K. Van Kley, *The Religious Origins of the French Revolution: From Calvin to the Civil Constitution, 1560–1791* (1996). Examines the manner in which debates within French Catholicism influenced the coming of the revolution.

M. Walzer (Ed.), *Regicide and Revolution: Speeches at the Trial of Louis XVI* (1974). An important and exceedingly interesting collection of documents with a useful introduction.

*The Napoleonic Wars spread savage destruction across Europe. The Spanish artist Francisco Goya (1794–1828) was horrified by the atrocities perpetrated by both sides during the guerrilla warfare that followed Napoleon's occupation of Spain in 1808. This painting, entitled "The Third of May" depicts French troops executing Spanish insurgents. Events such as this roused popular resistance in Spain where the British soon began to assist the insurgency. [Museo del Prado, Madrid, Spain. Scala/Art Resource, N.Y.]*

# The Age of Napoleon
# and the Triumph of Romanticism

## K E Y   T O P I C S

- Napoleon's rise, his coronation as emperor, and his administrative reforms
- Napoleon's conquests, the creation of a French Empire, and Britain's enduring resistance
- The invasion of Russia and Napoleon's decline
- The reestablishment of a European order at the Congress of Vienna
- Romanticism and the reaction to the Enlightenment

**B**y the late 1790s, there existed a general wish for stability in France, especially among property owners, who now included the peasants. The government of the Directory was not providing this stability. The one force that was able to take charge of the nation as a symbol of both order and popular national will was the army. The most politically astute of the army generals was Napoleon Bonaparte. He had been a radical during the early revolution, a victorious general in Italy, and a supporter of the attempt to suppress revolutionary disturbances after Thermidor. Furthermore, as a general, he was a leader in the French army, the institution seen most clearly to embody the popular values of the nation and the revolution.

...e in power, Napoleon consolidated many of ...achievements of the revolution. He also repudiated much of it by establishing an empire. Thereafter, his ambitions drew France into wars of conquest and liberation throughout the continent. For over a decade Europe was at war, with only brief periods of armed truce. In leading the French armies across the Continent, Napoleon spread many of the ideas and institutions of the revolution and overturned much of the old political and social order. He also provoked popular nationalism in opposition to his conquest. This new force and the great diplomatic alliances that arose against France eventually defeated Napoleon.

Throughout these Napoleonic years, new ideas and sensibilities, known by the term romanticism, grew across Europe. Many of the ideas had originated in the eighteenth century, but they flourished in the turmoil of the French Revolution and the Napoleonic Wars. The events and values of the revolution spurred the imagination of poets, painters, and philosophers. Some romantic ideas, such as romantic nationalism, supported the revolution; others, such as the emphasis on history and religion, opposed the values of the revolution.

# The Rise of Napoleon Bonaparte

The chief danger to the Directory came from the royalists, who hoped to restore the Bourbon monarchy by legal means. Many of the émigrés had returned to France. Their plans for a restoration drew support from devout Catholics and from those citizens disgusted by the excesses of the revolution. Monarchy seemed to promise stability. The spring elections of 1797 replaced most incumbents with constitutional monarchists and their sympathizers, thus giving them a majority.

To preserve the republic and prevent a peaceful restoration of the Bourbons, the antimonarchist Directory staged a coup d'état on 18 Fructidor (September 4, 1797). They put their own supporters into the legislative seats won by their opponents. They then imposed censorship and exiled some of their enemies. At the request of the Directors, Napoleon Bonaparte, the general in charge of the Italian campaign, had sent one of his subordinates to Paris to guarantee the success of the coup. In 1797, as in 1795, the army and Bonaparte had saved the day for the government installed in the wake of the Thermidorian Reaction.

Napoleon Bonaparte was born in 1769 to a poor family of lesser nobles at Ajaccio, Corsica. Because France had annexed Corsica in 1768, he went to French schools, pursued a military career, and in 1785 obtained a commission as a French artillery officer. He strongly favored the revolution and was a fiery Jacobin. In 1793 he played a leading role in recovering the port of Toulon from the British. In reward for his service, he was appointed a brigadier general. His previous radical associations threatened his career during the Thermidorian Reaction, but his defense of the new regime on 13 Vendémiaire won him another promotion and a command in Italy.

## Early Military Victories

By 1795 French arms and diplomacy had shattered the enemy coalition, but France's annexation of Belgium guaranteed continued fighting with Britain and Austria. The attack on Italy aimed at depriving Austria of the provinces of Lombardy and Venetia. In a series of lightning victories, Bonaparte crushed the Austrian and Sardinian armies. On his own initiative, and in many ways against the wishes of the government in Paris, he concluded the Treaty of Campo Formio in October 1797. The treaty took Austria out of the war and crowned Napoleon's campaign and independent policy with success. Before long, all of Italy and Switzerland had fallen under French domination.

In November 1797, the triumphant Bonaparte returned to Paris to be hailed as a hero and to confront France's only remaining enemy, Britain. He judged it impossible to cross the channel and invade England at that time. Instead, he chose to attack British interests through the eastern Mediterranean. He set out to capture Egypt from the Ottoman Empire. By this strategy he hoped to drive the British fleet from the Mediterranean, cut off British communications with India, damage British trade, and threaten the British Empire.

Even though Napoleon overran Egypt, the invasion was a failure. Admiral Horatio Nelson (1758–1805) destroyed the French fleet at Abukir on August 1, 1798. Cut off from France, the French army could then neither accomplish anything of importance in the Near East nor get home. To make matters worse, the situation in Europe was deteriorating. The invasion of Egypt had alarmed Russia, which had its own ambitions in the Near East. The Russians, the Austrians, and the Ottomans soon

*Napoleon Bonaparte used his military successes to consolidate his political leadership as First Consul and later as Emperor of France. In this heroic portrait Jacques-Louis David portrays Napoleon as a force of nature conquering not only the armies of the enemies of France but also the Alps. On the rocks in the foreground his name follows those of Hannibal and Charlemagne, other great generals who had led armies over the Alps. [Bildarchiv Preussischer Kulturbesitz]*

joined Britain to form the Second Coalition. In 1799 the Russian and Austrian armies defeated the French in Italy and Switzerland and threatened to invade France.

 ### The Constitution of the Year VIII

Economic troubles and the dangerous international situation eroded the already fragile support of the Directory. One of the Directors, the Abbé Siéyès, proposed a new constitution. The author of the pamphlet *What Is the Third Estate?* (1789) wanted to establish a vigorous executive body independent of the whims of electoral politics, a government based on the principle of "confidence from below, power from above." The change would require another coup d'état with military support. News of France's diplomatic misfortunes had reached Napoleon in Egypt. Without orders and leaving his doomed army

behind, he returned to France in October 1799. Although some people thought that he deserved a court-martial for desertion, he received much popular acclaim. He soon joined Siéyès. On 19 Brumaire (November 10, 1799), his troops drove out the legislators and ensured the success of the coup.

Siéyès appears to have thought that Napoleon could be used and then dismissed, but if so, he badly misjudged his man. The proposed constitution divided executive authority among three consuls. Bonaparte quickly pushed it aside, as he did Siéyès, and in December 1799, he issued the Constitution of the Year VIII. Behind a screen of universal male suffrage that suggested democratic principles, a complicated system of checks and balances that appealed to republican theory, and a Council of State that evoked memories of Louis XIV, the new constitution in fact established the rule of one man—the First Consul, Bonaparte. To find an appro-

*In this early-nineteenth-century cartoon, England, personified by a caricature of Williams Pitt, and France, personified by a caricature of Napoleon, are carving out their areas of interest around the globe. [Bettmann Archives]*

priate historical analogy, one must go back to Caesar and Augustus and the earlier Greek tyrants. The career of Bonaparte, however, pointed forward to the dictators of the twentieth century. He was the first modern political figure to use the rhetoric of revolution and nationalism, to back it with military force, and to combine those elements into a mighty weapon of imperial expansion in the service of his own power and ambition.

## The Consulate in France (1799–1804)

Establishing the Consulate, in effect, closed the revolution in France. The leading elements of the Third Estate—that is, officials, landowners, doctors, lawyers, and financiers—had achieved most of their goals by 1799. They had abolished hereditary privilege, and the careers thus opened to talent allowed them to achieve the wealth, status, and security for their property they sought. The peasants were also satisfied. They had gained the land they had always wanted and had destroyed oppressive feudal privileges as well. The newly established dominant classes were profoundly conservative. They had little or no desire to share their new privileges with the lower social orders. Bonaparte seemed just the person to give them security. When he submitted his constitution to the voters in a plebiscite, they overwhelmingly approved it.

### Suppressing Foreign Enemies and Domestic Opposition

Bonaparte quickly justified the public's confidence by making peace with France's enemies. Russia had already quarreled with its allies and left the Second Coalition. A campaign in Italy brought another victory over Austria at Marengo in 1800. The Treaty of Luneville early in 1801 took Austria out of the war and confirmed the earlier settlement of Campo Formio. Britain was now alone and, in 1802, concluded the Treaty of Amiens, which brought peace to Europe.

Bonaparte also restored peace and order at home. He used generosity, flattery, and bribery to win over some of his enemies. He issued a general amnesty and employed in his own service persons from all political factions. He required only that they be loyal to him. Some of the highest offices were occupied by persons who had been extreme radicals during the Reign of Terror, others by persons who had fled the Terror and favored constitutional monarchy, and still others by former high officials of the old monarchical government.

On the other hand, Bonaparte was ruthless and efficient in suppressing opposition. He established a highly centralized administration in which prefects directly responsible to the central government in Paris managed all departments. He employed secret police. He stamped out once and for all the royalist rebellion in the west and made the rule of

# Napoleon Describes Conditions Leading to the Consulate

*In late 1799 various political groups in France became convinced that the constitution that had established the Directory could not allow France to achieve military victory. They also feared domestic unrest and new outbreaks of the radicalism that had characterized the French Revolution during the mid-1790s. With the aid of such groups Napoleon Bonaparte seized power in Paris in November, 1799. Thereafter, under various political arrangements he governed France until 1814. He later gave his own version of the situation that brought him to power.*

✦ *What are the factors that Napoleon outlines as having created a situation in which the government of France required change? In his narration how does he justify the use of military force? How does he portray himself as a savior of political order and liberty?*

On my return to Paris I found division among all authorities, and agreement upon only one point, namely, that the Constitution was half destroyed and was unable to save liberty.

All parties came to me, confided to me their designs, disclosed their secrets, and requested my support; I refused to be the man of a party.

The Council of Elders summoned me; I answered its appeal. A plan of general restoration had been devised by men whom the nation has been accustomed to regard as defenders of liberty, equality, and property; this plan required an examination, calm, free, exempt from all influence and all fear. Accordingly, the Council of Elders resolved upon the removal of the Legislative Body to Saint-Cloud; it gave me the responsibility of disposing the force necessary for its independence. I believed it my duty to my fellow citizens, to the soldiers perishing in our armies, to the national glory acquired at the cost of their blood, to accept the command. . . .

I presented myself to the Council of Five Hundred, alone, unarmed, my head uncovered, just as the Elders had received and applauded me; I came to remind the majority of its wishes, and to assure it of its power.

The stilettos which menaced the deputies were instantly raised against their liberator; twenty assassins threw themselves upon me and aimed at my breast. The grenadiers of the Legislative Body whom I had left at the door of the hall ran forward, placed themselves between the assassins and myself. One of these brave grenadiers had his clothes pieced by a stiletto. They bore me out.

At the same moment cries of "Outlaw" were raised against the defender of the law. It was the fierce cry of assassins against the power destined to repress them.

They crowded around the president, uttering threats, arms in their hands; they commanded him to outlaw me. I was informed of this; I ordered him to be rescued from their fury, and six grenadiers of the Legislative Body secured him. Immediately afterwards some grenadiers of the Legislative Body charged into the hall and cleared it.

The factions, intimidated, dispersed and fled. . . .

Frenchmen, you will doubtless recognize in this conduct the zeal of a soldier of liberty, a citizen devoted to the Republic. Conservative, tutelary, and liberal ideas have been restored to their rights through the dispersal of the rebels who oppressed the Councils. . . .

*J. H. Stuart,* A Documentary Survey of the French Revolution *(New York: Macmillan, 1951), pp. 763–765.*

Paris effective in Brittany and the Vendée for the first time in many years.

Napoleon also used and invented opportunities to destroy his enemies. When a bomb plot on his life surfaced in 1804, the event provided an excuse to attack the Jacobins, though the bombing was the work of the royalists. In 1804 his forces violated the sovereignty of the German state of Baden to seize the Bourbon duke of Enghien (1772–1804). The duke was accused of participation in a royalist plot and put to death, though Bonaparte knew him to be innocent. The action was a flagrant violation of international law and of due process. Charles Maurice de Talleyrand-Périgord (1754–1838), Bonaparte's foreign minister, later termed the act "worse than a crime—a blunder," because it helped to provoke foreign opposition. On the other hand, it was popular with the former Jacobins, for it seemed to preclude the possibility of a Bourbon restoration. The executioner of a Bourbon was hardly likely to restore the royal family. The execution also seems to have put an end to royalist plots.

## Concordat with the Roman Catholic Church

A major obstacle to internal peace was the steady hostility of French Catholics. Refractory clergy continued to advocate counterrevolution. The religious revival that dated from the Thermidorian Reaction increased discontent with the secular state created by the revolution. Bonaparte regarded religion as a political matter. He approved its role in preserving an orderly society but was suspicious of any such power independent of the state.

In 1801, to the shock and dismay of his anticlerical supporters, Napoleon concluded a concordat with Pope Pius VII (r. 1800–1823). The settlement gave Napoleon what he most wanted. The agreement required both the refractory clergy and those who had accepted the revolution to resign. Their replacements received their spiritual investiture from the pope, but the state named the bishops and paid their salaries and the salary of one priest in each parish. In return, the church gave up its claims on its confiscated property.

The concordat declared, "Catholicism is the religion of the great majority of French citizens." This was merely a statement of fact and fell far short of what the pope had wanted: religious dominance for the Roman Catholic Church. The clergy had to swear an oath of loyalty to the state. The Organic Articles of 1802, which were actually distinct from

the concordat, established the supremacy of state over church. Similar laws were applied to the Protestant and Jewish communities as well, reducing still further the privileged position of the Catholic Church.

## The Napoleonic Code

In 1802 a plebiscite ratified Napoleon as consul for life, and he soon produced another constitution that granted him what amounted to full power. He thereafter set about reforming and codifying French law. The result was the Civil Code of 1804, usually known as the *Napoleonic Code*.

The Napoleonic Code safeguarded all forms of property and tried to make French society secure against internal challenges. All the privileges based on birth that had marked the Old Regime and that had been overthrown during the revolution remained abolished. Employment of salaried officials chosen on the basis of merit replaced the purchase of offices.

The conservative attitudes toward labor and women that had emerged during the revolutionary years, however, received full support. Workers' organizations remained forbidden, and workers had fewer rights than their employers. Within families, fathers were granted extensive control over their children and husbands over their wives. At the same time, laws of primogeniture remained abolished, and property was distributed among all children, males and females. Married women could only dispose of their own property with the consent of their husbands. Divorce remained more difficult for women than for men. French law before this code had been a patchwork that differed from region to region. Within that confused set of laws, women had had opportunities to assert and protect their interests. The universality of the Napoleonic Code ended those possibilities.

## Establishing a Dynasty

In 1804 Bonaparte seized on the bomb attack on his life to make himself emperor. He argued that establishing a dynasty would make the new regime secure and make further attempts on his life useless. Another new constitution was promulgated in which Napoleon Bonaparte was called Emperor of the French, instead of First Consul of the Republic. This constitution was also overwhelmingly ratified in a plebiscite.

*The coronation of Napoleon, December 2, 1804, as painted by Jacques-Louis David. Having first crowned himself, the emperor is shown about to place the crown on the head of Josephine. Napoleon instructed David to paint Pope Pius VII with his hand raised in blessing. [Giraudon/Art Resource, N.Y.]*

To conclude the drama, Napoleon invited the pope to Notre Dame to take part in the coronation. At the last minute, however, the pope agreed that Napoleon should place the crown on his own head. The emperor had no intention of allowing anyone to think that his power and authority depended on the approval of the church. Henceforth, he was called Napoleon I.

# Napoleon's Empire (1804–1814)

Between his coronation as emperor and his final defeat at Waterloo (1815), Napoleon conquered most of Europe in a series of military campaigns that astonished the world. France's victories changed the map of Europe. The wars put an end to the Old Regime and its feudal trappings throughout western Europe and forced the eastern European states to reorganize themselves to resist Napoleon's armies.

Everywhere Napoleon's advance unleashed the powerful force of nationalism. His weapon was the militarily mobilized French nation, one of the achievements of the revolution. Napoleon could put as many as 700,000 men under arms at one time, risk as many as 100,000 troops in a single battle, endure heavy losses, and return to fight again. He could conscript citizen soldiers in unprecedented numbers, thanks to their loyalty to the nation and to their remarkable leader. No single enemy could match such resources. Even coalitions were unsuccessful until Napoleon finally overreached himself and made mistakes that led to his own defeat.

## Conquering an Empire

The Peace of Amiens (1802) between France and Great Britain was merely a truce. Napoleon's unlimited ambitions shattered any hope that it might last. He sent an army to restore the rebellious colony of Haiti to French rule. This move

*Admiral Viscount Horatio Nelson (1758–1805) was the greatest naval commander of his age. From the battle of Abukir in 1798 to his death at the battle of Trafalgar in 1805, he won a series of brilliant victories that gave Britain mastery of the seas. [Bettmann Newsphotos]*

aroused British fears that he was planning the renewal of a French empire in America, because Spain had restored Louisiana to France in 1800. More serious were his interventions in the Dutch Republic, Italy, and Switzerland and his role in the reorganization of Germany. The Treaty of Campo Formio had required a redistribution of territories along the Rhine River, and the petty princes of the region engaged in a shameful scramble to enlarge their holdings. Among the results were the reduction of Austrian influence in Germany and the emergence of a smaller number of larger German states in the west, all dependent on Napoleon.

BRITISH NAVAL SUPREMACY    The British found these developments alarming enough to justify an ultimatum. When Napoleon ignored it, Britain declared war in May 1803. William Pitt the Younger

returned to office as prime minister in 1804 and began to construct the Third Coalition. By August 1805, he had persuaded Russia and Austria to move once more against French aggression. A great naval victory soon raised the fortunes of the allies. On October 21, 1805, the British admiral Horatio, Lord Nelson, destroyed the combined French and Spanish fleets at the Battle of Trafalgar just off the Spanish coast. Nelson died in the battle, but the British lost no ships. The victory of Trafalgar put an end to all French hope of invading Britain and guaranteed British control of the sea for the rest of the war.

NAPOLEONIC VICTORIES IN CENTRAL EUROPE    On land the story was different. Even before Trafalgar, Napoleon had marched to the Danube River to attack his continental enemies. In mid-October he forced a large Austrian army to surrender at Ulm and soon occupied Vienna. On December 2, 1805, in perhaps his greatest victory, Napoleon defeated the combined Austrian and Russian forces at Austerlitz. The Treaty of Pressburg that followed won major concessions from Austria. The Austrians withdrew from Italy and left Napoleon in control of everything north of Rome. He was recognized as king of Italy.

Napoleon also made extensive political changes in Germany. In July 1806, he organized the Confederation of the Rhine, which included most of the western German princes. The withdrawal of these princes from the Holy Roman Empire led Francis II of Austria to dissolve that ancient political body and henceforth to call himself Emperor of Austria.

Prussia, which had carefully remained neutral up to this point, was now provoked into war against France. Napoleon's forces quickly crushed the famous Prussian army at the battles of Jena and Auerstädt on October 14, 1806. Two weeks later, Napoleon was in Berlin. There, on November 21, he issued the Berlin Decrees forbidding his allies from importing British goods. On June 13, 1807, Napoleon defeated the Russians at Friedland and went on to occupy Königsberg, the capital of East Prussia. The French emperor was master of all Germany.

TREATY OF TILSIT    Unable to fight another battle and unwilling to retreat into Russia, Tsar Alexander I (r. 1801–1825) was ready to make peace. He and Napoleon met on a raft in the middle of the Niemen River while the two armies and the nervous king of Prussia watched from the bank. On

*Napoleon's victory at the battle of Austerlitz is considered his most brilliant. A French army of 73,000 crushed an Austro-Russian army of 86,000 under the command of the tsar and the emperor of Austria. [Giraudon/Art Resource, N.Y.]*

July 7, 1807, they signed the Treaty of Tilsit, which confirmed France's gains. Moreover, the treaty reduced the Prussian state to half its previous size, and only the support of Alexander saved it from extinction. Prussia openly and Russia secretly became allies of Napoleon in his war against Britain.

Napoleon organized conquered Europe much like the domain of a Corsican family. The great French Empire was ruled directly by the head of the clan, Napoleon. On its borders lay several satellite states carved out as the portions of the several family members. His stepson ruled Italy for him, and three of his brothers and his brother-in-law were made kings of other conquered states. Napoleon denied a kingdom only to his brother Lucien, of whose wife he disapproved. The French emperor expected his relatives to take orders without question. When

they failed to do so, he rebuked and even punished them. This establishment of the Napoleonic family as the collective sovereigns of Europe was unpopular and provoked political opposition that needed only encouragement and assistance to flare up into serious resistance.

### The Continental System

After the Treaty of Tilsit, such assistance could come only from Britain, and Napoleon knew that he must defeat the British before he could feel safe. Unable to compete with the British navy, he continued the economic warfare begun by the Berlin Decrees. He planned to cut off all British trade with the European continent and thus to cripple British commercial and financial power. He hoped to cause

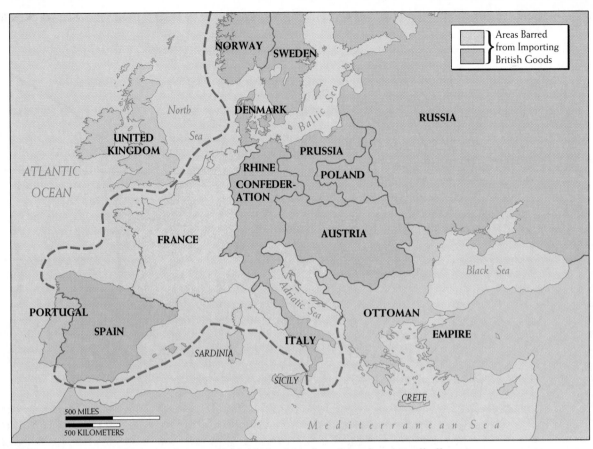

MAP 20–1 THE CONTINENTAL SYSTEM, 1806–1810 *Napoleon hoped to cut off all British trade with the European continent and thereby drive the British from the war.*

**Napoleon and the Continental System**

| | |
|---|---|
| 1806 | Napoleon establishes the Continental System prohibiting all trade with England |
| 1807 | The peace conference at Tilsit results in Russia joining the Continental System and becoming an ally of Napoleon |
| 1809 and 1810 | Napoleon at the peak of his power |
| 1810 | Russia withdraws from the Continental System and resumes relations with Britain; Napoleon plans to crush Russia militarily |
| 1812 | Napoleon invades Russia; the Russians adopt a scorched-earth policy and burn Moscow; the thwarted Napoleon deserts his dwindling army and rushes back to Paris |

domestic unrest and revolution, and thus to drive the British from the war. The Milan Decree of 1807 went further and attempted to stop neutral nations from trading with Britain.

Despite initial drops in exports and domestic unrest, the British economy survived. British control of the seas assured access to the growing markets of North and South America and of the eastern Mediterranean. At the same time, the Continental System did badly hurt the European economies. (See Map 20–1.) Napoleon rejected advice to turn his empire into a free-trade area. Such a policy would have been both popular and helpful. Instead, his tariff policies favored France, increased the resentment of foreign merchants, and made them less willing to enforce the system and more ready to engage in smuggling. It was in part to prevent smuggling that Napoleon invaded Spain in 1808. The resulting peninsular campaign in Spain and Portugal helped to bring on his ruin.

# Napoleon Advises His Brother to Rule Constitutionally

*As Napoleon conquered Europe, he set his relatives on the thrones of various conquered kingdoms and then imposed written constitutions on them. In this letter of November 1807, Napoleon sent his brother Jerome (1784–1860) a constitution for the Kingdom of Westphalia in Germany. The letter provides a good description of how Napoleon spread the political ideas and institutions of the French Revolution across Europe. Napoleon ignored, however, the possibility of nationalistic resentment that French conquest aroused even when that conquest brought more liberal political institutions. Such nationalism would be one of the causes of his downfall.*

✦ *What are the benefits that Napoleon believes his conquest and subsequent rule by his brother will bring to their new subjects? How does he believe these rather than military victory will achieve new loyalty? How does Napoleon suggest playing off the resentment of the upper classes to consolidate power? What is the relationship between having a written constitution such as Napoleon is sending his brother and the power of public opinion that he mentions toward the close of the letter?*

I enclose the constitution for your Kingdom. You must faithfully observe it. I am concerned for the happiness of your subjects, not only as it affects your reputation, and my own, but also for its influence on the whole European situation.

Don't listen to those who say that your subjects are so accustomed to slavery that they will feel no gratitude for the benefits you give them. There is more intelligence in the Kingdom of Westphalia than they would have you believe; and your throne will never be firmly established except upon the trust and affection of the common people. What German opinion impatiently demands is that men of no rank, but of marked ability, shall have an equal claim upon your favour and your employment, and that every trace of serfdom, or of a feudal hierarchy between the sovereign and the lowest class of his subjects shall be done away with. The benefits of the Code Napoleon, public trial, and the introduction of juries, will be the leading features of your Government. And to tell you the truth, I count more upon their effects, for the extension and consolidation of your rule, than upon the most resounding victories. I want your subjects to enjoy a degree of liberty, equality, and prosperity hitherto unknown to the German people. . . . Such a method of government will be a stronger barrier between you and Prussia than the Elbe, the fortresses, and the protection of France. What people will want to return under the arbitrary Prussian rule, once it has tasted the benefits of a wise and liberal administration? In Germany, as in France, Italy, and Spain, people long for equality and liberalism. I have been managing the affairs of Europe long enough now to know that the burden of the privileged classes was resented everywhere. Rule constitutionally. Even if reason, and the enlightenment of the age, were not sufficient cause, it would be good policy for one in your position; and you will find that the backing of public opinion gives you a great natural advantage over the absolute kings who are your neighbors.

*J. M. Thompson, ed.,* Napoleon's Letters *(London: Dent, 1954), pp. 190–191, as quoted in Maurice Hutt, ed.,* Napoleon *(Englewood Cliffs, N.J.: Prentice Hall, 1972), p. 34.*

# European Response to the Empire

Napoleon's conquests stimulated the two most powerful political forces in nineteenth-century Europe: liberalism and nationalism. The export of his version of the French Revolution directly and indirectly spread the ideas and values of the Enlightenment and the principles of 1789. Wherever Napoleon ruled, the Napoleonic Code was imposed, and hereditary social distinctions were abolished. Feudal privileges disappeared, and the peasants were freed from serfdom and manorial dues. In the towns, the guilds and the local oligarchies that had been dominant for centuries were dissolved or deprived of their power. New freedom thus came to serfs, artisans, workers, and entrepreneurs outside the privileged circles. The established churches lost their traditional independence and were made subordinate to the state. Church monopoly of religion was replaced by general toleration.

These reforms were not undone by the fall of Napoleon. Along with the demand for representative, constitutional government, they remained the basis of later liberal reforms. It also became clear, however, that Napoleon's policies were intended first for his own glory and that of France. The Continental System demonstrated that France, rather than Europe generally, was to be enriched by Napoleon's rule. Consequently, before long the conquered states and peoples grew restive.

## German Nationalism and Prussian Reform

The German response to Napoleon's success was particularly interesting and important. There had never been a unified German state. The great German writers of the Enlightenment, such as Immanuel Kant, Friedrich von Schiller, and Gotthold Lessing, were neither deeply politically engaged nor nationalistic.

At the beginning of the nineteenth century, the romantic movement had begun to take hold. One of its basic features in Germany was the emergence of nationalism. Nationalism went through two distinct stages. Initially, nationalistic writers emphasized the unique and admirable qualities of German culture, which, they argued, arose from the peculiar history of the German people. Such cultural nationalism prevailed until Napoleon's humiliation of Prussia at Jena in 1806.

At that point many German intellectuals began to urge resistance to Napoleon on the basis of German nationalism. The French conquest endangered the independence and achievements of all German-speaking people. Many nationalists were also critical of the German princes, who ruled selfishly and inefficiently and who seemed ever ready to lick the boots of Napoleon. Only a people united through its language and culture could resist the French onslaught. No less important in forging a German national sentiment was the example of France itself, which had attained greatness by enlisting the active support of the entire people in the patriotic cause. Henceforth many Germans sought to solve their internal political problems by attempting to establish a unified German state, reformed to harness the energies of the entire people.

After Tilsit, only Prussia could arouse such patriotic feelings. Elsewhere German rulers were either under Napoleon's thumb or actively collaborating with him. Defeated, humiliated, and diminished, Prussia continued to resist, however feebly. To Prussia fled German nationalists from other states, calling for reforms and unification that were, in fact, feared and hated by Frederick William III (r. 1797–1840) and the Junker nobility. Reforms came about despite such opposition because the defeat at Jena had made clear the necessity of new departures for the Prussian state.

The Prussian administrative and social reforms were the work of Baron vom Stein (1757–1831) and Count von Hardenberg (1750–1822). Neither of these reformers intended to reduce the autocratic power of the Prussian monarch or to put an end to the dominance of the Junkers, who formed the bulwark of the state and of the army officer corps. Rather, they aimed at fighting French power with their own version of the French weapons. As Hardenberg declared:

Our objective, our guiding principle, must be a revolution in the better sense, a revolution leading directly to the great goal, the elevation of humanity through the wisdom of those in authority. . . . Democratic rules of conduct in a monarchical administration, such is the formula . . . which will conform most comfortably with the spirit of the age.[1]

[1]Quoted in Geoffrey Brunn, *Europe and the French Imperium* (New York: Harper & Row, 1938), p. 174.

# Fichte Calls for the Regeneration of Germany

*Johann Gottlieb Fichte (1762–1814) began to deliver his famous Addresses to the German Nation late in 1807 as a series of Sunday lectures in Berlin. Earlier that year Prussia had been crushed by Napoleon's armies. In this passage from Fichte's concluding lecture, presented in early 1808, he challenged the younger generation of Germans to recognize the national duty that historical circumstances had placed on their shoulders. They might either accept their defeat and the consequent slavery or revive the German nation and receive the praise and gratitude of later generations. It is important to note that Fichte saw himself speaking to all Germans as citizens of a single cultural nation rather than as the subjects of various monarchs and princes.*

✦ *What are the conditions that Fichte portrays as the consequences of inaction? What do you think he meant by viewing Germany as "the regenerator and re-creator of the world"? To what extent do you think he is hoping that Germany may exert power and influence on the European scene similar to what France had exerted since 1792?*

Review in your own minds the various conditions between which you now have to make a choice. If you continue in your dullness and helplessness, all the evils of serfdom are awaiting you; deprivations, humiliations, the scorn and arrogance of the conqueror; you will be driven and harried in every corner, because you are in the wrong and in the way everywhere; until, by the sacrifice of your nationality and your language, you have purchased for yourselves some subordinate and petty place, and until in this way you gradually die out as a people. If, on the other hand, you bestir yourselves and play the man, you will continue in a tolerable and honorable existence, and you will see growing up among and around you a generation that will be the promise for you and for the Germans of most illustrious renown. You will see in spirit the German name rising by means of this generation to be the most glorious among all peoples; you will see this nation the regenerator and re-creator of the world.

It depends on you whether you want to be the end, and to be the last of a generation unworthy of respect and certain to be despised by posterity even beyond its due—a generation of whose history . . . your descendants will read the end with gladness, saying its fate was just; or whether you want to be the beginning and the point of development for a new age glorious beyond all your conceptions, and the generation from whom posterity will reckon the year of their salvation. Reflect that you are the last in whose power this great alteration lies.

*Johann Gottlieb Fichte, Addresses to the German Nation, ed. by George Armstrong Kelly (New York: Harper Torchbooks, 1968), pp. 215–216.*

Although the reforms came from the top, they wrought important changes in Prussian society.

Stein's reforms broke the Junker monopoly of landholding. Serfdom was abolished. The power of the Prussian Junkers, however, did not permit the total end of the system in Prussia as was occurring in the western principalities of Germany. In Prussia, peasants remaining on the land were forced to continue manorial labor, although they were free to leave the land if they chose. They could obtain the ownership of the land they worked only if they forfeited a third of it to the lord. The result was that

Junker holdings grew larger. Some peasants went to the cities to find work, others became agricultural laborers, and some did actually become small freeholding farmers. In Prussia and elsewhere, serfdom had ended, but new social problems had been created as a landless labor force was enlarged by the population explosion.

Military reforms sought to increase the supply of soldiers and to improve their quality. Jena had shown that an army of free patriots commanded by officers chosen on merit rather than by birth could defeat an army of serfs and mercenaries commanded by incompetent nobles. To remedy the situation, the Prussian reformers abolished inhumane military punishments, sought to inspire patriotic feelings in the soldiers, opened the officer corps to commoners, gave promotions on the basis of merit, and organized war colleges that developed new theories of strategy and tactics.

These reforms soon enabled Prussia to regain its former power. Because Napoleon strictly limited the size of the Prussian army to 42,000 men, however, universal conscription could not be introduced until 1813. Before that date, the Prussians evaded the limit by training one group each year, putting them into the reserves, and then training a new group the same size. Prussia could thus boast an army of 270,000 by 1814.

## The Wars of Liberation

SPAIN   In Spain more than elsewhere in Europe, national resistance to France had deep social roots. Spain had achieved political unity as early as the sixteenth century. The Spanish peasants were devoted to the ruling dynasty and especially to the Roman Catholic Church. France and Spain had been allies since 1796. In 1807, however, a French army came into the Iberian Peninsula to force Portugal to abandon its traditional alliance with Britain. The army stayed in Spain to protect lines of supply and communication. When a revolt broke out in Madrid in 1808, Napoleon used it as a pretext to depose the Spanish Bourbons and to place his brother Joseph (1768–1844) on the Spanish throne. Attacks on the privileges of the church increased public outrage. Many members of the upper classes were prepared to collaborate with Napoleon, but the peasants, urged on by the lower clergy and the monks, rose in a general rebellion.

In Spain, Napoleon faced a new kind of warfare. Guerilla bands cut lines of communication, killed stragglers, destroyed isolated units, and then disappeared into the mountains. The British landed an army under Sir Arthur Wellesley (1769–1852), later the duke of Wellington, to support the Spanish insurgents. Thus began the long peninsular campaign that would drain French strength from elsewhere in Europe and play a critical role in Napoleon's eventual defeat.

AUSTRIA   The French troubles in Spain encouraged the Austrians to renew the war in 1809. Since their defeat at Austerlitz, they had sought a war of revenge. The Austrians counted on Napoleon's distraction in Spain, French war weariness, and aid from other German princes. Napoleon was fully in command in France, however; and the German princes did not move. The French army marched swiftly into Austria and won the Battle of Wagram. The resulting Peace of Schönbrunn deprived Austria of much territory and three and a half million subjects.

Another spoil of victory was the Austrian archduchess Marie Louise (1791–1847), daughter of the emperor. Napoleon's wife, Josephine de Beauharnais (1763–1814), was forty-six and had borne him no children. His dynastic ambitions, as well as the desire for a marriage matching his new position as master of Europe, led him to divorce his wife and to marry the eighteen-year-old Austrian princess. Napoleon had also considered marrying the sister of Tsar Alexander but had received a polite rebuff.

## The Invasion of Russia

The failure of Napoleon's marriage negotiations with Russia emphasized the shakiness of the Franco-Russian alliance concluded at Tilsit. The alliance was unpopular with Russian nobles because of the liberal politics of France and because the Continental System prohibited timber sales to Britain. Only French aid in gaining Constantinople could justify the alliance in their eyes, but Napoleon gave them no help against the Ottoman Empire. The organization of the Grand Duchy of Warsaw as a Napoleonic satellite on the Russian doorstep and its enlargement in 1809 after the Battle of Wagram angered Alexander. Napoleon's annexation of Holland in violation of the Treaty of Tilsit, his recognition of the French Marshal Bernadotte (1763–1844) as the future King Charles XIV of Sweden, and his marriage to an Austrian princess further disturbed the tsar. At the end of 1810, Russia withdrew from the Continental

When their marriage failed to produce a male heir, Napoleon divorced his first wife, Josephine de Beauharnais (1763–1814). Many considered the action one aspect of Napoleon's betrayal of the Revolution, especially because he then married a daughter of the Habsburg emperor. This portrait is by F. P. Gerard. [Chateau, Fontainebleau, France. Giraudon/Art Resource]

Napoleon's second wife, Marie Louise (1791–1847), bore him a son. It was clear that Napoleon hoped to establish a new imperial dynasty in France. This portrait is by J. B. Isabey. [Chateau de Versailles, France. The Bridgeman Art Library]

System and began to prepare for war. (See Map 20–2.)

Napoleon was determined to end the Russian military threat. He amassed an army of more than 600,000 men, including a core of Frenchmen and more than 400,000 other soldiers drawn from the rest of his empire. He intended the usual short campaign crowned by a decisive battle, but the Russians disappointed him by retreating before his advance. His vast superiority in numbers—the Russians had only about 160,000 troops—made it foolish for them to risk a battle. Instead they followed a "scorched-earth" policy, destroying all food and supplies as they retreated. The so-called Grand Army of Napoleon could not live off the country, and the expanse of Russia made supply lines too

long to maintain. Terrible rains, fierce heat, shortages of food and water, and the courage of the Russian rear guard eroded the morale of Napoleon's army. Napoleon's advisers urged him to abandon the venture, but he feared that an unsuccessful campaign would undermine his position in the empire and in France. He pinned his faith on the Russians' unwillingness to abandon Moscow without a fight.

In September 1812, Russian public opinion forced the army to give Napoleon the battle he wanted despite the canny Russian General Kutuzov's (1745–1813) wish to avoid the fight and to let the Russian winter defeat the invader. At Borodino, not far west of Moscow, the bloodiest battle of the Napoleonic era cost the French 30,000 casualties

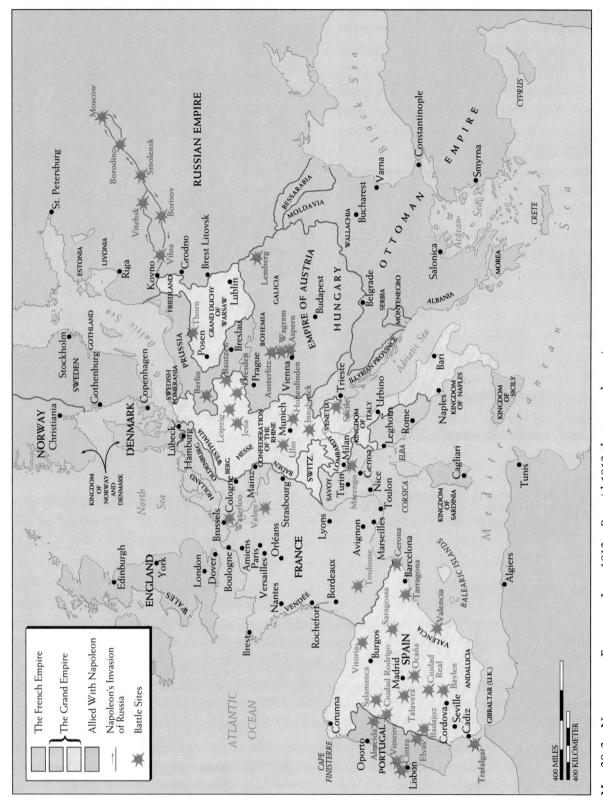

MAP 20–2   NAPOLEONIC EUROPE IN LATE 1812   By mid-1812 the areas shown in peach were incorporated into France, and most of the rest of Europe was directly controlled by or allied with Napoleon. But Russia had withdrawn from the failing Continental System, and the decline of Napoleon was about to begin.

**The French Empire**
**The Grand Empire**
**Allied With Napoleon**
**Napoleon's Invasion of Russia**
**Battle Sites**

and the Russians almost twice as many. Yet the Russian army was not destroyed. Napoleon won nothing substantial, and the battle was regarded as a defeat for him.

Fires, set by the Russians, soon engulfed Moscow and left Napoleon far from home with a badly diminished army lacking adequate supplies as winter came to a vast and unfriendly country. Napoleon, after capturing the burned city, addressed several peace offers to Alexander, but the tsar ignored them. By October, what was left of the Grand Army was forced to retreat. By December, Napoleon realized that the Russian fiasco would encourage plots against him at home. He returned to Paris, leaving the remnants of his army to struggle westward. Perhaps only as many as 100,000 of the original army of more than 600,000 lived to tell the tale of their terrible ordeal.

### European Coalition

Even as the news of the disaster reached the West, the final defeat of Napoleon was far from certain. He was able to put down his opponents in Paris and raise another 350,000 men. Neither the Prussians nor the Austrians were eager to risk another bout with Napoleon, and even the Russians hesitated. The Austrian foreign minister, Prince Klemens von Metternich (1773–1859), would have been glad to make a negotiated peace that would leave Napoleon on the throne of a shrunken and chastened France rather than see Europe dominated by Russia. Napoleon might have won a reasonable settlement by negotiation had he been willing to make concessions that would have split his jealous opponents. He would not consider that solution, however. As he explained to Metternich:

Your sovereigns born on the throne can let themselves be beaten twenty times and return to their capitals. I cannot do this because I am an upstart soldier. My domination will not survive the day when I cease to be strong, and therefore feared.[2]

In 1813 patriotic pressure and national ambition brought together the last and most powerful coalition against Napoleon. The Russians drove westward, and Prussia and then Austria joined them. All were assisted by vast amounts of British money. From the west Wellington marched his peninsular army into France. Napoleon's new army was inexperienced and poorly equipped. His generals had lost confidence and were tired. The emperor himself was worn out and sick. Still he waged a skillful campaign in central Europe and defeated the allies at Dresden. In October, however, he was decisively defeated by the combined armies of the enemy at Leipzig in what the Germans called the Battle of the Nations. At the end of March 1814, the allied army marched into Paris. A few days later, Napoleon abdicated and went into exile on the island of Elba, off the coast of northern Italy.

# The Congress of Vienna and the European Settlement

Fear of Napoleon and hostility to his ambitions had held the victorious coalition together. As soon as he was removed, the allies pursued their separate ambitions. The key person in achieving eventual agreement among them was Robert Stewart, Viscount Castlereagh (1769–1822), the British foreign secretary. Even before the victorious armies had entered Paris, he brought about the signing of the Treaty of Chaumont on March 9, 1814. It provided for the restoration of the Bourbons to the French throne and the contraction of France to its frontiers of 1792. Even more important was the agreement by Britain, Austria, Russia, and Prussia to form a Quadruple Alliance for twenty years to guarantee the peace terms and to act together to preserve whatever settlement they later agreed on. Remaining problems—and there were many—and final details were left for a conference to be held at Vienna.

### Territorial Adjustments

The Congress of Vienna assembled in September 1814 but did not conclude its work until November 1815. Although a glittering array of heads of state attended the gathering, the four great powers conducted the important work of the conference. The only full session of the congress met to ratify the arrangements made by the big four. The easiest problem facing the great powers was France. All the victors agreed that no single state should be allowed to dominate Europe, and all were determined to see

[2]Quoted in Felix Markham, *Napoleon and the Awakening of Europe* (New York: Macmillan, 1965), pp. 115–116.

MAP 20–3  THE GERMAN STATES AFTER 1815  *As noted, the German states were also reorganized.*

On these matters agreement was not difficult, but the settlement of eastern Europe sharply divided the victors. Alexander I of Russia wanted all Poland under his rule. Prussia was willing to give it to him in return for all of Saxony. Austria, however, was unwilling to surrender its share of Poland or to see Prussian power grow or Russia penetrate deeper into central Europe. The Polish–Saxon question brought the congress to a standstill and almost caused a new war among the victors. But defeated France provided a way out. The wily Talleyrand, now representing France at Vienna, suggested that the weight of France added to that of Britain and Austria might bring Alexander to his senses. When news of a secret treaty among the three leaked out, the tsar agreed to become ruler of a smaller Poland, and Frederick William III of Prussia accepted only part of Saxony. (See Map 20–3.) Thereafter, France was included as a fifth great power in all deliberations.

### The Hundred Days and the Quadruple Alliance

Unity among the victors was further restored by Napoleon's return from Elba on March 1, 1815. The French army was still loyal to the former emperor, and many of the French people thought that their fortunes might be safer under his rule than under that of the restored Bourbons. The coalition seemed to be dissolving in Vienna. Napoleon seized the opportunity, escaped to France, and was soon restored to power. He promised a liberal constitution and a peaceful foreign policy. The allies were not convinced. They declared Napoleon an outlaw (a new device under international law) and sent their armies to crush him. Wellington, with the crucial help of the Prussians under Field Marshal von Blücher (1742–1819), defeated Napoleon at Waterloo in Belgium on June 18, 1815. Napoleon again abdicated and was sent into exile on Saint Helena, a tiny Atlantic island off the coast of Africa, where he died in 1821.

The Hundred Days, as the period of Napoleon's return is called, frightened the great powers and made the peace settlement harsher for France. In addition to some minor territorial adjustments, the victors imposed a war indemnity and an army of occupation on France. Alexander proposed a Holy Alliance, whereby the monarchs promised to act together in accordance with Christian principles.

that France should be prevented from doing so again. The restoration of the French Bourbon monarchy, which was temporarily popular, and a nonvindictive boundary settlement were designed to keep France calm and satisfied.

The powers also built up a series of states to serve as barriers to any new French expansion. (See Political Transformations, page 702.) They established the kingdom of the Netherlands, including Belgium, in the north and added Genoa to Piedmont in the south. Prussia, whose power was increased by accessions in eastern Europe, was given important new territories along the Rhine River to deter French aggression in the west. Austria was given full control of northern Italy to prevent a repetition of Napoleon's conquests there. As for the rest of Germany, most of Napoleon's arrangements were left untouched. The venerable Holy Roman Empire, which had been dissolved in 1806, was not revived. In all these areas, the congress established the rule of legitimate monarchs and rejected any hint of the republican and democratic politics that had flowed from the French Revolution.

*Arthur Wellesley, the duke of Wellington, first led troops against Napoleon in Spain and later defeated him at the battle of Waterloo, June 18, 1815. Unlike his great naval contemporary, Nelson, he survived to become an elder statesman of Britain. [Bildarchiv Preussischer Kulturbesitz]*

Austria and Prussia signed; but Castlereagh thought it absurd and England abstained. The tsar, who was then embracing mysticism, believed his proposal a valuable tool for international relations. The Holy Alliance soon became a symbol of extreme political reaction.

The Quadruple Alliance among England, Austria, Prussia, and Russia was renewed on November 20, 1815. Henceforth, it was as much a coalition for the maintenance of peace as for the pursuit of victory over France. A coalition with such a purpose had not previously existed in European international relations. Its existence and later operation represented an important new departure in European affairs. Unlike the situation in the eighteenth century certain powers were determined to prevent the outbreak of future war. The experiences of the statesmen at Vienna were very different from those of their eighteenth century counterparts. They had seen the armies of the French Revolution change

major frontiers of the European states. They had witnessed Napoleon overturning the political and social order of much of the continent. They had seen their nations experience unprecedented military organization and destruction. They knew that war affected not a relatively few people in professional armies and navies but civilian populations and the entire social and political life of the continent. They were determined to prevent such upheavel and destruction from repeating itself.

Consequently, the chief aims of the Congress of Vienna were to prevent a recurrence of the Napoleonic nightmare and to arrange an acceptable settlement for Europe that might produce lasting peace. The leaders of Europe had learned that the previous peace treaties of the revolutionary era had failed and that the purpose of a treaty should be not to secure victory but to secure future peace. The shared purpose of the diplomats was to establish a framework for future stability not to punish a defeated France. The great powers through the Vienna Settlement framed international relations in such a manner that the major powers would respect that settlement and not as in the eighteenth century use military force to change it.

The Congress of Vienna succeeded remarkably in achieving these goals. France accepted the new situation without undue resentment in part because it was recognized as a great power in the new international order as well as the defeated enemy of the revolutionary and Napoleonic eras. The victorious powers settled difficult problems among themselves and lesser states reasonably. They established a new legal framework among states whereby treaties were made between states rather than between or among monarchs. The treaties remained in place when a monarch died. Furthermore, during the quarter century of warfare European leaders had come to calculate the nature of political and economic power in new ways that went beyond the simple vision of gaining a favorable balance of trade that had caused so many eighteenth-century wars. They took into account their natural resources, the technological structure of their economies, their systems of education, and the possibility of a general growth in agriculture, commerce, and industry whereby all states could prosper economically and not one at the expense of others.

The work of the congress has been criticized for failing to recognize and provide for the great forces that would stir the nineteenth century—nationalism

# POLITICAL TRANSFORMATIONS

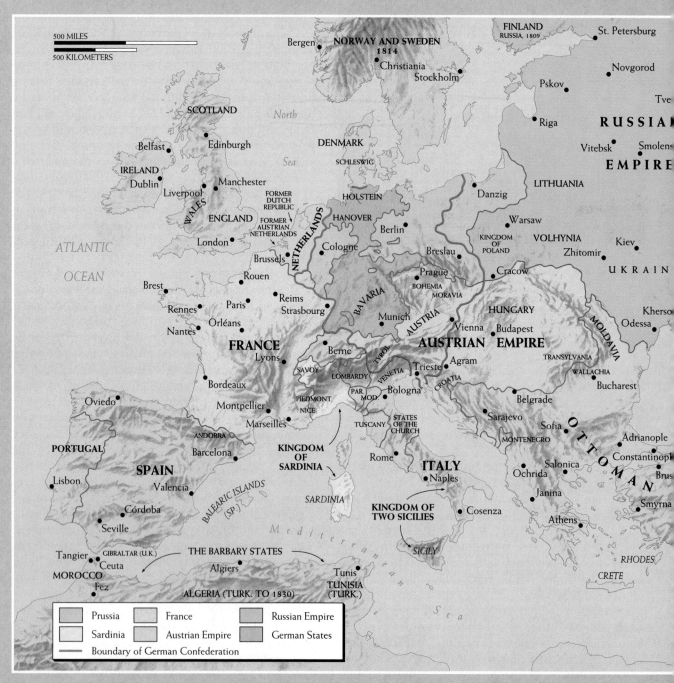

500 MILES

500 KILOMETERS

Bergen

**NORWAY AND SWEDEN**
**1814**

Christiania
Stockholm

**FINLAND**
RUSSIA, 1809

St. Petersburg

Novgorod

Tve

Pskov

Riga

**RUSSIA**

Vitebsk   Smolens

**EMPIRE**

**SCOTLAND**

*North*

Belfast   Edinburgh

**DENMARK**

SCHLESWIG

LITHUANIA

**IRELAND**
Dublin   Manchester
Liverpool

*Sea*

FORMER
DUTCH
REPUBLIC

HOLSTEIN

Danzig

Warsaw

**WALES**

**ENGLAND**

FORMER
AUSTRIAN
NETHERLANDS

HANOVER

Berlin

**KINGDOM
OF
POLAND**

**VOLHYNIA**

Kiev

London

**ATLANTIC**

Cologne

Breslau

Zhitomir

**UKRAIN**

Brussels

Prague

Cracow

**OCEAN**

Rouen

**BOHEMIA**
MORAVIA

Brest

Reims

**HUNGARY**

Kherso

Rennes   Paris
Strasbourg

Munich

Vienna
Budapest

Odessa

Orléans

**AUSTRIA**

**MOLDAVIA**

Nantes

**FRANCE**
Lyons

Berne

**TYROL**

**AUSTRIAN EMPIRE**

TRANSYLVANIA

WALLACHIA

SAVOY

LOMBARDY

VENETIA

Trieste   Agram

Bordeaux

PIEDMONT
NICE

PAR.
MOD.

Bologna

**CROATIA**

Bucharest

Oviedo

Montpellier

TUSCANY

STATES
OF THE
CHURCH

Belgrade

Sarajevo

Sofia

**OTTOMAN**

Adrianople

Marseilles

MONTENEGRO

**PORTUGAL**

ANDORRA

Barcelona

**KINGDOM
OF
SARDINIA**

Rome

**ITALY**
Naples

Ochrida

Janina

Constantinop

Brus

**SPAIN**

Lisbon

Valencia

*SARDINIA*

**KINGDOM OF
TWO SICILIES**

Cosenza

Athens

Smyrna

Córdoba

BALEARIC ISLANDS
(SP.)

Seville

*Mediterranean*

*SICILY*

*RHODES*

Tangier   GIBRALTAR (U.K.)
Ceuta

**THE BARBARY STATES**

*CRETE*

**MOROCCO**
Fez

Algiers

Tunis
**TUNISIA**
(TURK.)

ALGERIA (TURK. TO 1830)

*Sea*

| | Prussia | | France | | Russian Empire |
| | Sardinia | | Austrian Empire | | German States |
| — | Boundary of German Confederation |

MAP 20–4

# The Congress of Vienna Redraws the Map of Europe

The Congress of Vienna redrew the map of Europe in 1815, following a period of continuous warfare that had begun in 1792. Those wars had flowed from the political turmoil of the French Revolution followed by Napoleon's attempt to dominate the Continent. And indeed, several of Napoleon's military campaigns had redrawn the ancient boundaries of Europe, replacing ruling dynasties with members of Napoleon's family on thrones in Spain and the Italian peninsula.

The goals of the statesmen who gathered at Vienna were conservative in the sense that they hoped to restore legitimate dynasties to the thrones of Europe. Their goals were novel in that they hoped to establish a system of international relations that would sustain peace rather than foster the kinds of wars that had marked eighteenth-century state relations. A permanent peace would require monarchs to believe that they had more to gain by supporting each other's governments than by attacking each other.

France was restored to its traditional borders with virtually no recognition of its various conquests since 1792. The Dutch republic and former Austrian Netherlands were united into a single state known as the Netherlands. The German Confederation replaced the now defunct Holy Roman Empire, with power in the Confederation primarily divided between Prussia and Austria. England had been determined to maintain a relatively strong Prussia as a buffer against possible future Russian aggression into Europe as well as against an overly strong Austrian Empire. Poland remained partitioned among Prussia, Austria, and Russia with the last power dominating most of the formerly independent kingdom. The Austrian Empire continued to include a vast number of nationalities. The Congress of Vienna left Italy divided among a number of small local states with Austria dominating the northeast and Piedmont the northwest. Spain and Portugal were restored to their former dynasties. The Ottoman Empire continued to govern southeastern Europe but with a very weak grip that permitted Russia, England, and France to establish spheres of influence.

The boundary decisions of the Congress of Vienna gave virtually no recognition to the principle of nationality. Yet except for the revolutions in Greece in 1821 and in Belgium in 1830 and the achievement of serbian independence in 1830, the borders established by the Congress of Vienna held until the mid-1850s. In the following passage Metternich expresses his views on the obligation of monarchs to maintain political stability, and to resist forces of political change.

The first principle to be followed by the monarchs, united as they are by the coincidence of their desires and opinions, should be that of maintaining the stability of political institutions against the disorganized excitement which has taken possession of men's minds; the immutability of principles against the madness of their interpretation; and respect for laws actually in force against a desire for their destruction.

. . . .

Let [the Governments] in these troublous times be more than usually cautious in attempting real ameliorations, not imperatively claimed by the needs of the moment, to the end that good itself may not turn against them—which is the case whenever a Government measure seems to be inspired by fear.

Let them not confound concessions made to parties with the good they ought to do for their people, in modifying, according to their recognized needs, such branches of the administration as require it.

LE CONGRÈS.

*In this political cartoon of the Congress of Vienna, Tallyrand simply watches which way the wind is blowing, Castlereagh hesitates, while the monarchs of Russia, Prussia, and Austria form the dance of the Holy Alliance. The king of Saxony holds onto his crown and the republic of Geneva pays homage to the Kingdom of Sardinia. [Bildarchiv Preussischer Kulturbesitz]*

. . . .

Let them give minute attention to the financial state of their kingdoms, so that their people may enjoy, by the reduction of public burdens, the real, not imaginary, benefits of a state of peace.

Let them be just, but strong; beneficent, but strict.

Let them maintain religious principles in all their purity, and not allow the faith to be attacked and morality interpreted according to the *social contracts* or visions of foolish sectarians. . . .

In short, let the great monarchs strengthen their union, and prove to the world that if it exists, it is beneficent, and ensures the political peace of Europe: that it is powerful only for the maintenance of tranquillity at a time when so many attacks are directed against it; that the principles which they profess are paternal and protective, menacing only the disturbers of public tranquillity. . . .

To every great State determined to survive the storm there still remain many chances of salvation, and a strong union between the States on the principles we have announced will over come the storm itself.

*Prince Klemons von Metternich,* Memoirs of Prince Metternich, 1815–1829, *ed. Prince Richard Metternich (New York: Howard Fertig, 1970; photoreprint of a Scribner and Sons 1881 edition), vol. 3, pp. 473–476, as quoted in Brian Tierney and Joan Scott, eds.,* Western Societies: A Documentary History *(New York: Alfred A. Knopf, 1984), 2: 242.*

succeeded. The powers would have had to have been more than human to have anticipated future problems or to have yielded to forces of which they disapproved and which they believed threatened international peace and stability. It was unusual enough, indeed virtually unprecedented, to produce an international settlement that remained essentially intact for almost half a century and that allowed Europe to suffer no general war for a hundred years.

# The Romantic Movement

The years of the French Revolution and the conquests of Napoleon saw the emergence of a new and important intellectual movement throughout Europe. *Romanticism* in its various manifestations was a reaction against much of the thought of the Enlightenment. Romantic writers opposed what they considered the excessive scientific narrowness of the eighteenth-century *philosophes*. They accused the latter of subjecting everything to geometrical and mathematical models and thereby demeaning feelings and imagination. Romantic thinkers refused to conceive of human nature as primarily rational. They wanted to interpret both physical nature and human society in organic rather than mechanical terms and categories. The Enlightenment *philosophes* had often criticized religion and faith; the romantics, in contrast, saw religion as basic to human nature and faith as a means to knowledge.

Some historians, most notably Arthur O. Lovejoy, have warned against speaking of a single European-wide romantic movement. They have pointed out that a variety of such movements—occurring almost simultaneously in Germany, England, and France—arose independently and had their own particular courses of development. Such considerations have not, however, prevented the designation of a specific historical period, dated roughly from 1780 to 1830, as the *Age of Romanticism*, or the *romantic movement*.

Despite national differences, a shared reaction to the Enlightenment marked all of these writers and artists. They saw the imagination or some such intuitive intellectual faculty supplementing reason as a means of perceiving and understanding the world. Many of these writers urged a revival of Christianity, such as had permeated Europe during the Middle Ages. And unlike the *philosophes*, the romantics liked the art, literature, and architecture

and democracy. Such criticism is inappropriate, however. At the time there were relatively few nationalist pressures; the general desire across the continent was for peace. The settlement, like all such agreements, was aimed at solving past ills, and in that it

of medieval times. They were also deeply interested in folklore, folk songs, and fairy tales. The romantics were fascinated by dreams, hallucinations, sleepwalking, and other phenomena that suggested the existence of a world beyond that of empirical observation, sensory data, and discursive reasoning.

# Romantic Questioning of the Supremacy of Reason

Several historical streams fed the romantic movement. These included the individualism of the Renaissance and the Reformation, the pietism of the seventeenth century, and the eighteenth-century English Methodist movement. The latter influence encouraged a heartfelt, practical religion in place of dogmatism, rationalism, and deism. The sentimental novels of the eighteenth century, such as Samuel Richardson's (1689–1761) *Clarissa* (1747),

also paved the way for thinkers who would emphasize feeling and emotion. The so-called *Sturm und Drang,* "storm and stress," period of German literature and German idealist philosophy were important to the romantics. Two writers who were also closely related to the Enlightenment, however, provided the immediate intellectual foundations for romanticism. They were Jean-Jacques Rousseau and Immanuel Kant, both of whom raised questions about the sufficiency of the rationalism so dear to the *philosophes.*

## *Rousseau and Education*

It has already been pointed out in Chapter 18 that Jean-Jacques Rousseau, though sharing in the reformist spirit of the Enlightenment, opposed many of its other facets. What romantic writers especially drew from Rousseau was his conviction that society and material prosperity had corrupted

*In* A Philosopher in a Moonlit Churchyard, *the British artist Philip James de Loutherbourg captured many of the themes of the Romantic movement. The painting suggests a sense of history, a love of Gothic architecture, a sense of the importance of religion, and a belief that the world is essentially mysterious. [Yale Center for British Art]*

human nature. In his works, Rousseau had portrayed humankind as happy and innocent by nature and originally living in a state of equilibrium, able to do what it desired and desiring only what it was able to do. To become happy again, humankind must remain true to its natural being while still attempting to realize the new moral possibilities of life in society. In his *Social Contract* (1762), Rousseau had provided his prescription for the reorganization of political life that would achieve that goal.

Rousseau set forth his view on the individual's development toward the good and happy life in his novel *Émile* (1762), discussed in Chapter 19 in regard to his views on gender. Initially this treatise on education was far more influential than the *Social Contract*. In *Émile*, Rousseau stressed the difference between children and adults. He distinguished the stages of human maturation and urged that children be raised in maximum individual freedom. Each child should be allowed to grow freely, like a plant, and to learn by trial and error what reality is and how best to deal with it. The parent or teacher would help most by providing the basic necessities of life and warding off what was manifestly harmful. Beyond that, the adult should stay completely out of the way, like a gardener who waters and weeds a garden but otherwise lets nature take its course. As noted in Chapter 19, Rousseau thought that men and women because of their physical differences would naturally grow into social roles with different spheres of activity.

Rousseau thought that the child's sentiments as well as its reason should be permitted to flourish. To romantic writers, this concept of human development vindicated the rights of nature over those of artificial society. They thought that such a form of open education would eventually lead to a natural society. In its fully developed form, this view of life led the romantics to value the uniqueness of each individual and to explore childhood in great detail. Like Rousseau, the romantics saw humankind, nature, and society as organically interrelated.

### Kant and Reason

Immanuel Kant (1724–1804) wrote the two greatest philosophical works of the late eighteenth century: *The Critique of Pure Reason* (1781) and *The Critique of Practical Reason* (1788). He sought to accept the rationalism of the Enlightenment and still to preserve a belief in human freedom, immortality, and the existence of God. Against Locke and other philosophers who saw knowledge rooted in sensory experience alone, Kant argued for the subjective character of human knowledge. For Kant, the human mind did not simply reflect the world around it like a passive mirror; rather, the mind actively imposed on the world of sensory experience "forms of sensibility" and "categories of understanding." The mind itself generated these categories. In other words, the human mind perceives the world as it does because of its own internal mental categories. This meant that human perceptions were as much the product of the mind's own activity as of sensory experience.

Kant found the sphere of reality that was accessible to pure reason to be quite limited. He believed, however, that beyond the phenomenal world of sensory experience, over which "pure reason" was master, there existed what he called the "noumenal" world. This world was a sphere of moral and aesthetic reality known by "practical reason" and conscience. Kant thought that all human beings possessed an innate sense of moral duty or an awareness of what he called a *categorical imperative*. This term referred to an inner command to act in every situation as one would have all other people always act in the same situation. Kant regarded the existence of this imperative of conscience as incontrovertible proof of humankind's natural freedom. On the basis of humankind's moral sense, Kant postulated the existence of God, eternal life, and future rewards and punishments. He believed that these transcendental truths could not be proved by discursive reasoning. Still, he was convinced that they were realities to which every reasonable person could attest.

To many romantic writers, Kantian philosophy constituted a decisive refutation of the narrow rationality of the Enlightenment. Whether they called it "practical reason," "fancy," "imagination," "intuition," or simply "feeling," the romantics believed in the presence of a special power in the human mind that could penetrate beyond the limits of largely passive human understanding as set forth by Hobbes, Locke, and Hume. Most of them also believed that poets and artists possessed these powers in abundance. Other romantic writers appealed to the limits of human reason to set forth new religious ideas or political thought that was often at odds with Enlightenment writers.

# Romantic Literature

The term *romantic* appeared in English and French literature as early as the seventeenth century. Neo-classical writers then used the word to describe literature that they considered unreal, sentimental, or excessively fanciful. In the eighteenth century, the English writer Thomas Warton (1728–1790) associated romantic literature with medieval romances. In Germany, a major center of the romantic literary movement, Johann Gottfried Herder (1744–1803) used the terms *romantic* and *Gothic* interchangeably. In both England and Germany, the term came to be applied to all literature that did not observe classical forms and rules and that gave free play to the imagination.

As an alternative to such dependence on the classical forms, August Wilhelm von Schlegel (1767–1845) praised the "romantic" literature of Dante, Petrarch, Boccaccio, Shakespeare, the Arthurian legends, Cervantes, and Calderón. According to Schlegel, romantic literature was to classical literature what the organic and living were to the merely mechanical. He set forth his views in *Lectures on Dramatic Art and Literature* (1809–1811).

The romantic movement had peaked in Germany and England before it became a major force in France under the leadership of Madame de Staël (1766–1817) and Victor Hugo (1802–1885). So influential was the classical tradition in France that not until 1816 did a French writer openly declare himself a romantic. That was Henri Beyle (1783–1842), who wrote under the pseudonym Stendhal. He praised Shakespeare and Lord Byron and criticized his own countryman, the seventeenth-century classical dramatist Jean Racine (1639–1699).

## The English Romantic Writers

The English romantics believed that poetry was enhanced by freely following the creative impulses of the mind. In this belief, they directly opposed Lockean psychology, which regarded the mind as a passive receptor and poetry as a mechanical exercise of "wit" following prescribed rules. For William Blake and Samuel Taylor Coleridge, the artist's imagination was God at work in the mind. As Coleridge expressed his views, the imagination was "a repetition in the finite mind of the eternal act of creation in the infinite I AM." So conceived of, poetry could not be considered idle play. It was the highest of human acts, humankind's self-fulfillment in a transcendental world.

BLAKE    William Blake (1757–1827) considered the poet a seer and poetry to be translated vision. He thought it a great tragedy that so many people understood the world only rationally and could perceive no innocence or beauty in it. In the 1790s, he went through a deep personal depression that seems to have been related to his own inability to perceive the world as he believed it to be. The better one got to know the world, the more the life of the imagination and its spiritual values seemed to recede. Blake saw this problem as evidence of the materialism and injustice of English society. He was deeply impressed by the strong sense of contradiction between a true childlike vision of the world and conceptions of it based on experience.

COLERIDGE    Samuel Taylor Coleridge (1772–1834) was the master of Gothic poems of the supernatural, such as "Christabel," "The Ancient Mariner," and "Kubla Khan." "The Ancient Mariner" relates the story of a sailor cursed for killing an albatross. The poem treats the subject as a crime against nature and God and raises the issues of guilt, punishment, and the redemptive possibilities of humility and penance. At the end of the poem, the mariner discovers the unity and beauty of all things. Having repented, he is delivered from his awful curse, which has been symbolized by the dead albatross hung around his neck:

O happy living things! no tongue
Their beauty might declare:
A spring of love gushed from my heart,
And I blessed them unaware . . .
The self-same moment I could pray;
And from my neck so free
The Albatross fell off, and sank
Like lead into the sea.

Coleridge also made major contributions to romantic literary criticism in his lectures on Shakespeare and in *Biographia Literaria* (1817), which presents his theories of poetry.

WORDSWORTH    William Wordsworth (1770–1850) was Coleridge's closest friend. Together they published *Lyrical Ballads* in 1798 as a manifesto of a new poetry that rejected the rules of eighteenth-century criticism. Among Wordsworth's most important later poems is his "Ode on Intimations of Immortality" (1803), written in part to console Coleridge, who was suffering a deep personal crisis. Its subject is the loss of poetic vision, something Wordsworth also keenly felt then in himself. Nature, which he had worshiped, no longer spoke freely to him, and he feared that it might never speak to him again:

There was a time when meadow, grove, and
   stream,
The earth, and every common sight,
To me did seem
Appareled in celestial light,
The glory and the freshness of a dream.
It is not now as it hath been of yore—
Turn whereso'er I may,
By night or day,
The things which I have seen I now can
   see no more.

He had lost what he believed that all human beings lose in the necessary process of maturation: their childlike vision and closeness to spiritual reality. For both Wordsworth and Coleridge, childhood was the bright period of creative imagination. Wordsworth held a theory of the soul's preexistence in a celestial state before its creation. The child, being closer in time to its eternal origin and undistracted by worldly experience, recollects the supernatural world much more easily. Aging and urban living corrupt and deaden the imagination, making one's inner feelings and the beauty of nature less important. In his book-length poem *The Prelude* (1850), Wordsworth presented a long autobiographical account of the growth of the poet's mind.

LORD BYRON    A true rebel among the romantic poets was Lord Byron (1788–1824). In Britain, even most of the other romantic writers distrusted and disliked him. He had little sympathy for their views of the imagination. Outside England, however, Byron was regarded as the embodiment of the new person of the French Revolution. He rejected the old traditions (he was divorced and famous for his paramours) and championed the cause of personal liberty. Byron was outrageously skeptical and mocking, even of his own beliefs. In *Childe Harold's Pilgrimage* (1812), he created a brooding, melancholy romantic hero. In *Don Juan* (1819), he wrote with

Lord Byron may well have been the most famous European poet of the first quarter of the nineteenth century. This portrait by the contemporary artist Géricault captures the poet in a brooding, introspective mood. [Bildarchiv Preussischer Kulturbesitz]

ribald humor, acknowledged nature's cruelty as well as its beauty, and even expressed admiration for urban life.

### The German Romantic Writers

Much romantic poetry was also written on the Continent, but almost all major German romantics wrote at least one novel. Romantic novels often were highly sentimental and borrowed material from medieval romances. The characters of romantic novels were treated as symbols of the larger truth of life. Purely realistic description was avoided. The first German romantic novel was Ludwig Tieck's (1773–1853) *William Lovell* (1793–1795). It contrasts the young Lovell, whose life is built on love and imagination, with those who live by cold reason alone and who thus become an easy

Johann Wolfgang von Goethe (1749–1832), perhaps the greatest German writer of modern times, is portrayed here in the garb of a pilgrim against a Romantic background of classical ruins in the fields outside Rome. [Städelisches Kunstinstitut, Frankfurt/Artothek]

prey to unbelief, misanthropy, and egoism. As the novel rambles to its conclusion, Lovell is ruined by a mixture of philosophy, materialism, and skepticism, administered to him by two women whom he naïvely loves.

SCHLEGEL Friedrich Schlegel (1767–1845) wrote a progressive early romantic novel, *Lucinde* (1799), which attacked contemporary prejudices against women as capable of being little more than lovers and domestics. Schlegel's novel reveals the ability of the romantics to become involved in the social issues of their day. He depicted Lucinde as the perfect friend and companion, as well as the unsurpassed lover, of the hero. Like other early romantic novels, the work shocked contemporary morals by frankly discussing sexual activity and by describing Lucinde as equal in all ways to the male hero.

GOETHE Towering above all of these German writers stood the figure of Johann Wolfgang von Goethe (1749–1832). Perhaps the greatest German writer of modern times, Goethe defies any easy classification. Part of his literary production fits into the romantic mold, and part of it was a condemnation of romantic excesses. The book that made his early reputa-

tion was *The Sorrows of Young Werther*, published in 1774. This novel, like many others in the eighteenth century, is composed of a series of letters. The hero falls in love with Lotte, who was married to another man. The letters explore this relationship and display the emotional sentimentalism that was characteristic of the age. Eventually Werther and Lotte part, but in his grief over his abandoned love, Werther takes his own life. This novel became popular throughout Europe. Virtually all later romantic authors, and especially those in Germany, admired it because of its emphasis on feeling and on living outside the bounds of polite society.

Much of Goethe's early poetry was also erotic in nature. As he became older, however, Goethe became much more serious and self-consciously moral. He published many other works, including *Iphigenia at Tauris* (1787) and *Wilhelm Meister's Apprenticeship* (1792–1800) that explored how human beings come to live moral lives while still acknowledging the life of the senses.

Goethe's greatest masterpiece was *Faust*, a long dramatic work of poetry in two parts. Part I was published in 1808. It tells the story of Faust, who, weary of life, makes a pact with the Devil—he will exchange his soul for greater knowledge than other human beings possess. As the story progresses, Faust seduces a young woman named Gretchen. She dies but is received into heaven as the grief-stricken Faust realizes that he must continue to live.

In Part II, completed in the year of Goethe's death (1832), Faust is taken through a series of strange adventures involving witches and various mythological characters. This portion of the work has never been admired as much as Part I. At the conclusion, however, Faust dedicates his life, or what remains of it, to the improvement of humankind. In this dedication he feels that he has found a goal that will allow him to overcome the restless striving that first induced him to make the pact with the Devil. That new knowledge breaks the pact. Faust then dies and is received by angels.

In this great work, Goethe obviously was criticizing much of his earlier thought and that of contemporary romantic writers. He was also attempting to portray the deep spiritual problems that Europeans would encounter as the traditional moral and religious values of Christianity were abandoned. Yet Goethe himself could not reaffirm those values. In that respect, both he and his characters symbolized the spiritual struggle of the nineteenth century.

# Religion in the Romantic Period

During the Middle Ages, the foundation of religion had been the church. The Reformation leaders had appealed to the authority of the Bible. Then, later Enlightenment writers had attempted to derive religion from the rational nature revealed by Newtonian physics. Romantic religious thinkers, on the other hand, appealed to the inner emotions of humankind for the foundation of religion. Their forerunners were the mystics of Western Christianity. One of the first great examples of a religion characterized by romantic impulses—Methodism—arose in England.

## Methodism

Methodism originated in the middle of the eighteenth century as a revolt against deism and rationalism in the Church of England. The Methodist revival formed an important part of the background of English romanticism. The leader of the Methodist movement was John Wesley (1703–1791). His education and religious development had been carefully supervised by his remarkable mother, Susan-

John Wesley (1703–1791) was the founder of Methodism. He emphasized the role of emotional experience in Christian conversion. [The Bettmann Archive]

nah Wesley, who bore eighteen children in addition to John.

While at Oxford, Wesley organized a religious group known as the "Holy Club." He soon left England for missionary work in Georgia in America, where he arrived in 1735. While crossing the Atlantic, a group of German Moravians on the ship had deeply impressed him. These German pietists exhibited unshakable faith and confidence during a violent storm at sea, while Wesley despaired of his life. Wesley concluded that they knew far better than he the meaning of justification by faith. When he returned to England in 1738 after an unhappy missionary career, Wesley began to worship with Moravians in London. There, in 1739, he underwent a conversion experience that he described in the words, "My heart felt strangely warmed." From that point on, he felt assured of his own salvation.

Wesley discovered that he could not preach his version of Christian conversion and practical piety in Anglican Church pulpits. Therefore, late in 1739, he began to preach in the open fields near the cities and towns of western England. Thousands of humble people responded to his message of repentance and good works. Soon he and his brother Charles (1707–1788), who became famous for his hymns, began to organize Methodist societies. By the late eighteenth century, the Methodists had become a separate church. They ordained their own clergy and sent missionaries to America, where they eventually achieved their greatest success and most widespread influence.

Methodism stressed inward, heartfelt religion and the possibility of Christian perfection in this life. John Wesley described Christianity as "an inward principle . . . the image of God impressed on a created spirit, a fountain of peace and love springing up into everlasting life." True Christians were those who were "saved in this world from all sin, from all unrighteousness . . . and now in such a sense perfect as not to commit sin and . . . freed from evil thoughts and evil tempers."[3]

Many people, weary of the dry rationalism that derived from deism, found Wesley's ideal relevant to their own lives. The Methodist preachers emphasized the role of enthusiastic emotional experience as part of Christian conversion. After Wesley, reli-

[3]Quoted in Albert C. Outler, ed., *John Wesley: A Representative Collection of His Writings* (New York: Oxford University Press, 1964), p. 220.

*Friedrich Schleiermacher (1768–1834) was the most important protestant theologian of the first half of the nineteenth century. He stressed the importance of feelings in religious experience. [Bildarchiv Preussischer Kulturbesitz]*

gious revivals became highly emotional in style and content.

## New Directions in Continental Religion

Similar religious developments based on feeling appeared on the Continent. After the Thermidorian Reaction, a strong Roman Catholic revival took place in France. Its followers disapproved of both the religious policy of the revolution and the anticlericalism of the Enlightenment. The most important book to express these sentiments was *The Genius of Christianity* (1802) by Viscount François René de Chateaubriand (1768–1848). In this work, which became known as the "Bible of romanticism," Chateaubriand argued that the essence of religion was "passion." The foundation of faith in the church was the emotion that its teachings and sacraments inspired in the heart of the Christian.

Against the Newtonian view of the world and of a rational God, the romantics found God immanent in nature. No one stated the romantic religious ideal more eloquently or with greater impact on the modern world than Friedrich Schleiermacher

# Chateaubriand Describes the Appeal of a Gothic Church

*Throughout most of the eighteenth century, writers had harshly criticized virtually all aspects of the Middle Ages, then considered an unenlightened time. One of the key elements of romanticism was a new appreciation of all things medieval. In this passage from* The Genius of Christianity, *Chateaubriand praises the beauty of the Middle Ages and the strong religious feelings produced by stepping into a Gothic church. The description exemplifies the typically romantic emphasis on feelings as the chief foundation of religion.*

◆ *Why does the capacity of a Gothic church to carry Chateaubriand back in time add to its power of inducing a religious feeling? How does Chateaubriand unite the church with nature to emphasize its religious character? Is this vision of religion dependent upon the authority of an organized church or of sacred writings, such as the Bible?*

You could not enter a Gothic church without feeling a kind of awe and a vague sentiment of the Divinity. You were all at once carried back to those times when a fraternity of cenobites [a particular order of monks], after having meditated in the woods of their monasteries, met to prostrate themselves before the altar and to chant the praises of the Lord, amid the tranquility and the silence of the night. . . .

Everything in a Gothic church reminds you of the labyrinths of a wood; everything excites a feeling of religious awe, of mystery, and of the Divinity.

The two lofty towers erected at the entrance of the edifice overtop the elms and yew trees of the church yard, and produce the most picturesque effect on the azure of heaven. Sometimes their twin heads are illumined by the first rays of dawn; at others they appear crowned with a capital of clouds or magnified in a foggy atmosphere. The birds themselves seem to make a mistake in regard to them, and to take them for the trees of the forests; they hover over their summits, and perch upon their pinnacles. But, lo! confused noises suddenly issue from the tops of these towers and scare away the affrighted birds. The Christian architect, not content with building forests, has been desirous to retain their murmurs; and, by means of the organ and of bells, he has attached to the Gothic temple the very winds and thunders that roar in the recesses of the woods. Past ages, conjured up by these religious sounds, raise their venerable voices from the bosom of the stones, and are heard in every corner of the vast cathedral. The sanctuary reechoes like the cavern of the ancient Sibyl; loud-tongued bells swing over your head, while the vaults of death under your feet are profoundly silent.

*Viscount François René de Chateaubriand,* The Genius of Christianity, *trans. by C. I. White (Baltimore: J. Murphy, 1862), as quoted in Howard E. Hugo, ed.,* The Romantic Reader *(New York: Viking, 1957), pp. 341–342.*

# Romantic Views of Nationalism and History

A distinctive feature of romanticism, especially in Germany, was its glorification of both the individual person and individual cultures. Behind these views lay the philosophy of German idealism, which understood the world as the creation of subjective egos. J. G. Fichte (1762–1814), an important German philosopher and nationalist, identified the individual ego with the Absolute that underlies all existing things. According to him and similar philosophers, the world is truly the creation of humankind. The world is as it is because especially strong persons conceive of it in a particular way and impose their wills on the world and other people. Napoleon served as the contemporary example of such a great person. This philosophy has ever since served to justify the glorification of great persons and their actions in overriding all opposition to their will and desires.

## Herder and Culture

In addition to this philosophy, the influence of new historical studies lay behind the German glorification of individual cultures. German romantic writers went in search of their own past in reaction to the copying of French manners in eighteenth-century Germany, the impact of the French Revolution, and the imperialism of Napoleon. An early leader in this effort was Johann Gottfried Herder (1744–1803). Herder had early resented the French cultural preponderance in Germany. In 1778 he published an influential essay entitled "On the Knowing and Feelings of the Human Soul." In it, he vigorously rejected the mechanical explanation of nature so popular with Enlightenment writers. He saw human beings and societies as developing organically, like plants, over time. Human beings were different at different times and places.

Herder revived German folk culture by urging the collection and preservation of distinctive German songs and sayings. His most important followers in this work were the Grimm brothers, Jakob (1785–1863) and Wilhelm (1786–1859), famous for their collection of fairy tales. Believing that each language and culture were the unique expression of a people, Herder opposed both the concept and the use of a "common" language, such as French, and "universal" institutions, such as those imposed on

(1768–1834). In 1799 he published *Speeches on Religion to Its Cultured Despisers*. It was a response to Lutheran orthodoxy, on the one hand, and to Enlightenment rationalism, on the other. The advocates of both were the "cultured despisers" of real, or heartfelt, religion. According to Schleiermacher, religion was neither dogma nor a system of ethics. It was an intuition or feelings of absolute dependence on an infinite reality. Religious institutions, doctrines, and moral activity expressed that primal religious feeling only in a secondary, or indirect, way.

Although Schleiermacher considered Christianity the "religion of religions," he also believed that every world religion was unique in its expression of the primal intuition of the infinite in the finite. He thus turned against the universal natural religion of the Enlightenment, which he termed "a name applied to loose, unconnected impulses," and defended the meaningfulness of the numerous world religions. Every such religion was seen to be a unique version of the emotional experience of dependence on an infinite being. In so arguing, Schleiermacher interpreted the religions of the world in the same way that other romantic writers interpreted the variety of unique peoples and cultures.

# Hegel Explains the Role of Great Men in History

*Hegel believed that behind the development of human history from one period to the next lay the mind and purpose of what he termed the "World-Spirit," a concept somewhat resembling the Christian God. Hegel thought particular heroes from the past (such as Caesar) and in the present (such as Napoleon) were the unconscious instruments of that Spirit. In this passage from his lectures on the philosophy of history, Hegel explained how these heroes could change the course of history. All these concepts are characteristic of the romantic belief that human beings and human history are always intimately connected with larger, spiritual forces at work in the world. The passage also reflects the widespread belief of the time that the world of civic or political action pertained to men and that of the domestic sphere belonged to women.*

✦ *How might the career of Napoleon have inspired this passage? What are the antidemocratic implications of this passage? In this passage, do great men make history or do historical developments make great men? Why do you think Hegel does not associate this power of shaping history with women as well as men? In that regard, note how he relates history with political developments rather than with those of the private social sphere.*

Such are all great historical men—whose own particular aims involve those large issues which are the will of the World-Spirit. They may be called Heroes, inasmuch as they have derived their purposes and their vocation, not from the calm, regular course of things, sanctioned by the existing order, but from a concealed fount—one which has not attained to phenomenal, present existence—from that inner Spirit, still hidden beneath the surface, which, impinging on the outer world as on a shell, bursts it in pieces, because it is another kernel than that which belonged to the shell in question. They are men, therefore, who appear to draw the impulse of their life from themselves; and whose deeds have produced a condition of things and a complex of historical relations which appear to be only their interest, and their work.

Such individuals had no consciousness of the general Idea they were unfolding, while prosecuting those aims of theirs; on the contrary, they were practical, political men. But at the same time they were thinking men, who had an insight into the requirements of the time—what was ripe for development. This was the very Truth for their age, for their world; the species next in order, so to speak, and which was already formed in the womb of time. It was theirs to know this nascent principle; the necessary, directly sequent step in progress, which their world was to take; to make this their aim, and to expend their energy in promoting it. World-historical men—the Heroes of an epoch—must, therefore, be recognized as its clear-sighted ones; their deeds, their words are the best of that time.

G. W. F. Hegel, *The Philosophy of History*, trans. by J. Sibree (New York: Dover, 1956), pp. 30–31.

The philsopher J. G. Fichte (1762–1814), shown here in the uniform of a Berlin home guard. Fichte glorified the role of the great individual in history. [Bildarchiv Preussischer Kulturbesitz]

Friedrich Hegel (1770–1831). He is one of the most difficult and significant philosophers in the history of Western civilization.

Hegel believed that ideas develop in an evolutionary fashion that involves conflict. At any given time, a predominant set of ideas, which he termed the *thesis*, holds sway. The thesis is challenged by other conflicting ideas, which Hegel termed the *antithesis*. As these patterns of thought clash, a *synthesis* emerges that eventually becomes the new thesis. Then the process begins all over again. Periods of world history receive their character from the patterns of thought predominating during them.

Several important philosophical conclusions followed from this analysis. One of the most significant was the belief that all periods of history have been of almost equal value because each was, by definition, necessary to the achievements of those that came later. Also, all cultures are valuable because each contributes to the necessary clash of values and ideas that allows humankind to develop. Hegel discussed these concepts in *The Phenomenology of Mind* (1806), *Lectures on the Philosophy of History* (1822–1831), and other works, many of which were published only after his death. During his lifetime, his ideas became widely known through his university lectures at Berlin.

◆

*These various romantic ideas made a major contribution to the emergence of nationalism, which proved to be one of the strongest motivating forces of the nineteenth and twentieth centuries. The writers of the Enlightenment had generally championed a cosmopolitan outlook on the world. The romantic thinkers, however, emphasized the individuality and worth of each separate people and culture. A people or a nation was defined by a common language, a common history, a homeland that possessed historical associations, and common customs. This cultural nationalism gradually became transformed into a political creed. It came to be widely believed that every people, ethnic group, or nation should constitute a separate political entity, and that only when it so existed could the nation be secure in its own character.*

*The example of France under the revolutionary government and then Napoleon had demonstrated*

Europe by Napoleon. These, he believed, were forms of tyranny over the individuality of a people. Herder's writings led to a broad revival of interest in history and philosophy. Although initially directed toward the identification of German origins, such work soon expanded to embrace other world cultures as well. Eventually the ability of the romantic imagination to be at home in any age or culture spurred the study of non-Western religion, comparative literature, and philology.

## Hegel and History

The most important philosopher of history in the Romantic Period was the German, Georg Wilhelm

*This colored lithograph of G. W. F. Hegel shows him attired in the robes of a university professor. Hegel was the most important philosopher of history in the Romantic period. [Bildarchiv Preussischer Kulturbesitz]*

the power of nationhood. Other peoples came to desire similar strength and confidence. Napoleon's toppling of ancient political structures, such as the Holy Roman Empire, proved the need for new political organization in Europe. By 1815 these were the aspirations of only a few Europeans, but as time passed, such yearnings came to be shared by scores of peoples from Ireland to Ukraine. The Congress of Vienna could ignore such feelings, but for the rest of the nineteenth century, as will be seen in subsequent chapters, statesmen had to confront the growing reality of the power these feelings unleashed.

## Review Questions

1. How did Napoleon rise to power? What groups supported him? What were the stages by which he eventually made himself emperor? What were his major domestic achievements? Did his rule more nearly fulfill or betray the ideals of the French Revolution?
2. What regions made up Napoleon's realm and what status did each region have within it? How did Napoleon rule his empire? Did his administration show foresight or did the empire ultimately become a burden he could not afford?

3. Why did Napoleon decide to invade Russia? Why did the operation fail? Can Napoleon be considered a "military genius"? Why or why not? To what extent was his brilliance dependent on the ineptitude of his enemies?
4. Who were the principal personalities and what were the most significant problems of the Congress of Vienna? What were the results of the Congress and why were they significant?
5. Compare the role of feelings for romantic writers with the role of reason for Enlightenment writers. What questions did Rousseau and Kant raise about reason?
6. Why did poetry become important to romantic writers? How did the romantic concept of religion differ from Reformation Protestantism and Enlightenment deism? How did romantic writers use the idea of history?

# Suggested Readings

M. H. ABRAMS, *The Mirror and the Lamp: Romantic Theory and the Critical Tradition* (1958). A standard text on romantic literary theory that looks at English romanticism in the context of German romantic idealism.

M. H. ABRAMS, *Natural Supernaturalism: Tradition and Revolution in Romantic Literature* (1971). A brilliant survey of romanticism across western European literature.

J. S. ALLEN, *Popular French Romanticism: Authors, Readers, and Books in the Nineteenth Century* (1981). Relates romanticism to popular culture.

F. C. BEISER, *Enlightenment, Revolution, and Romanticism: The Genesis of Modern German Political Thought, 1790–1800* (1992). The best recent study of the subject.

L. BERGERON, *France Under Napoleon* (1981). An in-depth examination of Napoleonic administration.

J. F. BERNARD, *Talleyrand: A Biography* (1973). A useful account.

E. CASSIRER, *Kant's Life and Thought* (1981). A brilliant work by one of the major philosophers of this century.

D. G. CHANDLER, *The Campaigns of Napoleon* (1966). A good military study.

D. G. CHARLTON, *New Images of the Natural in France* (1984). An examination of the changing attitude toward nature in France during the romantic era.

K. CLARK, *The Romantic Rebellion* (1973). A useful discussion that combines both art and literature.

O. CONNELLY, *Napoleon's Satellite Kingdoms* (1965). The rule of Napoleon and his family in Europe.

A. D. CULLER, *The Victorian Mirror of History* (1985).

Studies in the writing of the nineteenth century with emphasis on romantic influences.

J. ENGELL, *The Creative Imagination: Enlightenment to Romanticism* (1981). An important book on the role of the imagination in romantic literary theory.

M. GLOVER, *The Peninsular War, 1807–1814: A Concise Military History* (1974). An interesting account of the military campaign that so drained Napoleon's resources in western Europe.

F. W. J. HEMMINGS, *Culture and Society in France: 1789–1848* (1987). Discusses French romantic literature, theater, and art.

H. HONOUR, *Romanticism* (1979). The best introduction to the subject in terms of the fine arts.

G. N. IZENBERG, *Impossible Individuality: Romanticism, Revolution, and the Origins of Modern Selfhood, 1787–1802* (1992). Explores the concepts of individualism in Germany, England, and France.

H. KISSINGER, *A World Restored: Metternich, Castlereagh and the Problems of Peace, 1812–1822* (1957). A provocative study by an author who became an American Secretary of State.

S. KÖRNER, *Kant* (1955). A clear introduction to a difficult thinker.

M. LEBRIS, *Romantics and Romanticism* (1981). A lavishly illustrated work that relates politics and romantic art.

G. LEFEBVRE, *Napoleon*, 2 vols., trans. by H. Stockhold (1969). The fullest and finest biography.

F. MARKHAM, *Napoleon and the Awakening of Europe* (1954). Emphasizes the growth of nationalism.

H. NICOLSON, *The Congress of Vienna* (1946). A good, readable account.

Z. A. PELCZYNSKI, *The State and Civil Society: Studies in Hegel's Political Philosophy* (1984). An important series of essays.

R. PLANT, *Hegel: An Introduction* (1983). Emphasis on his political thought.

R. PORTER AND M. TEICH (EDS.), *Romanticism in National Context* (1988). Essays on the phenomenon of romanticism in the major European nations.

B. M. G. REARDON, *Religion in the Age of Romanticism: Studies in Early Nineteenth-Century Thought* (1985). The best introduction to this important subject.

P. W. SCHROEDER, *The Transformation of European Politics, 1763–1848* (1994). A major synthesis of the diplomatic history of the period emphasizing the new departures of the Congress of Vienna.

S. B. SMITH, *Hegel's Critique of Liberalism: Rights in Context* (1989). An excellent introduction to Hegelian political thought.

C. TAYLOR, *Hegel* (1975). The best one-volume introduction.

J. M. THOMPSON, *Napoleon Bonaparte: His Rise and Fall* (1952). A sound biography.

A. WALICKI, *Philosophy and Romantic Nationalism: The*

*Case of Poland* (1982). Examines how philosophy influenced the character of Polish nationalism.

W. R. WARD, *The Protestant Evangelical Awakening* (1992). Examines the religious revivals of the eighteenth and nineteenth century from a transatlantic perspective.

B. YACK, *The Longing for Total Revolution: Philosophic Sources of Social Discontent from Rousseau to Marx and Nietzsche* (1986). A major exploration of the political philosophy associated with romanticism.

T. ZIOLKOWSKI, *German Romanticism and Its Institutions* (1990). An exploration of how institutions of intellectual life influenced creative literature.

*In 1830 Revolution again erupted in France as well as elsewhere on the continent. Eugène Delacroix's "Liberty Leading the People" was the most famous image recalling that event. Note how he portrays persons from different social classes and occupations joining the revolution led by the figure of Liberty. [Erich Lessing/Art Resource]*

# The Conservative Order and the Challenges of Reform (1815–1832)

## K E Y   T O P I C S

- The challenge of nationalism and liberalism to the conservative order in the early nineteenth century
- The domestic and international politics of the conservative order from the Congress of Vienna through the 1820s
- The wars of independence in Latin America
- The revolutions of 1830 on the Continent and the passage of the Great Reform Bill in Britain

*The close of the Congress of Vienna was followed by a decade in which conservative political forces controlled virtually all of Europe. In the international arena these forces sought to maintain peace and to prevent the outbreak of war that would unleash destruction and disorder. They did so through unprecedented forms of cooperation and mutual consultation. Domestically they sought to maintain the authority of monarchies and aristocracies after the turmoil wrought by the French Revolution and Napoleon. Two sets of critics challenged this conservative order. Nationalists wished to see the map of Europe drawn according to the boundaries of nationalities or ethnic groups. Liberals sought moderate political reform and freer*

*economic markets. The goals of nationalists and liberals threatened the dominance of landed aristocracies and the rule of monarchs who governed by virtue of dynastic inheritance rather than nationality. Still another challenge to the status quo came from the efforts of Europe's Latin American colonies to gain independence.*

*For the first fifteen years after the Congress of Vienna, the forces of conservatism were successful except for their failure to retain control of Latin America. Late in the 1820s, however, the conservatives faced stronger challenges. Thereafter, certain major liberal goals were achieved when a revolution occurred in France in 1830 and a sweeping reform bill passed through the British Parlia-*

*ment in 1832. During the same period, however, Russia and other countries in eastern and central Europe continued to resist political and social change.*

# The Challenges of Nationalism and Liberalism

Observers have frequently regarded the nineteenth century as the great age of *isms*. Throughout the Western world, secular ideologies began to take hold of the learned and popular imaginations in opposition to the political and social status quo. These included nationalism, liberalism, republicanism, socialism, and communism. Earlier in this century, a noted historian called all such words "trouble-breeding and usually thought-obscuring terms."[1] They are just that, if one uses them as an excuse to avoid thinking or if one fails to see the variety of opinions concealed beneath each of them.

## *The Emergence of Nationalism*

Nationalism proved to be the single most powerful European political ideology of the nineteenth and early twentieth centuries. It has reasserted itself in present-day Europe following the collapse of Communist governments in Eastern Europe and in the former Soviet Union. As a political outlook, nationalism was and is based on the relatively modern concept that a nation is composed of people who are joined together by the bonds of common language, customs, culture, and history and who, because of those bonds, should be administered by the same government. That is to say, nationalists in the past and the present contend that political and ethnic boundaries should coincide. Political units had not been so defined or governed earlier in European history. The idea came into its own during the late eighteenth and the early nineteenth centuries.

OPPOSITION TO THE VIENNA SETTLEMENT  Early-nineteenth-century nationalism directly opposed the principle upheld at the Congress of Vienna that legitimate monarchies or dynasties, rather than ethnicity, provide the basis for political unity. Nationalists naturally protested multinational states such as the Austrian and Russian empires. They also objected to peoples of the same ethnic group, such as Germans and Italians, dwelling in political units smaller than that of the ethnic nation. Consequently, nationalists challenged both the domestic and the international order of the Vienna settlement.

Behind the concept of nationalism usually, though not always, lay the idea of popular sovereignty, since the qualities of peoples rather than rulers determine national character. But this aspect of nationalism frequently led to confusion or conflict because of the presence of minorities. Within many territories where one national group has predominated, there have also existed significant minority ethnic enclaves whom the majority has had every intention of governing with or without their consent. In some cases, a nationalistically conscious group would dominate in one section of a country, but people of the same ethnicity in another region would not have nationalistic aspirations. The former might then attempt to impose their aspirations on the latter.

CREATING NATIONS  In point of fact, it was nationalists who actually created nations in the nineteenth century. During the first half of the century, a particular group of nationalistically minded writers or other intellectual elite, usually small, using the printed word spread a nationalistic concept of the nation. They were frequently historians who chronicled a people's past or writers and literary scholars who established a national literature by collecting and publishing earlier writings in the people's language. In effect, they gave a people a sense of their past and a literature of their own. As time passed, schoolteachers, by imparting a nation's official language and history, played an important role in spreading nationalistic ideas. These small groups of early nationalists established the cultural beliefs and political expectations upon which the later mass-supported nationalism of the second half of the century would grow.

The language to be used in the schools and in government offices was always a point of contention for nationalists. In France and Italy, official versions of the national language were imposed in the schools and replaced local dialects. In parts of Scandinavia and eastern Europe, nationalists attempted to resurrect from earlier times what they regarded as purer versions of the national language. Often these resurrected languages were virtually invented by modern scholars or linguists. This process of establishing national languages led to far

[1]Arthur O. Lovejoy, *The Great Chain of Being: A Study in the History of an Idea* (New York: Harper Torchbooks, 1963), p. 6.

more linguistic uniformity in European nations than had existed prior to the nineteenth century. Yet even in 1850 perhaps less than half of the inhabitants of France spoke official French.

Language could become such an effective cornerstone in the foundation of nationalism thanks in large measure to the emergence of the print culture discussed in Chapter 18. The presence of large numbers of printed books, journals, magazines, and newspapers "fixed" language in a more permanent fashion than did the spoken word. This uniform language found in printed works could overcome regional spoken dialects and establish itself as dominant. In most countries, spoken and written proficiency in the official printed language became a path to social and political advancement. The growth of a uniform language helped to persuade people who had not thought of themselves as constituting a nation that they did so.

MEANING OF NATIONHOOD   Nationalists used a whole variety of arguments and metaphors to express what they meant by *nationhood*. Some argued that gathering, for example, Italians into a unified Italy or Germans into a unified Germany, thus eliminating the petty dynastic states that governed those regions, would promote economic and administrative efficiency. Adopting a tenet from political liberalism, certain nationalist writers suggested that nations determining their own destinies resembled individuals exploiting personal talents to determine their own careers. Some nationalists claimed that nations, like biological species in the natural world, were distinct creations of God. Other nationalists claimed a place for their nations in the divine order of things. Throughout the nineteenth century, for example, Polish nationalists portrayed Poland as the suffering Christ among nations, thus implicitly suggesting that Poland, like Christ, would experience resurrection and a new life.

A significant difficulty for nationalism was, and is, determining which ethnic groups could be considered nations, with claims to territory and political autonomy. In theory, any of them could, but in reality nationhood came to be associated with groups that were large enough to support a viable economy, that had a history of significant cultural association, that possessed a cultural elite that could nourish and spread the national language, and that had the capacity to conquer other peoples or to establish and protect their own independence. Throughout the century many smaller ethnic

groups claimed to fulfill these criteria but could not effectively achieve either independence or recognition. They could and did, however, create domestic unrest within the political units they inhabited.

REGIONS OF NATIONALISTIC PRESSURE   During the nineteenth century, nationalists challenged the political status quo in six major areas of Europe. England had brought Ireland under direct rule in 1800, allowing the Irish to elect members to the British Parliament in Westminster. Irish nationalists, however, wanted independence or at least larger measures of self-government. The "Irish problem," as it was called, would haunt British politics for the next two centuries. German nationalists sought political unity for all German-speaking peoples, challenging the multinational structure of the Austrian Empire and pitting Prussia and Austria against each other. Italian nationalists sought to unify Italian-speaking peoples on the Italian peninsula and to drive out the Austrians. Polish nationalists, targeting primarily their Russian rulers, struggled to restore Poland as an independent nation. In eastern Europe, a whole host of national groups, including Hungarians, Czechs, Slovenes, and others sought either independence or formal recognition within the Austrian Empire. Finally, in southeastern Europe on the Balkan peninsula and eastward, national groups, including Serbs, Greeks, Albanians, Romanians, and Bulgarians, sought independence from Ottoman and Russian control. Although there were never disturbances in all six areas at one time, any one of them could erupt into turmoil. In each area, nationalist activity ebbed and flowed. The dominant governments often thought they needed only to repress the activity or ride it out until stability returned. Over the course of the century, however, nationalists changed the political map and political culture of Europe.

## Early-Nineteenth-Century Political Liberalism

The word *liberal* as applied to political activity entered the European and American vocabulary during the nineteenth century. Its meaning has varied over time. Nineteenth-century European conservatives often regarded as *liberal* almost anyone or anything that challenged their own political, social, or religious values. For twentieth-century Americans the word *liberal* carries with it meanings and connotations that have little or noth-

# Mazzini Defines Nationality

*No political force in the nineteenth century was stronger than nationalism. It eventually replaced dynastic political loyalty with loyalty based on ethnic considerations. In this passage, written in 1835, the Italian nationalist and patriot Giuseppe Mazzini (1805–1872) explains his understanding of the concept. Note how he combines a generally democratic view of politics with a religious concept of the divine destiny of nations.*

✦ *What are the specific qualities of a people that Mazzini associates with nationalism? How and why does Mazzini relate nationalism to divine purposes? How does this view of nationality relate to the goals of liberal freedom?*

The essential characteristics of a nationality are common ideas, common principles and a common purpose. A nation is an association of those who are brought together by language, by given geographical conditions or by the role assigned them by history, who acknowledge the same principles and who march together to the conquest of a single definite goal under the rule of a uniform body of law.

The life of a nation consists in harmonious activity (that is, the employment of all individual abilities and energies comprised within the association) towards this single goal. . . .

But nationality means even more than this. Nationality also consists in the share of mankind's labors which God assigns to a people. This mission is the task which a people must perform to the end that the Divine Idea shall be realized in this world; it is the work which gives a people its rights as a member of Mankind; it is the baptismal rite which endows a people with its own character and its rank in the brotherhood of nations. . . .

Nationality depends for its very existence upon its sacredness within and beyond its borders.

If nationality is to be inviolable for all, friends and foes alike, it must be regarded inside a country as holy, like a religion, and outside a country as a grave mission. It is necessary too that the ideas arising within a country grow steadily, as part of the general law of Humanity which is the source of all nationality. It is necessary that these ideas be shown to other lands in their beauty and purity, free from any alien mixture, from any slavish fears, from any skeptical hesitancy, strong and active, embracing in their evolution every aspect and manifestation of the life of the nation. These ideas, a necessary component in the order of universal destiny, must retain their originality even as they enter harmoniously into mankind's general progress.

The people must be the basis of nationality; its logically derived and vigorously applied principles its means; the strength of all its strength; the improvement of the life of all and the happiness of the greatest possible number its results; and the accomplishment of the task assigned to it by God its goal. This is what we mean by nationality.

Herbert H. Rown, ed., From Absolutism to Revolution, 1648–1848, 2nd ed. (New York: Macmillan; London: Collier-Macmillan Limited, 1969), pp. 277, 280.

ing to do with its significance to nineteenth-century Europeans. European conservatives of the last century saw liberals as more radical than they actually were; present-day Americans often think of nineteenth-century liberals as more conservative than they were.

POLITICAL GOALS Nineteenth-century liberals derived their political ideas from the writers of the Enlightenment, the example of English liberties, and the so-called principles of 1789 embodied in the French Declaration of the Rights of Man and Citizen. They sought to establish a political framework of legal equality, religious toleration, and freedom of the press. Their general goal was a political structure that would limit the arbitrary power of government against the persons and property of individual citizens. They generally believed that the legitimacy of government emanated from the freely given consent of the governed. The popular basis of such government was to be expressed through elected representative, or parliamentary, bodies. Most important, free government required that state or crown ministers be responsible to the representatives rather than to the monarch. Liberals sought to achieve these political arrangements through the device of written constitutions. Their desire was to see constitutionalism and constitutional governments installed across the Continent.

These goals may seem very limited, and they were. Responsible constitutional government, however, existed nowhere in Europe in 1815. Even in Great Britain, the cabinet ministers were at least as responsible to the monarch as to the House of Commons. Conservatives were suspicious of written constitutions, associating them with the French Revolution and Napoleonic regimes. They also were certain that all necessary political wisdom could not be reduced to writing.

Those who espoused liberal political structures often were educated, wealthy people who were excluded in one manner or another from the existing political processes. Because of their wealth and education, they felt their exclusion was unjustified. Liberals were often academics, members of the learned professions, and people involved in the rapidly expanding commercial and manufacturing segments of the economy. They believed in and were products of the career open to talent. The monarchical and aristocratic regimes as restored after the Congress of Vienna often failed to recognize sufficiently their new status and to provide for their economic and professional interests.

Although liberals wanted broader political participation, they did not advocate democracy. What they wanted was to extend representation to the propertied classes. Second only to their hostility to the privileged aristocracies was their general con-

tempt for the lower, unpropertied classes. Liberals transformed the eighteenth-century concept of aristocratic liberty into a new concept of privilege based on wealth and property rather than birth. As the French liberal theorist Benjamin Constant (1767–1830) wrote in 1814:

Those whom poverty keeps in eternal dependence are no more enlightened on public affairs than children, nor are they more interested than foreigners in national prosperity, of which they do not understand the basis and of which they enjoy the advantages only indirectly. Property alone, by giving sufficient leisure, renders a man capable of exercising his political rights.[2]

By the middle of the century, this widely shared attitude meant that throughout Europe liberals had separated themselves from both the rural and the urban working class, a division that was to have important consequences.

ECONOMIC GOALS The economic goals of nineteenth-century liberals also served to divide them from working people. The manufacturers of Great Britain, the landed and manufacturing middle class of France, and the commercial interests of Germany and Italy, following the Enlightenment ideas of Adam Smith, sought the removal of the economic restraints associated with mercantilism or the regulated economies of enlightened absolutists. They wanted to manufacture and sell goods freely. To that end, they favored the removal of international tariffs and internal barriers to trade. Economic liberals opposed the old paternalistic legislation that established wages and labor practices by government regulation or by guild privileges. They saw labor as simply one more commodity to be bought and sold freely.

Liberals wanted an economic structure in which people were at liberty to use whatever talents and property they possessed to enrich themselves. Such a structure, they contended, would produce more goods and services for everyone at lower prices and provide the basis for material progress.

Because the social and political circumstances of various countries differed, the specific programs of liberals also differed. In Great Britain, the monarchy was already limited and most individual liberties had been secured. With reform, Parliament could provide more nearly representative government.

[2]Quoted in Frederick B. Artz, *Reaction and Revolution, 1814–1832* (New York: Harper, 1934), p. 94.

# Benjamin Constant Discusses the Character of Modern Liberty

*In 1819 the French liberal theorist Benjamin Constant (1767–1830) delivered lectures on the character of ancient and modern liberty. In the passage given here, he emphasizes the close relationship of modern liberty to economic freedom and a free private life. He then ties the desire for a free private life to the need for representative government.*

✦ *According to Constant, what are the specific ways in which a modern citizen is free of government control and interference? What is Constant's defense of representative government? On the basis of this passage, why do you believe that Constant was opposed to democratic government?*

[Modern liberty] is, for each individual, the right not to be subjected to anything but the law, not to be arrested, or detained, or put to death, or mistreated in any manner, as a result of the arbitrary will of one or several individuals. It is each man's right to express his opinions, to choose and exercise his profession, to dispose of his property and even abuse it, to come and go without obtaining permission and without having to give an account of either his motives or his itinerary. It is the right to associate with other individuals, either to confer about mutual interests or profess the cult that he and his associates prefer or simply to fill his days and hours in the manner most conforming to his inclinations and fantasies. Finally, it is each man's right to exert influence on the administration of government, either through the election of some or all of its public functionaries, or through remonstrances, petitions, and demands which authorities are more or less obliged to take into account. . . .

Just as the liberty we now require is distinct from that of the ancients, so this new liberty itself requires an organization different from that suitable for ancient liberty. For the latter, the more time and energy a man consecrated to the exercise of his political rights, the more free he believed himself to be. Given the type of liberty to which we are now susceptible, the more the exercise of our political rights leaves us time for our private interests, the more precious we find liberty to be. From this . . . stems the necessity of the representative system. The representative system is nothing else than an organization through which a nation unloads on several individuals what it cannot and will not do for itself. Poor men handle their own affairs; rich men hire managers. This is the story of ancient and modern nations. The representative system is the power of attorney given to certain men by the mass of the people who want their interests defended but who nevertheless do not always have the time to defend these interests themselves.

*Benjamin Constant, Ancient and Modern Liberty, as translated and quoted in Stephen Holmes, Benjamin Constant and the Making of Modern Liberalism (New Haven, Conn.: Yale University Press, 1984), pp. 66, 74.*

Links between land, commerce, and industry were in place. France likewise had many structures favored by liberals. The Napoleonic Code gave them a modern legal system. They could justify calls for greater rights by appealing to the widely accepted "principles of 1789." As in England, representatives of the different economic interests had worked together. The problem for liberals in both countries was to protect civil liberties, define the respective powers of the monarch and the elected representative body, and to expand the electorate moderately while avoiding democracy.

The complex political situation in German-speaking Europe was different from that in France or Britain, and German liberalism differed accordingly from its French and British counterparts. Monarchs and aristocrats offered stiffer resistance to liberal ideas, leaving German liberals less access to direct political influence. A distinct social divide separated the aristocratic landowning classes, which filled the bureaucracies and officer corps, from the small middle-class commercial and industrial interests. There was little or no precedent for middle-class participation in the government or the military and no strong tradition of civil or individual liberty. From the time of Martin Luther through Kant and Hegel, freedom in Germany had meant conformity to a higher moral law rather than participation in politics.

Most German liberals favored a united Germany and looked either to Austria or Prussia as the instrument of unification. As a result they were more tolerant of strong state and monarchical power than other liberals. They believed a freer social and political order would emerge once unification had been achieved. Unfortunately, the monarchies in Austria and Prussia refused to cooperate with these dreams of unification, leaving German liberals frustrated and forcing them to be satisfied with more modest achievements such as the lowering of internal trade barriers.

RELATIONSHIP OF NATIONALISM AND LIBERALISM Nationalism was not necessarily or even logically linked to liberalism. Indeed, many aspects of nationalism were directly opposed to liberal political values. Some nationalists wished their own particular ethnic group to dominate minority national or ethnic groups within a particular region. This was true of the Hungarian Magyars, who sought political control over non-Magyar peoples living within the historical boundaries of Hungary. Nationalists also often defined their own national group in opposition to other national groups whom they might regard as cultural inferiors or as historical enemies. This darker side of nationalism would emerge starkly in the second half of the nineteenth century and would poison European political life early and late in the twentieth century. Further-

more, conservative nationalists might seek political autonomy for their own ethnic group but would have no intention of establishing liberal political institutions thereafter.

Nonetheless, although liberalism and nationalism were not identical, they were often compatible. By espousing the cause of representative government, civil liberties, and economic freedom, nationalist groups in one country could gain the support of liberals elsewhere in Europe who might not otherwise share their nationalist interests. Many nationalists in Germany, Italy, and much of the Austrian Empire adopted this tactic. Some nationalists took other symbolic steps to arouse sympathy. Nationalists in Greece, for example, made Athens their capital because they believed it would associate their struggle for independence with ancient Athenian democracy, which English and French liberals revered.

# Conservative Governments: The Domestic Political Order

Despite the challenges of liberalism and nationalism, the domestic political order established by the restored conservative institutions of Europe, particularly in Great Britain and eastern Europe, showed remarkable staying power. Not until World War I did their power and pervasive influence come to an end.

## Conservative Outlooks

The major pillars of nineteenth-century conservatism were legitimate monarchies, landed aristocracies, and established churches. The institutions themselves were ancient, but the self-conscious alliance of throne, land, and altar was new. Throughout the eighteenth century, these groups had engaged in frequent conflict. Only the upheavals of the French Revolution and the Napoleonic era transformed them into natural, if sometimes, reluctant, allies. In that regard, conservatism as an articulated outlook and set of cooperating institutions was as new a feature on the political landscape as nationalism and liberalism.

The more theoretical political and religious ideas of the conservative classes were associated with romantic thinkers, such as Edmund Burke (see Chapter 19) and Friedrich Hegel (see Chapter 20).

Conservatives shared other, less formal attitudes forged by the revolutionary experience. The execution of Louis XVI at the hands of a radical democratic government convinced most monarchs that they could trust only aristocratic governments or governments of aristocrats in alliance with the wealthiest middle-class and professional people. The European aristocracies believed that their property and influence would rarely be safe under any form of genuinely representative government. All conservatives spurned the idea of a written constitution unless they were permitted to promulgate the document themselves. Even then, some could not be reconciled to the concept.

The churches were equally apprehensive of popular movements except their own revivals. The ecclesiastical leaders throughout the Continent regarded themselves as entrusted with the educational task of supporting the social and political status quo. They also feared and hated most of the ideas associated with the Enlightenment, because those rational concepts and reformist writings enshrined the critical spirit and undermined revealed religion.

Conservative aristocrats retained their former arrogance but not their former privileges or their old confidence. They saw themselves as surrounded by enemies and as standing permanently on the defensive against the forces of liberalism, nationalism, and popular sovereignty. They knew they could be toppled by political groups that hated them. They understood that revolution in one country could spill over into another.

All of the nations of Europe in the years immediately after 1815 confronted problems arising directly from their entering an era of peace after a quarter-century of armed conflict. The war effort with its loss of life and property and its necessity of organizing people and resources had distracted attention from other problems. The wartime footing had allowed all the belligerent governments to exercise firm control over their populations. War had fueled economies and had furnished vast areas of employment in armies, navies, military industries, and expanded agricultural activities. The onset of peace meant that citizens could raise new political demands and that there must be a major economic adjustment to peacetime economies. Soldiers and sailors came home and required nonmilitary employment. The vast demand of the military effort on other industries subsided and caused unemploy-

*Prince Clemens von Metternich (1773–1859) epitomized nineteenth-century conservatism. [Royal Library, Windsor Castle]*

ment. The young were no longer growing up in a climate of war and could turn their minds to other issues. For all of these reasons the conservative statesmen who led every major government in 1815 confronted new pressures that would cause various degrees of domestic unrest and that would lead them to use differing degrees of repressive action.

## Liberalism and Nationalism Resisted in Austria and the Germanies

The early-nineteenth-century statesman who more than any other epitomized conservatism was the Austrian prince Metternich (1773–1859). This devoted servant of the Habsburg emperor had been, along with Britain's Viscount Castlereagh (1769–1822), the chief architect of the Vienna settlement. It was he who seemed to exercise chief control over the forces of the European reaction.

DYNASTIC INTEGRITY OF HABSBURG EMPIRE The Austrian government could make no serious compromises with the new political forces in Europe. To no other country were the programs of liberalism and nationalism potentially more dangerous. Germans and Hungarians, as well as Poles, Czechs, Slovaks, Slovenes, and other ethnic groups, peopled the Habsburg domains. Through puppet governments Austria also dominated the Italian peninsula.

So far as Metternich and other Austrian officials were concerned, the recognition of the political rights and aspirations of any of the various national groups would mean the probable dissolution of the empire. If Austria permitted representative government, Metternich feared that the national groups would fight their battles internally at the probable cost of Austrian international influence.

Pursuit of dynastic integrity required Austrian domination of the newly formed German Confederation to prevent the formation of a German national state that might absorb the heart of the empire and exclude the other realms governed by the Habsburgs. The Congress of Vienna had created the German Confederation to replace the defunct Holy Roman Empire. It consisted of thirty-nine states under Austrian leadership. Each state remained more or less autonomous, but Austria was determined to prevent any movement toward constitutionalism in as many of them as possible.

DEFEAT OF PRUSSIAN REFORM  An important victory for this holding policy came in Prussia in the years immediately after the Congress of Vienna. In 1815 Frederick William III (r. 1797–1840), caught up in the exhilaration that followed the War of Liberation, as Germans called the last part of their conflict with Napoleon, had promised some mode of constitutional government. After stalling on keeping his pledge, he formally reneged on it in 1817. Instead, he created a new Council of State, which, although it improved administrative efficiency, was not constitutionally based.

In 1819 the king moved further from reform. After a major disagreement over the organization of the army, his chief reform-minded ministers resigned, to be replaced with hardened conservatives. On their advice, in 1823 Frederick William III established eight provincial estates, or diets. These bodies were dominated by the Junkers and exercised only an advisory function. The old bonds

*In the fall of 1817, students from across Germany gathered near Wartburg castle to celebrate their sense of national identity. Such events frightened conservative political forces in the German states. [Bildarchiv Preussischer Kulturbesitz]*

linking monarchy, army, and landholders in Prussia had been reestablished. The members of this alliance would oppose the threats posed by the aspirations of German nationalists to the conservative social and political order.

STUDENT NATIONALISM AND THE CARLSBAD DECREES
Three southern German states—Baden, Bavaria, and Württemberg—had received constitutions after 1815 as their monarchs tried to secure wider political support. None of these constitutions, however, recognized popular sovereignty, and all defined *political rights* as the gift of the monarch. In the minds and hearts of many young Germans, however, nationalist and liberal expectations fostered by the defeat of the French armies remained alive.

The most important of these groups was composed of university students who had grown up during the days of the reforms of Stein and Hardenberg and the initial circulation of the writings of Fichte and other German nationalists. Many of them or their friends had fought Napoleon. When they went to the universities, they continued to dream of a united Germany. They formed *Burschenschaften*, or student associations. Like student groups today, these clubs served numerous social functions, one of which was to sever old provincial loyalties and replace them with loyalty to the concept of a united German state. It should also be noted that these clubs were often anti-Semitic.

In 1817 in Jena, one such student club organized a large celebration for the fourth anniversary of the Battle of Leipzig and the tercentenary of Luther's Ninety-five Theses. There were bonfires, songs, and processions as more than 500 people gathered for the festivities. The event made German rulers uneasy, for it was known that some republicans were involved with the student clubs.

Two years later, *in March 1819, a young man named Karl Sand (d. 1820), a* Burschenschaft member, assassinated the conservative dramatist August von Kotzebue (1761–1819). Sand, who was tried, condemned, and publicly executed, became a martyr in the eyes of some nationalists. Although the assassin had acted alone, Metternich decided to use the incident to suppress the student clubs and other potential institutions of liberalism.

In July 1819, Metternich persuaded representatives of the major German states to issue the Carlsbad Decrees, which dissolved the *Burschenschaften*. The decrees also provided for university inspectors and press censors. The next year the German Confederation promulgated the Final Act, which limited the subjects that might be discussed in the constitutional chambers of Bavaria, Württemberg, and Baden. The measure also asserted the right of the monarchs to

In May, 1820, Karl Sand, a German student and a member of a Burschenschaft, *was executed for his murder of the conservative playwright August von Kotzebue the previous year. In the eyes of many young German nationalists, Sand was a political martyr.* [Bildarchiv Preussischer Kulturbesitz]

# Metternich Discusses Sources of Political Unrest

*Metternich was the chief minister of the Austrian emperor and the statesman who most opposed change in Europe after the Congress of Vienna. In 1819 he was attempting to suppress political activity in the universities. As he explained in this letter, he did not fear students as such but rather the later adults who during their student hays had been taught liberal political ideas. He also saw lawyers as a greater source of potential political unrest than professors.*

✦ *According to Metternich, what is the difference between people who conspire against things and those who conspire against theories? What is his fear of the role of universities as a source of revolutionary disturbance? Why does he conclude by saying the greatest danger at present is the press?*

That the students' folly declines or tunes to some other side than that of politics does not surprise me. This is in the nature of things. The student, taken in himself, is a child, and the *Burschenshaft* [student fraternity] is an unpractical puppetshow. Then, I have never . . . spoken of students, but all my aim has been directed at the professors. Now, the professors, singly or united, are most unsuited to be conspirators. People only conspire profitably against things, not against theories. . . . Where they are political, they must be supported by deed, and the deed is the overthrow of existing institutions. . . .

This is what learned men and professors cannot manage, and the class of lawyers is better suited to carry it on. I know hardly one learned man who knows the value of property; while, on the contrary, the lawyer class is always rummaging about in the property of others. Besides, the professors are, nearly without exception, given up to theory; while no people are more practical than lawyers.

Consequently, I have never feared that the revolution would be engendered by the universities; but that at them a whole generation of revolutionaries must be formed, unless the evil is restrained, seems to me certain. I hope that the most mischievous symptoms of the evil at the universities may be met, and that perhaps from its own peculiar sources, for the measures of the Government will contribute to this less than the weariness of the students, the weakness of the professors, and the different direction which the studies may take. . . .

The greatest and consequently the most urgent evil now is the press.

*Memoirs of Prince Metternich, vol. 3, trans. by Mrs. Napier (New York: Scribner: 1880–1881), pp. 286–288.*

---

resist demands of constitutionalists. For many years thereafter, the secret police of the various German states harassed potential dissidents. In the opinion of the princes, these included almost anyone who sought even moderate social or political change.

## Post-War Repression in Great Britain

The years 1819 and 1820 marked a high tide for conservative influence and repression in western as well as eastern Europe. After 1815 Great Britain experienced two years of poor harvests. At the same time, discharged sailors and soldiers and out-of-work industrial workers swelled the ranks of the unemployed.

LORD LIVERPOOL'S MINISTRY AND POPULAR UNREST
The Tory ministry of Lord Liverpool (1770–1828) was unprepared for these problems of postwar dislocation. Instead, it sought to protect the interests

of the landed and other wealthy classes. In 1815 Parliament passed a Corn Law to maintain high prices for domestically produced grain through import duties on foreign grain. The next year Parliament abolished the income tax paid by the wealthy and replaced it with excise or sales taxes on consumer goods paid by both the wealthy and the poor. These laws continued a legislative trend that marked the abandonment by the British ruling class of its traditional role of paternalistic protector of the poor. In 1799 Parliament had passed the Combination Acts, outlawing workers' organizations or unions. During the war, wage protection had been removed. And many in the taxpaying classes called for the abolition of the Poor Law that provided public relief for the destitute and unemployed.

In light of these policies and the postwar economic downturn, it is hardly surprising that the lower social orders began to doubt the wisdom of their rulers and to call for a reform of the political system. Mass meetings calling for the reform of Parliament were held. Reform clubs were organized. Radical newspapers, such as William Cobbett's *Political Registrar*, demanded political change. In the hungry, restive agricultural and industrial workers the government could see only images of conti-

nental *sans-culottes* crowds ready to hang aristocrats from the nearest lamppost. Government ministers regarded radical leaders, such as Cobbett (1763–1835), Major John Cartwright (1740–1824), and Henry "Orator" Hunt (1773–1835), as demagogues who were seducing the people away from allegiance to their natural leaders.

The government's answer to the discontent was repression. In December 1816, an unruly mass meeting took place at Spa Fields near London. This disturbance provided Parliament an excuse to pass the Coercion Act of March 1817. These measures temporarily suspended habeas corpus and extended existing laws against seditious gatherings.

"PETERLOO" AND THE SIX ACTS   This initial repression, in combination with improved harvests, brought calm for a time to the political landscape. By 1819, however, the people were restive again. In the industrial north, many well-organized mass meetings were held to demand the reform of Parliament. The radical reform campaign culminated on August 16, 1819, with a meeting in Manchester at Saint Peter's Fields. Royal troops and the local militia were on hand to ensure order. As the speeches were about to begin, a local magistrate

*In August, 1819, local troops dispersed a political rally in Manchester, killing a number of the participants. The event became known as the "Peterloo Massacre."* [Bildarchiv Preussischer Kulturbesitz]

The French Bourbons were restored to the throne in 1815 but would rule only until 1830. This picture shows Louis XVIII, seated, second from left, and his brother, the Count of Artois, who would become Charles X, standing on the left. Notice the bust of Henry IV in the background, placed there to associate the restored rulers with their popular late-sixteenth–early-seventeenth-century forebear. [Bildarchiv Preussischer Kulturbesitz]

ordered the militia to move into the audience. The result was panic and death. At least eleven people in the crowd were killed; scores were injured. The event became known as the "Peterloo Massacre," a phrase that drew a contemptuous comparison with the victory at Waterloo.

Peterloo had been the act of the local Manchester officials, whom the Liverpool ministry felt it must support. The cabinet also decided to act once and for all to end these troubles. Most of the radical leaders were arrested and taken out of circulation. In December 1819, a few months after the German Carlsbad Decrees, Parliament passed a series of laws called the *Six Acts*. These (1) forbade large unauthorized, public meetings, (2) raised the fines for seditious libel, (3) speeded up the trials of political agitators, (4) increased newspaper taxes, (5) prohibited the training of armed groups, and (6) allowed local officials to search homes in certain disturbed counties. In effect, the Six Acts attempted to remove the instruments of agitation from the hands of radical leaders and to provide the authorities with new powers.

Two months after the passage of the Six Acts, the Cato Street Conspiracy was unearthed. Under the guidance of a possibly demented figure named Thistlewood, a group of extreme radicals had plotted to blow up the entire British cabinet. The plot was foiled. The leaders were arrested and tried, and four of them were executed. Although little more than a half-baked plot, the conspiracy helped further to discredit the movement for parliamentary reform.

## Bourbon Restoration in France

The abdication of Napoleon in 1814 opened the way for a restoration of Bourbon rule in the homeland of the great revolution. The new king was the former count of Provence and a brother of Louis XVI. The son of the executed monarch had died in prison. Royalists had regarded the dead boy as Louis XVII, and so his uncle became Louis XVIII (r. 1814–1824). This fat, awkward man had become a political realist during his more than twenty years of exile. He understood that he could not govern if he attempted to turn back the clock. France had undergone too many irreversible changes. Consequently, Louis XVIII agreed to become a constitutional monarch, but under a constitution of his own making.

THE CHARTER  The constitution of the French restoration was the Charter. It provided for a hereditary monarchy and a bicameral legislature. The monarch appointed the upper house; the lower house, the Chamber of Deputies, was elected according to a very narrow franchise with a high property qualification. The Charter guaranteed most of the rights enumerated by the Declaration of the Rights of Man and Citizen. There was to be religious toleration, but Roman Catholicism was designated as the official religion of the nation. Most important for thousands of French people at all social levels who had profited from the revolution, the Charter promised not to challenge the property rights of the current owners of land that had been confiscated from aristocrats and the church. With this provision,

Louis XVIII hoped to reconcile to his regime those who had benefitted from the revolution.

ULTRAROYALISM    This moderate spirit did not penetrate deeply into the ranks of royalist supporters whose families had suffered at the hands of the revolution. Rallying around the count of Artois (1757–1836), those people who were more royalist than the monarch now demanded their revenge. In the months after Napoleon's final defeat at Waterloo, royalists in the south and west carried out a White Terror against former revolutionaries and supporters of the deposed emperor. The king could do little or nothing to halt this bloodbath. Similar extreme royalist sentiment could be found in the Chamber of Deputies. The ultraroyalist majority elected in 1816 proved so dangerously reactionary that the king soon dissolved the chamber. The majority returned by the second election was more moderate. Several years of political give-and-take followed with the king making mild accommodations to liberals.

In February 1820, however, the duke of Berri, son of Artois and heir to the throne after his father, was murdered by a lone assassin. The ultraroyalists persuaded Louis XVIII that the murder was the result of his ministers' cooperation with liberal politicians, and the king responded with repressive measures. Electoral laws were revised to give wealthy electors two votes. Press censorship was imposed,

*Tsar Alexander I (r. 1801–1825). A mild reformer when he succeeded to the throne, Alexander became increasingly reactionary after 1815. [The Bettmann Archive]*

and people suspected of dangerous political activity were made subject to easy arrest. By 1821 the government placed secondary education under the control of the Roman Catholic bishops.

All these actions revealed the basic contradiction of the French restoration. By the early 1820s, the veneer of constitutionalism had worn away. Liberals were being driven out of politics and into a near-illegal status.

## The Conservative International Order

At the Congress of Vienna, the major powers—Russia, Austria, Prussia, and Great Britain—had agreed to consult with each other from time to time on matters affecting Europe as a whole. Such con-

**The Period of Political Reaction**

| | |
|---|---|
| 1814 | French monarchy restored |
| 1815 | Russia, Austria, Prussia form Holy Alliance |
| 1815 | Russia, Austria, Prussia, and Britain renew Quadruple Alliance |
| 1818 | Congress of Aix-la-Chapelle |
| 1819 (July) | Carlsbad Decrees |
| 1819 (August 16) | Peterloo Massacre |
| 1819 (December) | Great Britain passes Six Acts |
| 1820 (January) | Spanish revolution |
| 1820 (October) | Congress of Troppau |
| 1821 (January) | Congress of Laibach |
| 1821 (February) | Greek revolution |
| 1822 | Congress of Verona |
| 1823 | France helps crush Spanish revolution |

sultation was one of the new departures in international relations achieved by the Congress. The vehicle for this consultation was a series of postwar congresses, or conferences. Later, as differences arose among the powers, the consultations became more informal. This new arrangement for resolving mutual foreign policy issues was known as the *Concert of Europe*. It prevented one nation from taking a major action in international affairs without the assent of the others. The initial goal of the Concert of Europe was to maintain the balance of power against new French aggression and against the military might of Russia. The Concert of Europe continued to function, however, on large and small issues until the third quarter of the century. Its goal—a novel one in European affairs—was to maintain the peace. In that respect, although the great powers sought to maintain conservative domestic governments, they were making genuinely new departures in regulating their international relations.

## The Congress System

In the years immediately following the Congress of Vienna the new congress system of mutual cooperation and consultation functioned well. The first congress took place in 1818 at Aix-la-Chapelle. As a result of this gathering, the four major powers removed their troops from France, which had paid its war reparations, and readmitted that nation to good standing among European nations. Despite unanimity on these decisions, the conference was not without friction. Tsar Alexander I (r. 1801–1825) suggested that the Quadruple Alliance (see Chapter 20) agree to uphold the borders and the existing governments of all European countries. Castlereagh, representing Britain, flatly rejected the proposal. He contended that the Quadruple Alliance was intended only to prevent future French aggression. These disagreements appeared somewhat academic until a series of revolutions began in southern Europe in 1820.

## The Spanish Revolution of 1820

When the Bourbon Ferdinand VII (r. 1814–1833) was placed on his throne following Napoleon's downfall, he had promised to govern according to a written constitution. Once securely in power, however,

he ignored his pledge, dissolved the *Cortes* (the parliament), and ruled alone. In 1820 a group of army officers, who were about to be sent to suppress revolution in Spain's Latin American colonies, rebelled. In March Ferdinand once again announced that he would abide by the provisions of the constitution. For the time being, the revolution had succeeded.

Almost at the same time, in July 1820, revolution erupted in Naples, where the king of the Two Sicilies quickly accepted a constitution. There were other, lesser revolts in Italy, but none of them succeeded.

These events frightened the ever nervous Metternich. Italian disturbances were especially troubling to him. Austria hoped to dominate the peninsula to provide a buffer against the spread of revolution on its own southern flank. The other powers were divided on the best course of action. Britain opposed joint intervention in either Italy or Spain. Metternich turned to Prussia and Russia, the other members of the Holy Alliance formed in 1815, for support. The three eastern powers, along with unofficial delegations from Britain and France, met at the Congress of Troppau in late October 1820. Led by Tsar Alexander, the members of the Holy Alliance issued the Protocol of Troppau. This declaration asserted that stable governments might intervene to restore order in countries experiencing revolution. Yet even Russia hesitated to authorize Austrian intervention in Italian affairs. That decision was finally reached in January 1821 at the Congress of Laibach. Shortly thereafter Austrian troops marched into Naples and restored the king of the Two Sicilies to nonconstitutional government. Thereafter, Metternich attempted to foster policies that would improve the efficient administration of the various Italian governments so as to give them more direct local support.

The final postwar congress took place in October 1822 at Verona. Its primary purpose was to resolve the situation in Spain. Once again Britain balked at joint action. Shortly before the meeting, Castlereagh had committed suicide. George Canning (1770–1827), the new foreign minister, was much less sympathetic to Metternich's goals. At Verona, Britain, in effect, withdrew from continental affairs. Austria, Prussia, and Russia agreed to support French intervention in Spain. In April 1823, the French army crossed the Pyrenees and within a few months brutally suppressed the Spanish revolution and established its temporary occupation of the country which ended in 1827.

What did *not* happen in Spain, however, was as important for the new international order as what did happen. The intervention had not been used as an excuse to aggrandize French power or territory. The same had been true of all the interventions under the Congress system. Despite the conservative intention of the various interventions from the standpoint of domestic politics, they did not represent decisions taken by the great powers to achieve territorial conquest but rather the maintenance of the international order established at Vienna. Such a situation stood in sharp contrast to the various alliances to invade or confiscate territory that had occurred among the European powers during the eighteenth century and the wars of the French Revolution and Napoleon. It was just this new mode of international restraint through the formal and informal consultation that prevented war until the middle of the century and a general European war until 1914. As one historian has commented, "The statesmen of the Vienna generation . . . did not so much fear war because they thought it would bring revolution as because they had learned from bitter experience that war *was* revolution."[3]

There was a second diplomatic result of the Congress of Verona and the Spanish intervention. George Canning was much more interested in the fate of British commerce and trade than Castlereagh had been. Thus Canning sought to prevent the politics of European reaction from being extended to Spain's colonies in Latin America, which were then in revolt (to be discussed later). He intended to exploit these South American revolutions to break the old Spanish trading monopoly with its colonies and gain access for Britain to Latin American trade. To that end, the British foreign minister supported the American Monroe Doctrine in 1823, prohibiting further colonization and intervention by European powers in the Americas. Britain soon recognized the Spanish colonies as independent states. Through the rest of the century, British commercial interests dominated Latin America. In this fashion, Canning may be said to have brought to a successful conclusion the War of Jenkins's Ear (1739).

[3]Paul W. Schroeder, *The Transformation of European Politics, 1763–1848* (Oxford: Clarendon Press, 1994), p. 802.

## The Greek Revolution of 1821

While the powers were plotting conservative interventions in Italy and Spain, a third Mediterranean revolt erupted, in Greece. The Greek revolution became one of the most famous of the century, because it attracted the support and participation of many illustrious literary figures. Liberals throughout Europe, who were seeing their own hopes crushed at home, imagined that the ancient Greek democracy was being reborn. Lord Byron went to fight in Greece and in 1824 died in the cause of Greek liberty. Philhellenic societies were founded in nearly every major country.

The Greeks were rebelling against the Ottoman Empire. The weakness of that empire troubled Europe throughout the nineteenth century, raising what was known as "the Eastern question": What should the European powers do about Ottoman inability to assure political and administrative stability in its holdings in and around the eastern Mediterranean? Most of the major powers had a keen interest in those territories. Russia and Austria coveted land in the Balkans. France and Britain were concerned with the empire's commerce and with control of key naval positions in the eastern Mediterranean. Also at issue was access for Christians to the shrines in the Holy Land. The goals of the great powers often conflicted with the desire for independence of the many national groups in the Ottoman Empire. But because the powers had little desire to strengthen the empire, they were often more sympathetic to nationalistic aspirations there than elsewhere in Europe.

These conflicting interests, as well as mutual distrust, prevented any direct intervention in Greek affairs for several years. Eventually, however, Britain, France, and Russia concluded that an independent Greece would benefit their strategic interests and would not threaten their domestic security. In 1827 they signed the Treaty of London, demanding Turkish recognition of Greek independence, and sent a joint fleet to support the Greek revolt. In 1828 Russia sent troops into the Ottoman holdings in what is today Romania, ultimately gaining control of that territory in 1829 with the Treaty of Adrianople. The treaty also stipulated that the Turks would allow Britain, France, and Russia to decide the future of Greece. In 1830 a second Treaty of London declared Greece an independent kingdom. Two years later, Otto I (r. 1832–1862), the son of the king of Bavaria, was chosen to be the first king of the new Greek royal dynasty.

## Serbian Independence

The year 1830 also saw the establishment of a second independent state on the Balkan peninsula. Since the late eighteenth century, Serbia had sought independence from the Ottoman Empire. During the Napoleonic wars its fate had been linked to Russian policy and Russian relations to the Ottoman Empire. Between 1804 and 1813, a remarkable leader, Karageorge (1762–1817), had led a guerilla war against the Ottoman authorities. This ultimately unsuccessful revolution helped build national self-identity and attracted the interest of the great powers.

In 1815 and 1816, a new leader, Milos (1780–1860), succeeded in negotiating greater administrative autonomy for some Serbian territory, but a majority of Serbs lived outside the borders of this new entity. In 1830 the Ottoman sultan formally granted independence to Serbia, and by the late 1830s the major powers had also extended it their recognition. The political structure of the new nation, however, remained in doubt for many years after 1830.

In 1833 Milos, now a hereditary prince, pressured the Ottoman authorities to extend the borders of Serbia, which they did. These new boundaries pertained until 1878. Serbian leaders continued to seek additional territory, however, creating tensions with Austria. The status of minorities, particularly Muslims, within Serbian territory, also created tensions.

Beginning in the mid-twenties, Russia became Serbia's formal protector, despite the Austrian territory that separated them. In 1856 Serbia came under the collective protection of the great powers, but the special relationship between Russia and Serbia would continue until the First World War and would play a decisive role in the outbreak of that conflict.

## The Wars of Independence in Latin America

The wars of the French Revolution and more particularly those of Napoleon sparked movements for independence from European domination throughout Latin America. In less than two decades, between 1804 and 1824, France was driven from Haiti, Portugal lost control of Brazil, and Spain was forced to withdraw from all of its American empire except Cuba and Puerto Rico. Three centuries of Iberian colonial government over the South American continent came to an end. (See Map 21–1.)

Haiti achieved independence in 1804, following a slave revolt that began in 1794 led by Toussaint L'Ouverture (1746–1803) and Jean-Jacques Dessalines (1758–1806). Haiti's revolution, which involved the popular uprising of a repressed social group, proved to be the great exception in the Latin American drive for liberty from European masters. Generally speaking, on the South American continent it was the Creole elite—merchants, landowners, and professional people of Spanish descent—who led the movements against Spain and Portugal. Very few Native Americans, blacks, mestizos, mulattos, or slaves became involved in or benefitted from the end of Iberian rule. Indeed, the example of the Haitian slave revolt haunted the Creoles,

*Toussaint L'Ouverture (1743–1803) began the revolt that led to Haitian independence in 1804. [Historical Pictures/Stock Montage, Inc.]*

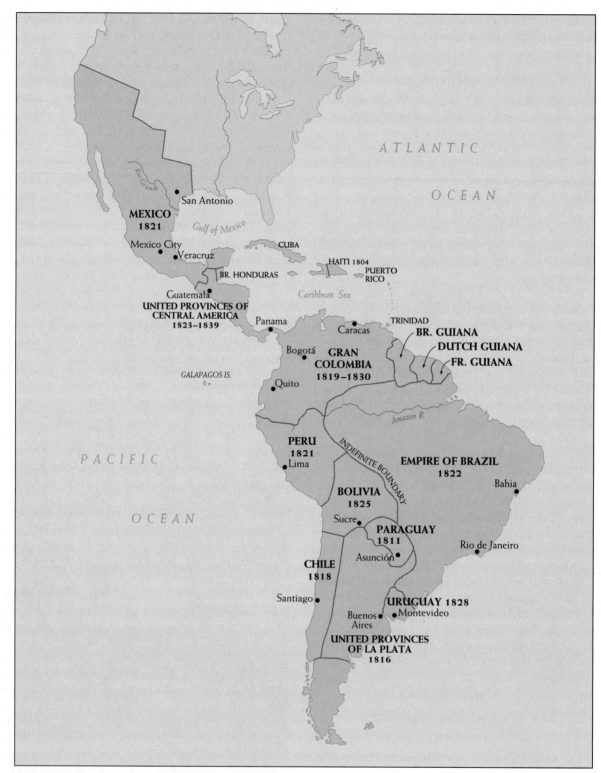

MAP 21–1   LATIN AMERICA IN 1830   *By 1830 Latin America had been liberated from European government. This map illustrates the early borders of the states of the region with the dates of their independence.*

as did the revolt of Indians in the Andes in 1780 and 1781. The Creoles were determined that any drive for political independence from Spain and Portugal should not cause social disruption or the loss of their existing social and economic privileges. In this respect, the Creole revolutionaries were not unlike American revolutionaries in the southern colonies who wanted to reject British rule but keep their slaves, or French revolutionaries who wanted to depose the king but not to extend liberty to the French working class.

CREOLE DISCONTENT  Creole discontent with Spanish colonial government had many sources. (The Brazilian situation will be discussed separately.) Latin American merchants wanted to trade more freely within the region and with North American and European markets. They wanted commercial regulations that would benefit them rather than Spain. They had also experienced increases in taxation by the Spanish crown.

Creoles were also deeply resentful of Spanish policies favoring *peninsulares*—whites born in Spain—for political patronage, including appointments in the colonial government, church, and army. The Creoles believed the *peninsulares* improperly secured all the best positions. Seen in this light, the royal patronage system represented another device with which Spain extracted wealth and income from America for its own people rather than its colonial subjects.

Creole leaders had read the Enlightenment *philosophes* and regarded their reforms as potentially beneficial to the region. They were also well aware of the events and the political philosophy of the American Revolution. Something more than reform programs and revolutionary example, however, was required to transform Creole discontent into revolt against the Spanish government. That transforming event occurred in Europe when Napoleon toppled the Portuguese monarchy in 1807 and the Spanish government in 1808 and then placed his own brother on the thrones of both countries. The Portuguese royal family fled to Brazil and established its government there. But the Bourbon monarchy of Spain stood, for the time being, wholly vanquished. That situation created an imperial political vacuum throughout Spanish Latin America and provided both the opportunity and the necessity for action by Creole leaders.

The Creole elite feared that a liberal Napoleonic monarchy in Spain would attempt to impose reforms in Latin America that would harm their economic and social interests. They also feared that a Spanish monarchy controlled by France would try to drain the region of the wealth and resources needed for Napoleon's wars. To protect their interests and to seize the opportunity to take over direction of their own political destiny, between 1808 and 1810 various Creole *juntas*, or political committees, claimed the right to govern different regions of Latin America. Many of them quite insincerely declared that they were ruling in the name of the deposed Spanish monarch Ferdinand VII. After the establishment of these local *juntas*, the Spanish would not again directly govern the continent; after ten years of politically and economically exhausting warfare, they were required to make Latin American independence permanent. The establishment of the *juntas* also ended the privileges of the *peninsulares*, whose welfare had always depended on the favors of the Spanish crown, and made positions in the government and army more easily available to Creoles.

SAN MARTÍN IN RÍO DE LA PLATA  The vast size of Latin America, its geographical barriers, its distinct regional differences, and the absence of an even marginally integrated economy meant there would be several different paths to independence. The first region to assert itself was the Río de la Plata, or modern Argentina. The center of revolt was Buenos Aires, whose citizens, as early as 1806, had fought off a British invasion against the Spanish commercial monopoly and thus had learned that they could look to themselves rather than Spain for effective political and military action. In 1810 the *junta* in Buenos Aires not only thrust off Spanish authority but also sent forces into both Paraguay and Uruguay in the cause of liberation from Spain and control by their own region. The armies were defeated, but Spanish control was nonetheless lost in the two areas. Paraguay asserted its own independence. Uruguay was eventually absorbed by Brazil.

The Buenos Aires government was not discouraged by these early defeats and remained determined to liberate Peru, the greatest stronghold of royalist power and loyalty on the continent. By 1814 José de San Martín (1778–1850) had become the leading general of the Río de la Plata forces. He organized a disciplined army and led his forces in a

*Simón Bolívar was the liberator of much of Latin America. He inclined toward a policy of political liberalism. [Bettmann/Hulton]*

daring march over the Andes Mountains. By early 1817, he had occupied Santiago in Chile, where the Chilean independence leader Bernardo O'Higgins (1778–1842) was established as supreme dictator. From Santiago, San Martín oversaw the construction and organization of a naval force that, in 1820, he employed to carry his army by sea to an assault on Peru. The next year, San Martín drove royalist forces from Lima and took for himself the title of Protector of Peru.

SIMÓN BOLÍVAR'S LIBERATION OF VENEZUELA   While the army of San Martín had been liberating the southern portion of the continent, Simón Bolívar (1783–1830) had been pursuing a similar task in the north. Bolívar had been involved in the organization of a liberating *junta* in Caracas, Venezuela, in 1810. He was a firm advocate of both independence and republican modes of government. Between 1811 and 1814, civil war broke out throughout Venezuela as both royalists, on one hand, and slaves and *llaneros* (Venezuelan cowboys), on the other, challenged the authority of the republican government. Bolívar had to go into exile first in Colombia and then in Jamaica. In 1816, with help from Haiti, he launched a new invasion against Venezuela. He first captured Bogotá, capital of New Granada (including

modern Colombia, Bolivia, and Ecuador), to secure a base for attack on Venezuela. The tactic worked. By the summer of 1821, Bolívar's forces had captured Caracas and he had been named president.

A year later, in July 1822, the armies of Bolívar and San Martín joined as they moved to liberate Quito. At a famous meeting of the two liberators in Guayaquil, a sharp disagreement occurred about the future political structure of Latin America. San Martín believed that monarchies were required; Bolívar maintained his republicanism. Not long after the meeting, San Martín quietly retired from public life and went into exile in Europe. Meanwhile, Bolívar purposefully allowed the political situation in Peru to fall into confusion, and in 1823 he sent in troops to establish his control. On December 9, 1824, at the Battle of Ayacucho, the Spanish royalist forces suffered a major defeat at the hands of the liberating army. The battle marked the conclusion of the Spanish effort to retain their American empire.

INDEPENDENCE IN NEW SPAIN   The drive for independence in New Spain, which included present-day Mexico as well as Texas, California, and the rest of the southwest United States, illustrates better than that in any other region the socially conservative outcome of the Latin American colonial revolutions. As elsewhere, a local governing *junta* was organized. Before it had undertaken any significant measures, however, a Creole priest, Miguel Hidalgo y Costilla (1753–1811), issued a call for rebellion to the Indians in his parish. They and other repressed groups of black and mestizo urban and rural workers responded. Father Hidalgo set forth a program of social change, including hints of changes in landholding. Soon he stood at the head of a loosely organized group of 80,000 followers, who captured several major cities and then marched on Mexico City. Hidalgo's forces and the royalist army that opposed them committed many atrocities. In July 1811, the revolutionary priest was captured and executed. Leadership of his movement then fell to José María Morelos y Pavón (1765–1815), a mestizo priest. Far more radical than Hidalgo, he called for an end to forced labor and for substantial land reforms. He was executed in 1815, ending five years of popular uprising.

The uprising and its demand for fundamental social reforms united all conservative political groups in Mexico, both Creole and Spanish. These groups were unwilling to undertake any kind of reform that might cause loss of their privileges. In 1820, however, they found their recently achieved security challenged from an unexpected source. As already explained, the revolution in Spain had forced Ferdinand VII to accept a liberal constitution. Conservative Mexicans feared that the new liberal monarchy would attempt to impose liberal reforms on Mexico. Therefore, for the most conservative of reasons, they rallied to a former royalist general, Augustín de Iturbide (1783–1824), who in 1821 declared Mexico independent of Spain. Shortly thereafter, Iturbide was declared emperor. His own regime did not last long, but an independent Mexico, governed by persons determined to resist any significant social reform, had been created.

BRAZILIAN INDEPENDENCE    Brazilian independence, in contrast to that of Spanish Latin America, came relatively simply and peacefully. As already noted, the Portuguese royal family, along with several thousand government officials and members of the court, took refuge in Brazil in 1807. Their arrival immediately transformed Rio de Janeiro into a court city. The prince regent João addressed many of the local complaints, equivalent to those of the Spanish Creoles, by, for example, taking measures that expanded trade. In 1815 he made Brazil a kingdom, which meant that it was no longer to be regarded merely as a colony of Portugal. This change was in many respects long overdue since Brazil was far larger and more prosperous than Portugal itself. Then, in 1820, a revolution occurred in Portugal, and its leaders demanded João's return to Lisbon. They also demanded the return of Brazil to colonial status. João, who had become João VI in 1816 (r. 1816–1826), returned to Portugal, but left his son Dom Pedro as regent in Brazil and encouraged him to be sympathetic to the political aspirations of the Brazilians. In September 1822, Dom Pedro embraced the cause of Brazilian independence against the recolonizing efforts of Portugal. By the end of the year, he had become emperor of an independent Brazil, which maintained an imperial form of government until 1889. Thus, in contrast to virtually all other nations of Latin America, Brazil achieved independence in a way that left no real dispute as to where the center of political authority lay.

Two other factors aided the peaceful transition to independence in Brazil. First, the political lead-

Father Miguel Hidalgo y Costilla (d. 1811) led an unsuccessful peasant revolt in 1810–1811 that marked the beginning of Mexico's struggle for independence. [Courtesy of the Organization of American States]

ers of Brazil were frightened by the destruction that had been unloosed in the Spanish American Empire by the wars of independence. They wanted to avoid that experience. Second, the political and social elite in Brazil had every intention of preserving slavery. The wars of independence elsewhere had generally led to the abolition of slavery or moved the independent states closer to abolition. Any attempt to gain independence from Portugal through warfare might have caused social as well as political turmoil that would open the slavery question.

CONSEQUENCES OF LATIN AMERICAN INDEPENDENCE
The era of the wars of independence left Latin America liberated from direct colonial control but economically exhausted and politically unstable. Only

Brazil prospered immediately. Independence there had come peacefully and resulted in the establishment of a clearly recognized political authority prepared to pursue policies desired by the economic elite. In contrast to Brazil, the new republics of the former Spanish Empire felt weak and vulnerable. Because the wars of independence had been largely civil wars, disaffected populations threatened all the new governments. Economic life contracted, and in 1830 overall production was lower than it had been in 1800. Mines had fallen into disrepair or had been flooded. Livestock had been confiscated or destroyed. There were few institutions to foster interregional trade or address the difficult terrain that impeded it. The disruption of old trade patterns reduced overseas trade. Funds for investment were scarce. Many wealthy *peninsulares* returned to Spain or went to Cuba. Consequently, Latin American governments and businesses looked to Britain for protection and for markets and capital investment.

MAP 21–2   CENTERS OF REVOLUTION, 1820–1831
*The conservative order imposed by the great powers in post-Napoleonic Europe was challenged by various uprisings and revolutions, beginning in 1820–1821 in Spain, Naples, and Greece, then later in the decade in Russia, Poland, France, and Belgium.*

# The Conservative Order Shaken in Europe

During the first half of the 1820s, the institutions of the restored conservative order had in general successfully resisted the forces of liberalism. The two exceptions to this success, the Greek Revolution and the Latin American wars of independence, both occurred on the periphery of the European world. Beginning in the middle of the 1820s, however, the conservative governments of Russia, France, and Great Britain faced new stirrings of political discontent. (See Map 21–2.) In Russia, the result was suppression; in France, revolution; and in Britain, accommodation.

## Russia: The Decembrist Revolt of 1825

Tsar Alexander I had come to the Russian throne in 1801 after a palace coup against his father, Tsar Paul (r. 1796–1801). After a brief flirtation with Enlightenment ideas, Alexander turned permanently away from reform. Both at home and abroad, he took the lead in suppressing liberalism and nationalism. There would be no significant challenge to tsarist autocracy until his death.

UNREST IN THE ARMY   As Russian forces drove Napoleon's army across Europe and then occupied defeated France, many Russian officers were exposed to the ideas of the French Revolution and the Enlightenment. Some of them, realizing how economically backward and politically stifled their own nation remained, developed reformist sympathies. Unable to express themselves openly because of Alexander's repressive policies, they formed secret societies. One of these, the Southern Society, was led by an officer named Pestel. It advocated representative government and the abolition of serfdom. Pestel himself even favored limited independence for Poland and democracy. Another secret society, the Northern Society, was more moderate. It favored constitutional monarchy and the abolition of serfdom but wanted protection for the interests of the aristocracy. Both societies were very small and often in conflict with each other. They agreed only that Russia's government must change. Sometime during 1825 they apparently decided to carry out a coup d'état in 1826.

DYNASTIC CRISIS   In late November 1825, Tsar Alexander I died unexpectedly. His death created two crises. The first was dynastic. Alexander had no direct heir. His brother Constantine, the next in line to the throne and at the time the commander of Russian forces in occupied Poland, had married a woman who was not of royal blood. He had thus

*When the Moscow regiment refused to swear allegiance to Nicholas, he ordered the cavalry and artillery to attack them. Although a total failure, the Decembrist Revolt came to symbolize the yearnings of all Russian liberals in the nineteenth century for a constitutional government. [Novosti/The Bridgeman Art Library]*

excluded himself from the throne and was more than willing to renounce any claim to it. Through a series of secret instructions made public only after his death, Alexander had named his younger brother, Nicholas (r. 1825–1855), as the new tsar.

Once Alexander was dead, the legality of these instructions became uncertain. Constantine acknowledged Nicholas as tsar, and Nicholas acknowledged Constantine. This family muddle continued for about three weeks, during which to the astonishment of all Europe Russia actually had no ruler. Then, during the early days of December, the army command reported to Nicholas the existence of a conspiracy among certain officers. Able to wait no longer for the working out of legal niceties, Nicholas had himself declared tsar, much to the delight of the by-now-exasperated Constantine.

The second crisis then proceeded to unfold. Several junior officers had indeed plotted to rally the troops under their command to the cause of reform. On December 26, 1825, the army was to take the oath of allegiance to Nicholas, who was less popular than Constantine and who was regarded as more conservative. Nearly all regiments took the oath. But the Moscow regiment, whose chief officers, surprisingly, were not secret society members, marched into the Senate Square in Saint Petersburg and refused to swear allegiance. Instead, they called for a constitution and the installation of Constantine as tsar. Attempts to settle the situation peacefully failed. Late in the afternoon, Nicholas ordered the cavalry and the artillery to attack the insurgents. More than sixty people were killed. Early in 1826 Nicholas himself presided over the commission that investigated the Decembrist Revolt and the secret army societies. Five of the plotters were executed and more than 100 others were exiled to Siberia.

Although the Decembrist Revolt completely failed, it was the first rebellion in modern Russian history whose instigators had had specific political goals. They wanted constitutional government and the abolition of serfdom. As the century passed, the Decembrists, in their political martyrdom, came to symbolize the yearnings of all the never very numerous Russian liberals.

THE AUTOCRACY OF NICHOLAS I    Although Nicholas was neither an ignorant nor a bigoted reactionary, he came to symbolize the most extreme form of nineteenth-century autocracy. Although he knew that economic growth and social improvement in Russia required reform, he was quite simply afraid of change. In 1842 he told his State Council, "There is no doubt that serfdom, in its present form, is a flagrant evil which everyone realizes, yet to attempt to remedy it now would be, of course, an evil more disastrous."[4] To remove serfdom would necessarily, in his view, have undermined the nobles' support of the tsar. So Nicholas turned his back on this and practically all other reforms. Literary and political censorship and a widespread system of secret police flourished throughout his reign. There was little attempt to forge even an efficient and honest administration. The only significant reform of his rule was a codification of Russian law, published in 1833.

OFFICIAL NATIONALITY    In place of reform, Nicholas and his closest advisers embraced a program called *Official Nationality*. Presiding over this program was Count S. S. Uvarov, minister of education from 1833 to 1849. Its slogan, published repeatedly in government documents, newspapers, journals, and schoolbooks, was "Orthodoxy, Autocracy, and Nationalism." The Russian Orthodox faith was to provide the basis for morality, education, and intellectual life. The church, which since the days of Peter the Great, had been an arm of the secular government, controlled the schools and universities. Young Russians were taught to accept their place in life and to spurn social mobility.

The program of autocracy championed the unrestrained power of the tsar as the only authority that could hold the vast expanse of Russia and its peoples together. Political writers stressed that only

[4]Quoted in Michael T. Florinsky, *Russia: A History and an Interpretation*, vol. 2 (New York: Macmillan, 1953), p. 755.

under the autocracy of Peter the Great, Catherine the Great, and Alexander I, had Russia prospered and exerted a major influence on world affairs.

Through the glorification of Russian nationality, Russians were urged to see their religion, language, and customs as a source of perennial wisdom that separated them from the moral corruption and political turmoil of the West. One result of this program was to leave serious Russian intellectuals profoundly alienated from the tsarist government.

REVOLT AND REPRESSION IN POLAND    Nicholas I was also extremely conservative in foreign affairs, as became apparent in Poland in the 1830s. Poland, which had been partitioned in the late eighteenth century and ceased to exist as an independent state, remained under Russian domination after the Congress of Vienna but was granted a constitutional government. Under this arrangement, the tsar was Poland's ruler. Both Alexander and Nicholas delegated their brother, the Grand Duke Constantine (1779–1831), to run Poland's government. Although both tsars frequently infringed on the constitution and quarreled with the Polish Diet, this arrangement held through the 1820s. Nevertheless, Polish nationalists continued to agitate for change.

In late November 1830, after news of the French and Belgian revolutions of that summer had reached Poland, a small insurrection of soldiers and students broke out in Warsaw. Disturbances soon spread throughout the rest of the country. On December 18, the Polish Diet declared the revolution to be a nationalist movement. Early the next month, the Diet voted to depose Nicholas as ruler of Poland. The tsar reacted by sending troops into the country and firmly suppressing the revolt. In February 1832, Nicholas issued the Organic Statute, declaring Poland to be an integral part of the Russian Empire. Although this statute guaranteed certain Polish liberties, these guarantees were systematically ignored. The Polish uprising had confirmed all the tsar's worst fears. Henceforth Russia and Nicholas became the *gendarme* of Europe, ever ready to provide troops to suppress liberal and nationalist movements.

## Revolution in France (1830)

The Polish revolt was the most distant of several disturbances that flowed from the overthrow of the Bourbon dynasty in France during July 1830. When

# Russia Reasserts Its Authority in Poland

*During 1830 Poland rebelled against Russian administration. The revolt failed after several months. Nicholas I then imposed even more direct and repressive control over Poland.*

✦ *In what variety of specific ways does this proclamation attempt to offend and repress Polish nationalism? What rights are given to the Poles? What evidence is there of any institutions being established to protect those rights? Is there anything in this proclamation aimed at gaining the support of some parts of the Polish population?*

Now that an end has been put by force of arms to the rebellion in Poland, and that the nation, led away by agitators, has returned to its duty, and is restored to tranquillity, we deem it right to carry into execution our plan with regard to the introduction of the new order of things, whereby the tranquillity and union of the two nations, which Providence has entrusted to our care, may be forever guarded against new attempts. . . . The kingdom of Poland, again subject to our sceptre, will regain tranquillity, and again flourish in the bosom of peace, restored to it under the auspices of a vigilant government. Hence we consider it one of our most sacred duties to watch with paternal care over the welfare of our faithful subjects, and to use every means in our power to prevent the recurrence of similar catastrophes, by taking from the ill-disposed the power of disturbing public tranquillity. . . .

Art. 1. The kingdom of Poland is forever to be reunited to the Russian empire and form an inseparable part of that empire. . . .

Art. 2. The Crown of the kingdom of Poland is hereditary in our person and in our heirs and successors, agreeably to the order of succession to the throne prescribed by all the Russians.

Art. 3. The Coronation of the Emperors of all the Russians and Kings of Poland shall be one and the same ceremonial which shall take place at Moscow, in the presence of a deputation from the kingdom of Poland, which shall assist at that solemnity with the deputies from the other parts of the empire. . . .

. . . .

Art. 5. The freedom of worship is guaranteed. . . . The Roman Catholic religion, being that of the majority of our Polish subjects, shall be the object of especial protection of the Government. . . .

. . . .

Art. 7. The protection of the laws is assured to all the inhabitants without distinction of rank or class. . . .

. . . .

Art. 13. Publication of sentiments by means of the press, shall be subjected to restrictions which will protect religion, the inviolability of superior authority, the interests of morals, and personal considerations. . . .

Art. 14. The kingdom of Poland shall proportionably contribute to the general expenditure and to the wants of the empire. . . .

. . . .

Art. 20. Our army in the empire and in the kingdom shall compose one in common, without distinction of Russian or Polish troops. . . .

Art. 21. Those of our subjects of the empire of Russia, who are established in the kingdom of Poland, who possess or shall possess, real property in that country, shall enjoy all the rights of natives. It shall be the same with those of our subjects in the kingdom of Poland, who shall establish themselves, and shall possess property, in the other provinces of the empire.

Published in Joseph Hordynaki, History of the Late Polish Revolution and the Events of the Campaign (Boston: Printed for Subscribers, 1833), pp. 424–428, as quoted in Alfred J. Bannan and Achilles Edelenyi, Documentary History of Eastern Europe (New York: Twayne Publishers, Inc., 1970), pp. 133–137.

Louis XVIII had died in 1824, his brother, the count of Artois, the leader of the ultraroyalist faction at the time of the restoration, succeeded him as Charles X (r. 1824–1830). The new king was a firm believer in rule by divine right.

THE REACTIONARY POLICIES OF CHARLES X   Charles X's first action was to have the Chamber of Deputies in 1824 and 1825 indemnify aristocrats who had lost their lands in the revolution. He did this by lowering the interest rates on government bonds to create a fund to pay an annual sum to the survivors of the *émigrés* who had forfeited land. Middle-class bondholders, who lost income, naturally resented this measure. In another action, Charles restored the rule of primogeniture, whereby only the eldest son of an aristocrat inherited the family domains. And, in support of the Roman Catholic Church, he enacted a law that punished sacrilege with imprisonment or death. Liberals disapproved of all of these measures.

In the elections of 1827 the liberals gained enough seats in the Chamber of Deputies to compel conciliatory actions from the king. He appointed a less conservative ministry. Laws against the press and those allowing the government to dominate education were eased. The liberals, however, wanted a genuinely constitutional regime and remained unsatisfied. In 1829 the king decided that his policy of accommodation had failed. He replaced his moderate ministry with an ultraroyalist ministry headed by the Prince de Polignac (1780–1847). The opposition, in desperation, opened negotiations with the liberal Orléanist branch of the royal family.

THE JULY REVOLUTION   In 1830 Charles X called for new elections, in which the liberals scored a stunning victory. Instead of accommodating the new Chamber of Deputies, the king and his ministers decided to attempt a royalist seizure of power. In June and July 1830, Polignac had sent a naval expedition against Algeria. Reports of its victory and the founding of a French empire in North Africa reached Paris on July 9. Taking advantage of the euphoria created by this victory, Charles X issued the Four Ordinances on July 25, 1830, staging what amounted to a royal coup d'état. These ordinances restricted freedom of the press, dissolved the recently elected Chamber of Deputies, restricted the franchise to the wealthiest people in the coun-

try, and called for new elections under the new royalist franchise.

The Four Ordinances provoked swift and decisive popular political reactions. Liberal newspapers called on the nation to reject the monarch's actions. The laboring populace of Paris, burdened since 1827 by an economic downturn, took to the streets and erected barricades. The king called out troops, and more than 1,800 people died during the ensuing battles in the city.

On August 2, Charles X abdicated and left France for exile in England. The Chamber of Deputies named a new ministry composed of constitutional monarchists. In an act that finally ended the Bourbon dynasty, it also proclaimed Louis Philippe (r. 1830–1848), the duke of Orléans, the new king of France.

In the Revolution of 1830, the liberals of the Chamber of Deputies had filled a power vacuum created by the popular Paris uprising and the failure of effective royal action. Had Charles X provided himself with sufficient troops in Paris, the outcome could have been quite different. Moreover, had the liberals, who favored constitutional monarchy, not acted quickly, the workers and shopkeepers of Paris might have attempted to form a republic. By seizing the moment, the middle class, the bureaucrats, and the moderate aristocratic liberals overthrew the restoration monarchy and still avoided a republic. These liberals feared a new popular revolution such as had swept France in 1792. They had no desire for another *sans-culottes* republic. A fundamental political and social tension thus underlay the new monarchy. The revolution had succeeded thanks to a temporary alliance between hard-pressed laborers and the prosperous middle class, but these two groups soon realized that their basic goals had been quite different.

MONARCHY UNDER LOUIS PHILIPPE   Politically the July Monarchy, as it was called, was more liberal than the restoration government. Louis Philippe was called the "king of the French" rather than "king of France." The tricolor flag of the revolution replaced the white flag of the Bourbons. The new constitution was regarded as a right of the people rather than as a concession of the monarch. Catholicism became the religion of *a majority of the people* rather than "the official religion." The new government was strongly anticlerical. Censorship was abolished. The franchise became some-

Ce Croquis ressemble à Louis Philippe?
vous Condamnerez doû!

Alors, il faudra Condamner celui là
qui ressemble au premier.

Puis Condamner pour cet autre
qui ressemble au second....

Et enfin, si vous étiez Conséquens,
vous ne sauriez absoudre Cette poire
qui ressemble aux Croquis précédens.

*Despite laws forbidding disrespect to the government, political cartoonists had a field day with Louis Philippe. Here, an artist emphasizes the king's resemblance to a pear and in the process attacks restraints on freedom of the press. [The Bettmann Archive]*

what wider but remained, on the whole, restricted. The king had to cooperate with the Chamber of Deputies; he could not dispense with laws on his own authority.

Socially, however, the Revolution of 1830 proved quite conservative. The hereditary peerage was abolished in 1831, but the everyday economic, political, and social influence of the landed oligarchy continued. Money was the path to power and influence in the government. There was much corruption.

Most important, the liberal monarchy displayed little or no sympathy for the lower and working classes. The Paris workers in 1830 had called for the protection of jobs, better wages, and the preservation of the traditional crafts rather than for the usual goals of political liberalism. The government of Louis Philippe ignored their demands and their plight. The laboring classes of Paris and the provincial cities seemed just one more possible source of disorder. In late 1831, troops suppressed a workers' revolt in Lyons. In July 1832, an uprising, which became known as the "July Days," occurred in Paris during the funeral of a popular Napoleonic general. Again the government called out troops,

and more than 800 people were killed or wounded. In 1834 a very large strike of silkworkers in Lyons was crushed. Such discontent might be smothered for a time, but without attention to the social and economic conditions creating it, new turmoil would eventually erupt.

### Belgium Becomes Independent (1830)

The July Days in Paris sent sparks to other political tinder on the Continent. The revolutionary fires first lighted in neighboring Belgium. The former Austrian Netherlands, Belgium, had been merged with the kingdom of Holland in 1815. The two countries differed in language, religion, and economy, however, and the Belgian upper classes never reconciled themselves to Dutch rule.

On August 25, 1830, disturbances broke out in Brussels following the performance of an opera about a rebellion in Naples against Spanish rule. To end the rioting, the municipal authorities and people from the propertied classes formed a provisional national government. When compromise between the Belgians and the Dutch failed, William of Holland (r. 1815–1840) sent troops and ships against Belgium. By November 10, 1830, the Dutch had been defeated. A national congress then wrote a liberal Belgian constitution, which was promulgated in 1831.

Although the major powers saw the revolution in Belgium as upsetting the boundaries established by the Congress of Vienna, they were not inclined to intervene to reverse it. Russia was preoccupied with the Polish revolt. Prussia and the other German states were suppressing small uprisings in their own domains. The Austrians were busy putting down disturbances in Italy. France under Louis Philippe favored an independent Belgium and hoped to dominate it. Britain felt that it could tolerate a liberal Belgium as long as it was free of foreign domination.

In December 1830, Lord Palmerston (1784–1865), the British foreign minister, gathered representatives of the powers in London. Through skillful negotiations he persuaded them to recognize Belgium as an independent and neutral state. In July 1831, Leopold of Saxe-Coburg (r. 1831–1865) became king of the Belgians. Belgian neutrality was guaranteed by the Convention of 1839 and remained an article of faith in European international relations for almost a century.

---

**Events Associated with Liberal Reform and Revolution**

| | |
|---|---|
| 1824 | Charles X becomes king of France |
| 1825 | Decembrist Revolt in Russia |
| 1828 | Repeal of restrictions against British Protestant Noncomformists |
| 1829 | Catholic Emancipation Act passed in Great Britain |
| 1830 (July 9) | News of French colonial conquest in Algeria reaches Paris |
| 1830 (July 25) | Charles X issues the Four Ordinances |
| 1830 (August 2) | Charles X abdicates; Louis Philippe proclaimed king |
| 1830 (August 25) | Belgian revolution |
| 1830 (November 29) | Polish revolution |
| 1832 | Organic Statute makes Poland an integral part of Russian Empire |
| 1832 | Great Reform Bill passed in Great Britain |

---

Both Belgium and Serbia gained independence in 1830, and ironically, diplomatic circumstances involving both led to World War I. The assassination of an Austrian archduke by a Serbian nationalist in Sarajevo triggered the war, and German violation of Belgian neutrality brought Britain into it.

## The Great Reform Bill in Britain (1832)

The revolutionary year of 1830 saw in Great Britain the election of a House of Commons that debated the first major bill to reform Parliament. The death of George IV (r. 1820–1830) and the accession of William IV (r. 1830–1837) required the calling of a Parliamentary election, held in the summer of 1830. Historians once believed that the July revolution in France influenced voting in Britain, but close analysis of the time and character of individual county and borough elections has shown otherwise. The passage of the Great Reform Bill, which became law in 1832, was the result of a series of events very different from those that occurred on the Continent. In Britain, the forces of conservatism and reform made accommodations with each other.

POLITICAL AND ECONOMIC REFORM    Several factors contributed to this spirit of accommodation. First, the commercial and industrial class was larger in Britain than in other countries. No matter what group might control the government, British prosperity required attention to their economic interests. Second, Britain's liberal Whig aristocrats, who regarded themselves as the protectors of constitutional liberty, represented a long tradition in favor of moderate reforms that would make revolutionary changes unnecessary. Early Whig sympathy for the French Revolution reduced their influence. After 1815, however, they reentered the political arena. Finally, British law, tradition, and public opinion all showed a strong respect for civil liberties.

In 1820, the year after the passage of the notorious Six Acts (discussed earlier), Lord Liverpool shrewdly moved to change his cabinet. The new members continued to favor generally conservative policies, but they also believed the government must accommodate itself to the changing social and economic life of the nation. They favored policies of greater economic freedom and repealed earlier Combination Acts that had prohibited labor organizations.

At the first meeting of the House of Commons following the passage of the Great Reform Bill, most seats were still filled by the gentry and the wealthy. But the elimination of "rotten boroughs" and the election of members from the new urban centers began to transform the House into a representative national body. [National Portrait Gallery, London]

CATHOLIC EMANCIPATION ACT   Economic considerations had generally led to these moderate reforms. English determination to maintain the union with Ireland brought about another key reform. England's relationship to Ireland was similar to that of Russia to Poland or Austria to its several national groups. In 1800, fearful that Irish nationalists might again rebel as they had in 1798 and perhaps turn Ireland into a base for a French invasion, William Pitt the Younger had persuaded Parliament to pass the Act of Union between Ireland and England. Ireland now sent 100 members to the House of Commons. Only Protestant Irishmen, however, could be elected to represent their overwhelmingly Roman Catholic nation.

During the 1820s, under the leadership of Daniel O'Connell (1775–1847), Irish nationalists organized the Catholic Association to agitate for Catholic emancipation. In 1828 O'Connell secured his own election to Parliament, where he could not legally take his seat. The British ministry of the duke of

Wellington realized that henceforth an entirely Catholic delegation might be elected from Ireland. If they were not seated, civil war might erupt across the Irish Sea. Consequently, in 1829 Wellington and Robert Peel steered the Catholic Emancipation Act through Parliament. Roman Catholics could now become members of Parliament. This measure, together with the repeal in 1828 of restrictions against Protestant nonconformists, ended the Anglican monopoly on British political life.

Catholic emancipation was a liberal measure passed for the conservative purpose of preserving order in Ireland. It included a provision raising the franchise in Ireland so that only the wealthier Irish could vote. Nonetheless, this measure alienated many of Wellington's Anglican Tory supporters in the House of Commons. The election of 1830 returned many supporters of parliamentary reform to Parliament. Even some Tories supported reform because they thought Catholic emancipation could have been passed only by a corrupt House of Com-

# Thomas Babington Macaulay Defends
## the Great Reform Bill

*Macaulay (1800–1859) was a member of the House of Commons, which passed the Great Reform Bill in 1831, only to have it rejected by the House of Lords before another measure was successfully enacted in 1832. His speeches in support of the bill reflect his views on the need for Parliament to give balanced representation to major elements in the population without embracing democracy. His arguments had wide appeal.*

✦ *Who does Macaulay think should be represented in Parliament? Why does he oppose universal suffrage? Why does he regard the Reform Bill as "a measure of conservation"?*

[The principle of the ministers] is plain, rational, and consistent. It is this,—to admit the middle class to a large and direct share in the Representation, without any violent shock to the institutions of our country. . . . I hold it to be clearly expedient, that in a country like this, the right of suffrage should depend on a pecuniary qualification. Every argument . . . which would induce me to oppose Universal Suffrage, induces me to support the measure which is now before us. I oppose Universal Suffrage, because I think that it would produce a destructive revolution. I support this measure, because I am sure that it is our best security against a revolution . . . I . . . do entertain great apprehension for the fate of my country. I do in my conscience believe, that unless this measure, or some similar measure, be speedily adopted, great and terrible calamities will befall us. Entertaining this opinion, I think myself bound to state it, not as a threat, but as a reason. I support this measure as a means of Reform: But I support it still more as a measure of conservation. That we may exclude those whom it is necessary to exclude, we must admit those whom it may be safe to admit. . . . All history is full of revolutions, produced by causes similar to those which are now operating in England. A portion of the community which had been of no account, expands and becomes strong. It demands a place in the system, suited, not to its former weakness, but to its present power. If this is granted, all is well. If this is refused, then comes the struggle between the young energy of one class, and the ancient privileges of another. . . . Such . . . is the struggle which the middle classes in England are maintaining against an aristocracy of mere locality.

Hansard's Parliamentary Debates, *3rd series, vol. 2, pp. 1191–1197.*

mons. The Tories, consequently, were badly divided, and the Wellington ministry soon fell. King William IV then turned to the leader of the Whigs, Earl Grey (1764–1845), to form a government.

LEGISLATING CHANGE  The Whig ministry soon presented the House of Commons with a major reform bill that had two broad goals. The first was to abolish "rotten boroughs," or boroughs that had very few voters, and to replace them with representatives for the previously unrepresented manufacturing districts and cities. Second, the number of voters in England and Wales was to be increased by about 50 percent through a series of new franchises. In 1831 the House of Commons narrowly defeated the bill. Grey called for a new election, in which a majority in favor of the bill was returned. The House of Commons passed the reform bill, but the House of Lords rejected it. Mass meetings were held throughout the country. Riots broke out in several cities.

Finally, William IV agreed to create enough new peers to give a third reform bill a majority in the House of Lords. Under this pressure the House of Lords yielded, and in 1832 the measure became law.

The Great Reform Bill expanded the size of the English electorate, but it was not a democratic measure. It increased the number of voters by more than 200,000, or almost 50 percent, but it kept a property qualification for the franchise. (Gender was also a qualification. No thought was given to enfranchising women.) Some members of the working class actually lost the right to vote because of the abolition of certain old franchise rights. New urban boroughs were created to allow the growing cities to have a voice in the House of Commons. Yet the passage of the reform act did not, as was once thought, constitute the triumph of middle-class interests in England. For every new urban electoral district a new rural district was also drawn, and the aristocracy was expected to dominate rural elections. What the bill permitted was a wider variety of property to be represented in the House of Commons.

The success of the reform bill was to reconcile previously unrepresented property owners and economic interests to the political institutions of the country. The act laid the groundwork for further orderly reforms of the church, municipal government, and commercial policy. By admitting into the political forum people who sought change and giving them access to the legislative process, it made revolution in Britain unnecessary. In this manner, Great Britain maintained its traditional institutions of government while allowing an increasingly diverse group of people to influence them.

◆

*Through the Congress System the major powers had responded to pressures on the Vienna Settlement without recourse to general warfare or territorial aggrandizement on the part of any state or collection of states. In the fifteen years between the conclusion of the Congress of Vienna and the Revolution of 1830 in France, with the exception only of the Greek revolution of 1821, no revolutionary disturbance had succeeded in Europe. In Russia,*
*the Decembrist Revolt of 1825 failed almost before it had begun. The only truly successful revolutionary activity during these years occurred in Latin America, where wars of independence ended Spain's centuries-old colonial domination.*

*Nonetheless, during the 1820s, liberal political ideas and some liberal political figures began to make inroads into the otherwise conservative domestic order. In 1830 revolution and reform again began to move across Europe. The French rejected the restored Bourbon monarchy and established a more liberal monarchy. Belgium also achieved independence with a liberal government. Perhaps most important, Great Britain moved slowly toward a more liberal position. During the 1820s, Great Britain had become unenthusiastic about a political role that placed it in opposition to all change. For its own commercial reasons, it favored independence for Latin America. Popular pressures at home led the British aristocratic leadership to enact a moderate reform bill in 1832. Thereafter, Britain would be viewed as the leading liberal state in Europe and one that would support nationalistic causes.*

## Review Questions

1. Define *nationalism*. What were the goals of nationalists? What were the difficulties they confronted in realizing those goals? Why was nationalism a special threat to the Austrian Empire? What areas saw significant nationalist movements between 1815 and 1830? Which were successful and which unsuccessful?

2. What were the tenets of *liberalism*? Who were the liberals and how did liberalism affect the political developments of the early nineteenth century? What relationship does liberalism have to nationalism?

3. What difficulties did the conservatives in Austria, Prussia, and Russia face in the years after the Napoleonic wars? How did they respond on both national and international levels? What were the aims of the Concert of Europe? How did international relations after the Congress of Vienna differ from the international relations of the eighteenth century?

4. What political changes took place in Latin America in the twenty years between 1804 and 1824? What were the main reasons for Creole discontent with Spanish rule and to what extent

were the Creole leaders influenced by Enlightenment political philosophy? Who were some of the primary leaders of Latin American independence and why were they successful?

5. Describe the constitution of the restored monarchy in France. Was the government truly constitutional? What did Charles X hope to accomplish? How much support did he have? What were the causes of the revolution of 1830? What did this revolution achieve, and at what cost?

6. Before 1820, Britain appeared to be moving down the same reactionary road as the other major powers. What factors led to a different outcome in Britain? What was the purpose of the Great Reform Bill? What did it achieve? Would you call it a "revolutionary" document?

# Suggested Readings

P. ALTER, *Nationalism* (1985). A useful brief introduction.

B. ANDERSON, *Imagined Communities*, rev. ed. (1991). A discussion of the forces that have fostered national identity.

M. BERDAHL, *The Politics of the Prussian Nobility: The Development of a Conservative Ideology, 1770–1848* (1988). A major examination of German conservative outlooks.

G. DE BERTIER DE SAUVIGNY, *Metternich and His Times* (1962). Sympathetic, but not uncritical, study of the forces of political conservatism.

G. DE BERTIER DE SAUVIGNY, *The Bourbon Restoration* (trans., 1966). Same as above.

R. J. BEZUCHA, *The Lyon Uprising of 1834: Social and Political Conflict in the Early July Monarchy* (1974). An excellent discussion of the tensions in France after the Revolution of 1830.

A. BRIGGS, *The Making of Modern England* (1959). Remains the best survey of English history during the first half of the nineteenth century.

M. BROCK, *The Great Reform Act* (1974). The standard work.

G. A. CRAIG, *The Politics of the Prussian Army, 1640–1945* (1955). A splendid study of the conservative political influence of the army on Prussian development.

D. DAKIN, *The Struggle for Greek Independence* (1973). An excellent explanation of the intricacies of the Greek independence question.

E. GELLNER, *Nations and Nationalism* (1983). A major theoretical work.

R. GILDEA, *Barricades and Borders: Europe 1800–1914* (1987). A useful survey.

L. GREENFELD, *Nationalism: Five Roads to Modernity* (1992). A major comparative study.

E. HALÉVY, *England in 1815* (1913). One of the most important and influential books written on nineteenth-century Britain.

E. J. HOBSBAWM, *The Age of Revolution, 1789–1848* (1962). A comprehensive survey emphasizing the social ramifications of the liberal democratic and industrial revolutions.

E. J. HOBSBAWM, *Nations and Nationalism since 1780: Programme, Myth, Reality*, rev. ed. (1992). The best recent introduction to the subject.

S. HOLMES, *Benjamin Constant and the Making of Modern Liberalism* (1984). An outstanding study of a major liberal theorist.

A. JARDIN AND A. J. TUDESQ, *Restoration and Reaction, 1815–1848* (1984). Surveys this period in France.

B. JELAVICH, *Russia's Balkan Entanglements, 1899–1914* (1991). Now the standard discussion of this topic.

C. JELAVICH AND B. JELAVICH, *The Establishment of the Balkan National States, 1804–1920* (1977). A standard, clear introduction.

W. B. KAUFMANN, *British Policy and the Independence of Latin America, 1802–1828* (1951). A standard discussion of an important relationship.

W. B. LINCOLN, *Nicholas I: Emperor and Autocrat of All the Russians* (1978). A serious scholarly treatment.

J. LYNCH, *The Spanish American Revolutions, 1808–1826* (1973). An excellent one-volume treatment.

C. A. MACARTNEY, *The Habsburg Empire, 1790–1918* (1971). An outstanding survey.

P. MANENT, *An Intellectual History of Liberalism* (1994). A penetrating, succinct study.

A. PALMER, *Alexander I: Tsar of War and Peace* (1974). An interesting biography that captures much of the mysterious personality of this ruler.

P. PILBEAM, *The 1830 Revolution in France* (1991). An account that emphasizes the restoration accommodation to various interest groups.

D. H. PINKNEY, *The French Revolution of 1830* (1972). The best account in English.

M. RAEFF, *The Decembrist Movement* (1966). An examination of the unsuccessful uprising, with documents.

N. V. RIASANOVSKY, *Nicholas I and Official Nationality in Russia, 1825–1855* (1959). A lucid discussion of the conservative ideology that made Russia the major opponent of liberalism.

C. A. RUUD, *Fighting Words: Imperial Censorship and the Russian Press, 1804–1906* (1982). Examines the government attempt to shape and control public opinion.

J. SHEEHAN, *German History, 1770–1866* (1989). A very long work that is now the best available survey of the subject.

C. TILLY, *Popular Contention in Great Britain, 1758–1834* (1995). A major study by one of the chief scholars of popular uprisings.

A. B. ULAM, *Russia's Failed Revolutionaries* (1981). Contains a useful discussion of the Decembrists as a background for other nineteenth-century Russian revolutionary activity.

P. S. WANDYCZ, *The Lands of Partitioned Poland, 1795–1918* (1974). The best study of Poland during the nineteenth century.

I. WOLOCH, *The New Regime: Transformations of the French Civic Order, 1789–1820s* (1994). An important overview of just what had and had not changed in France after the quarter-century of revolution and war.

# The West & the World

## THE ABOLITION OF SLAVERY IN THE TRANSATLANTIC ECONOMY

One of the most important developments during the age of Enlightenment and Revolution was the opening of a crusade to abolish chattel slavery in the transatlantic economy. The antislavery movement constituted the greatest and most extensive achievement of liberal reformers during the eighteenth and nineteenth centuries. Indeed, it marked the first time in the history of the world that a society actually tried to abolish slavery. This achievement came as the result of the impact of Christian ethics, Enlightenment ideals, slave revolts, revolutionary wars in America and Europe, civil war in the United States, and economic dislocation in the slave economies themselves. In 1750 almost no one seriously questioned the existence of slavery, but by 1888 the institution no longer existed in the transatlantic economy.

Chattel slavery—the ownership of one human being by another—had existed in the West as well as elsewhere in the world since ancient times and had received intellectual and religious justification throughout the history of the West. Both Plato and Aristotle provided arguments for slavery based on the assertion that persons in bondage were intended by nature to be slaves. Christian writers similarly accommodated themselves to the institution. They contended that the most harmful form of slavery was the enslavement of the soul to sin rather than the enslavement of the physical body. They also argued that genuine freedom was realized through one's relationship to God and that problems relating to the injustices of inequality would be solved in the hereafter. Christian scholastic thinkers in the Middle Ages had portrayed slavery as part of the natural and necessary hierarchy of the universe.

**Slavery Spreads to the Americas.** Although a vast slave trade existed throughout the Mediterranean world through the end of the Middle Ages, slavery was no longer a dominant institution on the European continent or within the European economy. The European encounter with America at the end of the fifteenth century radically transformed that situation. The American continent and the West Indies presented opportunities for achieving great wealth, but a major labor shortage existed in these regions. Eventually slavery provided the means to resolve this labor shortage.

The establishment and maintenance of slavery in the transatlantic economy drew Europeans and Americans into various relationships with Africa. About the same time as the encounter with America, Europeans made contact with areas of West Africa where slavery already existed. This region became the chief source of slaves imported into the Americas. Four centuries later, during the antislavery movement, Europeans would seek to change the African economy by ending its dependence on the slave trade. Those efforts led to the penetration of Africa by European traders, missionaries, and finally colonial forces and administrators.

Although at one time or another slaves labored throughout the Americas, the system of slavery became primarily identified with the plantation economy stretching from Maryland south to Brazil, where tropical products, initially primarily sugar, were produced by slave labor. This plantation economy existed from approximately the late sixteenth through the late nineteenth century. The slaves upon whose labor this economy was based included Native Americans enslaved within both the Spanish Empire and North America, and Africans forcibly imported into the Americas. Consequently, the slaves were virtually always of a different race from their masters. Race itself soon became part of the justification for the social hierarchy of the plantation world.

In and of itself the fact of slavery in the Americas was not unusual to the Western experience or to that of other societies in Africa or Asia. Slavery had existed at most times and places in human history. Far more unusual in the history of the West and for that matter in the experience of all other societies that had held and continued to hold slaves was the emergence after 1760 of an international movement to abolish chattel slavery in the transatlantic economy.

**The Crusade Against Slavery.** The eighteenth-century crusade against slavery originated in a profound change in the religious and intellectual outlooks on slavery among small but influential groups in both America and Europe. The entire thrust of Enlightenment reasoning to the extent that it challenged or questioned the wisdom of existing institutions gnawed away at the older defenses of slavery, most particularly the concept of an unchanging social hierarchy. Although some writers associated with the Enlightenment, including John Locke, were reluctant to question slavery and even defended it, the general Enlightenment rhetoric of equality stood in sharp contrast to the radical inequality of slavery. Montesquieu sharply satirized

After 1807 the British Royal Navy patrolled the West African coast attempting to intercept slave-trading ships. In 1846 the British ship HMS Albatross captured a Spanish slave ship, the Albanoz and freed the slaves. A British officer depicted the appalling conditions in the slavehold in this watercolor. [The Granger Collection]

slavery in *The Spirit of the Laws* (1748). Similarly, the emphasis of Adam Smith in *The Wealth of Nations* (1776) on free labor and efficiency of free markets undermined defenses of slavery.

Within much eighteenth-century literature there emerged a tendency to idealize primitive peoples living in cultures very different from those of Europe. Previously such peoples had been regarded as backward and rebellious. Now numerous writers portrayed them as embodying a lost human virtue. This expanding body of literature transformed the way many people thought about slavery and allowed some Europeans to look upon African slaves in the Americas as having been betrayed and robbed of an original innocence. Additionally, much eighteenth-century European ethical thinking, as well as later romantic poetry, emphasized empathy and feeling. In such a climate, attitudes toward slavery were transformed. Once considered to be the natural and deserved result of some deficiency in slaves themselves, slavery now grew to be regarded as undeserved and unacceptable. The same kind of ethical thinking led reformers to believe that by working against slavery, for virtually the first time defined as an unmitigated evil, they would realize their own highest ethical character.

Religious movements became the single most important cultural force to foster the antislavery crusade. The evangelical religious revival associated with Methodism and with other forms of Protestant preaching emphasized the conversion experience and the change of heart as a sign of having received salvation. In 1774 John Wesley, the founder of Methodism, attacked slaveholding in *Thoughts on Slavery*. Turning against slaveholding and slave trading by plantation owners and slave traders served to illustrate one clear example of such a change of heart. Some slave-holders and slave traders feared they might be endangering their own salvation by their association with the institution. John Newton, a former slave trader who underwent an evangelical conversion, wrote the hymn "Amazing Grace."

The initial religious protest against slavery originated among English Quakers, a radical Protestant religious group founded by George Fox in the seventeenth century. By the early eighteenth century it had solidified itself into a small but relatively wealthy sect in England. Members of Quaker congregations at that time actually owned slaves in the West Indies and participated in the transatlantic slave trade. During the Seven Years' War (1756–1763), however, many Quakers experienced economic hardship. Furthermore, the war created other difficulties for the English population as a whole. Certain Quakers decided the presence of the evil of slavery in the world explained these troubles. They then sought to remove this evil from their own lives and that of their congregations and began to take action against the whole system of slavery that characterized the transatlantic economy.

Just as the slave system was a transatlantic affair, so was the crusade against it. Quakers in both Philadelphia and England soon moved against the institution. The most influential of the early antislavery writers was Anthony Benezet, a Philadelphia Quaker, whose most important publications were *Some Considerations on the Keeping of Negroes* (1754) and *A Short Account of That Part of Africa Inhabited by the Negroes* (1762). The latter work emphasized the manner in which the slave trade degraded African society itself. Benezet also drew heavily upon Montesquieu. This may not be surprising because Enlightenment writers often admired the English Quakers as exemplifying a religion of tolerance and reason.

By the earliest stages of the American Revolution a small group of reformers, normally spearheaded by Quakers, had established an antislavery network. They published pamphlets, sermons, and books on the subject. The Society for the Relief of Free Negroes Illegally Held in Bondage, the first antislavery society in the world, was founded in Philadelphia in 1775 and when reorganized in 1784 as the Pennsylvania Abolition Society, Benjamin Franklin became its president.

In 1787 the Committee for the Abolition of the Slave Trade was organized in England. In France the *Société des Amis des Noirs* was founded in 1778.

The turmoil of the American Revolution and the founding of the American republic gave these groups the occasion for some of their earliest successes. Emancipation gradually, but nonetheless steadily, spread among the northern states. In 1787 the Continental Congress forbade the presence of slavery in the newly organized Northwest Territory north of the Ohio River. What is important so far as the crusade against slavery is concerned is the disappearance of slavery in approximately half of the new nation and the commitment not to extend it to an important new territory.

Despite these American developments, Great Britain became and remained the center for the antislavery movement. In 1772 a decision by the chief justice affirmed that slaves brought into Great Britain could not forcibly be removed. The decision, though of less immediate importance than some thought at the time, gave further impetus to the small but growing group of antislavery reformers.

During the early 1780s the antislavery reformers in Great Britain decided to work toward ending the slave trade rather than the institution of slavery. The horrors of the slave trade caught the public's attention in 1783 when the captain of the slave ship *Zong* threw more than 130 slaves overboard in order to collect insurance. For the reformers, attacking the trade rather than the institution appeared a less radical and a more achievable reform. To many , the slave trade appeared a more obvious crime than the holding of slaves which seemed a more nearly passive act. Furthermore attacking slavery itself involved serious issues of property rights which might alienate potential supporters of the abolition of the slave trade. The antislavery groups also believed that if the trade were ended, planters would have to treat their remaining slaves more humanely.

By the end of the 1780s the English Quakers were joined by evangelical Christians from the Church of England to form the Society for the Abolition of the Slave Trade. The most famous of the new leaders was William Wilberforce who, for the rest of his life, fought the slave trade. Year after year he introduced a bill to abolish the slave trade. Finally in 1807 he saw it passed.

*The Slave Revolt on the French Island of St. Dominique achieved the largest emancipation of slaves in the eighteenth century. In this print Toussant-L'Ouverture leads that revolt. [Corbis/Bettmann]*

**Slave Revolts.** While the British reformers worked for the abolition of the slave trade, slaves themselves in certain areas took matters into their own hands. The largest emancipation of slaves to occur in the eighteenth century came on the island of Saint Domingue (Haiti), France's wealthiest colony, as a result of the slave revolt of 1794 led by Toussaint L'Ouverture and Jean-Jacques Dessalines. The revolt in Haiti and Haiti's eventual independence in 1804 stood as a warning to slave owners throughout the West Indies. There would be other slave revolts such as those in Virginia led by Gabriel Prosser in 1800 and by Nat Turner in 1831, in South Carolina led by Denmark Vesey in 1822, in British controlled Demarra in 1823 and 1824 and in Jamaica in 1831. Each of these was brutally suppressed.

**Economic Pressures.** Through the conclusion of the Seven Years' War the West Indies interest group had been one of the most powerful in the British Parliament. During the second half of the eighteenth century and beyond, new and different economic interest groups began to displace the influence of that group. Within the West Indies themselves the planters were experiencing soil exhaustion and new competition from newly tilled islands controlled by France and other new islands opened for sugar cultivation. Some older plantations were being abandoned while others operated with low profitability. Now with the new islands under cultivation there was a glut of sugar on the market, and as a consequence the price was falling.

Under these conditions some British West Indies planters, for reasons that had nothing to do with religion or humanitarianism, began to favor curtailing that slave trade. Without new slaves, French planters would lack the labor they needed to exploit their islands. During the Napoleonic Wars, the British captured a number of the valuable French islands. In order to protect the planters on the older British West Indies islands, in 1805 the British cabinet issued Orders in Council, which forbade the importation of slaves into the newly acquired French islands. By 1807 the abolition sentiment was strong enough for Parliament to pass Wilberforce's measure prohibiting slave trading from any British port.

The suppression of this trade through the navy became one of the fundamental pillars of nineteenth-century British foreign policy. Throughout the rest of the Napoleonic era the British attempted to draw allies into a policy of forbidding the slave trade. They also attempted unsuccessfully to incorporate the abolition of the slave trade into the settlement of the Congress of Vienna. In addition, the British navy maintained squadrons of ships around the coast of West Africa to halt slave traders. Although the French and Americans also patrolled the West African coast, neither was deeply committed to ending the slave trade. Nonetheless, in 1824 the American Congress had made slave trading a capital offense.

The French invasion of Spain in 1808, as discussed in Chapter 21, provided the spark for the Latin American wars of independence. The leaders of these movements had been influenced by the liberal ideas of the Enlightenment and were thus generally predisposed to disapprove of slavery. The political groups seeking independence from Spain also sought the support of slaves by promises of emancipation. Furthermore, the newly independent nations needed good relations with Britain to support their economies and consequently most of them very quickly freed their slaves to gain such support. The actual freeing of slaves was gradual and often came some years after the emancipation legislation. Despite the gradual nature of this abolition, slavery would disappear by approximately the middle of the century from all of the newly independent nations of Latin America. The great exception was Brazil.

**Abolishing Slavery in the New World.** British reformers gradually recognized that the abolition of the slave trade had not actually improved the lot of slaves. In 1823 they adopted as a new goal the gradual emancipation of slaves. The chief voices calling for this change were those of William Wilberforce and Thomas Clarkson, who were active in founding the Abolition Society. The savagery with which West Indian planters put down slave revolts in 1823 and 1824 and again in 1831 strengthened the resolve of the antislavery reformers. By 1830 the reformers had abandoned the goal of gradual abolition and demanded the complete abolition of slavery. In 1833 after the passage of the Reform Bill in Great Britain they achieved that goal when Parliament abolished the right of British subjects to hold slaves. In the British West Indies, 750,000 slaves were freed within a few years.

The other old colonial powers in the New World tended to be much slower in their own abolition of slavery. Portugal did little or nothing about slavery in Brazil, and when that nation became independent of Portugal, its new government continued slavery. Portugal ended slavery elsewhere in its American possessions in 1836; the Swedes, in 1847; the Danes, in 1848; but the Dutch not until 1863. France had witnessed a significant antislavery movement throughout the first half of the century, but slavery was not abolished in its West Indian possessions until the revolution 1848.

During the first thirty years of the nineteenth century the institution of slavery revived and achieved strong new footholds in the transatlantic world. These areas were the lower south of the United States for the cultivation of cotton, Brazil for the cultivation of coffee, and Cuba for the cultivation of sugar. World demand for those products made the slave system economically viable in these regions. Consequently, despite the drive to emancipation, which had succeeded in the northern states of the United States slavery persisted in much of the Caribbean and in most of Latin America.

An antislavery movement had existed in the United States since the end of the eighteenth century, but it took on a new life in the early 1830s. The British abolition of slavery in the West Indies served as an inspiration to a new generation of American antislavery leaders, the most famous of whom was William Lloyd Garrison. He and other American abolitionists raised the question of slavery throughout the 1830s and 1840s. It was, however, the disposition of lands the United States had acquired in the Mexican War of 1847 that placed slavery at the heart of American political debate. For over a decade the question of slavery sharply divided Americans. The election of Lincoln in 1860 brought those sectional tensions to a head, and the American Civil War erupted in the spring of 1861. In 1862 Lincoln issued the Emancipation Proclamation, which ended slavery in the combatant states. The passage of the Thirteenth Amendment to the American Constitution in 1865 abolished slavery in the United States.

The end of slavery in the United Sates left both Cuba, the most important remaining possession of the Spanish Empire in the Americas, and Brazil with slave economies. In 1868 an insurgency against Spanish colonial policy broke out in Cuba and lasted for ten years. This war disrupted much of the Cuban economy and saw some planters move toward using free labor. The Spanish forces attacked other planters by freeing their slaves. In 1870 the Spanish government passed a measure for gradual emancipation of slaves in both Cuba and Puerto Rico. In subsequent years, the sugar economy collapsed, making slavery unprofitable. Abolitionist agitation grew in Spain, and slavery was abolished in its new world colonies in 1886.

Brazil, under British pressure, had effectively ended the slave trade in 1850, but the question of the abolition of slavery was postponed for many years. In 1871, as a result of abolitionist agitation and because the Emperor Pedro II opposed slavery, a law providing for an extremely gradual abolition of slavery was passed. During the next two decades abolitionist sentiment grew, and public figures from across the political spectrum voiced opposition to slavery. In 1888, Isabel Christiana, then regent while her father Pedro II was in Europe for medical treatment, signed a law abolishing slavery in Brazil without any form of compensation to the slave owners.

The abolition of slavery in Brazil ended a system of forced labor that had characterized the transatlantic economy for almost 400 years. Wherever slavery had existed, however, its presence left and would continue to leave long-term consequences for the realization of equality and social justice. The end of slavery consequently did not end the problems that slavery created in the transatlantic world.

**Africa and the End of Slavery.** The transatlantic slave trade itself had adversely affected the life of Africa both through the vast loss of population over the centuries as well as through the undermining of African society through the internal slave trade. Similarly, the crusade against transatlantic slavery had drawn Europeans much more deeply into the affairs of the African continent. The various efforts by antislavery groups began to impact Africa in the first half of the nineteenth century. Their goal was to transform the African economy by substituting new peaceful trade in tropical goods for the slave trade. The reformers hoped to spread both free trade and Christianity into Africa. "Christianity and civilization" and "Christianity and commerce" were popular slogan of the day. Missionaries and traders saw themselves as natural allies in the cause.

The first effort in this direction was the resettlement of black slaves or children of black slaves into Africa. In 1787 the British established a colony of poor free blacks from Britain in Sierra Leone. The effort went badly but a few years later former slaves once owned by British loyalists in America were settled there. Then former slaves from the Caribbean were brought to Sierra Leone. The colony became relatively successful only after 1807, when the British navy landed slaves rescued from captured slave trading ships. Sierra Leone though quite small became a place on the coast of West Africa where Christianity and commerce rather than the slave trade flourished. The French established a smaller experiment at Libreville in Gabon. The most famous and lasting attempt to resettle former black slaves in Africa was the establishment of Liberia by the efforts of the American Colonization Society after 1817. Liberia became an independent republic in 1847. All of these efforts to move former slaves back to Africa had only modest success, but they did affect the life of West Africa.

Other antislavery reformers were less interested in establishing outposts for the settlement of former slaves than in transforming the African economy itself. In 1841 the African Civilization Society under the leadership of Thomas Fowell Buxton sent a group of paddle-steamer ships up the Niger River in the hope of creating the basis for new trade with Africa. The goal was to establish free trade between Britain and Africa in which the manufactured goods of the former, most particularly textiles, would be exchanged for tropical agricultural goods produced by Africans. The expedition failed because most of its members died of disease. Yet the impulse to penetrate Africa for purposes of spreading trade and Christianity would continue for the rest of the century.

The antislavery movement marked the first of the intrusions of the European powers well beyond the coast of West Africa into the heart of the continent. After the American Civil War finally halted any large-scale demand for slaves from Africa, the antislavery reformers began to focus on ending the slave trade in East Africa and the Indian Ocean. This drive against slavery and the slave trade in Africa itself became one of the rationales for European interference in Africa during the second half of the century and served as one of the foundations for the establishment of the late-century colonial empires.

The crusade against slavery in the transatlantic economy eventually touched most of the world. It radically transformed the economies and societies of both North and South America. It led to a transformation of the African economy and eventually to a significant European presence in the life of African societies. Efforts to eradicate slavery, particularly the efforts by British reformers, caused the spread of the reform movement into Asia. Slavery was not abolished throughout the world, and antislavery societies still exist though they receive little publicity. But the abolition of slavery in the transatlantic world stands as one of the most permanent achievements of the forces of eighteenth-century Enlightenment and Revolution.

✦ *What were the justifications of slavery prior to the eighteenth century? What religious and intellectual developments led some Europeans and some Americans to question and criticize the institution of slavery? Why did anti-slavery reformers first concentrate on the abolition of the slave trade? How did both slavery and antislavery lead Americans and Europeans to become involved with Africa? How did that involvement change between approximately 1600 and 1870?*

*The social and political tensions of the second quarter of the nineteenth century erupted in a series of revolutionary upheavals that swept across much of Europe in 1848. In "The Uprising," the French artist Honoré Daumier recalled the drama of that year's revolution in Paris in a remarkable image of political and social protest. [Oil on canvas. 34$^1/_2$ x 44$^1/_2$ in. (87.6 x 113.0 mm.), Unsigned. Acquired 1925. The Phillips Collection.]*

# Economic Advance and Social Unrest (1830–1850)

## K E Y   T O P I C S

- The development of industrialism and its effects on the organization of
  labor and the family
- The changing role of women in industrial society
- The establishment of police forces and reform of prisons
- Early developments in European socialism
- The revolutions of 1848

By 1830 Europe was headed toward an industrial society. Only Great Britain had already attained that status, but the pounding of new machinery and the grinding of railway engines soon began to echo across much of the Continent. Yet what characterized the second quarter of the century was not the triumph of industrialism but the final protests of those economic groups who opposed it. Intellectually, the period saw the formulation of the major creeds supporting and criticizing the newly emerging society.

These were years of uncertainty for almost everyone. Even the most confident entrepreneurs knew that the trade cycle might bankrupt them in a matter of weeks. For the industrial workers and the artisans, unemployment became a haunting and recurring problem. For the peasants, the question was sufficiency of food. It was a period of self-conscious transition that culminated in 1848 with a continent-wide outbreak of revolution. People knew that one mode of life was passing, but no one knew what would replace it.

# Toward an Industrial Society

During the first half of the nineteenth century, industrial production of both manufacturing and consumer goods that had begun earlier in Great Britain began to spread across much of Europe. This slow but steady conversion of the European economy to industrial manufacturing generally took place in cities. Thus, it brought about new migrations of people from the countryside to urban settings and caused a painful reorganization in the lives of European workers. Many of those who possessed valuable preindustrial skills saw those skills displaced by machines. Industrialism and the accompanying urban growth no less than the political revolutions that derived from the French Revolution overturned the social order of the Old Regime.

## Britain's Industrial Leadership

The Industrial Revolution had begun in eighteenth-century Great Britain with the advances in textile production described in Chapter 16. Natural resources, adequate capital, native technological skills, a growing food supply, a social structure that allowed considerable mobility, and strong foreign and domestic demand for goods had given Britain an edge in achieving a vast new capacity for production in manufacturing. British factories and recently invented machines allowed producers to furnish customers with a greater number of products whose quality was higher and whose prices were lower than those of any competitors. The French Revolution and the wars of Napoleon had also finally destroyed the French Atlantic trade and had for two decades disrupted continental economic life. The Latin American wars of independence opened the markets of South America to British goods. In North America, both the United States and Canada demanded British products. Through its control of India, Britain commanded the markets of southern Asia.

The British textile industry was a vast worldwide economic network. Much of the raw cotton that fed the new British textile mills came from the plantations of the southern United States. The British textile industry was thus dependent on the labor of American slaves, though Britain itself had since 1807 been trying to end the slave trade. Then in turn the finished textiles were shipped all over the world along sea lanes protected by the British navy.

The wealth that Britain gained through textile production and its other industries of ironmaking, shipbuilding, china production, and the manufacture of other finished goods was invested all over the world but especially in the United States and Latin America. This enormous activity provided the economic foundation for British dominance of the world scene in the nineteenth century.

Despite the economic lag, the continental nations were beginning to make material progress. By the 1830s, in Belgium, France, and Germany, the number of steam engines in use was growing steadily. Exploitation of the coalfields of the Ruhr and the Saar basins had begun. Coke was replacing charcoal in iron and steel production.

Industrial areas on the Continent were generally less concentrated than in Britain, and large manufacturing districts, such as the British Midlands, did not yet exist there. Major pockets of production, such as Lyons, Rouen, Liège, and Lille, did exist in western Europe, but most continental manufacturing still took place in the countryside. New machines were integrated into the existing domestic system. The extreme slowness of continental imitation of the British example meant that at mid-century peasants and urban artisans remained more important politically than industrial factory workers.

## Population and Migration

While the process of industrialization spread, the population of Europe continued to grow on the base of the eighteenth-century population explosion. The number of people in France rose from 32.5 million in 1831 to 35.8 million in 1851. The population of Germany rose from 26.5 million to 33.5 million during approximately the same period. That of Britain grew from 16.3 million to 20.8 million. More and more of the people of Europe lived in cities. By mid-century, one-half of the population of England and Wales and one-quarter of the population of France and Germany had become town dwellers. Eastern Europe by contrast remained overwhelmingly rural with little industrial manufacturing.

The sheer numbers of human beings put considerable pressure on the physical resources of the cities. Migration from the countryside meant that existing housing, water, sewers, food supplies, and lighting were completely inadequate. Slums with indescribable filth grew, and disease, especially cholera, ravaged the population. Crime increased

*Cities all across the continent grew during the first half of the nineteenth century. Some developed with little planning into bewildering places. Others—as this Berlin street scene suggests—developed in ways more congenial to their residents, with neighborhoods that continued to combine workshops, stores, and residences. [Bildarchiv Preussischer Kulturbesitz]*

and became a way of life for those who could make a living in no other manner. Human misery and degradation in many early-nineteenth-century cities seemed to have no bounds.

The situation in the countryside was scarcely better. During the first half of the century, the productive use of the land remained the basic fact of life for most Europeans. The enclosures of the late eighteenth century, the land redistribution of the French Revolution, and the emancipation of serfs in Prussia and later in Austria (1848) and Russia (1861) commercialized landholding. Liberal reformers had hoped that the legal revolution in ownership would transform peasants into progressive, industrious farmers. Instead, most peasants had become conservative landholders without enough land to make agricultural innovations or, often, even to support themselves.

It is important to note the differing dates of rural emancipation across Europe. In England, France, and the Low Countries, persons living in the countryside could move freely between country and town. In Germany, eastern Europe, and Russia, such migration was difficult until after emancipation of the serfs. Even when emancipation did occur, as throughout Germany early in the century, it did not make migration simple. So from Germany eastward, the pace of industrialization was much slower in part because of the absence of a fluid market for free labor moving to the cities.

The specter of poor harvests still haunted Europe. The worst such experience of the century was the Irish famine of 1845–1847. Perhaps as many as half a million Irish peasants with no land or small plots simply starved when disease blighted the potato crop. Hundreds of thousands emigrated. By mid-century, the revolution in landholding had led to greater agricultural production. It also resulted in a vast uprooting of people from the countryside into cities and from Europe into the rest of the world. The countryside thus provided many of the workers for the new factories as well as people with few economic skills who slowly emigrated to cities in hope of finding work.

## Railways

Industrial advance itself had also contributed to this migration. The 1830s and 1840s were the great age of railway building. The Stockton and Darlington Line opened in England in 1825. By 1830 another major line had been built between Manchester and Liverpool and had several hundred passengers a day. Belgium had undertaken railway construction by 1835. The first French line opened in 1832, but serious construction came only in the 1840s. Germany entered the railway age in 1835. At mid-century, Britain had 9,797 kilometers of railway; France, 2,915; and Germany, 5,856.

The railroads, plus canals and improved regular roads, meant that people could leave the place of their birth more easily than ever before. The improvement in transportation also allowed cheaper and more rapid passage of raw materials and finished products.

Railways epitomized the character of the industrial economy during the second quarter of the century. They represented investment in capital goods rather than in consumer goods. There was consequently a shortage of consumer goods at cheap

*A view of one of the first French railways, the line between Paris and the suburb of Saint Germain. The line was built by Baron James de Rothschild of the famous banking family. [H. Roger Viollet]*

prices. This favoring of capital over consumer production was one reason that the working class often found itself able to purchase so little for its wages. The railways in and of themselves also brought about still more industrialization. Embodying the most dramatic application of the steam engine, they created a sharply increased demand for iron and steel and then for a more skilled labor force. The new iron and steel capacity soon permitted the construction of ironclad ships and iron machinery rather than ships and machinery made of wood. These great capital industries led to the formation of vast industrial fortunes that would be invested in still newer enterprises. Industrialism had begun to grow on itself.

## The Labor Force

The composition and experience of the early nineteenth-century labor force was varied. No single description could include all the factory workers, urban artisans, domestic system craftspeople, household servants, miners, countryside peddlers, farm workers, or railroad navvies. The workforce was composed of some persons who were reasonably well off, enjoying steady employment and decent wages. It also numbered the "laboring poor," who held jobs but who earned little more than subsistence wages. There were others, such as the women and children who worked naked in the mines of Wales, whose conditions of life shocked all of Europe when a parliamentary report in the early 1840s publicized them. Furthermore, the conditions of workers varied from decade to decade and from industry to industry within any particular decade.

Although historians have traditionally emphasized the role and experience of industrial factory workers, only the textile-manufacturing industry became thoroughly mechanized and moved into the factory setting during the first half of the century. Far more of the nonrural, nonagricultural workforce consisted of skilled artisans living in cities or small towns. They were attempting to maintain the value of their skills and control over their trades in the face of changing features of production. All these working people faced possible unemployment, with little or no provision for their security. They confronted during their lives the dissolution of many of the traditional social ties of custom and community.

### Proletarianization of Factory Workers and Urban Artisans

During the century, both artisans and factory workers underwent a process of proletarianization. This term is used to indicate the entry of workers into a wage economy and their gradual loss of significant ownership of the means of production, such as tools and equipment, and of control over the conduct of their own trades. The process occurred rapidly wherever the factory system arose. The factory owner provided the financial capital to construct the factory, to purchase the machinery, and to secure the raw materials. The factory workers contributed their labor for a wage. The process could also occur outside the factory setting if a new invention, such as a mechanical printing press, could do the work of several artisans within a workshop setting.

Factory workers also submitted to various kinds of factory discipline that was virtually always unpopular and difficult to impose. This discipline meant that the demands for smooth operation of the machinery largely determined work conditions. Closing of factory gates to late workers, fines for such lateness, dismissal for drunkenness, and public scolding of faulty laborers were attempts to create human discipline that would match the regularity of the cables, wheels, and pistons. The factory worker had no direct say about the quality of the product or its price.

For all the difficulties of factory conditions, however, the economic situation was often better than for the textile workers who resisted the factory mode of production. In particular, English handloom weavers, who continued to work in their homes, experienced decades of declining trade and growing poverty in their unsuccessful competition with power looms.

Urban artisans in the nineteenth century experienced proletarianization more slowly than factory workers, and machinery had little to do with the process. The emergence of factories in and of itself did not harm urban artisans. Many even prospered from the development. For example, the construction and maintenance of the new machines generated major demand for metalworkers, who consequently prospered. The actual erection of factories and the expansion of cities benefitted all craftspeople in the building trades, such as carpenters, roofers, joiners, and masons. The lower prices for machine-made textiles aided artisans involved in the making of clothing, such as tailors and hatters, by reducing the costs of their raw materials. Where the urban artisans encountered difficulty and where they found their skills and livelihood threatened were in the organization of production.

In the eighteenth century, a European town or city workplace had usually consisted of a few artisans laboring for a master. They labored first as apprentices and then as journeymen, according to established guild regulations and practices. The master owned the workshop and the larger equipment, and the apprentices and journeymen owned their tools. The journeyman could expect to become a master. This guild system had allowed considerable worker control over labor recruitment and training, pace of production, quality of product, and price.

In the nineteenth century, it became increasingly difficult for artisans to continue to exercise corporate or guild direction and control over their trades. The legislation of the French Revolution had outlawed such organizations in France. Across Europe,

A parliamentary report in the early 1840s revealed the deplorable conditions of women and children working underground in Welsh mines. The report had published illustrations of those conditions. This contemporary political cartoon draws upon those illustrations by portraying the wealthy and comfortable classes living a life based on the foundation of the misery of workers.
[The Granger Collection]

political and economic liberals disapproved of labor and guild organizations and attempted to ban them.

Other destructive forces were also at work. The masters often found themselves under increased competitive pressure from larger, more heavily capitalized establishments or from the introduction of machine production into a previously craft-dominated industry. In many workshops masters began to follow a practice, known in France as *confection*, whereby goods, such as shoes, clothing, and furniture, were produced in standard sizes and styles rather than by special orders for individual customers.

This practice increased the division of labor in the workshop. Each artisan produced a smaller part of the more-or-less uniform final product. Thus, less skill was required of each artisan, and the particular skills possessed by a worker became less valuable. Masters also tried to increase production and reduce costs by lowering the wages paid for piecework. Those attempts often led to work stoppages or strikes. Migrants from the countryside or small towns into the cities created, in some cases, a surplus of relatively unskilled workers. They were willing to work for lower wages or under less favorable and protected conditions than traditional artisans. This situation made it much more difficult for urban journeymen ever to hope to become masters with their own workshops in which they would be in charge. Increasingly, these artisans became lifetime wage laborers whose skills were simply bought and sold in the marketplace.

### *Working-Class Political Action: The Example of British Chartism*

By the middle of the century, such artisans, proud of their skills and frustrated in their social expectations, became the most radical political element in the European working class. From at least the 1830s onward, these artisans took the lead in one country after another in attempting to formulate new ways of protecting their social and economic interests.

By the late 1830s, significant numbers of people in the British working class linked the solution of their economic plight to a program of political reform known as *Chartism*. In 1836 William Lovett (1800–1877) and other London radical artisans formed the London Working Men's Association. In 1838 the group issued the Charter, demanding six specific reforms. The Six Points of the Charter included universal male suffrage, annual election of the House of Commons, the secret ballot, equal electoral districts, abolition of property qualifications for members of the House of Commons, and payment of salaries to members of the House of Commons.

For more than ten years, the Chartists, who were never tightly organized, agitated for their reforms. On three occasions the Charter was presented to Parliament, which refused to pass it. Petitions with millions of signatures were presented to the House of Commons. Strikes were called. The Chartists published a newspaper, the *Northern Star*. Feargus O'Connor (1794–1855), the most important Chartist leader, made speeches across Britain. Despite this vast activity, Chartism as a national movement failed. Its ranks were split between those who favored violence and those who wanted to use peaceful tactics. On the local level, however, the Chartists scored several successes and controlled the city councils in Leeds and Sheffield.

As prosperity returned after the depression of the late 1830s and early 1840s, many working people abandoned the movement. Chartists' demonstrations in 1848 fizzled. Nevertheless, Chartism was the first large-scale European working-class political movement. It had specific goals and largely working-class leadership. Eventually, several of the Six Points were enacted into law. Continental working-class observers saw in Chartism the kind of mass movement that workers must eventually adopt if they were to improve their situation.

# Family Structures and the Industrial Revolution

It is more difficult to generalize about the European working-class family structure in the age of early industrialism than under the Old Regime. Industrialism developed at such different rates across the Continent, and the impact of industrialism cannot be separated from that of migration and urbanization. Furthermore, industrialism did not touch all families directly. The structures and customs of many peasant families changed little for much of the nineteenth century.

Much more is known about the relationships of the new industry to the family in Great Britain than elsewhere. Many of the British developments foreshadowed those in other countries as the factory system spread.

## The Family in the Early Factory System

Contrary to the opinion historians and other observers once held, the adoption of new machinery and factory production did not destroy the working-class family. Before the late-eighteenth-century revolution in textile production in England, the individual family involved in textiles was the chief unit of production. The earliest textile inventions, such as the spinning jenny, did not change that situation. The new machine was simply brought into the home to spin the thread. It was the mechanization of weaving that led to the major change. The father who became a machine weaver was then employed in a factory. His work was thus separated from his home. Although one should not underestimate the changes and pressures in family life that occurred when the father left for the factory, the structure of early English factories allowed the father to preserve certain of his traditional family roles as they had existed before the factory system.

In the domestic system of the family economy, the father and mother had worked with their children in textile production as a family unit. They had trained and disciplined the children within the home setting. Their home life and their economic life were largely the same. Early factory owners and supervisors permitted the father to employ his wife and children as his assistants. Parental training and discipline were thus transferred from the home into the early factory. In some cases, in both Britain and France, whole families would move near a new factory so the family as a unit could work there. Those accommodations to family life nonetheless did not relieve any family members of having to face the new work discipline of the factory setting.

A major shift in this family and factory structure began in the mid-1820s in England and had been more or less completed by the mid-1830s. As spinning and weaving were put under one roof, the size of factories and of the machinery became larger. These newer machines required fewer skilled operators but many relatively unskilled attendants. Machine tending became the work of unmarried women and of children. Factory owners found that these workers would accept lower wages and were less likely than adult men to try to form worker or union organizations.

Factory wages for the more skilled adult males, however, became sufficiently high to allow some fathers to remove their children from the factory and to send them to school. The children who were now working in the factories as assistants were often the children of the economically depressed handloom weavers. The wives of the skilled operatives also usually did not work in the factories any longer. So, the original links of the family in the British textile factory that had existed for well over a quarter century largely disappeared. Men were supervising women and children who did not belong to their families.

CONCERN FOR CHILD LABOR It was at this point in the 1830s that workers became concerned about the plight of child-laborers, because parents were no longer exercising discipline over their own children in the factories. The English Factory Act of 1833 forbade the employment of children under age nine, limited the workday of children aged nine to thirteen to nine hours, and required that these children be given two hours of education a day paid for by the factory owner. The effect was further to divide work and home life. The workday for adults and older teenagers remained twelve hours. Younger children often worked in relays of four or six hours. Consequently, the parental link was thoroughly broken. The education requirement began the process of removing nurturing and training from the home and family to a school, where a teacher rather than the parents was in charge of education.

After passage of the English Factory Act, many of the British working class demanded shorter workdays for adults. They desired to reunite, in some manner, the workday of adults with that of their children, or at least to allow adults to spend more time with their children. In 1847 Parliament mandated a ten-hour workday. By present standards, this was long. At that time, however, it allowed parents and children more hours together as a domestic unit since their relationship as a work or production unit had ceased wherever the factory system prevailed. By the middle of the 1840s, in the lives of industrial workers, the roles of men as breadwinners and as fathers and husbands had become distinct in the British textile industry.

CHANGING ECONOMIC ROLE FOR THE FAMILY What occurred in Britain presents a general pattern for what would happen elsewhere with the spread of industrial capitalism and public education. The European family was passing from being the chief unit of both production and consumption to becoming the chief unit of consumption alone. This development did not mean the end of the family as an economic unit. Parents and children, however, now came to depend on sharing wages often derived from several sources rather than on sharing work in the home or factory.

Ultimately, the wage economy meant that families were less closely bound together than in the past. Because wages could be sent over long distances to parents, children might now move farther away from home. Once they moved far away, the economic link was, in time, often broken. On the other hand, when a family settled in an industrial city, the wage economy might, in that or the next generation, actually discourage children from leaving home as early as they had in the past. Children could find wage employment in the same city and then live at home until they had accumulated enough savings to marry and begin their own household. That situation meant that children often remained with their parents longer than in the past.

## Women in the Early Industrial Revolution

The industrial economy ultimately produced an immense impact on the home and family life of women. First, it took virtually all productive work out of the home and allowed many families to live on the wages of the male spouse. That transformation prepared the way for a new concept of gender-determined roles in the home and in domestic life generally. Women came to be associated with domestic duties, such as housekeeping, food preparation, child rearing and nurturing, and household management. Men came to be associated almost exclusively with breadwinning. Children were reared to match these expected gender patterns. Previously, this domestic division of labor into separate spheres had prevailed only among the relatively small middle class and the gentry. During the nineteenth century, that division came to characterize the working class as well.

### Opportunities and Exploitation in Employment

Because the early Industrial Revolution had begun in textile production, women and their labor were deeply involved from the start. While both spinning and weaving were still domestic industries, women

As textile production became increasingly automated in the nineteenth century, textile factories required fewer skilled workers and more unskilled attendants. To fill these unskilled positions, factory owners turned increasingly to unmarried women and widows, who worked for lower wages than men and were less likely to form labor organizations. [Bildarchiv Preussischer Kulturbesitz]

usually worked in all stages of production. Hand spinning was virtually always a woman's task. At first, when spinning was moved into factories and involved large machines, women often were displaced by men. Furthermore, the higher wages commanded by male cotton-factory workers allowed many married women not to work or to work only to supplement their husbands' wages.

WOMEN IN FACTORIES   With the next generation of machines in the 1820s, however, unmarried women rapidly became employed in the factories. But their new jobs often demanded fewer skills than those they had previously exercised in the home production of textiles. Women's factory work also required fewer skills than most work done by men. Tending a machine required less skill than actually spinning or weaving or acting as foreman. There was thus a certain paradox in the impact of the factory on women. Many new jobs were opened to them, but the level of skills was lowered.

# Women Industrial Workers Explain Their Economic Situation

*In 1832 there was much discussion in the British press about factory legislation. Most of that discussion was concerned with the employment of children, but the* Examiner *newspaper made the suggestion that any factory laws should not only address the problem of child labor but also in time eliminate women from employment in factories. That article provoked the following remarkable letter to the editor, composed by or on behalf of women factory workers, which eloquently stated the real necessity of such employment for women and the unattractive alternatives.*

✦ *What are the reasons these women enumerate to prove the necessity of their holding manufacturing jobs? What changes in production methods have led women from the home to the factory? How does the situation of these women relate to the possibility of their marrying? Compare the plight of these English working-class women with that of the French middle-class woman in the next document.*

Sir,

Living as we do, in the densely populated manufacturing districts of Lancashire, and most of us belonging to that class of females who earn their bread either directly or indirectly by manufactories, we have looked with no little anxiety for your opinion on the Factory Bill. . . . You are for doing away with our services in manufactories altogether. So much the better, if you had pointed out any other more eligible and practical employment for the surplus female labour, that will want other channels for a subsistence. If our competition were withdrawn, and short hours substituted, we have no doubt but the effects would be as you have stated, "not to lower wages, as the male branch of the family would be enabled to earn as much as the whole had done," but for the thousands of females who are employed in manufactories, who have no legitimate claim on any male relative for employment or support, and who have, through a variety of circumstance, been early thrown on their own resources for a livelihood, what is to become of them?

In this neighbourhood, hand-loom has been almost totally superseded by power-loom weaving, and no inconsiderable number of females, who must depend on their own exertions, or their parishes for support, have been forced, of necessity into the manufactories, from their total inability to earn a livelihood at home.

It is a lamentable fact, that, in these parts of the country, there is scarcely any other mode of employment for female industry, if we except servitude and dressmaking. Of the former of these, there is no chance of employment for one-twentieth of the candidates that would rush into the field, to say nothing of lowering the wages of our sisters of the same craft; and of the latter, galling as some of the hardships of manufactories are (of which the indelicacy of mixing with the men is not the least), yet there are few women who have been so employed, that would change conditions with the ill-used genteel little slaves, who have to lose sleep and health, in catering to the whims and frivolities of the butter-flies of fashion.

We see no way of escape from starvation, but to accept the very tempting offers of the newspapers, held out as baits to us, fairly to ship ourselves off to Van Dieman's Land [Tasmania] on the very delicate errand of husband hunting, and having safely arrived at the "Land of Goshen," jump ashore, with a "Who wants me?" . . .

The Female Operatives of Tødmorden

---

*The* Examiner, *February 26, 1832, as quoted in Ivy Pinchbeck,* Women Workers and the Industrial Revolution, 1750–1850 *(New York: Augustus M. Kelley, 1969), pp. 199–200.*

Moreover, almost always, the women in the factories were young single women or widows. Upon marriage or perhaps after the birth of the first child, young women usually found that their husbands earned enough money for them to leave the factory. Or they found themselves unwanted by the factory owners, who disliked employing married women because of the likelihood of pregnancy, the influence of their husbands, and the duties of child rearing. Widows might return to factory work because they then lacked their husbands' income.

WORK ON THE LAND AND IN THE HOME  In Britain and elsewhere by mid-century, industrial factory work still accounted for less than half of all employment for women. The largest group of employed women in France continued to work on the land. In England, they were domestic servants. Through western Europe, domestic industries, such as lace making, glove making, garment making, and other kinds of needlework, employed a vast number of women. In almost all such cases, their conditions of labor were harsh, whether they worked in their homes or in sweatshops. It cannot be overemphasized that all work by women commanded low wages and involved low skills. They had virtually no effective modes of protecting themselves from exploitation. The charwoman, a common sight across the Continent, symbolized the plight of working women.

The low wages of female workers in all areas of employment sometimes led to their becoming prostitutes to supplement their wage income. This situation prevailed across Europe throughout the century. In 1844 Louise Aston (1814–1871), a German political radical, portrayed this situation in a poem looking at the experience of a Silesian weaver as she confronts a factory owner upon whom her family depends to purchase the cloth they have woven:

The factory owner has come,
And he says to me: "My darling child,
I know your people
Are living in misery and sorrow;
So if you want to lie with me
For three or four nights,
See this shiny gold coin!
It's yours immediately."[1]

[1]As quoted in Lia Secci, "German Women Writers and the Revolution of 1848," in John C. Fout, ed., *German Women in the Nineteenth Century: A Social History* (New York: Holmes & Meier, 1984), p. 162.

Such sexual exploitation of women was hardly new to European society, but the particular pressures of the transformation of the economy from one of skilled artisans to unskilled factory workers made many women especially vulnerable.

## Changing Expectations in Working-Class Marriage

Movement to cities and entrance into the wage economy gave women wider opportunities for marriage. Cohabitation before marriage was not uncommon. Parents had less to do with arranging marriages than in the past. Marriage now usually meant that a woman would leave the workforce to live on her husband's earnings. If all went well, that arrangement might improve her situation. If the husband became ill or died, however, or if he deserted his wife, she would have to reenter the market for unskilled labor at an advanced age.

Despite these changes, many of the traditional practices associated with the family economy survived into the industrial era. As a young woman came of age, both family needs and her desire to marry still directed what she would do with her life. The most likely early occupation for a young woman was domestic service. A girl born in the country normally migrated to a nearby town or city for such employment, often living initially with a relative. As in the past, she would try to earn enough in wages to give her a dowry, so that she might marry and set up her own household. If she became a factory worker, she would probably live in a supervised dormitory. These dormitories helped attract young women into their employ by convincing parents that their daughters would be safe.

The life of young women in the cities was more precarious than earlier. There were fewer family and community ties. There were also perhaps more available young men. These men, who worked for wages rather than in the older apprenticeship structures, were more mobile, so that relationships between men and women often were more fleeting. In any case, illegitimate births increased; fewer women who became pregnant before marriage found the father willing to marry them.

Marriage in the wage industrial economy was also different in certain respects from marriage in earlier times. It still involved the starting of a separate household, but the structure of gender relationships within the household was different. Mar-

# A Young Middle-Class French Woman Writes to Her Father About Marriage

*Stéphanie Jullien was a young middle-class woman whose father wished her to marry a man who was courting her. She had already rejected one suitor and her father was greatly concerned about her future. In this letter, she explains to her father the matters that disturb her and make her wish to delay her decision. Ultimately, she did marry the man in question, and the marriage appears to have been happy.*

✦ *How does Stéphanie Jullien distinguish between the vocational and social opportunities available to a woman and those to a man? What are her expectations of a relationship with a husband? What does the letter also tell you about her sense of her relationship to her father? Compare this letter with the preceding letter by English working-class women. What problems do the women share? How are their lives different? What does a comparison of the two letters tell you about the difference in class experience in the early nineteenth century?*

You men have a thousand occupations to distract you: society, business, politics, and work absorb you, exhaust you, upset you. . . . As for us women who, as you have said to me from time to time, have only the roses in life, we feel more profoundly in our solitude and in our idleness the sufferings that you can slough off. I don't want to make a comparison here between the destiny of man and the destiny of woman: each sex has its own lot, its own troubles, its own pleasures. I only want to explain to you that excess of moroseness of which you complain and of which I am the first to suffer. . . . I am not able to do anything for myself and for those around me. I am depriving my brothers in order to have a dowry. I am not even able to live alone, being obliged to take from others, not only in order to live but also in order to be protected, since social convention does not allow me to have independence. And yet the world finds me guilty of being the only person that I am at liberty to be; not having useful or productive work to do, not having any calling except marriage, and not being able to look by myself for someone who will suit me, I am full of cares and anxieties. . . .

I am asking for more time [before responding to a marriage proposal]. It is not too much to want to see and know a man for ten months, even a year when it is a matter of passing one's life with him. There is no objection to make, you say. But the most serious and the most important presents itself: I do not love him. Don't think I am talking about a romantic and impossible passion or an ideal love, neither of which I ever hope to know. I am talking of a feeling that makes one want to see someone, that makes his absence painful and his return desirable, that makes one interested in what another is doing, that makes one want another's happiness almost in spite of oneself, that makes, finally, the duties of a woman toward her husband pleasures and not efforts. It is a feeling without which marriage would be hell, a feeling that cannot be born out of esteem, and which to me, however, seems to be the very basis of conjugal happiness. I can't feel these emotions immediately. . . . Let me have some time. I want to love, not out of any sense of duty, but for myself and for the happiness of the one to whom I attach my life, who will suffer if he only encounters coldness in me, when he brings me love and devotion.

*From the Jullien Family Papers, 39 AP 4, Archives Nationales, Paris, trans. by Barbara Corrado Pope, as quoted in Erna Olafson Hellerstein, Leslie Parker Hume, and Karen M. Offen, eds., Victorian Women: A Documentary Account of Women's Lives in Nineteenth-Century England, France, and the United States (Stanford, Calif.: Stanford University Press, 1981), pp. 247–248.*

riage was less an economic partnership. The husband's wages might well be able to support the entire family. The wage economy and the industrialization separating workplace from home made it difficult for women to combine domestic duties with work. When married women worked, it was usually in the nonindustrial sector of the economy. More often than not, it was the children rather than the wife who were sent to work. This may help explain the increase of births within marriages, as children in the wage economy usually were an economic asset. Married women worked outside the home only when family needs or illness or the death of a spouse forced them to do so.

In the home, working-class women were by no means idle. Their domestic duties were an essential factor in the family wage economy. If work took place elsewhere, someone had to be directly in charge of maintaining the home front. Homemaking came to the fore when a life at home had to be organized separate from the place of work. Wives were primarily concerned with food and cooking, but they often also were in charge of the family's finances. The role of the mother expanded when the children still living at home became wage earners. She was now providing home support for her entire wage-earning family. She created the environment to which the family members returned after work. The longer period of home life of working children may also have increased and strengthened familial bonds of affection between those children and their hardworking, homebound mothers. In all these respects, the culture of the working-class marriage and family tended to imitate the family patterns of the middle and upper classes, whose members had often accepted the view of separate gender spheres set forth by Rousseau and popularized in hundreds of novels, journals, and newspapers.

# Problems of Crime and Order

Throughout the nineteenth century, the political and economic elite in Europe were profoundly concerned about social order. The revolutions of the late eighteenth and early nineteenth centuries made them fearful of future disorder and threats to life and property. The process of industrialization and urbanization also contributed to this problem of order. Thousands of Europeans migrated from the countryside to the towns and cities. There they often encountered poverty or unemployment and general social frustration and disappointment. Cities became places associated with criminal activity and especially crimes against property, such as theft and arson. Throughout the first sixty years of the nineteenth century, crime appears to have increased slowly but steadily before more or less reaching a plateau.

Historians and social scientists are divided about the reasons for this rise in the crime rate. So little is known about crime in rural settings that comparisons with the cities are difficult. There are also many problems with crime statistics in the nineteenth century. No two nations kept them in the same manner. Different legal codes and systems of judicial administration were in effect in different areas of the Continent, thus giving somewhat different legal definitions of criminal activity. The result has been confusion, difficult research, and tentative conclusions.

## New Police Forces

From the propertied elite classes, two major views about containing crime and criminals emerged during the nineteenth century: prison reform and better systems of police. The result of these efforts was the triumph in Europe of the idea of a policed society. This concept means the presence of a paid, professionally trained group of law-enforcement officers charged with keeping order, protecting property and lives, investigating crime, and apprehending offenders. These officers are distinct from the army and are charged specifically with domestic security. It is to them that the civilian population normally turns for law enforcement. One of the key features of the theory of a policed society is that crime may be prevented by the visible presence of law-enforcement officers. These police forces, at least in theory, did not perform a political role, though in many countries that distinction was often ignored. Police forces also became one of the major areas of municipal government employment.

Such professional police forces did not really exist until the early nineteenth century. They differed from one country to another in both authority and organization, but their creation proved to be one of the main keys to the emergence of an orderly European society. The prefect of Paris set forth the chief principles that lay behind the founding of all of these new police units when he announced in 1828:

London policemen, 1850. Professional police forces did not exist before the early nineteenth century. The London police force was created by Parliament in 1828. [Mansell Collection]

Safety by day and night, free traffic movement, clean streets, the supervision of and precaution against accidents, the maintenance of order in public places, the seeking out of offences and their perpetrators. . . . The municipal police is a parental police.[2]

Professional police forces appeared in Paris in 1828. The same year the British Parliament passed legislation sponsored by Sir Robert Peel (1788–1850) that placed police on London streets. They were soon known as *bobbies* after the sponsor of the legislation. Similar police departments were deployed in Berlin after the Revolution of 1848. All of these forces were distinguished by an easily recognizable uniform. Police on the Continent were armed; those in Britain were not.

Although citizens sometimes viewed police with a certain suspicion, by the end of the century, most Europeans held friendly views toward police and regarded them as their protectors. Persons from the upper and middle classes felt their property to be more secure. Persons from the working class also frequently turned to the police to protect their lives and property and to aid them in other ways in emergencies. Of course, such was not the attitude toward political or secret police, who were hated and dreaded wherever governments created them.

[2]Quoted in Clive Emsley, *Policing and Its Context, 1750–1870* (London: Macmillan, 1983), p. 58.

## Prison Reform

Before the nineteenth century, European prisons were local jails or state prisons, such as the Bastille. Governments also sent criminals to prison ships, called *hulks*. Some Mediterranean nations sentenced prisoners to naval galleys, where, chained to their benches, they rowed until they died or were eventually released. Prisons inmates lived under wretched conditions. Men, women, and children were housed together. Persons guilty of minor offenses were left in the same room with those guilty of the most serious offenses.

Beginning in the late eighteenth century, the British government used the penalty of transportation for persons convicted of the most serious offenses. Transportation to the colony of New South Wales in Australia was regarded as an alternative to capital punishment and was used by the British until the middle of the nineteenth century, when the colonies began to object. Thereafter the British government established public works prisons in Britain to house long-term prisoners.

By the close of the eighteenth century and the early decades of the nineteenth century, reformers, such as John Howard (1726–1790) and Elizabeth Fry (1780–1845) in England and Charles Lucas (1803–1889) in France, exposed the horrendous conditions in prisons and demanded change. Reform came slowly because of the expense of constructing new prisons and a general lack of sympathy for criminals.

In many prisons, treadmills like these were the only source of exercise available to English prisoners. [Bildarchiv Preussischer Kulturbesitz]

In the 1840s, however, both the French and the English undertook several bold efforts at prison reform. These reform efforts would appear to indicate a shift in opinion whereby crime was seen not as an assault on order or on authority but as a mark of a character fault in the criminal. Thereafter part of the goal of imprisonment was to rehabilitate or transform the prisoner during the period of incarceration. The result of this change was the creation of exceedingly repressive prison systems designed according to the most advanced scientific modes of understanding criminals and criminal reform.

Europeans used various prison models originally established in the United States. All these experiments depended on separating prisoners from each other. One was known as the Auburn system after Auburn Prison in New York State. According to it, prisoners were separated during the night but could associate in work time during the day. The other was the Philadelphia system, in which prisoners were kept rigorously separated at all times.

The chief characteristics of these systems were an individual cell for each prisoner and long periods of separation and silence among prisoners. The most famous example of this kind of prison in Europe was Pentonville Prison near London. There each prisoner occupied a separate cell and was never allowed to speak to or see another prisoner. Each prisoner wore a mask when in the prison yard; in the chapel, each had a separate stall. The point of

the system was to turn the prisoner's mind in on itself to a mode of contemplation that would reform criminal tendencies. As time passed, the system became more relaxed because the intense isolation often led to mental collapse.

In France, imprisonment became more repressive as the century passed. The French constructed prisons similar to Pentonville in the 1840s. In 1875 the French also adopted a firm general policy of isolation of inmates in prison. Sixty prisons based on this principle were constructed by 1908. Prisoners were supposed to be trained in some kind of trade or skill while in prison so they could reemerge as reformed citizens.

The vast increase in repeat offenses led the French government in 1885 to declare transportation the penalty for repeated serious crimes. It did this long after the British had abandoned the practice. The French sent serious repeat offenders to places, such as the infamous Devil's Island off the coast of South America, literally to purge the nation of its worst criminals and to ensure that they would never return.

All of these attempts to create a police force and to reform prisons illustrate the new post-French Revolution concern about order and stability by European political and social elites. On the whole, by the end of the century, an orderly society had been established, and the new police and prisons had no small role in that development.

# Classical Economics

Economists whose thought largely derived from Adam Smith's *Wealth of Nations* (1776) dominated private and public discussions of industrial and commercial policy. Their ideas are often associated with the phrase *laissez-faire*. Although they thought that the government should perform many important functions, the classical economists favored economic growth through competitive free enterprise. They conceived of society as consisting of atomistic individuals whose competitive efforts met the demands of consumers in the marketplace. They believed that most economic decisions should be made through the mechanism of the marketplace. They distrusted government action, believing it to be mischievous and corrupt. The government should maintain a sound currency, enforce contracts, protect property, impose low tariffs and taxes, and leave the remainder of economic life to private initiative. The economists naturally assumed that the state would maintain enough armed forces and naval power to protect the nation's economic structure and foreign trade. The emphasis on thrift, competition, and personal industriousness voiced by the political economists appealed to the middle classes.

## Malthus on Population

The classical economists suggested complicated and pessimistic ideas about the working class. Thomas Malthus (1766–1834) and David Ricardo (1772–1823), probably the most influential of all these writers, suggested, in effect, that the condition of the working class could not be improved. In 1798 Malthus published the first edition of his *Essay on the Principle of Population*. His ideas have haunted the world ever since. He contended that population must eventually outstrip the food supply. Although the human population grows geometrically, the food supply can expand only arithmetically. There was little hope of averting the disaster, in Malthus's opinion, except through late marriage, chastity, and contraception, the last of which he considered a vice. It took three-quarters of a century for contraception to become a socially acceptable method of containing the population explosion.

Malthus contended that the immediate plight of the working class could only become worse. If wages were raised, the workers would simply produce more children, who would, in turn, consume both the extra wages and more food. Later in his life, Malthus suggested, in a more optimistic vein, that if the working class could be persuaded to adopt a higher standard of living, their increased wages might be spent on consumer goods rather than on more children.

## Ricardo on Wages

In his *Principles of Political Economy* (1817), David Ricardo transformed the concepts of Malthus into the Iron Law of Wages. If wages were raised, more children would be produced. They, in turn, would enter the labor market, thus expanding the number of workers and lowering wages. As wages fell, working people would produce fewer children. Wages would then rise, and the process would start all over again. Consequently, in the long run, wages would always tend toward a minimum level. These arguments simply supported employers in their natural reluctance to raise wages and also provided strong theoretical support for opposition to labor unions. The ideas of the economists were spread to the public during the 1830s through journals, newspapers, and even short stories, such as Harriet Martineau's (1802–1876) series entitled *Illustrations of Political Economy*.

## Government Policies Based on Classical Economics

The working class of France and Great Britain, needless to say, resented these attitudes, but the governments embraced them. Louis Philippe (1773–1850) and his minister François Guizot (1787–1874) told the French to go forth and enrich themselves. People who simply displayed sufficient energy need not be poor. A number of the French middle class did just that. The July Monarchy (1830–1848) saw the construction of major capital-intensive projects, such as roads, canals, and railways. Little, however, was done about the poverty in the cities and the countryside.

In Germany, the middle classes made less headway. The Prussian reformers after the Napoleonic wars, however, had seen the desirability of abolishing internal tariffs that impeded economic growth. In 1834 all the major German states, except Austria, formed the *Zollverein*, or free trading union. Classical economics had less influence in Germany because of the tradition dating from enlightened

*Harriet Martineau (1802–1876) popularized the ideas of the British classical economists, using moral tales to illustrate their principles. [The Bettmann Archive]*

whom the law should serve. The application of reason and utility would remove the legal clutter that prevented justice from being realized. He believed the principle of utility could be applied to other areas of government administration.

Bentham gathered round him political disciples who combined his ideas with those of classical economics. In 1834 the reformed House of Commons passed a new Poor Law that had been prepared by followers of Bentham. This measure established a Poor Law Commission that set out to make poverty the most undesirable of all social situations. Government poor relief was to be disbursed only in workhouses. Life in the workhouse was consciously designed to be more unpleasant than life outside. Husbands and wives were separated; the food was bad; and the enforced work was distasteful. The social stigma of the workhouse was even worse. The law and its administration presupposed that people would not work because they were lazy. The laboring class, not unjustly, regarded the workhouses as new "bastilles."

The second British monument to applied classical economics was the repeal of the Corn Laws in 1846. The Anti-Corn Law League, organized by manufacturers, had sought this goal for more than six years. The league wanted to abolish the tariffs protecting the domestic price of grain. That change would lead to lower food prices, which would then allow lower wages at no real cost to the workers. In turn, the prices on British manufactured goods could also be lowered to strengthen their competitive position in the world market.

The actual reason for Sir Robert Peel's repeal of the Corn Laws in 1846 was the Irish famine. Peel had to open British ports to foreign grain to feed the starving Irish. He realized that the Corn Laws could not be reimposed. Peel accompanied the abolition measure with a program for government aid to modernize British agriculture and to make it more efficient. The repeal of the Corn Laws was the culmination of the lowering of British tariffs that had begun during the 1820s. The repeal marked the opening of an era of free trade that continued until late in the century.

## Early Socialism

During the twentieth century, the socialist movement, in the form of either communist or social democratic political parties, constituted one of the

absolutism of state direction of economic development. The German economist Friedrich List (1789–1846) argued for this approach to economic growth during the second quarter of the century.

Britain was the home of the major classical economists, and their policies were widely accepted. The utilitarian thought of Jeremy Bentham (1748–1832) increased their influence. Although utilitarianism did not originate with him, Bentham sought to create codes of scientific law that were founded on the principle of utility, that is, the greatest happiness for the greatest number. In his *Fragment on Government* (1776) and *The Principles of Morals and Legislation* (1789), Bentham explained that the application of the principle of utility would overcome the special interests of privileged groups who prevented rational government. He regarded the existing legal and judicial systems as burdened by traditional practices that harmed the very people

major political forces in Europe. Less than 150 years ago, the advocates of socialism lacked any meaningful political following, and their doctrines appeared blurred and confused to most of their contemporaries.

The early socialists generally applauded the new productive capacity of industrialism. They denied, however, that the free market could adequately produce and distribute goods the way the classical economists claimed. In the capitalist order, the socialists saw primarily mismanagement, low wages, maldistribution of goods, and suffering arising from the unregulated industrial system. Moreover, the socialists thought that human society should be organized as a community rather than merely as a conglomerate of atomistic, selfish individuals.

## Utopian Socialism

Among the earliest people to define the social question were a group of writers called the *utopian socialists* by their later critics. They were considered *utopian* because their ideas were often visionary and because they frequently advocated the creation of ideal communities. They were called *socialists* because they questioned the structures and values of the existing capitalistic framework. In some cases, they actually deserved neither description. A significant factor in the experience of almost all these groups was the discussion and sometimes the practice of radical ideas in regard to sexuality and the family. People who might have been sympathetic to their economic concerns were profoundly unsympathetic to their views on free love and open family relationships.

SAINT-SIMONIANISM   Count Claude Henri de Saint-Simon (1760–1825) was the earliest of the socialist pioneers. As a young liberal French aristocrat, he had fought in the American Revolution. Later he welcomed the French Revolution, during which he made and lost a fortune. By the time of Napoleon's ascendancy, he had turned to a career of writing and social criticism.

Above all else, Saint-Simon believed that modern society would require rational management. Private wealth, property, and enterprise should be subject to an administration other than that of its owners. His ideal government would have consisted of a large board of directors organizing and coordinating the activity of individuals and groups to achieve social harmony. In a sense he was the ideological father of

technocracy. Not the redistribution of wealth but its management by experts would alleviate the poverty and social dislocation of the age.

When Saint-Simon died in 1825, he had persuaded only a handful of people that his ideas were correct. Nonetheless, Saint-Simonian societies were always centers for lively discussion of advanced social ideals. Some of the earliest debates in France over feminism took place within those societies. During the late 1820s and 1830s, the Saint-Simonians became well known for advocating sexuality outside marriage. Interestingly enough, several of Saint-Simon's disciples became leaders in the French railway industry during the 1850s.

OWENISM   The major British contributor to the early socialist tradition was Robert Owen (1771–1858), a self-made cotton manufacturer. In his early twenties, Owen became a partner in one of the largest cotton factories in Britain at New Lanark, Scotland. Owen was a firm believer in the environmentalist psychology of the Enlightenment. If human beings were placed in the correct surroundings, they and their character could be improved. Moreover, Owen saw no incompatibility between creating a humane industrial environment and making a good profit.

At New Lanark, he put his ideas into practice. Workers were provided with good quarters. Recreational possibilities abounded, and the children received an education. There were several churches, although Owen himself was a notorious freethinker on matters of religion and sex. In the factory itself, various rewards were given for good work. His plant made a fine profit. Visitors flocked from all over Europe to see what Owen had accomplished through enlightened management.

In numerous articles and pamphlets, as well as in letters to influential people, Owen pleaded for a reorganization of industry based on his own successful model. He envisioned a series of communities shaped like parallelograms in which factory and farm workers might live together and produce their goods in cooperation. During the 1820s, Owen sold his New Lanark factory and then went to the United States, where he established the community of New Harmony, Indiana. When quarrels among the members led to the community's failure, he refused to give up his reformist causes. He returned to Britain, where he became the moving force behind the organization of the Grand National Union. This was an attempt to draw all British trade unions into a single body. It collapsed with other labor organizations during the early 1830s.

FOURIERISM   Charles Fourier (1772–1837) was the French intellectual counterpart of Owen. He was a commercial salesperson who never succeeded in attracting the same kind of public attention as Owen. He wrote his books and articles and waited at home each day at noon, hoping to meet a patron who would undertake his program. No one ever arrived to meet him. Fourier believed that the industrial order ignored the passionate side of human nature. Social discipline ignored all the pleasures that human beings naturally seek.

Fourier advocated the construction of communities, called *phalanxes*, in which liberated living would replace the boredom and dullness of industrial existence. Agrarian rather than industrial production would predominate in these communities. Sexual activity would be relatively free, and marriage was to be reserved only for later life. Fourier also urged that no person be required to perform the same kind of work for the entire day. People would be both happier and more productive if they moved from one task to another. Through his emphasis on the problem of boredom, Fourier isolated one of the key difficulties of modern economic life.

Saint-Simon, Owen, and Fourier expected some existing government to carry out their ideas. They failed to confront the political difficulties of their envisioned social transformations. Other figures paid more attention to the politics of the situation. In 1839 Louis Blanc (1811–1882) published *The Organization of Labor*. Like other socialist writers, this Frenchman demanded an end to competition, but he did not seek a wholly new society. He called for political reform that would give the vote to the working class. Once so empowered, workers could use the vote to turn the political processes to their own economic advantage. A state controlled by a working-class electorate would finance workshops to employ the poor. In time, such workshops might replace private enterprise, and industry would be organized to ensure jobs. Blanc recognized the power of the state to improve life and the conditions of labor. The state itself could become the great employer of labor.

## Anarchism

Other writers and activists of the 1840s, however, rejected both industry and the dominance of government. These were the *anarchists*. They are usually included in the socialist tradition, although they do not exactly fit. Some favored programs of violence and terrorism; others were peaceful. Auguste Blanqui (1805–1881) was a major spokesperson for terror. He spent most of his adult life in jail. Seeking the abolition of both capitalism and the state, Blanqui urged the development of a professional revolutionary vanguard to attack capitalist society. His ideas for the new society were vague, but in his call for professional revolutionaries he foreshadowed Lenin.

Pierre Joseph Proudhon (1809–1865) represented the other strain of anarchism. In his most famous work, *What Is Property?* (1840), Proudhon attacked the banking system, which rarely extended credit to small property owners or the poor. He wanted credit expanded to allow such people to engage in economic enterprise. Society should be organized on the basis of mutualism, which amounted to a system of small businesses. There would be peaceful cooperation and exchange of goods among these groups. With such a social system, the state as it then existed would be unnecessary. His ideas later influenced the French labor movement, which was generally less directly political in its activities than the movements in Britain or Germany.

## Marxism

Too often the history of European socialism is regarded as a linear development leading naturally or necessarily to the late-century triumph of Marxism. Nothing could be further from the truth. Marxist socialist ideas did eventually triumph over much, though not all, of Europe, but only through competition with other socialist formulas. At midcentury, the ideas of Karl Marx were simply one more contribution to a heady mixture of concepts and programs criticizing the emerging industrial capitalist society. Marxism differed from its competitors in its claims to scientific accuracy, its rejection of reform, and its call for revolution, though the character of that revolution was not well defined.

Karl Marx (1818–1883) was born in the Rhineland. His family was Jewish, but his father had converted to Lutheranism, and Judaism played no role in his education. Marx's middle-class parents sent him to the University of Berlin, where he became deeply involved in Hegelian philosophy and radical politics. During 1842 and 1843, he edited the radical *Rhineland Gazette* (*Rheinische Zeitung*). Soon the German authorities drove him from his native land. He lived as an exile in Paris, then in Brussels, and finally, after 1849, in London.

PARTNERSHIP WITH ENGELS  In 1844 Marx met Friedrich Engels (1820–1895), another young middle-class German, whose father owned a textile factory in Manchester, England. The next year Engels published *The Conditions of the Working Class in England*, which presented a devastating picture of industrial life. The two men became fast friends. Late in 1847, they were asked to write a pamphlet for a newly organized and ultimately short-lived secret Communist League. The *Communist Manifesto*, published in German, appeared early in 1848. Marx, Engels, and the league had adopted the name *communist* because the term was much more self-consciously radical than socialist. *Communism* implied the outright abolition of private property rather than some less extensive rearrangement of society. A work of fewer than fifty pages, the Manifesto would become the most influential political document of modern European history, but that development lay in the future. At the time it was simply one more political tract. Moreover, neither Marx nor his thought had any effect on the revolutionary events of 1848.

SOURCES OF MARX'S IDEAS  The major ideas of the *Manifesto* and of Marx's later work, including *Capital* (vol. I, 1867), were derived from German Hegelianism, French socialism, and British classical economics. Marx applied to social and economic development Hegel's concept that thought develops from the clash of thesis and antithesis into a new intellectual synthesis. For Marx, the conflict between dominant and subordinate social groups generated conditions that led to the emergence of a new dominant social group. These new social relationships, in turn, generated new discontent, conflict, and development.

The French socialists provided Marx with a portrayal of the problems of capitalist society and had raised the issue of property redistribution. Both Hegel and Saint-Simon led Marx to see society and economic conditions as developing through historical stages. The classical economists had produced the analytical tools for an empirical, scientific examination of industrial capitalist society. Marx later explained to a friend:

*Karl Marx's socialist philosophy eventually triumphed over most alternative versions of socialism in Europe, but his monumental work has been subject to varying interpretations, criticisms, and revisions that continue to this day. [Bildarchiv Preussischer Kulturbesitz]*

What I did that was new was to prove: (1) that the existence of classes is bound up with particular historical phases in the development of production; (2) that the class struggle necessarily leads to the dictatorship of the proletariat; (3) that this dictatorship itself only constitutes the transition to the abolition of all classes and to a classless society.[3]

REVOLUTION THROUGH CLASS CONFLICT  In the *Communist Manifesto*, Marx and Engels contended that human history must be understood rationally and as a whole. History is the record of humankind's coming to grips with physical nature to produce the goods necessary for survival. That basic productive process determines the structures, values, and ideas of a society. Historically, the orga-

[3]Albert Fried and Ronald Sanders, eds., *Socialist Thought: A Documentary History* (Garden City, N.Y.: Anchor Doubleday, 1964), p. 295.

nization of the means of production has always involved conflict between the classes who owned and controlled the means of production and those classes who worked for them. That necessary conflict has provided the engine for historical development; it is not an accidental by-product of mismanagement or bad intentions. Thus, piecemeal reforms cannot eliminate the social and economic evils that are inherent in the very structures of production. A radical social transformation is required. The development of capitalism will make such a revolution inevitable.

In Marx's and Engels's eyes, the class conflict that had characterized previous Western history had become simplified during the early nineteenth century into a struggle between the bourgeoisie and the proletariat, or between the middle class and the workers. The character of capitalism ensured the sharpening of the struggle. Capitalist production and competition would steadily increase the size of the unpropertied proletariat. Large-scale mechanical production crushed both traditional and smaller industrial producers into the ranks of the proletariat. As the business structures grew larger and larger, the competitive pressures would squeeze out smaller middle-class units. Competition among the few remaining giant concerns would lead to more intense suffering for the proletariat.

As the workers suffered increasingly from the competition among the ever-enlarging firms, Marx contended, they would eventually begin to foment revolution. Finally, they would overthrow the few remaining owners of the means of production. For a time the workers would organize the means of production through a dictatorship of the proletariat. This would eventually give way to a propertyless and classless communist society.

This proletarian revolution was inevitable, according to Marx and Engels. The structure of capitalism required competition and consolidation of enterprise. Although the class conflict involved in the contemporary process resembled that of the past, it differed in one major respect. The struggle between the capitalistic bourgeoisie and the industrial proletariat would culminate in a wholly new society that would be free of class conflict. The victorious proletariat, by its very nature, could not be a new oppressor class: "The proletarian movement is the self-conscious, independent movement of the immense majority, in the interest of the immense majority."[4] The result of the proletarian victory would be "an association, in which the free development of each is the condition for the free development of all."[5] The victory of the proletariat over the bourgeoisie would represent the culmination of human history. For the first time in human history, one group of people would not be oppressing another.

The economic environment of the 1840s had conditioned Marx's analysis. The decade had seen much unemployment and deprivation. During the later part of the century, however, capitalism did not collapse as he had predicted, nor did the middle class become proletarianized. Rather, more and more people came to benefit from the industrial system. Nonetheless, within a generation Marxism had captured the imagination of many socialists, especially in Germany, and large segments of the working class. Marxist doctrines appeared to be based on the empirical evidence of hard economic fact. This scientific claim of Marxism helped the ideology as science became more influential during the second half of the century.

## 1848: Year of Revolutions

In 1848 a series of liberal and nationalistic revolutions erupted across the Continent. No single factor caused this general revolutionary ground-swell; rather, similar conditions existed in several countries. Severe food shortages had prevailed since

[4]Robert C. Tucker, ed., *The Marx–Engels Reader* (New York: W. W. Norton, 1972), p. 353.
[5]Ibid.

*During the February days of the French Revolution of 1848 crowds in Paris burned the throne of Louis Philippe. [Bildarchiv Preussischer Kulturbesitz]*

1846. Grain and potato harvests had been poor. The famine in Ireland was simply the worst example of a more widespread situation. The commercial and industrial economy was also depressed. Unemployment was widespread. All systems of poor relief were overburdened. These difficulties, added to the wretched living conditions in the cities, heightened the sense of frustration and discontent of the urban artisan and laboring classes.

The dynamic force for change in 1848 originated, however, not with the working classes but with the political liberals, who were generally drawn from the middle classes. Throughout the Continent, liberals were pushing for their program of more representative government, civil liberty, and unregulated economic life. The repeal of the English Corn Laws and the example of peaceful agitation by the Anti-Corn Law League encouraged them. The liberals on

the Continent wanted to pursue similar peaceful tactics. To put additional pressure on their governments, however, they began to appeal for the support of the urban working classes. The goals of the latter were improved working and economic conditions rather than a liberal framework of government. Moreover, the tactics of the working classes were frequently violent rather than peaceful. The temporary alliance of liberals and workers in several states overthrew or severely shook the old order; then the allies began to fight each other.

Finally, outside France, nationalism was an important common factor in the uprisings. Germans, Hungarians, Italians, Czechs, and smaller national groups in eastern Europe sought to create national states that would reorganize or replace existing political entities. The Austrian Empire, as usual, was the state most profoundly endangered by nationalism. At the same time, however, various national groups clashed with each other during these revolutions.

The immediate results of the 1848 revolutions were stunning. Never in a single year had Europe known so many major uprisings. The French monarchy fell, and many other thrones were badly shaken. Yet the revolutions proved a false spring for progressive Europeans. Without exception, the revolutions failed to establish genuinely liberal or national states. The conservative order proved stronger and more resilient than anyone had expected. Moreover, the liberal middle-class political activists in each country discovered that they could no longer push for political reform without also raising the social question. The liberals refused to follow political revolution with social reform and thus isolated themselves from the working classes. Once separated from potential mass support, the liberal revolutions became an easy prey to the armies of the reactionary classes.

## France: The Second Republic and Louis Napoleon

As had happened twice before, the revolutionary tinder first blazed in Paris. The liberal political opponents of the corrupt regime of Louis Philippe and his minister Guizot had organized a series of political banquets. These occasions were used to criticize the government and to demand further middle-class admission to the political process. The poor harvests of 1846 and 1847 and the resulting high food prices and unemployment brought working-class support to the liberal campaign. On February 21, 1848, the government forbade further banquets. A large one had been scheduled for the next day. On February 22, disgruntled Parisian workers paraded through the streets demanding reform and Guizot's ouster. The next morning the crowds grew, and by afternoon Guizot had resigned. The crowds had erected barricades, and numerous clashes had occurred between the citizenry and the municipal guard. On February 24, 1848, Louis Philippe abdicated and fled to England.

THE NATIONAL ASSEMBLY AND PARIS WORKERS  The liberal opposition, led by the poet Alphonse de Lamartine (1790–1869), organized a provisional government. They intended to call an election for an assembly that would write a republican constitu-tion. The various working-class groups in Paris had other ideas; they wanted a social as well as a political revolution. Led by Louis Blanc, they demanded representation in the cabinet. Blanc and two other radical leaders were made ministers. Under their pressure, the provisional government organized national workshops to provide work and relief for thousands of unemployed workers.

On Sunday, April 23, an election based on universal male suffrage chose the new National Assembly. The result was a legislature dominated by moderates and conservatives. In the French provinces, there had been much resentment against the Paris radicals. The church and the local notables still exercised considerable influence. Small landowning peasants feared possible confiscation of their holdings by Parisian socialists. The new conservative National Assembly had little sympathy for the expensive national workshops, which they incorrectly perceived to be socialistic.

Throughout May, government troops and the Parisian crowd of unemployed workers and artisans clashed. As a result, the assembly closed the workshops to new entrants and planned the removal of many enrolled workers. By late June, barricades again appeared in Paris. On June 24, under orders from the government, General Cavaignac (1802–1857), with troops drawn largely from the conservative countryside, moved to destroy the barricades and to quell potential disturbances. During the next two days, more than 400 people were killed. Thereafter, troops hunted down another 3,000 persons in street fighting. The drive for social revolution had ended.

EMERGENCE OF LOUIS NAPOLEON  The so-called June Days confirmed the political predominance of conservative property holders in French life. They wanted a state safe for small property. This search for social order received further confirmation late in 1848. The victor in the presidential election was Louis Napoleon Bonaparte (1808–1873), a nephew of the great emperor. For most of his life, he had been an adventurer living outside France. Twice he had attempted to lead a coup against the July Monarchy. The disorder of 1848 gave him a new opportunity to enter French political life. After the corruption of Louis Philippe and the turmoil of the early months of the Second Republic, the voters turned to the name of Bonaparte as a source of stability and greatness.

# Paris Workers Complain About the Actions of the Second Republic

*In the late spring of 1848 the government of the recently formed Second French Republic abolished the national workshops that it had created a few weeks earlier to provide aid for the unemployed. The first selection below illustrates the anger felt by the workers. The second selection describes the experience of a cabinet worker who had for a time enrolled in one of the workshops.*

✦ *Each of these statements reflects political disillusionment, but how does each reflect a different kind of disillusionment? How does the first statement reflect a sense of an expected economic reward for political action? How does the second statement reflect a belief in a political philosophy of cooperation among different classes or social groups?*

To the Finance Minister of the Republic

Are you really the man who was the first finance minister of the Republic, of the Republic won at the cost of blood thanks to the workers' courage, of this Republic whose first vow was to provide bread every day for all its children by proclaiming the universal right to work. Work, who will give it to us if not the state at a time when industry has everywhere closed its workshops, shops and factories? Yesterday martyrs for the Republic out on the barricades, today its defenders in the ranks of the national guard, the workers might consider it owed them something. . . .

Why do the national workshops so rouse your reprobation . . .? You are not asking for their reform, but for their total abolition. But what is to be done with this mass of 100,000 workers who are waiting each day for their modest pay, for the means of existence for themselves and their families? Are they to be left a prey to the evil influences of hunger and of the excesses that follow in the wake of despair?

A Letter to a Newspaper Editor

I live in the fauborg [working class neighborhood]; by trade I am a cabinet-maker and I am enrolled in the national workshops, waiting for trade to pick up again.

I went into the workshops when I could no longer find bread elsewhere. Since then people have said we were given charity there. But when I went in I did not think that I was becoming a beggar. I believed that my brothers who were rich were giving me a little of what they had to spare simply because I was their brother.

I admit that I have not worked very hard in the national workshops, but then I have done what I could. I am too old now to change my trade easily—that is one explanation. But there is another: the fact is that, in the national workshops, there is absolutely nothing to do.

*Roger Price, ed. and trans, 1848 in France (Ithaca, N.Y.: Cornell University Press, 1975), pp. 103–104.*

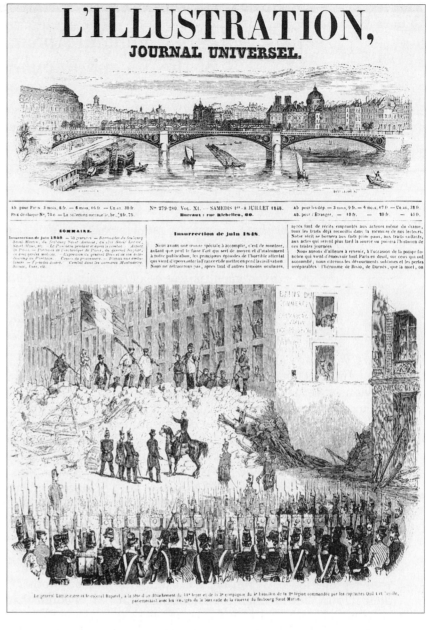

*During June 1848, troops moved against the insurrection in Paris. This edition of a French journal is reporting those events and illustrates a moment before a clash between troops and revolutionaries.*
*[Bildarchiv Preussischer Kulturbesitz]*

The election of the "Little Napoleon" doomed the Second Republic. Louis Napoleon was dedicated to his own fame rather than to republican institutions. He was the first of the modern dictators who, by playing on unstable politics and social insecurity, greatly changed European life. He constantly quarreled with the National Assembly and claimed that he, rather than they, represented the will of the nation. In 1851 the assembly refused to amend the constitution to allow the president to run for reelection. Consequently, on December 2, 1851, the anniversary of the great Napoleon's victory at Austerlitz, Louis Napoleon seized personal power. Troops dispersed the assembly, and the president called for new elections. More than 200 people died resisting the coup, and more than 26,000 persons were arrested throughout the country. Almost 10,000 persons who opposed the coup were transported to Algeria.

Yet, in the plebiscite of December 21, 1851, more than 7.5 million voters supported the actions of Louis Napoleon and approved a new constitu-

# Alexis de Tocqueville Laments the Coup of Napoleon III

*Alexis de Tocqueville (1805–1859) was one of the shrewdest political observers of the first half of the nineteenth century. He was deeply troubled by what he saw as a tendency in French politics to swing form democratic excesses to dictatorship. When Louis Napoleon carried out his coup in 1851, a new dictatorship was established in France. In this letter, de Tocqueville expresses his disappointment, anger, and concern about the future.*

✦ *Why does de Tocqueville blame both Louis Philippe and the revolutionaries for the emergence of Louis Napoleon? How does he portray Louis Napoleon as appealing to conservative groups in France? Why does he think it will require a foreign policy disaster to oust Louis Napoleon from power?*

. . . When I finally want to speak of our affairs, even to my best friends (. . .), a sadness so bitter and so profound seizes me that I have trouble continuing such distressing conversations or correspondence. . . . What has happened can be defined: the most odious conduct of revolutionaries has been employed to serve the grudges and above all to calm the fears of the conservation party. Indeed, one has to go back to the Committee of Public Safety and the Terror to find anything analogous in our history to what we are seeing now. . . . [De Tocqueville discusses arbitrary arrests and the exile without trial of persons to Algeria and Guiana.] But what is heartbreaking is to see the bulk of the nation applaud and feel that it is not suppressed, but supreme. Nothing shows two things more clearly: the first, the softening of souls, which the immoral government of Louis Philippe brought about; the second, the dreadful terror into which this violent, but above all mad, Revolution of February [1848] has thrown these souls, softened and ready to bear anything with joy and even to assist in anything provided that the phantom of socialism that disturbed their enjoyment by threatening their future would disappear.

Although this government has been established by one of the greatest crimes known in history [the coup of Louis Napoleon], nevertheless it will last a long enough time, unless it hastens itself to ruin. Its excesses, its wars, its corruption must make the country forget its fear of the socialist, which necessarily requires time. God be willing, in the meantime it will not find its end in a fashion nearly as prejudicial to us as to itself, in some mad foreign adventure. We know this only too well in France; governments never escape the law of their origins. This one, which arrives by means of the army, which can only endure by means of the army, which minds its popularity and even its reason for existing only in the memories of military glory, this government will be dragged fatally into wanting territorial expansion, spheres of influence, in other words, into war. This is, at least, what I fear, and what all sensible people dread with me. In war, it will surely find death, but perhaps then its death will cost us very dearly.

*Alexis de Tocqueville to Henry Reeve, January 9, 1852, as quoted in Alexis de Tocqueville, Selected Letters on Politics and Society, ed. by Roger Boesche, trans. by James Toupin and Roger Boesche (Berkeley: University of California Press, 1985), pp. 283–284.*

tion that consolidated his power. Only about 600,000 citizens dared to vote against him. A year later, in December 1852, an empire was proclaimed, and Louis Napoleon became Emperor Napoleon III. Again a plebiscite approved the action. For the second time in just over fifty years, France had turned from republicanism to caesarism.

FRENCH WOMEN IN 1848   The years between the February Revolution of 1848 and the Napoleonic coup of 1852 saw major feminist activity on the part of French women. Especially in Paris, women seized the opportunity of the collapse of the July Monarchy to voice demands for reform of their social conditions. They joined the wide variety of political clubs that emerged in the wake of the revolution. Some of these clubs particularly emphasized women's rights. Some women even tried unsuccessfully to vote in the various elections of 1848. Both middle-class and working-class women were involved in these activities. The most radical group of women called themselves the *Vesuvians*, after the volcano in Italy. They claimed it was time for the demands of women to come forth like pent-up lava. They demanded full domestic household equality between men and women, the right of women to serve in the military, and similarity in dress for both sexes. They also conducted street demonstrations. The radical character of their demands and actions lost them the support of more moderate women.

Certain Parisian women quickly attempted to use for their own cause the liberal freedoms that suddenly had become available. They organized the *Voix des femmes* (*The Women's Voice*), a daily newspaper that addressed issues of concern to women. The newspaper insisted that improving the lot of men would not necessarily improve the condition of women. They soon organized a society with the same name as the newspaper. Many of the women involved in the newspaper and society had earlier been involved in Saint-Simonian or Fourierist groups. Members of the *Voix des femmes* group were relatively conservative feminists. They cooperated with male political groups, and they urged the integrity of the family and fidelity in marriage. They furthermore warmly embraced the maternal role for women, but tried to use that social function to raise the importance of women in society. Because motherhood and child rearing are so important to a society, they argued, women must

receive better educations, the right to work, economic security, equal civil rights, property rights, and the right to vote. The provisional government made no move to enact these rights, although some members of the assembly supported the women's groups. The emphasis on family and motherhood represented in part a defensive strategy to prevent conservative women and men from accusing the advocates of women's rights of seeking to destroy the family and traditional marriage.

The fate of French feminists in 1848 was similar to that of the radical workers. They were thoroughly defeated, and their efforts wholly frustrated. Once the elections were held that spring, the new government expressed no sympathy for their causes. The closing of the national workshops adversely affected women workers as well as men and blocked one outlet that women had used to make their needs known. The conservative crackdown on political clubs closed another arena in which women had participated. Women were soon specifically forbidden to participate in political clubs either by themselves or with men. These repressive actions repeated what had happened to politically active French women and their organizations in 1793.

At this point, women associated with the *Voix des femmes* attempted to organize workers' groups to improve the economic situation for working-class women. Two leaders of this effort, Jeanne Deroin (d. 1894) and Pauline Roland (1805–1852), were arrested, tried, and imprisoned for these activities. The former eventually went into exile from France; the latter was sent off to Algeria during the repression after the coup of Louis Napoleon. By 1852 the entire feminist movement that had sprung up in 1848 had been thoroughly eradicated.

## The Habsburg Empire: Nationalism Resisted

The events of February 1848 in Paris immediately reverberated throughout the Habsburg domains. The empire was susceptible to revolutionary challenge on every score. Its government rejected liberal institutions. Its borders cut across national lines. Its society perpetuated serfdom. During the 1840s, even Metternich had urged reform, but none was forthcoming. In 1848 the regime confronted major rebellions in Vienna, Prague, Hungary, and Italy. It was also intimately concerned about the disturbances that broke out in Germany.

*When revolution broke out in Vienna, Metternich resigned his leadership of the government. [Bildarchiv Preussischer Kulturbesitz]*

THE VIENNA UPRISING   The Habsburg troubles began on March 3, 1848, when Louis Kossuth (1802–1894), a Magyar nationalist and member of the Hungarian Diet, attacked Austrian domination of Hungary, called for the independence of Hungary, and demanded a responsible ministry under the Habsburg dynasty. Ten days later, inspired by Kossuth's speeches, students led a series of major disturbances in Vienna. The army failed to restore order. Metternich resigned and fled the country. The feebleminded Emperor Ferdinand (r. 1835–1848) promised a moderately liberal constitution. Unsatisfied, the radical students then formed democratic clubs to press the revolution further. On May 17, the emperor and the imperial court fled to Innsbruck. The government of Vienna at this point lay in the hands of a committee of more than 200 persons primarily concerned with alleviating the economic plight of Viennese workers.

What the Habsburg government actually most feared was not the urban rebellions but a potential uprising of the serfs in the countryside. Already there had been isolated instances of serfs invading manor houses and burning records. Almost immediately after the Vienna uprising, the imperial government had emancipated the serfs in much of Austria. The Hungarian Diet also abolished serfdom in March 1848. These actions smothered the most serious potential threat to order in the empire. The emancipated serfs now had little

reason to support the revolutionary movement in the cities. These emancipations were one of the most important permanent results of the Revolutions of 1848.

THE MAGYAR REVOLT   The Vienna revolt had further encouraged the Hungarians. The Magyar leaders of the Hungarian March Revolution were primarily liberals supported by nobles who wanted their aristocratic liberties guaranteed against the central government in Vienna. The Hungarian Diet passed the March Laws, a series of laws that ensured equality of religion, jury trials, the election of a lower chamber, a relatively free press, and payment of taxes by the nobility. Emperor Ferdinand approved these measures because in the spring of 1848 he could do little else.

The Magyars also hoped to establish a separate Hungarian state within the Habsburg domains. They would retain considerable local autonomy while Ferdinand remained their emperor. As part of this scheme for a partially independent state, the Hungarians attempted to annex Transylvania, Croatia, and other eastern territories of the Habsburg Empire. That policy of annexation would have brought Romanians, Croatians, and Serbs under Magyar government. These national groups resisted the drive toward Magyarization, the most important element of which was the imposition upon them of the Hungarian language. The national groups now being

*Louis Kossuth, a Magyar nationalist, seeking to raise troops to fight for Hungarian independence during the revolutionary disturbances of 1848. [Bildarchiv Preussischer Kulturbesitz]*

repressed by the Hungarians believed that they had a better chance of maintaining their national or ethnic identity, their languages, and their economic self-interest under Habsburg control. In late March the Vienna government sent Count Joseph Jellachich (1801–1859) to aid the national groups who were rebelling against the rebellious Hungarians. By early September 1848, he was leading an invasion force against Hungary with the strong support of the national groups who were resisting Magyarization. These events in Hungary represented a prime example of the clash between liberalism and nationalism. The state that the Hungarian March Laws would have governed was liberal in political structure, but it would not have allowed autonomy to the non-Magyar peoples within its borders.

CZECH NATIONALISM    In the middle of March 1848, with Vienna and Budapest in revolt, Czech nationalists had demanded that Bohemia and Moravia be permitted to constitute an autonomous Slavic state within the empire similar to that just constituted in Hungary. Conflict immediately developed, however, between the Czechs and the Germans living in these regions. The Czechs summoned a congress of Slavs, including Poles, Ruthenians, Czechs, Slovaks, Croats, Slovenes, and Serbs, who met in Prague during early June. Under the leadership of Francis Palacky (1798–1876), this first Pan-Slavic Congress issued a manifesto calling for the national equality of Slavs within the Habsburg Empire. The manifesto also protested the repression of all Slavic peoples under Habsburg, Hungarian, German, and Ottoman

# The Pan-Slavic Congress Calls for the Liberation of Slavic Nationalities

*The first Pan-Slavic Congress met in Prague in June 1848. In this "manifesto" it called for the reorganization of the Austrian Empire and the political reorganization of most of the rest of eastern Europe. Its calls for changes in the national standing of the various Slavic peoples would have touched the Russian, Austrian, and Ottoman empires as well as some of the then un-united states of Germany. The national aspirations voiced in this document would affect Europe from that time to the present. It is also important to note that the authors recognize that the principle of nationality as adapted to the political life of Slavic peoples is relatively new in 1848.*

✦ *How did the authors of this manifesto apply the individual freedoms associated with the French Revolution to the fate of individual nations? What are the specific areas of Europe that these demands would have changed? What potential national or ethnic differences among the Slavic peoples does this manifesto ignore or gloss over?*

The Slavic Congress in Prague is something unheard-of, in Europe as well as among the Slavs themselves. For the first time since our appearance in history, we, the scattered members of a great race, have gathered in great numbers from distant lands in order to become reacquainted as brothers and to deliberate our affairs peacefully. We have understood one another not only through our beautiful language, spoken by eighty millions, but also through the consonance of our hearts and the similarity of our spiritual qualities. . . .

It is not only in behalf of the individual within the state that we raise our voices and make known our demands. The nation, with all its intellectual merit, is as sacred to us as are the rights of an individual under natural law. . . .

In the belief that the powerful spiritual stream of today demands new political forms and that the state must be re-established upon altered principles, if not within new boundaries, we have suggested to the Austrian Emperor, under whose constitutional government we, the majority [of Slavic peoples] live, that he transform his imperial state into a union of equal nations. . . .

. . . We raise our voices vigorously in behalf of our unfortunate brothers, the Poles, who were robbed of their national identity by insidious force. We call upon the governments to rectify this curse and these old onerous and hereditary sins in their administrative policy, and we trust in the compassion of all Europe. . . . We demand that the Hungarian Ministry abolish without delay the use of inhuman and coercive means toward the Salvic races in Hungary, namely the Serbs, Croats, Slovaks, and Ruthenians, and that they promptly be completely assured of their national rights. Finally, we hope that the inconsiderate policies of the Porte will no longer hinder our Slavic brothers in Turkey from strongly claiming their nationality and developing it in a natural way. If, therefore, we formally express our opposition to such despicable deeds, we do so in the confidence that we are working for the good of freedom. Freedom makes the peoples who hitherto have ruled more just and makes them understand that injustice and arrogance bring disgrace not to those who must endure it but to those who act in such a manner.

*From the "Manifesto of the First Pan-Slavic Congress," trans. by Max Riedlsperger from I. I. Udalzow, Aufzeichnungen über die Geschichte des nationalen und politischen Kampfes in Böhme im Jahre 1848 (Berlin: Rutten & Loening, 1953), pp. 223–226, as quoted in Stephen Fischer-Galati, ed., Man, State, and Society in East European History (New York: Praeger Publishers, 1970), pp. 156–159.*

domination. The document raised the vision of a vast East European Slavic nation or federation of Slavic states that would extend from Poland south and eastward through Ukraine and within which Russian interests would surely dominate. Although such a state never came into being, the prospect of a unified Slavic people freed from Ottoman and Habsburg control was an important political factor in later European history. Panslavism would become a tool that Russia would use in attempts to gain the support of nationalist minorities in eastern Europe and the Balkans and to bring pressure against both the Habsburg Empire and Germany.

On June 12, the day the Pan-Slavic Congress closed, a radical insurrection broke out in Prague. General Prince Alfred Windischgraetz (1787–1862), whose wife had been killed by a stray bullet, moved his troops against the uprising. The local middle class was happy to see the radicals suppressed, as they were by June 17. The Germans in the area approved the smothering of Czech nationalism. The policy of "divide and conquer" had succeeded.

REBELLION IN NORTHERN ITALY While repelling the Hungarian and Czech bids for autonomy, the Habsburg government also faced war in northern Italy. A revolution against Habsburg domination began in Milan on March 18. Five days later the Austrian commander General Count Joseph Wenzel Radetzky (1766–1858) retreated from the city. King Charles Albert of Piedmont (r. 1831–1849), who wanted to expand the influence of his kingdom in Lombardy (the province of which Milan is the capital), aided the rebels. The Austrian forces fared badly until July, when Radetzky, reinforced by new troops, defeated Piedmont and suppressed the revolution. For the time being, Austria had held its position in northern Italy.

Vienna and Hungary remained to be recaptured. In midsummer the emperor returned to the capital. A newly elected assembly was trying to write a constitution, while within the city the radicals continued to press for further concessions. The imperial government decided to reassert its control. When a new insurrection occurred in October, the imperial army bombarded Vienna and crushed the revolt. On December 2, Emperor Ferdinand, now clearly too feeble to govern, abdicated in favor of his young nephew Francis Joseph (r. 1848–1916). Real power now lay with Prince Felix Schwarzenberg (1800–1852), who intended to use the army with full force.

On January 5, 1849, troops occupied Budapest. By March the triumphant Austrian forces had imposed military rule over Hungary, and the new emperor repudiated the recent constitution. The Magyar nobles attempted one last revolt. In August Austrian troops reinforced by 200,000 soldiers happily furnished by Tsar Nicholas I of Russia (r. 1825–1855) finally crushed the Hungarian revolt. Croatians and other nationalities who had resisted Magyarization welcomed the collapse of the Hungarian revolt. The imperial Habsburg government had survived its gravest internal challenge because of the divisions among its enemies and its own willingness to use military force with a vengeance.

## Italy: Republicanism Defeated

The brief Piedmont–Austrian war of 1848 marked only the first stage of the Italian revolution. Many Italians hoped that King Charles Albert of Piedmont would drive Austria from the peninsula and thus prepare the way for Italian unification. The defeat of Piedmont was a sharp disappointment to them. Liberal and nationalist hopes then shifted to the pope. Pius IX (r. 1846–1878) had a liberal reputation. He had reformed the administration of the Papal States. Nationalists believed that some form of a united Italian state might emerge under the leadership of this pontiff.

In Rome, however, as in other cities, political radicalism was on the rise. On November 15, 1848, a democratic radical assassinated Count Pelligrino Rossi (r. 1787–1848), the liberal minister of the Papal States. The next day, popular demonstrations forced the pope to appoint a radical ministry. Shortly thereafter, Pius IX fled to Naples for refuge. In February 1849, the radicals proclaimed the Roman Republic. Republican nationalists from all over Italy, including Giuseppe Mazzini (1805–1872) and Giuseppe Garibaldi (1807–1882), two of the most prominent, flocked to Rome. They hoped to use the new republic as a base of operations to unite the rest of Italy under a republican government.

In March 1849, radicals in Piedmont forced Charles Albert to renew the patriotic war against Austria. After the almost immediate defeat of Piedmont at the Battle of Novara, the king abdicated in favor of his son, Victor Emmanuel II (r. 1849–1878). The defeat meant that the Roman Republic must defend itself alone. The troops that attacked Rome and restored the pope came from France. The French wanted to prevent the rise of a strong, unified state on their southern border. Moreover, protection of the pope was good domestic politics for the French Republic and its president, Louis Napoleon. In early June 1849, 10,000 French soldiers laid siege to Rome. By the end of the month, the Roman Republic had dissolved. Garibaldi attempted to lead an army north against Austria but was defeated. On July 3, Rome fell to the French forces, which stayed there to protect the pope until 1870.

Pius IX returned, having renounced his previous liberalism. He became one of the archconservatives of the next quarter century. Leadership toward Italian unification would have to come from another direction.

## Germany: Liberalism Frustrated

The revolutionary contagion had also spread rapidly through numerous states of Germany. Württemberg, Saxony, Hanover, and Bavaria all experienced insurrections calling for liberal government and greater German unity. The major revolution, however, occurred in Prussia.

REVOLUTION IN PRUSSIA   By March 15, 1848, large popular disturbances had erupted in Berlin. Frederick William IV (r. 1840–1861), believing that the trouble stemmed from foreign conspirators, refused to turn his troops on the Berliners. He even announced certain limited reforms. Nevertheless,

on March 18, several citizens were killed when troops cleared a square near the palace.

The monarch was still hesitant to use his troops forcefully, and there was much confusion in the government. The king also called for a Prussian constituent assembly to write a constitution. The next day, as angry Berliners crowded around the palace, Frederick William IV appeared on the balcony to salute the corpses of his slain subjects. He made further concessions and implied that henceforth Prussia would aid the movement toward German unification. For all practical purposes, the Prussian monarchy had capitulated.

Frederick William IV appointed a cabinet headed by David Hansemann (1790–1864), a widely respected moderate liberal. The Prussian constituent assembly, however, proved to be radical and democratic. As time passed, the king and his conservative supporters decided that they would ignore the assembly. The liberal ministry resigned and was replaced by a conservative one. In April 1849, the assembly was dissolved, and the monarch proclaimed his own constitution. One of its key elements was a system of three-class voting. All adult males were allowed to vote. They voted, however, according to three classes arranged by ability to pay taxes. Thus, the largest taxpayers, who constituted only about 5 percent of the population, elected one-third of the Prussian Parliament. This system prevailed in Prussia until 1918. In the finally revised Prussian constitution of 1850, the ministry was

*German revolutionaries behind a street barricade in Berlin prepare for an assault from forces loyal to King Frederick William IV, March 18–19, 1848. [The Bettmann Archive]*

## The Revolutionary Crisis of 1848–1851

### 1848

| | |
|---|---|
| February 22–24 | Revolution in Paris forces the abdication of Louis Philippe |
| February 26 | National workshops established in Paris |
| March 3 | Kossuth attacks the Habsburg domination of Hungary |
| March 13 | Revolution in Vienna |
| March 15 | The Habsburg emperor accepts the Hungarian March Revolution Laws in Berlin |
| March 18 | Frederick William IV of Prussia promises a constitution |
| | Revolution in Milan |
| March 19 | Frederick William IV is forced to salute the corpses of slain revolutionaries in Berlin |
| March 22 | Piedmont declares war on Austria |
| April 23 | Election of the French National Assembly |
| May 15 | Worker protests in Paris lead the National Assembly to close the national workshops |
| May 17 | Habsburg emperor Ferdinand flees from Vienna to Innsbruck |
| May 18 | The Frankfurt Assembly gathers to prepare a German constitution |
| June 2 | Pan-Slavic Congress gathers in Prague |
| June 17 | A Czech revolution in Prague is suppressed |
| June 23–26 | A workers' insurrection in Paris is suppressed by the troops of the National Assembly |
| July 24 | Austria defeats Piedmont |
| September 17 | General Jellachich invades Hungary |
| October 31 | Vienna falls to the bombardment of General Windisch-Graetz |

| | |
|---|---|
| November 15 | Papal minister Rossi is assassinated in Rome |
| November 16 | Revolution in Rome |
| November 25 | Pope Pius IX flees Rome |
| December 2 | Habsburg Emperor Ferdinand abdicates and Francis Joseph becomes emperor |
| December 10 | Louis Napoleon is elected president of the Second French Republic |

### 1849

| | |
|---|---|
| January 5 | General Windischgraetz occupies Budapest |
| February 2 | The Roman Republic is proclaimed |
| March 12 | War is resumed between Piedmont and Austria |
| March 23 | Piedmont is defeated, and Charles Albert abdicates the crown of Piedmont in favor of Victor Emmanuel II |
| March 27 | The Frankfurt Parliament completes a constitution for Germany |
| March 28 | The Frankfurt Parliament elects Frederick William IV of Prussia to be emperor of Germany |
| April 21 | Frederick William IV of Prussia rejects the crown offered by the Frankfurt Parliament |
| June 18 | The remaining members of the Frankfurt Parliament are dispersed by troops |
| July 3 | Collapse of the Roman Republic after invasion by French troops |
| August 9–13 | The Hungarian forces are defeated by Austria aided by Russian troops |

### 1851

| | |
|---|---|
| December 2 | Coup d'état of Louis Napoleon |

responsible to the king alone. Moreover, the Prussian army and officer corps swore loyalty directly to the monarch.

THE FRANKFURT PARLIAMENT   While Prussia was moving from revolution to reaction, other events were unfolding in Germany as a whole. On May 18, 1848, representatives from all the German states gathered in Saint Paul's Church in Frankfurt to revise the organization of the German Confederation. The Frankfurt Parliament intended to write a moderately liberal constitution for a united Germany. The liberal character of the Frankfurt Parliament alienated both German conservatives and the German working class. The offense to the conservatives was simply the challenge to the existing political order. The Frankfurt Parliament lost the support of the industrial workers and artisans by refusing to restore the protection once afforded by the guilds. The liberals were too attached to the concept of a free labor market to offer meaningful legislation to workers. This failure marked the beginning of a profound split between German liberals and the German working class. For the rest of the century, German conservatives would be able to play on that division.

As if to demonstrate its disaffection from workers, in September 1848, the Frankfurt Parliament called in troops of the German Confederation to suppress a radical insurrection in the city. The liberals in the parliament wanted nothing to do with workers who erected barricades and threatened the safety of property.

The Frankfurt Parliament also floundered on the issue of unification. Members differed over including Austria in the projected united Germany. The "large German [grossdeutsch] solution" favored inclusion, whereas the "small German [kleindeutsch] solution" advocated exclusion. The latter formula prevailed because Austria rejected the whole notion of German unification, which raised too many other nationality problems within the Habsburg domains. Consequently, the Frankfurt Parliament looked to Prussian rather than Austrian leadership.

On March 27, 1849, the parliament produced its constitution. Shortly thereafter, its delegates offered the crown of a united Germany to Frederick William IV of Prussia. He rejected the offer, asserting that kings ruled by the grace of God rather than by the permission of manmade constitutions. On his refusal, the Frankfurt Parliament began to dissolve. Not long afterward troops drove off the remaining members.

German liberals never fully recovered from this defeat. The Frankfurt Parliament had alienated the artisans and the working class without gaining any compensating support from the conservatives. The liberals had proved themselves to be awkward, hesitant, unrealistic, and ultimately dependent on the armies of the monarchies. They had failed to unite Germany or to confront effectively the realities of political power in the German states. The various revolutions did achieve an extension of the franchise in some of the German states and the establishment of conservative constitutions. The gains were not negligible, but they were a far cry from the hopes of March 1848.

✦

*The first half of the nineteenth century had witnessed enormous, unprecedented social change in Europe. The foundations of the industrial economy were laid. Virtually no existing institution was untouched by that emerging economy. Railways crossed the Continent. New consumer goods were available. Family patterns changed, as did the social and economic expectations of women. The crowding of cities presented new social and political problems. Issues of social order came to the fore with the new concern about crime and the establishment of new police forces. An urban working class became one of the chief facts of both political and social life. The ebb and flow of the business cycle caused increased economic anxiety for workers and property owners alike.*

*While all these fundamental social changes took place, Europe was also experiencing continuing political strife. The turmoil of 1848 through 1850 ended the era of liberal revolution that had begun in 1789. Liberals and nationalists had discovered that rational argument and small insurrections would not achieve their goals. The political initiative passed for a time to the conservative political groups. Nationalists henceforth were less romantic and more hardheaded. Railways, commerce, guns, soldiers, and devious diplomacy rather than language and cultural heritage became the future weapons of national unification. The working class also adopted new tactics and organization. The era of the riot and urban insurrection was also ending. In the future, workers would turn to trade unions and political parties to achieve their political and social goals.*

*Perhaps most important after 1848, the European middle class ceased to be revolutionary. It became increasingly concerned about protecting its property against radical political and social movements associated with socialism and, increasingly, as the century passed, with Marxism. The middle class remained politically liberal only so long as liberalism seemed to promise economic stability and social security for its own style of life.*

## Review Questions

1. What inventions were particularly important in the development of industrialism? What changes did industrialism make in society? Why were the years covered in this chapter so difficult for artisans? What is meant by "the proletarianization of workers"?

2. In what ways did the industrial economy change the working-class family? What roles and duties

did various family members assume? Most specifically, how did the role of women change in the new industrial era?

3. What were the goals of the working class in the new industrial society and how did they differ from middle-class goals? How do you explain the separation of working-class and middle-class goals?

4. How did police change in the nineteenth century and why were new systems of enforcement instituted? In what ways were prisons improved and how do you account for the reform movement that led to the improvements?

5. How would you define *socialism*? What were the chief ideas of the early socialists? How did the ideas of Karl Marx differ from earlier writers?

6. What factors, old and new, led to the widespread outbreak of revolutions in 1848? Were the causes in the various countries essentially the same or did each have its own particular set of circumstances? Why did these revolutions fail throughout Europe? What roles did liberals and nationalists play in these revolutions? Why did they sometimes clash?

# Suggested Readings

B. S. ANDERSON AND J. P. ZINSSER, *A History of Their Own: Women in Europe from Prehistory to the Present*, vol. II (1988). A wide-ranging survey.

I. BERLIN, *Karl Marx: His Life and Environment* (4th ed., 1996). A classic introduction.

P. BROCK, *The Slovak National Awakening* (1976). A standard work.

E. D. BROSE, *The Politics of Technological Change in Prussia: Out of the Shadow of Antiquity, 1809–1848* (1993). Examines the role of the various social groups in the economic growth and industrialization of Prussia.

R. B. CARLISLE, *The Proffered Crown: Saint-Simonianism and the Doctrine of Hope* (1987). The best treatment of the broad social doctrines of Saint-Simonianism.

A. CLARK, *The Struggle for the Breeches: Gender and the Making of the British Working Class* (1995). An examination of the manner in which industrialization made problematical various relationships between men and women.

W. COLEMAN, *Death Is a Social Disease: Public Health and Political Economy in Early Industrial France* (1982). One of the first works in English to study this problem.

I. DEAK, *The Lawful Revolution: Louis Kossuth and the Hungarians, 1848–1849* (1979). The most significant study of the topic in English.

J. ELSTER, *An Introduction to Karl Marx* (1985). Provides the best discussion of Marx's fundamental concepts.

T. HAMEROW, *Restoration, Revolution, and Reaction: Economics and Politics in Germany, 1815–1871* (1958). Traces the forces that worked toward the failure of revolution in Germany.

R. F. HAMILTON, *The Bourgeois Epoch: Marx and Engels on Britain, France, and Germany* (1991). Examines Marx's and Engels's observations against what is known to have been the situation in each nation.

J. F. C. HARRISON, *Quest for the New Moral World: Robert Owen and the Owenites in Britain and America* (1969). Now the standard work.

G. HIMMELFARB, *The Idea of Poverty: England in the Early Industrial Age* (1984). A major work covering the subject from the time of Adam Smith through 1850.

M. IGNATIEFF, *A Just Measure of Pain: The Penitentiary in the Industrial Revolution, 1750–1850* (1978). An important treatment of early English penal thought and practice.

K. KOLAKOWSKI, *Main Currents of Marxism: Its Rise, Growth, and Dissolution*, 3 vols. (1978). An important and comprehensive survey.

D. LANDES, *The Unbound Prometheus: Technological Change and Industrial Development in Western Europe from 1750 to the Present* (1969). The best one-volume treatment of technological development in a broad social and economic context.

W. L. LANGER, *Political and Social Upheaval, 1832–1852* (1969). A remarkably thorough survey strong in both social and intellectual history as well as political narrative.

R. MAGRAW, *A History of the French Working Class*, 2 vols. (1992). A major overview based on the most recent literature.

F. MANUEL, *The Prophets of Paris* (1962). Remains a stimulating treatment of French utopian socialism and social reform.

T. W. MARGADANT, *French Peasants in Revolt: The Insurrection of 1851* (1979). A study of the rural resistance to Louis Napoleon.

J. M. MERRIMAN, *The Agony of the Republic: The Repression of the Left in Revolutionary France, 1848–1851* (1978). A major study of how the Second French Republic and popular support for it were suppressed.

C. G. MOSES, *French Feminism in the Nineteenth Century* (1984). Includes important chapters on French feminism in 1848.

P. O'BRIEN, *The Promise of Punishment: Prisons in Nineteenth-Century France* (1982). An excellent treatment of the problems of life within the prison.

H. PERKIN, *The Origins of Modern English Society, 1780–1880* (1969). A provocative attempt to look at the society as a whole.

I. PINCHBECK, *Women Workers and the Industrial Revolution, 1750–1850* (1930, rep. 1969). A pioneering study that remains of great value.

D. H. Pinkney, *Decisive Years in France, 1840–47* (1986). A detailed and careful examination of the years leading up to the Revolution of 1848.

P. Robertson, *An Experience of Women: Pattern and Change in Nineteenth-Century Europe* (1982). A useful survey.

W. H. Sewell, Jr., *Work and Revolution in France: The Language of Labor from the Old Regime to 1848* (1980). A fine analysis of French artisans.

D. Sorkin, *The Transformation of German Jewry, 1780–1840* (1987). An examination of the decades of Jewish emancipation in Germany.

J. Sperber, *The European Revolution, 1841–1851* (1993). An excellent synthesis.

P. Stearns, *Eighteen Forty-Eight: The Tide of Revolution in Europe* (1974). A good discussion of the social background.

L. S. Strumingher, *Women and the Making of the Working Class: Lyon, 1830–1870* (1979). A local study from which broader generalizations can be made.

G. D. Sussman, *Selling Mother's Milk: The Wetnursing Business in France, 1715–1914* (1982). An examination of an important subject in the history of the family and of women.

D. Thompson, *The Chartists: Popular Politics in the Industrial Revolution* (1984). An important study.

E. P. Thompson, *The Making of the English Working Class* (1964). A classic work.

L. A. Tilly and J. W. Scott, *Women, Work, and Family* (1978). A useful and sensitive survey.

D. Valenze, *The First Industrial Woman* (1995). A remarkable study of the manner in which both women and the traditional work of women became marginalized in the process of industrialization.

A. S. Wohl, *Endangered Lives: Public Health in Victorian Britain* (1983). A wide-ranging examination of the health problems created by urbanization and industrialization.

G. Wright, *Between the Guillotine and Liberty: Two Centuries of the Crime Problem in France* (1983). A useful overview.

H. Zehr, *Crime and the Development of Modern Society: Patterns of Criminality in Nineteenth-Century Germany and France* (1976). An examination of crimes against property in urban society.

# Toward
# the Modern World

The century between approximately 1850 and 1945 may quite properly be regarded as the European era of world history. The nations of Europe achieved and exercised an unprecedented measure of political, economic, and military power across the globe. No less impressive than the extent of this influence was its brevity. By 1945 much of Europe, from Britain to the Soviet Union, literally lay in ruins. Within a few years, the United States and the Soviet Union would emerge as superpowers with which no European state could compete. Furthermore, nations throughout Asia, Africa, and Latin America that had once experienced direct or indirect European rule would soon thrust off their colonial status. Both the rise and the decline of European world dominance fostered violence, warfare, and human exploitation all over the globe.

The half century after 1850 witnessed political consolidation and economic expansion that paved the way for the momentary dominance of Europe. The skillful diplomats and armies of the conservative monarchies of Piedmont and Prussia united Italy and Germany by military force. As a major new political and economic power in central Europe, Germany loomed as a potential rival to Great Britain, France, and Russia. For a time, shrewd diplomacy and a series of complex alliances contained that rivalry. At the same time, while sorting out the new power relationships on the continent, the nations of Europe exported potential conflicts overseas. The result of this externalized rivalry was a period of imperialistic ventures. By the turn of the century, these had resulted in the outright partition of Africa into areas directly governed by Europeans, in the penetration of China by European merchants, administrators, and missionaries, and the direct rule of other parts of Asia.

What permitted this unprecedented situation to arise was the economic and technological base of late-nineteenth-century European civilization. Europeans possessed the productive capacity to dominate world markets. Their banks controlled or influenced vast amounts of capital throughout the world. Their engineers constructed and later often managed railways on all the continents. Their military technology, especially their navies, allowed them to back up economic power with armed force.

With the expansion of industrial power, new political ideologies came to the fore in Europe. Across the continent, socialists challenged the ideology of liberalism and spawned internal disputes that have influenced European political life to the present day. The supporters of nationalism, the other dominant political ideology, challenged the legitimacy of any political arrangement that was not based on ethnicity or failed to recognize it. Nowhere was nationalism a more troubling force than in the multinational Habsburg Empire.

In 1914 Europe's general dominance came to an abrupt end when war, growing out of imperialistic and nationalistic rivalry, erupted among its major states. That conflict may be regarded as the central event of the twentieth century. Its effects continue to influence the world today. The Austro–Hungarian monarchy collapsed. Germany became a republic. The revolutionary socialist government of the Bolsheviks replaced the imperial government of the Russian tsars.

Social turmoil and economic dislocation accompanied the political revolutions. The victorious nations of Britain, France, and Italy had lost millions of young men, and much of their wealth had been exhausted by wartime expenditures. The military and financial participation of the United States blocked the establishment of independent economic policy by the European powers. Continuing nationalistic resentments fostered by the Paris Peace Settlement of 1919, in combination with the political and economic pressures of the 1920s and 1930s, created stressful conditions from which arose the authoritarian movements of Italian Fascism and German Nazism. By 1939 the aggression of Germany and the hesitant response of the other major powers led again to the outbreak of war in Europe. From that conflict, Europe failed to reemerge as the dominant political or economic force in the world.

Two other developments also contributed to the end of the European era of world history. First, the principle of national self-determination, applied to Europeans in the 1919 settlement, was adopted by colonial peoples asserting their own right to national independence. Second, the demand for self-determination soon became linked to a critique of foreign capitalist domination of colonial economic life, a critique flowing directly from the spread of communist ideas throughout the colonial world after the Russian Revolution. Thus, the peoples of Asia, Africa, and Latin America adopted the European ideologies of nationalism and revolutionary socialism as a solution to their own problems, turning them against their source.  ✦

| | POLITICS AND GOVERNMENT | SOCIETY AND ECONOMY | RELIGION AND CULTURE |
|---|---|---|---|
| **1850–1890** | 1851 **Louis Napoleon seizes power in France** | 1850–1910 **Height of European outward migration** | 1850–1880 **Jewish emancipation in much of Europe** |
| | 1854–1856 **Crimean War** | 1853–1870 **Haussmann redesigns Paris** | 1853–1854 **Gobineau, *Essay on the Inequality of the Human Races*** |
| | 1861 **Proclamation of the kingdom of Italy** | 1857 **Bessemer steelmaking process** | 1857 **Flaubert, *Madame Bovary*** |
| | 1862 **Bismarck becomes prime minister of Prussia** | 1861 **Serfdom abolished in Russia** | 1859 **Darwin, *The Origin of Species*** |
| | 1864 **First International founded** | | 1864 **Pius IX, *Syllabus of Errors*** |
| | 1867 **Austro–Hungarian Dual Monarchy founded** | | |
| | 1868 **Gladstone becomes British prime minister** | | |
| | 1869 **Suez Canal completed** | | |

Charles Darwin

| | POLITICS AND GOVERNMENT | SOCIETY AND ECONOMY | RELIGION AND CULTURE |
|---|---|---|---|
| | 1870 **Franco–Prussian War; French Republic proclaimed** | 1870 **Education Act and first Irish Land Act, Britain** | 1867 **Mill, *The Subjection of Women*** |
| | 1871 **German Empire proclaimed; Paris Commune** | | 1869 **Disestablishment of the Irish Church** |
| | 1874 **Disraeli becomes British prime minister** | | 1871 **Darwin, *The Descent of Man*; Religious tests abolished at Oxford and Cambridge** |
| | 1875 **Britain gains control of Suez** | 1875 **Public Health and Artisan Dwelling Acts, Britain** | 1872 **Nietzsche, *The Birth of Tragedy*** |
| | 1880s **Britain establishes Protectorate in Egypt** | | 1873–1876 **Bismarck's *Kulturkampf*** |
| | 1881 **People's Will assassinates Alexander II; Three Emperors' League is renewed** | 1881 **Second Irish Land Act** | 1879 **Ibsen, *A Doll's House*** |
| | | | 1880s **Growing anti-Semitism in Europe** |
| | | | 1880 **Zola, *Nana*** |
| | 1882 **Italy, Germany, Austria form Triple alliance** | | 1883 **Mach, *The Science of Mechanics*** |
| | 1884–1885 **Germany forms African protectorates** | | |
| | 1888 **William II becomes German emperor** | 1886 **Daimler invents internal combustion engine** | 1883 **Nietzsche, *Thus Spake Zarathustra*** |
| **1890–1918** | 1894 **Dreyfus convicted in France; Nicholas II becomes tsar of Russia** | 1890s **Oil begins to have impact on world economy** | 1892 **Ibsen, *The Master Builder*** |
| | 1898 **Germany begins to build a battleship navy** | 1894 **Union of German Women's Organizations founded** | 1893 **Shaw, *Mrs. Warren's Profession*** |
| | 1902 **British Labour Party formed** | 1895 **Diesel engine invented** | 1896 **Herzl, *The Jewish State*** |
| | 1903 **Bolshevik–Menshevik split** | 1897 **German and Czech language equality in Austrian Empire; Russia mandates eleven-and-a-half hour workday** | 1899 **Bernstein, *Evolutionary Socialism*** |
| | 1904 **Britain and France in Entente Cordiale** | | 1900 **Freud, *The Interpretation of Dreams*; Key, *The Century of the Child*** |

| POLITICS AND GOVERNMENT | SOCIETY AND ECONOMY | RELIGION AND CULTURE |
|---|---|---|

**1890–1918 (cont.)**

**POLITICS AND GOVERNMENT**

1905 Revolution in Saint Petersburg suppressed; first Moroccan crisis

1906 Dreyfus conviction set aside

1908–1909 Bosnian crisis

1911 Second Moroccan crisis

1912 Third Irish Home Rule Bill passed

1912–1913 First and Second Balkan wars

1914–1918 World War I

1917 Russian Revolution; Bolsheviks seize power

**SOCIETY AND ECONOMY**

1901 National Council of French Women founded

1903 Third Irish Land Act; British Women's Social and Political Union founded; Wright brothers fly the first airplane

1906 Land redemption payments canceled for Russian peasants

1907 Women vote on national issues in Norway

1918 Vote granted to some British women

**RELIGION AND CULTURE**

1902 Lenin, *What Is to Be Done?*

1903 Shaw, *Man and Superman*

1905 Weber, *The Protestant Ethic and the Spirit of Capitalism*; Termination of the Napoleonic Concordat in France

1907 Bergson, *Creative Evolution*

1908 Sorel, *Reflections of Violence*

1910 Pope Pius X requires anti-Modernist oath

1914 Joyce, *Portrait of the Artist as a Young Man*

Signing of the Treaty of Versailles

**1918–1939**

**POLITICS AND GOVERNMENT**

1919 Paris Peace Conference; Weimar constitution proclaimed in Germany

1922 Mussolini takes power in Italy

1923 France invades the Ruhr; Hitler's Beer Hall *Putsch*; first Labour government in Britain

1924 Death of Lenin

1925 Locarno Agreements

1931 National Government formed in Great Britain

1933 Hitler appointed chancellor of Germany

1935 Nuremburg Laws; Italy invades Ethiopia

1936 Popular Front in France; purge trials in the Soviet Union; Spanish Civil War begins

1938 Munich Conference; *Kristallnacht* in Germany

1939 Germany invades Poland, starts World War II

**SOCIETY AND ECONOMY**

1920s Worldwide commodity crisis

1921 Soviet Union begins New Economic Policy

1922 French Senate rejects vote for women

1923 Rampant inflation in Germany

1926 General strike in Great Britain

1928 Britain extends full franchise to women

1928–1933 First Five-Year Plan and agricultural collectivization in the Soviet Union

1929 Wall Street crash

1932 Lausanne Conference ends German reparations

mid-1930s Nazis stimulate German economy through public works and defense spending

**RELIGION AND CULTURE**

1919 Barth, *Commentary on the Epistle to the Romans*

1920 Keynes, *Economic Consequences of the Peace*

1922 Joyce, *Ulysses*

1924 Hitler, *Mein Kampf*

1925 Woolf, *Mrs. Dalloway*

1927 Heidegger, *Being and Time*; Mann, *Buddenbrooks*

1927 Woolf, *To the Lighthouse*; Mann, *Magic Mountain*

1929 Woolf, *A Room of One's Own*

1936 Keynes, *General Theory of Employment, Interest, and Money*

1937 Orwell, *Road to Wigan Pier*

1938 Sartre, *Nausea*

*Prince Otto von Bismarck (1815–1898) was the most important statesman of the second half of the nineteenth century. He used warfare and shrewd diplomacy to lead Prussia to unify Germany. Having achieved this goal, he worked for the rest of his career to keep the peace. [Erich Lessing/Art Works]*

# The Age of Nation-States

## KEY TOPICS

- The unification of Italy and Germany
- The shift from empire to republic in France
- The emergence of dual monarchy in Austria–Hungary
- Reforms in Russia, including the emancipation of the serfs
- The emergence of Great Britain as the exemplary liberal state and its confrontation with Irish nationalists

*The revolutions of 1848 had collapsed in defeat for both liberalism and nationalism. Throughout the early 1850s, conservative regimes entrenched themselves across the Continent. Yet only a quarter century later, many of the major goals of early-nineteenth-century liberals and nationalists had been accomplished. Italy and Germany were each finally united under constitutional monarchies. The Habsburg emperor had accepted constitutional government and recognized the liberties of the Magyars of Hungary. In Russia, the tsar had emancipated the serfs. France was again a republic. Liberalism and even democracy flourished in Great Britain.*

*Paradoxically, most of these developments occurred under conservative leadership. Events within European*

*international affairs compelled some governments to pursue new policies at home as well as abroad. They had to find novel methods of maintaining the loyalty of their subjects. Some conservative leaders preferred to carry out a popular policy on their own terms, so that they, rather than the liberals, would receive credit. Other leaders acted as they did because they had no choice.*

## The Crimean War (1853–1856)

As has so often been true in modern European history, the impetus for change originated in war. The Crimean War (1853–1856) was rooted in the long rivalry between Russia and the Ottoman

Empire. Two disputes led to the conflict. First, the Ottoman Empire had recently granted Catholic France rather than Orthodox Russia the oversight of the Christian shrines in the Holy Land. Second, Russia wanted to extend its control over the Ottoman provinces of Moldavia and Walachia (now in Romania). The tsar's duty to protect Orthodox Christians in the Ottoman Empire furnished the pretext for the Russian aggression. Russia occupied the two provinces in the summer of 1853. The Ottoman Empire declared war on Russia in the autumn of that year.

The other great powers soon became involved, and a war among major European states resulted. Both France and Great Britain opposed Russian expansion in the eastern Mediterranean, where they had extensive naval and commercial interests. Napoleon III also thought that an activist foreign policy would shore up domestic support for his regime. On March 28, 1854, France and Britain declared war on Russia. Much to the disappointment of Tsar Nicholas I, Austria and Prussia remained neutral. The Austrians had their own ambitions in the Balkans, and, for the moment, Prussia followed Austrian leadership.

Both sides conducted the conflict ineptly. The ill-equipped and poorly commanded armies became bogged down along the Crimean coast of the Black Sea. In September 1855, after a long siege, the Russian fortress of Sevastopol finally fell to the French and British. In March 1856, a conference in Paris concluded the Treaty of Paris, which required Russia to surrender territory near the mouth of the Danube River, to recognize the neutrality of the Black Sea, and to renounce claims of protection over Christians in the Ottoman Empire. Even before the conference, Austria had forced Russia to withdraw from Moldavia and Walachia. The image of an invincible Russia that had prevailed across Europe since the close of the Napoleonic wars was shattered.

Also shattered was the Concert of Europe (see Chapter 21) as a means of dealing with international relations on the Continent. Following the successful repression of the 1848 uprisings, the great powers feared revolution less than they had earlier in the century, and consequently they displayed much less reverence for the Vienna settlement. As historian Gordon Craig once commented, "After 1856 there were more powers willing to fight

*During the Crimean War, Florence Nightingale of Great Britain organized nursing care for the wounded. [The Bettmann Archive]*

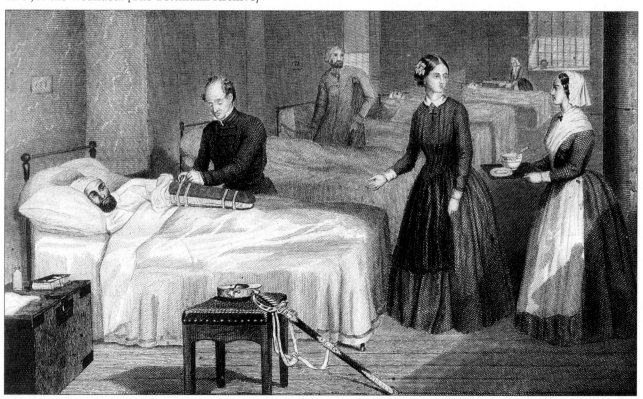

*A fortress near Sevastopol lies in ruins in August, 1855, following a bombardment during the Crimean War. [Bildarchiv Preussischer Kulturbesitz]*

to overthrow the existing order than there were to take up arms to defend it."[1] Napoleon III had little respect for the Congress of Vienna and favored redrawing the map along lines of nationality. Hoping to compensate for their failure to act during the Crimean War, the Austrians tried to assert more influence within the German Confederation. Prussia became increasingly discontented with a role in Germany subordinate to Austria's. Russia, which had been among the chief defenders of the Vienna settlement, now sought to overcome the disgrace of the 1856 Treaty of Paris. The mediocre display of British military prowess led that nation to hesitate about future continental involvement.

Consequently, for about twenty-five years after the Crimean War, European affairs were unstable, producing a period of largely unchecked adventurism in foreign policy. Without the restraining influence of the Concert of Europe, each nation believed that only the limits of its military power and its diplomatic influence should constrain its international ambitions. Moreover, foreign policy increasingly became an instrument of domestic policy. The

[1]*The New Cambridge Modern History*, vol. 10 (Cambridge, England: Cambridge University Press, 1967), p. 273.

two most significant achievements to result from this new international situation were the unifications of Italy and Germany. Those events, in turn, put further pressures on their neighbors.

## Italian Unification

Nationalists had long wanted to unite the small, absolutist principalities of the Italian peninsula into a single state. During the first half of the century, however, opinion differed about the manner and goals of Italian unification.

### Romantic Republicans

One approach to the issue was *romantic republicanism*. After the Congress of Vienna, secret republican societies were founded throughout Italy, the most famous of which was the *Carbonari* ("charcoal burners"). They were singularly ineffective.

Following the failure of nationalist uprisings in 1831, the leadership of romantic republican nationalism passed to Giuseppe Mazzini (1805–1872). He became the most important nationalist leader in all Europe and brought new emotional fervor to the

*Giuseppe Mazzini was a fervent republican nationalist. He aroused emotional support for Italian unity, but also frightened moderate Italians. [Bildarchiv Preussischer Kulturbesitz]*

cause. He once declared, "Nationality is the role assigned by God to a people in the work of humanity. It is its mission, its task on earth, to the end that God's thought may be realized in the world."[2] In 1831 he founded the Young Italy Society to drive Austria from the peninsula and establish an Italian republic.

During the 1830s and 1840s, Mazzini and his fellow republican Giuseppe Garibaldi (1807–1882) led insurrections. Both were deeply involved in the ill-fated Roman Republic of 1849. Throughout the 1850s, they continued to conduct what amounted to guerilla warfare. Because both men spent much time in exile, they became well known across the Continent and in the United States.

Republican nationalism frightened moderate Italians, who wanted to rid themselves of Austrian domination but not at the cost of establishing a

[2]Quoted in William L. Langer, *Political and Social Upheaval, 1832–1852* (New York: Harper Torchbooks, 1969), p. 115.

republic. For a time, these people had looked to the papacy as a possible vehicle for unification. That solution became impossible after the experience of Pius IX with the Roman Republic in 1849. Consequently, at mid-century, "Italy" remained a geographical expression rather than a political entity.

Yet between 1852 and 1860, the Italian peninsula was transformed into a nation-state governed by a constitutional monarchy. The process was carried out not by romantic republican nationalists but by Count Camillo Cavour (1810–1861), the moderately liberal prime minister of Piedmont. The method of unification was force of arms tied to secret diplomacy. The spirit of Machiavelli must have smiled over the enterprise.

## Cavour's Policy

Piedmont (officially styled the Kingdom of Sardinia), in northwestern Italy, was the most independent state on the peninsula. The Congress of Vienna had restored the kingdom as a buffer between French and Austrian ambitions. As we have seen, during 1848 and 1849, King Charles Albert of Piedmont, after having promulgated a conservative constitution, twice unsuccessfully fought Austria. Following the second defeat, he abdicated in favor of his son, Victor Emmanuel II (r. 1849–1878). In 1852 the new monarch chose as his prime minister Count Camillo Cavour.

A cunning statesman, Cavour had begun political life as a strong conservative but had gradually moved toward a moderately liberal position. He had made a fortune by investing in railroads, reforming agriculture on his own estates, and editing a newspaper. He was deeply imbued with the ideas of the Enlightenment, classical economics, and utilitarianism. Cavour was a nationalist of a new breed who had no respect for Mazzini's ideals. A strong monarchist, Cavour rejected republicanism. It was economic and material progress rather than romantic ideals that required a large, unified state on the Italian peninsula.

Cavour believed that if Italians proved themselves to be efficient and economically progressive, the great powers might decide that Italy could govern itself. He joined the Piedmontese Cabinet in 1850 and became premier two years later. He worked for free trade, railway construction, credit expansion, and agricultural improvement. He felt that such material and economic bonds, rather than fuzzy Romantic yearnings, must unite the Italians.

# Cavour Explains Why Piedmont Should Enter the Crimean War

*As prime minister of Piedmont, Cavour tried to prove that the Italians were capable of progressive government. In 1855, addressing the Parliament of Piedmont, he urged entry into the Crimean War, so that the other Europeans would consider Piedmont a military power. Earlier, politics in Italy had been characterized by petty absolute princes and romantic nationalist conspiracies, both of which Cavour scorned. He understood that in the nineteenth century a nation must possess good government, economic prosperity, and a strong army.*

✦ *Why does Cavour feel it necessary to condemn conspiracies as a political device? What does Cavour believe Italy must do to raise its reputation? Why is war the test of strength and character for Italy?*

The experience of recent years and previous centuries has proved (at least in my opinion) how little Italy has benefited by conspiracies, revolutions and disorderly uprisings. Far from helping her, they have been a tremendous calamity for this beautiful part of Europe. And not only, gentlemen, because individual people so often suffered from them, not only because revolutions became the cause or pretext for repression, but above all because continual conspiracies, repeated revolutions and disorderly uprisings damaged the esteem and, up to a certain point, the sympathy that other European peoples cherished for Italy.

Now, gentlemen, I believe that the principal condition for the improvement of Italy's fate, the condition that stands out above all others, is to lift up her reputation once more, so to act that all the peoples of the world, those governing and those governed, may do justice to her qualities. And for this two things are necessary: first, to prove to Europe that Italy has sufficient civic sense to govern herself freely and according to law, and that she is in a condition to adopt the very best forms of government; second, to prove that her military valor is as great as that of her ancestors.

You have done Italy one service by your conduct over the last seven years. You have shown Europe in the most luminous way that Italians are capable of governing themselves with wisdom, prudence, and trustworthiness. But it still remains for you to do Italy an equal, if not a greater, service; it is our country's task to prove that Italy's sons can fight valiantly on battlefields where glory is to be won. And I am sure, gentlemen, that the laurels that our soldiers will win in Eastern Europe will help the future state of Italy more than all that has been done by those people who hoped to regenerate her by rhetorical speeches and writings.

*As quoted in Denis Mack Smith, ed. and trans.,* The Making of Italy, 1796–1870 *(New York: Walker and Company, 1968), pp. 199–200.*

Cavour also recognized the need to capture the loyalties of those Italians who believed in other varieties of nationalism. He thus fostered the Nationalist Society, which established chapters in other Italian states to press for unification under the leadership of Piedmont. Finally, the prime minister believed that Italy could be unified only with the aid of France. The recent accession of Napoleon III in France seemed to open the way for such aid.

FRENCH SYMPATHIES   Cavour used the Crimean War to bring Italy into European politics. In 1855 Piedmont joined the conflict on the side of France and Britain and sent 10,000 troops to the front. This small but significant participation in the war allowed Cavour to raise the Italian question at the Paris conference. He left Paris with no diplomatic reward, but his intelligence and political capacity had impressed everyone. Cavour also gained the sympathy of Napoleon III. During the rest of the decade, he achieved further international respectability for Piedmont by opposing various plots of Mazzini, who was still attempting to lead nationalist uprisings. By 1858 Cavour represented a moderate liberal alternative to both republicanism and reactionary absolutism in Italy.

Cavour continued to bide his time. Then, in January 1858, an Italian named Orsini attempted to assassinate Napoleon III. The incident made the French emperor, who had once belonged to a nationalist group, newly concerned about the Italian issue. He saw himself continuing his more famous uncle's liberation of the peninsula. He also saw Piedmont as a potential ally against Austria. In July 1858, Cavour and Napoleon III met at Plombières in southern France. Riding alone in a carriage, with the emperor at the reins, the two men plotted to provoke a war in Italy that would permit them to defeat Austria. A formal treaty in December 1858 confirmed the agreement. France was to receive French-speaking Nice and Savoy from Piedmont for its aid.

WAR WITH AUSTRIA  In early 1859 tension grew between Austria and Piedmont as Piedmont mobilized its army. On April 22, Austria demanded that Piedmont demobilize. That demand allowed Piedmont to claim that Austria was provoking a war. France intervened to aid its ally. On June 4, the Austrians were defeated at Magenta, and on June 24 at Solferino. Meanwhile, revolutions had broken out in Tuscany, Modena, Parma, and the Romagna provinces of the Papal States.

With the Austrians in retreat and the new revolutionary regimes calling for union with Piedmont, Napoleon III feared too extensive a Piedmontese victory. On July 11, he independently concluded a peace with Austria at Villafranca. Piedmont received Lombardy, but Venetia remained under Austrian control. Cavour felt betrayed by France, but the war had driven Austria from most of northern Italy. Later that summer, Parma, Modena, Tuscany, and the Romagna voted to unite with Piedmont. (See Map 23–1.)

GARIBALDI'S CAMPAIGN  At this point, the forces of romantic republican nationalism compelled Cavour to pursue the complete unification of northern and southern Italy. In May 1860, Garibaldi landed in Sicily with more than 1,000 troops, who had been outfitted in the north. He captured Palermo and prepared to attack the mainland. By September he controlled the city and kingdom of Naples, probably the most corrupt example of Italian absolutism. Garibaldi had for more than two decades hoped to

*Giuseppe Garibaldi represented the forces of romantic Italian nationalism. The landing of his Redshirts on Sicily and their subsequent invasion of southern Italy in 1860 forced Cavour to unite the entire peninsula sooner than he had intended. [Bildarchiv Preussischer Kulturbesitz]*

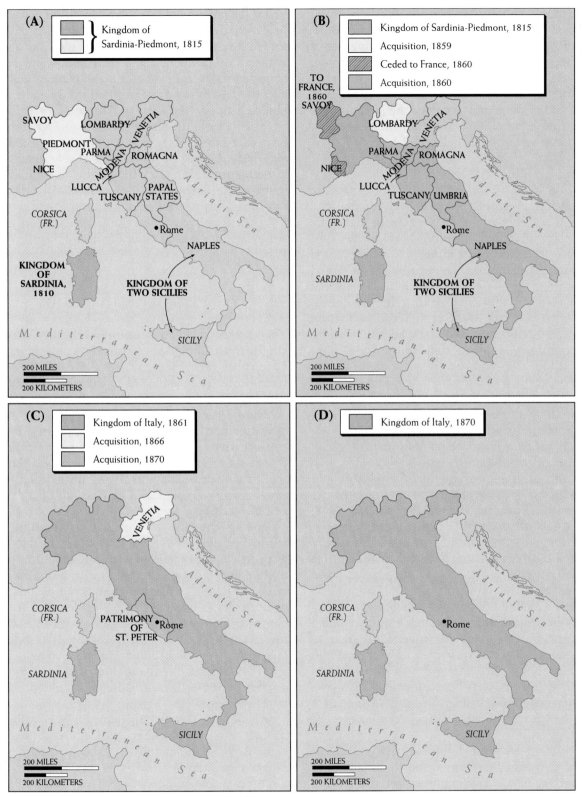

**MAP 23-1   THE UNIFICATION OF ITALY** *Beginning with the association of Sardinia and Piedmont by the Congress of Vienna in 1815, unification was achieved through the expansion of Piedmont between 1859 and 1870. Both Cavour's statesmanship and the campaigns of ardent nationalists played large roles.*

form a republican Italy, but Cavour forestalled him. He rushed Piedmontese troops south to confront Garibaldi. On the way, they conquered the rest of the Papal States except the area around Rome, which was protected for the pope by French troops. Garibaldi's nationalism won out over his republicanism, and he unhappily accepted the Piedmontese domination. In late 1860 Naples and Sicily voted to join the northern union forged by Piedmont.

### The New Italian State

In March 1861, Victor Emmanuel II was proclaimed king of Italy. Three months later Cavour died. The new state more than ever needed his skills because Italy had, in effect, been more nearly conquered than united by Piedmont. The republicans resented the treatment of Garibaldi. The clericals resented the conquest of the Papal States. In the south, armed resistance continued until 1866 against the imposition of Piedmontese-style administration. The economies of north and south Italy were incompatible. The south was rural, poor, and backward. The north was industrializing, and its economy was increasingly linked to the rest of Europe. The social structures of the two regions reflected those differences, with large landholders and peasants dominant in the south and an urban working class emerging in the north.

The political framework of the united Italy could not overcome these problems. The constitution, which was that promulgated for Piedmont in 1848, provided for a conservative constitutional monarchy. Parliament consisted of two houses: a senate appointed by the king, and a chamber of deputies elected on a narrow franchise. Ministers were responsible to the monarch, not to Parliament. These arrangements did not foster vigorous parliamentary life. Political leaders often simply avoided major problems. In place of efficient, progressive government, such as Cavour had brought to Piedmont, a system called *transformismo* developed; political opponents were "transformed" into government supporters through bribery, favors, or a seat in the cabinet. Italian politics became a byword for corruption.

Nor was unification complete. Many Italians believed that other territories should be added to their nation. The most important of these were Venetia and Rome. The former was gained in 1866 in return for Italy's alliance with Prussia in the Austro-Prussian War. Rome and the papacy continued to be guarded by French troops, first sent there in 1849, until the Franco-Prussian War of 1870 forced their withdrawal. The Italian state then annexed Rome and made it the capital. The papacy confined itself to the Vatican, and it remained hostile to the Italian state until the two sides concluded a treaty, the Lateran Accord of 1929.

By 1870 only the small province of Trent and the city of Trieste, both ruled by Austria, remained outside Italy. In and of themselves, these areas were not important, but they fueled the continued hostility of Italian nationalists toward Austria. The desire to liberate *Italia irredenta*, or "unredeemed Italy," was one reason for the Italian support of the Allies against Austria and Germany during World War I.

# German Unification

The construction of a united Germany was the single most important political development in Europe between 1848 and 1914. (See Map 23–2.) It transformed the balance of economic, military, and international power. Moreover, the method of its creation largely determined the character of the new German state. Germany was united by the conservative army, monarchy, and prime minister of Prussia, among whose chief motives was the outflanking of Prussian liberals. A unified Germany, sought for two generations by German liberals, was actually achieved for the most illiberal of reasons.

During the 1850s, German unification still seemed remote. The major states continued to trade with each other through the *Zollverein* (tariff union), and railways linked their economies. Frederick William IV of Prussia had given up thoughts of unification under Prussian leadership. Austria continued to oppose any closer union that might lessen its influence. Liberal nationalists had not recovered from the humiliating experiences of 1848 and 1849. What quickly modified this situation was a series of domestic political changes and problems within Prussia.

In 1858 Frederick William IV was adjudged insane, and his brother William assumed the regency. William I (r. 1861–1888), who became king in his own right in 1861, was less idealistic than his brother and more of a Prussian patriot. In the usual Hohenzollern tradition, his first concern was to strengthen the Prussian army. In 1860 his war minister and chief of staff proposed to enlarge the

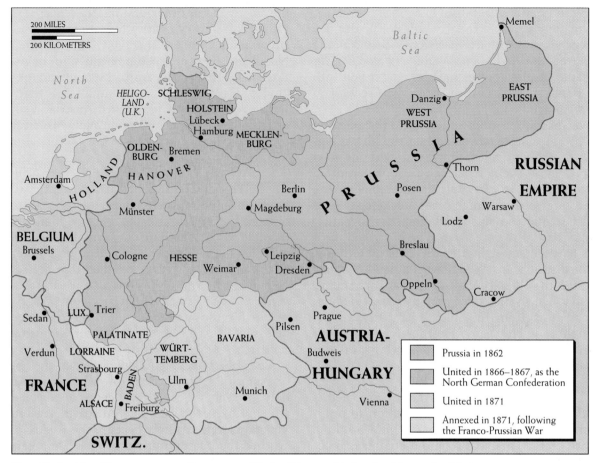

MAP 23–2   THE UNIFICATION OF GERMANY   *Under Bismarck's leadership, and with the strong support of its royal house, Prussia used diplomatic and military means, on both the German and international stages, to forcibly unify the German states into a strong national entity.*

army, to increase the number of officers, and to extend the period of conscription from two to three years. The Prussian Parliament, created by the Constitution of 1850, refused to approve the necessary taxes. The liberals, who dominated the body, sought to avoid placing additional power in the hands of the monarchy. For two years monarch and Parliament were deadlocked.

### Bismarck

In September 1862, William I turned for help to the person who, more than any other single individual, shaped the next thirty years of European history: Otto von Bismarck (1815–1898). Bismarck came from Junker (noble landlord) stock. He attended university, joined a *Burschenschaft* (a student society), and displayed an interest in German unification. Then he retired to his father's estate. During the

1840s he was elected to the provincial diet, where his stand was so reactionary as to disturb even the king. Yet he had made his mark. From 1851 to 1859, Bismarck served as the Prussian minister to the Frankfurt Diet of the German Confederation. Later he became Prussian ambassador to Russia and had just been named ambassador to France when William I appointed him prime minister of Prussia.

Although Bismarck had entered public life as a reactionary, he had mellowed into a conservative. He opposed parliamentary government but not a constitutionalism that provided for a strong monarch. He understood that Prussia—and later, Germany—must have a strong industrial base. His years in Frankfurt arguing with his Austrian counterpart had hardened his Prussian patriotism. In politics, he was a pragmatist who put more trust in power and action than in ideas. As he declared in his first speech as prime minister, "Germany is not looking to Prussia's liberalism but to her power. . . . The great questions of the day will not be decided by speeches and majority decisions—that was the mistake of 1848–1849—but by iron and blood."[3] Yet this same minister, after having led Prussia into three wars, spent the next nineteen years seeking to preserve peace.

Upon becoming prime minister in 1862, Bismarck immediately moved against the liberal Parliament. He contended that even without new financial levies, the Prussian constitution permitted the government to carry out its functions on the basis of previously granted taxes. Therefore, taxes could be collected and spent despite the parliamentary refusal to vote them. The army and most of the bureaucracy supported this interpretation of the constitution. In 1863, however, new elections sustained the liberal majority in the Parliament. Bismarck had to find some way to attract popular support away from the liberals and toward the monarchy and the army. He therefore set about uniting Germany through the conservative institutions of Prussia.

THE DANISH WAR (1864) Bismarck pursued a *kleindeutsch*, or small German, solution to unification: Austria was to be excluded from a united German state. This goal required complex diplomacy. The Schleswig–Holstein problem gave Bismarck the handle for his policy. These two northern duchies had long been ruled by the kings of Denmark without being part of Denmark itself. Their populations were a mixture of Germans and Danes. Holstein, where Germans predominated, belonged to the German Confederation. In 1863 the Danish Parliament moved to incorporate both duchies into Denmark. The smaller states of the German Confederation proposed an all-German war to halt this move. Bismarck wanted Prussia to act alone or only in cooperation with Austria. Together the two large states easily defeated Denmark in 1864.

The Danish defeat increased Bismarck's personal prestige, and over the next two years, he maneuvered Austria into war with Prussia. In August 1865, the two powers negotiated the Convention of Gastein, which put Austria in charge of Holstein and Prussia in charge of Schleswig. Bismarck then moved to mend other diplomatic fences. He had gained Russian sympathy by supporting the 1863 suppression of a Polish revolt, and he persuaded Napoleon III to promise neutrality in an Austro-Prussian conflict. In April 1866, Bismarck concluded a treaty with Italy promising that Italy would get Venetia if it attacked Austria in support of Prussia when war broke out. Now Bismarck had to provoke his war.

THE AUSTRO-PRUSSIAN WAR (1866) Constant Austro-Prussian tension had arisen over the administration of Schleswig and Holstein. Bismarck ordered the Prussian forces to be as obnoxious as possible to the Austrians. On June 1, 1866, Austria appealed to the German Confederation to intervene in the dispute. Bismarck claimed that the request violated the terms of the 1864 alliance and the Convention of Gastein. The Seven Weeks' War, which resulted in the summer of 1866, led to the decisive defeat of Austria at the Battle of Königgrätz in Bohemia.

The Treaty of Prague, which ended the conflict on August 23, was lenient toward Austria. Austria only lost Venetia, which was ceded to Napoleon III, who in turn ceded it to Italy. Austria refused to give Venetia directly to Italy because the Austrians had crushed the Italians during the war. The treaty and the military defeat permanently excluded the Habsburgs from German affairs. Prussia had thus established itself as the only major power among the German states.

THE NORTH GERMAN CONFEDERATION In 1867 the states of Hanover, Hesse, and Nassau, and the city of Frankfurt, which had all supported Austria during the war, were annexed by Prussia, and their rulers were deposed. All Germany north of the Main River now formed a federation under Prussian leadership, known as the North German Confederation. Each state retained its own local government, but all military forces were under federal control. The president of the federation was the king of Prussia, represented by his chancellor, Bismarck. There was a legislature consisting of two houses: a federal council, or *Bundesrat*, composed of members appointed by the governments of the states, and a lower house, or *Reichstag*, chosen by universal male suffrage.

Bismarck had little fear of this broad franchise, because he sensed that the peasants would vote for conservatives. Moreover, the *Reichstag* had little

[3]Quoted in Otto Pflanze, *Bismarck and the Development of Germany: The Period of Unification: 1815–1871* (Princeton, N.J.: Princeton University Press, 1963), p. 177.

real power, because the ministers were responsible only to the monarch. The *Reichstag* could not even originate legislation. All laws had to be proposed by the chancellor. The legislature did have the right to approve military budgets, but these were usually submitted to cover several years at a time. The constitution of the confederation, which after 1871 became the constitution of the German Empire, possessed some of the appearances but none of the substance of liberalism. Germany was in effect a military monarchy.

The spectacular success of Bismarck's policy overwhelmed the liberal opposition in the Prussian Parliament. The liberals were split between those who prized liberalism and those who supported unification. In the end, nationalism proved more attractive. In 1866 the Prussian Parliament retroactively approved the military budget that had been earlier disputed. Bismarck had crushed the Prussian liberals by making the monarchy and the army the most popular institutions in the country. The drive toward unification had achieved his domestic political goal.

### The Franco-Prussian War and the German Empire (1870–1871)

Bismarck now awaited an opportunity to complete unification by bringing the states of southern Germany into the confederation. Events in Spain gave him the excuse. In 1868 a military coup deposed the corrupt Bourbon queen of Spain, Isabella II (r. 1833–1868). In searching for a new monarch, the Spaniards chose Prince Leopold of Hohenzollern-Sigmaringen, a Catholic cousin of William I of Prussia. On June 19, 1870, Leopold accepted the Spanish crown with Prussian blessings. Bismarck knew that France would react strongly against the idea of a Hohenzollern Spain.

On July 2, the Spanish government announced Leopold's acceptance, and the French reacted as expected. France sent its ambassador Count Vincent Benedetti (1817–1900) to consult with William I, who was vacationing at Bad Ems. They discussed the matter at several meetings. On July 12, Leopold's father renounced his son's candidacy for the Spanish throne, fearing that the issue would cause war between Prussia and France. William was relieved that conflict had been avoided and that he had not had to order Leopold to renounce the Spanish throne.

There the matter might have rested had it not been for the impetuosity of the French and the guile of Bismarck. On July 13, the French government

| German and Italian Unification | |
|---|---|
| 1854 | Crimean War opens |
| 1855 | Cavour leads Piedmont into the war on the side of France and England |
| 1856 | Treaty of Paris concludes the Crimean War |
| 1858 | (January 14) Attempt to assassinate Napoleon III |
| 1858 | (July 20) Secret conference between Napoleon III and Cavour at Plombières |
| 1859 | War of Piedmont and France against Austria |
| 1860 | Garibaldi lands his forces in Sicily and invades southern Italy |
| 1861 | (March 17) Proclamation of the Kingdom of Italy |
| 1861 | (June 6) Death of Cavour |
| 1862 | Bismarck becomes prime minister of Prussia |
| 1864 | Danish-Prussian War |
| 1865 | Convention of Gastein |
| 1866 | Austro-Prussian War |
| 1866 | Venetia ceded to Italy |
| 1867 | North German Confederation formed |
| 1870 | (June 19–July 12) Crisis over Hohenzollern candidacy for the Spanish throne |
| 1870 | (July 13) Bismarck publishes the edited Ems dispatch |
| 1870 | (July 19) France declares war on Prussia |
| 1870 | (September 1) France defeated at Sedan and Napoleon III captured |
| 1870 | (September 4) French Republic proclaimed |
| 1870 | (October 2) Italian state annexes Rome |
| 1871 | (January 18) Proclamation of the German Empire at Versailles |
| 1871 | (March 28–May 28) Paris Commune |
| 1871 | (May 23) Treaty of Frankfurt ratified between France and Germany |

instructed Benedetti to ask William for assurances that he would tolerate no future Spanish candidacy for Leopold. The king refused but said that he might take the question under further consideration. Later that day he sent Bismarck, who was in Berlin, a telegram reporting the substance of the meeting. The chancellor, who desperately wanted a war with France to complete unification, had been disappointed by the peaceful resolution of the controversy. The king's telegram gave him a new opportunity to incite a war. Bismarck released an edited version of the dispatch. The revised Ems telegram made it appear that William had insulted the French ambassador. The idea was to goad France into declaring war.

The French government fell for Bismarck's bait and declared war on July 19. Napoleon III was sick and not eager for war, but his government believed that victory over the North German Confederation would give the empire renewed popular support. Once the conflict erupted, the southern German states, honoring treaties of 1866, enthusiastically joined Prussia against France, whose defeat was not long in coming. On September 1, at the Battle of Sedan, the Germans not only beat the French army but also captured Napoleon III. By late September Paris was besieged; it finally capitulated on January 28, 1871.

Ten days earlier, in the Hall of Mirrors at the Palace of Versailles, the German Empire had been proclaimed. During the war the states of southern Germany had joined the North German Confederation, and their rulers requested William to accept the imperial title of German emperor. The princes remained heads of their respective states within the new federation. From the peace settlement with France, Germany received the additional territory of Alsace and part of Lorraine.

Both the fact and the manner of German unification produced long-range effects in Europe. A powerful new state had been created in north central Europe. It was rich in natural resources and talented citizens. Militarily and economically, the German Empire would be far stronger than Prussia had been alone. The unification of Germany was also a blow to European liberalism, because the new state was a conservative creation. Conservative politics was now backed not by a weak Austria or an economically retrograde Russia but by the strongest state on the Continent.

The two nations most immediately affected by German and Italian unification were France and Austria. The emergence of the two new united states revealed the weakness of both France and the Habsburg Empire. Change had to come in each. France returned to republican government, and the Habsburgs came to terms with their Magyar subjects.

# France: From Liberal Empire to the Third Republic

Historians have traditionally divided the reign of Emperor Napoleon III (r. 1851–1870) into the years of the authoritarian empire and those of the liberal empire. The point of division is the year 1860. Initially, after the coup in December 1851, Napoleon III had controlled the legislature, strictly censored the press, and harassed political dissidents. His support came from the army, property owners, the French Catholic Church, and businesspeople. They approved the security he ensured for property, his protection of the pope, and his aid to commerce and railroad construction. The French victory in the Crimean War had further confirmed the emperor's popularity.

From the late 1850s onward, Napoleon III began to modify his policy. In 1860 he concluded a free trade treaty with Britain and permitted freer debate in the legislature. By the late 1860s, he had relaxed the press laws and had permitted labor unions. In 1870 he allowed the leaders of the moderates in the legislature to form a ministry, and he also agreed to a liberal constitution that made the ministers responsible to the legislature.

Napoleon III's liberal concessions sought to shore up domestic support to compensate for his failures in foreign policy. By 1860 he had lost control of the diplomacy of Italian unification. Between 1861 and 1867, he had supported a disastrous military expedition against Mexico led by Archduke Maximilian of Austria that ended in defeat and Maximilian's execution. In 1866 France had watched passively while Bismarck and Prussia reorganized German affairs. The war of 1870 against Germany had been the French government's last and most disastrous attempt to shore up its foreign policy and secure domestic popularity.

The Second Empire, but not the war, came to an inglorious end with the Battle of Sedan in September 1870. The emperor was captured, imprisoned, and then allowed to go to England, where he died in 1873. Shortly after news of the Sedan disaster reached Paris, a republic was proclaimed, and a Government of National Defense was established. Paris itself was soon under Prussian siege, and the government was transferred to Bordeaux. Paris finally surrendered in January 1871, but the rest of France had been ready to sue for peace long before.

## The Paris Commune

The division between the provinces and Paris became sharper after the fighting with Germany stopped. Monarchists dominated the new National Assembly elected in February. For the time being,

# The Paris Commune is Proclaimed

*In September 1870, the French Republic was proclaimed, and shortly there-
after a National Assembly was elected. Paris, which had held out against
Prussia longer than any other part of France, was hostile to the National
Assembly. On March 18, 1871, a revolt against the assembly occurred in
Paris. The National Guard of Paris sought to organize the city as a separate
part of France. Here is an excerpt of the proclamation of March 28 of Paris as
an autonomous commune separate from France. The rebellious Parisians
wanted all of France to be organized into a federation of politically
autonomous communes. This communal concept was directly opposed to that
of the large national state. Two months after this proclamation, the troops of
the assembly crushed the commune.*

✦ *How does this document interpret the French defeat at the hands of Prussia as a punishment? How does this declaration portray the proclamation of
the commune as a continuation of the French Revolution? What are the specific political goals and values of the commune according to this declaration?*

By its revolution of the 18th march, and the
spontaneous and courageous efforts of the
National Guard, Paris has regained its autonomy. . . . On the eve of the sanguinary and disastrous defeat suffered by France as the punishment it has to undergo for the seventy years of
the Empire, and the monarchical, clerical, parliamentary, legal and conciliatory reaction, our
country again rises, revives, begins a new life,
and retakes the tradition of the Communes of
old and of the French Revolution. This tradition, which gave victory to France, and earned
the respect and sympathy of past generations,
will bring independence, wealth, peaceful glory
and brotherly love among nations in the future.

Never was there so solemn an hour. The
Revolution which our fathers commenced and
we are finishing . . . is going on without bloodshed, by the might of the popular will. . . . To
secure the triumph of the Communal idea . . .
it is necessary to determine its general principles, and to draw up . . . the programme to be
realized. . . .

The Commune is the foundation of all political states, exactly as the family is the embryo
of human society. It must have autonomy; that
is to say, self-administration and self-government, agreeing with its particular genius, traditions, and wants; preserving, in its political,
moral, national, and special groups its entire
liberty, its own character, and its complete sovereignty, like a citizen of a free town.

To secure the greatest economic development, the national and territorial independence,
and security, association is indispensable; that
is to say, a federation of all communes, constituting a united nation.

The autonomy of the Commune guarantees
liberty to its citizens; and the federation of all
the communes increases, by the reciprocity,
power, wealth, markets, and resources of each
member, the profit of all. It was the Communal
idea . . . which triumphed on the 18th of March,
1871. It implies, as a political form, the Republic, which is alone compatible with liberty and
popular sovereignty.

*G. A. Kertesz, ed.,* Documents in the Political History of the European Continent, 1815–1939
*(Oxford: Clarendon Press, 1968), pp. 312–313.*

*The siege of Paris during the Franco-Prussian War led to extreme food shortages. Animals in the zoo were slaughtered and domestic dogs and cats were butchered to feed the hungry citizens. Sketches such as this one, made early in 1871, were published in London newspapers after being sent from Paris by balloon post. [The Granger Collection]*

the assembly gave executive power to Adolphe Thiers (1797–1877), who had been active in French politics since 1830. He negotiated a settlement with Prussia (the Treaty of Frankfurt) whereby France was charged a large indemnity and remained occupied by Prussian troops until the indemnity had been paid. France also lost Alsace and part of Lorraine. The treaty was officially ratified on May 23.

Many Parisians, having suffered during the siege, resented what they regarded as a betrayal by the monarchist National Assembly sitting at Versailles. The Parisians elected a new municipal government, called the Paris Commune, which was formally proclaimed on March 28, 1871. The Commune intended to administer Paris separately from the rest of France. At one time or another, political radicals and socialists of all stripes participated in the Paris Commune. The National Assembly moved rapidly in early April to surround Paris with an army. On May 8, this army bombarded the city. On May 21, the assembly's forces broke through the city's defenses. During the next seven days, the troops restored order to Paris and killed about 20,000 inhabitants. The communards claimed their own victims as well.

The short-lived Paris Commune quickly became a legend throughout Europe. Marxists regarded it as a genuine proletarian government that the French bourgeoisie had suppressed. This interpretation is mistaken. The Commune, though of shifting composition, was dominated by petty bourgeois members. The socialism of the Commune had its roots in Blanqui's and Proudhon's anarchism rather than in Marx's concept of class conflict. The goal of the Commune was not a worker's republic but a nation composed of relatively independent, radically democratic enclaves. Its suppression thus represented not only the protection of property but also the triumph of the centralized nation-state over an alternative political organization. Just as the armies of Piedmont and Prussia had united the small states of Italy and Germany, the army of the French National Assembly destroyed the particularistic political tendencies of Paris and, by implication, those of any other French community.

### The Third Republic

The National Assembly backed into a republican form of government indirectly and much against its

# Walter Bagehot Analyzes the Power of Napoleon III

*Walter Bagehot (1826–1877) was an astute English observer of continental politics and an important journalist. This passage, written in 1863, explains the manner in which Napoleon III had to please various elements of French society in order to retain his power.*

✦ *What did Bagehot mean by referring to Napoleon II as "the Crowned Democrat of Europe"? What did Bagehot see as the chief sources of Napoleon III's support? What accounted in each case for that support? Are there elements in Bagehot's analysis that would explain why Napoleon III would fall at the end of the decade once France had encountered military defeat?*

The Emperor is the Crowned Democrat of Europe. The position is no doubt one of great elevation and of enormous power, but it is also one full of peril and full of exigencies. "The Masses," though an effective, and under many circumstances, an almost resistless servant make a capricious, exacting, and relentless master. Both at home and abroad Napoleon III has a contract with the agencies that have made him what he is and that sustain him where he is, the terms of which must be rigidly fulfilled. At home he rules *over* the middle classes, *in defiance* of the educated classes, and *by the support* of the lower classes and the army. In ultimate resort he may be said to reign by the right of numbers and by the instrumentality of bayonets. It is true that he has done much—perhaps as much as lay in his power—to widen the basis of his throne, and to make all classes interested in maintaining him. He has tentatively and modestly allowed the intellectual classes to raise their heads; he has conciliated the *bourgeoisie* by the material prosperity which he has so sagaciously and indefatigably fostered; and he has canceled or moderated the hostility once felt towards him by the rich and great by convincing them that property was in habitual danger from the *Rouges* [Reds], and that he was the only hand that could avert that danger. So that beyond dispute the number of those who wish to overthrow him has largely diminished, and the number of those who desire to maintain him has largely increased, each year since 1852. Still it remains true that to retain his popularity and prestige with *FRANCE*, . . . he must be sedulous to please, or at all events careful not to offend, the populace, the peasantry, and the army.

The Collected Works of Walter Bagehot, *Norman St. John-Stevas, ed. vol. 4, (Cambridge, Mass.: Harvard University Press, 1968), p. 105.*

will. The monarchists, who constituted its majority, were divided in loyalty between the House of Bourbon and the House of Orléans. They could have surmounted this problem because the Bourbon claimant, the count of Chambord, had no children and agreed to accept the Orléanist heir as his successor. Chambord refused to become king, however, if France retained the revolutionary tricolor flag. Even the conservative monarchists would not return to the white flag of the Bourbons, which symbolized extreme political reaction.

While the monarchists quarreled among themselves, time passed, and events marched on. By September 1873, the indemnity had been paid, and the Prussian occupation troops had withdrawn. Theirs was ousted from office because he had displayed clear republican sentiments. The monarchists wanted a more sympathetic executive. They elected as president a conservative army officer, Marshal MacMahon (1808–1893), who was expected to prepare for a monarchist restoration. In 1875 the National Assembly, still monarchist in sentiment but unable to find a king, decided to regularize the political system. It adopted a law that provided for a Chamber of Deputies elected by universal male suffrage, a Senate chosen indirectly, and a president elected by the two legislative houses. This rather simple republican system had resulted from the bickering and frustration of the monarchists.

After numerous quarrels with the Chamber of Deputies, MacMahon resigned in 1879. His departure meant that dedicated republicans generally controlled the national government despite lingering opposition from the church, wealthy families, and a part of the army.

The political structure of the Third Republic proved much stronger than many citizens suspected at the time. It survived challenges for leadership from persons such as General Georges Boulanger (1837–1891), who would have imposed stronger executive authority. It also survived several scandals, such as those involving sales of awards of the Legion of Honor and widespread corruption of politicians by a company that tried to construct a canal in Panama, which made its politics appear increasingly sleazy to conservatives. The institutions of the republic, however, allowed new ministers to replace those whose corruption was exposed.

### The Dreyfus Affair

The greatest trauma of the Third Republic occurred over what became known as the "Dreyfus affair." On December 22, 1894, a French military court found Captain Alfred Dreyfus (1859–1935) guilty of passing secret information to the German army. The evidence against him was flimsy and was later revealed to have been forged. Someone in the officer corps had been passing documents to the Germans, and it suited the army investigators to accuse Dreyfus, who was Jewish. After Dreyfus had been sent to Devil's Island, a notorious prison in French Guiana, however, secrets continued to flow to the German army. In 1896 a new head of French counterintelligence reexamined the Dreyfus file and found evidence of forgery. A different officer was implicated, but a military court acquitted him of all charges.

*The prosecution of Captain Alfred Dreyfus, who is shown here standing on the right at his military trial, provoked the most serious crisis of the Third Republic. [The Bettmann Archive]*

By then the affair had provoked widespread and sometimes near-hysterical public debate. The army, the French Catholic Church, political conservatives, and vehemently antisemitic newspapers repeatedly contended that Dreyfus was guilty. Such anti-Dreyfus opinion was dominant at the beginning of the affair. In 1898, however, the novelist Émile Zola published a newspaper article entitled *"J'accuse"* (I accuse) in which he contended that the army had consciously denied due process to Dreyfus and had plotted to suppress or forge evidence. Zola was convicted of libel and received a one-year prison sentence, which he avoided by fleeing to England.

Zola was only one of numerous liberals, radicals, and socialists who had begun to demand a new trial for Dreyfus. Although these forces of the political left had come to Dreyfus's support rather slowly, they soon realized that his cause could aid their own public image. They portrayed the conservative institutions of the nation as having denied Dreyfus the rights belonging to any citizen of the republic. They also claimed, and properly so, that Dreyfus had been singled out, so that the guilty persons, who were still in the army, could be protected. In August 1898, further evidence of forged material came to light. The officer responsible for those forgeries committed suicide in jail, but a new military trial again convicted Dreyfus. The president of France immediately pardoned him, however, and eventually, in 1906, a civilian court set aside the results of both military trials.

The Dreyfus case divided France as no issue had done since the Paris Commune. By its conclusion, the conservatives were on the defensive. They had allowed themselves to persecute an innocent person and to manufacture false evidence against him to protect themselves from disclosure. They had also

embraced violent antisemitism. On the political left, radicals, republicans, and socialists developed an informal alliance, which outlived the fight over the Dreyfus case itself. These groups realized that republican institutions must be supported if the political left were to achieve its goals. Nonetheless, the political, religious, and racial divisions and suspicions growing out of the Dreyfus affair continued to divide the Third Republic until France's defeat by Germany in 1940.

## The Habsburg Empire

After 1848 the Habsburg Empire was a problem both to itself and for the rest of Europe. An ungenerous critic remarked that a standing army of sol-

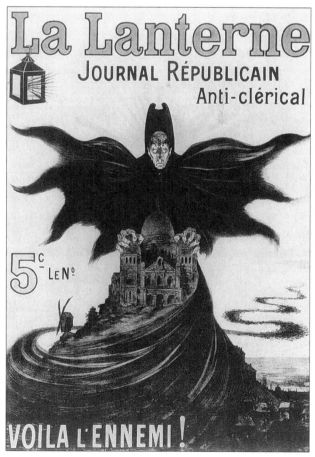

*Political discourse in the Third French Republic was harsh. The cover of this anticlerical journal presents the French Roman Catholic Church as the enemy of the nation. A menacing figure symbolizing the church holds the recently built Basilica of the Sacred Heart.* [The Bettmann Archive]

| Major Dates in the History of Third French Republic | |
|---|---|
| 1870 | Defeat by Prussia and proclamation of republic |
| 1871 | Paris Commune |
| 1873 | Prussian occupation troops depart |
| 1873 | Marshal MacMahon elected president |
| 1875 | Major political institutions of Third Republic organized |
| 1894 | Captain Dreyfus convicted |
| 1906 | Dreyfus's conviction set aside |

# The Austrian Prime Minister
# Explains the Dual Monarchy

*The multinational character of the Austrian Empire had long been a source of internal weakness and political discontent. After the defeat of Austria by Prussia in 1866, the Austrian government attempted to regain the loyalty of the Hungarians by making Hungary a separate kingdom within a dual monarchy, known thereafter as Austria-Hungary.*

✦ *How does the Austrian prime minister define the problems of nationality within the empire? Why does he distinguish Hungary from the other national groups who seek independence or association with another nation? What are the principles he claims lie behind the establishment of the dual monarchy?*

The dangers which Austria has to face are of a twofold nature. The first is presented by the tendency of her liberal-minded German population to gravitate toward that larger portion of the German-speaking people. . . . the second is the diversity of language and race in the empire. Of Austria's large Slav population, the Poles have a natural craving for independence after having enjoyed and heroically fought for it for centuries; while the other nationalities are likely at a moment of dangerous crisis to develop pro-Russian tendencies.

Now my object is to carry out a bloodless revolution—to show the various elements of this great empire that it is to the benefit of each of them to act in harmony with its neighbor. . . . But to this I have made one exception. Hungary is an ancient monarchy, more ancient as such than Austria proper. . . . I have endeavoured to give Hungary not a new position with regard to the Austrian empire, but to secure her in the one which she has occupied. The Emperor of Austria is King of Hungary; my idea was that he should revive in his person the Constitution of which he and his ancestors have been the heads. The leading principles of my plan are . . . the resuscitation of an old monarchy and an old Constitution; not the separation of one part of the empire from the other, but the drawing together of the two component parts by the recognition of their joint positions, the maintenance of their mutual obligations, their community in questions affecting the entire empire, and their proportional pecuniary responsibility for the liabilities of the whole State. It is no plan of separation that I have carried out: on the contrary, it is one of close union, not by the creation of a new power, but by the recognition of an old one. . . .

*Memories of Friedrich Ferdinand Count von Beust, Vol. I, ed. by Baron Henry de Worms (London: Remington, 1887), pp. xx–xxvi.*

diers, a kneeling army of priests, and a crawling army of informers supported the empire. In the age of national states, liberal institutions, and industrialism, the Habsburg domains remained primarily dynastic, absolutist, and agrarian. The Habsburg response to the revolts of 1848–1849 had been the reassertion of absolutism. Francis Joseph, who became emperor in 1848 and ruled until 1916, was honest and hardworking, but unimaginative. He reacted to events but rarely commanded them.

During the 1850s, Francis Joseph's ministers attempted to impose a centralized administration on the empire. The system amounted to a military and bureaucratic government dominated by German-speaking Austrians. The Vienna government abolished all internal tariffs in the empire. It divided Hungary, which had been so revolutionary in 1848, into military districts. The Roman Catholic Church acquired control of education. National groups, such as the Croats and Slovaks, who had supported the empire against the Hungarians, received no rewards for their loyalty. Although this domestic system of neo-absolutism provoked resentment and opposition, it eventually floundered because of setbacks in Habsburg foreign affairs.

Austrian refusal to support Russia during the Crimean War meant that the new tsar would no longer help preserve Habsburg rule in Hungary as Nicholas I had done in 1849. An important external prop of Habsburg power for the past half-century thus disappeared. The Austrian defeat in 1859 at the hands of France and Piedmont and the subsequent loss of territory in Italy confirmed the necessity for a new domestic policy. For seven years the emperor, the civil servants, the aristocrats, and the politicians tried to construct a viable system of government.

### Formation of the Dual Monarchy

In 1860 Francis Joseph issued the October Diploma, which created a federation among the states and provinces of the empire. There were to be local diets dominated by the landed classes and a single imperial parliament. The Magyar nobility of Hungary, however, rejected the plan.

Consequently, in 1861, the emperor issued the February Patent, which set up an entirely different form of government. It established a bicameral imperial parliament, or *Reichsrat*, with an upper chamber appointed by the emperor and an indirectly elected lower chamber. Again the Magyars refused to cooperate in a system designed to give political dominance in the empire to German-speaking Austrians. The Magyars sent no delegates to the legislature. Nevertheless, for six years, the February Patent governed the empire, and it prevailed in Austria proper until World War I. Ministers were responsible to the emperor, not the *Reichsrat*, and civil liberties were not guaranteed. Armies could be levied and taxes raised without parliamentary consent. When the *Reichsrat* was not in session, the emperor could simply rule by decree.

Meanwhile, negotiations continued secretly between the emperor and the Magyars. These produced no concrete result until the Prussian defeat of Austria in the summer of 1866 and the consequent exclusion of Austria from German affairs. The military disaster compelled Francis Joseph to come to terms with the Magyars. The subsequent *Ausgleich*, or Compromise, of 1867 transformed the Habsburg Empire into a dual monarchy, thereafter generally known as Austria–Hungary.

Francis Joseph was crowned king of Hungary in Budapest in 1867. Except for the common monarch, Austria and Hungary became almost wholly separate states. They shared ministers of foreign affairs, defense, and finance, but the other ministers were different for each state. There were also separate parliaments. Each year, sixty parliamentary delegates from each state met to discuss mutual interests. Every ten years, Austria and Hungary renegotiated their trade relationship. By this cumbersome machinery, unique in European history, the Magyars were reconciled to Habsburg rule. They had achieved the free hand they had long wanted in Hungary.

### Unrest of Nationalities

The Compromise of 1867 had introduced two different principles of political legitimacy into the two sections of the Habsburg Empire. In Hungary, political loyalty was based on nationality because Hungary had been recognized as a distinct part of the monarchy on the basis of nationalism. In effect, Hungary was a Magyar nation under the Habsburg emperor. In the rest of the Habsburg domains, the principle of legitimacy meant dynastic loyalty to the emperor. Many of the other nationalities wished to achieve the same type of settlement that the Hungarians had won, or to govern themselves, or to unite with fellow nationals who lived outside the empire. (See Map 23–3.)

Many of those other national groups—including the Czechs, the Ruthenians, the Romanians, and the Croatians—opposed the Compromise of 1867 that in effect had permitted the German-speaking Austrians and the Hungarian Magyars to dominate all other nationalities within the empire. The most vocal critics were the Czechs of Bohemia. They favored a policy of trialism, or triple monarchy, in which the Czechs would be given a position similar to that given the Hungarians. In 1871 Francis Joseph was willing to accept this concept. The Magyars, however, vetoed it lest they be forced to make similar concessions to their own subject nationalities. Furthermore, the Germans of Bohemia were afraid that the Czech language would be imposed on them and their children.

For more than twenty years, the Czechs were placated by generous patronage and posts in the bureaucracy. By the 1890s, however, Czech nation-

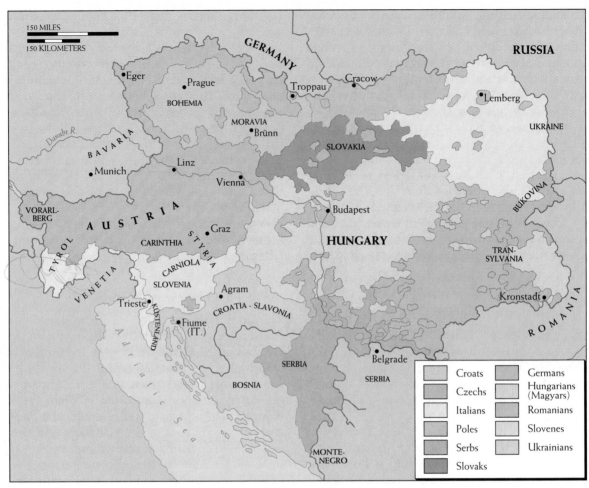

MAP 23–3 NATIONALITIES WITHIN THE HABSBURG EMPIRE *The patchwork appearance reflects the unusual problem of the numerous ethnic groups that the Habsburgs could not, of course, meld into a modern national state. Only the Magyars were recognized in 1867, leaving nationalist Czechs, Slovaks, and the others chronically dissatisfied.*

alism again became more strident. In 1897, Francis Joseph gave the Czechs and the Germans equality of language in various localities. Thereafter, the Germans in the Austrian *Reichsrat* opposed these measures by disrupting Parliament. The Czechs replied in kind. By the turn of the century, this obstructionism, which included the playing of musical instruments in the *Reichsrat*, had paralyzed parliamentary life. The emperor ruled by imperial decree through the bureaucracy. In 1907 Francis Joseph introduced universal male suffrage in Austria (but not in Hungary), but this action did not eliminate the chaos in the *Reichsrat*. In effect, by 1914 constitutionalism was a dead letter in Austria. It flourished in Hungary, but only because the

Magyars relentlessly exercised political supremacy over all other competing national groups except Croatia, which was permitted considerable autonomy.

There is reason to believe that nationalism became stronger during the last quarter of the nineteenth century. It was then that language became the single most important factor in defining a nation. The expansion of education made this possible. In all countries where nationalistic groups prospered, their membership was dominated by intellectuals, students, and educated members of the middle class, all of whom were literate in the literary version of particular national languages. Furthermore, it was during these same years, as will

*The coronation of Francis Joseph of Hungary in 1867 is depicted in this painting. The so-called* Ausgleich, *or Compromise, of 1867 transformed the Habsburg Empire into a dual monarchy in which Austria and Hungary became almost separate states except for defense and foreign affairs. [Bildarchiv der Österreichischen Nationalbibliothek, Vienna]*

be seen in Chapter 25, that racial thinking became important in Europe. Racial thought maintained there was a genetic basis for ethnic and cultural groups who had hitherto been generally defined by a common history and culture. Once language and race became the ways to define an ethnic or national group, the lines between such groups became much more sharply drawn.

The unrest of the various nationalities within the Habsburg Empire not only caused internal political difficulties, it also became a major source of political instability for all of central and eastern Europe. Each of the nationality problems normally had ramifications for both foreign and domestic policy. Both the Croats and the Poles wanted an independent state in union with their fellow nationals who lived outside the empire, and in the case of the Poles, with fellow nationals in the Russian Empire. Other national groups, such as Ukrainians, Romanians, Italians, and Bosnians, saw themselves as potentially linked to Russia, Romania, Serbia, Italy, or to a yet-to-be established south Slavic, or Yugoslav, state. Many of these nationalities looked to Russia to protect their interests or influence the government in Vienna. The Romanians were also concerned about the Romanian minority in Hungary. Serbia sought to expand its borders to include Serbs who lived within Habsburg or Ottoman territory. Out of these Balkan tensions emerged much of the turmoil that would spark the First World War. Many of the same ethnic tensions account for the warfare in the former Yugoslavia.

# Lord Acton Condemns Nationalism

*Lord Acton (1834–1902) was a major nineteenth-century English historian and commentator on contemporary religious and political events. In all his writings, he was deeply concerned with the character and preservation of liberty. His was one of the earliest voices to warn against the political dangers of nationalism.*

✦ *Why does Acton see the principle of nationality as dangerous to liberty? Why does he see nationalism as a threat to minority groups? Why does he see nationalism as a threat to democracy?*

The greatest adversary of the rights of nationality is the modern theory of nationality. By making the State and the nation commensurate with each other in theory, it reduces practically to a subject condition all other nationalities that may be within the boundary. It cannot admit them to an equality with the ruling nation which constitutes the State, because the State would then cease to be national, which would be a contradiction of the principle of its existence. According, therefore, to the degree of humanity and civilization in that dominant body which claims all the rights of the community, the inferior races are exterminated, or reduced to servitude, or outlawed, or put in a condition of dependence.

If we take the establishment of liberty for the realization of moral duties to be the end of civil society, we must conclude that those states are substantially the most perfect which, like the British and Austrian Empires, include various distinct nationalities without oppressing them. Those in which no mixture of races has occurred are imperfect; and those in which its effects have disappeared are decrepit. A State which is incompetent to satisfy different races condemns itself; a State which labors to neutralize, to absorb, or to expel them, destroys its own vitality; a State which does not include them is destitute of the chief basis of self-government. The theory of nationality, therefore, is a retrograde step in history. . . .

. . . [N]ationality does not aim either at liberty or prosperity, both of which it sacrifices to the imperative necessity of making the nation the mold and measure of the State. Its course will be marked with material as well as moral ruin, in order that a new invention may prevail over the works of God and the interests of mankind. There is no principle of change, no phrase of political speculation conceivable, more comprehensive, more subversive, or more arbitrary than this. It is a confutation of democracy, because it sets limits to the exercise of the popular will, and substitutes for it a higher principle.

*John Emerich Edward Dalberg-Acton, First Baron Acton,* Essays in the History of Liberty, *ed. by J. Rufus Fears (Indianapolis: Liberty Classics, 1985), pp. 431–433.*

---

The dominant German population of Austria proper was generally loyal to the emperor. A part of it, however, yearned to join the united German state being established by Bismarck. These nationalistic Austro-Germans often hated the non-German national groups of the empire, and many of them were antisemites. Such attitudes would influence the youth and young adulthood of Adolph Hitler.

For the next century of European and even world history, the significance of this nationalist unrest within the late-nineteenth-century Austrian Empire and its neighbors can hardly be overestimated. These nationality problems touched all three of the great central and eastern European empires—the German, the Russian, and the Austrian. All had large Polish populations, and Russia had many minority groups. Each nationality regarded its own aspirations and discontents as more important than the larger good or even survival of the empires that they inhabited. The weakness of the Ottoman

Empire allowed both Austria and Russia to compete in the Balkans for greater influence and thus further inflame nationalistic resentments. Such nationalistic stirrings affected the fate of all three empires from the 1860s through the outbreak of World War I. The government of each of those empires would be overturned during the war, and the Austrian Empire would disappear. Those same unresolved problems of central and eastern European nationalism would then lead directly to World War II. They continue to fester today.

# Russia: Emancipation and Revolutionary Stirrings

Russia changed remarkably during the last half of the nineteenth century. The government finally both addressed the long-standing problem of serfdom and undertook a broad range of administrative reforms. During the same period, however, radical revolutionary groups began to organize. These groups tried to draw the peasants into revolutionary activity and assassinated major government officials, including the tsar. The government's response was a new era of repression following the years of reform.

## Reforms of Alexander II

Russia's defeat in the Crimean War and its humiliation of the Treaty of Paris compelled the government to reconsider its domestic policies. Nicholas I had died in 1855 during the conflict. Because of extensive travel in Russia and an early introduction to government, his son Alexander II (r. 1855–1881) was familiar with the chief difficulties facing the

nation. The debacle of the war had made reform both necessary and possible. Alexander II took advantage of this turn of events to institute the most extensive restructuring of Russian society and administration since Peter the Great. Like Peter, Alexander imposed his reforms from the top.

ABOLITION OF SERFDOM  In every area of economic and public life, a profound cultural gap separated Russia from the rest of Europe. Nowhere was this more apparent than in the survival of serfdom. In Russia, the institution had changed very little since the eighteenth century, though every other nation on the Continent had abandoned it. Russian landowners still had a free hand with their serfs, and the serfs had little recourse against the landlords. In March 1856, at the conclusion of the Crimean War, Alexander II announced his intention to abolish serfdom. He had decided that only its abolition would permit Russia to organize its human and natural resources to maintain its status as a great power.

Serfdom had become economically inefficient. There was always the threat of revolt; the serfs forced into the army had performed poorly in the Crimean conflict. Moreover, nineteenth-century moral opinion condemned serfdom. Only Russia, Brazil, and certain portions of the United States among the Western nations still retained such forms of involuntary servitude. For five years, government commissions wrestled over how to implement the tsar's desire. Finally, in February 1861, against much opposition from the nobility and the landlords, Alexander II promulgated the long statute ending serfdom in Russia.

The actual emancipation statute proved to be a disappointment, however, because freedom was not accompanied by land. Serfs immediately received the personal right to marry without their landlord's permission as well as the rights to purchase and sell property freely, to engage in court actions, and to pursue trades. What they did not receive was free title to their land. They had to pay the landlords over a period of forty-nine years for allotments of land that were frequently too small to support them. They were also charged interest during this period. The serfs made the payments to the government, which had already reimbursed the landlords for their losses. The serfs would not receive title to the land until the debt was paid.

The procedures were so complicated and the results so limited that many serfs believed that real emancipation was still to come. The redemption payments led to almost unending difficulty. Poor harvests made it impossible for many peasants to keep up with the payments, and they fell increasingly behind in their debt. The situation was not remedied until 1906, when, during the widespread revolutionary unrest following the Japanese defeat of Russia in 1905, the government grudgingly completed the process of emancipation by canceling the remaining debts.

### REFORM OF LOCAL GOVERNMENT AND THE JUDICIAL SYSTEM

The abolition of serfdom required the reorganization of local government and the judicial system. The authority of village communes replaced that of the landlord over the peasant. The village elders settled family quarrels, imposed fines, issued internal passports, and collected taxes. Often, also, it was the village commune rather than individual peasants who owned the land. The nobility were permitted a larger role in local administration through a system of provincial and county *zemstvos*, or councils, organized in 1864. These councils were to oversee local matters, such as bridge and road repair, education, and agricultural improvement. Because the councils received inadequate funds, however, local government were never vitalized.

The flagrant inequities and abuses of the preemancipation judicial system could not continue. In 1864 Alexander II promulgated a new statute on the judiciary. For the first time, western European legal principles were introduced into Russia. These included equality before the law, impartial hearings, uniform procedures, judicial independence, and trial by jury. The new system was far from perfect. The judges were not genuinely independent, and the tsar could increase as well as reduce sentences. Certain offenses, such as those involving the press, were not tried before a jury. Nonetheless, the new courts were both more efficient and less corrupt than the old system.

*Life in Russian villages during the 1870s was very difficult. Tsar Alexander II abolished serfdom in 1861, but peasants were required to pay compensation to the government for 49 years and living standards remained dismal. This painting shows peasants waiting patiently outside a government office while officials inside take their time over lunch. [Bildarchiv Preussischer Kulturbesitz]*

**MILITARY REFORM** The government also reformed the army. Russia possessed the largest military force on the Continent, but it had floundered badly in the Crimean War. The usual period of service for a soldier was twenty-five years. Villages had to provide quotas of serfs to serve in the army. Often the recruiters simply appeared in the villages and seized serfs from their families. Once in the army, the recruits rarely saw their homes again. Life in the army was harsh, even by the brutal standards of most mid-century armies. In the 1860s, the army lowered the period of service to fifteen years and slightly relaxed discipline. In 1874 the enlistment period was lowered to six years of active duty, followed by nine years in the reserves. All males were subject to military service after the age of twenty.

**REPRESSION IN POLAND** Alexander's reforms became more measured shortly after the Polish Rebellion of 1863. As in 1830, Polish nationalists attempted to overthrow Russian dominance. Once again the Russian army suppressed the rebellion. Alexander II then moved to "russify" Poland. In 1864 he emancipated the Polish serfs to punish the politically restive Polish nobility. Russian law, language, and administration were imposed on all areas of Polish life. Henceforth, until the close of World War I, Poland was treated as merely another Russian province.

As the Polish suppression demonstrated, Alexander II was a reformer only within the limits of his own autocracy. His changes in Russian life failed to create new loyalty to or gratitude for the government among his subjects. The serfs felt that their emancipation had been inadequate. The nobles and the wealthier educated segments of Russian society resented the tsar's persistent refusal to allow them a meaningful role in government and policy making. Consequently, although Alexander II became known as the Tsar Liberator, he was never popular. He could be indecisive and closed-minded. These characteristics became more pronounced after 1866, when an attempt was made on his life. Thereafter Russia increasingly became a police state. This new repression fueled the activity of radical groups within Russia. Their actions, in turn, made the autocracy more reactionary.

## Revolutionaries

The tsarist regime had long had its critics. One of the most prominent was Alexander Herzen (1812–

| Major Dates in Late-Nineteenth-Century Russia | |
|---|---|
| 1855 | Alexander II becomes tsar |
| 1856 | Defeat in Crimean War |
| 1861 | Serfdom abolished |
| 1863 | Suppression of Polish rebellion |
| 1864 | Reorganization of local government |
| 1864 | Reform of judicial system |
| 1874 | Military enlistment period lowered |
| 1878 | Attempted assassination of military governor of Saint Petersburg |
| 1879 | Land and Freedom splits |
| 1881 | The People's Will assassinates Alexander II |
| 1881 | Alexander III becomes tsar |
| 1894 | Nicholas II becomes tsar |

1870), who lived in exile. From London, he published a newspaper called *The Bell*, in which he set forth reformist positions. The initial reforms of Alexander II had raised great hopes among Russian students and intellectuals, but they soon became discontented with the limited character of the reforms. Drawing on the ideas of Herzen and other radicals, these students formed a revolutionary movement known as *Populism*. They sought a social revolution based on the communal life of the Russian peasants. The chief radical society was called *Land and Freedom*.

In the early 1870s, hundreds of young Russians, including both men and women, took their revolutionary message into the countryside. They intended to live with the peasants, to gain their trust, and to teach them about the peasant's role in the coming revolution. The bewildered and distrustful peasants turned most of the youths over to the police. In the winter of 1877–1878, almost 200 students were tried. Most were acquitted or given light sentences, because they had been held for months in preventive detention and because the court believed that a display of mercy might lessen public sympathy for the young revolutionaries. The court even suggested that the tsar might wish to pardon those students given heavier sentences. The tsar refused and let it become known that he favored heavy penalties for all persons involved in revolutionary activity.

Thereafter the revolutionaries decided that the tsarist regime must be attacked directly. They adopted a policy of terrorism. In January 1878, Vera

# The People's Will Issues a Revolutionary Manifesto

*In the late 1870s, an extreme revolutionary movement appeared in Russia calling itself The People's Will. It advocated the overthrow of the tsarist government and the election of an Organizing Assembly to form a government based on popular representation. It directly embraced terrorism as a path toward its goal of the Russian people governing themselves. Members of this group assassinated Alexander II in 1881.*

✦ *Which of the group's seven demands might be associated with liberalism and which go beyond liberalism in their radical intent? Why does the group believe it must engage in terrorism as well as propaganda? Would there have been any reforms or steps toward reform that the Russian government might have taken that might have satisfied this group or dissuaded them from terrorist action?*

Although we are ready to submit wholly to the popular will, we regard it as none the less our duty, as a party, to appear before the people with our program. . . . It is as follows:

1. Perpetual popular representation, . . . having full power to act in all national questions.

2. General local self-government, secured by the election of all officers, and the economic independence of the people.

3. The self-controlled village commune as the economic and administrative unit.

4. Ownership of the land by the people.

5. A system of measures having for their object the turning over to the laborers of all mining works and factories.

6. Complete freedom of conscience, speech, association, public meeting, and electioneering activity.

7. The substitution of a territorial militia for the army.

. . . .

In view of the stated aim of the party its operations may be classified as follows:

1. Propaganda and agitation. Our propaganda has for its object the popularization, in all social classes, of the idea of a political and popular revolution as a means of social reform, as well as popularization of the party's own program. Its essential features are criticism of the existing order of things, and a statement and explanation of revolutionary methods. The aim of agitation should be to incite the people to protest as generally as possible against the present state of affairs, to demand such reforms as are in harmony with the party's purposes, and, especially, to demand the summoning of an Organizing Assembly. . . .

2. Destructive and terroristic activity. Terroristic activity consists in the destruction of the most harmful persons in the Government, the protection of the party from spies, and the punishment of official lawlessness and violence in all the more prominent and important cases in which such lawlessness and violence are manifested. The aim of such activity is to break down the prestige of Governmental power, to furnish continuous proof of the possibility of carrying on a contest with the Government, to raise in that way the revolutionary spirit of the people and inspire belief in the practicability of revolution, and, finally, to form a body suited and accustomed to warfare.

*Quoted in George Kennan,* Siberia and the Exile System, *vol. 2 (New York: The Century Co., 1891), pp. 495–499.*

*Tsar Alexander II (r. 1855–1881) was assassinated on March 1, 1881. The assassins first threw a bomb that wounded several Imperial guards. When the tsar stopped his carriage to see to the wounded, the assassins threw a second bomb, killing him. [Bildarchiv Preussischer Kulturbesitz]*

Zasulich (1849–1919) attempted to assassinate the military governor of Saint Petersburg. A jury acquitted her because the governor she had shot had a reputation for brutality. Some people also believed that Zasulich had a personal rather than a political grievance against her victim. Nonetheless, the verdict further encouraged the terrorists.

In 1879 Land and Freedom split into two groups. One advocated educating the peasants, and it soon dissolved. The other, known as *The People's Will*, was dedicated to the overthrow of the autocracy. Its members decided to assassinate the tsar himself. Several attempts failed, but on March 1, 1881, a bomb hurled by a member of People's Will killed Alexander II. Four men and two women were sentenced to death for the deed. All of them had been willing to die for their cause. The emergence of such dedicated revolutionary opposition was as

much a part of the reign of Alexander II as were his reforms. The limited character of those reforms convinced many Russians that the autocracy could never truly redirect Russian society.

The reign of Alexander III (r. 1881–1894) strengthened that pessimism. He possessed all the autocratic and repressive characteristics of his grandfather, Nicholas I, and none of the better qualities of his father, Alexander II. Some slight improvements were made to conditions in Russian factories, but Alexander III primarily sought to roll back his father's reforms. He favored the centralized bureaucracy over the *zemstvos*. He strengthened the secret police and increased press censorship. In effect, he confirmed all the evils that the revolutionaries saw as inherent in autocratic government. His son, Nicholas II (r. 1894–1917), who became tsar in 1894, would discover that autocracy could not survive the pressures of the twentieth century.

# Great Britain: Toward Democracy

While the continental nations became unified and struggled toward internal political restructuring, Great Britain continued to symbolize the confident liberal state. Britain was not without its difficulties and domestic conflicts, but it seemed able to deal with these through existing political institutions. The general prosperity of the third quarter of the century mitigated the social hostility of the 1840s. All classes shared a belief in competition and individualism. Even the leaders of trade unions during these years asked mainly to receive more of the fruits of prosperity and to have their social respectability acknowledged. Parliament itself remained an institution through which new groups and interests were absorbed into the existing political processes. In short, the British did not have to create new liberal institutions and then learn how to live within them.

## The Second Reform Act (1867)

By the early 1860s, most observers realized that the franchise would again have to be expanded. The prosperity and social respectability of the working class convinced many politicians that the workers deserved the vote. Organizations such as the Reform League, led by John Bright (1811–1889), were agitating for parliamentary action. In 1866 Lord Russell's Liberal ministry introduced a reform bill that was defeated by a coalition of traditional Conservatives and antidemocratic Liberals. Russell resigned, and the Conservative Lord Derby (1799–1869) replaced him. What then occurred surprised everyone.

The Conservative ministry, led in the House of Commons by Benjamin Disraeli (1804–1881), introduced its own reform bill in 1867. As the debate proceeded, Disraeli accepted one amendment after another and expanded the electorate well beyond the limits earlier proposed by the Liberals. When the final measure was passed, the number of voters had been increased from approximately 1,430,000 to 2,470,000. Britain had taken a major step toward democracy. Large numbers of male working-class voters had been admitted to the electorate.

Disraeli hoped that by sponsoring the measure, the Conservatives would receive the gratitude of the new voters. Because reform was inevitable, it was best for the Conservatives to enjoy the credit for it. Disraeli thought that eventually significant portions of the working class would support Conservative candidates who were responsive to social issues. He also thought that the growing suburban middle class would become more conservative. In the long run, his intuition proved correct. The Conservative Party has dominated British politics in the twentieth century.

The immediate election of 1868, however, dashed Disraeli's hopes. William Gladstone (1809–1898) became the new prime minister. Gladstone had begun political life in 1833 as a strong Tory, but over the next thirty-five years, he became steadily more liberal. He had supported Robert Peel, free trade, repeal of the Corn Laws, and efficient administration. As chancellor of the exchequer (finance minister) during the 1850s and early 1860s, he had lowered taxes and government expenditures. He had also championed Italian nationalism. Yet he had continued to oppose a new reform bill until the early 1860s. In 1866 he had been Russell's spokesperson in the House of Commons for the unsuccessful Liberal reform bill.

## Gladstone's Great Ministry (1868–1874)

Gladstone's ministry of 1868–1874 witnessed the culmination of classical British liberalism. Those institutions that remained the preserve of the aristocracy and the Anglican Church were opened to people from other classes and religious denominations. In 1870 competitive examinations for the civil service replaced patronage. In 1871 the purchase of officers' commissions in the army was abolished. The same year, Anglican religious requirements for the faculties of Oxford and Cambridge universities were removed. The Ballot Act of 1872 introduced voting by secret ballot.

The most momentous measure of Gladstone's first ministry was the Education Act of 1870. For the first time in British history, the government assumed the responsibility for establishing and running elementary schools. Previously, British education had been a task relegated to the religious denominations, which received small amounts of state support for the purpose. Henceforth, the government would establish schools where the efforts

*William Ewart Gladstone served in the British Parliament from the 1830s through the 1890s. Four times the Liberal Party prime minister, he was responsible for guiding major reforms through Parliament. [Bildarchiv Preussischer Kulturbesitz]*

*Benjamin Disraeli served as British prime minister from 1874 to 1880. He is regarded as the founder of modern British conservatism because of his efforts to convince the Conservative Party to accept a democratic electorate, which he believed would vote conservative more often than not. [Bildarchiv Preussischer Kulturbesitz]*

of religious denominations to establish them had proved inadequate.

All of these reforms were typically liberal. They sought to remove long-standing abuses without destroying existing institutions and to permit all able citizens to compete on the grounds of ability and merit. They tried to avoid the potential danger to a democratic state of an illiterate citizenry. These reforms also constituted a mode of state building, because they created new bonds of loyalty to the nation by abolishing many sources of discontent.

### Disraeli in Office (1874–1880)

The liberal policy of creating popular support for the nation by extending political liberty and reforming abuses had its conservative counterpart in concern for social reform. Disraeli succeeded Gladstone as prime minister in 1874, when the election pro-

duced sharp divisions among Liberal Party voters over religion, education, and the sale of alcohol.

The two men had stood on different sides of most issues for over a quarter century. Whereas Gladstone looked to individualism, free trade, and competition to solve social problems, Disraeli believed in paternalistic legislation. Disraeli also believed in state action to protect the weak. In his view, such paternalistic legislation would alleviate class antagonisms.

Disraeli talked a better line than he produced. He had few specific programs or ideas. The significant social legislation of his ministry stemmed primarily from the efforts of his Home Secretary, Richard Cross (1823–1914). The Public Health Act of 1875 consolidated previous sanitary legislation and reaffirmed the duty of the state to interfere with private property on matters of health and physical well-being. Through the Artisans Dwelling Act of 1875, the government became actively involved in providing housing for the working class. The same year, in an important symbolic gesture, the Conservative majority in Parliament gave new protection to British trade unions and allowed them to raise picket lines. The Gladstone ministry, although recognizing the legality of unions, had refused such protection.

## The Irish Question

In 1880 a second Gladstone ministry took office when an agricultural depression and an unpopular foreign policy undermined the Conservative government. In 1884, with Conservative cooperation, a third reform act gave the vote to most male farm workers. The major issue of the decade, however, was Ireland. From the late 1860s onward, Irish nationalists had sought to achieve home rule for Ireland, by which they meant Irish control of local government.

During his first ministry, Gladstone had addressed the Irish question through two major pieces of legislation. In 1869 he had disestablished the Church of Ireland, the Irish branch of the Anglican church. Henceforth, Irish Roman Catholics would not pay taxes to support the hated Protestant Church, to which few of the Irish belonged. Second, in 1870 the Liberal ministry sponsored a land act that provided compensation to those Irish tenants who were evicted and loans for those who wished to purchase their land. Throughout the 1870s, the Irish question continued to fester. Land remained the center of the agitation. Today Irish economic development seems more complicated and who owned the land seems less important than the methods of management and cultivation. Nevertheless, the organization of the Irish Land League in the late 1870s led to intense agitation and intimidation of landlords, who were often English. The leader of the Irish movement for a just land settlement and for home rule was Charles Stewart Parnell (1846–1891). In 1881 the second Gladstone ministry passed another Irish land act that strengthened tenant rights. It was accompanied, however, by a Coercion Act to restore law and order to Ireland.

By 1885 Parnell had organized eighty-five Irish members of the House of Commons into a tightly disciplined party that often voted as a bloc. They frequently disrupted Parliament to gain attention for the cause of home rule. They bargained with the two English political parties. In the election of 1885, the Irish Party emerged holding the balance of power between the English Liberals and Conservatives. Irish support could decide which party took office. In December 1885, Gladstone announced his support of home rule for Ireland. Parnell gave his votes to the formation of a Liberal ministry. The home rule issue then split the Liberal Party. In 1886 a group known as the Liberal Unionists joined with the Conservatives to defeat Gladstone's Home Rule Bill. Gladstone called for a new election, in which the Liberals were defeated. They remained permanently divided, and Ireland remained firmly under English administration.

The new Conservative ministry of Lord Salisbury (1830–1903) attempted to reconcile the Irish to English government through public works and administrative reform. The policy, which was tied to further coercion, had only marginal success. In 1892 Gladstone returned to power. A second Home Rule Bill passed the House of Commons but was defeated in the House of Lords. There the Irish

---

**Major Dates in Late-Nineteenth-Century Britain**

| | |
|---|---|
| 1867 | Second Reform Act |
| 1868 | Gladstone becomes prime minister |
| 1869 | Disestablishment of Church of Ireland |
| 1870 | Education Act and first Irish Land Act |
| 1871 | Purchase of army officers' commissions abolished |
| 1871 | Religious tests abolished at Oxford and Cambridge |
| 1872 | Ballot Act |
| 1874 | Disraeli becomes prime minister |
| 1875 | Public Health Act and Artisan Dwelling Act |
| 1880 | Beginning of Gladstone's second ministry |
| 1881 | Second Irish Land Act and Irish Coercion Act |
| 1884 | Third Reform Act |
| 1885 | Gladstone announces support of Irish home rule |
| 1886 | Home Rule Bill defeated and Lord Salisbury becomes the Conservative prime minister |
| 1892 | Gladstone begins his third ministry; second Irish Home Rule Bill defeated |
| 1903 | Third Irish Land Act |
| 1912 | Third Irish Home Rule Bill passed |
| 1914 | Provisions of Irish Home Rule Bill suspended because of the outbreak of World War I |

# William Gladstone Pleads for Irish Home Rule

*Since 1800 Ireland had been governed as part of Great Britain, sending representatives to the British Parliament in Westminster. Throughout the century, there had been tension and violent conflict between the Irish and their English governors. Agitation for home rule whereby the Irish would directly control many of their own affairs reached a peak in the 1880s. In 1886 William Gladstone introduced a Home Rule Bill into Parliament. The evening when Parliament voted on the measure Gladstone made a long speech, part of which is quoted here, asking Parliament to reject the traditions of the past and to grant Ireland this measure of independence. That night the Home Rule Bill of 1886 went down to defeat. The problem of Irish home rule continues to vex British politics today.*

✦ *Why did Gladstone support Irish home rule in 1886? How does he pose the issue as a matter of redeeming the reputation of England? How did the situation of nationalism that Gladstone confronted compare with that of the Austrian prime minister quoted earlier in this chapter?*

What is the case of Ireland at this moment? . . . Can anything stop a nation's demand, except its being proved to be immoderate and unsafe? But here are multitudes, and, I believe, millions upon millions, out-of-doors, who feel this demand to be neither immoderate nor unsafe. In our opinion, there is but one question before us about this demand. It is as to the time and circumstance of granting it. There is no question in our minds that it will be granted. . . .

. . . .

Ireland stands at your bar expectant, hopeful, almost suppliant. Her words are the words of truth and soberness. She asks a blessed oblivion of the past, and in that oblivion our interest is deeper than even hers. My right honourable Friend the Member [of Parliament] for East Edinburgh asks us tonight to abide by the traditions of which we are the heirs. What traditions? By the Irish traditions? Go into the length and breadth of the world, ransack the literature of all countries, find, if you can, a single voice, a single book, find, I would almost say, as

much as a single newspaper article, unless the product of the [present] day, in which the conduct of England towards Ireland is anywhere treated except with profound and bitter condemnation. Are these the traditions by which we are exhorted to stand? No; they are a sad exception to the glory of our country. They are a broad and black blot upon the pages of its history; and what we want to do is to stand by the traditions of which we are the heirs in all matters except our relations with Ireland, and to make our relations with Ireland to conform to the other traditions of our country. So we treat our traditions—so we hail the demand of Ireland for what I call a blessed oblivion of the past. She also asks a boon [a favor] for the future; and that boon for the future, unless we are much mistaken, will be a boon to us in respect of honour, no less than a boon to her in respect of happiness, prosperity, and peace. Such . . . is her prayer. Think, I beseech you, think well, think wisely, think, not for the moment, but for the years that are to come, before you reject this Bill.

*Quoted in Hans Kohn, ed.,* The Modern World: 1848 to the Present, *2nd ed. (New York: Macmillan; London: Collier-Macmillan Ltd., 1968), pp. 116, 118.*

question stood until after the turn of the century. The Conservatives sponsored a land act in 1903 that carried out the final transfer of land to tenant ownership. Ireland became a country of small farms. In 1912 a Liberal ministry passed the third Home Rule Bill. Under the provisions of the House of Lords Act of 1911, which curbed the power of that body, the bill had to pass the Commons three times over the Lords' veto to become law. The third passage occurred in the summer of 1914, but the implementation of the home rule provisions of the bill was suspended for the duration of World War I.

The Irish question affected British politics in a manner not unlike that of the Austrian nationalities problem. Normal British domestic issues could not be resolved because of the political divisions created by Ireland. The split of the Liberal Party proved especially harmful to the cause of further social and political reform. People who could agree about reform could not agree about Ireland, and the Irish problem seemed more important. Since the two traditional parties failed to deal with the social questions, by the turn of the century, a newly organized Labour Party began to fill the vacuum.

◆

*Between 1850 and 1875, the major contours of the political systems that would dominate Europe until World War I had been drawn. Those systems and political arrangements solved, so far as such matters can be solved, many of the political questions and problems that had troubled Europeans during the first half of the nineteenth century. The concept of the nation-state had on the whole triumphed. Support for governments no longer stemmed from loyalty to dynasties but from various degrees of citizen participation. Moreover, the unity of nations was no longer based on dynastic links but on ethnic, cultural, linguistic, and historical bonds. The parliamentary governments of western Europe were different from the autocracies of eastern Europe, but both political systems had been compelled to recognize the force of nationalism and the larger role of citizens in political affairs. Only Russia failed to make such concessions, but the emancipation of serfs had partly been a concession to a mode of popular opinion.*

*The major sources of future discontent would arise from the demands of labor to enter the political processes and the still unsatisfied aspirations of subject nationalities. Those two areas of unrest would trouble Europe for the next forty years and would eventually undermine the political structures created during the third quarter of the nineteenth century.*

# Review Questions

1. Why was it so difficult to unify Italy? What groups were urging unification? Who was Camillo Cavour and how did he achieve what others failed to do? What were Garibaldi's contributions to Italian unification?

2. Who was Otto von Bismarck and why did he try to unify Germany? What attempts had preceded Bismarck's efforts and why did they fail? What was Bismarck's policy of unification and why did he succeed? What effect did the unification of Germany have on the rest of Europe?

3. Discuss the transformation in France from the Second Empire of Napoleon III to the establishment of the Third Republic. Why did the Second Empire fall and what problems faced the new republic? Why did the Paris Commune become a legend throughout Europe? What effect did the Dreyfus affair have on the politics of the Third Republic?

4. Describe the government changes in Austria after 1848. What unique problems did Austria have? Were they solved? Why was nationalism a more pressing problem for Austria than for any other nation?

5. What reforms were instituted by Tsar Alexander II in Russia? Were they effective in solving some of Russia's domestic problems? Can Alexander II be regarded as a "visionary" reformer? Why or why not?

6. How would you contrast the British Liberal and Conservative parties between 1860 and 1890? Who were the leaders of each? What problems did they face in those years and what different solutions did they favor? Specifically, how did British politicians handle the Irish question? What are the parallels between England's relationship with Ireland and the nationality problem of the Austrian Empire?

# Suggested Readings

M. BENTLEY, *Politics Without Democracy, 1815–1914* (1984). A well-informed survey of British development.

R. BLAKE, *Disraeli* (1967). Remains the best biography.

J. BLUM, *Lord and Peasant in Russia from the Ninth to the Nineteenth Century* (1961). A clear discussion of emancipation in the later chapters.

G. Chapman, *The Dreyfus Affair: A Reassessment* (1955). A detached treatment of a subject that still provokes strong feelings.

G. Craig, *Germany, 1866–1945* (1978). An excellent survey.

S. Edwards, *The Paris Commune of 1871* (1971). A useful examination of a complex subject.

S. Elwitt, *The Making of the Third Republic: Class and Politics in France, 1868–1884* (1975). An excellent introduction.

S. Elwitt, *The Third Republic Defended: Bourgeois Reform in France, 1880–1914* (1986). A study that continues the survey of the previously listed volume.

E. Hobsbawm, *The Age of Empire, 1875–1914* (1987). A stimulating survey that covers cultural as well as political developments.

I. V. Hull, *The Entourage of Kaiser Wilhelm II, 1888–1918* (1982). An important discussion of the scandals of the German court.

R. A. Kann, *The Multinational Empire*, 2 vols. (1950). The basic treatment of the nationality problem of Austria-Hungary.

R. R. Locke, *French Legitimists and the Politics of Moral Order in the Early Third Republic* (1974). An excellent study of the social and intellectual roots of monarchist support.

A. J. May, *The Habsburg Monarchy, 1867–1914* (1951). Narrates in considerable detail and with much sympathy the fate of the dual monarchy.

J. F. McMillan, *Napoleon III* (1991). The best recent study.

N. M. Naimark, *Terrorists and Social Democrats: The Russian Revolutionary Movement Under Alexander III* (1983). Useful discussion of a complicated subject.

C. C. O'Brien, *Parnell and His Party* (1957). An excellent treatment of the Irish question.

J. P. Parry, *The Rise and Fall of Liberal Government in Victorian Britain* (1994). An outstanding study.

O. Pflanze, *Bismarck and the Development of Germany*, 3 vols. (1990). A major biography and history of Germany for the period.

A. Plessis, *The Rise and Fall of the Second Empire, 1852–1871* (1985). A useful survey of France under Napoleon III.

R. Shannon, *Gladstone: 1809–1865* (1982). Best coverage of his early career.

D. M. Smith, *The Making of Italy, 1796–1870* (1968). A narrative that incorporates the major documents.

D. M. Smith, *Cavour* (1984). An excellent biography.

A. J. P. Taylor, *The Habsburg Monarchy, 1809–1918* (1941). An opinionated but highly readable work.

R. Tombs, *The War Against Paris, 1871* (1981). Examines the role of the army in suppressing the Commune.

A. B. Ulam, *Russia's Failed Revolutionaries* (1981). A study of revolutionary societies and activities prior to the Revolution of 1917.

F. Venturi, *The Roots of Revolution* (trans., 1960). A major treatment of late-nineteenth-century revolutionary movements.

H. S. Watson, *The Russian Empire, 1801–1917* (1967). A far-ranging narrative.

H. U. Wehler, *The German Empire, 1871–1918* (1985). An important, controversial work.

J. Wertheimer, *Unwelcome Strangers: East European Jews in Imperial Germany* (1987). Examines the difficult position of Jews in Wilhelminian Germany.

C. B. Woodham-Smith, *The Reason Why* (1953). A lively account of the Crimean War and the charge of the Light Brigade.

T. Zeldin, *France: 1848–1945*, 2 vols. (1973, 1977). Emphasizes the social developments.

R. E. Zelnick, *Labor and Society in Tsarist Russia: The Factory Workers of Saint Petersburg, 1855–1870* (1971). An important volume that considers the early stages of the Russian industrial labor force in the era of serf emancipation.

Women only gradually gained access to secondary and university education during the second half of the nineteenth century and the early twentieth century. Young women on their way to school, the subject of this 1880 English painting, would thus have been a new sight when it was painted. [Sir George Clausen (RA) (1852–1944) "Schoolgirls, Haverstock Hill, signed and dated 1880, oil on canvas, 20$^1/_2$ x 30$^3/_8$ in. (52 x 77.2 cm), Yale Center for British Art/Paul Mellon Collection B1985.10.1]

# The Building of European Supremacy:
## Society and Politics to World War I

**Population Trends and Migration**

**The Second Industrial Revolution**
New Industries
Economic Difficulties

**The Middle Classes in Ascendancy**
Social Distinctions Within the Middle Classes

**Late-Nineteenth-Century Urban Life**
The Redesign of Cities
Urban Sanitation
Housing Reform and Middle-Class Values

**Varieties of Late-Nineteenth-Century Women's Experiences**
Social Disabilities Confronted by All
    Women
New Employment Patterns for Women

Working-Class Women
Poverty and Prostitution
Women of the Middle Class
The Rise of Political Feminism

**Jewish Emancipation**
Differing Degrees of Citizenship
Broadened Opportunities

**Labor, Socialism, and Politics to World War I**
Trade Unionism
Democracy and Political Parties
Marx and the First International
Great Britain: Fabianism and Early Welfare
    Programs
France: "Opportunism" Rejected
Germany: Social Democrats and Revisionism
Russia: Industrial Development and the Birth
    of Bolshevism

# K E Y   T O P I C S

- The transformation of European life by the Second Industrial Revolution
- Urban sanitation, housing reform, and the redesign of cities
- The condition of women in late-nineteenth-century Europe and the rise of political feminism
- The development of labor politics and socialism in Europe to the outbreak of World War I
- Industrialization and political unrest in Russia

The growth of industrialism between 1860 and 1914 increased Europe's productive capacity to unprecedented and unparalleled levels. Newly erected steel mills, railways, shipyards, and chemical plants reflected an expanding supply of capital goods in the second half of the nineteenth century. By the first decade of the new century, the age of the automobile, the airplane, the bicycle, the refrigerated ship, the telephone, the radio, the typewriter, and the electric light bulb had dawned.

The world's economies, based on the gold standard, became increasingly interdependent. European manufactured goods and financial capital flowed into markets all over the globe. In turn, Europeans imported foreign raw materials and foodstuffs. Within Europe itself, the countries toward the eastern part of the continent tended to import finished goods from the west and to export agricultural products.

During this half century, European political, economic, and social life assumed many of its current characteristics. Nation-states with large electorates, political parties, and centralized bureaucracies emerged. Business adopted large-scale corporate structures, and the labor force organized itself into trade unions. Increasing numbers of white-collar workers appeared. Urban life came to predominate throughout western Europe. Socialism became a major ingredient in the political life of all nations. The foundations of the welfare state and of vast military establishments were laid. Taxation increased accordingly.

Europe had also quietly become dependent on the resources and markets of the rest of the world. Changes in the weather conditions in Kansas, Argentina, or New Zealand might now affect the European economy. Before World War I, however, that dependence was concealed by Europe's industrial, military, and financial supremacy. Many Europeans assumed their supremacy to be natural and enduring, but the twentieth century would reveal it to have been temporary.

# Population Trends and Migration

The proportion of Europeans in the world's total population was apparently greater around 1900— estimated at about 20 percent—than ever before or since. The number of Europeans had risen from approximately 266 million in 1850 to 401 million in 1900 and 447 million in 1910. Thereafter, birth and death rates declined or stabilized in Europe and other developed regions, and population growth began to slow in those areas but not elsewhere. The result has been the demographic differential between the developed and undeveloped world— stable or slowly growing populations in developed countries and large, rapidly growing populations in undeveloped regions—that contributes to the world's present food and resource crisis.

Europe's peoples were on the move in the latter half of the century as never before. The mid-century emancipation of peasants lessened the authority of landlords and made legal movement and migration easier. Railways, steamships, and better

European emigrants from eastern Europe wait to board a ship that will carry them to the United States. Between 1846 and 1932, more than 50 million Europeans immigrated to the United States, Canada, South America, Australia, and South Africa. [Bilarchiv Preussischer Kulturbesitz]

roads increased mobility. Cheap land and better wages accompanied economic development in Europe, North America, Latin America, and Australia, enticing people to move.

Europeans migrated away from their continent in record numbers. Between 1846 and 1932, more than 50 million Europeans left their homelands. The major areas to benefit from this movement were the United States, Canada, Australia, South Africa, Brazil, and Argentina. At mid-century most of the emigrants were from Great Britain (especially Ireland), Germany, and Scandinavia. After 1885 migration from southern and eastern Europe rose. This exodus helped to relieve the social and population pressures on the Continent. The outward movement of peoples in conjunction with Europe's economic and technological superiority contributed heavily to the Europeanization of the world. Not since the sixteenth century had European civilization had such an impact on other cultures.

# The Second Industrial Revolution

During the third quarter of the nineteenth century, the gap that had long existed between British and continental economic development closed. The basic heavy industries of Belgium, France, and Germany underwent major expansion. In particular, the growth of all areas of German industry was stunning. German steel production surpassed that of Britain in 1893 and had almost doubled Britain's by the outbreak of World War I. This emergence of an industrial Germany was *the* major fact of European economic and political life at the turn of the century.

## New Industries

Initially the economic expansion of the third quarter of the century involved the spread of industries similar to those pioneered earlier in Great Britain. In particular, the expansion of railway systems on the Continent spurred economic growth. Thereafter, however, wholly new industries emerged. It is this latter development that is usually termed the *Second Industrial Revolution*. The first Industrial Revolution was associated with textiles, steam, and iron; by contrast, the second was associated with steel, chemicals, electricity, and oil.

In the 1850s, Henry Bessemer (1830–1898), an English engineer, discovered a new process, named after him, for manufacturing steel cheaply in large quantities. In 1860 Great Britain, Belgium, France, and Germany had produced 125,000 tons of steel. By 1913 the figure had risen to 32,020,000 tons.

The chemical industry also came of age during this period. The Solway process of alkali production replaced the older Leblanc process, allowing the recovery of more chemical by-products. The new process permitted increased production of sulfuric acid and laundry soap. New dyestuffs and plastics were also developed. Formal scientific research played an important role in this growth of the chemical industry, marking the beginning of a direct link between science and industrial development. As in so many other aspects of the Second Industrial Revolution, Germany was a leader in forging this link, fostering scientific research and education.

The most significant change for industry and eventually for everyday life involved the application of electrical energy to production. Electricity was the most versatile and transportable source of power ever discovered. It could be delivered almost anywhere to run either large or small machinery, making factory location more flexible and factory construction more efficient. The first major public power plant was constructed in 1881 in Great Britain. Soon electric poles, lines, and generating stations dotted the European landscape. Homes began to use electric lights. Streetcar and subway systems were electrified.

The internal combustion engine was invented in 1886. When the German engineer Gottlieb Daimler (1834–1900) put it on four wheels and obtained a French patent in 1887, the automobile was born. France initially took the lead in auto manufacture, but for many years the car remained a novelty item that only the wealthy could afford. It was the American, Henry Ford (1863–1947), who later made the automobile accessible to large numbers of people.

The automobile and new industrial and chemical uses for petroleum had, by the turn of the century, created the first significant demand for oil, and then as now Europe depended on imported supplies. The major oil companies were Standard Oil of the United States, British Shell Oil, and Royal Dutch Petroleum.

## Economic Difficulties

Despite the multiplication of new industries, the second half of the nineteenth century was not a period of uninterrupted or smooth economic

| Major Dates of the Second Industrial Revolution | |
|---|---|
| 1856–1870 | Passage of laws permitting joint stock companies: 1856, Britain; 1863, France; 1870, Prussia |
| 1857 | Bessemer process for making steel |
| 1873 | Beginning of major economic downturn |
| 1876 | Alexander Graham Bell invents the telephone |
| 1879 | Edison perfects the electric light bulb |
| 1881 | First electric power plant in Britain |
| 1886 | Daimler invents the internal combustion engine |
| 1887 | Daimler's first automobile |
| 1895 | Diesel engine invented |
| 1895 | Wireless telegraphy invented |
| 1890s | Decade of first major impact of petroleum |
| 1903 | Wright brothers make first successful airplane flight |
| 1909 | Ford manufactures the Model T |

growth. Both industry and agriculture generally prospered from 1850 to 1873, but in the last quarter of the century economic advance was slower. Bad weather and foreign competition put grave pressures on European agriculture. Although these problems for agriculture lowered consumer food prices, they also put a drag on the economy. Many of the emigrants who left Europe during these years came from the countryside or from the least industrialized parts of Europe.

Several large banks failed in 1873, and the rate of capital investment slowed. Some industries then entered a two-decade-long period of stagnation that many contemporaries regarded as a depression. Overall, however, the general standard of living in the industrialized nations improved in the second half of the nineteenth century. Prices and wages, as well as profits, both fell, so real wages generally held firm, and in some countries even rose. Yet many workers still lived and labored in abysmal conditions. There were pockets of *unemployment* (a word that was coined during this period), and strikes and other forms of labor unrest were common. The economic difficulties fed the growth of trade unions and socialist political parties.

The new industries produced consumer goods, and expansion in consumer demand brought the economy out of stagnation by the end of the cen-

tury. Lower food prices eventually allowed all classes to spend a marginally larger amount of their income on consumer goods. Urbanization naturally created larger markets. People living in cities simply saw more things they wanted to buy than they would have seen in the countryside. New forms of retailing and marketing appeared—department stores, chain stores, packaging techniques, mail-order catalogs, and advertising—simultaneously stimulating and feeding consumer demand. Overseas imperialism also opened new markets for European consumer goods.

# The Middle Classes in Ascendancy

The sixty years before World War I were the age of the middle classes. The London Great Exhibition of 1851 held in the Crystal Palace had displayed the products and the new material life they had forged. Thereafter, the middle classes became the arbiter of consumer taste. After the revolutions of 1848, the middle classes ceased to be a revolutionary group. Once the question of social and property equality had been raised, large and small property owners across the Continent moved to protect what they possessed against demands from socialists and other working-class groups.

## Social Distinctions Within the Middle Classes

The middle classes, never perfectly homogeneous, grew increasingly diverse. Their most prosperous members—the owners and managers of great businesses and banks—lived in splendor that rivaled and sometimes exceeded that of the aristocracy. Some, such as W. H. Smith (1825–1891), the owner of railway newsstands in England, were made members of the House of Lords. The Krupp family of Germany were pillars of the state and received visits from the German emperor and his court.

Only a few hundred families gained such wealth. Beneath them were the comfortable small entrepreneurs and professional people, whose incomes permitted private homes, large quantities of furniture, pianos, pictures, books, journals, education for their children, and vacations. Also in this group were the shopkeepers, schoolteachers, librarians, and others who had either a bit of property or a skill

# Paris Department Stores
# Expand Their Business

*The department store in Europe and the United States became a major institution of retailing in the last half of the nineteenth century. It was one of the reasons for the expansion in late-century consumer demand. This description, written by the Frenchman E. Levasseur in 1907, follows the growth of such stores in Paris and explains why they exerted such economic power. The reader will notice how many of their techniques of retailing are still used today.*

*✦ Why should the various French governments have favored the growth of department stores? Where did these stores stand in the process of economic production and sales? Why was the volume of sales so important? What kinds of people might have benefitted from the jobs available in these stores?*

It was in the reign of Louis Philippe [1830–1848] that department stores for fashion goods and dresses . . . began to be distinguished. The type was already one of other notable developments of the Second Empire; it became one of the most important ones of the Third Republic. These stores have increased in number and several of them have become extremely large. Combining in their different departments all articles of clothing, toilet articles, furniture and many other ranges of goods, it is their special object so to combine all commodities as to attract and satisfy customers who will find conveniently together an assortment of a mass of articles corresponding to all their various needs. They attract customers by permanent display, by free entry into the shops, by periodic exhibitions, by special sales, by fixed prices, and by their ability to deliver the goods purchased to customers' homes, in Paris and to the provinces. Turning themselves into direct intermediaries between the producer and the consumer, even producing sometimes some of their articles in their own workshops, buying at lowest prices because of their large orders and because they are in a position to profit from bargains, working with large sums, and selling to most of their customers for cash only, they can transmit these benefits in lowered selling prices. They can even decide to sell at a loss, as an advertisement or to get rid of out-of-date fashions.

The success of these department stores is only possible thanks to the volume of their business, and this volume needs considerable capital and a very large turnover. Now capital, having become abundant, is freely combined nowadays in large enterprises. . . . [The]he large urban agglomerations, the ease with which goods can be transported by the railways, the diffusion of some comforts to strata below the middle classes, have all favoured these developments. . . .

According to the tax records of 1891, these stores in Paris, numbering 12, employed 1,708 persons and rated their site values at 2,159,000 francs; the largest had then 542 employees. These same stores had, in 1901, 9,784 employees; one of them over 2,000 and another over 1,600; their site value was doubled.

*Sidney Pollard and Colin Holmes,* Documents of European Economic History, Vol. 3 *(London: Edward Arnold, 1972), pp. 95–96.*

*The Paris Exhibition of 1889, like other exhibitions held during the second half of the nineteenth century, allowed Europeans to see the vast array of consumer goods that had become available to them. [Bildarchiv Preussischer Kulturbesitz]*

derived from education that provided respectable, nonmanual employment.

Finally, there was a wholly new element—"white-collar workers"—who formed the lower middle class, or *petit bourgeoisie*. They included secretaries, retail clerks, and lower-level bureaucrats in business and government. They often had working-class origins and might even belong to unions, but they had middle-class aspirations and consciously sought to distance themselves from a lower-class lifestyle. They actively pursued educational opportunities and chances for even the slightest career advancement for themselves and more especially for their children. Many of them spent a considerable portion of their disposable income on consumer goods, such as stylish clothing and furniture, that were distinctively middle class in appearance.

Significant tensions and social anxieties marked relations among the various middle-class groups.

Small shopkeepers resented the power of the great capitalists, with their department stores and mail-order catalogs. There is some evidence that the professions were becoming overcrowded. People who had only recently attained a middle-class lifestyle feared losing it in bad economic times. Nonetheless, the decades immediately before the World War I saw the middle classes setting the values and goals for most of the society.

## Late-Nineteenth-Century Urban Life

Europe became more urbanized than ever in the latter half of the nineteenth century as migration to the cities continued. Between 1850 and 1911, urban dwellers rose from 25 to 44 percent of the population in France and from 30 to 60 percent of the population in Germany. Other western European countries experienced similar increases.

The rural migrants to the cities were largely uprooted from traditional social ties. They often faced poor housing, social anonymity, and, because they rarely possessed the right kinds of skills, unemployment. People from different ethnic backgrounds found themselves in proximity to one another and had difficulty mixing socially. Competition for jobs generated new varieties of political and social discontent, such as the anti-Semitism directed at the thousands of Russian Jews who had migrated to western Europe. Indeed, much of the political anti-Semitism of the latter part of the century had its roots in the problems generated by urban migration.

## The Redesign of Cities

The inward urban migration placed new social and economic demands on already strained city resources and gradually produced significant transformations in the patterns of urban living. National and municipal governments redesigned the central portions of many major European cities during the second half of the century. Previously, the central urban areas had been places where many people from all social classes both lived and worked. From the middle of the century onward, planners transformed these districts into areas where businesses, government offices, large retail stores, and theaters were located, but where fewer people resided. Commerce, trade, government, and leisure activities now dominated central cities.

THE NEW PARIS  The most famous and extensive transformation of a major city occurred in Paris. Like so many other European cities, Paris had expanded from the Middle Ages onward with little or no design or planning. Great public buildings and squalid hovels stood near each other. The Seine River was little more than an open sewer. The streets were narrow, crooked, and crowded. It was impossible to cross easily from one part of the city to another either on foot or by carriage. In 1850 a fully accurate map of the city did not even exist. Of more concern to the government of Napoleon III, the city's streets had for sixty years provided battlegrounds for urban insurrections that had on numerous occasions, most recently in 1848, toppled French governments.

Napoleon III personally determined that Paris must be redesigned. He appointed Georges Haussmann (1809–1891), who, as prefect of the Seine from 1853 to 1870, oversaw a vast urban reconstruction program. Whole districts were destroyed to open the way for the broad boulevards and streets that became the hallmark of modern Paris. Much, though by no means all, of the purpose of this street planning was political. The wide vistas were not only beautiful but also allowed for the quick deployment of troops to put down riots. The eradication of the many small streets and alleys removed areas where barricades could be and had been erected.

The project was also political in another sense. In addition to the new boulevards, parks such as the Bois de Boulogne and major public buildings such as the Paris Opera were also constructed or completed. These projects, along with the demolition and street building, created thousands of public jobs. Many other laborers found employment in the private construction that accompanied the public works.

Further rebuilding and redesign occurred under the Third Republic after the destruction that accompanied the suppression of the Commune. Many department stores, office complexes, and largely middle-class apartment buildings were constructed. By the late 1870s, mechanical trams were operating in Paris. After much debate, construction of a subway system (the *métro*) began in 1895, long after that of London (1863). New railway stations were also erected near the close of the century. This

| Growth of Major European Cities (FIGURES IN THOUSANDS) | | | |
|---|---|---|---|
| | 1850 | 1880 | 1910 |
| Berlin | 419 | 1,122 | 2,071 |
| Birmingham | 233 | 437 | 840 |
| Frankfurt | 65 | 137 | 415 |
| London | 2,685 | 4,470 | 7,256 |
| Madrid | 281 | 398 | 600 |
| Moscow | 365 | 748 | 1,533 |
| Paris | 1,053 | 2,269 | 2,888 |
| Rome | 175 | 300 | 542 |
| St. Petersburg | 485 | 877 | 1,962 |
| Vienna | 444 | 1,104 | 2,031 |
| Warsaw | 160 | 339 | 872 |

*The Eiffel Tower, shown under construction in this painting, was to become a symbol of the newly redesigned Paris and its steel structure a symbol of French industrial strength. [H. Roger Viollet]*

transport linked the refurbished central city to the suburbs.

In 1889 the Eiffel Tower was built, originally as a temporary structure for the international trade exposition of that year. Not all the new structures of Paris bespoke the impact of middle-class commerce and the reign of iron and steel, however. Between 1873 and 1914, the French Roman Catholic Church oversaw the construction of the Basilica of the Sacred Heart high atop Montmartre as an act of national penance for the sins that had led to French defeat in the Franco-Prussian War. Those two landmarks—the Eiffel Tower and the Basilica of the Sacred Heart—visibly symbolized the social and political divisions between liberals and conservatives in the Third Republic.

DEVELOPMENT OF SUBURBS   Commercial development, railway construction, and the clearing of slums displaced many city dwellers and raised urban land values and rents. Consequently, both the middle classes and the working class began to seek housing elsewhere. The middle classes looked for neighborhoods removed from urban congestion. The working class looked for affordable housing. The result, in virtually all countries, was the development of suburbs surrounding the city proper. These suburbs housed families whose breadwinners worked in the central city or in a factory located within the city limits. European suburbs, unlike those that developed in the United States, often

consisted of apartment buildings or private houses built closely together with small lawns and gardens.

The expansion of railways with cheap workday fares and the introduction of mechanical and later electric tramways, as well as subways, allowed tens of thousands of workers from all classes to move daily between the city and the outlying suburbs. For hundreds of thousands of Europeans, home and work became more physically separated than ever before.

## Urban Sanitation

The efforts of governments and of the increasingly conservative middle classes to maintain public order after 1848 led to a growing concern with the problems of public health and housing for the poor. A widespread feeling arose that only when the health and housing of the working class were improved would the middle-class health also be secure and the political order stable.

IMPACT OF CHOLERA   These concerns first manifested themselves as a result of the great cholera epidemics of the 1830s and 1840s. Unlike many other common deadly diseases of the day that touched only the poor, cholera struck all classes, impelling the middle class to demand a solution. Before the development of the bacterial theory of disease late in the century, physicians and sanitary reformers believed that cholera and other diseases

*Railways were an important part of late nineteenth-century middle-class life. They helped promote the development of suburbs, allowing breadwinners to commute into the city to work, leaving their families at home. They also promoted travel to the vacation spots that were being developed across Europe during this era. [Bildarchiv Preussischer Kulturbesitz]*

were spread through infection from miasmas in the air. These miasmas, the presence of which was marked by their foul odors, were believed to arise from filth. The way to get rid of the dangerous, foul-smelling air was to clean up the cities.

During the 1840s, many physicians and some government officials began to publicize the dangers posed by the unsanitary conditions associated with overcrowding in cities and with businesses such as basement slaughterhouses. In 1840 Louis René Villermé published his *Tableau de l'état physique et moral des ouvriers (Catalog of the Physical and Moral State of Workers)*. In 1842 Edwin Chadwick's (1800–1890) *Report on the Sanitary Condition of the Labouring Population* shocked the English public. In Germany, Rudolf Virchow (1821–1902) published similar findings. These and various other private and public commission reports closely linked the issues of wretched living conditions and public health. They also demonstrated that sanitary reform would remove the dangers. These reports, incidentally, now provide some of the best information available about working-class living conditions in the middle of the nineteenth century.

NEW WATER AND SEWER SYSTEMS   The proposed solution to the health hazard was cleanliness, to be achieved through new water and sewer systems. These facilities were constructed slowly, beginning usually in capital cities and then much later in

# A French Physician Describes a Working-Class Slum in Lille Before the Public Health Movement

*It is difficult to conceive of the world before the sanitation movement. The work of medical doctors frequently carried them into working-class areas of industrial cities rarely visited by other members of the middle class. Louis Villermé was such a French physician. He wrote extensive descriptions of the slums and the general living conditions of industrial workers. The passage here, published in 1840, describes a particularly notorious section of Lille, a major cotton-manufacturing town in northern France.*

✦ *What does this physician find most disturbing about the scene he describes? How is his description possibly designed to call forth sympathy and concern from a middle-class reader? How might the conditions described have led the poor of France toward socialism or radical politics? How would addressing the problems described have led to a larger role for government?*

The poorest live in the cellars and attics. These cellars . . . open onto the streets or courtyards, and one enters them by a stairway which is very often at once the door and the window. . . . Commonly the height of the ceiling is six or six and a half feet at the highest point, and they are only ten to fourteen or fifteen feet wide.

It is in these somber and sad dwellings that a large number of workers eat, sleep, and even work. The light of day comes an hour later for them than for others, and the night an hour earlier.

Their furnishings normally consist, along with the tools of their profession, of a sort of cupboard or a plank on which to deposit food, a stove . . . a few pots, a little table, two or three poor chairs, and a dirty pallet of which the only pieces are a straw mattress and scraps of a blanket. . . .

In their obscure cellars, in their rooms, which one would take for cellars, the air is never renewed, it is infected; the walls are plastered with garbage. . . . If a bed exists, it is a few dirty, greasy planks; it is damp and putrescent straw; it is a coarse cloth whose color and fabric are hidden by a layer of grime; it is a blanket that resembles a sieve. . . . The furniture is dislocated, worm-eaten, covered with filth. Utensils are thrown in disorder all over the dwelling. The windows, always closed, are covered by paper and glass, but so black, so smoke-encrusted, that the light is unable to penetrate . . . everywhere are piles of garbage, of ashes, of debris from vegetables picked up from the streets, of rotten straw; of animal nests of all sorts; thus, the air is unbreathable. One is exhausted, in these hovels, by a stale, nauseating, somewhat piquante odor, odor of filth, odor of garbage. . . .

And the poor themselves, what are they like in the middle of such a slum? Their clothing is in shreds, without substance, consumed, covered, no less than their hair, which knows no comb, with dust from the workshops. And their skin? . . . It is painted, it is hidden, if you wish, by indistinguishable deposits of diverse exudations.

Louis René Villermé, Tableau de l'état physique et moral des ouvriers employés dans les manufactures de coton, de laine et de soie *(Paris, 1840), as quoted and trans. in William H. Sewell, Jr.,* Work and Revolution in France: The Language of Labor from the Old Regime to 1848 *(Cambridge, England: Cambridge University Press, 1980), p. 224.*

*Urban slums such as this one in Glasgow, Scotland, aroused the concern of sanitary and housing reformers. [Service Photographique des Musées Nationaux, Paris/Photo R.M.N.]*

provincial cities. Some major urban areas did not have good water systems until after the turn of the century. Nonetheless, the building of these systems was one of the major health and engineering achievements of the second half of the nineteenth century. The sewer system of Paris was a famous part of Haussmann's rebuilding program. In London, the construction of the Albert Embankment along the Thames involved not only large sewers discharging into the river but gas mains and water pipes as well; all were encased in thick walls of concrete, one of the new building materials of the day, and granite. Wherever these sanitary facilities were installed, the mortality rate dropped considerably.

EXPANDED GOVERNMENT INVOLVEMENT IN PUBLIC HEALTH  This concern with public health led to an expansion of governmental power on various levels. In Britain the Public Health Act of 1848, in France the Melun Act of 1851, and various laws in the still-disunited German states, as well as later legislation, introduced new restraints on private life and enterprise. This legislation allowed medical officers and building inspectors to enter homes and other structures in the name of public health. Private property could be condemned for posing health hazards. Private land could be excavated for the construction of the sewers and water mains required to protect the public. New building regulations put restraints on the activities of private contractors.

Full acceptance at the close of the century of the bacterial theory of disease associated with the discoveries of Louis Pasteur (1822–1895) in France, Robert Koch (1843–1910) in Germany, and Joseph Lister (1827–1912) in Britain made cleanliness an even more prominent public concern. Throughout Europe, issues related to the maintenance of public health and the physical well-being of national populations repeatedly opened the way for new modes of government intervention in the lives of citizens.

## Housing Reform and Middle-Class Values

The information about working-class living conditions brought to light by the sanitary reformers also led to heated debates over the housing problem. The wretched dwellings of the poor were themselves a cause of poor sanitation and thus became a newly perceived health hazard. Furthermore, middle-class reformers and bureaucrats found themselves shocked by the domestic arrangements of the poor, whose large families might live in a single room lacking all forms of personal privacy. A single toilet facility might serve a whole block of tenements. After the revolutions of 1848, the overcrowding in housing and the social discontent that it generated were also seen to pose a political danger.

Middle-class reformers thus turned to housing reform to solve the medical, moral, and political dangers posed by slums. Proper, decent housing would foster a good home life, in turn leading to a healthy, moral, and politically stable population. As A. V. Huber, one of the early German housing reformers, declared:

Certainly it would not be too much to say that the home is the communal embodiment of family life. Thus the purity of the dwelling is almost as important for the family as is the cleanliness of the body for the individual. Good or bad housing is a question of life and death if ever there was one.[1]

Later advocates of housing reform, such as Jules Simon in France, saw good housing as leading to good family life and ultimately to strong patriotic feeling. It was widely believed that providing the poor and the working class with adequate, respectable, cheap housing would alleviate social and political discontent. It was also believed that the personal saving and investment required for owning a home would lead the working class to adopt the thrifty habits of the middle classes.

Private philanthropy made the first attack on the housing problem. Companies operating on low profit margins or making low-interest loans encouraged housing for the poor. Firms, such as the German Krupp armaments concern, seeking to ensure a contented, healthy, and stable workforce, constructed model housing projects and industrial communities.

By the mid-1880s, the migration into cities had made housing a political issue. Legislation in England in 1885 lowered the interest rates for the construction of cheap housing, and soon thereafter public authorities began public housing projects. In Germany, action on housing came later in the century through the initiative of local municipalities. In 1894 France made inexpensive credit available for constructing housing for the poor. None of these governments, however, adopted wide-scale housing experiments.

Nonetheless, by 1914 the housing problem had been fully recognized if not adequately addressed. The goal of housing reform across western Europe came to be to provide homes for the members of the working class that would allow them to enjoy a family life more or less like that of the middle class. Such a home would be in the form of a detached house or some kind of affordable city apartment with several rooms, a private entrance, and separate toilet facilities.

# Varieties of Late-Nineteenth-Century Women's Experiences

Late-nineteenth-century women, like late-nineteenth-century men, led lives that reflected their social rank. Yet, within each rank, the experience of women was distinct from that of men. Women remained, generally speaking, in positions of economic dependence and legal inferiority, whatever their social class.

## Social Disabilities Confronted by All Women

At the middle of the nineteenth century, virtually all European women faced social and legal disabilities in three areas: property rights, family law, and education. By the close of the century, there had been some improvement in each area.

WOMEN AND PROPERTY   Until the last quarter of the century in most European countries, married women could not own property in their own names no matter what their social class. For all practical purposes, upon marriage women lost to their husbands' control any property they owned or that they might inherit or earn by their own labor. Their legal identities was subsumed in their husbands', and they had no independent standing before the law. The courts saw the theft of a woman's purse as a theft of her husband's property. Because European society was based on private property and wage earning, these disabilities put married women at a great disadvantage. They limited their freedom to work, to save, and to move from one location to another.

Reform of women's property rights came very slowly. By 1882 Great Britain had passed the Married Woman's Property Act, which allowed married women to own property in their own right. In France, however, a married woman could not even open a savings account in her own name until 1895 and not until 1907 were married women granted possession of the wages they earned. In 1900 Germany allowed women to take jobs without their husbands' permission, but except for her wages, a German husband retained control of most of his

---

[1]Quoted in Nicholas Bullock and James Read, The Movement for Housing Reform in Germany and France, 1840–1914 (Cambridge, England: Cambridge University Press, 1985), p. 42.

wife's property. Similar laws prevailed elsewhere in Europe.

FAMILY LAW   Virtually all European family law also worked to the disadvantage of women. Legal codes actually required wives to "give obedience" to their husbands. The Napoleonic Code and the remnants of Roman law still in effect made women legal minors throughout Europe. Divorce was difficult everywhere for most of the century. In England before 1857, divorce required an act of Parliament. Thereafter, divorce could be procured, with difficulty, through the Court of Matrimonial Causes. Most nations did not permit divorce by mutual consent. French law forbade divorce between 1816 and 1884. Thereafter the chief recognized legal cause for divorce was cruelty and injury, which had to be proven in court. In Great Britain, adultery was the usual cause for divorce, but to obtain a divorce a woman had to prove her husband's adultery plus other offenses, whereas a man only had to prove his wife's adultery. In Germany, only adultery or serious maltreatment were recognized as reasons for divorce. Across Europe, some version of the double standard prevailed whereby extramarital sexual relations of husbands were tolerated to a greater degree than those of wives. Everywhere, divorce required legal hearings and the presentation of legal proof, making the process expensive and all the more difficult for women who did not control their own property.

The authority of husbands also extended to children. A husband could take children away from their mother and give them to someone else for rearing. Only the husband, in most countries, could permit his daughter to marry. In some countries, he could virtually force his daughter to marry the man of his choice. In cases of divorce and separation, the husband normally assumed authority over children no matter how he had treated them previously.

The issues surrounding the sexual and reproductive rights of women that have been so widely debated recently could hardly be discussed in the nineteenth century. Until well into the twentieth century, both contraception and abortion were illegal. The law surrounding rape normally worked to the disadvantage of women. Wherever they turned with their problems—whether to physicians or lawyers—women confronted an official or legal world almost wholly populated and controlled by men.

EDUCATIONAL BARRIERS   Throughout the nineteenth century, women had less access to education than men, and what was available to them was inferior to that available to men. Not surprisingly, the percentage of illiterate women exceeded that of men. Most women were educated only enough for the domestic careers they were expected to follow.

University and professional education remained reserved for men until at least the third quarter of the century. The University of Zurich first opened its doors to women in the 1860s. The University of London admitted women for degrees in 1878. Women's colleges were founded at Cambridge during the last quarter of the century. Women could take Oxford and Cambridge university examinations, but were not awarded degrees at Oxford until 1920 or at Cambridge until 1921. Women could not attend Sorbonne lectures until 1880. Just before the turn of the century, universities and medical schools in the Austrian Empire allowed women to matriculate, but Prussian universities did not admit women until after 1900. Russian women did not attend universities before 1914, but other institutions that awarded degrees were open to them. Italian universities proved themselves more open to both women students and women instructors than similar institutions elsewhere in Europe. In many countries, there were frequently more foreign than native women attending university classes. This was especially the case in Zurich, where many Russian women studied for medical degrees. Many of the American women who founded or taught in the first women's colleges in the United States studied at European universities.

The absence of a system of private or public secondary education for women prevented most of them from gaining the qualifications they needed to enter a university whether or not the university prohibited them. Considerable evidence suggests that educated, professional men feared their professions would be overcrowded if they admitted women. Women who attended universities and medical schools, like the young Russian women who studied medicine at Zurich, were sometimes labeled political radicals.

By the turn of the century, some men in the educated elites feared the challenge educated women posed to traditional gender roles in the home and workplace. Restricting women's access to secondary and university education helped bar them from social and economic advancement. Women would

*Women working in the London Central Telephone Exchange. The invention of the telephone opened new employment opportunities for women. [Mary Evans Picture Library]*

benefit only marginally from the expansion of professional employment that occurred during the late nineteenth and early twentieth centuries. Some women did enter the professions, most particularly medicine, but their numbers remained few. Most nations refused to allow women to become lawyers until after World War I.

School teaching at the elementary level, which had come to be seen as a "female job" because of its association with the nurturing of children, became a professional haven for women. Trained at institutions that were equivalent to normal schools, women schoolteachers at the elementary level were regarded as educated, but not as university educated. Secondary education remained largely the province of men.

The few women who pioneered in the professions and on government commissions and school boards or who dispersed birth control information faced grave social obstacles, personal humiliation, and often outright bigotry. These women and their male supporters were challenging that clear separation of life into male and female spheres that had emerged in middle-class European social life during the nineteenth century. Women themselves were often hesitant to support feminist causes or expanded opportunities for themselves because they had been so thoroughly acculturated into the recently stereotyped roles. Many women as well as men saw a real conflict between family responsibilities and feminism.

### New Employment Patterns for Women

During the decades of the Second Industrial Revolution, two major developments affected the economic lives of women. The first was a significant expansion in the variety of jobs available outside the better-paying learned professions. The second was a significant withdrawal of married women from the workforce. These two seemingly contradictory developments require some explanation.

AVAILABILITY OF NEW JOBS The expansion of governmental bureaucracies, the emergence of corporations and other large-scale businesses, and the vast growth of retail stores opened many new employment opportunities for women. The need for elementary school teachers, usually women, grew as governments adopted compulsory education laws. Technological inventions and innovations such as the typewriter and eventually the telephone exchange also fostered female employment. Women by the thousands became secretaries and clerks for governments and for private businesses. Still more thousands became shop assistants.

Although these jobs did open new and often somewhat better employment opportunities for women, they nonetheless required low-level skills and involved minimal training. They were occupied primarily by unmarried women or widows. Women were rarely to be found in more prominent positions.

Employers continued to pay women low wages, because they assumed, quite often knowing better, that a woman did not need to support herself independently but could expect additional financial support from her father or from her husband. Consequently, a woman who did need to support herself independently was almost always unable to find a job paying an adequate income—or a position that paid as well as one held by a man who was supporting himself independently.

WITHDRAWAL FROM THE LABOR FORCE   Most of the women filling these new service positions were young and unmarried. Upon marriage, or certainly after the birth of her first child, a woman normally withdrew from the labor force. She either did not work or she worked at some occupation that could be pursued in the home. This pattern was not new, but it had become significantly more common by the end of the nineteenth century. The kinds of industrial occupations that women had filled in the middle of the nineteenth century, especially textile and garment making, were shrinking. There were thus fewer opportunities for employment in those industries for either married or unmarried women. Employers in offices and retail stores preferred young, unmarried women whose family responsibilities would not interfere with their work. The

*These German women are operating lathes in a metalworking plant. It was rare for women to have such skilled jobs. [The Bettmann Archive]*

decline in the number of children being born also meant that fewer married women were needed to look after other women's children.

The real wages paid to male workers increased during this period, and so families had a somewhat reduced need for a second income. Also, thanks to improving health conditions, men lived longer than before, and so wives were less likely to be thrust into the workforce by the death of their husbands. The smaller size of families also lowered the need for supplementary wages. Working children stayed at home longer and continued to contribute to the family's wage pool.

Finally, the cultural dominance of the middle class established a pattern of social expectations, especially for wives. The more prosperous a working-class family became, the less involved in employment its women were supposed to be. Indeed, the less income-producing work a wife did, the more prosperous and stable the family was considered.

Yet behind these generalities stands the enormous variety of social and economic experience late-nineteenth-century women actually encountered. As might be expected, the chief determinant of these individual experiences was social class.

## Working-Class Women

Although the textile industry and garment making were much less dominant than earlier in the century, they continued to employ large numbers of women. The situation of women in the German clothing-making trades illustrates the kind of vulnerable economic situation that they could encounter as a result of their limited skills and the organization of the trade. The system of manufacturing mass-made clothes of uniform sizes in Germany was complex. It was designed to require minimal capital investment on the part of the manufacturers and to protect them from significant risk. A major manufacturer would arrange for the production of clothing through a putting-out system. He would purchase the material and then put it out for tailoring. The clothing was produced not in a factory but usually in numerous, independently owned, small sweatshops or by workers in their homes.

In Berlin in 1896, there were more than 80,000 garment workers, mostly women, who were so employed. When business was good and the demand strong, employment for these women was high. As the seasons shifted or business became poor, however, less and less work was put out, idling many of them. In effect, the workers who actually sewed the clothing carried much of the risk of the enterprise. Some women did work in factories, but they, too, were subject to layoffs. Furthermore, women in the clothing trade were nearly always in positions less skilled than those of the male tailors or the male middlemen who owned the workshops.

The expectation of separate social and economic spheres for men and women and the definition of women's chief work as pertaining to the home contributed mightily to the exploitation of women workers outside the home. Because their wages were regarded merely as supplementing their husbands', they became particularly vulnerable to the kind of economic exploitation that characterized the German putting-out system for clothing production and similar systems of clothing production elsewhere. Women were nearly always treated as casual workers everywhere in Europe.

## Poverty and Prostitution

A major but little recognized social fact of most nineteenth-century cities was the presence of a surplus of working women who did not fit the stereotype of wife or daughter supplementing a family's income. There were almost always many more women seeking employment than there were jobs. The economic vulnerability of women and the consequent poverty many of them faced were among the chief causes of prostitution. In any major late-nineteenth-century European city, there were thousands of prostitutes.

Prostitution was, of course, not new. It had always been one way for very poor women to find some income. In the late nineteenth century, however, it was closely related to the difficulty encountered by very poor women who were trying to make their way in an overcrowded female labor force. On the Continent, prostitution was generally legalized and was subject to governmental and municipal regulations. Those regulations were, it should be noted, passed and enforced by male legislatures and councils and were enforced by male police and physicians. In Great Britain, prostitution received only minimal regulation.

Many myths and misunderstandings have surrounded the subject of prostitution. The most recent studies of the subject in England emphasize

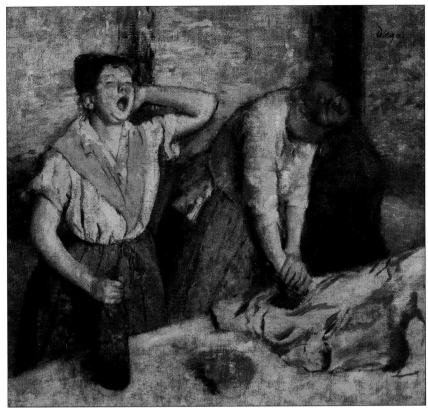

*Although new opportunities opened to them in the late nineteenth century, many working-class women, like these women ironing in a laundry, remained in traditional occupations. As the wine bottle suggests, alcoholism was a problem for women as well as for men engaged in tedious and boring work. The painting is by Edgar Degas (1834–1917). [Service Photographique des Musées Nationaux, Paris/Photo R.M.N.]*

that most prostitutes were active on the streets for a very few years, generally from their late teens to about age twenty-five. They often were very poor women who had recently migrated from nearby rural areas. Others were born in the towns where they became prostitutes. Certain cities—those with large army garrisons or naval ports or those, like London, with large transient populations—attracted many prostitutes. There were far fewer prostitutes in manufacturing towns, where there were more opportunities for steady employment and where community life was more stable.

Women who became prostitutes usually came from families of unskilled workers and had minimal skills and education themselves. Many had been servants. They also often were from broken homes or were orphaned. Contrary to many sensational late-century newspaper accounts, there were few child prostitutes. Furthermore, rarely were women seduced into prostitution by middle-class employers or middle-class clients, although working-class women were always potentially subject to such pressure. The customers of poor working-class prostitutes were primarily working-class men.

## Women of the Middle Class

A vast social gap separated poor working-class women from their middle-class counterparts. As their fathers' and husbands' incomes permitted, middle-class women participated in the vast expansion of consumerism and domestic comfort that marked the end of the nineteenth century and the early twentieth century. They filled their homes with manufactured items, including clothing, china, furniture, carpets, drapery, wallpaper, and prints. They enjoyed all the improvements of sanitation and electricity. They could command the services of numerous domestic servants. They moved into the fashionable new houses being constructed in the rapidly expanding suburbs.

THE CULT OF DOMESTICITY    For the middle classes the distinction between work and family, defined by gender, had become complete and constituted the model for all other social groups. Middle-class women, if at all possible, did not work. More than any other women, they became limited to the roles of wife and mother. As a result, they might enjoy great domestic luxury and comfort, but their lives,

*Family was central to the middle-class conception of a stable and respectable social life. This portrait of the Bellelli family is by Degas. Notice that the husband and father sits at his desk, suggesting his association with business and the world outside the home, whereas the wife and mother stands with their children, suggesting her domestic role. [Giraudon/Art Resource, N.Y.]*

talents, ambitions, and opportunities for applying their intelligence were markedly circumscribed.

Middle-class women became, in large measure, the product of a particular understanding of social life. Home life was to be very different from the life of business and the marketplace. The home was to be a private place of refuge, a view set forth in scores of women's journals across Europe.

As studies of the lives of middle-class women in northern France have suggested, this image of the middle-class home and of the role of women in the home is quite different from the one that had existed earlier in the nineteenth century. During the first half of the century, the spouse of a middle-

class husband might very well contribute directly to the business, handling accounts or correspondence. These women also frequently had little to do with rearing their children, leaving that task first to nurses and later to governesses. The reasons for the change over the course of the century are not certain, but it appears that men began to insist on doing business with other men. Magazines and books directed toward women began to praise motherhood, domesticity, religion, and charity as the proper work of women in accordance with the concept of separate spheres.

For middle-class French women, as well as for middle-class women elsewhere, the home came to

# The Virtues of a French Middle-Class Lady Praised

*One of the chief social roles assigned to middle-class French women was that of charitable activity. This obituary of Mme Émile Delesalle from a Roman Catholic Church paper of the late nineteenth century describes the work of this woman among the poor. It is a very revealing document because it clearly shows the class divisions that existed in the giving of charity. Also through the kinds of virtues it praises, it gave instruction to its women readers. Note the emphasis on home life, spirituality, and instruction of children in charitable acts.*

✦ *What assumptions about the character of women allowed writers to see charity as a particularly good occupation for women? What middle-class attitudes toward the poor are displayed in this passage? How did the assignment of charity work to women lead to their being excluded from other kinds of work and the learned professions?*

The poor were the object of her affectionate interest, especially the shameful poor, the fallen people. She sought them out and helped them with perfect discretion which doubled the value of her benevolent interest. To those whom she could approach without fear of bruising their dignity, she brought, along with alms to assure their existence, consolation of the most serious sort—she raised their courage and their hopes. To others, each Sunday, she opened all the doors of her home, above all when her children were still young. In making them distribute these alms with her, she hoped to initiate them early into practices of charity.

In the last years of her life the St. Gabriel Orphanage gained her interest. Not only did she accomplish a great deal with her generosity, but she also took on the task of maintaining the clothes of her dear orphans in good order and in good repair. When she appeared in the courtyard of the establishment at recreation time, all her protégés surrounded her and lavished her with manifestations of their profound respect and affectionate gratitude.

Bonnie G. Smith, Ladies of the Leisure Class: The Bourgeoises of Northern France in the Nineteenth Century *(Princeton, N.J.: Princeton University Press, 1981) pp. 147–148.*

---

be seen as the center of virtue, children, and the proper life. Marriages were usually arranged for some kind of family economic benefit. Romantic marriage was viewed as a danger to social stability. Most middle-class women in northern France married by the age of twenty-one. Children were expected to follow very soon after marriage, and the first child was often born within the first year. The rearing and nurturing of her children was a woman's chief task. She would receive no experience or training for any role other than that of dutiful daughter, wife, and mother.

Within the home, a middle-class woman performed major roles. She was largely in charge of the household. She oversaw virtually all domestic management and child care. She was in charge of the home as a unit of consumption, which is why so much advertising was directed toward women. All this domestic activity, however, occurred within the limits of the approved middle-class lifestyle that set strict limits on a woman's initiative. In her conspicuous position within the home and family, a woman symbolized first her father's and then her husband's worldly success.

RELIGIOUS AND CHARITABLE ACTIVITIES  The cult of domesticity in France and elsewhere assigned firm religious duties to women, which the Roman Catholic Church strongly supported. Women were expected to attend mass frequently and assure the religious instruction of their children. They were charged with observing meatless Fridays and with participating in religious observances. Prayer was a major part of their lives and daily rituals. They internalized those portions of the Christian religion that stressed meekness and passivity. In other countries as well, religion and religious activities became part of the expected work of women. For this reason, women were regarded by political liberals as especially susceptible to the influence of priests. This close association between religion and a strict domestic life for women was one of the reasons for later tension between feminism and religious authorities.

Another important role for middle-class women was the administration of charity. Women were judged especially qualified for this work because of their presumed innate spirituality and their capacity to instill domestic and personal discipline. Middle-class women were often in charge of clubs for poor youth, societies to protect poor young women, schools for infants, and societies for visiting the poor. Women were supposed to be particularly interested in the problems of poor women, their families, and their children. Quite often charity from middle-class women required the poor recipient to demonstrate good character. By the end of the century, middle-class women seeking to expand their spheres of activity became social workers for the church, for private charities, or for the government. These vocations were a natural extension of the roles socially assigned to them.

SEXUALITY AND FAMILY SIZE  The world of the middle-class wife and her family is now understood to have been much more complicated than was once thought. Neither they nor their families all conformed to the stereotypes. Recent studies have suggested that the middle classes of the nineteenth century enjoyed sexual relations within marriage far more than was once thought. Diaries, letters, and even early medical and sociological sex surveys indicate that sexual enjoyment rather than sexual repression was fundamental to middle-class marriages. Much of the inhibition about sexuality stemmed from the dangers of childbirth rather than from any dislike or disapproval of sex itself.

One of the major changes in this regard during the second half of the century was the acceptance of small family size among the middle classes. The birth rate in France dropped throughout the nineteenth century. It began to fall in England steadily from the 1870s onward. During the last decades of the century, various new contraceptive devices became available, which middle-class couples used. One of the chief reasons for the apparently conscious decision of couples to limit family size was to maintain a relatively high level of material consumption. Children had become much more expensive to rear, and at the same time, more material comforts had become available. Fewer children probably meant more attention for each of them, possibly bringing mothers and their children emotionally closer.

## The Rise of Political Feminism

As can be seen from the previous discussion, liberal society and its values neither automatically nor inevitably improved the lot of women. In particular, it did not give them the vote and access to political activity. Male liberals feared that granting the vote to women would benefit political conservatives, because women were thought to be unduly controlled by Roman Catholic priests. A similar apprehension existed about the alleged influence of the Anglican clergy over women in England. Consequently, anticlerical liberals often had difficulty working with feminists.

OBSTACLES TO ACHIEVING EQUALITY  But women also were often reluctant to support feminist causes. Political issues relating to gender were only one of several priorities for many women. Some were very sensitive to their class and economic interests. Others subordinated feminist political issues to national unity and nationalistic patriotism. Still others would not support particular feminist organizations because of differences over tactics. The various social and tactical differences among women led quite often to sharp divisions within the feminists' own ranks. Except in England, it was often difficult for working-class and middle-class women to cooperate. Roman Catholic feminists were uncomfortable with radical secularist feminists. There were other disagreements about which goals for improvement in women's legal and social conditions were most important.

Although liberal society and law presented women with many obstacles, they also provided feminists with many of their intellectual and political tools. As early as 1792 in Britain, Mary Wollstonecraft (1759–1797), in *The Vindication of the Rights of Woman*, had applied the revolutionary doctrines of the rights of man to the predicament of the members of her own sex (see Chapter 18). John Stuart Mill (1806–1873), with his wife Harriet Taylor (1804–1858), had applied the logic of liberal freedom to the position of women in *The Subjection of Women* (1869). The arguments for utility and efficiency so dear to middle-class liberals could be used to expose the human and social waste implicit in the inferior role assigned to women.

Furthermore, the socialist criticism of capitalist society often, though by no means always, included a harsh indictment of the social and economic position to which women had been relegated. The earliest statements of feminism arose from critics of the existing order and were often associated with people who had unorthodox opinions about sexuality, family life, and property. This hardened resistance to the feminist message, especially on the Continent.

These difficulties prevented continental feminists from raising the kind of massive public support or mounting the large demonstrations that feminists in Great Britain and the United States could. Everywhere in Europe, however, including Britain, the feminist cause was badly divided over both goals and tactics.

VOTES FOR WOMEN IN BRITAIN Europe's most advanced women's movement was in Great Britain. There Millicent Fawcett (1847–1929) led the moderate National Union of Women's Suffrage Societies. She believed Parliament would grant women the vote only when convinced that they would be respectable and responsible in their political activity. In 1908 this organization could rally almost half a million women in London. Fawcett's husband was a former Liberal Party cabinet minister and economist. Her tactics were those of English liberals.

Emmeline Pankhurst (1858–1928) led a different and much more radical branch of British feminists. Pankhurst's husband, who died near the close of the century, had been active in both labor and Irish nationalist politics. Irish nationalists had developed

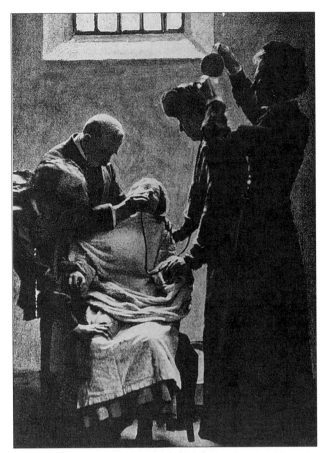

When British suffragettes went to prison, many of them went on hunger strikes. The response of the authorities was to force feed them by having physicians insert tubes down their throats through which liquid nourishment was pumped. Here Emmeline Pankhurst is undergoing this painful and humiliating experience. [Bildarchiv Preussischer Kulturbesitz]

numerous disruptive political tactics. Early labor politicians had also sometimes had confrontations with police over the right to hold meetings. In 1903 Pankhurst and her daughters, Christabel and Sylvia, founded the Women's Social and Political Union. For several years they and their followers, known derisively as *suffragettes*, lobbied publicly and privately for the extension of the vote to women. By 1910, having failed to move the government, they turned to the violent tactics of arson, window breaking, and sabotage of postal boxes. They marched en masse on Parliament. The Liberal government of Henry Asquith imprisoned many of the demonstrators and force-fed those who went on hunger strikes in jail. The government refused to

# An English Feminist Defends the Cause of the Female Franchise

*Frances Power Cobby (1822–1904) wrote widely on many religious and social issues of the second half of the century. She had been a feminist since early adulthood. In this letter to a British feminist magazine in 1884, she explains why women should seek the vote.*

✦ *What motives does Cobbe assign to the pursuit of the right to vote? Why does she emphasize the issue of "womanliness" as one that must not be allowed to undermine the cause of women? What is Cobbe's attitude toward violence? Why would later British advocates of votes for women turn to violent tactics?*

If I may presume to offer an old woman's counsel to the younger workers in our cause, it would be that they should adopt the point of view—that it is before all things our *duty* to obtain the franchise. If we undertake the work in this spirit, and with the object of using the power it confers, whenever we gain it, for the promotion of justice and mercy and the kingdom of God upon earth, we shall carry on all our agitation in a corresponding manner, firmly and bravely, and also calmly and with generous good temper. And when our opponents come to understand that this is the motive underlying our efforts, they, on their part, will cease to feel bitterly and scornfully toward us, even when they think we are altogether mistaken. . . .

The idea that the possession of political rights will destroy "womanliness," absurd as it may seem to us, is very deeply rooted in the minds of men; and when they oppose our demands, it is only just to give them credit for doing so on grounds which we should recognize as valid, *if their premises were true*. It is not so much that our opponents (at least the better part of them) despise women, as that they really prize what women now are in the home and in society so highly that they cannot bear to risk losing it by any serious change in their condition. These fears are futile and faithless, but there is nothing in them to affront us. To remove them, we must not use violent words, for every such violent word confirms their fears; but, on the contrary, show the world that while the revolutions wrought by men have been full of bitterness and rancor and stormy passions, if not of bloodshed, we women will at least strive to accomplish our great emancipation calmly and by persuasion and reason.

Letter to the *Woman's Tribune,* May 1, 1884, quoted in Frances Power Cobbe, *Life of Frances Power Cobbe by Herself,* vol. 2 *(Boston: Houghton Mifflin, 1894), pp. 532–533.*

---

extend the franchise. Only in 1918, and then as a result of their contribution to the war effort, did some British women receive the vote.

POLITICAL FEMINISM ON THE CONTINENT   The contrast between the women's movement in Britain and those in France and Germany shows how advanced the British women's movement was. In France, when Hubertine Auclert (1848–1914) began campaigning for the vote in the 1880s, she stood virtually alone. During the 1890s, several women's organizations emerged. In 1901 the National Council of French Women (CNFF) was organized among upper-middle-class women, but it did not support the vote for women for several years. French Roman Catholic feminists such as Marie Mauguet (1844–1928) supported the franchise. Almost all French feminists, however, rejected any form of violence. They also were never able to organize mass rallies. The leaders of French feminism believed that the vote could be achieved through careful legalism. In 1919 the French Chamber of Deputies passed a bill granting the vote to women, but in 1922 the French Senate defeated the bill. It was not until after World War II that French women received the right to vote.

In Germany, feminist awareness and action was even more underdeveloped. German law actually forbade German women from political activity. Because no group in the German Empire enjoyed extensive political rights, women were not certain that they would benefit from demanding them. Any such demand would be regarded as subversive not only of the state but also of society.

In 1894 the Union of German Women's Organizations (BDFK) was founded. By 1902 it was supporting a call for the right to vote. But it was largely concerned with improving women's social conditions, their access to education, and their right to other protections. The group also worked to see women admitted to political or civic activity on the municipal level. Their work usually included education, child welfare, charity, and public health. The German Social Democratic Party supported women's suffrage, but that socialist party was so disdained by the German authorities and German Roman Catholics that this support only served to make suffrage more suspect in their eyes. Women received the vote in Germany only in 1918, when the constitution of the Weimar Republic was promulgated after German defeat in war and revolution at home.

Throughout Europe in the years before World War I, women demanded rights widely and vocally. The tactics they used and the success they achieved, however, varied from country to country depending on political and class structures. Before World War I, only in Norway (1907) could women vote on national issues.

# Jewish Emancipation

The emancipation of European Jews from the narrow life of the ghetto into a world of equal or nearly equal citizenship and social status was a major accomplishment of political liberalism and had an enduring impact on European life. The process of emancipation, slow and never fully completed, began in the late eighteenth century and continued throughout the nineteenth. It moved at different paces in different countries.

## Differing Degrees of Citizenship

In 1782 Joseph II, the Habsburg emperor, issued a decree that placed the Jews of his empire under more or less the same laws as Christians. In France, the National Assembly recognized Jews as French citizens in 1789. During the turmoil of the Napoleonic wars, Jewish communities in Italy and Germany were allowed to mix on a generally equal footing with the Christian population. These various steps toward political emancipation were always somewhat uncertain and were frequently limited or partially repealed with changes in rulers or governments. Certain freedoms were granted only to be partially withdrawn later. Even in countries that had advanced some political rights, Jews could not own land and could be subject to special discriminatory taxes. Nonetheless, during the first half of the cen-

*The era of Jewish emancipation allowed more freedom to European Jews and a wider recognition of their faith and culture. This painting by G. E. Opitz portrays the dedication of a new synagogue in Alsace in 1820. [Jewish Museum, N.Y./Art Resource, N.Y.]*

tury, European Jews in western Europe and to a much lesser extent in central and eastern Europe began to gain significant rights that brought them equal or more nearly equal citizenship.

In Russia, however, the traditional modes of prejudice and discrimination continued unabated until World War I. Jews were treated as aliens under Russian rule. The government undermined Jewish community life, limited publication of Jewish books, restricted areas where Jews might live, required internal passports from Jews, banned Jews from many forms of state service, and excluded Jews from many institutions of higher education. The police and others were allowed to conduct *pogroms*—organized riots—against Jewish neighborhoods and villages.

### Broadened Opportunities

After the revolutions of 1848, European Jews saw a general improvement in their situation that lasted for several decades. In Germany, Italy, the Low Countries, and Scandinavia, Jews attained full rights of citizenship. After 1858 Jews in Great Britain could sit in Parliament. Austria–Hungary extended full legal rights to Jews in 1867. Indeed, from about 1850 to 1880, there was relatively little organized or overt prejudice toward Jews. They entered the professions and other occupations once closed to them. They participated fully in the literary and cultural life of their nations. They were active in the arts and

music. They became leaders in science and education. Jews intermarried freely with non-Jews as legal secular prohibitions against such marriages were repealed during the last quarter of the century.

Outside of Russia, Jewish political figures entered cabinets and served in the highest offices of the state. Politically, they often were aligned with liberal parties because these groups had championed equal rights. Later in the century, especially in eastern Europe, many Jews became associated with the socialist parties.

The prejudice that had been associated with Christian religious attitudes toward Jews seemed for a time to have dissipated, although it still appeared in Russia and other parts of eastern Europe. Hundreds of thousands of European Jews migrated from these regions to western Europe and the United States. Almost anywhere in Europe, Jews might encounter prejudice on a personal level. But in western Europe, including England, France, Italy, Germany, and the Low Countries, Jews felt fairly secure from the legalized persecution and discrimination that had so haunted them in the past.

That newfound security began to erode during the last two decades of the nineteenth century. Anti-Semitic voices began to be heard in the 1870s attributing the economic stagnation of the decade to Jewish bankers and financial interests. In the 1880s, organized anti-Semitism erupted in Germany as it did in France at the time of the Dreyfus Affair. As will be seen in the next chapter, these developments gave rise to the birth of Zionism, initially a minority movement within the Jewish community. Most Jewish leaders believed the attacks on Jewish life were merely temporary recurrences of older modes of prejudice; they felt their communities would remain safe under the liberal legal protections that had been extended over the course of the century. That analysis would be proved disastrously wrong during the second quarter of the twentieth century.

# Labor, Socialism, and Politics to World War I

The late-century industrial expansion wrought further changes in the life of the labor force. In all industrializing continental countries, the numbers of the urban proletariat rose. The proportion of artisans and highly skilled workers declined, and for the first time factory wage earners predominated. The number of people engaged in the unskilled work associated with shipping, transportation, and building also grew considerably.

Workers still had to look to themselves to improve their lot. After 1848, however, European workers stopped rioting in the streets to voice their grievances. They also stopped trying to revive the paternal guilds and similar institutions of the past. After mid-century, workers turned to new institutions and ideologies. Chief among these were trade unions, democratic political parties, and socialism.

## Trade Unionism

Trade unionism came of age as governments extended legal protections to unions during the second half of the century. Unions became fully legal in Great Britain in 1871 and were allowed to picket in 1875. In France, Napoleon III at first used troops against strikes, but as his political power waned, he allowed weak labor associations in 1868. The Third French Republic fully legalized unions in 1884. In Germany, unions were permitted to function with little disturbance after 1890. Union participation in the political process was at first marginal. As long as the representatives of the traditional governing classes looked after labor interests, members of the working class rarely sought office themselves.

Unions directed their mid-century organizational efforts toward skilled workers and the immediate improvement of wages and working conditions. By the close of the century, industrial unions for unskilled workers were being organized. With thousands of workers, these large unions met intense opposition from employers. They frequently had to engage in long strikes to convince employers to accept their demands. Europe suffered a rash of strikes in the prewar decade as unions sought to keep wages in line with inflation. Despite union advances, however, and the growth of union membership (in 1910 to approximately 3 million in Britain, 2 million in Germany, and 977,000 in France), most of Europe's labor force was never unionized in this period. What the unions did represent for workers was a new collective form of association for confronting economic difficulties and improving security.

## Democracy and Political Parties

Except for Russia, all the major European states adopted broad-based, if not perfectly democratic, electoral systems in the late nineteenth century. Great Britain passed its second voting reform act in 1867 and its third in 1884. Bismarck brought universal male suffrage to the German Empire in 1871. The French Chamber of Deputies was democratically elected. Universal male suffrage was adopted in Switzerland in 1879, in Spain in 1890, in Belgium in 1893, in the Netherlands in 1896, and in Norway in 1898. Italy finally fell into line in 1912. The broadened franchise meant that politicians could no longer ignore workers and discontented groups could now voice their grievances and advocate their programs within the institutions of government rather than from the outside.

The advent of democracy brought organized mass political parties like those already in existence in the United States to Europe for the first time. In the liberal European states with narrow electoral bases, most voters had been people of property who knew what they had at stake in politics. Organization had been minimal. The expansion of the electorate brought into the political processes many people whose level of political consciousness, awareness, and interest was quite low. This electorate had to be organized and taught the nature of power and influence in the liberal democratic state.

The organized political party—with its workers, newspapers, offices, social life, and discipline—was the vehicle that mobilized the new voters. The largest single group in these mass electorates was the working class. The democratization of politics presented the socialists with opportunities and required the traditional ruling classes to vie with the socialists for the support of the new voters.

During these years, socialism as a political ideology and plan of action opposed nationalism. The problems of class were supposed to be transnational, and socialism was supposed to unite the working classes across national borders. European socialists, however, badly underestimated the emotional drawing power of nationalism. Many workers had both socialist and nationalist sympathies, which were rarely in conflict with each other. When the out-

break of war in 1914 did bring them into conflict, however, nationalist feelings prevailed.

The major question for late-century socialist parties throughout Europe was whether the improvement of the lot of the working class would come about through revolution or democratic reform. This question sharply divided all socialist parties and most especially those whose leadership adhered to the intellectual legacy of Karl Marx.

### Karl Marx and the First International

Karl Marx himself made considerable accommodation to the new practical realities that developed

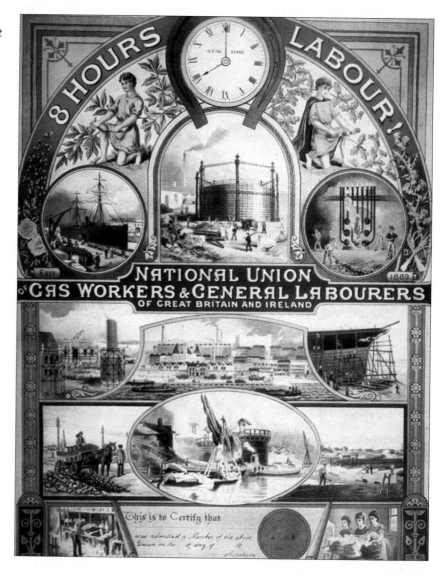

*Trade Unions continued to grow in late-century Great Britain. The effort to curb the unions eventually led to the formation of the Labour Party. The British unions often had quite elaborate membership certificates, such as this one for the National Union of Gas Workers and General Labourers of Great Britain and Ireland. [The Granger Collection]*

during the third quarter of the century. Although he continued to predict the disintegration of capitalism, his practical, public political activity reflected a somewhat different approach.

In 1864 a group of British and French trade unionists founded the International Working Men's Association. Known as the *First International*, its membership encompassed a vast array of radical political types, including socialists, anarchists, and Polish nationalists. In the inaugural address for the International, Marx supported and approved efforts by workers and trade unions to reform the conditions of labor within the existing political and economic processes. In his private writings he often criticized such reformist activity, but these writings were not made public until near the end of the century, and years after his death.

The violence involved in the rise and suppression of the Paris Commune (see Chapter 23), which Marx had declared a genuine proletarian uprising, cast a pall over socialism throughout Europe. British trade unionists, who in 1871 received legal protections, wanted no connection with the events in Paris. The French authorities used the uprising to suppress socialist activity. Under these pressures, the First International held its last European congress in 1873. It soon transferred its offices to the United States, where it was dissolved in 1876.

The short-lived First International had a disproportionately great impact on the future of European socialism. Throughout the late 1860s, the organization had gathered statistics, kept labor groups informed of mutual problems, provided a forum for the debate of socialist doctrine, and extravagantly proclaimed its own influence over contemporary events. From these debates and activities Marxism emerged as the single most important strand of socialism. Marx and his supporters defeated or drove out anarchists and advocates of other forms of socialism. The apparently scientific character of Marxism made it attractive—science was more influential than at any previous time in European history. German socialists, who were to establish the most powerful socialist party in Europe, were deeply impressed by Marx's thought and were the chief vehicle for preserving and developing it. The full development of German socialism also, however, involved the influence of non-Marxist socialists in Great Britain.

## Great Britain: Fabianism and Early Welfare Programs

Neither Marxism nor any other form of socialism made significant progress in Great Britain, the most advanced industrial society of the day. There trade unions grew steadily, and their members normally supported Liberal Party candidates. The "new unionism" of the late 1880s and the 1890s organized the dock workers, the gas workers, and similar unskilled groups. In 1892 Keir Hardie became the first independent working man to be elected to Parliament, but the small socialist Independent Labour Party founded a year later remained ineffective. Until 1901 general political activity on the part of labor remained quite limited. In that year, however, the House of Lords, through the Taff Vale decision, removed the legal protection previously accorded union funds. The Trades Union Congress responded by launching the Labour Party. In the election of 1906, the fledgling party sent twenty-nine members to Parliament. Their goals as trade unionists, however, did not yet include socialism. In this same period, the British labor movement became more militant. In scores of strikes before the war, workers fought for wages to meet the rising cost of living. The government took a larger role than ever before in mediating these strikes, which in 1911 and 1912 involved the railways, the docks, and the mines.

British socialism itself remained primarily the preserve of non-Marxist intellectuals. The Fabian Society, founded in 1884, was Britain's most influential socialist group. The society took its name from Q. Fabius Maximus, the Roman general whose tactics against Hannibal involved avoiding direct conflict that might lead to defeat. The name reflected the society's gradualist approach to major social reform. Its leading members were Sidney Webb (1859–1947) and Beatrice Webb (1858–1943), H. G. Wells (1866–1946), Graham Wallas (1858–1932), and George Bernard Shaw (1856–1950). Many Fabians were civil servants who believed that the problems of industry, the expansion of ownership, and the state direction of production could be achieved gradually, peacefully, and democratically. They sought to educate the country about the rational wisdom of socialism. They were particularly interested in modes of collective ownership on the municipal level, the so-called gas-and-water socialism.

*Beatrice and Sidney Webb, in a photograph from the late 1920s. These most influential British Fabian socialists wrote many books on governmental and economic matters, served on special parliamentary commissions, and agitated for the enactment of socialist policies. [UPI/Bettmann]*

The British government and the major political parties responded slowly to these various pressures. In 1903 Joseph Chamberlain (1836–1914) launched his unsuccessful tariff-reform campaign to match foreign tariffs and to finance social reform through higher import duties. The campaign badly split the Conservative Party. After 1906 the Liberal Party, led by Sir Henry Campbell-Bannerman (1836–1908) and after 1908 by Herbert Asquith (1852–1928), pursued a two-pronged policy. Fearful of losing seats in Parliament to the new Labour Party, they restored the former protection of the unions. Then, after 1909, with Chancellor of the Exchequer David Lloyd George (1863–1945) as its guiding light, the Liberal ministry undertook a broad program of social legislation. This included the establishment of labor exchanges, the regulation of certain trades, such as tailoring and lace making, and the National Insurance Act of 1911, which provided unemployment benefits and health care.

The financing of these programs brought the House of Commons into conflict with the Conservative-dominated House of Lords. The result was the Parliament Act of 1911, which allowed the Commons to override the legislative veto of the upper chamber. The new taxes and social programs meant that in Britain, the home of nineteenth-century liberalism, the state was taking on an expanded role in the life of its citizens. The early welfare legislation was only marginally satisfactory to labor, many of whose members still thought they could gain more from the direct action of strikes.

## France: "Opportunism" Rejected

At the turn of the century, Jean Jaurès (1859–1914) and Jules Guesde (1845–1922) led the two major factions of French socialists. Jaurès believed that socialists should cooperate with middle-class Radical ministries to ensure the enactment of needed social legislation. Guesde opposed this policy, arguing that socialists could not, with integrity, support a bourgeois cabinet that they were theoretically dedicated to overthrow. The government's response to the Dreyfus affair brought the quarrel to a head. In 1899, seeking to unite all supporters of Dreyfus, Prime Minister René Waldeck-Rousseau (1846–1904) appointed the socialist Alexander Millerand (1859–1943) to the cabinet.

The Second International had been founded in 1889 in a new effort to unify the various national socialist parties and trade unions. By 1904 the Amsterdam Congress of the Second International debated the issue of "opportunism," as such cabinet participation by socialists was termed. The Amsterdam Congress condemned "opportunism" in France and ordered the French socialists to form a single party. Jaurès accepted the decision. Thereafter French socialists began to work together, and by 1914 the recently united Socialist Party had become the second largest group in the Chamber of Deputies. But Socialist Party members would not again serve in a French cabinet until the Popular Front Government of 1936.

The French labor movement, with deep roots in anarchism, was uninterested in either politics or socialism. French workers usually voted socialist, but the unions themselves, unlike those in Great Britain, avoided active political participation. The

Confédération Générale du Travail, founded in 1895, regarded itself as a rival to the socialist parties. Its leaders sought to improve the workers' conditions through direct action. They embraced the doctrines of syndicalism, which had been most persuasively expounded by Georges Sorel (1847–1922) in *Reflections on Violence* (1908). This book enshrined the general strike as a device for generating worker unity and power. The strike tactic often conflicted with the socialist belief in aiding labor through state action. Strikes were common between 1905 and 1914, and the middle-class Radical ministry on more than one occasion used troops to suppress them.

## Germany: Social Democrats and Revisionism

The negative judgment rendered by the Second International against French socialist participation in bourgeois ministries reflected a policy of permanent hostility to nonsocialist governments previously adopted by the German Social Democratic Party, or SPD. The organizational success of this party, more than any other single factor, kept Marxist socialism alive during the late nineteenth and early twentieth centuries.

The Social Democratic Party had been founded in 1875. Its origins lay in the labor agitation of Ferdinand Lasalle (1825–1864), who sought worker participation in German politics. Wilhelm Liebknecht (1826–1900) and August Bebel (1840–1913), who were Marxists and opposed reformist politics, soon joined the party. Thus from its founding the SPD was divided between those who advocated reform and those who advocated revolution.

BISMARCK'S REPRESSION OF THE SPD   Twelve years of persecution under Bismarck forged the character of the SPD. The so-called Iron Chancellor believed that socialism would undermine German politics and society. He used an assassination attempt on William I in 1878, in which the socialists were not involved, to steer several antisocialist laws through the *Reichstag*. The measures suppressed the organization, meetings, newspapers, and other public activities of the SPD. Thereafter, to remain a socialist meant to remove oneself from the mainstream of respectable German life and possibly to lose one's job. The antisocialist legislation proved politically counterproductive. From the early 1880s onward,

the SPD steadily polled more and more votes in elections to the *Reichstag*.

As simple repression failed to isolate German workers from socialist loyalties, Bismarck undertook a program of social welfare legislation. In 1883 the German Empire adopted a health insurance measure. The next year saw the enactment of accident insurance legislation. Finally, in 1889 Bismarck sponsored a plan for old age and disability pensions. These programs, to which both workers and employers contributed, represented a paternalistic, conservative alternative to socialism. The state itself would organize a system of social security that did not require any change in the system of property holding or politics. Germany became the first major industrial nation to enjoy this kind of welfare program.

THE ERFURT PROGRAM   After forcing Bismarck's resignation, Emperor William II (r. 1888–1918) allowed the antisocialist legislation to expire, hoping to build new political support among the working class. Even under the repressive laws, members of the SPD could sit in the *Reichstag*. With the repressive measures lifted, the party needed to decide what attitude to assume toward the German Empire.

The answer came in the Erfurt Program of 1891, formulated under the political guidance of Bebel and the ideological tutelage of Karl Kautsky (1854–1938). In good Marxist fashion, the program declared the imminent doom of capitalism and the necessity of socialist ownership of the means of production. The party intended to pursue these goals through legal political participation rather than by revolutionary activity. Kautsky argued that because capitalism by its very nature must collapse, the immediate task for socialists was to work for the improvement of workers' lives rather than for the revolution, which was inevitable. So, although in theory the SPD was vehemently hostile to the German Empire, in practice the party functioned within its institutions. The SPD members of the *Reichstag* maintained clear political consciences by refusing to enter the cabinet (to which they were not invited anyway) and by refraining for many years from voting in favor of the military budget.

THE DEBATE OVER REVISIONISM   The dilemma of the SPD, however, generated the most important chal-

# The German Social Democratic Party Presents a Program

*After the Anti-Socialist Laws were repealed in 1891, the German Social Democratic Party could once more operate legally. Through the Erfurt Program of the same year the party again asserted a basically revolutionary program for the working class. In theory the Erfurt Program rejected the idea of compromising the goals of socialism with the existing social and economic structures of the German Empire. However, despite its rhetoric, as manifested in the following passage from the Erfurt Program, the SPD did not undertake revolutionary activity.*

✦ *Why did the SDP believe that socialism would increase production of goods and services? Why did it argue that the emancipation of the working class was equivalent to human emancipation? What elements of this program emphasize international as opposed to nationalistic goals.*

Private property in the means of production, which was formerly the means of securing to the producer the possession of his own product, has today become the means of expropriating peasants, handicraftsmen and small producers, and of putting the non-workers, capitalists and great landlords in possession of the product of the workers. Only the conversion of capitalistic private property in the means of production . . . into common property, and the change of the production of goods into a socialistic production, worked for and through society, can bring it about that production on a large scale, and the ever-growing productiveness of human labour, shall develop, for the hitherto exploited classes, from a source of misery and oppression, into a source of the highest well-being and perfect universal harmony.

This social change betokens the emancipation, not only of the proletariat, but of the whole human race, which is suffering under the present conditions. But it can only be the work of the working classes. . . .

The struggle of the working class against capitalistic exploitation is of necessity a political struggle. . . .

To give to this fight of the working class a conscious and unified form, and to show it its necessary goal—that is the task of the Social Democratic Party.

The interests of the working classes are the same in all countries with a capitalistic mode of production. . . . In recognition of this, the Social Democratic Party of Germany feels and declares itself to be one with the class-conscious workmen of all other countries.

The Social Democratic Party of Germany does not fight, accordingly, for new class-privileges and class rights, but for the abolition of class-rule and of classes themselves, for equal rights and equal duties of all, without distinction of sex or descent.

*Bertrand Russell,* German Social Democracy *(London: Longmans, Green, 1896), pp. 138–139.*

lenge within the socialist movement to the orthodox Marxist analysis of capitalism and the socialist revolution. The author of this socialist heresy, Eduard Bernstein (1850–1932), had spent over a decade of his life in Great Britain and was familiar with the Fabians. Bernstein questioned whether Marx and his later orthodox followers, such as Kautsky, had been correct in their pessimistic appraisal of capitalism and the necessity of revolution. In *Evolutionary Socialism* (1899), Bernstein pointed to conditions that did not meet orthodox Marxists' expectations. The standard of living was on the rise in Europe. Ownership of capitalist industry was becoming more widespread through stockholding. The middle class was not falling into the ranks of the proletariat and was not identifying its problems with those of the workers. The inner contradictions of capitalism as expounded by Marx had simply not developed. Moreover, the extension of the franchise to the working class meant that parliamentary methods might achieve revolutionary social change. For Bernstein, social reform through democratic institutions replaced revolution as the path to a humane socialist society.

Bernstein's doctrines, known as *revisionism*, generated heated debate among German socialists, who finally condemned them. His critics argued that evolution toward social democracy might be possible in liberal, parliamentary Britain, but not in authoritarian, militaristic Germany, with its basically powerless *Reichstag*. Nonetheless, while still calling for revolution, the SPD pursued a course of action similar to that advocated by Bernstein. Its trade union members, prospering within the German economy, did not want revolution. Its grass-roots members wanted to consider themselves patriotic Germans as well as good socialists. Its leaders feared any actions that might renew the persecution that they had experienced under Bismarck.

Consequently, the SPD worked for electoral gains, membership expansion, and short-term political and social reform. It prospered and became one of the most important institutions of imperial Germany. Even some middle-class Germans voted for it as a way to oppose the illiberal institutions of the empire. And in August 1914, after long debate among themselves, the SPD members of the *Reichstag* abandoned their former practice and unanimously voted for the war credits that would finance Germany's participation in World War I.

## Russia: Industrial Development and the Birth of Bolshevism

During the last decade of the nineteenth century, Russia entered the industrial age and confronted many of the problems that the more advanced nations of the Continent had experienced fifty or seventy-five years earlier. Unlike those other countries, Russia had to deal with major political discontent and economic development simultaneously. Russian socialism reflected that peculiar situation.

WITTE'S PROGRAM FOR INDUSTRIAL GROWTH    Alexander III (r. 1881–1894) and, after him, Nicholas II (r. 1894–1917) were determined that Russia should become an industrial power. Only by doing so, they believed, could the country maintain its European military position and diplomatic role. It was Sergei Witte (1849–1915) who led Russia into the industrial age. After a career in railways and other private business, he was appointed finance minister in 1892. Witte, who pursued a policy of planned economic development, protective tariffs, high taxes, the gold standard, and efficiency, epitomized the nineteenth-century modernizer. He established strong financial relationships with the French money market, which led to later diplomatic cooperation between Russia and France.

Witte favored heavy industries. Between 1890 and 1904, the Russian railway system grew from 30,596 to 59,616 kilometers. The 5,000-mile Trans-Siberian Railroad was almost completed. Coal output more than tripled during the same period. There was a vast increase in pig-iron production, from 928,000 tons in 1890 to 4,641,000 tons in 1913. During the same period, steel production rose from 378,000 to 4,918,000 tons. Textile manufacturing continued to expand and was still the single largest industry. The factory system began to be used more extensively throughout the country.

Industrialism brought considerable social discontent to Russia, as it had elsewhere. Landowners felt that foreign capitalists were earning too much of the profit. The peasants saw their grain exports and tax payments finance development that did not measurably improve their lives. A small but significant industrial proletariat emerged. At the turn of the century there were approximately three million factory workers in Russia. Their working and living conditions were poor by any standard. They enjoyed

# A Russian Social Investigator Describes the Condition of Children in the Moscow Tailoring Trade

*E. A. Oliunina was a young Russian woman who had been active among union organizers during the Revolution of 1905. Later, as a student at the Higher Women's Courses in Moscow, a school for women's postsecondary eduction, she began to investigate and to write about child garment workers. The clothes produced by these children might have ended up in Russian department stores that copied those in Paris, described in an earlier document in this chapter.*

✦ *Why might the parents of these children have allowed them to work in these sweatshops? Why was alcoholism such a prevalent problem? Why does Oliunina regard schools as the solution to this problem?*

Children begin their apprenticeship between the ages of twelve and thirteen, although one can find some ten- and eleven-year-olds working in the shops. . . .

Apprenticeship is generally very hard on children. At the beginning, they suffer enormously, particularly from the physical strain of having to do work well beyond the capacity of their years. They have to live in an environment where the level of morality is very low. Scenes of drunkenness and debauchery induce the boys to smoke and drink at an early age.

For example, in one subcontracting shop that made men's clothes, a fourteen-year-old boy worked together with twelve adults. When I visited there at four o'clock one Tuesday afternoon, the workers were half-drunk. Some were lying under the benches, others in the hallway. The boy was as drunk as the rest of them and lay there with a daredevil look on his face, dressed only in a pair of longjohns and a dirty, tattered shirt. He had been taught to drink at the age of twelve and could now keep up with the adults.

"Blue Monday" is a custom in most subcontracting shops that manufacture men's clothes. The whole workshop gets drunk, and work comes to a standstill. The apprentices do nothing but hang around. Many of the workers live in the workshop, so the boys are constantly exposed to all sorts of conversations and scenes. In one shop employing five workers and three boys, "Blue Monday" was a regular ritual. even the owner himself is prone to alcoholic binges. In these kinds of situations, young girls are in danger of being abused by the owner or his sons. . . .

In Russia, there have been no measures taken to improve the working conditions of apprentices. As I have tried to show, the situation in workshops in no way provides apprentices with adequate training in their trade. The young workers are there only to be exploited. Merely limiting the number of apprentices would not better their position, nor would it eradicate the influx of cheap labor. An incomparably more effective solution would be to replace apprenticeship with a professional educational system and well-established safeguards for child workers. However, the only real solution to the exploitation of unpaid child labor is to introduce a minimum wage for minors.

*Quoted in Victoria E. Bonnell,* The Russian Worker: Life and Labor Under the Tsarist Regime *(Berkeley: University of California Press, 1983), pp. 177, 180–181, 182–183.*

little state protection, and trade unions were illegal. In 1897 Witte did enact a measure providing for an $11^1/_2$-hour workday. But needless to say, discontent and strikes continued.

Similar social and economic problems arose in the countryside. Russian agriculture had not revived after the emancipation of the serfs in 1861. The peasants remained burdened with redemption payments, local taxes, excessive national taxes, and falling grain prices. Free peasants owned their land communally through the *mir*, or village. They farmed the land inefficiently through strip farming or the tilling of small plots. Many free peasants with too little land to support their families had to work on larger noble estates or for more prosperous peasant farmers, known as *kulaks*. Between 1860 and 1914, the population of European Russia rose from approximately 50 million to approximately 103 million people. Land hunger and intense discontent spread among the peasants. Uprisings in the countryside were a frequent problem.

New political departures accompanied the economic development. The membership and intellectual roots of the Social Revolutionary Party, founded 1901, reached back to the Populists of the 1870s. The new party opposed industrialism and looked to the communal life of rural Russia as a model for the future. In 1903 the Constitutional Democratic Party, or Cadets, was formed. This liberal party drew its members from people who participated in the local councils called *zemstvos*. Modeling themselves on the liberal parties of western Europe, the Cadets wanted a parliamentary regime with responsible ministries, civil liberties, and economic progress.

LENIN'S EARLY THOUGHT AND CAREER The situation of Russian socialists differed radically from that of socialists in other major European countries. Russia had no representative institutions and only a small working class. The compromises and accommodations achieved elsewhere were meaningless in Russia, where socialists believed that in both theory and practice they must be revolutionary. The repressive policies of the tsarist regime required the Russian Social Democratic Party, founded in 1898, to function in exile. The party members greatly admired the German Social Democratic Party and adopted its Marxist ideology.

The leading late-nineteenth-century Russian Marxist was Gregory Plekhanov (1857–1918), who wrote from exile in Switzerland. At the turn of the century, his chief disciple was Vladimir Ilyich Ulyanov (1870–1924), who later took the name of Lenin. The future leader of the Communist Revolution was the son of a high bureaucrat. His older brother, while a student in Saint Petersburg, had become involved in radical politics; arrested for participating in a plot against Alexander III, he was executed in 1887. In 1893 Lenin moved to Saint

*In this photograph taken in 1895, Lenin sits at the table among a group of other young Russian radicals from Saint Petersburg. [The Bettmann Archive]*

Petersburg, where he studied law. Soon he, too, was drawn to the revolutionary groups among the factory workers. He was arrested in 1895 and exiled to Siberia. In 1900, after his release, Lenin left Russia for the West. He spent most of the next seventeen years in Switzerland.

Once in Switzerland, Lenin became deeply involved in the organizational and policy disputes of the exiled Russian Social Democrats. They all considered themselves Marxists, but they differed on the meaning of a Marxist revolution for primarily rural Russia, and on how to structure their own party. Unlike the backward-looking Social Revolutionaries, the Social Democrats were modernizers who favored further industrial development. The majority believed that Russia must develop a large proletariat before the revolution could come. This same majority hoped to build a mass political party like the German SPD.

Lenin dissented from both positions. In *What Is to Be Done?* (1902), he condemned any accommodations, such as those practiced by the German SPD. He also criticized trade unionism that settled for short-term gains rather than true revolutionary change for the working class. Lenin further rejected the concept of a mass democratic party composed of workers. He declared that revolutionary consciousness would not arise spontaneously from the working class. Rather, "people who make revolutionary activity their profession" must carry that consciousness to the workers.[2] Only a small, tightly organized, elite party could possess the proper dedication to revolution and prove able to resist penetration by police spies. The guiding principle of that party should be "the strictest secrecy, the strictest selection of members, and the training of professional revolutionaries."[3] Within the context of turn-of-the-century European socialist debates, Lenin thus rejected both Kautsky's view that revolution was inevitable and Bernstein's view that it would arrive democratically. Lenin substituted the small, professional, nondemocratic revolutionary party for Marx's proletariat as the instrument of revolutionary change.

In 1903, at the London Congress of the Russian Social Democratic Party, Lenin forced a split in the party ranks. During much of the congress, he and

[2]*Quoted in Albert Fried and Ronald Sanders, eds.,* Socialist Thought: A Documentary History *(Garden City, N.Y.: Anchor Doubleday, 1964), p. 459.*

[3]*Fried, p. 468.*

---

### Major Dates in the Development of Socialism

| | |
|---|---|
| 1864 | International Working Men's Association (the First International) founded |
| 1875 | German Social Democratic Party founded |
| 1876 | First International dissolved |
| 1878 | German antisocialist laws passed |
| 1884 | British Fabian Society founded |
| 1889 | Second International founded |
| 1891 | German antisocialist laws permitted to expire |
| 1891 | German Social Democratic Party's Erfurt Program |
| 1895 | French *Confédération Générale du Travail* founded |
| 1899 | Eduard Bernstein's *Evolutionary Socialism* |
| 1902 | Formation of the British Labour party |
| 1902 | Lenin's *What Is to Be Done?* |
| 1903 | Bolshevik–Menshevik split |
| 1904 | "Opportunism" debated at the Amsterdam Congress of the Second International |

---

his followers lost many votes on various questions put before the body, but near the close they mustered a very slim majority. Thereafter Lenin's faction assumed the name *Bolsheviks*, meaning "majority," and the other, more moderate, democratic revolutionary faction came to be known as the *Mensheviks*, or "minority." There was, of course, a considerable public relations advantage to the name Bolshevik. (In 1912 the Bolsheviks organized separately.)

In 1905 Lenin complemented his organizational theory with a program for revolution in Russia. In *Two Tactics of Social Democracy in the Bourgeois-Democratic Revolution,* he urged the socialist revolution to unite the proletariat and the peasantry. Lenin grasped better than any other revolutionary the profound discontent in the Russian countryside. He believed that the tsarist government probably could not suppress an alliance of workers and peasants in rebellion.

Lenin's two principles—an elite party and a dual social revolution—guided later Bolshevik activity. The Bolsheviks ultimately seized power in November 1917, transforming the political landscape of the modern world. But they did so only after the turmoil of World War I had undermined support for the tsar and only after other political forces had toppled the tsarist government earlier in 1917. Between the turn of the century and World War I, the gov-

# Lenin Argues for the Necessity of a Secret and Elite Party of Professional Revolutionaries

*Social democratic parties in western Europe had mass memberships and generally democratic structures of organization. In this passage from* What Is to Be Done? *(1902), Lenin explains why the autocratic political conditions of Russia demanded a different kind of organization for the Russian Social Democratic Party. Lenin's ideas became the guiding principles of Bolshevik organization.*

✦ *What does Lenin mean by "professional revolutionaries"? Why are such revolutionaries especially needed in Russia? How does he reconcile his anti-democratic views to the goal of aiding the working class?*

I assert that it is far more difficult [for government police] to unearth a dozen wise men than a hundred fools. This position I will defend, no matter how much you instigate the masses against me for my "anti-democratic" views, etc. As I have stated repeatedly, by "wise men," in connection with organization, I mean *professional revolutionaries*, irrespective of whether they have developed from among students or working men. I assert: (1) that no revolutionary movement can endure without a stable organization of leaders maintaining continuity; (2) that the broader the popular mass drawn spontaneously into the struggle, which forms the basis of the movement and participates in it, the more urgent the need for such an organization, and the more solid this organization must be . . . ; (3) that such an organization must consist chiefly of people professionally engaged in revolutionary activity; (4) that in an autocratic state [such as Russia], the more we *confine* the membership of such an organization to people who are professionally engaged in revolutionary activity and who have been professionally trained in the art of combating the political police, the more difficult will it be to unearth the organization; and (5) the *greater* will be the number of people from the working class and from other social classes who will be able to join the movement and perform active work in it. . . .

The only serious organization principle for the active workers of our movement should be the strictest secrecy, the strictest selection of members, and the training of professional revolutionaries.

*Albert Fried and Ronald Sanders, eds.,* Socialist Thought: A Documentary History *(Garden City, N.Y.: Anchor Doubleday, 1964), pp. 460, 468.*

ernment of Nicholas II confronted political upheaval more or less successfully.

THE REVOLUTION OF 1905 AND ITS AFTERMATH   The quarrels among the exiled Russian socialists and Lenin's doctrines had no immediate influence on events in Russia. Industrialization proceeded and continued to stir resentment in many sectors. In 1903 Nicholas II dismissed Witte, hoping to quell the criticism. The next year Russia went to war against Japan, partly in hopes that the conflict would rally public opinion to the tsar. Instead, the Russians lost the war and the government faced an internal political crisis. The Japanese captured Port Arthur early in 1905. A few days later, on January 22, a priest named Father Gapon led several hundred workers to present a petition to the tsar for the improvement of industrial conditions. As the petitioners approached the Winter Palace in Saint Petersburg, the tsar's troops opened fire. About 100 people were shot down in cold blood, and many more were wounded on what became known as *Bloody Sunday*.

During the next ten months, revolutionary disturbances spread throughout Russia. Sailors mutinied, peasant revolts erupted, and property was attacked. The uncle of Nicholas II was assassinated. Liberal leaders of the Constitutional Democratic Party from the *zemstvos* demanded political reform. Student strikes occurred in the universities. Social Revolutionaries and Social Democrats agitated among urban working groups. In early October 1905, strikes broke out in Saint Petersburg, and for all practical purposes, worker groups, called *soviets*, controlled the city. Nicholas II recalled Witte and issued the October Manifesto, which promised Russia constitutional government.

Early in 1906, Nicholas II announced the election of a representative body, the Duma, with two chambers. He reserved to himself, however, ministerial appointments, financial policy, military matters, and foreign affairs. The April elections returned a very radical group of representatives. The tsar then dismissed Witte and replaced him with P. A. Stolypin (1862–1911), who had little sympathy for parliamentary government. Stolypin persuaded Nicholas to dissolve the Duma. A second assembly was elected in February 1907. Again cooperation proved impossible, and the tsar dissolved that Duma in June. A third Duma, elected in late

*On Bloody Sunday, January 22, 1905, troops of Tsar Nicholas II fired on a peaceful procession of workers who sought to present a petition at the Winter Palace in Saint Petersburg. After this event, there was little chance of reconciliation between the Tsarist government and the Russian working class. [Bildarchiv Preussischer Kulturbesitz]*

# Count Witte Warns Tsar Nicholas II

*After the events of Bloody Sunday in 1905, revolutionary disturbances shook the tsarist government. Count Sergei Witte had been Tsar Nicholas II's chief minister and had presided over much of the modernization effort undertaken in Russia. In light of the troubles spreading across the country, he warned his monarch of revolution if steps were not taken to halt the spread of discontent. He sent this memorandum to the tsar on October 9, 1905. In the months and years after receiving this memorandum, Tsar Nicholas and other ministers moved in a very different direction than that advocated by Witte.*

✦ *What were examples of the extremist ideas then affecting Russia and Europe to which Witte points? Why did he say that the actions of the government had been clumsy? What might have been policies of freedom taken by the tsar's government? Why might the policies of the Russian government after 1905 be described as too little and too late to stem the tide of social and political discontent?*

The basic watchword of the present-day movement of public opinion in Russia is freedom.

. . . . . . . . . . . . . . . . . . . . . . . . . . . . . . . .

We live in a time dominated wholly by extremist ideas. No one stops to consider whether a given idea is realizable. To impetuous minds everything seems attainable and realizable, simply and easily.

Such a mood among the public is the most dangerous sign of an imminent explosion. The ranks of those who fervently advocate the regeneration of all aspects of Russian life, but only through peaceful evolution, are growing thinner each day. Each day it is becoming more and more difficult for them to restrain the movement.

. . . . . . . . . . . . . . . . . . . . . . . . . . . . . . . .

The inconsistent and clumsy actions and the indiscriminate methods the administration resorted to in the past, and which continue to his day, have produced fatal results. The public is not only dissatisfied; it has nurtured a hatred for the government which grows from day to day. The government is not respected and not trusted. The most beneficial undertakings inspire protest. At the same time the public has come to feel confident of its importance and its powers, of its ability to withdraw support from the government and completely to capitulate. The daily course of events confirms public opinion as to the importance, ignorance, and bewilderment of the authorities.

. . . . . . . . . . . . . . . . . . . . . . . . . . . . . . . .

The government should give real rather than fictitious leadership to the country. . . .

Leadership demands above all else a clearly formulated goal, an ideological, high-principled goal accepted by everyone.

The public has set such a goal, a goal of great and completely invincible significance, for justice and truth are on its side. The government must therefore accept it. The watchword of freedom should become the watchword of all government activity. There is no other way to save the state.

The course of historical progress cannot be stemmed. The idea of civil freedom will triumph, if not by reform then by revolution. But in the latter case it will be regenerated from the ashes of an overthrown millennial past. A Russian rebellion, mindless and merciless, will sweep everything away, will crumble everything into dust.

*George Vernadsky, ed.,* A Source Book of Russian History from Early Times to 1917 *(New Haven: Yale University Press, 1972), 3: 703–704.*

condemning almost 700 to death. Before undertaking this repression, the minister, in November 1906, had canceled any redemptive payments that the peasants still owed the government from the emancipation of the serfs in 1861. He took this step to encourage peasants to assume individual proprietorship of their landholdings and to abandon the communal system associated with the *mirs*. Stolypin believed that farmers would be more productive working for themselves. Combined with a program to instruct peasants in better farming methods, this policy did improve agricultural production. The very small peasant proprietors who sold their land increased the size of the industrial labor force.

The moderate liberals who sat in the Duma approved of the new land measures. They liked the idea of competition and individual property ownership. The Constitutional Democrats wanted a more genuinely parliamentary mode of government, but they compromised out of fear of new revolutionary disturbances. Hatred of Stolypin was still widespread, however, among the country's older conservative groups, and industrial workers remained antagonistic to the tsar. In 1911 Stolypin was assassinated by a Social Revolutionary, who may have been a police agent in the pay of conservatives. Nicholas II found no worthy successor. His government simply continued to muddle along.

Meanwhile, at court the monk Grigory Efimovich Rasputin (1871?–1916) came into ascendancy because of his alleged power to heal the tsar's hemophilic son, the heir to the throne. The undue influence of this strange, uncouth man, as well as continued social discontent and conservative resistance to any further liberal reforms, rendered the position and the policy of the tsar uncertain after 1911. Once again, as in 1904, he and his ministers thought that some bold move on the diplomatic front might bring the regime the broad popular support that it so desperately needed.

1907 on the basis of a more conservative franchise, proved sufficiently pliable for the tsar and his minister. Thus, within two years of the 1905 Revolution, Nicholas II had recaptured much of the ground he had conceded.

Stolypin set about repressing rebellion, removing some causes of the revolt, and rallying property owners behind the tsarist regime. Early in 1907, special field courts-martial tried rebellious peasants,

*The years from 1860 through 1914 saw the emergence of two apparently contradictory developments in European social life. On one hand, the lifestyle of the urban middle classes came to dominate, becoming the model to which much of society aspired. The characteristics of this lifestyle included a relatively small family living in its own* house or large apartment, servants, and a wife who did not earn an income. The middle classes in general benefitted from the many material comforts generated by the Second Industrial Revolution.

During the same period, the forces of socialism and labor unions assumed a new and major role in European political life. Their leaders demanded greater social justice and a fairer distribution of the vast quantities of consumer goods being produced in Europe. Some socialists sought in one way or another to work within existing political systems. Others—most particularly those in Russia—advocated revolution. The growth in wealth and the availability of new goods and services magnified the injustices suffered by the poor and the contrast between them and the middle classes, contributing to the stridency of the demands of labor and the socialists. In Russia, the strains of the early stages of industrialization intensified social unrest. These strains, compounded by a humiliating defeat in a war against Japan, triggered the unsuccessful revolution of 1905.

The working class, however, was not alone in seeking change. Women, for the first time in European history, began in significant ways to demand a political role and to protest the gender inequalities embedded in law and family life. They were beginning to enter the professions in small numbers and were taking a significant role in the service economy, such as the new telephone companies. These changes, as much as the demands of socialists, would in time raise questions about the adequacy of the much admired late-nineteenth-century middle-class lifestyle.

## Review Questions

1. How was European society transformed by the Second Industrial Revolution? What new industries developed and which do you think had the greatest impact in the twentieth century? How do you account for European economic difficulties in the second half of the nineteenth century?
2. How would you describe living conditions in European cities during the late nineteenth century? Why were European cities redesigned during this period? In what ways were they redesigned? Why were housing and health key issues for urban reform? Be specific in your examples.

3. What was the status of European women in the second half of the nineteenth century? Why did they grow discontented with their lot? What factors led to change? To what extent had they improved their position by 1914? What tactics did they use in effecting change? Was the emancipation of women inevitable? How did women approach their situation differently from country to country?
4. What were the major characteristics of Jewish emancipation in the nineteenth century?
5. What was the status of the proletariat in 1860? Had it improved by 1914? What caused the growth in trade unions and organized mass political parties? Why were the debates over "opportunism" and "revisionism" important to the socialist parties?
6. Assess the value of industrialism for Russia. Were the tsars wise in attempting to modernize their country or would they have been better off leaving it as it was? How did Lenin's view of socialism differ from that of the socialists in western Europe?

## Suggested Readings

J. ALBISETTI, Schooling German Girls and Women: Secondary and Higher Education in the Nineteenth Century (1988). Contains much information on the subject beyond Germany.

H. ANDERSON, Utopian Feminism: Women's Movements in Fin-de-Siècle Vienna (1992). Examines movements to improve the status of women in the Austrian Empire.

I. M. ARONSON, Troubled Waters: The Origins of the 1881 Anti-Jewish Pogroms in Russia (1990). The best discussion of this subject.

L. R. BERLANSTEIN, The Working People of Paris, 1871–1914 (1985). Interesting and comprehensive.

N. BULLOCK AND J. READ, The Movement for Housing Reform in Germany and France, 1840–1914 (1985). An important and wide-ranging study of the housing problem.

C. M. CIPOLLA, The Economic History of World Population (1962). A basic introduction.

L. FRADER AND S. ROSE (EDS.), Gender and Class in Modern Europe (1996). A wide-ranging collection of essays.

J. FRANKEL AND S. ZIPPERSTEIN, Assimilation and Community: The Jews in Nineteenth-Century Europe (1992). A major collection of essays that ranges widely over the continent.

P. Gay, *The Dilemma of Democratic Socialism: Eduard Bernstein's Challenge to Marx* (1952). A clear presentation of the problems raised by Bernstein's revisionism.

P. Gay, *The Bourgeois Experience: Victoria to Freud*, vol. 1, *Education of the Senses* (1984). vol. 2, *The Tender Passion* (1986). A major study of middle-class sexuality.

D. F. Good, *The Economic Rise of the Hapsburg Empire, 1750–1914* (1985). The best available study.

A. Geifman, *Thou Shalt Kill: Revolutionary Terrorism in Russia, 1894–1917* (1993). An examination of political violence in late imperial Russia.

J. Harsin, *Policing Prostitution in Nineteenth-Century Paris* (1985). A major study of this very significant subject in French social history.

S. C. Hause, *Women's Suffrage and Social Politics in the French Third Republic* (1984). A wide-ranging examination of the question.

P. Hilden, *Working Women and Socialist Politics in France, 1880–1914* (1986). A study that traces both cooperation and tension between socialism and feminism in the French working class.

G. Himmelfarb, *Poverty and Compassion: The Moral Imagination of the Late Victorians* (1991). The best examination of late Victorian social thought.

E. J. Hobsbawm, *The Age of Capital* (1975). Explores the consolidation of middle-class life after 1850.

L. Holcombe, *Wives and Property: Reform of the Married Women's Property Law in Nineteenth-Century England* (1983). The standard work on the subject.

S. S. Holton, *Feminism and Democracy: Women's Suffrage and Reform Politics in Britain, 1900–1918* (1986). An excellent treatment of the subject.

P. Joyce, *Visions of the People: Industrial England and the Question of Class, 1848–1914* (1991). Based on important explorations of what actually occurred in the workplace.

S. Kern, *The Culture of Time and Space, 1880–1918* (1983). A lively discussion of the impact of the new technology.

S. Kern, *The Culture of Love: Victorians to Moderns* (1992). A major discussion of how Europeans have thought and behaved in regard to love, family, and sexuality.

K. Kolakowski, *Main Currents of Marxism: Its Rise, Growth, and Dissolution*, 3 vols. (1978). The sections on the last years of the nineteenth century and the early years of the twentieth are especially good.

D. Landes, *The Unbound Prometheus: Technological Change and Industrial Development in Western Europe from 1750 to the Present* (1969). Includes excellent discussions of late-nineteenth-century development.

A. MacLaren, *Sexuality and Social Order: The Debate over the Fertility of Women and Workers in France, 1770–1920* (1983). Examines the debate over birth control in France.

W. O. McCagg, Jr., *A History of Habsburg Jews, 1670–1918* (1989). An excellent examination of the political and economic life of the Jews under Habsburg rule.

G. L. Mosse, *German Jews Beyond Judaism* (1985). Sensitive essays exploring the relationship of Jews to German culture in the nineteenth and early twentieth centuries.

P. G. Nord, *The Republican Moment: Struggles for Democracy in Nineteenth-Century France* (1996). A major new examination of nineteenth-century French political culture.

D. Olsen, *The City As a Work of Art: London, Paris, Vienna* (1986). A splendidly illustrated survey of nineteenth-century urban growth and design.

H. Pelling, *The Origins of the Labour Party, 1880–1900* (1965). Examines the sources of the party in the activities of British socialists and trade unionists.

M. Perrot, *Workers on Strike: France, 1871–1890* (1987). A major exploration of the social and cultural dimensions of strikes.

D. H. Pinkney, *Napoleon III and the Rebuilding of Paris* (1958). A classic study.

T. Richards, *The Commodity Culture of Victorian England: Advertising and Spectacle, 1851–1914* (1990). A study of how consumers were persuaded of their need for new commodities.

H. Rogger, *Russia in the Age of Modernization and Revolution, 1881–1917* (1983). The best synthesis of the period.

H. Rogger, *Jewish Policies and Right-Wing Politics in Imperial Russia* (1986). A very learned examination of Russian anti-Semitism.

M. L. Rozenblit, *The Jews of Vienna, 1867–1914: Assimilation and Identity* (1983). Covers the cultural, economic, and political life of Viennese Jews.

C. E. Schorske, *German Social Democracy, 1905–1917* (1955). The classic study of the difficulties of the Social Democrats under the empire.

A. L. Shapiro, *Housing the Poor of Paris, 1850–1902* (1985). Examines what happened to working-class housing at the time of the remodeling of Paris.

B. G. Smith, *Ladies of the Leisure Class: The Bourgeoises of Northern France in the Nineteenth Century* (1981). Emphasizes the importance of the reproductive role of women.

R. A. Soloway, *Birth Control and the Population Question in England, 1877–1930* (1982). An important book that should be read with the MacLaren book.

N. Stone, *Europe Transformed* (1984). A sweeping survey that emphasizes the difficulties of late-nineteenth-century liberalism.

R. Stuart, *Marxism at Work: Ideology, Class, and French Socialism during the Third Republic* (1992). The most extensive examination of French Marxism during this period.

F. M. L. Thompson, *The Rise of Respectable Society: A Social History of Victorian Britain, 1830–1900* (1988). A major survey.

A. B. ULAM, *The Bolsheviks: The Intellectual and Political History of the Triumph of Communism in Russia* (1965). Early chapters discuss prewar developments and the formation of Lenin's doctrines.

A. M. VERNER, *The Crisis of Russian Autocracy: Nicholas II and the 1905 Revolution* (1990). A major study of this crucial event.

J. R. WALKOWITZ, *Prostitution and Victorian Society: Women, Class, and the State* (1980). A work of great insight and sensitivity.

E. WEBER, *Peasants into Frenchmen: The Modernization of Rural France, 1870–1914* (1976). An important and fascinating work on the transformation of French peasants into self-conscious citizens of the nation-state.

M. J. WIENER, *English Culture and the Decline of the Industrial Spirit, 1850–1980* (1981). The best study of the problem.

T. ZELDIN, *France, 1848–1945*, 2 vols. (1973, 1977). Covers many areas of French social life.

*The German physicist Albert Einstein's theory of relativity, published in 1905, set the fundamental theory of physics in a new direction. His work was part of a multi-faceted series of intellectual developments that changed and challenged much Western thought not only in science but also in literature, politics, and philosophy, redirecting Western thinking in ways that were often quite different from those of the Enlightenment. [Corbis-Bettmann]*

# The Birth of Modern European Thought

## KEY TOPICS

- The dominance of science in the thought of the second half of the nineteenth century
- The conflict of church and state over education
- The effect of modernism, psychoanalysis, and the revolution in physics on intellectual life
- Racism and the resurgence of anti-Semitism
- Late-nineteenth- and early-twentieth-century developments in feminism

During the same period that the modern nation-state developed and the Second Industrial Revolution laid the foundations for the modern material lifestyle, the ideas and concepts that have marked European thought for much of the present century took shape. Like previous intellectual changes, these arose from earlier patterns of thought. The Enlightenment provided late-nineteenth-century Europeans with a heritage of rationalism, toleration, cosmopolitanism, and appreciation of science. Romanticism led them to value feelings, imagination, national identity, and the autonomy of the artistic experience.

By 1900 these strands of thought had become woven into a new fabric. Many of the traditional intellectual signposts were disappearing. The death of God had been proclaimed. Christianity had undergone the most severe attack in its history. The picture of the physical world that had prevailed since Newton had undergone major modification. The work of Darwin and Freud had challenged the special place that Western thinkers had assigned to humankind. Writers began to question the value long ascribed to rationality. The political and humanitarian ideals of liberalism and socialism gave way to new, aggressive nationalism. At the turn of the century, European intellectuals were more daring than ever before, but they were also probably less certain and less optimistic.

Many of the new ideas shaking Europe were not particularly sympa-

*thetic to the women's movement, but women could use the challenge to tradition for their own ends. Small groups of European feminists also began to challenge in new ways the idea of separate gender spheres.*

# The New Reading Public

The social context of intellectual life changed in the latter half of the nineteenth century. For the first time in Europe, a mass reading public came into existence as more people than ever before became drawn into the world of print culture. In 1850 about half the population of western Europe and a much higher proportion of Russians were illiterate. Even those people who could technically read and write often did so poorly. That situation changed during the next half century.

### Advances in Primary Education

Literacy on the Continent improved steadily, as from the 1860s onward one government after another undertook state-financed education. Hungary provided elementary education in 1868; Britain, in 1870; Switzerland, in 1874; Italy, in 1877; and France, between 1878 and 1881. The already advanced education system of Prussia was extended in various ways throughout the German Empire after 1871. The attack on illiteracy proved most successful in Britain, France, Belgium, the Netherlands, Germany, and Scandinavia, where by 1900 approximately 85 percent or more of the people could read. Italy, Spain, Russia, Austria–Hungary, and the Balkans lagged well behind, with illiteracy rates of between 30 and 60 percent.

The new primary education in the basic skills of reading and writing and elementary arithmetic reflected and generated social change. Both liberals and conservatives regarded such minimal training as necessary for orderly political behavior by the newly enfranchised voters. They also hoped that literacy might help the poor to help themselves and might create a better, more productive labor force. This side of the educational crusade embodied the Enlightenment rationalist faith that right knowledge would lead to right action.

*Public education became widespread in Europe during the second half of the nineteenth century and women came to dominate the profession of schoolteaching, especially at the elementary level. This 1905 photograph shows English schoolchildren going through morning drills. [The Bettmann Archive]*

Literacy and its extension, however, soon became forces in their own right. The schoolteaching profession grew rapidly in numbers and prestige and, as noted in the previous chapter, became a major area for the employment of women. Those people who learned to read the little they were taught could continue to read much more on their own. They soon discovered that much of the education that led to better jobs and political influence was still open only to those who could afford it. Having created systems of primary education, the major nations had to give further attention to secondary education by the time of World War I. In yet another generation, the question would become one of democratic university instruction.

### Reading Material for the Mass Audience

The expanding literate population created a vast market for new reading material. There was a veritable explosion of printed matter of every variety. Advances in printing and paper technology lowered production costs. The number of newspapers, books, magazines, mail-order catalogs, and libraries grew rapidly. Cheap mass-circulation newspapers, such as *Le Petit Journal* of Paris and the *Daily Mail* and *Daily Express* of London, enjoyed their first heyday. Such newspapers carried advertising that alerted readers to the new consumer products made available through the Second Industrial Revolution. Other publishers produced newspapers with specialized political or religious viewpoints. The number of monthly and quarterly journals for families, women, and freethinking intellectuals increased. Probably more people with different ideas could get into print in the late nineteenth century than ever before in European history. And more people could read their ideas than ever before.

Because many of the new readers were only marginally literate and still ignorant about many subjects, the books and journals catering to them often were mediocre. The cheap newspapers prospered on stories of sensational crimes and political scandal and on pages of advertising. Religious journals depended on denominational rivalry. A brisk market existed for pornography. Newspapers with editorials on the front page became major factors in the emerging mass politics. The news could be managed, but in central Europe more often by the government censor than by the publisher.

Social and artistic critics were correct in pointing to the low level of public taste. Nevertheless, the new education, the new readers, and the hundreds of new books and journals permitted a monumental popularization of knowledge that has become a hallmark of the contemporary world. The new literacy was the intellectual parallel of the railroad and the steamship. People could leave their original intellectual surroundings since literacy is not an end in itself, but it leads to other skills and the acquisition of other knowledge.

# Science at Mid-Century

In about 1850 Voltaire would still have felt at home in a general discussion of scientific concepts. The basic Newtonian picture of physical nature that he had popularized still prevailed. Scientists continued to believe that nature operated as a vast machine according to mechanical principles. At mid-century, learned persons regarded the physical world as rational, mechanical, and dependable. Its laws could be ascertained objectively through experiment and observation. Scientific theory purportedly described physical nature as it really existed.

### Comte, Positivism, and the Prestige of Science

During the early nineteenth century, science had continued to establish itself as the model for all human knowledge. The French philosopher Auguste Comte (1798–1857), a late child of the Enlightenment and a one-time follower of Saint-Simon, developed a philosophy of human intellectual development that culminated in science. In *The Positive Philosophy* (1830–1842), Comte argued that human thought had developed in three stages. In the first or theological stage, physical nature was explained in terms of the action of divinities or spirits. In the second or metaphysical stage, abstract principles were regarded as the operative agencies of nature. In the final or positive stage, explanations of nature became matters of exact description of phenomena, without recourse to an unobservable operative principle.

Physical science had, in Comte's view, entered the positive stage, and similar thinking should penetrate other areas of analysis. In particular, Comte thought that positive laws of social behavior could be discovered in the same fashion as laws of physical nature. He is thus generally regarded as the father of sociology. Works like Comte's helped to

*Auguste Comte, the founder of Positivism. Comte argued that all natural phenomena, including the workings of human society, could be explained scientifically in terms of empirically derived natural laws. [Roger-Viollet]*

convince learned Europeans that genuine knowledge in any area must resemble scientific knowledge.

From the middle of the nineteenth century onward, the links of science to the technology of the Second Industrial Revolution made the general European public aware of science and technology as never before. The British Fabian socialist Beatrice Webb (1858–1943) recalled this situation from her youth:

Who will deny that the men of science were the leading British intellectuals of that period; that it was they who stood out as men of genius with international reputations; that it was they who were the self-confident militants of the period; that it was they who were routing the theologians, confounding the mystics, imposing their theories on philosophers, their inventions on capitalists, and their discoveries on medical men; whilst they were at the same time snubbing the artists, ignoring the poets, and even casting doubts on the capacity of the politicians?[1]

[1]*Beatrice Webb,* My Apprenticeship *(London: Longmans, Green, 1926), pp. 130–131.*

Her remarks would have applied in virtually every industrialized nation in Europe. During the third quarter of the century, writers spoke of a religion of science that would explain all nature without resort to supernaturalism. Popularizers, such as Thomas Henry Huxley (1825–1895) in Britain and Ernst Haeckel (1834–1919) in Germany, wrote and lectured widely on scientific topics. They argued that science held the answer to the major questions of life. They worked for government support of scientific research and for inclusion of science in the schools and universities.

### Darwin's Theory of Natural Selection

In 1859 Charles Darwin (1809–1882) published *The Origin of Species*, which carried the mechanical interpretation of physical nature into the world of living things. The book proved to be one of the seminal works of Western thought and earned Darwin the honor of being regarded as the "Newton of biology." Both Darwin and his book have been much misunderstood. He did not originate the concept of evolution, which had been discussed widely before he wrote. What he and Alfred Russel Wallace (1823–1913) did, working independently, was to formulate the principle of natural selection, which explained how species had changed or evolved over time. Earlier writers had believed that evolution might occur; Darwin and Wallace explained how it could occur.

Drawing on Malthus, the two scientists contended that more seeds and living organisms come into existence than can survive in their environment. Those organisms having some marginal advantage in the struggle for existence live long enough to propagate their kind. This principle of survival of the fittest Darwin called *natural selection*. The principle was naturalistic and mechanistic. Its operation required no guiding mind behind the development and change in organic nature. What neither Darwin nor anyone else in his day could explain was the origin of those chance variations that provided some living things with the marginal chance for survival. Only after 1900, when the work on heredity of the Austrian monk, Gregor Mendel (1822–1884), received public attention, did the mystery of those variations begin to be unraveled.

Darwin's and Wallace's theory represented the triumph of naturalistic explanation, which removed the idea of purpose from organic nature. Eyes were not made for seeing according to the rational

# Darwin Defends a Mechanistic View of Nature

*In the closing paragraphs of* The Origin of Species *(1859), Charles Darwin contrasted the view of nature he championed with that of his opponents. He argued that an interpretation of organic nature based on mechanistic laws was actually nobler than an interpretation based on divine creation. In the second edition, however, Darwin added the term Creator to these paragraphs.*

✦ *Why does Darwin believe a mechanistic creation suggests no less dignity than creation by God? How does the insertion of the term Creator change this passage? What is the grandeur that Darwin finds in his view of life?*

Authors of the highest eminence seem to be fully satisfied with the view that each species has been independently created. To my mind it accords better with what we know of the laws impressed on matter by the Creator, that the production and extinction of the past and present inhabitants of the world should have been due to secondary causes, like those determining the birth and death of the individual. When I view all beings not as special creations, but as the lineal descendants of some few beings which lived long before the first bed of the Cambrian [geological] system was deposited, they seem to me to become ennobled. . . .

It is interesting to contemplate a tangled bank, clothed with many plants of many kinds, with birds singing on the bushes, with various insects flitting about, and with worms crawling through the damp earth, and to reflect that these elaborately constructed forms, so different from each other, and dependent upon each other in so complex a manner, have all been produced by laws acting around us. These laws, taken in the largest sense, being Growth with Reproduction; Inheritance which is almost implied by reproduction; Variability from the indirect and direct action of the conditions of life, and from use and disuse: a Ratio of Increase so high as to lead to a Struggle for Life, and as a consequence to Natural Selection, entailing Divergence of Character and the Extinction of less-improved forms. Thus, from the war of nature, from famine and death, the most exalted object which we are capable of conceiving, namely the production of the higher animals, directly follows. There is grandeur in this view of life, with its several powers, having been originally breathed by the Creator into a few forms or into one; and that, whilst this planet has gone cycling on according to the fixed law of gravity, from so simple a beginning endless forms most beautiful and most wonderful have been, and are being evolved.

Charles Darwin, The Origin of Species and the Descent of Man *(New York: Modern Library, n.d.), pp. 373–374.*

---

wisdom and purpose of God but had developed mechanistically over time. Thus, the theory of evolution through natural selection not only contradicted the biblical narrative of the Creation but also undermined the deistic argument for the existence of God from the design of the universe. Moreover, Darwin's work undermined the whole concept of fixity in nature or the universe at large. The world was a realm of flux and change. The idea that physical and organic nature might be constantly changing allowed people in the late nineteenth century to believe that society, values, customs, and beliefs should also change.

In 1871 Darwin carried his work a step further. In *The Descent of Man*, he applied the principle of evolution by natural selection to human beings.

*In two works of seminal importance,* The Origin of Species *(1859) and* The Descent of Man *(1871), Charles Darwin articulated the theory of evolution by natural selection and applied that theory to human beings. The result was a storm of controversy that affected not only biology but also religion, philosophy, sociology, and even politics. [Bildarchiv Preussischer Kulturbesitz]*

Darwin was hardly the first person to treat human beings as animals, but his arguments brought greater plausibility to that point of view. He contended that humankind's moral nature and religious sentiments, as well as its physical frame, had developed naturalistically largely in response to the requirements of survival. Neither the origin nor the character of humankind on Earth, in Darwin's view, required the existence of a God for their explanation. Not since Copernicus had removed the Earth from the center of the universe had the pride of Western human beings received so sharp a blow.

Darwin's theory of evolution by natural selection was controversial from the moment of the publication of *The Origin of Species*. It encountered criticism from both the religious and the scientific communities. By the end of the century, scientists widely accepted evolution, but not yet Darwin's

mechanism of natural selection. The acceptance of the latter within the scientific community really dates from the 1920s and 1930s, when Darwin's theory was combined with the insights of modern genetics.

## Science and Ethics

Darwin's ideas remained highly controversial. They were widely debated in popular and scientific journals. He changed some of them in the course of his writings. At issue, however, was not only the correctness of the theory and the place of humankind in nature but also the role of science and scientists in society.

One area in which science came to have a new significance was in social thought and ethics. Certain philosophers modeled theories of ethics on science. They applied the concept of the struggle for survival to human social relationships. The phrase "survival of the fittest" pre-dated Darwin and reflected the competitive outlook of classical economics. Darwin's use of the phrase gave it the prestige associated with advanced science.

The most famous advocate of evolutionary ethics was Herbert Spencer (1820–1903), a British philosopher. Spencer, a strong individualist, believed that human society progressed through competition. If the weak received too much protection, the rest of humankind was the loser. In Spencer's work, struggle against one's fellow human beings became a kind of ethical imperative. The concept could be applied to justify the avoidance of aiding the poor and the working class or to justify the domination of colonial peoples or to advocate aggressive competition among nations. Evolutionary ethics and similar concepts, all of which are usually termed *social Darwinism*, often came close to saying that might makes right.

One of the chief opponents of such thinking was Thomas Henry Huxley, the great defender of Darwin. In 1893 Huxley declared that the physical cosmic process of evolution was at odds with the process of human ethical development. The struggle in nature held no ethical implications except to demonstrate how human beings should not behave.

Scientists and their admirers enjoyed a supreme confidence during the last half of the century. They genuinely believed that they had, for all intents and purposes, discovered all that might be discovered. The issues for science in the future would be the

# T. H. Huxley Criticizes Evolutionary Ethics

*T. H. Huxley (1825–1895) was a British scientist who had been among Darwin's strongest defenders. He was also an outspoken advocate for the advancement of science in the late nineteenth century. Huxley, however, became a major critic of social Darwinism, which attempted to deduce ethical principles from evolutionary processes involving struggle in nature. Huxley drew a strong distinction between the cosmic process of evolution and the social process of ethical development. He argued that human ethical progress occurred through combating the cosmic process. These passages are taken from* Evolution and Ethics *(1893).*

♦ *What does Huxley mean by the "cosmic process"? Why does he equate "social progress" with the "ethical process"? In this passage, does Huxley present human society as part of nature or as something that may be separate from nature?*

Men in society are undoubtedly subject to the cosmic process. As among other animals, multiplication goes on without cessation, and involves severe competition for the means of support. The struggle for existence tends to eliminate those less fitted to adapt themselves to the circumstances of their existence. The strongest, the most self-assertive, tend to tread down the weaker. But the influence of the cosmic process on the evolution of society is the greater the more rudimentary its civilization. Social progress means a checking of the cosmic process at every step and the substitution for it of another, which may be called the ethical process; the end of which is not the survival of those who may happen to be the fittest, in respect of the whole of the conditions which obtain, but of those who are ethically the best.

As I have already urged, the practice of that which is ethically best—what we call goodness or virtue—involves a course of conduct which, in all respects, is opposed to that which leads to success in the cosmic struggle for existence. In place of ruthless self-assertion it demands self-restraint; in place of thrusting aside, or treading down, all competitors, it requires that the individual shall not merely respect, but shall help his fellows; its influence is directed, not so much to the survival of the fittest, as to the fitting of as many as possible to survive. It repudiates the gladiatorial theory of existence.

It is from neglect of these plain considerations that the fanatical individualism of our time attempts to apply the analogy of cosmic nature to society. . . .

Let us understand, once for all, that the ethical progress of society depends, not on imitating the cosmic process, still less in running away from it, but in combating it.

T. H. Huxley, Evolution and Ethics *(London: Macmillan & Co., 1894), as quoted in Franklin L. Baumer,* Main Currents of Western Thought: Readings in Western European Intellectual History from the Middle Ages to the Present, *3rd ed., rev. (New York: Alfred A. Knopf, 1970), pp. 561–562.*

extension of acknowledged principles and the refinement of measurement. The turn of the century, however, held a much more brilliant and rapidly expanding horizon for science as a much more complicated picture of nature developed. Before examining those new departures, we must see how the cult of science affected religious thought and practice.

# Christianity and the Church Under Siege

The nineteenth century was one of the most difficult periods in the history of the organized Christian churches. Many European intellectuals left the faith. The secular, liberal nation-states attacked the political and social influence of the church. The expansion of population and the growth of cities challenged its organizational capacity to meet the modern age. Yet during all of this turmoil, the Protestant and Catholic churches still made considerable headway at the popular level.

## Intellectual Skepticism

The intellectual attack on Christianity arose on the grounds of its historical credibility, its scientific accuracy, and its pronounced morality. The *philosophes* of the Enlightenment had delighted in pointing out contradictions in the Bible. The historical scholarship of the nineteenth century brought new issues to the fore.

HISTORY In 1835 David Friedrich Strauss (1808–1874) published *The Life of Jesus*, in which he questioned whether the Bible provided any genuine historical evidence about Jesus. Strauss contended that the story of Jesus was a myth that had arisen from the particular social and intellectual conditions of first-century Palestine. Jesus' character and life represented the aspirations of the people of that time and place rather than events that had actually occurred. Other authors also published skeptical lives of Jesus.

During the second half of the century, scholars such as Julius Wellhausen (1844–1918) in Germany, Ernst Renan (1823–1892) in France, and William Robertson Smith (1847–1894) in Great Britain contended that human authors had written and revised the books of the Bible with the problems of Jewish society and politics in mind. The Bible was not an inspired book but had, like the Homeric epics, been written by normal human beings in a primitive society. This questioning of the historical validity of the Bible caused more literate men and women to lose faith in Christianity than any other single cause.

SCIENCE The march of science also undermined Christianity. This blow was particularly cruel because many eighteenth-century writers had led Christians to believe that the scientific examination of nature provided a strong buttress for their faith. William Paley's (1743–1805) *Natural Theology* (1802) and books by numerous scientists had enshrined this belief. The geology of Charles Lyell (1797–1875) suggested that the Earth was much older than the biblical records contended. By looking to natural causes to explain floods, mountains, and valleys, Lyell removed the miraculous hand of God from the physical development of the Earth. Darwin's theory cast doubt on the doctrine of the Creation. His ideas and those of other writers suggested that the moral nature of humankind could be explained without appeal to God. Finally, anthropologists, psychologists, and sociologists suggested that religion itself and religious sentiments were just one more set of natural phenomena.

MORALITY Other intellectuals questioned the morality of Christianity. The old issue of immoral biblical stories was again raised. Much more important, the moral character of the Old Testament God came under fire. His cruelty and unpredictability did not fit well with the progressive, tolerant, rational values of liberals. They also wondered about the morality of the New Testament God, who would sacrifice for his own satisfaction the only perfect being ever to walk the Earth. Many of the clergy began to ask themselves if they could honestly preach doctrines they felt to be immoral.

During the last quarter of the century, this moral attack on Christianity came from another direction. Writers like Friedrich Nietzsche (1844–1900) in Germany portrayed Christianity as a religion of sheep that glorified weakness rather than the strength life required. Christianity demanded a useless and debilitating sacrifice of the flesh and spirit rather than full-blooded heroic living and daring. Nietzsche once observed, "War and courage have accomplished more great things than love of neighbor."[2]

These widespread skeptical intellectual currents directly influenced only the upper levels of educated society. Yet they created a climate in which Christianity lost much of its intellectual respectability. Fewer educated people joined the clergy. More and more people found that they could lead their lives with little or no reference to Christian-

[2]*Walter Kaufmann, ed. and trans.,* The Portable Nietzsche *(New York: Viking, 1967), p. 159.*

# Matthew Arnold Contemplates the Loss of Religious Certainties

*In this poem, "Dover Beach," written in 1867, Matthew Arnold (1822–1888) portrays a man and a woman looking across the waters of the English Channel on a moonlit night. The speaker in the poem notes that Sophocles, the ancient Greek dramatist, had drawn lessons about the misery of life from the ebb and flow of the Aegean Sea. The speaker then compares the movement of the sea to the perceived withdrawal of the Christian faith from the lives of nineteenth-century men and women. Finally, he says that the world that seems so beautiful is really a place where there can be no certainty, love, light, or peace.*

✦ *What developments in the world of science might have shaken the faith of the speaker in this poem? What changes in European theology might also have changed his religious views? Why does the speaker associate this shaken faith with looking at nature as a realm without any higher religious meaning?*

The sea is calm tonight.
The tide is full, the moon lies fair
Upon the Straits;—on the French coast the
   light
Gleams and is gone; the cliffs of England
   stand,
Glimmering and vast, out in the tranquil
   bay.
Come to the window, sweet is the night air!
Only, from the long line of spray
Where the sea meets the moon-blanch'd
   land,
Listen! you hear the grating roar
Of pebbles which the waves draw back, and
   fling,
At their return, up the high strand,
Begin, and cease, and then again begin,
With tremulous cadence slow, and bring
The eternal note of sadness in.

Sophocles long ago
Heard it on the Aegean, and it brought
Into his mind the turbid ebb and flow
Of human misery; we

Find also in the sound a thought,
Hearing it by this distant northern sea.

The Sea of Faith
Was once, too, at the full, and round earth's
   shore
Lay like the folds of a bright girdle furl'd.
But now I only hear
Its melancholy, long, withdrawing roar,
Retreating, to the breath
Of the night-wind, down the vast edges
   drear
And naked shingles of the world.

Ah, love, let us be true
To one another! for the world, which seems
To lie before us like a land of dreams,
So various, so beautiful, so new,
Hath really neither joy, nor love, nor light,
Nor certitude, nor peace, nor help for pain;
And we are here as on a darkling plain
Swept with confused alarms of struggle and
   flight,
Where ignorant armies clash by night.

Matthew Arnold, "Dover Beach," in Donald J. Gray and G. B. Tennyson, eds., Victorian Literature: Poetry (New York: Macmillan, 1976), pp. 479–480.

ity. The secularism of everyday life proved as harmful to the faith as the direct attacks. This situation was especially prevalent in the cities, which were growing faster than the capacity of the churches to meet the challenge. There was not even enough room in urban churches for potential worshipers to sit. Whole generations of the urban poor grew up with little or no experience of the church as an institution or of Christianity as a religious faith.

## Conflict of Church and State

The secular state of the nineteenth century clashed with both the Protestant and the Roman Catholic churches. Liberals generally disliked the dogma and the political privileges of the established churches. National states were often suspicious of the supranational character of the Roman Catholic Church. The primary area of conflict between the state and the churches, however, was the expanding systems of education. Previously, most education in Europe had taken place in schools run by religious orders or denominations. The churches feared that future generations would emerge from the new state-financed schools without the rudiments of religious teaching. From 1870 through the turn of the century, religious education was heatedly debated in every major country.

GREAT BRITAIN    In Great Britain, the Education Act of 1870 provided for the construction of state-supported schools run by elected school boards, whereas earlier the government had given small grants to religious schools. The new schools were to be built in areas where the religious denominations did not provide satisfactory education. There was rivalry not only between the Anglican Church and the state but also between the Anglican Church and the Nonconformist denominations, that is, those Protestant denominations that were not part of the Church of England. There was intense local hostility among all these groups. The churches of all denominations had to oppose improvements in education because these increased the costs of their own schools. In the Education Act of 1902, the government decided to provide state support for both religious and nonreligious schools but imposed the same educational standards on each.

FRANCE    The British conflict was calm compared with that in France, which had a dual system of Catholic and public schools. Under the Falloux Law of 1850, the local priest provided religious education in the public schools. The conservative French Catholic Church and the Third French Republic were hostile to each other. Between 1878 and 1886, the government passed a series of educational laws sponsored by Jules Ferry (1832–1893). The Ferry Laws replaced religious instruction in the public schools with civic training. Members of religious orders could no longer teach in the public schools, the number of which was to be expanded. After the Dreyfus affair, the French Catholic Church again paid a price for its reactionary politics. The Radical government of Pierre Waldeck-Rousseau (1846–1904), drawn from pro-Dreyfus groups, suppressed the religious orders. In 1905 the Napoleonic Concordat was terminated, and church and state were totally separated.

GERMANY AND THE KULTURKAMPF    The most extreme example of church–state conflict occurred in Germany during the 1870s. At unification, the German Catholic hierarchy had wanted freedom for the churches guaranteed in the constitution. Bismarck left the matter to the discretion of each federal state, but he soon felt that the activity of the Roman Catholic Church and the Catholic Center Party threatened the political unity of the new German Empire. Through administrative orders in 1870 and 1871, Bismarck removed both Catholic and Protestant clergy from overseeing local education in Prussia and set education under state direction. This secularization of education represented the beginning of a concerted attack on the independence of the Catholic Church in Germany.

The "May Laws" of 1873, which applied to Prussia but not to the entire German Empire, required priests to be educated in German schools and universities and to pass state-administered examinations. The state could veto the appointments of priests. The legislation abolished the disciplinary power of the pope and the church over the clergy and transferred it to the state. When the bishops and many of the clergy refused to obey these laws, Bismarck used the police against them. In 1876 he had either arrested or driven from Prussia all the Catholic bishops.

In the end, Bismarck's Kulturkampf ("cultural struggle") against the Catholic Church failed. Not for the first time, Christian martyrs aided resistance to persecution. By the end of the 1870s, the chancellor had abandoned his attack. He had gained state control of education and civil laws governing marriage only at the price of provoking long-term Catholic resentment against the German state. The *Kulturkampf* was probably the greatest blunder of Bismarck's career.

## Areas of Religious Revival

The successful German Catholic resistance to the intrusions of the secular state illustrates the continuing vitality of Christianity during this period of intellectual and political hardship. In Great Britain, both the Anglican Church and the Nonconformist denominations experienced considerable growth in membership and raised vast sums of money for new churches and schools. In Ireland, the 1870s saw a widespread Catholic devotional revival. In France after the defeat by Prussia, priests organized special pilgrimages by train to shrines for thousands of penitents who believed that France had been defeated because of their sins. The cult of the miracle of Lourdes grew during these years. There were efforts by churches of all denominations to give more attention to the urban poor.

In effect, the last half of the nineteenth century witnessed the final great effort to Christianize Europe. It was well organized, well led, and well financed. It failed not from want of effort but because the population of Europe had simply outstripped the resources of the churches. This persistent liveliness of the churches accounts in part for the intense hostility of its enemies.

## The Roman Catholic Church and the Modern World

The most striking feature of Christian religious revival amidst turmoil and persecution was the resilience of the papacy. The brief hope for a liberal pontificate from Pope Pius IX (r. 1846–1878) vanished on the night in November 1848 when he fled the turmoil in Rome. In the 1860s, Pius IX, embittered by the process of Italian unification, launched a counteroffensive against liberalism in thought and deed. In 1864 he issued the *Syllabus of Errors*, which condemned all the major tenets of political liberalism and modern thought. He set the Roman Catholic Church squarely against contemporary science, philosophy, and politics.

In 1869 the pope summoned the First Vatican Council. The next year, through the political manipulations of the pontiff and against much opposition from many bishops, the council promulgated the dogma of the infallibility of the pope when speaking officially on matters of faith and morals. No earlier pope had gone so far. The First Vatican Council ended in 1870, when Italian troops invaded Rome at the outbreak of the Franco-Prussian War.

Pius IX died in 1878 and was succeeded by Leo XIII (r. 1878–1903). The new pope, who was sixty-eight years old at the time of his election, sought to make accommodation with the modern age and to address the great social questions. He looked to the philosophical tradition of Thomas Aquinas (1225–1274) to reconcile the claims of faith and reason.

The conflict between church and state disrupted German politics during the 1870s. In this contemporary cartoon Bismarck and Pope Pius IX seek to checkmate each other in a game of chess. [Bildarchiv Preussischer Kulturbesitz]

# Leo XIII Considers the Social Question in European Politics

*In his 1891 encyclical* Rerum Novarum, *Pope Leo XIII addressed the social question in European politics, providing the Catholic Church's answer to secular calls for social reforms. The pope denied the socialist claim that class conflict was the natural state of affairs. He urged employers to seek just and peaceful relations with workers.*

♦ *How does Leo XIII reject the concept of class conflict? What responsibilities does he assign to the rich and to the poor? Are these responsibilities equal? What kinds of social reform might emerge from these ideas?*

The great mistake that is made in the matter now under consideration is to possess oneself of the idea that class is naturally hostile to class; that rich and poor are intended by Nature to live at war with one another. So irrational and so false is this view that the exact contrary is the truth. . . . Each requires the other; capital cannot do without labour, nor labour without capital. Mutual agreement results in pleasantness and good order; perpetual conflict necessarily produces confusion and outrage. Now, in preventing such strife as this, and in making it impossible, the efficacy of Christianity is marvelous and manifold. . . . Religion teaches the labouring man and the workman to carry out honestly and well all equitable agreements freely made; never to injure capital, or to outrage the person of an employer; never to employ violence in representing his own cause, or to engage in riot or disorder; and to have nothing to do with men of evil principles, who work upon the people with artful promises and raise hopes which usually end in disaster and in repentance when too late. Religion teaches the rich man and the employer that their work people are not their slaves; that they must respect in every man his dignity as a man and as a Christian; that labour is nothing to be ashamed of, if we listen to right reason and to Christian philosophy, but is an honourable employment, enabling a man to sustain his life in an upright and creditable way; and that it is shameful and inhuman to treat men like chattels to make money by, or to look upon them merely as so much muscle or physical power. Thus, again, Religion teaches that, as among the workman's concerns are Religion herself and things spiritual and mental, the employer is bound to see that he has time for the duties of piety; that he be not exposed to corrupting influences and dangerous occasions; and that he be not led away to neglect his home and family or to squander his wages. Then, again, the employer must never tax his work people beyond their strength, nor employ them in work unsuited to their sex or age. His great and principal obligation is to give every one that which is just.

*As quoted in F. S. Nitti,* Catholic Socialism, *trans. by Mary Mackintosh (London: S. Sonnenschein, 1895), p. 409.*

Leo XIII's encyclicals of 1885 and 1890 permitted Catholics to participate in the politics of liberal states.

Leo's most important pronouncement on public issues was the encyclical *Rerum Novarum* (1891). In that document he defended private property, religious education, and religious control of the marriage laws; and he condemned socialism and Marxism. He also declared, however, that employers should treat their employees justly, pay them proper wages, and permit them to organize labor unions. He supported laws and regulations to protect the conditions of labor. The pope urged that modern society be organized according to corporate groups, including people from various classes, who might cooperate according to Christian principles. The corporate society, derivative of medieval social organization, was to be an alternative to both socialism and competitive capitalism. On the basis of Leo XIII's pronouncements, democratic Catholic parties and Catholic trade unions were founded throughout Europe.

Pius X, who reigned from 1903 to 1914 and who has been proclaimed a saint, hoped to resist the intrusions of modern thought and to restore traditional devotional life. Between 1903 and 1907, he condemned Catholic modernism, a movement of modern biblical criticism within the church, and in 1910 he required all priests to take an anti-Modernist oath. Pius X thus set the church once more squarely against the intellectual currents of the day, and the struggle between Catholicism and modern thought continued. Although Pius X did not strongly support the social policy of Leo XIII, the Catholic Church continued to permit its members to participate actively in social and political movements.

## Toward a Twentieth-Century Frame of Mind

The last quarter of the nineteenth century and the first decade of the twentieth century constituted the crucible of modern Western and European thought. During this period, the kind of fundamental reassessment that Darwin's work had previously made necessary in biology and in understanding the place of human beings in nature became writ large in other areas of thinking. Philosophers, scientists, psychologists, and artists began to portray physical reality, human nature, and human society in ways different from those of the past. Their new concepts challenged the major presuppositions of mid-nineteenth-century science, rationalism, liberalism, and bourgeois morality.

### Science: The Revolution in Physics

The changes in the scientific worldview originated within the scientific community itself. By the late 1870s, considerable discontent existed over the

*Marie Curie (1869–1934) and Pierre Curie (1859–1906) were two of the most important figures in the advance of physics and chemistry. Marie was born in Poland but worked in France for most of her life. She is credited with the discovery of radium, for which she was awarded the Nobel Prize in Chemistry in 1911. [Bildarchiv Preussischer Kulturbesitz]*

excessive realism of mid-century science. It was thought that many scientists believed that their mechanistic models, solid atoms, and absolute time and space actually described the real universe.

In 1883 Ernst Mach (1838–1916) published *The Science of Mechanics*, in which he urged that scientists consider their concepts descriptive not of the physical world but of the sensations experienced by the scientific observer. Scientists could describe only the sensations, not the physical world that underlay the sensations. In line with Mach, the French scientist and mathematician Henri Poincaré (1854–1912) urged that the concepts and theories of scientists be regarded as hypothetical constructs of the human mind rather than as descriptions of the true state of nature. In 1911 Hans Vaihinger (1852–1933) suggested that the concepts of science be considered "as if" descriptions of the physical world. By World War I, few scientists believed any longer that they could portray the "truth" about physical reality. Rather, they saw themselves as recording the observations of instruments and as setting forth useful hypothetical or symbolic models of nature.

X-RAYS AND RADIATION Discoveries in the laboratory paralleled the philosophical challenge to nineteenth-century science. With those discoveries, the comfortable world of supposedly "complete" nineteenth-century physics vanished forever. In December 1895, Wilhelm Roentgen (1845–1923) published a paper on his discovery of x-rays, a form of energy that penetrated various opaque materials. Major steps in the exploration of radioactivity followed within months of the publication of his paper.

In 1896 Henri Becquerel (1852–1908), through a series of experiments building on Roentgen's work, discovered that uranium emitted a similar form of energy. The next year, J. J. Thomson (1856–1940), working in the Cavendish Laboratory of Cambridge University, formulated the theory of the electron. The interior world of the atom had become a new area for human exploration, which continues to this day. In 1902 Ernest Rutherford (1871–1937), who had been Thomson's assistant, explained the cause of radiation through the disintegration of the atoms of radioactive materials. Shortly thereafter, he speculated on the immense store of energy present in the atom.

THEORIES OF QUANTUM ENERGY, RELATIVITY, AND UNCERTAINTY The discovery of radioactivity and discontent with the existing mechanical models led to revolutionary theories in physics. In 1900 Max Planck (1858–1947) pioneered the articulation of the quantum theory of energy, according to which energy is a series of discrete quantities, or packets, rather than a continuous stream. In 1905 Albert Einstein (1879–1955) published his first epoch-making papers on relativity in which he contended that time and space exist not separately but rather as a combined continuum. Moreover, the measurement of time and space depends on the observer as well as on the entities being measured.

In 1927 Werner Heisenberg (1901–1976) set forth the uncertainty principle, according to which the behavior of subatomic particles is a matter of statistical probability rather than of exactly determinable cause and effect. Much that only fifty years earlier had seemed certain and unquestionable about the physical universe had now become ambiguous.

The mathematical complexity of twentieth-century physics meant that, despite valiant efforts on the part of scientific writers, science would rarely again be successfully popularized. At the same time, through applied technology and further research in chemistry, physics, and medicine, science affected daily living more than ever before in human history. Scientists from the late nineteenth century onward became the most successful group of Western intellectuals in gaining the financial support of governments and private institutions for the pursuit of their research. They did so by relating the success of science to the economic progress, military security, and health of their various nations. In all those regards, science through pure research, medical knowledge, and technological change has affected modern life more significantly than any other intellectual activity.

## Literature: Realism and Naturalism

Between 1850 and 1914, the moral certainties of learned and middle-class Europeans underwent changes no less radical than their concepts of the physical universe. The realist movement in literature portrayed the hypocrisy, the physical and psychic brutality, and the dullness that underlay bourgeois life and society. The realist and naturalist writers brought scientific objectivity and observation to their work. By using the mid-century cult of science so vital to the middle class, they confronted readers with the harsh realities of life around them. Realism rejected the romantic idealization of nature, the poor, love, and polite society. Realist novelists portrayed the dark, degraded, and dirty side of life almost, some people thought, for its own sake.

An earlier generation of writers, including Charles Dickens (1812–1870) and Honoré de Balzac (1799–1850), had portrayed the cruelty of industrial life and of a society based wholly on money. Other authors, such as George Eliot (born Mary Ann Evans, 1819–1880), had paid close attention to the details of the scenes and the characters portrayed. There had, however, always been room in their works for imagination, fancy, and artistry. They had felt a better moral world possible through Christian values or humane efforts or, for Eliot, through an appreciation of humanity arising from Auguste Comte's thought.

The major figures of late-century realism examined the dreary and unseemly side of life without being certain whether a better life was possible. In good Darwinian fashion, they regarded and portrayed human beings as animals, subject to the passions, the materialistic determinism, and the pressures of the environment like any other animals. Most of them, however, also saw society itself as perpetuating evil.

FLAUBERT AND ZOLA    Critics have often considered Gustave Flaubert's (1821–1880) *Madame Bovary* (1857), with its story of colorless provincial life and a woman's hapless search for love in and outside of marriage, as the first genuinely realistic novel. It portrayed life without heroism, purpose, or even simple civility.

The author who turned realism into a movement was Émile Zola (1840–1902). He found artistic inspiration in Claude Bernard's (1813–1878) *An Introduction to the Study of Experimental Medicine* (1865). Zola argued that he could write an experimental novel in which he would observe and report the characters and their actions as the scientist might relate events within a laboratory experiment. He once declared, "I have simply done on living bodies the work of analysis which surgeons perform on corpses."[3] He believed that absolute physical and psychological determinism ruled human events in the same manner as determinism prevailed in the physical world.

Between 1871 and 1893, Zola published twenty volumes of novels exploring subjects normally untouched by writers. In *L'Assommoir* (1877), he discussed the problem of alcoholism, and in *Nana* (1880), he followed the life of a prostitute. In other works, he considered the defeat of the French army in 1870 and the social strife arising from attempts to organize labor. Zola refused to turn his pen or his readers' thoughts away from the most ugly aspects of life. Nothing in his purview received the light of hope or the aura of romance. Although polite critics faulted his taste and middle-class moralists condemned his subject matter, Zola enjoyed a wide following in France and elsewhere. As noted in Chapter 23, he took a leading role in the public defense of Captain Dreyfus.

[3]*Quoted in George J. Becker,* Documents of Modern Literary Realism *(Princeton, N.J.: Princeton University Press, 1963), p. 159.*

*Émile Zola of France was the master of the realistic novel. [Bettmann Archive]*

IBSEN AND SHAW    The Norwegian playwright Henrik Ibsen (1828–1906) carried realism into the dramatic presentation of domestic life. He sought to achieve new modes of social awareness and to strip away the illusory mask of middle-class morality. His most famous play is *A Doll's House* (1879). Its chief character, Nora, has a narrow-minded middle-class husband who cannot tolerate any independence of character or thought on her part. She finally confronts this situation, the play ending as she leaves him, slamming the door behind her. In *Ghosts* (1881), a respectable middle-class woman must deal with a son suffering from syphilis inherited from her husband. In *The Master Builder* (1892), an aging architect kills himself while trying to impress a young woman who perhaps loves him. Ibsen's works were extremely controversial. He had dared to attack sentimentality, the ideal of the female "angel of the house," and the cloak of respectability that hung so insecurely over the middle-class family.

One of Ibsen's greatest champions was the Irish writer George Bernard Shaw (1856–1950), who spent most of his life in England. During the late 1880s, Shaw vigorously defended Ibsen's work. He went on

*Henrick Ibsen's plays challenged middle-class values in one area of life after another. He particularly questioned the values surrounding marriage and the family. [Bildarchiv Preussischer Kulturbesitz]*

to make his own realistic onslaught against romanticism and false respectability. In *Mrs. Warren's Profession* (1893), a play long censored in England, he explored prostitution. In *Arms and the Man* (1894) and *Man and Superman* (1903), he heaped scorn on the romantic ideals of love and war, and in *Androcles and the Lion* (1913), he pilloried Christianity. Shaw added to the impact of his plays by writing long critical prefaces, in which he emphasized his social criticism.

These and many other realist writers believed it the duty of the artist to portray reality and the commonplace. In dissecting what they considered the "real" world, they helped to change the moral perception of the good life. They refused to let existing public opinion dictate what they wrote about or how they treated their subjects. By presenting their audiences with unmentionable subjects, they sought to remove the veneer of hypocrisy that had previously forbidden such discussion. They hoped to destroy social and moral illusions and to compel the public to face reality. That change in itself seemed good. Few of the realist writers who raised

these problems posed solutions to them. They often left their readers unable to sustain old values and uncertain about where to find new ones.

## Modernism

From the 1870s onward throughout Europe, a new multifaceted movement usually called *modernism* touched virtually all the arts. Like realism, modernism was critical of middle-class society and accepted morality. Modernism, however, whether in music, art, or literature, was not deeply concerned with social issues. What drove the modernists in every field was a concern for the aesthetic or the beautiful. The English essayist Walter Pater (1839–1903) set the tone of the movement when he declared in 1877 that art "constantly aspires to the condition of music."

Across the spectrum of the arts, modernists tried to break the received forms and to create new forms. To many contemporaries, the new forms seemed formless. Practitioners of the modern believed that each of the arts should and could influence the others. Painters gave their works musical titles, as did James Abbott McNeill Whistler (1834–1903) in *Nocturnes*. Musicians combined material from many sources. In his at first notorious and then famous ballet, *The Rite of Spring* (1913), Igor Stravinsky (1882–1971) combined jazz rhythms, dissonance, and anthropological theory. Pablo Picasso (1881–1973) and other artists associated with cubism constructed paintings that involved viewing objects from a variety of angles at the same time and drew inspiration from primitive masks they saw in Paris anthropological museums. In England, practitioners of what was called the *New Sculpture* mixed various materials in richly sensuous statues. Other sculptors rejected traditional forms entirely. For all of these artists, the immediate aesthetic experience of a work of art, whatever its medium, dominated other concerns.

Among the chief proponents of modernism in England were the members of the Bloomsbury Group, including authors Virginia Woolf (1882–1941) and Leonard Woolf (1880–1969), artists Vanessa Bell (1879–1961) and Duncan Grant (1885–1978), the historian and literary critic Lytton Strachey (1880–1932), and the economist John Maynard Keynes (1883–1946). These authors challenged what they regarded as the inherited values of their Victorian forebears. In *Eminent Victorians* (1918), Strachey used a series of biographical sketches less

*Virginia Woolf charted the changing sentiments of a world with most of the nineteenth-century social and moral certainties removed. In A Room of One's Own, quoted in the document selection on p. 906, she also challenged some of the accepted notions of feminist thought, asking whether women writers should bring to their work any separate qualities they possessed as women, and concluding that men and women writers should strive to share each other's sensibilities. [Hulton/Deutsch Collection Limited]*

**Dates of Major Works of Fiction**

| | |
|---|---|
| 1857 | Flaubert, *Madame Bovary* |
| 1877 | Zola, *L'Assommoir* |
| 1879 | Ibsen, *A Doll's House* |
| 1880 | Zola, *Nana* |
| 1881 | Ibsen, *Ghosts* |
| 1892 | Ibsen, *The Master Builder* |
| 1893 | Shaw, *Mrs. Warren's Profession* |
| 1894 | Shaw, *Arms and the Man* |
| 1901 | Mann, *Buddenbrooks* |
| 1903 | Shaw, *Man and Superman* |
| 1913 | Shaw, *Androcles and the Lion* |
| 1913 | Proust, first volume of *In Search of Time Past* |
| 1922 | Joyce, *Ulysses* |
| 1924 | Mann, *The Magic Mountain* |
| 1925 | Woolf, *Mrs. Dalloway* |
| 1927 | Woolf, *To the Lighthouse* |

to write history than to heap contempt on his subjects. Grant and Bell looked to the modern artists on the Continent for their models. Keynes eventually challenged much of the structure of nineteenth-century economic theory. In both personal practice and theory, all in the Bloomsbury Group rejected what they regarded as the repressive sexual morality of their parents' generation.

No one charted these changing sensibilities with more care and eloquence than Virginia Woolf. Her novels, such as *Mrs. Dalloway* (1925) and *To the Lighthouse* (1927), portrayed individuals seek-ing to make their way in a world with most of the nineteenth-century social and moral certainties removed.

On the Continent, one of the major practitioners of modernism in literature was Marcel Proust (1871–1922). In his seven-volume novel *In Search of Time Past* (*À la Recherche du temps perdu*, published between 1913 and 1927), he adopted a stream-of-consciousness format that allowed him to explore his memories. He would concentrate on a single experience or object and then allow his mind to wander through all the thoughts and memories it evoked. In Germany, Thomas Mann (1875–1955), through a long series of novels, the most famous of which were *Buddenbrooks* (1901) and *The Magic Mountain* (1924), explored both the social experience of middle-class Germans and how they dealt with the immediate intellectual heritage of the nineteenth century. In *Ulysses* (1922), James Joyce (1882–1941), who was born in Ireland but spent much of his life on the Continent, wholly transformed not only the novel, but also the structure of the paragraph. Joyce encountered enormous difficulty getting this novel published because of its challenging form and its frank sexuality.

Modernism in literature arose before World War I and flourished after the war, nourished by the turmoil and social dislocation it created. The war removed many of the old political structures and social expectations. After its appalling violence,

*James Joyce transformed the novel and drew his readers into new modes of realism. In 1922 Sylvia Beach published his highly controversial novel,* Ulysses. *Here, Joyce and Beach sit in her Paris bookstore, Shakespeare and Company, with a poster for* Ulysses *in the background. [Corbis-Bettmann]*

readers found themselves much less shocked by upheavals in literary forms and the moral content of novels and poetry.

### Friedrich Nietzsche and the Revolt Against Reason

During the second half of the century, philosophers began to question the adequacy of rational thinking to address the human situation. No late-nineteenth-century writer better exemplified this new attitude than the German philosopher Friedrich Nietzsche (1844–1900), who had been educated as a classical philologist rather than as an academic philosopher. His books remained unpopular until late in his life, when his brilliance had deteriorated into an almost totally silent insanity. He was wholly at odds with the predominant values of the age. At one time or another, he attacked Christianity, democracy, nationalism, rationality, science, and progress. He sought less to change values than to probe the sources of values in the human mind and character. He wanted not only to tear away the masks of respectable life but also to explore how human beings made such masks.

His first important work was *The Birth of Tragedy* (1872), in which he urged that the nonrational aspects of human nature were as important and noble as the rational characteristics. Here and elsewhere, he insisted on the positive function of instinct and ecstasy in human life. To limit human activity to strictly rational behavior was to impoverish human life and experience. In this work, Nietzsche regarded Socrates as one of the major contributors to Western decadence because of the Greek philosopher's appeal for rationality in human affairs. In Nietzsche's view, the strength for the heroic life and the highest artistic achievement arose from sources beyond rationality.

In later works, such as the prose poem *Thus Spake Zarathustra* (1883), Nietzsche criticized democracy and Christianity. Both would lead only to the mediocrity of sheepish masses. He announced the death of God and proclaimed the coming of the Overman (*Übermensch*), who would embody heroism and greatness. This latter term was frequently interpreted as some mode of superman or super race, but such was not Nietzsche's intention. He was highly critical of contemporary racism and anti-Semitism. He sought a return to the heroism that he

*Friedrich Nietzsche (1844–1900) became the most influential German philosopher of the late nineteenth century. His books, which challenged existing morality and values, have exerted a powerful influence on twentieth-century literature and philosophy. Detail from portrait by Kurt Stoeving, 1904. [Bildarchiv Preussischer Kulturbesitz]*

associated with Greek life in the Homeric age. He thought that the values of Christianity and of bourgeois morality prevented humankind from achieving life on a heroic level. Those moralities forbade too much of human nature from fulfilling and expressing itself.

Two of Nietzsche's most profound works are *Beyond Good and Evil* (1886) and *The Genealogy of Morals* (1887). Both are difficult books. Much of the former is written in brief, ambiguous aphorisms. Nietzsche sought to discover not what is good and what is evil but the social and psychological sources of the judgment of good and evil. He declared, "There are no moral phenomena at all, but only a moral interpretation of phenomena."[4] He dared to raise the question of whether morality itself was valuable: "We need a critique of moral values; the value of these values themselves must first be called in question."[5] In Nietzsche's view, morality was a human convention that had no independent existence apart from humankind. For Nietzsche, this discovery did not condemn morality but liberated human beings to create life-affirming instead of life-denying values. Christianity, utilitarianism, and middle-class respectability could, in good conscience, be abandoned. Human beings could, if they so willed, create a new moral order for themselves that would glorify pride, assertiveness, and strength rather than meekness, humility, and weakness.

In his appeal to feelings and emotions and in his questioning of the adequacy of rationalism, Nietzsche drew on the Romantic tradition. The kind of creative impulse that earlier Romantics had considered the gift of artists, Nietzsche saw as the burden of all human beings. The character of the

[4]The Basic Writings of Nietzsche, *ed. and trans. by Walter Kaufman (New York: The Modern Library, 1968), p. 275.*

[5]*Kaufman, p. 456.*

human situation that this philosophy urged on its contemporaries was that of an ever changing flux in which little or nothing but change itself was permanent. Human beings had to forge from their own inner will and determination the truth and values that were to exist in the world. Nietzsche's philosophy and that of other writers of the time questioned not only the rigid domestic and religious morality of the nineteenth century but also the values of toleration, cosmopolitanism, and benevolence that had been championed during the Enlightenment.

## The Birth of Psychoanalysis

A determination to probe beneath surface or public appearance united the major figures of late-nineteenth-century science, art, and philosophy. They sought to discern the various undercurrents, tensions, and complexities that lay beneath the smooth, calm surfaces of hard atoms, respectable families, rationality, and social relationships. As a result of their theories and discoveries, articulate, educated Europeans could never again view the surface of life with smugness or complacency or even much confidence. No single intellectual development more clearly and stunningly exemplified this trend than the emergence of psychoanalysis through the work of Sigmund Freud (1856–1939).

DEVELOPMENT OF FREUD'S EARLY THEORIES  Freud was born into an Austrian Jewish family that settled in Vienna. He originally planned to become a lawyer but soon moved to the study of physiology and then to medicine. In 1886 he opened his medical practice in Vienna, where he lived until driven out by the Nazis in 1938. Freud conducted all his research and writing from the base of his medical practice. His earliest medical interests had been psychic disorders, to which he sought to apply the critical method of science. In late 1885 he had studied for a few months in Paris with Jean-Martin Charcot (1825–1893), who used hypnosis to treat cases of hysteria. In Vienna, he collaborated with another physician, Josef Breuer (1842–1925), and in 1895 they published *Studies in Hysteria*.

In the mid-1890s, Freud changed the technique of his investigations. He abandoned hypnosis and allowed his patients to talk freely and spontaneously about themselves. Repeatedly, he found that they associated their particular neurotic symptoms with experiences related to earlier experiences, going back

Sigmund Freud forced a reconsideration of the role of rationality in human motivation. After Freud it was no longer possible to see reason as the sole determinant of behavior. [Bildarchiv Preussischer Kulturbesitz]

to childhood. He also noted that sexual matters were significant in his patients' problems. For a time, he thought that perhaps sexual incidents during childhood accounted for their illnesses.

By 1897, however, Freud had privately rejected this view. In its place he formulated a theory of infantile sexuality, according to which sexual drives and energy already exist in infants and do not simply emerge at puberty. For Freud, human beings were sexual creatures from birth through adulthood. He thus questioned in the most radical manner the concept of childhood innocence. He also portrayed the little-discussed or little-acknowledged matter of sexuality as one of the bases of mental order and disorder.

FREUD'S CONCERN WITH DREAMS  During the same decade, Freud also examined the psychic phenomena of dreams. Romantic writers had taken dreams seriously, but few psychologists had examined them scientifically. As a rationalist, Freud believed that the seemingly irrational content of dreams must have a reasonable, scientific explanation. His research led him to reconsider the general nature of the human mind. He concluded that dreams allow unconscious wishes, desires, and drives that had been excluded from everyday conscious life and experience to enjoy freer play in the mind. "The dream," he wrote, "is the (disguised) fulfillment of a (suppressed, repressed) wish."[6] During the waking hours, the mind represses or censors those wishes, which are as important to the individual's psychological makeup as conscious thought. In fact, Freud argued, unconscious drives and desires contribute to conscious behavior. Freud developed these concepts and related them to his idea of infantile sexuality in his most important book, *The Interpretation of Dreams*, published in 1900.

FREUD'S LATER THOUGHT    In later books and essays, Freud continued to maintain the significance of the human unconscious. He developed a new model of the internal organization of the mind. According to this model, the mind is an arena of struggle and conflict among three entities: the *id*, the *ego*, and the *superego*. The id consists of amoral, irrational, driving instincts for sexual gratification, aggression, and general physical and sensual pleasure. The superego embodies the external moral imperatives and expectations imposed on the personality by society and culture. The ego mediates between the impulses of the id and the asceticism of the superego. The ego allows the personality to cope with the inner and outer demands of its existence. Consequently, everyday behavior displayed the activity of the personality as its inner drives were partially repressed through the ego's coping with the external moral expectations as interpreted by the superego.

It has been a grave misreading of Freud to see him as urging humankind to thrust off all repression. He believed that excessive repression could lead to mental disorder but that civilization and the survival of humankind required some repression of sexuality and aggression.

Freud's work revolutionized the understanding of human nature. As his views gained adherents just before and after World War I, new dimensions of human life became widely recognized. Human beings were seen as attaining rationality rather than merely exercising it. Civilization itself came to be regarded as a product of repressed or sublimated aggressions and sexual drive.

In his acknowledgment of the role of instinct, will, dreams, and sexuality, Freud reflected the Romantic tradition of the nineteenth century. In other respects, however, he was a son of the Enlightenment. Like the *philosophes*, he was a realist who wanted human beings to live free of fear and illusions by rationally understanding themselves and their world. He saw the personalities of human beings as being determined by finite physical and mental forces in a finite world. He was hostile to religion and spoke of it as an illusion. Freud, like the writers of the eighteenth century, wished to see civilization and humane behavior prevail. More fully than those predecessors, however, he understood the immense sacrifice of instinctual drives required for civilized behavior. He understood how many previously unsuspected obstacles lay in the way of rationality. Freud believed that the sacrifice and struggle were worthwhile, but he was pessimistic about the future of civilization in the West.

DIVISIONS IN THE PSYCHOANALYTIC MOVEMENT Freud's work marked the beginning of the psychoanalytic movement. By 1910 he had gathered around him a small but able group of disciples. Several of his early followers soon moved toward theories of which the master disapproved. The most important of these dissenters was Carl Jung (1875–1961), a Swiss whom for many years Freud regarded as his most distinguished and promising student. Before World War I, the two men had, however, come to a parting of the ways. Jung had begun to question the primacy of sexual drives in forming human personality and in contributing to mental disorder. He also put much less faith in the guiding light of reason.

Jung believed that the human subconscious contained inherited memories from previous generations. These collective memories, as well as the personal experience of an individual, constituted his or her soul. Jung regarded human beings in the twentieth century as alienated from these useful collective memories. In *Modern Man in Search of a Soul* (1933) and other works, Jung tended toward mysticism and saw positive values in religion. Freud was highly critical of most of Jung's work. If Freud's thought derived primarily from the Enlightenment, Jung's was more dependent on romanticism.

[6]The Basic Writings of Sigmund Freud, *trans. by A. A. Brill (New York: The Modern Library, 1938), p. 235.*

By the 1920s, the psychoanalytic movement had become even more fragmented. Nonetheless, in its several varieties, it influenced not only psychology but also sociology, anthropology, religious studies, and literary theory. It has been one of the major tools of twentieth-century intellectuals in their efforts to understand themselves and their civilization. In recent years, psychoanalysis has confronted considerable criticism. Whether or not it survives as a model for understanding human behavior, however, there can be no question that it profoundly influenced the intellectual life of the twentieth century.

## Retreat from Rationalism in Politics

Nineteenth-century liberals and socialists agreed that rational principles could guide society and politics. Rational analysis could discern the problems of society and prepare solutions. They generally felt that once given the vote, individuals would behave according to their rational political self-interest. Improvement of society and the human condition would be possible through education. By the close of the century, these views had come under attack in both theory and practice. Political scientists and sociologists painted politics as frequently irrational. Racial theorists questioned whether rationality and education could affect human society at all.

WEBER During this period, however, one major social theorist was profoundly impressed by the role of reason in human society. The German sociologist Max Weber (1864–1920) regarded the emergence of rationalism throughout society as the major development of human history. Such rationalization displayed itself in both the development of scientific knowledge and the rise of bureaucratic organization.

Weber saw bureaucratization as the basic feature of modern social life. He used this view to oppose Marx's concept of the development of capitalism as the driving force in modern society. Bureaucratization involved the extreme division of labor as each individual began to fit himself or herself into a particular small role in much larger organizations. Furthermore, Weber believed that in modern society people derived their own self-images and sense of personal worth from their position in these organizations.

Weber also contended—again, in contrast to Marx—that noneconomic factors might account for major developments in human history. For exam-

*Max Weber considered bureaucratization as the basic feature of modern social life. In contrast to Marx and Freud, Weber stressed the role of the individual and of rationality in human affairs. [Bildarchiv Preussischer Kulturbesitz]*

ple, in his best-known essay, *The Protestant Ethic and the Spirit of Capitalism* (1905), Weber traced much of the rational character of capitalist enterprise to the ascetic religious doctrines of Puritanism. The Puritans, in his opinion, had accumulated wealth and worked for worldly success less for its own sake than to assure themselves that they stood among the elect of God. The theory has generated both much historical research and critical debate from its publication to the present.

THEORISTS OF COLLECTIVE BEHAVIOR In his emphasis on the individual and on the dominant role of rationality, Weber differed from many contemporary social scientists, such as Gustave LeBon (1841–1931), Émile Durkheim (1858–1917), and Georges Sorel (1847–1922) in France, Vilfredo Pareto (1848–1923) in Italy, and Graham Wallas (1858–1932) in England. LeBon was a psychologist who explored the activity of crowds and mobs. He believed that in crowd situations rational behavior was abandoned. Sorel argued in *Reflections on Violence* (1908) that people did not pursue rationally perceived goals but were led to action by collectively shared ideals. Durkheim and Wallas became deeply interested in the necessity of shared values and activities in a society. These elements, rather than a logical analysis of the social situation, bound human beings together. Instinct, habit, and affections instead of reason directed human social behavior. Besides playing down the function of reason in society, all of these theorists emphasized the role of collective groups in politics rather than that of the individual formerly championed by liberals.

## Racism

The same tendencies to question or even to deny the constructive activity of reason in human affairs and to sacrifice the individual to the group manifested themselves in theories of race. Racial thinking had long existed in Europe. Renaissance explorers had displayed considerable prejudice against nonwhite peoples. Since at least the eighteenth century, biologists and anthropologists had classified human beings according to the color of their skin, their language, and their stage of civilization. Late-eighteenth-century linguistic scholars had observed similarities between many of the European languages and Sanskrit. They then postulated the existence of an ancient race called the Aryans, who had spoken the original language from which the rest derived. During the romantic period, writers had called the different cultures of Europe races.

The debates over slavery in the European colonies and the United States had given further opportunity for the development of racial theory. In the late nineteenth century, however, race emerged as a single dominant explanation of the history and the character of large groups of people.

GOBINEAU  Count Arthur de Gobineau (1816–1882), a reactionary French diplomat, enunciated the first important theory of race as the major determinant of human history. In his four-volume *Essay on the Inequality of the Human Races* (1853–1854), Gobineau portrayed the troubles of Western civilization as being the result of the long degeneration of the original white Aryan race. He claimed it had unwisely intermarried with the inferior yellow and black races, thus diluting the qualities of greatness and ability that originally existed in its blood. Gobineau was deeply pessimistic because he saw no way to reverse the degeneration that had taken place.

Gobineau's essay remained little known for many years. In the meantime, a growing literature by anthropologists and explorers helped to spread racial thinking. In the wake of Darwin's theory, thinkers applied the concept of survival of the fittest to races and nations. The recognition of the animal nature of humankind made the racial idea all the more persuasive.

CHAMBERLAIN  At the close of the century, Houston Stewart Chamberlain (1855–1927), an Englishman who settled in Germany, drew together these strands of racial thought into the two volumes of his *Foundations of the Nineteenth Century* (1899). He championed the concept of biological determinism through race, but he was somewhat more optimistic than Gobineau. Chamberlain believed that through genetics the human race could be improved and even that a superior race could be developed.

# H. S. Chamberlain Exalts the Role of Race

*Houston Stewart Chamberlain's* Foundations of the Nineteenth Century *(1899) was one of the most influential works of the day to argue for the primary role of race in history. Chamberlain believed that most people in the world were racially mixed and that this mixture weakened those human characteristics most needed for physical and moral strength. As demonstrated in the passage here, he also believed that people assured of their racial purity could act with the most extreme self-confidence and arrogance. Chamberlain's views had a major influence on the Nazi Party in Germany and on others who wished to establish their alleged racial superiority for political purposes.*

♦ *What does Chamberlain mean by "Race" in this passage? How, in his view, does race, as opposed to character or environment, determine human nature? How might a nationalist use these ideas?*

Nothing is so convincing as the consciousness of the possession of Race. The man who belongs to a distinct, pure race, never loses the sense of it. The guardian angel of his lineage is ever at his side, supporting him where he loses his foothold, warning him like the Socratic Daemon where he is in danger of going astray, compelling obedience, and forcing him to undertakings which, deeming them impossible, he would never have dared to attempt. Weak and erring like all that is human, a man of this stamp recognises himself, as others recognise him, by the sureness of his character, and by the fact that his actions are marked by a certain simple and peculiar greatness, which finds its explanation in his distinctly typical and super-personal qualities. Race lifts a man above himself; it endows him with extraordinary—I might almost say supernatural—powers, so entirely does it distinguish him from the individual who springs from the chaotic jumble of peoples drawn from all parts of the world: and should this man of pure origin be perchance gifted above his fellows, then the fact of Race strengthens and elevates him on every hand, and he becomes a genius towering over the rest of mankind, not because he has been thrown upon the earth like a flaming meteor by a freak of nature, but because he soars heavenward like some strong and stately tree, nourished by thousands and thousands of roots—no solitary individual, but the living sum of untold souls striving for the same goal.

*Houston Stewart Chamberlain,* Foundations of the Nineteenth Century, vol. 1, *trans. by John Lees (London: John Lane, 1912), p. 269.*

Chamberlain brought anti-Semitism to prominence in racial theory. He pointed to the Jews as the major enemy of European racial regeneration. Chamberlain's book and the works on which it drew aided the spread of anti-Semitism in European political life. Also in Germany, the writings of Paul de Lagarde (1827–1891) and Julius Langbehn (1851–1907) emphasized the supposed racial and cultural dangers posed by the Jews to traditional German national life.

LATE-CENTURY NATIONALISM    Racial thinking was one part of a wider late-century movement toward more aggressive nationalism. Previously, nationalism had in general been a movement among European literary figures and liberals. The former had sought to develop what they regarded as the historically distinct qualities of particular national or ethnic literatures. The liberal nationalists had hoped to redraw the map of Europe to reflect ethnic boundaries. The drive for the unification of Italy and Germany had been major causes, as had been the liberation of Poland from foreign domination. The various national groups of the Habsburg Empire had also sought emancipation from Austrian domination.

From the 1870s onward, however, nationalism became a movement with mass support, well-financed organizations, and political parties. Nationalists often redefined nationality in terms of race and blood. The new nationalism opposed the internationalism of both liberalism and socialism. The ideal of nationality was used to overcome the pluralism of class, religion, and geography. The nation and its duties replaced religion in the lives of many secularized people. It sometimes became a secular religion in the hands of state schoolteachers, who were replacing the clergy as the instructors of youth. Nationalism of this aggressive racist variety would prove to be the most powerful ideology of the early twentieth century and would reemerge after the collapse of communism late in the century.

## Anti-Semitism and the Birth of Zionism

Political and racial anti-Semitism, which have cast such dark shadows across the twentieth century, developed in part from this atmosphere of racial thought and the retreat from rationality in politics. Religious anti-Semitism dated from at least the Middle Ages. Since the French Revolution, West European Jews had gradually gained entry into the civil life of Britain, France, and Germany. Popular anti-Semitism, however, continued to exist as the Jewish community was identified with money and banking interests. During the last third of the century, as finance capitalism changed the economic structure of Europe, many non-Jewish Europeans pressured by the changes became hostile toward the Jewish community.

ANTI-SEMITIC POLITICS   In Vienna, Mayor Karl Lueger (1844–1910) used anti-Semitism as a major attraction to his successful Christian Socialist Party. In Germany, the ultraconservative Lutheran chaplain Adolf Stoecker (1835–1909) revived anti-Semitism. The Dreyfus affair in France allowed a new flowering of hatred toward the Jews.

To this already ugly atmosphere, racial thought contributed the belief that no matter to what extent Jews assimilated themselves and their families into the culture of their country, their Jewishness—and thus their alleged danger to the society—would

*Theodor Herzl's visions of a Jewish state would eventually lead to the creation of Israel in 1948. [The Bettmann Archive/BBC Hulton]*

remain. According to racial thinkers, the problem of race was not in the character but in the blood of the Jew. An important Jewish response to this new, rabid outbreak of anti-Semitism was the launching in 1896 of the Zionist movement to found a separate Jewish state. Its founder was the Austro-Hungarian Theodor Herzl (1860–1904).

HERZL'S RESPONSE   The conviction in 1894 of Captain Dreyfus in France and the election of Karl Lueger in 1895 as mayor of Vienna, as well as personal experience of discrimination, deeply influenced Herzl. He became convinced that liberal politics and the institutions of the liberal state could not protect the Jews in Europe or ensure that they would be treated justly. In 1896 Herzl published *The Jewish State*, in which he called for the organization of a separate state in which all Jews might be assured of those rights and liberties that they should be enjoying in the liberal states of Europe. Furthermore, Herzl followed the tactics of late-century mass democratic politics by particularly direct-

# Herzl Calls for the Establishment of a Jewish State

*In 1896 Theodor Herzl published his pamphlet* The Jewish State. *Herzl had lived in France during the turmoil and anti-Semitism associated with the Dreyfus affair. He became convinced that only the establishment of a separate state for Jews would halt the various outbreaks of anti-Semitism that characterized late-nineteenth-century European political and cultural life. Following the publication of this pamphlet, Herzl began to organize the Zionist movement among Jews in both eastern and western Europe.*

✦ *Why does Herzl define what he calls the Jewish Question as a national question? What objections does he anticipate to the founding of a Jewish state? Why does he believe the founding of a Jewish state will be an effective move against anti-Semitism?*

The idea which I develop in this pamphlet is an age-old one: the establishment of a Jewish State.

The world resounds with outcries against the Jews, and this is what awakens the dormant idea.

. . . .

I believe I understand anti-Semitism, a highly complex movement. I view it from the standpoint of a Jew, but without hatred or fear. I think I can discern in it the elements of vulgar sport, of common economic rivalry, of inherited prejudice, of religious intolerance—but also of a supposed need for self-defense. To my mind, the Jewish Question is neither a social nor a religious one, even though it may assume these and other guises. It is a national question, and to solve it we must first of all establish it as an international political problem which will have to be settled by the civilized nations of the world in council.

We are a people, *one* people.

Everywhere we have sincerely endeavored to merge with the national communities surrounding us and to preserve only the faith of our fathers. We are not permitted to do so. . . .

. . . .

And will some people say that the venture is hopeless, because even if we obtain the land and the sovereignty only the poor people will go along? They are the very ones we need first! Only desperate men make good conquerors.

Will anybody say, Oh yes, if it were possible it would have been done by now?

It was not possible before. It is possible now. As recently as a hundred, even fifty years ago it would have been a dream. Today it is all real. The rich, who have an epicurean acquaintance with all technical advance, know very well what can be done with money. And this is how it will be: Precisely the poor and plain people, who have no idea of the power that man already exercises over the forces of Nature, will have the greatest faith in the new message. For they have never lost their hope of the Promised Land.

. . . .

Now, all this may seem to be a long-drawn-out affair. Even in the most favorable circumstances it might be many years before the founding of the State is under way. In the meantime, Jews will be ridiculed, offended, abused, whipped, plundered, and slain in a thousand different localities. But no; just as soon as we begin to implement the plan, anti-Semitism will immediately grind to a halt everywhere. . . .

Theodor Herzl, The Jewish State *(New York: The Herzl Press, 1970), pp. 27, 33, 109, as quoted in William W. Hallo, David B. Ruderman, and Michael Stanislawski, eds.,* Heritage: Civilization and the Jews Source Reader *(New York: Praeger, 1984), pp. 234–235.*

ing his appeal to the economically poor Jews who lived in the ghettos of eastern Europe and the slums of western Europe. The original call to Zionism thus combined a rejection of the anti-Semitism of Europe and a desire to realize some of the ideals of both liberalism and socialism in a state outside Europe.

# Women and Modern Thought

The ideas that so shook Europe from the publication of *The Origin of Species* through the opening of World War I raised questions about much of the European intellectual legacy. Religion, science, art, and society came under new forms of criticism. Yet these new ideas and intellectual movements produced at best mixed results for women. Within the often radically new ways of thinking about the world, views of women and their roles in society often remained remarkably unchanged.

## Antifeminism in Late-Century Thought

The influence of biology on the thinking of intellectuals during the late nineteenth century and their own interest in the nonrational side of human behavior led many of them to sustain what had become stereotyped views of women. The emphasis on biology, evolution, and reproduction led intellectuals to concentrate on women's mothering role. Their interest in the nonrational led them to reassert the traditional view that feeling and the nurturing instinct were basic to women's nature. Many late-century thinkers and writers of fiction also often displayed real fear and hostility toward women, portraying them as creatures susceptible to overwhelming and often destructive feelings and instincts. A genuinely misogynist strain emerged in late-century fiction and painting.

Much of the biological thought that challenged religious ideas and the accepted wisdom in science actually reinforced the traditional view of women as creatures weaker and less able than men. Darwin himself held such views of women, and he expressed them directly in his scientific writings. Medical thought of the late century similarly sustained these views. Whatever social changes were to be wrought through science, significant changes in the organization of the home and the relationship of men and women were not among them.

This conservative and hostile perception of women manifested itself in several ways within the scientific community. In London in 1860, the Ethnological Society excluded women from its discussions on the grounds that the subject matter of the customs of primitive peoples was unfit for women and that women were amateurs whose presence would lower the level of the discussion. T. H. Huxley, the great defender of Darwin, took the lead in this exclusion as he had in a previous exclusion of women from meetings of the Geological Society. Male scientists also believed women should not discuss reproduction or other sexual matters. Huxley, in public lectures, claimed to have found scientific evidence of the inferiority of women to men. Karl Vogt (1817–1895), a leading German anthropologist, held similar views about the character of women. Darwin would repeat the ideas of both Huxley and Vogt in his *Descent of Man*. Late Victorian anthropologists tended likewise to assign women, as well as nonwhite races, an inferior place in the human family. Despite their otherwise conservative views on gender, however, both Darwin and Huxley supported the expansion of education for women.

The position of women in Freud's thought has always been controversial. Many of his earliest patients, upon whose histories he developed his theories, were women. Critics have claimed, nonetheless, that Freud portrayed women as incomplete human beings who might be inevitably destined to unhappy mental lives. He saw the natural destiny of women as motherhood, and their greatest fulfillment the rearing of sons. The first psychoanalysts were trained as medical doctors, and their views of women reflected contemporary medical education, which, like much of the rest of the scientific establishment, tended to portray women as inferior. Distinguished women psychoanalysts, such as Karen Horney (1885–1952) and Melanie Klein (1882–1960), would later sharply challenge Freud's views on women, and other writers would try to establish a psychoanalytic basis for feminism. Nonetheless, the psychoanalytic profession would remain dominated by men, as would nonpsychoanalytic academic psychology. Since psychology would increasingly influence child-rearing practices and domestic relations law in the twentieth century, it would, ironically, give men a large impact in the one area of social activity that had been dominated by women.

The social sciences of the late nineteenth and early twentieth centuries similarly reinforced traditional gender roles. Virtually all major theorists believed that women's role in reproduction and child rearing demanded a social position inferior to men. Auguste Comte, whose thought in this area owed much to Rousseau, portrayed women as biologically and intellectually inferior to men. Herbert Spencer, although an advocate for improving women's lot, thought they could never achieve genuine equality with men. Émile Durkheim portrayed women as essentially creatures of feeling and family rather than of intellect. Max Weber favored improvements in the social condition of women but did not really support significant changes in their social roles or in their relationship to men. Virtually all of the early sociologists took a conservative view of marriage, the family, child rearing, and divorce.

## New Directions in Feminism

The close of the century witnessed a revival of feminist thought in Europe that would grow as the twentieth century passed. The role of feminist writers during these years was difficult. Many women's organizations, as seen in the previous chapter, concentrated on achieving the vote for women, but feminist writers and activists raised other questions as well. Women became more clearly conscious of their problems as women in a variety of ways, confronting them not only by seeking the vote. Some organizations forged new ways of thinking about women, redefining their relationships to men and the larger society. Few of these groups were large, and their victories were rare. Nonetheless, late in the last century and early in this one, they defined the issues that would become more fully and successfully explored after World War II.

SEXUAL MORALITY AND THE FAMILY    In various nations, middle-class women began to challenge the double standard of sexual morality and the traditional male-dominated family. Often this challenge took the form of action relating to prostitution.

Between 1864 and 1886, English prostitutes were subject to the Contagious Diseases Acts. The police in certain cities with naval or military bases could require any woman identified as or suspected of being a prostitute to undergo an immediate internal medical examination for venereal disease. Those found to have a disease could without legal recourse be confined for months to lock hospitals (women's hospitals for the treatment of venereal diseases). The law took no action against their male cus-

tomers. Indeed, the purpose of the laws were to protect men, presumably sailors and soldiers, not the women themselves, from infection.

These laws angered English middle-class women who believed that the working conditions and the poverty imposed on so many working-class women were the true causes of prostitution. They framed the issue in the context of their own efforts to prove that women were as human and rational as men and thus properly subject to equal treatment. They saw poor women being made victims of the same kind of discrimination that prevented themselves from entering the universities and professions. The Contagious Diseases Acts assumed that women were inferior to men and treated them as less than human and less than rational creatures. The laws literally took women's bodies from their own control and put them under the control of male customers, male physicians and male law enforcement personnel. They denied to poor women the freedoms that all men enjoyed in English society.

By 1869 the Ladies' National Association for the Repeal of the Contagious Diseases Acts, a distinctly middle-class organization led by Josephine Butler (1828–1906), began actively to oppose these laws. The group achieved the suspension of the acts in 1883 and their repeal in 1886. The issue of government and police regulation of prostitution roused similar movements in other nations, which adopted the English movement as a model. In Vienna during the 1890s, the General Austrian Women's Association, led by Auguste Ficke (1833–1916), combated the introduction of legally regulated prostitution, which would have put women under the control of police authorities. In Germany, women's groups divided between those who would have penalized prostitutes and those who saw them as victims of male society. By the turn of the century, the latter had come to dominate, although tensions between the groups would remain for some time.

The feminist groups that demanded the abolition of laws that punished prostitutes without questioning the behavior of their customers were challenging the double standard and, by extension, the traditional relationship of men and women in marriage. In their view, marriage should be a free union of equals with men and women sharing responsibility for their children. In Germany, the Mothers' Protection League (Bund für Mutterschutz) contended that both married and unmarried mothers required the help of the state, including leaves for pregnancy and child care. This radical group empha-

The Swedish feminist Ellen Key maintained that motherhood was so crucial to society that the support of mothers and children should be a government responsibility. [Hulton/Deutsch/Collection Limited]

torate in geology, who pioneered contraception clinics in the poor districts of London.

WOMEN DEFINING THEIR OWN LIVES   For Josephine Butler and Auguste Ficke, as well as other continental feminists, achieving legal and social equality for women would be one step toward transforming Europe from a male-dominated society to one in which both men and women could control their own destinies. Ficke wrote, "Our final goal is therefore not the acknowledgement of rights, but the elevation of our intellectual and moral level, *the development of our personality*."[7] Increasingly, feminists would concentrate on freeing and developing women's personalities through better education and government financial support for women engaged in traditional social roles, whether or not they had gained the vote.

Some women also became active within socialist circles. There they argued that the socialist transformation of society should include major reforms for women. Socialist parties usually had all-male leadership. Most male socialist leaders by the close of the century, including Lenin and later Stalin, were intolerant of demands for changes in the family or greater sexual freedom for either men or women. Nonetheless, socialist writings began to include calls for improvements in the economic situation of women that were compatible with more advanced feminist ideals.

It was within literary circles, however, that feminist writers often most clearly articulated the problems that they now understood themselves to face. Distinguished women authors as authors were actually doing, on a more or less equal footing, something that men had always done, leading some to wonder whether simple equality was the main issue. Virginia Woolf's *A Room of One's Own* (1929) became one of the fundamental texts of twentieth-century feminist literature. In it, she meditated first on the difficulties that women of both brilliance and social standing encountered in being taken seriously as writers and intellectuals. She concluded that a woman who wished to write required both a room of her own, meaning a space not dominated by male institutions, and an adequate independent income. But Woolf was concerned with more than asserting the right of women

sized the need to rethink all sexual morality. In Sweden, Ellen Key (1849–1926), in *The Century of the Child* (1900) and *The Renaissance of Motherhood* (1914), both widely read in Europe, maintained that motherhood was one of women's chief roles and was so crucial to society that the government, rather than husbands, should support mothers and their children.

Virtually all turn-of-the-century feminists in one way or another supported wider sexual freedom for women, often claiming that it would benefit society as well as improving women's lives. Many of the early advocates of contraception had also been influenced by social Darwinism. They hoped that limiting the number of children would allow a larger proportion of both healthy and intelligent children to survive. Such was the outlook of Marie Stopes (1880–1958), an Englishwoman with a doc-

[7]*Quoted in Harriet Anderson,* Utopian Feminism: Women's Movements in Fin-de-Siècle Vienna *(New Haven, Conn.: Yale University Press, 1992), p. 13.*

# Virginia Woolf Urges Women to Write

*In 1928 Virginia Woolf, the English novelist, delivered two papers at women's colleges at Cambridge University. Those papers provided the basis for* A Room of One's Own, *published a year later. In* A Room of One's Own, *Woolf discussed the difficulty a woman writer confronted in finding women role-models. She also outlined many of the obstacles that women faced in achieving the education, the time, and the income that would allow them to write. In this passage, which closes her essay, she urges women to begin to write so that future women authors will have models. She then presents an image of Shakespeare's sister who, lacking such models, had not written anything, but who through the collective efforts of women might in the future emerge as a great writer because she would have the literary models of the women Woolf addressed to follow and to imitate.*

✦ *How does Woolf's fiction of Shakespeare's sister establish a benchmark for women writers? What does Woolf mean by the common life through which women will need to work to become independent writers? Why does she emphasize the need for women to have both income and space if they are to become independent writers?*

A thousand pens are ready to suggest what you should do and what effect you will have. My own suggestion is a little fantastic, I admit; I prefer, therefore, to put it in the form of fiction.

I told you in the course of this paper that Shakespeare had a sister; but do not look for her in Sir Sidney Lee's life of the poet. She died young—alas, she never wrote a word. She lies buried where the omnibuses now stop, opposite the Elephant and Castle [a London intersection]. Now my belief is that this poet who never wrote a word and was buried at the cross-roads still lives. She lives in you and in me, and in many other women who are not here to-night, for they are washing up the dishes and putting the children to bed. But she lives; for great poets do not die; they are continuing presences; they need only the opportunity to walk among us in the flesh. This opportunity, as I think, it is now coming within your power to give her. For my belief is that if we live another century or so—I am talking of the common life which is the real life and not of the little separate lives which we live as individuals—and have five hundred [pounds income] a year each of us and rooms of our own; if we have the habit of freedom and the courage to write exactly what we think; if we escape a little from the common sitting-room and see human beings not always in their relation to each other but in relation to reality; and the sky, too, and the trees or whatever it may be in themselves; . . . if we face the fact, for it is a fact, that there is no arm to cling to, but that we go alone and that our relation is to the world of reality and not only to the world of men and women, then the opportunity will come and the dead poet who was Shakespeare's sister will put on the body which she has so often laid down. Drawing her life from the lives of the unknown who were her forerunners, as her brother did before her, she will be born. As for her coming without that preparation, without that effort on our part, without that determination that when she is born again she shall find it possible to live and write her poetry, that we cannot expect, for that would be impossible. But I maintain that she would come if we worked for her, and that so to work, even in poverty and obscurity, is worth while.

*Virginia Woolf,* A Room of One's Own *(London: The Hogarth Press, 1974), pp. 170–172.*

to participate in intellectual life. Establishing a new stance for feminist writers, she asked whether women as writers must imitate men or should bring to their endeavors separate intellectual and psychological qualities that they possessed as women. As she had challenged some of the literary conventions of the traditional novel in her fiction, she challenged some of the accepted notions of feminist thought in *A Room of One's Own*, and concluded that male and female writers must actually be able to think as both men and women and share the sensibilities of each. In this sense, she sought to open the whole question of gender definition.

By World War I, feminism in Europe, fairly or not, had become associated in the popular imagination with challenges to traditional gender roles and sexual morality and with either socialism or political radicalism. So when extremely conservative political movements arose between the world wars, their leaders often emphasized traditional roles for women and traditional ideas about sexual morality. Lenin and Stalin would follow a similar path in the Soviet political experiment.

✦

*By the opening of the twentieth century, European thought had achieved contours that seem familiar to us today. The study of science had led to virtually revolutionary changes in thinking about both biological and physical nature. Physicists had transformed the traditional views of matter and energy as they probed the mysteries of the atom. Research in evolutionary biology had revealed human beings as part of the natural order, not something distinct from it. In the minds of some writers, science was expected to provide human beings with a basis for new ethical knowledge and moral values. Christianity had experienced the strongest challenge in modern times. In part, this was a result of the strong new role for science, but also because of other intellectual changes arising from the study of history and philosophy and the goals of the politicians in secular national states.*

*Simultaneous with this struggle between religion and science, there arose a tendency among certain major nonreligious thinkers and writers to question the primacy of reason. Nietzsche and Freud in their different ways questioned whether human beings were primarily creatures of reason. Weber and other social and political theorists doubted*

*that politics could be entirely rational. All these developments challenged the rational values associated with the Enlightenment. The racial theorists questioned whether mind and character were as important as alleged racial characteristics carried in the blood.*

*Racial thinking also allowed Europeans to believe that they were somehow inherently superior to other peoples and cultures in the world. Such racial thinking fostered anti-Semitism in Europe and discrimination against other ethnic minority groups. Similar racial attitudes also informed the thinking of virtually all the colonial administrators of the European imperial powers.*

*The feminists of the turn of the century, more than any of their predecessors, demanded a rethinking of gender roles. They urged equal treatment for women under the law, but no less important, they contended that the relationship of men and women within marriage and the family required rethinking. They set forth much of the feminist agenda for the twentieth century.*

## Review Questions

1. How would you account for the dominance of science in the thought of the second half of the nineteenth century? What were some of the major changes in scientific outlook between 1850 and 1914? Comment especially on advances in physics. How would you define *positivism*? Describe Darwin's and Wallace's theory of natural selection. What effect did it have on theories of ethics, on Christianity, and on European views of human nature?

2. How and why did Christianity come under attack in the late nineteenth century? Discuss the politics of Pius IX, Leo XIII, and Pius X. Why was Leo XIII regarded as a liberal pope? How do you account for the resilience of the papacy during this period of attack on the church?

3. How had the social conditions of literature changed in the late nineteenth century? What was the significance of the explosion of literary matter? What was literary realism? How was it influenced by science? How did the realists undermine middle class morality? How did literary modernism differ from realism?

4. How did Nietzsche and Freud challenge traditional middle class and religious morality? Would

you describe Freud more as a product of the Enlightenment or of the Age of Romanticism?

5. How do you account for the fear and hostility many late-nineteenth-century intellectuals displayed toward women? How did Freud view the position of women? What were some of the social and political issues affecting women in the late nineteenth and early twentieth centuries and how did reformers confront them? What new directions did feminism take?

6. What was the character of late-nineteenth-century racism? How did it become associated with anti-Semitism? What personal and contemporary political experiences led Herzl to develop the idea of Zionism?

# Suggested Readings

J. L. ALTHOLZ, *The Churches in the Nineteenth Century* (1967). A useful overview.

R. ARON, *Main Currents in Sociological Thought*, 2 vols. (1965, 1967). An introduction to the founders of the science.

S. ASCHHEIM, *The Nietzsche Legacy in Germany 1890–1990* (1992). Examines the influence of Nietzsche.

S. AVINERI, *The Making of Modern Zionism: The Intellectual Origins of the Jewish State* (1981). An excellent introduction to the development of Zionist thought.

S. BARROWS, *Distorting Mirrors: Visions of the Crowd in Late Nineteenth-Century France* (1981). An imaginative examination of crowd psychology as it related to social tension in France.

M. D. BIDDIS, *Father of Racist Ideology: The Social and Political Thought of Count Gobineau* (1970). Sets the subject in the more general context of nineteenth-century thought.

D. BLACKBOURNE, *Marpingen: Apparitions of the Virgin Mary in Nineteenth-Century Germany* (1993). A major study of popular religious movements and the religious revival of the late century.

P. BOWLER, *Evolution: The History of an Idea* (1989). An outstanding survey of the subject.

O. CHADWICK, *The Secularization of the European Mind in the Nineteenth Century* (1975). The best treatment available.

D. G. CHARLTON, *Positivist Thought in France During the Second Empire, 1852–1870* (1959). A clear introduction to an important subject.

D. G. CHARLTON, *Secular Religions in France, 1815–1870* (1963). A clear introduction to an important subject.

C. M. CIPOLLA, *Literacy and Development in the West* (1969). Traces the explosion of literacy in the past two centuries.

A. DANTO, *Nietzsche As Philosopher* (1965). A helpful and well-organized introduction.

A. DESMOND AND J. MOORE, *Darwin* (1992). A brilliant biography.

J. EFRON, *Defenders of the Race: Jewish Doctors and Race Science in Fin-de-Siècle Europe* (1994). A study of the manner in which Jewish physicians responded to late-century anti-Semitic racial thought.

P. GAY, *Freud: A Life for Our Time* (1988). The new standard biography.

C. C. GILLISPIE, *The Edge of Objectivity* (1960). One of the best one-volume treatments of modern scientific ideas.

H. S. HUGHES, *Consciousness and Society: The Reorientation of European Social Thought, 1890–1930* (1958). A wide-ranging discussion of the revolt against positivism.

C. JUNGNICKEL AND R. MCCORMMACH, *Intellectual Mastery of Nature: Theoretical Physics from Ohm to Einstein*, 2 vols. (1986). A demanding but powerful exploration of the creation of modern physics.

J. KATZ, *From Prejudice to Destruction: Anti-Semitism, 1700–1933* (1980). An excellent and far-reaching analysis.

J. T. KLOPPENBERG, *Uncertain Victory: Social Democracy and Progressivism in European and American Thought* (1986). An extremely important comparative study.

T. A. KSELMAN, *Miracles and Prophesies in Nineteenth-Century France* (1983). A study of popular religion.

W. LACQUEUR, *A History of Zionism* (1989). The most extensive one-volume treatment.

B. LIGHTMAN, *The Origins of Agnosticism: Victorian Unbelief and the Limits of Knowledge* (1987). The best study of the subject.

E. MAYR, *The Growth of Biological Thought: Diversity, Evolution, and Inheritance* (1982). A major survey by a scientist of note.

W. J. MCGRATH, *Freud's Discovery of Psychoanalysis: The Politics of Hysteria* (1986). A study of the relationship of Freud's cultural and political background to his scientific thought.

J. MCMANNERS, *Church and State in France, 1870–1914* (1972). The standard treatment.

P. MEISEL, *The Myth of the Modern: A Study in British Literature and Criticism After 1850* (1987). A broad study.

J. R. MOORE, *History, Humanity, and Evolution* (1989). A collection of major essays on evolution that touch upon science, religion, and the question of evolution and women.

G. L. MOSSE, *Toward the Final Solution: A History of European Racism* (1978). A sound introduction.

R. NOLL, *The Jung Cult: Origins of a Charismatic Movement* (1994). A highly critical account of the origins of Jung's thought in nineteenth-century occult science.

R. PASCAL, *From Naturalism to Expressionism: German Literature and Society, 1880–1918* (1973). A helpful survey.

H. W. PAUL, *From Knowledge to Power: The Rise of the Science Empire in France, 1860–1939* (1985). An extensive survey of both scientific thought and institutions in France.

L. POLIAKOV, *The Aryan Myth: A History of Racist and Nationalist Ideas in Europe* (1971). The best introduction to the problem.

P. G. J. PULZER, *The Rise of Political Anti-Semitism in Germany and Austria* (rev. 1989). A sound discussion of anti-Semitism in the world of central European politics.

A. RABINBACH, *The Human Motor: Energy, Fatigue, and the Origins of Modernity* (1990). A broad study of the impact of metaphors of energy as related to the study of human nature.

C. E. SCHORSKE, *Fin de Siècle Vienna: Politics and Culture* (1980). Major essays on the explosively creative intellectual climate of Vienna.

W. SMITH, *Politics and the Sciences of Culture in Germany, 1840–1920* (1991). A major survey of the interaction between science and the various social sciences.

F. STERN, *The Politics of Cultural Despair: A Study in the Rise of the German Ideology* (1965). An important examination of antimodern and anti-Semitic thought in imperial Germany.

F. M. TURNER, *Contesting Cultural Authority: Essays in Victorian Intellectual Life* (1993). Essays that deal with the relationship of science and religion and the problem of faith for intellectuals.

J. P. VON ARX, *Progress and Pessimism: Religion, Politics, and History in Late Nineteenth Century Britain* (1985). A major study that casts much new light on the nineteenth-century view of progress.

C. WELCH, *Protestant Thought in the Nineteenth Century*, 2 vols. (1972, 1985). The most extensive study.

R. WOHL, *A Passion for Wings: Aviation and the Western Imagination, 1908–1918* (1994). An examination of the relationship of technology, art, and culture.

*India was "the jewel in the crown" of the British Empire, its most profitable and valued possession. This engraving from 1875 pictures the Prince of Wales entering the Indian town of Baroda on an elephant. [The Granger Collection]*

# Imperialism, Alliances, and War

## KEY TOPICS

- The economic, cultural, and strategic factors behind Europe's New Imperialism in the late nineteenth and early twentieth centuries
- The formation of alliances and the search for strategic advantage among Europe's major powers
- The origins and progress of World War I
- The Russian Revolution
- The peace treaties ending World War I

During the second half of the nineteenth century, and especially after 1870, Europe exercised unprecedented influence and control over the rest of the world. North and South America, as well as Australia and New Zealand, almost became part of the European world as great streams of European immigrants populated them. Until the nineteenth century, Asia (with the significant exception of India) and most of Africa had gone their own ways, having little contact with Europe. But in the latter part of that century, almost all of Africa was divided among a number of European nations. Europe also imposed its economic and political power across Asia. By the next century, European dominance had brought every part of the globe into a single world economy. Events in any corner of the world had significant effects thousands of miles away.

These developments might have been expected to lead to greater prosperity and good fortune. Instead, they helped to foster competition and hostility among the great powers of Europe and to bring on a terrible war that undermined Europe's strength and its influence in the world. The peace settlement, proclaimed as "a peace without victors," disillusioned idealists in the West. It treated Germany almost as harshly as Germany would have treated its foes if it had been victorious. Also, the new system failed to provide realistic and effective safeguards against a return to power of a vengeful Germany. The withdrawal of the United States into a disdainful isolation from world affairs destroyed the basis for keeping the peace on which the hopes of Britain and France relied. The frenzy for imperial expansion that seized Europeans in the late nineteenth cen-

*tury had done much to destroy Europe's peace and prosperity and its dominant place in the world.*

# Expansion of European Power and the New Imperialism

The explosive developments in nineteenth-century science, technology, industry, agriculture, transportation, communication, and military weapons provided the chief sources of European power. They made it possible for a few Europeans (or Americans) to impose their will on other peoples many times their number by force or the threat of force. Institutional as well as material advantages allowed westerners to have their way. The growth of national states that commanded the loyalty, service, and resources of their inhabitants to a degree previously unknown was a Western phenomenon. It permitted the European nations to deploy their resources more effectively than ever before.

The Europeans also possessed another, less tangible, weapon. They considered their civilization and way of life to be superior to all others. This gave them a self-confidence that was often unpleasantly arrogant and fostered their expansionist mood.

The expansion of European influence was not anything new. Spain, Portugal, France, Holland, and Britain had controlled territories overseas for centuries, but by the mid-nineteenth century, only Great Britain still had extensive holdings. The first half of the century was generally hostile to colonial expansion. Even the British had been sobered by their loss of the American colonies. The French acquired Algeria and part of Indochina, and the British added territory to their holdings in Canada, India, Australia, and New Zealand. The dominant doctrine of free trade, however, opposed political interference in other lands as economically unprofitable.

Britain ruled the waves and had great commercial advantages as a result of being the first country to experience the Industrial Revolution. Therefore, the British were usually content to trade and invest overseas without annexations. Yet they were prepared to interfere forcefully if a less industrialized country placed barriers in the way of their trade. Still, at mid-century, in Britain as elsewhere, most people opposed further political or military involvement overseas.

In the last third of the century, however, the European states swiftly spread their control over perhaps 10 million square miles and 150 million people—about one-fifth of the world's land area and one-tenth of its population. During this period, European expansion went forward with great speed and participation in it came to be regarded as necessary for a great power. The movement has been called the *New Imperialism*.

## The New Imperialism

The word *imperialism* is now so loosely used that it has almost lost real meaning. It may be useful to offer a definition that might be widely accepted: "the

*Queen Victoria (r. 1837–1901) works on state papers in 1893. Note the Indian attendant. The Queen was also Empress of India, which was by far the most important possession in the British Empire. [National Portrait Gallery, London]*

policy of extending a nation's authority by territorial acquisition or by establishing economic and political hegemony over other nations."[1] That definition seems to apply equally well to ancient Egypt and Mesopotamia and to the European performance in the late nineteenth century. But there were new elements in the latter case. Previous imperialisms had taken the form either of seizing land and settling it with the conqueror's people or of establishing trading centers to exploit the resources of the dominated area. The New Imperialism did not completely abandon these devices, but it also introduced new ones.

The usual pattern of the New Imperialism was for a European nation to invest capital in a "less industrialized" country, to develop its mines and agriculture, to build railroads, bridges, harbors, and telegraph systems, and to employ great numbers of natives in the process. They thereby transformed the local economy and culture. To safeguard its investments, the dominant European state would make favorable arrangements with the local government either by loaning the rulers money or by intimidating them.

If these arrangements proved inadequate, the dominant power would establish more direct political control. Sometimes this meant full annexation and direct rule as a colony, or it could be a protectorate status, whereby the local ruler became a figurehead controlled by the dominant European state and maintained by its military power. In other instances, the European state established "spheres of influence" in which it received special commercial and legal privileges without direct political involvement.

### Motives for the New Imperialism: The Economic Interpretation

The predominant interpretation of the motives for the New Imperialism has been economic, in the form given by the English radical economist J. A. Hobson (1858–1928) and later adapted by Lenin. As Lenin put it, "Imperialism is the monopoly stage of capitalism,"[2] the last stage of a dying system. Competition inevitably eliminates inefficient capitalists and, therefore, leads to monopoly. Powerful industrial and financial capitalists soon run out of prof-

itable areas of investment in their own countries and persuade their governments to gain colonies in "less developed" countries. Here they can find higher profits from their investments, new markets for their products, and safe sources of raw materials.

Facts do not support this viewpoint, however. The European powers did invest considerable capital abroad, but not in a way that fit the model of Hobson and Lenin. Britain, for example, made heavier investments abroad before 1875 than during the next two decades. Only a small percentage of British and European investments overseas, moreover, went to their new colonies. Most capital went into other European countries or to older, well-established areas like the United States, Canada, Australia, and New Zealand. Even when investments were made in new areas, they were not necessarily put into colonies held by the investing country.

The facts are equally discouraging for those who emphasize the need for markets and raw materials. Colonies were not usually important markets for the great imperial nations, and all these states were forced to rely on areas that they did not control as sources of vital raw materials. It is not even clear that control of the new colonies was particularly profitable, though Britain, to be sure, benefited greatly from its rule of India. It is also true that some European businesspeople and politicians hoped that colonial expansion would cure the great depression of 1873–1896.

Nevertheless, as one of the leading students of the subject has said, "No one can determine whether the accounts of empire ultimately closed with a favorable cash balance."[3] That is true of the European imperial nations collectively, but it is certain that for some of them, like Italy and Germany, empire was a losing proposition. Some individuals and companies, of course, made great profits from particular colonial ventures, but such people were able to influence national policy only occasionally. Economic motives certainly played a part, but a full understanding of the New Imperialism requires a search for other motives.

### Cultural, Religious, and Social Interpretations

Advocates of imperialism gave various justifications for it. Some argued that the advanced European

[1]American Heritage Dictionary of the English Language, 3rd ed. (New York: Houghton Mifflin, 1993), p. 681.

[2]V. I. Lenin, Imperialism, the Highest Stage of Capitalism (New York: International Publishers, 1939), p. 88.

[3]D. K. Fieldhouse, The Colonial Empires (New York: Delacorte, 1966), p. 393.

# Social Darwinism and Imperialism

*One of the intellectual foundations of the New Imperialism was the doctrine of "social Darwinism," a pseudoscientific application to nations and races of Darwin's ideas about biology. The impact of social Darwinism was substantial. In the following selection, an Englishman, Karl Pearson (1857–1936), attempts to connect concepts from evolutionary theory—the struggle for survival and the survival of the fittest—with the development of human societies.*

✦ *How does the author connect Darwin's ideas with the concept of human progress? Is it reasonable to equate biological species with human societies, races, or nations? How do the author's ideas justify imperial expansion? What arguments can you make against the author's assertions?*

History shows me one way, and one way only, in which a state of civilisation has been produced, namely, the struggle of race with race, and the survival of the physically and mentally fitter race.

This dependence of progress on the survival of the fitter race, terribly black as it may seem to some of you, gives the struggle for existence its redeeming features; it is the fiery crucible out of which comes the finer metal. You may hope for a time when the sword shall be turned into the ploughshare, when American and German and English traders shall no longer compete in the markets of the world for raw materials, for their food supply, when the white man and the dark shall share the soil between them, and each till it as he lists. But, believe me, when that day comes mankind will no longer progress; there will be nothing to check the fertility of inferior stock; the relentless law of heredity will not be controlled and guided by natural selection. Man will stagnate. . . .

The path of progress is strewn with the wreck of nations; traces are everywhere to be seen of the hecatombs of inferior races, and of victims who found not the narrow way to the greater perfection. Yet these dead peoples are, in very truth, the stepping stones on which mankind has arisen to the higher intellectual and deeper emotional life of today.

*Karl Pearson,* National Life from the Standpoint of Science, *2nd ed. (Cambridge, England: Cambridge University Press, 1907), pp. 21, 26–27, 64.*

---

nations had a duty to bring the benefits of their higher culture and superior civilization to more "backward" peoples. Religious groups demanded Western governments furnish political and even military support for Christian missionaries. Some politicians and diplomats supported imperialism as a tool of social policy. In Germany, for instance, some people suggested that imperial expansion would deflect public interest away from domestic politics and social reform. Yet Germany acquired few colonies, and such considerations played little if any role in its colonial policy.

In Britain, Joseph Chamberlain (1836–1914), the colonial secretary from 1895 to 1903, argued for the empire as a source of profit and economic security that would finance a great program of domestic reform and welfare. These arguments were not important as motives for British imperial expansion because they were made well after Britain had acquired most of its empire.

Another common and apparently plausible justification for imperialism was that colonies would attract a European country's surplus population. In fact, most European emigrants went to areas not controlled by their countries, chiefly to North and South America and Australia.

## Strategic and Political Interpretations: The Scramble for Africa

Strategic and political considerations were more important in bringing on the New Imperialism. The scramble for Africa in the 1880s is one example. (See Maps 26-1 and 26-2.)

GREAT BRITAIN   Britain was the only great power with extensive overseas holdings on the eve of the scramble. The completion of the Suez Canal in 1869 made Egypt vitally important to the British because it sat astride the shortest route to India. Under Disraeli, Britain purchased a major, but not a controlling, interest in the canal in 1875. When internal troubles threatened Egypt's stability in the 1880s, the British established control. Then, to protect Egypt, they advanced into the Sudan.

FRANCE AND SMALLER NATIONS   France became involved in North Africa in 1830 by sending an expedition to attack the pirates in Algiers. The French gradually extended their control, and thousands of Europeans settled in the country. By the 1880s, France was in full control of Algeria. In 1882, to prevent Tunisia from falling into Italy's hands, France took over that country also. The French also annexed much of West Africa, the Congo, and the island of Madagascar.

Soon smaller states like Belgium, Portugal, Spain, and Italy were acquiring new African colonies or expanding old ones. By the 1890s, their intervention had compelled Britain to expand northward from the Cape of Good Hope into what is now Zimbabwe and Zambia. Britain may have had significant strategic reasons for protecting the Suez and Cape routes to India, but France and the other European nations did not. Their motives were political as well as economic, for they equated political status (Britain was the chief model) with the possession of colonies. They therefore sought colonies to buttress their own importance.

GERMANY   Bismarck appears to have pursued an imperial policy, however briefly, from cold political motives. In 1884 and 1885, Germany declared protectorates over Southwest Africa (Namibia), Togoland, the Cameroons, and East Africa (Tanzania).

LA FRANCE VA POUVOIR PORTER LIBREMENT AU MAROC LA CIVILISATION LA RICHESSE ET LA PAIX

*France's imperialism always reflected its sense of its unique cultural superiority, and the French liked to think of themselves as benevolently sharing it with the colonial people they ruled. This magazine cover from 1911 shows the symbol of France bringing civilization, peace, and prosperity to Morocco. [The Granger Collection]*

None of these places was particularly valuable or of intrinsic strategic importance. Bismarck himself had no interest in overseas colonies and once compared them to fine furs worn by impoverished Polish nobles who had no shirts underneath. His concern lay in Germany's exposed position in Europe. On one occasion he said, "My map of Africa lies in Europe. Here is Russia, and there is France, and here in the middle are we. That is my map of Africa."[4] He acquired colonies chiefly to improve Germany's diplomatic position in Europe.

[4]*Quoted in J. Remak, The Origins of World War I, 1871–1914 (New York: Holt, Rinehart & Winston, 1967), p. 5.*

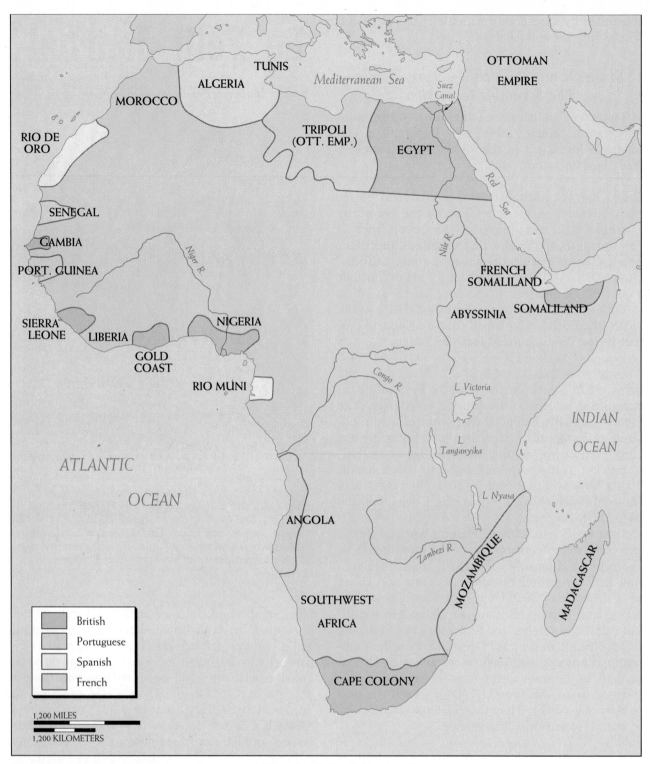

**MAP 26–1  IMPERIAL EXPANSION IN AFRICA TO 1880**  *Until the 1880s, few European countries held colonies in Africa, mostly on its fringes.*

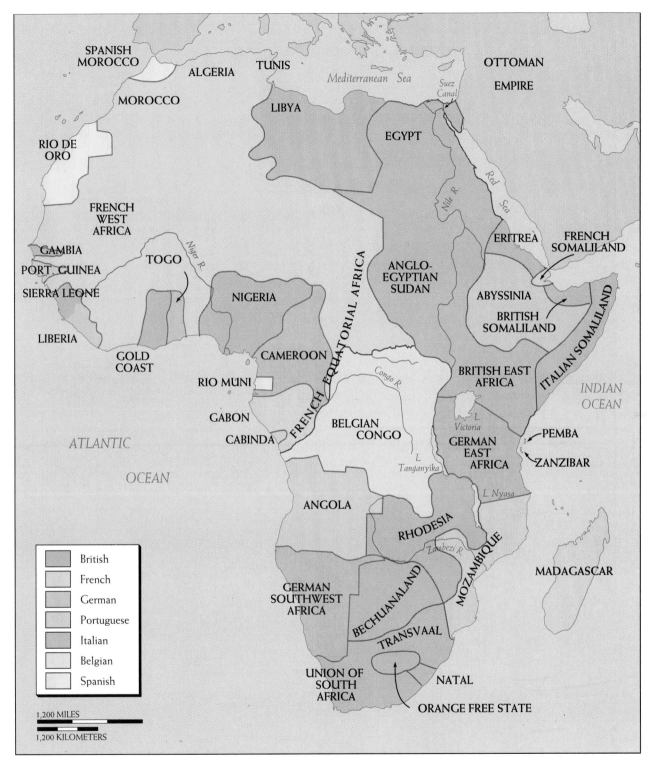

SPANISH
MOROCCO
ALGERIA          TUNIS                                    OTTOMAN
                          *Mediterranean Sea*      *Suez*   EMPIRE
MOROCCO                          LIBYA          *Canal*

RIO DE                                    EGYPT
ORO

FRENCH
WEST                                                           ERITREA      FRENCH
AFRICA                                                                      SOMALILAND
                          *Niger R.*                       ANGLO-
GAMBIA                            TOGO                      EGYPTIAN        ABYSSINIA
PORT. GUINEA                                               SUDAN                BRITISH
                                          NIGERIA                              SOMALILAND
SIERRA LEONE                                                                          ITALIAN SOMALILAND

LIBERIA                                                                        BRITISH EAST
            GOLD                    CAMEROON                                   AFRICA
            COAST                                      *Congo R.*                           INDIAN
                          RIO MUNI                                                          OCEAN
                                                      BELGIAN            *L.*
                          GABON                       CONGO             *Victoria*
*ATLANTIC*                CABINDA                                       GERMAN          PEMBA
                                                      *L.*              EAST            ZANZIBAR
    OCEAN                                              *Tanganyika*     AFRICA

                                                                       *L. Nyasa*
                          ANGOLA
                                                      RHODESIA
                                                *Zambezi R.*                    MADAGASCAR
| British                                          MOZAMBIQUE
| French              GERMAN
| German              SOUTHWEST     BECHUANALAND
| Portuguese          AFRICA
| Italian                               TRANSVAAL
| Belgian
| Spanish             UNION OF                      NATAL
                      SOUTH
1,200 MILES          AFRICA         ORANGE FREE STATE
1,200 KILOMETERS

MAP 26–2  PARTITION OF AFRICA, 1880–1914  *Before 1880 the European presence in
Africa was largely the remains of early exploration by old imperialists and did not
penetrate the heart of the continent. By 1914 the occupying powers included most
large European states; only Liberia and Abyssinia remained independent.*

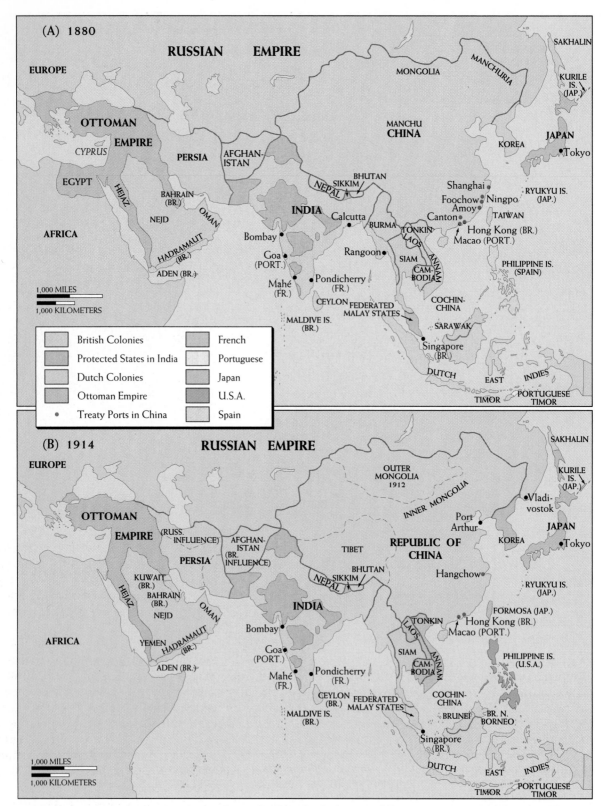

**(A) 1880**

RUSSIAN EMPIRE

EUROPE

MONGOLIA

MANCHURIA

SAKHALIN

KURILE IS. (JAP.)

OTTOMAN EMPIRE

*CYPRUS*

PERSIA

AFGHAN-ISTAN

MANCHU CHINA

KOREA

JAPAN

Tokyo

EGYPT

HEJAZ

BAHRAIN (BR.)

OMAN

NEPAL

SIKKIM

BHUTAN

Shanghai

RYUKYU IS. (JAP.)

AFRICA

NEJD

HADRAMAUT (BR.)

ADEN (BR.)

INDIA

Calcutta

Foochow

Amoy

Ningpo

Canton

TAIWAN

Bombay

BURMA

TONKIN

Hong Kong (BR.)

Macao (PORT.)

Goa (PORT.)

Rangoon

LAOS

SIAM

ANNAM

PHILIPPINE IS. (SPAIN)

Mahé (FR.)

Pondicherry (FR.)

CAM-BODIA

COCHIN-CHINA

1,000 MILES

1,000 KILOMETERS

CEYLON

FEDERATED MALAY STATES

SARAWAK

MALDIVE IS. (BR.)

Singapore (BR.)

DUTCH

EAST

INDIES

TIMOR

PORTUGUESE TIMOR

| British Colonies | French |
| Protected States in India | Portuguese |
| Dutch Colonies | Japan |
| Ottoman Empire | U.S.A. |
| • Treaty Ports in China | Spain |

**(B) 1914**

RUSSIAN EMPIRE

EUROPE

OUTER MONGOLIA 1912

INNER MONGOLIA

SAKHALIN

KURILE IS. (JAP.)

OTTOMAN EMPIRE

(RUSS. INFLUENCE)

AFGHAN-ISTAN (BR. INFLUENCE)

PERSIA

TIBET

REPUBLIC OF CHINA

Port Arthur

Vladi-vostok

JAPAN

KOREA

Tokyo

HEJAZ

KUWAIT (BR.)

BAHRAIN (BR.)

OMAN

NEPAL

SIKKIM

BHUTAN

Hangchow

RYUKYU IS. (JAP.)

AFRICA

NEJD

YEMEN

HADRAMAUT (BR.)

ADEN (BR.)

INDIA

Bombay

TONKIN

FORMOSA (JAP.)

Hong Kong (BR.)

Macao (PORT.)

Goa (PORT.)

LAOS

SIAM

ANNAM

PHILIPPINE IS. (U.S.A.)

Mahé (FR.)

Pondicherry (FR.)

CAM-BODIA

COCHIN-CHINA

CEYLON (BR.)

FEDERATED MALAY STATES

BRUNEI

BR. N. BORNEO

1,000 MILES

1,000 KILOMETERS

MALDIVE IS. (BR.)

Singapore (BR.)

DUTCH

EAST

INDIES

TIMOR

PORTUGUESE TIMOR

MAP 26–3   ASIA 1880–1914   *As in Africa, the decades before World War I saw imperialism spread widely and rapidly in Asia. Two new powers, Japan and the United States, joined the British, French, and Dutch in extending control both to islands and to the mainland and in exploiting an enfeebled China.*

918   *Toward the Modern World*

In the Spanish–American War of 1898, Spain was driven from the Western Hemisphere and Cuba came under U.S. influence. This lithograph shows the Ninth and Tenth Cavalry Regiments, composed of black Americans, engaged in the Battle of Quasimas, near Santiago, Cuba, on June 24, 1898. [The Granger Collection, New York]

He hoped that colonial expansion would divert French hostility against Germany. Also, German colonies in Africa could be used as a subtle weapon with which to persuade the British to be reasonable.

### The Irrational Element

Germany's annexations started a wild scramble by the other European powers to acquire what was left of Africa. By 1890 almost all the continent had been parceled out. Great powers and small had expanded into areas neither profitable nor strategic for reasons less calculating and rational than Bismarck's. "Empire in the modern period," D. K. Fieldhouse observed, "was the product of European power: its reward was power or the sense of power."[5]

Such motives were not new. They had been well understood by the Athenian spokesman at Melos in 416 B.C.E., whose words were reported by Thucydides: "Of the gods we believe and of men we know clearly that by a necessity of their nature where they have the power they rule."[6]

In Asia, the emergence of Japan as a great power frightened the other powers who were interested in China. (See Map 26–3.) The Russians were building a railroad across Siberia to Vladivostok and were afraid of any threat to Manchuria. Together with France and Germany, they applied diplomatic pressure that forced Japan out of the Liaotung Peninsula in northern China and its harbor, Port Arthur. All pressed feverishly for concessions in China. Fearing that China, its markets, and its investment opportunities would soon be closed to its citizens,

[5]Fieldhouse, p. 393.

[6]Thucydides, The Peloponnesian War, 5.105.2.

# Carl Peters Demands Colonies for Germany

*Germany was a late arrival in the competition for colonies. The territories still available were neither profitable nor attractive for settlement by Europeans. Carl Peters (1856–1918) was one of the growing number of Germans, who, nevertheless, were eager to acquire a colonial empire. He was the founder of German East Africa, now Tanzania. His arguments based on economic advantage and the prospects of German emigration proved to be absurd, but they provided a mask for less rational motives.*

✦ *What reasons does Peters give for Germany to seek colonies? What assumptions does he make about their advantages? Are those assumptions correct? What do you think were the most important motives for colonization to Peters and those who supported his policy?*

### Manifesto of the Society for German Colonization, April 1884

In the partition of the earth, as it has proceeded from the beginning of the fifteenth century up to our times, the German nation received nothing. All the remaining European culture-bearing peoples possess areas outside our continent where their languages and customs can take firm root and flourish. The moment that the German emigrant leaves the borders of the Reich behind him, he is a stranger sojourning on foreign soil. The German Reich, great in size and strength through its bloodily achieved unity, stands in the leading position among the continental European powers: her sons abroad must adapt themselves to nations which look upon us with either indifference or even hostility. For centuries the great stream of German emigration has been plunging down into foreign races where it is lost sight of. Germandom outside Europe has been undergoing a perpetual national decline.

This fact, so painful to national pride, also represents a great economic disadvantage for our *Volk*. Every year our Fatherland loses the capac-

the United States in 1899 proposed the Open Door Policy. This policy opposed foreign annexations in China and allowed entrepreneurs of all nations to trade there on equal terms. The support of Britain helped win acceptance of the policy by all the powers except Russia.

The United States had only recently emerged as a force in international affairs. After freeing itself of British rule and consolidating its independence during the Napoleonic wars, the Americans had busied themselves with westward expansion on the North American continent until the end of the nineteenth century. The Monroe Doctrine of 1823 had, in effect, made the entire Western Hemisphere an American protectorate. Cuba's attempt to gain independence from Spain was the spark for the new United States involvement in international affairs. Sympathy for the Cuban cause, American investments on the island, the desire for Cuban sugar, and concern over the island's strategic importance in the Caribbean all helped persuade the Americans to fight Spain.

Victory in the Spanish-American War of 1898 brought the United States an informal protectorate over Cuba and the annexation of Puerto Rico and drove Spain completely out of the Western Hemisphere. The Americans forced Spain to sell the Philippine Islands and Guam, and Germany bought the other Spanish islands in the Pacific. The Americans and the Germans also divided Samoa between them. The remaining Pacific Islands were taken by France and Britain. Hawaii had been under American influence for some time and was annexed in 1898. This burst of activity after the Spanish War made the United States an imperial and Pacific power.

Thus by the turn of the century, most of the world had come under the control of the industrialized West. The one remaining area of great vulner-

ity of approximately 200,000 Germans. The greatest amount of this capacity flows directly into the camp of our economic competitors and increases the strength of our rivals. Germany's imports of products from tropical zones originate in foreign settlements whereby many millions of German capital are lost every year to alien nations. German exports are dependent upon the discretion of foreign tariff policies. Our industry lacks an absolutely safe market for its goods because our *Volk* lacks colonies of its own.

The alleviation of this national grievance requires taking practical steps and strong action.

In recognition of this point of view, a society has been organized in Berlin with the goal of mobilizing itself for such steps and such action. The Society for German Colonization aims to undertake on its own, in a resolute and sweeping manner, carefully chosen colonization projects and thereby supplement the ranks of organizations with similar tendencies.

Its particular tasks will be:

1. to provide necessary sums of capital for colonization;
2. to seek out and lay claim to suitable districts for colonization;
3. to direct German emigrants to these regions.

Imbued as we are with the conviction that it is no longer permissible to hesitate in energetically mobilizing ourselves for this great national task, we venture to come before the German *Volk* with a plea for active support of the endeavors of our Society! The German nation has proven time and again its willingness to make sacrifices for general patriotic undertakings: may she also bring her full energies to play in the solution of this great historical task.

Every German whose heart beats for the greatness and the honor of our nation is entreated to come to the side of our Society. What is at stake is compensation for centuries of deprivation: to prove to the world that, along with the splendor of the Reich, the German *Volk* has inherited the old German national spirit of its forefathers!

*Carl Peters*, Die Grundung von Deutsch-Ostafrika [The Foundation of German East Africa] *(Berlin, 1906), pp. 43–45, as trans. in Ralph A. Austen,* Modern Imperialism *(Lexington, Mass.: D. C. Heath, 1969), pp. 62–63.*

# Emergence of the German Empire and the Alliance Systems (1873–1890)

Prussia's victories over Austria and France and its creation of a large, powerful German Empire in 1871 revolutionized European diplomacy. A vast new political unit had united the majority of Germans to form a nation of great and growing population, wealth, industrial capacity, and military power. Its sudden appearance created new problems and upset the balance of power that had been created at the Congress of Vienna. Britain and Russia ability was the Ottoman Empire. Its fate, however, was closely tied up with European developments and must be treated in that context.

retained their positions, though the latter had been weakened by the Crimean War.

Austria, however, had been severely weakened, and the forces of nationalism threatened it with disintegration. French power and prestige were badly damaged by the Franc–Prussian War and the German annexation of Alsace–Lorraine. The French were both afraid of their powerful new neighbor and resentful of their defeat and their loss of territory and France's traditional position as the dominant western European power.

## Bismarck's Leadership (1873–1890)

Until 1890 Bismarck continued to guide German policy. After 1871 he insisted that Germany was a satisfied power and wanted no further territorial gains, and he meant it. He wanted to avoid a new war that might undo his achievement. He tried to assuage French resentment by friendly relations and by supporting French colonial aspirations. He also prepared for the worst. If France could not be conciliated, it must be isolated. Bismarck sought to prevent an alliance between France and any other European power—especially Austria or Russia—that would threaten Germany with a war on two fronts.

WAR IN THE BALKANS    Bismarck's first move was to establish the Three Emperors' League in 1873. It brought together the three great conservative empires of Germany, Austria, and Russia. The league soon collapsed as a result of Austro–Russian rivalry in the Balkans that arose from the Russo–Turkish War that broke out in 1875. The tottering Ottoman Empire was held together chiefly because the European powers could not agree about how to partition it. Ottoman weakness encouraged Serbia and Montenegro to come to the aid of their fellow Slavs in Bosnia and Herzegovina when they revolted against Turkish rule. Soon the rebellion spread to Bulgaria.

Then Russia entered the fray and turned it into a major international crisis. The Russians hoped to pursue their traditional policy of expansion at Ottoman expense and especially to achieve their most cherished goal: control of Constantinople and the Dardanelles. Russian intervention also reflected the influence of the Pan-Slavic movement, which sought to unite all the Slavic peoples, even those under Austrian or Ottoman rule, under the protection of Holy Mother Russia.

The Ottoman Empire was weak and soon was forced to sue for peace. The Treaty of San Stefano of March 1878 was a Russian triumph. The Slavic states in the Balkans were freed of Ottoman rule, and Russia itself obtained territory and a large monetary indemnity. The terms of the settlement, however, alarmed the other great powers. Austria feared that the great Slavic victory and the powerful increase in Russian influence in the Balkans would threaten its own Balkan provinces. The British were alarmed both by the effect of the Russian victory on the European balance of power and by the possibility of Russian control of the Dardanelles, which would make Russia a Mediterranean power and threaten Britain's control of the Suez Canal. Disraeli was determined to resist, and British public opinion supported him. A music-hall song that became popular gave the language a new word for superpatriotism: *jingoism*.

We don't want to fight,
But by jingo if we do,
We've got the men,
We've got the ships,
We've got the money too!
The Russians will not have Constantinople!

THE CONGRESS OF BERLIN    Even before the Treaty of San Stefano, Disraeli sent a fleet to Constantinople. After the magnitude of Russia's appetite was known, Britain and Austria forced Russia to agree to an international conference at which the other great powers would review the provisions of San Stefano. The resulting Congress of Berlin met in June and July of 1878 under the presidency of Bismarck. The choice of site and presiding officer was a clear recognition of Germany's new importance and of Bismarck's claim that Germany wanted no new territory and sought to preserve the peace.

Bismarck referred to himself as an "honest broker," and the title was justified. He agreed to the congress simply because he wanted to avoid a war between Russia and Austria into which he feared Germany would be drawn with nothing to gain and much to lose. From the collapsing Ottoman Empire, he wanted nothing. "The Eastern Question," he said, "is not worth the healthy bones of a single Pomeranian musketeer."[7]

The decisions of the congress were a blow to Russian ambitions. Bulgaria, a Russian client, was reduced in size by two-thirds and was deprived of access to the Aegean Sea. Austria–Hungary was given Bosnia and Herzegovina to "occupy and administer," although those provinces remained formally under Ottoman rule. Britain received Cyprus, and France was encouraged to occupy Tunisia. These territories were compensation for the gains that Russia was permitted to keep. Germany asked for nothing but still earned Russian resentment. The Russians believed that they had saved Prussia in 1807 from complete dismemberment by Napoleon and had expected a show of German gratitude. They were bitterly disappointed, and the Three Emperors' League was dead.

All of the Balkan states were also annoyed by the Berlin settlement. Romania wanted Bessarabia, which Russia kept; Bulgaria wanted a return to the

[7]Quoted by Hajo Holborn, A History of Modern Germany, 1840–1945 (New York: Knopf, 1969), p. 239.

| 1869 | Suez Canal completed |
| 1875 | Britain gains control of Suez |
| 1882 | France controls Algeria and Tunisia |
| 1880s | Britain establishes protectorate over Egypt |
| 1884–1885 | Germany establishes protectorate over Southwest Africa (Namibia), Togoland, the Cameroons, and East Africa (Tanganyika) |
| 1898 | Spanish–American War United States acquires Puerto Rico, Philippines, and Guam; annexes Hawaiian Islands, establishes protectorate over Cuba |
| 1899 | United States proposes Open Door Policy in Far East |

Bismarck and the young Kaiser William II meet in 1888. The two disagreed over many issues, and in 1890 William dismissed the aged chancellor. [German Information Center]

borders of the Treaty of San Stefano; and Greece wanted a part of the Ottoman spoils. The major trouble spot, however, was in the south Slavic states of Serbia and Montenegro. They deeply resented the Austrian occupation of Bosnia and Herzegovina, as did many of the natives of those provinces. The south Slavic question, no less than the estrangement between Russia and Germany, was a threat to the peace of Europe.

GERMAN ALLIANCES WITH RUSSIA AND AUSTRIA   For the moment Bismarck could ignore the Balkans, but he could not ignore the breach in his eastern alliance system. With Russia alienated, he concluded a secret treaty with Austria in 1879. The resulting Dual Alliance provided that Germany and Austria would come to each other's aid if either were attacked by Russia. If either were attacked by another country, each promised at least to maintain neutrality.

The treaty was for five years and was renewed regularly until 1918. As the anchor of German policy, it was criticized at the time, and some have considered it an error in retrospect. It appeared to tie German fortunes to those of the troubled Austro-Hungarian Empire and thus to borrow trouble for Germany. And, by isolating the Russians, it pushed them to seek alliances in the West.

Bismarck was fully aware of these dangers but discounted them with good reason. He never allowed the alliance to drag Germany into Austria's Balkan quarrels. As he put it, in any alliance there is a horse and a rider, and he meant Germany to be the rider. He made it clear to the Austrians that the alliance was purely defensive and that Germany would never be a party to an attack on Russia. "For us," he said, "Balkan questions can never be a motive for war."[8]

Bismarck believed that monarchical, reactionary Russia would not seek an alliance either with republican, revolutionary France or with increasingly democratic Britain. In fact, he expected the news of the Austro–German negotiations to frighten Russia into seeking closer relations with Germany, and he was right. Russian diplomats soon approached him, and by 1881 he had concluded a renewal of the Three Emperors' League on a firmer basis. The three powers promised to maintain friendly neutrality in case any of them was

[8]Quoted in Remak, p. 14.

attacked by a fourth power. Other clauses included the right of Austria to annex Bosnia–Herzegovina whenever it wished and the support of all three powers for closing the Dardanelles to all nations in case of war.

The agreement allayed German fears of a Russian–French alliance and Russian fears of a combination of Austria and Britain against it, of Britain's fleet sailing into the Black Sea, and of a hostile combination of Germany and Austria. Most importantly, the agreement aimed to resolve the conflicts in the Balkans between Austria and Russia. Though it did not end such conflicts, it was a significant step toward peace.

THE TRIPLE ALLIANCE  In 1882 Italy, ambitious for colonial expansion and bothered by the French occupation of Tunisia, asked to join the Dual Alliance. The provisions of its entry were defensive and were directed against France. At this point, Bismarck's policy was a complete success. He was allied with three of the great powers and friendly with the other, Great Britain, which held aloof from all alliances. France was isolated and no threat. Bismarck's diplomacy was a great achievement, but an even greater challenge was to maintain this complicated system of secret alliances in the face of the continuing rivalries among Germany's allies. Despite another Balkan war that broke out in 1885 and that again estranged Austria and Russia, he succeeded.

Although the Three Emperors' League lapsed, the Triple Alliance (Germany, Austria, and Italy) was renewed for another five years. To restore German relations with Russia, Bismarck negotiated the Reinsurance Treaty of 1887, in which both powers promised to remain neutral if either was attacked. All seemed smooth, but a change in the German monarchy soon upset Bismarck's arrangements.

In 1888 William II (r. 1888–1918) came to the German throne. He was twenty-nine years old, ambitious, and impetuous. He was imperious by temperament and believed that he ruled by divine right. He had suffered an injury at birth that left him with a withered left arm. He compensated for this disability with vigorous exercise, a military bearing and outlook, and an often embarrassingly bombastic rhetoric.

Like many Germans of his generation, William II was filled with a sense of Germany's destiny as the leading power of Europe. He wanted to achieve

Admiral Alfred von Tirpitz (1849–1930). Tirpitz was responsible for building the German navy into a force capable of challenging the Royal Navy of Great Britain, reflecting Kaiser William II's desire to increase Germany's prominence among the great powers of Europe. [Bildarchiv Preussischer Kulturbesitz]

recognition of at least equality with Britain, the land of his mother and of his grandmother, Queen Victoria. To achieve a "place in the sun," he and his contemporaries wanted a navy and colonies like Britain's. These aims, of course, ran counter to Bismarck's limited continental policy. When William argued for a navy as a defense against a British landing in North Germany, Bismarck replied, "If the British should land on our soil, I should have them arrested." This was only one example of the great distance between the young emperor, or Kaiser, and his chancellor. In 1890 William used a disagreement over domestic policy to dismiss Bismarck.

As long as Bismarck held power, Germany was secure, and there was peace among the great European powers. Although he made mistakes and was not always successful, there was much to admire in his understanding and management of international relations in the hard world of reality. He had a clear and limited idea of his nation's goals. He resisted pressures for further expansion with few and insignificant exceptions. He understood and used the full range of diplomatic weapons: appeasement and deterrence, threats and promises, secrecy and openness. He understood the needs and hopes of other countries and, where possible, tried to help them satisfy them or used them to his own advantage. His system of alliances created a stalemate in the Balkans and ensured German security.

During Bismarck's time, Germany was a force for European peace and was increasingly understood to be so. This position would not, of course, have been possible without its great military power. It also required, however, the leadership of a statesman who was willing and able to exercise restraint and who understood what his country needed and what was possible.

## Forging of the Triple Entente (1890–1907)

FRANCO-RUSSIAN ALLIANCE   Almost immediately after Bismarck's retirement, his system of alliances collapsed. His successor was General Leo von Caprivi (1831–1899), who had once asked, "What kind of jackass will dare to be Bismarck's successor?" Caprivi refused the Russian request to renew the Reinsurance Treaty, in part because he felt incompetent to continue Bismarck's complicated policy and in part because he wished to draw Germany closer to Britain. The results were unfortunate, as Britain remained aloof and Russia was alienated.

Even Bismarck had assumed that ideological differences would prevent a Franco–Russian alliance. Political isolation and the need for foreign capital, however, unexpectedly drove the Russians toward France. The French, who were even more isolated, were glad to encourage their investors to pour capital into Russia if it would help produce an alliance and security against Germany. In 1894 a defensive Franco–Russian alliance against Germany was signed.

BRITAIN AND GERMANY   Britain now became the key to the international situation. Colonial rival-ries pitted the British against the Russians in central Asia and against the French in Africa. Traditionally, Britain had also opposed Russian control of Constantinople and the Dardanelles and French control of the Low Countries. There was no reason to think that Britain would soon become friendly to its traditional rivals or abandon its accustomed friendliness toward the Germans.

Yet within a decade of William II's accession, Germany had become the enemy in British minds. Before the turn of the century, popular British thrillers about imaginary wars portrayed the French as the invader; after the turn of the century, the enemy was always Germany. This remarkable transformation has often been attributed to economic rivalry between Germany and Britain, in which Germany made vast strides to challenge and even overtake British production in various materials and markets. Certainly, Germany made such gains and many Britons resented them. Yet the problem was not a serious cause of hostility, and it waned during the first decade of the century. The real problem lay in the foreign and naval policies of the German emperor and his ministers.

William II admired Britain's colonial empire and mighty fleet. At first, Germany tried to win the British over to the Triple Alliance, but when Britain clung to its "splendid isolation," German policy changed. The idea was to demonstrate Germany's worth as an ally by withdrawing support and even making trouble for Britain. This odd manner of gaining an ally reflected the Kaiser's confused feelings toward Britain, which mixed dislike and jealousy with admiration. These feelings were shared by many Germans, especially in the intellectual community. Like William, they were eager for Germany to pursue a "world policy" rather than Bismarck's limited one that confined German interests to Europe. They, too, saw England as the barrier to German ambitions. Their influence in the schools, the universities, and the press guaranteed popular approval of actions and statements hostile to Britain.

The Germans began to exert pressure against Britain in Africa by barring British attempts to build a railroad from Capetown to Cairo. They also openly sympathized with the Boers of South Africa in their resistance to British expansion. In 1896 William insulted the British by sending a congratulatory telegram to Paul Kruger (1825–1904), president of the Transvaal, for repulsing a British raid "without having to appeal to friendly powers for assistance," i.e., Germany.

In 1898 William began to realize his dream of a German navy with the passage of a naval law providing for nineteen battleships. In 1900 a second law doubled that figure. The architect of the new navy was Admiral Alfred von Tirpitz (1849–1930), who openly proclaimed that Germany's naval policy was aimed at Britain. His "risk" theory argued that Germany could build a fleet strong enough, not to defeat the British, but to do enough damage to make the British navy inferior to that of other powers like France or the United States. The theory was, in fact, absurd because as Germany's fleet became menacing, the British would certainly build enough ships to maintain their advantage, and Britain had greater financial resources than Germany.

The naval policy, therefore, was doomed to failure. Its main achievements were to waste German resources and to begin a great naval race with Britain. Eventually, the threat posed by the German navy so antagonized and alarmed British opinion that the British abandoned their traditional attitudes and policies.

At first, however, Britain was not unduly concerned. The British were embarrassed by the general hostility of world opinion during the Boer War (1899–1902), in which their great empire crushed a rebellion by South African farmers, and their isolation no longer seemed so splendid. The Germans had acted with restraint during the war. Between 1898 and 1901, Joseph Chamberlain, the colonial secretary, made several attempts to conclude an alliance with Germany. The Germans, confident that a British alliance with France or Russia was impossible, refused and expected the British to make greater concessions in the future.

THE ENTENTE CORDIALE   The first breach in Britain's isolation came in 1902, when it concluded an alliance with Japan to defend British interests in the Far East against Russia. Next, Britain abandoned its traditional antagonism toward France and in 1904 concluded a series of agreements with the French, collectively called the *Entente Cordiale*. It was not a formal treaty and had no military provisions, but it settled all outstanding colonial differences between the two nations. In particular, Britain gave France a free hand in Morocco in return for French recognition of British control over Egypt. The Entente Cordiale was a long step toward aligning the British with Germany's great potential enemy.

Britain's new relationship with France was surprising, but in 1904 hardly anyone believed that the British whale and the Russian bear would ever come together. The Russo-Japanese War of 1904–1905 made such a development seem even less likely because Britain was allied with Russia's enemy. But Britain had behaved with restraint, and the Russians were chastened by their unexpected and humiliating defeat. The defeat also led to the Russian Revolution of 1905. Although the revolution was put down, it weakened Russia and reduced British apprehensions about Russian power. The British were also concerned that Russia might again drift into the German orbit.

THE FIRST MOROCCAN CRISIS   At this point, Germany decided to test the new understanding between Britain and France and to press for colonial gains. In March 1905, Emperor William II landed at Tangier, made a speech in favor of Moroccan independence, and by implication asserted Germany's right to participate in Morocco's destiny. This was a challenge to France. Germany's chancellor, Prince Bernhard von Bülow (1849–1929), intended to show France how weak it was and how little support it could expect from Britain. He also hoped to gain significant colonial concessions.

The Germans demanded an international conference to show their power more dramatically. The conference met in 1906 at Algeciras in Spain. Austria sided with its German ally, but Spain, which also had claims in Morocco, Italy, and the United States, voted with Britain and France. The Germans had overplayed their hand, receiving trivial concessions, and the French position in Morocco was confirmed. German bullying had, moreover, driven Britain and France closer together. In the face of the threat of a German attack on France, Sir Edward Grey (1862–1933), the British foreign secretary, without making a firm commitment, authorized conversations between the British and French general staffs. Their agreements became morally binding as the years passed. By 1914 French and British military and naval plans were so mutually dependent that the two countries were effectively, if not formally, allies.

BRITISH AGREEMENT WITH RUSSIA   Britain's fear of Germany's growing naval power, its concern over German ambitions in the Near East (as represented by the German-sponsored plan to build a railroad from Berlin to Baghdad), and its closer relations with France made it desirable for Britain to become more friendly with France's ally, Russia. With French support, the British concluded an agreement with Russia in 1907 much like the Entente Cordiale with France. It settled Russo–British quarrels in central Asia and opened the door for wider cooperation. The Triple Entente, an informal, but powerful association of Britain, France, and Russia, was now ranged against the Triple Alliance. Italy was an unreliable ally, however, which meant that Germany and Austria–Hungary were encircled by two great land powers and Great Britain.

William II and his ministers had turned Bismarck's nightmare of the prospect of a two-front war with France and Russia into a reality. They had made it more horrible by adding Britain to their foes. The equilibrium that Bismarck had worked so hard to achieve was destroyed. Britain would no longer support Austria in restraining Russian ambitions in the Balkans. Germany, increasingly alarmed by a sense of being encircled, was less willing to restrain the Austrians for fear of alienating them, too. In the Dual Alliance of Germany and Austria, it had become less clear who was the horse and who was the rider.

Bismarck's alliance system had been intended to maintain peace, but the new alliance increased the risk of war and made the Balkans a likely spot for it to break out. Bismarck's diplomacy had left France isolated and impotent; the new arrangement associated France with the two greatest powers in Europe besides Germany. The Germans could rely only on Austria, and Austria's troubles made it less likely to provide aid than to need it.

# World War I

## The Road to War (1908–1914)

The weak Ottoman Empire still controlled the central strip of the Balkan Peninsula running west from Constantinople to the Adriatic. North and south of it were the independent states of Romania, Serbia, and Greece, as well as Bulgaria, technically still part of the empire but legally autonomous and practically independent. The Austro–Hungarian Empire included Croatia and Slovenia and since 1878 had "occupied and administered" Bosnia and Herzegovina.

Except for the Greeks and the Romanians, most of the inhabitants of the Balkans spoke variants of the same Slavic language and felt a cultural and historical kinship with one another. For centuries they had been ruled by Austrians, Hungarians, or Turks, and the growing nationalism that characterized late-nineteenth-century Europe made many of them eager for independence. The more radical among them longed for a union of the south Slavic, or Yugoslav, peoples in a single nation. They looked to independent Serbia as the center of the new nation and hoped to detach all the Slavic provinces (especially Bosnia, which bordered on Serbia) from Austria. Serbia believed that its destiny was to unite the Slavs at the expense of Austria, as Piedmont had united the Italians and Prussia the Germans.

In 1908 a group of modernizing reformers called the *Young Turks* brought about a revolution in the Ottoman Empire. Their actions threatened to revive the life of the empire and to interfere with the plans of the European jackals preparing to pounce on the Ottoman corpse. These events brought on the first of a series of Balkan crises that would eventually lead to war.

THE BOSNIAN CRISIS   In 1908 the Austrian and Russian governments decided to act quickly before Turkey became strong enough to resist. They struck a bargain in which Russia agreed to support the Austrian annexation of Bosnia and Herzegovina, in return for Austrian backing for opening the Dardanelles to Russian warships.

Austria, however, declared the annexation before the Russians could act. The British and French, eager for the favor of the Young Turks, refused to agree to the Russian demand for the opening of the Dardenelles. The Russians were humiliated and furious but too weak to do anything but protest. Their "little brothers," the Serbs, were frustrated and angered by the Austrian annexation of Bosnia, which they had hoped one day to annex themselves.

The Germans had not been warned in advance of Austria's plans and were unhappy because the action threatened their relations with Russia. Germany felt so dependent on the Dual Alliance, however, that it nevertheless assured Austria of its support. Austria had been given a free hand, and to some extent, German policy was being made in Vienna. It was a dangerous precedent. Also, the failure of Britain and France to support Russia strained the Triple Entente. This made it harder for them to oppose Russian interests in the future if they were to keep Russian friendship.

THE SECOND MOROCCAN CRISIS The second Moroccan crisis, in 1911, emphasized the French and British need for mutual support. When France sent an army to Morocco to put down a rebellion, Germany took the opportunity to "protect German interests" there as a means of extorting colonial concessions in the French Congo. To add force to their demands, the Germans sent the gunboat *Panther* to the Moroccan port of Agadir, purportedly to protect German citizens there. Once again, as in 1905, the Germans went too far. The *Panther's* visit to Agadir provoked a strong reaction in Britain. For some time Anglo–German relations had been growing worse, chiefly because of the intensification of the naval race. In 1907 Germany had built its first new dreadnought, a new type of battleship that Britain had launched in 1906. In 1908 Germany had passed still another naval law that accelerated the challenge to British naval supremacy.

These actions frightened and angered the British because they threatened the security of the island kingdom and its empire. The German actions also forced Britain to increase taxes to pay for new armaments just when the Liberal government in Britain was launching its expensive program of social legislation. Negotiations failed to persuade William II and Tirpitz to slow down naval construction.

In this atmosphere, the British heard of the *Panther's* arrival in Morocco. They wrongly believed that the Germans meant to turn Agadir into a naval base on the Atlantic. The crisis passed when France yielded some insignificant bits of the Congo and Germany recognized the French protectorate over Morocco. The main result was to increase British fear and hostility and to draw Britain closer to France. Specific military plans were formulated for a British expeditionary force to defend France in case of German attack, and the British and French navies agreed to cooperate. Without any formal treaty, the German naval construction and the Agadir crisis had turned the Entente Cordiale into an alliance, de facto. If Germany attacked France, Britain must defend the French, for its own security was inextricably tied up with that of France.

WAR IN THE BALKANS The second Moroccan crisis also provoked another crisis in the Balkans. Italy sought to gain colonies and to take its place among the great powers. It wanted Libya, which, though worth little before the discovery of oil in the 1950s, was at least available. Italy feared that the recognition of the French protectorate in Morocco would encourage France also to move into Libya. So, in 1911, Italy attacked the Ottoman Empire to preempt the French, defeated the faltering Turks, and forced Turkey to cede Libya and the Dodecanese Islands in the Aegean. The Italian victory demonstrated Turkish weakness and encouraged the Balkan states to try their luck. In 1912 Bulgaria, Greece, Montenegro, and Serbia jointly attacked the Ottoman Empire and won easily. (See Map 26–4.) After this First Balkan War, the victors fell out among themselves over the division of Macedonia, and in 1913 a Second Balkan War erupted. This time Turkey and Romania joined the other states against Bulgaria and stripped away much of what the Bulgarians had gained in 1878 and 1912.

After the First Balkan War, the alarmed Austrians were determined to limit Serbian gains and especially to prevent the Serbs from gaining a port on the Adriatic. This policy meant keeping Serbia out of Albania, but the Russians backed the Serbs, and tensions mounted. An international conference sponsored by Britain in early 1913 resolved the matter in Austria's favor and called for an independent kingdom of Albania. Austria, however, felt humiliated by the public airing of Serbian demands and the Serbs defied the powers and continued to occupy parts of Albania. Under Austrian pressure they eventually withdrew, but they returned to Albania in September 1913, after the Second Balkan War. Finally, in mid-October, Austria unilaterally issued an ultimatum, and Serbia again withdrew its forces from Albania.

During this crisis, many people in Austria had wanted an all-out attack on Serbia to remove its threat to the empire once and for all. Those demands had been resisted by Emperor Francis Joseph and the heir to the throne, Archduke Francis Ferdinand. At the same time, Pan-Slavic sentiment in Russia pressed Tsar Nicholas II to take a firm stand, but Russia once again let Austria have its way in its confrontation with Serbia. Throughout the crisis, Britain, France, Italy, and Germany restrained their allies, although each worried about seeming too reluctant to help its friends.

The lessons learned from this crisis of 1913 profoundly influenced behavior in the final crisis in 1914. The Russians had once again, as in 1908, been

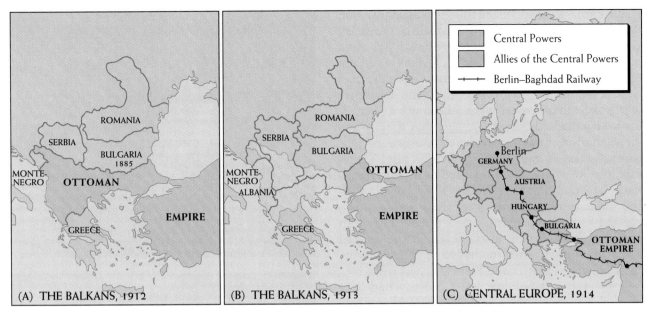

MAP 26-4  THE BALKANS, 1912–1913  *Two maps show the Balkans before (a) and after (b) the two Balkan wars; note the Ottoman retreat. In (c) we see the geographical relationship of the Central Powers and their Bulgarian and Turkish allies.*

embarrassed by their passivity; and their allies were more reluctant to restrain them again. The Austrians were embarrassed by the results of accepting an international conference and were determined not to do it again. They had gotten better results from a threat of direct force; they and their German allies did not miss the lesson.

## Sarajevo and the Outbreak of War (June–August 1914)

THE ASSASSINATION  On June 28, 1914, a young Bosnian nationalist shot and killed Archduke Francis Ferdinand, heir to the Austrian throne, and his wife as they drove in an open car through the Bosnian capital of Sarajevo. The assassin was a member of a conspiracy hatched by a political terrorist society called *Union or Death*, better known as the *Black Hand*. The chief of intelligence of the Serbian army's general staff had helped plan and prepare the crime. Though his role was not actually known at the time, it was generally believed throughout Europe that Serbian officials were involved. The glee of the Serbian press after the assassination lent support to that belief.

The archduke was not popular in Austria, and his funeral evoked few signs of grief. He had been known to favor a form of federal government for Austria that would have raised the status of the Slavs in the empire. This position alienated the conservatives among the Habsburg officials and the Hungarians. It also alarmed radical Yugoslav nationalists, who feared that Habsburg reform might end their dream of an independent south Slav state.

GERMANY AND AUSTRIA'S RESPONSE  News of the assassination produced outrage and condemnation everywhere in Europe except in Serbia. To those Austrians who had long favored an attack on Serbia as a solution to the empire's Slavic problem, the opportunity seemed irresistible. But it was never easy for the Dual Monarchy to make a decision. Conrad von Hötzendorf (1852–1925), chief of the Austrian general staff, urged an attack as he had often done before. Count Stefan Tisza (1861–1918), speaking for Hungary, resisted. Count Leopold von Berchtold (1863–1942), the Austro–Hungarian foreign minister, felt the need for strong action, but he knew that German support would be required in the likely event that Russia should decide to intervene to protect Serbia. He also knew that nothing could be done without Tisza's approval and that only German support could persuade the Hungarians to accept the policy of war. The question of peace or war against Serbia, therefore, had to be answered in Berlin.

William II and Chancellor Theobald von Bethmann-Hollweg (1856–1921) readily promised German support for an attack on Serbia. It has often been said that they gave the Austrians a "blank check," but their message was more specific than that. They urged the Austrians to move swiftly while the other powers were still angry at Serbia. They also made the Austrians feel that they would view a failure to act as evidence of Austria–Hungary's weakness and uselessness as an ally. Therefore, the Austrians never wavered in their determination to make war on Serbia. They hoped, with the protection of Germany, to fight Serbia alone, but they were prepared to risk a general European conflict. The Germans also knew that they risked a general war, but they too hoped to "localize" the fight between Austria and Serbia.

Some scholars believe that Germany had long been plotting war, and some even think that a specific plan for war in 1914 was set in motion as early as 1912. The vast body of evidence on the crisis of 1914, however, gives little support to such notions. The German leaders plainly reacted to a crisis that they had not foreseen and just as plainly made decisions in response to events. The fundamental decision to support Austria, however, made war difficult if not impossible to avoid. That decision was made by the emperor and chancellor without significant consultation with either their military or diplomatic advisers.

William II appears to have reacted violently to the assassination. He was moved by his friendship for the archduke and by outrage at an attack on royalty. A different provocation would probably not have moved him so much. Bethmann-Hollweg was less emotional but under severe pressure. To resist the decision would have meant flatly opposing the emperor. The powerful military circles favored by William suspected the chancellor of being "soft." It would have been difficult for him to take a conciliatory position.

Moreover, Bethmann-Hollweg, like many other Germans, feared for the future. Russia was recovering its strength and would reach a military peak in 1917. The Triple Entente was growing closer and more powerful, and Germany's only reliable ally was Austria. The chancellor recognized the danger of supporting Austria, but he believed it to be even more dangerous to withhold that support. If Austria did not crush Serbia, it would soon collapse before the onslaught of Slavic nationalism defended

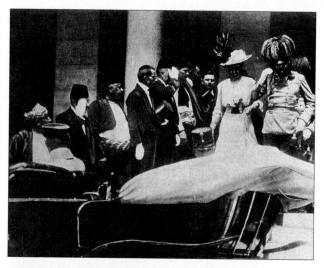

*Above: The Austrian Archduke Francis Ferdinand and his wife in Sarajevo on June 28, 1914. Later in the day the royal couple were assassinated by young revolutionaries trained and supplied in Serbia, igniting the crisis that led to World War I. Below: Moments after the assassination the Austrian police captured one of the assassins. [Brown Brothers]*

by Russia. If Germany did not defend its ally, the Austrians might look elsewhere for help. His policy was one of "calculated risk."

Unfortunately, the calculations proved to be incorrect. Bethmann-Hollweg hoped that the Austrians would strike swiftly and present the powers with a fait accompli while the outrage of the assassination was still fresh. And he felt that German support would deter Russian involvement. Failing that, he was prepared for a continental war against France and Russia. This policy depended on British neutrality; and the German chancellor convinced himself that the British could be persuaded to stand aloof.

The Austrians, however, were slow to act. They did not even deliver their deliberately unacceptable ultimatum to Serbia until July 24, when the general hostility toward Serbia had begun to subside. Serbia further embarrassed the Austrians by returning so soft and conciliatory an answer that even the mercurial German emperor thought it removed all reason for war. But the Austrians were determined not to turn back. On July 28, they declared war on Serbia, even though the army would not be ready to attack until mid-August.

THE TRIPLE ENTENTE'S RESPONSE  The Russians, previously so often forced to back off, responded angrily to the Austrian demands on Serbia. The most conservative elements of the Russian government opposed war, fearing that it would lead to revolution as it had in 1905. But nationalists, Pan-Slavs, and most of the politically conscious classes in general demanded action. The government responded by ordering partial mobilization, against Austria only. This policy was militarily impossible, but its intention was to put diplomatic pressure on Austria to refrain from attacking Serbia.

Mobilization of any kind, however, was a dangerous weapon because it was generally understood to be equivalent to an act of war. It was especially alarming to the German general staff. The possibility that the Russians might start mobilization before the Germans could move would upset the delicate timing of Germany's only battle plan, the Schlieffen Plan, which required an attack on France before the Russians were ready to act, and would put Germany in great danger. From this point on, the general staff pressed for German mobilization

## The Austrian Ambassador Gets a "Blank Check" from the Kaiser

*It was at a meeting at Potsdam on July 5, 1914 that the Austrian ambassador received from the Kaiser assurance that Germany would support Austria in the Balkans, even at the risk of war.*

- ✦ *Why did the Austrians need to consult the Germans?*
- ✦ *How did the Kaiser's response compare with German policy in recent crises?*
- ✦ *Was the check "written" by the Kaiser really blank?*
- ✦ *How important for the coming of the war was this meeting?*

After lunch, when I again called attention to the seriousness of the situation, the Kaiser authorised me to inform our gracious Majesty that we might in this case, as in all other, rely upon Germany's full support. He must, as he said before, first hear what the Imperial Chancellor has to say, but he did not doubt in the least that Herr von Bethmann Hollweg would agree with him. Especially as far as our action against Serbia was concerned. But it was his (Kaiser Wilhelm's) opinion that this action must not be delayed. Russia's attitude will no doubt be hostile, but to this he had been for years prepared, and should a war between Austria–Hungary and Russia be unavoidable, we might be convinced that Germany, our old faithful ally, would stand at our side. Russia at the present time was in no way prepared for war, and would think twice before it appealed to arms. But it will certainly set other powers on to the Triple Alliance and add fuel to the fire in the Balkans. He understands perfectly well that His Apostolic Majesty in his well-known love of peace would be reluctant to march into Serbia; but if we had really recognised the necessity of warlike action against Serbia, he (Kaiser Wilhelm) would regret if we did not make use of the present moment, which is all in our favour.

Outbreak of the World War: German Documents Collected by Karl Kautsky, Max Montgelas and Walther Schücking (eds.) (New York: Carnegie Endowment for International Peace, 1924), p. 76.

and war. The pressure of military necessity soon became irresistible.

France and Britain were not eager for war. France's president and prime minister were on their way back from a visit to Russia when the crisis flared on July 24. The Austrians had, in fact, timed their ultimatum precisely so that these two men would be at sea when it was delivered to the Serbs. Had they been in Paris, they might have tried to restrain the Russians. The French ambassador to Russia gave the Russians the same assurances, however, that Germany had given its ally. The British worked hard to resolve the crisis by traditional means: a conference of the powers. Austria, still smarting from its humiliation after the London Conference of 1913, would not hear of it. The Germans privately supported the Austrians but publicly took on a conciliatory tone in the hope of keeping the British neutral.

Soon, however, Bethmann-Hollweg came to realize what he should have known from the first. If Germany attacked France, Britain must fight. Until July 30, his public appeals to Austria for restraint were a sham. Thereafter, he sincerely tried to persuade the Austrians to negotiate and avoid a general war, but it was too late. The Austrians could not turn back without losing their own self-respect and the respect of the Germans.

On July 30, Austria ordered mobilization against Russia. Bethmann-Hollweg resisted the enormous pressure to mobilize, not because he had any further hope of avoiding war but because he wanted Russia to mobilize against Germany first and appear to be the aggressor. Only in that way could he win the support of the German nation for war, especially the support of pacifist Social Democrats. His luck was good for a change. The news of Russian general mobilization came only minutes before Germany would have mobilized in any case. The Schlieffen Plan went into effect. (See Map 26–5.) The Germans occupied Luxembourg on August 1 and invaded Belgium, which resisted, on August 3. The invasion of Belgium violated the treaty of 1839 in which the British had joined the other powers in guaranteeing Belgian neutrality. This factor undermined the considerable sentiment in Britain for neutrality and united the nation against Germany. Germany then invaded France, and on August 4, Britain declared war on Germany.

The Great War had begun. As Sir Edward Grey, the British foreign secretary, put it, the lights were

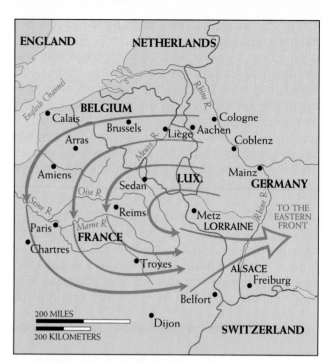

MAP 26–5 THE SCHLIEFFEN PLAN OF 1905 *Germany's grand strategy for quickly winning the war against France in 1914 is shown by the wheeling arrows on the map. The crushing blows at France were, in the original plan, to be followed by the release of troops for use against Russia on Germany's eastern front. The plan, however, was not adequately implemented, and the war on the Western Front became a long contest in place.*

going out all over Europe. They would come on again, but Europe would never be the same.

## Strategies and Stalemate: 1914–1917

Throughout Europe, jubilation greeted the outbreak of war. No general war had been fought since Napoleon, and few understood the horrors of modern warfare. The dominant memory was of Bismarck's swift and decisive campaigns, in which the costs and casualties were light and the rewards great. After the repeated crises of recent years and the fears and resentments they had created, war came as a release of tension. The popular press had increased public awareness of and interest in foreign affairs and had fanned the flames of patriotism. The prospect of war moved even a rational man of science like Sigmund Freud to say, "My whole libido goes out to Austria–Hungary."[9]

[9]*Quoted in Remak, p. 134.*

| | POPULATION (TOTAL) | SOLDIERS POTENTIALLY AVAILABLE | MILITARY EXPENDITURES (1913-1914 MILLIONS OF $) | BATTLESHIPS IN SERVICE OR BEING BUILT | CRUISERS | SUBMARINES | MERCHANT SHIPS (TONS) |
|---|---|---|---|---|---|---|---|
| GREAT BRITAIN | Overseas Emp. 390 Million 45,000,000 | 711,000 | 250,000,000 | 64 | 121 | 64 | 20,000,000 |
| FRANCE | Overseas Emp. 58 Million 40,000,000 | 1,250,000 | 185,000,000 | 28 | 34 | 73 | 2,000,000 |
| ITALY | Overseas Emp. 2 Million 35,000,000 | 750,000 | 50,000,000 | 14 | 22 | 12 | 1,750,000 |
| RUSSIA | 164,000,000 | 1,200,000 | 335,000,000 | 16 | 14 | 29 | 750,000 |
| BELGIUM | 7,500,000 | 180,000 | 13,750,000 | | | | |
| ROMANIA | 7,500,000 | 420,000 | 15,000,000 | | | | |
| GREECE | 5,000,000 | 120,000 | 3,750,000 | | | | |
| SERBIA | 5,000,000 | 195,000 | 5,250,000 | | | | |
| MONTENEGRO | 500,000 | | | | | | |
| UNITED STATES | 92,000,000 | 150,000 | 150,000,000 | 37 | 35 | 25 | 4,500,000 |
| GERMANY | 65,000,000 | 2,200,000 | 300,000,000 | 40 | 57 | 23 | 5,000,000 |
| AUSTRIA-HUNGARY | 50,000,000 | 810,000 | 110,000,000 | 16 | 12 | 6 | 1,000,000 |
| OTTOMAN EMPIRE | 20,000,000 | 360,000 | 40,000,000 | | | | |
| BULGARIA | 4,500,000 | 340,000 | 5,500,000 | | | | |

FIGURE 26–1  *Relative strengths of the combatants in World War I.*

Both sides expected to take the offensive, force a battle on favorable ground, and win a quick victory. The Triple Entente powers—or the Allies, as they called themselves—held superiority in numbers and financial resources as well as command of the sea. (See Figure 26-1.) Germany and Austria, the Central Powers, had the advantages of internal lines of communication and of having launched their attack first.

After 1905 Germany's only war plan was the one developed by Count Alfred von Schlieffen (1833–1913), chief of the German general staff from 1891 to 1906. (See Map 26-5.) It aimed at going around the French defenses by sweeping through Belgium to the Channel, then wheeling to the south and east to envelop the French and to crush them against the German fortresses in Lorraine. The secret of success lay in making the right wing of the advancing German army immensely strong and deliberately weakening the left opposite the French frontier. The weakness of the left was meant to draw the French into attacking the wrong place while the war was decided on the German right. As one keen military analyst has explained:

It would be like a revolving door—if a man pressed heavily on one side, the other side would spring round and strike him in the back. Here lay the real subtlety of the plan, not in the mere geographical detour.[10]

In the east, the Germans planned to stand on the defensive against Russia until France had been

[10]B. H. Liddell Hart, The Real War, 1914–1918 (Boston: Little, Brown, 1964; first published in 1930), p. 47.

crushed, a task they thought would take only six weeks.

The apparent risk, besides the violation of Belgian neutrality and the consequent alienation of Britain, lay in weakening the German defenses against a direct attack across the frontier. The strength of German fortresses and the superior firepower of German howitzers made that risk more theoretical than real. The true danger was that the German striking force on the right through Belgium would not be powerful enough to make the swift progress vital to success. Schlieffen is said to have died uttering the words, "It must come to a fight. Only make the right wing strong."

The execution of his plan, however, was left to Helmuth von Moltke (1848–1916), the nephew of Bismarck's most effective general. Despite Schlieffen's warning, Moltke (chief of staff 1906–1914) added divisions to the left wing and even weakened

the Russian front for the same purpose. As a result of this hesitant strategy and of theoretical mistakes by German commanders in the field, the Schlieffen Plan failed by a narrow margin.

THE WAR IN THE WEST   The French had also put their faith in the offensive, but with less reason than the Germans. They badly underestimated the numbers and effectiveness of the German reserves and overestimated the importance of the courage and spirit of their own troops. Courage and spirit, however, could not win against machine guns and heavy artillery. The French offensive on Germany's western frontier failed totally. This defeat probably was preferable to a partial success because it released troops for use against the main German army. As a result, the French and the British were able to stop the German advance on Paris at the Battle of the Marne in September 1914. (See Maps 26–6 and 26–7.)

Thereafter, the nature of the war in the west became one of position instead of movement. Both sides dug in behind a wall of trenches protected by barbed wire that stretched from the North Sea to Switzerland. Strategically placed machine-gun nests made assaults difficult and dangerous. Both sides, nonetheless, attempted massive attacks preceded by artillery bombardments of unprecedented and horrible force and duration. Still the defense was always able to recover and to bring up reserves fast enough to prevent a breakthrough.

Sometimes assaults that cost hundreds of thousands of lives produced advances of only hundreds of yards. The introduction of poison gas to resolve the problem proved ineffective. In 1916 the British introduced the tank, which eventually proved to be the answer to the machine gun, but the Allied command was slow to understand this, and until the end of the war, defense was supreme. For three years after its establishment, the western front moved only a few miles in either direction.

THE WAR IN THE EAST   In the east, the war began auspiciously for the Allies. The Russians advanced into Austrian territory and inflicted heavy casualties, but Russian incompetence and German energy soon reversed the situation. A junior German officer, Erich Ludendorff (1865–1937), under the command of the elderly General Paul von Hindenburg (1847–1934), destroyed or captured an entire Russian army at the Battle of Tannenberg and defeated another one at the Masurian Lakes. In 1915 the

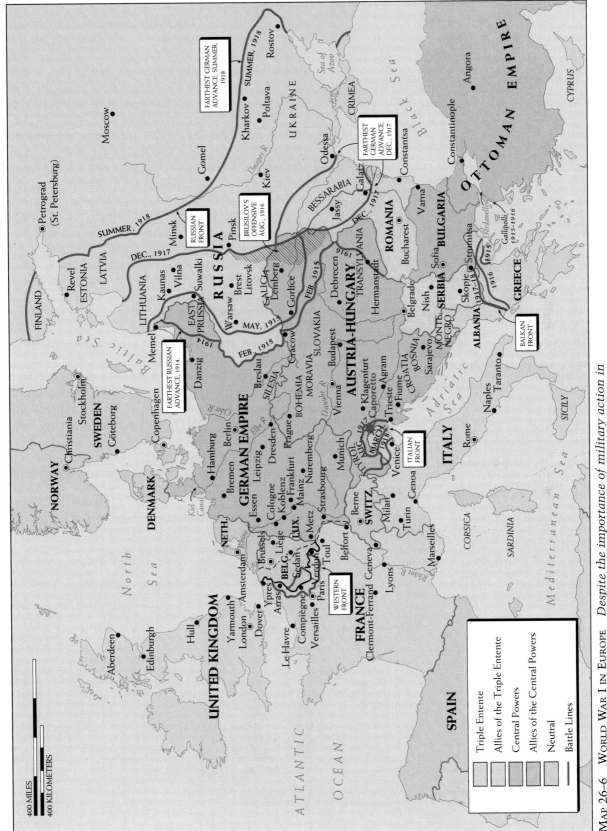

MAP 26-6 WORLD WAR I IN EUROPE *Despite the importance of military action in the Far East, in the Arab world, and at sea, the main theaters of activity in World War I were in the European areas.*

MAP 26–7  THE WESTERN FRONT 1914–1918  *This map shows the crucial western front in detail.*

Map legend:
- ① Farthest German Advance, Sept., 1914
- ② Nivelle's Offensive, Spring, 1917
- ③ Hindenburg Line (Stabilized Line) 1917–1918
- ④ German Gains, March–July, 1918
- ⑤ Major American Drives, Nov. 11, 1918
- ⑥ Armistice Line, Nov. 11, 1918

MEUSE–ARGONNE MAJOR AMERICAN DRIVES CUT THE GERMAN SUPPLY LINE AT SEDAN AND END THE WAR, NOV. 11, 1918.

*German infantrymen eating in a trench on the western front. Trenches, defended by barbed wire and machine guns, gave the defense the advantage in World War I and prevented breakthroughs. [Bildarchiv Preussischer Kulturbesitz]*

Central Powers pressed their advantage in the east and drove into the Baltic states and Russian Poland, inflicting more than two million casualties in a single year.

As the battle lines hardened, both sides sought new allies. Turkey (because of its hostility to Russia) and Bulgaria (the enemy of Serbia) joined the Central Powers.

Both sides bid for Italian support with promises of the spoils of victory. Because what the Italians wanted most was held by Austria, the Allies could promise more. In a secret treaty of 1915, they agreed to deliver to Italy after victory most of *Italia Irredenta* (i.e., the South Tyrol, Trieste, and some of the Dalmatian Islands) plus new colonies in Africa and a share of the Turkish Empire. By the spring of 1915, Italy was engaging Austrian armies. The Italian campaign weakened Austria and divided some German troops, but the Italian alliance was generally a disappointment to the Allies and never produced significant results. Romania joined the Allies in 1916 but was quickly defeated and driven from the war.

In the Far East, Japan honored its alliance with Britain and entered the war. The Japanese quickly overran the German colonies in China and the Pacific and used the opportunity to improve their own position against China.

Both sides also appealed to nationalistic sentiment in areas held by the enemy. The Germans supported nationalist movements among the Irish, the Flem-

*Armierungssoldaten beim Mittagessen.*

*British tanks moving toward the battle of Cambrai in Flanders late in 1917. Tanks were impervious to machine-gun fire. Had they been used in great numbers they might have broken the stalemate in the west. [Bildarchiv Preussischer Kulturbesitz]*

ings in Belgium, and the Poles and the Ukrainians under Russian rule. They even tried to persuade the Turks to lead a Muslim uprising against the British in Egypt and India and the French in North Africa.

The Allies made the same appeals with greater success. They sponsored movements of national autonomy for the Czechs, the Slovaks, the south Slavs, and the Poles that were under Austrian rule. They also favored a movement of Arab independence from Turkey. Guided by Colonel T. E. Lawrence (1888–1935), this last scheme proved especially successful later in the war.

In 1915 the Allies undertook to break the deadlock on the western front by going around it. The idea came chiefly from Winston Churchill (1874–1965), first lord of the British admiralty. He proposed to attack the Dardanelles and capture Constantinople. This policy would knock Turkey from the war, bring help to the Balkan front, and ease communications with Russia. The plan was daring but promis-

ing and, in its original form, presented little risk. British naval superiority and the element of surprise would allow the forcing of the straits and the capture of Constantinople by purely naval action. Even if the scheme failed, the fleet could escape with little loss.

Success depended on timing, speed, and daring leadership, but all of these were lacking. The execution of the attack was inept and overly cautious. Troops were landed, and as Turkish resistance continued, the Allied commitment increased. Before the campaign was abandoned, the Allies lost almost 150,000 men and diverted three times that number from more useful occupations.

RETURN TO THE WEST  Both sides turned back to the west in 1916. General Erich von Falkenhayn (1861–1922), who had succeeded Moltke in September 1914, sought success by an attack on the French stronghold of Verdun. His plan was not to take the

*The Allies promoted Arab efforts to secure independence from Turkey in an effort to remove Turkey from the war. Delegates to the peace conference of 1919 in Paris included British Colonel T. E. Lawrence, who helped lead the rebellion, and representatives from the Middle Eastern region. Prince Feisal, the third son of King Hussein, stands in the foreground of this picture; Colonel T. E. Lawrence is in the middle row, second from the right; and Brigadier General Nuri Pasha Said of Baghdad is second from the left. [The Bettmann Archive]*

fortress or to break through the French line but to inflict enormously heavy casualties on the French, who would have to defend Verdun against superior firepower from several directions. He, too, underestimated the superiority of the defense. The French were able to hold Verdun with comparatively few men and to inflict almost as many casualties as they suffered. The commander of Verdun, Henri Pétain (1856–1951), became a national hero, and "They shall not pass" became a slogan of national defiance.

The Allies tried to end the impasse by launching a major offensive along the River Somme in July. Aided by a Russian attack in the East that drew off some German strength and by an enormous artillery bombardment, they hoped at last to break

through. Once again, the defense was superior. Enormous casualties on both sides brought no result. On all fronts, the losses were great and the results meager. The war on land dragged on with no end in sight.

THE WAR AT SEA    As the war continued, control of the sea became more important. The British ignored the distinction between war supplies (which were contraband according to international law) and food or other peaceful cargo (which was not subject to seizure). They imposed a strict blockade meant to starve out the enemy, regardless of international law. The Germans responded with submarine warfare meant to destroy British shipping and to starve

| Major Campaigns and Events of World War I | |
| --- | --- |
| August 1914 | Germans attack in West |
| August–September 1914 | First Battle of the Marne |
| | Battles of Tannenberg and the Masurian Lakes |
| April 1915 | British land at Gallipoli, start of Dardanelles campaign |
| May 1915 | Germans sink British ship *Lusitania* |
| February 1916 | Germans attack Verdun |
| May–June 1916 | Battle of Jutland |
| February 1917 | Germans declare unrestricted submarine warfare |
| March 1917 | Russian Revolution |
| April 1917 | United States enters war |
| November 1917 | Bolsheviks seize power |
| March 1918 | Treaty of Brest–Litovsk |
| March 1918 | German offensive in the West |
| November 1918 | Armistice |

the British. They declared the waters around the British Isles a war zone, where even neutral ships would not be safe. Both policies were unwelcome to neutrals, and especially to the United States, which conducted extensive trade in the Atlantic. Yet the sinking of neutral ships by German submarines was both more dramatic and more offensive than the British blockade.

In May 1915, a German submarine torpedoed the British liner *Lusitania*. Among the 1,200 drowned were 118 Americans. President Woodrow Wilson (1856–1924) warned Germany that a repetition would have grave consequences; the Germans desisted for the time being rather than further anger the United States. This development gave the Allies a considerable advantage. The German fleet that had cost so much money and had caused so much trouble played no significant part in the war. The only battle it fought was at Jutland in the spring of 1916. The battle resulted in a standoff and confirmed British domination of the surface of the sea.

AMERICA ENTERS THE WAR  In December 1916, President Woodrow Wilson of the United States intervened to try to bring about a negotiated peace. Neither side, however, was willing to renounce war aims that its opponent found unacceptable. The war seemed likely to continue until one or both sides reached exhaustion.

Two events early in 1917 changed the situation radically. On February 1, the Germans announced the resumption of unrestricted submarine warfare, which led the United States to break off diplomatic relations. On April 6, the United States declared war on the Central Powers. One of the deterrents to an earlier American intervention had been the presence of autocratic tsarist Russia among the Allies. Wilson could conceive of the war only as an idealistic crusade "to make the world safe for democracy." That problem was resolved in March of 1917 by a revolution in Russia that overthrew the tsarist government.

# The Russian Revolution

The March Revolution in Russia was neither planned nor led by any political faction. It was the result of the collapse of the monarchy's ability to govern. Although public opinion had strongly supported Russian entry into the war, the conflict put far too great demands on the resources of the country and the efficiency of the tsarist government.

Nicholas II was weak and incompetent and was suspected of being under the domination of his German wife and the insidious peasant faith healer Rasputin, who was assassinated by a group of Russian noblemen in 1916. Military and domestic failures produced massive casualties, widespread hunger, strikes by workers, and disorganization in the army. The peasant discontent that had plagued the countryside before 1914 did not subside during the conflict. In 1916 the tsar adjourned the Duma, Russian's parliament, and proceeded to rule alone. All political factions were discontented.

## The Provisional Government

In early March 1917, strikes and worker demonstrations erupted in Petrograd, as Saint Petersburg had been renamed. The ill-disciplined troops in the city refused to fire on the demonstrators. The tsar abdicated on March 15. The government of Russia fell into the hands of members of the reconvened Duma, who soon formed a provisional government composed chiefly of Constitutional Democrats (Cadets) with Western sympathies.

At the same time, the various socialists, including both Social Revolutionaries and Social Democrats of the Menshevik wing, began to organize the workers into *soviets*, councils of workers and sol-

# The Outbreak of the Russian Revolution

*The great Russian Revolution of 1917 started with a series of ill-organized demonstrations in Petrograd early in March. The nature of these actions and the incompetence of the government's response are described in the memoirs of Maurice Paléologue (1859–1944), the French ambassador.*

✦ *What elements contributing to the success of the March Revolution emerge from this selection? Why might the army have been unreliable? Why did the two ambassadors think a new ministry should be appointed? What were the grievances of the revolutionaries? Why is there no discussion of the leaders of the revolution? What role did the emperor (tsar) play in these events?*

**Monday, March 12, 1917**

At half-past eight this morning, just as I finished dressing, I heard a strange and prolonged din which seemed to come from the Alexander Bridge. I looked out: there was no one on the bridge, which usually presents such a busy scene. But, almost immediately, a disorderly mob carrying red flags appeared at the end which is on the right bank of the Neva, and a regiment came towards it from the opposite side. It looked as if there would be a violent collision, but on the contrary the two bodies coalesced. The army was fraternizing with revolt.

Shortly afterwards, someone came to tell me that the Volhynian regiment of the Guard had mutinied during the night, killed its officers and was parading the city, calling on the people to take part in the revolution and trying to win over the troops who still remain loyal.

At ten o'clock there was a sharp burst of firing and flames could be seen rising somewhere on the Liteïny Prospekt which is quite close to the embassy. Then silence.

Accompanied by my military attaché, Lieutenant-Colonel Lavergne, I went out to see what was happening. Frightened inhabitants were scattering through the streets. There was indescribable confusion at the corner of the Liteïny. Soldiers were helping civilians to erect a barricade. Flames mounted from the Law Courts. The gates of the arsenal burst open with a crash. Suddenly the crack of machine-gun fire split the air: it was the reg-

diers. Initially, they allowed the provisional government to function without actually supporting it. As relatively orthodox Marxists, the Mensheviks believed that a bourgeois stage of development must come to Russia before the revolution of the proletariat could be achieved. They were willing to work temporarily with the Constitutional Democrats in a liberal regime, but they became estranged when the Cadets failed to control the army or to purge "reactionaries" from the government.

In this climate, the provisional government decided to remain loyal to the existing Russian alliances and to continue the war against Germany. The provisional government thus accepted tsarist foreign policy and associated itself with the source of much domestic suffering and discontent. Its fate was sealed by the collapse of the last Russian offensive in the summer of 1917. Disillusionment with the war, shortages of food and other necessities at home, and the growing demand by the peasants for land reform undermined the government. This occurred even after its leadership had been taken over by the moderate socialist Alexander Kerensky (1881–1970). Moreover, discipline in the army had disintegrated.

ulars who had just taken up position near the Nevsky Prospekt. The revolutionaries replied. I had seen enough to have no doubt as to what was coming. Under a hail of bullets I returned to the embassy with Lavergne who had walked calmly and slowly to the hottest corner out of sheer bravado.

About half-past eleven I went to the Ministry for Foreign Affairs, picking up Buchanan [the British ambassador to Russia] on the way.

I told Pokrovski [the Russian foreign minister] everything I had just witnessed.

"So it's even more serious than I thought," he said.

But he preserved unruffled composure, flavoured with a touch of scepticism, when he told me of the steps on which the ministers had decided during the night:

"The sitting of the Duma has been prorogued to April and we have sent a telegram to the Emperor, begging him to return at once. With the exception of M. Protopopov [the Minister of the Interior, in charge of the police], my colleagues and I all thought that a dictatorship should be established without delay; it would be conferred upon some general whose prestige with the army is pretty high, General Russky for example."

I argued that, judging by what I saw this morning, the loyalty of the army was already too heavily shaken for our hopes of salvation to be based on the use of the "strong hand," and that the immediate appointment of a min-istry inspiring confidence in the Duma seemed to me more essential than ever, as there is not a moment to lose. I reminded Pokrovski that in 1789, 1830, and 1848, three French dynasties were overthrown because they were too late in realizing the significance and strength of the movement against them. I added that in such a grave crisis the representative of allied France had a right to give the Imperial Government advice on a matter of internal politics.

Buchanan endorsed my opinion.

Pokrovski replied that he personally shared our views, but that the presence of Protopopov in the Council of Ministers paralyzed action of any kind.

I asked him:

"Is there no one who can open the Emperor's eyes to the real situation?"

He heaved a despairing sigh.

"The Emperor is blind!"

Deep grief was writ large on the face of the honest man and good citizen whose uprightness, patriotism and disinterestedness I can never sufficiently extol.

*Maurice Paléologue*, An Ambassador's Memoirs *(London: Doubleday & Company, Inc., Hutchinson Publishing Group Ltd., 1924), pp. 221–225. Reprinted by permission.*

### Lenin and the Bolsheviks

Ever since April, the Bolshevik wing of the Social Democratic Party had been working against the provisional government. The Germans, in their most successful attempt at subversion, had rushed the brilliant Bolshevik leader V. I. Lenin in a sealed train from his exile in Switzerland across Germany to Petrograd. They hoped that he would cause trouble for the revolutionary government.

Lenin saw the opportunity to achieve the political alliance of workers and peasants that he had dis-cussed before the war. In speech after speech, he hammered away on the theme of peace, bread, and land. The Bolsheviks demanded that all political power go to the *soviets*, which they controlled. The failure of the summer offensive encouraged them to attempt a coup, but the effort was a failure. Lenin fled to Finland, and his chief collaborator, Leon Trotsky (1879–1940), was imprisoned.

The failure of a right-wing countercoup gave the Bolsheviks another chance. Trotsky, released from prison, led the powerful Petrograd *soviet*. Lenin returned in October, insisted to his doubting col-

*Petrograd Munitions workers demonstrating in 1917. [Ria-Novosit/Sovfoto]*

leagues that the time was ripe to take power, and by the extraordinary force of his personality persuaded them to act. Trotsky organized the coup that took place on November 6 and that concluded with an armed assault on the provisional government. The Bolsheviks, almost as much to their own astonishment as to that of the rest of the world, had come to rule Russia.

### The Communist Dictatorship

The victors moved to fulfill their promises and to assure their own security. The provisional government had decreed an election for late November to select a Constituent Assembly. The Social Revolutionaries won a large majority over the Bolsheviks. When the assembly gathered in January, it met for only a day before the Red Army, controlled by the Bolsheviks, dispersed it. All other political parties also ceased to function in any meaningful fashion. In November and January, the Bolshevik government issued decrees that nationalized the land and turned it over to its peasant proprietors. Factory workers were put in charge of their plants. Banks were taken from their owners and seized for the state, and the debt of the tsarist government was repudiated. Property of the church reverted to the state.

The Bolshevik government also took Russia out of the war, which they believed benefited only capitalism. They signed an armistice with Germany in December 1917. On March 3, 1918, they accepted the Treaty of Brest–Litovsk, by which Russia yielded Poland, the Baltic states, and the Ukraine. Some territory in the Transcaucasus region went to Turkey. The Bolsheviks also agreed to pay a heavy war indemnity.

# Lenin Establishes His Dictatorship

*After the Bolshevik coup in October, elections for the Constituent Assembly were held in November. The results gave a majority to the Social Revolutionary Party and embarrassed the Bolsheviks. Using his control of the Red Army, Lenin closed the Constituent Assembly in January 1918, after it had met for only one day, and established the rule of a revolutionary elite and his own dictatorship. Here is the crucial Bolshevik decree.*

✦ *What reasons does Lenin give for closing the legitimately elected Constituent Assembly? What other reasons might he have had? What were the Soviets? Did they have a legitimate claim to the monopoly of political power? Was the dissolution of the assembly a temporary or permanent measure? What defense can be made for the Bolsheviks' action? Is it enough to justify that action?*

The Constituent Assembly, elected on the basis of lists drawn up prior to the October Revolution, was an expression of the old relation of political forces which existed when power was held by the compromisers and the Cadets. When the people at the time voted for the candidates for the Socialist-Revolutionary Party, they were not in a position to choose between the Right Socialist-Revolutionaries, the supporters of the bourgeoisie, and the Left Socialist-Revolutionaries, the supporters of Socialism. Thus the Constituent Assembly, which was to have been the crown of the bourgeois parliamentary republic, could not but become an obstacle in the path of the October Revolution and the Soviet power.

The October Revolution, by giving the power to the Soviets, and through the Soviets to the toiling and exploited classes, aroused the desperate resistance of the exploiters, and in the crushing of this resistance it fully revealed itself as the beginning of the socialist revolution . . . the majority in the Constituent Assembly which met on January 5 was secured by the party of the Right Socialist-Revolutionaries, the party of Kerensky, Avksentyev and Chernov. Naturally, this party refused to discuss the absolutely clear, precise, and unambiguous proposal of the supreme organ of Soviet power, the Central Executive Committee of the Soviets, to recognize the program of the Soviet power, to recognize the "Declaration of Rights of the Toiling and Exploited People," to recognize the October Revolution and the Soviet power. . . .

The Right Socialist-Revolutionary and Menshevik parties are in fact waging outside the walls of the Constituent Assembly a most desperate struggle against the Soviet power. . . .

Accordingly, the Central Executive Committee resolves: The Constituent Assembly is hereby dissolved.

*Reprinted from* A Documentary History of Communism: Communism in Russia, vol. 1, *Robert V. Daniels, ed., by permission of University Press of New England; pp. 91–92 "The Dissolution of the Constituent Assembly," Copyright © 1984 by the Trustees of the University of Vermont.*

These terms were a terribly high price to pay for peace, but Lenin had no choice. Russia was incapable of renewing the war effort, and the Bolsheviks needed time to impose their rule on a devastated and chaotic Russia. Moreover, Lenin believed that communist revolutions would soon occur

*Women munitions workers in England. World War I demanded more from the civilian populations than had previous wars, resulting in important social changes. The demands of the munitions industries and a shortage of men (so many of whom were in uniform) brought many women out of traditional roles at home and into factories and other war-related work. [Bettmann/Hulton]*

across Europe as a result of the war and the Russian example.

Until 1921 the new Bolshevik government met major domestic resistance. A civil war erupted between the "Red" Russians, who supported the revolution and the "White" Russians, who opposed it. In the summer of 1918, the Bolsheviks murdered the tsar and his family. Loyal army officers continued to fight the revolution and eventually received aid from the Allied armies. Under the leadership of Trotsky, however, the Red Army eventually overcame the domestic opposition. By 1921 Lenin and his supporters were in firm control.

# The End of World War I

The collapse of Russia and the Treaty of Brest–Litovsk were the zenith of German success. The Germans controlled eastern Europe and its resources, especially food, and by 1918 they were free to concentrate their forces on the western front.

These developments would probably have been decisive had they not been balanced by American intervention. Still, American troops would not arrive in significant numbers for about a year, and both sides tried to win the war in 1917.

An Allied attempt to break through in the west failed disastrously. Losses were heavy and the French army mutinied. The Austrians, supported by the Germans, defeated the Italians at Caporetto and threatened to overrun Italy, until they were checked with the aid of Allied troops. The deadlock continued, but time was running out for the Central Powers.

### Germany's Last Offensive

In March 1918, the Germans decided to gamble everything on one last offensive. (In this decision they were persuaded chiefly by Ludendorff, by then quartermaster-general, second-in-command to Hindenburg, but the real leader of the army.) The German army pushed forward and even reached the Marne again but got no farther. They had no more reserves, and the entire nation was exhausted. The Allies, on the other hand, were bolstered by the arrival of American troops in ever increasing numbers. They were able to launch a counteroffensive that proved to be irresistible. As the Austrian fronts in the Balkans and Italy collapsed, the German high command knew that the end was imminent.

Ludendorff was determined that peace should be made before the German army could be thoroughly defeated in the field and that the responsibility for ending the war should fall on civilians. For some time, he had been the effective ruler of Germany under the aegis of the emperor. He now allowed a new government to be established on democratic principles and to seek peace immediately. The new government, under Prince Max of Baden, asked for peace on the basis of the Fourteen Points that President Wilson had declared as the American war aims. These were idealistic principles, including self-determination for nationalities, open diplomacy, freedom of the seas, disarmament, and establishment of a league of nations to keep the peace. Wilson insisted that he would deal only with a democratic German government because he wanted to be sure that he was dealing with the German people and not merely their rulers.

### German Republican Government Accepts Defeat

The disintegration of the German army forced William II to abdicate on November 9, 1918. The majority branch of the Social Democratic Party proclaimed a republic to prevent the establishment of a soviet government under the control of their radical, Leninist wing, which had earlier broken away as the Independent Socialist Party. Two days later, this republican, socialist-led government signed the armistice that ended the war by accepting German defeat. The German people were, in general, unaware that their army had been defeated in the field and was crumbling. No foreign soldier stood on German soil. Many Germans expected a negotiated and mild settlement. The real peace was quite different and embittered the Germans. Many of them came to believe that Germany had not been defeated but had been tricked by the enemy and betrayed—even stabbed in the back—by republicans and socialists at home.

The victors rejoiced, but they also had much to mourn. The casualties on all sides came to about ten million dead and twice as many wounded. The economic and financial resources of the European states were badly strained. The victorious Allies, formerly creditors to the world, became debtors to the new American colossus, itself barely touched by the calamities of war.

The old international order, moreover, was dead. Russia was ruled by a Bolshevik dictatorship that preached world revolution and the overthrow of capitalism everywhere. Germany was in chaos. Austria–Hungary had disintegrated into a half dozen small states competing for the remains of the ancient empire. These kinds of changes affected the colonial peoples ruled by the European powers, and overseas empires would never again be as secure as they had seemed before the war. Europe was no longer the center of the world, free to interfere when it wished or to ignore the rest of the world if it chose. Four years of horrible war had shattered its easy confidence in material and moral progress. The memory of that war lived on to shake the nerve of the victorious Western powers as they faced the new conditions of the postwar world.

## The Settlement at Paris

The representatives of the victorious states gathered at Versailles and other Parisian suburbs in the first half of 1919. Wilson speaking for the United States, David Lloyd George (1863–1945) for

*The German delegation signs the peace treaty ending World War I in the Hall of Mirrors of the Palace of Versailles on June 28, 1919. This painting by Sir William Orpen, completed in 1921, now hangs in the Imperial War Museum in London. [Bildarchiv Preussischer Kulturbesitz]*

Britain, Georges Clemenceau (1841–1929) for France, and Vittorio Emanuele Orlando (1860–1952) for Italy made up the Big Four. Japan also had an important part in the discussions. The diplomats who met in Paris had a far more difficult task than those who had sat at Vienna a century earlier. Both groups attempted to restore order to the world after long and costly wars. At the earlier conference, however, Metternich and his associates could confine their thoughts to Europe. France had acknowledged defeat and was willing to take part in and uphold the Vienna settlement. The diplomats at Vienna were not much affected by public opinion; and they could draw the new map of Europe along practical lines determined by the realities of power and softened by compromise.

## Obstacles Faced by the Peacemakers

The negotiators at Paris in 1919 were less fortunate. They represented constitutional, generally democratic governments, and public opinion had become a mighty force. Though there were secret sessions, the conference often worked in the full glare of publicity. Nationalism had become almost a secular religion, and Europe's many ethnic groups could not be relied on to remain quiet while they were distributed on the map at the whim of the great powers. World War I, moreover, had been transformed by propaganda and especially by the intervention of Woodrow Wilson into a moral crusade to achieve a peace that would be just as well as secure. The Fourteen Points set forth the right of nationalities to self-determination as an absolute value; but in fact the map of Europe could not be drawn to match ethnic groups perfectly with their homelands. All these elements made compromise difficult.

Wilson's idealism, moreover, came into conflict with the more practical war aims of the victorious powers and with many of the secret treaties that had been made before and during the war. The British and French people had been told that Germany would be made to pay for the war. Russia had been promised control of Constantinople in return for recognition of the French claim to Alsace–Lorraine and British control of Egypt. Romania had been promised Transylvania at the expense of Hungary.

Some of the agreements contradicted others. Italy and Serbia had competing claims to the islands and shore of the Adriatic. During the war, the British had encouraged Arab hopes of an independent Arab state carved out of the Ottoman Empire. Those plans, however, contradicted the Balfour Declaration (1917), in which the British seemed to accept Zionist ideology and to promise the Jews a national home in Palestine. Both of these plans conflicted with an Anglo–French agreement to divide the Near East between themselves.

The continuing national goals of the victors presented further obstacles to an idealistic "peace without victors." France was painfully conscious of its numerical inferiority to Germany and of the low birth rate that would keep it inferior. So France was naturally eager to weaken Germany permanently and preserve French superiority. Italy continued to seek the acquisition of *Italia Irredenta*; Britain continued to look to its imperial interests; Japan pursued its own advantage in Asia. And the United States insisted on freedom of the seas, which favored American commerce, and on its right to maintain the Monroe Doctrine.

Finally, the peacemakers of 1919 faced a world still in turmoil. The greatest immediate threat appeared to be the spread of Bolshevism. While Lenin and his colleagues were distracted by civil war, the Allies landed small armies at several places in Russia to help overthrow the Bolshevik regime. The revolution seemed likely to spread as communist governments were established in Bavaria and Hungary. Berlin also experienced a dangerous communist uprising led by the "Spartacus group." The Allies were sufficiently worried by these developments to support their suppression by right-wing

military forces. They even allowed an army of German volunteers to operate against the Bolsheviks in the Baltic states.

Fear of the spread of communism affected the diplomats at Versailles, but it was far from dominant. The Germans played on such fears to get better terms, but the Allies, and especially the French, would not hear of it. Fear of Germany remained the chief concern for France. More traditional and more immediate interests governed the policies of the other Allies.

## The Peace

The Paris settlement consisted of five separate treaties between the victors and the defeated powers. Formal sessions began on January 18, 1919, and the last treaty was signed on August 10, 1920. (See Map 26–8.) Wilson arrived in Europe to unprecedented popular acclaim. Liberals and idealists expected a new kind of international order achieved in a new and better way, but they were soon disillusioned. "Open covenants openly arrived at" soon gave way to closed sessions in which Wilson, Clemenceau, and Lloyd George made arrangements that seemed cynical to outsiders.

The notion of "a peace without victors" became a mockery when the Soviet Union (as Russia was now called) and Germany were excluded from the peace conference. The Germans were simply presented with a treaty and compelled to accept it, fully justified in their complaint that the treaty had not been negotiated but dictated. The principle of national self-determination was violated many times, as was unavoidable. Still, the diplomats of the small nations were angered by their exclusion from decisions. The undeserved adulation accorded Wilson on his arrival gradually turned into equally undeserved scorn. He had not abandoned his ideals lightly but had merely given way to the irresistible force of reality.

THE LEAGUE OF NATIONS Wilson could make unpalatable concessions without abandoning his ideals because he put great faith in a new instrument for peace and justice, the League of Nations. Its covenant was an essential part of the peace treaty. The league was to be not an international government but a body of sovereign states who agreed to pursue common policies and to consult in the common interest, especially when war

**Austria-Hungary, 1914**

**Germany, 1914**

**Areas lost by Germany in 1919**

**Areas lost by Bulgaria**

**Areas lost by Russia**

**Areas lost by The Ottoman Empire**

MAP 26–8   WORLD WAR I PEACE SETTLEMENT IN EUROPE AND THE MIDDLE EAST   *The map of central and eastern Europe, as well as that of the Middle East, underwent drastic revision after World War I. The enormous territorial losses suffered by Germany, Austria–Hungary, the Ottoman Empire, Bulgaria, and Russia were the other side of the coin represented by gains for France, Italy, Greece, and Romania and by the appearance or reappearance of at least eight new independent states from Finland in the north to Yugoslavia in the south. The mandate system for former Ottoman territories outside Turkey proper laid foundations for several new, mostly Arab, states in the Middle East.*

threatened. The members promised to submit differences among themselves to arbitration, an international court, or the League Council. Refusal to abide by the results would justify league actions in the form of economic sanctions and even military intervention. The league was unlikely to be effective, however, because it had no armed forces at its disposal. Furthermore, any action required the unanimous consent of its council, consisting permanently of Britain, France, Italy, the United States, and Japan, as well as four other states that had temporary seats. The Covenant of the League bound its members to "respect and preserve" the territorial integrity of all its members; this was generally seen as a device to ensure the security of the victorious powers. The exclusion from the League Assembly of Germany and the Soviet Union further undermined its claim to evenhandedness.

COLONIES  Another provision of the covenant dealt with colonial areas. These were to be placed under the "tutelage" of one of the great powers under league supervision and encouraged to advance toward independence. This provision had no teeth, and little advance was made. Provisions for disarmament were equally ineffective. Members of the league remained fully sovereign and continued to pursue their own national interests. Only Wilson put much faith in its future ability to produce peace and justice. To get the other states to agree to the league, he approved territorial settlements that violated his own principles.

GERMANY  In the West, the main territorial issue was the fate of Germany. Although a united Germany was less than fifty years old, no one seems to have thought of undoing Bismarck's work and dividing it into its component parts. The French would have liked to set the Rhine-land up as a separate buffer state, but Lloyd George and Wilson would not permit it. Still, they could not ignore France's need for protection against a resurgent Germany. France received Alsace-Lorraine and the right to work the coal mines of the Saar for fifteen years. Germany west of the Rhine and fifty kilometers east of it was to be a demilitarized zone; Allied troops could stay on the west bank for fifteen years.

In addition to this physical barrier to a new German attack, the treaty provided that Britain and the United States would guarantee aid to France if it were attacked by Germany. Such an attack was made more unlikely by the permanent disarmament of Germany. Its army was limited to 100,000 men on long-term service, its fleet was reduced to a coastal defense force, and it was forbidden to have war planes, submarines, tanks, heavy artillery, or poison gas. As long as these provisions were observed, France would be safe.

THE EAST  The settlement in the East reflected the collapse of the great defeated empires that had ruled it for centuries. Germany lost part of Silesia, and East Prussia was cut off from the rest of Germany by a corridor carved out to give the revived state of Poland access to the sea. The Austro–Hungarian Empire disappeared entirely, giving way to five small successor states. Most of its German-speaking people were gathered in the Republic of Austria, cut off from the Germans of Bohemia and forbidden to unite with Germany.

The Magyars were left with the much-reduced kingdom of Hungary. The Czechs of Bohemia and Moravia joined with the Slovaks and Ruthenians to the east to form Czechoslovakia, and this new state included several million unhappy Germans plus Poles and Magyars. The southern Slavs were united in the kingdom of Serbs, Croats, and Slovenes, or Yugoslavia. Italy gained Trentino and Trieste. Romania was enlarged by receiving Transylvania from Hungary and Bessarabia from Russia. Bulgaria lost territory to Greece, Romania, and Yugoslavia. Russia lost vast territories in the west. Finland, Estonia, Latvia, and Lithuania became independent states, and most of Poland was carved out of formerly Russian soil. **Political Transformations,** p. 952, discusses the post-war status of former colonies under the mandate system.

REPARATIONS  Perhaps the most debated part of the peace settlement dealt with reparations for the damage done by Germany during the war. Before the armistice, the Germans promised to pay compensation "for all damages done to the civilian population of the Allies and their property." The Americans judged that the amount would be between $15 billion and $25 billion and that Germany would be able to pay that amount. France and Britain, however, worried about repaying their war debts to the United States, were eager to have Germany pay the full cost of the war, including pensions to survivors and dependents.

There was general agreement that Germany could not afford to pay such a huge sum, whatever it might be, and no sum was fixed at the conference. In the meantime, Germany was to pay $5 billion annually until 1921. At that time, a final figure would be set, which Germany would have to pay in thirty years. The French did not regret the outcome. Either Germany would pay and be bled into impotence, or Germany would refuse to pay and justify French intervention.

To justify these huge reparation payments, the Allies inserted the notorious Clause 231 into the treaty:

> The Allied and Associated Governments affirm, and Germany accepts, the responsibility of Germany and her allies for causing all the loss and damage to which the Allied and Associated Governments and their nationals have been subjected as a consequence of the war imposed upon them by aggression of Germany and her allies.

The Germans, of course, did not believe that they were solely responsible for the war and bitterly resented the charge. They had lost territories containing badly needed natural resources. Yet they were presented with an astronomical and apparently unlimited reparations bill. To add insult to injury, they were required to admit to a war guilt that they did not feel.

Finally, to heap insult upon insult, they were required to accept the entire treaty as it was written by the victors, without any opportunity for negotiation. Germany's Prime Minister Philipp Scheidmann (1865–1939) spoke of the treaty as the imprisonment of the German people and asked, "What hand would not wither that binds itself and us in these fetters?" But there was no choice. The Social Democrats and the Catholic Center Party formed a new government, and their representatives signed the treaty. These parties formed the backbone of the Weimar government that ruled Germany until 1933. They never overcame the stigma of accepting the Treaty of Versailles.

## Evaluation of the Peace

Few peace settlements have undergone more severe attacks than the one negotiated in Paris in 1919. It was natural that the defeated powers should object to it, but the peace soon came under bitter criticism in the victorious countries as well. Many of the French objected that the treaty tied French security to promises of aid from the unreliable Anglo–Saxon countries. In England and the United States, a wave of bitter criticism arose in liberal quarters because the treaty seemed to violate the idealistic and liberal aims that the Western leaders had professed.

It was not a peace without victors. It did not put an end to imperialism, but attempted to promote the national interests of the winning nations. It violated the principles of national self-determination by leaving significant pockets of minorities outside the borders of their national homelands.

THE ECONOMIC CONSEQUENCES OF THE PEACE  The most influential economic critic of the treaty was John Maynard Keynes (1883–1946), a brilliant British economist who took part in the peace conference. He resigned in disgust when he saw the direction it was taking. His book, *The Economic Consequences of the Peace* (1920), was a scathing attack, especially on reparations and the other economic aspects of the peace. It was also a skillful assault on the negotiators and particularly on Wilson, who was depicted as a fool and a hypocrite. Keynes argued that the Treaty of Versailles was both immoral and unworkable. He called it a Carthaginian peace, referring to the utter destruction of Carthage by Rome after the Third Punic War. He argued that such a peace would bring economic ruin and war to Europe unless it were repudiated.

Keynes's argument had a great effect on the British, who were already suspicious of France and glad of an excuse to withdraw from continental affairs. The decent and respectable position came to be one that supported revision of the treaty in favor of Germany. Even more important was the book's influence in the United States. It fed the traditional American tendency toward isolationism and gave powerful weapons to Wilson's enemies. Wilson's own political mistakes helped prevent American ratification of the treaty. Thus, America was out of the League of Nations and not bound to defend France. Britain, therefore, was also free from its obligation to France. France was left to protect itself without adequate means to do so for long.

Many of the attacks on the Treaty of Versailles are unjustified. It was not a Carthaginian peace. Germany was neither dismembered nor ruined. Reparations could be and were scaled down. Until the great world depression of the 1930s, the Ger-

*John Maynard Keynes served on the British delegation to the Paris peace conference of 1919. His denunciation of the Versailles Treaty helped undermine Western willingness to uphold its terms. [Hulton-Deutsch Collection Limited]*

mans recovered a high level of prosperity. Complaints against the peace should also be measured against the peace that the victorious Germans had imposed on Russia at Brest-Litovsk and their plans for a European settlement in case of victory. Both were far more severe than anything enacted at Versailles. The attempt at achieving self-determination for nationalities was less than perfect, but it was the best effort Europe had ever made to do so.

DIVISIVE NEW BOUNDARIES AND TARIFF WALLS  The peace, nevertheless, was unsatisfactory in important ways. The elimination of the Austro–Hungarian Empire, however inevitable, created several serious problems. Economically it was disastrous, for it separated raw materials from manufacturing areas and producers from their markets by new boundaries and tariff walls. In hard times, this separation created friction and hostility that aggravated other quarrels also created by the peace treaties. Poland contained unhappy German and Ukrainian minorities, and Czechoslovakia was a collection of nationalities that did not find it easy to live together as a nation. Disputes over territories in eastern Europe promoted further tension.

The peace was inadequate on another level as well. It rested on a victory that Germany did not admit. The Germans believed that they had been cheated rather than defeated. And the high moral principles proclaimed by the Allies undercut the validity of the peace, for it plainly fell far short of those principles.

# POLITICAL TRANSFORMATIONS

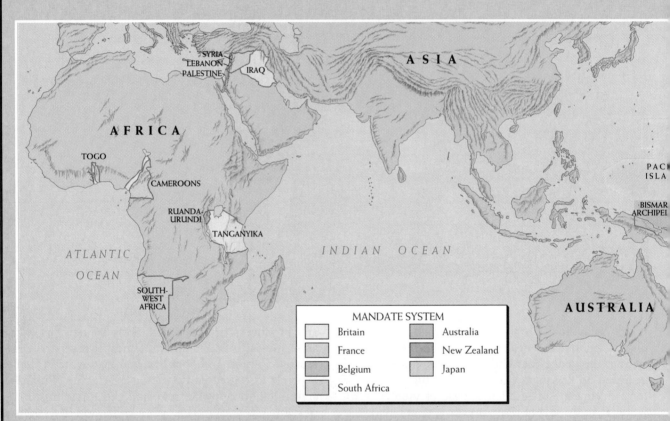

MAP 26–9

# The Mandate System: 1919 to World War II

The peace of Paris that ended the Great War of 1914–1918 had to deal with the colonial question created by prewar imperialism. The principle of self-determination and the general hostility toward imperialism and colonialism prevented the victorious powers from merely taking over the colonies of the defeated nations. But they were not willing to grant them independence. Instead the former colonies were placed as mandated territories under the "tutelage" of one of the great powers, and under league supervision they would be encouraged to advance toward independence.

Under the mandate system the old Ottoman Empire disappeared. The new republic of Turkey was limited to little more than Constantinople and Asia Minor. The former Ottoman territories of Palestine and Iraq came under British control; Syria and Lebanon were controlled by France. In Africa, Germany's former colonies were divided among Britain, France, and South Africa. The German Pacific possessions went to Australia, New Zealand, and Japan.

There was, in fact, very little advance toward independence, and the colonial system largely persisted under its new guise. Twenty years after the signing of the treaty, not even one mandate had achieved full independence. The blatant hypocrisy of the mandate system troubled some consciences in the colonial nations and lent support to those advocating an end to colonialism. Colonialism would remain a problem even after World War II. Article 22 of the Treaty of Versailles, establishing the mandate system, appears below:

## Article 22

To those colonies and territories which as a consequence of the late war have ceased to be under the sovereignty of the States which formerly governed them and which are inhabited by peoples not yet able to stand by themselves under the strenuous conditions of the modern world, there should be applied the principle that the well-being and development of such peoples form a sacred trust of civilization and that securities for the performance of this trust should be embodied in this Covenant.

The best method of giving practical effect to this principle is that the tutelage of such peoples should be entrusted to advanced nations who by reason of their resources, their experience or their geographical position can best undertake this responsibility, and who ware willing to accept it, and that this tutelage should be exercised by them as Mandatories on behalf of the League.

The character of the mandate must differ according to the stage of the development of the people, the geographical situation of the territory, its economic conditions, and other similar circumstances.

Certain communities formerly belonging to the Turkish Empire have reached a stage of development where their existence as independent nations can be provisionally recognised subject to the rendering of administrative advice and assistance by a Mandatory until such time as they are able to stand alone. The wishes of these communities must be a principal consideration in the selection of the Mandatory.

Other peoples, especially those of Central Africa, are at such a stage that the Mandatory must be responsible for the administration of the territory under conditions which will guarantee freedom of conscience and religion, subject only to the maintenance of public order and morals, the prohibition of abuses such as the slave trade, the arms traffic, and the liquor traffic, and the prevention of the establishment of fortifications or military and naval bases and of military training of the natives for other than police purposes and the defence of territory, and will also secure equal opportunities for the trade and commerce of other Members of the League.

*Georges Clemenceau, Woodrow Wilson, and David Lloyd George leaving the Palace of Versailles after signing the treaty. [Archive Photos]*

There are territories, such as South-West Africa and certain of the South Pacific Islands, which, owing to the sparseness of their population, or their small size, or their remoteness from the centres of civilisation, or their geographical contiguity to the territory of the Mandatory, and other circumstances, can be best administered under the laws of the Mandatory as integral portions of its territory, subject to the safeguards above mentioned in the interests of the indigenous population.

In every case of mandate, the Mandatory shall render to the Council an annual report in reference to the territory committed to its charge.

The degree of authority, control, or administration to be exercised by the Mandatory shall, if not previously agreed upon by the Members of the League, be explicitly defined in each case by the Council.

A permanent commission shall be constituted to receive and examine the annual reports of the Mandatories and to advise the Council on all matters relating to the observance of the mandates.

*Carnegie Endowment for International Peace," The Treaty of Versailles," art. 22,* The Treaties of Peace 1919–1923, vol. 1 (1924).

FAILURE TO ACCEPT REALITIES Finally, the great weakness of the peace was its failure to accept reality. Germany and Russia must inevitably play an important part in European affairs, yet they were excluded from the settlement and from the League of Nations. Given the many discontented parties, the peace was not self-enforcing; yet no satisfactory machinery for enforcing it was established. The League of Nations was never a serious force for this purpose. It was left to France, with no guarantee of support from Britain and no hope of help from the United States, to defend the new arrangements. Finland, the Baltic states, Poland, Romania, Czechoslovakia, and Yugoslavia were expected to be a barrier to the westward expansion of Russian communism and to help deter a revival of German power. Most of these states, however, would have to rely on France in case of danger, and France was simply not strong enough to protect them if Germany were to rearm.

The tragedy of the Treaty of Versailles was that it was neither conciliatory enough to remove the desire for change, even at the cost of war, nor harsh enough to make another war impossible. The only hope for a lasting peace was that Germany would remain disarmed while the more obnoxious clauses of the peace treaty were revised. Such a policy required continued attention to the problem, unity among the victors, and farsighted leadership; but none of these was consistently present during the next two decades.

◆

*The outburst of European imperialism in the last part of the nineteenth century brought the Western countries into contact with almost all the inhabited areas of the world. They intensified their activity in places where they had already been interested. The growth of industry, increased ease of transportation and communication, and the growth of a world economic system all brought previously remote and isolated places into the orbit of the West.*

*By the time of the outbreak of the war, European nations had divided Africa among themselves for exploitation in one way or another. The vast subcontinent of India had long been a British colony. The desirable parts of China were under European commercial control. Indochina was under French rule and the islands of the Pacific had been divided among the powers. Much of the Near East was under the nominal control of the Ottoman Empire, in its death throes and under European influence. The Monroe Doctrine made Latin America a protectorate of the United States. Japan, pushed out of its isolation, had itself become an imperial power at the expense of China and Korea.*

*But the world created by the New Imperialism did not last long. What began as yet another Balkan war involving the European powers became a general war that profoundly affected much of the rest of the world. As the terrible war of 1914–1918 dragged on, the real motives that had driven the European powers to fight gave way to public affirmations of the principles of nationalism and self-determination. The peoples under colonial rule took the public statements—and promises sometimes made to them in private—seriously and sought to win their independence and nationhood.*

*Mostly, they were disappointed by the peace settlement. The establishment of the League of Nations and the system of mandates in place of the previous system of open colonial rule changed little. The British Empire grew even larger as it inherited vast territories from the defeated German and the defunct Ottoman empires. The French retained and expanded their holdings in Africa, the Pacific, and the Near East. The Americans added to the islands they controlled in the Pacific. Japanese imperial ambitions were rewarded at the expense of China.*

*A glance at the new map of the world could give the impression that the old imperial nations, especially Britain and France, were more powerful than ever, but that impression would be superficial and misleading. The great western European powers had paid an enormous price in lives, money, and will for their victory in the war. Colonial peoples pressed for the rights that were proclaimed as universal by the West but denied to their colonies; and some influential minorities in the countries that ruled them sympathized with colonial aspirations for independence. Tension between colonies and their ruling nations was a cause of serious instability in the world created by the Paris treaties of 1919.*

## Review Questions

1. To what areas of the world did Europe extend its power after 1870? How and why did European

attitudes toward imperialism change after 1870? What features differentiate the New Imperialism from previous imperialistic movements? What features did they have in common?

2. What role in the world did Bismarck envisage for the new Germany after 1871? How successful was he in carrying out his vision? What was Bismarck's attitude toward colonies? Was he wise to tie Germany to Austria–Hungary?

3. Why and in what stages did Britain abandon its policy of "splendid isolation" at the turn of the century? Were the policies it pursued instead wise ones, or should Britain have followed a different course?

4. How did developments in the Balkans lead to the outbreak of World War I? What was the role of Serbia? Of Austria? Of Russia? What was the aim of German policy in July 1914? Did Germany want a general war?

5. Why did Germany lose World War I? Could Germany have won, or was victory never a possibility? Assess the settlement of Versailles. What were its benefits to Europe, and what were its drawbacks? Was the settlement too harsh or too conciliatory? Could it have secured lasting peace in Europe? How might it have been improved?

6. Why was Lenin successful in establishing Bolshevik rule in Russia? What role did Trotsky play? Was it wise policy for Lenin to take Russia out of the War?

# Suggested Readings

L. ALBERTINI, *The Origins of the War of 1914*, 3 vols. (1952, 1957). Discursive but invaluable.

M. BALFOUR, *The Kaiser and His Times* (1972). A fine biography of William II.

V. R. BERGHAHN, *Germany and the Approach of War in 1914* (1973). A work similar in spirit to Fischer's 1967 book (see below) but stressing the importance of Germany's naval program.

R. BOSWORTH, *Italy and the Approach of the First World War* (1983). A fine analysis of Italian policy.

L. CECIL, *Wilhelm II Prince and Emperor 1859–1900* (1989). The first part of a projected two-volume history of the kaiser.

S. B. FAY, *The Origins of the World War*, 2 vols. (1928). The best and most influential of the revisionist accounts.

M. FERRO, *The Great War, 1914–1918* (1973). A solid account of the course of World War I.

D. K. FIELDHOUSE, *The Colonial Experience: A Compara-tive Study from the Eighteenth Century* (1966). An excellent recent study.

F. FISCHER, *Germany's Aims in the First World War* (1967). An influential interpretation that stirred an enormous controversy by emphasizing Germany's role in bringing on the war.

F. FISCHER, *War of Illusions* (1975). A long and diffuse book that tries to connect German responsibility for the war with internal social, economic, and political developments.

I. GEISS, *July 1914* (1967). A valuable collection of documents by a student of Fritz Fischer. The emphasis is on German documents and responsibility.

O. J. HALE, *The Great Illusion 1900–1914* (1971). A fine survey of the period, especially good on public opinion.

M. B. HAYNE, *The French Foreign Office and the Origins of the First World War* (1993). An examination of the work of the influence on French policy of the professionals in the foreign service.

J. N. HORNE, *Labour at War: France and Britain, 1914–1918* (1991). An examination of a major issue on the home fronts.

J. JOLL, *The Origins of the First World War* (1984). A brief but thoughtful analysis.

P. KENNEDY, *The Rise of the Anglo-German Antagonism 1860–1914* (1980). An unusual and thorough analysis of the political, economic, and cultural roots of important diplomatic developments.

J. M. KEYNES, *The Economic Consequences of the Peace* (1920). The famous and influential attack on the Versailles treaty.

V. G. KIERNAN, *European Empires from Conquest to Collapse 1815–1960* (1981). A study of the course of modern European imperialism.

L. LAFORE, *The Long Fuse* (1965). A readable account of the origins of World War I that focuses on the problem of Austria–Hungary.

W. L. LANGER, *The Diplomacy of Imperialism* (1935). An excellent study of diplomatic history of the years 1890–1902.

W. L. LANGER, *European Alliances and Alignments*, 2nd ed. (1966). An admirable diplomatic history of the years 1871–1890.

D. C. B. LIEVEN, *Russia and the Origins of the First World War* (1983). A good account of the forces that shaped Russian policy.

E. MANTOUX, *The Carthaginian Peace* (1952). A vigorous attack on Keynes's view.

W. J. MOMMSEN, *Theories of Imperialism* (1980). A study of the debate on the meaning of imperialism.

G. SCHÖLLGEN, *Escape Into War? The Foreign Policy of Imperial Germany* (1990). A valuable collection of interpretive essays.

J. STEINBERG, *Yesterday's Deterrent* (1965). An excellent study of Germany's naval policy and its consequences.

Z. STEINER, *Britain and the Origins of the First World*

*War* (1977). A perceptive and informed account of the way British foreign policy was made before the war.

A. J. P. TAYLOR, *The Struggle for Mastery in Europe, 1848–1918* (1954). Clever but controversial.

L. C. F. TURNER, *Origins of the First World War* (1970).

Especially good on the significance of Russia and its military plans.

S. R. WILLIAMSON, JR., *Austria-Hungary and the Origins of the First World War* (1991). A valuable new study of a complex subject.

# The West & the World

## IMPERIALISM: ANCIENT AND MODERN

The concept of "empire" does not win favor today, and the word *imperialism*, derived from it, has carried an increasingly pejorative meaning since it was coined in the nineteenth century. Both words imply forcible domination by a nation or a state that exploits an alien people for its own benefit. Although, in our time, the charge of "imperialism" arises whenever a large and powerful nation influences weaker ones, exertion of influence alone is not imperialism. To be true to historical experience, one nation's actions toward another are imperialistic only if the dominant nation exerts both political and military control over the weaker one. In that sense, the last great empire in the modern world was the conglomeration of republics and ostensibly independent satellite states dominated by Russia prior to the USSR's collapse. But the Russians and the other imperial powers after World War II took no public pride in their domination. In our day, ruling an "empire" or engaging in "imperialism" is generally considered among the worst acts a nation can commit.

Such views are rare, perhaps unique, in the history of civilization. A major source for this opinion is the Christian religious tradition, especially parts of the New Testament that deprecate power and worldly glory and praise humility. But in fact, Christianity was not hostile to power and empire, for it took control of the Roman Empire in the fourth century C.E. and has lived comfortably with "empire" until our own century. The rise of democracy and nationalism in the last two centuries may have been more influential in changing attitudes toward imperialism because these move-

ments exalt the freedom and autonomy of a people. But perhaps the modern disdain for empire-building has its principal origins in the extraordinary horror of modern warfare and the historical knowledge that competition for empire has often led to war.

If, however, we are to understand the widespread experience of empire throughout history, we must be alert to the great gap that separates the views of most people throughout history from our current opinions. The earliest empires go back more than four thousand years to the valleys of the Nile and the Tigris–Euphrates, and empires arose later in China, Japan, India, Iran, and Central and South America, among other areas. Typically, they were led by rulers who were believed to be gods or the representatives of gods, or at least were godlike in their ability to rule over many people. To their own people they brought wealth and prosperity, power, and reflected glory, all considered highly desirable. No one appears to have questioned the propriety of conquering another people and taking their lands, property, and persons to benefit the conquerors. Empire seemed to be part of the order of things—good for the rulers, usually bad for the ruled.

**The Greeks: Ambiguities of Power.** In most respects the Greeks resembled other ancient peoples in their attitudes toward power, conquest, empire, and the benefits that came with them. Their Olympian gods held sway over Earth, heaven, and the underworld because of victorious wars over other deities, and they gloried in their

*Exile of the Israelites. In 1722 B.C.E. the northern part of Jewish Palestine, the kingdom of Israel, was conquered by the Assyrians. Its people were driven from their homeland and exiled all over the vast Assyrian empire. This wall carving in low relief comes from the palace of the Assyrian king Sennacherib at Nineveh. It shows the Jews with their cattle and baggage going into exile. [Erich Lessing/Art Resource, N.Y.*

rule. The heroes in the epic poems that formed the Greek system of values won glory and honor through battle, conquest, and rule over other people. They viewed the world as a place of intense competition in which victory and domination, which brought fame and glory, were the highest goals, while defeat and subordination brought ignominy and shame.

When the legendary world of aristocratic heroes gave way to the world of city-states (*poleis*), competition was elevated from contests among individuals, households, and clans to contests and wars among *poleis*. In 416 B.C.E., more than a decade after the death of Pericles (c. 490–429 B.C.E.), Athenian spokesmen explained to some

Melian officials their view of international relations: "Of the gods we believe, and of men we know, that by a necessity of their nature they always rule wherever they have the power." (Thucydides 5.105) Although their language was shockingly blunt, it reflected the views of most Greeks.

Yet this was also a dramatic presentation of the morally problematic status of the Athenian Empire. The Athenians' harsh statement would have struck a sympathetic chord among the Greeks. They appreciated power and the security and glory it can bring, but their own historical experience was different from that of other ancient nations. Their culture had been shaped by small, autonomous, independent city-states, and they considered freedom natural for people raised in such an environment. Citizens, they believed, should be free in their persons, free to maintain their own constitutions, laws, and customs, and their city-states should be free to conduct their own foreign relations and to compete for power and glory. The free, autonomous *polis*, they thought, was greater than the mightiest powers in the world, and the sixth-century B.C.E. poet Phocylides was prepared to compare it to the great Assyrian Empire: "A little *polis* living orderly in a high place is greater than block-headed Nineveh." (Fragment 5)

When *poleis* fought one another, the victor typically took control of a piece of border land that was usually the source of the dispute. They did not normally enslave the defeated enemy or annex and occupy its land. In these matters, as in many others, the Greeks distinguished themselves from alien peoples who did not speak Greek and were not shaped by the Greek cultural tradition. These people were called barbarians, *barbaroi*, because their speech sounded to the Greeks like "bar bar." Since they had not been raised as people in free communities, but lived as subjects to a ruler, they were, it seemed, slaves by nature. To the Greeks, then, dominating and enslaving such people was perfectly acceptable. Greeks, on the other hand, viewed themselves as naturally free, as they demonstrated by creating and living in the free institutions of the *polis*. To rule over such people, to deny them their freedom and autonomy, would be wrong. So the Greeks thought, but they did not always act accordingly. The early Spartans, for instance, had changed the status of the conquered Greeks of Laconia and Messenia to *Helots*, or slaves of the state.

The Greeks shared still another belief that interfered with the comfortable acceptance of great power and empire: They thought that any good thing amassed by humans to excess, beyond moderation, eventually led to *hybris*, a condition of wanton violence arising from arrogant pride in one's greatness. Those overcome by *hybris* were thought to have overstepped the limits established for human beings, to have shown contempt for the gods and, thereby, to have incurred *nemesis*, or divine anger and retribution. The great example to the Greeks of the fifth century of the workings of *hybris* and *nemesis* was the fate of Xerxes (r. 486–465 B.C.E.), Great King of the Persian Empire. His power became so great that it filled him with a blind arrogance that led him to try to extend his rule over the Greek mainland and thus brought disaster to himself and his people. When, therefore, the Athenians undertook the leadership of a Greek alliance after the Persian War, and that leadership brought them wealth and power and, in fact, turned into what was frankly acknowledged to be an empire, their response was ambiguous and contradictory. These developments were a source of pride and gratification, but also of embarrassment and, to some Athenians, shame.

The Macedonian conquest of the Greek city-states in 338 B.C.E. marked a return to an older attitude toward empire. Alexander the Great (r. 340–323 B.C.E.) conquered the vast Persian Empire, itself the successor of empires that had stretched from the Nile to the Indus valley. The death of Alexander led to its division and eventual absorption by the emergent Roman Empire by the second century B.C.E.

**The Romans: A Theory of Empire**  The Romans had fewer hesitations about the desirability of imperial power than the Greeks. Their culture, which arose from a world of farmers accustomed to hard work, deprivation, and subordination to authority, venerated the military virtues. Roman society valued power, glory, and the responsibilities of leadership, even domination, without embarrassment. In time the Romans formulated a theory of empire that claimed that Roman rule brought great advantages to its subjects: prosperity, justice, the rule of law, and, most valuable of all, peace. In the words of their great epic poet Vergil (70–19 B.C.E.), it was the Roman practice "To humble the arrogant and be sparing to their subjects." These claims had considerable foundation, and the Romans could not have ruled so vast an empire with a relatively small army for more than half a millennium if their subjects had not enjoyed these benefits. Some of the conquered had a different viewpoint, however. As one British chieftain put it in the first century C.E.: "They make a wilderness and call it peace."

**Muslims, Mongols, and Ottomans**  The rise of Islam in the seventh century C.E. produced a new kind of empire that derived its energy from religious zeal. Bursting out of Arabia, the Muslim

*The philosopher-emperor Marcus Aurelius was compelled to spend much of his time fighting against tribal invaders on Rome's northern frontiers. This relief from the triumphal arch dedicated to him in Rome (176-180) shows him mounted, on campaign. [Nimatallah/Art Resource]*

armies swiftly gained control of most of the territory held by the old Persian Empire, North Africa, and Spain.

In the twelfth and thirteenth centuries, the great Mongol Empire, at its height, dominated Eurasia from the Pacific to central Europe, ruling Russia for more than two centuries. As in most ancient empires, the Mongols demanded taxes and military service from the conquered. They also imposed their rule over the mighty and long-standing Chinese Empire, parts of India, and much of the Islamic world before their power declined.

Still another great empire that spanned Europe and Asia was that of the Ottomans, a Turkish people, originally from central Asia. In the fourteenth century, they established a kingdom in Anatolia (Asia Minor) and soon conquered the ancient Byzantine Empire, seizing Constantinople in 1453. In the next century, the Ottoman Empire dominated southeastern Europe, the Black Sea, North Africa from Morocco to Egypt, Palestine, Syria and Arabia, Mesopotamia and Iraq, and Kurdistan and Georgia in the Caucasus. As late as 1683, Ottoman armies threatened to take Vienna and push into western Europe. Over the next two centuries, however, Ottoman power declined as the European national states grew stronger. Russia, in particular, inflicted defeats that left Turkey in the late nineteenth century, "the sick man of Europe."

**European Expansion**   Europe, divided first by feudalism, then by the emergence of multiple nascent national states, had been the victim of Islamic imperial expansion during the Middle Ages, first at the hands of the Arabs, then the Turks. The crusades had produced small and transitory conquests. It was only in the late 1400s that Europeans began the economic and political expansion that culminated in their command of much of the planet by 1900. The first phase of European expansion involved the "discovery," exploration, conquest, exploitation, and settlement of the Americas. It was made possible by important developments in naval and military technology, the dynamism inherent in early commercial and financial capitalism, and the freedom to compete for wealth and power unleashed by the division into separate states.

Spain and Portugal took the lead, founding empires in central and South America, sometimes conquering existing empires ruled by native peoples. In Central America the Aztecs exacted labor and taxes from their subject peoples, using some of them as human sacrifices. In the Andes the Incas ruled a great empire that also required military service and forced labor from its subjects. Both Native American empires were overthrown by Spain, which then established a vast American empire whose resources, especially gold and silver, formed the basis of the great Spanish Empire in Europe. Portugal exploited the agricultural and mineral riches of Brazil using slaves imported from Africa.

The seventeenth century saw the establishment of European trading posts and then colonies on the Indian subcontinent and in the East Indies, chiefly by the Dutch, British, and French. In North America Spain held Mexico, Florida, and California. Of more lasting significance were French and British settlements in Canada and what was to become the United States. The British colonies, especially, represented a special kind of European overseas settlement in which concern for commerce was less important than the acquisition of land for farming.

The wars of the eighteenth century ultimately cleared North America and India of French competition, leaving both as British monopolies and important bases of what would become a worldwide British Empire. The largest and most populous empire in the history of the world, it included colonies of one sort or another on all the inhabited continents; the sun, as the saying went, never set on the British Empire. Whether European colonialism was profitable for the imperial powers is still controversial, but Great Britain certainly benefited more than the others. Unlike most colonial powers, the British imported great quantities of

natural resources from their colonies and carried on a high percentage of their trade with them. Even more singular, the British Empire included such self-governing areas as Canada, Australia, New Zealand, and South Africa, ruled by emigrants from Britain who remained loyal to the mother country and were willing to assist it in wartime. The jewel in Britain's imperial crown, as another saying went, was India. With a population of some 300,000,000, it contained perhaps 80 percent of the empire's subjects and provided much of the imperial profit.

At the height of its power in the mid-nineteenth century, it is remarkable how little money and effort Britain needed to spend to maintain these desired conditions. The cost of its armed services, including its great navy, during these years was only about 2 to 3 percent of its gross national product—a low figure compared with other nations, and incredibly low considering Britain's status as the world's greatest empire. The British army was the smallest among the European powers: By 1880

*The period in which the European imperial powers were compelled to abandon their colonies was sometimes difficult and painful for both sides. The French departure from Algeria, under French control for more than a century, was especially agonizing. This picture shows the Rue Michelet, one of Algiers' chief shopping streets, patrolled by armed troops in 1962. [AFP/Archive Photos]*

it numbered fewer than a quarter of a million men, less than half the size of France's and barely a quarter of Russia's.

France returned to its imperial pursuits after its defeat in the Napoleonic Wars, especially in North Africa and Southeast Asia, and in the last quarter of the century, Germany and Italy joined the competition for colonies. The latter part of the century brought the European partition of Africa and the establishment of European economic and political power throughout Asia. Modernized Japan, too, became a colonial power, modeling itself on the imperialist policies of the European powers. (See Chapter 26.)

By the next century, European dominance had created a single global economy and had made events in any corner of the world significant thousands of miles away. The possession of colonies became part of the definition of a great power, and competition for colonies helped bring on World War I.

**Toward Decolonization** The weakening of the European colonial powers in the World War II began the process of decolonization. The economic value of most colonies had proved to be much smaller than anticipated, and the colonial powers lacked both the capacity and the incentive to restore their former rule. Nationalist movements in the old colonies, moreover, would make such attempts costly and unpleasant. These movements flourished under the banner of national self-determination, self-government, and independence, ideas that came from and were cherished by the European colonial powers themselves. The example of Nazi Germany, moreover, had discredited theories of racial superiority that had justified much of European imperial rule. For European imperialism the handwriting was on the wall, although some colonial powers held on more fiercely than others. The French, for instance, fought at great cost—but in vain—to retain Algeria and Indo-China. By the 1970s a post-colonial world had emerged, and the concept of empire had become unclean.

✦ *What were the major ancient attitudes toward imperialism? What are the major modern attitudes? How do you account for the differences? What justifications and explanations have modern people used in connection with imperialism? Which do you think are the most important? Do you think ancient and modern reasons for imperialism are fundamentally different?*

*Anxiety over the spread of the Bolshevik Revolution was a fundamental factor of European politics during the 1920's. Much of this fear was the product of various Bolshevik propaganda images such as this poster which declares, "You have nothing to lose but your chains, but the world will soon be yours." Such declarations conjured fears among people in the rest of Europe of a political force determined to overturn their social, political, and economic institutions. [The Bridgeman Art Library]*

# Political Experiments of the 1920s

## KEY TOPICS

- Economic and political disorder in the aftermath of World War I
- The Soviet Union's far-reaching political and social experiment
- Mussolini and the Fascist seizure of power in Italy
- French determination to enforce the Versailles treaty
- First Labour government and general strike in Britain
- The development of authoritarian governments in all the successor states to the Austrian Empire except Czechoslovakia
- Reparations, inflation, political turmoil, and the rise of Nazism in the German Weimar Republic

Experimentation in politics and the pursuit of normality in economic life marked the decade following the conclusion of the Paris peace settlement, also known throughout the period as the Versailles settlement. These treaties, as examined in the last chapter, established a bold new experiment in European diplomatic relations. The Paris settlement instituted the League of Nations and imposed economic and military arrangements that fostered friction among all the powers and deep resentment in Germany. In the Soviet Union, the Bolsheviks, after seizing control of the government in 1917 and then winning the civil war, proceeded to reorganize every aspect of life in Russia. In Italy, the political turmoil and social strains of the postwar era resulted in the emergence of the authoritarian movement known as fascism. In Great Britain, the Labour Party came to power for the *first time, and most of Ireland became an independent nation. Through war and revolution the Habsburg Empire collapsed, and its peoples formed several small successor states, only one of which became a successful democracy. Germany, after suffering a humiliating military defeat, jettisoned the imperial monarchy and set out on the experiment of the Weimar Republic, which encountered numerous determined and violent opponents.*

*Many of these political experiments failed, and the economic and social normality so many Europeans sought proved elusive. By the close of the 1920s, the political path had been paved for the nightmares of brutally authoritarian governments and international aggression that were to mark the 1930s and 1940s. Yet many of the people who had survived the Great War had hoped and worked for a better outcome. Authoritarianism and aggression were not the inescapable destiny of Europe. They emerged from the failure to secure alternative modes of democratic political life and stable international relations and from the inability to achieve long-term economic prosperity.*

# Political and Economic Factors after the Paris Settlement

## New Governments

In 1919 experimental political regimes studded the map of Europe. From Ireland to Russia, new governments were seeking to gain the active support of their citizens and to solve the grievous economic problems caused by the war. In the Soviet Union, the Bolsheviks regarded themselves as forging a new kind of civilization, one built on achieving communism. To that end, they constructed a vast authoritarian state apparatus.

The situation was different elsewhere on the Continent. In many, though not all, countries, the turn to liberal democracy resulted in the right to vote being given to women and previously disenfranchised males. For the first time in European history, the governments handling diplomatic and economic matters were responsible to mass electorates. Even where the authoritarian, military empires of Germany and Austria–Hungary had previously held sway, democratically elected parliamentary governments took form. Their goals were substantially more modest and less utopian than those of the Bolsheviks. Yet to pursue parliamentary politics where

it had never been meaningfully practiced proved no simple task. The Wilsonian vision of democratic, self-determined nations foundered on the harsh realities of economics, aggressive nationalism, and revived political conservatism. Too often, nations that had been given democratic, parliamentary government lacked both the will and the political skill to make the new system work. Moreover, in many of the new democracies, important sectors of the citizenry believed that parliamentary politics was inherently corrupt or unequal to great nationalistic enterprises. Economics and politics had become more intimately connected than ever before. The economic and social anxieties of the electorate as well as nationalistic ambitions could and eventually did overcome political scruples.

## Demands for Revision of the Paris Settlement

The Paris peace treaties themselves became domestic political issues. Usually the objections arose from nationalistic concerns and resentments. Germany had been humiliated. The arrangements for reparations led to endless haggling over payments. Various national groups in the successor states of eastern Europe also felt that they had been treated unjustly or been denied self-determination. There were demands for further border adjustments. On the other side, the victorious powers, and especially France, often believed that the provisions of the treaty were not being adequately enforced. So, throughout the 1920s, calls either to revise or to enforce the Paris treaties contributed to domestic political turmoil across the Continent. Many political figures were willing to fish in these troubled international waters for a large catch of domestic votes.

## Postwar Economic Problems

Along with the move toward political experimentation and the demands for revision of the new international order, there existed a widespread desire to return to the economic prosperity of the prewar years. After 1918, however, it was impossible to restore in the economic realm what American President Warren Harding (1865–1923) would shortly term "normalcy." During the Great War, Europeans had turned the vast military and industrial power that they had created during the previous century against themselves and their civilization. What had been "normal" in economic and social life during the previous half century could not be reestablished.

More than 750,000 British soldiers had perished. The combat deaths for France and Germany were 1,385,000 and 1,808,000, respectively. Russia had lost no fewer than 1,700,000 troops. Hundreds of thousands more from other nations had also been killed. Still more millions had been wounded. These casualties represented not only the waste of human life and talent but also the loss of producers and consumers.

Another casualty of the conflict was the financial dominance and independence of Europe. At the opening of hostilities, Europe had been the financial and credit center of the world. At the close of the fighting, European states were deep in debt to each other and to the United States. The Bolsheviks had repudiated the debt of the tsarist government, much of which was owed to French creditors. Other nations could not pursue this revolutionary course. The Paris settlement had imposed heavy financial obligations on Germany and its allies. The United States refused to ask reparations from Germany but demanded repayment of war debts from its own allies.

On one hand, the reparation and debt structure meant that no nation was fully in control of its own economic life. On the other hand, the absence of international economic cooperation meant that more than ever individual nations felt compelled to pursue or to try to pursue selfish, nationalistic economic aims. It was perhaps the worst of all possible international economic worlds.

The market and trade conditions that had prevailed before 1914 had also changed radically. In addition to the unprecedented loss of human life, much of Europe's transport facilities, mines, and industry had been damaged or destroyed. Russia all but withdrew from the European economic order. The political reconstruction of eastern and central Europe into a multitude of small states broke up the trade region formerly encompassed by Germany and Austria–Hungary. Most of those new states had weak economies hardly capable of competing in modern economic life. The new political boundaries separated raw materials from the factories using them. Railway systems on which finished and unfinished products traveled might now lie under the control of two or more nations. Political and economic nationalism went together. Nations raised new customs barriers where before there had been none.

International trade also followed novel patterns. The United States became less dependent on European production and was now a major competitor. During the war, the belligerents had been forced to sell many of their investments on other continents to finance the conflict. As a consequence, European dominance over the world economy weakened. Slow postwar economic growth or even the decline of economic activity within colonies or former colonies lowered the international demand for European goods. The United States and Japan began to penetrate markets in Latin America and Asia that European producers and traders had previously dominated.

## New Roles for Government and Labor

Throughout Europe, the war had given labor new prominence. In every country, the unions had actively supported the war effort. They had ensured labor peace for wartime production. In turn, their members had received better wages, and their leaders had been admitted to high political councils. This wartime cooperation of unions and labor leaders with the various national governments destroyed the internationalism of the prewar labor movement. It also, however, meant that henceforth government could not ignore the demands of labor. After the war, many wages were lowered, but rarely to prewar levels. European workers intended to receive their just share of the fruits of their labor. Collective bargaining and union recognition brought on by the war were also there to stay. This improvement in both the status and the effective influence of labor was one of the most significant social and political changes to flow from World War I.

The social condition of workers seemed to be improving while that of the middle class seemed to be stagnating or declining. Throughout the 1920s, people from the various segments of the middle class remained suspicious of the new role of labor and of socialist political parties. This suspicion and fear of potential loss of property by the middle classes led them to seek to perpetuate the status quo and to fend off further social and economic advances by the working classes. Thus, the European middle classes, once the vanguard of the liberal revolution, became a generally conservative political force in the 1920s. Their conservatism deepened as fear of Bolshevism spread across the Continent.

# The Soviet Experiment Begins

The consolidation of the Bolshevik Revolution in Russia established the most extensive and durable of all the twentieth-century authoritarian governments that came to power in the political turmoil of World War I and its aftermath. The Communist Party of the Soviet Union retained power from 1917 until the end of 1991, and its presence influenced the political history of Europe during this century as did no other single factor. The Communist Party was neither a mass party nor a nationalistic one. Its early membership rarely exceeded 1 percent of the Russian population. For several years after 1917, it faced widespread domestic opposition, and the Communist leaders long felt that their hold on the country was insecure. Yet the Communists also regarded their government and their revolution not as local events in a national history but as epoch-making events in the history of the world and the development of humanity. Communism was an exportable commodity that could disrupt the political life of other nations, and throughout the history of the Soviet Union, its leaders sought to export its ideology and doctrines. Fear of communism and determination to stop its spread became one of the leading political forces in western Europe and the United States for most of the rest of the century.

## War Communism

Within the Soviet Union, the Red Army under the organizational direction of Leon Trotsky (1879–1940) eventually suppressed internal and foreign military opposition to the new government. The White Russian armies, which fought the Red Army for several years, could not adequately organize themselves, and Allied help was inadequate to defeat the Bolsheviks. The existence of a military threat allowed the Bolsheviks rapidly to pursue authoritarian policies. Within months of the revolution, a new secret police, known as the *Cheka*, appeared. Throughout the civil war, Lenin had declared that the Bolshevik Party, as the vanguard of the revolution, was imposing the dictatorship of the proletariat. Political and economic administration became highly centralized. All major decisions flowed from the top in a nondemocratic manner. Under the economic policy of *war communism*, the revolutionary government confiscated and then operated the banks, the transport system, and heavy industry. The state also seized grain from the peasants to feed the army and the workers in the cities. The fact of the civil war permitted the Bolsheviks to suppress resistance to this economic policy. Throughout the period of the civil war the government headed by Lenin carried out extensive repression of all actual or potential sources of opposition.

War communism aided the victory of the Red Army. The revolution had survived and triumphed. The policy, however, generated domestic opposition to the Bolsheviks, who in 1920 numbered only about 600,000 members. The alliance of workers and peasants forged by the slogan of "Peace, Bread, and Land" had begun to come apart at the seams. Many Russians were no longer willing to make the sacrifices demanded by the central party bureaucrats. In 1920 and 1921, large strikes occurred in many factories. Discontented peasants resisted the requisition of grain as they had since 1918. In March 1921, the Baltic fleet mutinied at Kronstadt. The Red Army crushed the rebellion with grave loss of life.

*During the civil war in the Soviet Union hunger and starvation haunted the countryside. Here a group of malnourished children posed for a photograph. [Bildarchiv Preussischer Kulturbesitz]*

Each of these incidents suggested that the proletariat itself was opposing the dictatorship of the proletariat as embodied in the Communist Party. Also, by late 1920 it had become clear that revolution was not going to erupt across the rest of Europe. For the time being, the Soviet Union would be a vast island of revolutionary socialism in the worldwide sea of capitalism.

## The New Economic Policy

Under these difficult conditions, Lenin made a crucial strategic retreat. In March 1921, following the Kronstadt mutiny and in the face of continuing peasant resistance to the requisition of grain needed to feed the urban population, he outlined the New Economic Policy, normally called NEP. Apart from what he termed "the commanding heights" of banking, heavy industry, transportation, and international commerce, the government would tolerate private economic enterprise. In particular, peasants could farm for profit. They would pay taxes like other citizens, but they could sell their surplus grain on the open market. The New Economic Policy was in line with Lenin's earlier conviction that the Russian peasantry held the key to the success of the revolution.

After 1921 the countryside did become more stable, and a more secure food supply seemed assured for the cities. Similar free enterprise flourished within light industry and domestic retail trade. The implementation of the New Economic Policy, however, was not fully successful, because there were virtually no consumer goods for the peasants to purchase with the money they received for their grain. Yet by 1927 industrial production had reached its 1913 level. The revolution seemed to have transformed Russia into a land of small, if frequently discontented, family farmers and owners of small, private shops and businesses.

## Stalin Versus Trotsky

The New Economic Policy had caused sharp disputes within the Politburo, the highest governing committee of the Communist Party. Some members considered the partial return to capitalism a betrayal of Marxist principles. These frictions increased when Lenin's firm hand disappeared. In 1922 he suffered a stroke and never again dominated party affairs. In 1924 Lenin died.

The resulting power vacuum led to an intense struggle for the leadership of the party. Two factions

After the Bolshevik Revolution there were many shortages in the cities of the new Soviet Union. This painting shows citizens buying and selling goods in a Moscow street market in the early 1920s. [Bildarchiv Preussischer Kulturbesitz]

emerged. One was led by Leon Trotsky; the other by Joseph Stalin (1879–1953), who had become general secretary of the party in 1922. Shortly before his death, Lenin had criticized both men but was especially harsh toward Stalin. Stalin's power base, however, lay with the party membership and in the day-to-day management of party affairs. Consequently, he was able to withstand the posthumous strictures of Lenin.

The issue between the two factions was power within the party, but the struggle was fought out over the question of Russia's path toward industrialization and the future of the communist revolutionary movement. Trotsky, speaking for what became known as the *left wing*, urged rapid industrialization financed through the expropriation of farm production. Agriculture should be collectivized, and the peasants should be made to pay for industrialization. Trotsky further argued that the revolution in Russia could succeed only if new revolutions took place elsewhere. Russia needed the skills and wealth of other nations to build its own

# Trotsky Urges the Use of Terror

*Leon Trotsky led the Red Army to victory in the civil war that followed the Bolshevik Revolution in 1918. He became a major opponent and later a victim of Stalin. In this 1920 discussion, he explains how terror and intimidation must be used to achieve communist revolution. He contends that capitalist society itself came to power through the use of force and that only force will allow the working class to establish its dominance. He argues there is no real moral argument against the use of terror and violence. In particular, he directs his remarks toward liberals who thought social change could be achieved by parliamentary means and against the German Marxist socialists, the Kautskians, who had argued that historical forces would bring about the revolution of the working class without the use of violence. These words of Trotsky help explain the fear of Bolshevism that swept across much of Europe immediately after World War I, a fear right-wing politicians manipulated during the 1920s and 1930s.*

✦ *How does Trotsky's justification of terror compare with that associated with the Reign of Terror during the French Revolution? How might the circumstances of the Russian civil war have led Trotsky to these views? Do you agree that the Communist terror advocated by Trotsky differed from the repressive police policies of the tsars?*

The problem of revolution, as of war, consists in breaking the will of the foe, forcing him to capitulate and to accept the conditions of the conqueror. The will, of course, is a fact of the physical world, but in contradistinction to a meeting, a dispute, or a congress, the revolution carries out its object by means of the employment of material resources—though to a lesser degree than war. The bourgeoisie itself conquered power by means of revolts, and consolidated it by the civil war. In the peace period, it retains power by means of a system

---

economy. As Trotsky's influence within the party waned, he also demanded that party members be permitted to criticize the policies of the government and the party. Trotsky was, however, a latecomer to the advocacy of open discussion. When he had controlled the Red Army, he had been an unflinching disciplinarian.

A faction known as the *right wing* opposed Trotsky. Its chief ideological voice was that of Nikolai Bukharin (1888–1938), the editor of *Pravda* (truth), the official party paper. Stalin was the major political manipulator of this group. In the mid-1920s, in the face of uncertain economic recovery, this faction pressed for the continuation of Lenin's NEP and for relatively slow industrialization. At the

time, this position represented an economic policy based largely on decentralized economic planning and the tolerance of modest free enterprise and small landholdings. Stalin emerged as the victor in these intraparty rivalries.

Stalin had been born in 1879 into a poor family. Unlike the other early Bolshevik leaders, he had not spent a long period of exile in western Europe and was much less intellectual and internationalist in his outlook. He was also much more brutal. As Commissar of Nationalities, Stalin's handling of various recalcitrant national groups within Russia after the revolution had shocked even Lenin, though not enough for Lenin to dismiss him. As the Party General Secretary, a post that

of repression. As long as class society, founded on the most deep-rooted antagonisms, continues to exist, repression remains a necessary means of breaking the will of the opposing side.

Even if, in one country or another, the dictatorship of the proletariat grew up within the external framework of democracy, this would by no means avert the civil war. The question as to who is to rule the country, i.e., of the life or death of the bourgeoisie, will be decided on either side, not by references to the paragraphs of the constitution, but by the employment of all forms of violence. . . .

The question of the form of repression, or of its degree, of course, is not one of "principle." It is a question of expediency. . . .

. . . Terror can be very efficient against a reactionary class which does not want to leave the scene of operations. *Intimidation* is a powerful weapon of policy, both internationally and internally. A victorious war, generally speaking, destroys only an insignificant part of the conquered army, intimidating the remainder and breaking their will. The revolution works in the same way: it kills individuals, and intimidates thousands. In this sense, the Red Terror is not distinguishable from the armed insurrection, the direct continuation of which it represents.

The State terror of a revolutionary class can be condemned "morally" only by a man who, as a principle, rejects (in words) every form of violence whatsoever—consequently, every war and every rising. For this one has to be merely and simply a hypocritical Quaker.

"But, in that case, in what do your tactics differ from the tactics of Tsarism?", we are asked by the high priests of Liberalism and Kautskianism.

You do not understand this, holy men? We shall explain to you. The terror of Tsarism was directed against the proletariat. The gendarmerie of Tsarism throttled the workers who were fighting for the Socialist order. Our Extraordinary Commissions shoot landlords, capitalists, and generals who are striving to restore the capitalist order. Do you grasp this—distinction? Yes? For us Communists it is quite sufficient.

*Leon Trotsky*, Terrorism and Communism 1920; *English trans.*, Dictatorship vs. Democracy: A Reply to Karl Kautsky, *New York: Workers' Party of America, 1922, pp. 54, 57–59, as quoted in Robert V. Daniels*, A Documentary History of Communism, *rev. ed., vol. 1 (Hanover, N.H., and London: University Press of New England, 1984), pp. 121–122.*

party intellectuals disdained as merely clerical, Stalin amassed power through his command of bureaucratic and administrative methods. He was neither a brilliant writer nor an effective public speaker. He did, however, master the crucial, if dull, details of party structure, including admission to the party and promotion within it. That mastery meant that he had the support of the lower levels of the party apparatus when he clashed with other leaders.

In the mid-1920s, Stalin expediently supported Bukharin's position on economic development. In 1924 he also enunciated, in opposition to Trotsky, the doctrine of "socialism in one country." He urged that socialism could be achieved in Russia alone. Russian success did not depend on the fate of revolutions elsewhere. Stalin thus nationalized the previously international scope of the Marxist revolution. He cunningly used his control over the Central Committee of the Communist Party to edge out Trotsky and his supporters.

By 1927 Trotsky had been removed from all his offices, expelled from the party, and exiled to Siberia. In 1929 he was forced out of Russia and eventually moved to Mexico, where he was murdered in 1940, presumably by one of Stalin's agents. With Trotsky defeated, Stalin was firmly in control of the Soviet state. It remained to be seen where he would take it and what "socialism in one country" would mean in practice.

# A Communist Woman Demands a New Family Life

*While Lenin sought to consolidate the Bolshevik revolution against internal and external enemies, there existed within the young Soviet Union a vast utopian impulse to change and reform virtually every social institution that had existed before the revolution or that was associated in the Communists' minds with capitalist society. Alexandra Kollontai (1872–1952) was a spokesperson of the extreme political left within the early Soviet Union. In Communist circles, there had been much speculation on how the end of bourgeois society might change the structure of the family and the position of women. In this passage, written in 1920, Kollontai states one of the most idealistic visions of this change. During the years immediately after the revolution, extreme rumors circulated in both Europe and America about sexual and family experimentation in the Soviet Union. Statements such as this fostered such rumors. Kollontai herself later became a supporter of Stalin and a Soviet diplomat.*

✦ *Why did Kollontai see the restructuring of the family as essential to the establishment of a new kind of communist society? Would these changes make people loyal to that society? What changes in society does the kind of economic independence she seeks for women presuppose? What kind of childhood might the children of this society expect to experience when they are the children of the state rather than of specific parents?*

There is no escaping the fact: the old type of family has seen its day. It is not the fault of the Communist State, it is the result of the changed conditions of life. *The family is ceasing to be a necessity of the State,* as it was in the past; on the contrary, it is worse than useless, since it needlessly holds back the female workers from more productive and far more serious work. . . . But on the ruins of the former family we shall soon see a new form

## The Third International

The success of the revolution in Russia and the outlook of its leaders divided socialist parties and socialist movements in the rest of Europe. As already noted, the early leaders of the Bolshevik Revolution believed they were beginning a new era of history and that their revolution would spread. Even after Stalin's declaration of "socialism in one country," the Soviet Union worked to expand communism.

In 1919 the Soviet Communists founded the Third International of the European socialist movement, better known as the *Comintern*. The Comintern wished to make the Bolshevik model of socialism, as developed by Lenin, the rule for all socialist parties outside the Soviet Union. In 1920, a year after its inception, the Comintern imposed its Twenty-one Conditions on any other socialist party that wished to join it. The conditions included acknowledgment of leadership from Moscow, rejection of reformist or revisionist socialism, and repudiation of previous socialist leaders. In effect, the Comintern sought to destroy all democratic socialism.

The decision whether to accept these conditions split every major European socialist party. As a result, separate communist and social democratic parties emerged in many countries. The communist parties modeled themselves after the Soviet party,

rising which will involve altogether different relations between men and women, and which will be *a union of affection and comradeship, a union of two equal members of the Communist society, both of them free, both of them independent, both of them workers*. No more domestic "servitude" of women. No more inequality within the family. No more fear on the part of the woman lest she remain without support or aid with little ones in her arms if her husband should desert her. The woman in the Communist city no longer depends on her husband but on her work. It is not her husband but her robust arms which will support her. There will be no more anxiety as to the fate of her children. The State of the Workers will assume responsibly for these. Marriage will be purified of all its material elements, of all money calculations, which constitute a hideous blemish on family life in our days. . . .

The woman who is called upon to struggle in the great cause of the liberation of the workers—such a woman should know that in the new State there will be no more room for such petty divisions as were formerly understood: "These are my own children, to them I owe all my maternal solicitude, all my affection; those are your children, my neighbour's children; I am not concerned with them. I have enough to do with my own." Henceforth the worker-mother, who is conscious of her social function, will rise to a point where she no longer differentiates between *yours* and *mine*; she must remember that there are henceforth only *our* children, those of the Communist State, the common possession of all the workers.

The Worker's State has need of a new form of relation between the sexes. The narrow and exclusive affection of the mother for her own children must expand until it embraces all the children of the great proletarian family. In place of the indissoluble marriage based on the servitude of woman, we shall see rise the free union, fortified by the love and mutual respect of the two members of the Workers' State, equal in their rights and in their obligations. In place of the individual and egotistic family there will arise a great universal family of workers, in which all the workers, men and women, will be, above all, workers, comrades.

*Alexandra Kollontai*, Communism and the Family, *as reprinted in Rudolf Schlesinger, ed. and trans.*, The Family in the USSR *(London: Routledge and Kegan Paul, 1949), pp. 67–69.*

and Moscow dictated their policies. The social democratic parties attempted to pursue both social reform and liberal parliamentary politics. Throughout the 1920s and early 1930s, the communists and social democrats fought each other more intensely than they fought either capitalism or conservative political parties. Their fierce conflict was one of the fundamental features of the interwar European political landscape.

These policies of the Comintern directly and importantly affected the rise of the Fascists and the Nazis in western Europe. It is difficult to exaggerate the fears that Soviet political rhetoric and Communist Party activity roused throughout Europe during the 1920s and 1930s. These fears, often exaggerated, were repeatedly manipulated by conservative and right-wing political groups. The presence of separate communist parties in western Europe meant that right-wing politicians always had a convenient target that they could justly accuse of seeking to overthrow the existing government and to impose Soviet-style political and economic experiments in their respective nations. Furthermore, right-wing politicians continued to accuse the democratic socialist parties of supporting policies that might facilitate a communist takeover. The division of the European political left also meant that right-wing political movements rarely had to confront a united left-wing opposition.

# The Third International Issues
# Conditions of Membership

*After the Russian Revolution, the Russian Communist Party organized the Third Communist International. Any communist party outside the Soviet Union was required to accept these Twenty-one Conditions, adopted in 1920, to join the International. In effect, this program demanded that all such parties adopt a distinctly revolutionary program. They also needed to cease operating as legal parties within their various countries. By this means, the Soviet Union sought to achieve leadership of the socialist movement throughout Europe. The non-Russian socialist parties quickly split into social democratic parties that remained independent of Moscow and communist parties that adopted the policy imposed by the Russian Communist Party.*

◆ *What are the major forms of revolutionary agitation that these conditions assume? Why was the Russian Communist Party willing to forgo all alliances with other socialist parties that would not declare and rename themselves Communist? How could this document and the organization it established be used by conservative and right-wing political groups elsewhere in Europe?*

1. The daily propaganda and agitation must bear a truly communist character and correspond to the program and all the decisions of the Third International. All the organs of the press that are in the hands of the party must be edited by reliable communists who have proved their loyalty to the cause of the proletarian revolution. . . .

4. The obligation to spread communist ideas includes the particular necessity of persistent, systematic propaganda in the army. . . .

5. It is necessary to carry on systematic and steady agitation in the rural districts. . . .

. . . . . . . . . . . . . . . . . . . . . . . . . . . . .

14. Every party that desires to belong to the Communist International must give every possible support to the Soviet Republics in their struggle against all counterrevolutionary forces. . . .

. . . . . . . . . . . . . . . . . . . . . . . . . . . . .

16. All decisions of the congresses of the Communist International . . . are binding on all parties affiliated to the Communist International. . . .

17. In connection with all this, all parties desiring to join the Communist International must change their names. Every party that wishes to join the Communist International must bear the name: Communist party of such-and-such country. This question as to name is not merely a formal one, but a political one of great importance. The Communist International has declared a decisive war against the entire bourgeois world and all the yellow social democratic parties. Every rank-and-file worker must clearly understand the difference between the communist parties and the old official "social democratic" or "socialist" parties which have betrayed the cause of the working class.

18. Members of the party who reject the conditions and thesis of the Communist International, on principle, must be expelled from the party.

*Helmut Gruber, ed.,* International Communism in the Era of Lenin: A Documentary History *(Garden City, N.Y.: Doubleday, 1972), pp. 241–246.*

Lenin and Trotsky (saluting) in Red Square in Moscow in 1919, from a documentary film made by Herman Axelbank. Trotsky's organizational skill was largely responsible for the Red Army's victory in the Russian civil war of 1918–1920. By 1921, as a result of war, revolution, and civil war, the Russian economy had all but collapsed. [United Press International Photo]

# The Fascist Experiment in Italy

Italy witnessed the first authoritarian political experiment in western Europe that arose in part from fears of the spread of Bolshevism. From the Italian fascist movement of Benito Mussolini (1883–1945) came the general term *fascist*, frequently used to describe a number of right-wing dictatorships that arose across Europe between the wars.

Both historians and political scientists disagree about the exact meaning of *fascism* as a political term. Most scholars agree, however, that the government regimes regarded as fascist were antidemocratic, anti-Marxist, antiparliamentary, and frequently anti-Semitic. These governments claimed to hold back the spread of Bolshevism, which because of Soviet rhetoric and the activity of domestic communist parties seemed at the time a real threat. They sought to make the world safe for the middle class, small businesses, owners of moderate amounts of property, and small farmers. The fascist regimes rejected the political inheritance of the French Revolution and of nineteenth-century liberalism. Fascist movements were invariably nationalistic in response to the feared international expansion of communism.

Fascists believed that normal parliamentary politics and parties sacrificed national honor and greatness to petty disputes. They wanted to overcome the class conflict of Marxism and the party conflict of liberalism by consolidating the various groups and classes within the nation for great national purposes. As Mussolini declared in 1931, "The fascist conception of the state is all-embracing, and outside of the state no human or spiritual values can exist, let alone be desirable."[1] The fascist governments were usually single-party dictatorships characterized by terrorism and police surveillance. These fascist dictatorships, in contrast to the Communist Party of the Soviet Union, were rooted in the base of mass political parties.

## The Rise of Mussolini

The Italian *Fasci di Combattimento*, or "Bands of Combat," was founded in 1919 in Milan. Its mem-

[1] *Quoted in Denis Mack Smith*, Italy: A Modern History *(Ann Arbor: University of Michigan Press, 1959), p. 412.*

bers came largely from Italian war veterans who felt that the Paris conference had cheated Italy of the hard-won fruits of victory. They especially resented Italy's failure to gain Fiume (now Rijeka) on the northeast coast of the Adriatic Sea. They also feared the spread of socialism and the effects of inflation.

Their leader, Benito Mussolini, had been born the son of a blacksmith. He had worked as a schoolteacher and a day laborer before becoming active in Italian socialist politics. By 1912 he had become editor of the socialist newspaper *Avanti* (meaning "forward"). In 1914 Mussolini broke with the socialists and supported Italian entry into the war on the side of the Allies. His interventionist position lost him the editorship of *Avanti*. He then established his own paper, *Il Popolo d'Italia* (the people of Italy). Later he served in the army and was wounded. In 1919, although of some prewar political stature, Mussolini was simply one of many Italian politicians, and his *Fasci* organization was just one more small political group in a country full of them. As a politician, Mussolini was an opportunist par excellence. He could change his ideas and principles to suit every new occasion. Action for him was always more important than thought or rational justification. His one real goal was political survival.

POSTWAR ITALIAN POLITICAL TURMOIL   Postwar Italian politics was a muddle. During the conflict, the Italian Parliament had virtually ceased to function, and it allowed ministers to rule by decree. Many Italians, however, were already dissatisfied with the parliamentary system. Italian nationalists—not just Mussolini's followers—felt that Italy had not been treated as a great power at the peace conference and had not received the territories it deserved.

The main spokesperson for this discontent was the extreme nationalist writer Gabriele D'Annunzio (1863–1938). In 1919 he seized Fiume with a force of patriotic Italians. He was eventually driven out, but D'Annunzio had shown how a nongovernmental military force could be put to political use. Moreover, the use of force against D'Annunzio embarrassed the Italian government and made it appear less patriotic than the ultranationalists.

Between 1919 and 1921, Italy also experienced considerable internal social turmoil. Many industrial strikes occurred, and workers occupied factories. Peasants seized uncultivated land from large estates. Parliamentary and constitutional government seemed incapable of dealing with this unrest. The Socialist Party had captured a plurality of seats in the Chamber of Deputies in the 1919 election. The sharp division between socialists and communists had not yet emerged, and so the Socialist Party included many people who were soon to become communists. A new Catholic Popular Party had also done well in the election. Both appealed to the working and agrarian classes. Neither party, however, would cooperate with the other; parliamentary deadlock resulted. Under these conditions, many Italians honestly and still others conveniently believed that the social upheaval and political paralysis would lead to a communist revolution.

*Mussolini poses with supporters the day after the Black Shirt March on Rome had intimidated the king of Italy into making him prime minister. [Bildarchiv Preussischer Kulturbesitz]*

# Mussolini Heaps Contempt on Political Liberalism

*The political tactics of the Italian Fascists wholly disregarded the liberal belief in the rule of law and the consent of the governed. In 1923 Mussolini explained why the Fascists so hated and repudiated these liberal principles. Note his emphasis on the idea of the twentieth century as a new historical epoch requiring a new kind of politics and his undisguised praise of force in politics.*

✦ *Who would be some nineteenth-century liberal political leaders included in Mussolini's attack? Why might Mussolini's audience have been receptive to these views? What events or developments within liberal states allowed Mussolini to portray liberalism as so corrupt and powerless?*

Liberalism is not the last word, nor does it represent the definitive formula on the subject of the art of government. . . . Liberalism is the product and the technique of the 19th century. . . . It does not follow that the Liberal scheme of government, good for the 19th century, for a century, that is, dominated by two such phenomena as the growth of capitalism and the strengthening of the sentiment of nationalism, should be adapted to the 20th century, which announces itself already with characteristics sufficiently different from those that marked the preceding century. . . .

I challenge Liberal gentlemen to tell if ever in history there has been a government that was based solely on popular consent and that renounced all use of force whatsoever. A government so constructed there has never been and never will be. Consent is an ever-changing thing like the shifting sand on the sea coast. It can never be permanent: It can never be complete. . . . If it be accepted as an axiom that any system of government whatever creates malcontents, how are you going to prevent this discontent from overflowing and constituting a menace to the stability of the State?

You will prevent it by force. By the assembling of the greatest force possible. By the inexorable use of this force whenever it is necessary. Take away from any government whatsoever force—and by force is meant physical, armed force—and leave it only its immortal principles, and that government will be at the mercy of the first organized group that decides to overthrow it. Fascism now throws these lifeless theories out to rot. . . . The truth evident now to all who are not warped by [liberal] dogmatism is that men have tired of liberty. They have made an orgy of it. Liberty is today no longer the chaste and austere virgin for whom the generations of the first half of the last century fought and died. For the gallant, restless and bitter youth who face the dawn of a new history there are other words that exercise a far greater fascination, and those words are: order, hierarchy, discipline. . . .

Know then, once and for all, that Fascism knows no idols and worships no fetishes. It has already stepped over, and if it be necessary it will turn tranquilly and step again over, the more or less putrescent corpse of the Goddess of Liberty.

*Benito Mussolini, "Force and Consent" (1923), as trans. in Jonathan F. Scott and Alexander Baltzly, eds.,* Readings in European History Since 1814 *(New York: F. S. Crofts, 1931), pp. 680–682.*

EARLY FASCIST ORGANIZATION  Initially, Mussolini was uncertain of the direction of the political winds. He first supported the factory occupations and land seizures. Never one to be concerned with consistency, however, he soon reversed himself. He had discovered that many upper-class and middle-class Italians, pressured by inflation and fearing the loss of their property, had no sympathy for the workers or the peasants. They wanted order rather than some vague social justice that might harm their own interests.

Consequently, Mussolini and his Fascists took direct action in the face of the government inaction. They formed local squads of terrorists who disrupted Socialist Party meetings, beat up Socialist leaders, and intimidated Socialist supporters. They attacked strikers and farm workers and protected strikebreakers. Conservative land and factory owners were grateful. The officers and institutions of the law simply ignored the crimes of the Fascist squads. By early 1922 the Fascists had turned to intimidation through arson, beatings, and murder against local officials in cities such as Ferrara, Ravenna, and Milan. They controlled the local government in much of northern Italy.

MARCH ON ROME  In the election of 1921, Italian voters sent Mussolini and thirty-four of his followers to the Chamber of Deputies. Their importance grew as the local Fascists gained more direct power. The movement now had hundreds of thousands of supporters. In October 1922, the Fascists, dressed in their characteristic black shirts, began a march on Rome, which became known as the *Black Shirt March*. King Victor Emmanuel III (r. 1900–1946), because of both personal and political concerns, refused to sign a decree that would have authorized the army to stop the marchers. Probably no other single decision so ensured a Fascist seizure of power. The cabinet resigned in protest. On October 29, the monarch telegraphed Mussolini in Milan and asked him to become prime minister. The next day, Mussolini arrived in Rome by sleeping car and greeted his followers as head of the government when they entered the city.

Technically, Mussolini had come into office by legal means. The monarch had the constitutional authority to appoint the prime minister. Mussolini, however, had no majority or even near majority in the Chamber of Deputies. Behind the legal facade of his coming to power lay months of terrorist disruption and intimidation and the threat of the Fascist march itself. The non-Fascist politicians, whose ineptitude had prepared the way for Mussolini, believed that his ministry, like others since 1919, would be brief. They did not comprehend that he was not a traditional Italian politician.

## The Fascists in Power

Mussolini had not really expected to be appointed prime minister. He moved cautiously to shore up his support and to consolidate his power. His success was the result of the impotence of his rivals, his own effective use of his office, his power over the masses, and his sheer ruthlessness. On November 23, 1922, the king and Parliament granted Mussolini dictatorial authority for one year to bring order to local and regional government. Wherever possible, Mussolini appointed Fascists to office.

REPRESSION OF OPPOSITION  Late in 1924, under Mussolini's guidance, Parliament changed the election law. Previously, parties had been represented in the Chamber of Deputies in proportion to the popular vote cast for them. According to the new election law, the party that gained the largest popular vote (if at least 25 percent) received two-thirds of the seats in the chamber. Coalition government, with all its compromises and hesitant policies, would no longer be necessary. In the election of 1924, the Fascists won a great victory and complete control of the Chamber of Deputies. They used that majority to end legitimate parliamentary life. A series of laws passed in 1925 and 1926 permitted Mussolini, in effect, to rule by decree. In 1926 all other political parties were dissolved. By the close of that year, Mussolini had transformed Italy into a single-party dictatorial state.

Their growing dominance over the government had not, however, diverted the Fascists from their course of violence and terror. Fascists were put in charge of the police force, and the terrorist squads became a government militia. In late 1924 their thugs murdered Giacomo Matteotti (1885–1924), a leading noncommunist socialist leader and member of Parliament. He had persistently criticized Mussolini and had exposed the criminality of the fascist movement. In protest against the murder, most opposition deputies withdrew from the Chamber of Deputies. That tactic gave Mussolini an even freer hand. The deputies were refused readmission.

*With the Lateran Accord of February 11, 1929, Mussolini made peace with the Roman Catholic Church, gaining respectability for his regime. Cardinal Gasparri, sitting on Mussolini's right, signed the agreement for the Vatican. [Archive Photos]*

PARALLEL STRUCTURE OF PARTY AND GOVERNMENT
The parallel organizations of the party and the government sustained support for the regime. For every government institution, there was a corresponding party organization. The Fascist Party thus dominated the political structure at every level. When all other political parties were outlawed, the citizens had to look to the Fascists in their community for political favors. They also knew the high price of opposition. By the late 1920s, the Grand Council of the party, which Mussolini controlled, had become an organ of the state. It decided who would stand for election to the Chamber of Deputies and on which policies the chamber would vote.

The party used propaganda to great effect. A cult of personality surrounded Mussolini. His skills in oratory and his general intelligence allowed him to hold his own with both large crowds and prominent individuals, foreign as well as Italian. Many respectable Italians tolerated and even admired Mussolini because they believed that he had saved them from Bolshevism. Those who did have the courage to oppose him were usually driven into exile, and some, like Matteotti, were murdered.

ACCORD WITH THE VATICAN Mussolini made one important domestic departure that brought him significant political dividends. Through the Lateran Accord of February 1929, the Roman Catholic Church and the Italian state made peace with each other. Ever since the armies of Italian unification had seized papal lands in the 1860s, the church had been hostile to the state. The popes had remained secluded in the Vatican after 1870. The agreement of 1929 recognized the pope as the temporal ruler of Vatican City. The Italian government agreed to pay an indemnity to the papacy for the territory it had confiscated. The state also recognized Catholicism as the religion of the nation, exempted church property from taxes, and allowed church law to govern marriage. The Lateran Accord brought further respectability to Mussolini's authoritarian regime.

# Joyless Victors

France and Great Britain, with the aid of the United States, had won the war. France became the strongest military power on the Continent. Britain had escaped with almost no physical damage. Both nations, however, had lost vast numbers of young men in the conflict. Their economies were weakened, their overseas investments and power much diminished. Compared with events in Russia and Italy, the interwar political development of the two major democracies seems rather tame. Neither experienced a revolution or a shift to authoritarian government. Yet this surface calm was largely illusory. Both France and Britain were troubled democracies. To neither did victory in war bring the good life in peace.

## France: The Search for Security

At the close of World War I, as after Waterloo, the revolution of 1848, and the defeat of 1871, the French voters elected a doggedly conservative Chamber of Deputies. The preponderance of military officers in blue uniforms among its members led to the nickname of the "Blue Horizon Chamber." The overwhelmingly conservative character of the chamber was registered in 1920 when it defeated Georges Clemenceau's bid for the presidency. The crucial factor had been, of all things, the alleged leniency of the Paris treaties and Clemenceau's failure to establish a separate Rhineland state. The deputies wanted to achieve future security against Germany and Russian communism. They intended to make as few concessions to domestic social reform as possible. The 1920s were marked by frequent changes of ministries and drift in domestic policy. The political turnstile remained ever active. Between the end of the war and January 1933, France was governed by no fewer than twenty-seven different cabinets.

New Alliances   During the first five years after the conclusion of the Paris settlement, France accepted its role as the leading European power. The French plan was to enforce strictly the clauses of the treaty that were meant to keep Germany weak and also to build a system of eastern alliances to replace the prewar alliance with Russia. In 1920 and 1921, three eastern states that had much to lose from revision of the Versailles treaty—Czechoslovakia, Romania, and Yugoslavia—formed the Little Entente. Before long, France made military alliances with these states and with Poland. A border dispute with Czechoslovakia prevented the Poles from joining the Little Entente, but Poland's independence depended on the maintenance of the Paris settlement.

This new system of eastern pacts was the best France could do, but it was far weaker than the old Franco–Russian alliance. Even combined, the new states were no match for the former power of tsarist Russia, and they were neither united nor reliable. Poland and Romania were more concerned about Russia than about Germany, and the main target of the Little Entente was Hungary. If one of these states was threatened by a resurgent Germany, it could not rely on the others to come to its aid.

The formation of this new alliance system heightened the sense of danger and isolation felt by the two excluded powers, Germany and the Soviet Union. In 1922, while the European states were holding an economic conference at Genoa, the Russians and the Germans met at nearby Rapallo and signed a treaty of their own. It established diplomatic and economic relations that proved useful to each of them. Although the treaty contained no secret political or military clauses, other governments suspected that such arrangements did exist. And it is now known that the Germans did help train the Russian army, and their own army got valuable experience in the use of tanks and planes in the Soviet Union. Rapallo confirmed the French in their belief that Germany would not live up to the terms of the Versailles treaty and helped move them to strong action.

Quest for Reparations   In early 1923 the Allies, and France in particular, declared Germany to be in technical default of its reparations payments. Raymond Poincaré (1860–1934), France's powerfully nationalistic prime minister, decided to teach the

The French invasion of the German Ruhr began a crisis that brought strikes and rampant inflation in Germany. Here French troops have commandeered a German locomotive during one of the strikes. [UPI/Bettmann Newsphotos]

Germans a lesson and to force them to comply. On January 11, 1923, to ensure receipt of the hard-won reparations, the French government ordered its troops to occupy Germany's borderland Ruhr mining and manufacturing district. In response, the German government ordered passive resistance. This policy amounted to calling a general strike in the largest industrial region of Germany. Confronted with this tactic, Poincaré sent French civilians to run the German mines and railroads. France prevailed.

The Germans paid, but France's victory was costly. The English were alienated by the French heavy-handedness and took no part in the occupation. They became more suspicious of France and more sympathetic to Germany. The cost of the Ruhr occupation, moreover, vastly increased French as well as German inflation and hurt the French economy. The Ruhr invasion demonstrated how the uncertainties surrounding the Versailles treaty could harm even the nations whom it was intended to benefit.

In 1924 Poincaré's conservative ministry gave way to a coalition of leftist parties, the so-called *Cartel des Gauches*, led by Edouard Herriot (1872–1957). The new cabinet recognized the Soviet Union and adopted a more conciliatory policy toward Germany. This policy was the work of Aristide Briand (1862–1932), who was foreign minister for the remainder of the decade. He championed the League of Nations and tried to persuade France that its military power did not give it unlimited influence in the foreign affairs of Europe.

Under the leftist coalition, a mild inflation also occurred. It had begun under the conservatives but picked up intensity in 1925. When the value of the franc fell sharply on the international money market in 1926, Poincaré returned to office as head of a national government of several parties. The value of the franc recovered somewhat, and inflation cooled. For the rest of the 1920s, the conservatives remained in power, and France enjoyed a general prosperity that lasted until 1931, longer than in any other nation.

## Great Britain: Economic Confusion

World War I profoundly changed British politics if not the political system. In 1918 Parliament expanded the electorate to include all men aged twenty-one and women aged thirty. (In 1928 the age for women voters was also lowered to twenty-one.) The prewar structure of parties and leadership also shifted. A coalition cabinet of Liberal, Conservative, and Labour ministers had directed the war effort. The wartime ministerial participation of the Labour Party helped dispel its radical image. For the Liberal Party, however, the conflict brought further division.

Until 1916 Liberal Prime Minister Herbert Asquith (1852–1928) had presided over the cabinet. As disagreements over war management developed, he was ousted by fellow Liberal David Lloyd George (1863–1945). The party split sharply between followers of the two men. In 1918, against the wishes of both the Labour Party and the Asquith Liberals, Lloyd George decided to maintain the coalition through the tasks of the peace conference and the domestic reconstruction. In December 1918, the wartime coalition, now minus its Labour members, won a stunning victory at the polls. Lloyd George, however, could thereafter remain prime minister only as long as his dominant Conservative partners wished to keep him.

During the election campaign, there had been much talk about creating "a land fit for heroes to live in." It did not happen. Except for the three years immediately after the war, the British economy was depressed throughout the 1920s. There was no genuine postwar recovery. Unemployment never dipped below 10 percent and often hovered near 11 percent. There were never fewer than a million workers unemployed. Government insurance programs to cover unemployed workers, widows, and orphans were expanded. There was no similar meaningful expansion in the number of jobs available. From 1922 onward, accepting the "dole" with little expectation of future employment became a wretched and degrading way of life for scores of thousands of poor British families.

THE FIRST LABOUR GOVERNMENT   In October 1922, the Conservatives replaced Lloyd George with Andrew Bonar Law (1858–1923), one of their own. A Liberal would never again be prime minister. Stanley Baldwin (1867–1947) soon replaced Law, who had fallen victim to throat cancer. Baldwin decided to attempt to cure Britain's economic plight by abandoning free trade and imposing protective tariffs. The voters rejected that policy in 1923. In the election, the Conservative Party lost its majority in the House of Commons, but only votes from both Liberal and Labour party members could provide an alternative majority.

Labour had elected the second largest group of members to the Commons. Consequently, in

December 1923, King George V (r. 1910–1936) asked Ramsay MacDonald (1866–1937) to form the first Labour ministry in British history. The Liberal Party did not serve in the cabinet but provided the necessary votes in the House of Commons to give Labour a working majority.

The Labour Party was socialistic in its platform, but democratic and distinctly nonrevolutionary. The party had expanded beyond its early trade-union base. MacDonald himself had opposed World War I and for a time had also broken with the party. His own version of socialism owed little, if anything, to Marx. His program consisted of plans for extensive social reform rather than for the nationalization or public seizure of industry. A sensitive politician, if not a great leader, MacDonald understood that the most important task facing his government was proving to the nation that the Labour Party was both respectable and responsible. His nine months in office achieved that goal, if little else of major importance. The establishment of Labour as a viable governing party signaled the permanent demise of the Liberal Party. It has continued to exist, but the bulk of its voters have drifted into either the Conservative or the Labour ranks.

THE GENERAL STRIKE OF 1926   The Labour government fell in the autumn of 1924 over charges of inadequate prosecution of a communist writer. Stanley Baldwin returned to office, where he remained until 1929. The stagnant economy remained uppermost in the public mind. Business and political leaders continued to believe that all would be well if they could restore the prewar conditions of trade. A major element in these conditions had been the gold standard as the basis for international trade. In 1925 the Conservative government returned to the gold standard, abandoned during the war, in hopes of recreating the former monetary stability. The government, however, set the conversion rate for the pound too high against other currencies and thus, in effect, raised the price of British goods to foreign customers.

To make their products competitive on the world market, British management attempted to lower prices by cutting wages. The coal industry was the sector most directly affected by the wage cuts. It was inefficient and poorly managed and had been in trouble since the end of the war.

Labor relations in the coal industry long had been unruly. In 1926, after cuts in wages and a breakdown in negotiations, the coal miners went on strike. Soon thereafter, in May 1926, sympathetic

Stanley Baldwin was the Conservative Party prime minister during the general strike of 1926. His solid, calm appearance suggested to many voters the qualities most needed in their government. [UPI/Bettmann Newsphotos]

workers in other industries engaged in a general strike lasting nine days. There was much tension but little violence. In the end, the miners and the other unions capitulated. With such high levels of unemployment, organized labor was in a weak position. After the general strike, the Baldwin government attempted to reconcile labor primarily through new housing and reforms in the poor laws. Despite the economic difficulties of these years, the actual standard of living of most British workers, including those receiving government insurance payments, actually improved.

EMPIRE   World War I also modified Britain's imperial position. The aid given by the dominions, such as Canada and Australia, demonstrated a new independence on their part. Empire was a two-way proposition. The idea of self-determination as applied to Europe filtered into imperial relationships. In India, the Congress Party, led by Mohandas Gandhi (1869–1948), was beginning to attract widespread support. The British started to talk more about eventual self-government for India. Moreover, during the 1920s the government of India achieved the right to impose tariffs to protect its own industry rather than for the advantage of British manufacturers. British textile producers no longer had totally free access to the vast Indian market.

IRELAND   A new chapter was written in the unhappy relations between Britain and Ireland

# Stanley Baldwin Reflects on the British General Strike

*After halting much economic activity for more than a week in 1926, the British general strike came to a peaceful conclusion. Stanley Baldwin, who was the Conservative Prime Minister at the time, thought the outcome spoke well for British character and British freedom. In examining the impact of the strike, he was particularly concerned to present British institutions in a favorable light, as contrasted with the new social order then emerging in the Soviet Union. He hoped that communist doctrines would not come to influence the British labor movement.*

✦ *In discussing the general strike, how did Baldwin seek to downplay the strife and class conflict present in the event? How did Baldwin appeal to patriotism to overcome political and social divisions in the wake of the strike? How do the language and rhetoric of this Prime Minister of a liberal democracy compare with the language and rhetoric of contemporary leaders of authoritarian political movements also presented in this chapter?*

It may have been a magnificent demonstration of the solidarity of labour, but it was at the same time a most pathetic evidence of the failure of all of us to live and work together for the good of all. . . . But if that strike showed solidarity, sympathy with the miners—whatever you like—it showed something else far greater. It proved the stability of the whole fabric of our own country, and to the amazement of the world not a shot was fired. We were saved by common sense and the good temper of our own people. We have been called a stupid people; but the moment the public grasped that what was at stake was not the solidarity of labour nor the fate of the miners, but the life of the State, then there was a response to the country's need deep and irresistible. And mark this: in my view there was that feeling in the country because the leaders of the strike and the men who were on strike felt it in their innermost hearts, too. They felt a conflict of loyalties. They knew that same conflict was raging in the breasts of thousands of men who had fought for their country ten years ago. Many of the strikers were uneasy in their minds and their consciences, because the British workman, as I known him, does not like breaking contracts, as so many of them did. I do not think

many of them like stopping food supplies and shutting down the Press. I sometimes amuse myself with wondering what their language would have been like if these things had been done by the Government. And, after all, when all has been said about England, about the mistakes we make, and about our stupidity, and about how much better they do things in Russia, yet how many of those men or any of us, would prefer to have been born and brought up in any country in the world but this, or to send our children to be brought up there. In these postwar years, in spite of the depression, in spite of all our troubles, never before has the wealth of this country, through the taxes and the rates, been so distributed to those less fortunate and for the provision of those thrown out of work. . . .

I want to see out British Labour movement free from alien and foreign heresy. I want to see it pursued and developed on English lines, led by English men. The temptations that beset the growth of these vast organizations [the labour unions], in many respects as they are today outside the law, controlling multitudes of men and large sums of money—the temptation to set such a machine in motion and make people follow it is great indeed.

*Stanley Baldwin, Our Inheritance (London: Hodder and Stroughton, 1928), pp. 222–224.*

*Eamon De Valera inspects troops of the Irish Republican Army during the Irish Civil War. [Archive Photos]*

during and after the war. In 1914 the Irish Home Rule Bill had passed Parliament, but its implementation was postponed until after the war. As the war dragged on, Irish nationalists determined to wait no longer. On Easter Monday in April 1916, a nationalist uprising occurred in Dublin. It was the only rebellion of a national group to occur against any government engaged in the war. The British suppressed it in less than a week, but then made a grave tactical blunder. They executed the Irish nationalist leaders who had been responsible for the uprising. Overnight those rebels became national martyrs. Leadership of the nationalist cause quickly shifted from the Irish Party in Parliament to the extremist *Sinn Fein*, or "Ourselves Alone," movement.

In the election of 1918, the Sinn Fein Party won all but four of the Irish parliamentary seats outside Ulster. They refused to go to the Parliament at Westminster. Instead they constituted themselves into a *Dail Eireann*, or Irish Parliament. On January 21, 1919, they declared Irish independence. The military wing of Sinn Fein became the Irish Republican Army (IRA). The first president was Eamon De Valera (1882–1975), who had been born in the United States. What amounted to a guerrilla war broke out between the IRA and the British army supported by auxiliaries known as the Black and Tans. There was intense bitterness and hatred on both sides.

In late 1921, the two governments began secret negotiations. In the treaty concluded in December 1921, the Irish Free State took its place beside the earlier dominions in the British Commonwealth: Canada, Australia, New Zealand, and South Africa. The six counties of Ulster, or Northern Ireland,

were permitted to remain part of what was now called the United Kingdom of Great Britain and Northern Ireland, with provisions for home rule. No sooner had the treaty been signed than a new civil war broke out between Irish moderates and diehards. The moderates supported the treaty; the diehards wanted to abolish the oath to the British

| Major Political Events of the 1920s | |
|---|---|
| 1919 (August) | Constitution of the Weimar Republic promulgated |
| 1920 | *Kapp Putsch* in Berlin |
| 1921 (March) | Kronstadt mutiny leads Lenin to initiate his New Economic Policy |
| 1921 (December) | Treaty between Great Britain and the Irish Free State |
| 1922 (April) | Treaty of Rapallo between Germany and the Soviet Union |
| 1922 (October) | Fascist march on Rome leads to Mussolini's assumption of power |
| 1923 (January) | France invades the Ruhr |
| 1923 (November) | Hitler's Beer Hall *Putsch* |
| 1923 (December) | First Labour government in Britain |
| 1924 | Death of Lenin |
| 1925 | Locarno Agreements |
| 1926 | General strike in Britain |
| 1928 | Kellogg–Briand Pact |
| 1929 (January) | Trotsky expelled from the Soviet Union |
| 1929 (February) | Lateran Accord between the Vatican and the Italian state |

monarch and establish a totally independent republic. The second civil war continued until 1923. De Valera, who supported the diehards, resigned the presidency and organized resistance to the treaty. In 1932 he was again elected president. The next year, the Dail Eireann abolished the oath of allegiance to the monarch.

During World War II, the Irish Free State remained neutral. In 1949 it declared itself the wholly independent republic of Eire.

# Trials of the Successor States in Eastern Europe

Only the barest outline can be given of the dreary political story of the successor states of eastern Europe. They were termed the *successor states* because they succeeded all or portions of the overturned German, Austrian–Hungarian, and Russian empires. Their story is significant because except for Austria after 1956 the interwar era provided those lands with their only modern experience of political independence before the revolutions of 1989 toppled their communist regimes.

It had been an article of faith among nineteenth-century liberals sympathetic to nationalism that only good could flow from the demise of Austria–Hungary, the restoration of Poland, and the establishment of nation-states throughout eastern Europe. These new states were to embody the principle of national self-determination and to provide a buffer against the westward spread of Bolshevism. They were, however, in trouble from the beginning.

Both France and Great Britain had long experience in liberal democratic government. Their primary challenges during the 1920s lay in responding to economic pressures and allowing new groups, such as the Labour Party, to share political power. In Germany, Poland, Austria, Czechoslovakia, and the other successor states, the challenge for the 1920s was to make new parliamentary governments function in a satisfactory and stable manner. Before the war, the elected parliaments of both Germany and Austria–Hungary had not exercised genuine political power. The question after the war became whether those groups that had previously sat powerless in parliaments could assume both power and responsibility. Another question was how long conservative political groups and institutions, such as the armies, would tolerate or cooperate with the liberal experiments.

## Economic and Ethnic Pressures

All the new states faced immense postwar economic difficulties. None of them possessed the kind of strong economy that nation-states such as France and Germany had developed in the nineteenth century. Indeed, political independence disrupted the previous economic relationships that each of them had developed as part of one of the prewar empires. None of the new states was financially independent; except for Czechoslovakia, all of them depended on foreign loans to finance economic development. Nationalistic antagonisms often prevented these states from trading with each other, and as a consequence, most became highly dependent upon trade with Germany. The successor states of eastern Europe were poor and overwhelmingly rural nations in an industrialized world. The depression hit them especially hard, because they had to import finished goods for which they paid with agricultural exports whose value was falling sharply.

Finally, throughout eastern Europe the collapse of the old German, Russian, and Austrian empires allowed various ethnic groups—large and small—to pursue nationalistic goals unchecked by any great power or central political authority. The major social and political groups in these countries were generally unwilling to make compromises lest they undermine their nationalist identity and independence. Each state included minority groups who wanted to be independent or to become part of a different nation in the region. Again except for Czechoslovakia, all of these states succumbed to some form of domestic authoritarian government.

It is important to recognize these interwar economic difficulties and nationalistic pressures because many of them seem to be reemerging in the region in the 1990s. Indeed, to a considerable extent, the breakup of Yugoslavia and Czechoslovakia, the present turmoil in the former Soviet Union, and the efforts at political reorganization in the rest of the areas dominated by the Soviet Union constitute one more attempt by the peoples of eastern Europe to achieve political and economic stability in the wake of the upheaval in that region caused by the events surrounding World War I.

## Poland: Democracy to Military Rule

The nation whose postwar fortunes probably most disappointed liberal Europeans was Poland. For more than 100 years, the country had, as a result of the late-eighteenth-century partitions, been erased from the map. Restoration of an independent Poland had been one of Woodrow Wilson's Fourteen Points. When the country was finally reconstructed in 1919, nationalism proved an insufficient bond to overcome political disagreements stemming from class differences, diverse economic interests, and regionalism. The new Poland had been constructed from portions governed by Germany, Russia, and Austria for over a century. Each of those regions of partitioned Poland had different administrative systems and laws, different economies, and different degrees of experience with electoral institutions. A vast number of small political parties bedeviled the new Polish Parliament. The constitution assigned too little power to the executive. In 1926 Marshal Josef Pilsudski (1857–1935) carried out a military coup. Thereafter he ruled in effect personally until his death, when the government passed into the hands of a group of his military followers.

## Czechoslovakia: Successful Democratic Experiment

Only one central European successor state escaped the fate of self-imposed authoritarian government. Czechoslovakia possessed a strong industrial base, a substantial middle class, and a tradition of liberal values. During the war, Czechs and Slovaks had cooperated to aid the Allies. They had learned to work together and to trust each other. After the war, the new government had broken up large estates in favor of small peasant holdings. In the person of Thomas Masaryk (1850–1937), the nation possessed a gifted leader of immense integrity and fairness. The country had a real chance of becoming a viable modern nation-state.

Czechoslovakia encountered discontent among its smaller national groups, including the German population of the Sudetenland, which the Paris settlement had placed within Czech borders. The parliamentary regime might have been able to deal with this problem, but extreme German nationalists in the Sudetenland looked to Hitler for aid. For his part, the German dictator wished to expand into eastern Europe. In 1938, at Munich, the great powers first divided liberal Czechoslovakia to appease Hitler's aggressive instincts and then watched passively as he occupied the country.

*Thomas Masaryk was the first president of the Czechoslovak Republic, which was the only successful democratic state in eastern Europe during the interwar period. [Bildarchiv Preussischer Kulturbesitz]*

## Hungary: Turmoil and Authoritarianism

Hungary was one of the defeated powers of World War I. In that defeat it achieved its long-desired separation from Austria, but at a high political and economic price. In Hungary during 1919, Bela Kun (1885–1937), a communist, established a short-lived Hungarian Soviet Republic, which received support from the socialists as well. The Allies authorized an invasion by Romanian troops to remove the Communist danger. The Hungarian landowners then established Admiral Miklós Horthy (1858–1957) as regent, a position he held until 1944. After the collapse of the Kun government, thousands of Hungarians were either executed or imprisoned. It was in part in reaction to Kun's cooperation with socialists that Lenin ordered the Comintern to reject such cooperation in the future. Kun himself was later murdered by Stalin in purges of the late 1930s.

There was also deep resentment in Hungary over the territory it had lost in the Paris settlement. The largely agrarian Hungarian economy suffered from a general stagnation. During the 1920s, the effective ruler of Hungary was Count Stephen Bethlen

(1874–1947). He presided over a government that was parliamentary in form but aristocratic in character. In 1932 he was succeeded by General Julius Gömbös (1886–1936), who pursued anti-Semitic policies and rigged elections. No matter how the popular vote turned out, the Gömbös party controlled Parliament. After his death in 1936, anti-Semitism lingered in Hungarian politics.

### Austria: Political Turmoil and Nazi Conquest

The situation in Austria was little better. A quarter of the eight million Austrians lived in Vienna. Viable economic life was almost impossible, and the Paris settlement forbade union with Germany. Throughout the 1920s, the leftist Social Democrats and the conservative Christian Socialists contended for power. Both groups employed small armies to terrorize their opponents and to impress their followers.

In 1933 the Christian Socialist Engelbert Dollfuss (1892–1934) became chancellor. He tried to steer a course between the Austrian Social Democrats and the German Nazis, who had surfaced in Austria. In 1934 he outlawed all political parties except the Christian Socialists, the agrarians, and the paramilitary groups, which composed his own Fatherland Front. He used troops against the Social Democrats, but was shot later that year during an unsuccessful Nazi coup. His successor, Kurt von Schuschnigg (1897–1977) presided over Austria until Hitler annexed it in 1938.

### Southeastern Europe: Royal Dictatorships

In southeastern Europe, revision of the arrangements in the Paris settlement was less of an issue. Parliamentary government floundered there nevertheless. Yugoslavia had been founded by the Corfu Agreement of 1917 and was known as the Kingdom of the Serbs, Croats, and Slovenes until 1929. Throughout the interwar period, the Serbs dominated the government and were opposed by the Croats. The two groups clashed violently, but the Serbs had the advantage of having had an independent state with an army prior to World War I, whereas the Croats and Slovenes had been part of the Austro–Hungarian Empire. The Croats generally were Roman Catholic, better educated, and accustomed to reasonably incorrupt government administration. The Serbs were Orthodox, somewhat less well educated, and considered to be corrupt administrators by the Croats. Furthermore, though each group predominated in certain areas of the country, each national group had isolated enclaves in other parts of the nation. Bosnia-Herzegovina, in addition to Serbs and Croats, had a significant Muslim population. The Slovenes, Muslims, and other small national groups often played the Serbs and the Croats off against each other. All of the political parties except the small Communist Party represented a particular ethnic group rather than the nation of Yugoslavia. The violent clash of nationalities eventually led to a royal dictatorship in 1929 under King Alexander I (r. 1921–1934), himself a Serb. He outlawed political parties and jailed popular politicians. Alexander was assassinated in 1934, but the authoritarian government continued under a regency for his son.

Other royal dictatorships were imposed elsewhere in the Balkans: in Romania by King Carol II (r. 1930–1940), and in Bulgaria by King Boris III (r. 1918–1943). They regarded their own illiberal regimes as preventing the seizure of power by more extreme antiparliamentary movements and as quieting the discontent of the varied nationalities within their borders. In Greece, the parliamentary monarchy floundered amidst military coups and calls for a republic. In 1936 General John Metaxas (1871–1941) instituted a dictatorship that for the time being ended parliamentary life in Greece.

The fate of the eastern European successor states disappointed those who had hoped that political liberty would result from the dissolution of the Habsburg Empire and from the restoration of an independent Poland. By the early 1930s, in most of those states, the authoritarianism of the Habsburgs had been replaced by that of other rulers. Meanwhile, Germany conducted the most momentous democratic experiment between the wars. There, after a century of frustration and disappointment, Germans had constructed a liberal state. It was in Germany that parliamentary democracy and its future in Western civilization faced its major trial.

# The Weimar Republic in Germany

The German Weimar Republic was born amidst the defeat of the imperial army, the revolution of 1918 against the Hohenzollerns, and the hopes of German Liberals and Social Democrats. Its name derived from the city of Weimar, in which its constitution was written and promulgated in August

1919. While the constitution was being debated, the republic, headed by the Social Democrats, accepted the humiliating terms of the Versailles treaty, that part of the Paris settlement that applied to Germany. Although it had signed only under the threat of an Allied invasion, the republic was nevertheless permanently associated with the national disgrace and the economic burdens of the treaty.

Throughout the 1920s, the government of the republic was required to fulfill the economic and military provisions imposed by the Paris settlement. It became all too easy for German nationalists and military figures whose policies had brought on the tragedy and defeat of the war to blame the young republic and the socialists for the military defeat and its grievous social and political results. In Germany, more than in other countries, all political groups shared the desire to revise the treaty, though they differed about the means. Some wished to oppose its provisions whenever good tactical opportunities arose; others simply assumed a position of total opposition to the treaty. Because of those revisionist desires, there were different degrees of loyalty among Germans to the political arrangements of the Weimar Constitution, which many of them associated with the Paris settlement.

## Constitutional Flaws

The Weimar Constitution was in many respects a highly enlightened document. It guaranteed civil liberties and provided for direct election, by universal suffrage, of the *Reichstag* and the president. It also contained, however, certain crucial structural flaws that eventually allowed its liberal institutions to be overthrown. It provided for proportional representation for all elections. This system made it relatively easy for small parties to gain seats in the *Reichstag*. Ministers were technically responsible to the *Reichstag*, but the president appointed and removed the chancellor. Perhaps most important, Article 48 allowed the president, in an emergency, to rule by decree. The constitution thus permitted a temporary presidential dictatorship.

## Lack of Broad Popular Support

Beyond the burden of the Paris settlement and these potential constitutional pitfalls, the Weimar Republic did not command the sympathy or loyalty of many Germans. No social revolution had accompanied the new political structure. Many important political figures favored a constitutional monarchy. The schoolteachers, civil servants, and judges of the republic were generally the same people who had served the kaiser and the empire. Before the war, they had distrusted or even hated the Social Democratic Party, which figured so prominently in the establishment and the politics of the republic.

The officer corps was also deeply suspicious of the government and profoundly resentful of the military provisions of the peace settlement. Its leaders and other nationalistic Germans perpetuated the myth that the German army had surrendered on foreign soil only because it had been stabbed in the back by civilians at home. Thus, many Germans in significant social and political positions wanted both to revise the peace treaty and to modify the system of government. The early years of the republic only reinforced those sentiments.

Major and minor humiliations as well as considerable economic instability impinged on the new government. In March 1920, the right-wing *Kapp Putsch*, or "armed insurrection," erupted in Berlin. Led by a conservative civil servant and supported by army officers, the attempted coup failed. But the *putsch* collapsed only after the government had fled the city and German workers had carried out a general strike. In the same month, strikes took place in the Ruhr. The government sent in troops. Such extremism from both the left and the right would haunt the republic for all its days.

In May 1921, the Allies presented a reparations bill for 132 billion gold marks. The German republican government accepted this preposterous demand only after new Allied threats of occupation. Throughout the early 1920s, there were numerous assassinations or attempted assassinations of important republican leaders. Violence marked the first five years of the republic.

## Invasion of the Ruhr and Inflation

Inflation brought on the major crisis of this period. Borrowing to finance the war and the continued postwar deficit spending generated an immense rise in prices. Consequently, the value of the German currency fell. By early 1921 the German mark traded against the American dollar at a ratio of 64 to 1, compared with a ratio of 4.2 to 1 in 1914. German bankers contended that the mark could not be stabilized until the reparations issue had been solved. In the meantime, the printing presses kept

In 1923 Germany suffered from cataclysmic inflation. Paper money became worthless and children used packets of it as building blocks. [Bettmann/Hulton]

pouring forth paper money, used to redeem government bonds as they fell due.

The French invasion of the Ruhr in January 1923 and the German response of economic passive resistance produced cataclysmic inflation. The Weimar government subsidized the Ruhr labor force, who had laid down their tools. Unemployment soon spread from the Ruhr to other parts of the country, creating a new drain on the treasury and also reducing tax revenues. The printing presses by this point had difficulty providing enough paper currency to keep up with the daily rise in prices. In November 1923, an American dollar was worth more than 800 million German marks. Money was literally not worth the paper it was printed on. Stores were unwilling to exchange goods for the worthless currency, and farmers withheld produce from the market.

The social and economic consequences of the great inflation of 1923 were disastrous for many Germans. Middle-class savings, pensions, and insurance policies were wiped out, as were investments in government bonds. Simultaneously, debts and mortgages could be paid off. Speculators in land, real estate, and industry made great fortunes. Union contracts generally allowed workers to keep up with rising prices. Farmers who supplied food to the cities did well, as did food stores whose proprietors benefitted from the barter that took place. The inflation thus was not a disaster to everyone. To the middle class and the lower middle class, however, the inflation was another trauma coming hard on the heels of the military defeat and the peace treaty. Only when the social and economic upheaval of these months is grasped can the later German desire for order and security at almost any cost be comprehended.

## Hitler's Early Career

Late in 1923 Adolf Hitler (1889–1945) made his first major appearance on the German political scene. In 1889 he had been born the son of a minor Austrian customs official. By 1907 he had gone to Vienna, where his hopes of becoming an artist were soon dashed. He lived off money sent by his widowed mother and later off his Austrian orphan's allowance. He also painted postcards for further income and worked as a day laborer. In Vienna, he became acquainted with Mayor Karl Lueger's (1844–1910) Christian Social Party, which prospered on an anti-Semitic ideology.

Hitler also absorbed the rabid German nationalism and extreme anti-Semitism that flourished in Vienna. He came to hate Marxism, which he associated with Jews. During World War I, Hitler fought in the German army and was wounded; he was promoted to the rank of corporal and awarded the Iron Cross for bravery. The war gave him his first sense of purpose.

After the conflict, Hitler settled in Munich. There he became associated with a small nationalistic, anti-Semitic political party, which in 1920 adopted the name of National Socialist German Workers' Party, better known simply as the *Nazis*. The same year, the group began to parade under a red and white banner with a black swastika. It issued a platform, or program, known as the *Twenty-five Points*. These called for the repudiation of the Versailles treaty, the unification of Austria and Germany, the exclusion of Jews from German citizenship, agrarian reform, the prohibition of land speculation, the confiscation of war profits, state administration of the giant cartels, and the replacement of department stores with small retail shops.

Originally, the Nazis had called for a broad program of nationalization of industry in an attempt to

*In this painting, which reflects the mood of social and political disillusionment that prevailed in much of Europe in the 1920s, George Grosz satirized conservative and right-wing groups in Weimar Germany, including the army, the courts, the newspapers, and the Nazi Party. [Bildarchiv Preussischer Kulturbesitz]*

many, people and land, land and people—that man is a Socialist.[2]

This definition, of course, had nothing to do with traditional German socialism. The "socialism" that Hitler and the Nazis had in mind was not state ownership of the means of production but the subordination of all economic enterprise to the welfare of the nation. It often implied protection for small economic enterprise. Increasingly, the Nazis discovered that their party appealed to virtually any economic group that was experiencing pressure and instability. They often tailored their messages to the particular local problems confronting these groups in different parts of Germany. The Nazis especially found considerable support among war veterans who faced economic and social displacement in Weimar society.

Soon after the promulgation of the Twenty-five Points, the storm troopers, or SA (*Sturmabteilung*), were organized under the leadership of Captain Ernst Roehm (1887–1934). It was a paramilitary organization that initially provided its members with food and uniforms and eventually paid them as well. In the mid-1920s, the SA adopted its infamous brown-shirted uniform. The storm troopers were the chief Nazi instrument for terror and intimidation before the party came into control of the government. They were a law unto themselves. They attacked socialists and communists. The organization was a means of preserving military discipline and values outside the small army permitted by the Paris settlement. The existence of such a private party army was a sign of the potential for violence in the Weimar Republic. It also represented widespread contempt for the law and the institutions of the republic. In response to the Nazi forces, both the Social Democrat and the Communist parties also organized paramilitary organizations, but in neither size nor discipline could they rival the Nazis. These paramilitary forces greatly weakened the Weimar Republic.

The social and economic turmoil following the French occupation of the Ruhr and the German inflation provided the fledgling Nazi Party with an opportunity for direct action against the Weimar Republic, which seemed incapable of giving Germany military or economic security. Because of his immense oratorical skills and organizational abilities, Hitler personally dominated the Nazi Party.

[2]Quoted in Alan Bullock, Hitler: A Study in Tyranny, rev. ed. (New York: Harper & Row, 1962), p. 76.

compete directly with the Marxist political parties for the vote of the workers. As the tactic failed, the Nazis redefined the meaning of the word *socialist* in their name so as to suggest a *nationalistic* outlook. In 1922 Hitler said:

Whoever is prepared to make the national cause his own to such an extent that he knows no higher ideal than the welfare of his nation; whoever has understood our great national anthem, *Deutschland, Deutschland, Über Alles* ["Germany, Germany, Over All"], to mean that nothing in the wide world surpasses in his eyes this Ger-

# The National Socialist German Workers' Party Issues Its Platform

*In 1920 the young Nazi Party issued its platform, known as the* Twenty-five Points. *This early statement of its goals reflected its attempt to appeal to Germans, who resented the Versailles Treaty, who found themselves in a situation of economic insecurity, and who had embraced anti-Semitism.*

✦ *What elements of the Versailles Treaty would the authors of this platform have found most objectionable? Why does this platform place such emphasis on definition of citizenship? To what social groups do the points of this platform seek to appeal?*

1. We demand the union of all Germans to form a Great Germany on the basis of self-determination enjoyed by nations.

2. We demand equality of rights for the German people in its dealings with other nations, and abolition of the peace treaties of Versailles and Saint-Germain.

3. We demand land and territory (colonies) for the nourishment of our people and for settling our excess population.

4. None but members of the nation may be citizens of the state. None but those of German blood, whatever their creed, may be members of the nation. No Jew, therefore, may be a member of the nation.

5. Anyone who is not a citizen of the state may live in Germany only as a guest and must be regarded as being subject to foreign laws.

. . . . . . . . . . . . . . . . . . . . . . . . . . . . . . . .

7. We demand that the state shall make it its first duty to promote the industry and livelihood of citizens of the state. If it is not possible to nourish the entire population of the state, foreign nationals (non-citizens of the state) must be excluded from the Reich.

. . . . . . . . . . . . . . . . . . . . . . . . . . . . . . . .

10. It must be the first duty of each citizen of the state to work with his mind or with his body. The activities of the individual may not clash with the interests of the whole, but must proceed within the frame of the community and be for the general good.

. . . . . . . . . . . . . . . . . . . . . . . . . . . . . . . .

15. We demand extensive development of provision for old age.

16. We demand creation and maintenance of a healthy middle class, immediate communalization of wholesale business premises, and their lease at a cheap rate to small traders, and that extreme considerations shall be shown to all small purveyors to the state, district authorities, and smaller localities.

. . . . . . . . . . . . . . . . . . . . . . . . . . . . . . . .

22. We demand abolition of a paid army and formation of a national army

. . . . . . . . . . . . . . . . . . . . . . . . . . . . . . . .

*Raymond E. Murphy, ed.,* National Socialism, *U. S. Department of State, Publication 1864 (Washington, 1943), pp. 222–224.*

On November 9, 1923, Hitler and a band of followers, accompanied by General Ludendorff, attempted a *putsch* at a beer hall in Munich, which was unsuccessful. When the local authorities crushed the uprising, sixteen Nazis were killed. Hitler and Ludendorff were arrested and tried for treason. The general was acquitted. Hitler employed the trial to make himself into a national figure. In his defense, he condemned the republic, the Versailles treaty, the Jews, and the weakened condition of his adopted country. He was convicted and sentenced to five years in prison. He actually spent only a few months in jail before being paroled. During this time, he dictated *Mein Kampf*, or "my struggle." Another result of the brief imprisonment was his decision to seize political power by legal methods.

During a Nazi Party rally in Nuremberg in 1927, Adolf Hitler stops his motorcade to receive the applause of the surrounding crowd. In the late 1920s the Nazi movement was only one of many bringing strife to the Weimar Republic. [Bildarchiv Preussischer Kulturbesitz]

## The Stresemann Years

Elsewhere, the officials of the republic were trying to repair the damage from the inflation. Gustav Stresemann (1878–1929) was primarily responsible for the reconstruction of the republic and for giving it a sense of self-confidence. As chancellor from August to November 1923, Stresemann abandoned the policy of passive resistance in the Ruhr. The country simply could not afford it. Then, with the aid of the banker Hjalmar Schacht (1877–1970), he introduced a new German currency. The rate of exchange was one trillion of the old German marks for one new *Rentenmark*.

Stresemann also moved against challenges from both the left and the right. He supported the crushing of both Hitler's abortive *putsch* and smaller Communist disturbances. In late November 1923, he resigned as chancellor and became foreign minister, a post that he held until his death in 1929. He continued to exercise considerable influence over the affairs of the republic.

In 1924 the Weimar Republic and the Allies agreed to a new system of reparation payments. The Dawes Plan, submitted by the American banker Charles Dawes, lowered the annual payments and allowed them to vary according to the fortunes of the German economy. The last French troops left the Ruhr in 1925. (See Map 27–1.)

The same year, Friedrich Ebert (1871–1925), the Social Democratic president of the republic, died. Field Marshal Paul von Hindenburg (1847–1934), a military hero and a conservative monarchist, was elected as his successor. He governed in strict accordance with the constitution, but his election suggested that German politics had become more conservative. It looked as if conservative Germans had become reconciled to the republic. This conservatism was in line with the prosperity of the later 1920s. The new political and economic stability meant that foreign capital flowed into Germany, and employment rose smartly. In the steel and chemical industries, large combines spread. The prosperity helped to broaden acceptance of and appreciation for the republic.

In foreign affairs, Stresemann was conciliatory. He fulfilled the provisions of the Paris settlement, even as he attempted to revise it by diplomacy. He was willing to accept the settlement in the west but was a determined, if sometimes secret, revisionist in the east. He aimed to recover German-speaking territories lost to Poland and Czechoslovakia and possibly to unite with Austria, chiefly by diplomatic means. The first step, however, was to achieve respectability and economic recovery. That goal required a policy of accommodation and "fulfillment," for the moment at least.

## Locarno

These developments gave rise to the Locarno Agreements of October 1925. The spirit of conciliation led foreign secretary Austen Chamberlain (1863–1937) for Britain and Aristide Briand for France to accept Stresemann's proposal for a fresh start. France and Germany both accepted the western frontier established at Paris as legitimate. Britain and Italy agreed to intervene against whichever side violated the frontier or if Germany sent troops into the demilitarized Rhineland. Significantly, no such agreement was reached about Germany's eastern frontier. The Germans signed treaties of arbitration with Poland and Czechoslovakia, however, and France strengthened its ties with the Little Entente. France supported German membership in the League of Nations and agreed to withdraw its occupation troops from the Rhineland in 1930, five years earlier than specified at Paris.

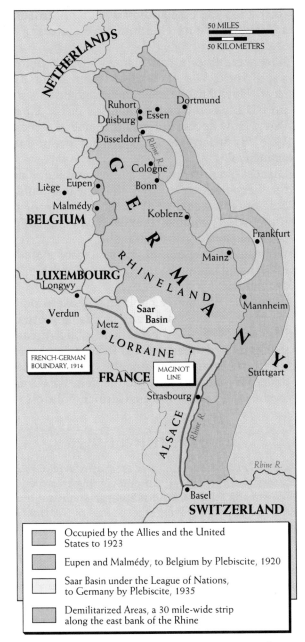

MAP 27–1  GERMANY'S WESTERN FRONTIER  *The French–Belgian–German border area between the two world wars was sensitive. Despite efforts to restrain tensions, there were persistent difficulties related to the Ruhr, Rhineland, Saar, and Eupen–Malmédy regions that required strong defenses.*

Locarno pleased everyone. Germany was pleased to have achieved respectability and a guarantee against another Ruhr occupation, as well as the possibility of revision in the east. Britain was pleased to be allowed to play a more evenhanded role. Italy was glad to be recognized as a great power. The French were happy, too, because the Germans voluntarily accepted the permanence of their western frontier, also guaranteed by Britain and Italy, while France maintained its allies in the east.

The Locarno Agreements brought a new spirit of hope to Europe. Germany's entry into the League of Nations was greeted with enthusiasm. Chamberlain and Dawes received the Nobel Peace Prize in 1925, and Briand and Stresemann were awarded it in 1926. The spirit of Locarno was carried even further when the leading European states, Japan, and the United States signed the Kellogg–Briand Pact in 1928, renouncing "war as an instrument of national policy."

The joy and optimism were not justified. France had merely recognized its inability to coerce Germany without help. Britain had shown its unwillingness to uphold the Paris settlement in the east. Austen Chamberlain declared that no British government would ever "risk the bones of a British grenadier" for the Polish corridor. Germany remained unreconciled to the eastern settlement. It continued its clandestine military connections with the Soviet Union, which had begun with the Treaty of Rapallo, and planned to continue to press for revision of the Paris settlement.

In both France and Germany, moreover, the conciliatory politicians represented only a part of the nation. In Germany, especially, most people continued to reject Versailles and regarded Locarno as only an extension of it. When the Dawes Plan ran out in 1929, it was replaced by the Young Plan. Named after the American businessman Owen D. Young (1874–1962), who devised it on behalf of the Allies, this plan lowered the reparation payments, put a limit on how long they must be made, and removed Germany entirely from outside supervision and control. The intensity of the outcry in Germany against the continuation of any reparations showed how far the Germans were from accepting their situation.

Despite these problems, major war was by no means inevitable. Europe, aided by American loans, was returning to prosperity. German leaders like Stresemann would unquestionably have continued to press for change, but they would certainly not have resorted to force, much less to a general war. Continued prosperity and diplomatic success might have won the loyalty of the German people for the Weimar Republic and moderate revisionism. But the Great Depression of the 1930s brought new forces into play.

*At the close of the 1920s, Europe appeared finally to have emerged from the difficulties of the World War I era. The Soviet Union, regarded in the West as a communist menace, was isolated by the other powers and had withdrawn into its own internal power struggles. Elsewhere, the initial resentments over the Versailles peace settlement seemed to have abated. The major powers were cooperating. Democracy was still functioning in Germany. The Labour Party was about to form its second ministry in Britain. France had settled into a less assertive international role. Mussolini's Fascism seemed to have little relevance to the rest of the Continent. The successor states had not fulfilled the democratic hopes of the Paris conference, but their troubles were their own.*

*The European economy seemed finally to be on an even keel. The frightening inflation of the early years of the decade was over, and unemployment had eased. American capital was flowing into the Continent. The reparation payments had been systematized by the Young Plan. Yet both this economic and political stability proved illusory and temporary. What brought them to an end was the deepest economic depression in the modern history of the West. As the governments and electorates responded to the economic collapse, the search for liberty gave way in more than one instance to a search for security. The political experiments of the 1920s gave way to the political tragedies of the 1930s.*

## Review Questions

1. How did the Bolshevik Revolution pose a challenge to the rest of Europe? Why did Lenin institute the New Economic Policy? Was it successful? Could the Russian Revolution have succeeded without Lenin? How did Lenin's policies lead to divisions among western socialist parties?
2. Discuss the rise of Joseph Stalin. How did he overcome the opposition of Trotsky and establish himself as head of the Soviet state?
3. Define *fascism*. How and why did the fascists succeed in obtaining power in Italy? What tactics did they use? To whom did they appeal? To what extent does Mussolini deserve the credit for his success? Was there a difference between the right-wing Fascist dictatorship of Mussolini and the left-wing Communist dictatorship of Stalin?
4. Why were Britain and France "joyless victors" after World War I? What weakness did each have? How did World War I change British politics? Discuss the decline and fall of the Liberal Party. How successful was the general strike of 1926? By what stages did Ireland win its independence?
5. Discuss France's foreign policy problems after the Versailles treaty. By what means could it best obtain security? Was the invasion of the Ruhr wise? Should France have signed the Locarno pact?
6. Why did all but one of the successor states in eastern and central Europe fail to establish viable democracies?
7. Could the Weimar Republic have taken root in Germany, or was its failure inevitable? Between 1919 and 1929, what were the republic's greatest strengths and weaknesses? To what extent did its fate depend on personalities rather than on underlying trends? Why did the Versailles Treaty loom so large in domestic German politics?

## Suggested Readings

I. BANAC, *The National Question in Yugoslavia: Origins, History, Politics* (1984). An outstanding treatment of the reorganization of eastern European political life.

R. BESSEL, *Political Violence and the Rise of Nazism: The Storm Troopers in Eastern Germany, 1925–1934* (1984). A study of the uses of violence by the Nazis.

K. D. BRACHER, *The German Dictatorship* (1970). A comprehensive treatment of both the origins and the functioning of the Nazi movement and government.

A. BULLOCK, *Hitler: A Study in Tyranny*, rev. ed. (1964). The best biography of Hitler.

E. H. CARR, *A History of Soviet Russia*, 14 vols. (1950–1978). An extensive study by a historian sympathetic to the Soviet policies of the time.

S. F. COHEN, *Bukharin and the Bolshevik Revolution: A Political Biography, 1888–1938* (1973). An interesting examination of Stalin's chief opponent on the Communist right.

I. DEUTSCHER, *The Prophet Armed* (1954), *The Prophet Unarmed* (1959), and *The Prophet Outcast* (1963). A major biography of Trotsky.

G. FELDMAN, *The Great Disorder: Politics, Economics, and Society in the Germany Inflation, 1914–1924* (1993). The best work on the subject.

O. FIGES, *Peasant Russia, Civil War: The Volga Country-*

side in *Revolution (1917–1921)* (1989). An important study of the Russian Civil War in a single district.

L. FISCHER, *The Life of Lenin* (1964). A sound biography by an American journalist.

P. FUSSELL, *The Great War and Modern Memory* (1975). A brilliant account of the literature arising from World War I during the 1920s.

P. GAY, *Weimar Culture: The Outsider as Insider* (1968). A sensitive analysis of the intellectual life of Weimar.

H. J. GORDON, *Hitler and the Beer Hall Putsch* (1972). An excellent account of the event and the political situation in the early Weimar Republic.

N. GREENE, *From Versailles to Vichy: The Third Republic, 1919–1940* (1970). A useful introduction to a difficult subject.

H. GRUBER, *International Communism in the Era of Lenin: A Documentary History* (1967). An excellent collection of difficult-to-find documents.

H. GRUBER, *Red Vienna: Experiment in Working-Class Culture, 1919–1934* (1991). A discussion of social democratic policies in Vienna after the fall of the Habsburgs.

J. HELD (ED.), *The Columbia History of Eastern Europe in the Twentieth Century* (1992). Individual essays on each of the nations.

B. JELAVICH, *History of the Balkans*, vol. 2 (1983). The standard work.

L. JONES, *German Liberalism and the Dissolution of the Weimar Party System, 1918–1933* (1988). A major study of the parties that failed during the experiment of the Weimar Republic.

P. KENEZ, *The Birth of the Propaganda State: Soviet Methods of Mass Mobilization, 1917–1929* (1985). An examination of how the Communist government inculcated popular support.

B. KENT, *The Spoils of War: The Politics, Economics, and Diplomacy of Reparations, 1918–1932* (1993). A comprehensive account of the intricacies of the reparations problem of the 1920s.

B. LINCOLN, *Red Victory: A History of the Russian Civil War* (1989). An excellent narrative account.

A. LYTTLETON, *Seizure of Power* (1973). A good narrative of the Italian Fascist rise to power.

C. S. MAIER, *Recasting Bourgeois Europe: Stabilization in France, Germany, and Italy in the Decade After World War I* (1975). An important interpretation written from a comparative standpoint.

A. MARWICK, *The Deluge: British Society and the First World War* (1965). Full of insights into both major and more subtle minor social changes.

M. MCAULEY, *Bread and Justice: State and Society in Petrograd, 1917–1922* (1991). A study that examines the impact of the Russian Revolution and Leninist policies on a major Russian city.

E. NOLTE, *Three Faces of Fascism* (1963). An important, influential, and difficult work on France, Italy, and Germany.

R. PIPES, *The Formation of the Soviet Union*, 2nd ed. (1964). A study of internal policy with emphasis on Soviet minorities.

R. PIPES, *The Unknown Lenin: From the Secret Archive* (1996). A collection of previously unpublished documents that indicate the repressive character of Lenin's government.

J. F. POLLARD, *The Vatican and Italian Fascism 1929–32: A Study in Conflict* (1985). Provides the background to the Lateran pacts.

J. ROTHSCHILD, *East Central Europe Between the Two World Wars* (1974). A detailed and authoritative survey.

S. A. SCHUKER, *The End of French Predominance in Europe: The Financial Crisis of 1924 and the Adoption of the Dawes Plan* (1976). An excellent study of a complicated issue.

H. SETON-WATSON, *Eastern Europe Between the Wars, 1918–1941* (1946). Somewhat dated, but still a useful work.

D. P. SILVERMAN, *Reconstructing Europe After the Great War* (1982). Examines the difficulties faced by the major powers.

D. M. SMITH, *Italy: A Modern History*, rev. ed. (1969). Good chapters on the Fascists and Mussolini.

D. M. SMITH, *Italy and Its Monarchy* (1989). A major treatment of an important neglected subject.

R. J. SONTAG, *A Broken World, 1919–1939* (1971). An exceptionally thoughtful and well-organized survey.

M. STEINBERG, *Sabers and Brownshirts: The German Students' Path to National Socialism, 1918–1935* (1977). An interesting study of the recruitment of young Germans.

A. J. P. TAYLOR, *English History, 1914–1945* (1965). Lively and opinionated.

M. TRACTENBERG, *Reparations in World Politics: France and European Economic Diplomacy, 1916–1923* (1980). Points to the special role of reparations in French calculations.

R. TUCKER, *Stalin as Revolutionary, 1879–1929: A Study in History and Personality* (1973). A useful and readable account of Stalin's rise to power.

N. TUMARKIN, *Lenin Lives: The Lenin Cult in Soviet Russia* (1983). An interesting work on the uses of Lenin's reputation after his death.

E. G. WALTERS, *The Other Europe: Eastern Europe to 1945* (1988). An excellent introduction to the problems in the region.

T. WILSON, *The Downfall of the Liberal Party, 1914–1935* (1966). A close examination of the surprising demise of a political party in Britain.

E. WISKEMANN, *Fascism in Italy: Its Development and Influence* (1969). A comprehensive treatment.

R. WOHL, *The Generation of 1914* (1979). An important work that explores the effect of the war on political and social thought.

*Thousands of German troops listen to a speech by Hitler at a Nuremberg rally in 1936. [Corbis-Bettmann]*

# Europe and the Great Depression of the 1930s

## K E Y   T O P I C S

- Financial collapse and depression in Europe
- The emergence of the National Government in Great Britain and the Popular Front in France in response to the political pressures caused by the depression
- The Nazi seizure of power, the establishment of a police state, and the imposition of racial laws in Germany
- Planned industrialism, agricultural collectivization, and purges in the Soviet Communist Party and army under Stalin

*In Europe, unlike in the United States, the 1920s had not been "roaring." Economically, it had been a decade of insecurity, of a search for elusive stability, of a short-lived upswing, followed by collapse in finance and production. The Great Depression that began in 1929 was the most severe downturn ever experienced by the capitalist economies. High unemployment, low production levels, financial instability, and shrinking trade arrived and would not depart. Capitalist business and political leaders despaired over the failure of the market mechanism to save them. Marxists and indeed many other observers thought that the final downfall of capitalism was at hand.*

*European voters looked for new ways out of the doldrums, and politicians sought escapes from the pressures that the depression had brought on them. One result of the fight for economic security was the establishment of the Nazi dictatorship in Germany. Another was the piecemeal construction of what has since become known as the mixed economy; that is, governments became directly involved in economic decisions alongside business and labor. In both cases, most of the political and economic guidelines of nineteenth-century liberalism were abandoned for good. Two other casualties of these years were decency and civility in political life.*

# Toward the Great Depression

Three factors combined to bring about the intense severity and the extended length of the Great Depression. First, there was a financial crisis that stemmed directly from the war and the peace settlement. Second, a crisis arose in the production and distribution of goods in the world market. These two problems became intertwined in 1929 and, so far as Europe was concerned, reached the breaking point in 1931. Finally, both of these difficulties became worse because neither the major western European nations nor the United States offered strong economic leadership or acted responsibly. Without cooperation or leadership in the Atlantic economic community, the economic collapse in finance and production simply lingered and deepened.

## The Financial Tailspin

Most European nations emerged from World War I with inflated currencies. Immediately after the armistice, the unleashed demand for consumer and industrial goods drove up prices. The price and wage increases generally subsided after 1921. Yet the problem of maintaining the value of their national currencies still haunted political leaders—and was intensified after the German financial disaster of 1923. The frightening German example of uncontrolled inflation helped explain the later refusal of most governments to run budget deficits when the depression struck. They feared inflation as a source of social instability and political turmoil the way that European governments since World War II have feared unemployment.

REPARATIONS AND WAR DEBTS  Reparation payments and international war-debt settlement further complicated the picture. Here France and the United States were the stumbling blocks. France had twice paid reparations as a defeated nation, once after 1815 and again after 1871. As a victor, it now intended both to receive reparations and to finance its postwar recovery through them. The 1923 invasion of the Ruhr demonstrated French determination on this question.

The United States was no less determined to be repaid for the wartime loans it had made to its allies. Moreover, the European Allies owed various debts to each other. It soon became apparent that

German reparations were to provide the means by which other European nations intended to repay all these debts. Most of the money that the Allies collected from each other eventually went to the United States.

In 1922 Great Britain announced that it would insist on payment for its own loans only to the extent that the United States required payments from Britain. The American government, however, would not relent. The reparations and the war debts made normal business, capital investment, and international trade difficult and expensive for the European nations. Governments exercised various controls over credit, trade, and currency. Currency speculation drew funds away from capital investment in productive enterprise. The monetary problems reinforced the general tendency toward high tariff policies. If a nation imported too many goods from abroad, it might have difficulty meeting those costs and the expenses of debt or reparation payments. The financial and money muddle thus discouraged trade and production and, in consequence, hurt employment.

AMERICAN INVESTMENTS  In 1924 the Dawes Plan reorganized the administration and transfer of reparations, which procedures in turn smoothed the debt repayments to the United States. Thereafter, private American capital flowed into Europe and especially into Germany. Much of this money, which provided the basis for Europe's brief prosperity after 1925, was in the form of short-term loans.

In 1928 this lending began to contract as American money was withdrawn from European investments into the booming New York stock market. In the Wall Street crash of October 1929—the result of

| Major Dates of the Economic Crisis | |
| --- | --- |
| 1923 | German inflation following French invasion of Ruhr |
| 1924 | Dawes Plan on reparations |
| 1929 (June) | Young Plan on reparations |
| 1929 (October) | Wall Street crash |
| 1931 (May) | Collapse of Kreditanstalt in Vienna |
| 1931 (June) | Hoover announces moratorium on reparations |
| 1932 | Lausanne Conference ends reparations |

*Crowds gathered on Wall Street in New York on October 29, 1929, the day the stock market crashed. The Great Depression in the United States dried up American capital previously available for investment in Europe. [Brown Brothers]*

virtually unregulated financial speculation—huge amounts of money were lost. United States banks had made large loans to customers, who then invested the money in the stock market. When stock prices collapsed, the customers could not repay the banks. Consequently, within the United States all kinds of credit that had been available shrank severely or disappeared, and many banks failed. Thereafter, little American capital was available for investment in Europe. Furthermore, loans already made to Europeans were not renewed, as American banks strove to cover domestic shortages.

THE END OF REPARATIONS   When the credit to Europe began to run out, a major financial crisis struck the continent. In May 1931, the *Kreditanstalt*, a major bank in Vienna, collapsed. It was a primary lending institution for much of central and eastern Europe. The German banking system came under severe pressure and was saved only through government guarantees. It became clear, however, that in this crisis Germany would be unable to make its next reparation payment as stipulated in the 1929 Young Plan. As the German difficulties mounted, American President Herbert Hoover (1874–1964) announced in June 1931 a one-year moratorium on all payments of international debts.

The Hoover moratorium was a prelude to the end of reparations. Hoover's action was a sharp blow to the French economy, for which the flow of reparations had continued to be important. The French agreed to the moratorium most reluctantly but really had little alternative because the German economy had all but collapsed. The Lausanne Conference in the summer of 1932 in effect ended the era of reparations. The next year, the debts owed to the United States were settled either through small token payments or simply through default. Nevertheless, the financial politics of the 1920s had done its damage.

## Problems in Agricultural Commodities

In addition to the dramatic financial turmoil and collapse, a less dramatic, but equally fundamental, downturn occurred in production and trade. The 1920s saw the market demand for European goods shrink relative to the Continent's capacity to produce goods. This meant idle factories and fewer jobs. Part of this problem originated within Europe, and part outside. In both instances, the difficulty arose from agriculture. Better methods of farming, improved strains of wheat, expanded tillage, and more extensive transport facilities all over the globe vastly increased the world supply of grain. World wheat prices fell to record lows. This development was, of course, initially good for consumers. The collapse in grain prices, however, meant lower incomes for European farmers and especially for those of central and eastern Europe.

Also, higher industrial wages raised the cost of the industrial goods used by farmers or peasants. The farmers could not purchase those products. Moreover, farmers began to have difficulty paying off their mortgages and normal annual operational debts. They normally borrowed money to plant their fields, expecting to pay the debt when the crops were sold. The fall in commodity prices made it difficult for the farmers to repay those debts.

These farm problems became especially pressing in eastern Europe. Immediately after the war, the new governments there had undertaken land-reform programs. The democratic franchise in the successor states had opened the way for considerable redistribution of tillable soil. In Romania and Czechoslovakia, large amounts of land changed hands. This occurred to a lesser extent in Hungary and Poland.

These new small farms, however, proved to be inefficient, and the farmers who worked them were unable to earn sufficient incomes. Protective tariffs often prevented the export of grain among European countries. The credit and cost squeeze on eastern European farmers and on their counterparts in Germany played a major role in their disillusionment with liberal politics. For example, farmers in Germany were a major source of political support for the Nazis.

Outside Europe, similar problems affected other producers of agricultural commodities. The prices that they received for their products plummeted. Government-held reserves of agricultural commodities accumulated to record levels. This glut involved the supplies of wheat, sugar, coffee, rubber, wool, and lard. The people who produced these goods in underdeveloped nations in Asia, Africa, and Latin America could no longer make enough money to buy finished goods from industrial Europe. As world credit collapsed, the economic position of these commodity producers worsened. Commodity production had simply outstripped world demand.

The collapse in the agricultural prices and the financial turmoil resulted in stagnation and depression for European industry. European coal, iron, and textiles had depended largely on international markets. Unemployment spread from these industries to those producing finished consumer goods. The persistent unemployment in Great Britain and to a lesser extent in Germany during the 1920s had already meant "soft" domestic markets in those countries. The policies of reduced government spending with which the governments confronted the depression further weakened domestic demand. By the early 1930s, the Great Depression was growing on itself.

## Depression and Government Policy

The Great Depression did not mean absolute economic decline. Nor did it mean that everyone was out of a job. People with work always well outnumbered those without work. New economic sectors such as production of automobiles, radios, synthetics, and the service industries around them did develop. But the economic downturn made people extremely anxious. People in nearly all walks of life feared that their own economic security and lifestyle would suffer next. The depression also frustrated social and economic expectations. People with jobs frequently improved their standard of living or were promoted much more slowly than might have been the case under sound economic conditions. They were working, but in their own eyes they seemed to be going nowhere. Their anxieties created a major source of social discontent.

The governments of the late 1920s and the early 1930s were not well fitted in either structure or ideology to confront these problems. The Keynesian theory of governments' spending the economy out of depression was not yet available. John Maynard Keynes's (1883–1946) *General Theory of Employment, Interest, and Money* was not published until 1936. Before Keynes, orthodox economic policy called for cuts in government spending to prevent inflation. Eventually, the market mechanism was supposed to bring the economy back to prosperity.

Nonetheless, the length and severity of the depression, plus direct political pressure from the new mass electorates, led governments across Europe to interfere with the economy as never before. Government participation in economic life was not new. One need only recall the mercantilistic policies of the seventeenth and eighteenth centuries and the government encouragement of railway building in the nineteenth century. From the early 1930s onward, however, government involvement increased rapidly. Private economic enterprise became subject to new trade, labor, and currency regulations. The political goals of restoring employment and providing for defense established new state-related economic priorities. As in the past, state intervention generally increased as one moved from west to east across the Continent. These new economic policies usually also involved further political experimentation.

# Confronting the Great Depression in the Democracies

The Great Depression ended the business-as-usual attitude that had marked the political life of Great Britain and France during the late 1920s. In Britain, the emergency led to a new coalition government and the abandonment of economic policies considered sacred for a century. The economic stagnation in France proved to be the occasion for a bold political and economic program sponsored by the parties of the left. The relative success of the British venture gave the nation new confidence in the democratic processes; the new departures in France created social and political hostilities that undermined faith in republican institutions.

## *Great Britain: The National Government*

In 1929 a second minority Labour government, headed by Ramsay MacDonald, took office. As the number of British unemployed rose to more than 2.5 million workers in 1931, the ministry became divided over what to do. MacDonald believed that the budget should be slashed, government salaries reduced, and unemployment benefits cut. This was a bleak program for a Labour government. MacDonald's strong desire to make the Labour Party respectable led him to reject more radical programs. Many of the cabinet ministries resisted MacDonald's proposals. They refused to take income away from the poor and the unemployed. The prime minister requested the resignations of his entire cabinet and arranged for a meeting with King George V.

Everyone assumed that the entire Labour ministry was about to leave office. However, to the surprise of his party and the nation, MacDonald did not resign. At the urging of the king and probably of his own ambition, MacDonald formed a coalition ministry, called the *National Government*, composed of Labour, Conservative, and Liberal ministers. The bulk of the Labour Party believed that their leader had sold them out. In the election of 1931, the National Government received a comfortable majority. After the election, however, MacDonald, who remained prime minister until 1935, was little more than a tool of the Conservatives. They held a majority in their own right in the House of Commons, but the appearance of a coalition was useful for imposing unpleasant programs.

The National Government took three decisive steps to attack the depression. First, to balance the budget, it raised taxes, cut insurance benefits to the unemployed and the elderly, and lowered government salaries. Its leaders argued that the fall in prices that had taken place meant that those reductions did not appreciably cut real income. Second, in September 1931, Britain went off the gold standard. The value of the British pound on the international money market fell by about 30 percent. This move somewhat stimulated exports. Third, in 1932 Parliament passed the Import Duties Bill, which placed a 10 percent *ad valorem* tariff (a tax levied in proportion to the value of each imported good) on all imports except those from the empire. In the context of previous British policy, these steps were extraordinary. Gold and free trade, the hallmarks of almost a century of British commercial policy, were abandoned.

# George Orwell Observes a Woman in the Slums

*Although Great Britain was beginning to emerge from the Great Depression by the late 1930s, much poverty and human degradation remained. This scene, described in 1937 by the social critic and novelist George Orwell (1903–1950), captures a glimpse of the sadness and hopelessness that many British citizens experienced every day of their lives.*

✦ *How does Orwell's descriptive language evoke sympathy for the woman he portrays? What economic conditions led to such poverty? What class attitudes does Orwell begin to explore in this passage?*

The train bore me away, through the monstrous scenery of slag-heaps, chimneys, piled scrap-iron, foul canals, paths of cindery mud crisscrossed by the prints of clogs.... As we moved slowly through the outskirts of the town we passed row after row of little grey slum houses running at right angles to the embankment. At the back of one of the houses a young woman was kneeling on the stones, poking a stick up the leaden waste-pipe which ran from the sink inside, and which I suppose was blocked. I had time to see everything about her—her sacking apron, her clumsy clogs, her arms reddened by the cold.... She had a round pale face, the usual exhausted face of the slum girl who is twenty-five and looks forty, thanks to miscarriages and drudgery; and it wore, for the second in which I saw it, the most desolate, hopeless expression I have ever seen. It struck me then that we are mistaken when we say that "It isn't the same for them as it would be for us," and that people bred in the slums can imagine nothing but the slums. For what I saw in her face was not the ignorant suffering of an animal. She knew well enough what was happening to her—understood as well as I did how dreadful a destiny it was to be kneeling there in the bitter cold, on the slimy stones of a slum backyard, poking a stick up a foul drain-pipe.

*George Orwell, The Road to Wigan Pier (New York: Berkley Medallion Books, 1967; originally printed in 1937), p. 29.*

---

The policies of the National Government produced significant results. Great Britain avoided the banking crisis that hit other countries. By 1934 industrial production had expanded beyond the level for 1929. Britain was the first nation to restore that level of production. Of course, the mediocre British industrial performance of the 1920s made the British task easier. The government also encouraged lower interest rates. This, in turn, led to the largest private housing boom in British history. Industries related to housing and the furnishing of homes prospered.

Those people who were employed generally improved their standard of living. Nonetheless, the hard core of unemployment remained. In 1937 the number of jobless had fallen to just below 1.5 million. That same year, when George Orwell (1903–1950) described the laboring districts of Britain in *The Road to Wigan Pier*, the poverty and the idle days without work of the people he met dominated his picture.

Britain had entered the depression with a stagnant economy and left the era with a stagnant economy. Yet the British political system was not fundamentally challenged. There were demonstrations by the unemployed, but social insurance, though hardly generous, did support them. To the employed citizens of the country, the National Government seemed to pursue a policy that avoided the extreme wings of both the Labour and the Conservative parties. When MacDonald retired in 1935, Stanley Baldwin again took office. He was succeeded in

1937 by Neville Chamberlain (1869–1940). The new prime minister is today known for the disastrous Munich agreement, but when he took office, he was considered one of the more progressive thinkers on social issues in the Conservative Party.

One movement in Britain did flirt with the extreme right-wing politics of the Continent. In 1932 Sir Oswald Mosley (1896–1980) founded the British Union of Fascists. He had held a minor position in the second Labour government and was disappointed by its feeble attack on unemployment. Mosley urged a program of direct action through a new corporate structure for the economy. His group wore black shirts and attempted to hold mass meetings. Even at the height of his popularity, he gained only a few thousand adherents. Thereafter his anti-Semitism began to alienate supporters, and by the close of the decade, he was little more than a political oddity.

## France: The Popular Front

The timing of the Great Depression in France was the reverse of that in Britain. It came later and lasted longer. Only in 1931 did the economic slide begin to affect the French economy. Even then, unemployment did not become a major problem. Rarely were more than half a million French workers without jobs. In one industry after another, however, wages were lowered. The government raised tariffs to protect French goods and especially French agriculture. Ever since that time, French farmers have enjoyed unusual protection by the government. These measures helped maintain the home market but did little to overcome industrial stagnation. Relations between labor and management were tense.

The first political fallout of the depression was the election of another Radical coalition government in 1932. Fearful of contributing to inflation as they had after 1924, the Radicals pursued a generally deflationary policy. In the same year that the new ministry took office, reparation payments upon which the French economy depended had stopped. As the economic crisis tightened, normal parliamentary and political life became difficult and confused.

RIGHT-WING VIOLENCE   Outside the Chamber of Deputies, politics grew ugly. Various right-wing groups with authoritarian tendencies became active. These leagues included the *Action Française*, founded before World War I in the wake of the Dreyfus affair, and the *Croix de Feu* or "Cross of Fire," composed of army veterans. These and similar groups had a total of more than two million members. Some of them wanted a monarchy; others favored what would have amounted to military rule. They were hostile to parliamentary government, socialism, and communism. They wanted what they regarded as the greater good and glory of France to be set above the petty machinations of political parties. They thus resembled the Fascists and the Nazis.

The activities and propaganda of these leagues weakened loyalty to republican government and made French political life more bitter and vindictive. They also led to an incident of extraordinary havoc that produced important long-range political consequences.

The incident grew out of the Stavisky affair, the last of those curious scandals that punctuated the political fortunes of the Third Republic. Serge Stavisky (d. 1934) was a small-time gangster who appears to have had good connections within the government. In 1933 he became involved in a fraudulent bond scheme. When finally tracked down by the police, he committed suicide in January 1934. The official handling of the matter suggested a political cover-up. It was alleged that people in high places wished to halt the investigation. To the right wing in France, the Stavisky incident symbolized all the seaminess, immorality, and corruption of republican politics.

On February 6, 1934, a large demonstration of the right-wing leagues took place in Paris. The exact purpose and circumstances of the rally remain uncertain, but the crowd did attempt to march on the Chamber of Deputies. Violence erupted between right and left political groups, and between them and the police. Fourteen demonstrators were killed; scores of others were injured. It was the largest disturbance in Paris since the Commune of 1871.

In the wake of the night of February 6, the Radical ministry of Édouard Daladier (1884–1970) resigned and was replaced by a national coalition government composed of all living former premiers. The Chamber of Deputies permitted the ministry to deal with economic matters by decree. The major result of the right-wing demonstrations, however, was a political self-reassessment by the parties of the left. Radicals, Socialists, and Communists began to realize that a right-wing coup might be possible in France.

# The Right Wing Attacks
# the Third French Republic

*The Stavisky affair provided new opportunity for various French right-wing political groups to criticize the liberal institutions of the Third Republic. In this proclamation of January 7, 1934, one such organization, the* Camelots du Roi, *accused one minister, and by implication all French politicians, of having aided Stavisky in a fraudulent bond scheme. The minister did later resign, but he was not directly implicated in the theft. Also, the reader should note how this proclamation invites the people of Paris to demonstrate against the Chamber of Deputies and to take the law into their own hands. The violence of the night of February 6, 1934, resulted from such invitations to right-wing demonstrations.*

✦ *Why was the Third French Republic so vulnerable to attacks concerning corruption? What are the specific charges in this manifesto? How does this manifesto exemplify appeals to nonparliamentary political action? How could such a manifesto be regarded as fostering political violence in France?*

To the People of Paris,

At a time when the Government and the Parliament of the Republic declare themselves incapable of balancing our budget, and continue to defend the topsy-turvy foundations of their regime; when they refuse to reduce the burden of taxation and are actually inflicting more taxes on the French people a scandal breaks out. This scandal shows that, far from protecting the savings of the people, the Republican Authorities have given free course to the colossal rackets of an alien crook. A minister, M. Dalimier, by his letters of 25 June and 23 September 1932, deliberately provided an instrument which enabled the thief Stavisky to rob the insurance companies and the Social Insurance Fund of over half a milliard francs. He has been urged to resign; but he has refused to do so. He should be in prison together with his pals Stavisky and Dubarry [another person implicated in the plot]; instead of which, he continues to be a member of the Government whose duty it is to inquire into this affair. Dalimier is not alone; we can see behind him a crowd of other ministers and influential members of Parliament, all of whom have, in one way or another, favored the adventurer's rackets, especially by instructing the police to leave him alone, and by suspending during many years the legal proceedings that should have been taken against him. There is no law and no justice in a country where magistrates and the police are accomplices of criminals. The honest people of France who want to protect their own interests, and who care for the cleanliness of public life, are forced to take the law into their own hands.

At the beginning of this week, Parliament will reassemble and we urge the people of Paris to come in large numbers before the Chamber of Deputies, to cry "Down with Thieves" and to clamour for honesty and justice.

*Sidney Pollard and Colin Holmes, Documents of European Economic History, vol. 3 (London: Edward Arnold, 1973), p. 369.*

## Emergence of Socialist–Communist Cooperation

Between 1934 and 1936, the French left began to make peace within its own ranks. This was not easy. French Socialists, led by Léon Blum (1872–1950), had been the major target of the French Communists since the split over joining the Comintern in 1920. Only Stalin's fear of Hitler as a danger to the Soviet Union made this new cooperation possible. Despite deep suspicions on all sides, the Popular Front of all left-wing parties had been established by July 1935. Its purpose was to preserve the republic and press for social reform.

The election of 1936 gave the Popular Front a majority in the Chamber of Deputies. The Socialists were the largest single party for the first time in French history. They organized the cabinet as they had long promised they would do when they constituted the majority party of a coalition. Léon Blum assumed the premiership on June 5, 1936. From the early 1920s, this Jewish intellectual and humanitarian had opposed the Communist version of socialism. Cast as the successor to Jean Jaurès (1859–1914), who had been assassinated in 1914, Blum pursued socialism in the context of democratic, parliamentary government.

**Blum's Government**  During May 1936, before the Popular Front came to power, strikes had begun to spread throughout French industry. Immediately after assuming office on June 6, the Blum government faced further spontaneous work stoppages involving over half a million workers who had occupied factories in sit-down strikes. These were the most extensive labor disturbances in the history of the Third Republic. They aroused new fears in the conservative business community, already frightened by the election of the Popular Front.

Blum acted swiftly to bring together representatives of labor and management. On June 8, he announced the conclusion of an accord that reorganized labor–management relations in France. Wages were immediately raised between 7 and 15 percent, depending on the job involved. Employers were required to recognize unions and to bargain collectively with them. Workers were given annual, paid two-week vacations. The forty-hour week was established throughout French industry. Blum hoped to overcome labor hostility to French society, to establish a foundation for justice in labor–management relations, and to increase the domestic consumer demand of the nation.

| Depression Years in Great Britain and France | |
|---|---|
| 1929 | Second Labour government comes to power in Britain with Ramsay MacDonald as prime minister |
| 1931 | Formation of National Government in Britain |
| 1931 | British government goes off the gold standard |
| 1932 | Oswald Mosley founds British Union of Fascists |
| 1933–1934 | Stavisky affair in France |
| 1934 (February 6) | Right-wing riots in Paris |
| 1935 | Stanley Baldwin becomes British prime minister |
| 1936 (June 5) | Popular Front government in France under Blum |
| 1936 (June 8) | Labor accord in France |
| 1937 | Neville Chamberlain becomes British prime minister |
| 1938 | Popular Front replaced by Radical ministry in France |

Blum followed his labor policy with other bold departures. He raised the salaries of civil servants and instituted a program of public works. Government loans were extended to small industry. Spending on armaments was increased, and some armament industries were nationalized. A National Wheat Board was set up to manage the production and sale of grain. Initially, Blum had promised to resist devaluation of the franc. By the autumn of 1936, however, international monetary pressure forced him to devalue. He did so again in the spring of 1937. The devaluations came too late to help French exports.

These moves enraged the conservative banking and business community. In March 1937, they brought enough influence to bear on the ministry to cause Blum to halt the program of reform. It was not taken up again. Blum's Popular Front colleagues considered the pause in reform an unnecessary compromise. In June 1937, Blum resigned. The Popular Front ministry itself held on until April 1938, when it was replaced by a Radical ministry under Daladier. Not until 1939 did French industrial production reach the level of 1929.

By the close of the 1930s, citizens from all walks of life had begun to wonder if the republic was worth preserving. The left remained divided. Businesspeople found the republic inefficient and too much subject to socialist pressures. The right wing hated the republic in principle. When the time came in 1940 to defend the republic, too many French citizens were not sure that it was worth defending.

# Germany: The Nazi Seizure of Power

The most remarkable political event caused by the uncertainty and turmoil of the Great Depression was the coming to power of the National Socialists (Nazis) in Germany. By the late 1920s, the Nazis were a major presence in the Weimar Republic, but were not yet real contenders for political dominance. The financial crisis, economic stress, and social anxiety associated with the onset of the depression rapidly changed that situation. All the fragility of the Weimar constitution stood exposed, and the path opened for the most momentous and far-reaching event of the decade, the Nazi seizure of power.

### Depression and Political Deadlock

The outflow of foreign, especially American, capital from Germany beginning in 1928 undermined the economic prosperity of the Weimar Republic. The resulting economic crisis brought parliamentary government to an end. In 1928 a coalition of center parties and the Social Democrats governed. All went reasonably well until the depression struck. Then the coalition partners disagreed sharply on economic policy. The Social Democrats refused to reduce social and unemployment insurance. The more conservative parties, remembering the inflation of 1923, insisted on a balanced budget. The coalition dissolved in March 1930.

To resolve the parliamentary deadlock in the *Reichstag*, President von Hindenburg appointed Heinrich Brüning (1885–1970) as chancellor. Lacking a majority in the *Reichstag*, Brüning governed through emergency presidential decrees as authorized by Article 48 of the constitution. The party divisions in the *Reichstag* prevented the parliament from overriding the decrees. The Weimar Republic was thus transformed into an authoritarian regime.

German unemployment rose from 2,258,000 in March 1930 to more than 6,000,000 in March 1932. There had been persistent unemployment during the 1920s, but nothing of such magnitude or duration. The economic downturn and the parliamentary deadlock worked to the advantage of the more extreme political parties. In the election of 1928, the Nazis had won only 12 seats in the *Reichstag*, and the Communists had won 54 seats. After the election of 1930, the Nazis held 107 seats and the Communists 77.

For the Nazis, politics meant the capture of power by terror and intimidation as well as by legal elections. All decency and civility in political life vanished. Thousands of unemployed joined the storm troopers (SA), which had 100,000 members in 1930 and almost one million in 1933. The SA freely and viciously attacked Communists and Social Democrats, who also went on fighting each other. The Nazis held mass rallies that resembled religious revivals. They gained powerful supporters and sympathizers in business, military, and newspaper circles. Some intellectuals were also sympathetic. The Nazis transformed this new enthusiasm born of economic despair and nationalistic frustration into impressive electoral results.

### Hitler Comes to Power

For two years Brüning governed with the confidence of his president, von Hindenburg. The economy did not improve, however, and the political situation deteriorated. In 1932 the eighty-three-year-old president stood for reelection. Hitler ran against him and forced a runoff. The Nazi leader got 30.1 percent of the first vote, and 36.8 percent in the runoff. Although Hindenburg remained in office, the results of the poll convinced him that Brüning no longer commanded sufficient confidence from conservative German voters.

On May 30, 1932, Hindenburg dismissed Brüning and the next day appointed Franz von Papen (1878–1969) as chancellor. The new chancellor was one of a small group of extremely conservative advisers on whom the aged Hindenburg had become increasingly dependent. Others included the president's son and several military figures. With the continued paralysis in the *Reichstag*, their influence over the president virtually amounted to control of the government. Thus, only a handful of people made the crucial decisions of the next several months.

*Hitler's mastery of the techniques of mass politics and propaganda—including huge staged rallies like this one in 1938—was an important factor in his rise to power.* [Bildarchiv Preussischer Kulturbesitz]

Papen and the circle around the president wanted to find some way to draw the Nazis into cooperation with them without giving any effective power to Hitler. The government needed the mass popular support that only the Nazis seemed able to generate. The Hindenburg circle decided to convince Hitler that the Nazis could not come to power on their own. Papen removed the ban on Nazi meetings that Brüning had imposed. Furthermore, he called a *Reichstag* election for July 1932. The Nazis won 230 seats and polled 37.2 percent of the vote. As the price for his entry into the cabinet, Hitler demanded appointment as chancellor. Hindenburg refused. The government called another election in November, partly to wear down the Nazis' financial resources, which it did. The Nazis lost 34 seats, and their popular vote dipped to 33.1 percent. The advisers around Hindenburg still refused to appoint Hitler to office.

In November 1932, Papen resigned, and the next month General Kurt von Schleicher (1882–1934)

became chancellor. Fear of civil war between the left and the right mounted. Schleicher tried to build a broad-based coalition of conservative groups and trade unionists. The prospect of such a coalition, including groups from the political left, frightened the Hindenburg circle even more than the prospect of Hitler. They did not trust Schleicher's motives, which have never been clear. Consequently, they persuaded Hindenburg to appoint Hitler as chancellor. To control Hitler and to see that he did little mischief, the Hindenburg circle appointed Papen as vice-chancellor and named other traditional conservatives to the cabinet. On January 30, 1933, Adolf Hitler became the chancellor of Germany.

Hitler had come into office by legal means. All the proper legal forms and procedures had been observed. This was important, for it permitted the civil service, the courts, and the other agencies of the government to support him in good conscience. He had forged a rigidly disciplined party structure

*The* Reichstag *fire in 1933 provided Hitler an excuse to consolidate his power. [Bildarchiv Preussischer Kulturbesitz]*

and had mastered the techniques of mass politics and propaganda. He understood how to touch the raw social and political nerves of the electorate. His support appears to have come from across the social spectrum and not simply from the lower middle class, as was once thought to be the case. Pockets of resistance appeared among Roman Catholic voters in the country and small towns. Otherwise, support for Hitler was particularly strong among groups such as farmers, war veterans, and the young, who had especially suffered from the insecurity of the 1920s and the depression of the early 1930s. Hitler promised them security against communists and socialists, effective government in place of the petty politics of the other parties, and

an uncompromising nationalist vision of a strong, restored Germany.

German big business once received much of the credit for the rise of Hitler. There is little evidence, however, that business contributions made any crucial difference to the Nazis' success or failure. Hitler's supporters were frequently suspicious of business and giant capitalism. They wanted a simpler world and one in which small property would be safe from both socialism and large-scale capitalist consolidation. These people looked to Hitler and the Nazis rather than to the Social Democrats because the latter, though concerned with social issues, never appeared sufficiently nationalistic. The Nazis won out over other conservative nationalistic parties because, unlike those conservatives, the Nazis did address the problem of social insecurities.

## Hitler's Consolidation of Power

Once in office, Hitler moved with almost lightning speed to consolidate his control. This process had three facets: the capture of full legal authority, the crushing of alternative political groups, and the purging of rivals within the Nazi Party itself.

On February 27, 1933, a mentally ill Dutch communist set fire to the *Reichstag* building in Berlin. The Nazis quickly claimed that the fire proved the existence of an immediate communist threat against the government. To the public, it was plausible that the communists might attempt some action against the state now that the Nazis were in power. Under Article 48, Hitler issued an Emergency Decree suspending civil liberties and proceeded to arrest communists or alleged communists. This decree was not revoked for as long as Hitler ruled Germany.

In early March, another *Reichstag* election took place. The Nazis still received only 43.9 percent of the vote and won 288 seats. The arrest and removal of all Communist deputies, however, and the political fear aroused by the fire enabled Hitler to control the *Reichstag*. On March 23, 1933, the *Reichstag* passed an Enabling Act that permitted Hitler to rule by decree. Thereafter there were no legal limits on his exercise of power. The Weimar constitution was never formally repealed or amended. It had simply been supplanted by the February Emergency Decree and the March Enabling Act.

Perhaps better than anyone else, Hitler understood that he and his party had not inevitably come to power. In a series of complex moves, Hitler outlawed or undermined any German institution that might have served as a rallying point for opposition. In early May 1933, the Nazi Party, rather than any government agency, seized the offices, banks, and newspapers of the free trade unions and arrested their leaders. In late June and early July, all other German political parties were outlawed. By July 14, 1933, the National Socialists were the only legal party in Germany. During the same months, the Nazis moved against the governments of the individual federal states in Germany. By the close of 1933, all major institutions of potential opposition had been eliminated.

*Joseph Goebbels (1897–1945) was in charge of Nazi propaganda. [Bildarchiv Preussischer Kulturbesitz]*

The final element in Hitler's consolidation of power involved the Nazi Party itself. By late 1933 the SA, or storm troopers, consisted of approximately one million active members and a larger number of reserves. The commander of this party army was Ernst Roehm (1887–1934), a possible rival to Hitler himself. The German army officer corps, on whom Hitler depended to rebuild the national army, were jealous of the SA leadership. So, to protect his own position and to shore up support with the regular army, on June 30, 1934, Hitler personally ordered the murder of key SA officers, including Roehm. Between June 30 and July 2, more than 100 persons were killed, including former chancellor General Kurt von Schleicher and his wife. The German army, the only institution that might have prevented the murders, did nothing.

A month later, on August 2, 1934, President Hindenburg died. Thereafter Hitler combined the offices of chancellor and president. He was now the sole ruler of Germany and of the Nazi Party.

# Josef Goebbels Explains How to Use Radio for Political Propaganda

*Radio produced a communications revolution during the interwar years. It also created an entirely new industry while many other areas of the economy stagnated. Radio, as popular at that time as television is today, also became an important political instrument. Most of the early radio stations were governed-owned and controlled. Political leaders could address their nations as they never could before. Communication became instant and could enter every home with a radio. Radio, unlike newspapers, did not depend upon the literacy of its audience. Shortly after coming into power, Josef Goebbels (1897–1945), who was in charge of Nazi propaganda, discussed the role of radio in the new Nazi order. Note how he urges his listeners, who were broadcasters, never to be boring. All radio broadcasting had to be interesting to audiences so they would be receptive to its political messages.*

◆ *Why does Goebbels emphasize the Nazi monopoly on broadcasting? What new attitudes did Goebbels want radio to bring to its audience? What advantages did radio have over newspapers as a propaganda device?*

We make no bones about the fact that the radio belongs to us and to no one else. And we will place the radio in the service of our ideology [*Idee*] and [. . .] no other ideology will find expression here. . . . The radio must subordinate itself to the goals which the Government of the national revolution has set itself. The Government will give the necessary instructions. . . .

I consider radio to be the most modern and the most crucial instrument that exists for influencing the masses. I also believe—one should not say that out loud—that radio will in the end replace the press. . . .

First, principle: At all costs avoid being boring. I put that before *everything*. . . . So do not think that you have the task of creating the correct attitudes, of indulging in patriotism, of blasting out military music and declaiming patriotic verse—no, that is not what this new orientation is all about. Rather you must help to bring forth a nationalist art and culture which is truly appropriate to the pace of modern life and to the mood of the times. The correct attitudes must be conveyed but that does not mean they must be boring. And simply because you have the task of taking part in this national enterprise you do not have *carte blanche* to be boring. You must use your imagination, an imagination which is based on sure foundations and which employs all means and methods to bring to the ears of the masses the new attitude in a way which is modern, up to date, interesting, and appealing; interesting, instructive but not schoolmasterish. Radio must never go down with the proverbial disease—the intention is clear and it puts you off.

I am placing a major responsibility in your hands for you have in your hands the most modern instrument in existence for influencing the masses. By means of this instrument you are the creators of public opinion. If you carry this out well we shall win over the people and if you do it badly in the end the people will once more desert us. . . .

J. Noakes and G. Pridham, eds., Nazism 1919–1945, vol. 2, State, Economy and Society 1933–39, A Documentary Reader, *Exeter Studies in History*, No. 8 (Exeter: University of Exeter, 1984), p. 386.

# The Nazis Pass Their Racial Legislation

*Anti-Semitism was a fundamental tenet of the Nazi Party and became a major policy of the Nazi government. This comprehensive legislation of September 15, 1935, carried anti-Semitism into all areas of public life and into some of the most personal areas of private life as well. It was characteristically entitled the Law for the Protection of German Blood and Honor. Hardly any aspect of Nazi thought and action shocked the non-German world as much as this policy toward the Jews.*

✦ *How would this legislation have affected the normal daily interaction between Jews and non-Jews in Germany? Why are there specific prohibitions against mixed marriages and sexual relations between Jews and non-Jews? How does this legislation separate German Jews from the symbols of German national life?*

Imbued with the knowledge that the purity of German blood is the necessary prerequisite for the existence of the German nation, and inspired by an inflexible will to maintain the existence of the German nation for all future times, the Reichstag has unanimously adopted the following law, which is now enacted:

Article I: (1) Any marriages between Jews and citizens of German or kindred blood are herewith forbidden. Marriages entered into despite this law are invalid, even if they are arranged abroad as a means of circumventing this law.

(2) Annulment proceedings for marriages may be initiated only by the Public Prosecutor.

Article II: Extramarital relations between Jews and citizens of German or kindred blood are herewith forbidden.

Article III: Jews are forbidden to employ as servants to their households female subjects of German or kindred blood who are under the age of forty-five years.

Article IV: (1) Jews are prohibited from displaying the Reich and national flag and from showing the national colors.

(2) However, they may display the Jewish colors. The exercise of this right is under state protection.

Article V: (1) Anyone who acts contrary to the prohibition noted in Article I renders himself liable to penal servitude.

(2) The man who acts contrary to the prohibition of Article II will be punished by sentence to either a jail or penitentiary.

(3) Anyone who acts contrary to the provisions of Articles III or IV will be punished with a jail sentence up to a year and with a fine, or with one of these penalties.

Article VI: The Reich Minister of Interior, in conjunction with the Deputy to the Führer and the Reich Minister of Justice, will issue the required legal and administrative decrees for the implementation and amplification of this law.

Article VII: This law shall go into effect on the day following its promulgation, with the exception of Article III, which shall go into effect on January 1, 1936.

Louis L. Snyder, ed. and trans., Documents of German History (New Brunswick, N.J.: Rutgers University Press, 1958), pp. 427–428.

## The Police State and Anti-Semitism

Terror and intimidation had been major factors in the Nazi march to office. As Hitler consolidated his power, he oversaw the organization of a police state. The chief vehicle of police surveillance was the SS (*Schutzstaffel*, or "protective force"), or security units, commanded by Heinrich Himmler (1900–1945). This group had originated in the mid-1920s as a bodyguard for Hitler and had become a more elite paramilitary organization than the much larger SA. In 1933 there were approximately 52,000 members of the SS. It was the instrument that carried out the blood purges of the party in 1934. By 1936 Himmler had become head of all police matters in Germany and stood second only to Hitler in power and influence.

The police character of the Nazi regime was all-pervasive, but the people who most consistently experienced the terror of the police state were the German Jews. Anti-Semitism had been a key plank of the Nazi program. It was anti-Semitism based on biological racial theories stemming from late-nineteenth-century thought rather than from religious discrimination. Before World War II, the Nazi attack on the Jews went through three stages of increasing intensity. First, in 1933, shortly after assuming power, the Nazis excluded Jews from the civil service. They also tried to enforce boycotts of Jewish shops and businesses, but these won little public support.

Second, in 1935, a series of measures known as the *Nuremberg Laws* robbed German Jews of their citizenship. All persons with at least three Jewish grandparents were defined as Jews. The professions and the major occupations were closed to them. Marriage and sexual intercourse between Jews and non-Jews were prohibited. Legal exclusion and humiliation of the Jews became the order of the day.

Then the persecution of the Jews increased again in 1938. Business careers were forbidden to them. In November 1938, under orders from the Nazi Party, thousands of Jewish stores and synagogues were burned or otherwise destroyed on what became known as *Kristallnacht*. The Jewish community itself was required to pay for the damage because the government confiscated the insurance money. In many other ways, large and petty, German Jews were harassed. This persecution allowed the Nazis to inculcate the rest of the population with the concept of a master race of pure German "Aryans" and also to display their own contempt for civil liberties.

Finally, after the war broke out, Hitler decided in 1941 and 1942 to destroy the Jews in Europe. More than six million Jews, mostly from eastern European nations, died as a result of that staggering decision, unprecedented in its scope and implementation.

*In early November, 1938, the Nazi authorities in Germany increased their persecution of Jews. On what has come to be called* Kristallnacht, *Nazis destroyed Jewish businesses and burned synagogues. [Bildarchiv Preussischer Kulturbesitz]*

Deutsche, verteidigt Euch
gegen die jüdische
Greuelpropaganda,
kauft
nur bei Deutschen!

Germans defend
yourselves against jewish
atrocity propaganda

buy only at German shops!

Deutsche!
Wehret Euch!
Kauft nicht bei Juden!

*Soon after seizing power, the Nazi government began harassing German Jewish businesses. Non-Jewish German citizens were urged not to buy merchandise from shops owned by Jews. [Bildarchiv Preussischer Kulturbesitz]*

## Nazi Economic Policy

Besides consolidating power and pursuing anti-Semitic policies, Hitler still had to confront the Great Depression. German unemployment had helped propel him to power. The Nazis attacked this problem with a success that astonished and frightened Europe. By 1936, while the rest of the European economy remained stagnant, the specter of unemployment and other difficulties associated with the Great Depression no longer haunted Germany.

As far as the economic crisis was concerned, Hitler had become the most effective political leader in Europe. This success was a most important source of the internal strength and support for his tyrannical regime. The Nazi success against the Great Depression gave the regime considerable contemporary credibility. Behind the direction of both business and labor stood the Nazi terror and police. The Nazi economic experiment proved that by sacrificing all political and civil liberty, destroying a free trade-union movement, preventing the private

exercise of capital, and ignoring consumer satisfaction, full employment to prepare for war and aggression could be achieved.

Nazi economic policies maintained private property and private capitalism, but subordinated all significant economic enterprise and decisions about prices and investment to the goals of the state. Hitler reversed the deflationary policy of the cabinets that had preceded him. He instituted a massive program of public works and spending. Many of these projects related directly or indirectly to rearmament. The government sponsored canal building, land reclamation, and the construction of a large highway system with clear military uses. The government returned some unemployed workers to farms if they had originally come from there. Other laborers were not permitted to change jobs.

In 1935 renunciation of the military provisions of the Versailles treaty led to open rearmament and expansion of the army with little opposition, as will be explained in Chapter 29. These measures essentially restored full employment. In 1936 Hitler instructed Hermann Göring (1893–1946), who had

# Hitler Rejects the Emancipation of Women

*According to Nazi ideology, women's place was in the home producing and rearing children and supporting their husbands. In this speech, Hitler urges this view of the role of women. He uses anti-Semitism to discredit those writers who had urged the emancipation of women from their traditional roles and occupations. Hitler returns here to the "separate spheres" concept of the relationship of men and women. His traditional view of women was directed against contrary views that were associated with the Soviet experiment during the interwar years. This Nazi outlook on women and the family should be contrasted with the view set forth by the young Bolshevik Alexandra Kollontai in the document in Chapter 27. Ironically, once World War II began, the Nazi leadership demanded that women leave the home and work in factories to support the war effort.*

✦ *What are the social tasks Hitler assigns to women? Why does he associate the emancipation of women with Jews and intellectuals? How does he attempt to subordinate the lives of women to the supremacy of the state?*

The slogan "Emancipation of women" was invented by Jewish intellectuals and its content was formed by the same spirit. In the really good times of German life the German woman had no need to emancipate herself. She possessed exactly what nature had necessarily given her to administer and preserve; just as the man in his good times had no need to fear that he would be ousted from his position in relation to the woman. . . .

If the man's world is said to be the State, his struggle, his readiness to devote his powers to the service of the community, then it may perhaps be said that the woman's is a smaller world. For her world is her husband, her family, her children, and her home. But what would become of the greater world if there were no one to tend and care for the smaller one? How could the greater world survive if there were no one to make the cares of the smaller world

headed the air force since 1933, to undertake a Four-Year Plan to prepare the army and the economy for war. The government determined that Germany must be economically self-sufficient. Armaments received top priority. This economic program satisfied both the yearning for social and economic security and the desire for national fulfillment.

With the crushing of the trade unions in 1933, strikes became illegal. There was no genuine collective bargaining. The government handled labor disputes through compulsory arbitration. It also required workers and employers to participate in the Labor Front, an organization intended to demonstrate that class conflict had ended. The Labor Front sponsored a "Strength Through Joy" program that provided vacations and other forms of recreation for the labor force.

## Women in Nazi Germany

Hitler and other Nazis thought there were naturally separate social spheres for men and women. Men belonged in the world of action, women in the home. The two spheres should not mix. Women who sought to liberate themselves and to adopt roles traditionally followed by men in public life were considered symptoms of cultural decline. Respect for women should arise from their function as wives and mothers.

These attitudes stood in direct conflict with many of the social changes that German women, like women elsewhere in Europe, had experienced during the first three decades of the twentieth century. German women had become much more active and assertive. More of them worked in fac-

the content of their lives? No, the greater world is built on the foundation of this smaller world. This great world cannot survive if the smaller world is not stable. Providence has entrusted to the woman the cares of that world which is her very own, and only on the basis of this smaller world can the man's world be formed and built up. The two worlds are not antagonistic. They complement each other, they belong together just as man and woman belong together.

We do not consider it correct for the woman to interfere in the world of the man, in his main sphere. We consider it natural if these two worlds remain distinct. To the one belongs the strength of feeling, the strength of the soul. To the other belongs the strength of vision, of toughness, of decision, and of the willingness to act. In the one case this strength demands the willingness of the woman to risk her life to preserve this important cell and to multiply it, and in the other case it demands from the man the readiness to safeguard life.

The sacrifices which the man makes in the struggle of his nation, the woman makes in the preservation of that nation in individual cases. What the man gives in courage on the battle field, the woman gives in eternal self-sacrifice, in eternal pain and suffering. Every child that a woman brings into the world is a battle, a battle waged for the existence of her people. . . .

So our women's movement is for us not something which inscribes on its banner as its programme the fight against men, but something which has as its programme the common fight together with men. For the new National Socialist national community acquires a firm basis precisely because we have gained the trust of millions of women as fanatical fellow-combatants, women who have fought for the common life in the service of the common task of preserving life. . . .

Whereas previously the programmes of the liberal, intellectualist women's movements contained many points, the programme of our National Socialist Women's movement has in reality but one single point, and that point is the child, that tiny creature which must be born and grow strong and which alone gives meaning to the whole life-struggle.

*J. Noakes and G. Pridham, eds.,* Nazism, 1919–1945, vol. 2, State, Economy and Society, 1933–39: A Documentary Reader, *Exeter Studies in History No. 8 (Exeter: University of Exeter, 1984), pp. 449–450.*

Young women among an enthusiastic crowd extend the Nazi salute at a party rally in 1938. Nazi ideology encouraged women to favor traditional domestic roles over employment in the workplace and to bear many children. The onset of the war, however, forced the government to recruit women workers. [Bildarchiv Preussischer Kulturbesitz]

*The Volkswagen, which first appeared in 1938, was intended to provide inexpensive transportation for German workers. This advertisement declares that saving five marks a week is all it takes to buy one. [Bildarchiv Preussischer Kulturbesitz]*

tories or were independently employed, and they had begun to enter the professions. Under the Weimar constitution, they voted. Throughout the Weimar period, there was also a lively discussion of issues surrounding women's emancipation. The Nazis saw many of these developments as signs of cultural weakness. They urged a much more traditional role for women in their new society. Nazi writers portrayed women as wives and mothers first and foremost.

The Nazis' point of view brought them the support of women of a conservative outlook and women who were following traditional roles as housewives, confirming the choices these women had made about the direction of their lives. In a period of high unemployment, the Nazi attitude also appealed to many men because it discouraged women from competing with men in the work-place. Such competition had begun during World War I and was regarded by many Nazis as an indication of the social confusion that had followed the German defeat.

The Nazi discussion of the role of women was also deeply rooted in the racism of Nazi ideology. Nazi writers argued that the superiority of the pure German race depended on the purity of the blood of each and every individual. It was the special task of German women in their role as mothers to preserve racial purity. Hitler particularly championed this view of women. They were to breed strong sons and daughters for the German nation. Nazi journalists often compared the role of women in childbirth to that of men in battle. Each served the state in particular social and gender roles. In both cases, the good of the nation was more important than that of the individual.

Most Nazis who discussed the role of women relegated them to the home. They also attacked feminist outlooks. They wanted women to bear many children. They believed the declining German birth rate was the result of emancipated women having spurned their natural and proper role as mothers. The Nazis established special medals for women who bore large families. They also sponsored schools that taught women how to care for and rear children.

The Nazis also intended women to be educators of the young. In that role, women were the special protectors of German cultural values. Through cooking, dress, music, and stories, mothers were to instill a love for the nation in their children. As consumers for the home, women were to support German-owned shops, to buy German-produced goods, and to boycott Jewish merchants.

Nazi ideology permitted women to be employed, but work was regarded as secondary to their being wives and mothers living in the home. The Nazis recognized that in the midst of the depression many women would need to work, but the party urged them to pursue employment that was "natural" to their character as women. These tasks included agricultural labor, teaching, nursing, social service, and domestic service. The Nazis seem to have achieved female political support because the party assigned to women roles in which most German women actually found themselves. Despite some variation throughout the decade, however, in 1939, 37 percent of German women were employed, the same as in 1928. Thereafter, the war effort forced the government to recruit women into the German work force.

A few Nazi feminists hoped that women could achieve new standing in the Nazi order. They appealed to ancient German history to prove that German men and women had once been equal. They also contended that only by allowing a broader role to women could Nazi society actually attain major achievements. They argued that if sons were not reared to respect their mothers, then those mothers could not carry out their role as educators of children for the nation. It would appear that most of these Nazi feminists were professional women who hoped both to support the party and to maintain their position in German society. They had only minimal influence on the policies of the party and none on the major leaders.

# Italy: Fascist Economics

The Fascists had promised to stabilize Italian social and economic life. Discipline was a substitute for economic policy and creativity. During the 1920s, Mussolini undertook vast public works, such as draining the Pontine Marshes near Rome for settlement. The government subsidized the shipping industry and introduced protective tariffs. Mussolini desperately sought to make Italy self-sufficient. He embarked on the "battle of wheat" to prevent foreign grain from appearing in products on Italian tables. Wheat farming in Italy expanded enormously. These policies, however, did not keep the Great Depression from affecting Italy. Production, exports, and wages fell. Even the increased wheat production backfired. So much poor marginal

*Mussolini was determined to make Italy a self-sufficient food producer. In July 1938, he stood on a threshing platform at a farm rally, stripped to the waist in the hot sun, to declare that Italy would never turn to other nations for grain. [Archive Photos]*

land that was expensive to cultivate came into production that the domestic price of wheat, and thus of much other food, actually rose.

### Syndicates

Both before and during the depression, the Fascists sought to steer an economic course between socialism and a liberal *laissez-faire* system. Their policy was known as *corporatism*. It was a planned economy linked to the private ownership of capital and to government arbitration of labor disputes. Major industries were first organized into syndicates representing labor and management. The two groups negotiated labor settlements within this framework and submitted differences to compulsory government arbitration. The Fascists contended that class conflict would be avoided if both labor and management looked to the greater goal of productivity for the nation.

Whether this arrangement favored workers or managers is still in dispute. From the mid-1920s, however, Italian labor unions lost the right to strike and to pursue independent economic goals. In that respect, management clearly profited.

### Corporations

After 1930 these industrial syndicates were further organized into entities called *corporations*. These bodies included all industries relating to a major area of production, such as agriculture or metallurgy, from raw materials through finished products and distribution. Twenty-two such corporations were established to encompass the whole economy. In 1938 Mussolini abolished the Italian Chamber of Deputies and replaced it with a Chamber of Corporations.

This vast organizational framework did not increase production; instead, bureaucracy and corruption proliferated. The corporate state allowed the government to direct much of the nation's economic life without a formal change in ownership. Consumers and owners could no longer determine what was to be produced. The Fascist government gained further direct economic power through the Institute for Industrial Reconstruction, which extended loans to businesses in financial difficulty. The loans, in effect, established partial state ownership.

How corporatism might have affected the Italian economy in the long run is unknown. In 1935 Italy invaded Ethiopia, and economic life was put on a formal wartime footing. The League of Nations imposed economic sanctions, urging member nations to refrain from purchasing Italian goods. The sanctions had little effect. Thereafter taxes rose. During 1935 the government imposed a forced loan on the citizenry by requiring property owners to purchase bonds. Wages continued to be depressed. As international tensions increased during the late 1930s, the Italian state assumed more and more direction over the economy. The order that Fascism brought to Italy had not proved to be the order of prosperity. It had brought economic dislocation and a falling standard of living.

# The Soviet Union: Central Economic Planning and Party Purges

While the capitalist economies of western Europe floundered in the doldrums of the Great Depression, the Soviet Union began a tremendous industrial advance. Like similar eras of past Russian economic progress, the direction and impetus came from the top. Stalin far exceeded his tsarist predecessors in the intensity of state coercion and terror he brought to the task. Russia achieved its stunning economic growth during the 1930s only at the cost of literally millions of human lives and the degradation of still other millions. Stalin's economic policy clearly proved that his earlier rivalry with Trotsky had been a political power struggle rather than one over substantial ideological differences.

### The Decision for Rapid Industrialization

Through 1927 Lenin's New Economic Policy (NEP), as championed by Bukharin with Stalin's support, had charted the course of Soviet economic development. The government permitted private ownership and enterprise to flourish in the countryside to ensure an adequate food supply for the workers in the cities. Though the industrial production level of 1913 had been achieved by 1927, industrial growth had slowed. During 1927 the Party Congress decided to push for rapid industrialization. This policy, which began in 1928, marked a sharp departure from NEP.

The industrial achievement of the Soviet Union between 1928 and World War II is one of the most

ДЛЯ БЛАГА СОВЕТСКОГО НАРОДА ПОСТРОИМ НОВЫЕ ЭЛЕКТРОСТАНЦИИ!

striking accomplishments of the twentieth century. The Russian economy grew more rapidly than that of any other nation in the Western world during any similar time period.

By even the conservative estimates of Western observers, Soviet industrial production rose approximately 400 percent between 1928 and 1940. The production of iron, steel, coal, electrical power, tractors, combines, railway cars, and other heavy machinery was emphasized. Few consumer goods were produced. The labor for this development was supplied internally. Capital was raised from the export of grain even at the cost of internal shortages. The technology was generally borrowed from already industrialized nations. This paralleled the manner in which the tsarist government had pursued industrialization in the late nineteenth century.

Unlike the tsarist drive toward an industrial economy, however, Stalin's organizational vehicle for industrialization was a series of five-year plans starting in 1928. The State Planning Commission, or Gosplan, oversaw the program. It set goals for production and organized the economy to meet them. The task of coordinating all facets of production was immensely difficult and complicated. Deliveries of materials from mines or factories had to be assured before the next unit could carry out its part of the plan. There was many a slip between the cup and the lip. The troubles in the country-side were harmful. The government and Communist Party undertook a vast program of propaganda to sell the five-year plans to the Russian people and to elicit cooperation. The industrial labor force, however, soon became subject to the same regimentation that was being imposed on the peasants.

By the close of the 1930s, the results of the three five-year plans were truly impressive and probably allowed the Soviet Union to survive the German invasion. Industries that had never before existed in Russia now challenged and in some cases, such as tractor production, surpassed their counterparts in the rest of the world. Large, new industrial cities had been built and populated by hundreds of thousands of people. The social and human cost of this effort had, however, been astounding.

### The Collectivization of Agriculture

The decision to industrialize rapidly brought enormous consequences for Soviet agriculture. Under NEP, a few farmers, the *kulaks*, had become prosperous. They probably numbered less than 5 percent of the rural population. They and other farmers were discontented with their situation, because there were few consumer goods to purchase with the cash they received for their crops. They had frequently withheld grain from the market in the 1920s and did so again during 1928 and 1929. Food

*Russian farmers attend a rally to celebrate the arrival of new tractors at their collective farm. [Bildarchiv Preussischer Kulturbesitz]*

shortages then occurred in the cities, and the government worried about potential unrest.

During these troubled months, Stalin came to a momentous decision. Agriculture must be collectivized to produce enough grain for food and export, to achieve control over the farm sector of the economy, and to free peasant labor for the factories in the expanding industrial sector. The implementation of this program of collectivization, which basically embraced Trotsky's earlier economic position, unleashed a second Russian revolution and unprecedented violence in the countryside.

In 1929 Stalin ordered party agents into the countryside to confiscate any hoarded wheat. The *kulaks* were blamed for the grain shortages. As part of the general plan to erase the private ownership of land and to collectivize farming, the government decided to eliminate the *kulaks* as a class. The definition of

a *kulak*, however, soon embraced anyone who opposed Stalin's policy. Peasants and farmers of all levels of wealth resisted collectivization. The stubborn peasants were determined to keep their land. They sabotaged collectivization by slaughtering more than 100 million horses and cattle between 1929 and 1933. The situation in the countryside amounted to open warfare. Peasant resistance caused Stalin to call a brief halt to the process in March 1930. He justified the slowdown on the grounds of "dizziness from success."

Soon thereafter the drive to collectivize the farms was renewed with vehemence, and the costs remained very high. As many as ten million peasants were killed, and millions of others were dragged off to collective farms or labor camps. Initially, because of the turmoil on the land, agricultural production fell. There was famine in 1932 and

1933. Milk and meat remained scarce because of the livestock slaughter. Yet Stalin persevered. The uprooted peasants were moved to thousand-acre collective farms. The state provided the machinery for these units through machine-tractor stations. The state monopoly in heavy farm machines was a powerful weapon.

Collectivization changed Russian farming dramatically. In 1928 approximately 98 percent of Russian farmland consisted of small peasant holdings. Ten years later, despite all opposition, more than 90 percent of the land had been collectivized, and the quantity of farm produce directly handled by the government had risen by 40 percent. Those shifts in control meant that the government now

*Collective farmers bringing grain to a shipment center. Note that horse-drawn wagons are the only form of transport in this picture; there are no trucks or tractors. [Bildarchiv Preussischer Kulturbesitz]*

# Stalin Calls for the Liquidation of the Kulaks as a Class

*The core of Stalin's agricultural policy undertaken in the late 1920s and early 1930s was the eradication of private farms and their replacement with large collective farms. The greatest obstacle to this policy was the kulaks, peasants who owned substantial farms. In this remarkable speech of 1929, Stalin first explains why small peasant farming must be replaced with collective farms to achieve an adequate food supply for the cities and the industrial sector of the population. He then calls for the liquidation of the kulaks as a class. As might be expected, the kulaks resisted collectivization by destroying crops and farm animals. In turn, Communist Party agents killed millions of peasants to achieve collectivization.*

◆ *What were the goals of the collectivization of farms in the Soviet Union? How did the kulaks stand in the way of collectivization? How does Stalin dehumanize the kulaks as people by discussing them entirely as a class and as part of the capitalistic system?*

Can we advance our socialized industry at an accelerated rate as long as we have an agricultural base, such as is provided by small-peasant farming, which is incapable of expanded reproduction, and which, in addition, is the predominant force in our national economy? No, we cannot. . . .

What, then, is the solution? The solution lies in enlarging the agricultural units, in making agriculture capable of accumulation, of expanded reproduction, and in thus transforming the agricultural bases of our national economy.

. . . [T]he *socialist* way [to enlarge farming units], which is to introduce collective farms and state farms in agriculture, the way which leads to the amalgamation of the small-peasant farms into large collective farms, employing machinery and scientific methods of farming, and capable of

---

controlled the food supply. The farmers and peasants could no longer determine whether there would be stability or unrest in the cities. Stalin and the Communist Party had won the battle of the wheat fields, but they had not solved the problem of producing enough grain. That difficulty would plague the Soviet Union until its collapse in 1991 and remains a problem for the new Commonwealth of Independent States.

## Foreign Reactions and Repercussions

Many foreign contemporaries looked at the Soviet economic experiment naïvely. While the capitalist world lay in the throes of the Great Depression, the Soviet economy had grown at a pace never realized in the West. The American writer Lincoln Steffens

(1866–1936) reported after a trip to Russia, "I have seen the future and it works." Beatrice and Sidney Webb, the British Fabian Socialists, spoke of "a new civilization" in the Soviet Union. These and similar observers ignored the shortages in consumer goods and the poor housing. More important, they had little idea of the social cost of the Soviet achievement. Millions of human beings had been killed and millions more uprooted. The total picture of suffering and human loss during those years will probably never be known; however, the deprivation and sacrifice of Soviet citizens far exceeded anything described by Marx and Engels in relation to nineteenth-century industrialization in western Europe.

The internal difficulties caused by collectivization and industrialization led Stalin to make an important shift in foreign policy. In 1934 he began

developing further, for such agricultural enterprises can achieve expanded reproduction. . . .

The characteristic feature in the work of our Party during the past year is that we, as a Party, as the Soviet power,

(a) have developed an offensive along the whole front against the capitalist elements in the countryside;

(b) that this offensive, as you know, has brought about and is bringing about very palpable, *positive* results.

What does this mean? It means that we have passed from the policy of *restricting* the exploiting proclivities of the kulaks to the policy of *eliminating* the kulaks as a class. . . .

Until recently the Party adhered to the policy of *restricting* the exploiting proclivities of the kulaks. . . .

. . . Could we have undertaken such an offensive against the kulaks five years or three years ago? Could we then have counted on success in such an offensive? No, we could not. That would have been the most dangerous adventurism. It would have been playing a very dangerous game at offensive. We would certainly have failed, and our failure would have strengthened the position of the kulaks. Why? Because we still lacked a wide network of state and collective farms in the rural districts which could be used as strongholds in a determined offensive against the kulaks. Because at that time we were not yet able to *substitute* for the capitalist production of the kulaks the socialist production of the collective farms and state farms. . . .

. . . Now we are able to carry on a determined offensive against the kulaks, to break their resistance, to eliminate them as a class and substitute for their output the output of the collective farms and state farms. Now, the kulaks are being expropriated by the masses of poor and middle peasants themselves, by the masses who are putting solid collectivization into practice. Now, the expropriation of the kulaks in the regions of solid collectivization is no longer just an administrative measure. Now, the expropriation of the kulaks is an integral part of the formation and development of the collective farms. Consequently it is now ridiculous and foolish to discourse on the expropriation of the kulaks. You do not lament the loss of the hair of one who has been beheaded.

*Stalin, "Problems of Agrarian Policy in the USSR," speech at a conference of Marxist students of the agrarian question, December 27, 1929, in* Problems of Leninism, *pp. 391–393, 408–409, 411–412, as quoted in Robert V. Daniels,* A Documentary History of Communism, *rev. ed. (Hanover, N.H., and London: University Press of New England, 1984), pp. 224–227.*

to fear that the nation might be left isolated against future aggression by Nazi Germany. The Soviet Union was not yet strong enough to withstand such an attack. So that year he ordered the Comintern to permit communist parties in other countries to cooperate with noncommunist parties against Nazism and Fascism. This reversed the Comintern policy established by Lenin as part of the Twenty-one Conditions in 1919. The new Stalinist policy allowed the formation of the Popular Front Government in France.

### The Purges

Stalin's decisions to industrialize rapidly, to move against the peasants, and to reverse the Comintern policy aroused internal political opposition. They were all departures from the policies of Lenin. In 1929 Stalin forced Bukharin, the fervent supporter of NEP and his own former ally, off the Politburo. Little detailed information is known about further opposition, but it seems to have existed among lower-level party followers of Bukharin and other opponents of rapid industrialization. In 1933 Stalin began to fear that he might lose control over the party apparatus and that effective rivals to his power might emerge. These fears were probably produced as much by his own paranoia as by real plots. Nevertheless, they resulted in the Great Purges, one of the most mysterious and horrendous political events of the twentieth century. The purges were not understood at the time and have not been fully comprehended either inside or outside the former Soviet Union to the present day.

*By the mid 1930s Stalin's purges had eliminated many leaders and other members from the Soviet Communist Party. This photograph of a meeting of a party congress in 1936 shows a number of the surviving leaders with Stalin, who sits fourth from the right in the front row. To his left is Vyacheslav Molotov, long-time foreign minister. The first person on the left in the front row is Nikita Khrushchev, who headed the Soviet Union in the late 1950s and early 1960s [ITAR-TASS/SOVFOTO]*

On December 1, 1934, Sergei Kirov (1888–1934), the popular party chief of Leningrad (formerly and now again Saint Petersburg) and a member of the Politburo, was assassinated. In the wake of the shooting, thousands of people were arrested, and still more were expelled from the party and sent to labor camps. At the time, it was believed that Kirov had been murdered by opponents of the regime. Direct or indirect complicity in the crime became the normal accusation against the persons whom Stalin attacked. It is now almost certain that Stalin himself authorized Kirov's assassination because he was afraid of the Leningrad leader.

The purges after Kirov's death were just the beginning of a larger process. Between 1936 and 1938, a series of spectacular show trials were held in Moscow. Previous high Soviet leaders, including former members of the Politburo, publicly confessed to political crimes. They were convicted and executed. It is still not certain why they made their palpably false confessions. Other leaders and lower-level party members were tried in private and shot. Hundreds of thousands of people received no trial at all. The purges touched persons in all areas of party life. No one can explain why some were executed, others sent to labor camps, and still others left unmolested.

After the civilian party members had been purged, the prosecutors turned against the army. Important officers, including heroes of the civil war, were shot. Within the party itself, hundreds of thousands of members were expelled, and applicants for membership were removed from the rolls. The exact numbers of executions, imprisonments, and expulsions are unknown but certainly ran into the millions.

The trials and purges astonished Western observers. Nothing like it had been seen before. Political murders and executions were not new, but the absurd confessions were novel. The scale of the political turmoil was also unprecedented. The Russians themselves did not believe or comprehend what was occurring. No national emergency or crisis existed. There were only accusations of sympathy for Trotsky, of complicity in Kirov's murder, of plots against the long-dead Lenin, or of other nameless crimes.

If a rational explanation is to be sought, it probably lies in Stalin's fears for his own power. In effect, the purges created a new party structure absolutely subservient and loyal to him. The "old Bolsheviks" of the October Revolution were among his earliest targets. They and others active in the first years of the revolution knew how far Stalin had moved from Lenin's policies. New, younger members replaced the party members executed or expelled. The newcomers had little knowledge of old Russia or of the ideals of the original Bolsheviks. They had not been loyal to Lenin, to Trotsky, or to any other Soviet leader except Stalin himself.

✦

*By the middle of the 1930s, dictators of the right and the left had established themselves across much of Europe. Political tyranny was hardly new to Europe, but several factors combined to give these rulers unique characteristics. They drew their immediate support from well-organized political parties. Except for the Bolsheviks, these were mass parties. The roots of support for the dictators lay in nationalism, the social and economic frustration of the Great Depression, and political ideologies that promised to transform the social and political order. As long as the new rulers seemed successful, they did not lack support. Many citizens believed that these leaders had ended the pettiness of everyday politics.*

*After coming to power, the dictators possessed a practical monopoly over mass communications. Through armies, police forces, and party discipline, they also monopolized terror and coercive power. They could propagandize large populations and compel people to obey them and their followers. Finally, as a result of the Second Industrial Revolution, they commanded a vast amount of technology and a capacity for immense destruction. Earlier rulers in Europe may have shared the ruthless ambitions of Hitler, Mussolini, and Stalin, but they had lacked the ready implements of physical force to impose their wills.*

*Mass political support, the monopoly of police and military power, and technological capacity meant that the dictators of the 1930s held more extensive sway over their nations than any other group of rulers who had ever governed on the Continent. Soon the issue would become whether they would be able to maintain peace among themselves and with their democratic neighbors.*

## Review Questions

1. Explain the causes of the Great Depression of the 1930s. Why was it more severe and longer-lasting than previous depressions? Could it have been avoided?

2. Compare the relative success of Britain's National Government and France's Popular Front in dealing with their respective economic problems. How would you account for the differences? Why did France's Third Republic have so few supporters?

3. How did the Great Depression affect Germany? Discuss Hitler's rise to power between 1929 and 1934. Was his dictatorship inevitable? Was his seizure of power due more to personalities than to impersonal forces?

4. Discuss Hitler's economic policies. Why were they successful? Compare and contrast his economic policies with those used in Britain, Italy, and France. Why were some nations more successful than others in addressing the Great Depression?

5. What were the characteristics of a "police state"? How necessary is terror and intimidation in the consolidation of an authoritarian regime? How did Hitler, Mussolini, and Stalin use terror to achieve their goals?

**6.** Why did Stalin decide that Russia had to industrialize rapidly? Why did this require the collectivization of agriculture? What obstacles stood in the way of collectivization, and how did Stalin overcome them? What were the causes of the purges in the Soviet Union? What groups became the special targets of the purges?

## Suggested Readings

W. S. ALLEN, *The Nazi Seizure of Power: The Experience of a Single German Town, 1930–1935*, rev. ed. (1984). A classic treatment of Nazism in a microcosmic setting.

K. E. BAILES, *Technology and Society Under Lenin and Stalin: Origins of the Soviet Technical Intelligentsia, 1917–1941* (1978). An important study of the people who actually put the programs of modernization into place.

N. BRANSON AND M. HEINEMANN, *Britain in the Nineteen Thirties* (1971). Primarily considers the social and economic problems of the day.

M. BURLEIGH AND W. WIPPERMAN, *The Racial State: Germany 1933–1945* (1991). Emphasizes the manner in which racial theory influenced numerous areas of policy.

D. CARROLL, *French Literary Fascism: Nationalism, Anti-Semitism, and the Ideology of Culture* (1995). A study of right-wing political theoriest in France.

J. COLTON, *Léon Blum: Humanist in Politics* (1966). One of the best biographies of any twentieth-century political figure.

R. CONQUEST, *The Great Terror: Stalin's Purges of the Thirties* (1968). Remains the most useful treatment of the subject to date.

R. CONQUEST, *The Harvest of Sorrow: Soviet Collectivization and the Terror-Famine* (1986). A study of how Stalin used starvation against his own people.

G. CRAIG, *Germany, 1866–1945* (1978). An important survey.

R. W. DAVIES, *The Socialist Offensive: The Collectivization of Soviet Agriculture, 1929–1930* (1980). Examines the crucial years when Stalin moved against the *kulaks*.

I. DEUTSCHER, *Stalin: A Political Biography*, 2nd ed. (1967). A major biography.

B. EICHENGREEN, *Golden Fetters: The Gold Standard and the Great Depression, 1919–1939* (1992). A remarkable study of the role of the gold standard in the economic policies of the interwar years.

S. FITZPATRICK, *Stalin's Peasants: Resistance and Survival in the Russian Village after Collectivization* (1994). A pioneering study.

R. GELLATELY, *The Gestapo and German Society: Enforcing Racial Policy, 1933–1945* (1990). A discussion of how the police state supported Nazi racial policies.

R. F. HAMILTON, *Who Voted for Hitler?* (1982). An important examination of voting patterns.

E. C. HELMREICH, *The German Churches Under Hitler: Background, Struggle, and Epilogue* (1979). A useful study.

J. JACKSON, *The Politics of Depression in France, 1932–1936* (1985). A detailed examination of the political struggles prior to the Popular Front.

J. JACKSON, *The Popular Front in France: Defending Democracy, 1934–1938* (1988). An extensive recent treatment.

H. JAMES, *The German Slump: Politics and Economics, 1914–1936* (1986). A difficult but informative examination of the German experience of the Great Depression.

C. KINDLEBERGER, *The World in Depression, 1929–1939* (1973). An account by a leading economist whose analysis is comprehensible to the layperson.

E. MENDELSOHN, *The Jews of East Central Europe Between the World Wars* (1983). An excellent survey of the subject.

I. MUELLER, *Hitler's Justice: The Courts of the Third Reich* (1991). An account of how German courts cooperated with the Nazis.

D. J. K. PEUKERT, *Inside Nazi Germany: Conformity, Opposition, and Racism in Everyday Life* (1987). An excellent discussion of life under Nazi rule.

P. PULZER, *Jews and the German State: The Political History of a Minority, 1848–1933* (1992). A detailed study by a major historian of European minorities.

R. PROCTOR, *Racial Hygiene: Medicine Under the Nazis* (1988). An exploration of how medical science contributed to racism.

L. J. RUPP, *Mobilizing Women for War: German and American Propaganda, 1939–1945* (1978). Although concentrating on a later period, it includes an excellent discussion of general Nazi attitudes toward women.

D. SCHOENBAUM, *Hitler's Social Revolution: Class and Status in Nazi Germany* (1966). A fascinating analysis of Hitler's appeal to various social classes.

D. M. SMITH, *Mussolini's Roman Empire* (1976). A general description of the Fascist regime in Italy.

W. D. SMITH, *The Ideological Origins of Nazi Imperialism* (1986). A study that links Nazi expansionist thought to earlier German foreign policy.

A. SOLZHENITSYN, *The Gulag Archipelago*, 3 vols. (1974–1979). A major examination of the labor camps under Stalin by one of the most important contemporary writers.

R. SOUCY, *French Fascism: The Second Wave, 1933–1939* (1995). A study of the right-wing leagues.

J. STEPHENSON, *The Nazi Organization of Women* (1981). Examines the attitude and policies of the Nazis toward women.

H. A. Turner, Jr., *German Big Business and the Rise of Hitler* (1985). An important major study of the subject.

H. A. Turner, Jr., *Hitler's Thirty Days to Power* (1996). A narrative of the events leading directly to the Nazi seizure of power.

E. Weber, *The Hollow Years: France in the 1930s* (1995). Examines France between the wars.

L. Yahil, *The Holocaust: The Fate of the European Jewry, 1932–1945* (1990). A major recent study of this fundamental subject in twentieth-century history.

Reference should also be made to the works cited in Chapters 27 and 29.

# Global Conflict, Cold War, and New Directions

The people of Europe and the United States regarded the great conflict of 1914–1918 as a "world war," but by far the largest part of the fighting and suffering was confined to the European continent. The second great political and military upheaval of the twentieth century, the war of 1939–1945, was truly global in scope and even more devastating than the first. Heavy fighting took place in Africa and Asia as well as in Europe. The people of every inhabited continent were involved. Battle casualties were many, and the assault on civilians was unprecedented. Massive aerial bombardment of cities began with the German attack on Britain in 1940 and concluded with the use of the new and terrifying atomic weapons against Japan in 1945. The cost of World War II in life and property was even greater than that of World War I.

After World War II, the hopes of many for peace and stability rested with a new international organization, the United Nations. Unlike the League of Nations, which the United States had never joined, the new organization included all the victorious powers and came to include almost all the nations of the world. Its success, however, depended on cooperation among the great powers, which grew elusive as the war drew to an end.

The coalition of victors had been threatened from the start by differences between the political and economic systems of the Soviet Union and the Western nations and their mutual suspicion. The Western powers' insistence on free, democratic elections in the liberated states of eastern Europe was incompatible with the Soviet Union's desire to secure control over the areas on its western border. Disputes over Poland, the Balkan states, and Ger-

many led to a division of Germany and of all Europe into East and West. Thus began a period of competition and sometimes open hostility called the *Cold War*. The division hardened with the formation of the North Atlantic Treaty Organization (NATO) in 1949 and the Warsaw Pact in 1955. From that time through the mid-1980s, the former allies faced each other across what Winston Churchill called an "Iron Curtain," with ever increasing collections of deadly weapons and with continuing tension, occasionally relaxed by hopes for cooperation.

The Cold War quickly spread to Asia, where the Communist Party under Mao Tse-tung gained control of China and allied itself with the Soviet Union. They supported the communist regime in North Korea against South Korea, which was in turn supported by the United States and its allies. Later, the same alignment influenced the emerging conflict in Vietnam. By the 1960s, however, a split between the Chinese and the Russians became apparent and international relations became even more complex. During the 1970s, the sharp exchanges of the Cold War gave way to a period of hesitant cooperation under the American policy known as *détente*. Negotiation replaced confrontation between the United States and the Soviet Union.

Throughout the postwar era, the influence of the United States touched Europe as never before. The NATO alliance, trade relations, and an enormous annual wave of tourists brought Americans into a series of close relationships with Europeans. At the same time, the nations of Western Europe began to forge new economic links among themselves through the establishment of the European Economic Community (EEC), founded in 1957. By the opening of the 1990s, the members of the EEC looked forward to unprecedented economic cooperation and unhindered movement of peoples and goods across their borders.

From the late 1940s through the mid-1980s, the peoples of the Soviet bloc, including the Soviet Union and its Eastern European neighbors, had lived under authoritarian political systems dominated by communist parties. Their economies were centrally controlled. In 1956 in Poland and Hungary and in 1968 in Czechoslovakia, the Soviet Union had demonstrated either politically or militarily its determination to dominate and control its Eastern European satellites. The activities of the Solidarity trade union movement in Poland began to challenge that dominance. The imposition of martial law in Poland in 1981 suppressed that challenge for a time. Then, in 1985, Mikhail Gorbachev began to lead the Soviet Union in new directions, instituting policies of economic and political liberation. The year 1989 saw popular uprisings throughout Eastern Europe against the political domination of the Communist Party and the Soviet Union. In the wake of these revolutions, Germany became reunited. In 1991, after an unsuccessful attempt by conservative forces to turn back reform, the communist government of the Soviet Union collapsed and the nation broke up into its constituent republics, loosely federated in the Commonwealth of Independent States. With these events, a fundamentally new era in European history began.  ✦

| | POLITICS AND GOVERNMENT | SOCIETY AND ECONOMY | RELIGION AND CULTURE |
|---|---|---|---|
| **1939–1960** | 1939 World War II begins<br>1941 Japan attacks Pearl Harbor, US enters war | 1945–1951 Attlee ministry establishes the Welfare State in Great Britain | 1940 Koestler, *Darkness at Noon* |

Churchill, Roosevelt, Stalin at Yalta

| | POLITICS AND GOVERNMENT | SOCIETY AND ECONOMY | RELIGION AND CULTURE |
|---|---|---|---|
| | 1942 Battle of Stalingrad<br>1944 Normandy invasion<br>1945 Yalta Conference; Germany surrenders; atomic bombs dropped on Japan; Japan surrenders; United Nations founded<br>1946 Churchill gives Iron Curtain speech<br>1947 Truman Doctrine<br>1948 Communist takeover in Czechoslovakia and Hungary; State of Israel proclaimed<br>1948–1949 Berlin blockade<br>1949 NATO founded; East and West Germany emerge as separate states<br>1950–1953 Korean War<br>1953 Death of Stalin<br>1954 French defeat at Dien Bien Phu<br>1955 Warsaw Pact founded<br>1956 Khrushchev denounces Stalin; Polish Communist Party crisis; Suez crisis; Soviet invasion of Hungary | 1947 Marshall Plan to rebuild Europe instituted<br><br>1949 Europe divided into Eastern and Western blocs<br>1950s and 1960s Increase in agricultural production<br><br>1957 European Economic Community founded | 1942 Lewis, *The Screwtape Letters*<br>1943 Sartre, *Being and Nothingness*<br><br>1947 Camus, *The Plague*; Gramsci, *Letters from Prison*<br><br>1949 de Beauvoir, *The Second Sex*; Crossman, *The God That Failed*<br><br>1958 Pasternak forbidden to accept Nobel Prize for *Dr. Zhivago*; John XXIII becomes pope |

| POLITICS AND GOVERNMENT | SOCIETY AND ECONOMY | RELIGION AND CULTURE |
|---|---|---|

**1960–1980**

| | | |
|---|---|---|
| 1960 Khruschev aborts Geneva summit | 1960s Rapid growth of student population in universities; migration of workers from eastern and southern to northern and western Europe; migration of non-European workers to northern and western Europe | 1960s The Beatles take world by storm |
| 1961 Berlin Wall erected | | |
| 1962 Cuban Missile Crisis | | |
| 1963 Test Ban Treaty | | |
| 1963–1973 Major US involvement in Vietnam | | |
| 1964–1982 Brezhnev era in Soviet Union | | |
| 1967 Six Days' War between Israel and Arab states | | |
| 1968 Soviet invasion of Czechoslovakia | | |

The Beatles

| | | |
|---|---|---|
| | | 1962–1965 Second Vatican Council |
| | | 1963 Solzhenitsyn, *One Day in the Life of Ivan Denisovich*; Robinson, *Honest to God* |
| | | 1968 Student rebellion in Paris |
| 1973 Yom Kippur War between Israel and Egypt | 1972 Club of Rome founded | |
| 1975 Helsinki Accords | 1973–1974 Arab oil embargo | 1974 Solzhenitsyn expelled from Soviet Union |
| 1978 Camp David Accords; Solidarity founded in Poland | | 1978 John Paul II becomes pope |
| 1979–1988 Soviet troops in Afghanistan | | |

**1980–1997**

| | | |
|---|---|---|
| 1981–1983 Martial law in Poland | 1980s and 1990s Internal migration from Eastern to Western Europe; racial and ethnic tensions in Western Europe | 1980s Growth of the environmental movement |
| 1982 Israel invades Lebanon | | 1990s Expanding influence of Roman Catholic Church in independent eastern Europe |
| 1985 Gorbachev comes to power in the Soviet Union | 1986 Chernobyl nuclear disaster | |
| 1987 Major US–Soviet arms limitation treaty; Palestinian *intifada* begins on West Bank | 1990s Changes in Eastern Europe and Soviet Union open way for economic growth and new trade relations across Europe | 1990s Feminists continue the critical tradition of Western culture |
| 1989 Revolutions sweep across Eastern Europe | | |
| 1990 German reunification; Yugoslavia breaks up | | |
| 1991 Persian Gulf War; civil war in former Yugoslavia; August coup in Moscow; Gorbachev resigns; Soviet Union dissolved | | |
| 1992 Ascendancy of Yeltsin in Russia | | |
| 1993 Israel and PLO recognize one another | | |
| 1995 Bosnia recognized as independent | | |
| 1997 Hong Kong returns to China | | |

In the spring of 1943, when only a fraction of the many Jews whom the Germans imprisoned in the Warsaw Ghetto were still alive, about a thousand of them took up hidden arms to offer what they knew would be a doomed resistance. Before the fighting was over the Germans suffered many casualties and had to call for reinforcements. [Archive Photos]

# World War II

# KEY TOPICS

- The origins of World War II
- The course of the war
- Racism and the Holocaust
- The impact of the war on the people of Europe
- Relationships among the victorious allies and the preparations for peace

The more idealistic survivors of World War I, especially in the United States and Great Britain, thought of it as "the war to end all wars" and a war "to make the world safe for democracy." Only thus could they justify the horrible slaughter, expense, and upheaval of that terrible conflict. How appalled they would have been had they known that only twenty years after the peace treaties a second great war would break out that would be more terribly global than the first. In this war, the democracies would be fighting for their lives against militaristic, nationalistic, authoritarian, and totalitarian states in Europe and Asia, and they would be allied with the communist Soviet Union in the struggle. The defeat of the militarists and dictators would not bring the peace they longed for, but a Cold War. In this Cold War, the European states would become powers of the second class, subordinate to the two new superpowers, partially or fully non-European: the Soviet Union and the United States.

## Again the Road to War (1933–1939)

World War I and the Versailles treaty themselves had only a marginal relationship to the world depression of the 1930s. In Germany, however, where the reparations settlement had contributed to the vast inflation of 1923, economic and social discontent focused on the Versailles settlement as the cause of all ills. Throughout the late 1920s, Adolf Hitler and the Nazi Party had denounced Versailles as the source of all Germany's trouble. The economic woes of the early 1930s seemed to bear them out. Nationalism and attention to the social question, along with party discipline, had been the sources of Nazi success. They continued to influence Hitler's foreign policy after he became chancellor in January 1933. Moreover, the Nazi destruction of the Weimar constitution and of political opposition meant that Hitler himself totally dominated German foreign policy. Consequently, it is important to know what his goals were and how he planned to achieve them.

## Hitler's Goals

From the first expression of his goals in a book written in jail, *Mein Kampf* or "my struggle," to his last days in the underground bunker in Berlin where he killed himself, Hitler's racial theories and goals were at the center of his thought. He meant to go far beyond Germany's 1914 boundaries, which were the limit of the vision of his predecessors. He meant to bring the entire German people—the *Volk*—understood as a racial group, together into a single nation.

The new Germany would include all the Germanic parts of the old Habsburg Empire, including Austria. This virile and growing nation would need more space to live, or "*Lebensraum,*" which would be taken from the Slavs, who, according to Nazi theory, were a lesser race, fit only for servitude. The new Germany would be purified by the removal of the Jews, another inferior race in Nazi theory. The plans required the conquest of Poland and Ukraine as the primary areas for the settlement of Germans and for the provision of badly needed food. Neither *Mein Kampf* nor later statements of policy were blueprints for action. Hitler was a brilliant improviser who exploited opportunities as they arose. He never lost sight of his goal, however, which would almost certainly require a major war.

GERMANY REARMS   When Hitler came to power, Germany was far too weak to permit a direct approach toward reaching his aims. The first problem he set out to resolve was to shake off the fetters of Versailles and to make Germany a formidable military power. In October 1933, Germany withdrew from an international disarmament conference and also from the League of Nations. Hitler argued that because the other powers had not disarmed as they had promised, it was wrong to keep Germany helpless. These acts alarmed the French but were merely symbolic. In January 1934, Germany signed a nonaggression pact with Poland that was of greater concern to France, for it undermined France's chief means of containing the Germans. At last, in March 1935, Hitler formally renounced the disarmament provisions of the Versailles treaty with the formation of a German air force, and soon he reinstated conscription, which aimed at an army of half a million men.

THE LEAGUE OF NATIONS FAILS   Hitler's path was made easier by growing evidence that the League of Nations could not keep the peace and that collective security was a myth. In September 1931, Japan occupied Manchuria, provoking an appeal to the League of Nations by China. The league responded by sending out a commission under a British diplomat, the earl of Lytton (1876–1951). The Lytton Report condemned the Japanese for resorting to force, but the powers were unwilling to impose sanctions. Japan withdrew from the league and kept control of Manchuria.

When Hitler announced his decision to rearm Germany, the league formally condemned that action, but it took no steps to prevent Germany's rearming. France and Britain opposed German rearmament, but they felt unable to object forcefully because they had not carried out their own promises to disarm. Instead, they met with Mussolini in June 1935 to form the so-called Stresa Front, promising to use force to maintain the status quo in Europe. This show of unity by the three powers was short-lived, however. Britain, desperate to maintain superiority at sea, violated the spirit of the Stresa accords and sacrificed French security needs to make a separate naval agreement with Hitler. This pact allowed him to rebuild the German fleet to 35 percent of the British navy. Italy's expansionist ambitions in Africa soon brought it into conflict with the Western powers. Hitler had taken a major step toward his goal without provoking serious opposition.

## Italy Attacks Ethiopia

In October 1935, Mussolini, using a border incident as an excuse, attacked Ethiopia. This attack made

# Hitler Describes His Goals in Foreign Policy

*From his early career, Hitler had certain long-term general views and goals. They were set forth in his* **Mein Kampf** *(my struggle), which appeared in 1925, and included consolidation of the German Volk (people), more land for the Germans, and contempt for such "races" as Slavs and Jews. Here are some of Hitler's views on land.*

✦ *What is the basic principle on which Hitler's policy is founded? How does he justify his plans for expansion? What reasons does he give for hostility to France and Russia? What is the basis for Hitler's claim of a right of every man to own farmland? Was that a practical goal for Germany in the 1930s? Was there any way for Hitler to achieve his goals without a major war?*

The National Socialist movement must strive to eliminate the disproportion between our population and our area—viewing this latter as a source of food as well as a basis for power politics—between our historical past and the hopelessness of our present impotence. . . .

. . . .

The demand for restoration of the frontiers of 1914 is a political absurdity of such proportions and consequences as to make it seem a crime. Quite aside from the fact that the Reich's frontiers in 1914 were anything but logical. For in reality they were neither complete in the sense of embracing the people of German nationality, nor sensible with regard to geomilitary expediency. . . .

As opposed to this, we National Socialists must hold unflinchingly to our aim in foreign policy, namely, to secure for the German people the land and soil to which they are entitled on this earth. . . .

. . . The soil on which some day German generations of peasants can beget powerful sons will sanction the investment of the sons of today, and will some day acquit the responsible statesmen of blood-guilt and sacrifice of the people, even if they are persecuted by their contemporaries. . . .

Much as all of us today recognize the necessity of a reckoning with France, it would remain ineffectual in the long run if it represented the whole of our aim in foreign policy. It can and will achieve meaning only if it offers the rear cover for an enlargement of our people's living space in Europe. . . .

If we speak of soil in Europe today, we can primarily have in mind only Russia and her vassal border states. . . .

. . . See to it that the strength of our nation is founded, not on colonies, but on the soil of our European homeland. Never regard the Reich as secure unless for centuries to come it can give every scion of our people his own parcel of soil. Never forget that the most sacred right on this earth is a man's right to have earth to till with his own hands, and the most sacred sacrifice the blood that a man sheds for this earth.

*Adolf Hitler,* Mein Kampf, *trans. by Ralph Manheim (Boston: Houghton, Mifflin, 1943), pp. 646, 649, 652, 653, 656.*

the impotence of the League of Nations and the timidity of the Allies even clear. Mussolini's purpose was to avenge a humiliating defeat that the Italians had suffered in 1896, to begin the restoration of Roman imperial glory, and, perhaps, to distract Italian public opinion from domestic problems.

France and Britain were eager to appease Mussolini in order to offset the growing power of Germany. They were prepared to allow him the substance of conquest if he would only maintain Ethiopia's formal independence. For Mussolini, however, the form was more important than the substance. His attack outraged opinion in the West, and the French and British governments were forced to at least appear to resist.

The League of Nations condemned Italian aggression and, for the first time, voted economic sanctions. It imposed an arms embargo that limited loans and credits to and imports from Italy. Britain and France were afraid of alienating Mussolini, however, and so they refused to embargo oil, the one economic sanction that could have prevented Italian victory. Even more important, the British fleet allowed Italian troops and munitions to use the Suez Canal. The results of this wavering policy were disastrous. The League of Nations and collective security were totally discredited, and Mussolini was alienated as well. He now turned to Germany, and by November 1, 1936, he could speak publicly of a Rome–Berlin "Axis."

### Remilitarization of the Rhineland

No less important a result of the Ethiopian affair was its effect on Hitler's evaluation of the strength and determination of the Western powers. On March 7, 1936, he took his greatest risk yet, sending a small armed force into the demilitarized Rhineland. This was a breach not only of the Versailles treaty but of the Locarno Agreements of 1925 as well—agreements Germany had made voluntarily. It also removed a crucial element of French security. France and Britain had every right to resist; and the French especially had a claim to retain the only element of security left to them after the failure of the Allies to guarantee France's defense. Yet neither power did anything but register a feeble protest with the League of Nations. British opinion would not permit support for France, and the French would not act alone. They were paralyzed by internal division and by military doctrine that concentrated on defense and shunned the offensive. Both countries were further weakened by a growing pacifism.

In retrospect, the Allies lost a great opportunity in the Rhineland to stop Hitler before he became a serious menace. The failure of his gamble, taken against the advice of his generals, might have led to his overthrow; at the least, it would have made German expansion to the east dangerous if not impossible. Nor is there much reason to doubt that the French army could easily have routed the tiny German force in the Rhineland. As the German general Alfred Jodl (1890–1946) said some years later, "The French covering army would have blown us to bits."[1]

A Germany that was rapidly rearming and had a defensible western frontier presented a completely new problem to the Western powers. Their response was the policy of "appeasement." It was based on the assumption that Germany had real grievances and that Hitler's goals were limited and ultimately acceptable. They believed that the correct policy was to negotiate and make concessions before a crisis could lead to war.

Behind this approach was the universal dread of another war. Memories of the horrors of the last war were still vivid, and the prospect of aerial bombardment made the thought of a new war even more terrifying. A firmer policy, moreover, would have required rapid rearmament. British leaders especially were reluctant to pursue this path because of the expense and the widespread belief that the arms race had been a major cause of the last war. As Germany armed, the French huddled behind their newly constructed defensive wall, the Maginot Line, and the British hoped for the best.

### The Spanish Civil War

The new European alignment that found the Western democracies on one side and the fascist states on the other was made clearer by the Spanish Civil War, which broke out in July 1936. (See Map 29–1.) In 1931 the monarchy had collapsed, and Spain became a democratic republic. The new government followed a program of moderate reform that antagonized landowners, the Catholic Church, nationalists, and conservatives without satisfying the demands of peasants, workers, Catalan separatists, or radicals. Elections in February 1936 brought to power a Spanish Popular Front government ranging from republicans of the left to communists and anarchists. The losers, especially the Falangists, the Spanish fascists, would not accept defeat at the polls. In July, General Francisco Franco (1892–1975) led an army from Spanish Morocco against the republic.

[1]Quoted in W. L. Shirer, The Collapse of the Third Republic (New York: Simon & Schuster, 1969), p. 281.

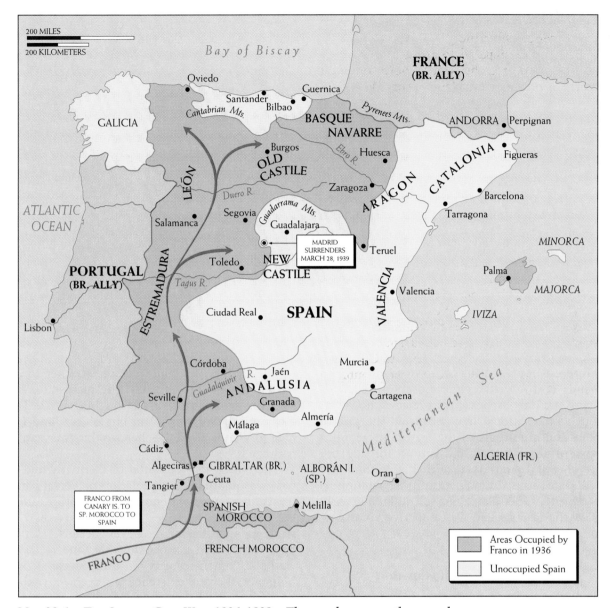

MAP 29–1   THE SPANISH CIVIL WAR, 1936–1939   *The purple area on the map shows the large portion of Spain quickly overrun by Franco's insurgent armies during the first year of the war. In the following two years, progress came more slowly for the fascists as the war became a kind of international rehearsal for the coming World War II. Madrid's fall to Franco in the spring of 1939 had been preceded by that of Barcelona a few weeks earlier.*

Thus began the Spanish Civil War, which lasted almost three years, cost hundreds of thousands of lives, and provided a training ground for World War II. Germany and Italy supported Franco with troops, airplanes, and supplies. The Soviet Union sent equipment and advisers to the republicans. Liberals and leftists from Europe and America volunteered to fight in the republican ranks against fascism.

The civil war, fought on blatantly ideological lines, profoundly affected world politics. It brought Germany and Italy closer together, leading to the Rome–Berlin Axis Pact in 1936. Japan joined the Axis powers that year in the Anti-Comintern Pact, ostensibly directed against international communism but really a new and powerful diplomatic alliance. Western Europe, especially France, had a

General Francisco Franco led an uprising against the duly elected government of Spain in 1936, producing a bloody civil war. Here he marches through the city of Burgos, in northern Spain. [Mary Evans Picture Library]

great interest in preventing Spain from falling into the hands of a fascist regime closely allied with Germany and Italy. Appeasement reigned, however. Although international law permitted the sale of weapons and munitions to the legitimate republican government, France and Britain forbade the export of war materials to either side, and the United States passed new neutrality legislation to the same end. When Barcelona fell to Franco early in 1939, the fascists had won effective control of Spain.

### Austria and Czechoslovakia

Hitler made good use of his new friendship with Mussolini. He had always planned to annex his native Austria. In 1934 the Nazi Party in Austria assassinated the prime minister and tried to seize power. Mussolini had not yet allied with Hitler and was suspicious of German intentions. He quickly moved an army to the Austrian border, thus preventing German intervention and causing the coup to fail.

In 1938 the new diplomatic situation encouraged Hitler to try again. He perhaps hoped to achieve his goal by propaganda, bullying, and threats, but the Austrian Chancellor Kurt Schuschnigg (1897–1977) refused to be intimidated. Schuschnigg announced a plebiscite for March 13, in which the Austrian people themselves could decide whether to unite with Germany. To forestall the plebiscite, Hitler sent his army into Austria on March 12. To his great relief, Mussolini did not object, and Hitler rode to Vienna amid the cheers of his Austrian sympathizers.

The *Anschluss*, or union of Germany and Austria, was another clear violation of Versailles. The treaty, however, was now a dead letter, and the West remained passive. The *Anschluss* had great strategic significance, however, because Germany now surrounded Czechoslovakia, one of the bulwarks of French security, on three sides.

In fact, the very existence of Czechoslovakia was an affront to Hitler. It was democratic and pro-Western; it had been created partly as a check on Germany and was allied both to France and to the Soviet Union. It also contained about 3.5 million Germans who lived in the Sudetenland near the German border. These Germans had belonged to the dominant nationality group in the old Austro-Hungarian Empire and resented their new minority position. Supported by Hitler and led by Konrad Henlein (1898–1945), the chief Nazi in Czechoslovakia, they made ever increasing demands for privileges and autonomy within the Czech state. The Czechs made many concessions, but Hitler did not really want to improve the lot of the Sudeten Germans. He wanted to destroy Czechoslovakia. He told Henlein, "We must always demand so much that we can never be satisfied."[2]

As pressure mounted, the Czechs grew nervous. In May 1938, they received false rumors of an imminent attack by Germany and mobilized their army. The French, British, and Russians all warned that they would support the Czechs. Hitler, who had not planned an attack at that time, was forced to publicly deny any designs on Czechoslovakia. The public humiliation infuriated him, and he planned a military attack on the Czechs. The affair stiffened Czech resistance, but it frightened the French and British. The French, as had become the rule, deferred to British leadership. The British prime minister was Neville Chamberlain (1869–1940), a man thoroughly committed to the policy of appeasement. He was determined not to allow Britain to go to war again. He pressed the Czechs to make further concessions to Germany, but no concession was enough.

On September 12, 1938, Hitler made a provocative speech at the Nuremberg Nazi Party rally. His rhetoric led to rioting in the Sudetenland, and the Czechs declared martial law. German intervention seemed imminent. Chamberlain, aged sixty-nine, who had never flown before, made three flights to Germany between September 15 and September 29 in an attempt to appease Hitler at Czech expense and thus to avoid war. At Hitler's mountain retreat,

[2] Quoted in Alan Bullock, Hitler, A Study in Tyranny (New York: Harper & Row, 1962), p. 443.

Berchtesgaden, on September 15, Chamberlain accepted the separation of the Sudetenland from Czechoslovakia. And he and the French premier, Édouard Daladier (1884–1970), forced the Czechs to agree by threatening to abandon them if they did not. A week later, Chamberlain flew yet again to Germany only to find that Hitler had raised his demands. He wanted cession of the Sudetenland in three days and immediate occupation by the German army.

## Munich

Chamberlain returned to England, and France and Britain prepared for war. At Chamberlain's request and at the last moment, Mussolini proposed a conference of Germany, Italy, France, and Britain. It met on September 29 at Munich. Hitler received almost everything he had demanded. (See Map 29–2.) The Sudetenland, the key to Czech security, became part of Germany, thus depriving the Czechs of any chance of self-defense. In return, Hitler agreed to spare the rest of Czechoslovakia. He promised, "I have no more territorial demands to make in Europe." Chamberlain returned to England with the Munich agreement and told a cheering crowd that he had brought "peace with honour. I believe it is peace for our time."

Even in the short run, the appeasement of Hitler at Munich was a failure. Czechoslovakia did not survive. Soon Poland and Hungary tore more territory from it, and the Slovaks demanded a state of

On September 29–30, 1938, Hitler met with the leaders of Britain and France at Munich to decide the fate of Czechoslovakia. The Allied leaders abandoned the small democratic nation in a vain attempt to appease Hitler and avoid war. Hitler sits in the center of the picture. To his right is Prime Minister Neville Chamberlain of Britain. [Ullstein Bilderdienst]

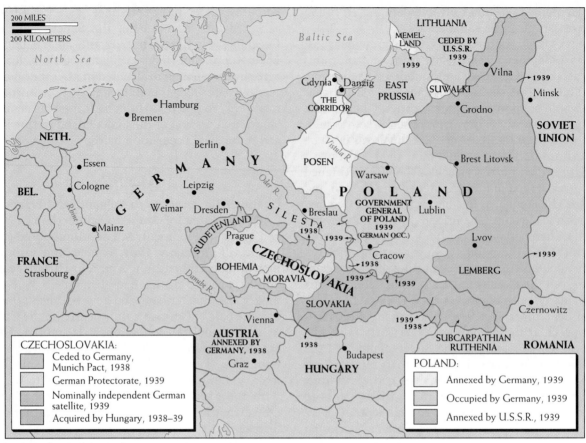

MAP 29–2 PARTITIONS OF CZECHOSLOVAKIA AND POLAND, 1938–1939 *The immediate background of World War II is found in the complex international drama unfolding on Germany's eastern frontier in 1938 and 1939. Germany's expansion inevitably meant the victimization of Austria, Czechoslovakia, and Poland. With the failure of the Western powers' appeasement policy and the signing of a German–Soviet pact, the stage for the war was set.*

their own. Finally, on March 15, 1939, Hitler broke his promise and occupied Prague, putting an end to the Czech state and to illusions that his only goal was to restore Germans to the Reich. Defenders of the appeasers have argued that their policy was justified because it bought valuable time in which the West could prepare for war. But that argument was not made by the appeasers themselves, who thought that they were achieving peace, nor does the evidence support it.

If the French and the British had been willing to attack Germany from the west while the Czechs fought in their own defense, their efforts might have been successful. High officers in the German army were opposed to Hitler's risky policies and might have overthrown him. Even failing such developments, a war begun in October 1938 would have forced Hitler to fight without the friendly neutrality

and material assistance of the Soviet Union—and without the resources of eastern Europe that became available to him as a result of appeasement and Soviet cooperation. If, moreover, the West ever had a chance of concluding an alliance with the Soviet Union against Hitler, the exclusion of the Russians from Munich and the appeasement policy helped destroy it. Munich remains an example of short-sighted policy that helped bring on war in disadvantageous circumstances because of the very fear of war and the failure to prepare for it.

Hitler's occupation of Prague discredited appeasement in the eyes of the British people. In the summer of 1939, a Gallup Poll showed that three-quarters of the British public believed it worth a war to stop Hitler. Though Chamberlain himself had not lost all faith in his policy, he felt he had to respond to public opinion, and he responded to excess.

# Churchill's Response to Munich

*In the parliamentary debate that followed the Munich conference at the end of September 1938, Winston Churchill was one of the few critics of what had been accomplished. In the following selections from his speech, he expresses his concerns.*

✦ *What was decided at Munich? Why were the representatives of Czechoslovakia not at the meeting? Why did Chamberlain think the meeting was successful? Munich was the high point of the policy called* appeasement. *How would its advocates defend this policy? Churchill was a leading opponent of appeasement. What are his objections to it?*

I will begin by saying what everybody would like to ignore or forget but which must nevertheless be stated, namely, that we have sustained a total and unmitigated defeat, and that France has suffered even more than we have.

. . . .

We really must not waste time after all this long Debate upon the difference between the positions reached at Berchtesgaden, at Godesberg and at Munich. They can be very simply epitomized if the House will permit me to vary the metaphor. One pound was demanded at the pistol's point. When it was given, £2 were demanded at the pistol's point. Finally, the dictator consented to take £1 17s. 6d. and the rest in promises of good will for the future.

. . . .

All is over. Silent, mournful, abandoned, broken, Czechoslovakia recedes into the darkness. She has suffered in every respect by her association with the Western democracies and with the League of Nations, of which she has always been an obedient servant.

. . . .

We have been reduced in those five years from a position of security so overwhelming and so unchallengeable that we never cared to think about it. We have been reduced from a position where the very word "war" was considered one which could be used only by persons qualifying for a lunatic asylum. We have been reduced from a position of safety and power—power to do good, power to be generous to a beaten foe, power to make terms with Germany, power to give her proper redress for her grievances, power to stop her arming if we chose, power to take any step in strength or mercy or justice which we thought right—reduced in five years from a position safe and unchallenged to where we stand now.

. . . .

The responsibility must rest with those who have had the undisputed control of our political affairs. They neither prevented Germany from rearming, nor did they rearm ourselves in time. They quarreled with Italy without saving Ethiopia. They exploited and discredited the vast institution of the League of Nations and they neglected to make alliances and combinations which might have repaired previous errors, and thus they left us in the hour of trial without adequate national defense or effective international security.

. . . .

We are in the presence of a disaster of the first magnitude which has befallen Great Britain and France. Do not let us blind ourselves to that. It must now be accepted that all the countries of Central and Eastern Europe will make the best terms they can with the triumphant Nazi power. The system of alliances in Central Europe upon which France has relied for her safety has been swept away, and I can see no means by which it can be reconstituted. The road down the Danube Valley to the Black Sea, the road which leads as far as Turkey, has been opened.

Winston S. Churchill, Blood, Sweat, and Tears *(New York: G. P. Putnam's Sons, 1941), pp. 55–56, 58, 60–61.*

Poland was the next target of German expansion. In the spring of 1939, the Germans put pressure on Poland to restore the formerly German city of Danzig and to allow a railroad and a highway through the Polish Corridor to connect East Prussia with the rest of Germany. When the Poles would not yield, the usual propaganda campaign began, and the pressure mounted. On March 31, Chamberlain announced a Franco–British guarantee of Polish independence. Hitler appears to have expected to fight a war with Poland but not with the Western allies, for he did not take their guarantee seriously. He had come to hold their leaders in contempt. He knew that both countries were unprepared for war and that large segments of their populations were opposed to fighting for Poland.

Moreover, France and Britain had no means of getting effective help to the Poles. The French, still dominated by the defensive mentality of the Maginot Line, had no intention of attacking Germany. The only way to defend Poland was to bring Russia into the alliance against Hitler, but a Russian alliance posed many problems. Each side was profoundly suspicious of the other. The French and the British were hostile to communism; and since Stalin's purge of the Red Army, they were skeptical of the military value of a Russian alliance. Besides, the Russians could not help Poland without being given the right to enter Poland and Romania. Both nations, suspicious of Russian intentions, and with good reason, refused to grant these rights. As a result, Western negotiations for an alliance with Russia made little progress.

### The Nazi–Soviet Pact

The Russians had at least equally good reason to hesitate. They resented being left out of the Munich agreement. They were annoyed by the low priority that the West gave to negotiations with Russia compared with the urgency with which they dealt with Hitler. They feared, quite rightly, that the Western powers meant them to bear the burden of the war against Germany. As a result, they opened negotiations with Hitler, and on August 23, 1939, the world was shocked to learn of a Nazi–Soviet nonaggression pact.

Its secret provisions, which were easily guessed and soon carried out, divided Poland between the two powers and allowed Russia to occupy the Baltic states and to take Bessarabia from Romania. The most bitter ideological enemies had become allies.

| The Coming of World War II | |
|---|---|
| 1919 (June) | The Versailles treaty |
| 1923 (January) | France occupies the Ruhr |
| 1925 (October) | The Locarno Agreements |
| 1931 (Spring) | Onset of the Great Depression in Europe |
| 1931 (September) | Japan occupies Manchuria |
| 1933 (January) | Hitler comes to power |
| 1935 (October) | Germany withdraws from the League of Nations |
| 1935 (March) | Hitler renounces disarmament, starts an air force, and begins conscription |
| 1935 (October) | Mussolini attacks Ethiopia |
| 1936 (March) | Germany reoccupies and remilitarizes the Rhineland |
| 1936 (July) | Outbreak of the Spanish Civil War |
| 1936 (October) | Formation of the Rome–Berlin Axis |
| 1938 (March) | *Anschluss* with Austria |
| 1938 (September) | The Munich conference and partition of Czechoslovakia |
| 1939 (March) | Hitler occupies Prague; France and Great Britain guarantee Polish independence |
| 1939 (August) | The Nazi–Soviet pact |
| 1939 (September 1) | Germany invades Poland |
| 1939 (September 3) | Britain and France declare war on Germany |

Communist parties in the West changed their line overnight from the ardent advocacy of resistance to Hitler to a policy of peace and quiet. Ideology gave way to political and military reality. The West offered the Russians immediate danger without much prospect of gain. Hitler offered Stalin short-term gain without immediate danger. There could be little doubt about Stalin's decision.

The Nazi–Soviet pact sealed the fate of Poland, and the Franco–British commitment guaranteed a general war. On September 1, 1939, the Germans invaded Poland. Two days later, Britain and France declared war on Germany. World War II had begun.

# World War II (1939–1945)

World War II has a better claim to its name than its predecessor, for it was truly global. Fighting took place in Europe and Asia, the Atlantic and the

German troops march down the Champs-Elysées in Paris in September, 1940, after the rapid collapse of French defenses. [Roger Viollet/Gamma Liaison, Inc.]

Pacific oceans, the Northern and Southern hemispheres. The demand for the fullest exploitation of material and human resources for increased production, the use of blockades, and the intensive bombing of civilian targets made the war of 1939 even more "total"—that is, comprehensive and intense—than that of 1914.

### The German Conquest of Europe

The German attack on Poland produced swift success. The new style of "lightning warfare," or *Blitzkrieg*, employed fast-moving, massed armored columns supported by airpower. The Poles had no tanks and few planes, and their defense soon collapsed. The speed of the German victory astonished the Russians, who hastened to collect their share of the booty before Hitler could deprive them of it.

On September 17, Russia invaded Poland from the east, dividing the country with the Germans. Stalin then forced the encircled Baltic countries to allow the Red Army to occupy them. By 1940 Esto-

nia, Latvia, and Lithuania had become puppet republics within the USSR (Union of Soviet Socialist Republics, or the Soviet Union). In June 1940, the Russians forced Romania to cede Bessarabia. In November 1940, the Russians invaded Finland, but the Finns resisted fiercely for six months. Although they were finally worn down and compelled to yield territory and bases to Russia, the Finns remained independent. Russian expansionism and the poor performance of the Red Army in Finland may well have encouraged Hitler to invade the Soviet Union in June 1941, just twenty-two months after the 1939 treaty.

Until the spring of 1940, the western front was quiet. The French remained behind the Maginot Line while Hitler and Stalin swallowed Poland and the Baltic states. Britain hastily rearmed, and the British navy blockaded Germany. Cynics in the West called it the *phony war*, or *Sitzkrieg*, but Hitler shattered the stillness in the spring of 1940. In April, without warning and with swift success, the Germans invaded Denmark and Norway. Hitler's northern front was secure, and he now had both air and naval bases closer to Britain. A month later, a combined land and air attack struck Belgium, the Netherlands, and Luxembourg. German airpower and armored divisions were irresistible. The Dutch surrendered in a few days; the Belgians, though aided by the French and the British, gave up less than two weeks later.

The British and French armies in Belgium were forced to flee to the English Channel to seek escape on the beaches of Dunkirk. The heroic efforts of hundreds of Britons manning small boats saved more than 200,000 British and 100,000 French soldiers. Casualties, however, were high and valuable equipment was abandoned.

The Maginot Line ran from Switzerland to the Belgian frontier. Until 1936 the French had expected the Belgians to continue the fortifications along their German border. After Hitler remilitarized the Rhineland without opposition, the Belgians lost faith in their French alliance and proclaimed their neutrality, leaving the Maginot Line exposed on its left flank. Hitler's swift advance through Belgium therefore circumvented France's main line of defense.

The French army, poorly and hesitantly led by aged generals who did not understand how to use tanks and planes, collapsed. Mussolini, eager to claim the spoils of victory when it was clearly safe to do so, invaded southern France on June 10. Less than a week later, the new French government, under the ancient hero of Verdun, Marshal Henri Philippe Pétain (1856–1951), asked for an armistice. In two months Hitler had accomplished what Germany had failed to achieve in four years of bitter fighting in the previous war.

*A member of the Royal Observation Corps watches for German planes on England's south coast during World War II. [The Hulton-Deutsch Collection Limited]*

*The close cooperation between Prime Minister Winston Churchill of Britain and President Franklin Roosevelt of the United States greatly helped to assure the effective cooperation of their two countries in World War II.*

## The Battle of Britain

The fall of France left Britain isolated, and Hitler expected the British to come to terms. He was prepared to allow Britain to retain its empire in return for a free hand for Germany on the Continent. The British had never been willing to accept such an arrangement and had fought the long and difficult war against Napoleon to prevent the domination of the Continent by a single power. If there was any chance that the British would consider such terms, it disappeared when Winston Churchill (1874–1965) replaced Chamberlain as prime minister in May of 1940.

Churchill had been an early and forceful critic of Hitler, the Nazis, and the policy of appeasement. He was a descendant and biographer of the duke of Marlborough (1650–1722), who had fought to prevent the domination of Europe by Louis XIV in the eighteenth century. Churchill's sense of history, his feeling for British greatness, and his hatred of tyranny and love of freedom made him reject any thought of compromise with Hitler. His skill as a speaker and a writer enabled him to inspire the British people with his own courage and determination and to undertake what seemed a hopeless fight. Hitler and his allies, including the Soviet Union, controlled all of Europe. Japan was having its way in Asia. The United States was neutral, dominated by isolationist sentiment, and determined to avoid involvement outside the Western Hemisphere.

One of Churchill's greatest achievements was establishing a close relationship with the American President Franklin D. Roosevelt (1882–1945). Roosevelt found ways to help the British despite strong political opposition. In 1940 and 1941, before the United States was at war, America sent military supplies, traded badly needed warships for leases on British naval bases, and even convoyed ships across the Atlantic to help the British survive.

As weeks passed and Britain remained defiant, Hitler was forced to contemplate an invasion, and that required control of the air. The first strikes by the German air force (*Luftwaffe*), directed against the airfields and fighter planes in southeastern England, began in August 1940. If these attacks had continued, Germany might soon have gained control of the air and, with it, the chance of a successful invasion.

In early September, however, seeking revenge for some British bombing raids on German cities, the *Luftwaffe* switched its main attacks to London. For two months, London was bombed every night. Much of the city was destroyed and about 15,000 people were killed. The theories of victory through airpower alone, however, proved false. Casualties were much less than expected, and morale was not shattered. In fact, the bombings united the British people and made them more resolute.

The Royal Air Force (RAF) inflicted heavy losses on the *Luftwaffe*. Aided by the newly developed radar and an excellent system of communications, the British Spitfire and Hurricane fighter planes destroyed more than twice as many enemy planes as were lost by the RAF. Hitler had lost the Battle of Britain in the air and was forced to abandon his plans for invasion.

## The German Attack on Russia

The defeat of Russia and the conquest of the Ukraine to provide *Lebensraum*, or "living space," for the German people had always been a major goal for Hitler. Even before the assault on Britain, he had informed his staff of his intention to attack Russia as soon as conditions were favorable. In December 1940, even while the bombing of England continued, he ordered his generals to prepare for an invasion of Russia by May 15, 1941. (See Map 29–3.) He apparently thought that a *Blitzkrieg* victory in the East would also destroy any further British hope of resistance.

Operation Barbarossa, the code name for the invasion of Russia, was aimed at destroying Russia before winter could set in. Success depended in part on an early start, but here Hitler's Italian alliance proved costly. Mussolini was jealous of Hitler's success and annoyed by the treatment he had received from the German dictator. His invasion of France was a fiasco even though the main French forces were being simultaneously crushed by the Germans. Hitler did not allow Mussolini to annex French territory in Europe or North Africa. Mussolini instead launched an attack against the British in Egypt and drove them back some sixty miles. Encouraged by this success, he also invaded Greece from his base in Albania (which he had seized in 1939). His purpose was revealed by his remark to his son-in-law, Count Ciano: "Hitler always faces me with a *fait accompli*. This time I

MAP 29–3   AXIS EUROPE, 1941   *On the eve of the German invasion of the Soviet Union, the Germany–Italy Axis bestrode most of western Europe by annexation, occupation, or alliance—from Norway and Finland in the north to Greece in the south and from Poland to France. Britain, the Soviets, a number of insurgent groups, and, finally, America, had before them the long struggle of conquering this Axis "fortress Europe."*

am going to pay him back in his own coin. He will find out in the newspapers that I have occupied Greece."[3]

[3]*Quoted in Gordon Wright,* The Ordeal of Total War, 1939–1945 *(New York: Harper & Row, 1968), pp. 35–36.*

In North Africa, however, the British counterattacked and drove the Italians back into Libya. The Greeks themselves pushed into Albania. In March 1941, the British sent help to the Greeks, and Hitler was forced to divert his attention to the Balkans and Africa. General Erwin Rommel (1891–1944),

*Mussolini inspecting Italian troops at the Florence train station in October 1940 as he awaits a visit from Hitler. Mussolini's military reverses in North Africa and the Balkans would divert German resources in 1941 and delay the beginning of Hitler's planned invasion of Russia. [Popperfoto]*

later to earn the title of "Desert Fox," went to Africa and soon drove the British out of Libya and back into Egypt. In the Balkans, the German army swiftly occupied Yugoslavia and crushed Greek resistance. The price, however, was a delay of six weeks. The diversion caused by Mussolini's vanity proved to be costly the following winter in the Russian campaign.

Operation Barbarossa was launched against Russia on June 22, 1941, and it almost succeeded. Despite their deep suspicion of Germany (and the excuse later offered by apologists for the Soviet Union that the Nazi–Soviet pact was meant to give Russia time to prepare), the Russians were taken quite by surprise. Stalin appears to have panicked. He had not fortified his frontier, nor did he order his troops to withdraw when attacked. In the first two days, 2,000 Russian planes were destroyed on the ground. By November, Hitler had gone further into Russia than Napoleon. The German army stood at the gates of Leningrad, on the outskirts of Moscow, and on the Don River. Of the 4.5 million troops with which the Russians had begun the fighting, they had lost 2.5 million; of their 15,000 tanks, only 700 were left. Moscow was in panic, and a German victory seemed imminent.

Yet the Germans could not deliver the final blow. In August, they delayed their advance while Hitler decided strategy. The German general staff wanted to drive directly for Moscow and take it before winter. This plan probably would have brought victory. Unlike in Napoleon's time, Moscow was the hub of the Russian system of transportation. Hitler, however, diverted a significant part of his forces to the south. By the time he was ready to return to the offensive near Moscow, it was too late. Winter devastated the German army, which was neither dressed nor equipped to face it.

## An Observer Describes the Mass Murder of Jews in Ukraine

*After World War II some German officers and officials were put on trial at Nuremberg by the victorious powers for crimes they were charged with having committed in the course of the war. The following selections from the testimony of a German construction engineer who witnessed the mass murder of Jews at Dubno in the Ukraine on October 5, 1942, reveal the brutality with which Hitler's attempt at a "final solution of the Jewish problem" was carried out.*

✦ *Why did the German government commit these atrocities? Why were they directed chiefly at Jews? Was there a cost to Germany in pursuing such a policy? Why did ordinary Germans participate?*

On October 5, 1942, when I visited the building office at Dubno, my foreman told me that in the vicinity of the site, Jews from Dubno had been shot in three large pits, each about 30 metres long and 3 metres deep. About 1,500 persons had been killed daily. All the 5,000 Jews who had still been living in Dubno before the pogrom were to be liquidated. As the shooting had taken place in his presence, he was still much upset.

Thereupon, I drove to the site accompanied by my foreman and saw near it great mounds of earth, about 30 metres long and 2 metres high. Several trucks stood in front of the mounds. Armed Ukrainian militia drove the people off the trucks under the supervision of an S.S. man. The militiamen acted as guards on the trucks and drove them to and from the pit. All these people had the regulation yellow patches on the front and back of their clothes, and thus could be recognized as Jews.

My foreman and I went directly to the pits. Nobody bothered us. Now I heard rifle shots in quick succession from behind one of the earth

---

Given precious time, Stalin restored order and built defenses for the city. Even more important, troops arrived from Siberia, where they had been placed to check a possible Japanese attack. In November and December, the Russians counterattacked. The Blitzkrieg had turned into a war of attrition, and the Germans began to have nightmares of duplicating Napoleon's retreat.

### Hitler's Plans for Europe

Hitler often spoke of the "new order" that he meant to impose after he had established his Third Reich (Empire) throughout Europe. The first two German empires were those of Charlemagne in the ninth century and Bismarck in the nineteenth. Hitler predicted that his own would last for a thousand years.

If his organization of Germany before the war is a proper guide, he had no single plan of government but relied frequently on intuition and pragmatism. His organization of conquered Europe had the same patchwork characteristics. Some conquered territory was annexed to Germany; some was not annexed but administered directly by German officials; other lands were nominally autonomous but were ruled by puppet governments.

Hitler's regime was probably unmatched in history for carefully planned terror and inhumanity. His plan of giving *Lebensraum* to the Germans was to be accomplished at the expense of people he deemed inferior. Hitler established colonies of Germans in parts of Poland, driving the local people from their land and employing them as cheap labor. He had similar plans on an even greater scale for

mounds. The people who had got off the trucks—men, women and children of all ages—had to undress upon the orders of an S.S. man, who carried a riding or dog whip. They had to put down their clothes in fixed places, sorted according to shoes, top clothing and underclothing. I saw a heap of shoes of about 800 to 1,000 pairs, great piles of underlinen and clothing.

Without screaming or weeping, these people undressed, stood around in family groups, kissed each other, said farewells, and waited for a sign from another S.S. man, who stood near the pit, also with a whip in his hand. During the fifteen minutes that I stood near I heard no complaint or plea for mercy. I watched a family of about eight persons, a man and a woman both about fifty with their children of about one, eight and ten, and two grown-up daughters of about twenty to twenty-nine. An old woman with snow-white hair was holding the one-year-old child in her arms and singing to it and tickling it. The child was cooing with delight. The couple were looking on with tears in their eyes. The father was holding the hand of a boy about ten years old and speaking to him softly; the boy was fighting his tears. The father pointed to the sky, stroked his head, and seemed to explain something to him.

At that moment the S.S. man at the pit shouted something to his comrade. The latter counted off about twenty persons and instructed them to go behind the earth mound. Among them was the family which I have mentioned. I well remember a girl, slim and with black hair, who, as she passed close to me pointed to herself and said "23." I walked around the mound and found myself confronted by a tremendous grave. People were closely wedged together and lying on top of each other so that only their heads were visible. Nearly all had blood running over their shoulders from their heads. Some of the people shot were still moving. Some were lifting their arms and turning their heads to show that they were still alive. The pit was already two-thirds full. I estimated that it already contained about 1,000 people.

*From the* Nuremberg Proceedings, *as quoted in Louis L. Snyder.* Documents of German History *(New Brunswick: Rutgers University Press, 1958), pp. 462–464.*

Russia. The Russians would be driven eastward to central Asia and Siberia; they would be kept in check by frontier colonies of German war veterans. European Russia would be settled by Germans.

Hitler's long-range plans included germanization as well as colonization. In lands inhabited by people racially akin to the Germans, like the Scandinavian countries, the Netherlands, and Switzerland, the natives would be absorbed into the German nation. Such peoples would be reeducated and purged of dissenting elements, but there would be little or no colonization. He even had plans, only slightly realized, of adopting selected people from the lesser races into the master race. One of these plans involved bringing half a million Ukrainian girls into Germany as servants and finding German husbands for them; about 15,000 were actually sent to Germany.

In the economic sphere, Hitler regarded the conquered lands merely as a source of plunder. From eastern Europe, he removed everything useful, including entire industries. In Russia and Poland, the Germans simply confiscated the land. In the West, the conquered countries were forced to support the occupying army at a rate several times above the real cost. The Germans used the profits to buy up everything useful and desirable, stripping the conquered peoples of most necessities. The Nazis were frank about their policies. One of Hitler's high officials said, "Whether nations live in prosperity or starve to death interests me only insofar as we need them as slaves for our culture."[4]

[4]*Quoted in Wright, p. 117.*

*These are some of the dead at the Nordhausen concentration camp, which was liberated by the American army in April 1945. The Nazis set up their first concentration camps in Germany in 1933 to hold opponents of their regime. After the conquest of Poland, new camps were established there as part of the "final solution," the extermination of the Jews. About six million Jews were murdered in these camps. Even in those camps not dedicated to extermination—in which political prisoners and "undesirables" such as Gypsies, homosexuals, and Jehovah's Witnesses were held—conditions were brutal in the extreme, and tens of thousands died. The crimes of the Nazi regime have no precedent in human history. [National Archives]*

## Racism and the Holocaust

The most horrible aspect of the Nazi rule in Europe arose not from military or economic necessity but from the inhumanity and brutality inherent in Hitler's racial doctrines. He considered the Slavs *Untermenschen*, subhuman creatures like beasts who need not be thought of or treated as people. In parts of Poland, the upper and professional classes were entirely removed—either jailed, deported, or killed. Schools and churches were closed; marriage was controlled by the Nazis to keep down the Polish birth rate; and harsh living conditions were imposed.

In Russia, things were even worse. Hitler spoke of his Russian campaign as a war of extermination. Heinrich Himmler, head of Hitler's elite SS guard, planned to eliminate thirty million Slavs to make room for the Germans; he formed extermination squads for the purpose. The number of Russian prisoners of war and deported civilian workers who died under Nazi rule may have reached six million.

Hitler had special plans for the Jews. He meant to make all Europe *Judenrein*, or "free of Jews." For a time he thought of sending them to the island of Madagascar. Later he arrived at the "final solution of the Jewish problem": extermination. The Nazis built extermination camps in Germany and Poland and used the latest technology to achieve the most efficient means of killing millions of men, women, and children simply because they were Jews. Before the war was over, perhaps six million Jews had died in what has come to be called the *Holocaust*. Only about a million remained alive, those mostly in pitiable condition.

World War II was unmatched in modern times in cruelty. When Stalin's armies conquered Poland and entered Germany, they raped, pillaged, and deported millions to the East. The British and American bombing of Germany killed thousands of civilians, and the dropping of atomic bombs on Japan inflicted terrible harm on civilian populations. The bombings, however, were thought of as acts of war that would help defeat the enemy. Stalin's atrocities were not widely known in the West at the time or even today.

The victorious Western allies were shocked by what they saw when they came on the Nazi extermination camps and their pitiful survivors. Little wonder that they were convinced that the effort of resistance to the Nazis and all the pain it had cost were well worth it.

## Japan and America's Entry into the War

The American government was very pro-British. The various forms of assistance that Roosevelt gave Britain would have justified a German declaration of war. Hitler, however, held back. The U.S. government might not have overcome isolationist sentiment and entered the war in the Atlantic if war had not been thrust on America in the Pacific.

Since the Japanese conquest of Manchuria in 1931, American policy toward Japan had been suspicious and unfriendly. The outbreak of the war in Europe emboldened the Japanese to accelerate their drive to dominate Asia. They allied themselves with Germany and Italy, made a treaty of neutrality with the Soviet Union, and penetrated Indochina at the expense of defeated France. They also continued their war in China and planned to gain control of Malaya and the East Indies at the expense of beleaguered Britain and the conquered Netherlands. The only barrier to Japanese expansion was the United States.

The Americans had temporized, unwilling to cut off vital supplies of oil and other materials for fear of provoking a Japanese attack on Southeast Asia and Indonesia. The Japanese occupation of Indochina in July 1941 changed that policy, which had already begun to stiffen. The United States froze Japanese assets and cut off oil supplies; the British and Dutch did the same. Japanese plans for expansion could not continue without the conquest of the Indonesian oil fields and Malayan rubber and tin.

In October, a war faction led by General Hideki Tojo (1885–1948) took power in Japan and decided to risk a war rather than yield. On Sunday morning, December 7, 1941, while Japanese representatives were discussing a settlement in Washington, Japan launched an air attack on Pearl Harbor, Hawaii, the chief American naval base in the Pacific. The technique was similar to the one Japan had used against the Russian fleet at Port Arthur in 1904, and it caught the Americans equally by surprise. Much of the American fleet and many airplanes were destroyed; the American capacity to wage war in the Pacific was negated for the time being. The next day, the United States and Britain declared war on

*The successful Japanese attack on the American base at Pearl Harbor in Hawaii on December 7, 1941, together with simultaneous attacks on other Pacific bases, brought the United States into war against the Axis powers. This picture shows the battleships USS* West Virginia *and USS* Tennessee *in flames as a small boat rescues a man from the water. [US Army Photograph]*

Japan. Three days later, Germany and Italy declared war on the United States.

## The Tide Turns

The potential power of the United States was enormous, but America was ill prepared for war. Though conscription had been introduced in 1940, the army was tiny, inexperienced, and poorly supplied. American industry was not ready for war. The Japanese swiftly captured Guam, Wake Island, and the Philippine Islands. Also, they attacked Hong Kong, Malaya, Burma, and the Dutch East Indies. By the spring of 1942, they controlled these places and the Southwest Pacific as far as New Guinea. They were poised for an attack on Australia, and it seemed that nothing could stop them.

In 1942 the Germans also advanced deeper into Russia and almost reached the Caspian Sea in their drive for Russia's oil fields. In Africa, too, Axis fortunes were high. Rommel drove the British back into Egypt toward the Suez Canal until he was stopped at El Alamein, only seventy miles from Alexandria. Relations between the democracies and their Soviet ally were not close. German submarine warfare was threatening British supplies. The Allies were being thrown back on every front, and the future looked bleak.

The first good news for the Allied cause in the Pacific came in the spring of 1942. A naval battle in the Coral Sea sank many Japanese ships and gave security to Australia. A month later, the United States defeated the Japanese in a fierce air and naval battle off Midway Island; they thus blunted the chance of another assault on Hawaii and did enough damage to halt the Japanese advance. Soon American Marines landed on Guadalcanal in the Solomon Islands and began to reverse the momentum of the war. The war in the Pacific was far from over, but the check to Japan allowed the Allies to concentrate their efforts first in Europe.

More than twenty nations located all over the world were opposed to the Axis powers. The main combatants, however, were Great Britain, the Soviet Union, and the United States. The two Western democracies cooperated to an unprecedented degree, but suspicion between them and the Soviet Union continued. The Russians accepted all the aid they could get. Nevertheless, they did not trust their allies, complained of inadequate help, and demanded that the democracies open a "second front" on the mainland of Europe.

In 1942 American preparation and production were inadequate for an invasion of Europe. German submarines made the Atlantic unsafe for crossing by the vast numbers of troops needed for an invasion. Not until 1944 were conditions right for the invasion, but in the meantime other developments forecast the doom of the Axis.

ALLIED LANDINGS IN AFRICA, SICILY, AND ITALY    In November 1942, an Allied force landed in French North Africa. (See Map 29-4.) Even before that landing, British Field Marshal Bernard Montgomery (1887–1976), after stopping Rommel at El Alamein, had begun a drive to the west. Now, the American General Dwight D. Eisenhower (1890–1969) had pushed eastward through Morocco and Algeria. The two armies caught the German army between them in Tunisia and crushed it. The Allies now controlled the Mediterranean and could attack southern Europe.

In July and August 1943, the Allies took Sicily. Mussolini was driven from power, but the Germans occupied Italy. The Allies landed in Italy, and Marshal Pietro Badoglio (1871–1956), the leader of the new Italian government, went over to their side, declaring war on Germany. Churchill had spoken of Italy as the "soft underbelly" of the Axis, but the Germans there resisted fiercely. Still the need to defend Italy diverted the Germans' energy and resources and left them vulnerable on other fronts.

BATTLE OF STALINGRAD    The Russian campaign became especially demanding. In the summer of 1942, the Germans resumed the offensive on all fronts but were unable to get far except in the south. (See Map 29-5.) Their goal was the oil fields near the Caspian Sea. Stalingrad on the Volga was a key point on the flank of the German army in the south. Hitler was determined to take the city and Stalin to hold it. The Battle of Stalingrad raged for months with unexampled ferocity. The Russians lost more men in this one battle than the Americans lost in combat during the entire war, but their heroic defense prevailed. Because Hitler again overruled his generals and would not allow a retreat, an entire German army was lost at Stalingrad.

Stalingrad marked the turning point of the Russian campaign. Thereafter, the Americans provided material help. Even more important, increased production from their own industry, which had been moved to or built up in the safety of the central and eastern regions of the USSR, allowed the Russians

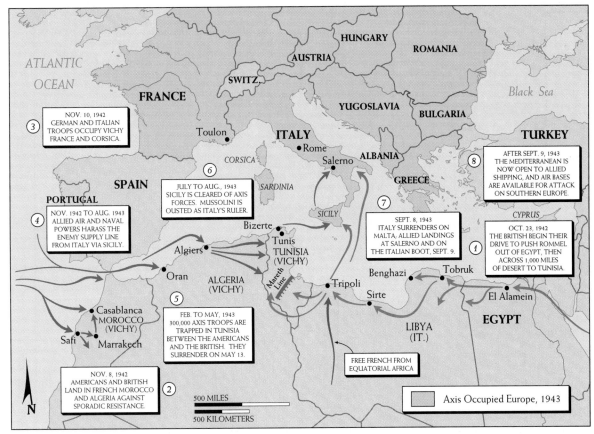

MAP 29–4   NORTH AFRICAN CAMPAIGNS, 1942–1945   *Control of North Africa would give the Allies access to Europe from the south. The map illustrates this theater of the war from Morocco to Egypt and the Suez Canal.*

*Russian soldiers, in their heroic defense of Stalingrad, dug trenches from building to building in the city. The German defeat at Stalingrad in February 1943 marked the turning point of the Russian campaign. Thereafter the Russians advanced inexorably westward. [Archive Photos]*

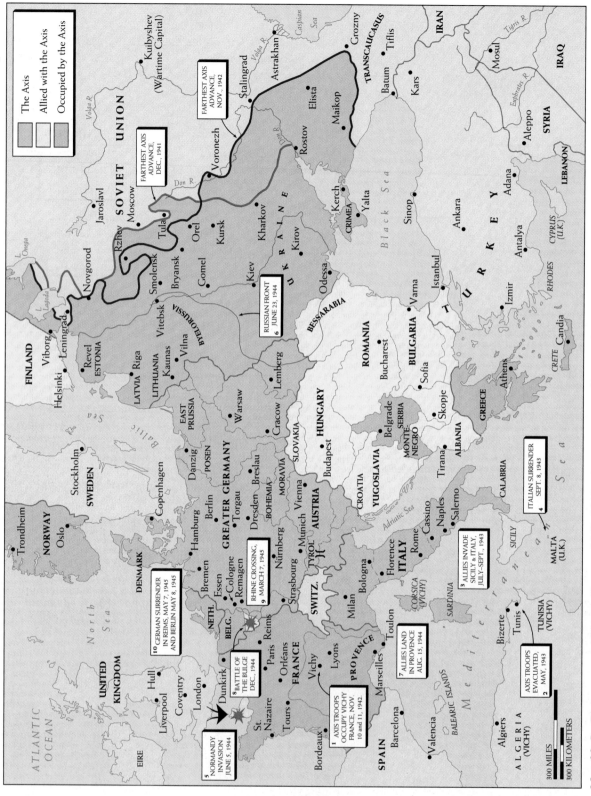

**MAP 29–5** DEFEAT OF THE AXIS IN EUROPE, 1942–1945 *Here we see some major steps in the progress toward Allied victory against Axis Europe. From the south through Italy, the west through France, and the east through Russia, the Allies gradually conquered the Continent to bring the war in Europe to a close.*

to gain and keep the offensive. As the Germans' resources dwindled, the Russians inexorably advanced westward.

STRATEGIC BOMBING  In 1943 the Allies also gained ground in production and logistics. The industrial might of the United States began to come into full force, and new technology and tactics greatly reduced the submarine menace.

In the same year, the American and British air forces began a series of massive bombardments of Germany by night and day. The Americans were more committed to the theory of "precision bombing" of military and industrial targets vital to the enemy war effort, and so they flew the day missions. The British considered precision bombing impossible and therefore useless. They preferred indiscriminate "area bombing" aimed to destroy the morale of the German people; this kind of bombing could be done at night. Neither kind of bombing had much effect on the war until 1944, when the Americans introduced long-range fighters that could protect the bombers and allow accurate missions by day.

By 1945 the Allies had virtually cleared the skies of German planes and could bomb at will. Concentrated attacks on industrial targets, especially communications centers and oil refineries, did extensive damage and helped to shorten the war. Terror bombing continued, too, with no useful result. The bombardment of Dresden in February 1945 was especially savage and destructive. It was much debated within the British government and has raised moral questions since. Whatever else it accomplished, the aerial war over Germany did take a heavy toll of the German air force and diverted vital German resources away from other military purposes.

## The Defeat of Nazi Germany

On June 6, 1944 ("D-Day"), American, British, and Canadian troops landed in force on the coast of Normandy. The "second front" was opened. General

*Allied troops landed in Normandy on D-Day, June 6, 1944. This photograph, taken two days later, shows long lines of men and equipment moving inland from the beach to reinforce the troops leading the invasion. [Archive Photos]*

Dwight D. Eisenhower, the commander of the Allied armies, faced a difficult problem. The European coast was heavily fortified. Amphibious assaults, moreover, are especially vulnerable to changes of wind and weather. Success depended on meticulous planning, advance preparation by heavy bombing, and feints to mask the point of attack. The German defense was strong, but the Allies were able to establish a beachhead and then to break out of it. In mid-August, the Allies landed in southern France to put more pressure on the enemy. By the beginning of September, France had been liberated.

THE BATTLE OF THE BULGE   All went smoothly until December, when the Germans launched a counter-attack in Belgium through the Ardennes Forest. Because the Germans were able to push forward into the Allied line, this was called the Battle of the Bulge. Although the Allies suffered heavy losses, the Bulge was the last gasp for the Germans in the West. The Allies soon recovered their momentum and pushed eastward. They crossed the Rhine in March of 1945, and German resistance rapidly crumbled. This time there could be no doubt that the Germans had lost the war on the battlefield.

THE CAPTURE OF BERLIN   In the East, the Russians swept forward no less swiftly despite fierce German resistance. By March 1945, they were near Berlin.

Because the Allies insisted on unconditional surrender, the Germans fought on until May. Hitler and his intimates committed suicide in an underground bunker in Berlin on May 1, 1945. The Russians occupied Berlin by agreement with their Western allies. The Third Reich had lasted a dozen years instead of the thousand predicted by Hitler.

## Fall of the Japanese Empire

The war in Europe ended on May 8, 1945, and by then victory over Japan was also in sight. The original Japanese attack on the United States had been a calculated risk against the odds. Japan was inherently weaker than the United States. The longer the war lasted, the more American superiority in industrial production and population counted.

AMERICANS RECAPTURE THE PACIFIC ISLANDS   In 1943 the American forces, still small in number, began a campaign of "island hopping." They did not try to recapture every Pacific island held by the Japanese but selected major bases and strategic sites along the enemy supply line. (See Map 29–6.) Starting from the Solomon Islands, they moved northeast toward Japan itself. By June 1944, they had reached the Mariana Islands, usable as bases for bombing the Japanese in the Philippines, China, and Japan itself.

*In April 1945, Americans invaded the heavily armed and fortified Japanese island of Okinawa, less than 400 miles from the Japanese home islands. Japanese resistance was strong, and the fighting was unbelievably fierce. In this picture, American Marines move forward in heavy fighting. [Bildarchiv Preussischer Kulturbesitz]*

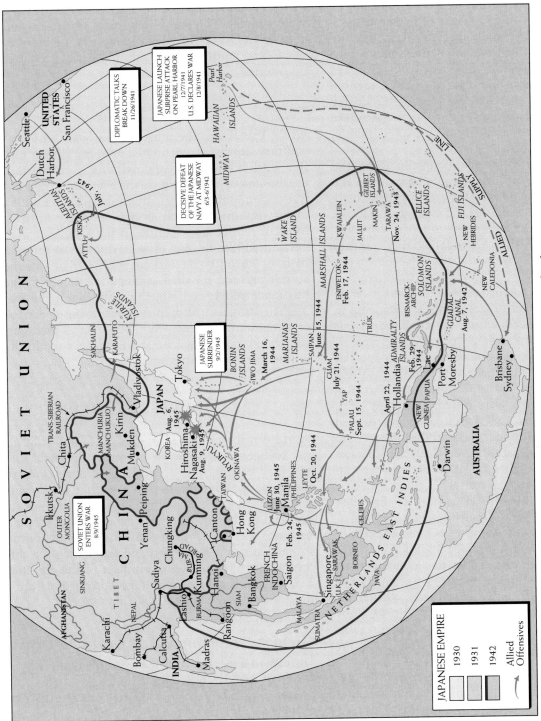

**MAP 29–6 WORLD WAR II IN THE PACIFIC** As in Europe, the Pacific war involved Allied recapture of areas that had been quickly taken earlier by the enemy. The enormous area represented by the map shows the initial expansion of Japanese holdings to cover half the Pacific and its islands, as well as huge sections of eastern Asia, and the long struggle to push the Japanese back to their homeland and defeat them by the summer of 1945.

In October of the same year, the Americans recaptured most of the Philippines and drove the Japanese fleet back into its home waters. In 1945 Iwo Jima and Okinawa fell, despite a determined Japanese resistance that included kamikaze attacks, suicide missions in which specially trained pilots deliberately flew their explosive-filled planes into American warships. From these new bases, closer to Japan, the American bombers launched a terrible wave of bombings that destroyed Japanese industry and disabled the Japanese navy. Still the Japanese government, dominated by a military clique, refused to surrender.

Confronted with Japan's determination, the Americans made plans for a frontal assault on the Japanese homeland. They calculated it might cost a million American casualties and even greater losses for the Japanese. At this point, science and technology presented the Americans with another choice.

THE ATOMIC BOMB   Since early in the war, a secret program had been in progress. Its staff, made up in significant part of exiles from Hitler's Europe, was working to use atomic energy for military purposes. On August 6, 1945, an American plane dropped an atomic bomb on the Japanese city of Hiroshima. The city was destroyed, and more than 70,000 of its 200,000 residents were killed. Two days later, the Soviet Union declared war on Japan and invaded Manchuria. The next day, a second atomic bomb fell, this time on Nagasaki. Even then, the Japanese cabinet was prepared to resist further, to face an invasion rather than give up.

The unprecedented intervention of Emperor Hirohito (r. 1926–1989) finally forced the government to surrender on August 14. Even then they made the condition that Japan could keep its emperor. Although the Allies had continued to insist on unconditional surrender, President Harry S. Truman (1884–1972), who had come to office on April 12, 1945, on the death of Franklin D. Roosevelt, accepted the condition. Peace was formally signed aboard the USS *Missouri* in Tokyo Bay on September 2, 1945.

Revulsion and horror at the use of atomic bombs as well as hindsight arising from the Cold War have made the decision to use the bomb against Japanese cities controversial. Some have suggested that the bombings were unnecessary to win the war and that their main purpose was to frighten the Russians into a more cooperative attitude after the war.

Others have emphasized the bureaucratic, almost automatic nature of the decision, once it had been decided to develop the bomb. To the decision makers and their contemporaries, however, matters were simpler. The bomb was a way to end the war swiftly and save American lives. The decision to use it was conscious, not automatic, and required no ulterior motive.

### The Cost of War

World War II was the most terrible war in history. Military deaths are estimated at some fifteen million, and at least as many civilians were killed. If deaths linked indirectly to the war, from disease, hunger, and other causes, are included, the number of victims might reach as high as forty million. Most of Europe and significant parts of Asia were devastated. Yet the end of so terrible a war brought little opportunity for relaxation. The dawn of the atomic age and the dramatic end it brought to the war made people conscious that another major war might extinguish humanity. Everything depended on concluding a stable peace, but even as the fighting ended, conflicts among the victors made the prospects of a lasting peace doubtful.

# The Domestic Fronts

World War II represented an effort at total war by all the belligerents. Never in European or world history had so many men and women and so many resources been devoted to military effort. One result was the carnage that occurred on the battlefields, at sea, and in the air. Another was an unprecedented organization of civilians on the various home fronts. Each domestic effort and experience was different, but few escaped the impact of the conflict. Everywhere there were shortages, propaganda campaigns, and new political developments.

### Germany: From Apparent Victory to Defeat

Hitler had expected to defeat all his enemies by a series of rapid strokes, or *Blitzkrieg*. Such campaigns would have required little change in Germany's society and economy. During the first two years of the war, in fact, Hitler demanded few important sacrifices from the German people. Spending on domestic projects continued, and food was plentiful; the economy as a whole was not on a full wartime footing. Germany's failure to quickly overwhelm the Soviet Union changed everything. Food could no longer be imported from the East in needed quantities, Germany had to mobilize for total war, and the government demanded major sacrifices from the people.

A great expansion of the army and of military production began in 1942. As minister for armaments and munitions, Albert Speer (1905–1981) directed the economy, and Germany met its military needs instead of making consumer goods. The government sought the cooperation of major German business enterprises to aid the growth of wartime production. Between 1942 and late 1944, the output of military products tripled; as the war went on, more men were drafted from industry into the army, and military production suffered.

As the manufacture of armaments replaced the production of consumer goods, shortages of everyday products became serious. Prices and wages were controlled, but the standard of living of German workers fell. Burdensome food rationing began in April 1942, and shortages were severe until the Nazi government seized more food from the occupied regions of Europe. To preserve their own home front, the Nazis passed on the suffering to their defeated neighbors.

By 1943 there were also serious labor shortages. The Nazis required German teenagers and retired men to work in the factories, and increasing numbers of women joined them. To achieve total mobilization, the Germans closed retail businesses, raised the age of women eligible for compulsory service, shifted non-German domestic workers to wartime industry, moved artists and entertainers into military service, closed theaters, and reduced such basic public services as mail and railways. Finally, the Nazis compelled thousands of people from conquered lands to do forced labor in Germany.

Hitler assigned women a special place in the war effort. The celebration of motherhood continued, with an emphasis on women who were the mothers of important military figures. Films portrayed ordinary women who became especially brave and patriotic during the war and remained faithful to their husbands who were at the front. Women were thereby shown as mothers and wives who sent their sons and husbands off to war. The government pictured other wartime activities of women as the natural fulfillment of their maternal roles. As air raid wardens, they protected their families; as factory workers in munitions plants, they aided their sons on the front lines. Women working on farms were providing for their soldier sons and husbands; as housewives, they were helping to win the war by conserving food and managing their households frugally. Finally, by their faithful chastity, German women were protecting racial purity. They were not to marry or to engage in sexual relations with men who were not Germans.

The war years also saw an intensification of political propaganda on the domestic front beyond what occurred in other countries. Hitler and other Germans genuinely believed that weak domestic support had led to Germany's defeat in World War I; they were determined that this situation would not happen again. Nazi propaganda blamed the outbreak of the war on the British and the Jews and its prolongation on the policies of Germany's opponents. It also stressed the power of Germany and the inferiority of its foes.

Propaganda Minister Josef Goebbels (1897–1945) used both radio and films to boost the Nazi cause. Movies of the collapse of Poland, Belgium, Holland, and France were shown in Germany to demonstrate German military might. Throughout the conquered territories, the Nazis used the same mass media to frighten inhabitants about the possible consequences of an Allied victory. Later in the war, the ministry broadcast exaggerated claims of Nazi victories. As the German armies were checked on the battlefield, especially in Russia, propaganda became a substitute for victory. To stiffen German resolve, propaganda now aimed to frighten Germans about the consequences of defeat.

After May 1943, when the Allies began their major bombing offensive over Germany, the German people had much to fear. One German city after another was devastated, but German morale was not undermined. The bombing may even have increased German resistance by seeming to confirm the regime's propaganda about the ruthlessness of Germany's opponents.

World War II increased the power of the Nazi Party in Germany. Every area of the economy and society came under the direct influence or control of the party. The Nazis were determined that they, rather than the traditionally honored German officer corps, would profit from the new authority that the war effort was giving to the central government. Throughout the war years, there was virtually no serious opposition to Hitler or his ministers. In 1944 a small group of army officers attempted to assassinate Hitler; the effort failed, and there were few indications of significant popular support for this act.

The war brought great changes to Germany, but what transformed the country was the experience of vast physical destruction, invasion, and occupation. Hitler and the Nazis had brought Germany to such a complete and disastrous defeat that only a new kind of state with new political structures could emerge.

## France: Defeat, Collaboration, and Resistance

The terms of the 1940 armistice between France, under Pétain, and Germany, signed June 22, allowed the Germans to occupy more than half of France, including the Atlantic and English Channel coasts. To prevent the French from continuing the fight from North Africa, and even more to prevent them from turning their fleet over to Britain, Hitler left southern France unoccupied until November 1942. Marshal Pétain set up a dictatorial regime at the resort city of Vichy and followed a policy of close collaboration with the Germans in hopes of preserving as much autonomy as possible.

Some of the collaborators believed that the Germans were sure to win the war and wanted to be on the victorious side. A few sympathized with the ideas and plans of the Nazis. Many conservatives regarded the French defeat as a judgment on what they saw as the corrupt, secularized, liberal ways of the Third Republic. Most of the French

The Allied campaign of aerial bombardment did terrible damage to German cities. This photograph shows the devastation it delivered to the city of Cologne on the Rhine. [UPI/Bettmann]

were not active collaborators but were helpless and demoralized by defeat and the evidence of German power.

Many conservatives and extreme rightists saw in the Vichy government a way to reshape the French national character and to halt the decadence they associated with political and religious liberalism. The Roman Catholic clergy, who had lost power and influence under the Third Republic, gained status under Vichy. The church supported Pétain, and his government restored religious instruction in the state schools and increased financial support for Catholic schools. Vichy adopted the church's views on the importance of family and spiritual values. The government forbade divorce during the first three years of marriage and made subsequent divorce difficult; large families were encouraged and subsidized.

The Vichy regime also encouraged an intense, chauvinistic nationalism. It exploited the long-standing prejudice against foreigners working in France and fostered resentment even against French men and women who were not regarded as genuinely "French." The chief victims were French Jews. Anti-Semitism was not new in France, as the Dreyfus affair had demonstrated. Even before Germany undertook Hitler's "final solution" in 1942, the French had begun to remove Jews from positions of influence in government, education, and publishing. In 1941 the Germans began to intern Jews living in occupied France; soon they carried out assassinations and imposed large fines collectively on the Jews of the occupied zone. In the spring of 1942, they began to deport Jews from France, ultimately more than 60,000, to the extermination camps of eastern Europe. The Vichy government had no part in these decisions, but it made no protest, and its own anti-Semitic policies made the whole process easier to carry out.

A few French, most notably General Charles de Gaulle (1890–1969), fled to Britain after the defeat of France. There they organized the French National Committee of Liberation, or "Free French." Until the end of 1942, the Vichy government controlled French North Africa and the navy, but the Free French began operating in central Africa. From London, they broadcast hope and defiance to their compatriots in France.

Serious internal resistance to the German occupiers and to the Vichy government, however, began to develop only late in 1942. The Germans tried to force young people in occupied France to work in German factories; some of them joined the Resistance, but the number of all the resisters was small. Many were deterred by fear of harsh punishment by the Germans. Some disliked the violence inevitably connected with resistance to a powerful ruthless nation. So long as it appeared the Germans would win the war, moreover, resistance seemed imprudent and futile. For these reasons, the organized Resistance never attracted vast numbers of followers; well under 5 percent of the adult French population appears to have been involved.

By early 1944, the tide of battle had shifted. The Allies seemed sure to win, and the Vichy government would clearly not survive; only then did a large-scale active movement of resistance assert itself. General de Gaulle spoke confidently for Free France from his base in London and urged the French people to resist their conquerors and the German lackeys in the Vichy government. Within France, Resistance groups joined forces to plan for a better day. From Algiers on August 9, 1944, the Committee of National Liberation declared the authority of Vichy illegitimate. Soon French soldiers joined in the liberation of Paris and established a government for Free France. On October 21, 1945, France voted to end the Third Republic and adopted a new constitution as the basis of the Fourth Republic. The French people had experienced defeat, disgrace, deprivation, and suffering in the war. Hostility and bitter quarrels over who had done what during the occupation and under Vichy divided them for decades.

### Great Britain: Organization for Victory

On May 22, 1940, the British Parliament gave the government emergency powers. Together with others already in effect, this measure allowed the government to institute compulsory military service, food rationing, and various controls over the economy.

To deal with the crisis facing them, all British political parties joined in a national government under Winston Churchill. Churchill and the British war cabinet moved as quickly as possible to mobilize the nation. Perhaps the most pressing immediate need was the production of airplanes to fight the Germans in the Battle of Britain. This effort was led by Lord Beaverbrook (1879–1964), one of Britain's most important newspaper publishers. The demand

*Winston Churchill walks through the rubble-strewn streets of London after the city had experienced a night of German bombing. Despite many casualties and widespread devastation, the German bombing of London did not break British morale or prevent the city from functioning. [UPI/Bettmann Newsphotos]*

for more planes and other armaments inspired a massive campaign to reclaim scrap metal. Wrought-iron fences, kitchen pots and pans, and every conceivable kind of scrap metal were collected for the war effort. This was only one successful example of the many ways the civilian population was enthusiastically engaged in the struggle.

By the end of 1941, British production had already surpassed Germany's. To meet the heavy demands on the labor force, factory hours were extended, and many women were brought into the workforce. Unemployment disappeared, and the working classes had more money to spend than they had enjoyed for many years. To avoid inflation caused by increased demand for an inadequate supply of consumer goods, savings were encouraged,

and taxes were raised to absorb the excess purchasing power.

The "blitz" air attacks of the winter and spring of 1940–1941 were the most immediate and dramatic experience of the war for the British people themselves. The German air raids killed thousands of people and left many others homeless. Once the bombing began, many families removed their children to the countryside. Ironically, the rescue effort improved the standard of living of many of the children, for the government paid for their food and medication. Gas masks were issued to thousands of city dwellers, who were frequently compelled to take shelter from the bombs in the London subways.

After the spring of 1941, Hitler needed most of his air force on the Russian front, but the bombing of Britain continued, killing more than 30,000 people by the end of the war. Terrible as it was, this toll was much smaller than the number of Germans killed by Allied bombing in the war. In England, as in Germany, however, the bombing, far from breaking the people's spirit, may well have made them more determined.

The British made many sacrifices. Transportation facilities were strained simply from carrying enough coal for domestic heating and for running factories. Food and clothing for civilians were scarce, and the government adopted strict rationing to achieve a fair distribution. Every scrap of land was farmed, increasing the productive portion by almost four million acres. Gasoline was scarce, and so private vehicles almost vanished.

The British established their own propaganda machine to influence the Continent. The British Broadcasting Company (BBC) sent programs to every country in Europe in the local language to encourage resistance against the Nazis. At home, the government used the radio to unify the nation. Soldiers at the front heard the same programs as their families at home. The most famous program, second only to Churchill's speeches, was *It's That Man Again*, a humorous broadcast filled with imaginary figures that the entire nation came to treasure.

Strangely, for the broad mass of the population, the standard of living improved during the war. The general health of the nation also improved for reasons that are still not clear. These improvements should not be exaggerated, but they did occur, and many connected them with the active involvement of the government in the economy and in the lives of the citizens. This wartime experience may have contributed to the Labour Party's victory in 1945; many feared that a return to Conservative Party rule would also mean a return to the economic problems and unemployment of the 1930s.

## The Soviet Union: "The Great Patriotic War"

The war against Germany came as a great surprise to Stalin and the Soviet Union. The German attack violated the 1939 pact with Hitler and put the government of the Soviet Union on the defensive militarily and politically. It showed the failure of Stalin's foreign policy and the ineptness of his preparation for war. He claimed that the pact had given the nation an extra year and a half to prepare for war, but this was clearly a lame and implausible excuse in light of the ease of Germany's early victories. Within days, German troops occupied much of the western Soviet Union. The Communist government feared that Soviet citizens who had been conquered by the Germans, many of them not ethnic Russians, might welcome the conquerors as liberators; these Soviet citizens had been harshly oppressed by the Stalinist regime.

No nation suffered greater loss of life or more extensive physical destruction during World War II than the Soviet Union. Perhaps as many as sixteen million people were killed, and vast numbers of Soviet troops were taken prisoner. Hundreds of cities and towns and well over half of the industrial and transportation facilities of the country were devastated. From 1942 thousands of Soviet prisoners worked in German factories as forced labor. The Germans also served their own war effort with grain, mineral resources, and oil confiscated from the Soviet Union.

Stalin conducted the war as virtual chief of the armed forces, and the State Committee for Defense provided strong central coordination. In the decade before the war, Stalin had already made the Soviet Union a highly centralized state; he had tried to manage the entire economy from Moscow through the five-year plans, the collectivization of agriculture, and the purges. The country was thus already on what amounted to a wartime footing long before the conflict erupted. When the war began, millions of citizens entered the army, but the army itself did not grow in influence at the expense of the state and the Communist Party, that is, of Stalin. He was suspicious of the generals, though he had presumably eliminated officers of doubtful loyalty in the purges of the late 1930s. As the war continued, however, the army gained some degree of independence, and eventually the generals were no longer subservient to party commissars. The army thus gained some freedom of action. It was, however, still sharply limited by the power of Stalin and by the nature of Soviet government and society.

Soviet propaganda was different from that of other nations. Because the Soviet government distrusted the loyalty of its citizens, it confiscated radios to prevent the people from listening to German or British propaganda. In cities, the government broadcast to the people over loudspeakers in place of radios. During the war, Soviet propaganda emphasized Russian patriotism rather than traditional Marxist themes that stressed class conflict. The struggle against the Germans was called "The Great Patriotic War."

Great Russian novels of the past were republished; more than half a million copies of Tolstoy's *War and Peace* were printed during the siege of Leningrad (Saint Petersburg). Other authors wrote straightforward propaganda fostering hatred of the Germans. Serge Eisenstein (1898–1948), the great filmmaker, produced a vast epic entitled *Ivan the Terrible*, which glorified this brutal tsar of the Russian past. Composers, such as Dimitri Shostakovich (1906–1975), produced scores that sought to contribute to the struggle and evoke heroic emotions. The most important of these was Shostakovich's *Seventh Symphony*, also known as the *Leningrad Symphony*.

The pressure of war led Stalin to make peace with the Russian Orthodox Church, allowing church leaders to enter the Kremlin. Stalin hoped that this new policy would give him more support at home and permit the Soviet Union to be viewed more favorably in eastern Europe, where the Orthodox Church predominated.

Within occupied portions of the western Soviet Union, an active resistance movement arose against the Germans. The swiftness of the German invasion had stranded thousands of Soviet troops behind German lines. Many were shipped to Germany as prisoners of war, but others escaped and carried on guerrilla resistance warfare behind enemy lines. Stalin supported partisan forces in lands held by the enemy for two reasons. He wanted to cause as much difficulty as possible for the Germans, and Soviet-sponsored resistance reminded the peasants in the conquered regions that the Soviet government, with its policies of collectivization, had not disappeared. Stalin feared that the peasants' hatred of the Communist government might lead them to collaborate with the invaders. When the Soviet army moved westward toward the end of the war, it incorporated the partisans into the regular army.

As its armies reclaimed the occupied areas and then moved across eastern and central Europe, the Soviet Union established itself as a world power second only to the United States. Stalin had entered the war a reluctant belligerent, but he emerged a major victor. In that respect, the war and the extraordinary patriotic effort and sacrifice it generated consolidated the power of Stalin and the party more

effectively than the political and social policies of the previous decade.

## Preparations for Peace

The split between the Soviet Union and its wartime allies should cause no surprise. As the self-proclaimed center of world communism, the Soviet Union was openly dedicated to the overthrow of the capitalist nations. This message, however, was muted when the occasion demanded. On the other side, the Western allies were no less open about their hostility to communism and its chief purveyor, the Soviet Union. Although they had been friendly to the early stages of the 1917 Russian Revolution, they had intervened to try to overthrow the Bolshevik regime during the civil war resulting from the Revolution. The United States did not grant formal recognition to the USSR until 1933. The Western powers' exclusion of the Soviets from the Munich conference and Stalin's pact with Hitler

| Major Campaigns and Events of World War II | |
| --- | --- |
| September 1939 | Germany and the Soviet Union invade Poland |
| November 1939 | The Soviet Union invades Finland |
| April 1940 | Germany invades Denmark and Norway |
| May 1940 | Germany invades Belgium, the Netherlands, Luxembourg, and France |
| June 1940 | Fall of France |
| August 1940 | Battle of Britain begins |
| June 1941 | Germany invades the Soviet Union |
| July 1941 | Japan takes Indochina |
| December 1941 | Japan attacks Pearl Harbor; United States enters war against Axis Powers |
| June 1942 | Battle of Midway Island |
| November 1942 | Battle of Stalingrad begins |
| July–August 1943 | Allies take Sicily, land in Italy |
| June 1944 | Allies land in Normandy |
| May 1945 | Germany surrenders |
| August 1945 | Atomic bombs dropped on Hiroshima and Nagasaki |
| September 1945 | Japan formally surrenders |

did nothing to improve relations between them during the war.

Nonetheless, the need to cooperate against a common enemy and strenuous propaganda efforts helped improve Western feeling toward the Soviet ally. Still, Stalin remained suspicious and critical of the Western war effort, and Churchill was determined to contain the Soviet advance into Europe. Roosevelt perhaps had been more hopeful that the Allies could continue to work together after the war, but even he was losing faith by 1945. Differences in historical development and ideology, as well as traditional conflicts over political power and influence, soon dashed hopes of a mutually satisfactory peace settlement and continued cooperation to uphold it.

## The Atlantic Charter

In August 1941, even before the Americans were at war, Roosevelt and Churchill had met on a ship off Newfoundland and agreed to the Atlantic Charter. This broad set of principles in the spirit of Wilson's Fourteen Points provided a theoretical basis for the peace they sought. When Russia and the United States joined Britain in the war, the three powers entered a purely military alliance in January 1942, leaving all political questions aside. The first political conference was the meeting of foreign ministers in Moscow in October 1943. The ministers reaffirmed earlier agreements to fight on until the enemy surrendered unconditionally and to continue cooperating after the war in a united-nations organization.

## Tehran: Agreement on a Second Front

The first meeting of the leaders of the "Big Three" (as the USSR, Britain, and the United States were known) took place at Tehran, the capital of Iran, in 1943. Western promises to open a second front in France the next summer (1944) and Stalin's agreement to join in the war against Japan when Germany was defeated created an atmosphere of goodwill in which to discuss a postwar settlement. Stalin wanted to retain what he had gained in his pact with Hitler and to dismember Germany. Roosevelt and Churchill were conciliatory, but they made no firm commitments.

The most important decision was the one that chose Europe's west coast as the main point of attack instead of the Mediterranean. That meant, in retrospect, that Soviet forces would occupy eastern Europe and control its destiny. At Tehran in 1943, the Western allies did not foresee this clearly, for the Russians were still fighting deep within their own frontiers, and military considerations were still paramount.

CHURCHILL AND STALIN   By 1944 the situation was different. In August, Soviet armies were before Warsaw, which had revolted against the Germans in expectation of liberation. But the Russians halted, allowing the Polish rebels to be annihilated while they turned south into the Balkans. They gained control of Romania and Hungary, advances that centuries of expansionist tsars had only dreamed of achieving. Alarmed by these developments, Churchill went to Moscow and met with Stalin in October. They agreed to share power in the Balkans on the basis of Soviet predominance in Romania and Bulgaria, Western predominance in Greece, and equality of influence in Yugoslavia and Hungary. These agreements were not enforceable without American approval, and the Americans were known to be hostile to such un-Wilsonian devices as "spheres of influence."

GERMANY   The three powers easily agreed on Germany—its disarmament, denazification, and division into four zones of occupation by France and the Big Three. Churchill, however, began to balk at Stalin's demand for $20 billion in reparations as well as forced labor from all the zones, with Russia to get half of everything. These matters were left to fester and cause dissension in the future.

EASTERN EUROPE   The settlement of eastern Europe was an equally thorny problem. Everyone agreed that the Soviet Union deserved to have friendly neighboring governments, but the West insisted that they also be autonomous and democratic. The Western leaders, especially Churchill, were not eager to see eastern Europe fall under Russian domination. They were also, especially Roosevelt, committed to democracy and self-determination.

Stalin, however, knew that independent, freely elected governments in Poland and Romania could not be counted on to be friendly to Russia. He had already established a puppet government in Poland in competition with the Polish government-in-exile in London. Under pressure from the Western leaders, however, he agreed to reorganize this government and include some Poles friendly to the West in it. He also signed a Declaration on Liberated Europe promising self-determination and free democratic elections. Stalin may have been eager to avoid conflict before the war with Germany was over. He was always afraid that the Allies would make a separate peace with Germany and betray him. And he probably thought it worth endorsing some hollow principles as the price of continued harmony. In any case, he wasted little time violating these agreements.

## Yalta

The next meeting of the Big Three was at Yalta in the Crimea in February 1945. The Western armies had not yet crossed the Rhine, but the Soviet army was within a hundred miles of Berlin. (See Map 29–7.) The war with Japan continued, and no atomic explosion had yet taken place. Roosevelt, faced with a prospective invasion of Japan and heavy losses, was eager to bring the Russians into the Pacific war as soon as possible. As a true Wilsonian, he also suspected Churchill's determination to maintain the British Empire and Britain's colonial advantages. The Americans thought that Churchill's plan to set up British spheres of influence in Europe would encourage the Russians to do the same and lead to friction and war. To encourage Russian participation in the war against Japan, Roosevelt and Churchill made extensive concessions to Russia of Sakhalin and the Kurile islands, in Korea, and in Manchuria.

Again in the tradition of Wilson, Roosevelt laid great stress on a united-nations organization: "Through the United Nations, he hoped to achieve a self-enforcing peace settlement that would not require American troops, as well as an open world without spheres of influence in which American enterprise could work freely."[5] Soviet agreement on these points seemed well worth concessions elsewhere.

## Potsdam

The Big Three met for the last time in the Berlin suburb of Potsdam in July 1945. Much had changed

[5]*Robert O. Paxton,* Europe in the Twentieth Century *(New York: Harcourt Brace Jovanovich, 1975), p. 487.*

MAP 29–7   YALTA TO THE SURRENDER   *"The Big Three"—Roosevelt, Churchill, Stalin—met at Yalta in the Crimea in February of 1945. At the meeting, concessions were made to Stalin concerning the settlement of Eastern Europe because Roosevelt was eager to bring the Russians into the Pacific war as soon as possible. This map shows the positions held by the victors when Germany surrendered.*

since the prior conference. Germany had been defeated, and news of the successful experimental explosion of an atomic weapon reached the American president during the meetings. The cast of characters was also different. President Truman replaced the deceased Roosevelt, and Clement Attlee (1883–1967), leader of the Labour Party that had defeated Churchill's Conservatives in a general election, replaced Churchill as Britain's spokesperson during the conference. Previous agreements

*This photograph shows the leaders of the Big Three at Potsdam. By the summer of 1945, only Stalin (right) remained of the original leaders of the major Allies. Roosevelt and Churchill had been replaced by Harry Truman (center) and Clement Atlee. [UPI/Bettmann]*

were reaffirmed, but progress on undecided questions was slow.

Russia's western frontier was moved far into what had been Poland and included most of German East Prussia. In compensation, Poland was allowed "temporary administration" over the rest of East Prussia and Germany east of the Oder–Neisse river line, a condition that became permanent. In effect, Poland was moved about a hundred miles west, at the expense of Germany, to accommodate the Soviet Union. The Allies agreed that Germany would be divided into occupation zones until the final peace treaty was signed. Germany remained divided until 1990.

A Council of Foreign Ministers was established to draft peace treaties for Germany's allies. Growing disagreements made the job difficult, and Italy, Romania, Hungary, Bulgaria, and Finland did not sign treaties until February 1947. The Russians were dissatisfied with the treaty that the United States made with Japan in 1951 and signed their own agreements with the Japanese in 1956. These disagreements were foreshadowed at Potsdam.

◆

*The second great war of the twentieth century (1939–1945) grew out of the unsatisfactory resolution of the first. In retrospect, the two wars appear to some people to be one continuous conflict, a kind of twentieth-century "Thirty Years' War,"*

*with the two main periods of fighting separated by an uneasy truce. To others, that point of view oversimplifies and distorts the situation by implying that the second war was the inevitable result of the first and its inadequate peace treaties. The latter opinion seems more sound, for, whatever the flaws of the treaties of Paris, the world suffered an even more terrible war than the first because of failures of judgment and will on the part of the victorious democratic powers.*

*The United States, which had become the wealthiest and potentially the strongest nation in the world, disarmed almost entirely and withdrew into a shortsighted and foolish isolation. Therefore, it could play no important part in restraining the angry and ambitious dictators who brought on the war. Britain and France refused to face the threat posed by the Axis powers until the most deadly war in history was required to put it down. If the victorious democracies had remained strong, responsible, and realistic, they could easily have remedied whatever injustices or mistakes arose from the treaties without endangering the peace.*

*The second war itself was so plainly a world war that little need be said to indicate its global character. There is good reason to think that if the Japanese occupation of Manchuria in 1931 was not technically a part of that war, it was a significant precursor. Moreover, there was Italy's attack on the African nation of Ethiopia in 1935; the Italian,*

German, and Soviet interventions in the Spanish Civil War (1936–1939); and Japan's attack on China in 1937. These acts revealed that aggressive forces were on the march around the globe and that the defenders of the world order lacked the will to stop them. The formation of the Axis among Germany, Italy, and Japan guaranteed that when the war came it would be fought around the world.

There was fighting and suffering in Asia, Africa, the Pacific islands, and Europe; and men and women from all the inhabited continents took part in it. The use of atomic weapons brought the frightful struggle to a close. Still, what are called conventional weapons did almost all the damage; their level of destructiveness threatened the survival of civilization, even without the use of atomic or nuclear devices.

This war ended not with unsatisfactory peace treaties but with no treaty at all in the European arena, where the war had begun. The world quickly split into two unfriendly camps: the western, led by the United States, and the eastern, led by the Soviet Union. This division, among other things, hastened the liberation of former colonial territories. The bargaining power of the new nations that emerged from them was temporarily increased as the two rival superpowers tried to gain their friendship or allegiance. It has become customary to refer to these nations as "the Third World," with the former Soviet Union and the United States and their respective allies being the first two. The passage of time has shown that the differences among Third World nations are so great as to make the term all but meaningless.

The surprising treatment received by the defeated powers of the second war was also largely the result of the emergence of the Cold War. Instead of holding them back, the Western powers installed democratic governments in Italy, West Germany, and Japan, took them into the Western alliances designed to contain communism, and helped them recover economically. Japan and Germany are now among the richest nations in the world, and Italy is more prosperous than it has ever been.

By the last decade of the twentieth century, Japan had become one of the greatest industrial, commercial, and financial powers in the world and a major investor in the American economy. Its manufacturers have offered stiff competition to their counterparts in the United States and Western Europe, provoking concern and calls for protective tariffs.

Germany, divided between East and West by the war, never ceased to hope for eventual unification. The startling events of 1989, in which the Soviet Union gave up its hold over Eastern Europe, made unification suddenly possible, and it occurred in 1990. One result of this unification has been to open again a question that lay behind the two great wars of the twentieth century—the place of a unified Germany in Europe.

# Review Questions

1. What were Hitler's foreign policy aims? Was he bent on conquest in the east and dominance in the west, or did he simply want to return Germany to its 1914 boundaries?

2. Why did Britain and France adopt a policy of appeasement in the 1930s? What were its main features? Did the appeasers buy the West valuable time to prepare for war by their actions at Munich in 1938?

3. How was Hitler able to defeat France so easily in 1940? Why was the air war against Britain a failure? Why did Hitler invade Russia? Why did the invasion ultimately fail? Could it have succeeded?

4. Why did Japan attack the United States at Pearl Harbor? What was the significance of American intervention in the war? Why did the United States drop atomic bombs on Japan? Did Presi-

dent Truman make the right decision when he ordered the bombs used?

5. What impact did World War II have on the civilian population of Europe? How did experiences on the domestic front of Great Britain differ from those of Germany and France? What impact did "the Great Patriotic War" have on the people of the Soviet Union? Did the Soviet Union's participation in World War II solidify Stalin's hold on power?

6. What was Hitler's "final solution" to the Jewish problem? Why did Hitler want to eliminate Slavs as well? Some historians have looked at the twentieth century and have seen a period of great destruction as well as of great progress. Is this truly a "century of Holocaust"? Discuss the ramifications of these questions.

# Suggested Readings

A. ADAMTHWAITE, *France and the Coming of the Second World War, 1936–1939* (1977). A careful account making good use of the French archives.

J. ADLER, *The Jews of Paris and the Final Solution: Communal Response and Internal Conflicts, 1940–1944* (1987). Written by a former member of the French Resistance.

E. R. BECK, *Under the Bombs: The German Home Front, 1942–1945* (1986). An interesting examination of a generally unstudied subject.

A. BULLOCK, *Hitler: A Study in Tyranny*, rev. ed. (1964). A brilliant biography.

W. S. CHURCHILL, *The Second World War*, 6 vols. (1948–1954). The memoirs of the great British leader.

H. FEIS, *From Trust to Terror: The Onset of the Cold War, 1945–1950* (1970). The best general account.

H. W. GATZKE, *Stresemann and the Rearmament of Germany* (1954). An important monograph.

M. GILBERT AND R. GOTT, *The Appeasers*, rev. ed. (1963). A revealing study of British policy in the 1930s.

M. GILBERT, *The Holocaust: A History of the Jews of Europe During the Second World War* (1985). The best and most comprehensive treatment.

M. HARRISON, *Soviet Planning in Peace and War, 1938–1945* (1985). An examination of the Soviet wartime economy.

J. KEEGAN, *The Second World War* (1990). A lively and penetrating account by a master military historian.

M. KNOX, *Mussolini Unleashed* (1982). An outstanding study of Fascist Italy's policy and strategy in World War II.

G. KOLKO, *The Politics of War* (1968). An interesting example of the revisionist school that finds the causes of the Cold War in economic considerations and emphasizes American responsibility.

W. L. LANGER AND S. E. Gleason, *The Challenge of Isolation* (1952). American foreign policy in the 1930s.

D. C. LARGE (ED.), *Contending with Hitler: Varieties of German Resistance in the Third Reich* (1992). Essays that examine the efforts of resistance to Hitler and their limits.

B. H. LIDDELL HART, *History of the Second World War*, 2 vols. (1971). A good military history.

S. MARKS, *The Illusion of Peace* (1976). A good discussion of European international relations in the 1920s and early 1930s.

V. MASTNY, *Russia's Road to the Cold War* (1979). Written by an expert on the Soviet Union and Eastern Europe.

W. MURRAY, *The Change in the European Balance of Power 1938–1939* (1984). A brilliant study of the relationship between strategy, foreign policy, economics, and domestic politics in the years before the war.

W. MURRAY AND A. R. Millett, *Calculation, Net Assessment and the Coming of World War II* (1992). An important study of the role of military intelligence.

N. RICH, *Hitler's War Aims*, 2 vols. (1973–1974). The best study of the subject in English.

M. SHERWIN, *A World Destroyed: The Atomic Bomb and the Grand Alliance* (1975). An analysis of the role of the atomic bomb in the years surrounding the end of World War II.

R. J. SONTAG, *A Broken World 1919–1939* (1971). An excellent survey.

A. J. P. TAYLOR, *The Origins of the Second World War* (1966). A lively, controversial, even perverse study.

H. THOMAS, *The Spanish Civil War*, 3rd ed. (1986). The best account in English.

C. THORNE, *The Approach of War 1938–1939* (1967). A careful analysis of diplomacy.

P. WANDYCZ, *The Twilight of French Eastern Alliances, 1926–1936* (1988). A well-documented account of the diplomacy of central and eastern Europe in a crucial period.

G. L. WEINBERG, *A World at Arms: A Global History of World War II* (1994). A thorough and excellent narrative account.

G. WRIGHT, *The Ordeal of Total War 1939–1945* (1968). An excellent survey.

The wall constructed in 1961 separating East and West Berlin became the single most important symbol of the Cold War. Along the wall there was a series of check points where troops were stationed to control the very limited flow of people between the sections of the divided city. Here a U.S. Army officer (left) and an Eastern German officer face each other at the Friedrichstrasse checkpoint. [UPI/Corbis-Bettmann]

# Europe and the Soviet–American Rivalry

## KEY TOPICS

- The origins of the Cold War and the division of Europe into Eastern and Western blocs following World War II
- Decolonization and the conflicts in Korea and Vietnam
- The Middle East and the Cold War
- Political and economic developments in Western Europe during the Cold War
- Polish protests against Soviet domination of Eastern Europe

*From the end of World War II in 1945 until the collapse of the Soviet Union and its subject regimes in Eastern Europe during the late 1980s, the Soviet Union and the United States—two nuclear-armed superpowers—confronted each other in a simmering conflict known as the Cold War. While it lasted, this conflict dominated global politics and threatened the peace of Europe, which stood at its center, divided between the US-dominated NATO (North Atlantic Treaty Organization) and the Soviet-dominated Warsaw Pact.*

*Undertaking an active role in Europe and the rest of the world was a major shift in the foreign policy for the United States, reflecting its leaders' awareness of the dangers to which the country had been exposed when it retreated from the world scene after World War I. Moving to oppose what it regarded as the expansion of Soviet power and communist influence across the globe, the United States assumed a position of military, political, and economic leadership. This policy of active international leadership prompted the Marshall Plan, the formation of NATO, and military interventions in Korea and Vietnam.*

*The Cold War rapidly became globalized as regional conflicts outside of Europe became drawn into the orbit of the US–Soviet rivalry. Most particularly as the nations of Europe retreated from empire, the rivalry between the two superpowers expanded into a contest for dominance in the post-colonial world. Superpower intervention aggravated local conflicts on every continent. Southeast Asia in particular developed into a battleground. In its efforts to limit communism, the United States became embroiled in bitter wars in Korea and Vietnam. The struggle between Israel and the Arab nations was likewise an arena of superpower conflict.*

*The Communist government of the Soviet Union, established in 1917 and consolidated under Stalin's dictatorship, underwent many changes and attempts at redirection after World War II. The turmoil of World War I had allowed the Soviet Union to come into existence; the turmoil of World War II permitted it to establish hegemony over eastern Europe. From the late 1940s through the 1980s, the Soviet Union tried to retain dominance in Eastern Europe and to challenge the United States around the globe.*

*The Soviet Union pursued two not always compatible foreign policy goals. One was to lead the international communist movement, dedicated to the overthrow of capitalism throughout the world. The other was to secure its own national interests, which sometimes put it at odds with communist movements elsewhere. Eventually, harsh rivalries emerged between the Soviet Union and other communist nations, most notably the People's Republic of China. The leaders of the Soviet Union, meanwhile, failed to build lasting support for their goals, either internally or in their eastern European dependencies. Nonetheless, the Soviet Union maintained its position as a superpower and its Cold War antagonism to the United States through the opening years of the 1980s.*

# The Emergence of the Cold War

The tense relationship between the United States and the Soviet Union started in the closing months of World War II. Some scholars attribute the hardening of the atmosphere between the two countries to Harry Truman's assumption of the presidency in April 1945, after the death of the more sympathetic Franklin Roosevelt, and to the American possession of an effective atomic bomb. Evidence suggests, however, that Truman was trying to carry Roosevelt's policies forward and that Roosevelt himself had become distressed by Soviet actions in Eastern Europe. Nor did Truman use the atomic bomb to try to keep Russia out of the Pacific. On the contrary, he worked hard to ensure Russian intervention against Japan at the end of the war. In part, the new coldness among the Allies arose from the mutual feeling that each had violated previous agreements. The Russians were plainly asserting permanent control of Poland and Romania under puppet communist governments. The United States, on the other hand, was taking a harder line on the extent of German reparations to the Soviet Union.

## *The Lines Are Drawn: the Iron Curtain*

In retrospect, however, it is unlikely that friendlier styles on either side could have avoided a split that rested on basic differences of ideology and interest. The Soviet Union's attempt to extend its control westward into central Europe and the Balkans and southward into the Middle East was a continuation of the policy of tsarist Russia. It had been Britain's traditional role to try to restrain Russian expansion into these areas, and it was not surprising that the United States should inherit that task as Britain's power waned.

The Americans made no attempt to roll back Soviet power where it existed. (See Map 30–1.) At the time, American military forces were the greatest in their history, American industrial power was unmatched in the world, and atomic weapons were an American monopoly. In less than a year from the war's end, Americans reduced their forces in Europe

MAP 30–1   TERRITORIAL CHANGES AFTER WORLD WAR II   *The map shows the shifts in territory following the defeat of the Axis. No treaty of peace formally ended the war with Germany.*

from 3.5 million to half a million. The speed of the withdrawal reflected pressure to "get the boys home" but was also fully in accord with America's peacetime plans and goals. Those goals included support for self-determination, autonomy, and democracy in the political sphere; and free trade, freedom of the seas, no barriers to investment, and the Open Door in the economic sphere. They reflected American principles and they served American interests well. As the strongest, richest nation in the world—the one with the greatest industrial plant and the strongest currency—the United States would benefit handsomely if an international order based on such goals were established.

American hostility to colonial empires created tensions with France and Britain, but these were minor. The main conflict was with the Soviet Union. From the Soviet perspective, extending the borders of the USSR and dominating the formerly independent states of Eastern Europe would provide needed security and would be a proper compensation for the fearful losses the Soviet people had endured in the war. The Soviets could thus see American resistance to their expansion as a threat to their security and their legitimate aims. American objections over Poland and other states could be seen as attempts to undermine regimes friendly to Russia and to encircle the Soviet Union with hostile neighbors. This point of view might also be seen to justify Russian attempts to overthrow regimes friendly to the United States in Western Europe and elsewhere.

The growth in France and Italy of large, popular communist parties plainly taking orders from Moscow led the Americans to believe that Stalin was engaged in a worldwide plot to destroy capitalism and democracy by subversion. Without reliable evidence about Stalin's intentions, it is impossible to be certain if these suspicions were justified, but most people in the West certainly thought them plausible. Rivalry between the Soviet Union and the United States dominated international relations for the next three decades. In the flawed world of reality, it is hard to see how it could have been otherwise. The important question then was whether the conflict would take a diplomatic or a military form.

Evidence of the new mood of hostility among the former allies was not long in coming. In February 1946, both Stalin and his foreign minister, Vyacheslav Molotov (1890–1986), gave public speeches in which they spoke of the Western democracies as enemies. A month later, Churchill gave a speech in Fulton, Missouri, in which he viewed Russian actions in Eastern Europe with alarm. He spoke of an Iron Curtain that had descended on Europe, dividing a free and democratic West from an East under totalitarian rule. He warned against Communist subversion and urged Western unity and strength as a response to the new menace. In this atmosphere, difficulties grew.

## Early Frustrations of the United Nations

Toward the end of the war, one of Roosevelt's major goals had been the formation of the United Nations. He hoped this new international body would provide a forum for negotiation and consultation

## Churchill Invents the Iron Curtain

*In 1946 Winston Churchill chose an American audience (at Westminster College in Fulton, Missouri) for the speech that contributed the expression* Iron Curtain *to the language. More important, it defined the existence of what came to be known as the* Cold War *between the communist and the democratic camps.*

✦ *Why do you think Churchill chose to deliver this address to an American audience? What events and concerns arising at the end of World War II and in the months immediately following had led Churchill to these conclusions? Would Churchill's description have been more accurate had he delivered this speech five years later? Why or why not?*

A shadow has fallen upon the scenes so lately lighted by the Allied victory. Nobody knows what Soviet Russia and its Communist international organization intends to do in the immediate future, or what are the limits, if any, to their expansive and proselytizing tendencies. . . .

From Stettin in the Baltic to Trieste in the Adriatic, an iron curtain has descended across the Continent. Behind that line lie all the capitals of the ancient states of central and eastern Europe. Warsaw, Berlin, Prague, Vienna, Budapest, Belgrade, Bucharest and Sofia; all these famous cities and the populations around them lie in the Soviet sphere and all are subject in one form or another, not only to Soviet influence but to a very high and increasing measure of control from Moscow. Athens alone, with its immortal glories, is free to decide its future at an election under British, American, and French observation. The Russian-dominated Polish government has been encouraged to make enormous and wrongful inroads upon Germany, and

mass expulsions of millions of Germans on a scale grievous and undreamed of are now taking place. The Communist parties, which were very small in all these eastern states of Europe, have been raised to preeminence and power far beyond their numbers and are seeking everywhere to obtain totalitarian control. Police governments are prevailing in nearly every case, and so far except in Czechoslovakia, there is no true democracy. . . .

. . . I do not believe that Soviet Russia desires war. What they desire is the fruits of war and the indefinite expansion of their power and doctrines. . . .

. . . If the western democracies stand together in strict adherence to the principles of the United Nations Charter, their influence for furthering these principles will be immense and no one is likely to molest them. If, however, they become divided or falter in their duty, and if these all-important years are allowed to slip away, then indeed catastrophe may overwhelm us all.

*"Winston Churchill's Speech at Fulton," in* Vital Speeches of the Day, *vol. 12 (New York: City News Publishing), March 15, 1946, pp. 331–332.*

*President Harry Truman greets Secretary of State George Marshall returning from Europe. Truman and Marshall were the architects of American foreign policy during the early years of the Cold War. [Archive Photos]*

among the nations of the world and would have sufficient military muscle to intervene against aggression. By committing itself to this organization and providing it a home, the United States, in contrast to its inward retreat following World War I, signaled its readiness to accept the responsibilities of a world power.

The United States had taken the leading role in devising the organization of the United Nations, formally founded in February 1945. It was organized around two governing bodies: a large General Assembly in which all member nations sat, and a smaller Security Council. The Security Council soon emerged as the dominant body. It had five permanent members—Great Britain, France, China, the Soviet Union, and the United States—and two temporary members drawn from among the UN's other member states. Each of the five permanent members—the major allied powers of World War II—had the right to veto any measure brought to the Security Council.

By the late 1940s, hopes that the United Nations would resolve the world's major conflicts had been disappointed. Like the League of Nations, the UN was (and is) dependent on voluntary contributions of money and troops. The UN Charter, moreover, forbids interference in the internal affairs of nations, and many of the problems of the late 1940s were internal in nature. Finally, during the late 1940s and throughout the 1950s, the Soviet Union repeatedly used its veto in the Security Council,

frustrating the ability of the United Nations to resolve problems.

The attempt to deal with the problem of atomic energy was an early victim of the Cold War and the paralysis of the United Nations. The Americans proposed a plan to place the manufacture and control of atomic weapons under international control, but the Russians balked at requirements for on-site inspection and for limits on veto power in the United Nations. The plan fell through. The United States continued to develop its own atomic weapons in secrecy, and the Russians did the same. By 1949, with the help of information obtained by Soviet spies in Britain and the United States, the Soviet Union had exploded its own atomic bomb, and the race for nuclear weapons was on.

### "Containment" in American Foreign Policy

The resistance of westerners to what they increasingly perceived as Soviet intransigence and communist plans for subversion and expansion took clearer form in 1947.

THE TRUMAN DOCTRINE   Since 1944, civil war had been raging in Greece between the royalist government restored by Britain and insurgents supported by the communist countries, chiefly Yugoslavia. In 1947 Britain informed the United States that it was financially no longer able to support the Greeks. On March 12, President Truman asked Congress for

# The Truman Doctrine Declared

*In 1947 the British informed the United States that they could no longer support the Greeks in their fight against a Communist insurrection supported from the outside. On March 12 of that year, President Truman asked Congress for legislation in support of both Greece and Turkey, which was also in danger. The principle behind that request, which became known as the Truman Doctrine, appears in the following selections from Truman's speech to the Congress.*

✦ *How does Truman relate the goals of the Second World War to the emerging Cold War with the Soviet Union? What are the qualities that Truman associates with free governments and how were those absent in the Soviet Union and the nations of eastern Europe under its domination? How does this speech establish guidelines that might be applied to U.S. policy in parts of the world beyond Greece?*

One of the primary objectives of the foreign policy of the United States is the creation of conditions in which we and other nations will be able to work out a way of life free from coercion. This was a fundamental issue in the war with Germany and Japan. Our victory was won over countries which sought to impose their will, and their way of life, upon other nations.

To insure the peaceful development of nations, free from coercion, the United States has taken a leading part in establishing the United Nations. The United Nations is designed to make possible lasting freedom and independence for all its members. We shall not realize our objectives, however, unless we are willing to help free peoples to maintain their free institutions and their national integrity against aggressive movements that seek to impose upon them totalitarian regimes. . . .

At the present moment in world history nearly every nation must choose between alternative ways of life. The choice is too often not a free one.

One way of life is based upon the will of the majority, and is distinguished by free institutions, representative government, free elections, guaranties of individual liberty, freedom of speech and religion, and freedom from political oppression.

The second way of life is based upon the will of a minority forcibly imposed upon the majority. It relies upon terror and oppression, a controlled press and radio, fixed elections, and the suppression of personal freedoms.

I believe that it must be the policy of the United States to support free peoples who are resisting attempted subjugation by armed minorities or by outside pressures.

I believe that we must assist free peoples to work out their own destinies in their own way.

I believe that our help should be primarily through economic and financial aid, which is essential to economic stability and orderly political processes.

*Senate Committee on Foreign Relations,* A Decade of American Foreign Policy: Basic Documents 1941–1949 *(1950), pp. 1235–1237.*

legislation that would provide funds to support Greece and also Turkey, then under Soviet pressure to yield control of the Dardanelles, and Congress complied. In a speech to Congress that gave these actions much broader significance, the president set forth what came to be called the *Truman Doctrine*. He advocated a policy of support for "free people who are resisting attempted subjugation by armed minorities or by outside pressures," by implication anywhere in the world.

THE MARSHALL PLAN   American aid to Greece and Turkey took the form of military equipment and advisers. For Western Europe, where postwar poverty and hunger fueled the menacing growth of communist parties, the Americans devised the European Recovery Program. Named the *Marshall Plan* after George C. Marshall (1880–1959), the secretary of state who introduced it, this program provided broad economic aid to European states on condition only that they work together for their mutual benefit. The Soviet Union and its satellites were invited to participate. Finland and Czechoslovakia were willing to do so, and Poland and Hungary showed interest. The Soviets, however, fearing that American economic aid would attract many satellites out of their orbit, forbade them to take part.

The Marshall Plan was a great success in restoring prosperity to Western Europe and in setting the stage for Europe's unprecedented postwar economic growth. In addition to the vast program of American economic aid, the strong Christian Democratic movement which dominated the politics of Italy, France, and West Germany also worked to keep Communist influence at bay outside the Soviet sphere in Eastern Europe. (See the later section in the chapter.)

## Soviet Assertion of Domination of Eastern Europe

From the Western viewpoint, this policy of "containment" was a new and successful response to the Soviet and communist challenge. The Soviet Union viewed the matter differently. For the Soviets, the determination to control Eastern Europe had both historical and ideological roots. Western European powers had invaded the lands of the Soviet Union once in the nineteenth century (under Napoleon) and already twice in the twentieth. For its part,

tsarist Russia had governed Poland for over a century and had intervened at the request of the Austrian Empire to put down the Hungarian revolution in 1848. Russia's interests in the lands around the Black Sea were long-standing. Given this history and the Soviet Union's extraordinary losses in World War II, it is not surprising that Soviet leaders would seek to use their Eastern European satellites as a buffer against future invasions.

To Stalin, containment may have looked like a renewed attempt by the West to isolate and encircle the USSR. His answer was to put an end to all multiparty governments behind the Iron Curtain and to replace them with thoroughly communist regimes completely under his control. He also called a meeting of all communist parties around the world at Warsaw in the autumn of 1947. There they organized the Communist Information Bureau (Cominform), a revival of the old Comintern, dedicated to spreading revolutionary communism throughout the world. In Eastern Europe the Soviet Union found numerous supporters who were willing to carry out Stalin's policies. For a time Communism appears to have been a popular ideology among some segments of the population who had opposed the various rightwing movements before the war and who had fought German Nazism during the war. In Western Europe the establishment of the Cominform meant the era of the popular front during which communists had cooperated with noncommunist parties was officially over. Communist leaders in the West who favored friendship, collaboration, and reform were replaced by hard-liners who attempted to sabotage the new structures.

In February 1948, Stalin gave a dramatic and brutal display of his new policy in Prague. The communists expelled the democratic members of what had been a coalition government and murdered Jan Masaryk (1886–1948), the foreign minister and son of the founder of Czechoslovakia, Thomas Masaryk. President Eduard Benes (1884–1948) was also forced to resign, and Czechoslovakia was brought fully under Soviet rule.

During the late 1940s, the Soviet Union moved to dominate the other subject governments in Eastern Europe. It required them to impose Stalinist policies, including one-party political systems, close military cooperation with the Soviet Union, collectivization of agriculture, Communist Party domination of universities and other institutions of education, and attacks on the church. Long-time

# The Church and the Communist Party Clash over Education in Hungary

*Throughout Eastern Europe, the Roman Catholic Church became one of the strongest opponents of the postwar communist governments. It raised issues relating to church schools, free worship, participation in church-sponsored organizations, and the erection of new church buildings. One of the harshest clashes took place in Hungary. Following are two statements that illustrate the opposing positions of the church and the party. Cardinal Mindszenty (1892–1975) was later imprisoned and became one of the best-known political prisoners in Eastern Europe.*

✦ *How does Mindszenty relate the position of church-supported schools to the nature and rights of parenthood? How does he compare the actions of the Communist Party to those of Hitler? How does the minister of public worship set party members against the church? How does he attempt to place loyalty to the party above private beliefs? What does the Communist Party fear from religious education and participation in religious activities on the part of its members or their children?*

## Statement of Josef Cardinal Mindszenty, May 20, 1946

The right of the Church to schools is entirely in concord with the right of parents to educate their children. What is incumbent upon the parents in all questions of natural life is incumbent upon the Church with regard to the supernatural life. Parents are prior to the state, and their rights were always and still are, acknowledged by the Church. The prerogative of parents to educate their children cannot be disputed by the state, since it is the parents who give life to the child. They feed the child and clothe it. The child's life is, as it were, the continuation of theirs. Hence it is their

---

Communist Party officials were purged and subjected to show trials like those that had taken place in Moscow during the late 1930s. The catalyst for this harsh tightening probably was the success of Marshal Josip "Broz" Tito (1892–1980), the leader of communist Yugoslavia, in freeing his country from Soviet domination. Stalin feared other Eastern European states might follow the Yugoslav example and moved to prevent them from doing so.

## The Postwar Division of Germany

These Soviet actions, especially those in Czechoslovakia, increased American determination to go ahead with its own arrangements in Germany.

DISAGREEMENTS OVER GERMANY  During the war, the Allies had never decided how to treat Germany after its defeat. At first they all agreed it should be dismembered, but differed on how. By the time of Yalta, Churchill had come to fear Russian control of Eastern and Central Europe and began to oppose dismemberment.

The Allies also differed on economic policy. The Russians proceeded swiftly to dismantle German industry in the Eastern Zone, but the Americans acted differently in the Western Zone. (See Map 30–2.) They concluded that following the Soviet policy would require the United States to support Germany economically for the foreseeable future. It would also cause political chaos and open the way for communism. They preferred, therefore, to try to make Germany self-sufficient, and this meant restoring rather than destroying its industrial capacity. To the Soviets, the restoration of a powerful industrial Germany, even in the Western Zone only,

right to demand that their children are educated according to their faith and their religious outlook.

It is their right to withhold their children from schools where their religious convictions are not only disregarded but even made the object of contempt and ridicule. It was this parental right which German parents felt was violated when the Hitler government deprived them of their denominational schools. The children came home from the new schools like little heathens, who smiled derisively or laughed at the prayers of their parents.

You Hungarian parents will likewise feel a violation of your fundamental rights if your children can no longer attend the Catholic schools solely because the dictatorial State closes down our schools by a brutal edict or renders their work impossible.

### Statement of the Hungarian Communist Minister of Public Worship, June 7, 1950

We must start a vast work of enlightenment, and in the first place explain to our party colleagues and also to all workers that any father who sends his child to religion classes, places it in the hands of the enemy and entrusts his soul and thinking to the enemies of peace and imperialistic warmongers.

A part of our working people believes that participation of children in religious instruction is a private matter which has nothing to do with the political conviction of their parents. They are wrong. To send children to a reactionary pastor for religious instruction, is a political movement against the People's Democracy, whether intentional or not. . . .

In carrying out the basic principles, religion within the party is no private matter, but we must make a difference between plain party members and party officials, and must not in any case make party membership dependent on the fact whether our party members are religious. In the first place, we must expect from our party officials, our leading men, that they do not send their children to religious instruction courses, do not take part in religious ceremonies and train their wives in the spirit of communistic conception.

Also, we must patiently endeavor to enlighten our members, and ensure through training and propaganda that they realize; "In going to Church, taking part in processions, sending our children to religious instruction, we unconsciously further the efforts of clerical reaction."

*Colman J. Barry, ed.*, Readings in Church History *(Westminster, Md.: The Newman Press, 1965), pp. 496–498.*

---

was frightening and unacceptable. The same difference of approach hampered agreement on reparations. The Soviets claimed the right to the industrial equipment in all the zones, and the Americans resisted their demands.

BERLIN BLOCKADE  Disagreement over Germany produced the most heated of postwar debates. When the Western powers agreed to go forward with a separate constitution for the western sectors of Germany in February 1948, the Soviets walked out of the joint Allied Control Commission. In the summer of that year, the Western powers issued a new currency in their zone. Berlin, though well within the Soviet zone, was governed by all four powers. The Soviets feared the new currency, which was circulating in Berlin at better rates than their own. They chose to seal the city off by closing all railroads and highways to West Germany. Their purpose was to drive the Western powers out of Berlin.

The Western allies responded to the Berlin blockade with an airlift of supplies to the city that lasted almost a year. In May 1949, the Russians were forced to back down and to open access to Berlin. The incident, however, was decisive. It increased tensions and suspicions between the opponents and hastened the separation of Germany into two states. West Germany formally became the German Federal Republic in September 1949, and the eastern region became the German Democratic Republic a month later. Ironically, Germany had been dismembered in a way no one had planned or expected. The two Germanies and the divided city of Berlin, isolated within East Germany, would remain central fixtures in the geopolitics of the Cold War.

MAP 30–2  OCCUPIED GERMANY AND AUSTRIA  *At the war's end, defeated Germany, including Austria, was occupied by the victorious Allies in the several zones shown here. Austria, by prompt agreement, was reestablished as an independent, neutral state, no longer occupied. The German zones hardened into an "East" Germany (the former Soviet zone) and a "West" Germany (the former British, French, and American zones). Berlin, within the Soviet zone, was similarly divided.*

## NATO and the Warsaw Pact

Meanwhile, the nations of Western Europe had been coming closer together. The Marshall Plan encouraged international cooperation. In March 1948, Belgium, the Netherlands, Luxembourg, France, and Britain signed the Treaty of Brussels, providing for cooperation in economic and military matters. In April 1949, these nations joined with Italy, Denmark, Norway, Portugal, and Iceland to sign a treaty with Canada and the United States that formed the North Atlantic Treaty Organization (NATO). NATO committed its members to mutual assistance in case any of them was attacked. The NATO treaty formed the West into a bloc. A few years later, West Germany, Greece, and Turkey joined the alliance. For the first time in history, the United States was committed to defend allies outside the Western Hemisphere.

A series of bilateral treaties providing for close ties and mutual assistance in case of attack gov-

*The Allied airlift in action during the Berlin blockade. Every day for almost a year Western planes supplied the city until Stalin lifted the blockade in May 1949.* [Bildarchiv Preussischer Kulturbesitz]

erned Soviet relations with the states of Eastern Europe. In 1949 these states formed the Council of Mutual Assistance (COMECON) to integrate their economies. Unlike the NATO states, the Eastern alliance system was under direct Soviet domination through local Communist parties controlled from Moscow and overawed by the presence of the Red Army. The Warsaw Pact of May 1955, which included Albania, Bulgaria, Czechoslovakia, East Germany, Hungary, Poland, Romania, and the Soviet Union, merely gave formal recognition to the system that existed. Europe was divided into two unfriendly blocs. The Cold War had taken firm shape in Europe. (See Map 30–3.)

The strategic interests and ambitions of the United States and the Soviet Union would not, however, permit the Cold War to be limited to the European continent. Major flash points would erupt around the world during the following decades, most particularly in the Middle East and in Asia. The establishment of a communist government in Cuba after 1959 would bring the conflict to the American hemisphere as well. In each case the Cold War rivalry drew what might otherwise have been regional conflicts into the realm of superpower strategic concerns. Furthermore, many of these

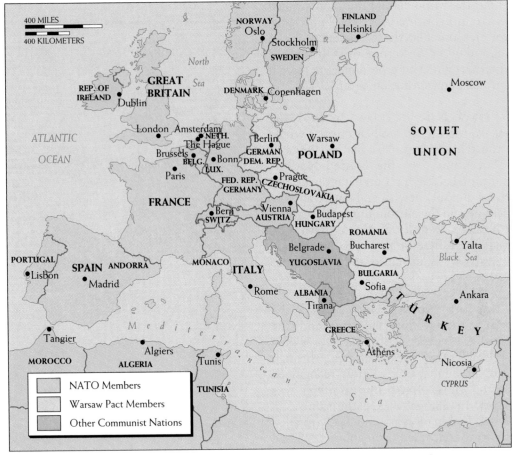

MAP 30–3   MAJOR EUROPEAN ALLIANCE SYSTEMS   *The North Atlantic Treaty Organization, which includes both Canada and the United States, stretches as far east as Turkey. By contrast, the Warsaw Pact nations were the contiguous communist states of Eastern Europe, with the Soviet Union, of course, as the dominant member.*

regional conflicts have continued in one form or another after the end of the Cold War.

## The Creation of the State of Israel

One of the areas of ongoing regional conflict that became a major point of Cold War rivalry was the Middle East. Following World War I Great Britain had exercised the chief political influence in the region under various postwar mandates. In the wake of World War II both the Zionist movement seeking to establish an independent Jewish state and Arab nationalists seeking to achieve self-determination challenged British authority and influence.

BRITISH BALFOUR DECLARATION   The modern state of Israel was the achievement of the world Zionist movement, founded in 1897 by Theodore Herzl and later led by Chaim Weizmann (1874–1952). The British Balfour Declaration of 1917 had favored establishing a national home for the Jewish people in Palestine. Between the wars, thousands of Jews, mainly from Europe, immigrated to the area, then governed by Great Britain under a mandate of the League of Nations. During the interwar period, the *Yishuv*, or Jewish community in Palestine, developed its own political parties, press, labor unions, and educational system. There were many conflicts with the Arabs already living in Palestine, who considered the Jewish settlers intruders. The British rather unsuccessfully tried to mediate those clashes.

This situation might have prevailed longer in Palestine except for the outbreak of World War II and Hitler's attempt to exterminate the Jewish population of Europe. The Nazi persecution united

Jews throughout the world behind the Zionist ideal of a Jewish state in Palestine. Also, the knowledge of Nazi atrocities touched the conscience of the United States and other Western powers. It seemed morally right that something be done for Jewish refugees from Nazi concentration camps.

THE UNITED NATIONS RESOLUTION   In 1947 the British turned over to the United Nations the whole problem of the relationship of Arabs and Jews in Palestine. That same year, the United Nations passed a resolution calling for a division of the territory into two states, one Jewish and one Arab. The Arabs in Palestine and the surrounding area resisted the United Nations resolution. Not unnaturally, they resented the influx of new settlers. Many Palestinian Arabs were displaced and themselves became refugees.

ISRAEL DECLARES INDEPENDENCE   In May 1948, the British official withdrew from Palestine and, the *Yishuv* declared the independence of a new Jewish state called Israel. The United States, through President Truman, almost immediately recognized the new nation, whose first prime minister was David Ben-Gurion (1886–1973). On the same day, Lebanon, Syria, Jordan, Egypt, and Iraq invaded Israel. The fighting continued throughout 1948 and 1949. By the end of its war of independence against the Arabs, Israel had expanded its borders beyond the limits originally set forth by the United Nations. (See Map 30–4.) It had also ceded the Old City of Jerusalem, but retained control of the New City. By 1949 Israel had secured its existence but not the acceptance of its Arab neighbors. So long as Egypt, Jordan, Syria, Lebanon, and Saudi Arabia, to name those closest, withheld diplomatic recognition, the peace amounted to little more than an armed truce.

The Arab–Israeli conflict would inevitably draw in the superpowers. The dispute directly involved Europe because many of the citizens of Israel had emigrated from Europe, and Europe, like the United States, is highly dependent on oil from Arab countries. Furthermore, both the United States and the Soviet Union believed they had major strategic as well as economic interests in the region.

By 1949 the United States had established itself as a firm ally of Israel. Gradually, after that date the Soviet Union would begin to furnish aid of various kinds to the Arab nations. The bipolar tensions that

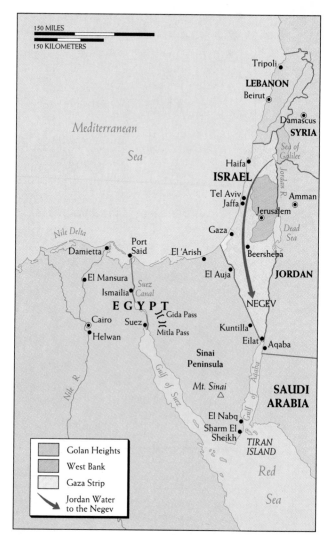

MAP 30–4   ISRAEL AND ITS NEIGHBORS IN 1949   *The territories gained by Israel in 1949 did not secure peace in the region. In fact, the disposition of those lands and the Arab refugees who live there has constituted the core of the region's unresolved problems to the present day.*

had settled over Europe were thus transferred to the Middle East.

## The Korean War

While early stages of the Cold War took place in Europe and the Arab–Israeli conflict developed in the Middle East, the United States found itself confronting armed aggression in Asia. As part of a UN police action, it intervened militarily in Korea, following the same principle of containment that directed its actions in Europe.

Between 1910 and 1945, Japan, as an Asian colonial power, had occupied and exploited Korea, but by the close of World War II, the Japanese had been driven out. Under the direction of the United States, Japan was politically reconstructed as a democracy. The United States then committed itself, as a cornerstone of its postwar policy, to maintain a democratic Japan.

The Japanese Empire, however, still had to be dealt with. The United States and the Soviet Union presided over the division of Korea into two parts with the thirty-eighth parallel of latitude as the line of separation. It was expected that the country would eventually be reunited. By 1948, however, two separate states had been organized: the Democratic People's Republic of Korea under Kim Il Sung in the North and the Republic of Korea under Syngman Rhee (1875–1965) in the South. The former was supported by the Soviet Union and the latter by the United States.

Numerous border clashes occurred between the two states. In late June 1950, forces from North Korea invaded South Korea by crossing the thirty-eighth parallel. (See Map 30–5.) The United States intervened and was soon supported by a United Nations mandate. Great Britain, Turkey, and Australia sent token forces. The troops were commanded by General Douglas MacArthur (1880–1964). The Korean police action was technically a United Nations venture to halt aggression. (It had been made possible by a boycott by the Soviet ambassador to the United Nations at the time of the key vote.) For the United States, the point of the Korean conflict was to contain the spread and to halt the aggression of communism.

General MacArthur's forces initially repelled the North Koreans and then pushed them almost to Manchuria. Late in 1950, however, the Chinese, responding to the pressure against their border, sent troops to support North Korea. The American forces had to retreat. The US policymakers believed that the Chinese, who since 1949 had been under the communist government of Mao Tse-tung (1893–1976), were simply the puppets of the Soviet Union. American policymakers conceived of the communist world as a single unit directed from Moscow. Accordingly, the movement of forces into South Korea was viewed as another example of communist pressure against a noncommunist state, similar to that previously confronted in Europe. Today it is clear there was much tension between

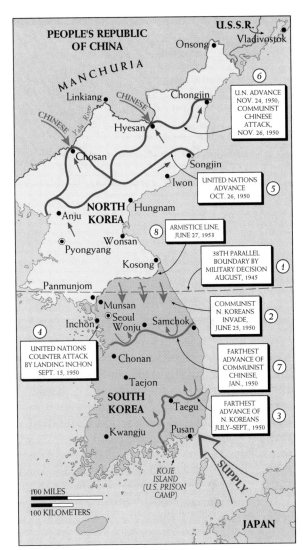

MAP 30–5  KOREA, 1950–1953  *The North Korean invasion of South Korea in 1950 and the bitter three-year war to repulse the invasion and stabilize a firm boundary near the thirty-eighth parallel are outlined here. The war was a dramatic application of the American policy of "containment" of communism.*

Moscow and the People's Republic of China, but those difficulties were little known or appreciated at the time.

For more than two years the war dragged on. Eventually, a border near the thirty-eighth parallel was restored. In 1952 General Dwight D. Eisenhower (1890–1969) was elected president of the United States. Early in his term of office, on June 16, 1953, his administration concluded an armistice ending the Korean War. American troops would, however, remain stationed in Korea for the rest of the century. The Korean peninsula remains one of the flash points of the cold War where regional conflict could still occur between North and South Korea.

In Korea, limited military action had halted and contained the military advance of a communist nation. The lessons of the Cold War learned in Europe appeared to have been successfully applied to Asia. The American government's faith in a policy of containment was confirmed. The Korean conflict transformed the Cold War into a global encounter and rivalry that ranged well beyond the borders of Europe.

The formation of NATO and the Korean conflict capped the first round of the Cold War. Stalin's death in 1953 and the armistice in Korea the same year fostered hopes that international tensions might ease. In early 1955 Soviet occupation forces left Austria after that nation agreed to neutral status. Later that year the leaders of France, Great Britain, the Soviet Union, and the United States held a summit conference at Geneva. Nuclear weapons and the future of divided Germany were the chief items on the agenda. The hopefulness inspired by this gathering of leaders to discuss so many grave issues was dubbed "the spirit of Geneva." Despite public displays of friendliness, however, the meeting produced few substantial agreements on major problems. The spirit of Geneva was short-lived, and the rivalry and polemics of the Cold War soon resumed.

# The Khrushchev Era in the Soviet Union

## *The Last Years of Stalin*

Many Russians had hoped that the end of World War II would signal a lessening of Stalinism. No other nation had suffered greater losses or more deprivation than the Soviet Union. Its people expected some immediate reward for their sacrifice and heroism. They desired a reduction in the scope of the police state and a redirection of the economy away from heavy industry to consumer products. They were disappointed. Stalin did little or nothing to modify the character of the regime he had created. The police remained ever-present. The cult of personality expanded, and the central bureaucracy continued to grow. Heavy industry was still favored over production for consumers, and agriculture continued to be troubled. Stalin's personal authority over the party and the nation remained unchallenged. The Cold War stance of the United States simply served to confirm Stalin in his ways.

By late 1952 and early 1953, Stalin appeared ready to unloose a new series of purges. In January 1953, a group of Jewish physicians was arrested and charged with plotting the deaths of important leaders. Claims of an extensive conspiracy appeared in the press. All these developments were similar to the events preceding the purges of the 1930s, which had been directed against both Communist Party members and the military. Then, quite suddenly, in the midst of this new furor, on March 6, 1953, Stalin died. The circumstances surrounding his death are unclear.

For a time, no single leader replaced Stalin. Rather the Presidium (the renamed Politburo) pursued a policy of collective leadership. Gradually, however, power and influence began to devolve on Nikita Khrushchev (1894–1971), who in 1953 had been named party secretary. Three years later, Khrushchev himself became premier. His rise ended collective leadership, but he never commanded the extraordinary powers of Stalin.

## *Khrushchev's Domestic Policies*

During the 1930s and 1940s, Stalin had placed his mark and control on virtually every aspect of Soviet politics, life, and culture. With his death in 1953, the Soviet system had to deal with his legacy.

The Khrushchev era, which lasted until the autumn of 1964, witnessed a marked retreat from Stalinism, though not from authoritarianism. Indeed, Stalin's rule had been so repressive that it left considerable room for his successors to relax their grip while still maintaining tyranny. Politically, the demise of Stalinism meant that shifts in leadership and party structure would occur by means other than purges.

In retrospect, Khrushchev's attempts at reform display some similarities to Gorbachev's later *perestroika* policies of the 1980s (discussed in Chapter 31). Both promised relief from the most repressive aspects of the Soviet state; both encountered opposition from more conservative, entrenched Communist Party leaders. From the time Khrushchev was removed from power in 1964 until Gorbachev's rise, however, the leaders of the Soviet Union, while avoiding the excesses of Stalinism, returned to repressive authoritarianism.

INTELLECTUAL LIFE UNDER KHRUSHCHEV  Intellectuals were somewhat freer to express their opinions. This so-called thaw in the cultural life of the country was closely related to the premier's interest in the opinions of experts on problems of industry and agriculture. He often went outside the usual bureaucratic channels in search of information and new ideas. Novels such as dissident Aleksandr Solzhenitsyn's (b. 1918) *One Day in the Life of Ivan Denisovich* (1963) could be published. However, Boris Pasternak (1890–1960), the author of *Dr. Zhivago* (1957), another novel critical of the government, was not permitted to accept the Nobel Prize for literature in 1958. The intellectual liberalization of Soviet life during this period should not be overestimated. It was favorable only in comparison with what had preceded it and with the decline in freedom of expression after Khrushchev's fall.

ECONOMIC EXPERIMENTS  Khrushchev's economic policy also differed somewhat from Stalin's. By 1953 the economy had recovered from the strains and destruction of the war, but consumer goods and housing remained in short supply and maintaining adequate supplies of food continued to be a problem. Khrushchev favored efforts to meet the demand for consumer goods. He also made some moves to decentralize economic planning and execution. During the late 1950s, he often boasted that Soviet production of consumer goods would over-take that of the West, but while steel, oil, and electric-power production continued to grow, the consumer sector improved only marginally.

Khrushchev was trying to move the country in too many directions at once. The Soviet Union's ambitious space program put the first artificial satellite—Sputnik—into orbit in 1957, but that effort and the ever growing defense budget made great demands on the nation's productive resources.

Khrushchev strongly redirected Stalin's agricultural policy. He recognized that in spite of the collectivization of the 1930s the Soviet Union still did not have an agricultural system capable of feeding its own people. He removed many of the most restrictive regulations on private cultivation. The machine tractor stations were abandoned. Existing collective farms were further amalgamated. The government undertook an extensive "virgin lands" program to increase the land available for wheat cultivation by hundreds of thousands of acres. The initial effect of this program was to increase grain production to new records, but inappropriate farming techniques caused soil erosion on the newly farmed lands within a few years, reducing yields. The agricultural problem simply continued to grow, forcing the Soviet Union to import vast quantities of grain from the United States and other countries. These American grain exports were an important facet of the policy of détente that marked relations between the Soviet Union and the United States for much of the 1970s (discussed later in this chapter).

## The Secret Speech of 1956

In February 1956, Krushchev made an extraordinary departure from expected practice by directly attacking the policies of the Stalin years. At the Twentieth Congress of the Communist Party, Khrushchev made a secret speech (later published outside the Soviet Union) in which he denounced Stalin and his crimes against socialist justice during the purges of the 1930s. The speech caused shock and consternation in party circles, but it also opened the way for genuine, if limited, internal criticism of the Soviet government and for many of the changes in intellectual and economic life already discussed. Gradually, the strongest supporters of Stalinist policies were removed from the presidium. By 1958 all Stalin's former supporters were gone, but none had been executed.

# Khrushchev Denounces the Crimes of Stalin: The Secret Speech

*In 1956 Khrushchev denounced Stalin in a secret speech to the Party Congress. The* New York Times *published a text of that speech smuggled from Russia.*

✦ *What are the specific actions on the part of Stalin that Khrushchev denounced? Why does Khrushchev pay so much attention to Stalin's creation of the concept of an "enemy of the people"? Why does Khrushchev draw a distinction between the actions of Stalin and those of Lenin?*

Stalin acted not through persuasion, explanation, and patient cooperation with people, but by imposing his concepts and demanding absolute submission to his opinion. Whoever opposed this concept or tried to prove his viewpoint and the correctness of his position was doomed to removal from the leading collective [group] and to subsequent moral and physical annihilation. . . .

Stalin originated the concept of "enemy of the people." This term automatically rendered it unnecessary that the ideological errors of a man or men engaged in a controversy be proved; this term made possible the usage of the most cruel repression violating all norms of revolutionary legality, against anyone who in any way disagreed with Stalin, against those who were only suspected of hostile intent, against those who had bad reputations.

This concept "enemy of the people" actually eliminated the possibility of any kind of ideological fight or the making of one's views known on this or that issue, even those of a practical character. In the main, and in actuality, the only proof of guilt used, against all norms of current legal science, was the "confession" of the accused himself; and, as a subsequent probing proved, "confessions" were acquired through physical pressures against the accused. . . .

Lenin used severe methods only in the most necessary cases, when the exploiting classes were still in existence and were vigorously opposing the revolution, when the struggle for survival was decidedly assuming the sharpest forms, even including civil war.

Stalin, on the other hand, used extreme methods and mass repressions at a time when the revolution was already victorious, when the Soviet State was strengthened, when the exploiting classes were already liquidated and Socialist relations were rooted solidly in all phases of national economy, when our party was politically consolidated and had strengthened itself both numerically and ideologically. It is clear that here Stalin showed in a whole series of cases his intolerance, his brutality and his abuse of power. Instead of proving his political correctness and mobilizing the masses, he often chose the path of repression and physical annihilation, not only against actual enemies, but also against individuals who had not committed any crimes against the party and the Soviet Government. . . .

*The* New York Times, *June 5, 1956, pp. 13–16.*

Khrushchev's speech had repercussions well beyond the borders of the Soviet Union. Communist leaders in Eastern Europe took it as a signal that they could govern with greater leeway than before. Khrushchev's attack on Stalin, they believed, might allow them to retreat, not from communism certainly, but from the Stalinist policies that had been required of them since the late

1940s. Indeed, Krushchev's 1956 speech was simply the first of a number of important and extraordinary events of that year.

# The Crises of 1956: The Middle East

In 1956, a major international crisis erupted in the Middle East as a result of the actions of Arab nationalists.

In 1952 a group of Egyptian army officers led by Gamal Abdel Nasser (1918–1970) had seized power in Egypt. Nasser established himself as a dictator, and more important for the stability of the region, as a spokesperson for militant Arab nationalism and activist opposition to the existence of the state of Israel. Strong hatred of all the old imperial powers also marked his policies and rhetoric.

## The Suez Intervention

In July 1956 President Nasser nationalized the Suez Canal, until then controlled by British and French interests. Now, Egyptian control of the Suez Canal threatened the access of Great Britain and France to Persian Gulf oil supplies, essential to their industrial economies. In October 1956 war broke out between Egypt, then receiving arms from the Soviet Union, and the eight-year-old state of Israel, closely tied to the West. Britain and France seized the opportunity to intervene. Although they justified their actions as a way to separate the combatants, their real motive was to regain control of the Suez Canal and to reassert their influence in the region. France was at war over its continuing control of Algeria. Prime Minister Anthony Eden, for his part, saw in the nationalist Nasser a Middle Eastern version of Hitler seeking to aggrandize himself. Israel joined with France and Britain. This alliance helped Israel fend off certain Arab guerrilla attacks but also associated Israel with the former imperial powers.

Although the Suez intervention was a military success, with Israel seizing the Sinai, and Britain and France landing troops in the canal zone, the operation ended in a humiliating diplomatic defeat. The United States refused to support the Anglo–French action, and the Soviet Union protested in the most severe terms. The Anglo–French forces had to be withdrawn, and control of the canal remained with Egypt. After 1956 a United Nations peacekeeping force separated the armies of Israel and Egypt with Israel withdrawing from the Sinai.

The Suez intervention proved that without the support of the United States the nations of Western Europe could no longer use military force to impose their will on the rest of the world. Also,

The Suez Canal was repaired in 1957 after the Egyptians had sunk ships to block the canal during the Anglo-French-Israeli invasion in 1956. [Archive Photos]

the United States and the Soviet Union showed that they would restrain their allies from undertaking actions that might result in a wider conflict. At the same time the Arab–Israeli conflict remained unresolved with no official Arab recognition of the existence of Israel. The Middle East would remain a major flash point of the Cold War and beyond.

# The Crises of 1956: Eastern Europe

The autumn of 1956 also saw important developments in Eastern Europe based in large measure on miscalculations about the real meaning of Khruschev's secret speech attacking Stalin. Events in Poland and Hungary demonstrated the limitations on independent action among the Soviet-bloc nations.

## Poland's Efforts Toward Independent Action

When the prime minister of Poland died, the Polish Communist Party leaders refused to accept as his successor the person designated by Moscow. Tensions were so high that the Soviet leaders even visited Warsaw to make their opinions known. In the end, Wladyslaw Gomulka (1905–1982) emerged as the new communist leader of Poland. The choice of the Polish communists, he also proved acceptable to the Soviets because he promised continued economic and military cooperation and, most important to the Soviets, continued Polish membership in the Warsaw Pact. Within those limits, he moved to halt the collectivization of Polish agriculture and to improve the relationship between the communist government and the Polish Roman Catholic Church. This resolution more or less allowed the Polish Communist Party to manage its

*In Budapest in October 1956, street battles raged for several days until Soviet tanks put down the Hungarian revolt. [Darolle/Sygma]*

own affairs, leading another Eastern European country to seek similar autonomy.

### Uprising in Hungary

In late October, as the Polish problem was nearing resolution, Hungarians in Budapest demonstrated in sympathy for the Polish people. Hungary's communist government moved to stop the demonstrations, and street fighting erupted. The Hungarian Communist Party then installed a new government headed by former premier Imre Nagy (1896–1958).

Nagy, although a communist, sought greater independence for Hungary. He demanded more than had Gomulka in Poland and appealed to noncommunist groups in Hungary for support. He wanted Soviet troops withdrawn, leading to the creation of a neutral Hungary. Nagy even went so far as to call for Hungarian withdrawal from the Warsaw Pact. These demands were wholly unacceptable to the Soviet Union. In early November, Soviet troops invaded Hungary, deposed Nagy (who was later executed), and imposed Janos Kadar (1912–1989) as premier.

The Polish and Hungarian disturbances had several results. They did not end pressure for more independence in Eastern Europe, but they showed the limits of the Soviet Union's tolerance for independence within its bloc notwithstanding Khrushchev's criticisms of Stalinism. They also demonstrated that the countries of Eastern Europe would not be permitted to imitate Austrian neutrality. It should also be noted that the Suez intervention had provided an international diversion permitting the Soviet Union freer action within its sphere of influence. Finally,

the failure of the United States to take any action in the Hungarian uprising demonstrated the hollowness of American domestic political rhetoric about liberating the captive nations of Eastern Europe.

## Later Cold War Confrontations

The events of 1956 in the Middle East and Eastern Europe solidified the position of the United States and the Soviet Union as superpowers. In different ways and to differing degrees, the two superpowers had demonstrated this new political reality to their allies. The nations of Western Europe would be able to make independent policy among themselves within Europe, but were generally curtailed from independent action on the broader international scene. For approximately twenty-five years the nations of Eastern Europe would be permitted virtually no autonomous actions in either the domestic or the international sphere.

### Collapse of the 1960 Paris Summit Conference

After 1956 the Soviet Union began to talk about "peaceful coexistence" with the United States. With the 1957 launch of Sputnik, the Soviet Union appeared to have achieved enormous technological superiority over the West. In 1958 the two countries began negotiations toward limiting the testing of nuclear weapons. The same year, however, the Soviet Union demanded the formal diplomatic recognition of East Germany and then announced that the status of West Berlin must be changed and the Allied occupation forces withdrawn. These demands were refused, but they had made the situation in Germany and most particularly in Berlin the center of East–West tension. In 1959 matters relaxed sufficiently for several Western leaders to visit Moscow and for Soviet Premier Khrushchev to tour the United States. A summit meeting was scheduled for May 1960, and US President Eisenhower was to go to Moscow.

The Paris Summit Conference of 1960 proved anything but a repetition of the friendly days of the 1955 meeting in Geneva. Just before the gathering, the Soviet Union shot down an American U-2 aircraft that was flying reconnaissance over Soviet territory. Khrushchev demanded an apology from Eisenhower for this air surveillance. Eisenhower accepted full responsibility for the surveillance policy but refused to issue any apology. Khrushchev then refused to take part in the summit conference, just as the participants arrived in the French capital. The conference was thus aborted, and Eisenhower's proposed trip to the Soviet Union never took place.

The Soviets did not scuttle the summit meeting on the eve of its opening simply because of the American spy flights. They had long been aware of these flights and had other reasons for protesting them when they did. First, they had not wanted to protest until they had shot down a plane, which they had not been able to do, because they feared their military technology would seem weak despite Sputnik. Second, Khrushchev had hoped that the leaders of Britain, France, and the United States would be sufficiently divided over the future of Germany so as not to present a united front at the summit. When these divisions failed to develop, the conference was of little use to him. Third and most important, by 1960 the communist world itself had split between the Soviets and the Chinese. The latter were portraying the Russians as lacking sufficient revolutionary zeal. Destroying the summit was, in part, a way to demonstrate the Soviet Union's hard-line attitude toward the capitalist world.

*President John Kennedy of the United States and Premier Nikita Khrushchev of the Soviet Union met in Vienna in 1961. The discussions were very difficult, leaving both leaders with feelings of distrust. [Sovfoto/Eastfoto]*

## The Berlin Wall

The aborted Paris conference opened the most difficult period of the Cold War. In 1961 the new US president, John F. Kennedy (1917–1963), and Premier Khrushchev met in Vienna. The conference was inconclusive, but the American president left wondering if the two nations could avoid war.

Throughout 1961 thousands of refugees from East Germany crossed the border into West Berlin. The western sector of the city was the single point in Eastern Europe where persons living under Soviet dominance might escape to a free political climate. This outflow of people was both a political embarrassment to East Germany and a detriment to its economy. For the Soviet Union, this movement of people indicated its inability to control events in Eastern Europe.

In August 1961, the East Germans, with the support of the Soviet Union, took decisive action. They erected a concrete wall along the border between East and West Berlin, shutting the two parts of the city off from each other. Crossing from one part to the other was possible only at designated checkpoints and only for people with proper papers. The United States protested and sent Vice President Lyndon Johnson to Berlin to reassure its citizens, but the wall remained until the collapse of East Germany in 1989, becoming a major symbol of the Cold War era. In June, 1963, President Kennedy himself appeared in Berlin making a famous speech in which he declared, *"Ich bin ein Berliner"* ("I am a Berliner"). Despite speeches and symbolic support from the West, the wall halted the flow of refugees and brought the United States' commitment to West Germany into doubt.

## The Cuban Missile Crisis

The most dangerous days of the Cold War occurred during the Cuban missile crisis of 1962, which represented another facet of the globalization of the Cold

*The Berlin Wall, erected in August 1961, came to symbolize the tensions of the Cold War era. [Bildarchiv Preussischer Kulturbesitz]*

War, on this occasion into the Americas. The nation of Cuba lies less than 100 miles from the United States. In 1957 Fidel Castro (b. 1926) launched a major communist insurgency in Cuba, which, on New Year's day, 1959, toppled the dictatorship of Flugencio Batista (1901–1973). Thereafter Castro established a communist government and Cuba became an ally of the Soviet Union. These events caused enormous concern within the United States.

In 1962 the Soviet Union began to place nuclear missiles on the island. Now concern turned to confrontation. The American government, under President Kennedy, blockaded Cuba, halted the shipment of new missiles, and demanded the removal of existing installations. After an extremely tense week, during which communications between Washington and Moscow were permeated with admonitions and threats, the Soviets backed down

and the crisis ended. This adventurism in foreign policy undermined Khrushchev's credibility in the ruling circles of the Soviet Union and caused other non-European communist regimes to question the Soviet Union's commitment to their security and survival. One result was to increase the influence of the People's Republic of China in communist circles. The Soviet backdown over Cuba also convinced Soviet military leaders of the need to strengthen their forces so that in any future confrontation their forces would be as strong as or stronger than those of the United States.

If the Cuban missile crisis had led to war, the United States could have launched missiles over Europe or from European bases into the Soviet Union. The crisis thus threatened Europe directly, but it was the last major Cold War confrontation to do so. In 1963 the United States and the Soviet

*In the summer of 1968, Soviet tanks rolled into Czechoslovakia, ending that country's experiment in liberalized communism. This picture shows defiant, flag-waving Czechs on a truck rolling past a Soviet tank in the immediate aftermath of the invasion. [Archive Photos]*

Union concluded a Nuclear Test Ban Treaty. This agreement marked the beginning of a lessening in the tensions between the two powers. The German problem subsided somewhat in the late 1960s as West Germany, under Premier Willy Brandt (1913–1992), moved to improve its relations with the Soviet Union and Eastern Europe. By 1964 many Russian leaders and people lower in the Communist Party had concluded that Khrushchev had tried to do too much too soon and had done it poorly. On October 16, 1964, after defeat in the Central Committee of the Communist Party, Khrushchev resigned.

Khrushchev was replaced by Alexei Kosygin (1904–1980) as premier and Leonid Brezhnev (1906–1982) as party secretary. Brezhnev eventually emerged as the dominant figure. He would roll back virtually all of Khrushchev's modest steps toward liberalization and reform.

## Brezhnev and the Invasion of Czechoslovakia

The events in Poland and Hungary of 1956 demonstrated the refusal of the Soviet Union to tolerate significant independence in its Eastern European neighbors. In 1968, during what became known as the *Prague Spring*, the government of Czechoslovakia, under Alexander Dubcek (1921–1992), began to experiment with a more liberal communism. Dubcek expanded freedom of discussion and other intellectual rights at a time when they were being suppressed in the Soviet Union. In the summer of 1968, the Soviet government sent troops into Czechoslovakia and installed communist leaders more to its own liking.

At the time of the invasion, Soviet Party Chairman Brezhnev, in what came to be termed the

# The Warsaw Pact Justifies the Invasion of Czechoslovakia

*In 1968 the Soviet Union and its Warsaw Pact allies invaded Czechoslovakia to halt the political liberalization being carried out by that portion of the Czech Communist Party led by Alexander Dubcek. Their intention was to place other, less liberal communists into power. This invasion provided the occasion for the declaration of the Brezhnev doctrine, according to which the Warsaw Pact members had the right to interfere in the internal affairs of their communist neighbors.*

✦ *On what grounds does the Soviet Union justify its invasion of Czechoslovakia? Why does this justification invoke to the possibility of the Czechs' involvement with foreign enemies? What limits does this justification place on political experimentation in Eastern European nations dominated by the Soviet Union? How could the principles of this justification be applied to other nations under Soviet control?*

Tass [the Soviet Government news agency] is authorized to state that [Communist] party and Government leaders of the Czechoslovak Socialist Republic have asked the Soviet Union and other allied states to render the fraternal Czechoslovak people urgent assistance, including assistance with armed forces. This request was brought about by the threat that has arisen to the socialist system existing in Czechoslovakia and to the statehood established by the Constitution—the threat emanating from the counterrevolutionary forces that have entered into a collusion with foreign forces hostile to socialism.

The events in Czechoslovakia and around her were repeatedly the subject of exchanges of views between leaders of fraternal socialist countries, including the leaders of Czechoslovakia. These countries are unanimous in that the support, consolidation and defense of the people's socialist gains is a common internationalist duty of all the socialist states. . . .

The Soviet Government and the Governments of the allied countries—the People's Republic of Bulgaria, the Hungarian People's Republic, the German Democratic Republic, the Polish People's Republic—proceeding from the principles of inseparable friendship and cooperation and in accordance with the existing contractual commitments, have decided to meet the above-mentioned request for rendering necessary help to the fraternal Czechoslovak people.

The decision is fully in accord with the right of states to individual and collective self-defense envisaged in treaties of alliance concluded between the fraternal socialist countries. This decision is also in line with vital interests of our countries in safeguarding European peace against forces of militarism, aggression and revenge, which have more than once plunged the peoples of Europe into wars.

Soviet armed units, together with armed units of the above-mentioned allied countries, entered the territory of Czechoslovakia on Aug. 21 [1968]. They will be immediately withdrawn from the Czechoslovak Socialist Republic as soon as the obtaining threat to the gains of socialism in Czechoslovakia, the threat to the security of the socialist countries, is eliminated and lawful authorities find that further presence of these armed units there is no longer necessary.

The actions which are being taken are not directed against any state and in no measure infringe state interests of anybody. They serve the purpose of peace and have been prompted by concern for its consolidation.

*The* New York Times, *December 5, 1989, p. A15.*

*Brezhnev Doctrine*, declared the right of the Soviet Union to interfere in the domestic politics of other communist countries. Whereas the Truman Doctrine of 1947 had supported democratic governments and resisted further communist penetration in Europe, the Brezhnev Doctrine of 1968 sought to sustain the communist governments of Eastern Europe and to prevent any liberalization in the region. No further direct Soviet interventions occurred in Eastern Europe after 1968, yet the invasion of Czechoslovakia had profound effects throughout the communist world. It made clear that any political experimentation involving greater liberalization could trigger Soviet military repression.

The invasion of Czechoslovakia was the last major Soviet military intervention in Europe related to the issues surrounding the Cold War. Elsewhere in the world the US–Soviet rivalry produced other major conflicts. These were related to the process of European retreat from colonial empires.

## The European Retreat from Empire

The first two decades of the Cold War took place against the backdrop of the breakup of the great European empires. At the onset of World War II, many of the nations of Europe were still imperial powers. Great Britain, France, Russia, the Netherlands, Belgium, Italy, and Portugal governed millions of non-Europeans. One of the most striking and significant postwar developments was the decolonization of these imperial holdings and the consequent emergence of the so-called Third World political bloc. (See Political Transformations, p. 1096.) The one exception to this decolonization movement was the vast Asiatic empire of the Soviet Union that had been established by the tsars.

### The Effects of World War II

Decolonization since 1945 has been a direct result of both the war itself and the rise of indigenous nationalist movements within the European colonial world. World War II drew the military forces of the colonial powers back to Europe. The Japanese conquests of Asia helped force the European powers from that area. After the military and political dislocations of the war came the postwar economic collapse, which left the European colonial powers unable to afford to maintain their positions abroad.

The war aims of the Allies had also undermined colonialism. It was difficult to fight against tyranny in Europe while maintaining colonial dominance abroad. Within the colonies, nationalist movements of varying strength had arisen. These movements were often led by gifted people who had been educated in Europe. They used the values and political ideologies they had learned in Europe to develop effective critiques of the colonial situation. Such leadership, as well as the frequently blatant injustice imposed on colonial peoples, helped make the nationalist movements effective.

Europe's retreat from empire was also encouraged by the postwar policy of the United States, which opposed the continuation of European empires, and by the emergence of the civil rights movement. Under the leadership of Reverend Martin Luther King, Jr., the US civil rights movement echoed many of the values and ideologies that would drive the European powers' retreat from empire. In Chapter 31 we consider the global democratization movement in the late twentieth century, including the civil rights movement (see the West and the World).

### Major Areas of Colonial Withdrawal

There was a wide variety in decolonization. In some cases, decolonization proceeded systematically; in others, the European powers simply beat a hasty retreat. In 1947 Britain left India, which, as a result of internal disputes, including religious differences, broke into two states, India and Pakistan. In 1948 Burma and Sri Lanka (formerly Ceylon) became independent. During the 1950s, the British tried to prepare colonies for self-government. Ghana (formerly the Gold Coat) and Nigeria—which became self-governing in 1957 and 1960, respectively—were the major examples of planned decolonization. In other areas, such as Malta and Cyprus, the British withdrawal occurred under the pressure of militant nationalist movements.

The smaller colonial powers had much less choice. The Dutch were forced from their East Indies possessions, which became independent as Indonesia, in 1950. In 1960 the Belgian Congo, now Zaire, became independent in the midst of great turmoil. For a considerable time, as will be seen, France tried to maintain its position in Southeast Asia but met defeat in 1954. It was similarly driven from North Africa. President de Gaulle carried out a policy of referendums on independence within the remaining French colonial possessions. By the late 1960s, only Portugal remained a traditional colonial power. Following a revolution in Portugal in 1974, its African colonies of Mozambique and Angola were finally liberated in 1974 and 1975 respectively.

Today in the various republics of the former Soviet Union, non-Europeans are seeking to establish their own political independence separate from the political control of Moscow. It is too early to say what will be the outcome of the various separatist movements in those republics.

# France, the United States, and Vietnam

The problem of decolonization was one of the factors that helped to transfer the Cold War rivalry that had developed in Europe to other continents. French decolonization in particular became an integral part of the Cold War and led directly to the long military involvement of the United States in the Southeast Asian country of Vietnam.

## Resistance to French Colonial Rule

During the years of the Korean conflict, another war was being fought in Asia between France and the Viet Minh nationalist movement in Indochina. France, in its push for empire, had occupied this territory (which contained Laos, Cambodia, and Vietnam) between 1857 and 1883. France had administered the area and had invested heavily in it, but the economy of Indochina remained overwhelmingly agrarian. During World War I, tens of thousands of Indochinese troops supported France. The

French also educated many people from the colony. Neither the military aid the Indochinese provided France nor their Western education, however, prevented the French colonial rulers from discriminating against their subjects.

HO CHI MINH'S LEADERSHIP  By 1930, Ho Chi Minh (1892–1969) had organized a movement against French colonial rule into the Indochinese Communist Party. Ho had traveled throughout the world and had held jobs in several places in Europe before World War I. He and other Indochinese had lobbied at the Versailles conference in 1919 to have the principle of self-determination applied to their country. In 1920 he was part of the wing of the French Socialist Party that formed the French Communist Party. In 1923 he was sent to Moscow. By 1925 he had formed the Vietnam Revolutionary Youth. After organizing the Indochinese Communist Party, he traveled in Asia and spent considerable time in the Soviet Union. Throughout the 1930s, however, the French succeeded in suppressing most activities by the Communist Party in their colony.

World War II provided new opportunities for Ho Chi Minh and other nationalists. When Japan invaded, it found the pro-Vichy French colonial administration ready to collaborate. Thus, action against the Japanese thereafter meshed quite neatly with action against the French. It was during these wartime actions that Ho Chi Minh established his position as a major nationalist leader. He was a communist to be sure, but he was first and foremost a nationalist. Most important, he had achieved his position in Vietnam during the war without the support of the Chinese communist movement.

In September 1945, Ho Chi Minh declared the independence of Vietnam under the Viet Minh, a coalition of nationalists soon dominated by the communists. There was considerable internal Vietnamese resistance to this claim of political control. The opposition arose from religious groups and non-Communist nationalists. After the war, the French immediately took advantage of these divisions to set up a government favorable to their own interests. The United States, in line with its wartime anticolonialist position, urged the French to make some kind of accommodation with Ho Chi Minh.

In 1946 France and the Viet Minh reached an armistice. It was short-lived; in 1947 full-fledged

# POLITICAL
# TRANSFORMATIONS

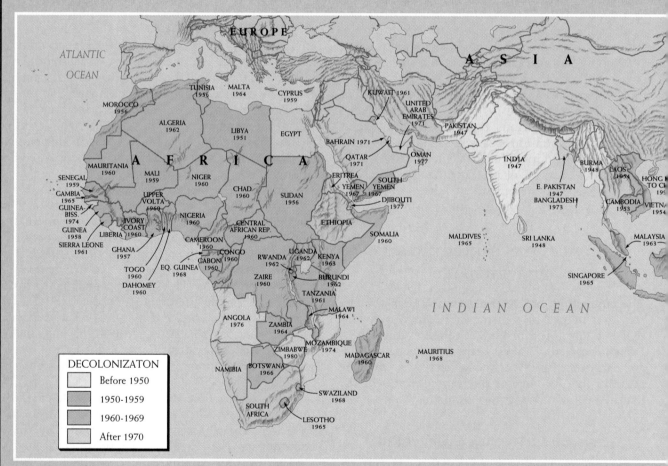

MAP 30–6

# Decolonization in Asia and Africa

For more than two centuries before World War II European powers had dominated or directly ruled large parts of Africa and Asia. The United States had ruled the Philippines from 1898 to 1946. After World War I, many of the colonial peoples had argued unsuccessfully for their independence at the Paris Peace Conference in 1919. Prior to World War II nationalist political movements came to the fore in a number of these colonial empires. After the war, nationalist movements burgeoned throughout most of the colonial world.

The costs of fighting World War II meant the European powers had less wealth with which to govern their colonies. In addition, the principles of the victorious Allies in Europe were inconsistent with colonialism, as was the foreign policy of the United States, now the dominant western power. In Asia, Japan's defeat meant that its armies and officials withdrew from areas that it had conquered earlier in the century. The movement for independence in India that had arisen in the 1920s finally brought about the British retreat from India in 1947. Pakistan and Burma achieved independence in 1947 and 1948 respectively, and Holland left its East Indies colonies in 1950 when Indonesia was organized as a nation. The nationalist movements among the French-governed peoples of Indochina resulted first in war between them and the French and later brought about the long American intervention in Vietnam.

The colonial retreat from Africa took place much more slowly. In North Africa, Morocco and Tunisia became independent in 1956, but France retreated from Algeria only in 1962, after a prolonged civil war. In West Africa the Gold Coast became Ghana in 1957. Thereafter most of West and Central Africa became independent states by the mid-1960s. But Portugal abandoned Angola only in 1976.

The development of these former colonies in the second half of the twentieth century has followed two quite distinct paths. The more recent history of the independent states in Africa has in general been marked by political instability and much poverty. Asia has been an area of general political stability and remarkable economic growth, which has challenged the economies of both the United States and Western Europe.

In the following passage, representatives to the 1945 Fifth Pan-African Congress meeting in Manchaster, England, set forth their demand for freedom.

### Declaration to the Colonial Powers

The delegates believe in peace. How could it be otherwise, when for centuries the African peoples have been the victims of violence and slavery? Yet if the Western world is still determined to rule mankind by force, then Africans, as a last resort, may have to appeal to force in the effort to achieve freedom, even if force destroys them and the world.

We are determined to be free. We want education. We want the right to earn a decent living; the right to express our thoughts and emotions, to adopt and create forms of beauty. We demand for Black Africa autonomy and independence so far and no further than it is possible in this One World for groups and peoples to rule themselves subject to inevitable world unity and federation.

We are not ashamed to have been an age-long patient people. We continue willingly to sacrifice and strive. But we are unwilling to starve any longer while doing the world's drudgery, in order to support by our poverty and ignorance a false aristocracy and a discarded imperialism.

We condemn the monopoly of capital and the rule of private wealth and industry for private profit alone. We welcome economic democracy as the only real democracy.

Therefore, we shall complain, appeal and arraign. We will make the world listen to the fact of our condition. We will fight in every way we can for freedom, democracy, and social betterment.

*Molefi Kete Asante and Abus S. Abarry,* African Intellectual Heritage: A Book of Sources *(Philadelphia: Temple University Press, 1996), pp. 520–521.*

Ho Chi Minh (1892–1969), center, and advisers meet during the war against the French in 1954. [Black Star]

war broke out. The next year, the French established a friendly Vietnamese government under Bao Dai (b. 1911). It was to be independent within a loose union with France. This arrangement would have meant very limited independence and was clearly unacceptable to both the Viet Minh and most other nationalists.

Until 1949 the United States had showed minimal concern about the Indochina War. The defeat of Chiang Kai-shek (1887–1975), however, and the establishment of the Communist People's Republic of China in 1949 dramatically changed its outlook. The United States now saw the French colonial war against Ho Chi Minh as an integral part of the Cold War conflict. The French government, hoping for US support, worked to maintain that point of view. Early in 1950 the United States recognized the Bao Dai government. At about the same time, the Soviet Union and the People's Republic

of China recognized the government of Ho Chi Minh. Indochina was thus transformed from a colonial battleground into an area of Cold War confrontation.

In May 1950, the United States announced that it would supply financial aid to the French war effort. Between that time and 1954, more than $4 billion flowed from the United States to France. Despite this aid, the French position deteriorated. At this point, the U.S. government was badly divided, but it decided against military intervention.

### The Geneva Settlement and Its Aftermath

During early 1954 the French army was engaged in a fierce battle at Dien Bien Phu. The French unsuccessfully sought American air support for their garrison there. During the late spring of 1954 while the battle raged, a conference opened at Geneva to settle the Indochina conflict. In the midst of this conference the French garrison at Dien Bien Phu fell. In early June Pierre Mendès-France (1907–1982), having campaigned on a platform to end the war, became the French premier. By late June a complicated peace accord had been secured.

The Geneva conference proved a most unsatisfactory gathering. To one degree or another, all the major powers were involved in the proceedings, but they did not sign the agreements. Technically, the agreements were between the armed forces of France and those of the Viet Minh. The precedents for such arrangements were the surrender of the German army in 1945 and the Korean armistice of 1953.

NORTH AND SOUTH VIETNAM   The Geneva conference provided for the division of Vietnam at the seventeenth parallel of latitude. This was to be a temporary border. By 1956 elections were to be held to reunify the country. North of the parallel, centered in Hanoi, the Viet Minh were in charge; below it, centered in Saigon, the French were in charge. The prospect of elections meant that theoretically both groups could function politically in the terri-

tory of the other. In effect, the conference attempted to transform a military conflict into a political one.

The United States was less than happy about the results of the Geneva discussions. Its first major response came in September 1954, with the formation of the Southeast Asia Treaty Organization (SEATO). This collective security agreement in some respects paralleled the European NATO alliance. It did not, however, involve the integration of military forces achieved in NATO, nor did it include all the major states of the region. Its membership consisted of the United States, Great Britain, France, Australia, New Zealand, Thailand, Pakistan, and the Philippines.

By 1955 American policymakers had begun to think about the Indochina region, and more especially Vietnam, largely in terms of the Korean example. The US government assumed that the government being established in North Vietnam was, like the government of North Korea, basically a communist puppet. The same year, French troops began to withdraw from South Vietnam. As they left, the various Vietnamese political groups began to fight for power.

*In French Indo-China which became North and South Vietnam under the armistice of 1954, Communist forces took over the northern region. Here, a crowd in Hanoi watches as Communist troops occupy the city. [UPI/Corbis-Bettman]*

**THE UNITED STATES AND THE DIEM GOVERNMENT**
The United States stepped into this turmoil with military and economic aid. Among the Vietnamese politicians, it chose to support Ngo Dinh Diem (1901–1963). He was a strong noncommunist nationalist who had not collaborated with the French. The Americans hoped that he would become a leader around whom a noncommunist Vietnamese nationalist movement might rally. Because the United States had been publicly and deeply committed to the French, however, any government it supported would be, and was, viewed with suspicion by Vietnamese nationalists. In October 1955, Diem established a Republic of Vietnam in the territory for which the Geneva conference had made France responsible. By 1956 the United States was training troops and government officials, paying salaries, and providing military equipment.

In the meantime, Diem announced that he and his newly established government were not bound by the Geneva agreements and that elections would not be held in 1956. The American government, which had not signed the Geneva documents, supported his position. Diem undertook an anticommunist campaign, attacking many citizens who had earlier resisted the French. This was the beginning of a program of political repression that characterized his regime and those that followed.

There was a long series of ordinances that gave Diem's government extraordinary power over its citizens. Diem alienated the peasants by restoring rents to landlords and generally strengthening large landowners. He abolished elected village councils and replaced them with his own officials, who had often come from the North. In fact, Diem's major base of political support lay with the more than one million Vietnamese who had migrated to the South after 1954.

By 1960 Diem's policy had created considerable internal resistance in South Vietnam. In that year, the National Liberation Front was founded, with the goals of overthrowing Diem, unifying the country, reforming the economy, and ousting the Americans. It was anticolonial, nationalist, and communist. Its military arm was called the Viet Cong. Sometime in the late 1950s, the government of North Vietnam began to aid the insurgent forces of the South. (See Map 30–7.) The Viet Cong and their supporters carried out a program of widespread terrorism and political disruption. They imposed an informal government through much of the coun-

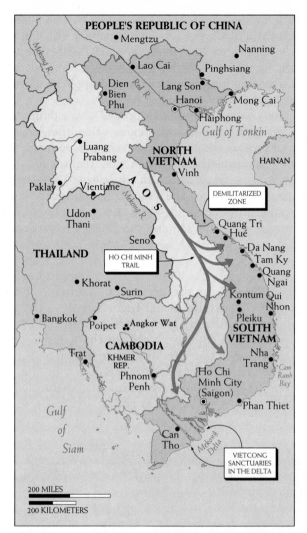

MAP 30–7 VIETNAM AND ITS NEIGHBORS *This map identifies important locations in the long and complex struggle centered in Vietnam.*

tryside. Many peasants voluntarily supported them; others supported them from fear of reprisals.

In addition to the communist opposition, Diem faced mounting criticism from noncommunist citizens. The Buddhists agitated against the Roman Catholic president. The army was less than satisfied with him. Diem's response to all these pressures was further repression and dependence on an ever smaller group of advisers.

### The US Involvement

The Eisenhower and early Kennedy administrations in the United States continued to support Diem while demanding reforms in his government. The American military presence grew from somewhat more than 600 people in early 1961 to more than 16,000 troops in late 1963. The political situation in Vietnam became increasingly unstable. On November 1, 1963, Diem was overthrown and murdered in an army coup. The United States was deeply involved in this plot. Kennedy and his advisers hoped that if the Diem regime were eliminated, the path would be opened to establish a new government in South Vietnam capable of generating popular support. Thereafter, the political goal of the United States was to find a leader who could fill this need. It finally settled on Nguyen Van Thieu (b. 1923), who governed South Vietnam from 1966 to 1975.

President Kennedy was assassinated on November 22, 1963. His successor, Lyndon Johnson, continued and vastly expanded the commitment to South Vietnam. In August 1964, after an attack on an American ship in the Gulf of Tonkin, the first bombing of North Vietnam was authorized. In February 1965, major bombing attacks began, and continued, with only brief pauses, until the early weeks of 1973. The land war grew year by year until, at its peak, more than 500,000 Americans were stationed in South Vietnam.

In 1969 President Richard Nixon began a policy known as *Vietnamization*, which was gradual withdrawal from Vietnam while slowly turning over the full military effort to the South Vietnamese army.

*United States armed forces patrol in Vietnam. At the war's peak, more than 500,000 American troops were stationed in South Vietnam. The United States struggled in Vietnam for more than a decade, seriously threatening its commitment to Western Europe. [C. Simonpietri/SYGMA]*

The war, which grew out of a power vacuum left by decolonization, had a major impact on the entire Western world. For a decade after the Cuban missile crisis, the attention of the United States was largely diverted from Europe. American prestige suffered, and the American commitment to Western Europe came into question. Moreover, the American policy in Southeast Asia made many Europeans wonder about the basic wisdom of the American government. Many young Europeans—and not a few Americans—born after World War II came to regard the United States not as a protector of liberty but as an ambitious, aggressive, and cruel power trying to keep colonialism alive after the end of the colonial era.

# The Middle East After Suez

In many respects the ongoing conflicts of the Middle East also represented part of the process of decolonization. Here, the political instability of the region arose from the political vacuum left by Britain's retreat from what had been a major sphere of direct and indirect influence.

## *The 1967 Six Days' War*

After the unsuccessful Suez intervention of 1956 an uneasy peace continued in the region. Meanwhile, the Soviet Union increased its influence in Egypt, and the United States did the same in Israel. Both great powers supplied weapons to their friends in the area. Then, in 1967, President Nasser took actions that, as in 1956, disrupted the stability of the region. Nasser calculated, mistakenly, that the Arab nations could defeat Israel, by then nearly two decades old. He began to mass troops in the Sinai Peninsula and attempted to close the Gulf of Aqaba to Israeli shipping. Nasser also demanded the withdrawal of the UN peacekeeping force. Diplomatic activity failed to stem the crisis and the Arab attempt to isolate Israel.

On June 5, 1967, the armed forces of Israel, under the direction of Defense Minister Moshe Dayan (1915–1981), attacked Egyptian airfields rather than endure additional provocation by Egypt. Almost immediately, Syria and Jordan entered the war on the side of Egypt. Yet, by June 11, the Six Days' War was over, and Israel had won a stunning victory.

Drawn-out peace negotiations had begun in Paris in the spring of 1968, but it was not until January 1973 that a ceasefire was finally arranged. The troops of the United States were pulled back, and prisoners of war held in North Vietnam were returned. Thereafter, violations of the ceasefire occurred on both sides. In early 1975 an evacuation of South Vietnamese troops from the northern part of their country turned into a complete rout as they were attacked by the troops of North Vietnam. On April 30, 1975, Saigon fell to the troops of the Viet Cong and North Vietnam. The Second Indochina War had ended.

The Second Indochina War was, in effect, a continuation of the first war, which the French had lost. The United States saw the conflict as part of the Cold War and as a repetition of what had occurred in Korea. Aggression from the North had to be halted. It was hoped too, that the military power of the United States might buy time so that a strong nationalist, noncommunist regime could be established in South Vietnam.

The military forces of Egypt lay in shambles. Moreover, Israel had occupied the entire Egyptian Sinai Peninsula, as well as the West Bank region along the Jordan River that had been part of the state of Jordan. This victory marked the height of Israeli power and prestige.

## Egyptian Policy Under Anwar el-Sadat

In 1970 President Nasser died. He was succeeded by Anwar el-Sadat (1918–1981). Sadat's first task was to shore up his support at home. The existing tensions between Israel and the defeated Egypt, of course, continued, and the Soviet Union still poured weapons into Egypt. Sadat, however, deeply distrusted the Soviets and in 1972 he ordered them to leave Egypt.

Sadat and his advisers also felt that only another war with Israel could return to Egypt the lands lost in 1967. In October 1973, on the Jewish holy day of Yom Kippur, the military forces of Egypt and Syria launched an attack across the Suez Canal into Israeli-held territory. The invasion came as a complete surprise to the Israelis. Initially, the Egyptian forces made considerable headway. Then the Israeli army thrust back the invasion. In November 1973, a truce was signed between the forces in the Sinai. Although Israel had successfully repelled the Egyptians, the cost in lives and prestige because of the surprise nature of the Egyptian attack was very high.

The Yom Kippur War added a major new element to the Middle East problem. In the fall of 1973, when the war broke out, the major Arab oil-producing states shut off the flow of oil to the United States and Europe. This dramatic move was an attempt to force the Western powers to use their influence to moderate the policy of Israel. The threat of the loss of oil was particularly frightening to Europeans, whose industry depends on it. At that time (prior to the development of the North Sea oil fields), Western Europe depended almost entirely on Middle Eastern oil.

In November 1977, President Sadat of Egypt, in a dramatic personal gesture, flew to Israel. He addressed the Israeli Parliament and held discussions with Prime Minister Menachem Begin (1913–1992), although the two states were still technically at war. In effect, for the first time the head of a major Arab state recognized the existence of Israel. Previously, all contacts had taken place through either the United Nations or other third parties.

## The Camp David Accords and the PLO

The Sadat initiative, roundly condemned in many Arab quarters, resulted in direct conversations. The most important occurred at Camp David in the United States with President Carter as moderator. The Camp David Accords of September 1978 have provided one framework for continuing negotiations on Middle East questions.

In early 1981 Prime Minister Begin's coalition was reelected, but in October of that year President Sadat was assassinated by Muslim extremists. Sadat's death cast doubt on the long-range stability of the Camp David process. Further strains appeared in late December 1981, when the Israeli Parliament suddenly annexed the Golan Heights while the attention of most of the Western world was on the crisis in Poland.

Until 1986 no other Arab states entered into formal negotiations with Israel. The major stumbling block to an agreement had been the Palestinian refugee problem. The Palestine Liberation Organization (PLO) was then and remains the major representative for the refugees. The PLO demanded a separate Palestinian state; the government of Israel steadily refused to recognize the PLO. Israel also believed that virtually any independent Palestinian state would be a threat to its own independence and ultimate survival.

## Lebanon and the Intifada

For years, Lebanon had served as a base for PLO terrorists' attacks on Israel. In 1982, in order to destroy the PLO bases and to disperse the PLO leadership, Israeli troops invaded Lebanon. They were largely successful. At the same time, however, the fragile Lebanese state, long racked by civil war, virtually collapsed. For a few months in 1983, the United States stationed marines in Lebanon. After a terrorist bombing killed more than 300 troops, the marines were withdrawn. In 1985 Israeli troops withdrew. Syrian troops remained and battled with the various Lebanese factions and their armies. Various radical Arab factions held British, French, and American citizens as hostages to attempt to put pressure on their governments. Lebanon has remained a center of political and social disorder.

In 1983 Begin, who was in ill health, resigned as prime minister of Israel. He was succeeded by a series of coalition governments. One of the most important developments in the region has been the *intifada*, the Arab uprising against Israeli rule that began in 1987 on the West Bank. This area was conquered in the 1967 war, but it has neither been annexed to Israel nor made independent. The Israelis have responded to the political and social unrest and the frequent local revolts on the West Bank since 1987 with increasing and often deadly force. Their actions have generated intense controversy both in Israel and the world community.

A series of events beginning in 1988 that led to unexpected and complicated diplomatic developments can only be summarized here. Late in 1988 the PLO, led by Yasir Arafat (b. 1929), publicly stated that Israel had a right to exist and that it would henceforth refrain from terrorist activity. Earlier that year, the PLO had declared the existence of a Palestinian state in the West Bank and Gaza.

In 1990 Iraq invaded Kuwait. In the months following, the United States organized a worldwide coalition to drive Iraq from Kuwait. That coalition included the Soviet Union, all the major European powers, Japan, Israel, Saudi Arabia, and other Arab states. Among the Arabs, only Jordan and the PLO supported Iraq. During a brief war in 1991, the coalition drove Iraq from Kuwait. The result was viewed not only as a defeat for Iraq but as a defeat for the entire radical Arab cause. Thereafter Saudi Arabia and other wealthy Arab states either decreased or ended their financial support of the PLO. The full details of those arrangements are still not fully public, but by the end of 1991, the PLO found itself increasingly isolated within the Arab world. Furthermore, events in the Soviet Union that will be discussed in the next chapter removed effective Soviet support from the PLO as well.

During the early 1990s, the United States sponsored peace talks in the Middle East. By early 1993 the Israeli government decided to permit meetings between the PLO and Israelis. Several months of secret negotiations followed, sponsored by Norway. In September 1993, Israel and the PLO signed a formal agreement recognizing each other and agreeing to Palestinian self-government in Gaza and the city of Jericho. The agreement came as a general surprise to the entire world community. Signed in Washington, DC, on September 14, 1993, it left most details to further negotiation. It has, nonetheless, transformed the diplomatic situation in the Middle East. Israel and various of the Arab states have since moved toward formal diplomatic recognition. Radical groups among both the Israelis and the Palestinians have opposed the agreement and carried out terrorist action to disrupt its implementation. In 1995 an Israeli assassinated Prime Minister Rabin, who had favored the peace process. In 1996 political groups in Israel, highly skeptical of the peace process, elected a coalition of political parties who elected Benyamin Netanyahu as prime minister.

Of the various flash points of the Cold War, the Middle East remains the most volatile, though new tensions could also loom on the Korean peninsula. The Arab–Israeli conflict pre-dated the Cold War, and the US–Soviet rivalry shaped the character of the conflict during four decades. The situation in the Middle East, whatever its ultimate outcome, is now transforming itself outside the economic and political structures of the Cold War.

In 1993 the leaders of Israel and the Palestine Liberation Organization signed a peace accord in Washington, D.C. Here, Prime Minister Yitzhak Rabin of Israel and PLO Chairman Yasir Arafat shake hands as President Bill Clinton of the United States looks on. [Reuters/Gary Hershorn/Archive Photos]

## Western European Political Developments During the Cold War

For the decades spanning the Cold War, the US involvement in Vietnam, the ongoing pressures of Middle Eastern conflict, and the continuing Soviet domination of Eastern Europe, the nations of Western Europe achieved unprecedented economic prosperity and maintained liberal democratic governments. All of them confronted the problems associated both with decolonization and with maintaining economic growth. France, in addition, faced a difficult path to long-term political stability.

After the war, except for Portugal and Spain, which remained dictatorships until the mid-1970s, the nations of Western Europe followed the path of liberal democracy. Their leaders realized, however, that the prewar democratic political structures had been insufficient to ensure peace, stability, material prosperity, and domestic liberty for their peoples. It had become clear that democracy required a social and economic base as well as a political structure. Most Europeans came to feel it was the duty of government to assure economic prosperity and social security. Success at doing so, they believed, would stave off the kind of turmoil that had brought on tyranny and war and that could lead to communism.

### Christian Democratic Parties

Except for the British Labour Party, the vehicles of the new postwar politics were not, as might have been expected, the democratic socialist parties. On the whole, those parties did not prosper after the onset of the Cold War. They stood opposed by both communists and groups more conservative than themselves. Rather, the new policies were introduced by various Christian democratic parties, usually leading coalition governments.

These parties were a major new feature of postwar politics. They were largely Roman Catholic in leadership and membership. Catholic parties had previously existed in Europe. From the late nineteenth century through the 1930s, however, they had been very conservative and had protected the social, political, and educational interests of the church. They had traditionally opposed communism but proposed few positive programs of their own. The postwar Christian democratic parties of Germany, France, and Italy, however, were progressive. They accepted democracy and advocated social reform. They welcomed non-Catholic members. Democracy, social reform, economic growth, and anticommunism were their hallmarks.

The events of the war years largely determined the political leadership of the postwar decade. On the Continent, those groups and parties, including communist parties, that had been active in the resistance against Nazism and Fascism held an initial advantage. After 1947, however, in a policy quite naturally favored by the United States, communists were systematically excluded from all Western European governments.

The most immediate postwar domestic problems included not only those created by the physical damage of the conflict but often also those that had existed in 1939. The war, however, although it may not have ended those prewar difficulties, opened new opportunities for solving them.

Margaret Thatcher, Britain's first woman prime minister, took office in 1979. She moved against trade unions and promoted a more nearly free-market economy. [Peter Marlow/SYGMA]

### Economic Concerns

Within Western Europe, with the exception of France, the economy dominated all other political issues from the end of World War II onward. The most remarkable success story of those years was what became known as the "economic miracle" of West Germany. That nation, under both Christian Democratic and Social Democratic ministries, achieved unprecedented levels of prosperity. In Great Britain, the Labour ministry of Clement Attlee, which governed from 1945 to 1950, introduced the welfare state and nationalized several major industries. In 1997, after eighteen years of Conservative government, the Labour Party returned to power but on a platform of much more limited state intervention. From the 1960s through the 1970s, clashes between unions and business became commonplace. When Margaret Thatcher (b. 1925), the first woman prime minister of Great Britain, took office in 1979, she moved strongly against the unions and pressed for a more nearly free market economy.

### The Search for Stability in France

For more than a decade after World War II France experienced a lack of consistent leadership and much political turmoil at the top of its political structure. Many of its problems arose from its postcolonial struggles in Indochina and Algeria.

Shortly after the war, French citizens ratified a constitution that established the Fourth Republic. Charles de Gaulle, who had led the forces of Free

*Charles de Gaulle returned to power as president of France in 1958 during the turmoil of the war in Algeria. He extricated France from Algeria, imposed the constitution that established the Fifth Republic, and for ten years led France on a determinedly independent course. [Bildarchiv Preussischer Kulturbesitz]*

thousands of workers went on strike. After assuring himself the support of the army, de Gaulle made a brief television speech to rally his followers. Soon they, too, came into the streets to demonstrate in support of de Gaulle and stability. The strikes ended and police moved against the student groups. The government, to prevent more unrest, quickly moved to improve the wages and benefits of workers. The events of May 1968 revealed the fragility of the Fifth Republic, but they also showed that the many citizens who had benefitted from France's postwar economic progress had enough stake in the status quo to fear and prevent disruption.

In 1969 President de Gaulle resigned after some minor constitutional changes he had proposed were rejected in a referendum. French political life became remarkably stable thereafter. In contrast to de Gaulle, his various successors, most importantly Valéry Giscard d'Estaing (b. 1926), a Gaullist, and François Mitterand (1916–1996), a Socialist, strongly supported European unification. Mixed electoral results have required the various French political parties to learn to cooperate and accommodate themselves to each other.

# Toward Western European Unification

Western European nations have taken unprecedented steps toward economic cooperation and unity during the past four decades. This process arose originally from American encouragement in response to the Soviet domination of Eastern Europe and from the Western European states' own sense that they lacked effective political power. There were also domestic political and economic considerations at work. France, for example, championed economic integration because it needed to expand its intra-European trade and feared that otherwise the resurgent German economy would dominate the Continent. For many years Great Britain resisted joining the effort because of anxiety over loss of its own economic and political independence and its position as leader of the British Commonwealth.

## Postwar Cooperation

The movement toward unity could have occurred in at least three ways: politically, militarily, or eco-

France during the war, grew disgusted with the politicians of the new republic and left government. He returned to power in 1958 during the turmoil and unrest that accompanied France's war in Algeria. He imposed a new constitution establishing the Fifth French Republic and led a strategic retreat from Algeria that culminated in Algerian independence in 1962.

For ten years de Gaulle led France according to his own priorities. Those included hostility to the United States and Great Britain, maintenance of an independent French nuclear capacity, and a tense relationship with NATO. In May 1968, however, he faced a domestic upheaval that nearly toppled his government. The troubles began among student groups in Paris but quickly spread. Hundreds of

nomically. The economic path was taken largely because the other paths were blocked. In 1949, ten European states organized the Council of Europe, which meets in Strasbourg, France. Its organization involved foreign ministers and a Consultative Assembly elected by the parliaments of the participants. The Council of Europe was and continues to be only an advisory body. Some had hoped that the council might become a parliament of Europe, but during the early 1950s none of the major states was willing to surrender any sovereignty to the newly organized body. The initial failure of the council to foster significant political cooperation ruled out for the time being the political or parliamentary routes to unification.

Between 1950 and 1954, there was some interest in a more thorough integration of the military forces of NATO. When the Korean War broke out, the United States began to urge the rearmament of West Germany. The German forces would provide Western Europe with further protection against possible Soviet aggression while the United States was involved in Korea. France, however, continued to fear a German army. In 1951 the French government suggested the creation of a European Defense Community that would constitute a supranational military organization. This organization would have required a permanent British commitment of forces to the Continent to help France counter any future German threat. The proposal was considered for some time, but in 1954 the French Parliament itself vetoed it. In 1955 West Germany was permitted to rearm and to enter NATO. Supranational military organization had not been achieved.

Economic cooperation, unlike military and political cooperation, involved little or no immediate loss of sovereignty. Furthermore, it brought material benefits to all the states involved, increasing popular support for their governments.

The Marshall Plan of the United States created the Organization for European Economic Cooperation (OEEC). This vehicle was set up to require common planning and cooperation among the participating countries and to discourage a return to prewar economic nationalism. The OEEC and NATO, as well as other economic organizations tied to the Marshall Plan, gave the countries involved new experience in working with each other and demonstrated the productivity and efficiency that resulted from cooperative action.

Among European leaders and civil servants, the opinion was widespread that only through the abandonment of economic nationalism could the newly organized democratic states avoid the economic turmoil that had proved such fertile ground for dictatorship. Economic cooperation carried the possibility of greater efficiency, prosperity, and employment. The leading proponents of this viewpoint were Robert Schuman (1886–1963), the foreign minister of France; Konrad Adenauer (1876–1967), the chancellor of the Federal Republic of Germany; Alcide De Gasperi (1881–1954), the prime minister of Italy; and Paul-Henri Spaak (1899–1972), the prime minister of Belgium. Among major civil servants and bureaucrats, Jean Monnet (1885–1981) of France was the leading representative.

In 1950 Schuman proposed that coal and steel production in Western Europe be organized on an integrated, cooperative basis. The next year, France, West Germany, Italy, and the "Benelux" countries (Belgium, the Netherlands, and Luxembourg) organized the European Coal and Steel Community. Its activity was limited to a single sector of the economy, but that sector affected almost all other industrial production. An agency called the *High Authority* administered the plan. The authority was genuinely supranational, and its members could not be removed during their appointed terms. The Coal and Steel Community prospered. By 1955, coal production had grown by 23 percent; iron and steel production was up by almost 150 percent. The community both benefitted from and contributed to the immense growth of material production in Western Europe during this period. Its success reduced the suspicions of government and business groups about coordination and economic integration.

### The European Economic Community

It took more than the prosperity of the European Coal and Steel Community to draw European leaders toward further unity. The unsuccessful Suez intervention and the resulting diplomatic isolation of France and Britain persuaded many Europeans that only through unified action could they exert any significant influence on the two superpowers or control their own destinies. So, in 1957, through the Treaty of Rome, the six members of the Coal and Steel Community agreed to form a new organization: the European Economic Community (EEC). The members of the *Common Market*, as the EEC soon came to be called, envisioned more than

*The move to achieve economic unity within Europe by eliminating all internal trade barriers and restrictive trade policies has encountered organized resistance. These French farmers are demonstrating against EEC policies. [Gamma-Liaison]*

a free-trade union. They sought to achieve the eventual elimination of tariffs, a free flow of capital and labor, and similar wage and social benefits in all the participating countries. The chief institutions of the EEC were a Council of Foreign Ministers and a High Commission, composed of technocrats. The former came to be the dominant body.

The Common Market achieved a stunning degree of success during its early years. By 1968, well ahead of schedule, all tariffs among the six members had been abolished. Trade and labor migration among the members grew steadily. Moreover, non-member states began to copy the EEC and later to seek membership. In 1959 Britain, Denmark, Norway, Sweden, Switzerland, Austria, and Portugal formed the European Free Trade Area. By 1961, however, Great Britain had decided to seek Common Market membership. Twice, in 1963 and

1967, British membership was vetoed by President de Gaulle of France. He felt that Britain was too closely tied to the United States to support the EEC wholeheartedly.

The French veto of British membership demonstrated the major difficulty facing the Common Market during the 1960s. The Council of Ministers, representing the individual national interests of member states, came to have more influence than the High Commission. Political as well as economic factors increasingly entered into decision making. France particularly was unwilling to compromise on any matter that it regarded as pertaining to its sovereignty. On more than one occasion, President de Gaulle demanded enactment of his own policies and refused French participation under any other conditions. This attitude caused major problems over agricultural policy.

Despite the French actions, the Common Market survived and continued to prosper. In 1973 Great Britain, Ireland, and Denmark became members. Discussions continued on further steps toward integration, including proposals for a common currency. Throughout the late 1970s, however, and into the 1980s, there was a loss of momentum. Norway and Sweden, with relatively strong economies, declined to join. Although in 1982 Spain, Portugal, and Greece applied for membership and were eventually admitted, sharp disagreements and a sense of stagnation within the EEC continued.

### The European Union

After this decade of disagreement and loss of direction, the leaders of the EEC reached an important decision in early 1988. They targeted the year 1992 for achieving a virtual free-trade zone throughout the EEC, entailing the elimination of the remaining trade barriers and other restrictive trade policies. In 1991 the leaders of the EEC signed the Treaty of Maastricht, which made a series of specific proposals leading to a unified currency and to a strong central bank. This treaty was submitted to referendums in several European states. It initially failed to be adopted in Denmark and only narrowly passed in France and Great Britain, making clear that it could not be enforced without wider popular support. When the treaty took effect in November 1993, the EEEC was renamed the European Union.

The troubles of the Treaty of Maastricht illustrate a new and important phase in the process of achieving European unity. Until recently, the process had been carried out primarily by political leaders and by bureaucrats in the individual governments and in the EEC's High Commission in Brussels. As the prospect of unity has become stronger, however, the people of Europe have begun to raise issues that relate to the democratic nature of the emerging political entity they are being asked to join. They clearly favor close cooperation and perhaps union, but they are unwilling to see it defined only by politicians and bureaucrats. They wish to see a wider European market, but they want that market to be genuinely free and not overregulated. Two major political concerns also confront the European Union. It must decide how to relate to the host of newly independent states in Eastern Europe whose economies and governments are less strong than those of the present members of the Union. Second, considerable concern exists in Europe about the profound influence of Germany and the German economy in the European Union. Germany, now unified, constitutes both the largest nation and largest economy of Europe. Europeans are concerned that the further development of the European Union not constitute the foundation for German economic and political domination of the continent.

# Protest and Repression: The Brezhnev Era in the Soviet Union and Eastern Europe

While Western Europe moved toward unity and experienced democracy and considerable prosperity during the seventies and early eighties, the Soviet Union and Eastern Europe saw some significant protests against communist government, but protests that were quickly repressed.

### Dissidents

Under Brezhnev, the Soviet government became markedly more repressive at home, suggesting a return to Stalinist policies. Intellectual freedoms were curtailed, and intellectuals were given little direct access to the government leadership. In 1974 the government expelled novelist Aleksandr Solzhenitsyn. It also began to harass Jewish citizens, creating bureaucratic obstacles for those who wanted to emigrate to Israel.

The internal repression gave rise to a dissident movement. Certain Soviet citizens dared to criticize the regime in public and to carry out small demonstrations against the government. They accused the government of violating the human rights provision of the 1975 Helsinki Accords (described in the next section). The dissidents included several prominent citizens, such as the Nobel Prize-winning physicist Andrei Sakharov (1921–1989). The Soviet government responded with further repression.

In 1977 the constitution of the Soviet Union was changed to combine the offices of president and party secretary. Brezhnev became president, and thus head of the state as well as of the party. He held more personal power than any Soviet leader since Stalin.

## Foreign Policy and Relations with the United States

Soviet foreign policy under Brezhnev combined attempts to reach an accommodation with the United States with continued efforts to expand Soviet influence and maintain Soviet leadership of the communist movement.

### The United States and Détente

Although the Soviet Union sided with North Vietnam in its war with the United States, its support was restrained. Under President Richard Nixon (1969–1974), the United States began a policy of détente with the Soviet Union and the two countries concluded agreements on trade and mutual reduction of strategic arms. Despite these agreements, Soviet spending on defense, and particularly on its navy, continued to grow, damaging the consumer sectors of the economy. Nixon resigned the presidency in 1974 as a result of the Watergate scandal.

During Gerald Ford's subsequent presidency (1974–1977), the United States and the Soviet Union both signed the Helsinki Accords, recognizing the Soviet sphere of influence in Eastern Europe. The signers of the accords, including the Soviet Union, also committed themselves to recognize and protect the human rights of their citizens. President Jimmy Carter (1977–1981), a strong advocate of human rights, sought to induce the Soviet Union to comply with this commitment, cooling relations between the two countries. Relations hardened further when the Soviet Union invaded Afghanistan in 1979.

INVASION OF AFGHANISTAN   Although the Soviet Union already had a presence in Afghanistan, the Brezhnev government, for reasons that remain unclear, felt it had to send in troops to ensure its influence in central Asia. The 1979 invasion brought a sharp response from the United States. The US Senate refused to ratify a second Strategic Arms Limitation agreement that President Carter had signed earlier that year. The United States also embargoed grain shipments to the Soviet Union and boycotted the 1980 Olympic Games in Moscow. As Soviet forces bogged down in Afghanistan, the invasion grew increasingly unpopular within the Soviet Union.

RELATIONS WITH THE REAGAN ADMINISTRATION   Brezhnev died in 1982, early in the administration of President Ronald Reagan (1981–1989) in the United States. Under Reagan, the United States relaxed its grain embargo and placed less emphasis on human rights. At the same time, however, Reagan intensified Cold War rhetoric. More important, he sharply increased US military spending, slowed arms limitation negotiations, successfully deployed a major new missile system in Europe, and proposed the Strategic Defense Initiative (dubbed *Star Wars* by the press), involving a high-technology defense in space against nuclear attack. The Star Wars proposal, although very controversial in the United States, was a major issue in later arms control negotiations between the Soviet Union and the United States. Combined with the Reagan defense spending, Star Wars forced the Soviet Union to increase defense spending when it could ill afford to do so, contributing to the economic problems that helped bring about its collapse. (See Chapter 31.)

### Communism and Solidarity in Poland

Events in Poland in the late 1970s—a time when the Soviet government was becoming increasingly rigidified and involved in Afghanistan—challenged both the authority of the Polish Communist Party and the influence of the Soviet Union.

After 1956 the Polish Communist Party, led by Wladyslaw Gomulka (1905–1982), made peace with the Roman Catholic Church, halted land collectivization, established trade with the West, and participated in cultural exchange programs with noncommunist nations. Poland was plagued, however, by chronic economic mismanagement and persistent shortages of food and consumer goods. In 1970 food shortages led to a series of strikes, the most famous of which occurred in the shipyards of Gdansk. In December 1970, the Polish authorities broke the strike at the cost of a number of workers' lives. These events led to the departure of Gomulka. His successor was Edward Gierek (b. 1913).

In the decade after 1970, the Polish economy made very little progress. Food and other consumer goods remained in short supply. In early July 1980, the Polish government raised meat prices, leading to hundreds of protest strikes across the country. On August 14, workers occupied the Lenin shipyard at Gdansk. The strike soon spread to other shipyards, transport facilities, and factories connected

# The Premier of Poland Announces the Imposition of Martial Law

*On December 13, 1981, General Wojciech Jaruzelski, the premier of Poland and the head of the Polish Communist Party, announced the imposition of martial law. The action was taken after months of liberal reform in Poland led by the independent trade union Solidarity. The government turned to military rule out of fear that the political activity of Solidarity would endanger the rule of the Communist Party in Poland. The announced reason for the imposition of martial law was to prevent disorder.*

✦ *What events in Poland had led to this imposition of martial law? How did Jaruzelski use fear of disorder to justify his action? Why did both the Polish Communist government and the Soviet Union so fear the activities of Solidarity? Are there any indications in this statement that Jaruzelski may have feared a Soviet invasion of Poland if the Polish Communist government did not itself take action?*

Our country is on the edge of the abyss. Achievements of many generations, raised from the ashes, are collapsing into ruin. State structures no longer function. New blows are struck each day at our flickering economy. Living conditions are burdening people more and more.

Through each place of work, in many Polish people's homes, there is a line of painful division. The atmosphere of unending conflict, misunderstanding and hatred sows mental devastation and damages the traditions of tolerance.

Strikes, strike alerts, protest actions have become standard. Even students are dragged into it. . . .

With our aims, it cannot be said that we [the Communist Party government] did not show good will, moderation, patience, and sometimes there was probably too much of it. It cannot be said the Government did not honor the social agreements [made with Solidarity in 1980 at Gdansk]. We even went further. The initiative of the great national understanding was backed by the millions of Poles. It created a chance, an opportunity to deepen the system of democracy of people ruling the country, widening reforms. Those hopes failed.

Around the negotiating table there was no leadership from Solidarity. Words said in Random and in Gdansk [strike calls and political demands from Solidarity] showed the real aims of its leadership. These aims are confirmed by everyday practice, growing aggressiveness of the extremists, clearly aiming to take apart the Polish state system.

How long can one wait for a sobering up? How long can a hand reached for accord meet a fist? I say this with a broken heart, with bitterness. It could have been different in our country. It should have been different. But if the current state had lasted longer, it would have led to a catastrophe, to absolute chaos, to poverty and starvation. . . .

I declare that today the army Council of National Salvation has been constituted, and the Council of State obeying the Polish Constitution declared a state of emergency at midnight on the territory of Poland. . . .

*The* New York Times, *December 14, 1981, p. 16.*

with the shipbuilding industry. The most important leader to emerge from among the strikers was Lech Walesa (b. 1944). He and the other strike leaders refused to negotiate with the government through any of the traditionally government-controlled unions. The Gdansk strike ended on August 31 after the government promised the workers the right to organize an independent union. The agreement with the government guaranteed both the new union—called Solidarity—and the Polish Roman Catholic Church the right of access to the news media, including television.

Less than a week later, on September 6, Gierek was dismissed as the head of the Polish Communist Party. He was replaced by Stanislaw Kania (b. 1927). Later in September, the Polish courts recognized Solidarity as an independent union, and the state-controlled radio for the first time in thirty years broadcast a Roman Catholic mass.

The summer of 1981 saw events that were no less remarkable occurring within the Polish Communist Party itself. For the first time in any European communist state, secret elections for the party congress were permitted with real choices among the candidates. Poland remained a nation governed by a single party, but for the time being, real debate was permitted within the party congress.

This extraordinary Polish experiment came to a rapid close in late 1981. General Wojciech Jaruzelski (b. 1923) became head of the Polish Communist Party, and the army moved into the center of Polish events. In December 1981, martial law was declared. The government moved against Solidarity and arrested several of its leaders. The Polish military leaders succeeded for the time being with this political repression. They acted to preserve their own position and perhaps to prevent a Soviet invasion similar to the one in Czechoslovakia in 1968. The Polish Communist Party proved unsuccessful, however, in addressing Poland's major economic problems. Martial law would continue in effect until late in the 1980s.

By the time of Brezhnev's death in 1982, the entire Soviet system had grown rigid and seemed hardly capable of meeting the needs of its people or pursuing a successful foreign policy. Until the middle of the 1980s, however, virtually no observers expected rapid change in the Soviet Union or its satellites. The nations of Eastern Europe were expected to continue with one-party governments, their aspirations for self-determination smothered, and with only limited possibilities for independent political action. The political situation that had lasted forty years, it was assumed, would endure into the future. Almost no one anticipated the vast changes that were imminent throughout both the Soviet Union and Eastern Europe.

*The quarter century following the conclusion of World War II saw the relative decline of European power. The United States and the Soviet Union emerged as two economic and military superpowers. They confronted each other across the globe at one crisis point after another in a long-lasting conflict called the Cold War. In Europe, the point of confrontation was often the divided city of Berlin. The United States voiced concern about Eastern Europe but was never willing to exert significant influence in that region.*

*There were, however, other pressure points throughout the world. In Asia, the United States twice intervened. First, it led the United Nations police action in Korea. Second, it became involved in the long war over the political future of Vietnam. The revolution in Cuba and the establishment there of a communist government provided another point of tension, which in 1962 provoked the Cuban missile crisis, the most dangerous confrontation of the postwar era. In the Middle East, both the Soviet Union and the United States became involved in the Arab–Israeli conflict.*

*Following almost two decades of tension and crises, the United States and the Soviet Union entered upon two decades of negotiation that culminated in a significant arms reduction treaty. The Cold War ended in the late 1980s as major structural and policy changes shook the Soviet Union and led eventually to its collapse.*

| Major Dates of the Brezhnev Era | |
| --- | --- |
| 1974 | Solzhenitsyn expelled |
| 1975 | Helsinki Accords |
| 1979 | Soviet invasion of Afghanistan |
| 1980 | US Olympic Games boycott |
| 1981 | Martial law declared in Poland in response to Solidarity |
| 1982 | Death of Brezhnev |

*In the midst of this superpower rivalry, Western Europe achieved new levels of economic prosperity and political stability. Its nations established the European Economic Community (the European Union since 1991), and have moved steadily, if with difficulty, toward economic cooperation.*

## Review Questions

1. How did Europe come to be dominated by the United States and the Soviet Union after 1945? Trace the stages of the Cold War. Why were 1956 and 1962 particularly crucial years?
2. How would you define the policy of "containment"? Give some specific examples of how this policy was instituted by the United States throughout the world from 1945 to 1982.
3. How did Khrushchev's policies and reforms change the Soviet state after the repression of Stalin? Why did many people inside and outside the Soviet Union regard Khrushchev as reckless?
4. After World War II, Europe "achieved unprecedented economic prosperity and maintained liberal democratic governments." How did Western Europe move toward political unity? To what extent were the domestic policies of Charles de Gaulle important for maintaining political stability in France?
5. Trace the process of European decolonization. Why did the nations of Europe give up their empires? Was the retreat orderly? How did the United States become involved in Vietnam? What was the effect of the Vietnam War on Europe?
6. Discuss the origin of problems that led to Arab–Israeli conflict in the Middle East after 1948. Why are the Camp David Accords historically important? What are the most recent peace initiatives in the region?
7. What internal political pressures did the Soviet Union experience in the 1970s and early 1980s? What steps did the Soviet government take to repress those protests?

## Suggested Readings

F. Ansprenger, *The Dissolution of Colonial Empires* (1989). A broad survey.

K. L. Baker, R. J. Dalton, and K. Hildebrandt (Eds.), *Germany Transformed: Political Culture and the New Politics* (1981). Useful essays on the functioning of the political structures of West Germany.

C. D. Black and G. Duffy (Eds.), *International Arms Control Issues and Agreements* (1985). A discussion of arms issues as they stood at the close of the Cold War.

E. Bottome, *The Balance of Terror: Nuclear Weapons and the Illusion of Security, 1945–1985* (1986). An examination of the role of nuclear weapons in the Cold War climate.

T. Buchanan and M. Conway, *Political Catholicism in Europe, 1918–1965* (1996). Examines the background of Christian democracy.

M. E. Chamberlain, *Decolonization: The Fall of the European Empires* (1985). A useful treatment.

R. V. Daniels, *Year of the Heroic Guerilla: World Revolution and Counterrevolution in 1968* (1989). A worldwide examination of the events of that year.

A. W. DePorte, *Europe Between the Superpowers: The Enduring Balance* (1979). Remains a significant study.

R. Emerson, *From Empire to Nation: The Rise to Self-assertion of Asian and African Peoples* (1960). An important early discussion of the origins of decolonization.

B. B. Fall, *The Two Vietnams: A Political and Military Analysis*, rev. ed. (1967). A discussion by a journalist who spent many years on the scene.

H. Feis, *From Trust to Terror: The Onset of the Cold War, 1945–1950* (1970). The best general account.

J. L. Gaddis, *The United States and the Origins of the Cold War, 1941–1947* (1992). The most important recent discussion.

S. Hoffman, *Decline or Renewal? France Since the Popular Front: Government and the People, 1936–1986* (1988). A broad survey by a major scholar.

D. Holloway, *The Soviet Union and the Arms Race* (1985). Excellent treatment of internal Soviet decision making.

P. Jenkins, *Mrs. Thatcher's Revolution: The Ending of the Socialist Era* (1988). The best work on the subject.

W. W. Kulski, *DeGaulle and the World: The Foreign Policy of the Fifth Republic* (1968). A straightforward treatment of de Gaulle's drive toward French and European autonomy.

D. Kunz, *The Economic Diplomacy of the Suez Crisis* (1991). An examination of the economic factors leading to the Suez intervention.

R. F. Leslie, *The History of Poland Since 1863* (1981). An excellent collection of essays that provide the background for later events in Poland.

F. Lewis, *Europe: Road to Unity* (1992). A discussion of contemporary Europe by a thoughtful journalist.

L. Martin (Ed.), *Strategic Thought in the Nuclear Age* (1979). A collection of useful essays on an issue that lay at the core of the American relationship to Western Europe.

D. McKay, *Rush to Union: Understanding the European Federal Bargain* (1996). Examines the background of the Maastricht treaty.

L. P. Morris, *Eastern Europe Since 1945* (1984). Concentrates on the political and economic organization of the Soviet-dominated states.

J. ROTHSCHILD, *Return to Diversity: A Political History of East Central Europe Since World War II* (1989). A clear, well-organized introduction.

L. SCHAPIRO, *The Communist Party of the Soviet Union* (1960). A classic analysis of the most important institution of Soviet Russia.

Z. SCHIFF AND E. YA'ARI, *Intifada: The Palestinian Uprising—Israel's Third Front* (1990). An analysis of recent developments.

H. SIMONIAN, *The Privileged Partnership: Franco–German Relations in the European Community (1969–1984)* (1985). An important examination of the dominant roles of France and Germany.

A. ULAM, *Expansion and Coexistence: The History of Soviet Foreign Policy, 1917–1967* (1968). A classic treatment.

A. ULAM, *The Communists: The Story of Power and Lost Illusions: 1948–1991* (1992). The best account to date of the days of communist strength and collapse.

M. WALKER, *The Cold War and the Making of the Modern World* (1994). A major new survey.

H. WALLACE (ED.), *Policy-Making in the European Union* (1996) A useful introduction to the institutions of European integration.

L. WESCHLER, *Solidarity: Poland in the Season of Its Passion* (1982). A discussion of the early activities of Solidarity.

# The West & the World

## GLOBAL DEMOCRATIZATION

The past two decades have witnessed a remarkable political phenomenon throughout the world. On one continent after another there has been a movement toward the expansion of democratic political rights. Authoritarian political regimes of both the left and the right have undergone internal reform or have collapsed. Dictatorships, military governments, one-party communist states, and governments based on legalized racial discrimination have fallen, to be replaced in an unprecedented manner by more nearly democratic governments. This process of political change, usually termed *democratization*, involves the expansion of the numbers of people who participate in the selection of executive leaders and legislative representatives, the orderly change in or confirmation of leadership through elections, the participation of a wider spectrum of citizens in the political processes, and a lessening of the extent of governmental control over the daily lives of citizens. The movement has also tended to involve a shift from regulated to free market economies. In some nations the process has gone further than in others, but at no time in history have so many nations around the world seen such an extension of democratic government.

**The Postwar World** The developments of the past two decades must be seen against the backdrop of democratic achievements that followed World War II. The Atlantic Charter drawn up by the United States and Great Britain in 1942 asserted a democratic vision of the postwar world that was first realized among the defeated nations. The three major Axis powers, Germany, Italy, and Japan, had possessed dictatorial governments, but after the war, the victorious Allies imposed democracy on them. In then West Germany the Allies created democratic structures. A referendum in Italy held under the auspices of the Allies saw the Italian people choose a republican form of government over the old monarchy. In Japan the United States presided over the establishment of democratic institutions that preserved the ceremonial position of the emperor. All three nations soon became among the most stable democracies in the world.

Elsewhere, the years immediately following World War II were less hopeful. The nations of Eastern Europe fell under the political and military domination of the Soviet Union. Soviet-controlled Communist Party governments were established in East Germany, Czechoslovakia, Poland, Hungary, Bulgaria, and Rumania. Soviet armies stood ready to keep those repressive governments in power. In Yugoslavia, Marshall Tito's more or less independent communist government resisted Stalin but was still authoritarian in character. On the Iberian peninsula the older dictatorships of Antonio Salazar and General Francisco Franco continued to hold sway. In 1967 Greece fell under military rule.

From the late 1940s through the 1970s, Latin America was studded with various forms of dictatorial regimes, usually, although not always, dominated by the military. There were exceptions to this rule. Costa Rica, for example, had a successful democracy but generally in Latin America the drift was toward repressive government. In Cuba, a communist dictatorship governed after 1957. During the 1960s and 1970s, military governments controlled a number of major Latin American nations, including Brazil, Chile, and Argentina, as well as several of the region's smaller nations. Older, often family-dominated dictatorships dominated Haiti, the Dominican Republic, Nicaragua, and Paraguay. Mexico was governed by a one-party system that observed democratic procedures but actually allowed voters very little choice. One of the ongoing justifications of these various authoritarian regimes was the necessity to oppose possible communist insurrections sponsored from Cuba. Salazar in Portugal and Franco in Spain had long used similar appeals to the dangers of communism to defend their nondemocratic governments.

In South Africa, the policy of apartheid, which was imposed formally after the Afrikaner-led National Party achieved power in 1948, established a racially divided society in which a white minority held virtually all effective political and social power. Black South Africans enjoyed no effective political rights.

It is also important to note that the process of decolonization, which saw the withdrawal of European powers from their colonial empires, generally failed to fulfill early democratic expectations. India, after the withdrawal of the British authority in 1947, became the world's largest democracy. But the story was different elsewhere. In sub-Saharan Africa during the late 1950s and 1960s, a number of former European colonies initially opted for democratic government. Tragically, and often violently, however, many of them later declined into brutal dictatorships of one variety or another. Across northern postcolonial Africa, authoritarian governments arose whose power often resided in the military or in the use of popular voting to confirm authoritarian power. In the former French colonies of Southeast Asia, stable democratic governments failed to establish themselves, and in North Vietnam a communist government prevailed. Nonetheless the early democratic vision of the postcolonial world remained, and has continued to remain, as a kind of ideal toward which groups opposing the authoritarian governments could point.

As a result of these developments, during the late 1960s and early 1970s some observers believed that the rest of the century might see only a few functioning democracies survive. Democracy at that time appeared secure in North America above the Mexican border, in Western Europe, Japan, Israel, and a few other isolated nations. The rest of the world seemed condemned to authoritarianism either of military dictatorship or of one-party government.

The political pessimists were proved wrong not in a single case but around the globe.

**Influence of the Civil Rights Movement**  The movement toward an expansion of political par-

The bus boycott in Montgomery, Alabama during 1956 stands as one of the key moments in the civil rights movement in the United States. Here Reverend Martin Luther King Jr. (center) is shown riding in the front of a Montgomery bus with Reverend Glenn Smiley of Texas. Before the boycott, black Americans in the segregated areas of the nation were required to ride in the back of the bus. [UPI/Corbis-Bettmann]

ticipation that culminated in the past two decades of steady democratization was influenced by the American civil rights movement which began in the 1950's. On May 17, 1954, the United States Supreme Court, in the decision of *Brown* v. *Board of Education of Topeka,* declared unconstitutional the segregation of black and white schoolchildren. A year later, the Court ordered the desegregation of schools with "all deliberate speed." For the next ten years, the struggle over school integration and civil rights for black Americans stirred the nation. Various southern states tried to resist school desegregation. In 1957, when hostile crowds and the governor of Arkansas physically blocked the entrance of black students to an all-white high school in Little Rock, President Eisenhower reluctantly sent troops into the city to integrate the schools. Resistance to desegregation continued in various forms in other southern states.

While the battle raged over the schools, an awakened civil rights movement among American blacks began to protest segregation in other areas of national life. In 1955 Reverend Martin Luther King, Jr. (1929–1968) organized a boycott in Montgomery, Alabama, to protest segregation on buses. The Montgomery bus boycott marked the beginning of the use of civil disobedience to fight racial discrimination in the United States. Drawing upon the ideas of Henry David Thoreau and the experience of Gandhi in India, the leaders of the civil rights movement went to jail rather than obey laws they believed to be unjust.

In 1963 a march on Washington by tens of thousands of supporters of civil rights legislation gave dramatic testimony to the growth and moral force of the movement. The next two years witnessed the passage of landmark legislation—the Civil Rights Act of 1964, which desegregated public accommodations, and the Voting Rights Act of 1965, which cleared the way for large numbers of African-Americans to vote. The results of that legislation as well as of continuing protests in areas of housing and job discrimination brought black citizens nearer to the mainstream of American life than ever before, though much still remains to be done.

The problems of race relations continue to plague the social life of the United States. Although African Americans have made much progress toward access to education and to public office, especially in urban areas, they continue to lag behind other Americans economically and in their prospects for good health. Furthermore, as other groups, particularly Hispanic Americans, began to enter the political process in the 1980s and to raise issues on behalf of their own communities, the issues surrounding racial relations in the nation became more complicated. In 1992 one of the most destructive riots in American history—triggered by the acquittal of police officers who had been videotaped beating an African American they were arresting—devastated parts of Los Angeles, bringing to the fore continuing problems with race relations in the United States. The presidential campaigns of 1992 and 1996 conspicuously ignored the problem of race relations.

**The Mediterranean**   In Western Europe, the next area that witnessed major movement toward democratization was the Mediterranean. The failure of an aging political leadership to provide for new authoritarian successors fostered the coming of democracy to Portugal with the death in 1970 of Salazar, the country's long-time dictator. Four years after his death an army revolt led to the beginning of a democratic movement that soon brought free elections. In 1976 General Franco died in Spain. His fascist regime was followed, as he had decreed, by a monarchy. The new king, Juan Carlos, rejected a continuation of authoritarian rule. He understood that Spain could achieve a new political and economic status in Europe and domestic and political stability only if it moved toward democratic government resembling that of other states in the region. His determination to bring democratic government to Spain made his succession stable and lasting. Very quickly a functioning multiparty system developed in Spain.

In some cases, unsuccessful military ventures by authoritarian regimes opened the way to democratic government. Portugal under Salazar, in an attempt to retain colonial rule, had long been involved in an unwinnable war in Angola that undermined support for his rule. In 1974 the Greek military government collapsed after an unsuccessful confrontation with Turkey over the future of Cyprus. A civilian government replaced it, and in a 1975 referendum, the Greek people decided against restoration of the monarchy.

Another important factor turning these nations toward democracy was that the European Economic Community (now the European Union) restricted membership to democracies. It had become clear by the mid-1970s that however slowly the integration of the community might take place, participation in it was a necessity for any European nation hoping for ongoing prosperity.

**Latin America**  The first breakthrough toward democracy in Latin America occurred in Brazil, where the military had governed since 1964. The leaders of that government argued that the country's economy could not yet support democracy and that the military could best sustain order and foster economic growth. Once in power and inevitably drawn deeply into the daily political deals and compromises associated with governing, the military itself became itself divided and politicized. By the mid-1970s, some officers began to feel that the military, to maintain its institutional independence and to avoid responsibility for the economic difficulties that followed the oil shocks of the early 1970s, should disentangle itself from politics. In other words, by expanding political life and allowing civilian leadership, military leaders hoped to avoid the appearance of political incompetence and the onus of political responsibility. Furthermore, the managers of major Brazilian corporations, which had prospered during the early years of military rule, wanted a larger political role. The military, however, did not want to turn power over immediately to groups that it believed might foster instability, and the business groups agreed to a slow transition to democracy. During 1974, the military allowed some free legislative elections, which saw victories by opposition groups. Thereafter the military slowly continued to open up the political process, allowing elections for the presidency in 1985. Thus under the paternalistic eye of the military, which continues to monitor the process carefully, the largest and most populous nation on the continent had made a transition to democracy.

In Argentina, by contrast, the military government, which had freely used terror, collapsed in the wake of the Argentine defeat at the hands of the British in the War of the Malvinas (Falkland Islands) of 1982. President Raul Alfonsin was elected in 1983, and since then the nation has made generally steady progress toward democracy.

In Chile a military government had ruled since 1973, when Augusto Pinochet led a coup that overthrew the democratically elected socialist president Salvador Allende. During the late 1980s, Pinochet's government began a very slow process of liberalization. When Pinochet left office in 1990, a civilian government was elected. In sharp contrast to the previous regime, the new government addressed human rights issues. As in Brazil, the developments in Chile took place under the watchful eye of military authorities. And as in Spain and Portugal, the turn to democracy reflected the difficulty authoritarian governments encounter when they need to transfer leadership from one generation to another.

Elsewhere in Latin America the tide of democracy has continued to rise. Dictatorships and one-party governments, including the Sandinista government in Nicaragua, have generally given way to democratic governments, although the long-term stability of some of them is uncertain. In the case of Nicaragua, the US government actively supported forces opposed to the Sandinistas.

In some quarters in Latin America, unfortunately, democracy is under challenge. The government of Peru, in the face of a radical insurrection, has taken the form of a presidential dictatorship. In Colombia, pressure from drug merchants has led the government to adopt nondemocratic measures. The situation in Mexico has become quite complicated as its government faces pressures to allow a genuine multiparty system and to reform widespread corruption. In 1994 one of the presidential candidates was assassinated, and the government faced a major armed insurgency from rebels in a southern province. The pressures to reform Mexican politics and to modify one-party rule are very real, but it is unclear whether those pressures will succeed.

**Asia**  Worldwide communications technology has often contributed to recent efforts toward democratization, particularly in Asia. Today, it is simply more difficult for repressive governments to hide their repression or to prevent opponents from communicating with the outside world through radio, television, e-mail, or fax machines.

In Asia, the eighties saw an expansion of democracy in South Korea, which, although noncommunist, had been ruled by a single party. The well-publicized repressive actions of the government discouraged international trade, which had grown increasingly important for South Korea's expanding economy. As a result, and although there is much progress still to be made, the one-party government has begun to involve opposition groups to some extent in the electoral and governing processes. High officials responsible for military and police attacks on South Korean citizens have been tried, convicted, and sentenced to very heavy sentences.

In the Philippines, the Marcos dictatorship was overthrown in 1985 after an opposition leader was assassinated in a public place with the world press watching. Corazon Aquino, the wife of the assassinated opposition leader, took office as elected president in 1986. Despite severe strains, the new democratic government has so far, as of this writing, endured, and in 1992 free elections permitted a peaceful transition of power.

**South Africa**  In South Africa, the late 1980s and early 1990s witnessed a remarkable example of a political party slowly surrendering monopoly power. The Afrikaner government came under enormous stress as years of economic sanctions injured the commercial life of the nation. South African blacks refused to cooperate with the government and engaged in various kinds of both peaceful and violent protest. Young South African blacks made it clear their generation would actively resist apartheid.

Under the leadership of F. W. DeKlerk in 1990, the Nationalist Party freed Nelson Mandela, the black nationalist political leader who had been imprisoned since 1962, and began serious negotiations with him and other opposition leaders. A 1992 referendum in which only white South Africans voted approved constitutional equality for all races. By 1994 elections were held in which, for the first time, South Africans of all races participated, and which brought Mandela and his party to power. The process of democratization was marked by violence from extremists on both sides, but the process has been steady and both the legal and political structures of apartheid have been removed.

**Eastern Europe**  Despite democratization achieved elsewhere, it was generally assumed that the

*The first multi-racial elections held in 1994 in South Africa symbolized, more than any other single moment, the end of apartheid and the achievement of genuine political change. [Haviv/SABA Press Photos, Inc.]*

authoritarian governments of Eastern Europe and the Soviet Union would survive indefinitely. For that reason the events of the 1980s and early 1990s in that region of the world were all the more astounding. Beginning in 1985 Mikhail Gorbachev undertook a number of reformist policies in the Soviet Union. They included experiments with forms of free market economy, greater freedom of discussion, and political restructuring. He also decided not to interfere in the political developments of Eastern Europe as the Soviet Union had done in 1956 in Hungary and in 1968 in Czechoslovakia. During 1989 all of the Communist Party regimes in Eastern Europe collapsed with amazing rapidity. Democratic governments embracing free market policies emerged in place of single-party governments and planned economies. These new governments, however, face very difficult economic challenges and severe political pressure from resurgent ethnic nationalism that could divert them from the democratic course. As the experiences of these countries attest, the collapse of authoritarian governments and the movement toward democratic structures is rarely smooth. It often involves periods of considerable instability that may result in governments perhaps less repressive than those of the past but still not fully democratic.

Gorbachev's momentous actions apparently reflected his belief that the Soviet Union could no longer afford the cost of its military repression of Eastern Europe or of operations like the disastrous war in Afghanistan. He also understood that, thanks again largely to worldwide communications, the Soviet people were aware of the difference between their standard of living and that of the people living in the democratic, market-oriented nations of Western Europe, North America, and Asia.

In the Soviet Union itself by the late 1980s Gorbachev had clearly lost control of the process he had fostered. After the Communist Party voted away its own political monopoly, Gorbachev began to side with more conservative political groups. In August 1991 a conservative coup attempted to remove him. Following that coup, Boris Yeltsin, a Russian leader far more democratic in outlook than Gorbachev, came to the fore. The Soviet Union itself dissolved, the Commonwealth of Independent States (CIS), a very loose confederation of the constituent republics of the former Union, was proclaimed, and Yeltsin himself was elected president of the Russian Republic and was reelected in 1996.

The drive toward greater democracy throughout the world remains both incomplete and uncertain. Communist dictatorships remain in power in Cuba, North Korea, and Vietnam. The People's Republic of China, still dominated by the Chinese Communist Party, repressed a drive toward democracy in 1989 with a massacre of protesters in Tiananmen Square and continues to have a poor record on human rights. In Iraq, Iran, Saudi Arabia, and other parts of the Middle East, nondemocratic governments still prevail as is also the case in Indonesia. In much of Africa the early attempts at democracy have given way to various modes of dictatorship and civil unrest.

In the new democracies of Eastern Europe enormous challenges remain. In virtually all of them, the economic situation remains difficult, and it is uncertain that they can withstand the possible social or political turmoil that may result. The extent of democracy differs from nation to nation. Impatient voters or military leaders may turn to older authoritarian structures. Yet the most recent elections in the region have witnessed the victory even if sometimes narrow of groups pressing for further political and economic reform. The future is anything but certain or easy, yet it would appear that much of the world has opted for seeking to achieve a democratic future.

✦ *How did the Allied victory in World War II prepare the way for a major movement toward democracy? Which parts of the world were most affected? What events in the United States constitute part of the story of the expansion of democractic institutions? How did the movement of colonial peoples in Africa and Asia against European domination contribute to democratization? Why did democracy spread in eastern Europe and the former Soviet Union? What factors accounted for that transformation?*

*The collapse of Communist Party governments in Eastern Europe and the Soviet Union is the most important of the closing years of this century. It was accompanied by the destruction of the public symbols of those governments. Throughout the region gigantic statues of Communist Party leaders were torn down. Here in former East Berlin the head of a large statue of Lenin hangs from a crane during the demolition process, November 1991. [Patrick Piel/Gamma-Liaisson, Inc.]*

# Toward a New Europe and the Twenty-first Century

## KEY TOPICS

- Unprecedented prosperity and the expansion of the consumer society in Western Europe
- Demographic trends, migrations, and growing ethnic tensions
- Intellectual and social movements since World War II
- *Perestroika* and *glasnost* in the Soviet Union
- The collapse of communism in Eastern Europe and the Soviet Union
- The civil war in Yugoslavia

The second half of the twentieth century has witnessed remarkable social and intellectual changes in European life. One of the most important of these, the formation of the European Economic Community and subsequent European Union, was discussed in the previous chapter. Other important transformations, overshadowed by the Soviet–American rivalry, occurred quietly and with little notice.

Western Europe experienced unprecedented economic growth. Much of Western Europe and even the popular culture of Eastern Europe became "Americanized." Consumers enjoyed more goods and services than ever before. A second agricultural revolution made Europe still more urban, with fewer people living on the land. The role of women in the workplace and in society at large became more important than during any previous era of history. A distinct youth culture blossomed, affecting both political and intellectual life. The Roman Catholic Church reformed itself more radically than at any time since the Council of Trent in the sixteenth century. Secular intellectuals found themselves compelled to wrestle with the problems posed by communism. And science was making remarkable advances in virtually every area of research. The effects of technology and industrialism, however, created growing concern for the environment in Europe and the United States.

The last decades of the twentieth century saw an astonishing and largely unexpected political transformation that will bring still further social and economic change. The communist governments of the Soviet Union and its Eastern European subject states collapsed in a manner and with a rapidity that amazed the entire world. As a result, Germany again became united, the nations of Eastern Europe became independent, civil war has raged in Yugoslavia, and the Soviet Union has been replaced by a Commonwealth of Independent States. A new Europe has clearly emerged after a period of flux and redirection that in recent history can only be compared with the period immediately after World War I or World War II.

## European Society in the Second Half of the Twentieth Century

The sharp division of Europe into a democratic West and communist East for most of the second half of the twentieth century makes generalizations about social and economic developments difficult. Prosperity in the West contrasted with the conditions of consumer goods shortages in the Eastern economies, which were managed for the benefit of the Soviet Union. Most of the developments discussed in this chapter have taken place in Western Europe. However, with the collapse of communism many of the trends that dominated Western Europe are now beginning to realize themselves in Eastern Europe as well.

### The "Americanization" of Europe

During the past half century, the United States has exerted enormous influence on Europe and most especially Western Europe. After the war, the US

Many American fast-food and retail chains are now appearing in Eastern Europe as well as Western Europe. This Pizza Hut is in Moscow. [Wolfgang Kaehl]

government, through the Marshall Plan, rebuilt the Western European economies. The United States was the leader of the NATO alliance. Over the decades, hundreds of thousands of American military personnel have been stationed in Europe. Thousands of American students have studied in Europe, and millions of American tourists have flocked there.

The term *Americanization*, which has appeared in European publications, refers in part to this economic and military influence, but it also refers to concerns about cultural loss. Many Europeans feel that American popular entertainment and economic enterprises threaten to extinguish some of the unique qualities of their various nations and regions. American banks and other financial institutions as well as law firms often have European branches. Large American corporations such as the McDonald's fast-food chain have established a presence in European cities from Dublin to Moscow. American liquor companies and distilleries now sell their goods in Europe. Styles of clothing, such as blue jeans, first popular in America, are now equally popular in Europe. Shopping centers and supermarkets, first pioneered in America, are displacing neighborhood shopping areas. American television programs and movies are readily available. Perhaps most impressive is the manner in which American rock music has come to dominate much of the European popular cultural scene. As a result, Americans and Europeans admire the same movie stars and popular entertainers.

Furthermore, as Europe moves toward greater economic cooperation, English seems to be emerging as the most common language of business and even of some academic fields. And it is American influence, not British, that lies behind this trend.

This Americanization is, of course, relative. The United States is not the only economic power impinging on Europe. Asian nations, particularly Japan, also have enormous presence. In Europe, as in the United States, the electronic merchandise that fills many stores today is often manufactured in Japan or elsewhere in Asia. Nonetheless, the infiltration of American values, products, and popular culture has been a major feature of European social life during the past half century. Europeans have frequently regretted or criticized this development, but it has become a major fact of European social life.

## A Consumer Society

Although European economies have been under pressure during the 1990s, most of the last half century has witnessed an extraordinary expansion in the consumer sector. This expansion was limited almost entirely to Europe outside the Soviet bloc.

The consumer orientation of the Western European economy emerged as one of the most important characteristics differentiating it from Eastern Europe. Those differences produced important political results. Throughout the Soviet Union and the nations it dominated in Eastern Europe, economic planning overwhelmingly favored capital investment and military production. Those nations produced inadequate food for their people and a very

low level of consumer goods. Long lines for food and nonfood staples such as shoes and clothing were common; automobiles were a luxury; housing was inadequate. The quality of all consumer goods was low.

By contrast, the last fifty years has seen a steady increase in the availability of consumer goods elsewhere in Europe. By the early 1950s, Western Europeans enjoyed an excellent food supply that has only improved over the years. The variety of fresh foods and vegetables available to western consumers has increased, as has the variety of frozen foods. And in a sign of the strength of Western Europe's consumer economy, if not the healthfulness of its diet, the number of fast food outlets has also expanded markedly.

Western Europe has enjoyed a similarly great expansion of virtually all other kinds of consumer goods and services. The number of automobiles increased and they have become widely accessible. The number of people owning refrigerators, washing machines, electric ranges, televisions, and now microwaves, videocassette recorders, computers, compact disc players, and other small electronic consumer items has grown rapidly. A wide variety of everyday clothing has become available, from woolen goods to blue jeans and sneakers. Like their American counterparts, Western Europeans now have a whole gamut of products, such as disposable diapers and prepared baby foods, to help them raise their children. They take foreign vacations year round, prompting the expansion of ski resorts in the Alpine countries and beach resorts on the Mediterranean.

This vast expansion of consumerism, which, as noted in Chapter 16, began in the eighteenth century, became a defining characteristic of Western Europe in the late twentieth century. It stood in marked contrast to the consumer shortages in Eastern Europe. Yet through even the limited number of radios, televisions, movies, and videos available to them, people in the East grew increasingly aware of the discrepancy between their lifestyle and that of the West. They saw Western consumerism clearly linked to democratic governments, free societies, and economic policies that favored the free market and only limited government planning. Thus the expansion of consumerism in the West, deplored by many commentators and Christian moralists, helped generate the discontent that brought down the communist governments of Eastern Europe and the Soviet Union.

## Population Changes

The wars of the twentieth century, from Ireland to the Soviet Union, killed millions of people in Europe. Yet despite these losses—in combat, from the slaughter of civilians, and from the hunger and deprivation associated with war—Europe's population has grown over the course of the century. Growth rates have varied over time and from country to country, but the overall increase has been substantial. Between 1913 and 1985, estimates suggest that Europe's population grew by more than 44 percent.[1] Elsewhere the pace was even higher. Whereas in the first decade of the century Europeans accounted for approximately 20 percent of the world's population, today they account for only about 11 percent. This shift in population has changed Europe's place in the world and accounts in part for the growing pressure on natural resources from non-European and non-Western regions.

The largest European population expansion in history took place during the twenty years after World War II. During that period, there were no wars to decimate the population, and Europe experienced a material prosperity, especially in the West, that it had not known previously in its history. Europeans today live more closely together than in earlier eras. Population density rose from 66 people per square kilometer in 1920 to 101 in 1985, and the trend has continued. The most densely populated regions are the Netherlands, Belgium, England, western Germany, and Italy.

The chief factors behind this remarkable population growth are increased life expectancy and a reduced infant mortality rate, both resulting from medical advances and improved living standards. In effect, a greater percentage of European children survive infancy than before and then go on to live longer than their predecessors. Despite regional variations and a persistently longer life expectancy for women than men, life expectancy has now increased almost uniformly across Europe.

Equally striking has been the decline in Europe's birthrate over the course of the century. Birth control information and contraceptives became widely available from the 1920s on. Although a "baby boom" did occur in the decade and a half following World War II, it was closely associated with the prosperity of those years. The European birthrate reached a peak in 1964 and has declined since then to much lower levels. The advent of the birth control pill during the 1960s contributed directly to this trend. Possibly also contributing to it was the legalization of abortion in many Western European countries. Abortion was generally already legal in Eastern Europe and the Soviet Union.

Effective and widely available contraception has combined with changing social attitudes to reduce the size of the European family significantly. Around the turn of the century, families with five or more children were not uncommon. Near the close of the century, the two-child family has become the norm. Evidence suggests that average family size is becoming still smaller in the 1990s.

## Modern European Household Structures

Despite the media attention devoted to unconventional lifestyles, the half century following World War II has actually seen an increase in the number of married people in Europe. Before then, a significant number of women remained single all their lives, but many fewer do so now. Women are also marrying at a younger age than before, particularly in Eastern and Southern Europe. Overall, more people in the last half century have married, and have married at an earlier age, than in all of previous European history.

At the same time, many of the traditional ideas and expectations surrounding marriage have changed. Family size is smaller, and divorce rates have risen over the course of the century. Divorce laws have eased throughout Europe, although not until after 1980 in the nations of Southern Europe, where the Roman Catholic Church is influential.

In the Scandinavian countries, more children are born out of wedlock. In many cases, the parents live together, but are not married. Such arrangements, as well as single motherhood, have been made economically feasible by government-sponsored programs directed toward the care of children. Despite the attention such arrangements have received, they have not become the norm anywhere in Europe.

## The Movement of Peoples

Many people have migrated from, to, and within Europe during the past half century.

[1]The information on population and most of the other statistical information in this chapter is taken from Gerold Ambrosius and William H. Hubbard, A Social and Economic History of Twentieth-Century Europe (Cambridge, Mass.: Harvard University Press, 1989).

*Immigration has heightened ethnic and racial tensions throughout Europe. In 1982 major riots erupted in the south of London among immigrants to England from the West Indies. [Stuart Franklin/SYGMA]*

EXTERNAL MIGRATION   In the decade and a half after 1945, approximately a half million Europeans each year settled elsewhere in the world. This was the largest outward migration since the 1920s, when the rate had been approximately 700,000 persons annually. A major difference between the post-World War II emigration and that of the second half of the nineteenth century was that the earlier migrants had mostly been from rural areas whereas the later migrants often included educated city dwellers.

Decolonization in the postwar period contributed to an inward flow of European colonials from overseas. The most dramatic example of this phenomenon was the more than one million French colonials who moved to France after the end of the Algerian War. British citizens returned from various parts of the British Empire; Dutch came back to the Netherlands from Indonesia; and Portuguese returned from Mozambique and Angola.

Decolonization also provoked a migration of non-European inhabitants of the former colonies to Europe. Great Britain, for example, received thousands of immigrants from India and Pakistan as well as from some of its former African colonies. France received many immigrants from its former colonies in Indochina and the Arab world. This influx has been a source of social tension and conflict. In Great Britain, for example, racial tension was high during the 1980s, with angry clashes between the police and non-European immigrants. France has had similar difficulties, which have contributed to the emergence there of the National Front, an extreme right-wing group led by Jean-Marie LePen. This group has drawn strength from the racial and ethnic tensions that have developed as a tight job market provokes resentment among some working-class voters toward North African immigrants.

INTERNAL MIGRATION    World War II and its aftermath created a vast refugee problem. Millions of people were displaced from their homes. Many cities in Germany and in Central and Eastern Europe had been bombed or overrun by invading armies. Hundreds of thousands of foreign workers had been moved into Germany to contribute to the war effort. There were thousands of prisoners of war. Some of these people were returned to their homeland willingly; others, unwillingly. Changes in borders after the war also caused many people to move or be moved. For example, Poland, Czechoslovakia, and Hungary removed millions of ethnic Germans from their territories and sent them to Germany. Hundreds of thousands of Poles were transferred within Poland's new borders and out of territory taken over by the Soviet Union. Before the construction of the Berlin Wall in 1961, an estimated three million East Germans migrated to West Germany.

Once the Cold War set in, Soviet domination made it impossible for Eastern Europeans to migrate to other parts of Europe, whether for political or economic reasons. As a result, until the collapse of the Soviet Empire, most internal migration in Europe after the immediate postwar years occurred outside the communist bloc.

The major motivation for internal migration from the late 1950s onward was economic opportunity. The prosperous nations of northern and western Europe had jobs that paid good wages and provided excellent benefits, often financed in part by the governments. Germany made labor agreements with countries in southern Europe to facilitate labor migration into Germany. Thus, there was a flow of workers from the poorer countries of Turkey, Greece, Yugoslavia, Italy, Spain, and Portugal into the wealthier countries of France, West Germany, Switzerland, and the Benelux nations. The establishment of the European Economic Community in 1957 made this movement of labor much easier.

The migration of workers into northern Europe grew to substantial proportions after 1960. Several hundred thousand workers would enter France and Germany each year. Virtually all these migrants settled in cities. The migrants usually were welcomed in the host countries during years of prosperity. When, however, European economies began to slow in the mid-1980s, these guest workers, as they were sometimes called, met increasing resentment. In Germany during the early 1990s, these workers who had originally been invited into the country became targets of hostile assaults.

In the late 1980s, politics again became a major factor in European migration. The pressure of thousands of refugees seeking to escape from Eastern Europe to the West contributed to the collapse of the communist governments of Eastern Europe in 1988 and 1989. Since 1989 people from all regions of Eastern Europe have migrated to Western European nations. The civil war in the former Yugoslavia has also created many refugees. Europe has been in recession, however, and the new migrants are generating tension, resentment, and strife. Several nations have taken legal and administrative steps to restrict migration.

URBAN EXPANSION    Since at least the eighteenth century, European populations have shifted from the countryside toward cities. This trend has become even more pronounced in the last half century. Today, except for Albania, at least one-third of the population of every European nation lives in large cities. In Western Europe, city dwellers are approximately 75 percent of the population.

In nations that were already heavily urbanized, the process has continued, although at a slower rate. In other nations, such as those surrounding the Mediterranean and in Eastern Europe, the process since World War II has been much more rapid.

The general effect of this urban growth has been to increase the size of cities that were already large. London, Paris, Rome, Athens, and Istanbul have, for example, experienced continued growth. The capital cities of Austria, Denmark, Finland, Greece, and Hungary embrace as much as 20 percent of their national populations. In Mediterranean Europe, the growth of metropolitan areas has been almost uncontrolled, putting enormous pressure on city services such as water, electricity, sanitation, and police, as well as housing and medical facilities. Similarly, urban growth in Eastern and Mediterranean Europe has often been accompanied by serious pollution.

## A Second Agricultural Revolution

Never in history has so much food in so many varieties been available in Europe; however, never have fewer Europeans been involved in agriculture—

approximately 10 percent. This development is, of course, the reverse process of the growth of cities. Agriculture remains, however, a major element in the European economy and one that has experienced major changes in the past half century.

The years of the Great Depression and World War II saw a steep drop in agricultural production in Europe. The farm sector was naturally among the hardest hit as the worldwide commodities crisis spread. The two decades after the war, however, saw a remarkable recovery and increase in production and productivity. European farming became more mechanized. New kinds of fertilizers were introduced, and better methods were developed to control diseases that afflicted crops. Although not without problems—in the Netherlands, for example, the use of fertilizers has raised growing environmental concerns—these changes have roughly doubled European agricultural production. The result has been nothing less than a second agricultural revolution.

The agricultural policies of the European Economic Community sought to foster medium-sized farms. The communist governments of Eastern Europe sought to create large collective farms. Agricultural policies in Eastern Europe were mostly ineffective, but collectivization did increase the amount of land tilled. Across Europe, the amount of land under cultivation expanded until the 1970s.

One result of changes in landholding has been the disappearance of the peasant in Western Europe. In France, for example, there are now virtually no peasants, whereas before World War II they still constituted most of the farming population.

## The Welfare State

The Great Depression, the rise of authoritarian states, and the experience of World War II, which saw larger groups of people involved in a war effort than ever before, led to a marked change in thinking about social welfare in Europe. The result was the emergence of the modern European welfare state.

The forces that created the welfare state are complex and differed from country to country. Before World War II, except in Scandinavia, there were two basic models for social legislation: the German and the British. Bismarck had introduced some forms of social insurance in Germany during the 1880s. His purpose was to undermine the influence of the German Social Democratic Party. In effect, he had the imperial German government provide workers with social insurance and thus some sense of social security while denying them significant political participation. In early-twentieth-century Great Britain, where all classes had access to the political system, social insurance was targeted toward the very poor. According to both approaches, workers should be insured against the risks arising from disease, injury on the job, and old age. Although various legislative efforts had been made to address unemployment, it was assumed to be only a short-term problem and often one that workers brought on themselves. People higher up in the social structure were assumed to be able to look out for themselves and not to need help.

After World War II, the concept emerged that social insurance against predictable risks was a right and should be universally available to all citizens. This concept had been most famously set forth in Great Britain by William B. Beveridge (1879–1963) in 1942. Paradoxically, making coverage universal, as Beveridge recommended, was attractive to conservatives as well as socialists. If medical care, old age pensions, and other benefits were available to all, they would not be seen as a device for redistributing income from one portion of the population to another.

The first European nation to begin the creation of a welfare state was Great Britain during the Labour Party ministry of Clement Attlee (1883–1967). The most important element of this early legislation was the creation of the National Health Service. Similar health care legislation was not adopted in France and Germany until the 1970s because the governments of those countries initially refused to consider making coverage universal.

The spread of welfare legislation (including various forms of unemployment insurance) within Western Europe was closely related to the Cold War as well as to domestic political and economic policy. The communist states were promising their people enormous social security as well as full employment. The capitalists states came to believe that they must respond in their own way by producing similar security for their people. But in fact, the social security of the communist states was often more a matter of rhetoric than reality.

The systems of government-furnished services now found across Europe in varying forms are beginning to encounter resistance. The payment systems on which they are based assume a growing population. As the proportion of the population consuming the services of the welfare state—the sick, the injured, and the elderly—increases relative to the able-bodied employed population that pays for them, the costs of those services rise. The significant leveling off of population growth in Europe thus places the now expected benefits of the welfare state in some peril.

# New Patterns in the Work and Expectations of Women

The decades since World War II have witnessed striking changes in the work patterns and the social expectations of women. In all social ranks, women have begun to assume larger economic and political roles. More women have entered the "learned professions" and are filling more major managerial positions than ever before in European history.

## More Married Women in the Work Force

One of the patterns firmly established at the turn of the century has reversed itself. The number of married women in the work force has sharply risen.

Both middle-class and working-class married women have sought jobs outside the home. Because of the rather low birthrate in the 1930s, there were not many young single women to be employed in the years just after the war. Married women entered the job market to replace them. Some factories changed their work shifts to accommodate the needs of married women. Consumer conveniences and improvements in health care also made it easier for married women to enter the work force by reducing somewhat the demands of child care on their time.

In the twentieth century, children have no longer been expected to make substantial contributions to family income. They now spend large amounts of their time in compulsory schools. When families need more income than one worker can provide, both parents will work, bringing many married women with children into the workforce. Such financial necessity led many married women back to work. Considerable evidence also suggests that married women began to work to escape the boredom of housework and to find company among other adult workers.

## New Work Patterns

The work pattern of European women has been far more consistent in the twentieth century than it had been in the nineteenth. Single women enter the work force after their schooling and continue to

*In Europe, as in the United States, women have gained access to new roles and opportunities. Geraldine Bridgewater was the first woman to hold a seat on the London Stock Exchange. [Gamma-Liaison]*

work after marriage. They might stop working to care for their young children, but return to work when the children begin school. Several factors crated this new pattern, but women's increasing life expectancy is one of the most important.

When women died relatively young, child rearing filled a large proportion of their lives. As a longer life span has shortened that proportion, women throughout the West are seeking ways to lead satisfying lives after their children have grown. The late twentieth century work pattern for women has also been shaped by decisions regarding when to have children and how many children to have. The age at which women have decided to bear children has risen, to the early twenties in Eastern Europe and to the late twenties in Western Europe. In urban areas, childbearing is later and the birthrate lower than elsewhere.

Many women have begun to choose to limit sharply the number of children they bear or to forgo childbearing and child rearing altogether. Both of these decisions leave many years free for developing careers and for staying in the work force.

## Women in the New Eastern Europe

Many paradoxes surround the situation of women in Eastern Europe now that it is no longer governed by communists. Under communism, women generally enjoyed social equality as well as a broad spectrum of government-financed benefits. A significant proportion (normally well over 50 percent) of women worked in these societies both because they could and because it was expected of them. There were, however, no significant women's movements since they, like all independent associations, were regarded with suspicion.

The new governments of the region are free, but have so far shown little concern toward women's issues. Indeed, the economic difficulties faced by the new governments may endanger the funding of various health and welfare programs that benefit women and children. For example, a free market economy may limit the extensive maternity benefits to which Eastern European women were previously entitled. Moreover, the high proportion of women in the work force could leave them more vulnerable than men to the region's economic troubles. Women may well find themselves being laid off before men and hired into new jobs later and at possible lower pay than men.

# Transformations in Knowledge and Culture

The realms of knowledge and culture have rapidly transformed themselves in the twentieth century. Institutions of higher education have reached out to an increasingly large and diverse student body, making knowledge more widely available than ever before. Also, intellectual movements, such as existentialism, have challenged many traditional intellectual attitudes. Concerns about the environment have also brought new issues to the fore. Throughout this ferment, representatives of the Christian faith have tried to keep the message of their religion relevant.

## Communism and Western Europe

Throughout this century, Western Europe has had organized communist parties as well as groups of intellectuals sympathetic to communism. The relationship of these groups to the Western European political experience must be seen in a context that goes back to the Bolshevik victory itself. That event in 1917 cast all pre-World War I European socialism into disarray. The Western European socialist movement rapidly divided into independent democratic socialist parties and Soviet-dominated communist parties that followed the directions of the Third International. Throughout the 1920s and 1930s, those two groups fought against each other with only rare moments of cooperation, as during the French Popular Front in 1936. European left-wing intellectuals divided between those who supported socialism and those who supported communism. The results of those divisions and debates have continued to influence Western European political life through the 1990s.

THE INTELLECTUALS During the 1930s, as liberal democracies floundered during the Great Depression and as right-wing regimes spread across the Continent, communism appeared to many people at the time as a vehicle for protecting humane and even liberal values. Throughout Europe, students in the universities were often affiliated with the Communist Party. They and older intellectuals visited the Soviet Union and praised Stalin's achievements. Some of these intellectuals did not know of Stalin's terror; others simply closed their eyes to it, some-

*George Orwell (1903–1950), shown here with his son, was an English writer of socialist sympathies who wrote major works opposing Stalin and communist authoritarianism. [Bildarchiv Preussischer Kulturbesitz]*

how believing that humane ends might come from inhumane methods; still others actually defended Stalinist terror. During the late 1920s and the 1930s, communism became for some Europeans little less than a substitute religion. One group of former communists, writing after World War II, described their attraction and later disillusionment with communism in a book entitled *The God That Failed* (1949).

Four events proved crucial to the disillusionment of the intellectuals. These were the great public purge trials of 1936 and later, the Spanish Civil War (1936–1939), the Nazi–Soviet pact of 1939, and the Soviet invasion of Hungary in 1956. Arthur Koestler's (1905–1983) novel *Darkness at Noon* (1940) recorded a former communist's view of the purges. George Orwell, who had never been a com-

munist but who had sympathized, presented his disappointment with Stalin's policy in Spain in *Homage to Catalonia* (1938). The Nazi–Soviet pact destroyed the image of Stalin as an opponent of fascism. Other intellectuals, such as the French philosopher Jean-Paul Sartre, continued to put faith in the Soviet Union through the war, but the Hungarian Revolution cooled his ardor. The later invasion of Czechoslovakia simply confirmed a general disillusionment with Soviet policies on the part of even left-wing Western European intellectuals.

Yet disillusionment with the Soviet Union or with Stalin did not in all cases mean disillusionment with Marxism or with radical socialist criticism of European society. Some writers and social critics looked to the establishment of alternative communist governments based on non-Soviet models. During the decade after World War II, Yugoslavia provided the example of such a different path. Beginning in the late 1950s, radical students and a few intellectuals found inspiration in the Chinese Revolution. Other groups hoped for the development of a European Marxist system. Among the more important contributors to this non-Soviet tradition was the Italian communist Antonio Gramsci (1891–1937) and his work *Letters from Prison* (published posthumously in 1947). The thinking of such non-Soviet Communists became very important to Western European Communist parties, such as the Italian party, which hoped to gain office democratically.

Another way to accommodate Marxism within mid-twentieth-century European thought was to redefine the basic message of Marx himself. During the 1930s, a considerable body of Marx's previously unprinted essays was published. These books and articles, written before the *Communist Manifesto* of 1848, are quite abstract and philosophical. They make the "young Marx" appear to belong more nearly to the humanist than to the revolutionary tradition of European thought. Since World War II, these works, including *Philosophic Manuscripts of 1844* and *German Ideology*, have been widely read. Today many people are more familiar with them than with the *Manifesto* or *Capital*. They have allowed some people to consider themselves sympathetic to Marxism without also seeing themselves as revolutionaries or supporters of the Soviet Union. With the collapse of the communist governments of Eastern Europe and the Soviet Union, it is now unclear what influence Marxism will continue to have on European intellectual life in the future.

THE RISE AND FALL OF EUROCOMMUNISM During the 1970s and early 1980s, a form of Marxism known as *Eurocommunism* appeared to be developing in Western Europe. This new Marxist alternative tried to accommodate Western European communist parties to the political realities of their positions in successfully functioning liberal democracies. The chief architect of this strategy was Enrico Berlinguer (1922–1984), the leader of the Italian Communist Party, which was the largest and best organized in Western Europe. The strategy was carried farther in Italy than in any other state.

Berlinguer's policy, known as the historic compromise, represented a major break not only with the previous stand of the Italian Communist Party but also with the Moscow-dominated communist movement. With the "compromise," Berlinguer announced the willingness of the Italian Communist Party to enter a coalition government with the Christian democrats and noncommunist parties. Thus, the Italian communists in effect renounced revolution as the path to political power. They also agreed to participate in a government that they would not dominate or control. The Italian Communist Party also promised that as a partner in the coalition or as the governing party, should it be elected, it would govern constitutionally and would respect individuals' civil liberties. Further, it urged continued Italian participation in NATO and criticized the crackdown on Solidarity in Poland.

Berlinguer's historic compromise was never put to the test in Italy. There is little evidence voters believed the communists would keep their word once in power. The Italian communists reached their electoral peak in the early 1980s. When Berlinguer died in 1984, no strong successor emerged. The importance of Eurocommunism may have been overestimated at the time; yet it marked still another development in the evolution of the communist movement in the West and in its attempts to separate itself from the Soviet model.

Western European communist parties found their position entirely transformed during the second half of the 1980s. Radical reform began in the Soviet Union, communist governments collapsed in Eastern Europe, and Western electorates became more conservative. In the wake of these developments, Western Europe's communist parties reorganized themselves and, often with great irony considering the struggles of the 1930s, dropped the term "communist" and relabeled themselves as some form of "socialist" party.

## Existentialism

The intellectual movement that perhaps best captured the predicament and mood of mid-twentieth-century European culture was *existentialism*. Like the modern Western mind in general, existentialism, which has been termed the "philosophy of Europe in the twentieth century," was badly divided; most of the philosophers associated with it disagreed with each other on major issues. The movement represented in part a continuation of the revolt against reason that began in the nineteenth century.

ROOTS IN NIETZSCHE AND KIERKEGAARD Friedrich Nietzsche, discussed in Chapter 25, was one of the major forerunners of existentialism. Another was the Danish writer Soren Kierkegaard (1813–1855), who wrote during the second quarter of the nineteenth century but received little attention until after World War I. Kierkegaard was a rebel against both the Hegelian philosophy and the Lutheran Christianity he encountered in Denmark. In works such as *Fear and Trembling* (1843), *Either/Or* (1843), and *Concluding Unscientific Postscript* (1846), he maintained that the truth of Christianity could not be contained in creeds, doctrines, and church organizations. It could be grasped only in the living experience of those who faced extreme human situations.

Kierkegaard also criticized Hegelian philosophy and, by implication, all modes of academic rational philosophy. Its failure, he felt, was the attempt to contain all of life and human experience within abstract categories. Kierkegaard spurned this faith in the power of mere reason. "The conclusions of passion," he once declared, "are the only reliable ones."[2]

The intellectual and ethical crisis of World War I brought Kierkegaard's thought to the fore and also created new interest in Nietzsche's critique of reason. The war led many people to doubt whether human beings were actually in control of their own destiny. Its destructiveness challenged faith in human rationality and improvement. Indeed, the war's most terrible weapons were the products of rational technology. The pride in rational human achievement that had characterized much nine-

[2]*Quoted in Walter Kaufman, ed.,* Existentialism from Dostoevsky to Sartre *(Cleveland: The World Publishing Company, 1962), p. 18.*

# Sartre Discusses the Character of His Existentialism

*Jean-Paul Sartre, dramatist, novelist, and philosopher, was the most important French existentialist. In the first paragraph of this 1946 statement, Sartre asserted that all human beings must experience a sense of anguish or the most extreme anxiety when undertaking a major commitment. That anguish arises because consciously or unconsciously they are deciding whether all human beings should make the same decision. In the second paragraph, Sartre argued that the existence or nonexistence of God would make no difference in human affairs. What humankind must do is to discover the character of its own situation by itself.*

✦ *How might the experiences of Fascism in Europe and the fall of France to the Nazis have led Sartre to emphasize the need of human beings to chose? Why does Sartre believe existentialism must necessarily be related to atheism? Why did Sartre regard existentialism as optimistic?*

The existentialist frankly states that man is in anguish. His meaning is as follows—When a man commits himself to anything, fully realizing that he is not only choosing what he will be, but is thereby at the same time a legislator deciding for the whole of mankind—in such a moment a man cannot escape from the sense of complete and profound responsibility. There are many, indeed, who show no such anxiety. But we affirm that they are merely disguising their anguish or are in flight from it. Certainly, many people think that in what they are doing they commit no one but themselves to anything: and if you ask them, "What would happen if everyone did so?" they shrug their shoulders and reply, "Everyone does not do so." But in truth, one ought always to ask oneself what would happen if everyone did as one is doing; nor can one escape from that disturbing thought except by a kind of self-deception. The man who lies in self-excuse, by saying, "Everyone will not do it" must be ill at ease in his conscience, for the act of lying implies the universal value which it denies. By its very disguise his anguish reveals itself.

. . . . . . . . . . . . . . . . . . . . . . . . . . . . . . .

Existentialism is nothing else but an attempt to draw the full conclusions from a consistently atheistic position. Its intention is not in the least that of plunging men into despair. And if by despair one means—as the Christians do—any attitude of unbelief, the despair of the existentialist is something different. Existentialism is not atheist in the sense that it would exhaust itself in demonstration of the nonexistence of God. It declares, rather, that even if God existed that would make no difference from its point of view. Not that we believe God does exist, but we think that the real problem is not that of His existence; what man needs is to find himself again and to understand that nothing can save him from himself, not even a valid proof of the existence of God. In this sense existentialism is optimistic. It is a doctrine of action, and it is only by self-deception, by confusing their own despair with ours that Christians can describe us as without hope.

*Jean-Paul Sartre,* Existentialism and Humanism, *trans. by Philip Mairet (London: Methuen), in Walter Kaufman, ed.,* Existentialism from Dostoevsky to Sartre *(New York: Meridian Books, 1956), pp. 292, 310–311.*

Jean-Paul Sartre (1905–1980) and Simone de Beauvoir (1908–1986) were two leading mid-century French intellectuals. His was a major voice in the existentialist movement, and she wrote extensively on the social position, experience, and psychology of women. [Bildarchiv Preussischer Kulturbesitz]

teenth-century European civilization lay in ruins. The sunny faith in rational human development and advancement had not withstood the extreme experiences of war.

QUESTIONING OF RATIONALISM  Existentialist thought came to thrive in this climate and received further support from the trauma of World War II. The major existential writers included the Germans Martin Heidegger (1889–1976) and Karl Jaspers (1883–1969) and the French Jean-Paul Sartre (1905–1980) and Albert Camus (1913–1960). Their books are often very difficult and in some cases simply obscure. Although they frequently disagreed with each other, they all, in one way or another, questioned the primacy of reason and scientific understanding as ways of coming to grips with the human situation. Heidegger went so far as to argue, "Thinking only begins at the point where we have come to know that Reason, glorified for centuries, is the most obstinate adversary of thinking."[3]

The romantic writers of the early nineteenth century had also questioned the primacy of reason, but they did so in a much less radical manner than the existentialists. The romantics emphasized the imagination and intuition, but the existentialists dwelled primarily on the extremes of human experience. Death, dread, fear, and anxiety provided their themes. The titles of their works illustrate their sense of foreboding and alienation: *Being and Time* (1927) by Heidegger; *Nausea* (1938) and *Being and Nothingness* (1943) by Sartre; *The Stranger* (1942) and *The Plague* (1947) by Camus. The touchstone of philosophic truth became the experience of the individual under extreme conditions.

According to the existentialists, human beings are compelled to formulate their own ethical values and cannot depend on traditional religion, rational philosophy, intuition, or social customs for ethical guidance. The opportunity and need to define values endow humans with a dreadful freedom.

The existentialists largely were protesting against a world in which reason, technology, and politics produced only war and genocide. Their thought reflected the uncertainty of social institutions and ethical values in the era of the two world wars. Since the 1950s, however, their works and ideas have found their way into university curriculums around the world, making them objects of study, if not the source of intellectual ferment they had been. They will probably continue to be sub-

[3]*Quoted in William Barrett,* Irrational Man *(Garden City, N.Y.: Doubleday, 1962), p. 20.*

jects of philosophy and literature classes, but it is unlikely that they will again achieve their former popularity.

European intellectuals were attracted to communism and existentialism before and just after World War II, but in 1960s, the turmoil over Vietnam and the youth rebellion brought other intellectual and social issues to the fore. Even before the collapse of communism, these had begun to redirect European intellectual interests.

## Expansion of the University Population and Student Rebellion

As rapid changes in communications technology have vastly expanded access to information, increasing numbers of Europeans have received some form of university education. At the turn of the century, no more than a few thousand people were enrolled in universities in any major European country. By the 1980s that figure had risen to hundreds of thousands, though university education is still less common in Europe than in the United States. Higher education is now available to people from a variety of social and economic backgrounds and, for the first time, readily available to women.

This expanding population of university-educated people is closely related to a surge of intense self-criticism among Europeans. Millions of citizens have acquired the critical intellectual skills and familiarity with critical writers that in previous centuries were usually the preserve of small literate elites. Television has given critical voices an even wider audience. Indeed, in Great Britain, the Open University uses television to provide university training to thousands of people.

Previously known only to a privileged few, the "student experience"—leaving home and settling for several years in a community composed primarily of late adolescents—has come to be widely shared. Since World War II, it has become a major feature of European society.

The expanding student population in Europe and elsewhere required an increase also in the number of university teachers. As a result, there have been more scientists, historians, economists, literary critics, and other professional intellectuals during the last seventy-five years than in all previous human history. Not since the early years of the Reformation have university intellectuals exerted such widespread influence. The major intellectual developments of the seventeenth, eighteenth, and nineteenth centuries took place primarily outside the university. In the twentieth century, the university has become the most likely home for the intellectual. And the symbol of success for a writer in almost any field has been the inclusion of his or her work in the university curriculum.

One of the most striking and unexpected results of this rising population of students and intellectuals was the student rebellion of the 1960s. This development is still not well understood. Student uprisings began in the early 1960s in the United States and assumed major proportions as opposition grew to the war in Vietnam. The student rebellion then spread into Europe and other parts of the world. It was almost always associated with a radical political critique of the United States, although in Eastern Europe some resentment was directed toward the Soviet Union. The movement was generally antimilitarist. In addition to their political concerns, students questioned middle-class values, traditional sexual mores, and traditional family life.

The student movement reached its peak in 1968, the year that students in the United States demonstrated against US involvement in Vietnam. In the same year, students at the Sorbonne in Paris instigated a serious challenge to the government of Charles de Gaulle, and in Czechoslovakia, students were in the forefront of the liberal socialist experiment. These protests ultimately failed to have an immediate effect on the policies of the governments at which they were directed. The United States remained in Vietnam for several more years. De Gaulle's government survived the challenge of May 1968. The Soviets suppressed the Czech experiment.

By the early 1970s, the era of student rebellion seemed to have passed. Students remained active in European movements against nuclear weapons and particularly against the placement of American nuclear weapons in Germany and elsewhere in Europe. From the middle of the 1970s, however, although often maintaining a radical political stance, they generally abandoned the kind of disruptive protests that marked the 1960s.

## Students and Popular Music

Nothing has so characterized both student and youth culture in the second half of the twentieth

*The Russian rock group "Dynamic" performs in Moscow in 1987. Rock music has been a hallmark of European and American culture since the 1960s. In the 1970s and 1980s rock music and its lyrics emerged as a major vehicle for cultural and political criticism in Eastern Europe and the Soviet Union. [ITAR-TASS/SOVFOTO]*

century as rock music, which first emerged in the 1950s. Now part of the fabric of contemporary European life, rock music abounds on radio and television. The lyrics of the Beatles, the British rock group that became wildly popular on both sides of the Atlantic in the 1960s, may be by now the most widely dispersed poetry in the history of the world. Rock had a universality that appealed across national and cultural borders. It did as much to create a more uniform European culture as advertising or the economic freedom provided by the European Economic Community.

Rock music became part of a continuing critique of contemporary society. Many lyrics emphasized the need for love, the anguish of isolation, a desire for sexual liberation, and hopes for community and peace. During the 1960s, rock music in the West was an integral feature of the antiwar movement and a vehicle for expressing discontent with the older generation. In the 1970s and 1980s, it emerged as a major vehicle for cultural and political criticism in Eastern Europe and the Soviet Union. Rock stars came to symbolize daring and even heroism. Their music emphasized subjectivity and individualism. Lyrics directly criticized communist governments, as in this example from "Get Out of Control," sung at a rock concert in Leningrad in 1986:

We were watched from the days of kindergarten.
Some nice men and kind women
Beat us up. They chose the most painful places

And treated us like animals on the farm.
So we grew up like a disciplined herd.
We sing what they want and live how they want
And we look at them downside up, as if we're trapped.
We just watch how they hit us
Get out of control!
Get out of control!
And sing what you want
And not just what is allowed
We have a right to yell![4]

This song later became popular throughout Eastern Europe. Sentiments like these were common in popular songs and undoubtedly contributed to the dramatic changes that swept through the region.

## Environmentalism

After World War II, shortages of consumer goods created a demand that fueled postwar economic reconstruction and growth into the 1950s and 1960s. In these expansive times, there was little room for public debate about the ethics of economic expansion and efficiency and their effects on the environment. Concerns about pollution began to emerge in the 1970s, and by the 1980s environmentalists had developed real political clout.

[4]"Get Out of Control," by Daniel Ash, © 1992 Momentum Music Ltd. (PRS). All rights o/b/o Momentum Music Ltd. administered by WB Music Corp. for the Western Hemisphere. All Rights Reserved. used by permission. Warner Bros. Publications US Inc. Miami, FL 33014.

*Pollution of waterways poses danger to human health in many parts of Europe and has been one of the conditions giving rise to the European environmental movement. Here, a German factory pours its refuse and chemicals into a river. Such pollution has been a particular problem in the former Soviet block nations. [Frischmuth/Argo/SABA Press Photos, Inc.]*

Among the most important of these were the Club of Rome, founded in 1972, and the German Greens. The Greens formed a political party in 1979 that immediately became an electoral force. During these same years concern for environmental issues, such as global warming and the pollution of water and the atmosphere with substances endangering human health commanded the attention of governments outside Europe and the agencies of the United Nations.

Several developments lay behind this new concern about dangers to the environment. The Arab oil embargo of 1973–1974 pressed home two key messages to Europeans and to other nations in the Northern Hemisphere: first, natural resources are limited, and second, supplies of several critical resources could only come from foreign countries. By the 1970s, too, the environmental consequences of three decades of economic expansion were becoming increasingly apparent. Fish were dying in

the Thames River in England. Industrial pollution was destroying the rivers of Germany and France. Acid rain had begun to kill trees throughout Germany. Finally, long-standing apprehensions about nuclear weapons merged with concerns about their environmental effects, strengthening antinuclear groups and generating opposition to the placement of nuclear weapons in Europe.

The German Green movement originated among the radical student groups of the late 1960s. It shared with them an anticapitalist point of view, holding business responsible for pollution. The Greens and other European environmental groups also assumed a strong antinuclear position. Unlike the students of the 1960s, the Greens avoided violence and mass demonstrations, seeking, instead, to enter the electoral process directly. They succeeded in electing a few representatives to the West German Parliament as well as to local offices.

## World Leaders Point to the Problems of the Environment

*In 1989 leaders of the major industrialized nations, including the United States, Japan, Canada, the United Kingdom, France, Germany, and Italy, gathered in Paris for an annual summit meeting. In this statement, they addressed themselves to the problem of preserving and cleaning up the environment.*

✦ *What evidence is cited for a world environmental crisis? Why does the crisis require international cooperation? How did the signers of this statement see environmental issues related to economic issues?*

There is growing awareness throughout the world of the necessity to preserve better the global ecological balance. This includes serious threats to the atmosphere, which could lead to future climate changes. We note with great concern the growing pollution of air, lakes, rivers, oceans and seas; acid rain; dangerous substances; and the rapid desertification and deforestation. . . .

Decisive action is urgently needed to understand and protect the Earth's ecological balance. We will work together to achieve the common goals of preserving a healthy and balanced global environment in order to meet shared economic and social objectives. . . .

We urge all countries to give further impetus to scientific research on environmental issues, to develop necessary technologies and to make clear evaluations of the economic costs and benefits. . . .

In this connection, we ask all countries to combine their efforts in order to improve observation and monitoring on a global scale. . . .

We believe that international cooperation also needs to be enhanced in the field of technology and technology transfer in order to reduce pollution. . . .

We believe that industry has a crucial role in preventing pollution at the source, in waste minimization, in energy conservation, and in the design and marketing of cost-effective clean technologies. The agricultural sector must also contribute to tackling problems such as water pollution, soil erosion and desertification. . . .

Environmental protection is integral to issues such as trade, development, energy, transport, agriculture and economic planning. Therefore, environmental considerations must be taken into account in economic decision-making.

*The New York Times, July 17, 1989, p. A7.*

---

The 1986 disaster at the Chernobyl nuclear reactor in the Soviet Union heightened concern about environmental issues and raised questions that no European government could ignore. The Soviet government had to confront deaths and injuries at the site and had to relocate tens of thousands of people. Clouds of radioactive fallout spread westward across Europe. Environmentalists had always contended that their issues tran-scended national borders. The Chernobyl fire proved them right.

In the wake of Chernobyl, virtually all European governments, East and West, began to respond to environmental concerns. Some observers believe the environment may become a major political issue across the Continent. In Western Europe, environmental groups command a significant share of votes. Economic and political integration opens the possibility of transnational cooperation on environmental matters. As the European Economic Community solidifies, the EEC and its member nations will likely move to impose environmental regulations on business and industry. The nations of Eastern Europe face the daunting task of cleaning up vast areas polluted by industrial development during the communist era and devising policies that combine environmental protection with economic growth.

### Feminism

Since World War II, European feminism, although less highly organized than American feminism, has set forth a new agenda. The most widely read postwar work on women's issues was undoubtedly Simone de Beauvoir's (1908–1986) *The Second Sex*, published in 1949. In that work, de Beauvoir explored the difference it had made in her life to be a woman rather than a man. She was very much a part of the French intellectual establishment and thus wrote from a privileged position. Over the years, however, she and other European feminists came to argue that at all levels, European women experienced distinct social and economic disadvantages. In the courts, divorce and family laws favored men. European feminists also called attention to the social problems that were particular to women, including spousal abuse.

In contrast to earlier feminism, recent feminism has been less a political movement pressing for specific rights than a social movement offering a broader critique of European culture. More radical European feminists have asserted that their society, as presently organized, inherently represses women. They have been equally critical of all political parties—from conservative to socialist—that avoid a full airing of women's issues. Several new feminist publications appeared during the 1970s, many of which are still publishing. These include *Courage, Emma—Magazine by Women for Women*, and *Spare Rib*. A statement in *Spare Rib*, an English magazine, captures the spirit of these publications:

*Spare Rib* aims to reflect women's lives in all their diverse situations so that they can recognize themselves in its pages. This is done by making the magazine a vehicle for their writing and their images. Most of all, *Spare Rib* aims to bring women together and support them in taking control of their lives.[5]

[5]*Quoted in Bonnie S. Anderson and Judith P. Zinsser, A History of Their Own: Women in Europe from Prehistory to the Present, Vol. 2 (New York: Harper Perennial, 1988), p. 412.*

This emphasis on women controlling their own lives may be the most important element of recent feminism. Whereas in the past feminists sought and in significant measure gained legal and civil equality with men, they have now turned their attention to the pursuit of personal independence and issues that are particular to women.

The women's movement and the environmental movement have come to play a significant, new role in European politics and culture. The collapse of communism in Eastern Europe has raised questions about socialism and challenged the credibility of the cultural criticism it has generated. Feminist and environmental groups now provide the continuing critique of society that had been the role of socialist parties. In this sense, feminism is an important manifestation of the critical tradition that has long been part of Western culture.

# The Christian Heritage

In most ways, Christianity has continued to be as hard-pressed during the twentieth century as it had been in the late nineteenth. Material prosperity, political ideologies, environmentalism, gender politics, and simple indifference to religion have replaced religious faith as the dominant factor in many people's lives. Despite the loss of much of their popular support and former legal privileges, however, the European Christian churches still exercise considerable social and political influence. In Germany, the churches were one of the few major institutions not wholly subdued by the Nazis. Lutheran clergy, such as Martin Niemöller and Dietrich Bonhoeffer (1906–1945), were leaders of the opposition to Hitler. After the war, in Poland and elsewhere in Eastern Europe, the Roman Catholic Church actively opposed the influence of communism.

In Western Europe, religious affiliation provided much of the initial basis for the Christian democratic parties. Across Europe, the churches have raised critical questions about colonialism, nuclear weapons, human rights, and other moral issues. Consequently, even in this most secular of all ages, Christian churches have influenced many issues of state and society.

### Neo-Orthodoxy

Liberal theologians of the nineteenth century often softened the concept of sin and portrayed human

*Pope John Paul II, elected in 1978, is the first non-Italian pope since 1522. He has reasserted traditional Roman Catholic practices and values while also emphasizing the Church's commitment to social justice. [Gamma-Liaison]*

Kierkegaard provided the basis for a real knowledge of humankind's need for God.

This view challenged outright much nineteenth-century writing about human nature. Barth's theology, which came to be known as *neo-Orthodoxy*, proved very influential throughout the West in the wake of new disasters and suffering.

## Liberal Theology

Neo-Orthodoxy did not, however, sweep away liberal theology, which had a strong advocate in Paul Tillich (1886–1965). This German-American theologian tended to regard religion as a human rather than a divine phenomenon. Whereas Barth saw God as dwelling outside humankind, Tillich believed that evidence of the divine had to be sought in human nature and human culture.

Other liberal theologians, such as Rudolf Bultmann (1884–1976), continued to work on the problems of naturalism and supernaturalism that had troubled earlier writers. Bultmann's major writing took place before World War II but was popularized thereafter in Anglican Bishop John Robinson's *Honest to God* (1963). Another liberal Christian writer from Britain, C. S. Lewis (1878–1963), attracted millions of readers during and after World War II. This layman and scholar of medieval literature often expressed his thoughts on theology in the form of letters and short stories. His most famous work is *The Screwtape Letters* (1942). In recent years, however, there have been few major Protestant voices in European religious thought.

## Roman Catholic Reform

Among Christian denominations, the most significant postwar changes have been in the Roman Catholic Church. Pope John XXIII (r. 1958–1963) initiated these changes, the most extensive in Catholicism for more than a century and, some would say, since the Council of Trent in the sixteenth century. In 1959 Pope John summoned the Twenty-first Ecumenical Council (the first had been called by Emperor Constantine in the fourth century), which came to be called Vatican II. The council finished its work in 1965 under John's successor, Pope Paul VI (r. 1963–1978). Among many changes in Catholic liturgy, the council ended the practice of celebrating the mass in Latin, instead requiring it to be recited in the vernacular. It also permitted

nature as not very far removed from the divine. The horror of World War I destroyed that optimistic faith, leaving many Europeans feeling that evil had stalked the continent.

The most important Christian response to this experience appeared in the theology of Karl Barth (1886–1968). In 1919 this Swiss pastor published *A Commentary on the Epistle to the Romans*, which reemphasized the transcendence of God and the dependence of humankind on the divine. Barth portrayed God as wholly other than, and different from, humankind. In a sense, Barth was returning to the Reformation theology of Luther, but the work of Kierkegaard had profoundly influenced his reading of the reformer. Barth, like the Danish writer, regarded the lived experience of men and women as the best testimony to the truth of his theology. Those extreme moments of life described by

# Pope John Paul II Discusses International Social Justice

*Pope John Paul II issued his encyclical* The Social Concerns of the Church *in 1988. In the passages given here, he attempted to set concerns for justice among developed and developing nations into the larger context of Christian moral theology.*

✦ *How does the pope relate the fate of poorest nations to the international system of trade and finance? What evidence is there that the pope did not favor radical social action on the part of Roman Catholic clergy? How does this encyclical illustrate the pope's concerns for non-European parts of the world?*

The Church's social doctrine is not a "third way" between liberal capitalism and Marxist collectivism, nor even a possible alternative to other solutions less radically opposed to one another: rather, it constitutes a category of its own. Nor is it an ideology, but rather the accurate formulation of the results of a careful reflection on the complex realities of human existence, in society and in the international order, in the light of faith and of the Church's tradition. Its main aim is to interpret these realities, determining their conformity with or divergence from the lines of the Gospel teaching on man and his vocation, a vocation which is at once earthly and transcendent; its aim is thus to guide Christian behavior. It therefore belongs to the field, not of ideology, but of theology and particularly moral theology.

. . . . . . . . . . . . . . . . . . . . . . . . . . . . .

The international trade system today frequently discriminates against the products of the young industries of the developing countries and discourages the producers of raw materials. There exists, too, a kind of international division of labor, whereby the low-cost products of certain countries which lack effective labor laws or which are too weak to apply them are sold in other parts of the world at considerable profit for the companies engaged in this form of production, which knows not frontiers. . . .

. . . . . . . . . . . . . . . . . . . . . . . . . . . . .

. . . [H]umanity today is in a new and more difficult phase of its genuine development. It needs a greater degree of international ordering, at the service of the societies, economies and cultures of the whole world.

. . . . . . . . . . . . . . . . . . . . . . . . . . . . .

It is desirable, for example, that nations of the same geographical area should establish forms of cooperation which will make them less dependent on more powerful producers; they should open their frontiers to the products of the area; they should examine how their products might complement one another; they should combine in order to set up those services which each one separately is incapable of providing; they should extend cooperation to the monetary and financial sector.

. . . . . . . . . . . . . . . . . . . . . . . . . . . . .

The Church well knows that no temporal achievement is to be identified with the Kingdom of God, but that all such achievements simply reflect and in a sense anticipate the glory of the Kingdom, the Kingdom which we await at the end of history, when the Lord will come again. But that expectation can never be an excuse for lack of concern for people in their concrete personal situations and in their social, national, and international life, since the former is conditioned by the latter, especially today.

*The* New York Times, February 20, 1988, *p. 4.*

freer relations with other Christian denominations and gave more power to bishops. In recognition of the growing importance to the church of the world outside Europe and North America, Pope Paul also appointed several cardinals from nations of the former colonial world, transforming the church into a truly world body.

In contrast to these liberal changes, however, Pope Paul and his successors have firmly upheld the celibacy of priests, maintained the church's prohibition on contraception, and opposed moves to open the priesthood to women. The church's unyielding stand on clerical celibacy has caused many men to leave the priesthood and many men and women to leave religious orders. The prohibition on contraception has caused resentment among the laity.

The current pope, John Paul II, was elected in 1978 after the death of John Paul I, whose reign lasted only 34 days. John Paul II, the former Karol Wojtyla, archbishop of Cracow in Poland, was the youngest pope to be elected in more than a century. He has pursued a three-pronged policy. First, he has maintained a traditional policy in doctrinal matters, stressing the authority of the papacy and attempting to limit doctrinal and liturgical experimentation. Second, he has encouraged the expansion of the church in the non-Western world, stressing the need for social justice but limiting the political activity of priests.

Finally, he took a firm and important stand against communism and directly contributed to the spirit of freedom in Eastern Europe that brought an end to the communist regimes. As a cardinal in Poland he had clashed with Poland's communist government. After his election, he visited Poland, lending support to the activities of the Solidarity movement. There is no question that his Polish origins helped make him an important factor in the popular resistance to Eastern Europe's communist governments that developed during the 1980s. In this respect, his actions, both public and private, opened a new chapter in the relationship between church and state in modern Europe.

# The Collapse of European Communism

The events of the past decade in Eastern Europe and the former Soviet Union are among the most important of this century. They occurred rapidly and quite unexpectedly. They will influence not only the political future of Europe but also its economic and social life. In 1980 most observers believed that the Soviet Union would remain a major military power and dominate Eastern Europe indefinitely. Although internal forces had long been undermining Soviet authority, what brought those forces to a head and began the dramatic collapse of the Soviet Empire was the accession to power of Mikhail S. Gorbachev (b. 1931).

## Gorbachev Redirects the Soviet Union

Brezhnev died in 1982, followed by the deaths, in office, of his immediate successors, Yuri Andropov (1914–1984) and Constantin Chernenko (1911–1985). In 1985 Mikhail S. Gorbachev came to power. In what proved to be the last great attempt to reform the Soviet system and eliminate its repressive Stalinist heritage, he immediately set about making the most remarkable changes that the Soviet Union had witnessed since the 1920s. This attempt ultimately failed, but the reforms Gorbachev initiated unloosed forces that within seven years would force him to retire and would end both communist rule and the Soviet Union as it had existed since the Bolshevik Revolution of 1917. The backdrop for these events was the stagnation of the Soviet economy, the lost war in Afghanistan, and the absence of open political life.

By the early 1980s, the Soviet Union stood in a paradoxical situation. Militarily, it was stronger than it had ever been. After backing down during the Cuban missile crisis, the Soviet government had poured resources into a military buildup, leaving the nonmilitary side of the economy stagnant and neglected. With progress in all but military technology slowed, the country's overall rate of economic growth declined. Shortages in all kinds of consumer goods were extensive, and both absenteeism at work and alcoholism among the populace were high. When Ronald Reagan began the military buildup in the United States in the 1980s (discussed in Chapter 30), the leaders of the Soviet Union felt challenged to respond in kind, but it appears that they simply could not afford to do so.

Gorbachev had been known in his earlier administrative career for impatience with the inefficiencies of the Soviet system. He believed that only drastic change could restore the Soviet Union's political and economic health. Russian and Soviet history are replete with figures who sought to impose reform from above, and Gorbachev assumed a role in that tradition. It should be noted, however, that he never repudiated socialism or much of the intellectual framework of Soviet communism. He hoped to rejuvenate the original Bolshevik vision, which he believed had been undermined by corruption and political terror. Unlike other strong leaders in the Russian tradition, Gorbachev quickly unleashed political and social forces far beyond his control and was ultimately overwhelmed by them.

ECONOMIC PERESTROIKA    Initially, Gorbachev and his supporters moved to challenge the way the party and bureaucracy had traditionally managed the Soviet government and economy. Under the policy of *perestroika*, or "restructuring," they proposed major economic and political reforms. A target of this effort was the various centralized economic ministries, which were considerably reduced in size. A larger role was allowed for private enterprise on the local level. By early 1990, in a clear abandonment of traditional Marxist ideology, Gorbachev had begun to advocate private ownership of property. Throughout 1990 he and his advisers considered policies to liberalize the economy and move it rapidly toward a free market.

During these same years, Gorbachev confronted troubling labor discontent. A major strike by miners occurred in July 1989 in Siberia. Gorbachev had to settle their grievances quickly because the economy desperately needed their output. He promised them better wages and wider political liberties.

Within the Soviet context, Gorbachev's approach was genuinely radical. It challenged centralized planning and centralized Communist Party control. He and his supporters were also exceedingly critical of the corruption and inefficiencies in the economy and the party bureaucracy. The results of their policies, however, were not what they had hoped. They did implement many organizational changes, but for all intents the Soviet economy, instead of growing, experienced stagnation and even decline. Shortages of food, consumer goods, and housing became chronic. Old-fashioned communists blamed these results on the abandonment of centralized planning. Democratic critics blamed overly slow reform and urged a more rapid move to a free market economy.

The failure of Gorbachev's economic policies affected his political policies. To some extent, he pursued bold political reform because of the absence of economic progress.

GLASNOST    Within the Soviet context, Gorbachev allowed an extraordinarily broad public discussion and criticism of Soviet history and Soviet Communist Party policy. This development was termed *glasnost*, or openness. Such communist figures from the 1920s as Bukharin, who had been purged by Stalin, once again received official public recognition for their positive contributions to Soviet history. Within factories, workers were permitted to criticize party officials and the economic plans of the party and the government. Censorship was relaxed and free expression encouraged. Dissidents were released from prison. In the summer of 1988, Gorbachev presided over a party congress that witnessed very full debates.

At the same time, national minorities voiced increasing demands for political autonomy. Throughout its history, the Soviet Union had remained a vast empire of diverse peoples and nationalities. Some of those groups had been conquered under the tsars; others, such as the Baltic states, had been incorporated into the Soviet Union under Stalin. *Glasnost* quickly brought to the fore the discontents of all such peoples, no matter how or when they had been incorporated into the Soviet state. Gorbachev proved particularly inept in addressing these ethnic complaints.

POLITICAL PERESTROIKA    Gorbachev soon moved from *glasnost* to *perestroika* in the political arena. In 1988 a new constitution was adopted, permitting openly contested elections. After real political campaigning, a new experience for the Soviet Union, the Congress of People's Deputies was elected in 1989. One of the new members of the congress was Andrei Sakharov (1921–1989), the dissident physicist who had been persecuted under Brezhnev. Lively debate took place in the Supreme Soviet when it met. This body formally elected Gorbachev as president in 1989.

During that same year, in a series of events closely related to developments in the Soviet Union, Soviet domination and communist rule in Eastern Europe came to an abrupt end.

## 1989: Year of Revolution in Eastern Europe

As seen in Chapter 30, the Soviet Union maintained tight control over Eastern Europe throughout the Cold War era. Twice it intervened with military forces to halt political experiments: in

Hungary in 1956 and in Czechoslovakia in 1968. At the time of the 1968 invasion, Soviet Party Chairman Brezhnev, in what came to be termed the *Brezhnev Doctrine*, declared the right of the Soviet Union to intervene in the domestic politics of other communist countries. After 1968 the Soviet Union did not again send troops into an Eastern European country. In 1981, however, Poland's communist government itself imposed martial law to suppress the Solidarity trade union movement and prevent Soviet military intervention. This self-imposed martial law marked, in effect, the third use of military force to prevent reform in a Soviet-dominated Eastern European nation. Until Gorbachev began his radical changes in the Soviet Union, reform seemed unlikely anywhere in Eastern Europe.

SOLIDARITY REEMERGES IN POLAND   During the mid-1980s, Poland's government relaxed martial law, although Jaruzelski remained in control. By 1984 several leaders of Solidarity had been released from prison, and in defiance of the conditions of their release, began again to work for free trade unions and democratic government. An active underground press developed, and several new dissenting political organizations emerged. Poland's economy continued to deteriorate, demonstrating there, as elsewhere, the inability of communist governments to deliver economic growth and prosperity.

During 1987 the government released the last of its Solidarity prisoners in a sweeping amnesty. In 1988 new strikes occurred that even the leaders of Solidarity had not anticipated. This time, the communist government was unable to reimpose control. After consultations between the government and Solidarity, the union was legalized. Lech Walesa again came into the public spotlight, now as a kind of mediator between the government and the more independent elements of the trade union movement he had founded.

Jaruzelski began some political reforms with the tacit consent of the Soviet Union. He repealed martial law and promised free elections to a parliament with increased powers. When elections were held, in 1989, the communists lost overwhelmingly to Solidarity candidates. Late in the summer, Jaruzelski, unable to find a communist who could forge a majority coalition in Parliament, turned to Solidarity. On August 24, 1989, after negotiating with Lech Walesa, Jaruzelski named Tadeusz Mazowiecki (b. 1927) the first noncommunist prime minister of Poland since 1945. The appointment was made with the express approval of Gorbachev.

THE SOVIET STANCE TOWARD REVOLUTIONARY DEVELOPMENTS   The establishment in August 1989 of a Solidarity government in Poland had been the result of almost a decade of struggle. Within a few months of that event, however, Communist Party governments had fallen throughout Soviet-dominated Eastern Europe. Except in Romania, the transitions were relatively peaceful.

None of these revolutions could have taken place without the refusal of the Soviet Union to intervene militarily as it had done in 1956 and 1968. As events unfolded, it became clear that Gorbachev would not come to the aid of the old-line communist governments and party leaderships in Eastern Europe. In October 1989, he formally renounced the Brezhnev Doctrine. For the first time since the end of World War II, the people of Eastern Europe could shape their own political destiny without the almost certain military intervention of the Soviet Union. Once they realized the Soviets would stand back, thousands of ordinary citizens took to the streets to denounce Communist Party domination and to assert their desire for democracy.

The generally peaceful character of most of these revolutions was not inevitable. It may, in part, have resulted from the shock with which much of the world responded to the violent repression of prodemocracy protesters in Beijing's Tiananmen Square by the People's Republic of China in the late spring of 1989. The Communist Party officials of Eastern Europe and the Soviet Union clearly decided at some point in 1989 that they could not risk offending world opinion with a similar attack on democratic demonstrators.

HUNGARY MOVES TOWARD INDEPENDENCE   Of the Eastern European nations, Hungary had for some time shown the greatest national economic independence of the Soviet Union. The Hungarian government had emphasized the production of food and consumer goods. It had also permitted a small stock exchange. During the early months of 1989, as events unfolded in Poland, the Hungarian communist government began to take other independent actions. In January its parliament passed legislation to permit independent political parties. Soon there-

# Why Historical Truth Became Important to Dissidents in Eastern Europe

*G. M. Tamás is a leader of an opposition party in present-day Hungary. In this passage, he explores how Eastern European and Soviet dissidents used the rights guaranteed in the Helsinki Accords of 1975 to document the repression of the communist regimes. He contends that telling these truths and bearing witness helped both to spread information and to embarrass the communist governments by showing how they violated what they had signed.*

✦ *How did the right to free expression become so closely related to the telling of historical truth? What does Tamás mean by "the right to historical truth"? What was the importance of the Helsinki Accords in creating it? Why did the dissidents believe more strongly in the value of the rights guaranteed in the Helsinki Accords than did some people in the West?*

The first, most important human right for dissident intellectuals was the right to freedom of expression. But freedom of expression meant a licence to tell the truth, especially the truth about the Communist system, the truth about the martyrdom of East European peoples under the Gulag regime. The moral attitude which emerged from this simple idea of uncensored truth-telling was that of *bearing witness:* so the chief genre of dissident writing is neither philosophical treatise nor poetry, but *testimony*. Martyrs are . . . witnesses. The eloquence of their martyrdom, where the whole community was martyred, created a new symbolic community: the community of those who suffered and lived to tell and were ready to suffer again for the right to tell.

The irresistible force of this surge of testimony was lethal, because in spite of denial, a sometimes almost psychotic refusal to know, everyone half-consciously knew that it was true. . . .

In the struggle for the right to historical truth, for the right to bear witness (where history and morals, strangely, become one), dissidents were harassed, persecuted and punished. They continued to document these new abuses—one of the chief tasks of the dissident movement was to write its own chronicle, a testimony this time on the fate of the witnesses themselves. They did not at first demand the usual fundamental human rights: their emphasis was on the Word. They did not set up political parties or organize conspiracies. They wanted to expose unspeakable, even unimaginable crimes and show the continuity of the Great Terror through the servility and mendacity of their present. The rulers were told that

after the government opened the Hungarian border with Austria and permitted free travel between the two nations, opening the first breach in the Iron Curtain. One immediate result was the movement of thousands of East Germans into Austria through Hungary. From Austria, they proceeded into West Germany.

Not long thereafter, various political changes occurred in Hungary. In May, Premier Janos Kadar,

who had been installed after the Soviet intervention in 1956, was voted from office by the Parliament. Hungarians demonstrated their determination to validate this change when thousands of people gave an honorary burial to the body of Hungarian Premier Imre Nagy, who had been executed in 1958. The Hungarian Communist Party changed its name to the Socialist Party and permitted the emergence of other opposition political parties. In the communiqués they had signed guaranteed the right to free speech, peaceful assembly and the like. "Why, therefore, cannot people say what they believe to be the truth?" . . .

In the West, little of this passion for historico-moral truth was understood. But the West's shaky faith in the universality of its basic principles (human and civil rights) was challenged by the East European dissidence: people putting themselves at risk for the pious and dull commonplaces of the Helsinki accords. The unasked-for support for Western constitutional principles by trustworthy people, made so by their willingness to suffer for those principles, gave a new distinction to a certain idea of natural right; the dissidents' behaviour forced the ideas of the American Revolution on to the political agenda after two hundred years. There was a universalist discourse common to both systems, and the debate conducted within it was won by the West and its allies, the dissidents. No *Realpolitik* could ever have won that controversy.

The irresistible force of this surge of testimony was lethal, because in spite of denial, a sometimes almost psychotic refusal to know, everyone half-consciously knew that it was true. . . .

In the struggle for the right to historical truth, for the right to bear witness (where history and morals, strangely, become one), dissidents were harassed, persecuted and punished. They continued to document these new abuses—one of the chief tasks of the dissident movement was to write its own chronicle, a testimony this time on the fate of the witnesses

themselves. They did not at first demand the usual fundamental human rights: their emphasis was on the Word. They did not set up political parties or organize conspiracies. They wanted to expose unspeakable, even unimaginable crimes and show the continuity of the Great Terror through the servility and mendacity of their present. The rulers were told that the communiqués they had signed guaranteed the right to free speech, peaceful assembly and the like. "Why, therefore, cannot people say what they believe to be the truth?" . . .

In the West, little of this passion for historico-moral truth was understood. But the West's shaky faith in the universality of its basic principles (human and civil rights) was challenged by the East European dissidence: people putting themselves at risk for the pious and dull commonplaces of the Helsinki accords. The unasked-for support for Western constitutional principles by trustworthy people, made so by their willingness to suffer for those principles, gave a new distinction to a certain idea of natural right; the dissidents' behaviour forced the ideas of the American Revolution on to the political agenda after two hundred years. There was a universalist discourse common to both systems, and the debate conducted within it was won by the West and its allies, the dissidents. No *Realpolitik* could ever have won that controversy.

*G. M. Tamás, "The Legacy of Dissent: How Civil Society Has Been Seduced by the Cult of Privacy," The Times Literary Supplement, May 14, 1993, p. 15.*

October, Hungary promised free elections. By 1990 a coalition of democratic parties controlled the parliament and governed the country.

THE BREACH OF THE BERLIN WALL AND GERMAN REUNIFICATION No part of Europe had so come to symbolize the tensions of the Cold War as the divided Germanies. The Berlin Wall had been erected in 1961 to halt the outflow of East Germans to the West. In the autumn of 1989, as tens of thousands of East Germans moved into West Germany through Hungary and then Austria, popular demonstrations erupted in many German cities. The most important demonstrations occurred in Leipzig. The streets filled with people demanding democracy and an end to Communist Party rule.

Adding to the pressure of the popular demonstrations, Gorbachev told the leaders of the East

*The opening of the Berlin Wall in November, 1989, more than any other event, symbolized the collapse of the communist governments in Eastern Europe. [R. Bossu/SYGMA]*

German Communist Party that the Soviet Union would no longer support them. With startling swiftness, the communist leaders of the East German government, including Premier Erich Honecker (b. 1912), resigned, making way for a younger generation of Communist Party leaders. These new leaders, who remained in office for only a matter of weeks, promised political and economic reform. They convinced few East Germans, however, and the emigration to the West continued. In November 1989, in one of the most emotional moments in European history since 1945, the government of East Germany ordered the opening of the Berlin Wall. That week, tens of thousands of East Berliners crossed into West Berlin to celebrate, to visit their families, and to shop with money provided by the West German government. Shortly thereafter, free travel began between East and West Germany. (See Map 31–1.)

Further political change occurred in East Germany. For all intents, the Communist Party had become thoroughly discredited. Enormous corruption among party officials was exposed. The East German Communist Party changed its name and claimed that henceforth it would be a social democratic party. Free elections in 1990 brought

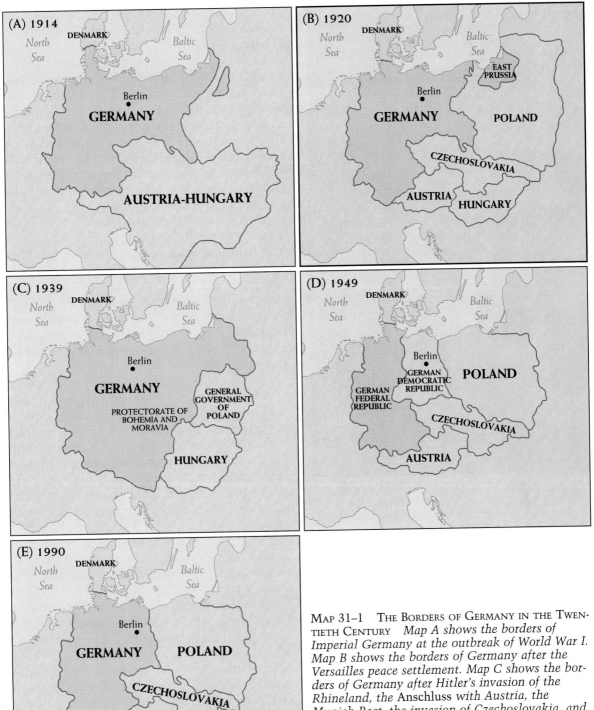

(A) 1914

*North Sea*
DENMARK
*Baltic Sea*
Berlin •
GERMANY
AUSTRIA-HUNGARY

(B) 1920

*North Sea*
DENMARK
*Baltic Sea*
EAST PRUSSIA
Berlin •
GERMANY
POLAND
CZECHOSLOVAKIA
AUSTRIA
HUNGARY

(C) 1939

*North Sea*
DENMARK
*Baltic Sea*
Berlin •
GERMANY
GENERAL GOVERNMENT OF POLAND
PROTECTORATE OF BOHEMIA AND MORAVIA
HUNGARY

(D) 1949

*North Sea*
DENMARK
*Baltic Sea*
Berlin •
GERMAN FEDERAL REPUBLIC
GERMAN DEMOCRATIC REPUBLIC
POLAND
CZECHOSLOVAKIA
AUSTRIA

(E) 1990

*North Sea*
DENMARK
*Baltic Sea*
Berlin •
GERMANY
POLAND
CZECHOSLOVAKIA
AUSTRIA

MAP 31–1   THE BORDERS OF GERMANY IN THE TWEN-
TIETH CENTURY   *Map A shows the borders of
Imperial Germany at the outbreak of World War I.
Map B shows the borders of Germany after the
Versailles peace settlement. Map C shows the bor-
ders of Germany after Hitler's invasion of the
Rhineland, the Anschluss with Austria, the
Munich Pact, the invasion of Czechoslovakia, and
the invasion of Poland. Map D illustrates the divi-
sion of Germany into the German Federal Repub-
lic (West Germany) and the German Democratic
Republic (East Germany) in the aftermath of
World War II. Map E illustrates the borders of Ger-
many after reunification in 1990.*

*Vaclav Havel, now president of the Czech Republic, led the revolution that overthrew the communist government of his nation and has since become a powerful advocate of political democracy and moderation in Eastern Europe. [Gamma-Liaison]*

become a forgone conclusion, accepted by the United States, the Soviet Union, Great Britain, and France.

In the closing months of 1989 and the opening weeks of 1990, it became clear that the citizens of the two Germanies were determined to reunify. With the collapse of Communist Party government in East Germany, there was no longer a viable distinction between the two Germanies. With the communists in confusion, the forces of national self-determination came to the fore. The rapidity of German reunification, however, was to sow the seeds of new problems.

THE "VELVET REVOLUTION" IN CZECHOSLOVAKIA
The hard-line wing of the Czechoslovak Communist Party had been restored to power by the Soviet invasion of 1968. This wing of the party then removed the communist leaders of the 1968 Prague Spring from public life and retained virtually unquestioned authority for twenty years. Any opponents were likely to find themselves imprisoned for their activities.

Late in 1989, in a series of events dubbed the "velvet revolution," communist rule in Czechoslovakia quickly unraveled. In November 1989, under popular pressure from street demonstrations and well-organized political opposition, the Communist Party began to retreat from office. The patterns were similar to those occurring elsewhere. The old leadership resigned, and younger communists replaced them. The changes they offered were inadequate.

The popular new Czech leader who led the forces against the party was Vaclav Havel (b. 1936), a playwright of international standing who had been frequently imprisoned by the government. Havel and the group he represented, which called itself *Civic Forum*, negotiated a series of changes with the government. These included an end to the political dominance of the Communist Party (which had been written into the constitution), inclusion of noncommunists in the government, elimination of traditional Marxist education, removal of travel restrictions, and relaxation of censorship.

Early in December, the tottering communist government acknowledged that the invasion of 1968 had been a mistake. The Soviet Union and other Warsaw Pact states did likewise. Shortly thereafter, Civic Forum succeeded in forcing the resignation of Gustav Husak (b. 1913), who had been president of Czechoslovakia since 1968, and in guaranteeing

into the East German Parliament a conservative majority that sought rapid unification with West Germany.

The revolution in East Germany, more than those elsewhere in Europe, had broad ramifications for international relations. Within days of the first dramatic events in East Germany, the issue of the reunification of the Germanies confronted West Germany and the other Western nations. Helmut Kohl (b. 1930), the Chancellor of West Germany, proposed a tentative plan for reunification. Soon thereafter Kohl became the leading force in moving toward full unification. Late in 1989 the ministers of the European Economic Community accepted in principle the unification of Germany. By February 1990, some form of reunification had

a free election for his successor. On December 28, 1989, Alexander Dubcek returned to public office as chairman of the Parliament. The next day, Havel was elected president.

VIOLENT REVOLUTION IN ROMANIA   The most violent upheaval of 1989 occurred in Romania, where President Nicolae Ceauşescu (1918–1989) had governed without opposition for almost a quarter century. Romania was a one-party state with totally centralized economic planning. Ceauşescu, who had been at odds with the Soviet government for some time, maintained his Stalinist regime in the face of Gorbachev's reforms. He was supported by an army and a smaller security force loyal to himself. He had also placed his closest relatives into major political positions where they personally profited through corrupt practices.

On December 15, troubles erupted in the city of Timisoara in western Romania. The security forces sought to arrest a clergyman who had tried to protect the rights of ethnic Hungarians within Romania's borders. Over the next two days, the Romanian security forces opened fire on demonstrators in Timisoara. Casualties ran into at least the hundreds and quite possibly higher. A few days later, demonstrators in Bucharest publicly shouted against Ceauşescu at a major rally, and by December 22 the city was in full revolt. Fighting, with many casualties, broke out between the army, which supported the revolution, and the security forces loyal to Ceauşescu. The revolutionaries gained control of the television station and broadcast reports of the spreading revolution. Ceauşescu and his wife attempted to flee the country but were captured, secretly tried, and executed by firing squad on December 25. With Ceauşescu's death, the shooting between the army and security forces ended. The provisional government in Bucharest announced that the first free elections since the end of World War II would take place in the spring of 1990. During the early months there were many demonstrations, both for and against the new government. Political turmoil continued for some time.

## The Collapse of the Soviet Union

Gorbachev clearly believed, as shown by his behavior toward Eastern Europe in 1989, that the Soviet Union could no longer afford to support communist governments in that region or intervene to

### Major Events in the Revolutions of 1989

| | |
|---|---|
| January 11 | Independent parties permitted in Hungary |
| April 5 | Solidarity legalized in Poland and free elections accepted by government |
| May 2 | Hungary dismantles barriers along its borders |
| May 8 | Janos Kadar removed from office in Hungary |
| May 17 | Polish government recognizes Roman Catholic Church |
| June 4 | Solidarity victory in Polish parliamentary elections |
| July 25 | Solidarity asked to join coalition government |
| August 24 | Solidarity member appointed premier in Poland |
| October 18 | Erich Honecker removed from office in East Germany |
| October 23 | Hungary proclaims itself a republic |
| October 25 | Gorbachev renounces Brezhnev Doctrine |
| November 9 | Berlin Wall opened |
| November 17 | Large antigovernment demonstration in Czechoslovakia crushed by police |
| November 19 | Czechoslovak opposition groups organize into Civic Forum and demand resignation of Communist leaders responsible for 1968 invasion |
| November 24 | Czechoslovak communist leadership resigns |
| December 1 | New Czechoslovak communist leaders denounce 1968 invasion; Soviet Union and Warsaw Pact express regret over 1968 invasion |
| December 3 | Czechoslovak government announces ministry with noncommunist members |
| December 16–17 | Massacre of civilians in Timisoara, Romania |
| December 22 | Ceauşescu government overthrown in Romania with many casualties |
| December 25 | Announcement of Ceauşescu's execution |
| December 28 | Alexander Dubcek elected chairman of Czechoslovak Parliament |
| December 29 | Vaclav Havel elected president of Czechoslovakia |

# Gorbachev Proposes the Soviet Communist Party Abandon Its Monopoly of Power

*On February 5, 1990, President Mikhail Gorbachev proposed to the Central Committee of the Soviet Communist Party that it abandon its position as the single legal party as provided in Article 6 of the Soviet constitution. His proposal followed similar actions by several of the communist parties of Eastern Europe. From the time of Lenin through Brezhnev, the Soviet Communist Party portrayed itself as the sole vanguard of the revolution. Gorbachev argued that it should abandon that special role and compete for political power with other political parties. Within two years, the party was no longer in power.*

✦ *Why did Gorbachev argue that the Soviet Communist Party must reform itself? To what extent did Gorbachev in this speech actually abandon traditional Communist Party goals? How did he think the Soviet Communist Party could function in a pluralistic political system?*

The main thing that now worries Communists and all citizens of the country is the fate of perestroika, the fate of the country and the role of the Soviet Communist Party at the current, probably most crucial, stage of revolutionary transformation.

. . . .

[It is important to understand] . . . that the party will only be able to fulfill the mission of political vanguard if it drastically restructures itself, masters the art of political work in the present conditions and succeeds in cooperating with forces committed to perestroika.

The crux of the party's renewal is the need to get rid of everything that tied it to the authoritarian-bureaucratic system, a system that left its mark not only on methods of work and inter-relationships within the party, but also on ideology, ways of thinking and notions of socialism.

The [newly proposed] platform says: our ideal is a humane, democratic socialism, expressing the interests of the working class and all working people; and relying on the great legacy of Marx, Engels and Lenin, the Soviet Communist Party is creatively, developing socialist ideals to match present-day realities and with due account for the entire experience of the 20th century.

The platform states clearly what we should abandon. We should abandon the ideological dogmatism that became ingrained during past decades, outdated stereotypes in domestic policy and outmoded views on the world revolutionary process and world development as a whole.

We should abandon everything that led to the isolation of socialist countries from the mainstream of world civilization. We should abandon the understanding of progress as a permanent confrontation with a socially different world. . . .

The party's renewal presupposes a fundamental change in its relations with state and economic bodies and the abandonment of the practice of commanding them and substituting for their functions.

The party in a renewing of society can exist and play its role as vanguard only as a democratically recognized force. This means that its status should not be imposed through constitutional endorsement.

The Soviet Communist Party, it goes without saying, intends to struggle for the status of the ruling party. But it will do so strictly within the framework of the democratic process by giving up any legal and political advantages, offering its program and defending it in discussions, cooperating with other social and political forces, always working amidst the masses, living by their interests and their needs.

*The* New York Times, *February 6, 1990, p. A16.*

uphold their authority. He was beginning to advance a similar view of the nature of the authority of the Communist Party within the Soviet Union.

### RENUNCIATION OF COMMUNIST POLITICAL MONOPOLY

During this period, Gorbachev tried to establish a new political structure with a strong presidency, eventually to be filled by election in the Supreme Soviet. He was also trying to build a political base outside the Soviet Communist Party. In early 1990 he formally proposed to the Central Committee of the Soviet Communist Party that the party abandon its monopoly of power. After intense debate, the Committee adopted his proposal, abandoning the Leninist position that only a single elite party could act as the vanguard of the revolution and forge a new Soviet society. Gorbachev seems not to have wanted wholly to abandon communism and most assuredly not socialism, but he did want to open the political process to genuine competition. He was determined, however, that the Soviet Union should remain a single strong state with a powerful central government.

### NEW POLITICAL FORCES

By this time, however, Gorbachev was not the only player in the Soviet Union's new political scene. He soon found himself, more than in the past, reacting to events rather than controlling them. In 1990 he experienced a sharp drop in popularity from which he never recovered.

Gorbachev confronted challenges from three major political forces by 1990. One consisted of those groups—considered conservative in the Soviet context—whose members wanted to preserve the influence of the Communist Party and the Soviet army. They were deeply disturbed by the country's economic stagnation and political and social turmoil. They still appeared to control significant groups in the economy and society. During late 1990 and early 1991, Gorbachev, who himself seems to have been disturbed by the nation's turmoil, began to appoint members of these factions to key positions in the government. In other words, Gorbachev seemed to be making a strategic retreat. He apparently believed that only these more conservative forces would give him the support he needed.

Gorbachev made this calculation because he was now facing opposition from members of a second group, those who wanted much more extensive and rapid change. Their leading spokesman was Boris Yeltsin (b. 1931). He and those supporting him wanted to move quickly to a market economy and a more democratic government. Like Gorbachev, Yeltsin had come up through the ranks of the Communist Party and had then become disillusioned with its policies. Throughout the late 1980s, he had been critical of Gorbachev. In 1990 he was elected president of the Russian Republic, the largest and most important of the Soviet Union's constituent republics. In the new political climate, that position gave him a firm political base from which to challenge Gorbachev's authority and increase his own.

The third force that came into play from 1989 onward was regional unrest in some of the republics of the Soviet Union. These republics had experienced considerable discontent in the past, but it had been repressed by military or Communist Party action. Initially, the greatest unrest came from the three Baltic republics of Estonia, Latvia, and Lithuania. These had been independent republics until the eve of World War II. In accord with secret arrangements in the Soviet–German nonaggression pact of 1939, they had been turned over to the Soviet Union. That prewar pact with Nazi Germany provided the only legal basis for the Soviet Union's continued control over them.

During 1989 and 1990, the parliaments of the Baltic republics tried in various ways to increase their independence from the Soviet Union, and Lithuania actually declared independence. Discontent also arose in the Soviet Islamic republics in central Asia. Riots broke out in Azerbaijan and Tajikistan. Throughout 1990 and 1991, Gorbachev sought to negotiate new constitutional arrangements between the republics and the central government. His failure in this effort may in time be seen as the most important reason for the rapid collapse of the Soviet Union.

### THE AUGUST 1991 COUP

The turning point in all of these events came in August 1991, when the conservative forces that Gorbachev had brought into the government attempted a coup. Armed forces occupied Moscow, and Gorbachev himself was placed under house arrest while on vacation in the Crimea. The forces of political and economic reaction—led by people who, at the time, were associated with Gorbachev—had at last attempted to seize control. The day of the coup, Boris Yeltsin

Lithuanians demonstrate for independence in 1990. As the Gorbachev reform era came to a close, the various republics of the former Soviet Union began to demand independence. [Lehtikuva Oy/Woodfin Camp & Associates]

After the failed coup in August, 1991, Boris Yeltsin soon displaced Mikhail Gorbachev as leader of the new Commonwealth of Independent States. Here they appeared jointly before the parliament of the collapsing Soviet Union. [Gamma]

climbed on a tank in front of the Russian Parliament building to denounce the coup and ask for the help of the world in maintaining the Soviet Union's movement toward democracy.

Within two days, the coup collapsed. Gorbachev returned to Moscow, but in humiliation, having been victimized by the groups to whom he had turned for support. One of the largest public demonstrations in all Russian history, perhaps the largest, celebrated the failure of the coup in Moscow. From that point on, Yeltsin steadily became the dominant political figure in the nation. In the months immediately after the coup, the Communist Party, compromised by its participation in the coup, totally collapsed as a political force. The constitutional arrangements between the central government and the individual republics were revised. On December 25, 1991, the Soviet Union ceased to exist, Gorbachev left office, and the Commonwealth of Independent States came into being.

CRUSHING THE RUSSIAN PARLIAMENT  Boris Yeltsin emerged as the strongest leader within the new commonwealth. As president of Russia, he was the head of the largest and most powerful of the new states. His popularity was high both in Russia and in the commonwealth in 1992, but by 1993, he faced serious economic and political problems. Opposition to Yeltsin personally and to his policies of economic and political reform grew in the Russian Parliament. The members of this parliament were mostly former communists who wanted to slow or halt the movement toward reform. Relations between the president and the parliament reached an impasse, crippling the government. In September 1993, Yeltsin suspended parliament, which responded by deposing him. Parliament's leaders tried to incite popular uprisings against Yeltsin in Moscow. The military, however, backed Yeltsin, and he eventually surrounded the parliament building with troops and tanks. On

*In October, 1993, President Boris Yeltsin ordered the military to bombard the Russian parliament building. More than a hundred people were killed. [SYGMA]*

October 4, 1993, after proparliament rioters rampaged through Moscow, Yeltsin ordered the tanks to attack the parliament building, crushing the revolt.

These actions temporarily consolidated Yeltsin's position and authority. All the major Western powers, deeply concerned by the turmoil in Russia, supported him. In December 1993, Russians voted for a new parliament and approved a new constitution. The constitution strictly limits parliamentary authority and gives the president strong powers. Russia's future, however, remains insecure. The crushing of parliament left Yeltsin far more dependent than before on the military. And the country's continuing economic problems breed unrest. In the December elections, for example, radical nationalists who are openly intolerant of non-Russian ethnic groups and who advocate rebuilding Russia's empire made an uncomfortably strong showing, nearly capturing more seats in the new parliament than supporters of Yeltsin.

When the newly elected Russian Parliament gathered early in 1994, tension between it and Yeltsin immediately developed. Nationalists and former communists cooperated to force Yeltsin to moderate his reformist, market-oriented economic program. Furthermore, early in 1994 the parliament granted amnesty both to the parliamentary leaders imprisoned after the attack on the parliament building the previous October and to the leaders of the 1991 coup against Gorbachev. Thereafter much political infighting took place, with a proliferation of political parties, the old Communist Party again coming to the fore as a significant force. Yet in 1996 Yeltsin, who by then was in very poor health, won reelection, and the movement toward political reform and a market economy has continued.

THE UNITED STATES AND THE COLLAPSE OF THE SOVIET UNION  The vast changes occurring in the Soviet Union were of enormous significance to the United States. In 1988 Vice President George Bush (b. 1924) was elected to succeed President Reagan and was immediately confronted by the transformations of the politics of both the Soviet Union and Eastern Europe. Bush worked to keep the NATO alliance intact though some observers had begun to question its future utility. He also worked to develop a close diplomatic relationship with the emerging leadership of the new Russia. In the fall of 1990, in response to the invasion of Kuwait by Iraq, Bush initiated the largest mobilization of American troops since the Vietnam War. Using the United Nations as a forum, he forced a broad worldwide coalition against Iraq's aggression. In this effort, Bush gained the cooperation of the Russian government as well as support from traditional American allies. In early 1991 the coalition launched "Operation Desert Storm" and forced Iraq out of Kuwait. During the Cold War such cooperation would have been impossible.

In 1992 Governor William Clinton of Arkansas was elected president and was reelected in 1996. Under his leadership the US government has continued the difficult effort to develop a relationship with the new Commonwealth of Independent States. The Clinton administration has moved toward a policy of embracing the gradual expansion of NATO to include, in some manner, states of the former Warsaw Pact. At the same time, the United States has attempted to assure the Commonwealth of Independent States that such an expansion will not harm their interests. (We return to this issue later in this chapter.) The Clinton administration has also steadily supported the leadership of Yeltsin as the most likely policy for further reform in the former Soviet Union. At present the major challenge facing US policy will be what direction it will take when Yeltsin is no longer president.

## The Future of the Commonwealth of Independent States

The Commonwealth of Independent States is a loosely organized federation of eleven of the fifteen former Soviet Republics, of which Russia is the largest and most powerful. (See Map 31–2.) What will eventually develop within this new commonwealth is uncertain, and the rapid changes of recent years makes prediction both difficult and foolhardy. Several issues, however, should be noted.

First, very real differences and disagreements exist among these states. The status of the federation is thus quite shaky. Many republics include ethnic minorities that are sometimes the dominant group in other republics. Persecution of these minorities is thus a source of conflict both within and between republics. As conflicts arise, the parties involved may seek military aid from other

MAP 31–2   THE COMMONWEALTH OF INDEPENDENT STATES   *In December 1991, the Soviet Union broke up into its fifteen constituent republics. Eleven of these are now loosely joined in the Commonwealth of Independent States. Those not in the CIS are Estonia, Latvia, Lithuania, and Georgia.*

republics. Russia has already used these conflicts to play groups off against each other to gain influence within the commonwealth. Ethnic Russians themselves form a significant minority in many republics, including the independent Baltic states. Associated as they are with the former Soviet rulers, they have often been badly treated. It is uncertain how long the Russian Republic will tolerate this situation. The treatment of these ethnic Russian minorities, in other words, could provide Russia with a pretext for leaving troops in the Baltic states or even reasserting control over the territories of what had been the Soviet (and tsarist) Empire.

Second, the economy of the commonwealth as a whole as well as of each of the individual republics remains weak. All the consumer shortages that existed before 1991 still exist. It is uncertain what level of economic aid Western countries will be willing to supply to help the democratic experiment survive.

Third, certain conservative institutions remain. The secret police still exists and is largely subject to its own direction. The former Soviet army also still exists, although it is under much strain as the various republics vie for control of its weapons and attempt to claim the allegiance of troops on their soil.

# Aleksandr Solzhenitsyn Ponders the Future of Russian Democracy

*Aleksandr Solzhenitsyn, the foremost Russian novelist of his generation, was one of the most outspoken critics of the communist government of the Soviet Union. He was eventually expelled from the Soviet Union and lived for many years in the United States. After the collapse of the Soviet Union and of the Soviet communist government, he returned to live in Russia. In recent years he has been highly critical of the new Russian government. In January 1997, he published a column in the* New York Times *outlining his criticism.*

✦ *What are Solzhenitsyn's chief criticisms of the structure of the new Russian government? Why does he believe that it is not proper to be regarded as democratic? Why does he put such emphasis on the necessity of establishing structures of local self-government? Why does he believe corruption could undermine future movement toward democracy in Russia?*

What is known today as "Russian democracy" masks a Government of a completely different sort. Glasnost—freedom of the press—is only an instrument of democracy, not democracy itself. And to a great extent freedom of the press is illusory, since the owners of newspapers erect strict taboos against discussion of issues of vital importance, while in the outlying parts of the country newspapers get direct pressure from the province authorities.

Democracy in the unarguable sense of the word means the rule of the people—that is a system in which the people are truly in charge of their daily lives and can influence the course of their own historical fate. There is nothing of the sort in Russia today.

In August 1991, the "councils of people's deputies," though only window dressing under the rule of the Communist Party, were abolished throughout the country. Since then, the

---

Fourth, the general situation is volatile; the present leaders could quickly become unpopular and new ones could surface. The important question is whether subsequent leaders will support democracy or favor some new kind of authoritarian government.

Finally, many common political terms—"liberal" and "conservative," for example—have special meanings when used in the context of Russia and the Commonwealth of Independent States. The meaning of these terms bears little relationship to their meaning in Western politics. In fact, almost all the major political figures within the commonwealth are former communists. Much of the political conflict is thus a struggle among these former communists to retain power and office in a new political framework.

## The Collapse of Yugoslavia and Civil War

The communist government of Yugoslavia had long been distinct from those of the other Eastern bloc nations dominated by the Soviet Union. The country's leader, Marshal Tito, had acted independently of Stalin in the late 1940s. Thereafter, Yugoslavia pursued a foreign policy that was independent of the Soviet Union. After Tito's death in 1980, Yugoslavia began a decade of growing instability that has culminated in a major civil war.

Yugoslavia was created after World War I. Its borders included six major national groups—Serbs, Croats, Slovenes, Montenegrins, Macedonians, and Bosnians (Muslims)—among whom there have been ethnic disputes for centuries. (See Map 31–3.) The Croats and Slovenes are Roman Catholic and

united resistance of the President's machine, the Government, State Duma [Parliament], leaders of the political parties and majority of governors has prevented the creation of any agencies of local self-government.

Legislative assemblies do exist at the regional level but are entirely subordinate to the governors, if only because they are paid by the province's executive branches. (The election of governors is only a recent development and far from widespread; most governors were appointed by the President.)

There exists no legal framework or financial means for the creation of local self-government; people will have no choice but to achieve it through social struggle. All that really exists is the government hierarchy, from the President and national Government on down.

. . . The Constitution of 1993, which was passed hastily and not in a manner to inspire confidence, groans under the weight of the President's power. The rights it allocates to the State Duma are exceedingly constrained.

. . . . . . . . . . . . . . . . . . . . . . . . . . . . . . .

. . . This system of centralized power cannot be called a democracy.

. . . . . . . . . . . . . . . . . . . . . . . . . . . . . . .

It could be said that throughout the last 10 years of frenetic reorganization our Government has not taken a single step unmarked by ineptitude. Worse, our ruling circles have not shown themselves in the least morally superior to the Communists who preceded them. Russia has been exhausted by crime, by the transfer into private hands of billions of dollars' worth of the nation's wealth. Not a single serious crime has been exposed, nor has there been a single public trial. The investigatory and judicial systems are severely limited in both their actions and their resources.

. . . . . . . . . . . . . . . . . . . . . . . . . . . . . . .

The destructive course of events over the last decade has come about because the Government, while ineptly imitating foreign modes, has completely disregarded the country's creativity and particular character as well as Russia's centuries-old spiritual and social traditions. Only if those paths are freed up can Russia be delivered from its near fatal condition.

*The* New York Times, *January 4, 1997, p. 23.*

use the Latin alphabet. The Serbs, Montenegrins, and Macedonians are Eastern Orthodox and use the Cyrillic alphabet. The Bosnians are Islamic. Most members of each group reside in a region with which they are associated historically—Serbia, Croatia, Slovenia, Montenegro, Macedonia, and Bosnia–Herzegovina—and these regions constituted individual republics within Yugoslavia. Many Serbs, however, live in areas outside Serbia proper.

Tito succeeded in muting these ethnic differences by encouraging a cult of personality around himself and by a complex arrangement of political power sharing. In addition to the central government, each state had its own government. After Tito's death, Yugoslavia encountered serious economic difficulties that undermined the authority of

the central government. Because the presidency rotated among the leaders of the six republics, however, no strong leader could emerge to deal with the country's problems.

In the late 1980s, the old ethnic differences came to the fore again in Yugoslav politics. Nationalist leaders—most notably Slobodan Miloŝevic (b. 1941) in Serbia and Franjo Tudjman (b. 1922) in Croatia—gained increasing authority. The Serbs contended that Serbia did not exercise sufficient influence in Yugoslavia and that Serbs living in Yugoslavia but outside Serbia encountered systematic discrimination, especially from Croats. The Croats and Slovenes believed they could prosper economically if a market economy were pursued more rapidly. Ethnic tension and violence soon resulted. During the summer of 1990, in the wake of the changes in

MAP 31–3 THE ETHNIC COMPOSITION OF BOSNIA–HERZEGOVINA, CROATIA, AND SERBIA IN THE FORMER YUGOSLAVIA *The rapid changes in Eastern Europe during the close of the 1980s have brought to the fore various long-standing ethnic tensions in the former Yugoslavia. This map shows national and ethnic borders and major ethnic enclaves within areas generally dominated by a single ethnic group.* [Source: CIA]

the former Soviet bloc nations, Slovenia and Croatia declared independence from the central Yugoslav government. Within a year, their independence was recognized by several European nations, including, most importantly, Germany. Recognition from the full European community soon followed.

From this point on, violence escalated steadily. Serbia—concerned about Serbs living in Croatia and about the loss of lands and resources there—was determined to maintain a unitary Yugoslav state that it would dominate. Croatia was equally determined to secure independence. Croatian Serbs demanded safeguards against discrimination and violence, providing the Serbian army with a pretext to move against Croatia. By June 1991, full-fledged war had erupted between the two republics. Serbia accused Croatia of reviving fascism, while Croatia accused Serbia of maintaining a Stalinist regime. At its core, however, the conflict is ethnic and as such highlights the potential for violent ethnic conflict within the former Soviet Union.

The conflict took a new turn in 1992 as Croatian and Serbian forces determined to divide Bosnia–Herzegovina. The Muslims in Bosnia—who had lived alongside Serbs and Croats in the region for generations—soon became crushed between the opposing forces. The Serbs in particular, pursuing a policy called "ethnic cleansing," a euphemism redolent of some of the worst horrors of World War II, have killed or forcibly moved large numbers of Bosnian Muslims.

More than any other single event, the unremitting bombardment of Sarajevo, the capital of Bosnia–Herzegovina, brought the violence of the Yugoslav civil war to the attention of the world. In long negotiations the United Nations attempted unsuccessfully to mediate the conflict and imposed sanctions, which had little impact. Early in 1994, however, a shell exploded in the marketplace in Sarajevo, killing dozens of people. Thereafter, NATO issued an ultimatum threatening to bomb Serbian military positions if the Serbs did not withdraw their artillery from around Sarajevo. The ulti-

*An elderly parishioner walks through the ruins of Saint Mary's Roman Catholic Church in Sarajevo. The church was destroyed by Serb shelling in May, 1992. [Reuters/Bettmann]*

matum, and the military actions taken to enforce it—the first such actions in NATO history—were successful. Serb forces did withdraw from the city.

The events of the civil war came to a head in 1995 when NATO forces carried out strategic air strikes. Later that year, under the leadership of the United States, the leaders of the warring forces completed a peace agreement in Dayton, Ohio. The agreement was of great complexity, but recognized an independent Bosnia. The terms of the agreement are to be enforced by the presence of NATO troops, including those from the United States. Thus far an uncertain peace has been established in the former Yugoslavia, though there is considerable political discontent in each of its constituent states and the future remains uncertain.

## Problems in the Wake of the Collapse of Communism

The collapse of communism in Eastern Europe and the Soviet Union has presented Europe with new problems and new opportunities. The opportunities include the possibility of establishing democratic governments and market economies throughout the region. They also include the restoration of civil liberties in countries where they have not been known for over half a century. If the countries of the former Soviet bloc reorganize their economies successfully, their citizens may come to enjoy the kinds of consumer goods—and the standard of living these goods make possible—that have been available in West-

# Vaclav Havel Ponders the Future of Europe

*In October 1993, Vaclav Havel, the president of the Czech Republic, gave an address in which he outlined many of the problems confronting Europe in the wake of the collapse of communism. The setting of the speech was the General Assembly of the Council of Europe, and so his general theme was European unity. In particular, he discussed what he regarded as the danger of resurgent ethnic nationalism. Elsewhere in the speech, he observed that twice in this century nationalism had caused major wars in Europe. He was seeking to convince European leaders and nationalist groups to think differently about their interests in the future and to create a European rather than a particular national ethos. Its remarks remain relevant.*

✦ *What are the values around which Havel believes European nations might integrate and unify themselves? How does he portray special interests as undermining cooperation? What are the special dangers that he associates with the appearance of new forms of nationalism?*

All of us—whether from the west, the east, the south, or the north of Europe—can agree that the common basis of any effort to integrate Europe is the wealth of values and ideas we share. Among them are respect for the uniqueness and the freedom for each human being, the principles of a democratic and pluralistic political system, a market economy, and a civic society with the rule of law. All of us respect the principle of unity in diversity and share a deter-mination to foster creative cooperation between the different nations and ethnic, religious, and cultural groups—and the different spheres of civilization—that exist in Europe. . . .

Despite general agreement on the values upon which European integration should stand, this process today, . . . has encountered a number of obstacles. . . .

There are many reasons for this state of affairs, but I feel strongly that they all have one

ern Europe for decades. Realizing these opportunities, however, is unlikely to be a rapid process and will require enormous patience. In all of the nations of Eastern Europe as well as the Soviet Union the communist parties, sometimes under new names, continue to function and have succeeded in electing numerous officials. Nonetheless, the preponderance of recent elections have seen victories by reform-minded groups.

The problems in the new political and economic situation are enormous. Unemployment is widespread throughout the former Soviet Union and Eastern Europe. The plants and factories that the communist governments built are obsolete. Many also are so polluting that they have left the former communist nations with some of the worst environmental problems in the world. These nations also now recognize that, by the standards of West-ern Europe, they are very poor. As a result, hundreds of thousands of people have migrated from Eastern to Western Europe looking for work. In Western countries such as Germany, however, Eastern European immigrants, like those from elsewhere in the world, have encountered resentment, opposition, and physical violence. Responding to these ethnic tensions, Western countries have taken steps to restrict immigration.

The nations of Western Europe, facing considerable public resentment over the costs already incurred from the collapse of communism, are hesitant to send economic aid to the East. This is especially true in Germany, where the costs of unification have been and continue to be very high. Many citizens of the former West Germany are angry about the state aid that has been directed to the former East Germany. It has become clear to the

thing in common: the erroneous belief that the great European task before us is a purely technical, a purely administrative, or a purely systematic matter. . . .

To put it more succinctly: Europe today lacks an ethos; it lacks imagination, it lacks generosity, it lacks the ability to see beyond the horizon of its own particular interests, be they partisan or otherwise. . . . Europe does not appear to have achieved a genuine and profound sense of responsibility for itself as a whole, and thus for the future of all those who live in it. . . .

The former Yugoslavia is the first great testing ground for Europe in the era that was initiated by the end of the cold war. . . .

Another one consists in how we deal with the temptation to open the back gate to the demons of nationalist collectivism with an apparently innocent emphasis on minority rights and on the right of minorities to self-determination. At first sight, this emphasis would seem harmless and beyond reproach. But one real consequence could be new unrest and tension, because demands for self-determination inevitably lead to questioning the integrity of the individual states and the inviolability of their present borders, and even the validity of all postwar treaties. Attempts of

this kind are dangerous chiefly because they look not to the future, but to the past, for they call in question the very principle of civil society and the indivisible rights of the individual, as well as the certainty that only democracy, individual rights and freedoms, and the civil principle can guarantee the genuinely full development of even that aspect of one's identity represented by membership in a nationality. . . .

If various Western states cannot rid themselves of their desire for a dominant position in their own sphere of interests, if they don't stop trying to outwit history by reducing the idea of Europe to a noble backdrop against which they continue to defend their own petty concerns, and if the post-Communist states do not make radical efforts to exorcise the ghosts their newly won freedom has let loose, then Europe will only with great difficulty be able to respond to the challenge of the present and fulfill the opportunities that lie before it.

*Vaclav Havel, Address to the General Assembly of the Council of Europe, October 9, 1993,* New York Review of Books, November 18, 1993, p. 3.

---

Kohl government that the economic integration of the former East Germany will be more difficult and will take longer than was envisioned in the heady days of 1989 and 1990. Other parts of Europe are also experiencing an economic downturn or very low growth and believe they lack the resources to aid the Eastern Europeans. Western Europeans are also grappling with another issue—how should the former communist economies relate to the European Economic Community? Many Eastern Europeans want rapid economic integration, but Western European leaders fear Eastern Europe's economic difficulties could threaten prosperity in the West.

The political challenges created by the collapse of communism are no less great than the economic. Civil war has raged in Yugoslavia. Ethnic violence has already erupted in the former Soviet Union,

where nuclear weapons are still available. The Czechs and the Slovaks, unable to establish a stable, unified state, divided Czechoslovakia into two separate nations in 1993. The liberty made possible by the end of the communist governments has thus far tended to be used in pursuit of ethnic goals, leading almost inevitably to domestic political turmoil. Except for Romania, Bulgaria, and Greece, all of the nations between Germany and the Commonwealth of Independent States have existed as distinct political units within more or less their present borders only since World War I, although many of the national groups in them enjoyed some form of political autonomy decades or centuries earlier. Moreover, between World War I and 1989, all of them found themselves under either fascist or communist government at one time or another. After World War II, West Germany and Austria developed strong democratic institutions, but elsewhere this did not happen. The key question is whether democratic governments can survive in the midst of the resulting disorder, economic stagnation, and competing ethnic claims or whether they will succumb to some form of illiberal alternative.

The collapse of European communism has broader implications as well. It has closed the era in the development of European socialism that began with the adoption of Marxist thought by German socialists in the 1870s. From that time, Marxism dominated European socialist thought. The Bolshevik victory in the Russian Revolution seemed to validate it, and the policies of Lenin and Stalin sought to extend it in Europe and elsewhere. Now the Soviet Union and the communist governments of Eastern Europe—heirs to the Bolshevik Revolution—lie in ruins with the economies they built in collapse. As a result, Marxist socialism has been discredited, and socialism in general may find itself on the defensive. Other groups, as we have seen—feminists and environmentalists, for example—may now provide the kind of social criticism that had previously flowed from socialism. To play a role in the new era taking shape in Europe, socialists must come to grips with the benefits of markets, economic decentralization, and political democracy.

On another front, the collapse of European communism has profoundly altered international relations within Europe. The demise of the Warsaw Pact has brought the future of NATO to the fore. The primary function of this alliance had been to deter a Soviet attack on Western Europe. As that danger has receded, the purpose of the alliance has become somewhat unclear. Many argue that NATO should be kept as an instrument to preserve international order. Its failure to play an effective role in ending the Yugoslav civil war, however, has raised doubts that it could counter the kinds of problems Europe may face in the future. Much debate now centers on the possible admission of some Eastern European nations, once members of the Warsaw Pact, into NATO. Poland, the Czech Republic, and Hungary would like membership in NATO to protect themselves from possible future Russian aggression and to integrate themselves more fully into the West European economy. Russia has indicated its disapproval of the expansion of NATO. At present it appears that NATO will expand but very carefully attempting to take account of Russian concerns. (See the West and the World, Part VI, for a discussion of global democratization during the late twentieth century.)

*Although recent transformations in Europe have been rapid and stunning, they are securely embedded in the context of Western civilization. The concern for constitutional government has again come to the fore. The church has played a major role in the revolutionary changes in Eastern Europe. The Western penchant for critical self-examination survived in Soviet-dominated Europe, at first secretly in intellectual circles, then emerging publicly in the political debates that followed the revolutions of 1989.*

*The desire of Eastern Europeans to share in the prosperity of Western Europe has been key to recent events. It would, however, be a mistake to explain the collapse of European communism only in terms of economic stagnation and consumer dissatisfaction. For more than forty years, the citizens of Eastern Europe were denied the broad array of civil liberties that are almost taken for granted in Western Europe and the United States. Lacking religious freedom, a free press, the right to free speech, the possibility of free assembly, and the security of law and judicial procedure, they lived under the shadow of police surveillance and arbitrary arrest. Individuals could not travel freely, workers could not organize independent unions, and even the most harmless associations, like hobby clubs, singing groups, and jazz ensembles, raised political suspicion. Communist governments jailed writers who voiced opposition and party officials who advocated reform. They repressed religious expression and imposed martial law when threatened with rebellion.*

*When the people of Eastern Europe took to the streets in the summer and autumn of 1989, when Romanian students fell before the bullets of government troops, when citizens of Moscow resisted the August 1991 coup, they carried banners and shouted slogans demanding democracy, fundamental political liberties, and human rights. This desire for constitutional government and respect for human dignity are a fundamental part of the Western heritage, however much they have been denied or compromised over the centuries in different parts of the West.*

Twice in the first half of the twentieth century, nationalism in Europe contributed to the outbreak of worldwide conflict. In the second half of the century, militant nationalism appeared remarkably to have disappeared as a significant force in European politics. In Eastern Europe, the long years of Soviet domination suppressed nationalism and ethnic conflict. Recently, however, militant nationalism has reemerged, unleashed by the collapse of communism. Europe once again faces the challenge of containing this threatening force and the ethnic strife that accompanies it. It is simply too early to predict whether the civil war in Yugoslavia will be replicated elsewhere, or whether it will be seen as a warning of the dangers of nationalism and ethnic rivalry.

Before the end of World War II, class conflict had also characterized much of European society. The recent prosperity in Western Europe, however, has brought changes in the region's economic structure and reduced class strife. Many serious social problems nonetheless persist. Unemployment and the social strains of economic dislocation have not disappeared. Homeless people walk the streets of Europe as they do in the United States. The presence, in Europe, of workers from Pakistan, India, Turkey, and North Africa has heightened racial and ethnic tensions. And nobody can predict the political turmoil that might result from another serious worldwide economic downturn. The kind of class conflict that marked Europe's past, however, is clearly less evident than it was.

Indeed, the development of technology may come to be seen as a more important historical force in this century than was class struggle. For some observers, technology is only an enemy and a threat to the environment. Yet science has touched in a positive manner the lives of more people than might have been imagined even fifty years ago. And it will be from scientific understanding that the problems of the environment and resource shortages will be resolved. Rationalism has never been more a factor in everyday life, despite the continuing concern of some intellectuals over its limitations.

These persistent features of European life—concern for constitutionalism, tension between church and state, pursuit of science and rationalism, and a penchant for self-criticism—have not ensured that its civilization, as well as the results flowing from it, will be morally good. Rather they have meant that Western civilization has possessed in itself the possibility of correcting and redirecting itself and of raising questions about what are the good life and the good society. The possibility of asking those questions is necessary before the desired improvement and reform can be attained. Perhaps the chief carriers of Western culture today are those who within its midst most criticize it and demand that it justify itself.

## Review Questions

1. In what specific ways has Europe been "Americanized" in the second half of the twentieth century? How do you account for the trend toward a consumer society in the West? What population changes and migration patterns have marked the period since World War II and how have they affected Europe's economy and society?

2. How have women's social and economic roles changed in the second half of the twentieth century? What tensions and difficulties have new work patterns created for women? What changes and problems have women faced amidst the political instability in Eastern Europe?

3. Discuss the changes in the pursuit and diffusion of knowledge in the twentieth century. What has been the effect of the communications revolution? Of the boom of universities? Has Western intellectual life become more unified or less so? Why?

4. Discuss the contributions of Nietzsche and Kierkegaard to existentialism. What does Sartre mean when he says that existentialism is a philosophy of anguish and despair? How is existentialism a response to the various crises of the twentieth century?

5. Trace the collapse of communism in Eastern Europe and the Soviet Union. How important was Gorbachev in transforming the political and economic atmosphere of the Soviet Union? Why did he fail? Compare and contrast the revolutions of 1989 with the revolutions of 1848.

6. How did Marshal Tito maintain political stability in Yugoslavia after 1945? Why have violence and civil war steadily escalated there in the 1990s? What are some of the problems and opportunities that the collapse of communism has presented to Europe?

# Suggested Readings

G. Ambrosius and W. H. Hubbard, *A Social and Economic History of Twentieth-Century Europe* (1989). The best one-volume treatment of the subject.

B. S. Anderson and J. P. Zinsser, *A History of Their Own: Women in Europe from Prehistory to the Present*, vol. 2 (1988). A broad-ranging survey.

T. G. Ash, *The Uses of Adversity* (1989). Important essays on Central European culture and politics prior to the events of 1989.

T. G. Ash, *The Magic Lantern: The Revolution of '89 Witnessed in Warsaw, Budapest, Berlin and Prague* (1990). Essays by a longtime observer of Central Europe.

P. Baldwin, *The Politics of Social Solidarity: Class Bases of the European Welfare State 1875–1975* (1990). An excellent analysis of the political forces that allowed the welfare state to come into being.

I. Banac (Ed.), *Eastern Europe in Revolution* (1992). Excellent articles on the events of 1989 and afterward.

J. H. Billington, *Russia Transformed: Breakthrough to Hope, Moscow, August, 1991* (1992). A thoughtful essay on the attempted coup.

E. Bramwell, *Ecology in the 20th Century: A History* (1989). Traces the environmental movement to its late-nineteenth-century origins.

W. M. Brinton and A. Rinzler (Eds.), *Without Force or Lies: Voices from the Revolutions of Central Europe, 1989–90* (1990). Selections by major spokespeople for political change and reform.

A. Brown, *The Gorbachev Factor* (1996). Reflections by a thoughtful observer.

R. Crossman (Ed.), *The God That Failed* (1949). Essays by former communist intellectuals.

P. Desai, *Perestroika in Perspective: The Design and Dilemmas of Soviet Reform* (1989). A thoughtful essay on Gorbachev's reforms.

A. N. Dragnich, *Serbs and Croats: The Struggle in Yugoslavia* (1992). An introduction to the historical roots of the current struggle.

M. Ellman and V. Kontorovich, *The Disintegration of the Soviet Economic System* (1992). An overview of the economic strains that the Soviet Union experienced during the 1980s.

B. Gwertzman and M. T. Kaufman (Eds.), *The Collapse of Communism* (1991). A collection of contemporary news accounts.

B. Gwertzman and M. T. Kaufman (Eds.), *The Decline and Fall of the Soviet Empire* (1992). Another collection of contemporary news accounts.

W. F. Hanrieder, *Germany, America, and Europe: Forty Years of German Foreign Policy* (1989). A major survey.

M. J. Hogan (Ed.), *The End of the Cold War: Its Meaning and Implications* (1992). A collection of essays by contributors from a wide political spectrum.

H. S. Hughes, *Sophisticated Rebels: The Political Culture of European Dissent, 1968–1987* (1988). A series of thoughtful essays on recent cultural critics.

K. H. Jarausch, *The Rush to German Unity* (1994) Examines the events and background of the reunification of Germany.

L. Johnson, *Central Europe: Enemies and Neighbors and Friends* (1996). Examines the various nations of central Europe with an eye to the recent changes in the region.

T. Judt, *Past Imperfect: French Intellectuals, 1944–1956* (1992). An important study on French intellectuals and communism.

R. G. Kaiser, *Why Gorbachev Happened* (1992). A useful overview.

W. Laqueur, *Soviet Realities: Culture and Politics from Stalin to Gorbachev* (1990). Essays on developments in Soviet intellectual life.

C. Lemke and G. Marks (Eds.), *The Crisis of Socialism in Europe* (1992). Essay on the difficulties now confronted by socialism.

R. Maltby (Ed.), *Passing Parade: A History of Popular Culture in the Twentieth Century* (1989). A collection of essays on a topic just beginning to receive scholarly attention.

Z. A. Medvedev, *Gorbachev* (1986). The best available biography for his early career.

R. Medvedev and C. Chiesa, *Time of Change: An Insider's View of Russia's Transformation* (1989). An effort to explain recent changes through analysis of Soviet society and political structures.

P. H. Merkl, *German Unification in the European Context* (1993). The first major essay on the impact of German unity.

G. Montefiore, *Philosophy in France Today* (1983). A good introduction to one of the major centers of contemporary thought.

J. Morrison, *Boris Yeltsin* (1992). A useful biography.

B. Nahaylo and V. Swoboda, *Soviet Disunion: A History of the Nationalities Problem in the USSR* (1990). A discussion of one of the major areas of political difficulty today.

D. Oberdorfer, *The Turn: How the Cold War Came to an End: The United States and the Soviet Union 1983–1990* (1992). A major narrative by a Washington journalist.

M. Poster, *Existential Marxism in Postwar France* (1975). An excellent and clear work.

P. Pulzer, *German Politics, 1945–1995* (1996). An important overview.

S. P. Ramet, *Social Currents in Eastern Europe: The Sources and Meaning of the Great Transformation* (1991). A broad survey of Eastern European social life and popular culture on the eve of the revolutions of 1989.

S. P. Ramet (Ed.), *The Religious Policy in the Soviet Union* (1993). Essays on an important subject that has often received little attention.

D. Remnick, *Lenin's Tomb: The Last Days of the Soviet Empire* (1993). An excellent account by an American journalist working in the Soviet Union.

G. Ross, *Workers and Communists in France: From Popular Front to Eurocommunism* (1982). A useful survey.

J. Rothschild, *Return to Diversity: A Political History of East Central Europe Since World War II* (1989). A clear, well-organized introduction.

J. Ruscoe, *The Italian Communist Party, 1976–1981: On the Threshold of Government* (1982). Examines the party at the height of its influence.

H. A. Turner, *Germany from Partition to Reunification* (1992). The best brief introduction.

# INDEX

*The alphabetical arrangement is letter-by-letter. Page numbers in italic refer to illustrations.*

# H